D1505661

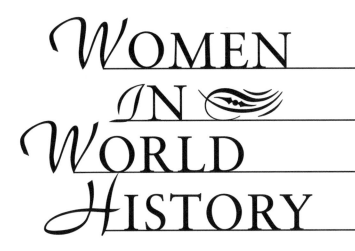

WOMEN IN WORLD HISTORY

A Biographical Encyclopedia

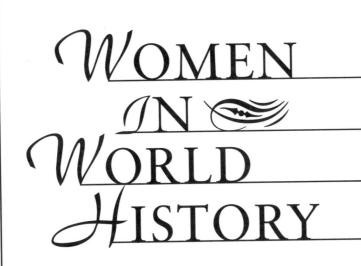

WOMEN IN WORLD HISTORY

A Biographical Encyclopedia

VOLUME
5
Ead-Fur

Anne Commire, Editor
Deborah Klezmer, Associate Editor

YORKIN PUBLICATIONS

GALE GROUP

Detroit
New York
San Francisco
London
Boston
Woodbridge, CT

Yorkin Publications

Anne Commire, *Editor*
Deborah Klezmer, *Associate Editor*
Barbara Morgan, *Assistant Editor*

Eileen O'Pasek, Gail Schermer, Patricia Coombs, James Fox,
Catherine Cappelli, Karen Rikkers, *Editorial Assistants*
Karen Walker, *Assistant for Genealogical Charts*

Special acknowledgment is due to Peg Yorkin who made this project possible.

Thanks also to Karin and John Haag, Bob Schermer, and to
the Gale Group staff, in particular Dedria Bryfonski, Linda Hubbard, John Schmittroth, Cynthia Baldwin,
Tracey Rowens, Randy Bassett, Christine O'Bryan, Rebecca Parks, and especially Sharon Malinowski.

The Gale Group

Sharon Malinowski, *Senior Editor*
Rebecca Parks, *Editor*
Linda S. Hubbard, *Managing Editor*
Margaret A. Chamberlain, *Permissions Specialist*
Mary K. Grimes, *Image Cataloger*

Mary Beth Trimper, *Production Director*
Evi Seoud, *Assistant Production Manager*

Cynthia Baldwin, *Product Design Manager*
Tracey Rowens, *Cover and Page Designer*

Barbara Yarrow, *Graphic Services Manager*
Randy Bassett, *Image Database Supervisor*
Robert Duncan and Michael Logusz, *Imaging Specialists*
Christine O'Bryan, *Graphics Desktop Publisher*

Dan Bono, *Technical Support*

Library of Congress Catalog Card Number Pending
A CIP record is available from the British Library

ISBN 0-7876-4064-6
Printed in the United States of America.

Library of Congress Cataloging-in-Publication Data

Women in world history : a biographical encyclopedia / Anne Commire, editor, Deborah Klezmer, associate editor.
    p. cm.
    Includes bibliographical references and index.
    ISBN 0-7876-3736-X (set). — ISBN 0-7876-4064-6 (v. 5)
    ISBN 0-7876-4065-4 (v. 6) — ISBN 0-7876-4066-2 (v. 7) — ISBN 0-7876-4067-0 (v.8) — ISBN 0-7876-4068-9 (v. 9)
    1. Women—History Encyclopedias.2. Women—Biography Encyclopedias.
    I. Commire, Anne. II. Klezmer, Deborah.
        HQ1115.W6 1999
        920.72'03—DC21

10 9 8 7 6 5 4 3 2

Eadburgh (c. 773–after 802)

*Queen of the West Saxons. Name variations: Eadburg; Eadburga. Born around 773; died after 802 in Pavia, Italy; daughter of Offa II, king of West Mercia, and Queen Cynethryth (fl. 736–796); possibly sister of *Etheldreda (d. around 840); married King Brihtric (Beorhtric) of the West Saxons, around 789 (died 802).*

Eadburgh, daughter of King Offa II and the notorious Queen *Cynethryth, was born a Saxon princess of West Mercia in England. Around 789, she married King Brihtric of the West Saxons. As queen, she gained significant power at the new court, for Brihtric entrusted her with many of the duties of ruling, and the couple seem to have been fairly close. A highly intelligent woman, Eadburgh was also reportedly a ruthless queen, involved in intrigues and power plays. She was accused of poisoning several court officials whom she disliked. In 802, she accidentally murdered her husband when he drank from a cup of poisoned wine that Eadburgh had prepared for one of his favorites, of whom she was jealous.

Widowed and friendless, Eadburgh was required to leave the court. She was so unpopular, it is reported, that the West Saxons would not grant the title of queen to any monarch's wife after Eadburgh. But she did not leave empty-handed; instead, she stole much of the West Saxon treasury and fled to the court of Charlemagne, king of the Franks. Charlemagne, proba-

bly unsure of what to do with a murderous Saxon queen, supposedly asked her to choose either himself or his son for a husband. After Eadburgh chose the son because the king was too old, Charlemagne replied that, if she had chosen him, he would have married her to his son; since she made the wrong choice, however, she could have neither.

Charlemagne did secure for her the position of abbess at a Frankish convent, a move that took her out of harm's way and off his hands, or so he thought. She had been at the abbey only a short while before she was caught with a lover. Charlemagne had little recourse but to banish the scandalous abbess from his kingdom, allowing her only one servant. Eadburgh ended her days in Pavia, Italy, probably surviving on charity. Although it is clear that she was disliked by her subjects, it is not clear how much of the evil attributed to her during her reign she actually committed.

Laura York,
Riverside, California

Eadburh

*Saxon noblewoman. Name variations: Eadburga. Possibly daughter of Wigmund and Elfleda; others say daughter of Coenwulf; married Ethelred the Great, ealdorman of the Gainis; children: *Elswitha (d. 902).*

Eadgifu.

Variant of Edgifu.

Eadgyth.

Variant of Edgitha or Edith.

Eadgyth Swanneshals (c. 1012–?)

*Mistress of Harold II Godwineson. Name variations: Edith; Edith of the Swan's Neck; Eadgyth Swan-neck. Born around 1012; some sources list her as the daughter of *Emma of Normandy (c. 985–1052) and Ethelred II the Unready, king of England; mistress of Harold II Godwineson (c. 1022–1066), king of England (d. 1066); children: (with Harold) *Gyseth (fl. 1070); Godwine; Edmund; Magnus; Gunhild, a nun at Wilton; Ulf (b. December 1066).*

Eadgyth Swanneshals found her ex-lover, Harold II Godwineson on the field where he lay dead after falling at the Battle of Hastings (October 14, 1066). He had been pierced through the eye with an arrow. Eadgyth identified the corpse by birthmarks known only to her and arranged for the king's burial in Waltham Abbey. Because

Eadgyth Swanneshals, finding the body of Harold II.

she is also known as Edith of the Swan's Neck, Eadgyth is often confused with Harold's wife *Edith (fl. 1063).

Eadhild.

Variant of Edhild.

Eady, Dorothy (1904–1981)

British-born Egyptian archaeologist and noted expert on the civilization of Pharaonic Egypt who believed that she was the reincarnation of an ancient Egyptian temple priestess. Name variations: Om Seti; Omm Seti; Omm Sety; Bulbul Abd el-Meguid. Born

Dorothy Louise Eady in Blackheath, East Greenwich, London, on January 16, 1904; died in Araba el-Madfuna near Abydos, Egypt, on April 21, 1981; daughter of Reuben Ernest Eady and Caroline Mary (Frost) Eady; married Imam Abd el-Meguid (divorced 1936); children: son, Sety.

Even by the flexible standards of British eccentricity, Dorothy Eady was *extremely* eccentric. She was born in a London suburb into a lower-middle-class family (her father was a master tailor) during the Edwardian era, and her life changed dramatically when at age three she fell down a flight of stairs and was declared dead by the family physician. An hour later, when the doctor returned to prepare the body for the funeral home, he found little Dorothy sitting up in bed, playing. Soon after, she began to speak to her parents of a recurring dream of life in a huge columned building. In tears, the girl insisted, "I want to go home!" All of this remained puzzling until she was taken at age four to the British Museum. When she and her parents entered the Egyptian galleries, the little girl tore herself from her mother's grip, running wildly through the halls, kissing the feet of the ancient statues. She had found her "home"—the world of ancient Egypt.

Although unable to afford a higher education, Eady did her best to discover as much as she could about the ancient civilization. Visiting the British Museum frequently, she was able to persuade such eminent Egyptologists as Sir E.A. Wallis Budge to informally teach her the rudiments of the ancient Egyptian hieroglyphs. When the opportunity came for her to work in the office of an Egyptian magazine published in London, Eady seized the chance. Here, she quickly became a champion of modern Egyptian nationalism as well as of the glories of the Pharaonic age. At the office, she met an Egyptian named Imam Abd el-Meguid, and in 1933—after dreaming of "going home" for 25 years—Eady and Meguid went to Egypt and married. After arriving in Cairo, she took the name Bulbul Abd el-Meguid. When she gave birth to a son, she named him Sety in honor of the long-dead pharaoh.

The marriage was soon in trouble, however, at least in part because Eady increasingly acted as though she were living in ancient Egypt as much as, if not more than, the modern land. She told her husband, and all who cared to listen, that around 1300 BCE there had been a girl of 14, Bentreshyt, daughter of a vegetable seller and ordinary soldier, who had been chosen to be an apprentice virgin priestess. The stunningly beautiful Bentreshyt caught the eye of Pharaoh Sety I by whom she became pregnant. Rather than implicate the sovereign in what would have been considered an act of pollution with an off-limits temple priestess, Bentreshyt committed suicide. The heartbroken Pharaoh Sety, deeply moved by her deed, vowed never to forget her. Eady was convinced that she was the reincarnation of the young priestess Bentreshyt and began to call herself Omm Sety in Arabic ("Mother of Sety").

Alarmed and alienated by her behavior, Imam Abd el-Meguid divorced Eady in 1936, but she took this development in stride and, convinced that she was now living in her true home, never returned to England. To support her son, Eady took a job with the Department of Antiquities where she quickly revealed a remarkable knowledge of all aspects of ancient Egyptian history and culture. Although regarded as highly eccentric, Eady was an accomplished professional, extremely efficient at studying and excavating ancient Egyptian artifacts. She was able to intuit countless details of ancient Egyptian life and rendered immensely useful practical assistance on excavations, puzzling fellow Egyptologists with her inexplicable insights. On excavations, she would claim to remember a detail from her previous life then give instructions like, "Dig here, I remember the ancient garden was here"; they would dig and uncover remains of a long-vanished garden.

In her journals, kept secret until after her death, Eady wrote about the numerous dream visitations by the spirit of her ancient lover, Pharaoh Sety I. She noted that at age 14, she had been ravished by a mummy. Sety—or at least his astral body, his *akh*—visited her at night with increasing frequency over the years. Studies of other reincarnation accounts often note that in these seemingly passionate affairs a royal lover is often involved. Eady usually wrote of her pharaoh in a matter-of-fact way, such as, "His Majesty drops in for a moment but couldn't stay—he was hosting a banquet in Amenti (heaven)."

Eady's contributions to her field were such that in time her claims of memory of a past life, and her worship of ancient gods like Osiris, no longer bothered her colleagues. Her knowledge of the dead civilization and the ruins that surrounded their daily lives earned the respect of fellow professionals who took full advantage of the countless instances when her "memory" enabled them to make important discoveries, the inspiration for which could not be rationally explained.

In addition to providing this invaluable assistance during excavations, Eady systematically organized the archaeological discoveries that she and others made. She worked with the Egyptian archaeologist Selim Hassan, assisting him with his publications. In 1951, she joined the staff of Professor Ahmed Fakhry at Dahshur. Assisting Fakhry in his exploration of the pyramid fields of the great Memphite Necropolis, Eady supplied knowledge and editorial experience that proved invaluable in the preparation of field records and of the final published reports when they eventually appeared in print. In 1952 and 1954, Eady's visits to the great temple at Abydos convinced her that her long held conviction that she had been a priestess there in a previous life was absolutely true.

In 1956, after pleading for a transfer to Abydos, she was able to work there on a permanent assignment. "I had only one aim in life," she said, "and that was to go to Abydos, to live in Abydos, and to be buried in Abydos." Though scheduled to retire in 1964 at age 60, Eady made a strong case to be retained on the staff for an additional five years. When she finally did retire in 1969, she continued to reside in the impoverished village of Araba el-Madfuna next to Abydos where she had long been a familiar figure to archaeologists and tourists alike. Having to support herself on a negligible pension of about $30 a month, she lived in a succession of mud-brick peasant houses shared by cats, donkeys, and pet vipers. She subsisted on little more than mint tea, holy water, dog vitamins, and prayer. Extra income came from the sale to tourists of her own needlepoint embroideries of the Egyptian gods, scenes from the temple of Abydos, and hieroglyphic cartouches. Eady would refer to her little mud-brick house as the "Omm Sety Hilton."

Just a short walk from the temple, she spent countless hours there in her declining years, describing its beauties to tourists and also sharing her vast fund of knowledge with visiting archaeologists. One of them, James P. Allen, of the American Research Center in Cairo, described her as a patron saint of Egyptology, noting, "I don't know of an American archaeologist in Egypt who doesn't respect her."

In her last years, Eady's health began to falter as she survived a heart attack, a broken knee, phlebitis, dysentery and several other ailments. Thin and frail but determined to end her mortal journey at Abydos, she looked back on her highly unusual life, insisting, "It's been more than worth it. I wouldn't want to change anything." When her son Sety, who was working at the time in Kuwait,

invited her to live with him and his eight children, Eady declined his offer, telling him that she had lived next to Abydos for over two decades and was determined to die and be buried there. Dorothy Eady died on April 21, 1981, in the village next to the sacred temple city of Abydos. In keeping with ancient Egyptian tradition, her tomb at the western side of her garden had at its head a carved figure of Isis with her wings outspread. Eady was certain that after her death her spirit would journey through the gateway to the West to be reunited with the friends she had known in life. This new existence had been described thousands of years earlier in the *Pyramid Texts,* as one of "sleeping that she may wake, dying that she may live."

SOURCES:

Cott, Jonathan. "Walk Like an Egyptian," in *Omni.* Vol. 9, no. 10. July 1987, pp. 66–74 and 118.

————, and Hanny El Zeini. *The Search for Omm Sety: A Story of Eternal Love.* Garden City, NY: Doubleday, 1987.

Dawson, Warren R., and Eric P. Uphill. *Who Was Who in Egyptology.* 3rd rev. ed. London: Egypt Exploration Society, 1995.

Eady, Dorothy. *A Dream of the Past.* Cairo: Egyptian State Tourist Department, 1949.

————. *Flowers from a Theban Garden.* Cairo: Impr. Misr S. A. E., 1939.

Eady, Dorothy Louise. *Omm Sety's Abydos.* Edited by Daniel Kolos. Mississauga, Ontario: Benben Publications, [1982].

"Omm Seti," in *The Times* [London]. April 29, 1981, p. 20.

Omm Sety, and Hanny El Zeini. *Abydos: Holy City of Ancient Egypt.* Los Angeles: L L Company, 1981.

Wren, Christopher S. "Om Seti: She Belongs among Pharaonic Ruins," in *The New York Times Biographical Service.* April 1979, pp. 512–513.

RELATED MEDIA:

"Omm Sety and Her Egypt," BBC documentary by Julia Cave, 1981.

John Haag,
Assistant Professor of History,
University of Georgia, Athens, Georgia

Eagels, Jeanne (1894–1929)

American stage actress, best known for her portrayal of Sadie Thompson, who died from a drug overdose in her early 30s. Born Jeannine Eagels in Kansas City, Missouri, on June 26, 1894; died in New York City on October 3, 1929; one of four children of Edward (a carpenter) and Julia (Sullivan) Eagels; married Morris Dubinsky (manager of a theater troupe), around 1910 (divorced); married Edward Harris Coy (a stockbroker and former football star), in 1925 (divorced 1928); children: (first marriage) one son who was put up for adoption.

Selected stage appearances: debuted as Puck in A Midsummer Night's Dream (1901); appeared as

Miss Renault in Jumping Jupiter *at the New York Theater (1911), Olga Cook in* The "Mind-the-Paint" Girl *at the Lyceum (1912), Dorothy Ainslie in* The Crinoline Girl *on tour (1914–15), Miriam in* The Outcast *on tour (1915–16), Kate Merrywether in* The Great Pursuit *at the Schubert (1916), Lady Clarissa in* Disraeli *opposite George Arliss on tour (1916), Lucy White in* The Professor's Love Story *and Mrs. Reynolds in* Hamilton, *both at the Knickerbocker (1917), Ruth Atkins in* Daddies *at the Belasco (1918), Mary Darling Furlong in* A Young Man's Fancy *at the Playhouse (1919), Eugenie de Corlaix in*

In the Night Watch *at the Century (1921), Sadie Thompson in* Rain *at the Maxine Elliott Theater (1922–24), Simone in* Her Cardboard Lover *at the Empire (1927).*

Selected filmography: The House of Fear *(1915);* The World and the Woman *(1916);* The Fires of Youth *(1917);* Under False Colors *(1917);* The Cross Bearers *(1918);* Man Woman and Sin *(1927);* The Letter *(1929);* Jealousy *(1929).*

Actress Jeanne Eagels was in her late 20s when she achieved a hard-won dream of stardom

Jeanne
Eagels

as Sadie Thompson in the 1922 Broadway production of *Rain*. She died only seven years later of alcoholism and drug addiction. ***Marilyn Monroe** has often been regarded as Eagels' modern-day counterpart. John D. Williams, who directed Eagels in *Rain* and wrote her obituary for *The New York Times*, maintained that she was "one of the two or three highest types of interpretative acting intelligences" he had ever met.

Eagels was born in Kansas City in 1894. She made her first appearance on stage at age seven, in a local production of *A Midsummer Night's Dream*. At 15, she ran away from home and joined a theater troupe with which she toured the midwest for two years. During this time, she married and had a son, who was put up for adoption after the short-lived marriage dissolved. By 1911, Eagels had made her way to New York, where she took small roles in *Jumping Jupiter* (1911), *The "Mind-the-Paint" Girl* (1912), and *Crinoline Girl* (1914). Determined to become a serious actress, she is said to have turned down an opportunity to become a Ziegfeld star.

In 1915, Eagels made the first of a series of movies for the fledgling Pathé Film Company (based in New York), while continuing to appear on stage at night. Her last Pathé film, *The Cross Bearers* (1918), coincided with her first Broadway hit, *Daddies*. The latter was produced by David Belasco who had spotted her in a small role and found her magnetic: "Her eyes were hard and bitter but shining with ambition," he later wrote. "Thousands of girls have come to me, but never such a girl as Jeanne Eagels, with the air of a *Duse, the voice of an earl's daughter, and the mien of a tired, starved little alley cat." By this time, however, Eagels was already an alcoholic and experimenting with heroin. She was also developing into a diva and angrily walked out on *Daddies* halfway through the run, without a word to anyone involved. "Never deny. Never explain," she once told a reporter. "Say nothing and become a legend."

Eagels managed to hold her career together through several more Broadway shows. Her breakthrough role came in 1922 as the good-natured and tough prostitute Sadie Thompson in *Rain*, a dark, bitter play by John Colton, based on a story by Somerset Maugham. Reviews were glowing, including Stark Young's in the *New Republic*. "Miss Eagels has pathos and a wit of her own," he wrote, "and an oddly likable and wistful effect of naturalness. And she has from the moment she comes on the stage the gift of being entertaining, which is at the bottom of all good acting everywhere." The show ran for two years

on Broadway, and Eagels toured with it for an additional five. (*Rain* was filmed in 1928 with ***Gloria Swanson**; it was remade in 1932 with ***Joan Crawford** and in 1957, under the title *Miss Sadie Thompson*, with ***Rita Hayworth**.) During the tour, Eagels entered into a second disastrous marriage, with Edward Harris Coy.

It was not until 1927 that Eagels found another role that suited her: the part of Simone in *Her Cardboard Lover*, opposite Leslie Howard. By this time, her substance abuse was taking its toll. The *Boston Transcript* described her performance as shaky, "all fidget and misgiving." While the show was on tour, she began to miss performances and was finally fined and suspended from stage work for 18 months by the Actors' Equity union. Eagels packed up for Hollywood, where Paramount signed her to a contract despite the fact that she was now 30 (old by early 20th-century standards) and an addict. Her first talkie, *The Letter* (1929), earned good notices. She went on to make *Jealousy* (1929), with Fredric March, in which her performance was adequate despite her failing health. In September 1929, Eagels spent ten days in a New York hospital, where she underwent an operation for an eye infection. She died of a drug overdose on October 3 in the office of her doctor. Eagels lay in state at Frank Campbell's Funeral Home at Broadway and 66th Street. Her final film *Jealousy* was playing at Lowe's Theater across the street.

RELATED MEDIA:

Jeanne Eagels (109 min. film), starring ***Kim Novak**, Jeff Chandler, and ***Agnes Moorehead**, produced by Columbia, 1964.

Barbara Morgan,
Melrose, Massachusetts

Eakins, Susan Hannah (1851–1938)

American painter and wife of artist Thomas Eakins. Name variations: *Susan Hannah Macdowell. Born Susan Hannah Macdowell in Philadelphia, Pennsylvania, on September 21, 1851; died in Philadelphia on December 27, 1938; daughter and fifth of eight children of William H. (a noted engraver) and Hannah Trimble (Gardner) Macdowell; sister of Elizabeth Macdowell; studied at the Philadelphia Academy of Fine Arts, 1876–82; married Thomas Eakins (1844–1916, a painter), on January 19, 1884; no children.*

The work of painter Susan Hannah Eakins was long ignored. Her first solo exhibition—a collection of over 50 oils and watercolors—was held at the Pennsylvania Academy of the Fine Arts in 1973, 35 years after her death. Her husband Thomas Eakins, now recognized as one of

America's finest painters though his reputation was by no means secure in his own day, maintained that she was one of the best female artists in America. Neither Susan's position as a gifted and promising painter before her marriage, nor her husband's claim, brought her the attention in her lifetime that she would receive posthumously.

One of eight children of **Hannah Gardner Macdowell** and William H. Macdowell, a distinguished engraver and a decided liberal, Susan Eakins was raised in a progressive and artistic environment. She and her sister **Elizabeth Macdowell** were encouraged in their interest in art and had a studio in the attic of the Macdowell home. In 1876, Susan visited the Haseltine Galleries, curious to see Thomas Eakins' scandalous painting of a surgical operation, *The Gross Clinic*; though impressed, she was too shy to approach the artist who was in attendance. Instead, she entered the Philadelphia Academy of Fine Arts (PAFA), intent on studying with Thomas; she would also study under Christian Schussele.

During her studies at PAFA from 1876 to 1882, Susan exhibited intermittently and won several prizes. The Charles Toppan draughtsmanship prize (1882) followed the Mary Smith Prize for best PAFA woman artist (1879), an award later bestowed on such eminent artists as *Cecilia Beaux, *Emily Sartain, and *Alice Barber Stephens. After her official matriculation at the academy, Eakins stopped exhibiting. It was not until 1905 that one of her paintings, an 1877 portrait of her teacher Christian Schussele, was again exhibited at the academy.

After her 1884 marriage to Thomas, Susan's primary concern became her husband's art, but reports that she had completely relinquished her own work are untrue. According to **Susan P. Casteras**, a leading authority on the artist, there was no friction or sense of rivalry between the two artists, who maintained separate studios in the Eakins' family house that they shared with Thomas' father. Both accepted and encouraged the other's work, although Susan Eakins' efforts to promote her husband are more well known. While he was still in charge of instruction at the Philadelphia Academy, she shielded him from household business and saw to it that all his free time could be devoted to his work. Eakins, who was said to possess a remarkable buoyancy of spirit and rollicking sense of fun, entertained her husband's students and friends, answered his correspondence, and supervised the shipping of his works to exhibitions (most of his paintings were returned unsold). She stood by him through controversy over his teaching methods

Susan Hannah Eakins, *painting by Thomas Eakins, 1899.*

and his dismissal from the academy, supposedly for removing the loincloth from a male model in a women's life class. It is rumored that she also knew of and endured her husband's affair with his childhood friend and sometimes model **Mary Adeline Williams**, who came to live with the couple in 1900. A portrait painted around 1899 reveals a troubled Eakins who appears old beyond her years.

Susan Eakins was primarily a portraitist who specialized in unsentimental domestic scenes depicting one or two subjects sitting while reading or knitting. During her student days, many of her portraits were of family and friends, characterized by the focus and the convincing anatomy of the figures, especially the faces and hands. During her middle period, the three decades of her marriage, Eakins began to consolidate the technical lessons she had learned from her husband into her own work. Thomas' influences are seen in her thin and broadly brushed backgrounds, against which the figures are solidly built up. Her palette—predominately warm, earthy, somber colors—also conformed to Thomas' color schemes. Susan Eakins often used her husband as a subject. Among her most poignant images of him is a drawing, executed towards the end of his life, in which he is depicted, old and tired, stroking a cat, one of the many animals in the household.

After Thomas' death in 1916, Susan Eakins' style changed radically. The solidity of her forms weakened, often into comparatively shapeless masses, as she became freer and more fluent. Her palette gave way to cooler hues, and she occasionally made use of vivid blues, reds, and brilliant yellows. Casteras regarded the quality of Eakins' later work as erratic, and remarked on a new freedom from the tragic element that had permeated her earlier work. Susan Eakins continued to paint until her 86th year, when a fall rendered her too weak and dizzy to continue. On December 27, 1938, she died of arteriosclerosis in the home in which her husband had spent his childhood and they had shared their married life. Although her first love was painting, Susan Eakins was also an accomplished pianist and an amateur photographer.

SOURCES:
Baigell, Matthew. *Dictionary of American Artists.* NY: Harper and Row, 1979.

Casteras, Susan P. *Susan Macdowell Eakins.* Exhibition Catalogue, Pennsylvania Academy of the Fine Arts, 1973.

Flam, Jack. "Eakins in Light and Shadow," in *American Heritage.* Vol. 42, no. 5. September 1991, pp. 57–68.

Wilmerding, John, ed. *Thomas Eakins.* Washington, DC: Smithsonian, 1994.

Barbara Morgan,
Melrose, Massachusetts

Ealdgyth.

Variant of Edith.

Ealdgyth

(fl. 1016)

Queen of the English. Name variations: Algitha; Edith. Flourished around 1016; married Sigeferth, a Danish thane; married Edmund II Ironside (c. 989–1016), king of the English (r. 1016), around July 1015; children: Edmund (1016–?); Edward the Exile also

known as Edward the Aetheling (1016–1057). Her sons were possibly twins.

Ealdgyth married Sigeferth. Following his death, she married Edmund II Ironside around July 1015, bringing with her as dowry the submission of Five Boroughs of the Danish Confederacy. For this reason, the marriage incurred the wrath of Edmund's brother-in-law Edric. It is said that the following year, along with her brother, Ealdgyth arranged for the murder of her second husband.

Ealhswith or Ealhswyth (d. 902).

See Elswitha.

Eames, Clare (1896–1930)

American actress. Born in Hartford, Connecticut, on August 5, 1896; died on November 8, 1930, at age 34; daughter of Hayden Eames and Clare (Hamilton) Eames; educated in Cleveland, Ohio, and Paris, France; niece of famous opera singer Emma Eames; studied for the stage under Sarah Cowell Le Moyne and at the Academy of Dramatic Art; married Sidney Howard (1891–1939, Pulitzer Prize-winning playwright), in 1922 (separated 1928, divorced March 1930); children: daughter Clare Jenness Howard.

Clare Eames, the niece of opera star *Emma Eames, first appeared on stage at the Greenwich Village Theater in *The Big Scene* on April 18, 1918. In March 1921, Eames attracted considerable attention when she performed at the Ritz Theater in the title role of John Drinkwater's *Mary Stuart.* That September, she was given the lead in Sidney Howard's first play, *Swords,* a poetic melodrama of the Italian Renaissance, at the National Theater in New York. Soon after, Eames married Howard and starred in several of his plays, most notably *Neb McCobb's Daughter.*

In 1924, at the 48th Street Theater in New York, Eames co-starred with James K. Hackett in *Macbeth,* portrayed Hedda Tesman in *Hedda Gabler,* and Proserpine Garnett in *Candida.* In 1926, she appeared as the Empress *Carlota (1840–1927) in *Juarez and Maximilian.* Eames made her London debut in September 13, 1927, playing Christina in *The Silver Cord* at the St. Martin's Theater. After returning to New York in 1928, she appeared as Nurse Wayland in *The Sacred Flame* at the Henry Miller Theater, the same role she would play at the Playhouse in London (February 1929) in her last performance. Eames divorced Howard in March 1930 and died in November of that year in a nursing home in London at age 34.

Eames, Emma (1865–1952)

Shanghai-born American lyric soprano. Born Emma Hayden Eames on August 13, 1865, in Shanghai, China; died on June 13, 1952, in New York, New York; daughter of Emma (Hayden) Eames and Ithama Bellows Eames (a lawyer); aunt of *Clare Eames (1896–1930); studied with Clara Munger and Annie Payson Call in Boston and with Mathilde Marchesi in Paris; married Julian Story (an American painter), in August 1891 (divorced 1907); briefly married to Emilio de Gogorza (an American opera singer), in 1911 (separated).

Debuted at Covent Garden (1891); debuted at Metropolitan Opera (1891) where she would sing over 250 performances (until 1909); taught singing in New York City (1936–52); owned two houses in Europe, a townhouse in Paris, and a castle in Tuscany.

On August 13, 1865, Emma Eames was born in Shanghai to Emma Hayden Eames and Ithama Bellows Eames, a lawyer who worked in the international courts of China. When Emma was five, because of her mother's ill health, the Eames family moved back to Bath, Maine, in 1870, and Emma was raised primarily by her Puritanical maternal grandparents. As a teenager, she began her musical training under the tutelage of her mother in Portland. She was singing for hire in Boston churches by age 17, and by age 20 she was in Paris with her mother, studying under *Mathilde Marchesi with the help of loans.

Fellow student *Nellie Melba managed to block Eames' debut at the Théâtre Royale la Monnaie in Brussels, Belgium. Instead, Eames made her debut starring in Charles Gounod's *Roméo et Juliette* opposite Jean de Reszke at the Paris Opéra in March 1889, the year Melba took on the same role at Covent Garden. The critic for Paris' *Figaro* lavishly praised Eames: "Twenty years old, tall, svelte, the figure and the profile of Diana, the nose fine and the nostrils quivering, the carmine mouth exhaling the breath of life, the face a pure oval lit by big eyes full of impudence and candor at the same time, the expression astonishingly mobile, the forehead high and crowned by a mass of blond fleece, the arms superb attached to the charming shoulders—such is Mlle Emma Hayden Eames . . . such is the new Juliette." When Melba joined the Paris Opéra company a year later and caused further havoc

for Eames, Eames branded the experience a "nightmare" and left.

Despite her continued rivalry with Melba, Eames sang more than a dozen leading roles in eight seasons at Covent Garden. She also sang 21 roles in more than 250 performances during 16 seasons at the Metropolitan Opera. She performed the first Met productions of Mascagni's *Cavalleria rusticana* and *Iris*, and made her way with great assurance into the Wagnerian repertory as early as 1891. She is remembered as a singer whose style was characterized by the Marchesi method, despite the fact that Eames broke publicly with Mathilde Marchesi, calling her a "Prussian drill-master."

Emma Eames

Considered something of a prima donna for her regal bearing, Eames was admired for her singing but resented offstage. Some, like George Bernard Shaw, found her acting cold and colorless. "I never saw such a well-conducted person as Miss Eames," he wrote of her. "She casts her propriety like a Sunday frock over the whole stage." An extremely disciplined worker, Eames was never able to fully overcome a lack of ease in the upper register. She made over 50 recordings between 1905 and 1911 that document her ability, but acoustical recording did not well serve her vocal talents. Dedicated and determined, Eames made a great impact on American opera in the early 20th century. She retired in 1916, age 51. From 1936 until her death in 1952, she taught in New York City.

SUGGESTED READING:
Eames, Emma Hayden. *Memories and Reflections.* NY: D. Appleton, 1927.

John Haag,
Assistant Professor of History,
University of Georgia, Athens, Georgia

Eanfleda (626–?)

Queen of Northumbria. Name variations: Eanfled; Eanflæd; Eanfled of Deira. Born on April 17, 626; death date unknown; daughter of *Ethelberga of Northumbria (d. 647) and Edwin (Eadwine), king of Northumbria (585?–633); married Oswy (Oswin,

Oswio), king of Northumbria; children: Ecgfrith, king of Northumbia; Elfwine (d. 679); *Ostrith (d. 697); Elflaed (d. 714).

Baptized in infancy by Bishop Paulinus, Eanfleda was the first Northumbrian to receive the rite. Along with her husband Oswy, who succeeded her father as king, she continued to champion Christianity, and the royal couple placed their one-year-old daughter *Elflaed under the tutelage of *Hilda of Whitby. When Elflaed became abbess of Whitby in 680, Eanfleda shared the rule with her daughter.

Earhart, Amelia (1897–1937)

America's most famous woman pilot from 1928, when she became the first woman in the world to cross the Atlantic in an airplane, until 1937 when she disappeared in the Pacific Ocean on a round-the-world flight. Born on July 24, 1897, in Atchison, Kansas; lost over the Pacific on July 2, 1937, on a flight between Lae, New Guinea, and Howland Island; daughter of Edwin (a lawyer) and Amy (Otis) Earhart; sister of Muriel Earhart Morrisey (1900–1998) who had taught in Medford, Massachusetts, public schools for many years; graduate of Hyde Park (Chicago) High School, 1915; attended Ogantz School in Philadelphia, 1916–17, Columbia University, 1919–20, 1924–25; married George Palmer Putnam, on February 7, 1931; no children.

Lived with grandparents in Atchison, Kansas (until 1909); joined her parents in Des Moines, Iowa; moved with family to St. Paul, Minnesota (1915), then to Springfield, Illinois; when parents separated, accompanied her mother to Chicago, where she finished high school, then attended school in Philadelphia (1916–17); worked as a volunteer nurse in a military hospital in Toronto (1917–18); moved to Northampton, Massachusetts (1918); attended university in New York City (1919–20); joined her parents in Los Angeles (1920–24), where she became a licensed pilot; moved to Boston (1924), working at a settlement house and flying on weekends; became the first woman to cross the Atlantic by air (1928).

Honors and awards included: 381st Aero Squadron pilot wings; Aero Club of France gold medal, Legion of Honor (France); Cross of the Order of Leopold (Belgium); Order of Virtutea Aviation (Rumania); American Women's Association award; Columbia Broadcasting System medal; Comité France-Amérique medal; Distinguished Flying Cross (U.S.); National Geographic Society's gold medal; society of Woman Geographers' gold medal; Harmon Trophies (1932 and 1935) as American's Outstanding Air Woman; medals from the cities of Chicago, New York, Philadelphia, and the Commonwealth of Massachusetts.

Subsequent record flights included: an altitude record in an autogiro, in which she became the first person to cross the U.S. and return (1931); first woman to fly solo across the Atlantic; fastest non-stop transcontinental flight by a woman (1932); broke her own transcontinental speed record (1933); first person to fly solo across the Pacific from Hawaii to California; first person to fly solo from Los Angeles to Mexico; broke Mexico City-Newark, N.J. speed record (1935); set speed record for east-west Pacific crossing from Oakland to Honolulu (1937).

A tireless and effective advocate of commercial aviation and equal rights for women, Amelia Earhart toured the United States lecturing on behalf of her convictions and established numerous records for distance and speed flights. The continual search for a solution to her unexplained disappearance has kept her name legendary in the history of American aviation.

In an astounding career of just nine years between 1928 and 1937, Amelia Earhart became America's and the world's most famous woman aviator. She was an unknown social worker in a settlement house in Boston and weekend amateur pilot when she became the first woman to cross the Atlantic in an airplane. Named captain of the flight for the publicity it was intended to engender, she was actually a mere passenger while two men acted as pilot and mechanic. Yet from this inauspicious introduction to fame, the amateur pilot became a professional and one of the ten most famous women in the world in less than a decade.

In 1900, the seven-year-old Earhart, speeding down a snow-covered hill in Kansas on her sled, took aim, lowered her head, closed her eyes and went straight between the legs of a horse crossing her path. On that day and on all of the daringly dangerous flights for distance and speed records during the rest of her life, she combined courage and determination with a reckless belief in her own abilities. When her luck gave out on the last flight, an attempt to encircle the globe at the equator, her disappearance only added to her fame, changing her status from that of hero to a legend in the annals of American aviation pioneers.

Amelia Earhart was born to Edwin and **Amy Otis Earhart** in Atchison, Kansas, in the home of her maternal grandparents, Alfred and **Amelia Harres Otis**, on July 24, 1897. While her parents were residing in Kansas City, Missouri, Amelia and her younger sister, **Muriel Earhart (Morrisey)**, spent all but the summer months at the Otis home in Atchison. She attended a private day school there until 1909 when her parents settled in Des Moines, Iowa, and Amelia and Muriel went to live with them. Her grandfather Otis, a banker, church warden, and U.S. District Court judge, harbored doubts about the ability of his son-in-law to care for a wife and children, doubts that proved justified. Edwin

Earhart, a handsome, intelligent and charming man whom Amelia adored, was an alcoholic, demoted and transferred by the railroad in 1913 to St. Paul, Minnesota, where Amelia attended high school and endured a year of real poverty. Fired from his position in St. Paul, Edwin made a desperate move to Springfield, Illinois, in 1914 but failed to find work and left his wife and daughters there soon after to live with his sister in Kansas City. Amelia moved again with her mother and sister to Chicago, where she was graduated from Hyde Park High School in 1915. There she had asked her classmates to sign a pe-

Amelia Earhart

tition requesting the firing of an inept teacher, hired through nepotism. But preferring to enjoy the lack of discipline and work, her fellow students refused, their disapproval isolating Amelia for her determined stand on principle. They described her in the yearbook as "A.E.—the girl in brown [her favorite color] who walks alone." This and the disappointment, humiliation, and poverty she suffered from her father's losing battle with alcoholism left her with a permanent mistrust of emotional dependency on others and a desire for financial security.

In 1916, Amelia's mother received an inheritance from Amelia Harres Otis that enabled her to send Amelia to Ogantz School in Philadelphia, an exclusive high school and junior college, where she proved an apt scholar and student leader. At Christmas of 1917, when Amelia went to Toronto to visit Muriel and her mother, she saw her first war wounded. Refusing to return to Ogantz, she enlisted as a volunteer nurse's aid at the Spadina Military Hospital, where she witnessed the suffering of Canadian soldiers, victims of tuberculosis and mustard gas in the World War I trenches of France. She remained until the winter of 1918, by which time she had become a convinced, lifelong pacifist. After the first in a series of sinusitis infections that were to plague her for the rest of her life, she left Toronto in 1918 to join her mother and sister in Northampton, Massachusetts, where Muriel was preparing to enter Smith College and Amelia took a course in auto mechanics. In the fall of 1919, Amelia entered Columbia University in New York City where she enrolled as a premedical student while auditing additional courses in French literature, but after one year she left for Los Angeles to join her parents, who had reconciled.

In December 1920, Earhart saw her first air show and after one brief ride as a passenger decided to become a pilot. She came home that night to announce to her family, "I think I'd like to fly," while secretly knowing "I'd die if I didn't." She began her lessons a month later with a woman instructor, **Neta Snook**, and passed her test for a license on December 15, 1921. To pay for her lessons and later, with the help of her mother, to buy an airplane, Amelia worked as a file clerk, office assistant, photographer, and truck driver. But by 1924, after being hospitalized with a recurring sinus infection and with her parents again separating, she sold the plane to pay her debts and bought a car in which she drove her mother to Boston, where Muriel was teaching school.

Amelia brought with her a collection of notes and newspaper clippings indicating strong feminist beliefs although she said little about them at the time. The collection centered on women's accomplishments—film directors in Europe, a Texas champion pistol shot, the first Indian to practice law in Great Britain, a new city manager and a speech by the president of an advertising club. She returned to Columbia University for another year but lacked funds to continue and joined her mother and sister in Boston. There, she was a part-time English teacher to immigrants, then a volunteer and later staff member at a settlement house for immigrant children. She resumed flying, buying a small interest in a new airfield and acting as a demonstrator and sales representative for Winfield Kinner, who had built the plane she had owned in Los Angeles. Now known to other aviators in the Boston area and a member of the local chapter of the National Aeronautics Association, in 1928 she came to the attention of George Palmer Putnam of Putnam and Sons who had published Charles Lindbergh's story of his 1927 solo trans-Atlantic flight. Putnam found in Earhart the woman he wanted to emulate Lindbergh—a "Lady Lindy" who would cross the Atlantic in a plane called "Friendship" as a symbol of English-American amity. Although nominally captain of the flight, Amelia was in fact merely a passenger while two men (Wilmer Stultz and Louis Gordon) piloted the plane from Newfoundland to Wales. She later described herself as "just baggage," but the ensuing publicity made her internationally famous. G.P. Putnam had created his "Lady Lindy," a title she loathed. Within weeks, with Putnam as her editor, she completed an account of the flight, *Twenty Hours, Forty Minutes: Our Flight in the Friendship*, published by Putnam and Sons.

In the two years after her return to the United States, she set an altitude record in an autogiro, then became the first person to fly that aircraft across the continent and back. She also became aviation editor of *Cosmopolitan* magazine and endorsed advertising of various products in contracts arranged by Putnam. In 1932, she made the trans-Atlantic flight she wanted—a solo crossing in a single-engine Vega, a plane now on display at the Smithsonian Institution's National Air and Space Museum in Washington, D.C. Soon after this flight, she wrote a book about it, *The Fun of It*. She followed this with record after record, transcontinental nonstop speed flights in 1932 and 1933, and in 1935 became the first person to fly solo across the Pacific from Hawaii to California. "It's easier to hit a continent than an island," she said. Before the year ended, she became the first person to fly solo from Los Angeles to Mexico City and set a speed record for a non-stop flight from Mexico City to Newark, New Jersey. To do this, she chose the most dangerous route, across the Gulf of Mexico, ignoring the advice of friend and test pilot Wiley Post.

There can be little doubt that Putnam, whom she married in 1931, was primarily responsible for the publicity that kept Earhart constantly in the public eye. Without him, her innate modesty and desire for privacy might have relegated her to the role of a competent amateur, known only to her colleagues. But Putnam used her courage, intelligence, determination and charisma to build her into a national hero. Their relationship was a complex one of mutual respect combined with a natural tension existing between persons of different styles and different goals.

Along with her second book, Putnam arranged for her to write magazine articles on her flights which popularized commercial aviation; they appeared in such varied publications as *National Geographic, Forum and Century, American, Outdoor Life, Sportsman Pilot,* and *The New York Times Sunday Magazine.* She also licensed franchises for lines of luggage and clothing bearing the Earhart name and which in fact she herself designed. Putnam also set up for her an exhausting schedule of nation-wide lectures as part of his continual campaign to generate publicity and keep her name before the public. Earhart was a ready partner, cooperating in all but Putnam's most outrageous schemes, because the publicity brought her the money she needed to continue flying.

The luggage she designed was sensible, and the clothing line was popular. She welcomed the opportunity to speak on behalf of jobs and political rights for all women and backed her faith in the future of commercial aviation by working for one airline and founding another. And although Putnam's efforts to manipulate the press frequently left newspaper reporters irate, Earhart invariably charmed them with her wit, patience, and intelligence. Proving a master of evasion when questioned about her personal life, she always gave them enough material for a story, a gift that made her known as "good copy" among journalists.

On the lecture circuit, Earhart became a celebrated speaker. During the winter months when flight conditions were hazardous, she drove a 12-cylinder Franklin automobile from city to city across the country, giving as many as 31 lectures in 29 towns in as many days, often arriving before dawn and facing a schedule of either a luncheon or dinner lecture, sometimes both, as well as interviews with local reporters before leaving late in the evening for the next engagement. These lectures and interviews were not only her chief means of support but also the platform from which she advocated her beliefs, equal rights—both political and economic—for women, and the development of commercial aviation.

A feminist who liked men while objecting to the idea of male superiority, Earhart claimed many influential friends from widely different circles—Franklin D. and *Eleanor Roosevelt, *Anne Lindbergh, comedian-columnist Will Rogers, director of the Bureau of Air Commerce Eugene Vidal, explorer Roy Chapman Andrews, pilots Wiley Post, *Jacqueline Cochran, and Paul Mantz, and publisher of the *New York Herald Tribune,* *Helen Rogers Reid. Although a reluctant joiner of groups, she accepted membership in those representing her interest—for equal rights for women, the National Women's Party; for women in science and exploration, the Society of Woman Geographers; for women in business, Zonta. And, to increase opportunities for women in aviation, she became a founding member of the Ninety-Nines, an international association of women pilots. In addition, she actively sought jobs for other women pilots and wrote countless letters of recommendation for them.

I may have to keep some place where I can go to be myself now and then, for I cannot guarantee to endure at all times the confinement of even an attractive cage.

—Amelia Earhart to George Putnam, on the eve of their marriage

The demanding speaking and flying schedules laid down by her husband led Earhart to fame and a successful career but left her little time to upgrade her skills as a pilot. She was certainly a competent flier—one instructor even called her "a natural"—but had neither the patience nor time for acquiring technical skills in navigation and communications. On March 17, 1937, attempting the second lap—from Hawaii to Howland Island in the mid-Pacific—of a planned east-west, round-the-world flight at the equator, she crashed on take-off in Honolulu, damaging her new twin-engine Lockheed Electra, a plane in which she had had inadequate flight training.

The plane was shipped back to the Lockheed factory in Los Angeles where Putnam and

Earhart spent the next few weeks raising money for repairs from new backers and old friends. Changing weather conditions necessitated an entirely new flight plan, starting again in Los Angeles but heading this time eastward, flying first to Miami, then along the South American coast, across the Atlantic to Africa, and on to India, Southeast Asia, and Australia. On May 21, the Electra now repaired, she took off from Oakland on her second attempt.

Accompanied by navigator Fred Noonan, Earhart completed 22,000 miles of the flight, reaching Lae, New Guinea. But plagued by mechanical breakdowns of her Electra, lack of sleep, insect bites, sunburn, and constant nausea and diarrhea, she was physically and emotionally exhausted. In a brief trans-Pacific telephone call to Putnam, she also reported "personnel trouble," possibly referring to a resumption of drinking by Noonan, her gifted navigator who had been fired by Pan American Airlines for alcoholism.

On July 2, 1937, 22 days before her 40th birthday and somewhere between Lae and Howland Island in the mid-Pacific, Earhart's Electra disappeared. Without a knowledge of Morse code, without a trailing antenna that she disliked using and deliberately left behind in Miami, and with conflicting instructions on which wave length to use on her radio-telephone, she was unable to reply to messages sent by a Coast Guard cutter at Howland Island—messages that might have saved her life. The most extensive search for a single plane ever made by the U.S. Navy failed to locate the plane or its crew. More than half a century later, the search continues, by numerous individuals determined to solve the mystery of her disappearance.

SUGGESTED READING:

Backus, Jean. *Letters from Amelia*. Boston, MA: Beacon Press, 1982.

Earhart, Amelia. *20 Hrs. 40 Min.* NY: Putnam, 1929.

———. *The Fun of It.* NY: Brewer, Warren and Putnam, 1932.

———. *Last Flight.* NY: Harcourt Brace, 1937.

Lovell, Mary S. *The Sound of Wings: The Life of Amelia Earhart.* NY: St. Martin's Press, 1989.

Rich, Doris L. *Amelia Earhart, a Biography.* Washington and London: Smithsonian Institution Press, 1989.

Ware, Susan. *Still Missing: Amelia Earhart and the Search for Modern Feminism.* NY: Norton, 1993.

BOOKS ON UNCONFIRMED THEORIES ABOUT EARHART'S DISAPPEARANCE:

Briand, Paul, Jr. *Daughters of the Sky.* NY: Duell, Sloan and Pearce, 1960.

Brink, Randall. *Lost Star: The Search for Amelia Earhart.* NY: Doubleday, 1966.

Goerner, Fred. *The Search for Amelia Earhart.* NY: Doubleday, 1966.

Strippel, Dick. *Amelia Earhart: The Myth and the Reality.* NY: Exposition Press, 1972.

Doris L. Rich,
author of *Amelia Earhart: A Biography* (Smithsonian Institution Press, 1989) and *Queen Bess: Daredevil Aviator* (Smithsonian Institution Press, 1993)

Earle, Alice Morse (1851–1911)

American writer and antiquarian. Born Mary Alice Morse in Worcester, Massachusetts, on April 27, 1851; died in Hempstead, Long Island, New York, on February 16, 1911; daughter of Edwin and Abigail Mason Clary Morse; educated at Worcester High School and at Dr. Gannett's boarding school, Boston; married Henry Earle, in April 1874; children: four.

Selected writings: The Sabbath in Puritan New England *(1891);* China Collecting in America *(1892);* Customs and Fashions in Old New England *(1893);* Costumes of Colonial Times *(1894); (editor)* Diary of Anna Green Winslow: A Boston School Girl of 1771 *(1894);* Colonial Dames and Goodwives *(1895);* The Life of Margaret Winthrop *(1895);* Colonial Days in Old New York *(1896);* Curious Punishments of Bygone Days *(1896);* Historic New York *(1897);* Chap Book Essays *(1897);* Home Life in Colonial Days *(1898);* In Old Narragansett: Romances and Realities *(1898);* Child Life in Colonial Days *(1899);* Stage-Coach and Tavern Days *(1900);* Old Time Gardens *(1901);* Sun Dials and Roses of Yesterday *(1902);* Two Centuries of Costume in America, 1620–1820 *(2 vols., 1903).*

Alice Morse Earle, whose books on the customs and everyday life in colonial America are meticulously researched and lively in style, did not embark on a writing career until she was nearly 40 years old. In the 12 years that followed her first publication in 1891, she more than made up for lost time, authoring, editing, and contributing to the publication of 17 books and over 30 articles dealing with various aspects on American colonialism. Her books are considered valuable resources for discovering America's domestic past.

Earle was born in Worcester, Massachusetts, and grew up in a house described as "a veritable museum" of fine antiques. In 1874, she married Henry Earle and moved to his home in Brooklyn Heights, New York, where she would live until her death. Her early life was devoted to her husband and four children, with little thought to history or writing. It wasn't until after the death of her husband that her family, especially her father, began to encourage her to write professionally. Her first book, *The Sabbath in Puritan New England,* grew out of an article originally written for *Youth's Companion* and later published in expanded form by *Atlantic Monthly.* Her popularity increased with each of her subsequent publications, helped along by the celebration of the Revolutionary centennial in 1876, which rekindled an interest in early American history. Earle, however, never sacrificed scholarship or historical integrity to meet the demands of her public, although she was criticized for occasionally repeating material from one volume to the next. Her research was of the highest quality, conducted through various libraries and historical societies, and she utilized primary source material such as diaries, letters, wills, newspapers, journals, and court records.

Earle's particular interest in the importance of women in the settlement of the colonies is illustrated in *Colonial Dames and Good Wives* (1895), which concentrates on the roles of women in America from the first settlements to the American Revolution. Written at a time when little attention was paid to the presence of women in American history, the book recreates the domestic and social lives of colonial women, using diaries and journals written by women throughout the country. In several other works, such as *Diary of Anna Green Winslow; A Boston School Girl of 1771* (1894) and *The Life of Margaret Winthrop* (1895), Earle focuses on specific personalities to reveal the economic and social circumstances of women of the era.

Earle's *Home Life in Colonial Days* (1898), perhaps the most widely read and referred to of her books, provides a comprehensive account of the ways in which colonists lived and raised their families. Beginning with the types of homes lived in by the early settlers and how these homes were constructed, Earle then devotes chapters to food, drink, clothing, gardens, and even the evolution of lighting in colonial homes from pine-knots to whale-oil lamps. Most of the book is devoted to the plethora of domestic tasks that were executed by colonial women.

Earle considered *Two Centuries of Costume in America, 1620–1820* (1903) to be her finest work. The two volumes that comprise this study of American fashion, from the settlement of New England to the early years of the American republic, are invaluable to students of American history, design, and art history. Critics have praised the work for its glossary of terms and more than 350 illustrations. The most outstanding of these are the portraits Earle used to illustrate examples of the clothing worn by the colonists and to note the gradual changes in styles through the years.

Opposite page

Amelia

Earhart

Active in the Daughters of the American Revolution and the Society of Colonial Dames, Earle also supported the women's suffrage movement. In 1909, she nearly drowned when the ship on which she was sailing to Egypt was struck by another vessel and wrecked near the Nantucket lightship. Her health failed following the incident, and she died on February 16, 1911, on Long Island, New York.

COLLECTIONS:

Alice Morse Earle's papers are at the American Antiquarian Society, Worcester, Massachusetts, and in the Sophia Smith College, Smith College, Northampton, Massachusetts.

Barbara Morgan,
Melrose, Massachusetts

Earle, Sylvia (b. 1935).

See Mead, Sylvia Earle.

Earle, Victoria (1861–1907).

See Matthews, Victoria Earle.

East Franks, queen of.

See Liutgard (d. 885).

Eastern Jewel (1906–1948).

See Yoshiko Kawashima.

Eastlake, Elizabeth (1809–1893)

English writer. Name variations: Lady Elizabeth Eastlake. Born Elizabeth Rigby in Norwich, England, on November 17, 1809; died on October 2, 1893; daughter and sister of well-known surgeons; married Sir Charles Lock Eastlake (1793–1865, an English painter and art critic), in 1849.

After the death of her surgeon father when she was 12, Lady Elizabeth Eastlake lived in Heidelberg with her mother for two years, before returning to England. In 1836, her first article, a criticism of Goethe, was published. From 1842 on, as an art critic and woman of letters, she was a regular contributor to the *Quarterly Review,* for which she contributed an infamous commentary on *Jane Eyre* and the **Brontës.* That same year, she and her mother moved to Edinburgh, where she joined the social circle of critic John Wilson ("Christopher North"). After traveling in Germany and Russia, Eastlake also published *A Residence on the Shores of the Baltic* (1844).

When she was 40, Eastlake married Sir Charles Lock Eastlake, an eminent painter, and she took to painting during the couple's annual treks to Italy. Following her husband's death in Pisa in 1865, Eastlake edited her husband's work and that of her father; she also translated many works on art and completed the last volume, *The History of Our Lord in Art,* for **Anna Jameson's four-volume series, following Jameson's death.

SUGGESTED READING:

Eastlake, Lady. *The Journals and Correspondence of Lady Eastlake.* Edited by C. Eastlake Smith. 1895.

Eastman, Crystal (1881–1928).

See Balch, Emily Greene for sidebar.

Eastman, Linda.

See McCartney, Linda.

Eastwood, Alice (1859–1953)

Canadian-born American botanist and naturalist who was a pioneer in the environmental movement in California. Born on January 19, 1859, in Toronto, Canada; died in San Francisco, California, on October 30, 1953; daughter of Colin Skinner Eastwood and Eliza Jane (Gowdey) Eastwood; had one sister and brother; never married.

Much of Alice Eastwood's childhood was difficult. She lost her mother when she was six and was separated from her brother, who was left with relatives while her father retired to parts unknown to make the fortune that had so far eluded him. Alice and her sister were placed in Toronto's Oshawa Convent, a gloomy setting that provided little in the way of intellectual stimulation for a bright young girl interested in nature. A French priest at the convent taught Alice much about gardening, however. Friendship with a nun and the responsibilities of watching over her younger sister kept Alice occupied, and her characteristic optimism buoyed her spirits even in the darkest hours of her early life.

When Eastwood was 14, her father suddenly reappeared. Having established himself as a storekeeper in Denver, Colorado, he offered his daughters a home there. Alice jumped at the opportunity and quickly settled in, becoming an excellent pupil at East Denver High School. Once again financial stresses buffeted the Eastwood family, and Alice had to work while attending school. Her father hoped that she would quit school to earn money for the family, but she continued her studies and graduated as valedictorian in 1879. She then embarked on a teaching career at East Denver High School.

Although Alice Eastwood quickly earned a reputation as an excellent teacher and was respected by her students, she eagerly anticipated summer vacations when she would spend as much time as possible in the high Rockies—by train, buckboard stage, horseback, and on foot—identifying wildflowers and collecting specimens for her herbarium. Soon her enthusiasm for exploration became so well known locally that the railroad builder David Moffat issued her a free rail pass; Alice reciprocated his generous support by naming a plant she had discovered, *Penstemon moffatii,* in his honor.

When the famous English naturalist Alfred Russel Wallace visited Denver in 1887 and insisted that he wanted to explore nearby Gray's Peak, Eastwood was presented as the person best equipped to be his guide. The famous scientist in his 60s and the unknown amateur naturalist still in her 20s enjoyed three wonderful days in the mountains, spending their nights in rough miners' cabins and making it to the summit of Gray's Peak. Wallace, writing in his autobiography *My Life,* noted that he had found many new alpine plants on this adventure. Alice later recalled with equal enthusiasm, "We luxuriated here in plants that were altogether new to me."

By 1890, supported by a small but assured income from real-estate sales and rentals made by her and her father, Eastwood resigned from her teaching job. She now devoted her full time to her true love, botany. She toured California and met with botanists there who encouraged her to move to that state to continue her collecting activities. In 1892, she returned to California, settling in San Francisco where she accepted a modest assistantship at the California Academy of Sciences. Eastwood also took on the task of founding and directing the activities of the California Botanical Club. By 1894, she had succeeded *Katharine Brandegee as curator of the Herbarium at the Academy. Never interested in calling attention to her own achievements, she stated, "My desire is to help, not to shine."

From the start of her life in California, Eastwood undertook extensive field work. She explored little-known regions like the inner south Coast Ranges, where she discovered a number of hitherto uncatalogued plants and flowers. Hardy and energetic as well as enthusiastic, Eastwood investigated on foot many regions of California, often making friends with the men and women she met on lonely, isolated ranches. When she encountered ill and hungry women and their impoverished children, Eastwood always stopped to share her provisions with them; upon returning to San Francisco, she sent food and clothing back to the needy families she had met. "To me human beings are as interesting as the plants," she wrote, "and there were situations . . . that were unusual because of the isolation."

Although she was a bold explorer capable of traveling anywhere on her own, Eastwood was not a loner by nature. She enjoyed the company of others who loved nature and was a loyal member of the "Hill Tribe," a group of San Franciscans who enjoyed roaming about nearby Mt. Tamalpais on Sundays. Clad in a buttoned denim skirt she had designed herself, with a heavy cotton nightgown as a bustle, she walked four miles an hour, never tiring, while carrying her heavy plant presses on her back. When exploring the Sierras, she was a member of a men's hiking group, the Cross Country Club. Among the mountains she climbed were Mt. Shasta and Mt. Whitney, the latter with members of the Sierra Club.

By 1905, Eastwood had accumulated a first-rate botanical collection for the California Academy of the Sciences. Something told her to separate out the irreplaceable specimens and keep these in one place where she could easily find them in an emergency. That emergency came on April 18, 1906, when the San Francisco earthquake and fire devastated the city. Although her part of town did not feel the quake as much as other areas, Alice went to the Academy's building after breakfast and, finding it partially demolished and threatened by fire from nearby ruins, managed to get into the front hall. Making it to the herbarium on the sixth floor proved to be a considerable challenge in the wrecked building. Eastwood went up, as she described in a letter to the journal *Science,* "chiefly by holding on to the iron railing and putting [her] feet between the rungs."

Unable to save any books or any of her own possessions, "except my favorite lens, without which I should feel helpless," she was nevertheless able to rescue 1,211 botanical specimens by pitching them out the window. The military forbade possessions being taken out of the stricken area, but Eastwood pleaded that an exception be made for her specimens and the Academy's files that she had transported out via private conveyance. With the help of friends, the precious items were taken first to Russian Hill, and, when that seemed threatened, they were moved to Fort Mason.

During this time, Eastwood neglected the safety of her own home, which burned to the ground. She lost all her books, pictures and "many treasures that I prized highly" but took this in stride, remarking, "I regret nothing for I am rich in friends and things seem of small account." In a narrative of the disaster she wrote for the Academy, Eastwood said that she did not "feel the loss to be mine, but it is a great loss to the scientific world and an irreparable loss to California. My own destroyed work I do not lament, for it was a joy to me while I did it."

At age 47, Eastwood set out to recreate the botanical collection that had been destroyed. She returned to the valleys and mountains to recollect the lost specimens, and hopefully find a few new ones as well. Since there was no money for this project, she used her own small income. From this point until her death almost a half-century later, she did her share to rebuild the lost library of the Academy by purchasing books for it whenever she received gifts of money for her birthday. With the Academy hard hit by the disaster, the fate of its herbarium remained in limbo. Eventually, Eastwood obtained a job as a staff assistant while the situation at the Academy remained unresolved. But she had hope in its ultimate destiny, working as an unpaid researcher at the botany department of the University of California in Berkeley as well as visiting the National Herbarium in Washington, D.C., the New York Botanical Gardens, and the Gray Herbarium at Harvard.

Convinced she needed to add additional data to her growing collection, Eastwood traveled to Europe to check original plant specimens. Since the Academy was financially hard-pressed and no funds were available, she used her savings. At London's Museum of Natural History, she met scientists who knew and respected her work, and she also made important discoveries at the Royal Botanic Gardens at Kew and the Paris Natural History Museum. On the way back home, Eastwood received the call for which she had been hoping: the California Academy of Sciences had chosen her to rebuild its herbarium. They now had a choice plot of land in Golden Gate Park. In North American Hall, the Academy's new headquarters, Eastwood established a highly popular floral exhibition. Along with its excellent library, the herbarium quickly established itself as a major center of botanical research. From its founding in 1912 to 1949, Alice Eastwood added an astonishing 340,000 specimens to the herbarium, many of which she discovered and named.

With her cheerful personality and immense knowledge of plants and flowers, Eastwood became a key personality in the California horticultural scene, founding and leading several organizations, including the California Botany Club, the California Horticultural Society, and the California Spring Blossom and Wildflower Association. San Francisco's Businessmen's Garden Club enthusiastically voted her its "Sweet-heart." Convinced that scholarship and public education were two sides of the same coin, Eastwood published a wide variety of articles on cultivated plants for both popular garden magazines and scholarly journals. She was an unchallenged expert on regional plants and flowers, and California nursery workers were often heard to say, "If you do not know what it is, send it to Miss Eastwood."

Continuing to display enormous energy in her 70s and 80s, Alice Eastwood only rarely made concessions to her age. One such came in 1929 when she took on an assistant, John Thomas Howell. Until that time, she alone had taught the Academy's botanical classes. Though at times she accepted riding in an automobile driven by Howell as a substitute for her walking to places to collect specimens, Eastwood always maintained that ideally there was "no way so good for a knowledge of the plants as walking through a region." Despite her great scholarly knowledge and immense prestige in the world of botany, she remained at heart an unpretentious individual who enjoyed reading Henry James novels, the *Saturday Evening Post,* and mystery stories with equal pleasure. She loved to talk about memorable meals she had eaten, and enjoyed making jellies, preserves and pickles for herself and her many friends.

As Alice Eastwood became the "grand old lady" of the California Academy of Sciences, many honors were heaped upon her. These included a redwood grove in her name at Prairie Creek Redwoods State Park, a fuchsia named for her, as well as an Alice Eastwood lilac and an Alice Eastwood orchid. A rare California shrub, *Eastwoodia elegans,* and two botanical genera, *Eastwoodia* and *Aliciella,* were all named in her honor. She retired in 1949, at age 90, receiving the title of Curator Emeritus. The next year, 1950, she flew to Sweden to serve as honorary president of the Seventh International Botanical Congress. In a high point of her stay in Stockholm, the tiny, indomitable woman was seated in the chair of the great Linnaeus, the founder of biological nomenclature. Alice Eastwood remained extremely active during the last years of her life, passing on her wide knowledge to the younger generation, including a precocious ten-year-old boy, Peter S. Raven, with whom she compared field notes. Raven went on to become a world-famous botanist, evolutionary biologist, and director of the Missouri Botanical Garden in St. Louis. Eastwood continued participating in botanical circles in San Francisco until her death in that city on October 30, 1953.

SOURCES:

Bonta, Marcia. "Alice Eastwood," in *American Horticulturist*. Vol. 62, no. 10. October 1983, pp. 10–15.

Bonta, Marcia Myers. *Women in the Field: America's Pioneering Women Naturalists*. College Station: Texas A&M University Press, 1991.

Jackson, Nancy Beth. "Through Politicking for Plants, He Made His Garden Grow," in *The New York Times*. August 4, 1998, p. B11.

Moore, Patricia Ann. "Cultivating Science in the Field: Alice Eastwood, Ynes Mexia and California Botany" (Ph.D. Thesis, University of California, Los Angeles, 1996).

Nobles, Connie H. "Alice Eastwood (1859–1953), Botanist," in Benjamin F. Shearer and Barbara S. Shearer, eds. *Notable Women in the Life Sciences: A Biographical Dictionary*. Westport, CT: Greenwood Press, 1996, pp. 102–106.

Ross, Michael Elsohn. *Flower Watching with Alice Eastwood*. Minneapolis, MN: Carolrhoda Books, 1997.

Schwartz, Joel S. "Alice Eastwood (1859–1953)," in Louise S. Grinstein et al., eds., *Women in the Biological Sciences: A Biobibliographic Sourcebook*. Westport, CT: Greenwood Press, 1997, pp. 124–137.

Smith, Michael L. *Pacific Visions: California Scientists and the Environment, 1850–1915*. New Haven, CT: Yale University Press, 1987.

Warner, Nancy J. "Taking to the Field: Women Naturalists in the Nineteenth-Century West" (M.S. Thesis, Utah State University, 1995).

Wilson, Carol Green. *Alice Eastwood's Wonderland: The Adventures of a Botanist*. San Francisco, CA: California Academy of Sciences, 1955.

John Haag,
Assistant Professor of History,
University of Georgia, Athens, Georgia

Easty, Mary.

See Witchcraft Trials in Salem Village.

Eaton, Margaret O'Neale (c. 1799–1879).

See Eaton, Peggy.

Eaton, Peggy (c. 1799–1879)

Well-known and controversial figure of her day—implicated in the fall of Andrew Jackson's first Cabinet, the ascension of Martin Van Buren to the presidency, and the political eclipse of John C. Calhoun—who has been uniformly denied significance in histories of the American early republic. Name variations: Margaret O'Neale or O'Neill Eaton; Peggy O'Neill, O'Neal, or O'Neale; Margaret O'Neale Timberlake Buchignani Eaton. *(Like many aspects of Eaton's life, even her naming is contested. Though in a self-justifying autobiography written late in life she claims that no one called her by the familiar "Peggy," sources confirm that friends and enemies alike used this nickname. In her autobiography, she also anglicizes her maiden name to "O'Neil," though "O'Neale" is the name that appears on deeds signed by her father in the office of* the Recorder of Deeds in the District of Columbia; *other authors use "O'Neill" and "O'Neal." Though Eaton married Antonio Buchignani after John H. Eaton's death, after her divorce she won the right to resume using "Eaton.")* Born Margaret O'Neale in Washington City (present-day Washington D.C.) sometime in December 1799; died in the same city on November 9, 1879, after a short illness; eldest daughter of William O'Neale (an innkeeper) and **Rhoda Howell O'Neale** (sister of Richard Howell, governor of New Jersey); had three brothers, William, Robert and John, and two sisters, Mary and Georgianna; tutored at home; attended Mrs. Hayward's school in Washington until her early teens; spent one winter at Madame Nau's (or Madame Day's) school in New York City; married John Bowie Timberlake, on July 18, 1816 (died at sea, 1828); married John Henry Eaton, on January 1, 1829 (died 1856); married Antonio Buchignani, in June 1859; children: (first marriage) William Timberlake (1817–1818); **Virginia Timberlake**; **Margaret Timberlake Randolph** (b. 1824).

Grew up in Washington in the Franklin House, an inn for politicians; married John Bowie Timberlake (1816) and continued working in parents' taproom; met Senator John Henry Eaton, a guest at the inn (1818) and formed a ten-year relationship with him while husband at sea; following death of husband, married John Henry Eaton (1829); husband appointed secretary of war by President Jackson (1829), beginning "The Petticoat War," which lasted until 1831, ending with John Eaton's resignation; served in Florida as the governor's lady (1834–35) and in Spain as ambassador's wife (1835–40); returned to America (1840); widowed (1856); married Antonio Buchignani (1859), later divorced; wrote her autobiography (1873).

⌈W⌋hen historians go to write about Gen. Jackson's administration in the future and in the libraries find his life by James Parton, I desire to put this little volume in that he may hear the other side before going to write the history of that great man and his Cabinet.

—Peggy Eaton

"Pity me, my friends, I was born and raised in Washington!" declares Peggy Eaton in her autobiography, written in Philadelphia near the end of her life and published 50 years after her death. The drama is typical of Eaton, who seemed to enjoy center stage and whatever spotlight life offered. Sources on her are sparse—mostly historical novels—and, aside from her book, Eaton left few personal papers. Lacking any scholarly studies, historians must depend, then, on Eaton for her account, which is undoubtedly the way she would have wanted it.

Not only was Margaret O'Neale Eaton born in Washington, she spent most of her life there, and indeed her personal history is intimately tied to the city's growth. Both she and Washington were infants in 1799, the year Eaton claims, and most historians accept, as her birth year. With typical flair, she places the occasion of her birth in political context. According to family legend, two weeks after delivering this first child, Mrs. O'Neale sat up in bed to queue her husband's hair so he could march in George Washington's funeral procession. Eaton's mother Rhoda Howell had lived in Trenton, New Jersey, until the previous year, when she and her husband relocated to Washington City. A beautiful, refined, deeply religious woman, Rhoda also came from a well-placed family, for she was the sister of Richard Howell, governor of New Jersey. Surely she married "down" when she accepted William O'Neale's proposal. A cooper and tanner, with Ulster antecedents, he appears in accounts of Eaton's life as the prototypical Irish descendant—genial, talkative, gregarious. He was probably a "climber," too. For years, he boasted of his friendship with General Washington, but though William had been a major in the army, any acquaintance with Washington probably stemmed from William's present vocation as innkeeper.

William and Rhoda ran the Franklin House, a brick building (rare in turn-of-the-century Washington) in the First Ward, on I Street, between the president's house and Georgetown. "A wilderness city," Washington City at the time consisted of little more than a large and drafty, white-gray limestone president's house (in which *Abigail Adams was hanging her laundry) at one end of Pennsylvania Avenue and the Senate Wing of the Capitol at the other. The present-day Mall was a pasture cut by a sewage ditch. However, rough as the physical surroundings appeared, in the early 1800s Washington already had a formidable social structure in place.

Because of the city's crudeness and lack of housing, members of Congress and other officials rarely brought their wives and families to Washington during their terms of service, preferring to "bach" together at a public hostelry. The O'Neales' Franklin House was the only hotel in town for some years, and, even as other establishments opened, it remained the preeminent one. In contrast to the boarding houses which bedded several gentlemen of the government in one room (a custom that the Southerners especially deplored), the O'Neales offered separate rooms, transportation to and from the Capitol, and sumptuous meals. In addition, to men far from home, the growing O'Neale family provided a warm, convivial atmosphere.

Peggy Eaton and her various biographers present a cautiously acceptable picture of her as an adored child, her father's favorite and spoiled by the attentions of her many "uncles." It seems natural to suppose that the hotel guests, separated from their own children, would make much of a pretty, outgoing, little girl. Though Eaton had three brothers and two sisters, history has not heard much from them, so probably they did not get the attention from the boarders that she did. Certainly, Eaton had an uncommonly familiar way about men as she grew older, which bespeaks a childhood spent learning to maneuver among males.

Eaton attended Mrs. Hayward's school until her early teen years. According to Peggy, her father wanted the best education for his child, and she was well educated for a daughter of her time. The curriculum at Mrs. Hayward's included: "Orthography, reading, writing, arithmetic, bookkeeping, English grammar, composition, belles lettres, history, chronology, geography, the use of Globes and Maps, topography, drawing and painting." However, life in her father's taproom, which adjoined the hotel, provided her most useful learning. Not only did numbers of government workers and officials stay in the hotel, but in addition the barroom attracted many of the men who lived elsewhere. O'Neale's tavern was widely known as a political meeting place, and doubtless young Peggy observed many deals and discussions. By the time she reached puberty, her good looks and opportunities for contact with, and ease around, men ensured that Eaton was precocious when it came to knowledge of politics and sex.

Even when trying to project herself in her writing as a prim, well-bred innocent, Eaton proudly declared, "While I was still in pantalets and rolling hoops with other girls I had the attentions of men, young and old, enough to turn a girl's head." According to her own account, the nephew of the secretary of the navy poisoned himself with laudanum over her, the adjutant general of the U.S. Army proposed (though "all the wooings of December could not win May"), and Major Belton and Captain Root nearly fought a duel for her—all before her 16th birthday.

When her father, alerted by the crash of an unsteady flower pot, aborted her elopement with

Peggy
Eaton

Major Belton, he promptly packed her off to a New York school, variously called Madame Nau's and Madame Day's. Away from Washington for the first time, Eaton was miserable. However, she became good friends with **Julia Dickinson,** daughter of New Jersey's governor, and the circumstances of her matriculation made Eaton a romantic figure among her classmates. Her father asked New York Governor DeWitt Clinton to keep an eye on her, but despite such gubernatorial surveillance, Eaton saw one of her erstwhile suitors daily. The school's headmistress proved to be a sympathetic romantic and permitted parlor visits between Eaton and Captain Root. They planned another elopement, but Eaton abruptly fell out of love with her hapless swain—"I loved Root up to a certain moment, and then the hate I suddenly acquired for him was quite as delicious as the love I had borne." Homesick and repentant, she wrote her father: "Dear Father: For the Lord's sake come and take me home; and if you will do so I will promise to be the best girl you ever saw, and I assure you that under no circumstance shall either Root or Branch take me away from you." This feeble pun worked, and Peggy came home to Washington.

At 16, Eaton had achieved the beauty that would garner so much attention, both laudatory and condemnatory. Though descriptions of her vary, she seems to have possessed a fine, full figure and dark eyes surrounded by heavy lashes and curls of a dark brown bordering on red. She had not been home from school long when, according to her own account, she looked out of a window and spotted a young navy purser, John Bowie Timberlake. Eaton remarked to her mother, "Come here, mother. Here is my husband riding on horseback." Whether or not this demonstration of Peggy's prescience happened, she claims to have become engaged to the handsome blond sailor that evening, and they married three weeks later on July 18, 1816. (Popular stereotypes aside, 16 was an uncommonly young age for a girl to wed, even in the "frontier" town of Washington.)

Unfortunately, Eaton's choice of husband proved disappointing. John Timberlake drank heavily, and his fecklessness as a purser precluded his continuing at sea. Their son William was born the next year but died of a fever six months later. Another child, Virginia, followed, giving her parents great satisfaction, but in other ways their life together continued to deteriorate. William O'Neale bought his son-in-law a store to run, which Timberlake promptly bankrupted, forcing the young couple to move back into the family hotel. The situation steadily worsened with his proximity to the innkeeper's alcohol.

In 1818, John Henry Eaton, a senator from Tennessee, arrived at the Franklin House. Despite his centrality to Peggy Eaton's life and story, John Eaton's character and personality remain shadowy in most versions of what came to be known as the "Eaton Affair." At 28, he was one of the youngest senators in the country; contemporary observers describe a man possessed of light auburn hair, fine hazel eyes, and a countenance and bearing that signaled serene dignity.

John Eaton came to Washington from a thriving Tennessee law practice, with a family fortune increased by canny land speculation. In the war of 1812, he served a short and unremarkable stint as a private soldier. Washington City knew him when he arrived for his affiliation with, and as biographer of, General Andrew Jackson, with whom he had a long personal and political association. As a senator, John stood up for his friend Jackson during the invasion of Florida, defending him against those who tried to portray "Old Hickory" as a bloodthirsty madman. A young widower in 1818, John Eaton began a long tenure in Washington that would culminate ten years later with Jackson's presidential win in the election of 1828. John quickly ingratiated himself with the O'Neale-Timberlake menage. To help Timberlake recover some of the money he had lost as purser, John introduced a petition in Congress for his reimbursement. Despite three readings he initiated, the bill did not pass. When Timberlake, long idled by his bankruptcy, confessed that he wanted to go to sea again, John secured a post for him on the USS *Shark*. At the same time, he came to the aid of William O'Neale, who also faced bankruptcy. John found a buyer for the hotel, who renamed it Gadsby's. William and Rhoda started over, opening a small boarding house financed by—John Eaton.

In 1823, Andrew Jackson came to Washington, not to the former Franklin House but to the O'Neales' new, smaller Indian Queen, in preparation for his presidential run in 1824. There he came to know the O'Neales and wrote to his wife *Rachel Jackson that though the whole family was "amiable," his particular favorite was "Mrs. Timberlake," who "plays on the Piano Delightfully, & every Sunday evening entertains her pious mother with Sacred music to which we are invited." Though Jackson received a plurality of the popular vote in the 1824 election, he lost the presidency to John Quincy Adams, who benefitted from votes given him by Henry Clay. When Clay was appointed secretary of state, cries went up about "a corrupt bargain," thus ensuring Adams a single term and Clay no chance at the highest office in the land.

During this time, except for some trips back to Tennessee, John Eaton stayed with the O'Neales in their hotel. When Andrew and Rachel Jackson came to town, they stayed with the O'Neales as well. Timberlake remained at sea, stopping with his wife long enough to father another daughter, Margaret, born in 1824. During these short leaves, Timberlake enjoyed a close friendship with the Tennessee senator and, as his fiscal irresponsibility continued, depended on John's influence for subsequent posts. He even gave John Eaton power of attorney over his finances to build his family a house. Perhaps most important for later events, during these years Peggy Timberlake and John Eaton began to appear in public together. Washington hostesses soon knew that, like it or not, when they invited the increasingly important senator to an event, they got Mrs. Timberlake as well. Many hostesses did not like it, but only a few had position enough to afford offending the man closest to Andrew Jackson. *Elizabeth Monroe had, and she forbade the White House drawing rooms to John Eaton.

Apparently Peggy and John supplied Washington with gossip for several seasons, until 1828, a momentous year—Andrew Jackson was elected president, and John Timberlake died at sea. Though he died of natural causes, rumor whipped around Washington that Timberlake had cut his own throat in despair over his wife's infidelity. Soon after the election, John Eaton wrote to his friend, the president-elect, detailing the current slanders and expressing a wish to marry Peggy and "snatch her from that injustice of City gossipers who attend to everybody's reputation to the neglect of their own." However, he was aware that such a move would generate more talk—"The impossibility of escaping detraction and slander was too well credenced to me in the abuse of those more meritorious and deserving than I ever could hope to be"—and gently hinted that, despite his honorable intentions, the timing might not be right for such a move.

Jackson reacted promptly and succinctly, "Marry her and you will be in a position to defend her." John Eaton did—on January 1, 1829—while Washington murmured and whispered. ❧ Margaret Bayard Smith, Washington observer and no friend to Peggy, wrote in her crisp style, "Tonight Gen'l Eaton, the bosom friend and almost adopted son of Gen'l Jackson is to be married to a lady whose reputation, her previous connection with him both before and after her husband's death, has totally destroyed."

Days later, a delegation of Washington insiders paid a call on the president-elect and advised him that, though no doubt John Eaton should receive a post of some importance in the new administration, Jackson should not give him a Cabinet position which would force Peggy Eaton into direct social contact with the prominent ladies of Washington. When Jackson pressed for details, the men admitted that

"ladies" would not receive a woman of Mrs. Eaton's reputation. Jackson reacted ferociously. "Do you suppose that I have been sent here by the people to consult the ladies of Washington," he said, "as to the proper persons to compose my Cabinet?" A few days after his inaugural, Jackson appointed John Eaton secretary of war. The other members of the Cabinet included John C. Calhoun as vice-president; Calhoun supporters Samuel D. Ingham as secretary of treasury, John Branch as secretary of navy, and John Berrien as attorney general; and Jackson supporters Martin Van Buren as secretary of state, and William Barry as postmaster general.

Jackson's ire and stubbornness make emotional sense in light of his recent campaign for president. His opponents had made much political hay over Jackson's marriage to Rachel Robards, which took place before she formally divorced her first husband. Though the couple regularized their union a few years later, the campaign rhetoric depicted Rachel as an "adulteress" and whore. Apparently, Jackson kept the sordid details of the campaign from his wife. A few days before the Jacksons' departure for Washington, Rachel Jackson died, and popular legend has it that she died of a broken heart, either after seeing an opposition flyer or overhearing a conversation that portrayed her as a scarlet woman. Jackson arrived in Washington with a ready-made grudge against those whose nattering tongues had slandered his dead wife's name.

In some ways it is hard to discern whether society's reaction stemmed from Peggy Eaton's sexual past or her "publican" origins. Certainly the latter reason has merit. Though the accusations of Peggy's immorality centered on John Eaton, he seems not to have suffered any censure. The Washington upper-crust certainly showed skittishness over the coming of "the common

❧ **Smith, Margaret Bayard** (1778–1844)
American reporter of Washington social and political scene.
Born Margaret Bayard in Philadelphia, Pennsylvania, on February 20, 1778; died in Washington, D.C., in 1844; daughter of Colonel John Bayard of the Revolutionary Army; married Samuel Harrison Smith, in 1800.

Margaret Bayard Smith was the author of *A Winter in Washington; or, the Seymour Family* (2 vols. 1827) and *What is Gentility?* (1830); she was also a frequent contributor to *Sarah Josepha Hale's *Lady's Book* magazine.

man" into their midst in the person of Andrew Jackson. To a group of people who feared a world turned upside down by democracy, what could have appeared more emblematic (and threatening) than the meteoric social rise of a coarse and vulgar barmaid on the coattails of a military bumpkin? Her ally, Postmaster General William Barry, described her as "a daughter of a tavern-keeper belonging to the democracy," who "moved into the fashionable world . . . touch[ing] the pride of the self-constituted great."

The upstart needed a lesson. Most of the "ladies" of Washington—Cabinet wives and other hostesses—decided to freeze Eaton out. They would not attend events that she attended, not accept any of her invitations, and certainly not extend any. The first shot in what came to be known as the "Petticoat War" was fired at the Inaugural Ball, where the wives of the administration, led by **Floride Calhoun**, wife of John C. who was widely considered the probable successor to Jackson, cut Peggy Eaton dead. Floride enlisted **Emily Donelson**, the young bride of Andrew Jackson Donelson, the president's adopted son and secretary and herself the official White House hostess, Mrs. Ingham, Mrs. Branch, and Berrien's daughters. The only Cabinet wife who sided with Eaton was **Mrs. William Barry**.

Soon after the unpleasantness began, Jackson received a letter from Dr. Ely, a cleric in Philadelphia, charging Eaton with a variety of offenses, some of them quite extreme. Ely began by stating that Peggy Eaton had a notorious reputation from girlhood and that the respectable folk of Washington had long barred their houses to her. He related that a gentleman, the morning after the British minister's ball, had said at the breakfast table that "Mrs. Eaton brushed by him last night pretending not to know him; she had forgotten the time when she slept with him." As regards John Eaton, Ely claimed that John and Peggy had traveled and lodged together before their marriage and that Peggy had instructed the servants to call her children by the surname "Eaton" instead of "Timberlake." In addition, Ely asserted that while her husband was at sea, Mrs. Timberlake had suffered a miscarriage as a result of a driving accident. According to Ely's supposedly impeccable but unnamed sources, the physician arrived to find Mrs. Timberlake, attended by her mother, and together they joked that he was too late to see "a little Eaton."

Andrew Jackson's letter of refutation was longer than his inaugural address. In it, he dismissed most of the charges as baseless gossip, citing his own and Rachel's good opinion of Peggy

and his personal knowledge of Timberlake's devotion to his wife and to his friend John Eaton. The miscarriage story he dismissed out of hand as contrary to all good sense. Jackson took the accusations seriously enough to employ his own investigators to scour the hotel registers looking for incriminating entries (they found none) and to collect depositions attesting to Peggy Eaton's good character. In all, 93 pages of Jackson's papers are devoted to refuting these charges.

In the meantime, through a visit to Ely, John Eaton had discovered that a Washington minister, a Dr. Campbell, was the source of the miscarriage story. When Jackson confronted the cleric, Campbell attributed the tale to a doctor long dead. According to Jackson, Campbell asserted positively that the miscarriage had occurred in 1821. However, faced with proof that Timberlake had been in Washington during that year, the parson changed his mind and the date, to Jackson's disgust. In September 1829, Jackson called a Cabinet meeting to review all the evidence, written and verbal, in his possession. He also delivered the verdict—"She is as chaste as a virgin!"—effectively, in his mind, closing the case.

However, the "Eaton malaria" continued. Washington's social life underwent a massive transformation. The intricate calling rounds Washington women executed in their husbands' interests ground down. Many were afraid to move for fear of offending someone important. Martin Van Buren, a widower, led the Peggy supporters. Not only did he call on the Eatons, the only man in the Cabinet besides Barry to do so, and they on him, but he gave several parties and balls in their honor, embarrassing the other members of the president's Cabinet by tendering them invitations he knew they must refuse. He also enlisted some of the European diplomats, in America without their wives, to host social events and invite the Eatons. At one of these soirees, the wife of the Dutch minister, **Madame Huygens**, made a scene when she discovered she had been placed next to Peggy Eaton at table. Jackson decided her remarks constituted an insult to the United States, and only Van Buren's diplomacy averted an international incident.

The opposition suffered the initial casualties in the "Petticoat War." Jackson gave a dinner with mandatory attendance and placed Eaton at his right side, demonstrating that all the furor had only endeared her to him. Emily Donelson, after a prolonged tussle with her Uncle Andrew, during which she steadfastly refused to receive Peggy Eaton, either left for, or was sent back to, Tennessee, replaced as White House host by

Mary Ann Lewis, daughter of Eaton supporter William B. Lewis.

More seriously, as Van Buren's star rose, Calhoun's fell. Initially, Calhoun took the stand that, though he harbored no personal animus against John Eaton, this purely social matter fell strictly under his wife's control. Jackson grew increasingly impatient with this excuse and soon suspected that Calhoun had concocted the whole affair to destroy his administration. Jackson had always ascribed the attacks against Peggy to the machinations of unscrupulous politicians; at first, he accused Henry Clay of engineering them, but because of Floride's insistence on her position, John Calhoun fell under presidential suspicion. Soon it came out that John Calhoun had condemned General Jackson's actions in Florida and that he was the anonymous author of South Carolina's position on nullification—an early "states' rights" position that protected slavery and, even the 1820s, was perceived as a threat to the sanctity of the Union, an ideal especially close to Jackson's heart. Though these differences between John Calhoun and Andrew Jackson had long roots, the Eaton affair brought them to the surface and further polarized the president and members of his Cabinet.

By the spring of 1831, the Washington situation looked desperate. Jackson could accomplish nothing with his frozen Cabinet. Contemporary Washington observers fully realized the implications of the Eaton affair. John Quincy Adams cynically remarked, "The Administration party is split up into a blue and a green faction upon this point of morals but the explosion has been hitherto deferred. Calhoun leads the moral party, Van Buren the frail sisterhood; and he is notoriously engaged in canvassing for the Presidency by paying court to Mrs. Eaton." Daniel Webster, sage of American politics, displayed his famed prescience: "It is odd, but the consequence of this desperate turmoil in the social and fashionable world may determine who shall succeed the present chief magistrate."

Martin Van Buren suggested a way out—he would resign, perhaps forcing the troublemakers to resign as well. John Eaton protested that since he and his family had caused the trouble, he should be the one to resign. In the end, they both did. Newspapers outside Washington did not know what to make of this development, unaware of the role Secretary Eaton's wife had played. Berrien, Branch, and Ingham were slow to take the hint, and in the end Jackson had to force them to step down. The three politicians went back to their hometowns and embarked on a bitter writing campaign, tearing into Jackson and John Eaton and bringing Peggy Eaton's name into print and national prominence for the first time.

The newspapers had a field day. **Queena Pollack**'s extensively researched 1931 historical novel, *Peggy Eaton: Democracy's Mistress,* presents a comprehensive and colorful account of the volcanic reaction of the national press and the electorate's reaction. Pro- and anti-Peggy groups erupted in every major city. Editors portrayed Peggy Eaton as "Bellona—Goddess of War" when the story of her brush with the Dutch minister's wife came out. Writers speculated that a woman controlled the White House, poisoning the president's mind. Political observers even attributed John Eaton's late Cabinet post to his wife's wiles, and the administration suffered from comparisons to corrupt European courts of old. Soon elements of the American press regularly referred to Eaton as "The American Pompadour" (***Jeanne-Antoinette Poisson, duchesse de Pompadour**).

In her autobiography, Eaton is oddly reticent about this time. Her purpose in writing her story 60 years after these events was to refute portrayals of her as a strumpet or a schemer in books and articles about the Jackson era. Eaton treats this episode only as the saga of a wronged woman, ignoring all the political ramifications. She spends most of the book painting a picture of herself, from childhood on, as a pure and pious Christian, well regarded by all who really knew her and the subsequent stories about her all lies constructed from base political motives. In her zeal to justify her life, she commits some easily confirmed historical errors, which, coupled with the saintly portrait she presents and her disavowal of her own political actions and motivations, seriously call into question the validity of her hindsight view of history. Because of these flaws, historians have either dismissed Eaton's story as politically insignificant or perpetuated the early "objective" depictions of her as a loose woman and political dupe.

In the meantime, while the newspapers were trumpeting the newly revealed events of the last two years, Jackson chose another Cabinet and got on with the business of government. John C. Calhoun's hopes of succeeding Jackson as president were dashed. His later political career is notable chiefly for his central role in the Southern secessionist movement. On the other hand, Martin Van Buren's loyalty and his "sacrifice" of his position endeared him to "Old Hickory," and he became Andrew Jackson's vice-president and successor. Never again did Peggy and John Eaton occupy so prominent a place in American politics. They remained in Washington for a short time, until John was appointed governor of Florida. The Eatons occupied the governor's mansion until John accepted the post of ambassador to Spain. The Eatons served there with Peggy's daughters for five years, and Peggy was, by all accounts, a tremendous hit, enjoying a close relationship with ◄❦ **Maria Christina I** (1806–1878). The family returned to Washington where Eaton became a prominent Washington host and John practiced law. When her daughter Margaret and son-in-law John Randolph died, Eaton adopted their four children.

In 1856, John Henry Eaton died, leaving Peggy Eaton a well-off and respectable personage in the Capital. In 1859, she again shocked her world by marrying her grandchildren's dancing master, a young Italian immigrant named Antonio Buchignani who, at 20, was 40 years younger than his wife. For five years, they defied the social predictions and lived happily, moving from Washington to New York City, but then Antonio ran off with Eaton's fortune and her granddaughter Emily. Peggy divorced him and resumed the last name "Eaton."

Now in financially straitened circumstances, she and her grandson John moved to Philadelphia, where he was able to get a government job. While they were there, James Parton published his *Life of Andrew Jackson*, which portrayed Peggy as a saucy barmaid. The pastor of her church, Reverend Charles Deems, to whom she turned for advice in dealing with these attacks, advised her to write her memoirs in refutation. She did so in 1873 and then entrusted them to him, to be published at her death. Unfortunately, because of Deems' death, they would not appear until 1932. Later that year, she and John moved back to Washington, where she lived in seclusion until the press, and then the Washington public, rediscovered her. She spent her final years giving occasional press interviews and being treated as a grande dame of American politics.

Margaret O'Neale Timberlake Buchignani Eaton died in the city she loved, on November 9, 1879. During her last morning of life, she repeated in a "clear, firm voice" the hymn "I Will Not Live Alway." At high noon, she died. Her purported last words were, "I am not afraid to die, but this is such a beautiful world to leave."

SOURCES:
Bassett, John Spencer. *The Life of Andrew Jackson.* NY: Doubleday, Page, 1916.

Bowers, Claude G. *The Party Battles of the Jackson Period.* Boston, MA: Houghton Mifflin, 1922.

Eaton, Margaret. *The Autobiography of Peggy Eaton.* NY: Scribner, 1932.

Nevin, David. "To the President, Peggy Eaton was Chaste Indeed," in *Smithsonian.* Vol. 23. May 1992, pp. 84–97.

Parton, James. *Life of Andrew Jackson.* Vol. III. NY: Mason Brothers, 1860.

Pollack, Queena. *Peggy Eaton: Democracy's Mistress.* NY: Minton, Balch, 1931.

Poore, Perley Benjamin. *Perley's Reminiscences of Sixty Years on the National Metropolis.* 2 vols. Philadelphia, PA: Hubbard Brothers, 1886.

Remini, Robert V. *Andrew Jackson and the Course of American Freedom, 1822–1832.* Vol. II. NY: Harper & Row, 1981.

Smith, Margaret Bayard. *The First Forty Years of Washington Society.* NY: Scribner, 1906.

SUGGESTED READING:
Adams, Samuel Hopkins. *The Gorgeous Hussy.* NY: Grossett and Dunlap, 1934.

Dillon, Mary. *The Patience of John Morland.* NY: Doubleday, Page, 1909.

James, Marquis. *Andrew Jackson: Portrait of a President.* NY: Bobbs-Merrill, 1937.

Keats, Charles B. *Petticoat War in the White House: A Novelized Biography of Peggy O'Neill.* NY: Heritage Hall, 1973.

Lewis, Alfred Henry. *Peggy O'Neal.* Philadelphia, PA: The American News Company, 1903.

Phillips, Leon. *That Eaton Woman: In Defense of Peggy O'Neale Eaton.* Barre, MA: Barre Publications, 1974.

COLLECTIONS:
Adams, John Quincy. *The Adams Papers.* Published by the Adams Manuscript Trust through the Massachusetts Historical Society, Boston, MA, Reel 15.

Bayard Papers and Jackson Papers, Library of Congress.

RELATED MEDIA:
The Gorgeous Hussy (VHS, 105 minutes), highly fictionalized account, starring ***Joan Crawford**, Lionel Barrymore, Melvyn Douglas, James Stewart, Robert Taylor and Franchot Tone, directed by Clarence Brown, Metro-Goldwyn-Mayer, 1936.

Catherine A. Allgor,
Assistant Professor of History,
Simmons College, Boston, Massachusetts

Eberhardt, Isabelle (1877–1904)

Swiss-born author, traveler and adventurer who ventured into little-known areas of North Africa in the guise of a Muslim man and, through her writings, presented an often romanticized vision of Muslim life to her European readers. Name variations: (pseudonyms) Nicolas Podolinsky and Si Mahmoud Saadi. Born Isabelle Wilhelmine Marie Eberhardt on February 17, 1877, in Geneva, Switzerland; died in a flash flood in Ain Sefra, Algeria, on October 21, 1904; illegitimate daughter of Nathalie Eberhardt de Moerder (a Prussian aristocrat) and Alexander Trophimowsky

Maria Christina I. See Isabella II for sidebar.

(a tutor, scholar and anarchist); educated by father at home; married Slimène Ehnni, on October 17, 1901, in Marseilles, France; no children.

Raised in an eccentric family in Geneva and encouraged to wear male clothing from a young age; traveled to Algeria with her mother and contributed essays on North African life to Parisian magazines (1897); participated in a riot against French colonialism and was forced to return to Geneva to avoid arrest (March 1898); after father's death, returned to North Africa (1899); presented herself as a Muslim man, Si Mahmoud Saadi, and traveled to the souf region of Southern Algeria; sojourned briefly in Marseilles and Paris, attempting to launch her career as a writer (1899–1900); returned to Algeria and met future husband, Slimène Ehnni, a non-commissioned officer in the French forces in Algeria; initiated into the Qadryas, a Sufi Islamic order; was almost assassinated by a member of a rival Islamic order (1901); expelled from Algeria (1901) and permitted to return only after securing French citizenship through marriage to Ehnni; worked under General Hubert Lyautey, engaged in espionage for French forces planning an incursion into Morocco (1903); killed in a flash flood in Ain Sefra, Algeria (1904).

Selected publications—in French: Dans l'ombre chaude de l'Islam *(1905);* Notes de route *(1908);* Pages d'Islam *(1920);* Trimardeur *(1922);* Amara le forçat *(1923);* Mes Journaliers *(1923);* Contes et Paysages *(1925);* Au pays des sables *(1944). In English translation:* The Passionate Nomad *(1987);* Vagabond *(1988). Articles in French in various periodicals under the pseudonyms Nicolas Podolinsky and Mahmoud Saadi.*

The flash flood that swept through Ain Sefra, Algeria, on October 21, 1904, took the town by surprise. No rain had fallen for a long time, but precipitation in the mountains caused a build-up of water that swept downwards towards the unsuspecting town, cascading out of the river bed and destroying everything in its path. The next day, when the torrent had subsided, French soldiers stationed in Ain Sefra dug through the rubble searching for the bodies of victims. Beneath the fallen beams of one house, they discovered a figure attired in the garb of an Arab cavalryman. But this was no Arab, nor even a man, but a female journalist and sometime spy for the French military, Isabelle Eberhardt. The iconoclastic path that took Isabelle Eberhardt from her birthplace in Switzerland to death in the water and debris of Ain Sefra a scant 27 years later would make her more fa-

mous—and infamous—after her demise than she had ever been during her brief life.

Eberhardt was born on February 17, 1877, in Geneva, Switzerland, the illegitimate daughter of **Nathalie Eberhardt de Moerder,** the widow of a Russian general, and Alexander Trophimowsky, the erstwhile tutor of the de Moerder children and a former Russian Orthodox priest. Although Trophimowsky's paternity was never openly acknowledged, he acted as a father to young Isabelle, her older brother Augustin, who may also have been Trophimowsky's child, and the three de Moerder children. De Moerder and Trophimowsky raised their children in a villa they had purchased on the outskirts of Geneva. Perhaps fearful that their adulterous relationship (Trophimowsky had a wife and children in Russia) would affront the bourgeois morality of Geneva, the couple lived a reclusive life. The children were rarely allowed off the villa grounds and were educated at home by Trophimowsky, who imbued them with his anarchistic beliefs, in addition to training them in several languages.

Eberhardt's parents treated her more as a boy than a girl, and, from an early age, Eberhardt abetted this adoption of a male persona. Visitors to the villa understandably mistook young Isabelle for a boy when they saw her attired in men's clothes performing traditionally masculine tasks such as chopping wood. Trophimowsky also stipulated that, for her own protection, Eberhardt could visit Geneva only if she wore male clothing. As a teenager, Eberhardt had herself photographed in the uniform of a French sailor and in the garb of an Arab man. For her earliest journalistic efforts, she adopted a masculine pseudonym. Thus, Eberhardt's later transvestism was not merely a device to facilitate her entrée into Muslim society, but also a natural outgrowth of her upbringing.

Eberhardt's fascination with North Africa also developed in her childhood. She studied classical Arabic and read the Koran with her father. She and her brother Augustin devoured the orientalist novels of Pierre Loti set in the "exotic" Middle East and dreamed of journeying to North Africa themselves. While Augustin was able to visit Algeria briefly, Isabelle, for the time being, contented herself with establishing a correspondence under the male pseudonym "Mahmoud Saadi," with Abou Naddara, an Egyptian intellectual living in Paris. Under her own name, she also corresponded with Eugène Letord, a lonely French officer stationed in southern Algeria who had advertised in the newspapers for a pen pal.

In May 1897, Eberhardt and her mother left Geneva for Bône, Algeria, where some acquaintances of the family helped the two women settle in. The move may have been motivated by a desire to escape the increasingly repressive atmosphere of their Geneva home, dominated by the paranoid Trophimowsky, or by concern for Mme de Moerder's failing health. Although Algeria had been a French colony since 1830, the European community there had remained aloof from the native population. Eberhardt's acquaintance in Algeria, a European woman named **Cécile David,** captured the typical attitude of the *colons* (the colonial residents of Algeria) when she wrote to Eberhardt, "My dear Isabelle, what a filthy race these Arabs are!"

Eberhardt and her mother did not share these feelings, however. They quickly moved out of their comfortable residence in the European quarter of Bône and into rooms in the Arab section. Mme de Moerder soon converted to Islam. (Eberhardt, who never acknowledged Trophimowsky's paternity, believed that her father had been a Russian Muslim and thus saw no need for a formal conversion to Islam for herself.) Eberhardt also fashioned the identity that would shape her life in North Africa from this point until her death seven years later. She presented herself as "Mahmoud Saadi," an Arabic male student. Attired in North African men's clothing, Eberhardt roamed freely throughout the Arab sections of Bône, soon becoming fluent in colloquial Arabic. Her experiences formed the basis for several essays published in Parisian journals under the pen name Nicolas Podolinsky.

On November 28, 1897, this interesting life came to an abrupt halt when Mme de Moerder died of heart failure. For several months, Eberhardt remained alone in Bône, apparently too numbed by her mother's death either to return to Switzerland or to reestablish her life in Algeria on a new footing. In March 1898, however, Eberhardt joined in a riot against the French authorities in Algeria. Although she had disguised herself as Mahmoud Saadi, she feared that the colonial government would discover her allegiance to the Muslim rioters and arrest her. Eberhardt quietly slipped out of Bône and returned to Geneva.

The situation at the family villa in Geneva was not happy. Trophimowsky and Eberhardt's half-brother Vladimir had been living in paranoid seclusion, their only occupation the tending of cactus plants grown in hothouses on the villa grounds. Shortly after Eberhardt's return, the always unstable Vladimir committed suicide.

Trophimowsky, already gravely ill with cancer, lingered on until May 1899. Although Eberhardt apparently nursed him devotedly, she also found time during this interlude in Geneva to become briefly engaged to a young Turkish diplomat attached to the embassy in Paris.

Trophimowsky had attempted to provide financially for Eberhardt and her brother Augustin after his death. However, members of both the Trophimowsky and de Moerder families in Russia quickly challenged these arrangements. Eberhardt would never benefit financially from her parents' deaths; her share of the estate was soon eaten up by legal costs. From this point on, money worries haunted her. Indeed, a mere two years later, Eberhardt summed up her situation as total poverty: "No food, no money and no heat," she wrote in her diary. "I have begun to make a point of going to people's houses to *eat,* for the sole purpose of keeping fit, something that would have been *anathema* in the old days."

Soon after her father's death, with a small sum of money held in her own name, Eberhardt returned to North Africa, this time to Tunisia. Again adopting masculine garb, she presented herself as a Muslim student traveling, as was the custom, from one *zawiya* (home of a holy man) to another, across the North African desert. Eberhardt claimed that her masculine disguise successfully hid her sex and nationality from her Muslim companions. She wrote, in reference to a Tunisian tax collector with whom she traveled and worked, "Si Larbi never suspected that I was a woman, he called me his brother Mahmoud, and I shared his nomadic life and his work for two months." It seems more likely, however, as many of Eberhardt's contemporaries recognized and as most of her later biographers have argued, that few of the men with whom she associated in such close quarters could have failed to discern her true identity. If her male companions neglected to raise the issue with Eberhardt, it was probably owing more to their tact, discretion, and tolerance for eccentric behavior than to the efficacy of her disguise. A French friend later confirmed that the Algerians with whom she associated, "knew that this svelte cavalier in her immaculate white burnous and soft red leather boots was a woman. The innate courtesy of the Arabs is such that in her presence none of them ever made any allusion, even by so much as a wink, to a quality she did not want to acknowledge."

One question that has tantalized Eberhardt's biographers has been the nature of her

Isabelle
Eberhardt

sexuality. Certainly sexual opportunities in North Africa were much more varied and more readily available than in straight-laced Geneva. Dressed as a Muslim man, Eberhardt enjoyed access to areas and experiences that would have been forbidden to her as a European woman.

Eberhardt apparently had a taste for the seedier areas of town, where quick and anonymous sexual encounters were the norm. As Mahmoud Saadi, she visited brothels, although only as an observer, not as a participant. Despite her penchant for men's clothes and for experiences generally reserved only for men, it appears that Eberhardt was heterosexual.

In addition to her transvestism, Eberhardt took advantage of differing cultural norms to engage in other forms of behavior usually closed off to European women. She smoked *kef* (hashish), as well as ordinary tobacco cigarettes, to both of which substances she appears to have been addicted. What little money Eberhardt possessed would often be used to purchase those substances rather than food or rent. Despite her adherence to Islam, Eberhardt was also a hard drinker and often finished an evening in a drunken stupor or a *kef*-induced haze. She justly feared that people viewed her as merely a "drunken, plate-smashing degenerate." Such excesses eventually took their toll on Eberhardt's health and physical appearance. Her devotion to narcotics and alcohol rather than food made her painfully thin (some biographers speculate that she was anorexic) and by her mid-20s she had lost most of her teeth.

As for myself, all I want is a good horse as a mute and loyal companion, a handful of servants hardly more complex than my mount, and a life as far away as possible from the hustle and bustle I happen to find so sterile in the civilised world where I feel so deeply out of place.

—Isabelle Eberhardt

Eberhardt's lifestyle also proved to be incompatible with her dream of becoming a great writer. Her plans to author a novel set in North Africa and to continue her travel writing languished under the spell of *kef* and alcohol. In late 1899, however, concerned about her lack of artistic productivity as well as by her diminishing financial resources, Eberhardt returned to Europe. Dividing her time between Paris and Marseilles, where her newly married brother Augustin had settled, Eberhardt furthered her connections in the French literary world and also managed to complete her novel and start another.

The siren song of North Africa, however, soon proved too strong to be resisted. In July 1900, Eberhardt arrived in Algiers and from there soon set off for El Oued, an oasis town in the southern part of Algeria. At some point during that journey, she met "the great love of my life," Slimène Ehnni, a noncommissioned officer in a *spahi* regiment stationed in El Oued. The *spahis* were a French army unit. Although the soldiers were Algerians, they had been greatly Europeanized through their contact with the French military. Ehnni, unlike most Algerians, was even a French citizen. Their love affair, as recorded by Eberhardt, was heightened by the exotic romance of the desert. Attempting to keep their relationship secret, the two would ride their horses to a palm-studded oasis outside the town, make love, and then spend the night on the sand under the desert sky, wrapped in their burnouses against the cold.

Ehnni was a Sufi Muslim and a member of the Qadriya order, an 11th-century sect with strong mystical beliefs. Eberhardt, too, soon became an initiate of the Qadriya order, an unusual honor for a European and even more so for a woman. As a Qadriya, Eberhardt enjoyed the rare pleasure of participating in a *fantasia,* two days of pageantry, festivities and equestrianship in the desert for the purpose of welcoming one of the spiritual leaders of the order.

Eberhardt's Qadriya status may also have led to a dramatic attempt on her life. With her fellow Qadriya initiates, Eberhardt journeyed from El Oued to rendezvous with one of their religious leaders as he set forth on a pilgrimage. At a resting point in the village of Béhima, Eberhardt was seated, her head down as she scrutinized a letter to be translated. Suddenly she felt a sharp blow to her head and two more on her arm and realized that a man she had never seen before was attacking her with a saber. The attacker was pulled off by two Qadriyas. When Eberhardt asked what she had done to him to provoke the attack, he answered, "Nothing, you've never done anything to me, I don't know you, but I have to kill you." The attacker, however, proved to be an initiate of a rival Sufi order, and this may have been the motivating factor in his attempted assassination of Eberhardt.

At the trial of Eberhardt's assailant, however, the French authorities portrayed the crime as arising from completely different motives. Increasingly nervous about growing anti-French sentiment among Algerian Muslims, the colonial authorities depicted the attack as an assault on a European Christian by a Muslim fanatic. With a harsh sentence for Eberhardt's assailant, they hoped to deter other Islamic militants from attacks on Europeans. Eberhardt's attacker—following the lead of his counsel—deflected this argument in his testimony. He claimed to have known that Eberhardt was a Muslim and testified that because Eberhardt had disgraced Islam through her transvestism and dissolute living he felt compelled to assassinate her. The court, however, found him guilty and sentenced him to hard labor for life, a draconian sentence. Eberhardt was appalled at this harsh punishment and even lodged an appeal on behalf of her attacker. She wrote that "Abdallah [her assailant] was the instrument of people who had an interest—real or imagined—in getting rid of me." In part because of Eberhardt's advocacy, Abdallah's sentence was commuted to ten years.

Eberhardt even came to believe that the attack might have been divinely ordained for the purpose of allowing her to become a *maraboute* (Muslim holy woman). Eberhardt claimed that the desire to follow a religious path had struck her "out of the blue" on the day Abdallah was jailed. She confided to her diary her belief that she would "have no trouble reaching a spiritual goal like that." Although her "unlimited devotion" to Islam appears genuine, it is doubtful that Muslim society would have accepted an eccentric and dissolute European as a religious leader.

Although the colonial authorities had used Eberhardt's mishap and Abdallah's trial to strike a blow against the perceived threat of Islamic fanaticism, they too were longing to be rid of this strange woman who mingled with Muslims and wore men's clothing. The French authorities had kept a close watch on Eberhardt since her first visit to Algeria. Her lifestyle immediately made her suspect in the eyes of the conservative colonial authorities. The head of the Arab Bureau in El Oued had written upon first meeting Eberhardt that in addition to her espousing "quite advanced ideas" she was "a neurotic and unhinged, and I'm inclined to think that she has come to El Oued principally to satisfy unhindered her dissolute tastes and her penchant for natives in a place where there are few Europeans." However, the French authorities also feared that Eberhardt, with her journalistic connections, was involved in press attacks against the colonial government and French army in Algeria. Although Eberhardt protested her loyalty to France, claiming to be "just a dreamy eccentric anxious to lead a free, nomadic life," the colonial government expelled her from Algeria immediately after the completion of Abdallah's trial. Since Eberhardt was officially a citizen of Russia, not of France, she had no legal recourse.

Eberhardt returned dejectedly to her brother Augustin and his family in Marseilles. She was desolate at being separated from Ehnni and from the land she loved. Her one hope was to marry Ehnni, whose French citizenship (which carried with it the right to live in French territory, including Algeria) would be extended to his wife

should he marry. The military authorities had initially forbidden Ehnni from marrying, but after Eberhardt appealed directly to the colonial minister in Paris they relented. The two married in Marseilles on October 17, 1901, Eberhardt dressed, for once, in women's clothes and a wig to hide her shorn head. She warned Ehnni that she did not envision their union as the traditional Muslim marriage; she wrote, "I am also your brother Mahmoud, the servant of God before I am the servant that being an Arab wife entails. And I do *not want*, you understand, you to prove unworthy of the beautiful dreams I have for us both."

Ehnni resigned his army post, and the newly married couple returned happily to Algeria. As a result of letters written to the Algerian press at the time of the trial, Eberhardt made several new acquaintances in Franco-Algerian literary circles. One of these, the journalist Victor Barrucand, was to play a prominent role in popularizing Eberhardt's writings and building up the myth of the "passionate nomad" associated with Eberhardt after her untimely death. In late 1903, Barrucand also mentioned Eberhardt to General Hubert Lyautey, army commander in the southwestern part of Algeria who was planning a military incursion into neighboring Morocco. Lyautey realized immediately that Eberhardt, with her knowledge of Islam and Algerian culture, as well as her journalistic experience, would be the perfect spy for the French military in areas closed off to most Europeans. Eberhardt traveled throughout the Moroccan border region writing articles about the political situation and about the local peoples for French journals and also providing Lyautey with crucial information. By autumn 1904, however, Eberhardt's always fragile health had curtailed her espionage activities as well as her writing. Exhausted, she headed for the town of Ain Sefra and its hospital.

Although her relationship with her husband had apparently been deteriorating for some time, owing perhaps to Eberhardt's prolonged absences on reconnaissance missions for Lyautey, Ehnni rejoined her in Ain Sefra. He later recalled the events of October 21, 1904, when the flash flood inundated Ain Sefra:

> We were on the balcony of my room on the first floor. Suddenly there was a roar like a procession of wagons. It came nearer. I didn't understand. The weather was calm. There was no rain, no storm. In a minute, the water came down the river bed, rising up like a wall, running like a galloping horse, at least two meters high, dragging along trees, furniture, bodies of animals and men. I saw

the danger and we fled. The torrent caught us up in it. How did I get out? I've no idea. My wife was carried away.

After Eberhardt's body had been recovered, General Lyautey ordered his troops to search the ruins of Ain Sefra for any of her manuscripts or other writings. The scraps that were eventually discovered were forwarded to Barrucand, Eberhardt's self-appointed literary executor. Barrucand decided to rework her fragments into a romantic novel set in the exotic Sahara. The resulting book, *Dans l'ombre chaude d'Islam* (In the Warm Shadow of Islam), published in November 1905, was an instant success, going into three editions and selling over 13,000 copies. Barrucand, who listed himself as co-author of the work, reaped the financial windfall from this bestseller and from subsequent publications of Eberhardt's other writings which he compiled and edited.

Barrucand's presentation of Eberhardt as a sensuous, passionate, and free-spirited adventurer ensured her in death the celebrity denied to her in life. And, in many respects, this glamorous portrayal of Eberhardt is accurate. Yet, her life was also one of poverty, physical hardship, and loneliness. Isabelle Eberhardt was, indeed, as she described herself, "a nomad who has no country besides Islam and neither family nor close friends[;] I shall wend my way through life until it is time for that everlasting sleep inside the grave."

SOURCES:

Clancy-Smith, Julia. "The 'Passionate Nomad' Reconsidered," in *Western Women and Imperialism*. Nupur Chaudhuri and Margaret Strobel, eds. Bloomington: Indiana University Press, 1992.

Eberhardt, Isabelle. *The Passionate Nomad: The Diary of Isabelle Eberhardt*. Boston, MA: Beacon Press, 1987.

Hart, Ursula Kingsmill. *Two Ladies of Colonial Algeria*. Athens, OH: Ohio University Center for International Studies, 1987.

Kobak, Annette. *Isabelle: The Life of Isabelle Eberhardt*. London: Chatto & Windus, 1988.

Mackworth, Cecily. *The Destiny of Isabelle Eberhardt*. London: Routledge & Kegan Paul, 1951.

COLLECTIONS:

Isabelle Eberhardt archive at Aix-en-Provence, France.

Mary A. Procida,
Visiting Assistant Professor of History,
Temple University, Philadelphia, Pennsylvania

Eberhart, Mignon G. (1899–1996)

American writer of mystery, crime, suspense, romance and historical fiction. Born on July 6, 1899, in Lincoln, Nebraska; died on October 8, 1996, in Greenwich, Connecticut; daughter of William Thomas and Margaret Hill (Bruffey) Good; attended Nebraska Wesleyan University, 1917–20; married Alanson C. Eberhart (a civil engineer), on December 29, 1923 (divorced); married John P. Hazen Perry, in 1946 (divorced); remarried Alanson C. Eberhart, 1948.

Awards: Scotland Yard Prize (1930), for While the Patient Slept; D.Litt., Nebraska Wesleyan University (1935); Mystery Writers of America Grand Master award (1970); Malice Domestic Lifetime Achievement award (1994).

Selected writings: (mystery novels; all published by Random House, New York City, except as noted) The Patient in Room 18 (Doubleday, New York City, 1929, rev. ed., Popular Library, New York City, 1972); While the Patient Slept (Doubleday, 1930); The Mystery of Hunting's End (Doubleday, 1930); From This Dark Stairway (Doubleday, 1931); Murder by an Aristocrat (Doubleday, 1932, published in England as Murder of My Patient, John Lane, 1934); The White Cockatoo (Doubleday, 1933); The Dark Garden (Doubleday, 1933, published in England as Death in the Fog, John Lane [London], 1934); The House on the Roof (Doubleday, 1935); Fair Warning (Doubleday, 1936); Danger in the Dark (Doubleday, 1936); The Pattern (Doubleday, 1937, published as Pattern of Murder, Popular Library, 1948); Hasty Wedding (Doubleday, 1938); The Glass Slipper (Doubleday, 1938); Brief Return (Collins, London, 1939); The Chiffon Scarf (Doubleday, 1939); The Hangman's Whip (Doubleday, 1940); Strangers in Flight (Bantam, 1940, enlarged edition published as Speak No Evil, Random House, 1941); With This Ring (1941); Wolf in Man's Clothing (1942); The Man Next Door (1943); Unidentified Woman (1943); Escape the Night (1944); Wings of Fear (1945); The White Dress (1946); Five Passengers from Lisbon (1946); Another Woman's House (1947); House of Storm (1949); Hunt with the Hounds (1950); Never Look Back (1951); Dead Men's Plans (1952); The Unknown Quantity (1953); Man Missing (1954); Postmark Murder (1956); Another Man's Murder (1957); Melora (1959, published as The Promise of Murder, Dell, 1961); Jury of One (1960); The Cup, the Blade, or the Gun (1961, published in England as The Crime at Honotassa, Collins, 1962); Enemy in the House (1962); Run Scared (1963); Call after Midnight (1964); R.S.V.P. Murder (1965); Witness at Large (1966); Woman on the Roof (1968); Message from Hong Kong (1969); El Rancho Rio (1970); Two Little Rich Girls (1971); The House by the Sea (1972); Murder in Waiting (1973); Danger Money (1975); Family Fortune (1976); Nine O'Clock Tide (1978); The Bayou Road (1979); Casa Madrone (1980); Family Affair (1981); Next of Kin (1982); The Patient in Cabin C (1984); The Alpine

Condo Cross Fire *(1984)*; A Fighting Chance *(1986)*; Three Days for Emeralds *(1988)*.

Collected works: The Cases of Susan Dare *(short stories, Doubleday, 1934)*; Mignon G. Eberhart Omnibus *(includes* The Patient in Room 18, While the Patient Slept, *and* Murder by an Aristocrat, *Grosset, 1936)*; Mignon G. Eberhart's Mystery Book *(includes* Speak No Evil *and* With This Ring, *World Publishing, 1945)*; Five of My Best: Deadly Is the Diamond, Bermuda Grapevine, Murder Goes to Market, Strangers in Flight, Express to Danger *(Hammond, London, 1949)*; Deadly Is the Diamond and Three Other Novelettes of Murder *(includes* Deadly Is the Diamond, Bermuda Grapevine, The Crimson Paw, *and* Murder in Waltz Time, *Random House, 1958)*; The Crimson Paw *(Hammond, 1959)*.

Other: (with Fred Ballard) 320 College Avenue *(French, New York, 1938); (with Robert Wallsten)* Eight O'Clock Tuesday *(first produced in New York City, 1941, French, 1941); also author of* The Murder of Dr. Harrigan *(story for film of the same title), 1936.*

Mignon G. Eberhart wrote her first mystery novel in 1929 and her last, 59 books later, in 1988. During more than half a century, Eberhart earned a place for herself as one of the most popular writers in the mystery genre. Her heroines, such as Sarah Keate and Susan Dare, were arresting and courageous. Appearing in 1929 in *The Patient in Room 18,* before even Miss Marple, Keate was one of the mystery genre's first female sleuths. Because of her plucky heroines, Eberhart was often seen as following in the footsteps of *Mary Roberts Rinehart, but she soon became known in her own right as a writer whose best work often combined a gothic atmosphere, a budding romance, and a "whodunit" mystery. She is considered to have influenced writers such as the best-selling **Mary Higgins Clark.** Eberhart's novels were also well received at the time of their publication, drawing high praise from both the reading public and reviewers. Often dubbed "America's *Agatha Christie,"** Eberhart was once described by *Gertrude Stein** as "one of the best mystifiers in America," and she counted President Harry S. Truman among her fans. In the 1990s, six of her earliest novels were republished by the University of Nebraska Press.

Many critics have referred to Eberhart's work as "escape" fiction. Marvin Lachman of *The Armchair Detective,* for example, wrote after the republication of *The Patient in Room 18,* "it is for someone seeking old-fashioned escape," and in the *St. James Guide to Crime and Mystery Writers,* **Joanne Harack** classified Eberhart's writing as "escape/fantasy adventures." Eberhart disagreed with such statements, however. "Escapes are for people who are lazy readers," Eberhart stated in a Cleveland *Plain Dealer* interview in 1975. "The mystery reader is highly intelligent, and he likes to participate in the book." To ensure the kind of accuracy that an intelligent reader demands, Eberhart's prewriting work included drawing up floor plans so that "she does not have someone entering a window that did not exist two chapters before," as Pat Hobeck noted in the *Plain Dealer.* A frequent traveler, she was able to incorporate many exotic locales, such as Hong Kong, Lisbon, and the Caribbean into her work. She also planned clues that led to evidence "that a district attorney could use." Eberhart was original for her time period as well in that she explored the underlying psychological processes of characters' thoughts and motivations.

Eberhart began writing in the early 1920s. After the publication of a novella in a detective magazine, she went on to publish her first mystery novel, *The Patient in Room 18,* in 1929. She wrote murder mysteries right from the start. "You just can't write a detective story without at least one murder," she said in 1939 in a *Plain Dealer* interview. "Nobody is going to read 300 pages just to find out what became of Lady Emily's jewels." In her first novel, Eberhart introduced nurse and amateur detective Sarah Keate, "a worthy successor to Rinehart's 'Miss Pinkerton,'" as Lachman called her. Keate narrates the mystery but shares the detection duties with private investigator Lance O'Leary; both characters would reappear six more times. Nurse Sarah is both tough (she served in a combat hospital during World War I) and delicate (she has trouble saying the word "legs" in front of other people). Though O'Leary is the one who is more threatened by physical danger, Keate contributes with what *Publishers Weekly* calls her "acerbic wit and derring-do."

The Patient in Room 18 has a hospital setting, and Keate herself is a prime suspect in the murder and radium robbery that takes place there. Upon publication, the novel immediately drew enthusiastic reviews. "The story is one of the best of its kind that we have had the good luck to read this year," wrote a critic for the *Saturday Review of Literature.* Though the novel fell into the genre of Golden Age detection stories in which clues mattered most in the solving of the crime, the detective story was not the only aspect of the book that readers and critics enjoyed. A *Bookman* review pointed to its "novel background," and a reviewer in the *Times Literary Supplement* commented that "the non-detective parts of this story are excellent."

A subsequent Keate story, *While the Patient Slept,* published the next year, further solidified Eberhart's reputation as a writer of suspense. Eberhart also won the Scotland Yard prize for this novel, "deservedly," according to Will Cuppy of *Books.* In this novel, Keate is working as a private nurse at Federie House when her patient is murdered, and she and O'Leary must track down the killer. A reviewer for *Bookman* said, "This book places detective fiction on a higher level than ever before and is heartily recommended to fans." Like *The Patient in Room 18,* described by the *New York Times* as a "good, creepy yarn," *While the Patient Slept* builds what would become the trademark Eberhart atmosphere. Eugene Rynall in the *Saturday Review of Literature* wrote of the setting, "Federie House, with it somber ruggedness on an almost deserted road, with its mysterious turrets, its darkened draperies, its heavily carpeted floors, and its sinister occupants, is an almost perfect setting for a mystery story."

Nurse Sarah Keate also saw success in the movies. Six of Eberhart's novels, four of which were Keate stories, were adapted into films in the 1930s. Eberhart also wrote one story expressly for film, *The Murder of Dr. Harrigan,* released in 1939, and, with a collaborator, she adapted another mystery into a play titled *Eight O'Clock Tuesday,* which ran on Broadway in the early 1940s. Along with these ventures into other media, Eberhart continued writing superior mystery novels. *The Dark Garden,* published in 1933, was her first novel that did not feature Keate and O'Leary. Cuppy, who reviewed Eberhart's books favorably for almost 20 years, found this novel to have "exciting gradations," a "vigorous, impressive climax," and to be "plotted most lucidly. . . . It ought to get your unanimous vote," he concluded. Other reviewers agreed on the quality of this novel.

Eberhart's next mystery, *The White Cockatoo,* garnered mixed reviews. Isaac Anderson, a long-time reviewer for the *New York Times,* found it to be disappointing. "Sarah Keate, the redhaired nurse who played a leading part in Mrs. Eberhart's other mystery stories does not appear in this book," he noted. "It might have been better if she had." For her next novel, however, Anderson had nothing but compliments for Eberhart again; "'The House on the Roof,'" he wrote, "is a Class A mystery, which is precisely what we have learned to expect from Mrs. Eberhart." Like Cuppy, Anderson recommended the great majority of Eberhart's books for almost two decades.

Over the next 50 years, Eberhart continued to do what she did best: write exciting, atmospheric murder mysteries. She introduced another female serial character, Susan Dare, who wrote mystery fiction. Harack found these stories to be "rather more successful" than those featuring Sarah Keate. Eberhart also created the baker James Wickwire. *New York Times* writer Anthony Boucher, however, found Eberhart's use of a male protagonist to be "a surprisingly unprofessional error," claiming that "[Eberhart] alienates her usual devotees by concentrating on a new male protagonist."

Eberhart continued writing mysteries until she was in her 80s. Her 57th novel, *The Alpine Condo Cross Fire,* was called "neat entertainment" in a *Publishers Weekly* review, which also praised Eberhart's "deft delivery." In 1995, the University of Nebraska Press began reissuing six of Eberhart's early novels. After rereading *The Patient in Room 18* Lachman noted that Eberhart "has more than nostalgia going for her. There is atmosphere and an aura of mystery and dread." A *Publishers Weekly* writer found that the "suspense steadily builds" to a "satisfying denouement" in *While the Patient Slept,* commenting also on the atmosphere of "darkness and decay." "Eberhart's timing and gothic atmosphere are second to none," wrote the *Publishers Weekly* contributor. "[Sarah's] return is a welcome addition to the distinguished ranks of other silver-streaked gumshoes."

Eberhart was one of the masters of the mystery field. Writing about *Postmark Murder,* published in 1956, a *New Yorker* reviewer described Eberhart as "one of the most thorough and ingenious plotters in the trade." Yet Eberhart's affinity for writing mysteries seemed to have gone beyond the words she put on paper and to extend to the whole field itself. Her *New York Times* obituary quoted Eberhart as saying, "My real love is for the brotherhood and sisterhood of the genre. I love mystery writers as a breed, and am so glad to belong."

SOURCES:
Armchair Detective, fall, 1995, p. 415.
Bookman, May 29, 1929, p. 30; March 30, 1930, p. 28.
Books, February 16, 1930, p. 18; October 8, 1933, p. 15.
The New Yorker, April 7, 1956, p. 164.
The New York Times, May 19, 1929, p. 24; January 15, 1933, p. 15; November 17, 1957, p. 55.
Plain Dealer (Cleveland, OH), April 27, 1975.
Publishers Weekly, July 5, 1985, p. 66; February 6, 1995, p. 80.
St. James Guide to Crime and Mystery Writers. 4th ed. Detroit, MI: St. James Press, 1996.

Saturday Review of Literature, May 18, 1929, p. 1028; March 15, 1930, p. 830.

Times Literary Supplement, June 6, 1929, p. 458; July 14, 1995, p. 8.

OBITUARY AND OTHER SOURCES:

The New York Times, October 9, 1996, p. D19.

Washington Post, October 11, 1996, p. B6.

COLLECTIONS:

Eberhart's manuscripts are housed at the Mugar Memorial Library at Boston University.

RELATED MEDIA:

Several of Eberhart's novels were adapted as films of the same title, including *While the Patient Slept* and *The White Cockatoo,* both 1935, *Murder by an Aristocrat,* 1936, and *The Patient in Room 18,* 1938. The novel *Hasty Wedding* was made into a film titled *Three's a Crowd,* 1945; *From This Dark Stairway* was made into a film titled *The Dark Stairway,* 1938; *The Great Hospital Mystery* was based on an unidentified story by Eberhart, 1937; *Mystery of Hunting's End* was adapted as a film titled *Mystery House,* 1938.

Eberle, Abastenia St. Leger

(1878–1942).

> *See Huntington, Anna Hyatt for sidebar.*

Eberle, Emilia (b. 1964).

> *See Comaneci, Nadia for sidebar.*

Ebner-Eschenbach, Marie

(1830–1916)

Austrian novelist and poet. Name variations: Countess Dubsky; Baroness von Ebner-Eschenbach. Born Countess Dubsky at Castle Zdislavic, in Moravia, on September 13, 1830; died in 1916; daughter of Count Dubsky; married Moritz von Ebner-Eschenbach (Austrian field marshal), in 1848; no children.

Marie Ebner-Eschenbach grew up in Vienna and on the family estate of Zdislavic in Moravia. She was an infant when her mother died, and her meticulous education was provided by her two stepmothers. In 1848, she married her cousin, the Austrian captain Moritz von Ebner-Eschenbach, who would subsequently attain the rank of field marshal. He was assigned to military posts, and the couple lived in Vienna, then Kolsterbruck, then Vienna once again. Baroness von Ebner-Eschenbach began her writings as a playwright, despite family disapproval, hoping for a career at the Vienna Burghtheater. Her drama *Maria von Schottland* (***Mary Stuart** in Scotland) was produced at the Karlsruhe theater in 1860, but her next few plays, including *Marie Roland* (***Madame Roland**), proved less successful.

Ebner-Eschenbach then turned to fiction. A distinguished author, she wrote a number of novels depicting the life in Bohemia: *Die Prinzessin von Banalien* (1872), *Bozena* (1876), and *Das Gemeindekind* (Child of the Community, 1887). She also wrote of the Austrian aristocracy in *Lotti, die Uhrmacherin* (1883), *Zwei Comtessen* (Two Countesses, 1885), *Unsühnbar* (1890), and *Glaubenslos?* (1893). In 1875, she published the story of a dog *Krambambuli,* one of her best-known books, and in 1880 produced a book of *Parables, Fairy Tales and Poems.*

Ebner-Eschenbach became a grande dame of Viennese society. Her humor, power of description, elegance of style, and masterly insight into character gave her a foremost place among German writers of her time. On the occasion of her 70th birthday, the University of Vienna conferred upon her the degree of doctor of philosophy. Her friends included ***Betty Paoli** and ***Enrica von Handel-Mazzetti.**

Eboli, princess of (1540–1592).

> *See Mendoza, Ana de.*

Ebtekar, Massoumeh (1960—)

Iranian vice president.

In August 1997, Massoumeh Ebtekar, a U.S.-educated lecturer, was named one of the seven vice presidents of Iran by the nation's newly chosen moderate president Mohammad Khatami. She was also named to head the Organization for the Protection of the Environment. Ebtekar was the first woman to serve in a top government post since Iran's 1979 Islamic revolution. At the time, two other women occupied senior government posts; there were also 13 women in Parliament.

Ecgwynn (d. around 901)

Saxon woman. Name variations: Ecgwyn. Died around 901; daughter of a shepherd; mistress of Edward I the Elder (c. 870–924), king of the English (r. 899–924); children: Aethelstan or Ethelstan (895–939), king of the English (r. 924–939); Alfred (died young); *Edith (d. 937, who married Sihtric, king of York).

Ecker, Heidemarie Rosendahl (b. 1948).

> *See Rosendahl, Heidemarie.*

Eckert, Bärbel (b. 1955).

> *See Wöckel-Eckert, Bärbel.*

Eckford, Elizabeth (b. 1942).

See Bates, Daisy (b. 1914) for sidebar.

Eckhardt-Gramatté, S.C.

(1899–1974)

Russian-born Canadian composer and violinist. Name variations: Sophie or Sophie-Carmen; Sonia Friedman-Gramatté or Gramatte; Sonia de Friedman-Kochevskoy. Born Sophie-Carmen de Friedman on January 6, 1899, probably in Moscow; died in Stuttgart, Germany, on December 2, 1974; daughter of Catherina de Kochevskaya (a music instructor) and Nicolas de Friedman; studied at the Paris Conservatoire with Alfred Brun, Guillaume Rémy, Vincent d'Indy, Camille Chevillard, and Bronislav Huberman; married Walter Gramatté, on December 13, 1920 (died of tuberculosis in 1929); married Ferdinand Eckhardt (an art historian), in 1934.

Won the Composition Prize of the Musikverein for her Piano Concerto No. 2 *(1948) and the Austrian State Prize for her* Triple Concerto *(1950); won first prize in the International Competition for Women Composers (1961). The S.C. Eckhardt-Gramatté Competition was named for her.*

Sophie-Carmen Eckhardt-Gramatté, later known as Sonia, was born in Russia in 1899 and had an eventful childhood. Her mother **Catherina de Kochevskaya** separated from her husband Nicholas de Friedman before Sophie was born. Fearing de Friedman would kidnap her little girl, Catherina sent Sophie-Carmen from Moscow to England where the child spent four years with foster parents in a Tolstoian colony located in the Cotswold Hills, Gloucestershire. From England, Sophie moved to Paris with her mother and began to take piano instruction. Between 1905 and 1909, Sophie-Carmen, not yet a teenager, wrote *Alphabet Pieces* and *Little Pieces*. Although she did not play the violin, she was accepted at the Paris Conservatoire as a violin student where her teachers were Alfred Brun, Guillaume Rémy, Vincent d'Indy, and Camille Chevillard. By the age 11, Sophie was concertizing throughout Europe alternately as a pianist and a violinist. She left the conservatory in 1913.

Eckhardt-Gramatté moved to Berlin with her mother and sister in 1914. For a time, she earned a living for the family by playing in cafes. **Suzanne Joachim-Chaigneau**, the daughter-in-law of the great Joseph Joachim, gave the young musician one of Joachim's violins and arranged a scholarship sponsored by Franz von Mendelssohn, a descendent of the composer. For six years, Eckhardt-Gramatté appeared in a number of recitals. Though her patrons wanted her to continue as a concert artist, she preferred to devote her time and energy to composing, and by 1920 she was immersed in composing large works. That same year, she married the German expressionist painter Walter Gramatté and was known as Sonia Friedman-Gramatté.

The couple moved to Barcelona in 1924, where Pablo Casals became Eckhardt-Gramatté's mentor. She performed frequently in Spain. In 1927, Leopold Stokowski heard of Eckhardt-Gramatté and asked to audition her. She was engaged to perform with the Philadelphia Orchestra, an appearance that was postponed when her husband died of tuberculosis in 1929. When she finally came to America in 1930, she received rave reviews. Deciding, nonetheless, to devote her time to composing rather than concertizing, Eckhardt-Gramatté returned to Berlin and enrolled as a pupil of Max Trapp at the Prussian Academy of Music. In 1934, she married Ferdinand Eckhardt, an Austrian art historian. Five years later, the couple moved to Vienna following the completion of her studies. In Vienna, she began to sign her name as S.C. Eckhardt-Gramatté. After the war, she was commissioned to write a piece for the Salzburg Festival and the *Violin Concerto No. 2* published in 1952 was the result. When Eckhardt-Gramatté's husband became director of the Winnipeg Art Gallery in 1953, she moved with him despite her career. Her home in Winnipeg soon became a gathering place for musicians. In 1959, she wrote a *Duo Concertante* for cello and piano for the University Music Festival in Saskatoon, and other commissions followed.

Eckhardt-Gramatté wrote highly individualized music. With the exception of three years' study with Max Trapp, she developed her skills almost completely on her own. Her style is very distinctive and listeners tend to either love or disdain her music. As she moved from the restrictive and competitive European milieu to the open frontier in Canada, her abilities grew. In addition to her talent as a composer, Eckhardt-Gramatté was an excellent violinist and teacher. Her approach to teaching violin was innovative, and she developed a technique for piano called the Natural Piano Technique.

SOURCES:

Cohen, Aaron I. *International Encyclopedia of Women Composers.* 2 vols. NY: Books and Music (USA), 1987.

Sadie, Stanley, ed. *New Grove Dictionary of Music and Musicians.* 20 vols. NY: Macmillan, 1980.

"Sophie Carmen Eckhardt-Gramatte: A Portrait," in *Musicanada*. October 1969, pp. 8–9

John Haag,
Assistant Professor of History,
University of Georgia, Athens, Georgia

Edburga (d. 960)

*Nun at Nunnaminster. Died on June 15, 960; interred at Pershore Abbey, Worcester, England; daughter of *Edgifu (d. 968) and Edward I the Elder (c. 870–924), king of the English (r. 899–924).*

Eddy, Mary Baker (1821–1910)

American founder of the Christian Science church and movement and author of its spiritual textbook, Science and Health with Key to the Scriptures. *Name variations: Mary Glover; Mary Patterson. Born Mary Morse Baker on July 16, 1821, in Bow, New Hampshire; died on December 3, 1910, at her home outside Boston, in Chestnut Hill, Massachusetts; youngest of six children of Abigail (Ambrose) Baker and Mark Baker (a farmer); given informal and sporadic schooling; married George Washington Glover, in 1843 (died 1844); married Daniel Patterson, in 1853 (died 1873); married Asa Gilbert Eddy, in 1877 (divorced 1882); children: George Washington Glover II (b. 1844); Ebenezer Foster Eddy (adopted, 1888).*

Raised in rural New Hampshire; as a child, suffered from chronic health problems; as an adult, experimented with various medical treatments and healing systems; "discovered" religious truths with the power to heal sickness (1866); began to write and teach classes on Christian healing (1866–72); wrote and published Science and Health *(1872–75); obtained legal charter for Massachusetts Metaphysical College (1881); published several books on Christian Science and founded bimonthly journal (1883–88); dissolved college and moved from Boston to New Hampshire (1889); organized Mother Church of Christian Science in Boston (1892); became pastor emeritus of church and published manual for its operation (1895); successfully battled a series of lawsuits and challenges to her position (1896–1909); returned to live in Boston and founded the* Christian Science Monitor *(1908).*

Selected publications: Science and Health with Key to the Scriptures *(1875) and a number of other writings collected together as* Prose Works *(1896), including her autobiography,* Retrospection and Introspection *(1891).*

The Christian Science Church was born on the day that its founder, Mary Baker Eddy, slipped on an icy street in Lynn, Massachusetts. With injuries to her head, neck, and back that left her racked with pain, the 45-year-old Eddy initially feared that she would be permanently disabled, or even die. Only three days after her accident, however, on Sunday, February 4, 1866, she not only regained her health but made the spiritual discovery that determined the course of the remainder of her life and defined her historical legacy.

The founding of Christian Science was also the result of a lifetime of experiences, revealing as much about the society in which Mary Baker Eddy lived as about her life. In some respects, her life mirrors the passage of the 19th century. Born in 1821, she grew up in a small New Hampshire town governed by New England Puritans, with their view of an angry God. She died in 1910 in her home outside Boston, the city in which, by then, the Mother Church of Christian Science stood as a lavish testament to the forceful leadership of its founder, who had established a new and quite unique American religious tradition. Although she spent virtually her entire life in New England, the 90 years of Mary Baker Eddy's life took her far beyond the world into which she had been born.

The foundation for her interest in Christian healing was laid by the circumstances of childhood. Born to **Abigail Ambrose Baker** and Mark Baker, a New England farmer, the child they named Mary Morse Baker had recurring health problems that often kept her from attending school in her early years. Although socially isolated, she had an active mind; she read widely on her own, wrote poetry, and was guided and encouraged in her reading by an older brother.

Christian teachings were important in the Baker home, where Mary's parents held steadfast, and often conflicting, religious beliefs. Abigail Baker saw God as kind, loving, and active in human lives, while her husband viewed a much more judgmental Supreme Being. When Eddy was eight years old, she confided to her mother that she sometimes heard voices calling her name. Seeing the experience as parallel to that of the young Samuel in the Old Testament who became a Biblical prophet, Abigail counseled her daughter to reply as Samuel had done, with the words, "Speak Lord, for thy servant heareth." The voices continued over a period of about a year, in what Eddy was to view later as the earliest important event in her religious life. The outlook of Christian Science that she would develop was at some level also a repudiation of the fierce and unyielding religious vision that her father had attempted to force on her.

In 1843, Mary was 22 when she married George Washington Glover, a successful builder from the South, and moved with him to South Carolina. Within seven months, Glover suffered a series of business setbacks and died of yellow fever, leaving her a young widow without any means of financial support. Eddy returned to the home of her parents and gave birth to a son, George Washington Glover II, three months later.

For months following the birth, Eddy was physically ill, emotionally depressed, and financially impoverished. Over the next few years, she looked without success for a way to support her child on her own but was forced to rely on family and friends. In 1853, when her son was nine years old, she married Daniel Patterson, a dentist. For reasons that are not entirely clear, the child did not join his mother in her home with her new husband but continued to live with the family that had cared for him since his early childhood. Eventually he moved west with them, losing contact with his mother over the next decade, and was not reunited with her for more than 25 years.

From my very childhood I was impelled, by a hunger and thirst after divine things,—a desire for something higher and better than matter, and apart from it,—to seek diligently for the knowledge of God as the one great and ever-present relief from human woe.

—Mary Baker Eddy

In the dark period lasting from her marriage in 1853 to her founding of Christian Science in 1866, Eddy was frequently ill and in need of emotional and financial support, needs her husband could not fulfill. Desperate for some relief from her physical maladies, she embarked on a search for healing that included experimentation with homeopathic remedies and hydropathic therapy, following the same path as many other men and women—especially women—of her time who lacked confidence in the curative methods offered by traditional physicians.

Homeopathy, based on the principle that "like cures like," minimized the use of drugs and had achieved a wide following. Hydropathy, a technique known as the "water cure" that rejected the use of drugs altogether, was said to offer a more natural approach to healing. Followers drank water and submitted to cold-water body wraps and special baths intended to purge the system and relieve pain.

By the time Eddy reached the Vail Hydropathic Institute to undergo the water cure in 1862, she had been sick for six years with "spinal inflammation" and related distress. Viewing the treatment as her last great hope, she worried that she would have nowhere else to turn if it failed. The treatment did fail, but she learned from a fellow patient about a gifted healer, Phineas Quimby, of Portland, Maine, who was having great success curing conditions similar to hers. Quimby would not travel to New Hampshire to evaluate her condition as Eddy wished, but he agreed to see her if she came to Portland. Convinced that her choice lay between Portland and Quimby or home and death, Eddy traveled to Portland.

Quimby's approach to mental healing relieved Eddy's physical distress, excited her intellectual curiosity, and changed her understanding and experience of sickness forever. Over the next three years, while she was both Quimby's patient and student, he insisted that his method of healing was a science—the same science, in fact, that Jesus had used in his healing ministry—just as she would claim for her own institution a decade later. In his healing practice, Quimby made no use of medicine or physical manipulation of the body, but cured by listening to his patients. At the root of his approach was the belief that sickness was an error of the mind that could be corrected by replacing a false belief in sickness with a true belief in health and wholeness.

During the nearly 30 years that Phineas Quimby developed his ideas on the mind-body connection (years that also included work as a mesmerist), he wrote extensively about his science and its foundation in the Christian gospel. The existence of these writings have made it difficult for historians to accept Mary Baker Eddy's version of Christian Science as an entirely separate entity; the similarities between her words and those of her mentor are too significant to overlook. Supporters of Eddy have tried to argue that it is the Quimby manuscripts that should be looked at with suspicion, not Eddy's writings, but they have yet to make a convincing case. While the debate remains important, it also tends to overshadow a far more significant part of the story: while the founder of Christian Science might well have owed more to her association with Phineas Quimby than she was willing to acknowledge, the religious empire that she founded was her own creation. Quimby possessed neither the temperament nor the genius of a religious leader, and so it was left to his avid follower to turn the raw materials of Quimby's approach into the finely nuanced religious system that Christian Science became.

Although she sought to minimize the importance of her relationship with Quimby, Mary Baker Eddy was to acknowledge later that her years as his patient and pupil helped to prepare her for the revelation she experienced less than a month after his death. Bedridden after her fall on the icy streets of Lynn, Massachusetts, she was alone on a Sunday afternoon when she picked up her Bible and started to read about the healing ministry of Jesus. As she read, she began to understand the words of the scriptures in an entirely new way, and, as her understanding grew, she found her body being healed of its injuries. In her view, the Thursday-to-Sunday sequence of events was symbolic of the religious character of her recovery: just as Jesus had moved from the Last Supper to death on the cross and a Sunday resurrection, she had come close to death on Thursday only to be given new life on Sunday through her "discovery" of Christian Science. *Science and Health*, the foundational text of Christian Science, was not to be published until nine years later, but the events of

Mary Baker Eddy

that weekend were to remain the "falling apple" that showed the founder of the faith the secret of Christian healing.

Eddy's discovery of Christian Science did not solve her most immediate problems. She was estranged from her second husband, from whom she was to divorce in 1873, and had to find some way to support herself. Although she began to teach and write about her "science of divine metaphysical healing," her ideas did not immediately earn her a steady income. After *Science and Health* was first published in 1875, her fortunes began to change. Continuing to promote her ideas through public lectures and classes, she attracted a growing following over the next decade, resulting in her decision to open the Massachusetts Metaphysical College for students of the movement. Chartered by the Massachusetts state legislature in 1881, the college opened its doors in May 1882. The college was very much a one-woman operation, with Eddy serving as the sole teacher of the sole class it offered, and as author of the sole textbook.

In 1877, she had married one of her followers and students, Asa Gilbert Eddy, but the marriage, apparently a happy one, lasted only five years. Asa died in 1882. Known to her following now as Mary Baker Eddy, she continued to run her school and expanded on her ideas developed for *Science and Health* by publishing a number of other writings and establishing the bimonthly *Journal of Christian Science*. As the movement drew notice outside of the Boston area, she won further recognition and followers, particularly in New York and Chicago.

As the movement grew, however, so did discord within its ranks. By the late 1880s, Eddy was forced to find some way to cope with former students who became angry defectors and organized against her cause. Divisions within the movement became so serious that she dissolved both the Christian Scientist Association, formed in 1876, and the Massachusetts Metaphysical College, and withdrew from public leadership. While in self-imposed exile, she began to undertake what was, in effect, her comeback as head of the movement.

After 1888, Eddy seldom made public appearances, but she spent the remaining 22 years of her life privately arranging the pieces of the denominational structure that was to survive her. The two most prominent institutions of Christian Science, the Mother Church in Boston and the *Christian Science Monitor* newspaper, were both founded during these two decades.

But the fame and accomplishments of these latter years also aroused a new round of controversy. Legal battles, critical newspaper reports, and a cutting parody of her ideas by the novelist Mark Twain succeeded in making Eddy's last 15 years far from peaceful. Fighting to preserve her position and protect her church from external threats, she was also putting in place the mechanisms that would assure its future viability. In 1894, a year before she retired as pastor of the church, Mary Baker Eddy "ordained" the Bible and *Science and Health* as her permanent pastoral replacements, a shrewd move that assured no other figure would ever have the opportunity to become the kind of charismatic leader she had been. In the years that followed, Eddy moved preemptively on a number of occasions to protect the church and safeguard her own singular status. In 1895, for example, she published the *Manual for the Mother Church,* a document that placed her permanent stamp on the church's operations.

As advancing age forced Eddy to plan for the time when she would no longer guide the church, she learned through painful experience how few people there were that she could trust and depend on. During the 1880s, she had tried without success to reestablish a relationship with her son, George Glover, but mother and son had little in common, and Eddy did not find in him the necessary qualities of a religious leader. In 1888, she made a surprising move by adopting one of her advisors, Ebenezer Foster, then 41 years old, in a legal action that was to secure Foster the right to succeed her. Eddy's enthusiasm for the arrangement quickly waned, however, as she realized that "Bennie" did not share her total devotion to the movement. As evidence mounted that Foster-Eddy could not be depended upon to handle church matters in ways his adoptive mother would wish, the relationship became increasingly strained, and he was eventually banished from her inner circle. At the time of her death, both Foster-Eddy and George Glover were to receive lump-sum inheritances from her, but without winning access to the bulk of what was by then a significant fortune.

The failure of her family to live up to her expectations, combined with the defection over the years of several close advisors, made Eddy wary in her old age. Tightening her control on the church, she demanded fierce loyalty from those immediately around her, but she also appears to have inspired great devotion, and there were many friends and admirers who voluntarily stayed close. On December 3, 1910, she died after a brief illness, at age 89, nearly 45 years after she had begun to formulate Christian Science. Throughout those years, she had insisted that disease and death could be conquered through spiritual growth and insight, and believers in the principles of Christian Science did not view the death of the founder as a contradiction of those principles. Their spiritual mother had "passed from their sight" in their view, but her words and wisdom lived on in the church she had built.

While the Christian Science Church is in many ways a product of the culture in which its founder lived, Mary Baker Eddy alone was responsible for making it an enduring institution. The critical forces that shaped it as a movement—Eddy's experience of illness, her journey through the world of alternative medicine, and her rejection of Puritan beliefs—were not unique, but Eddy's response to them was unique. Other Americans shared her interest in the mind-body connection, but no one took it to comparable heights. She was an organizational genius of extraordinary energy, and the church has survived on her strength.

SOURCES:

Eddy, Mary Baker. *Prose Works*. Boston: First Church of Christ, Scientist, 1925.

———. *Science and Health with Key to the Scriptures*. Boston: First Church of Christ, Scientist, 1971.

Peel, Robert. *Mary Baker Eddy: The Years of Discovery*. NY: Holt, Rinehart and Winston, 1966.

———. *Mary Baker Eddy: The Years of Authority*. NY: Holt, Rinehart and Winston, 1977.

———. *Mary Baker Eddy: The Years of Trial*. NY: Holt, Rinehart and Winston, 1971.

SUGGESTED READING:

Braden, Charles. *Spirits in Rebellion*. Dallas, TX: Southern Methodist University Press, 1984.

Cather, Willa, and Georgine Milmine. *The Life of Mary Baker G. Eddy and the History of the Christian Science Church*. University of Nebraska, 1993 (first published in 1909).

Cayleff, Susan E. *Wash and Be Healed: The Water Cure Movement and Women's Health*. Philadelphia, PA: Temple University Press, 1987.

Gottschalk, Stephen. *The Emergence of Christian Science in American Religious Life*. Berkeley, CA: University of California Press, 1973.

Judah, J. Stillson. *The History and Philosophy of Metaphysical Movements in America*. Philadelphia, PA: Westminster Press, 1967.

COLLECTIONS:

Mary Baker Eddy's personal papers are not available to the public. Her published writings, however, are widely available in local libraries and in the Christian Science Reading Rooms run by the Church of Christ, Scientist.

Kathleen M. Joyce,
Assistant Professor in the Department of Religion
at Duke University, Durham, North Carolina

Eden, Emily (1797–1869)

English political host and author whose paintings and writings depict the splendors and hardships of life in imperial India during the 1830s and 1840s. Born on March 4, 1797, in London, England; died on August 5, 1869, in London, England; daughter of William Eden, 1st Baron Auckland, and Eleanor Elliot; educated privately; never married; no children.

Emily Eden accompanied her brother George, the British governor-general of India, on a two-and-a-half-year tour through Northern India in 1837. To impress the local princes and rajahs with the power of British imperialism, they traveled with a ten-mile-long procession of camels, elephants, horses, carriages, bamboo carts, soldiers and camp followers. Twelve thousand people strong, this cavalcade could travel only about two hours in the early morning before the sun became too strong. Emily Eden, the witty and learned daughter of a politically well-connected Whig family, commented wryly on her participation in this gigantic daily parade:

> We feel so certain that people who live in houses, and get up by a fire at a reasonable hour and then go quietly to breakfast, would think us raving mad, if they saw nine Europeans of steady age and respectable habits, going galloping every morning at sunrise over a sandy plain, followed by quantities of black horsemen, and then by ten miles of beasts of burden carrying things which, after all, will not make the nine madmen even decently comfortable.

Certainly nothing in Emily Eden's early life had led her to believe that she would spend five years in India (despite the fact that one of her uncles was Lord Minto, an early governor-general of India). Eden was a daughter of **Eleanor Elliot Eden** and William Eden, a retired diplomat and the 1st Baron Auckland. Born in London, she was tutored at home by a series of governesses. Eden was quite well-educated, especially for a woman of her day, and was avidly involved in the political life of Britain.

Her older brother, George, who had assumed the title of Lord Auckland upon the death of his father, was a well-connected Whig. In 1818, after their mother died, Emily and her younger sister **Fanny Eden** set up housekeeping for George, a lifelong bachelor. George served as commissioner of Greenwich Hospital and in 1834 was appointed First Lord of the Admiralty. The Edens' home became a meeting place for Whig politicians, and Emily Eden was an active and equal participant in the lively political discussions among her brother's colleagues.

In 1835, the prime minister, Lord Melbourne, appointed Lord Auckland governor-general of India, a prestigious and potentially lucrative position but one that required residence in India. Although reluctant to leave her stimulating life in England and leery of any long sea voyages, Emily Eden resolved to accompany her dearly loved brother to India. Fanny Eden, too, agreed to make the journey.

Prior to the opening of the Suez Canal, the trip from England to India around the Cape of Good Hope took approximately five months. The Edens arrived in Calcutta, the seat of British administration in India, in March 1836. Although Lord Auckland was often occupied with official government business, his position also required that he and his sisters, as his hostesses, participate in many social activities. Emily and Fanny Eden presided weekly at official dinners, "Open Houses," balls and "At Homes" at Government House in Calcutta.

As Emily Eden revealed to her many correspondents back in England, she intensely disliked her new life in India. She found the British inhabitants dull and gossipy. The weather was oppressive, especially as the Edens had arrived at the beginning of Calcutta's hottest season. Eden wrote, "I have not been able yet to live five minutes, night or day, without the *punkah* [large ceiling fan], and we keep our blinds all closed as long as there is a ray of sun." The heat and humidity, aided by the insects, caused books, clothing and furniture to rot. Eden was uninterested in Indian culture and viewed the Indians with "aversion." Her brother was so occupied with governmental responsibilities that she rarely saw him. In sum, Eden averred, "I cannot abide India, and that is the truth."

In 1837, however, the Edens abandoned their boring Calcutta routine and embarked on their two-and-a-half-year tour through Northern India. The official purpose of the trip was to impress the Indian rulers in the region with the power of British imperialism and to solidify friendly relations with Ranjit Singh, ruler of the Punjab. Emily Eden's trenchant and witty letters to her sister describing this trip, which were published in 1866 under the title *Up the Country,* describe the magnificence and pomp associated with British imperial power in the mid-19th century. Eden, however, was also a shrewd observer of the incongruities of imperialism. Describing a ball at Simla, the Himalayan retreat that would become the fashionable summer capital of the British Empire in India, Eden wrote:

Twenty years ago no European had ever been here, and there we were, with the band playing and eating salmon from Scotland. [W]e, 105 Europeans, [were] surrounded by at least 3,000 mountaineers, who, wrapped in their hill blankets, looked on at what we call our polite amusements, and bowed to the ground if a European came near them. I sometimes wonder they do not cut all our heads off, and say nothing more about it.

The ten-mile-long procession of elephants and soldiers that made up the governor-general's entourage probably succeeded in its purpose of impressing the local princes and rajahs. At *durbars* (formal ceremonies for the governor-general to meet with the local ruler), Lord Auckland and his sisters received elaborate presents from the Indian princes. They were obliged by law, however, to turn these gifts over to the East India Company, nominal ruler of British India. Eden captured many of these local rulers in sketches and paintings, which were later published as a highly praised book entitled *Portraits of the Princes and People of India.*

Lord Auckland's tenure as governor-general ended on a disastrous note. A contingent of British soldiers, sent to Afghanistan to forestall Russian advances that might threaten the British presence in India, were massacred by the Afghans. The new prime minister, Robert Peel, recalled Lord Auckland to England in 1841. Emily Eden apparently retained a deep-rooted enmity against her brother's successor for many years after.

Back in England, Emily, Fanny and George continued to live together at their house in London. After yet another change in government, Lord Auckland was again appointed First Lord of the Admiralty. Emily Eden's voracious interest in politics continued unabated, but her health, damaged by the years in India, worsened. After her brother and sister died within a few months of each other, Emily Eden became a chronic invalid. In 1859, however, she published her first novel, a comic work entitled *The Semi-Detached House,* which was followed in 1860 by another satirical book, *The Semi-Attached Couple.* Although she rarely left her house, leading figures in the Whig Party continued to visit Eden to pay their respects and to seek her advice.

Emily Eden died at Eden Lodge on August 5, 1869. Through her writings and paintings, she memorialized an imperial lifestyle that was fast receding in the face of railroads, limited-liability companies and hotels. Her works preserved for posterity what Eden called the "contrasts of public grandeur and private discomfort

Opposite page

𝒢 *ertrude*

ℰ *derle*

[that] will probably be seen no more, on a scale of such magnificence."

Mary A. Procida,
Visiting Assistant Professor of History,
Temple University, Philadelphia, Pennsylvania

Ederle, Gertrude (1906—)

American swimmer and winner of three medals at the 1924 Olympics before becoming the first woman to swim the English Channel, who set many international freestyle swimming records over short and long distance. Name variations: Trudie or Trudy. Pronunciation: ED-ur-LEE. Born Gertrude Caroline Ederle on October 23, 1906, in New York City; daughter of Henry and Gertrude Ederle (German immigrants and owners of a delicatessen on Amsterdam Avenue in New York); never married; no children.

Three-time medal-winner in the 1924 Olympics and record-setting swimmer of the English Channel in 1926. Records: 100 meters (1:12.5 on October 11, 1923); 150 yards (1:42.5 on March 1, 1925); 200 meters (2:45.2 on April 4, 1923); 220 yards (2:46.8 on April 4, 1923); 300 yards (3:58.4 on February 28, 1925); 400 meters (5:53.2 on September 4, 1922); 440 yards (5:54.6 on September 4, 1922); 500 yards (6:45.2 on September 4, 1922); 500 meters (7:22.2) and 880 yards (13:19.0) on September 4, 1922. Metropolitan New York junior 100-meter freestyle championship (1921); Olympic bronze medals in 100-meter and 400-meter freestyle, and gold medal in 4x100-meter freestyle relay team (1924). English Channel swim in 14 hours 31 minutes (1926).

America's Roaring '20s represents a decade of rebellion, personified by the short-skirted flappers and remembered for the consumption of spirits made illegal by passage of the 18th Amendment banning the manufacture and sale of alcoholic beverages. It is remembered more for its show of social excess than for the broader political questions raised by the appearance of women dancing the Charleston, going to speakeasies, and drinking and smoking in mixed company. The automobile, meanwhile, was providing a new level of mobility and opportunities to leave chaperons behind, helping to give rise to the so-called sexual revolution, along with the efforts of advanced thinkers like *Margaret Sanger and her American Birth Control League. It was also America's Golden Age of sports, a period when people knew more about Ruth, Gehrig, and Rockne than Hoover, Coolidge, and Harding. Before the decade was over Red Grange would be featured on the cover of *Time* magazine, and New York City would hold a

tickertape parade that registered the triumph of a new kind of female athlete, the swimmer Gertrude Ederle.

In the 1920s, swimming was still so novel as a competitive sport for women that, on the day Ederle completed her swim of the English Channel, the *London Daily News* carried a story claiming that women would always be the physically weaker sex. Strenuous activity was still believed by many to be harmful to women and their potential offspring. Ederle's achievements helped to dispel these views in a field of athletics previously dominated by men, while she set records of achievement that were to hold for many years.

Gertrude "Trudie" Ederle was born on October 23, 1906, in New York City, the second child of Henry and Gertrude Ederle, German immigrants who operated a small delicatessen on Amsterdam Avenue. Young Trudie showed early promise while swimming at her family's summer cottage in Highland, New Jersey. At age 13, in 1919, she joined the Women's Swimming Association on New York's Lower East Side.

*S*he was the catalyst that took thousands of women to the beaches and pools of America, as swimming became one of the leading women's sports in the United States.

—Janet Woolum

The Women's Swimming Association had been founded by *Charlotte Epstein, who led the organization in promoting sports for women for more than 20 years. Epstein wanted the same opportunities in sports for women that men enjoyed, and she helped many young women achieve dreams. Before 1914, James Sullivan was president of the Amateur Athletic Union (AAU) and held to the traditional view that the physical frailties of women should bar them from participating in strenuous physical activities. In 1914, after Sullivan died, Epstein worked with the AAU to get an agreement to sponsor meets and to register female swimmers. She also attempted to coerce colleges and universities to change their swimming policies but with less success.

Epstein, hoping to improve Ederle's self-esteem, had encouraged the young girl to join the Women's Swimming Association after she had dropped out of school. (Trudie's sister **Margaret Ederle** also swam there, but she did not show similar promise.) Within a year, Ederle had won the national championships in both the 220-yard and 440-yard swim. In 1922, the first sign of her approaching stardom occurred when she came in first in a field of 51 swimmers, including the British champion ✥➤ **Hilda James**, in a three-and-a-half-mile race across New York Bay to win the J.P. Day Cup. This was Ederle's initial race over a distance of more than 220 yards, and after her victory she went on to set at least nine amateur world records in distances of 100–500 meters.

In 1924, Ederle's growing prowess led to her selection for the American Olympic team. In the Paris Olympics, she earned three medals: bronze medals in the 100-meter and 400-meter freestyle and a gold medal as part of the winning 4x100-meter freestyle relay team, whose other members were **Euphrasia Donnelly**, ✥➤ **Ethel Lackie**, and ✥➤ **Mariechen Wehselau**.

By 1925, Ederle had decided to turn professional and swim the English Channel. In preparation, on June 15, 1925 she swam 21 miles from New York's Battery to Sandy Hook in New York's Lower Bay, in 7 hours 11 minutes, becoming the first woman to finish that course. That same year, her first attempt at swimming the English Channel failed six miles from the end because of cramping. Ederle did not want to quit, but her coach Jabez Wolffe had her physically removed from the water for fear that she might drown. Critics took this event as confirmation that women were physically inferior to men, while some publications discussed Ederle's strength as a detriment to her femininity, citing experts who held that you could not be a true woman and participate in such strenuous events. Humility, piety, domesticity and submissiveness were held as the prevailing characteristics of the ideal woman, and long-distance swimming was not within those boundaries.

The following year, Ederle's successful swim across the English Channel placed her name in the history books, as the sixth swimmer and first woman ever to accomplish the feat. The first long-distance swimmer to successfully complete the course had been Britain's Matthew Webb in 1875, followed by another Briton, Thomas W. Burgess, in 1911, and by Americans Henry Sullivan and Charles Toth and Argentinean Enrique Tiraboschi in 1923. Ederle's swim from Cape Gris-Nez, France, began in the early morning hours of August 6, 1926, at 7:09 AM, with her body greased with lard by her sister Margaret. Almost 15 hours later, at 9:40 PM, when most of England had settled in for the evening, she arrived at Kingsdorn, near Dover. A storm had closed the area to all normal shipping throughout the day, and she had to swim through rain that began in the early afternoon, with increasing winds that made the sea choppy by early evening. Ederle's trainer, father, sister, and others, who were tracking her progress in a tug named the *Alsace*, tried to get Ederle to stop on at least two occasions, but she refused. In later interviews, she maintained that she finished the swim for her mother, who sent periodic radiograms that were read to her from the boat by her supporters. Throughout the day, the crew aboard the *Alsace* also sang patriotic songs, including the National Anthem, to help keep her spirits high. With Burgess, one of the former channel swimmers, serving as her coach, Ederle swam the 30–35 miles in 14 hours 31 minutes, setting a new record and breaking the previous male record by nearly two hours. Her success received front page coverage throughout the United States, England, France, and Germany. Newspapers now characterized her as courageous and determined, and praised her for her endurance and stamina as well her modesty, generosity, and poise.

Congratulatory notes arrived by the thousands. Some simply commended her while others extended invitations to be a speaker at banquets or attend special ceremonies like German Day, held on October 31. Huge crowds greeted Ederle on her return to France, on her visit to her grandmother in Germany, and on her arrival in New York City in late August 1926. Newspapers called her "Queen of the Waves," while Tom Robinson, the swim coach at Northwestern University, declared to news reporters that Ederle's swim marked a triumph over corsets and petticoats that had long kept women out of the pools and out of the gyms. Her record for a woman's channel swim would stand until 1964.

In New York, Ederle was welcomed by the mayor at City Hall and treated to a tickertape parade, but her triumph was to prove fleeting. Though her agent, Dudley Malone, lined up appearances for her throughout the nation, other news events soon caught the imagination of a fickle public. Moreover, Ederle discovered that she did not like all the public attention. Always shy, she was uncomfortable with the scrutiny, and in 1928 she suffered a nervous breakdown.

In the early 1930s, Ederle endured another setback when she fell and injured her back. The spinal injury required that she wear a back brace for more than four years before she could return to swimming. By 1933, her swimming was also blamed for causing permanent deafness. Living with friends in New York City, she finally returned to swimming as a coach for deaf children. Her quiet life was interrupted on only two later occasions, when she was elected in 1965 to the International Swimming Hall of Fame, and

James, Hilda (1904—)
British swimmer. Born in 1904.

Hilda James won the silver medal in the 4x100-meter freestyle at the Antwerp Olympic Games in 1920.

Lackie, Ethel (1907—)
American swimmer. Born on February 10, 1907.

American swimmer Ethel Lackie not only won the gold medal for the 4x100-meter relay in Paris in 1924, she also won the gold medal in the 100-meter freestyle.

Wehselau, Mariechen (1906—)
American swimmer. Born on April 15, 1906.

Mariechen Wehselau won the gold medal in the 4x100-meter freestyle in Paris in 1924; she also won the silver in the 100-meter freestyle.

when she was inducted in 1980 into the Women's Sports Hall of Fame. Her accomplishments served as an inspiration to many other women who followed after her. In 1926, a writer for *The New York Times* may have described her achievement the best, calling her record-breaking channel swim a "triumph for femininity."

SOURCES:
Associated Press and Grolier. *The Olympic Story: Pursuit of Excellence.* NY: Franklin Watts, 1979.
Besford, Pat. *Encyclopedia of Swimming.* NY: St. Martin's Press, 1971.
"Gertrude Ederle Swims the Channel," in *The New York Times.* August 7, 1926.
Guttmann, Allen. *Women's Sports: A History.* NY: Columbia University Press, 1991.
Markel, Robert, Nancy Brooks, and Susan Markel. *For the Record: Women in Sports.* NY: World Almanac Publications, 1985.
The New York Times. August 6–10, 1926.
Woolum, Janet. *Outstanding Women Athletes.* Phoenix, AZ: Oryx Press, 1992.

Leslie Heaphy,
Assistant Professor of History
at Kent State University, Stark Campus, Kent, Ohio

Edflaed (c. 900–?)
West Saxon nun. Born around 900; interred at Wilton Abbey, Wiltshire, England; daughter of Edward I the Elder (c. 870–924), king of the English (r. 899–924), and *Elflaed (d. 920).

Edgeworth, Maria (1768–1849)
Irish author who wrote influential treatises on education in the early 19th century, as well as pioneering

*works in the genres of regional fiction and children's literature. Born on January 1, 1768 [earlier sources cite 1767] in Oxon, England; died at her family estate, Edgeworthtown, in County Longsford, Ireland, on May 22, 1849; eldest daughter of Richard Lovell Edgeworth (an inventor and educator) and **Anna Maria (Elers) Edgeworth**; educated at a girls' boarding school in Derby, England, until 15, then at home by her father; never married; no children.*

Mother died when she was seven; returned to her family estate in Ireland at 15; published her first works on education (1795–98); wrote her best-known work, Castle Rackrent (1800); wrote several dozen volumes of children's stories, romances, plays, treatises on education, and novels about rural Irish life; supervised the Edgeworthtown estate after the death of her father (1817).

Selected writings: Letters for Literary Ladies (1795); Practical Education (1798); Castle Rackrent (1800); Leonora (1806); Tales of Fashionable Life (1809, 1812: 6 vols.); Memoirs of Richard Lovell Edgeworth (1820); Helen (1834); Orlandino (1848).

In July of 1782, a coach made its way along the rutted roads of County Longsford in Ireland. Gazing out the window, young Maria Edgeworth saw a forlorn landscape, dotted with ramshackle peasant's cottages, filthy streets, and the decaying mansions of absentee landlords. At age 15, she and her family were coming home to Edgeworthtown, their family's estate. What Maria saw when she arrived looked nothing like the grand world of England where she had been living for the past seven years. Long abandoned, the Edgeworth mansion had been battered by time, sadly in need of repair. And the surrounding lands and cottages, where peasants did the work that supported the estate, were in even worse condition, suffering from years of poverty, neglect, and the greed of unscrupulous overseers.

There is no picture of me. My face has nothing remarkable in it of any kind nor has it any expression such as you would expect; therefore I would rather you took your idea of me from my writings.

—**Maria Edgeworth**

Gazing at this tattered scene, none would have imagined that Edgeworthtown would soon become one of the most celebrated spots on Europe's literary landscape, that writers and reformers from around the world would one day find their way to this remote place in the Irish countryside. This remarkable transformation was made possible by one of the great collaborations in lit-erary history, the partnership of Richard Edgeworth and his daughter, a woman who was called by her contemporaries "the Great Maria."

Maria's father was born on the family estate in Ireland, into the privileged class of English Protestant landlords who had taken over the country from the native Catholics two centuries earlier. While a student at Oxford, Richard fell in love with the daughter of a family friend, Anna Maria Elers. The two eloped and, when a son was born a year later, Richard ended his formal studies. But he spent the rest of his life learning, spurred on by a voracious curiosity, a remarkable talent for mechanical invention, and a self-confidence that many thought spilled over into egotism. One of his inventions brought him to the attention of Erasmus Darwin, the great poet, scientist, and grandfather of the evolutionist, Charles Darwin. Erasmus invited Richard to join the Lunar Society, a gathering of the most progressive scientists and philosophers in England at that time.

While Richard's intellectual life was stimulating, his marriage to Anna Maria was troubled. She apparently took little interest in his ideas, a gulf that was probably widened by his disastrous experiment with their son. Fascinated by Rousseau's romantic educational theories, Richard tested them on his own child. Rousseau was a great believer in the goodness of a child's natural instincts and encouraged parents not to damage these impulses with early education or discipline. Accordingly, Richard gave his son free rein through his early childhood, with terrible consequences. The boy became unbearably rude and unruly, forcing his father to abandon the experiment and reexamine his theory of education.

Born two years after the Edgeworths' first child, Maria experienced a different kind of neglect, the product not of deliberate experiment but of unhappy circumstances. She received little attention from her parents, who were preoccupied by their crumbling marriage and her mother's failing health. Anna Maria died when Maria was seven. Within four months, her father married **Honora Sneyd**, a beautiful and accomplished young Irishwoman who shared his interest in educational reform. Honora taught her new stepdaughter some important lessons. According to biographer **Elisabeth Inglis-Jones**, it was here that Maria learned "obedience and the scrupulous neatness and orderliness in whatever she did," traits that would mark her character for the rest of her life. But Maria was soon sent off to an English boarding school, separated from her family for most of the next seven years.

These were trying years for Maria. The school was designed to polish the social skills of upper-class girls, preparing them for marriage, but she felt too unattractive to ever win the heart of a suitor. She was short at 4'7". And, according to Inglis-Jones, "her pale narrow face looked altogether too small for her big, beaky nose and wide mouth." Making matters worse, she suffered inflammations of her eyes that contorted her entire face, and even threatened blindness.

Racked by insecurity, Maria's only refuge was her correspondence with her father. Perhaps hoping to compensate for his neglect, he wrote her long letters, instructing and encouraging her. Anxious to draw out her imagination, he asked her to write stories for him, thus awakening the talent that would one day make her famous. Edgeworth enjoyed these assignments and soon found that she could gain the attention of her classmates by improvising fanciful tales. From this point on, words became her way of winning the approval of the world in general, and her father in particular.

In 1782, Maria's life changed course dramatically. Honora Sneyd died of consumption, on her death bed encouraging Richard to take her sister, **Elizabeth**, as his new wife. Though some in English society considered the new match a scandal, Richard complied with Honora's last request just a few months after her funeral. At the same time, he resolved to make a fresh start with his lands and with his family, devoting his talents to his children's education and to the restoration of his estate along progressive lines. That summer, he reunited his family at their ancestral home in Edgeworthtown.

Although the house was badly dilapidated, Maria hardly noticed, entranced as she was by this sudden attention from her father. With his new wife absorbed much of the time in caring for a new set of Edgeworth babies, Richard looked to his eldest daughter, the plain but eloquent Maria, for a partner in his intellectual pursuits. He carefully supervised her education and, in turn, enlisted her in the education of her growing flock of younger brothers and sisters. This sense of purpose, and the intense bond of affection and intellectual partnership that grew between Maria and her father, dispelled her insecurity, replacing it with what Richard called "an inordinate desire to be beloved." For the rest of his life, Richard used Maria's need for his affection as a way to inspire her to write.

Undaunted by his failed attempt to create a natural man out of his first son, Richard continued his interest in educational reform. He and Maria spent long hours discussing the newest pedagogical theories, trying them out on the Edgeworth children and carefully noting the results. He even "gave" Maria one of her younger brothers to supervise as her own special project, granting her the chance to test the educational ideas they were developing. Using their family as a laboratory, the father and daughter team were pioneers in the field of experimental education, summarizing their findings in a work they called *Practical Education* (1798). While Richard had been working on these ideas for many years, much of the writing was done by Maria.

The Edgeworths argued that parents and educators should learn to see their children as individuals, each one with unique talents and needs. Children learn best, they found, when they are motivated by a love of learning and a desire to win the affection of their teachers, rather than by the fear of stern discipline. And their attentions are more easily engaged in practical, hands-on learning, than in the rote memorization of dead

Maria
Edgeworth

languages. Finally, they insisted that the education of girls was particularly in need of reform, that they were as capable as boys of learning all branches of knowledge and should be given an equal chance to do so. All of these ideas sound like modern-day common sense, but they were controversial innovations at the time. Maria's writings on education were avidly read and discussed by parents and educators all across Britain and Europe, and soon made the Edgeworths the most widely respected authorities on education in the early 19th century.

Maria also published *The Parent's Assistant,* a volume of children's tales designed to illustrate the Edgeworths' educational theories. These stories, the first of her many volumes of "wee-wee tales," transformed the fledgling field of children's literature. Like other children's stories written at the time, Maria's stories were extremely moralistic, written primarily to teach children right and wrong. But Maria learned how to instruct without sacrificing the art of storytelling. True to the Edgeworth tradition of experimental education, she did this by testing each story out with the audience of her brothers and sisters, noting what they liked and what bored them, and revising accordingly. As a result, she was one of the first adults to write stories that truly appealed to the mental world of children, teaching them by enchanting them.

While Maria was becoming one of Europe's leading experts on childhood education, she was receiving another, quite different education of her own at Edgeworthtown. Her father made her a partner in the running of his estate. After years of neglecting his land, Richard was determined to apply humane and scientific principles to his job as a landlord. He introduced many agricultural innovations and improved his tenants' living conditions. While most Protestant landlords took advantage of their Catholic tenants, he was a broad-minded man who preached religious toleration and treated all his tenants equally. Maria accompanied her father each day as he made his rounds, kept all of the estate's books, and helped him deal with a steady stream of tenants, beggars, and middle men. Few women of her day had such an opportunity to learn about the practical affairs of business and to observe such a wide spectrum of the human condition.

A keen and compassionate observer, Maria created a new form of fiction to record her observations about life in rural Ireland. In 1800, she published *Castle Rackrent,* a humorous short novel about the ruinous mismanagement of an Irish estate by generations of proud but in-

competent landlords. Told from the perspective of a "loyal" old servant, *Rackrent* captured the rich flavor of Irish dialect and culture, and the conflicts of class and religion endemic to Irish society. Though Maria and her father did not think much of the book at the time, critics consider it to be her masterpiece, its influence echoed in the works of Thackeray, Turgenev, and Cooper. Maria's sharp eye for manners, dialect and other traits of the Irish peasantry made her the founder of a new genre of "regional" literature. When Sir Walter Scott published the first of his popular tales about life in his native Scotland a few years later, he explained that his goal was "to emulate the admirable Irish portraits drawn by Miss Edgeworth."

In 1802, Maria traveled abroad in the company of her father and his wife. In London, Edinburgh, and even in Paris, where most of her works had appeared in translation, she was surprised to find herself at the center of attention. At social gatherings and literary salons, artists and aristocrats clamored for a sight of the great writer. From a distance, many were surprised at her physical appearance; her enormous talents seemed mismatched with her tiny frame, plain face, and, as one observer put it, her "look of utmost reserve and modesty." But those thoughts were soon dispelled when they drew close enough to hear her conversation and found her to be remarkably eloquent, witty, and charming. Her admirers' only regret was that she so often deferred to her father, who dominated the conversation and basked in his daughter's limelight.

The feeling that Edgeworth overshadowed his daughter, obstructing a clear view of her, has frustrated literary critics ever since. Some think that his constant presence in Maria's life damaged her art. Because she so often placed her fiction in the service of his educational theories, they charge that he encouraged her to be more moralistic than she might otherwise have been. Too eager to drive home one of his points, they say, she sometimes sacrificed the complexity and subtlety of her art.

Yet others feel that the collaboration was essential to Maria's work. Richard spent long hours discussing his daughter's new works with her and listening to her read them around the family hearth each night. He edited each line carefully and wrote introductions to many of her volumes. Perhaps most important of all, he urged her to keep writing, despite all the other distractions of her duties at Edgeworthtown. In some cases, when Maria's inspiration ran dry, he even suggested lengthy passages, which she dutifully inserted into her stories. Richard's defenders say that his own contributions fit seamlessly into Maria's work. After years of conversation and friendship, it seems, the two spoke with a single voice. Maria certainly felt this way. The only reason she wrote, she often said, was to please her father.

Though Richard loved his daughter's company as much as she loved his, he looked forward to the day when she would be married. During their stay in Paris, that opportunity came at last. A Swedish count named Edelcrantz proposed and asked her to return with him to live in the Swedish court. Maria was taken aback. She seems never to have allowed herself to dream of having a life partner, other than her father. Besides, though Edelcrantz was gallant and distinguished, she hardly knew this man. And, worst of all, to accept this offer she would have to leave Ireland, losing the inspiration and protection of her loving, bustling family at Edgeworthtown. In the end, Maria turned down what she sensed would be her only offer of marriage. For years, she brooded over the decision, but there is no evidence to suggest that she ultimately regretted it.

Home at Edgeworthtown in 1804, Maria poured out a remarkable stream of writing. For more than a decade, she published at least one, and as many as seven new volumes each year. Responding to popular demand, she continued to write educational tales for children and more serious treatises on education for adults. Drawing on her brief flurry of exposure to high society, she also produced a number of novels she called *Tales of Fashionable Life*. Invariably, these romances tried to make a moral point. Though Maria considered herself "as fond of novels as you can be," she worried that the genre too often acted "on the constitution of the mind as dreams do on that of the body." She strove to write novels that would instruct as they entertained. In *The Absentee* (1812), for example, she continued to explore the social and economic injustices of Ireland's negligent landlords. And in *Harrington* (1817), she attacked the problem of anti-Semitism in English society.

These happy and productive years came to a close in 1817, with the death of her father. For Maria, the loss was profound, and, as might be expected, the torrent of her literary output slowed to a trickle without his counsel and encouragement. For several years, she worked on the completion of his memoirs, a project he had begun and, on his deathbed, had asked her to complete. In the early 1820s, Edgeworth returned to England, again enjoying the accolades of her contemporaries, this time without her father to interrupt. She particularly enjoyed her growing friendship with Sir Walter Scott and paid an extended visit to his plantation in Scotland.

One of the most successful writers of her day, Edgeworth was able to support herself on her own income, despite a penchant for giving generously to worthy causes and lavishing gifts on her family members. But in 1826, she learned that her family estate was deep in debt, on the verge of being seized by creditors. Since her father's death, Edgeworthtown had been supervised by Maria's oldest living brother, Lovell. He had carried on the family tradition of commitment to education, founding a well-known school for boys in the nearby town. But he had expensive tastes and no head for business. The school, the home, and lands that had been in the family for centuries, and the annuities that Maria's father had set aside to support his large family, were now about to be lost by Lovell's recklessness. In desperation, he confessed his predicament to Maria, and she agreed, at age 56, to take over supervision of Edgeworthtown. Through years of hard work and careful management, she succeeded in saving the estate and restoring the family's financial stability.

As time healed the wound caused by the loss of her father, Maria felt "the delightful warmth of creation" returning to her. Though her art had to take a back seat while she struggled to save the family estate, she still succeeded in producing several volumes of children's stories. And in 1834, she completed her last novel, *Helen*. For the next 15 years, she continued to write occasional short stories, watch over affairs at Edgeworthtown, advocate for the poor during the Irish famine, and entertain the many poets and reformers who made their way to her door. She died in 1849, at the age of 81.

Now, Maria Edgeworth is best known for her depictions of the Irish peasantry, particularly in her masterpiece, *Castle Rackrent*. But a growing number of literary critics and historians believe that she should also be remembered for some of the other accomplishments that made her one of the most celebrated authors of her time. A re-examination of the full range of her writings, they suggest, will remind us that Edgeworth also made important contributions to the development of the novel, helped create a new children's literature, and made a major contribution to the history of educational thought.

SOURCES:

Harden, Elizabeth. *Maria Edgeworth*. Boston, MA: Twayne, 1984.

Inglis-Jones, Elisabeth. *The Great Maria: A Portrait of Maria Edgeworth*. Westport, CT: Greenwood Press, 1959.

Newcomer, James. *Maria Edgeworth*. Lewisburg: Bucknell University Press, 1973.

Ernest Freeberg,
historian, Bath, Maine

Edgeworth David, Mrs. (1856–1951).

See David, Caroline Edgeworth.

Edgifu (902–951)

*Queen of France and countess of Meaux. Name variations: Eadgifu; Edgiva or Edgive; Ogive or Odgive d'Angleterre. Born in 902 (some sources cite 896); died in 951; daughter of Edward I the Elder (c. 870–924), king of the English (r. 899–924), and *Elflaed (d. 920); married Charles III the Simple (879–929), king of France (r. 898–923), in 917; married Herbert of Vermandois, count of Meaux; children: (first marriage) Louis IV (918–954), king of France (r. 936–954).*

Edgifu (d. 968)

*Queen of the English. Name variations: Eadgifu; Edgiva. Born before 905; died on August 25, 968; interred at Canterbury Cathedral, Canterbury, Kent, England; daughter of Sigehelm, ealdorman of Kent; became second wife of Edward I the Elder (c. 870–924), king of the English (r. 899–924), around 905; children: *Edgifu (c. 917–?); *Edburga (d. 960); Edmund I the Magnificent (921–946), king of the English (r. 939–946); Edred or Eadred (c. 923–955), king of the English (r. 946–955).*

Edgifu (c. 917–?)

*Queen of Arles. Born around 917; date of death unknown; daughter of Edward I the Elder (c. 870–924), king of the English (r. 899–924), and *Edgifu (d. 968); married Louis II, prince of Aquitaine and king of Arles. (Some sources claim that she married Ebalus the Bastard, count of Poitou.)*

Edgitha (c. 912–946)

*West Saxon princess and German empress. Name variations: Eadgyth; Edith. Born around 912; died on January 26, 946, in Germany; interred at St. Maurice Cathedral, Magdeburg, Germany; daughter of Edward I the Elder (c. 870–924), king of the English (r. 899–924), and Elflaed (d. 920); stepdaughter of *Edgifu (d. 968); half-sister of English kings Ethelstan (r. 924–939), Edmund (r. 939–946), and Eadred (r. 946–955); niece of *Ethelflaed (869–918) and *Elfthrith (d. 929); became first wife of Otto I the Great (912–973), king of Germany (936–973), Holy Roman emperor (r. 962–973), and duke of Saxony, in 929 or 930; children: son Liudolf, duke of Swabia; daughter *Liutgard of Saxony (d. 953), duchess of Lorraine. (Otto also had an illegitimate son William, future archbishop of Mainz, from an early liaison with a Slav woman of noble birth.)*

Edgitha was the daughter of *Elflaed and Edward the Elder and the half-sister of English king Ethelstan, whose mother *Ecgwynn had been Edward's mistress. To shore up alliances, Ethelstan married Edgitha to the German emperor Otto I the Great. As her wedding gift, Otto offered her the town of Magdeburg, an important commercial crossroad. After Magdeburg was destroyed by the Magyars, Edgitha rebuilt the town, and upon her death in 946 she was buried there. When Otto died in 973, he was buried next to her. Otto's second wife was *Adelaide of Burgundy (931–999), the mother of Otto II.

Edgiva.

Variant of Edgifu.

Edgiva or Edgive (902–951).

See Edgifu.

Edgren, Anne Charlotte (1849–1892)

Swedish novelist, dramatist, and duchess of Cajanello. Name variations: Anne Charlotte Leffler; Anne Edgren-Leffler; Duchess di Cajanello; (pseudonym) Carlot. Born Anne Charlotte Leffler in Stockholm, Sweden, on October 1, 1849; died in Naples, Italy, on October 21, 1892; daughter of C.O. Leffler; sister of Gösta Mittag-Leffler (a professor of mathematics at the University of Stockholm); married Gustav Edgren, in 1872 (separated about 1884, divorced 1889); married Pasquale del Pezzo (an Italian mathematician), duke of Cajanello, in 1890.

Anne Charlotte Edgren, a prominent 19th-century Swedish writer, won an eminent position in the world of letters for her style, skill, and realistic portrayal of upper-class life. As the only daughter of a Swedish rector, she experienced a comfortable and commonplace childhood. From her mother, who was also the daughter of a cleric, she inherited her literary tendencies and was encouraged toward writing by her parents and three devoted brothers, although they thought it best to restrain her from publishing her early efforts. Once her talent was developed, Anne Edgren's first book, a collection of stories entitled *Händelsvis* (*By Chance*), appeared in 1869, under the pseudonym "Carlot."

In 1872, she entered into a marriage, probably of convenience, with Gustav Edgren, secretary of the prefecture in Stockholm. Although the alliance was harmonious at first, by about 1884 she was separated from her husband, who did not share her advanced views. Until the time of her engagement to Gustav, Anne Charlotte had never visited the theater and was ignorant of stage technique. Nevertheless, her dramatic instincts belied her lack of training, and she became a successful playwright. In 1873, Edgren's drama *Skådespelerskan* (*The Actress*) was produced anonymously and held the stage in Stockholm for an entire winter; this was followed by *Pastorsadjunkten* (*The Curate*) in 1876 and *Elfvan* (*The Elf*) in 1880, the latter being even more successful. The theme of all her dramas centered on the struggle of a woman's individuality within the confines of her life.

Edgren's first work to be published under her own name came in 1882 with *Ur Lifvet* (*From Life*), a series of realistic sketches of the upper circles of Swedish society. The collection was extremely well received. Her works were translated into Danish, Russian, and German, and Edgren became widely known as one of the most talented of Swedish writers. In 1883, a second volume of *From Life* appeared and was followed in 1889 with yet another volume under the same title. These later stories showed an unprecedented boldness of thought and expression, placing Edgren among the ranks of the radicals. *Sanna Kvinnor* (*Ideal Women*), a drama directed against exaggerated femininity, appeared in 1883 and was well received in Germany as well as in Sweden. She also wrote *Hur Man Gör Godt* (*How We Do Good*) in 1885 and *Kampen für Lyckan* (*The Struggle for Happiness*) in 1888, the latter in collaboration with *Sophia Kovalevskaya.

In company with her brother, Professor Gösta Mittag-Leffler, Edgren attended a Mathematical Congress in Algiers in the early part of 1888. Upon her return through Italy, she met a friend of her brother's, Pasquale del Pezzo, subsequently duke of Cajanello, who was a mathematician and professor at the University of Naples. Edgren was married to the duke in 1890, following the dissolution of her marriage

with Gustav. Later that year, she published a romance, *Kvinlighet och Erotik* (*Womanliness and Erotics*), which attracted a great deal of attention, and other dramas, including *Familjelycka* (*Domestic Happiness*) and *En Räddande Engel* (*A Rescuing Angel*), which proved to be her greatest dramatic success. Her last book (1892) was a biography of her close friend Sophia Kovalevskaya. An English translation (1895) by A. de Furnhjelm and A.M. Clive Bayley contains a biographical note on Edgren by **Lily Wolffsohn**, based on private sources. Anne Charlotte Edgren died suddenly in Naples on October 21, 1892, while at the height of her creative powers. Her biography, written by *Ellen Key, was published in 1893.

SUGGESTED READING:

Key, Ellen. *Anne Charlotte Leffler*. Stockholm, 1893.

Edgyth.

Variant of Edith.

Edhild (d. 946)

*West Saxon princess. Name variations: Eadhild; Edhilda. Died on January 26, 946; daughter of Edward I the Elder (c. 870–924), king of the English (r. 899–924), and *Elflaed (d. 920); married Hugh the Great also known as Hugh the White (c. 895–956), count of Paris and duke of Burgundy, in 926. Hugh the Great's second wife was *Hedwig (c. 915–965).*

Edib, Halide (c. 1884–1964).

See Adivar, Halide Edib.

Edinburgh, duchess of.

See Marie Alexandrovna (1853–1920).

Edinger, Tilly (1897–1967)

German-born American scientist, a major world figure in vertebrate paleontology, who essentially established the field of paleoneurology. Born Johanna Gabrielle Ottilie Edinger in Frankfurt am Main, Germany, on November 13, 1897; died in Cambridge, Massachusetts, on May 27, 1967; daughter of Ludwig Edinger (1855–1918, professor of neurology at the University of Frankfurt) and Anna (Goldschmidt) Edinger; sister of Friedrich (Fritz) Edinger and Dorothea (Dora) Edinger; received doctorate from University of Frankfurt, 1921; never married; no children.

Born Johanna Gabrielle Ottilie Edinger into a highly assimilated German-Jewish family of

Tilly Edinger

The year 1918 was particularly traumatic for the patriotic Edinger family. Ludwig died in January, and Germany was defeated in November. As good German *Bürgers,* none of the Edingers could then have imagined that within 15 years, because they were Jews, they would be demonized as "un-German aliens" and forced to flee their beloved homeland. But in time the horrors of modern German history would determine the course of Tilly Edinger's career and life.

An excellent student, she graduated from Frankfurt's elite Schillerschule. As a typical German university student spending semesters at several institutions—the universities of Heidelberg, Munich, and finally Frankfurt am Main—she originally intended to major in geology. Upon discovering that there were few positions for women in this field, however, she switched to zoology. When told that this field, too, was virtually closed to women, she refused to be discouraged and signed up for courses in the specialized area she had wished to study in the first place—vertebrate paleontology. Edinger received her doctorate in 1921 from the University of Frankfurt; her dissertation topic was a detailed study of the skull and cranial cavity of Nothosaurus, a long-extinct marine reptile of the Triassic era.

Soon, however, Edinger's scientific interests shifted to her late father's area of neurology. Her time was now occupied with work in paleontology, and in 1927 her growing reputation in the field was recognized when she was appointed curator of the vertebrate collection at Frankfurt's Senckenberg Museum. Her financial independence, due to her family's wealth, made it possible for her to accept this prestigious but unpaid position. Her intensive research during the 1920s made it clear that there was a need for a direct study of fossil mammal brains on the basis of casts made from their cranial cavities. Since brain tissues do not fossilize, casts of the inside of the skull make it possible for experts to reconstruct a reasonable facsimile of the long-dead animal's brain structure. Up to that time, little research had been done in this field. As the quality of Edinger's scientific papers became apparent to those who read them, the importance of this new area of science for a study of the evolution of animal intelligence became apparent to the world scientific community. Within a few years, her probing and systematic work had earned her an international scientific reputation.

In 1929, Edinger published a major study of fossil brains, *Die fossilen Gehirne.* Just as her achievements began to bring recognition, a time

Frankfurt am Main's wealthy *Grossbürgertum* (upper bourgeoisie), young Tilly enjoyed the privileges of the doomed world of pre-1914 Europe: servants, long and leisurely vacations, and a sense of security. A serious health impediment, congenital deafness, did little to rein in her curiosity. Because her parents encouraged her intellectual growth and could afford books, travel and every aspect of high culture, her path to an academic career was open if not assured. Tilly's father Ludwig Edinger, a professor of neurology at the University of Frankfurt, was a distinguished medical researcher and one of the founders of the field of comparative neurology. After his death, the city of Frankfurt am Main named a street after him. Tilly's mother **Anna Edinger** (1863–1929) was descended from the influential Warburg family of bankers; though she concentrated on home life, Anna was socially conscious and active in welfare work. After her death, she was honored with a bronze bust in the municipal park.

of chaos and moral disintegration descended on Germany. The onset of the world economic depression (1929–30) led to a rapid deterioration of social and political stability, the most dramatic manifestation of which was the rapid growth of Adolf Hitler's National Socialist movement. The Nazis viewed many as foes to be extirpated, but Germany's Jews, linked in millions of minds to the suspect ideals of liberal bourgeois democracy, invariably came at the top of their list.

After the Nazi takeover in 1933, Edinger did not leave Germany. Like many German Jews, she thought of herself as a German citizen of the Jewish faith and believed—or at least hoped—that the storm would blow over. But Nazism grew more virulent with time, although for purely tactical reasons Nazi anti-Semitic policies blew alternately hot and cold. In Edinger's case, a workable modus vivendi emerged on her job. Nazi anti-Semitism was rapidly purging German public life of Jews, but she was able to retain her post of curator at the Senckenberg Museum. Although the museum's director was a Nazi, he clearly recognized Edinger's value to his institution and created a situation that made it possible for her to continue to work there for more than five years under the Hitler regime. The stratagem was one of removing her name from the door of her office, and allowing her to leave the premises whenever there were visitors. This precariously "normal" situation ended in 1938, when a heightened ferocity of the Nazi war on German Jews led to her discovery and expulsion from the museum.

Long realizing that being Jewish in Germany was a hopeless situation, Edinger had already obtained a visa to immigrate to the United States. But the waiting list was long, and by the time of the violent Kristallnacht pogrom of November 1938 she still could not depart from Germany. Concerned colleagues at Harvard offered her a post-graduate fellowship so that she could emigrate immediately, but the snag was that she would have to return to Germany after the fellowship's expiration and also be forced to relinquish her place in the quota. A better situation soon emerged when the Harvard Corporation offered her a tenured faculty appointment. Nevertheless, her quota number was still not due, and in May 1939 Edinger was able to leave Germany for a temporary stay in England, the basis for this being the permanent immigration status that had earlier been granted her by U.S. authorities. Her brother Friedrich (Fritz) was not as fortunate; unable to escape Nazi Germany, he died in the Holocaust.

Safe from Nazi persecution but penniless, Edinger eked out a living in London by working as a translator and living frugally. By now, war had descended on the European Continent, and she was relieved to arrive in Cambridge, Massachusetts, in 1940 to resume her scientific work. Thanks to the intercession of Alfred Sherwood Romer, director of Harvard's Museum of Comparative Zoology, Edinger became a research associate at the museum. Except for a year of teaching comparative zoology at Wellesley College, she would remain at the museum for the rest of her life. Research work best fitted Edinger's health situation, for she was extremely hard of hearing; as a result, classroom teaching presented its own obstacles.

For more than two decades, Edinger's work flourished at Harvard. Her studies of fossil brains, the first systematic work in the field, proved that the evolution of the brain in animals should be studied directly from fossils rather than from a hierarchy of separate living species, each of which had adopted its own mode of life in modern times. A vigorous polemicist, in her publications she often attacked orthodox thinking in her field as being outmoded and just plain wrong. In her work on the horse brain, she convincingly showed that an enlarged forebrain had evolved several times, independently among advanced mammal groups, and no single evolutionary scale could be seen as embracing all of them.

Her work made a strong case for viewing brain evolution in terms of the varying ecologies and adaptations among mammals; she also provided convincing evidence of how rates and styles of change varied significantly in different lineages. In 1948, she published the results of her pathbreaking investigations in a major work, *The Evolution of the Horse Brain*.

Because of Edinger's pioneering work, by the 1950s paleoneurology had become one of the most exciting subdisciplines of vertebrate paleontology. Her research found recognition through fellowships awarded her by the Guggenheim Foundation and the American Foundation of University Women. Edinger was honored by her fellow scientists in 1964 when she was elected president of the Society of Vertebrate Paleontology. Other signs of the universal respect her work had earned included the honorary doctorates awarded by Wellesley College and in Germany by the universities of Giessen and Frankfurt am Main. Despite the suffering inflicted in Germany during the 1930s, including the murder of her brother, Edinger insisted on distinguishing between the good and the bad in her native country's people and culture. She remained loyal to her home city of Frankfurt am Main, visited it on several occasions and was deeply moved by the honorary degree that she received from its university in 1964.

Edinger enjoyed her postwar visits to Frankfurt, and in 1967 looked forward to another visit on the occasion of the 150th anniversary of the founding of the Senckenberg Museum. But her lifelong hearing difficulties proved to be a fatal handicap in the spring of that year when, unaware of its dangerous proximity, she was struck by an automobile near her home in Cambridge on May 26, 1967. She died of her injuries the following day.

To honor her, a Tilly Edinger Fund was established for the purchase of books on vertebrate paleontology at the Harvard Museum of Comparative Zoology. She was remembered by Stephen Jay Gould as a major scientist with a strong personality, "feisty, strong-willed, opinionated, and warm-hearted—a most engaging, if sometimes trying, combination." Another colleague recalled her "warmth of emotion [which] would, on occasion, rouse her violently against things or persons which she disliked—notably editing and editors! But in general this emotional warmth erupted in friendship and affection, and won her hosts of friends. Typical was her spirit as a refugee. Like many in those days, she found herself here in position and finances far below the status which she had formerly enjoyed. Did Tilly complain? Far from it! She became an enthusiastic American citizen, to whom her 'Uncle Sam' was almost a living person, and her gratitude to Harvard and affection for the Museum were without bounds."

SOURCES:

Aldrich, Michele L. "Women in Geology," in G. Kass-Simon et al., eds. *Women of Science: Righting the Record*. Bloomington: Indiana University Press, 1990, pp. 42–71.

Bailey, Martha J. *American Women in Science: A Biographical Dictionary*. Denver: ABC-CLIO, 1994.

"Edinger, Tilly, Ph.D.," in *Encyclopedia of American Biography*. New Series, Vol. 39. NY: American Historical Society, 1969, pp. 248–250.

"Famous Horseologists—Tilly Edinger (1897–1967)," in *Pony Express: Florida Fossil Horse Newsletter*. Vol. 2, no. 4. December 1993, pp. 2–3.

Gould, Stephen Jay. "Edinger, Tilly," in Barbara Sicherman et al., eds. *Notable American Women, The Modern Period: A Biographical Dictionary*. Cambridge, MA: The Belknap Press of Harvard University Press, 1980, pp. 218–219.

Hoffer, Helmut. "In Memoriam Tilly Edinger," in *Gegenbaurs Morphologisches Jahrbuch*. Vol. 113, No. 2, 1969, pp. 303–313.

Lang, Harry G., and Bonnie Meath-Lang. *Deaf Persons in the Arts and Sciences: A Biographical Dictionary*. Westport, CT: Greenwood Press, 1995.

Olson, Everett C. *Vertebrate Paleozoology*. NY: Wiley-Interscience, 1971.

Romer, Alfred Sherwood. "Tilly Edinger," in *Society of Vertebrate Paleontology News Bulletin*. No. 81. October 1967, pp. 51–53.

———. *Vertebrate Paleontology*. 3rd ed. Chicago: University of Chicago Press, 1966.

COLLECTIONS:

Edinger Family Papers, Leo Baeck Institute, New York City.

Tilly Edinger Papers, Archives of the Museum of Comparative Zoology, Harvard University, Cambridge, Massachusetts.

John Haag,
Assistant Professor of History,
University of Georgia, Athens, Georgia

Edip, Halide (c. 1884–1964).

See Adivar, Halide Edib.

Edissa (fl. 475 BCE).

See Esther.

Edith.

Variant of Edgitha.

Edith (d. 871)

Abbess of Pellesworth. Name variations: Editha, abbess of Polesworth. Died in 871; interred at Polesworth Abbey, Warwickshire; daughter of Ecgbert also known as Egbert III (c. 775–839), king of Wessex, Kent, and the English (r. 802–839), and *Redburga; sister of Ethelwulf (Æthelwulf), king of Wessex and England (r. 839–858); Ethelstan (d. around 851), king of Kent.

Edith (c. 912–946).

See Edgitha.

Edith (d. 937)

Queen of York and abbess of Pellesworth. Name variations: Saint Edith; abbess of Polesworth. Died in 937; illegitimate daughter of Edward I the Elder, king of the English (r. 899–924), and *Ecgwynn (d. around 901); married Sihtric, king of York, on January 30, 926 (some sources cite July 30, 925), in Tamworth, Staffordshire, England; children: Amlaib; Gofraid; Olaf Cuarán, king of Dublin and York; possibly Gyda.

Edith, the illegitimate daughter of Edward I the Elder, king of the English, and *Ecgwynn, married Sihtric, king of York, on January 30, 926. Following the death of her husband, she became a nun at Pellesworth Abbey, then transferred to Tamworth Abbey in Gloucestershire where she was elected abbess. She was canonized as a saint; her feast day is on July 15.

Edith (c. 961–984)

West Saxon nun and saint. Name variations: Saint Edith; Eadgyth. Born around 961 in Kemsing, Kent, England; died on September 16, 984, in Wilton, Wiltshire, England; illegitimate daughter of Edgar (944–975), king of the English (r. 959–975), and Wulfthryth (c. 945–1000, his mistress).

Edith was born in Kemsing, Kent, around 961, the illegitimate daughter of Edgar, king of the English, and his mistress ***Wulfthryth**. Wulfthryth retired to the monastery of Wilton, where Edith was raised and took the veil. Edith remained in the monastery until her death, at age 23, in 984. Her feast day is on September 16.

Edith (fl. 1009)

West Saxon princess. Flourished in 1009; daughter of Aethelred or Ethelred II the Unready (c. 968–1016), king of the English (r. 979–1013, deposed, 1014–1016), and *Elfgifu (c. 963–1002); married Eadric or Edric Streona, ealdorman of Mercia (r. 1007–1017), in 1009 (executed on December 25, 1017); married Thurkil the Tall; children: (first marriage) daughter (name unknown, who married Ethelgar and was the mother of Siward and Ealdred); (second marriage) Harold.

Edith (c. 1025–1075)

Queen of the English. Name variations: Ealdgyth; Eadgyth; Edgyth. Born around 1025; died on December 18, 1075, in Winchester, Hampshire, England; interred at Westminster Abbey; daughter of Godwin or Godwine (d. 1053), earl of Wessex, and *Gytha; sister of Harald or Harold II Godwineson (c. 1022–1066), king of the English (r. 1066); married Edward III the Confessor (c. 1002–1066), king of the English (r. 1042–1066), on January 23, 1045; children: none.

Edith was the daughter of ***Gytha** and Godwine, earl of Essex. She married Edward III the Confessor, king of the English, in 1045, receiving Winchester and Exeter as her morning gift. Edith is said to have planned the murder of Gospatric, one of the king's thegns, in 1064, at the instigation of her brother Tostig, earl of Northumberland. She founded a church at Wilton, which was consecrated in 1065, and on the death of her husband retired to Winchester.

Edith (fl. 1040)

Lady Allerdale. Name variations: Ealdgyth. Daughter of Uchtred, earl of Northumberland, and *Elfgifu (daughter of Ethelred II the Unready); married Maldred Dunkeld (brother of Duncan I, king of Scotland), lord of Allerdale; children: Gospatric Dunkeld (b. around 1040), earl of Northumberland; Maldred of Allerdale.

Edith (fl. 1063)

Queen of the English. Name variations: Aldgyth; Algytha; Eadgyth; Ealdgyth. Flourished around 1063; died after 1070; daughter of Aelfgar or Elfgar, earl of Mercia, and Elfgifu (daughter of Morcar and Ealdgyth); married Griffith also known as Gruffydd ap Llywelyn, ruler of All Wales, around 1050 (killed in 1063); married Harald or Harold II Godwineson (c. 1022–1066), king of the English (r. 1066), in January 1066, in London; children: (first marriage) Nesta Ferch; Maredudd, king of Powys; Ithell; (second marriage) Harold (b. 1066).

In 1063, provoked by Welsh incursions, Harold II Godwineson, king of England, marched against Gruffydd ap Llywelyn, ruler of All Wales. After Gruffydd was killed by his own people, Harold turned the reins of government over to Gruffydd's brothers, Bleddyn and Rhiwallon, who swore fealty oaths to him. Harold then wed Gruffydd's enchanting widow Edith in order to secure the alliance of her brothers, Morcar and Edwin. When Harold died at the Battle of Hastings in October 1066, it was another woman sometimes called Edith, his mistress Edith of the Swan's Neck also known as ***Eadgyth Swanneshals**, who identified his body.

Edith Matilda (1080–1118).

See Empress Matilda (1102–1167) for sidebar on Matilda of Scotland.

Edith of the Swan's Neck (c. 1012–?).

See Eadgyth Swanneshals.

Edla (fl. 900s)

Swedish mistress. Paramour of Olof or Olaf Sköttkonung or Skötkonung, king of Sweden (r. 994–1022); children: Emund the Old, king of Sweden (r. 1050–1060); Astrid Olafsdottir. Olaf's wife was *Astrid of the Obotrites (c. 979–?).

Edmonds, Emma (1841–1898)

Canadian-American nurse who, disguised as a man, served the Union Army during the American Civil War as a nurse, courier, and spy. Name variations: Sarah Edwards; Sarah Emma Evelyn Edmonson;

Emma Edmonds; Frank Thompson; Mrs. Sarah Emma E. Seelye. Born Sarah Emma Evelyn Edmonson in Magaguadavic, New Brunswick province, Canada, in December 1841; died on September 5, 1898, in La Porte, Texas; daughter of Isaac Edmonson (a farmer) and Elizabeth (Betsy) Leeper; attended Oberlin College in Oberlin, Ohio; married Linus H. Seely (an "e" was added after marriage, creating "Seelye"), on April 27, 1867; children: Linus B., Homer, Alice Louise; (adopted children) George Frederick, Charles Finney.

Disguised as a man, joined the Union Army at the outbreak of the American Civil War (1860), first duty was that of male nurse; later acted as postman, postmaster, courier, and spy for the Federal Secret Service; following military service, wrote memoirs and supported various charities.

During the American Civil War, one soldier served as a dispatch courier, male nurse, and spy for the Federal Secret Service. That same soldier was a Canadian expatriate, a teenager, and a woman. Disguised as a man, Emma Edmonds joined the Union Army to fight in the Civil War.

Sarah Emma Evelyn Edmonson was born in December 1841 in Magaguadavic, New Brunswick province, Canada, one of six children of Isaac and **Betsy Edmonson**, who were potato farmers. Life was often difficult in the Edmonson family. Authoritarian and strongly patriarchal, Isaac was cruel and demeaning to Betsy and had a general resentment toward women. With a farm to run, he desired sons to handle the heavy work. Betsy gave him five daughters, with the only son being sickly and epileptic. Emma was their last child, thereby dashing any hope for a healthy male sibling. This seemed to add to Isaac's disgust with Emma, and she was often browbeaten by her tyrannical and quick-tempered father.

I felt called to go and do what I could for the defense of the right; if I could not fight, I could take the place of someone who could, and thus add one more soldier to the ranks.

—Emma Edmonds

In order to gain her father's approval, Emma took it upon herself to work, play, and think like a boy. Her duties around the farm were performed with physical gusto, and she excelled at equestrian skills, hunting, and fishing. Despite her best efforts, Isaac remained unimpressed and disappointed in his youngest child.

While still a girl, Emma received a gift from a traveling peddler. *Fanny Campbell, The Female Pirate Captain: A Tale of the Revolution!* was a novel about a girl who masquerades as a man to rescue her boyfriend from pirates. Emma idealized the heroine who had the bravery not only to seek out her lover but to experience the adventure and excitement of the then masculine world. The images within this novel, along with the expectations of her father, would leave a lasting impression.

Throughout her teenage years, Emma resisted conventional dating practices, along with any romantic social situations involving boys. This did not deter her father from arranging her marriage to an older, local farmer. Appalled, she desperately sought a way out. With the covert help of her mother, Emma was secreted out of town to stay with a family friend in the town of Salisbury, 100 miles away.

In her new home, Emma changed her last name to Edmonds and was schooled in the millinery trade, eventually becoming so successful that she and a partner opened their own hat shop. Her prosperity was short-lived, as her father got wind of her whereabouts and seemed sure to retrieve her. Again, she had to escape. She disappeared, evidently without informing her business partner or friends as to her destination, and resurfaced in Saint John, New Brunswick, sporting both a new appearance and name. Her hair was cut short, and she was dressed in men's clothing. In order to elude her father's wrath and live the fantasy of Fanny Campbell, Emma had become Frank Thompson.

Edmonds had worn male clothing for years, both as a practicality of heavy farm work and to gain acceptance from her father. Thus, she was accustomed to this mode of dress and may have found it more comfortable than typical female garb of the period. Though small in stature, her body had been made strong by years spent as a farmhand. This, along with a flat bosom, made for a convincing male disguise.

In her new role as an ambitious young man, Edmonds found a job selling Bibles and religious books door-to-door. She was quite successful in applying her trade throughout New Brunswick and later relocated to the United States, perhaps to satisfy her desire for travel and adventure. While tensions escalated among the states, Edmonds made Flint, Michigan, her home.

But Emma's peaceful life in Flint was not to last as the Confederacy attacked Fort Sumter on April 12, 1861. Three days later, President Abraham Lincoln made a public proclamation requesting 75,000 militia; the Civil War had begun. As bands played and flags waved, the streets of Flint were swept up in the war hysteria. While Edmonds could have easily returned to her native Canada, she felt compelled to consider an alternative. "I was not able to decide for myself," she wrote, "so I carried this question to the Throne of Grace, and found a satisfactory answer there." With God and her loyalties in agreement, Emma decided to serve in the military.

At the time, entry into the Union Army required no physical examination. However, there was a height requirement of 5'8¼", which Edmonds did not meet, being only 5'6". Though bitterly disappointed, she reapplied the following month. Demand for recruits had become so great by then that the recruiting agents overlooked shortcomings and signed up as many men as possible. Accepted into the Union Army, Edmonds was sent to Fort Wayne, Detroit, for basic training. On May 25, 1861, ironically the same day that draft boards received more stringent regulations regarding the selection of new recruits, Emma Edmonds became Private Frank Thompson, Union Army nurse.

Emma
Edmonds

Her assignment as a male nurse may have been the result of Emma's small size, though descriptions of her demeanor suggest that her stature was irrelevant. Fellow soldiers described her as "dependable as well as conscientious" and "ready for duty, brave, willing and cheerful." Perhaps most flattering was the comrade who noted Edmonds as being a "strong, healthy and robust soldier." Such praise would follow her throughout her varied military service.

Emma arrived in Washington on June 10, 1861, with the Second regiment of Michigan Volunteers. There she continued her military drills and began nursing training. She had the good fortune to acquire Damon Stewart as her bunk mate. They had been friends in Flint before the war began, and his companionship was a comfort to her in this new and strange environment.

Emma and the Union Army would experience their first major military engagement at the Battle of Bull Run. On July 21, 1861, Union and Confederate forces clashed near the town of Manassas, Virginia. Although both forces were relatively inexperienced, the North suffered from poor timing and overconfidence. The South, getting the upper hand, began to drive the Union into a retreat that soon digressed into a headlong panic. Expecting a decisive Union victory, picnicking Washingtonians, who had taken up spectating points on the neighboring hillsides, now vied for space on the crowded roads and bridges leading to the safe haven of Washington. During the battle, Edmonds tended to the wounded and dodged sniper fire to obtain needed supplies. She stayed with the wounded until the advancing Rebels compelled her to join the retreat. Despite the Union loss, Emma met her first battlefield experience with the courage and professionalism of a model soldier.

The Battle of Bull Run became a rout to the Confederacy and a wake up call to the Union. The Federal troops were reorganized to form the Army of the Potomac, commanded by General George B. McClellan. The general spent the remainder of the summer and the following winter retraining his new army.

It was during this hiatus that Edmonds would make an important friendship. James V. (an alias) had been a childhood friend from New Brunswick. He was now Lieutenant James V. of the Army of the Potomac, whom Emma describes with the highest respect, honor, and warmth. Her memoirs state plainly that the lieutenant did not recognize his transformed schoolmate, and they proceeded to develop a "new

friendship." While this scenario is certainly possible, it's unlikely that the lieutenant didn't see past Emma's charade, especially when considering how deeply she was touched by him. In any event, their relationship became a mutual asset in the face of the impending hostilities. Another friendly acquaintance was that of Colonel Poe, her new regiment commander. The colonel seemed to favor Emma, making her letter carrier and later postmaster to the entire brigade. As in the case with Lieutenant James V., the nature of their relationship was suspicious.

The spring of 1862 found the refurbished Army of the Potomac ready for action. The plan was to land at the Union-held Fort Monroe at the mouth of the James River and push northwest up the Virginia peninsula to Richmond, the Confederate capital. Heavy rains and food shortages plagued the troops as they plodded up the peninsula. Edmonds continued delivering the mail, while fighting a case of malaria developed in the swampy and soggy conditions. Upon returning from one of her rounds, she received horrible news: Lieutenant James V. had been killed by a sniper while delivering orders to the outer picket line. "Now he was gone," she wrote in her memoirs, "and I was left alone with a deeper sorrow in my heart than I had ever known before." Her reaction added support to their suspected, deeper relationship, and helped to explain her next rash and dangerous decision.

A Federal spy had been captured and executed in Richmond, and someone was needed to take his place. Edmonds applied for the post and was sent to Washington for interviews and evaluations. Having been found worthy of the position, she returned to her regiment as a sworn member of the Federal Secret Service.

Her first assignment was to infiltrate the Rebel lines at Yorktown and take note of fortifications and troop numbers. To pose as a black male worker, she used walnut juice to darken her skin, shaved her head, donned a black wig, and wore "real plantation style" clothing. She had no trouble sneaking past the Rebel lines and freely walked throughout the Yorktown fortifications. A Confederate officer found this idle black to be suspicious and ordered Emma to the gun barriers where she spent an exhaustive day in heavy labor on the fortifications. That evening, she bribed a black worker for his job and spent the next two days carrying water to the Rebel troops. This gave her an excellent opportunity to observe the camp and to listen in on camp talk. On the evening of the third day, after gathering sufficient information, Edmonds volunteered to bring water to the outer pickets. She slipped into the night and quietly crossed the line to Union ground. Along with descriptions of armaments and troop estimates, Edmonds' report included overheard conversations claiming that Yorktown could not be held if attacked. This proved to be correct, for as the Union readied their attack the Confederates quietly pulled out of Yorktown.

The Federal advance toward Richmond was slower than expected, due in part to the heavy rains, but also to the reticence of General McClellan. Inaccurate intelligence reports convinced the general that he was badly outnumbered when in fact the Union had a numerical advantage. Disappointed by their lack of progress, one of McClellan's officers nicknamed him "the Virginia Creeper." For her second spy mission, Edmonds was to enter a Rebel camp and discover how they interpreted the Union's slow advance.

Disguised as an Irish peddler woman, Edmonds set out toward the Rebel line, forging through rain swollen rivers and swamps. Soaking wet from her travels, she became ill and spent the next three days in the swamp, incapacitated. Finally, she stumbled upon an abandoned house that contained food and, to her surprise, a dying Confederate officer. She fed both herself and the officer, then stayed with him until he died. Emma agreed to honor his final wish; to inform his friends at the Rebel camp about his fate. She touched up her peddler disguise and walked straight into the Rebel headquarters.

Her act worked flawlessly, enabling her to casually eavesdrop on the camp scuttlebutt. She then sought out the friend of the officer whose death she had witnessed. Grateful for the information, he asked if Edmonds would lead them back to retrieve his comrade's body and loaned her a horse for the escort. As they tended to the corpse, Edmonds was asked to check for any sign of Yankees further down the road. She casually rode in that direction but did not stop until she found the Union Army.

The peninsula campaign became a bitter failure for the North. Numerous battles had been fought, bringing Richmond within reach of the Union. Yet General McClellan's fear of the thousands of nonexistent "ghost" troops sacrificed the Union's momentum and advantage. McClellan pulled back to Harrison's Landing on the James River, appealing to Lincoln for more new troops. On August 3, 1862, McClellan and his Army of the Potomac were ordered to leave the peninsula.

For Edmonds, the campaign had brought her the challenge of Secret Service work and the loss of her bunkmate. Damon Stewart had been badly injured and was sent home to Flint. Despite this loss, she dutifully continued her nursing and courier work when not involved in espionage. While still suffering a lingering illness from her mission in the swamps, Edmonds was also severely bitten and kicked by her horse while tending a wounded officer. As the Army of the Potomac prepared to leave for Alexandria and Aquia Creek, she returned to Washington to convalesce.

Instead of going back to her regiment when she recovered, Edmonds was first ordered on a series of spy missions. Disguised as a black female cook, she entered Confederate headquarters and obtained information on troop numbers and locations. She also procured written orders describing the proposed capture of Washington the following day. All told, Edmonds "visited the rebel generals three times at their own camp-fires, within a period of ten days, and came away with valuable information, unsuspected and unmolested."

Back once again with the Army of the Potomac, Edmonds took part in three more battles in 1862. In the Second Battle of Bull Run, August 29, she again spied as a black woman. She then served as a nurse during the Battle of Antietam on September 17, the single bloodiest day in American history with more than 23,000 casualties. Finally, during the Battle of Fredericksburg on December 13, Edmonds served as orderly to her friend General (formerly colonel) Poe.

Throughout this time, Edmonds was suffering from an escalating medical condition. Injuries received during the peninsula campaign when she was kicked by her horse, and more recently during the Second Battle of Bull Run when she was thrown from her horse, caused "frequent hemmorhaging [sic] from the lungs." The degree of her loyalty was such that she avoided medical care for fear of exposing her gender. Her strong sense of duty would come at great personal expense. When her friend General Poe was transferred to the Ninth Corps, Western Department in Kentucky, Edmonds asked to be transferred with him. There she would take part in two final covert missions.

While disguised as a male Confederate sympathizer in Lebanon, Kentucky, Edmonds happened upon a wedding party and mingled with the guests. She caught the attention of a Rebel captain who was suspicious of this healthy young man who was not serving the military. Despite her most imaginative arguments, the captain persisted and shanghaied Emma into the Confederate cavalry. As they departed the following day because of the impending advance of the Union, Edmonds and her new Rebel comrades encountered a party of Federal cavalry. During the resulting skirmish, she was able to slip away to the Union side of the fray. As the tide of the battle shifted, Edmonds found herself opposing, face to face, the Confederate officer who had enlisted her. With military professionalism, she "discharged the contents of my pistol in his face." As the Union infantry arrived to assist, the Confederates fled.

Edmonds' final spy mission took place in Union-held Louisville, Kentucky. In order to expose Confederate sympathizers, she disguised herself as a young Canadian man who wished to support the Rebel cause, and she found a job as a clerk in a dry goods store. The employer, impressed with her naive, farm-boy act, turned out to be a Confederate sympathizer who happily assisted her in entering the Confederate service. When Edmonds finally ended the charade, one Confederate sympathizer and three spies had been exposed. But Edmonds' health continued to decline, and she was under more pressure to seek medical treatment. Her plight became serious when General Poe's commission expired, leaving him chief engineer on a general's staff. Without her friend's support, and feeling "that I would certainly die if I did not leave immediately," Edmonds went "AWOL" from the army in April 1863.

She first traveled to Oberlin, Ohio, where she rested and recuperated. In a transformation as sudden and unexpected as the first, Frank Thompson became Emma Edmonds. For the remainder of her life, she would keep her female identity. As she recuperated, she wrote her memoirs. Published as *Nurse and Spy in the Union Army* by S. Emma E. Edmonds, it became a best-seller at 175,000 copies, the profits of which Edmonds contributed to Civil War charities. For the remainder of the war, she volunteered her nursing skills to the war injured.

Later, Edmonds returned to Ohio and briefly attended Oberlin College. Not long after, she received a proposal of marriage from Linus H. Seely, a carpenter from Emma's native New Brunswick, Canada. They had met after her army service while Edmonds was a volunteer nurse in Harper's Ferry. On April 27, 1867, Emma and Linus were wed in Cleveland, Ohio. As had happened so often in her life, Edmonds was dissatisfied with the name she now carried. Citing personal aesthetics, she added an "e" to

her new married name, creating "Seelye." The couple moved often, working in diverse fields such as farming, orphanage management, and carpentry. They had three children, all of whom died young. Through adoption, they acquired two boys who survived to adulthood.

Since her war years, Emma had suffered chronic illnesses that were attributed to her army service. This often put a strain on her family budget, since she did not receive a military pension. While in the midst of just such a financial and medical hardship, Edmonds found the justification not only to apply for her well-earned pension but to attempt to clear her military record of the "AWOL" charge. Through correspondence with her former military companions, Edmonds gathered statements and affidavits that attested to her army service. A general reaction of surprise if not shock was felt by the men who fought beside her. Eventually, most accepted her as an endeared and respected veteran, prompting her to attend the 1884 regimental reunion in Flint, Michigan.

Following years of legislative persistence, Emma finally received a proper honorable discharge from the army, along with her monthly military pension. In April of 1897, while living in La Porte, Texas, she was accepted into the George B. McClellan Post No. 9 of the Grand Army of the Republic (GAR). Upon her death, September 5, 1898, Emma E. Seelye was buried by her GAR post in La Porte cemetery. On Memorial Day, 1901, her body was moved to the GAR plot in Washington Cemetery, Houston, Texas. That same year, in a tribute while addressing the veterans of the Second Michigan, Colonel Frederick Schneider said of his comrade Emma Edmonds:

> No war ever developed so much bravery and devotion among women as did the great Civil War of 1861–1865. But none of the many instances recorded have surpassed the record for pure, unselfish patriotism and zeal for the cause of humanity, daring bravery and heroic fortitude as that of Sarah Emma Edmonds, Frank Thompson of Company F, in the summing up of whose life, find an extraordinary amount of patriotic devotion to the cause of her adopted country in the greatest crisis of its history, and nearly her whole life devoted to the alleviation of human suffering and the whole world made better from her having lived in it.

SOURCES:

Bowman, John S., ed. *The Civil War Almanac*. NY: World Almanac, 1983.

Dannett, Sylvia G.L. *She Rode With the Generals*. NY: Thomas Nelson, 1960.

Denney, Robert E. *The Civil War Years; A Day-by-Day Chronicle of the Life of a Nation.* NY: Sterling, 1992.

Edmonds, S. Emma E. *Nurse and Spy in the Union Army.* Hartford, CT: W.S. Williams, 1865.

Faust, Patricia L., ed. *Historical Times Illustrated Encyclopedia of the Civil War.* NY: Harper & Row, 1986.

James, Edward T., ed. *Notable American Women 1607-1950.* Vol. I of IV. Cambridge, MA: Belknap Press of Harvard University Press, 1971.

National Geographic Society (U.S.). *National Geographic Atlas of the World.* 6th ed. Washington DC: National Geographic Society, 1992.

Rawley, James A. *Turning Points of the Civil War.* Lincoln: University of Nebraska Press, 1966.

Stevens, Bryna. *Frank Thompson: Her Civil War Story.* NY: Macmillan, 1992.

Talmadge, Marian, and Iris Gilmore. *Emma Edmonds; Nurse and Spy.* NY: Putnam, 1970.

Ward, Geoffrey C. *The Civil War: An Illustrated History.* NY: Alfred A. Knopf, 1990.

Matthew Lee,
freelance writer, Colorado Springs, Colorado

Edmonds, Helen Woods (1901–1968).

See Kavan, Anna.

Edmonds, Sarah (1841–1898).

See Edmonds, Emma.

Edmondstone, Isabel (d. ca. 1410).

See Stewart, Isabel.

Edmonson, Sarah E.E. (1841–1898).

See Edmonds, Emma.

Edmonton Grads (1915–1940)

Most successful basketball team in Canadian history.

When J. Percy Page, who would eventually be voted lieutenant-governor of Alberta, began to coach the girls of McDougall High in Edmonton, Alberta, Canada, the team was so successful that the girls decided to remain together after graduation. "Short on flash, long on execution," the all-woman Edmonton Grads monopolized the basketball courts from 1915 to 1940, winning an extraordinary 502 out of 522 games. Traveling 125,000 miles around the world, they took on all comers. This collection of stenographers, school teachers, housewives, and file clerks competed in 27 games in four Olympics; participated in 13 Canadian ladies championships, winning all of them; and triumphed in 114 of the 120 games played for the Underwood Trophy (the North American championship in ladies' basketball). They also played nine official games against men's teams, winning all but two. Fifty women played for the team over the years,

including the 1922 team of **Daisy Johnson, Nellie Perry, Eleanor Mountifield, Dorothy Johnson, Connie Smith**, and **Winnie Martin**. None of the Grads were ever paid.

SOURCES:

Batten, Jack. *Champions: Great Figures in Canadian Sport.* Toronto: New Press, 1971.

Edney, Patience (1911–1996).

See Darton, Patience.

Edonne

Queen of the Franks. Married Childebert III (683–711), king of all Franks (r. 695–711).

Edvina, Louise (1878–1948)

Canadian soprano. Born Lucienne Juliette Martin on May 28, 1878, in Montreal, Canada; died in London, England, on November 13, 1948; studied with Jean de Reszke; married James Matthews Buxton, in 1898 (died); married the Honorable Cecil Edwardes, in 1901 (died); married Major Nicholas Rothesay Stuart Wortley, in 1919 (died).

Debuted at Covent Garden (1908) and Metropolitan Opera (1915); made six recordings for HMV (1921); retired in Cannes (1926).

Louise Edvina grew up in Vancouver before going to Paris to study voice with Jean de Reszke. She made her debut as Marguerite in *Faust* at Covent Garden in 1908, then performed in Paris, Brussels, Stockholm, Monte Carlo, Chicago, Boston, and Montreal. When World War I interrupted her operatic career, she gave a number of benefit concerts. "Her limpid and even voice with its pure sensuous quality held great charm," wrote one critic. If Edvina was faulted, it was for her lack of temperament in such fiery masterworks as *Tosca, I Gioielli della Madonna*, and *Francesca da Rimini*. She preferred roles like Marguerite which were more suited to her talents. All three of Edvina's marriages ended in widowhood. In 1921, she made six recordings for HMV, including her admired portrayals of Louise and Tosca, which were reissued. Edvina retired in 1926 in Cannes where she operated an antique shop until World War II.

John Haag,
Athens, Georgia

Edwards, Amelia B. (1831–1892)

English author and Egyptologist. Born Amelia Ann Blandford Edwards in London, England, on June 7,

*1831; died of influenza in Weston-super-Mare, Somersetshire, England, on April 15, 1892; daughter of one of the duke of Wellington's officers; cousin of *Matilda Barbara Betham-Edwards (1836–1919), a writer on French life; educated at home by her mother; studied music under Mrs. Mounsey Bartholomew; never married; no children.*

At a very early age, Amelia Edwards displayed considerable literary and artistic talent. She became a contributor to various magazines and newspapers and wrote eight novels, the most successful of which were *Debenham's Vow* (1870) and *Lord Brackenbury* (1880). But her most important contribution would not be in the field of literature.

Edwards visited Egypt in the winter of 1873–74. Profoundly impressed by the new openings for archaeological research, she learned the hieroglyphic characters and accumulated a considerable collection of Egyptian antiquities. In 1877, she wrote and illustrated *A Thousand Miles up the Nile,* the most comprehensive book on the subject of Egyptian history and hieroglyphics at the time. But Edwards was horrified by the unskilled hands that were destroying Egyptian antiquities and was determined to bring the problem to the attention of the public. Ultimately, in 1882, she was largely instrumental in founding the Egypt Exploration Fund, of which she became joint honorary secretary with Reginald Stuart Poole. She now abandoned her other literary work, writing only on Egyptology.

During the winter of 1889–90, at the request of 25 college presidents and such men as James Russell Lowell, John Greenleaf Whittier, Oliver Wendell Holmes, and William Dean Howells, she came to America on a speaking tour. The substance of her lectures was published in volume form in 1891 as *Pharaohs, Fellahs, and Explorers.* Shortly before her death the following year, Edwards received a civil list pension from the British government. She bequeathed her valuable collection of Egyptian antiquities to University College, London, together with a sum to found a chair of Egyptology.

Edwards, Henrietta Muir

(1849–1933)

Canadian journalist, suffragist, and organizer. Name variations: often listed as one of the Alberta Five also known as the Famous Five. Born Henrietta Muir in Montreal, Quebec, Canada, on December 19, 1849; died in 1933; married Dr. Oliver C. Edwards, in 1876.

Born into a wealthy family in 1849, Henrietta Muir was educated in Canada, Europe, and the United States. As an acclaimed painter of florals and miniatures, in 1875 she founded the Working Girls' Association in Montreal (a forerunner of the YWCA); the organization ran a 60-room boarding house and provided women with vocational education and employment opportunities. Seven years after her 1876 marriage to Dr. Oliver C. Edwards, Henrietta moved with her husband to Fort Qu'Appelle, Saskatchewan. In 1890, the couple moved to Ottawa. While there, Henrietta helped to found the National Council of Women and the Victoria Order of Nurses with **Lady Aberdeen** (1857–1939). In 1903, Henrietta moved to Fort Macleod where she compiled a handbook on the legal status of women in Alberta. In later years, she acted as the convenor of laws for the National Council of Women and the president of the Alberta Provincial Council.

In the 1920s, along with *Emily Murphy, *Nellie McClung, *Louise McKinney, and *Irene Parlby, Henriette Muir Edwards launched a court case challenging the historical prohibition of women holding public office. While the Canadian constitution grants this privilege to "persons," in 1928 the Canadian Supreme Court unanimously decided that women were not considered persons under the law and could not hold office. "Women are persons in matters of pains and penalties, but are not persons in matters of rights and privileges," went the 1876 British Common Law ruling. Edwards and the others took the matter to the British Privy Council, then the highest court of appeal in Canada, which reversed the decision. Shortly after, the first woman was appointed to the Canadian Senate. Every year since 1979, in Commemoration of the Persons Case, Status of Women Canada recognizes the contributions of the Famous Five with the Governor General's Award at which outstanding Canadian women are honored.

In December 1997, Honourable **Hedy Fry,** secretary of state (Multiculturalism), joined with **Jean Augustine,** Member of Parliament for Etobicoke-Lakeshore, and **Isabel Metcalfe,** president of the Ottawa chapter of the Calgary-based Famous 5 Foundation, to celebrate the unanimous passage of a motion in the House of Commons that recommended the Famous 5 Foundation statue be placed on Parliament Hill. The motion was spearheaded by Canadian Heritage Minister **Sheila Copps** and presented in the House by Augustine, chair of the National Liberal Women's Caucus.

Edwards, India (1895–1990)

American political party leader. Born in Chicago, Illinois, in 1895; died in 1990; moved to Nashville, Tennessee, as a child; attended school in St. Louis, Missouri; married a man named Moffett, in 1924 (divorced 1931); married Herbert Edwards (chief of the international motion pictures division of the office of International Information and Cultural Affairs of the Department of State), in 1942; children: (first marriage) India Moffett; John Holbrook Moffett (killed in action, 1944).

India Edwards, daughter of a suffragist, held the post of executive director of the women's division of the Democratic National Committee, succeeding *Margaret Woodhouse. Following a 20-year stint as an editorial staff member of the *Chicago Tribune* (1915–42), Edwards joined the Democratic National Committee in 1944. During her tenure, she helped to organize a nationwide campaign to publicize the aims and importance of the UN. "It was largely through the public understanding, enthusiasm, and support aroused by such efforts as those exerted under the leadership of Mrs. [Charles W.] Tillett and Mrs. Edwards," declared the *Democratic Digest*, "that the charter was so promptly ratified by the United States Senate." Edwards was prominent and effective during the 1948 re-election campaign for Harry S. Truman; following his election, she successfully lobbied the president to appoint women to public office, including *Georgia Neese Clark, first female treasurer of the United States, *Eugenia Anderson, first female ambassador, and *Perle Mesta, minister to Luxemburg.

SUGGESTED READING:

Rothe, Anna, ed. *Current Biography, 1949.* NY: H.W. Wilson, 1950.

Edwards, Margaret (b. 1939).

See Grinham, Judith for sidebar.

Edwards, Matilda Betham (1836–1919).

See Betham-Edwards, Matilda.

Edwards, Sarah (1841–1898).

See Edmonds, Emma.

Edwards, Teresa (1964—)

African-American basketball player. Born on July 19, 1964, in Cairo, Georgia; only daughter and one of five children of Mildred Edwards; graduated from Cairo High School, 1982; attended the University of Georgia.

Selected championships and honors: (team) three gold medals, Olympic Games (1984, 1988, 1996), two gold medals, World Championships (1986 and 1990), bronze medal, World Championships (1984), gold medal, Pan American Games (1987), two gold medals, Goodwill Games (1986 and 1990), bronze medal, Pan American Games (1991), bronze medal Olympic Games (1992); (individual) two-time All-American (1985 and 1986), two-time USA Basketball Female Athlete of the Year (1987 and 1990).

Called "the Michael Jordan of women's basketball," Teresa Edwards has had a professional career that rivals her male counterparts. A member of the gold-medal U.S. teams at the 1984, 1988, and 1996 Olympics, and a bronze medalist at the 1992 Olympics, Edwards is the first American, man or woman, to play basketball in four consecutive Olympic Games. During the 1990s, the 5'11" guard also played professionally in Italy and Japan, where she earned upwards of $200,000 a year as a starter for the Nagoya, Japan, team sponsored by Mitsubishi.

Edwards grew up in a single-parent home in Cairo, Georgia, the only girl among four boys. Although her mother did not approve of women playing sports, Teresa was a regular in the sandlot baseball, football, and basketball games with the locals. She played in her first structured basketball program in seventh grade and progressed rapidly through the ranks. After achieving high school All-American, she attended the University of Georgia on an athletic scholarship, where she was All-American in 1985 and 1986. While still in college, she also played on the 1984 U.S. Olympic team, bringing home a gold medal.

Edwards left college just short of her degree requirements to play professionally overseas. She has admitted that the long seasons away were difficult, and she was frequently lonely and homesick. "But, my god, if it hadn't been for the professional leagues, my best years as a player would have been wasted," she says. "I got so much better after college." Indeed, she did. In addition to her performance on the Olympic teams, she also played on gold medal teams in the U.S. World Championship, the Pan American Games, and the Goodwill Games.

Edwards went on to play for the American Basketball League's Atlanta Glory. Despite her fame, friends claim that Edwards has remained down-to-earth and accessible. While her own lifestyle is modest, she has used her money to help out her younger brothers with college and to buy a house for her mother. In 1989, she finished the requirements to earn her bachelor's degree in recreation, and when not traveling she lives near her hometown of Cairo, Georgia, where friends and neighbors named a street in her honor. "Values are important to her," says **Theresa Grentz**, the coach of the 1992 U.S. Olympic women's basketball team. "Her humility and the simplicity of her life made her very special to be around."

Edwards, Valaida (c. 1903–1956).

See Snow, Valaida.

Efflatoun, Inji.

See Egyptian Feminism.

Efimova, Nina Simonovich (b. 1877).

See Simonovich-Efimova, Nina.

Efthryth (d. 929).

See Elfthrith.

Efua Kobiri (fl. 1834–1884).

See Yaa Asantewaa for sidebar on Afua Koba.

Egerszegi, Krisztina (1974—)

Hungarian swimmer. Born on August 16, 1974, in Budapest, Hungary.

Won silver medal in 100-meter backstroke and gold in 200-meter backstroke in Seoul Olympics (1988); won gold medals in 400-meter individual medley, 200-meter backstroke, and 100-meter backstroke in Barcelona Olympics (1992); won gold medal in the 200-meter backstroke in Atlanta Olympics (1996).

Known as the queen of the backstroke, Krisztina Egerszegi held the world record at 2:06.62 in the 200-meter backstroke. Egerszegi began swimming at age 13; since *Eger* means mouse, she was dubbed the Little Mouse. At the 1987 European championships, she finished fourth and fifth. The following year, in the Seoul Olympics, 14-year-old Egerszegi was the youngest swimming gold medalist ever, taking gold in the 200-meter backstroke; she also won a silver in 100-meter backstroke. In 1991, she won two world titles, breaking world records at the 100 and 200-meter backstroke. In 1992, in the Barcelona Olympics, she won three individual gold medals in the 400-meter individual medley, the 200-meter backstroke, and the 100-meter backstroke. When she took the gold medal in the 200 meter backstroke with a time of 2:07.83 in the Atlanta Olympics in 1996, she became the first swimmer since *Dawn Fraser* to win three gold medals in the same event, a record that went unbroken for 32 years. Only 21 at the time, Egerszegi was the youngest triple champion in history. She also holds distinction as the first woman swimmer to win five individual golds.

Egervári, Márti (b. 1956).

See Comaneci, Nadia for sidebar.

Eglah (fl. 1000 BCE)

Biblical woman. One of David's wives and mother of his son, Ithream (2 Sam. 3:5; 1 Chr. 3:3)

Egmont, countess of.

See Anna of Egmont (1533–1558).

Egorova, Lyubov (1966—).

Russian Nordic skiing champion. Name variations: Ljubov or Ljubova Yegorova. Born on May 5, 1966, in Tomsk, Russia; married with children.

Won silver medals in the 5 km and 30 km and gold medals in the 10 km, 15 km, and 4x100 km in the Winter Olympics in Albertville (1992); won a silver medal in the 15 km and gold medals in the 5km, 10km, and 4x100 km in the Winter Olympics in Lillehammer (1994).

The Soviet Union long held sway in women's cross-country events. In the 1964 Olympics, **Claudia Boyarskikh** took first place in all three Nordic events. Four years later, **Galina Kulakova** appeared on the scene, earning four gold, two silver, and two bronze Olympic medals from 1968 to 1980. Her teammate, **Raisa Smetanina**, continued the pattern from 1976 to 1988, winning three Olympic gold medals, five silver medals, and one bronze, thus, tying for the most decorated competitor in the history of the Winter Games.

Following the breakup of the Soviet Union, Lyubov Egorova won six gold medals at two Winter Olympics (1992 and 1994) in the 5-, 10-, 15-, 30-, and 4x100-kilometer Nordic cross-country skiing events using the classic technique. In 1992, representing Russia's Unified Team, she took gold in the 10-, 15-, and 4x100-km and silver in the 5- and 30-km in Albertville, becoming the most successful woman athlete in a single winter games. (Another member of the Unified Team, 23-year-old **Elena Välbe**, won a gold medal and four bronzes in the same events.) In 1994, at the Winter Olympics in Lillehammer, Norway, Egorova did it again, adding three more golds and two silvers in cross-country events.

In February 1997, at the Nordic World championships, Egorova won another gold medal but was disqualified when her doping test came back positive for a stimulant known as Promanthan, a drug had that had just been added to the doping list the previous November. Instead, Välbe moved up to first. Egorova openly admitted using the drug, absolved her Russian coaches who did not know that the drug was on the list, and claimed that she took an old tablet by mistake. She was adamant that none of her coaches be blamed for the situation.

Egypt, queen of.

See Mer-neith (fl. c. 3100 BCE).
See Hatshepsut (c. 1515–1468 BCE).
See Tiy (c. 1400–1340 BCE).
See Mutnedjmet (c. 1360–1326 BCE).
See Berenice I (c. 345–275 BCE).
See Arsinoe II Philadelphus (316–270 BCE).
See Berenice II of Cyrene (c. 273–221 BCE).
See Arsinoe III (fl. c. 250–210/05 BCE).
See Cleopatra I (c. 210–176 BCE).
See Cleopatra II (c. 183–116 BCE).
See Cleopatra III (c. 155–101 BCE).
See Cleopatra IV (c. 135–112 BCE).
See Cleopatra Selene (c. 130–69 BCE).
See Cleopatra Berenice III (c. 115–80 BCE).
See Berenice IV (d. 55 BCE).
See Cleopatra VII (69–30 BCE).

Egyptian Feminism (1800–1980)

For over a century and a half, women and men of Egypt have addressed the need for sexual equality in their country, through political organizations, feminist journals, and demonstrations that have made women's voices increasingly heard.

Europeans and Americans commonly assume that the women's rights movement is native only to their own cultures. In truth, however, women throughout the world have long struggled for equality. Western influence on the international women's movement has generally occurred in two ways. European women have worked with their sisters in foreign countries to create change, and European colonial rule has at times sparked rebellion and revolt in which women played a prominent role. Egyptian feminism reflects both these trends. The feminist movement which began in the 19th century was spurred largely by greater contact with Europe. Then, following World War I, when Egyptians revolted against colonial rule, women joined the nationalist effort, fighting and dying to liberate their country. In the process, they gained new freedoms, greater respect, and enhanced political and economic influence.

Women were a significant force in Egyptian society long before Europe had any influence in the country. Tomb paintings thousands of years old often depict women the same size as men, signifying equality according to the iconography of the ancient art, which includes female figures performing as swimmers and acrobats. Ancient Egypt was ruled by many queens, including *Nefertiti, *Hatshepsut, and in later times *Cleopatra (VII) and *Zenobia, queen of Palmyra. In Egyptian religion, goddesses like Hathor, Mut (the goddess of truth), and Isis had roles almost equal to the gods, influencing many spheres of human activity. Even after 1517, when Egypt was annexed by the Ottoman Empire and converted to Islam, its society retained a high regard for women, with their status only somewhat diminished.

For much of their history, Egyptians considered their culture superior to that of Europeans. In medieval times, when Europe had few cities and hardly any roads, Cairo and Alexandria were thriving cities under centrally administered governments, and Egyptian ships were making their way from the Red Sea across the Indian Ocean to procure the silks, spices, and other luxury goods available from India and China. Classical Greek and Roman manuscripts were a staple in Egyptian libraries and centers of learning long before they ever reached the lands to the north.

In 1798, Egypt's sense of superiority was shattered by the armies of Napoleon Bonaparte, which occupied the land for three years. Napoleon brought 120 scholars and scientists into the country to make comprehensive studies of its ancient civilization, and the Institut d'Egypte was established to probe its antiquities, languages, agriculture, and medical knowledge. A French-language journal, *Courier de l'Égypte*, was published, as well as an encyclopedia, *Description de l'Égypte*, introduced between 1809–29. The French occupation ended with their defeat by the British navy at Abukir, after which the British vied for control of the country with the Ottoman Empire, which maintained a nominal suzerainty while the British actually took control.

Muhammed Ali, who ruled from 1805 to 1849, instituted many of the reforms that gave the country the foundations of a modern state, including in particular the improvement of female education. Up to this time, the daughters of the rich were educated at home, while girls from poorer families attended *kuttabs*, where they learned the Qu'ran as well as some reading and writing. In 1832, Muhammed Ali established the first school for poorer girls, followed by missionary efforts in 1846. After 1841, the power of

Muhammed Ali was restricted by a treaty with the British, whose influence increased under the reign of Khedive Ismail Pasha (1863–1879). Many male Egyptian students were meanwhile returning from studies abroad, usually in France, with new ideas about instituting social reforms, including many related to the position of women.

In the stormy days of 1919 [the women] descended in large bodies into the streets, those of the more respectable classes still veiled and shrouded in their loose black coats, whilst the courtesans from the lowest quarters of the city, who had also caught the contagion [of political unrest], disported themselves unveiled and arrayed in less discreet garments. In every turbulent demonstration women were well to the front. They marched in procession—some on foot, some in carriages shouting 'independence' and 'down with the English' waving national banners.

—Sir Valentine Chirol, *The Egyptian Problem*

Centuries-old customs, predating the country's conversion to Islam, supported the segregation of women in Egypt. The religious laws spelled out by the Qu'ran actually gave Muslim women more rights in terms of property than those enjoyed by European women, but it did not alter the customs of polygamy and seclusion. Among the wealthy, the system was upheld through the harem, a term that can signify both a portion of a house set aside for women and children to live, and a man's wife or wives. When women left the harem, they remained separate by donning veils. Since the support of numerous wives and children was expensive, the harem, seclusion, and veiling all became status symbols of the wealthy, helping to perpetuate the system. Among the poor, men and women lived crammed together in one-room quarters, with peasant women working in the fields alongside the men. In urban working-class areas, women also took jobs outside the home.

By the late 19th century, several Egyptian male leaders were advocating an end to female segregation. Sayyed Jamal al-din al-Afghani (1839–1897) was an early feminist. Born in Iran, he lived in India, Afghanistan, Turkey, Egypt, Russia, and Europe, often forced to move when his radical beliefs led to his expulsion. Al-

Afghani believed that science and technology held the key to Arab independence from Europe, and changing society, especially women's social status, was central to his reform plan. Rifaa Rafii el-Tahtawi (1801–1871) demanded education for women and changes in a system that was inherently unjust to them. His views were spelled out in *A Guide to Education of Girls and Boys,* published in 1872. Many of these reformers held that women's inferior status had resulted from misinterpretations of Islam and called for a return to fundamental religious tenets. Sheik Muhammed Abduh (1849–1905) denounced polygamy as a practice counter to fundamental Islamic beliefs and condemned concubinage as slavery. His flexible interpretation of the Qu'ran greatly influenced the entire Muslim world. A disciple of Abduh, Kasim Amin (1865–1908), wrote *Tahrir al Mara* (Women's Emancipation) in 1899. Amin argued that seclusion, veiling, arranged marriages, and divorce were un-Islamic, views he reiterated in *al-Mara al Jadida* (The New Woman).

Begun by men, the debate on women's emancipation was being co-opted by women at the turn of the century. ❧ **Malak Hifni Nassif** (1886–1918), using the pen-name Bahissat el Badia ("Searcher in the Desert"), wrote articles about education, seclusion, marriage, and divorce. In 1900, she was one of the first women in the country to qualify as a teacher. Nassif moved with her husband from Cairo to the fringes of the desert, where she came to idealize the village life she discovered. Urban upper-class women, Nassif felt, spent lives of useless idleness. She wanted them to be more involved in the upbringing of their children and encouraged them in breastfeeding and the care and education of their offspring, rather than leaving such tasks to servants. Nassif's goals were mainly social, and she cared little about Egyptian nationalism or politics; her main objection to colonialism was the intermarriage of Egyptian men to foreign women. She felt that foreign women dominated their husbands and that the children of these unions were not true Egyptians.

Some of Nassif's ideas, which now seem outdated, were revolutionary by the standards of the time. In 1911, she appeared before the Egyptian Legislative Assembly to put forth her ten-point program for women's emancipation, which included elementary schooling for all girls, and the introduction of hygiene, first aid, and economics as standard school subjects. She also wanted a limited number of girls trained in the medical and teaching professions, to serve the needs of women. Her assumptions that women should fulfill certain "natural tasks" centered around home and family were typical of the time, even among Europeans. Women did not begin to be admitted to teaching and medical institutions in Europe until the end of the 19th century.

In early 20th-century Egypt, feminist issues were widely discussed by women and men alike, and contemporary press accounts engendered much debate. Feminist articles were first published in French, the language in use among upper-class Egyptians, then appeared in Arabic, widening the scope of the debate. Before World War I, there were 15 Arabic-language magazines specializing in women's issues. All but one were founded and edited by women, indicating not only the level of interest in feminism, but the number of women professionals capable of producing the literature.

One young girl greatly influenced by these works was ❧▶ **Hidiya Afifi Barakat** (1898–1969), daughter of Ahmad Pasha Afifi, a magistrate connected with the royal palace. Educated at the French convent of Notre Dame de la Mère, Hidiya was forced, according to Muslim custom, to withdraw into seclusion at age 13. In May 1918, when she married Bahieddine Barakat, a professor of law at Cairo University, she had never laid eyes on her husband until their wedding night. Despite this traditional background, her new family was revolutionary in outlook. Her husband was closely related to the Egyptian nationalist leader Sa'ad Pasha Zaghlul, who opposed British rule, and when the uprising against the British began to engulf all of Egypt, she became involved. Dressed in flowing robes, Barakat would take the train for Upper Egypt carrying shopping baskets packed with anti-British pamphlets. Schoolteachers met her at every station, ready to distribute the subversive literature, while the British remained unsuspecting of the diminutive gentlewoman swathed in veils. Had she been caught, she would have been sentenced to death like a number of other nationalists, and her bravery earned her the nickname "little soldier."

Barakat also proved to be a skillful organizer, who took over the philanthropic association Mabarrat Muhammed Ali al-Kabir, founded by two princesses, and developed it into the largest and most active women's organization in the country, involving a network of clinics, dispensaries, and hospitals. In 1919, she helped create the Société de la Femme Nouvelle, which set up girls' schools and established child-care centers and orphanages, which were especially success-

❧▶ Nassif, Malak Hifni (1886–1918)

Egyptian feminist. Name variations: Nasif; (pseudonym) Bahithat al-Badiya, Badiyya, or Bahissat el Badia. Born in Cairo, Egypt, in 1886; died in 1918; married and moved to the desert.

Malak Hifni Nassif was an influential Egyptian writer whose ten-point program for improving Egyptian women's position became the standard for women's demands in the pre-World War I era.

❧▶ Barakat, Hidiya Afifi (1898–1969)

Egyptian feminist. Name variations: Hidiya Hanim Barakat, Hidiya Afifi. Born in Cairo, Egypt, in 1898; died in Cairo in 1969; married Bahieddine Barakat, a professor of law at Cairo University.

Long regarded as a leading Egyptian feminist, Hidiya Afifi Barakat was known as the "little soldier" during the Revolution of 1919. She organized The Société de la Femme Nouvelle, which concentrated on education for girls, and the Mabarra, which was concerned with clinics and women's health care.

Egyptian Women's Magazines
Founded Before 1914

Year	Founder	Magazine
1892	Hind Nawfal	al-Fatah
1898	Alexandra Avierinoh	Anis al-jalis
1901	Ibrahim Ramzi	al-Mar'a fi-al Islam
1901	Anisa 'Ata Allah	al-Mar'a
1901	Sa'diya Sa'd ad-Din	Shajarat ad-durr
1902	Maryam Sa'd	az-Zahra
1902	Rujina 'Awwad	as-Sa'ada
1903	Ruza Antun	Majallat as-sayyi-dat wa-al-banat
1904	Esther Moyel	al'A'ila
1906	Labiba Hashim	Fata ash-sharq
1908	Malaka Sa'd	al-Jins al-latif
1908	Fatima Rashid	Majallat tarqiyat al-mar'a
1909	Anjilina Abu Shi'r	Murshid al-atfal
1912	Fatima Tawfiq	al-Jamila
1913	Sarah Mihiya	Fata an-nil

ful in the countryside. Barakat's strategy, along with her co-workers was to ask a wealthy landowner to donate land for a project, and then consult with the village headman. Village support of the clinic or school would then be assured, as the headman would not want to affront the landowner, who was his superior. By 1961, Mabarra had created 12 hospitals, and in a 20-year period more than 13 million patients were treated in its medical facilities.

Like Hidiya Barakat, *Huda Shaarawi (1879–1947) came from a wealthy family, was cloistered and married at a young age, and then became politically active. Her husband, Ali Shaarawi, was a founding member of the Wafd Party which fought for Egyptian independence, a cause that drew the couple together. Huda Shaarawi sponsored many charitable projects and worked for legislation related to women. In 1910, she opened a school for girls, and in 1919, she risked her life in organizing huge groups of women to protest against British rule. She was also founder of the Egyptian Feminist Union, the main women's organization for many decades.

Egypt's Revolution of 1919 engulfed rich and poor, female and male. When the British exiled Zaghlul Pasha and other rebels in an attempt to quash the rebellion, they only fed the flames of revolt. As men were arrested, interned, and killed, women took their place in the front lines. As *Nawal El-Saadawi wrote:

> They went onto the rural roads, side by side with the men, cut the telephone wires and disrupted the railway lines in order to paralyze the movement of the British troops. Some of them participated in storming the improvised camps and jails in which many of those who had led the uprisings or participated in them had been imprisoned. Women were killed or injured when British troops fired on them. Some of them are known such as **Shafika Mohammed, Hamida Khalil, Sayeda Hassan, Fahima Riad** and **Aisha Omar**. But hundreds of poor women lost their lives without anybody being able to trace their names.

In 1922, the British allowed the Egyptians limited sovereignty. Although the rebellion had clearly demonstrated the value of women's participation in national life, full acknowledgement of their role was slow in coming. Inevitably, however, their social status began to change. When Egypt's new constitution was drafted in 1924, many women hoped to attain the right to vote, but Egyptian feminists were divided over the importance of political rights. While Shaarawi's Egyptian Feminist Union worked to secure more educational opportunities and to end polygamy, seclusion, child marriage, and easy divorce, these remained abstract issues for most women. Since only the rich could afford more than one wife, harem life did not seem so burdensome to poor women who worked in the fields, sold goods on the street, or carried water

from the communal well. Class differences thus led to a diminution of feminist fervor during the 1930s and early 1940s.

But the social forces that slowed Egyptian feminism eventually helped to revive it. Between World Wars I and II, as people flocked to Cairo, Alexandria, and many provincial towns in search of jobs, a growing middle class emerged, better educated and more prosperous than ever before. Women, who had especially benefitted from increased education, were now more aware of their second-class status. As they realized that their concerns would not be addressed without their own elected representatives, the right to vote became their rallying point. *Doria Shafik (1908–1975) founded the Bint al-Nil Union (Daughter of the Nile) in March 1948, expressly to fight for the right to vote. Bint al-Nil's appeal was strongest to the growing number of teachers, clerical workers, nurses, and other professionals, rejecting programs of the Egyptian Feminist Union which were viewed as elitist. Largely due to Shafik's rallies and protests, Egypt's women won the vote in 1956, only 11 years after it was attained by Frenchwomen, in 1945.

Shafik represented a middle-of-the-road approach to feminism, compared to the more radical views that began to emerge among Egypt's Marxists and Communists. Marxism was unusual in Egypt's conservative society, but some were drawn to its philosophy and espousal of equal status for the sexes. ☙▶ Inji Efflatoun was a leader in the radical wing of Egyptian feminism. Born into a family of Cairo landowners, she had a middle-class upbringing in a French-speaking household and did not become fluent in Arabic until years later. While a student at a French *lycée* in Cairo, she began to take private lessons from Kamil al Tilmisani, a Trotskyite from a very poor background, who soon exploded Efflatoun's middle-class views of the world, expounding on the need for equal opportunity for rich and poor, male and female. Efflatoun discovered leftist books, engaged in endless discussions, and became a Marxist, believing in revolution, not parliamentary process, as the only effective means of change.

Another radical feminist was ☙▶ Latifa al-Zayyat (1923—) born to a lower-middle-class family in Damietta, who came to Cairo to be educated at age 12. Al-Zayyat had long been interested in politics but was discouraged by existing political parties, which at that point were not addressing the issue of British colonial rule, and saw the middle class as too cowardly to implement change. In 1942, at age 18, she was drawn to the Marxists at the university because they did not discriminate on the basis of sex, class, or race.

The Egypt of young Marxists like Efflatoun and al-Zayyat in the 1940s was a much different country than had been the case only a few decades earlier. World War II had accelerated social change, and what had once been a largely agrarian nation was now highly urban. In the crowded cities, a large proletariat had emerged, which was seen by Communists as an ideal environment in which to promote their agenda. Women were avidly recruited by the party and educated in Marxist philosophy before being sent out to distribute leaflets, demonstrate outside factories, and agitate on campuses.

In theory, Marxism espoused women's equality, but in practice the Communists did a poor job of implementing policies to improve their status, and male Communists have been accused of being particularly chauvinistic. The Marxists did gain ground, however, when they concentrated on ending British occupation of Egypt to the exclusion of most all other causes on their agenda. When social issues were addressed, establishing trade unions was the next priority. Unfortunately for radical leaders like Efflatoun and al-Zayyat, however, trade unions were overwhelmingly male. Women radicals postponed their agenda and worked hard to foster other forms of change, their attitude summed up by Latifa al-Zayyat:

> It is a luxury to think of the liberation of women . . . when you see your brothers, fathers, and children strangled, scorned, and exploited by foreigners and local men and women of the local upper classes. It is only when civilization reaches a certain level that the problems of women, children, and minorities become important.

Radical feminists lived in fear of arrest and imprisonment, which was not uncommon. The Egyptian Communist movement was never large and was often factionalized, its organization inept at times, and its theories abstract. Eventually, women like Efflatoun and al-Zayyat did expand the outlook on women's issues, and with the passage of time their demands came to be seen as more middle-of-the-road.

In 1952, the socialist government of Gamal Abdel Nasser came to power, and under his leadership British control of Egypt finally ended. Although Nasser was an "Arab socialist," his government was not always tolerant of divergent views from the left or right, and the women's movement found itself co-opted by the government. The voices of moderates like Shafik, as

Efflatoun, Inji

Egyptian feminist. Name variations: Inge Aflatun. Born in Cairo into a family of landowners; introduced to Marxist ideas as a student at a French lycée in Cairo.

Inji Efflatoun became active in the Communist Party and agitated for women's rights as well as freedom from colonial rule.

Zayyat, Latifa al- (1923—)

Writer and novelist who worked for greater emancipation for Egyptian women. Name variations: Zayat; az-Zayyat, as-Zayyat. Born in Damietta, Egypt, in 1923; came to Cairo in 1936 to be educated; became a Marxist after she began studying at the University of Cairo in 1942.
Works include: The Open Door (1960), Old Age and Other Stories (1980).

Latifa al-Zayyat earned a B.A., M.A., and Ph.D. from Cairo University before turning her attention to teaching English at the Women's College of Ain Shams University in Cairo. She has been active in politics at both the university and national level since her student days. As both a leftist and a feminist, she continues to be outspoken in her objection to the oppressive inroads of the political right as regards women's freedom. In her literature, most notably in *The Open Door* (1960), she addresses these inequalities. Al-Zayyat has also written extensive literary criticism.

SOURCES:
Buck, Claire, ed. *The Bloomsbury Guide to Women's Literature*. NY: Prentice Hall, 1992.
Schipper, Mineke, ed. *Unheard Words*. London: Allison and Busby, 1984.

Crista Martin,
freelance writer, Boston, Massachusetts

well as radicals like Efflatoun and al-Zayyat, were still. After Nasser's death in 1970, a greater tolerance for diversity surfaced, but by then political debate was beginning to focus around issues of Islamic fundamentalists, who generally mistrusted all Western ideas. Their interests do not represent all Egyptians, however, and Egyptian women have continued to be galvanized by the debate surrounding the status of women. In 1979, when the Personal Status Law, protecting the benefits of divorced women, was rescinded, women came together in widespread protests that resulted in the reinstatement of the law, and The Committee for the Defense of the Rights of the Woman and the Family was formed to ensure the rights it guaranteed would not be terminated.

SOURCES:
Badran, Margot. "Independent Women: More Than a Century of Feminism in Egypt," in *Arab Women: Old Boundaries, New Frontiers*. Edited by Judith E.

Tucker. Bloomington, IN: Indiana University Press, 1993, pp. 129–148.

Baer, Gabriel. *Studies in the Social History of Modern Egypt*, Chicago, IL: The University of Chicago Press, 1969.

Botman, Selma. "The Experience of Women in the Egyptian Communist Movement, 1939–1954," in *Women's Studies Int. Forum.* Vol 11, no. 2, 1988, pp. 117–126.

———. *The Rise of Egyptian Communism, 1939–1970.* Syracuse, NY: Syracuse University Press, 1988.

Davis, Eric. "Ideology, Social Class and Islamic Radicalism in Modern Egypt," in *From Nationalism to Revolutionary Islam.* Edited by Amir Arjomand. Albany, NY: State University of New York Press, 1984, pp. 134–157.

El-Saadwi, Nawal. *The Hidden Face of Eve—Women in the Arab World.* London: Zed Press, 1980.

Ismael, Tareq Y., and Rifa'at El-Sa'id. *The Communist Movement in Egypt, 1920–1988.* Syracuse, NY: Syracuse University Press, 1990.

Hunter, F. Robert. *Egypt Under the Khedives 1805–1879: From Household Government to Modern Bureaucracy.* Pittsburgh, PA: University of Pittsburgh Press, 1984.

Jayadena, Kumar. *Feminism and Nationalism in the Third World.* London: Zed Books, 1986.

Khater, Akran, and Cynthia Nelson. "Al-Harakah al-Nissaiyah: The Women's Movement and Political Participation in Modern Egypt," in *Women's Studies International Forum.* Vol. 11, no. 5, 1988, pp. 465–483.

Marsot, Afaf Lutfi al-Sayyid. "The Revolutionary Gentlewomen in Egypt," in *Women in the Muslim World.* Edited by Lois Beck and Nikki Keddie. Cambridge, MA: Harvard University Press, 1978, pp. 261–276.

Nelson, Cynthia. "Changing Roles of Men and Women: Illustrations from Egypt," in *Anthropological Quarterly.* Vol. 41, 1968, pp. 57–77.

Philipp, Thomas. "Feminism and Nationalist Politics in Egypt," in *Women in the Muslim World.* Edited by Lois Beck and Nikki Keddie. Cambridge, MA: Harvard University Press, 1978, pp. 277–293.

Shaarawi, Huda. *Harem Years. The Memoirs of an Egyptian Feminist (1879–1924).* Transl. and edited by Margot Badran. NY: The Feminist Press, 1987.

Karin Loewen Haag,
freelance writer, Athens, Georgia

Egyptian Singers and Entrepreneurs (fl. 1920s)

Group of accomplished women who shifted the venue of their musical talents from private homes into theaters and nightclubs, owned and operated thriving entertainment businesses, became recording and radio stars, and led in the formation of mainstream entertainment for modern Arab life.

Munira al-Mahdiyya (c. 1895–1965). Born in Zaqazig around 1895; died in 1965; married and divorced five times. Ran away from home to perform in Cairo; became famous for her nationalist, anti-colonial songs which were recorded and widely distrib-uted; founded her own theater company after the British tried to ban her from the stage.

Tauhida (?–1932). Birth date unknown; died in 1932. Owner and operator of the nightclub Alf Laila wa Laila, one of the earliest in the Azbakiyya area of Cairo, established in 1897; one of the first women to move from singing to club ownership and management.

Na'ima al-Masriyya. Na'ima became a performer out of economic necessity when she was divorced by her husband. A popular star on radio, recordings, and stage, she owned and operated the Alhambra, an enormously popular club and casino.

Badi'a Masabnik. Born in Syria in the 1890s; moved to Cairo in 1921; married Najib al-Rihani, in 1923; left him in 1926 and founded her own music hall, the Sala Badi'a. Known and loved as a recording artist throughout the Arab world, she sponsored the careers of many other female performers.

Fathiyya Ahmad (c. 1898–1975). Born around 1898; died in 1975; daughter of a Qur'an reciter who began her theatrical career around 1910; married a wealthy landowner; two children. Popular singer and manager of the Sala Badi'a, who was also a widely recorded vocalist until her retirement in 1950.

Although Westerners often assume that all Arab women's lives are confined by rigid social custom, many have, in fact, been influential in many sectors of society for hundreds, even thousands of years. A group of female entertainers who emerged in Egypt at the dawn of the 20th century challenged the stereotype. Their role was not unusual, as women have long been performers in the Arab world. What was unusual was their entrepreneurship which redefined the position of the female star. These women moved from performing in harems to theater stages. They founded and operated nightclubs and theaters to showcase their talents. They quickly adopted emerging technologies, making recordings and performing on the radio. These women not only carved a new niche for their gender in Egyptian life, but they also made Egyptian entertainment pre-eminent in the Arab world.

Discovering the facts about any entertainer can often be difficult. Dates of birth as well as personal details are grudgingly given. *Greta Garbo*'s desire to conceal her private life was legendary, and many performers throughout the world emulated her example to some extent. When discussing Egyptian female performers, other factors enter the picture. Most of these women came from the poorer classes and had no records of their birth. Social pressure also explains the garbled data available, because in Europe, as well as the Middle East, female performers were often regarded as "fallen women." Thus, they sometimes changed the facts to improve their social status. In the case of the celebrated *Um Kalthum (c. 1898–1975), for example, her father always insisted that his unmarried daughter be addressed as Mrs. Um Kalthum when she began to appear in Cairo. A poor peasant from the provinces, he did not think it was fitting for an unmarried woman to appear in public, a view widely shared in Egypt at the time. When Um Kalthum finally married, she withheld the information for some time before announcing it to fans.

The career of **Munira al-Mahdiyya** (c. 1895–1965) was typical of Cairo's outstanding group of entrepreneurial entertainers. Born in the provincial town of Zaqazig, Munira became enamored of musical performances at an early age, sneaking out of her house to hear popular singers. Her determination to perform drew her from the provinces to Cairo. By 1913, Munira al-Mahdiyya was featured nightly at a famous coffee house, the Nuzhat al-Nufus, and she also sang at the Alhambra and the Eldorado, both popular nightclubs. She became particularly well-known for nationalist songs, written by herself and others, that gave voice to the rising popular resentment against British colonialism during and after World War I. In response to her public defiance, the British closed the Nuzhat al-Nufus coffeehouse, forcing al-Mahdiyya to seek work in a theater. Ironically, the action resulted in the blossoming of her career. She formed her own theatrical troupe and became its manager, negotiating with composers, lyricists, and singers, planning schedules and meeting payrolls. Her Egyptian nationalism remained unabated, and politicians and journalists flocked to her performances. When commercial recordings were introduced, al-Mahdiyya became one of the first to take advantage of the new medium, making some of the earliest recordings of Egyptian popular music. Her nationalist sentiments attracted a wide audience throughout Egypt and the Arab world. She was a great commercial success, and many followed in her footsteps. Her personal life remained daring and unconventional: in her long lifetime, she married and divorced five men.

Sweeping cultural change also played a part in the success of women like Munira al-Mahdiyya. Long an agrarian society, Egypt became more and more urbanized in the 20th century. In the past, female singers or `awailim had performed in private only for the very wealthy. Some lived as perma-

nent members of wealthy households. The population influx into urban centers like Cairo and Alexandria created a need for cheap mass entertainment, just as it did in Europe and America. By the beginning of World War I in 1914, few of the old style `awailim were still performing, and in their place came more ambitious and enterprising female stars. A maze of cafés, music halls, and nightclubs were built in an area in Cairo that became known as the Azbakiyya Garden, and a theater district sprang up, offering theatrical performances that were enormously popular with the public. Two performers who moved aggressively into the new type of mass entertainment were **Tauhida** (?–1932) and **Na'ima al-Masriyya**. Both were older performers whose careers predated World War I.

Tauhida, a Syrian immigrant who worked as a singer and dancer, had married an Egyptian of Greek extraction who managed her career. In 1897, the couple opened one of the earliest modern nightclubs, called Alf Laila wa Laila, featuring Tauhida playing the `ud, a popular Arab musical instrument. After her husband died, Tauhida continued to perform and operate the club until her own death in 1932. Though she made few, if any, commercial recordings, she was a much-loved figure in the entertainment world.

Here, as in Europe, among these favoured mortals, the women hold their own against the men in number and estimation.

—Georg Ebers

A stipulation in Tauhida's standard contract demonstrates the special problems faced by women in a traditional society as they moved into the public social arena. Although she usually performed in her own club, the clause stated that she could not be required to drink more than five glasses of cognac with patrons on any one evening, a device she no doubt found necessary; also she probably wished to signal to her public that she was a respectable figure. In their past appearances in private homes, Egyptian women performers had often been accompanied by their husbands, or a male member of the family, to protect their virtue. Once these women moved onto theater and nightclub stages, they crossed an undefined social boundary. As was also the case in the West, taverns and brothels existed side-by-side with nightclubs and music halls. Mass entertainment sometimes involved prostitution, drunkenness, gambling, and drug use. Socializing with patrons was good for business, but the border between respect and over-familiarity could easily be crossed, especially in a society with women in so few public roles. Because women like Tauhida demanded respect from patrons and fans, public esteem for these performers rose over the decades and became the norm. In fact, few individuals enjoyed greater respect in Egypt than its female entertainers.

The career of Na'ima al-Masriyya parallels that of Tauhida's. Born in a lower-middle-class Cairo neighborhood, she became a singer out of necessity when her husband divorced her. For Arab men, divorce was then notoriously easy to obtain, but wives cast aside were usually disgraced and destitute. Na'ima supported herself by teaming up with two neighborhood women to sing at local weddings. Soon, she was performing in music halls in Egypt's provincial cities, before moving back to Cairo where she appeared in the main theater district. By 1927, Na'ima al-Masriyya had accumulated a considerable fortune when she purchased the Alhambra, a casino and nightclub she managed while singing and performing as a recording artist. Through her success, Na'ima al-Masriyya helped to reshape the concept of respectability, forcing the public to alter its rigid standards for single women.

Badi'a Masabnik, a much more colorful and flamboyant figure, was adored by her fans. Born in Syria in the 1890s, she performed as a singer and dancer in Syria, Egypt, and throughout the Mideast, and remained quite open about the series of wealthy lovers who financed her career. In 1921, Badi'a starred in Najib al-Rihani's theatrical troupe in Cairo, and in 1923 she married al-Rihani, though the union proved to be of short duration. On tour in North Africa, she discovered al-Rihani in the arms of a French actress. Without a word, she packed her bags and left the troupe starless. By 1926, the marriage had ended, and Badi'a opened her own music hall in Cairo. Called Sala Badi'a, the club not only featured the owner but performers she had trained. Many Egyptian performers first appeared on her stage: **Laila Murad, Fraid al-Atrash, Najat `Ali,** and **Nadira**. When Badi'a went on tour throughout the Mideast, her friend and colleague, **Fathiyya Ahmad** (c. 1898–1975), managed the club in her absence. Famous in her own right, Ahmad was both an excellent manager and a good drawing card, and both women profited from the association. Ever inventive, Badi'a also inaugurated largely popular matinees for women only, held when the club's male patrons were at work. Matinees for women soon became a feature of clubs throughout Egypt.

The career of the more conventional Fathiyya Ahmad demonstrates the upward mobility that was increasingly available to Egypt's beloved female stars. The daughter of a Qur'an reciter, Ahmad had ventured out of a traditional background onto the stage. Her theatrical career began in Cairo in 1910, and she was an instant success. When she married a wealthy landowner in the early 1920s, it was a sign of the increasing social acceptance of female entertainers. Economics had propelled many of these women onstage, and class background as well as their public lives removed them from candidacy as wives of middle- or upper-class men. But as public adulation grew, this prejudice began to wane. As the wife of a wealthy man, Ahmad no longer had to perform, but she clearly enjoyed the spotlight, despite the fact that she was shy and quiet. Though she always maintained a respectable demeanor, she had no qualms about associating with the flamboyant Badi'a, another example of the ability of these women to make their own rules. As a performer, manager, and recording star, Fathiyya Ahmad was a much-loved figure until her retirement in 1950.

Moving aggressively into the business world, taking advantage of the new technologies to reach a wider mass audience, these women demonstrated an entrepreneurial spirit best measured when songs began to be broadcast in homes, coffeehouses, and grocery stores. The voices of Badi'a, Fathiyya Ahmad, Na'ima al-Masriyya, and Munira al-Mahdiyya dominated the air waves, and were soon heard throughout the Middle East. They enjoyed enormous success, dominating the entertainment field and earning more than male performers. As the 20th century progressed, public adulation became almost frenzied. For decades, the radio broadcasts on the first Thursday of every month of Egypt's most famous singer, Um Kalthum, virtually brought the Arab world to a halt. As the center of the impact these women had on Arab entertainment, Cairo is probably best compared to another music mecca, Nashville, except that Cairo's eventual audience was much larger, as it included the entire Middle East.

In the Middle East, where Westerners tend to measure progress politically rather than artistically, some of the greatest progress has been made by women through the arts and entertainment. By creating roles for themselves, roles that had never before existed in the Arab world, these women ultimately set new standards, offering all members of their sex a new prominence and dignity.

SOURCES:

Badran, Margot. "Independent Women: More Than a Century of Feminism in Egypt," in *Arab Women: Old Boundaries, New Frontiers*. Edited by Judith E. Tucker. Bloomington, IN: Indiana University Press, 1993, pp. 129–148.

Baer, Gabriel. *Studies in the Social History of Modern Egypt*, Chicago, IL: University of Chicago Press, 1969.

Baron, Beth. "Artists and Entrepreneurs: Female Singers in Cairo during the 1920s," in *Women in the Muslim World*. Edited by Lois Beck and Nikki Keddie. Cambridge, MA: Harvard University Press, 1978, pp. 292–309.

Early, Evelyn Aleen. "Getting It Together: *Baladi* Egyptian Businesswomen" in *Arab Women: Old Boundaries, New Frontiers*. Edited by Judith E. Tucker. Bloomington, IN: Indiana University Press, 1993, pp. 84–101.

El-Saadwi, Nawal. *The Hidden Face of Eve—Women in the Arab World*, London: Zed Press, 1980.

Khater, Akran, and Cynthia Nelson. "Al-Harakah Al-Nissaiyah: The Women's Movement and Political Participation in Modern Egypt," in *Women's Studies International Forum*. Vol. 11, no. 5, 1988, pp. 465–483.

Marsot, Afaf Lutfi al-Sayyid. "The Revolutionary Gentlewomen in Egypt," in *Women in the Muslim World*. Edited by Lois Beck and Nikki Keddie. Cambridge, MA: Harvard University Press, 1978, pp. 261–276.

Nelson, Cynthia. "Changing Roles of Men and Women: Illustrations from Egypt," in *Anthropological Quarterly*. Vol. 41, 1968, pp. 57–77.

Philipp, Thomas. "Feminism and Nationalist Politics in Egypt," in *Women in the Muslim World*. Edited by Lois Beck and Nikki Keddie. Cambridge, MA: Harvard University Press, 1978, pp. 277–293.

Karin Loewen Haag,
freelance writer, Athens, Georgia

Ehre, Ida (1900–1989)

Austrian-born, German-Jewish actress and theater director who founded the Hamburger Kammerspiele, one of West Germany's most innovative theaters. Born in Prerau, Moravia, Austria-Hungary (now Prerov, Czech Republic), on July 9, 1900; died in Hamburg, Germany, on February 16, 1989; married Bernhard Heyde (a physician), in 1928; children: daughter, Ruth Heyde.

A survivor of the Holocaust, Ida Ehre was one of only a small number of Jews who chose to remain in Germany after 1945. She became one of the best known and most respected theater personalities in West Germany, and her life and artistic career was long and full of drama both on and off the stage.

Born into a religiously observant Jewish family in Moravia in the Habsburg monarchy of Austria-Hungary, young Ida Ehre received her dramatic training at Vienna's Academy for Music and the Performing Arts. She began her professional acting career in 1918 in provincial Austrian theaters in towns like Bielitz, in Silesia (now Bielsko-Biala, Poland), appearing in the title role in Goethe's *Iphigenie*. Her abilities were quickly recognized, and within a few years she had advanced to leading theaters in Bonn, Königsberg, Mannheim and Stuttgart. In 1928, Ehre married a physician, Dr. Bernhard Heyde, and soon a daughter, Ruth, was born to the couple.

By the early 1930s, Ehre and her family had settled in the great port city of Hamburg, where her husband became director of a hospital. Her acting career blossomed, and she hoped to someday combine her acting work with directing and managing her own theater. These dreams were threatened in 1933 when the Nazi dictatorship was born and Jews like Ehre began to lose their jobs in both public and private employment. But until 1938, when the National Socialist authorities banned all public performances by Jews, she was one of the star performers at Berlin's Lessing Theater, which maintained a vigorous Jewish cultural presence in the German capital. Ehre's non-Jewish husband remained fiercely loyal to her, providing physical protection and emotional support to both Ida and their "half-Aryan" daughter Ruth.

By 1939, conditions for Germany's Jews had become intolerable, and the Heyde family made plans to emigrate. Bernhard Heyde resigned from his hospital directorship, and, in late August 1939, the family of three set sail for an uncertain future in Chile. Their timing could not have been worse, for the German attack on Poland which began World War II on September 1 necessitated the return of their vessel to its home port of Hamburg.

Although her husband and daughter lived in constant fear of Ida being arrested and sent to be "resettled" (i.e., murdered) in the East, it was not until 1943 that the Gestapo came for her. Ida was about to be placed on the train to Auschwitz when her husband's protestations to Gestapo officials brought about the desired result. Although she would be incarcerated in a prison camp near Hamburg, her own tenacity and her husband's continuing protests kept her from being sent to a death camp. As the Jewish partner in a "privileged mixed marriage," Ida Ehre survived because Nazi officials did not wish to create scenes that would weaken German civilian morale during the war. The courage of her husband made it possible for her to survive Nazi racism, and the family lived through not only Adolf Hitler's genocidal fury but also the terrible air raids of 1943 and the final blood-letting of spring 1945. In 1945, she and her family began to rebuild their lives. Virtually all of her Jewish friends and acquaintances who had not escaped Germany before 1942 had been murdered in the Holocaust. Her mother and sister Bertha had died in the "model ghetto" of Theresienstadt/Terezin.

Now in her mid-40s, Ehre was determined to resume her career in the theater. In June 1945, she approached British occupation authorities for permission to open and operate a theater company. After receiving clearance, she secured a venue, recruited actors and staff, and attended to countless small but necessary details. Hamburg was a city in ruins, but on December 10, 1945, a scant seven months after Germany's capitulation, Ehre's dream was realized. Naming her theater the Hamburg Chamber Players (Hamburger Kammerspiele), a venerable and honored name in local theater history, Ehre fought off depression by working 12-, 14- and 16-hour days. For the next four decades, she served not only as her company's director (*Intendantin*) but also as its producer and stage manager (*Regisseurin*). Besides this immense work load, she appeared in leading roles in many plays.

Determined to bring to her audiences the kind of plays that could not be seen during 12 years of Nazi dictatorship, Ehre constantly looked for innovative theater works. Opening in a building that the Nazis had "Aryanized" from its Jewish owners, the Hamburg Chamber Players signalled their determination to bring German theater back in touch with an outside world. On their first night, Ehre's ensemble presented the German premiere of *Leuchtfeuer* (original title: *Thunder Rock*), a work by the American playwright Robert Ardrey.

Within a short time, Ehre's theater was regularly presenting some of the newest and most challenging plays of the day, including German premiere performances of works by such eminent playwrights as Jean Anouilh, Max Frisch, Jean-Paul Sartre and Thornton Wilder. The most moving premiere took place in 1947 when Hamburg-born Wolfgang Borchert's antiwar drama *Draussen vor der Tür* (*The Man Outside*) was introduced. Fatally ill while he wrote his play, Borchert had died in a Basel hospital the day before its first performance in his home city.

In addition to her theater in Hamburg, Ehre often appeared on other German stages as well. She was particularly celebrated for her interpre-tations of Mother Courage in Bertolt Brecht's play of the same name, as well as in the roles of Mrs. Warren in George Bernard Shaw's *Mrs. Warren's Profession* and Amanda Wingfield in Tennessee Williams' *The Glass Menagerie*. Starting in 1947, Ehre began to take roles in German films, and by the 1960s she was regularly appearing in major dramatic roles on German television. She was always willing to invest her time and energy in furthering the careers of talented actors, actresses, and stage managers who had yet to become famous; these included such later stars as Helmut Käutner, **Hilde Krahl**, Wolfgang Liebeneiner, Eduard Marks, John Olden, Hans Quest, and Hermann Schomberg.

As a Holocaust survivor living in Germany, Ehre was determined to remind Germans of the burdens their recent history had placed on their shoulders. An active member of the Hamburg and West German Jewish communities, she often spoke out in public on crucial issues of racial and ethnic hatred. In the mid-1980s, she demonstrated her support for the West German peace movement by staging—and starring in—*Die Friedensfrau* (*The Woman of Peace*), Walter Jens' update of Aristophanes' classic *Lysistrata*.

As one of the best-known and most eloquent citizens of the German Federal Republic, Ida Ehre received many awards, including the Schiller Prize of the City of Mannheim, the Grand Federal Cross for Achievement, and the Arts and Sciences medal of the city of Hamburg. Hamburg's university also awarded her an honorary doctorate as well as a professorship. She published the first edition of her autobiography in 1985.

In November 1988, Ehre was chosen to read Paul Celan's classic Holocaust poem "Death Fugue" as part of an hour-long nationally televised Bundestag ceremony to commemorate the 40th anniversary of the notorious 1938 Nazi anti-Jewish Kristallnacht pogrom. Overcome, Ehre was photographed covering her face, emotionally distraught, after her recitation before the German legislative body. The photograph became internationally famous because her distress had been misinterpreted as a response not to the poem, but rather to the memorial address given by the Speaker of the Bundestag, Philipp Jenninger, a poorly crafted presentation that was widely interpreted as a defense of Nazi racism. (It was not, but Jenninger had to resign his post due to the controversy raised by his clumsy comments on Adolf Hitler's "fascination" for countless millions of Germans.) Ida Ehre died in Hamburg on February 16, 1989.

SOURCES:

"Aufbrüche und Katastrophen: Zur Geschichte der Hamburger Kammerspiele," in *Neue Zürcher Zeitung.* June 3, 1996, p. 20.

Ehre, Ida. *Gott hat einen grösseren Kopf, mein Kind.* New ed. Reinbek bei Hamburg: Rowohlt Verlag, 1988.

"Ida Ehre," in *Daily Telegraph* [London]. February 24, 1989, p. 21.

"Ida Ehre," in *Variety.* March 1, 1989.

"Ida Ehre, 88, Is Dead; West German Actress," in *The New York Times Biographical Service.* February 1989, p. 167.

Italiaander, Rolf, ed. *Mutter Courage und ihr Theater: Ida Ehre und die Hamburger Kammerspiele.* Hamburg: Freie Akademie der Künste, 1965.

Johnson, Daniel. "Bonn's Speaker Resigns over His 'Nazi' Speech," in *Daily Telegraph* [London]. November 12, 1988, p. 9.

Schütt, Peter. "Theater für den Frieden," in *Theater der Zeit.* Vol. 41, no. 6, 1986, p. 71.

John Haag,
Assistant Professor of History,
University of Georgia, Athens, Georgia

Ehrengarde Melusina von der Schulenburg, baroness Schulenburg

(1667–1743).

See Schulenburg, Ehrengard Melusina von der.

Ehrensvärd, Thomasine Gyllembourg

(1773–1856).

See Heiberg, Johanne for sidebar.

Ehrig, Andrea (b. 1961).

See Schöne, Andrea Mitscherlich.

Eibenschütz-Dernbourg, Ilona

(1872–1967)

Hungarian pianist. Name variations: Ilona Eibenschütz. Born in Budapest, Hungary, on May 8, 1872; died in London, England, on May 21, 1967; student of Clara Schumann.

Ilona Eibenschütz-Dernbourg is chiefly remembered as a student of *Clara Schumann. She was one of a group of students, fortunate enough to study with Schumann, who passed on a unique style of piano playing which traced back to the early 19th century when the instrument evolved. Eibenschütz-Dernbourg was also directly exposed to the thinking of Johannes Brahms, a friend and close associate of Schumann's, who listened attentively to all of Schumann's students, commenting on their progress. Eibenschütz-Dernbourg played many of Brahms' works in public at a time when they were considered both modern and difficult to understand. Returning to London to concertize and teach,

she passed on the valuable legacy of both Schumann and Brahms.

John Haag,
Athens, Georgia

Eilberg, Amy (1954—)

American who became the first woman to be ordained a rabbi within the Conservative branch of Judaism. Born in Philadelphia, Pennsylvania, on October 12, 1954; daughter of Joshua Eilberg and Gladys Eilberg; graduated summa cum laude from Brandeis; M.A. in Talmud from the Jewish Theological Seminary, 1978; graduate degree in social work, Smith College, 1984; married Howard Schwartz.

Completed Talmudic studies (1978) but had to wait until 1985 before Conservative rabbis finally voted to allow women to be ordained, thus confirming her as the first female Conservative rabbi in history.

Amy Eilberg was born in 1954 in Philadelphia, Pennsylvania, and her strong family background prepared her for the struggles she would face as a religious pioneer. Her mother **Gladys Eilberg**, a social worker, described the family as being "Jewish culturally and philosophically down to our gut in every way." Her father Joshua Eilberg, a lawyer who served in the U.S. House of Representatives, spent countless hours involved in various Jewish causes, including support for Israel, the plight of Jews in the Soviet Union, and the prosecution of Nazi war criminals. From her mother, young Amy heard stories about the pogroms her family had endured in tsarist Russia earlier in the century, including a hallowed family story about her maternal grandmother talking cossacks out of killing her husband. Fortified by a strong sense of tradition, Amy Eilberg was already on a path of social activism by the time she was in her teens. As a leader in Conservative Judaism's United Synagogue Youth (USY), she traveled to the Soviet Union with a USY group that visited Jewish "refuseniks," men and women who had been denied exit visas for Israel.

When Eilberg began her studies at Brandeis University in 1972, she was determined to integrate her traditional Judaism with the contemporary egalitarian views that had become so central to young people's thinking in the United States during the 1960s. Jewish feminism, too, was growing rapidly as both an ideology and a movement during these years, and Eilberg and other young Jewish women at Brandeis were strongly influenced by its ideals and aspirations. During her first year there, she was active in transforming Conservative religious services to include full participation by women. Eilberg received her education at a time when women were seeking equality in the Jewish religious arena. In September 1971, a group of mostly Conservative Jewish women founded Ezrat Nashim. This organization hoped to achieve reform by acting as an internal critic of male-dominated religious traditions. As a vigorous "loyal opposition," some of these women participated in public events hitherto reserved for male rabbis alone, such as their dramatic appearance at the Conservative Rabbinal Assembly convention in March 1972.

Eilberg was deeply influenced by an event that took place in 1973 at the First National Jewish Women's Conference. On that occasion, pioneering Jewish feminist and theorist **Rachel Adler** publicly prayed with *tallit* (prayer shawl) and *tefillin* (phylacteries). Hallowed traditions—and some said *halacha*, the traditional Jewish legal system—had long held that women need not wear these during services. Adler's action challenged traditions that exempted women from these obligations, presumably due to a notion that by their very nature women were different from (and inferior to) men.

After hearing of Adler's deed, Eilberg decided that she too would wear the *tallit* and *tefillin* as a way of "rejecting the concept that simply by virtue of being a woman, I was exempt and therefore excluded from a certain set of central activities." From this point on, she marked herself as a religious activist by leading services and reading from the Torah. She also spent considerable time and energy teaching other young women to do these liturgical tasks.

Eilberg graduated from Brandeis summa cum laude. By the time she enrolled at New York's Jewish Theological Seminary in 1976, she had decided to become a rabbi even though the issue of the ordination of women had not yet been resolved within the leadership hierarchy of American Conservative Judaism. There were some encouraging signs for her in the mid-1970s. In June 1972, *Sally Jane Priesand became the first female ordained rabbi in the United States. Whereas Priesand had become a rabbi within the traditions of Reform Judaism, the somewhat more traditional vision of Judaism found in the Reconstructionist wing of the faith was also willing to ordain women as rabbis during these years, and in 1974 **Sandy Eisenberg Sasso** was ordained as the first female Reconstructionist rabbi.

Throughout the 1970s, the issue of women's ordination flared as rabbis heatedly debated its pros and cons within America's Conservative Jewish community. Passionate feminists within Conservative circles made their case vociferously, refusing to take "no" for an answer. Using the national media skillfully, they were able to have their case presented in *The New York Times* and other national elite media, pointing out that women who felt frustrated in Conservative pararabbinic jobs had abandoned Conservative Judaism in order to become rabbis in Reform and Reconstructionist synagogues. Convinced that Conservative Judaism would accept women as rabbis and confident in her own strengths as a pioneer, Eilberg continued her studies at the Jewish Theological Seminary, where she completed a master's degree in Talmud in 1978. She spent the year after graduation teaching in Israel, then returned to the United States to work on another graduate degree, in social work, which she received from Smith College in 1984.

Try as they might to make the issue of female rabbis disappear from public view, the male leaders of Conservative Judaism could not wish it away. For more than a decade, from 1972 to 1985, a holding action took place that depended on "shifting alliances, studies undertaken, commissions formed, hearings held, motions tabled, and votes counted." Amy Eilberg and others like her, who wished to remain in the fold of Conservative Judaism but who also demanded their full rights as women in the religious community, finally prevailed. Although the deeply divided faculty of the Jewish Theological Seminary had suspended consideration of the issue in 1979, the issue did not disappear from view and by 1983 that institution's faculty counted a solid majority favoring the admission of women as candidates for ordination into its rabbinical school. With support from Chancellor Gerson Cohen, who had been in favor of female rabbis since the late 1970s, the seminary faculty voted affirmatively on this issue in October 1983, the vote being 34 to 8 with one abstention and about half a dozen absent, presumably to register their protest.

Despite the positive changes that were taking place at the Jewish Theological Seminary in the early 1980s, considerable resistance to the idea of female rabbis remained during this period among members of the all-male Rabbinical Assembly, the international governing body of Conservative rabbis. One tactic of the reform faction, to create "instant" Conservative female rabbis by allowing Reform female rabbis to transfer over to Conservative Judaism, failed to receive a passing vote in the Rabbinical Assembly conventions of 1983 and 1984, because a three-fourths majority was required to approve individual candidates for membership within that body. Opposition weakened significantly after the sea change that occurred at the Jewish Theological Seminary in the fall of 1983, and in early 1985 Amy Eilberg, who had never lost hope of serving as·a Conservative rabbi, saw her dreams realized.

At its February 1985 convention, the Rabbinical Assembly voted on a measure to automatically admit all seminary graduates to membership in their body. Being in the form of a constitutional amendment that required only a two-thirds majority in order to pass, the measure was enacted by a vote of 636 to 267. At a time when there were already 71 female Reform rabbis, Conservative Judaism now could point to Amy Eilberg as its first woman rabbi. She was ordained in May 1985 after receiving her degree from the Jewish Theological Seminary, and in July of the same year Eilberg was officially designated a member of the Rabbinical Assembly. She was quickly joined in that organization by **Beverly Magidson** and **Jan Kaufman**, also pioneer female rabbis. Enjoying the strong support of her parents and her husband Rabbi Howard Schwartz during her years of preparation to enter the rabbinate, Amy Eilberg worked at several posts over the next decade including that of chaplain at the Methodist Hospital of Indiana in Indianapolis, as a community rabbi at the Jewish Welfare Federation, and at the Jewish Healing Center in San Francisco, California.

SOURCES:

Cantor, Aviva. "Rabbi Eilberg," in *Ms.* Vol. 14, no. 6. December 1985, pp. 45–46.

Eilberg, Amy. "Rites of Passage in Judaism: A Comparative Study of Jewish and Eriksonian Theories of Human Development" (M.S. Thesis, Smith College School for Social Work, 1984).

"End of a Vigil," in *Time.* Vol. 125, no. 8. February 25, 1985, p. 61.

Estep, Kimberly K. "Amy Eilberg," in Frank Northen Magill, ed. *Great Lives from History: American Women Series.* Vol. 2. Pasadena, CA: Salem Press, 1995, pp. 569–572.

Golinkin, David. "The Movement for Equal Rights for Women in Judaism as Reflected in the Writings of Rabbi David Aronson," in *American Jewish Archives.* Vol. 47, no. 2. Fall–Winter, 1995, pp. 243–260.

Lerner, Anne Lapidus. "'Who Hast Not Made Me a Man': The Movement for Equal Rights for Women in American Jewry," in *American Jewish Year Book.* Vol. 77, 1977, pp. 3–38.

Nadell, Pamela S. "Rabbis," in Paula E. Hyman and Deborah Dash Moore, eds. *Jewish Women in America: An Historical Encyclopedia.* Vol. 2. NY: Routledge, 1997, pp. 1115–1120.

Rudavsky, Tamar, ed. *Gender and Judaism: The Transformation of Tradition.* NY: New York University Press, 1995.

Schneider, Carl J., and Dorothy Schneider. *In Their Own Right: The History of American Clergywomen.* NY: Crossroad Publishers, 1997.

Schwartz, Shuly Rubin. "Conservative Judaism," in Paula E. Hyman and Deborah Dash Moore, eds., *Jewish Women in America: An Historical Encyclopedia.* 2 vols. NY: Routledge, 1997, pp. 275–278.

Weinik, Susan Aimee. "Amy Eilberg will be Conservative Judaism's First Woman Rabbi," in *People.* Vol. 23. April 29, 1985, pp. 50–51.

John Haag,
Assistant Professor of History,
University of Georgia, Athens, Georgia

Einstein-Maríc, Mileva

(1875–1948)

Serbian mathematician and first wife of Albert Einstein who did the computations for his theory of relativity and other important papers, but whose contributions went unmentioned after their collaboration ceased, while his scientific contributions never again achieved the level reached during the marriage. Name variations: Einstein-Maric. Born Mileva Maríc in Titel, in the Serbian part of the former Austro-Hungarian Empire, on December 19, 1875; died in Zurich, Switzerland, on August 4, 1948; daughter of a civil servant in the Hungarian army and a mother who came from a wealthy family; early evidence of brilliance in mathematics led to her admittance, as the sole female student, to a boys' gymnasium in Zagreb; attended university in Switzerland; married Albert Einstein, on January 6, 1903; children: a daughter, Liserele or Lieserl (b. 1902), whose fate is unknown, and two sons, Hans Albert (b. May 14, 1904) and Eduard (b. July 28, 1910).

Went to Zurich to attend university (c. 1894); met Albert Einstein (1896); left her studies at the Polytechnic (1901); provided the mathematical calculations for the paper that initially bore her name as co-author, that would later win her husband the Nobel Prize in physics (1905); remained in Zurich after Albert moved to Berlin (1914); received the money awarded with the Nobel Prize (1922).

The famous equation $E=mc^2$ in which Albert Einstein demonstrated that mass and energy are equivalent is one of the major scientific breakthroughs of the 20th century, and the theory of relativity which he derived from it made the name Einstein a household word. But few are aware of the contributions made to these great works by the physicist's first wife, the mathematician Mileva Einstein-Maríc. Given how thoroughly she has been forgotten, it is interesting to compare the careers of this couple with their contemporaries, Pierre and *Marie Curie, central figures in 20th-century science, who also worked together. In 1905, the Curies shared the Nobel Prize for chemistry, but Pierre was always one to advertise his wife's intellectual gifts, and, after his tragic early death, the further research done by her left no doubt as to the power of Marie Curie's own achievements. In the case of Mileva Einstein-Marić, the situation remains more cloudy. For one thing, Albert Einstein showed no inclination after his early years to share any credit with his first wife, although there are many indications that Mileva Einstein-Marić made the calculations that were a deeply significant contribution to the formulation of his theory of relativity; in particular, mathematics were known not to be Einstein's strong suit.

Everything I have done and accomplished I owe to Mileva. She is my genial source of inspiration, my protective angel against the sins in life and even more so in science. Without her I would not have started my work let alone finished it.

—Albert Einstein in a letter to Mileva Einstein-Marić's father

Mileva Marić was born on December 19, 1875, in Titel, in the multicultural Austro-Hungarian Empire, the daughter of Serbs who were familiar with German language and culture. Mileva's father was a civil servant in the Hungarian army, and her mother came from a wealthy family. Recognized early by her parents as extremely gifted, Mileva attended several secondary schools before gaining admittance as a private student to an all-male gymnasium, or high school, in Zagreb. Her mathematical abilities led to her study of physics, and at age 19 she went to Switzerland, one of the few countries that then allowed women to take university courses. After studying medicine for one term, she concentrated on mathematics and physics.

Up to this time in history, the sciences had consisted of an odd mix of professionals and dabblers and were far less exclusive than would later be the case. It was only when science began to surpass the humanities in prestige that they became male dominated. Women had long participated in science, but few chose it as a professional career.

Given the general attitude that women did not belong in higher education, women pioneers in any area of study faced special challenges because of their sex. Professors tended not to believe that female students seriously wanted to study for their doctorates, for instance, and few thought about taking them on as assistants. In pursuing mathematics and physics, Marić had no female models.

Although Switzerland was ahead of other European countries in allowing women to pursue a university education, a woman who entered one of these institutions found her career opportunities far from assured. Barely a generation ahead of Mileva, **Emilie Kempin-Spyri** became the first woman in the world to achieve a doctorate in jurisprudence at the University of Zurich in 1887, but the practice of law was contingent on being a voting citizen, and women were not allowed to vote. Despite a move to the United States where she founded the First Woman Law College, Kempin-Spyri's career became a tragic example of thwarted circumstances leading eventually to bankruptcy and a breakdown.

In 1896, one of Mileva Marić's classmates at the Polytechnic in Zurich was Albert Einstein, who came there after studying in Germany and Italy. Albert's attendance at lectures was sporadic as he preferred to spend his time in the physics laboratory, and Mileva appeared to be the more dedicated and determined student. In July 1900, Albert received a teaching degree and began giving private lessons and working at various local schools to support himself. By this time, he and Mileva were deeply involved, and she began to lobby their professor to offer Albert an assistantship. Whether she gave any thought to asking for this position for herself is not known. What is known is that Professor Weber did not consider Albert—who had received the lowest marks on his final of any degree candidate—a particularly promising student. In August 1901, Weber's indifference to Albert may have played a role in Mileva's decision to stop her research and leave the Polytechnic. The couple had agreed that they would marry as soon as one of them obtained a job, and from this point forward Albert's needs came first in Mileva's life. In January 1902, she gave birth to a daughter, Liserele. Nothing is known of the child's fate, although she may have been given up for adoption. (**Michele Zackheim** argues that she was born severely retarded and died of scarlet fever at 21 months.) Mileva and Albert finally married a year later, on January 6, 1903.

Einstein-Marić remained part of a group called Academic Olympia—composed of her husband, the Habicht brothers, Maurice

Solovine, and Michele Angelo Besso—which met regularly to study and read philosophical and scientific works. During this time, Einstein-Maríc worked with Paul Habicht on the construction of a machine to measure small electrical currents, and Albert did the work of describing the apparatus for a patent application. When the patent was approved, the apparatus appeared under the name Einstein-Habicht (Patent No. 35693). When one of the Habicht brothers asked Mileva why her name was not included, she replied with a pun on the name Einstein, "What for, we are both only one stone." By this decision, however, the record of her contribution to the project was lost, a fact that was made worse when her husband published two more articles related to the project, further appropriating work that had been his wife's by using his name only.

One reason Albert did not always stress his wife's academic abilities was perhaps that he valued other traits. Writing to his friend Michele Besso, about his recent marriage, he said, "I am now a married man, and my wife and I lead an extremely agreeable life. She occupies herself perfectly with everything, cooks very well, and is always cheerful." To be fair to the physicist, it should be remembered that domesticity was considered to be a female's highest field of endeavor during this period, and the description would have been considered a high compliment.

On May 14, 1904, Einstein-Maríc gave birth to the couple's first son, Hans Albert. Now wife and mother, she also continued to collaborate scientifically with Albert, who made no secret at the time of her assistance with his work, stating over and over, "My wife does my mathematics." Since mathematics is the language of science, those who "speak" the language of mathematics fluently are better understood by the scientific community than those who cannot, and Einstein's dislike of mathematics was well known. Hermann Minkowski, a former professor of Einstein's and a great mathematician, is said to have told Max Born after Einstein's theory of relativity was published, "This was a big surprise for me because Einstein was quite a lazybones and wasn't at all interested in mathematics." Notes Desanka Trbuhovic-Gjuric of Mileva:

> In her work, she was not the co-creator of his ideas, something no one else could have been, but she did examine all his ideas, then discussed them with him and gave mathematical expression to his ideas about the extension of Planck's quantum theory and about the special theory of relativity. . . . Mileva Einstein-Maríc was the first person

Mileva Einstein-Maríc, with Albert Einstein, 1911.

to tell Albert Einstein after the completion of his paper: this is a great, very great and beautiful work, whereupon he sent it to the journal *Annalen der Physik* in Leipzig.

In 1905, five articles by Albert Einstein appeared in the Leipzig *Annalen der Physik*. Two of them, including his dissertation, were written in Zurich. The other three, published in Vol. XVII of *Annalen der Physik*, were written with his wife while he was employed at the Bern patent office. For one of these papers, "Einen die Erzeugung und Verwandlung des Lichtes betreffenden heuristischen Gesichtspunkt," he would later receive the Nobel Prize. The theory of relativity was continued in another, "Elektrodynamik bewegter Körper." According to Abram F. Joffe, the famous Russian physicist who was a member of the editorial team for *Annalen der Physik*, the original manuscripts for these papers, as well as a third, were co-signed by Einstein-Maríc. Unfortunately, the original manuscripts may no longer exist. A reward of $11,500,000 was offered to the person who could present them to the Library of Congress, and the fate of the co-signed manuscripts was discussed in a *New York Times* article on February 15, 1944, but no trace of the papers has ever been found.

The extent of the contributions of Einstein-Maríc to her husband's work is suggested, if not verified, by what followed. Many have noted that the period in Switzerland was the most intellectually productive time of Einstein's life. After the age of 26, his work never reached the same level as his earlier research. His friend, David Reichenstein, notes: "It is strange how fruitful that short period of his life was. Not only his special theory of relativity but a lot of other basic papers bear the date 1905." One of Einstein's biographers, Leopold Infeld, echoes: "His most important scientific work he wrote as a little civil servant in the Patent Office in Bern." Finally, Peter Michelmore, who had a great deal of information directly from the famous physicist, states: "Mileva helped him solve certain mathematical problems. She was with him in Bern and helped him when he was having such a hard time with his theory of relativity." In 1905, Einstein-Maríc felt no hesitancy about her own contribution when she wrote to her father, saying, "A short while ago we finished a very important work which will make my husband world famous."

How was the record of Einstein-Maríc's contribution to the theory of relativity lost? There are several explanations. In the first place, when the single name of Einstein was used, her contribution was glossed over. How her name became deleted after appearing as co-author on some of the original papers is not known. What is obvious, however, is that Albert Einstein did not protest the deletion, and, as his career blossomed, he never discussed her contributions. In later years, the dissolution of their marriage may have been a factor. In 1922, when he was awarded the Nobel Prize, Einstein did seem to make a personal acknowledgement that he was in his first wife's debt, when he gave all the prize money to Mileva. This may also have been due to the fact that he had failed to pay child support for several years. In public, he once acknowledged at a congress, "Ever since the mathematicians have taken up my theory of relativity, I don't understand it myself."

In 1904, after the birth of their first son, Mileva asked her brother, who was also studying in Zurich, to help babysit so she could check her husband's computations. Following the publication of his earth-shaking paper in 1905, Albert became a professor at the University of Zurich and the family's income improved, but Mileva still took in student boarders to make ends meet. A mathematician from the University of Zagreb remembers Mileva doing her husband's mathematical problems past midnight, after a long day of household chores. Still she was happy because her husband was successful.

On July 28, 1910, the couple's life changed when they had a second son, Eduard, who was to be plagued by physical and emotional problems throughout his life. By 1911, when the family moved to Prague, the marriage was no longer happy. After their return to Zurich in 1912, Ein-stein-Maríc complained in a letter to her friend, **Helene Kaufler**, on March 17, 1913, that her husband no longer had time for her or the children.

In April 1914, Einstein accepted a position in Berlin as the director of the Kaiser Wilhelm Institute for Physics and was made a member of the Prussian Academy of Sciences. Mileva had no friends or family in Berlin and chose not to follow him. As the guns of August signalled the start of World War I, Albert advised her to stay in Switzerland with the children as it was a neutral country. By then, however, he had another reason for this advice; he had found another woman. Albert sent money only intermittently, and then not enough.

With the two children as her responsibility, lacking food and clothing, Mileva was forced to ask a friend for a loan. When Albert came to Zurich a year later, Einstein-Maríc knew that her husband had moved in with a cousin of his, **Elsa (Einstein)**. He gave no hint that he and Mileva had any future together.

The following years grew increasingly difficult. Because of the devaluation of German currency, Albert did not have the money to take care of his family. At age 19, Eduard became psychotic. Einstein-Maríc devoted herself to his care, knowing that his disease was probably inherited through Albert's mother. The illness was a tremendous financial burden; to meet expenses, she taught physics at a secondary school.

Albert Einstein eventually obtained a divorce in 1919 and married his cousin that same year; Elsa died in 1936. By the late 1920s, he had stopped referring to his first marriage, while Einstein-Maríc's troubles continued. Her brother, captured in Russia during World War I, never returned from military imprisonment; one sister became mentally ill and died, and the second died in 1938; her father, having survived three of his four children, is said to have died of heartbreak. Einstein-Maríc lived until August 4, 1948, when she died in a Zurich clinic, described by her biographer at that time as, "an impoverished old woman, pushed aside even by the clinic personnel."

SOURCES:
Bernstein, Jeremy. "A Critic at Large: The Einstein-Besso Letters," in *The New Yorker*. Vol. 64, no. 2. February 27, 1989, pp. 86–92.

Highfield, Robert, and Paul Carter. *The Private Lives of Albert Einstein*. London: Faber & Faber, 1993.

Joffe, Abram F. *Meetings with Physicists: My Reminiscences of Foreign Physicists*. Moscow: State Publishing House of Physics and Mathematics Literature, 1960.

Renn, Jürgen, and Robert Schulmann. *Albert Einstein/ Mileva Marić: The Love Letters*. Princeton, NJ: Princeton University Press, 1992.

Stachel, John, ed. *The Collected Papers of Albert Einstein: The Early Years 1879–1907*. Vol. I. Princeton, NJ: Princeton University Press, 1987.

Sugimoto, Kenji. *Albert Einstein: A Photographic Biography*. Translated by Barbara Harshav. NY: Schocken Books, 1989.

Trbuhovic-Gjuric, Desanka. *Im Schatten Albert Einsteins: Das tragische Leben der Mileva Einstein-Marić*. Bern, Switzerland: Paul Haupt, 1983.

Troemel-Ploetz, Senta. "Mileva Einstein-Marić: The Woman Who Did Einstein's Mathematics," in *Women's Study International Forum*. Vol. 13, no. 5, 1990, pp. 415–432.

———. "Mileva Einstein-Marić. The Woman Who Did Einstein's Mathematics," in *Index on Censorship*. Vol. 19, no. 9. October 1990, pp. 33–36.

White, Michael, and John Gribbin. *Einstein—A Life in Science*. NY: Simon & Schuster, 1993.

SUGGESTED READING:

Gabor, Andrea. *Einstein's Wife: Work and Marriage in the Lives of Five Great Twentieth-Century Women*. Penguin, 1996.

Zackheim, Michele. *Einstein's Daughter: The Search for Lieserl*. Riverhead Books, 1999.

John Haag,
Assistant Professor of History,
University of Georgia, Athens, Georgia

Eirene.

Variant of Irene.

Eisenblätter, Charlotte (1903–1944)

German anti-Nazi activist who was a member of the underground organization led by Robert Uhrig. Name variations: Charlotte Eisenblatter or Eisenblaetter. Born in Berlin, Germany, on August 7, 1903; executed in Berlin on August 25, 1944; had seven siblings.

Charlotte Eisenblätter was born in Berlin as the youngest child of a large working-class family. Unable to afford a higher education, she read constantly and worked as an office messenger, then later as a secretary. At age 15, she joined the Socialist youth movement and, through her membership in its "Friends of Nature" organization, was able to hike through the beautiful German countryside on weekends and vacations. An intelligent, socially aware woman who had experienced poverty firsthand, Eisenblätter gravitated toward other revolutionary organizations close to the Communist Party of Germany, including its sports unit. Here she made many friends with whom she would retain close connections even after the rise of German Nazism.

The National Socialist seizure of power in 1933 destroyed the German Communist Party

Charlotte Eisenblätter

but individual anti-Nazi resistance cells continued a precarious and increasingly risky existence. Eisenblätter joined an extensive anti-Nazi network led by Robert Uhrig (1903–1944), and, by the time World War II began in September 1939, she had become a seasoned underground activist. She fully recognized the dangers involved in such activities but persisted in her illegal tasks which included the typing and reproduction of anti-Nazi literature. Eisenblätter risked her life when in 1941 she provided room and board for Alfred Kowalke, a German Communist leader who moved to Berlin from the Nazi-occupied Netherlands.

In February 1942, she was arrested and sent to Ravensbrück, the Nazi concentration camp for women. Opened in 1939, by 1942 Ravensbrück had become a site of intense suffering and arbitrary death for many thousands of women from Nazi Germany and German-occupied Europe. By the time of its liberation in 1945, more than 92,000 women had died at Ravensbrück as the victims of shootings, hangings, and beatings as well as cold, hunger and illness due to medical neglect.

Two years later, on February 15, 1944, Eisenblätter was finally indicted for high treason and after a farcical judicial procedure was sentenced to death. Along with her colleague from the Uhrig resistance group, **Elfriede Tygor**, Charlotte Eisenblätter was executed at Berlin's notorious Plötzensee prison on August 25, 1944. In a moving letter to her family and friends written a day before the trial that she knew would lead to her death, Eisenblätter reminded them that her life, while not long in years, had been a rich one, particularly because of the countless hours spent in the circle of her many friends. Calling on them to "remember me in love and do not mourn me," she wished them good health so that they could one day "assist in the reconstruction of our Fatherland." She also reminded them, "as much as I love life, I will die gladly for the ideas I cherish." One of Charlotte's older sisters was not able to come to grips with her loss, consequently taking her own life upon receiving news of the execution.

Charlotte Eisenblätter's name was universally recognized in the German Democratic Republic as that of an exemplary martyr of the militant anti-Nazi working class. She was honored with a postage stamp issued by the GDR post office on September 3, 1959, to raise funds for the preservation of the national memorial at the site of the Ravensbrück concentration camp.

SOURCES:

Kraushaar, Luise. *Berliner Kommunisten im Kampf gegen den Faschismus 1936 bis 1942: Robert Uhrig und Genossen.* Berlin: Dietz Verlag, 1981.

———. *Deutsche Widerstandskämpfer 1933–1945: Biographien und Briefe.* 2 vols. Berlin: Dietz Verlag, 1970.

Partington, Paul G. *Who's Who on the Postage Stamps of Eastern Europe.* Metuchen, NJ: Scarecrow Press, 1979.

Zorn, Monika. *Hitlers zweimal getötete Opfer: Westdeutsche Endlösung des Antifaschismus auf dem Gebiet der DDR.* Freiburg im Breisgau: Ahriman-Verlag, 1994.

John Haag,
Assistant Professor of History,
University of Georgia, Athens, Georgia

Eisenhower, Mamie (1896–1979)

American first lady from 1953 to 1961. Born Mary Geneva Doud on November 14, 1896, in Boone, Iowa; died on November 1, 1979, in Washington, D.C.; second of four daughters of John Sheldon (a meat packer) and Elivera (Carlson) Doud; married Dwight David Eisenhower (1890–1969, president of the U.S.), on July 1, 1916, in Denver, Colorado; children: Dwight D. Eisenhower (1921–1924); John Seldon Doud Eisenhower (b. 1923, attended West Point, served as ambassador to Belgium, and is now a historian).

Opposite page

ℳamie and

𝒟wight 𝒟.

ℰisenhower

Life on the road for Mamie Eisenhower began at the age of nine, when her father moved the family from Boone, Iowa, to Denver, Colorado, then later bought a home in San Antonio, Texas. Mamie, named Mary Geneva for an aunt, was always called by her nickname. She met Lieutenant Dwight D. Eisenhower on a family visit to Fort Sam Houston, where he was Officer of the Day, assigned to escort visitors around the facility. She thought he was "the spiffiest looking man I ever talked to . . . big, blond, and masterful," and he found her "vivacious" and "saucy in the look about her face." They were married nine months later, just shy of her 20th birthday, and settled into two rooms in the officers' barracks at Fort Houston, the first of 33 homes they would live in during 53 years of marriage. She would later remark that she had lived in "everything but an igloo."

As her husband's military career moved forward, Mamie traveled from post to post whenever possible, learning to pack up and move at a moment's notice. The couple had two sons: Dwight, who died of scarlet fever at age three, and John. In 1922, Mamie sailed with her husband to Camp Faillard in the Panama Canal Zone, where they lived in a house on stilts, sharing occupancy with bats and tarantulas. Convinced her husband would one day be a great soldier, Mamie developed a self-sacrificing attitude, which left her husband "free from personal worries," she said, "to conduct his career as he saw fit."

Mamie described the December 7, 1941, attack on Pearl Harbor that signaled the start of America's involvement in World War II as one of "the most terrible nights of her life," second only to the night of her son's death. During the war, she lived in Washington at the Wardman Park Hotel, worked for the USO, and did not see her husband for a three-year stretch. After the war, the couple moved to New York, where Dwight Eisenhower served as president of Columbia University for a short time before becoming supreme commander of the North Atlantic Treaty Organization (NATO) and moving the family to Paris.

Eisenhower's distinguished war record made him a national hero and a natural for a presidential run in 1952. Since he had no political affiliation, and Mamie had never voted, there was a brief skirmish between parties before the GOP won him for their candidate. Though she had no interest in politics, Mamie accompanied him on a 77-stop train tour, appearing beside him on the platform, smiling and silent, once in bathrobe and curlers.

After he took office in 1953, Mamie organized the White House. Everything was planned to the last detail, from the "Mamie pink" table decorations to the entrances for state dinners. A meticulous housekeeper, she made surprise "white glove" inspections and trained the staff to walk around the edges of a room after it was vacuumed because she wanted to avoid footprints on the carpeting. Her flouncy dresses and bob hairstyle, with the trademark bangs, somewhat belied her status. As a general's wife, she had been accustomed to having aides attend to her wishes. As first lady, she demanded the same kind of attention. "When I go out," she ordered, "I am to be escorted to the diplomatic entrance by an usher. And when I return, I am to be met at the door and escorted upstairs."

The first lady suffered with rheumatic heart problems and from Mèniere's disease, an inner-ear disorder that causes dizziness. She often stumbled when walking, which gave rise to rumors of alcoholism. Mamie Eisenhower was also claustrophobic and plagued by headaches and asthma, necessitating a great deal of rest. She once advocated that every woman over 50 should spend one day a week in bed.

As first lady, Mamie did not take on any social or civic causes, preferring to dedicate herself to her husband and making the White House comfortable for those who visited. When the president suffered a heart attack in 1955, she moved into the hospital to be near him and personally answered every one of the letters he received. During his second term, she protected his health by giving state luncheons instead of dinners and by putting visitors up at Blair House, instead of in the White House guest quarters.

The Eisenhowers retired to Gettysburg, Pennsylvania, where, in 1966, they celebrated their 50th wedding anniversary. In 1968, they attended their grandson David's marriage to **Julie Nixon**, the daughter of Eisenhower's vice-president Richard Nixon. During Eisenhower's final illness, Mamie once again took up residence at Walter Reed Hospital to be close to him. After his death in 1969, she continued to work for his causes and promote his name. She attended the dedication of Eisenhower Hall at West Point in 1974, helped christen the super-carrier U.S.S. *Dwight D. Eisenhower* in 1977, and supported Eisenhower College at Seneca Falls, New York, where she attended graduation ceremonies each year.

Mamie Eisenhower died of cardiac arrest two weeks shy of her 83rd birthday. She is

buried next to her husband and their infant son in the chapel of the Eisenhower Library in Abilene, Kansas.

SOURCES:

Healy, Diana Dixon. *America's First Ladies: Private Lives of the Presidential Wives*. NY: Atheneum, 1988.

Melick, Arden Davis. *Wives of the Presidents*. Maplewood, NJ: Hammond, 1977.

Paletta, LuAnn. *The World Almanac of First Ladies*. NY: World Almanac, 1990.

SUGGESTED READING:

Eisenhower, Susan. *Mrs. Ike: Memories and Reflections on the Life of Mamie Eisenhower*. Farrar, Straus, 1996.

Barbara Morgan,
Melrose, Massachusetts

Eisenschneider, Elvira

(1924–c. 1944)

German anti-Nazi activist who parachuted into Nazi Germany and was later captured. Born on April 22, 1924, in Fischbach near Kirn on the Nahe (county Birkenfeld); death date unknown because all traces of her disappear after her capture in 1944; daughter of Paul Eisenschneider (a militant anti-Nazi).

Elvira Eisen-schneider

Elvira Eisenschneider was born into a politically militant family in rural Germany; both of her parents were Communist activists. At the age of ten, she witnessed the brutality of German Fascism when Nazis entered their home to search for her father Paul Eisenschneider, a member of the anti-Nazi underground. When her mother refused to reveal her husband's whereabouts, Nazi Brownshirts savagely beat her, smashing six vertebrae in her spine and crippling her for life. Mother and daughter fled to France and eventually to the Soviet Union where in 1936 they received news that Paul had been arrested by the Nazis while carrying out his underground work.

Elvira Eisenschneider grew up at the international children's home in Ivanovo, where Soviet authorities provided room and board for the sons and daughters of persecuted Communists of various nations. Here she learned Russian and became a militant revolutionary, joining the Komsomol, the Soviet children's organization. At the time of Nazi Germany's attack on the USSR in June 1941, Eisenschneider had begun her studies at Moscow's Institute of International Literature. Abandoning her academic aspirations, she took a course in emergency nursing and became a member of the medical staff that accompanied the many thousands of refugees from the war zone. She resettled in the city of Tsheliabinsk and began to resume her interrupted studies at the local college of technology.

Despite her youth, Eisenschneider believed that she could help the anti-Nazi cause, hastening the day when the German dictatorship was smashed and individuals like her father could be liberated from the terrors of Hitler's concentration camps. In 1942, she volunteered her services to Soviet military authorities, insisting that she could carry out sabotage assignments deep in the heart of Nazi Germany. Trained in intelligence and sabotage work, she parachuted into Nazi territory in the summer of 1943. Eisenschneider was captured in the spring of 1944, after almost a year of successfully carrying out her assignments. All traces of her vanish at this point, but it is clear that she was killed by her captors, most likely soon after her capture and interrogations. Tragically, after almost eight years' incarceration, her father Paul Eisenschneider died around the same time; he was murdered at the Mauthausen concentration camp in Austria on April 19, 1944.

In the German Democratic Republic, Elvira Eisenschneider was universally recognized as an exemplary martyr of the militant anti-Nazi German working class. She was honored with a postage stamp issued by the GDR post office on February 6, 1961, to raise funds for the preservation of the national memorials at the Buchenwald, Ravensbrück and Sachsenhausen concentration camps.

SOURCES:

Kraushaar, Luise. *Deutsche Widerstandskämpfer 1933–1945: Biographien und Briefe*. 2 vols. Berlin: Dietz Verlag, 1970.

Partington, Paul G. *Who's Who on the Postage Stamps of Eastern Europe*. Metuchen, NJ: Scarecrow Press, 1979.

Zorn, Monika. *Hitlers zweimal getötete Opfer: Westdeutsche Endlösung auf dem Gebiet der DDR*. Freiburg im Breisgau: Ahriman-Verlag, 1994.

John Haag,
Assistant Professor of History,
University of Georgia, Athens, Georgia

Eisler, Charlotte (1894–1970)

Austrian musician who emerged from the shadow of her famous composer husband to create a distinguished musical career of her own. Born Charlotte Demant in Tarnopol, Austria-Hungary (now Ternopol, Ukraine), on January 2, 1894; died in Vienna on August 3, 1970; married Hanns Eisler (1898–1962), a composer (divorced 1934); children: Georg Eisler (1928–1998, an Expressionist painter).

Born in the provincial town of Tarnopol in the final decade of the 19th century, Charlotte Demant experienced extraordinary musical, intellectual and political transformations in her lifetime. Like many Austrians yearning for broader horizons, she studied music in Vienna with several of the geniuses to be found there during the period between 1900 and 1938. Her Viennese teachers included Anton von Webern and Edward Steuermann. At first her musical talent took a vocal form, but in some of her Lieder recitals Demant revealed her considerable pianistic abilities by serving as her own piano accompanist.

While moving in the musical circle of the composer Arnold Schönberg, Demant met a brilliant young composer, four years her junior, named Hanns Eisler (1898–1962) who became her husband. Both she and Hanns were as radical in their political orientation as they were in their musical views; the shattering experiences of World War I and the emergence of what was seen as a new Socialist commonwealth in Soviet Russia in 1917 made them highly sympathetic to Communism. Charlotte became a member of the minuscule Austrian Communist Party in the early 1920s and remained loyal to Marxist ideals for the rest of her life. Although compatible musically and politically, the Eislers began to drift apart emotionally by the late 1920s despite the birth of a son, Georg Eisler, in 1928. When Hanns went to Berlin in 1925, Charlotte remained in Vienna, and the couple saw each other only occasionally from that point on, both artists concentrating on the pursuit of their own individual careers.

The onset of Nazi dictatorship in Germany in 1933 resulted in Hanns Eisler's return to Vienna, but irreconcilable differences in their relationship led to a divorce between the two in 1934. Charlotte never remarried. She spent her time and energy on raising her son, continuing her musical career, and engaging in dangerous underground political work for the now-banned Communist movement. In 1936, fearing a Nazi takeover in Austria, Charlotte Eisler immigrated with her son to the Soviet Union. While she worked in Moscow at the Soviet State Music Publishing House, editing among other works the vocal compositions of Gustav Mahler, her young son Georg was enrolled at the German-language Karl Liebknecht School. By 1938, the arbitrary savagery of Stalin's purges had made life precarious for Charlotte and her son. His school had been closed, and she was informed that her visa to remain in the Soviet Union was no longer valid. Mother and son were fortunate in being able to emigrate from the Soviet Union, first for a time to Czechoslovakia, and then on to England.

Settled in Manchester, Eisler resumed her musical career in a country that was in many ways culturally alien to her. She performed successfully throughout the United Kingdom both as a singer and pianist. Eisler's son Georg, who would return to Austria after World War II to win international recognition as an Expressionist painter, for a time lived away from his mother with a Quaker family. In September 1946, Charlotte Eisler returned to war-devastated Vienna (her son had already returned some months earlier). She resumed her interrupted career and soon received an appointment at the municipal Music Conservatory as a professor of piano. Eisler became a mainstay of musical Vienna in the next two decades, presenting many live concerts and recitals over the radio.

By the 1960s, Charlotte Eisler was seen by many Viennese as one of the few remaining active survivors of their city's pre-1938 cultural life. As one of a handful of intellectual emigrés who had returned after 1945, Eisler began to be appreciated by a younger generation of Austrian musicians and music lovers for both artistic and personal reasons. With her immense knowledge of the Second Vienna School of Berg, Schönberg and Webern—much of it based on firsthand experiences—Eisler became a major link in the chain of Austrian cultural continuity. Because of the years she had spent in exile in the United Kingdom, she was also regarded as an expert on contemporary British music, particularly that of Benjamin Britten. Charlotte Eisler died in Vienna on August 3, 1970.

SOURCES:

Betz, Albrecht. *Hanns Eisler, Political Musician.* Translated by Bill Hopkins. Cambridge, UK: Cambridge University Press, 1982.

Blake, David, ed. *Hanns Eisler: A Miscellany.* NY: Harwood Academic Publishers, 1995.

Brockhaus, Heinz Alfred. *Hanns Eisler.* Leipzig: VEB Breitkopf & Härtel, 1961.

Pass, Walter, Gerhard Scheit, and Wilhelm Svoboda. *Orpheus im Exil: Die Vertreibung der österreichischen Musik von 1938 bis 1945.* Vienna: Verlag für Gesellschaftskritik, 1995.

John Haag,
Assistant Professor of History,
University of Georgia, Athens, Georgia

Eisler, Elfriede (1895–1961).

See Fischer, Ruth.

Eisner, Lotte (1896–1983)

German-born French film critic and one of the major film historians of the 20th century, who argued that German Expressionist cinema must be viewed as a major element in the evolution of modern film art. Name variations: (during World War II) Louise Escoffier. Born Lotte Henriette Eisner in Berlin, Germany, on March 6, 1896; died in Paris, France, on November 26, 1983; daughter of Hugo Eisner and Margarethe Feodora (Aron) Eisner (died in a concentration camp in 1942); University of Rostock, Ph.D. in art history, 1924; never married; no children.

Lotte Eisner was born in Berlin into a wealthy, assimilated Jewish family in the closing years of the 19th century. Three days after her birth, the Lumiére Cinematographe made its first public appearance in London, marking the international birth of motion pictures, a phenomenon with which Eisner's life and career would be closely linked. Her father, a textile merchant, created a prosperous and cultured environment in which his daughter experienced various aspects of the art world from her earliest years. After a leisurely course of study at a number of German universities, she received her Ph.D. in art history in 1924 from the University of Rostock, with a dissertation topic about ancient Greek vase paintings.

Although qualified to pursue an academic career, Eisner decided to enter the exciting world of Berlin journalism. While still a student, she had already been contributing articles on art and theater subjects to noted journals and newspapers including *Die literarische Welt* and the *Berliner Tageblatt.* In 1927, a chance encounter at a party would forever change Eisner's life. She met Dr. Hans Feld, a journalist and critic with Berlin's *Film-Kurier,* the world's first film journal to be published on a daily basis, who suggested that she join the staff. Eisner began writing for *Film-Kurier* in 1927, thus becoming Germany's first female film critic to work on a full-time professional basis.

Along with Hans Feld and other *Film-Kurier* contributors like Willy Haas and Béla Balázs, Lotte Eisner was determined not only to inform her readers of new trends in cinema, but to raise their artistic appreciation for what was still in the 1920s a relatively new art form. While *Film-Kurier,* the German film industry's main newspaper, was a practical guide to the mundane problems of film production, the journal also saw itself as part of an intellectual crusade centered "upon furthering experiments, the young avant-garde, and following a film-political line of a widening cultural horizon." Eisner's *Film-Kurier* articles were closely linked to the journal's crusade for better German films. Thoroughly enjoying the exhilarating artistic environment of Berlin, Lotte Eisner met regularly with most of the creative talent of that great metropolis including world-renowned film directors like Fritz Lang and G.W. Pabst. She also became acquainted with the path-breaking Soviet Russian director Sergei Eisenstein. Artists of other disciplines, too, became part of Lotte Eisner's circle of friends, which included the playwright Bertolt Brecht, renowned director Max Reinhardt, and actresses such as *Louise Brooks, *Asta Nielsen, Lupu Pick, and *Leni Riefenstahl (before she emerged as a film director).

In 1933, Adolf Hitler's Nazis seized power in Germany. Almost immediately journals like *Film-Kurier* that were branded as "un-German" and "Jewish-infected" found themselves "Aryanized" and purged of their Jewish and liberal staffs. Both Hans Feld and Lotte Eisner emigrated from Germany, with Feld settling in London and Eisner choosing Paris, where her younger sister **Stephanie Eisner** had recently settled. The transition from respected film authority in Berlin to an insecure life as a refugee from Nazism in a foreign country was not easy for Eisner, but she was able to support herself by working as a secretary, translator, and freelance researcher. With her well-established reputation as a critic, she also found work as a film correspondent for a number of French journals as well as English-language periodicals, including *Film Culture, Sight and Sound,* and *World Film News.*

While in Paris in 1934, Eisner met a French journalist and film enthusiast named Henri Langlois (1914–1977) who had hopes of creating a major film archive and research center, which in later years was to emerge as the world-famed Cinémathèque Française. Immediately sharing his vision, Lotte Eisner became an indispensable collaborator with Langlois as he lobbied tirelessly to find support for his project. Eisner and Langlois worked together throughout the next years at his organization, the Cercle du Cinéma, which made it possible for him to share with a growing group of enthusiasts his own unique private collection of silent films. In the fall of 1939, their dreams of a great film center went up in smoke as World War II began. German refugees in France, including Lotte Eisner, were arrested and interned by panicked French authorities despite the fact that virtually all of them were ardent anti-Nazis, with the overwhelming majority of them being Jewish refugees from Hitlerite racism as well. Along with many others, Eisner was taken to the infamous Gurs concentration camp, where she remained for three months.

With her life at risk during the German occupation of France, Lotte Eisner began an underground existence that was to last four years. With forged identity papers that turned her into "Louise Escoffier," she chose to live in Départment Lot in the Vichy-controlled part of France. Besides saving her own life, Eisner was able to successfully hide a number of important films entrusted to her by Henri Langlois, who feared the Germans would find and destroy them. Boldly, she lived her life under the noses of the Gestapo and French collaborators, even working for a while in the kitchen of a restaurant at Figcac.

The end of the Nazi occupation made it possible for Eisner to return to Paris, where she immediately rejoined Langlois. From 1945 to her retirement in 1974, Eisner worked as archivist and chief curator of Langlois' now expanding Cinémathèque Française. An indefatigable enthusiast for films, she spent three decades arranging programs for film retrospectives, festivals, exhibitions and collections. Working closely with Langlois, Eisner was successful in tracking down and saving thousands of films that were in imminent danger of complete physical deterioration. Eisner was also able to collect a staggering number of costumes, set designs,

scripts and other film memorabilia that Henri Langlois turned into his brilliant exhibitions, which eventually found a fitting permanent home at the Musée du Cinéma at the Palais de Chaillot. Eisner genuinely enjoyed being involved in the hunt for film artifacts, and one of the proudest moments of this aspect of her busy career took place when she came back to Paris from a trip to Rome with the cart that *Giulietta Masina had pulled in the film *La Strada.*

Relying on her sharp mind and excellent memory as well as on a journalist's ability to write quickly and clearly, Eisner published a large number of essays and reviews in the journal *Revue du cinéma* (later *Cahiers du cinéma*), starting in 1945. More important, she began to plan a number of ambitious book-length research projects. The first of these, which was initially published in France in 1952 and which appeared in an English-language translation as *The Haunted Screen* in 1969, was her masterful study of the films influenced by the spirit of German Expressionism. Relying not only on her vast sum of knowledge of films that included firsthand contacts with directors and actors in pre-Nazi Berlin, Eisner also drew upon her early training as an art historian for additional insights into the aesthetics of the film art.

Other highly acclaimed film history books by Eisner appeared during the next years, including definitive studies of the director F.W. Murnau (1964) and Fritz Lang (1977). Her study of Lang was of value, not only because of her 50-year friendship with the director but also because, unlike her previous books that were written in French, this volume was written in German so that Lang, who was still alive, could read the text carefully and annotate proofs of the manuscript with his own comments and suggested changes—which he did up to the time of his death.

Rooted in France after a period of many decades there, and profoundly embittered by her mother Margarethe's death in the Theresienstadt concentration camp in 1942, Eisner remained alienated from Germany until the final years of her life. She began resolving her deeply ambivalent feelings toward her German homeland by working on memoirs entitled *Ich hatte einst ein schönes Vaterland* (*I Once Had a Beautiful Fatherland*), a book that would be published posthumously in 1984. Starting in the early 1970s, however, she entered into a series of friendships with Werner Herzog and other members of a new generation of brilliant young German film directors. On their visits to France, Herzog and other German film personalities visited the physically frail but mentally alert Eisner in her small, exquisite apartment in the Paris suburb of Neuilly sur Seine, which she had over the years transformed into a virtual modern salon for many of Europe's most talented cinema artists.

In her final years, Lotte Eisner enjoyed not only the friendship and admiration of many of the most talented film personalities of Europe, but also became the object of public acclaim from her adopted French homeland. In 1965, she was awarded the Prix Armand Tallier for her study of F.W. Murnau, followed in 1967 by the award of the title Chevalier des Arts et des Lettres. In March 1983, she became a Chevalier of the Legion of Honor. At the time of her death in November 1983, France's Minister of Culture Jack Lang declared the passing of Lotte Eisner to be "a great loss for the French cinema" which would be "felt with profound sadness by her numerous friends in the film world."

SOURCES:

Becker, Klaus. *Friedrich Wilhelm Murnau: Ein grosser Filmregisseur der 20er Jahren.* Kassel: Stadtsparkasse Kassel, 1981.

Eisner, Lotte H. *Fritz Lang.* NY: Da Capo Press, 1986.

———. *The Haunted Screen: Expressionism in the German Cinema and the Influence of Max Reinhardt.* Translated by Roger Greaves. Berkeley, CA: University of California Press, 1973.

———. *Murnau.* Revised and enlarged edition, Berkeley: University of California Press, 1973.

———, and Martje Grohmann. *Ich hatte einst ein schönes Vaterland: Memoiren.* Munich: Deutscher Taschenbuch Verlag, 1988.

Hake, Sabine. *The Cinema's Third Machine: Writing on Film in Germany 1907–1933.* Lincoln: University of Nebraska Press, 1993.

Horowitz, S.M. *Lotte Eisner in Germany.* NY: New Yorker Films, 1980.

"Lotte Eisner," in *The Times* [London]. December 3, 1983, p. 8.

Passek, Jean Loup, Jacqueline Brisbois, and Lotte H. Eisner. *Vingt ans de cinema allemand, 1913–1933: Catalogue.* Paris: Centre national d'art et de culture Georges Pompidou, 1978.

RELATED MEDIA:

"The German Film: A Conversation with Lotte Eisner," conducted by Harold Reynolds. Los Angeles: Pacifica Radio Archive BC 0181, 1986.

John Haag,
Assistant Professor of History,
University of Georgia, Athens, Georgia

Eji (c. 1360–1326 BCE).

See Mutnedjmet.

Ekaterina.

Variant of Catherine.

Ekejiuba, Felicia Ifeoma (1872–1943).

See Okwei of Osomari.

Elder, Kate (fl. 1881)

American legend of the frontier days. Name variations: Kate Fisher. Flourished in 1881; friend of John "Doc" Holliday.

Kate Elder, also referred to as Kate Fisher, is known to history as a prostitute and friend of John "Doc" Holliday, a tubercular gambler, gunfighter, and erstwhile dentist. Holliday and his close friend Wyatt Earp took part in the Gunfight at O.K. Corrall in Tombstone, Arizona Territory, in October 1881. During the six-minute shootout, two of the eight men involved were killed. In the film *Gunfight at O.K. Corral,* *Jo Van Fleet portrays Elder under the character name of Fisher.

Elder, Louisine (1855–1929).

See Cassatt, Mary for sidebar on Havemeyer, Louisine Elder.

Elder, Ruth (1904–1977)

Student pilot who attempted to become first airplane passenger to cross the Atlantic. Born in Florida in 1904; died in San Francisco, California, in 1977; married six times.

Ruth Elder enjoyed brief notoriety following her attempt to become the first airplane passenger to cross the Atlantic. In September 1927, on the heels of Charles Lindbergh's famous solo flight, she and a male pilot set out from Tampa, Florida, in a plane called the *American Girl.* They ran into trouble 250 miles short of the coast of Spain, when an oil leak forced them to deliberately crash in the ocean. Fortunately, the plane landed near a Dutch ship that was able to rescue them. Elder was cited for her daring in ceremonies in Paris and at the White House, where she was heralded as the "Miss America of Aviation." She was soon upstaged, however, by *Amelia Earhart, who not only made a successful transatlantic flight in June 1928 but was a licensed pilot as well. Elder went on to an undistinguished movie career and six marriages.

Elders, Joycelyn (1933—)

African-American physician and the first black woman appointed to the post of U.S. surgeon general. Born Minnie Joycelyn Jones in Schaal, Arkansas, on August 13, 1933; eldest daughter and one of eight children of Curtis (a sharecropper) and Haller Jones; Philander Smith College, Little Rock, Arkansas, B.A., 1952; Uni-

Joycelyn
Elders

*versity of Arkansas Medical
School, M.D., 1960, M.S. in biochemistry, 1967; married Oliver Elders (a
basketball coach); children: two sons.*

Having vowed to become "the voice and vision of the poor and the powerless," Joycelyn Elders was confirmed as the 16th surgeon general
of the United States in September 1993, succeeding *Antonia Novello. The first black woman
ever appointed to the post, Elders was an outspoken advocate of reproductive rights, contracep-
tives, safe sex, and the decriminalization of drugs,
issues that the American public has not always
been comfortable with in open forum. Unfortu-

nately, Elder's pronouncements were frequently as controversial as her views, and after a
series of uncensored statements that embarrassed the White House, she was removed from
office 15 months into her term.

Elders is the eldest of eight children of
sharecroppers and grew up in a three-room
cabin in Schaal, Arkansas, without electricity or
indoor plumbing. At the age of 15, she entered
the University of Arkansas on a scholarship
from the United Methodist Church and, following her graduation in 1952, joined the Army as a
first lieutenant. After the service, she used the
G.I. Bill to attend the University of Arkansas

Medical School, where she was the only woman to graduate in the class of 1960. After serving her internship and residency, she went on to earn an M.S. degree in biochemistry from the University of Arkansas Medical School, after which she joined the faculty there as an assistant professor of pediatrics. She became a full professor in 1976 and two years later was board certified as a pediatric endocrinologist.

It was during the 1970s that Elders first met Bill Clinton, then governor of Arkansas, when he attended the funeral for her brother Bernard, who had been murdered by a psychologically unstable man who was obsessed with Bernard's wife. In 1987, Clinton appointed her director of Arkansas' department of public health. Even then, Elders was not one to mince words. At a press conference following her appointment, after she had announced her intention to combat Arkansas' soaring teenage pregnancy rate by establishing school-based health clinics, she was asked if the clinics would dispense condoms. "Well, I'm not going to put them on their lunch trays, but yes," she replied. Later, when recounting the incident to Paul Hendrickson of the *Washington Post* (February 16, 1993), Elders recalled that Clinton's face had turned bright red. "I realized I'd just dropped my governor in an ocean of Jell-O," she said.

In 1992, impressed with Elders' track record in Arkansas, particularly in the areas of early childhood screening and immunization, prenatal care for women, and HIV testing and counseling, president-elect Clinton offered her the post of surgeon general. At the time, she reminded the president of her past record. "Governor, you didn't really know five years ago what you were buying," she told him. "Now you know exactly what you're getting if you're gonna name me surgeon general."

Even Elders' confirmation hearing was problematic, with concern over her removal as a member of the board of directors of the National Bank of Arkansas in a scandal involving mismanagement, questions about whether she should be responsible for Social Security taxes on wages earned by a nurse retained by her husband to care for his aged mother, and accusations of "double-dipping" (as a member of **Hillary Rodham Clinton**'s health-care task force, she earned a consulting fee from the federal government while still employed as Arkansas' public health director). Other critics, especially conservative women's and religious groups, attacked her past efforts to promote sex education, contraception, and abortion rights, citing some of her more un-

restrained remarks, including her reference to the Roman Catholic Church as a "celibate, male-dominated" institution, and her pointing out the absurdity of offering teen-agers driver's education while ignoring health education. "We taught them what to do in the front seat of a car. Now it's time to teach them what to do in the back seat."

Even after Elders' nomination reached the Senate floor for confirmation, Republican opponents delayed the floor vote until after the congressional summer recess, insisting that they needed more time to examine her views and the allegations against her. She was finally confirmed and sworn in on September 8. "I felt it was more a mechanism to try to destroy me than anything else," Elders said about the confirmation process. "When it was all over I remember thinking, 'I came to Washington, D.C., like prime steak, and after being here a while I feel like poor-grade hamburger.'"

Almost immediately upon taking office, Elders was raising hackles again, reiterating her support for widespread availability of condoms, and telling *The New York Times* (September 14, 1993) that the conservatives' opposition to sex education and preventative measures was due to an underlying "fear of sex," and an accompanying belief "that fornication must be punished and that teenage pregnancy and the bad things that happen after are the natural punishment." A short time later, she departed from White House policy by advocating a so-called "sin tax" on alcohol as well as tobacco. Then in December 1993, she suggested that it might be a good idea to study the potential impact of the legalization of drugs, a position that, once again, embarrassed the White House. While Clinton had for some time turned a deaf ear to Elders' off-hand remarks, his tolerance level was beginning to dip. In 1994, following a statement suggesting that masturbation should be taught in schools, Elders lost her job.

Amid the swirl of controversy that surrounds her, it is easy to lose sight of Elders' ongoing commitment to improving health care in this country. Dozens of awards attest to her accomplishments, among them the Arkansas Democrat's Woman of the Year award, the National Governors' Association Distinguished Service Award, The American Medical Association's Dr. Nathan Davis Award, the De Lee Humanitarian Award, and the National Coalition of 100 Black Women's Candace Award for Health Science. Elders is a prolific writer and has authored more than 150 articles on children's growth patterns and hormone-related illnesses. She is also the recipient of more than a half-dozen honorary degrees, including one from Yale University.

In comparison to her public life, Elders' personal life is almost humdrum. Married for over 30 years to Oliver Elders, a retired high school basketball coach, and the mother of two grown sons, Elders shuns social occasions claiming that she is almost phobic about being around a crowd of people.

Harkening back to the statement that cost her her job, Elders is writing a serious book about masturbation, which she sees as a useful weapon against disease and unwanted pregnancies. Entitled *The Dreaded "M" Word*, the book maintains that masturbation can help prevent the spread of sexually transmitted diseases, including AIDS. "Masturbation has never given anyone a disease; it's never gotten anyone pregnant," she contends, as her detractors once again gear up for battle.

SOURCES:

Graham, Judith, ed. *Current Biography 1994*. NY: H.W. Wilson, 1994.

Rosellini, Lynn. "Joycelyn Elders is master of her domain," in *U.S. News & World Report*. November 3, 1997.

SUGGESTED READING:

Elders, Joycelyn, M.D., and David Chanoff. *From Sharecropper's Daughter to Surgeon General of the United States*. NY: Morrow, 1996.

Barbara Morgan,
Melrose, Massachusetts

Eldershaw, Flora (1897–1956).

See Barnard, Marjorie for sidebar.

Eldershaw, M. Barnard (1897–1987).

See Barnard, Marjorie.

Eldredge, Sara Willis (1811–1872).

See Fern, Fanny.

Eldridge, Florence (1901–1988)

American actress. Name variations: Mrs. Fredric March. Born Florence McKechnie on September 5, 1901, in Brooklyn, New York; died on August 1, 1988, in Santa Monica, California; daughter of James and Clara Eugenie McKechnie; graduate of Girls' High School, Brooklyn; married Fredric March (an actor), on May 30, 1927 (died 1975); children: Penelope March, and Anthony March (both adopted).

Selected theatrical roles: made first New York appearance in chorus of Rock-a-Bye Baby *(Astor Theater, 1919); appeared as Dolly McKibble in* Pretty Soft *(Morosco Theater, 1919), Margaret Nichols in Am-* bush *(Garrick Theater, 1921), Annabelle West in* The Cat and the Canary *(National Theater, 1922), the Step-daughter in* Six Characters in Search of an Author *(Princess Theater, 1922), Nadine Morand in* The Love Habit *(Bijou Theater, 1923), Alma Lowery in* The Dancers *(Broadhurst Theater, 1923), Evelyn Gardner in* Cheaper to Marry *(49th Street Theater, 1924), the Girl in* Bewitched *(National Theater, 1924), Louise in* Young Blood *(Ritz Theater, 1925), Daisy Fay in* The Great Gatsby *(Ambassador Theater, 1926), Mation Taylor in* A Proud Woman *(Maxine Elliott Theater, 1926), Alice Reynolds in* Off Key *(Belmont Theater, 1927); toured for the Theater Guild in* Arms and the Man, The Silver Cord, Mr. Pim Passes By, *and* The Guardsman *(1928–29); appeared as Alexa in* An Affair of State *(Broadhurst Theater, 1930); was in* Private Lives *(1931); appeared as Julie Rodman in* Days to Come *(Vanderbilt Theater, 1936), Prue in* Your Obedient Husband *(Broadhurst Theater, 1938), Irma Gunther in* The American Way *(Center Theater, 1939), Carlotta Thatcher in* Hope for a Harvest *(Guild Theater, 1941), Mrs. Antrobus in* The Skin of Our Teeth *(Plymouth Theater, 1942), Annie Jones in* Years Ago *(Mansfield Theater, 1946), Miss Leonora Graves in* Now I Lay Me Down to Sleep *(Broadhurst Theater, 1950), Mrs. Stockmann in* An Enemy of the People *(Broadhurst Theater, 1950), Rose Griggs in* The Autumn Garden *(Coronet Theater, 1951), Mary Cavan Tyrone in* Long Day's Journey into Night *(Helen Hayes Theater, 1956, and Theater of Nations Festival, Sarah Bernhardt Theatre, Paris, 1957).*

Filmography: Six Cylinder Love *(1923);* The Studio Murder Mystery *(1929);* Charming Sinners *(1929);* The Greene Murder Case *(1929);* The Divorcee *(1930);* The Matrimonial Bed *(1930);* Thirteen Women *(1932);* Dangerously Yours *(1933);* The Great Jasper *(1933);* The Story of Temple Drake *(1933);* A Modern Hero *(1934);* Les Miserables *(1935);* Mary of Scotland *(1936);* Another Part of the Forest *(1948);* An Act of Murder *(1948);* Christopher Columbus *(1949);* Inherit the Wind *(1960).*

A highly respected actress and half of a famous theatrical couple, Florence Eldridge was born in Brooklyn and made her New York debut in the chorus of Jerome Kern's musical *Rock-a-Bye Baby* (1919). Within three years' time, she was the toast of Broadway. Eldridge's performance in *Ambush* (1921) was acclaimed as "one of the brightest chapters in the season's theatrical history," and her stature increased with subsequent roles in *The Cat and the Canary* (1922), *Six Characters in Search of an Author* (1922), and *The Love Habit* (1923). In 1926, on the

Florence Eldridge as Mary Tyrone in Long Day's Journey into Night *(starring Fredric March).*

toon in theatrical columns of two trapeze artists missing each other's grip in mid-air over the caption: "Oops, sorry!" Duet performances in the plays *The American Way* (1939) and *Hope for a Harvest* (1941) were better received. One critic called the pair's casting in *The Skin of Our Teeth* (1943), as "nothing short of inspired. . . . March plays . . . with immense power, and Miss Eldridge is right behind him in giving a parable of human sympathy and warmth."

Eldridge had one of her greatest stage successes as Mary Tyrone in Eugene O'Neill's autobiographical *Long Day's Journey into Night* (1956), for which she received the New York Drama Critics Award for Best Actress. March won a Tony for his role opposite her. In 1960, the couple appeared together in the film *Inherit the Wind* (for which March received an Oscar), and in 1965 they toured Egypt, Greece, Italy, and the Middle East for the U.S. State Department, giving concert readings.

Florence Eldridge outlived her husband, who died in 1975, by more than a decade. She died in California on August 1, 1988.

SOURCES:

Current Biography. NY: H.W. Wilson, 1943.

Katz, Ephraim. *The Film Encyclopedia.* NY: HarperCollins, 1994.

Wilmeth, Don B., and Tice L. Miller, eds. *Cambridge Guide to American Theatre.* NY: Cambridge University Press, 1993.

Barbara Morgan,
Melrose, Massachusetts

brink of stardom, she met and fell in love with actor Fredric March, and the two were married in Mexico in 1927. In lieu of a honeymoon, they went on tour with the Theater Guild's first traveling repertory company.

In 1928, the couple headed to California, where he had the lead in *The Royal Family* and then signed a film contract with Paramount. Eldridge embarked on her own film career, often starring with her husband, notably in *Les Miserables* (1935) and *Mary of Scotland* (1936). After the marriage, Eldridge put her husband's career first. In time, she limited herself to one picture a year in order to preserve the couple's home life, which was based in the East. The Marches spent winters in Manhattan so that their two adopted children could attend the same school and have the same friends year after year.

In 1938, Eldridge played opposite March in the play *Your Obedient Husband*, which was a loud failure and closed in a week. So great was the couple's chagrin that they placed a small car-

Eleanor.

Variant of Helena or Leonor.

Eleanor (c. 1413–1472), countess of Northumberland.

See Beaufort, Joan (1379–1440) for sidebar on Neville, Eleanor.

Eleanor, the Maid of Brittany (1184–1241)

English royal. Name variations: Damsel of Brittany; Pearl of Brittany; Eleanor of Brittany; Eleanor Plantagenet. Born in 1184; died on August 12, 1241, at Corfe Castle, Dorset, England; buried first at St. James's Church in Bristol, before exhumation and reburial at Amesbury, Wiltshire, England; daughter of Geoffrey Plantagenet (1158–1186), duke of Brittany, and Constance of Brittany (1161–1201); granddaughter of *Eleanor of Aquitaine (1122–1204).

Known as the Damsel, the Pearl, or the Maid of Brittany, Eleanor was born in 1184, the daughter of Geoffrey, duke of Brittany, and *Constance of Brittany. She was also the niece of King John of England and the sister of Arthur, count of Brittany. Because of contention for the throne between Arthur and John (1199–1202), Eleanor was imprisoned by her uncle John. She died in 1241.

Eleanor Balliol (fl. 1230).

See Balliol, Eleanor.

Eleanor Balliol (c. 1255–?).

See Balliol, Margaret.

Eleanor d'Arborea (c. 1360–c. 1404)

Ruler of Sardinia who created the Carta de Logu. Name variations: Eleanora of Arborea; Eleanor di Arborea; Leonora. Born around 1360 in Arborea (on Sardinia); died around 1404 on Sardinia; daughter of Mariano IV (ruler of Sardinia); married Brancoleone de Oria (a Spanish noble); children: unknown.

Eleanor was born into the ruling house of Sardinia, a large island located west of Italy which was claimed by Aragon as part of its kingdom. She married Brancoleone de Oria, a Spanish noble. Eleanor's brother Ugono succeeded their father, but he ruled during a time of civic strife and economic hardship; discontented Sardinian citizens rebelled against the childless Ugono in 1383 and killed him. Eleanor ascended the throne and through her leadership managed to put down the revolt and began to restore peace. When an Aragonese army led by Alphonso IV invaded Sardinia, hoping to secure its submission to Aragonese rule by force during this period of internal struggle, Eleanor proved herself a capable military ruler once more. Galvanizing her troops to defend their island against the foreigners, she at last defeated Alphonso's army and drove it from Sardinia.

Eleanor established peace once again and reigned for another 20 years. Among other accomplishments, she restored economic prosperity. Her most lasting achievement by far, however, was the creation of a complete code of law, the Carta de Logu, which was adopted in 1421. This legal code remained in effect until the 18th century.

Laura York,
Riverside, California

Eleanor de Bohun (1366–1399).

See Bohun, Eleanor.

Eleanor Desmier (1639–1722).

See Desmier, Eleanor.

Eleanor de Warrenne (c. 1250–?)

*English noblewoman. Name variations: Eleanor Percy. Born around 1250; daughter of John de Warrenne (c. 1231–1304), 3rd earl of Warrenne and Surrey, and *Alice le Brun (d. 1255); married Henry Percy (d. 1272); children: Henry Percy, 1st baron Percy (d. 1315).*

Eleanor Gonzaga (1493–1543).

See Gonzaga, Eleonora.

Eleanor Gonzaga (1534–1594).

See Eleonora of Austria.

Eleanor Gonzaga (1567–1611).

See Medici, Eleonora de.

Eleanor I Gonzaga (1598–1655).

See Gonzaga, Eleonora I.

Eleanor II Gonzaga (1628–1686).

See Gonzaga, Eleonora II.

Eleanor Habsburg (1498–1558).

See Eleanor of Portugal.

Eleanor of Albuquerque (1374–1435)

*Queen of Aragon. Name variations: Leonor of Albuquerque. Born in 1474; died on December 16, 1435 (some sources cite 1455); daughter of *Beatrice of Portugal (c. 1347–1318) and Sancho (b. 1373), count of Albuquerque; married Fernando also known as Ferdinand I of Antequera (b. 1380), king of Aragon (r. 1412–1416); children: Alfonso also known as Alphonso V (1396–1458), king of Aragon (r. 1416–1458); Juan also known as John II of Trastamara (1398–1479), king of Navarre and Aragon (r. 1458–1479); Enrique or Henry (1399–1445); Sancho (1400–1417); *Leonora of Aragon (1405–1445, who married Duarte I, king of Portugal, 1391–1438); Pedro or Peter (1409–1438); *Maria of Aragon(1403–1445, who married John II, king of Leon and Castile).*

Eleanor of Aquitaine (1122–1204)

Europe's most famous medieval queen who wielded power and influence as queen of France and England, and was also an important patron of 12th-century troubadour poetry and courtly love literature. Pronunciation: ACK-ee-taine. Name variations: Al-

iénor. Born in 1122 in Bordeaux, France; died at the abbey of Fontevrault or Fontevraud, Anjou, France, on April 1, 1204; interred at Fontevraud Abbey, Maine-et-Loire, France; daughter of William X (b. 1099), duke of Aquitaine and count of Poitou, and Aénor of Châtellerault (d. 1130); sister of ◀❧ Aelith de Poitiers (c. 1123–?); married Louis VII, king of France (r. 1137–1180), in Bordeaux, in 1137 (marriage annulled 1152); married Henry Plantagenet, count of Anjou, later Henry II, king of England (r. 1154–1189), in 1152 (died in Chinon, 1189); children: (first marriage) Marie de Champagne (1145–1198); Alice (1150–c. 1197), countess of Blois; (second marriage) William (1153–1156); Henry (1155–1183), count of Anjou and duke of Normandy; *Matilda of England (1156–1189); Richard I the Lionheart (1157–1199), king of England (r. 1189–1199); Geoffrey (1158–1186), duke of Brittany and earl of Richmond; Eleanor of Castile (1162–1214); Joanna of Sicily (1165–1199); John also known as John Lackland (1166–1216), king of England (r. 1199–1216).

Became queen of France at age 15 (1137); went on Second Crusade with Louis VII (1147); held influential literary court with her daughter Marie de Champagne; marriage to Louis annulled (1152); married Henry II of England (1152); incited her sons to rebel against Henry II (1173); imprisoned under "house arrest" (1173–89); governed as regent for Richard I (1189–94); traveled across Pyrenees at age 78 to obtain marriage alliance; died peacefully at abbey of Fontevrault (1204).

By the 12th century, the political power of medieval queens was beginning to decrease. Centralization of Europe's medieval kingdoms led to a growth of bureaucratic officers and institutions which contributed to a greater separation of the queen's household from the king's. Instead of coordinating and controlling the royal finances, as they had done in the past, medieval queens were increasingly pushed out of participating in the management of royal government. While this was true for most of Europe's royal wives, there was one exception: Eleanor of Aquitaine.

Eleanor of Aquitaine was born in 1122 at Bordeaux, the birthplace of European troubadours (medieval lyric poets) and the literature of courtly love. The daughter of William X of Aquitaine and ◀❧ Aénor of Châtellerault, Eleanor grew up surrounded by wealth and culture. Her grandfather, William IX, duke of Aquitaine, was one of the earliest troubadour poets on record, and Eleanor inherited not only his sarcastic wit and charm but also his love of poetry. In her later years, Eleanor was to be an extremely influential patron and protector of medieval poets. Little is known of Eleanor's mother who died when Eleanor was eight years old. Her father, however, had a significant impact on Eleanor's childhood. Tall, strong and quarrelsome, Duke William was—like his father before him—a well-educated, cultured man who patronized troubadours at his court. From her father, Eleanor inherited a strong will, a sense of independence and, more important, his lands. Most of her childhood was spent traveling through the duchy of Aquitaine with her father, where she was able to observe him interacting with the vassals and peasants who occupied some of the richest lands in France. Like all young women from the aristocracy, Eleanor was given an education. She was taught to read and write Latin as well as her own Provençal dialect. These were happy and influential years for her.

In 1137, however, Eleanor's life changed radically when her father died, at age 38, while on pilgrimage to the shrine of St. James at Compostella in Spain. Eleanor was now the richest heiress in Europe. The lands she inherited from her father stretched from the Pyrenees to the Loire and were larger than those held by the king of France. Her father had appointed the

❧▶ **Aelith de Poitiers** (c. 1123–?)

French noblewoman. Name variations: Petronilla. Born around 1123; death date unknown; daughter of William X, duke of Aquitaine, and *Aénor of Châtellerault (d. 1130); sister of *Eleanor of Aquitaine (1122–1204).

❧▶ **Aénor of Châtellerault** (d. 1130)

Duchess of Aquitaine. Name variations: Aenor of Chatellerault; Anor; Aenor Aimery; Eleanor of Châtellerault. Born after 1107 (some sources cite 1103); died in Talmont, France, in 1130; daughter of Aimery, viscount of Châtellerault, and Dangereuse (mistress of William IX, duke of Aquitaine); married William X (1099–1137), duke of Aquitaine, in 1121; children: *Eleanor of Aquitaine (1122–1204); *Aelith de Poitiers (born around 1123 and sometimes referred to as Petronilla); William de Poitiers (died in infancy, 1130).

Aénor of Châtellerault was the daughter of **Dangereuse** (La Maubergeonne) who had been abducted by William IX, duke of Aquitaine, and kept in a tower. She married William X, duke of Aquitaine, in 1121, and had two daughters: ***Eleanor of Aquitaine** and ***Aelith de Poitiers**. Aénor died when her children were quite young.

Eleanor of Aquitaine and Henry II, as portrayed in tomb effigies in a French abbey.

French king, Louis VI, as her guardian, and King Louis knew that marriage to a woman such as Eleanor expanded not only a nobleman's territories but increased his economic and political power as well. Like virtually every other medieval noblewoman, 15-year-old Eleanor had very little choice as to the man she would marry. Shortly after her father's death, King Louis arranged for her betrothal to his own son, Louis (VII).

The king's son, unlike his father (who was popularly known as "Louis the Fat"), was a well-built, slender young man with blue eyes and long blond hair. Young Louis was the king's second son and consequently had been destined for a career in the church. After his older brother died from an accident, however, Louis was named as his father's successor and was removed from the monastery where he had spent his early childhood. Perhaps it was Louis' monastic upbringing which earned him the name "Louis the Pious." For much of the rest of his life, he was torn between his love for the quiet solitude of the cloister and his duty toward France. Humble and intelligent, he fell deeply in love with Eleanor as soon as he saw her. The young heiress was tall, gracious and regal, and her wit and charm easily captivated the 16-year-old prince. They were married soon after they met, on July 25, 1137, in the cathedral of Saint André at Bordeaux.

At 15, Eleanor of Aquitaine was now not only the richest landholder in Europe, but she was also the wife of the heir to the French throne. One month after her marriage, the old king died and she became queen of France. The newly crowned monarchs moved to Paris, where young King Louis continued his father's policy of extending royal authority throughout France. Eleanor's early years at the French royal court were spent learning Parisian French and listening to the lectures given by nearby university students. The first years of their marriage appeared happy, although Eleanor was becoming increasingly worried because she had not yet become pregnant. She was aware, as were all medieval queens, that one of her most important duties was to give birth to the next heir. She finally visited the king's confessor, Abbe Suger, who advised her to pray for an end to her barren state. Her prayers were answered in 1145 when she gave birth to a daughter, whom she christened *Marie (de Champagne), as thanks to the Virgin Mary who had so blessed her.

Shortly after, Pope Eugenius III asked King Louis to go on a crusade to the Holy Land. Louis, understandably, felt deeply about his duty to take up the cross and straightaway began to prepare for his journey. Eleanor also expressed a strong desire to participate, and, consequently, in June 1147 the king and queen left France for the Holy Land. It was not unusual for women to accompany their husbands on crusade, and, in the early expeditions, many women helped build fortifications, haul supplies and weapons, and some of them even fought on occasion. Nonetheless, Eleanor's company of 300 women soon gave rise to unfounded rumors and legends that likened them to the Amazons. The crusaders' first stop was Constantinople, where Eleanor was captivated by the bright clothes, the vitality, and the exotic sights, smells and sounds of Byzantine culture. Their next port of call was Antioch, where Eleanor's young uncle, Raymond of Poitiers, provided them with entertainment and protection.

An incomparable woman; beautiful yet gracious, strong-willed yet kind, unassuming yet sagacious.

—Roger of Devizes

Eleanor was feted by Raymond, and the time they spent together was thoroughly enjoyable for both. Her obvious preference for her uncle's company, however, inevitably led Louis to misinterpret their relationship, and rumors of an affair between the two did nothing to allay the king's suspicions. It was a difference in plans that finally led to an irrevocable breach between the king and queen. Raymond suggested that they combine forces and attempt to recover Montferrand from the Turks. Louis, however, refused to embark on an any military campaigns until he had made a pilgrimage to Jerusalem. Eleanor sided with her uncle, and, when Louis angrily announced that he was proceeding to Jerusalem immediately, Eleanor refused to accompany him. Louis asserted his authority and, displaying his famous temper, forcibly dragged Eleanor from her uncle's palace.

Louis' behavior was entirely unacceptable to Eleanor, who refused to be bullied by anyone, and the couple were never close again. When they fi-

nally reached Jerusalem, the king's forces attempted to storm Damascus and failed. Beaten and dejected, Louis and Eleanor returned home to France in the spring of 1149. Although their marriage was clearly failing, they attempted a brief reconciliation, and in the summer of 1150 Eleanor gave birth to a second daughter, ◄❧ **Alice.** Her failure to provide a male heir to the throne, however, widened the rift between them, and they began to quarrel more frequently. The end finally came when they were granted an annulment on March 21, 1152, on the grounds of consanguinity. Eleanor's lands were returned to her, and, unlike the circumstances of her first marriage, she chose her second husband herself.

Her sights were set on Henry Plantagenet, count of Anjou and duke of Normandy (future Henry II of England), whom she had met the previous summer. Although she had made her decision, Eleanor was still in danger of being unable to carry it out. Medieval heiresses, especially rich ones like Eleanor, were in peril whenever they traveled about the countryside. Unscrupulous suitors had no qualms about capturing a rich heiress and forcing her into marriage. Eleanor herself narrowly escaped capture from no less than two overanxious swains when she returned home to Bordeaux shortly after her first marriage ended. She was successful in eluding them, however, and at age 29 married 18-year-old Henry Plantagenet in May 1152, two months after her annulment from Louis.

Although 11 years her junior, red-haired and blue-eyed Henry was her intellectual and physical equal. Throughout his life, he exhibited a relentless energy that suited his strong, stocky physique. Like Eleanor, he could read and write Latin as well as French and Provençal. With this marriage and their combined lands, they now controlled the entire area of Western France. When Henry succeeded Stephen of Blois as king of England in 1154, Eleanor was able to add queen of England to her illustrious list of titles.

During the early years of their marriage, Eleanor was actively involved in political life. She and Henry traveled continuously in both France and England, crossing the Channel frequently to dispense justice throughout their sprawling empire. Henry was determined to restore law and order in England after the past 25 years of civil war, and both he and Eleanor worked to improve the efficiency of English government by creating new bureaucratic institutions. Eleanor acted as regent for her husband in England whenever he was in France, and, as the feudal lord of Aquitaine and Poitou, she as-

❧► **Alice** (1150–c. 1197)

Countess of Blois. Name variations: Alisa; Alix; Alice Capet. Born in 1150; died around 1197; daughter of Louis VII, king of France (r. 1137–1180), and ***Eleanor of Aquitaine*** *(1122–1204); sister of* ***Marie de Champagne*** *(1145–1198); married Thibaut or Theobald V, count of Blois, around 1164; children: Louis Blois; Isabel de Blois; and possibly* ***Marguerite, countess of Blois*** *(r. 1218–1230).*

sumed the governance of those lands for 65 years. Historian **Amy Kelly** has aptly summarized the first decade of their marriage:

> They had founded a dynasty, established an empire, fortified its frontiers with strong castles, made it proof against arms, filled it with treasure, and enlivened it with learning and the arts. Abruptly, invincibly, they had altered the map, the balance of power, and the destiny of peoples.

During these busy years, Eleanor also fulfilled what was perhaps the most important task of a medieval queen: to produce an heir to the throne. Between 1152 and 1166, Eleanor gave birth to a child almost every year. Of the eight children from her marriage to Henry, only one did not survive into adulthood, while two of her sons became future kings (Richard the Lionheart and John), and two of her daughters future queens (✤➤ **Eleanor of Castile** and ✤➤ **Joanna of Sicily**). She rarely saw her children during their early years, although she later grew to depend and look upon Richard as her favorite.

While she divided her time between France and England, Eleanor's favored residence was in her beloved Aquitaine which centered upon her court at Poitiers. Here, she established what became one of the most famous and influential cultural centers in 12th-century Europe. With her daughter Marie de Champagne, Eleanor gathered together a brilliant circle of poets and troubadours. Both mother and daughter were significant patrons of a new form of vernacular literature that emphasized love and chivalry while utilizing feudal and religious imagery. The literature of courtly love, as it came to be known, concentrated on the love of a young knight for a married noblewoman who, while ostensibly rejecting his amorous overtures, nonetheless imposes various trials upon him which he cheerfully endures in order to prove his love for her. Unlike the majority of medieval literature, courtly love exalted women and promoted the notion that love for a woman was not destructive (as church fathers taught) but was the inspiration for heroic deeds. Although courtly love literature was restricted to women of the upper classes, it provided an alternative to the misogyny which pervaded the majority of medieval literature. Eleanor and her daughter encouraged the development of this new literature and patronized some of the most famous 12th-century poets and troubadours including Bernard de Ventadour, Bertran de Born, *Marie de France, and Chretien de Troyes. It was at Marie de Champagne's court that Andreas Capellanus formulated his code of rules for courtly love, the *Ars Amandi* (*The Art of Love*). According to the rule, men were required to act courteously, avoid vulgar language, dress well and be well-groomed, all of which were completely new ideas for the knightly class. The courts of Eleanor and Marie were centers of female influence where women held the balance of power. Their influence on European culture lasted well beyond the 12th century.

While Eleanor was successfully ruling over her lands in France, Henry II was faced with his own political problems which centered on his attempts to dominate the church in England. By 1170, the situation reached a breaking point when Thomas Becket, the archbishop of Canterbury, was murdered at the altar of his own cathedral by four of Henry's officials. Relations between the queen and her husband had also begun to deteriorate after the birth of her last child, John, in 1166. Not only did the king begin to restrict her governing powers, but he publicly flaunted his adulterous relationship with his mistress, *Rosamund Clifford. According to later medieval legend, Eleanor was supposed to have hired a sorcerer to drain the blood of her rival.

The king was also experiencing difficulty maintaining amicable relations with his sons. In 1169, he divided his vast empire among three of them (John, the youngest, was excluded, thus earning him the nickname "Lackland"), and in 1170 he crowned his eldest son Henry as king-elect. Unfortunately, young Henry reacted by complaining that his new title was an empty one and that his father was preventing him from assuming independent rule over his lands. Matters came to a head in 1173 when young Henry rebelled against his father with the full support of Eleanor and his two brothers, Richard and Geoffrey. The rebellion was quickly suppressed, and Henry II graciously pardoned his sons for their attempt to seize his crown. The king, however, was not willing to forgive Eleanor who had been captured, while dressed as a man, trying to escape. For a brief time, Henry considered divorcing her, but then he realized that he would lose her lands in Aquitaine and Poitou by taking such action. Failing to coerce her into retiring into a nunnery, he placed his 53-year-old wife in prison. For the next 15 years, Eleanor of Aquitaine was kept in close confinement (or "house arrest") in Salisbury Castle where she was allowed out periodically to attend family gatherings or to receive homage from her Aquitaine vassals.

Despite her situation, Henry was never able to break his wife's strong and independent spirit.

➤ **Eleanor of Castile** See *Blanche of Castile* for sidebar.

➤ **Joanna of Sicily.** See *Berengaria of Navarre* for sidebar.

His policy of playing his sons off against one another proved successful until 1186, when the aging king was no longer able to cope with their political maneuverings. In 1188, Richard allied himself with the French king Phillip II Augustus and by the summer of 1189 the king, tired and ill, was forced to capitulate to their demands. He died shortly after, a broken man.

For Eleanor, her husband's death signalled the end of her long imprisonment and the resurgence of her political power when she assumed the regency for her son Richard. An English chronicler described her position:

Queen Eleanor, who for many years had been under close guard, was entrusted with the power of acting as regent for her son. Indeed he issued instructions to the princes of the realm, almost in the style of a general edict, that the queen's word should be law in all matters.

Eleanor took her duties seriously and traveled throughout England transacting court and financial business, as well as receiving oaths of homage to her favorite son. As a former prisoner, one of her first acts as regent was to free all unjustly imprisoned English women and men.

Katharine Hepburn as Eleanor of Aquitaine and Peter O'Toole as Henry II in The Lion in Winter.

Despite his great popularity, Richard the Lionheart spent virtually all of his ten-year reign outside England. One month after his coronation, he set off to fight in the Third Crusade, leaving Eleanor behind in England to rule in his absence. At 67, the aging queen had lost neither her boundless energy nor her political savvy. She arranged for the marriage of Richard to *Berengaria of Navarre and personally went to retrieve the bride at Pamplona. Richard had now been away for three years, but on his way home to England he was captured by Duke Leopold of Austria who demanded a huge ransom for his release. Only a woman of Eleanor's fortitude and dedication would have been successful in coaxing the amount of money that was needed from Richard's already over-burdened English subjects. After obtaining the vast sum of money, the queen traveled in person to deliver it and accompany her son home. Celebrations for the king's return centered on his second coronation in 1194 which Eleanor had arranged. One month later, however, Richard left England for Normandy, leaving the archbishop of Canterbury at the head of the government. Eleanor accompanied her son to France, and neither of them ever set foot in England again.

Eleanor retired to her favorite abbey at Fontevrault where she lived a peaceful life for the next five years. Fontevrault was known as a safe-haven for widows and ill-used wives of the aristocracy, and throughout her life Eleanor supported the monastery with large gifts and endowments. This peaceful existence was disrupted in 1199 when Richard was wounded during a siege at Châlus. The elderly queen rushed to the deathbed of her favorite son and held him in her arms as he died. Grief-stricken, Eleanor was unable to mourn peacefully as she was concerned to secure the succession of her youngest son, John. Although Richard had designated John as his successor, John's right to the throne was challenged by his 12-year-old nephew Arthur, count of Brittany. Eleanor traveled throughout her French lands, ensuring support for John, and, with the support of his mother and the majority of the English and Norman barons, he was crowned king of England on May 27, 1199.

One year later, in an effort to secure the Angevin dynasty that she had been so influential in building, Eleanor arranged and supervised the marriage of her granddaughter, *Blanche of Castile, to the French dauphin Louis (IX). In order to fulfill her goal, the 78-year-old queen crossed the Pyrenees in winter to fetch the young bride. Upon her return to France, she was still unable to rest peacefully as she was determined to defend Aquitaine against her grandson, Arthur of Brittany, who attempted to claim it for France. She successfully withstood a siege at Mirebeau until John appeared and finally took Arthur prisoner in 1202. Eleanor was finally able to retire to Fontevrault, where she died peacefully two years later in April 1204, at age 82.

SOURCES:

Kelly, Amy. *Eleanor of Aquitaine and the Four Kings.* NY: Vintage Books, 1958.

Rosenberg, M.V. *Eleanor of Aquitaine.* Boston, MA: Houghton Mifflin, 1937.

Seward, Desmond. *Eleanor of Aquitaine.* NY: Dorset Press, 1978.

SUGGESTED READING:

Owen, D.D.R. *Eleanor of Aquitaine: Queen and Legend.* Blackwell Publications, 1993.

Warren, W.L. *Henry II.* Berkeley, CA: University of California Press, 1973.

RELATED MEDIA:

King John by William Shakespeare.

The Lion in Winter (134 min.), film starring *Katharine Hepburn as Eleanor of Aquitaine and Peter O'Toole as Henry II, directed by Anthony Harvey, 1968.

Margaret McIntyre,
Instructor in Women's History,
Trent University, Peterborough, Ontario, Canada

Eleanor of Aragon (1358–1382)

*Queen of Castile and Leon. Name variations: Leonor or Leonora of Aragon. Born on February 20, 1358, in Santa Maria del Puig, Spain; died in Cuellar, Castile and Leon, Spain, on September 13, 1382; daughter of Peter IV the Ceremonious, king of Aragon (r. 1336–1387), and *Eleanor of Sicily (d. 1375); became first wife of Juan also known as John I (1358–1390), king of Castile and Leon (r. 1379–1390), on June 18, 1375; children: Enrique also known as Henry III (1379–1406), king of Castile and Leon (r. 1390–1406); Fernando also known as Ferdinand I of Antequera (1380–1416), king of Aragon (r. 1412–1416). John I's second wife was *Beatrice of Portugal (1372–after 1409).*

Eleanor of Aragon (1405–1445).

See Leonora of Aragon.

Eleanor of Austria (1498–1558).

See Eleanor of Portugal.

Eleanor of Castile (1162–1214).

See Blanche of Castile (1188–1252) for sidebar.

Eleanor of Castile (1202–1244).

See Blanche of Castile (1188–1252) for sidebar.

Eleanor of Castile (1241–1290)

Paragon of medieval queenship, who was an active partner of her husband Edward I, accompanying him to the Holy Land on Crusade, to Gascony and Wales, while also bearing 15 children. Name variations: *Eleanora of Castile; Eleanor the Faithful.* Born in late 1241 in Castile; died at Harby, Nottinghamshire, on November 28, 1290; daughter of Ferdinand III (1199–1252), king of Castile and Leon (r. 1217–1252) and Joanna of Ponthieu, Countess Aumale (d. 1279); became first wife of Edward I Longshanks (1239–307), king of England (r. 1272–1307), in 1254; children: Eleanor Plantagenet (1264–1297, who married Alphonso III, king of Aragon); Joan (1265–1265); John (1266?–1271); Katherine (1271–1271); Henry (1267–1274); Joan of Acre (1272–1307), countess of Gloucester; Alphonso (1273–1284); Margaret (1275–1318), duchess of Brabant; Berengaria (1276–c. 1279); Mary (1278–1332, became a nun); Isabel (1279–1279); ◀ Alice (1280–1291); Elizabeth (1282–1316), countess of Hereford and Essex; Edward II (1284–1327), king of England (r. 1307–1327, who married *Isabella of France [1296–1358]); Beatrice (c. 1286–?); Blanche (1290–1290).

Eleanor of Castile was the only daughter of the five children born to Ferdinand III of Castile and Leon (1201–1252) and his second wife ◀ Joanna of Ponthieu (d. 1279). The chroniclers and historians who recorded the middle ages rarely paid as much attention to women as they did to men, even when those women were

---

◆▶ Alice (1280–1291)

English princess. Name variations: *Alice Plantagenet.* Born on March 12, 1280, in Woodstock, Oxfordshire, England; died in 1291, age 11; daughter of Edward I Longshanks, king of England (r. 1272–1307), and *Eleanor of Castile (1241–1290).

◆▶ Joanna of Ponthieu (d. 1279)

Queen of Castile and Leon. Name variations: *Joan of Ponthieu; Joan de Ponthieu; Jean de Ponthieu; Jeanne de Dammartin; Countess Aumale.* Birth date unknown; died in 1279; daughter of William of Ponthieu (though some sources cite Simon de Dammartin, count of Ponthieu and Aumale) and *Alais of France (b. 1160, daughter of Louis VII of France); became second wife of Fernando also known as St. Ferdinand or Ferdinand III (1199–1252), king of Castile and Leon (r. 1217–1252), in 1237; children: Fernando, count of Aumale; *Eleanor of Castile (1241–1290); Luis; Simon; Juan.

---

of royal birth. As a consequence, the birth and early childhood of Eleanor of Castile remain sketchy. Although contemporaries did not record the date of Eleanor's birth, recent scholarship has uncovered enough information about her life to deduce that she was probably born sometime in late 1241.

The first attention that contemporaries seem to have paid to Eleanor was in 1254, when plans for her marriage to Edward (I Longshanks), heir to the English throne, became known. In 1252, Eleanor's half-brother, Alphonso X the Wise, had succeeded to the Castilian throne upon the death of his father, Ferdinand III. Almost immediately Alphonso promoted his claims to the wealthy province of Gascony, which at that time belonged to the king of England, Henry III. While Alphonso's claims were questionable and his ability to drive the English out of Gascony doubtful, in 1253 Henry III was facing increasing financial difficulties and did not want to engage in a long and expensive war with Castile over Gascony.

In 1253, therefore, Henry III and Alphonso X began diplomatic negotiations concerning Gascony which resulted in an alliance between the two kingdoms, to be sealed by the marriage of Eleanor to the English prince. It is quite possible that this diplomatic solution—an alliance with England sealed by a marriage—was what Alphonso X had in mind when he first made his claims on Gascony. An alliance with England could protect him against other aggressive neighbors and would at the same time allow him to provide well for his half-sister's future. English envoys finished negotiating the terms of the treaty with Alphonso in April 1254. In June, Henry III sent Edward in "great pomp and splendor" to Spain to receive knighthood and be wed. Alphonso welcomed the young prince and satisfied himself that Edward was suitable to wed his sister. Then in October 1254, he knighted Edward, and the young couple—Edward was 15 and Eleanor was around 13—were married at Burgos, beginning one of the happiest royal marriages in English history.

Soon after, the newlyweds left Castile and traveled to Gascony where Eleanor met her father-in-law Henry III, who had not attended the wedding. She remained in Gascony for almost a year, until, in late 1255, she and her household journeyed northwards for her first glimpse of England. The princess, without Edward, who had stayed behind in Gascony, landed at Dover with such a large retinue that some of the English looked upon her arrival with suspicion. So large was her household, which was composed largely of Spaniards, that one contemporary, Matthew Paris, wrote, "fears were entertained that the country would be forcibly taken possession of by them."

These fears, if they actually existed, were minimized by the king, who apparently had developed a fondness for his young daughter-in-law. He ordered that Eleanor should be received with all honor and reverence at London as well as other places. The Londoners responded enthusiastically. They rode out to meet her dressed in holiday clothes and mounted on richly decorated horses. The city itself rang out with bells and songs, and the townspeople staged processions, illuminations, and other special events to welcome and honor the young woman who would someday be their queen.

When Eleanor entered her apartments, she found them hung with palls of silk and tapestry, "like a temple," and even the floor was covered with arras. The English did not cover the walls and floors of their living quarters with tapestries and carpets, which caused Matthew Paris, a critic of such ostentation, to remark that while "this was done . . . in accordance with the custom of the Spaniards," it showed excessive pride and excited the laughter and derision of the English. One can imagine, though, the 14-year-old princess' gratefulness to her father-in-law for providing her with familiar surroundings when she was so far removed from her native Castilian culture. Even in the last years of life, Eleanor kept herself surrounded with tapestries, even weaving some herself.

Matthew Paris was not the only critic of Eleanor's arrival in England. There were those who were disturbed by Henry III's evident fondness for the foreigners. His desire to please Eleanor and her entourage and the conspicuous displays he ordered to welcome them to England astonished and dismayed many. Watching the favors that their king heaped upon the new princess and her entourage, the English feared that Henry held his own people in less esteem than almost any other. Many were suspicious of the foreigners because they felt that their own fortunes would suffer. A large part of this distrust was the result of events that had transpired before Eleanor's arrival in England. When the last royal bride, Henry III's wife **Eleanor of Provence** (c. 1222–1291), had appeared in England, she had brought with her an entourage much larger than that of Eleanor of Castile. Eleanor of Provence's relatives and compatriots quickly found themselves appointed to a number of important positions in the English government. This provoked a reaction among the English nobility against the queen's relatives especially and against foreigners in general, a distrust that was still evident in England when Eleanor of Castile arrived. Throughout her life, Eleanor showed the political savvy and wisdom that made her a valuable part of the English political scene. She quite consciously worked to avoid rekindling the earlier xenophobia by adopting a much more judicious policy with her appointments and patronage. Most of those advanced in the queen's court were women who were not appointed to places of high government office. Moreover, most of the relatives patronized and promoted by Eleanor had some former connection to England.

Between 1255 and 1270, Eleanor is mentioned only briefly. During the Baron's Revolt in 1264–65, Henry III was captured by a faction of rebellious nobles and had to hand over Prince Edward as a hostage. Eleanor, who had already given birth to two children, was at that time sequestered in Windsor Castle, awaiting the birth of her third child, Joan, who was born in January 1265. To protect them from possible harm during the rebellion, in June of that year, Henry III ordered Eleanor and Joan to leave England and stay in France until the troubles with the rebels were over. Not long after Eleanor departed, Edward escaped his captors, raised an army in support of the Crown, and in August defeated the rebel barons at the battle of Evesham. Unfortunately, in September 1265, Joan fell ill and died.

One of the most important functions of a queen was to provide for the succession by producing children—preferably sons. In this aspect, Eleanor was remarkably successful. Eleanor had 12 more children during the next 19 years. Her last, Edward of Caernarvon, the future Edward II, was born in April 1284. She gave birth to 15 in all, but in an age of high infant mortality, only six—❧▶ **Eleanor Plantagenet** (1264–1297), *****Joan of Acre** (1272–1307), *****Margaret** (1275–1318), *****Mary** (1278–1332), ❧▶ **Elizabeth Plantagenet** (1282–1316), and Edward (1284–1327)—survived her.

In 1268, Eleanor of Castile took up the cross and in 1270 accompanied Edward on a Crusade to the Holy Land. Her decision to accompany her husband on Crusade was unusual but not unprecedented. Women had gone on crusade ever since the First Crusade in 1096, often with their husbands, but not always. For instance, *****Eleanor of Aquitaine** (1122–1204) had accompanied her first husband, Louis VII of

❧▶
See sidebar on the following page

❧▶ **Eleanor Plantagenet** (1264–1297)

*Queen of Aragon. Name variations: Princess Eleanor; Countess of Bar. Born on June 17, 1264, at Windsor Castle, Windsor, Berkshire, England; died on October 12, 1297 (some sources cite 1298), at Ghent, Flanders, Belgium; interred at Westminster Abbey, London; daughter of Edward I Longshanks, king of England (r. 1272–1307), and *Eleanor of Castile (1241–1290); married Alfonso also known as Alphonso III the Liberal (1265–1291), king of Aragon (r. 1285–1291), on August 15, 1290, at Westminster Abbey; married Henry de Bar (d. 1302), count de Bar, around 1293 in Champagne, France; children: (second marriage) Lady Eleanor of Bar; Joan of Bar (b. 1295); Edward I, count of Bar (b. 1294).*

❧▶ **Elizabeth Plantagenet** (1282–1316)

*Duchess of Hereford and Essex. Name variations: Elizabeth Bohun. Born in August 1282 in Rhuddlan Castle, Caernarvon, Gwynedd, Wales; died on May 5, 1316, in England; daughter of Edward I Longshanks, king of England (r. 1272–1307), and *Eleanor of Castile (1241–1290); married John I, count of Holland and Zeeland, on January 18, 1297 (died 1299); married Humphrey Bohun (1276–1322), 4th earl of Hereford, 3rd of Essex, on November 14, 1320; children: (second marriage) ten, including John (1306–1335), 5th earl of Hereford, 4th of Essex; Humphrey (c. 1309–1361), 6th earl of Hereford; Edward; William (c. 1312–1360), 1st earl of Northampton; *Eleanor Bohun, countess of Ormonde; and *Margaret (Bohun) Courtenay.*

France, on crusade in 1147, and *Ida of Austria** had gone on her own in 1101. Even with these precedents, Eleanor's decision to make the arduous journey reveals much about her devotion to the church and to her husband. The trip to the Holy Land was difficult, and the rigors of military campaign and camp life could be harsh.

It was during this Crusade that Eleanor became involved in an episode that has become part of English historical folklore. In 1272, Edward I Longshanks was camped outside the town of Acre, alone in his chamber, when a Muslim attacked him with a poisoned dagger. Edward, known for his fighting ability and swift reflexes, fought with the assassin and in the ensuing scuffle managed to kill him. During the melee, however, he was wounded in the forearm with the dagger. According to popular legend, Eleanor rushed to her wounded husband and courageously sucked the poison out of the wound on his arm, thus saving his life. This

story, while accurate in its portrayal of the genuine affection and devotion that husband and wife felt for each other, is most likely merely a product of later embellishment. Eleanor's real role during the attack on Edward shows her no less devoted to him, but less integral to his survival and recovery. Walter of Guisborough, who wrote about the incident, maintained that after several treatments Edward's wound began to fester. An English doctor said that he could cure him, but that his remedy would be painful. Fearing for his life, Edward agreed to the doctor's solution, which was to cut away the decayed flesh from the wound. Eleanor, who was present, began weeping and had to be escorted from the room by her brother-in-law, Edmund, and other of Edward's close friends, Edward telling them that "it was better that she, rather than the whole of England, should weep."

In 1272, Henry III died. Upon hearing the news, Edward and Eleanor left the Holy Land and returned to England. As queen, Eleanor continued to bear Edward children and accompany him on diplomatic missions and military campaigns. Even as queen, though, Eleanor's activities are shadowy and little better recorded than her earlier life. Financial records compiled for her household expenses during the last year of her life reveal that Eleanor of Castile was a cultured woman. She never lost her fondness for tapestries or fine furnishings, maintaining trading contacts as far away as Syria for the pieces that adorned her chambers and the spices that graced her table. She possessed a library of romances, the popular literary form of the day, and employed scribes to copy and write these and other books and paid painters to illuminate them. She even persuaded the archbishop of Canterbury to write a scholarly work for her. There are also references to her playing a game called Four Kings, probably a four-handed variant of chess.

As queen, Eleanor of Castile possessed landed wealth in her own right. She was expected to be able to live off her lands and estates, which were extensive and brought her about 4,500 li. per year. Eleanor, though, apparently found it difficult to run her large and constantly moving household on this income. As a result, like many other large landholders of the period, she and her estate officials resorted to harsh measures to maximize the income from her lands. In the years after Eleanor's death in 1290, the queen's tenants complained about the extortionate and high-handed activities of these estate managers. One charge held that one of Eleanor's lesser officials had seized a house from its owners, imprisoned them unjustly, and dumped their baby in its cradle in the middle of the road. In another instance, the men of the queen's manor of Havering recalled how she had arbitrarily limited local hunting rights by extending her own hunting rights. A number of tenants had tried to resist the queen in this case, but they were imprisoned for three days for their efforts and forced to wait until after the queen's death to reassert their complaint. Such was the queen's reputation as a landowner towards the end of her life that a popular rhyme had been composed which criticized the more acquisitive aspects of the king and queen: "The king he wants to get our gold/ The queen would like our lands to hold."

While Eleanor cannot be released of her responsibility for the actions of her officials, some of the blame for her harsh reputation as a landlord can be laid at the feet of the men who managed her estates. One of the queen's stewards was an unpopular clerk named Hugh Cressingham. Cressingham had a reputation for thoroughness and high-handedness which undoubtedly caused the queen's tenants and peasants to regard him bitterly. His success in the queen's household brought a more important position in the king's service, and eventually Edward I appointed him treasurer of Scotland. As treasurer, Cressingham's well-established tactics quickly earned him the hatred of the Scots, and, when they rebelled in 1297, he was killed, skinned, and a sword strap made from his hide. While Cressingham is the most notorious of Eleanor's officials, and a few others had similar reputations, on the whole they were no more grasping and ambitious than officials of the king's household or those of any other great noble.

In 1290, Eleanor of Castile died at the age of 49 at Harby in Nottinghamshire, and the king lost his most devoted and trusted partner. The reaction of Edward I at her death shows the depth of his devotion. The king was on his way north to adjudicate a succession dispute in Scotland in late 1290 when word reached him that Eleanor had taken ill. He rushed south to her bedside to be with her in her last illness, and after her death was disconsolate, putting aside state business for months while he grieved over his loss. He made arrangements to have her body divided and buried in three separate tombs. The practice of dividing corpses was not unusual at this time, although it would be forbidden by the pope in 1299. Her entrails were buried at Lincoln; her heart taken to London and buried in a tomb at Blackfriars; and after the long journey south, her body laid to rest in an elaborate gilded tomb in Westminster Abbey.

Edward I also commissioned a series of memorial crosses that were to be erected at each site where the queen's funeral cortege stopped to rest for the night on its journey to Westminster. Altogether there were 12 magnificent crosses erected from Lincoln to London and all were complete by 1294. The cost of the tombs and crosses is impressive—almost 2,200 li.—and is further evidence of Edward's grief. The death of Eleanor of Castile in 1290 robbed Edward I of his life's companion, a woman who had given him 16 children, traveled with him on crusade, and who, throughout their 36 years of marriage, had been a paragon of medieval queenship. In 1299, Edward married *Margaret of France, the daughter of the king of France, and had two more sons and two more daughters; he named the youngest Eleanor (1306–1311).

SOURCES:

Paris, Matthew. *Matthew of Paris's English History from the Year 1235 to 1273.* Translated by J.A. Giles. 3 volumes. London. 1854.

Parsons, John C. "The Year of Eleanor of Castile's Birth and Her Children by Edward I," in *Mediaeval Studies.* Vol. 46, 1984.

———. *The Court and Household of Eleanor of Castile in 1290.* Toronto. 1977.

Prestwich, Michael. *Edward I.* Berkeley and Los Angeles. 1988.

Douglas C. Jansen, Ph.D.,
Medieval History, University of Texas, Austin, Texas

Eleanor of Castile (1307–1359)

*Queen-consort of Aragon. Name variations: Leonor of Castile; Leonor de Castilla; Infanta of Castile. Born in 1307; murdered in 1359 at the Château de Catroheriz; daughter of Ferdinand IV, king of Castile and Leon (r. 1296–1312), and *Constance of Portugal (1290–1313); married Prince Jaime of Aragon, on October 18, 1319; became second wife of Alfonso or Alphonso IV (d. 1359), king of Aragon (r. 1327–1336), on February 5, 1329; children: Ferran; Juan (Joan).*

Eleanor of Castile was born in 1307, the daughter of Ferdinand IV, king of Castile, and *Constance of Portugal. She was the sister of Castilian king, Alphonso XI. In 1319, her father betrothed Eleanor to the crown prince of Aragon, Prince Jaime. This union quickly ended in failure, however, because shortly after the nuptials, the groom announced that he intended to take religious vows. Ten years later, Eleanor's brother Alphonso arranged her marriage to Jaime's widowed younger brother, Alphonso IV, king of Aragon.

Eleanor gave birth to two sons, Ferran and Juan (Joan), and dedicated much of her energy to securing properties and power for them, as the crown would pass to their elder half-brother, Peter IV the Ceremonius (also known as Pedro IV), Alphonso IV's son by his first wife, *Teresa d'Entenza. Reluctant to resist his determined wife, Alphonso conferred several cities and other incomes upon the sons, despite widespread criticism and protest in the kingdom. According to Aragonese custom, the properties should have remained part of the royal patrimony to be inherited by Peter.

In other words, the Aragonese resented Eleanor's influence over her irresolute husband. Eleanor and her stepson were fierce foes. He saw that she was persuading his father to give away parts of the royal patrimony, and she understood Peter to be the main obstacle to satisfying her ambitions for her sons. No fool, Eleanor sneaked back to Castile when Alphonso became fatally ill in 1336, not even waiting for the king to die.

Gathering allies, Eleanor and her sons battled to keep Peter IV from stripping them of their holdings. Negotiation succeeded where war failed, and the Aragonese finally agreed that Ferran and Joan could retain the properties, although at their death, the estates would revert to the king's possession. Meanwhile, Eleanor became enmeshed in the Castilian civil war between Peter the Cruel and Enrique of Trastámara. She sided too early with Enrique, the eventual victor. In 1358 one of Peter the Cruel's allies brutally assassinated Joan and the following year the Castilian king arrested and killed Eleanor. Peter IV murdered Ferran, Eleanor's surviving son, in 1363.

SOURCES:
Estow, Clara. *Pedro the Cruel of Castile, 1350–1369.* NY: Brill, 1995.

Kendall W. Brown,
Professor of History, Brigham Young University, Provo, Utah

Eleanor of Châtellerault (d. 1130).

See Eleanor of Aquitaine for sidebar on Aénor of Châtellerault.

Eleanor of Gonzaga I (1598–1655).

See Gonzaga, Eleonora I.

Eleanor of Gonzaga II (1628–1686).

See Gonzaga, Eleonora II.

Eleanor of Montfort (1215–1275)

English princess, countess of Leicester, and rebel. Name variations: Eleanor of England; Eleanor de Montfort; Eleanor Plantagenet. Born in 1215 in Gloucester, Gloucestershire, England; died on April 13, 1275, at Montargis convent in France; buried in Montargis, France; daughter of John also known as John Lackland, king of England (r. 1199–1216), and Isabella of Angoulême (1186–1246); married William Marshal, 2nd earl of Pembroke, in 1224 (died 1231); married Simon V of Montfort (c. 1208–1265), earl of Leicester, on January 7, 1239 (died 1265); children: Harry or Henry Montfort (1239–1265); Bran; Guy; Amauric; Richard; *Eleanor of Montfort (1252–1282).

Eleanor of Montfort was the last child born to King John of England and *Isabella of Angoulême. She was made countess of Leicester and, as a young woman, married one of her father's baronial supporters, William Marshal of Pembroke. He died when she was only 16. Apparently she had not enjoyed her brief time as a wife, for the young Eleanor, who was not notably pious, took a vow of perpetual chastity on his death. Yet when she met Simon of Montfort, the English noble who had emerged as the leader of the pro-baronial alliance against her brother, now King Henry III, she fell in love with him. They married in 1239.

The marriage was annulled because of her vow of chastity, however, and they were forced to travel to Rome to get a dispensation from the pope to legitimize their union. They seem to have been a close, intimate couple; in their years together, Eleanor gave birth to five sons and one daughter. Eleanor and Simon remained together for 27 years, during which Eleanor was an important aid in Simon's political and military schemes, probably due to her close ties to the house of Simon's enemy, Henry III.

Simon died in battle in 1265. Grief-stricken, Eleanor was forced to flee for her life, smuggling her children and a personal fortune in gold and jewels to safety in France. Probably tired of the adventures and trials of being an outlaw, the countess retired to a convent at Montargis where she died at age 60.

Laura York,
Riverside, California

Eleanor of Montfort (1252–1282)

Princess of Wales. Name variations: Eleanor de Montfort; (nickname) The Demoiselle. Born in 1252 in Kenilworth, Warwickshire, England; died in childbirth in June 1282 in Wales; buried in Llanfaes, Gwynedd, Wales; daughter of Simon of Montfort and Eleanor of Montfort (1215–1275), countess of Leicester; married Llewellyn ap Gruffydd (Llywelyn III), prince of Wales, on October 13, 1278; children: Gwenllian (b. 1282).

The daughter of Simon of Montfort and *Eleanor of Montfort (1215–1275), Eleanor was born into the chaos of her parents' rebellion against King Henry III of England. She was only 13 when her father died while leading the baronial army at the Battle of Evesham. Henry had sworn to imprison Eleanor and her mother to avoid any opportunities for further rebellion, even though the elder Eleanor was his own sister. Mother and daughter escaped to France to avoid imprisonment, and the younger Eleanor remained at the convent of Montargis until about 1276, when she was sent to Wales to marry the Welsh prince Llewellyn ap Gruffydd. The marriage had actually been arranged 11 years earlier by her father Simon of Montfort, but the constant warfare between Wales and England prevented Llewellyn from marrying Eleanor for a decade.

The new English king Edward I was opposed to this marriage between his greatest Welsh enemy and a member of the rebellious Montfort family, despite the fact that he and Eleanor were cousins. Edward had pirates in his employ capture the ship on which Eleanor was sailing, and she was kept imprisoned, though in some luxury, for two years. Llewellyn was forced to swear fealty to Edward in order to free his bride, and in 1278 they were finally married. Eleanor, now about 26, spent the next four years acting as a peacemaker. She used her familial ties to the English royal house and her close relationship with her husband to convince the parties to cease the warring for power over Wales which was destroying lands and families. She had some positive effect on the conflict but unfortunately died at age 30 in giving birth to a daughter.

SOURCES:

Costain, Thomas. *The Three Edwards*. NY: Popular Library, 1958.

Gies, Frances, and Joseph Gies. *Women in the Middle Ages*. NY: Harper and Row, 1978.

Laura York,
Riverside, California

Eleanor of Navarre (1425–1479)

*Queen of Navarre. Name variations: Leonor; Eleanor Trastamara; Eleanor de Foix. Born on February 2, 1425 (some sources cite 1426), in Aragon; died on February 12, 1479, in Tudela, Navarre, Spain; daughter of Juan II also known as John II, king of Aragon (r. 1458–1479), and *Blanche of Navarre (1385–1441); sister of Blanche of Navarre (1424–1464), queen of Castile and Leon; half-sister of Ferdinand of Aragon (who married *Isabella I [1451–1504]); married Gaston de Foix also known as Gaston IV, count of Foix, on July 30, 1436 (died 1470 or 1472); children: (in*

order of birth) Maria de Foix; Gaston, prince of Viane or Viana; Jeanne de Foix; Jean; Pierre; Margareta de Foix; Catherine de Foix; Eleanor de Foix; Jaime; Anne de Foix.

Eleanor, a princess of Navarre, was the daughter of King John II of Aragon and *Blanche of Navarre (1385–1441). As a young woman, she married the French count Gaston de Foix. On her mother's death in 1441, Eleanor's brother Charles (or Carlos), prince of Viana, inherited the small but prosperous kingdom of Navarre, although their father John took over as regent. Eleanor moved to France to reside on her husband's estates in Foix, and she gave birth to ten children, four sons and six daughters. John, who despised his son Charles, soon disinherited Eleanor's brother in favor of Eleanor and her husband Gaston, which greatly pleased Eleanor.

However, though she was queen in name, Eleanor of Navarre was unable to exert the authority of a ruler because her father refused to allow her to govern. Her deposed brother and her elder sister ☙➤ Blanche of Navarre (1424–1464) rebelled against their father and demanded Charles' reinstatement as the rightful heir to Navarre. John refused, and Eleanor therefore found herself struggling for power against her father as well as her brother, sister, and most of the political and religious leaders on the Spanish peninsula, who supported Charles. Her only ally was her husband Gaston, who led the armed struggle for his wife's inheritance. Her efforts to secure the throne led to years of warfare and civil strife, while her father retained control of Navarre. She spent much of her time trying to rid herself of her sister Blanche, whom Charles had named as his heir. In 1464, Blanche was kidnapped and imprisoned; soon she was murdered, probably on Eleanor's orders.

☙➤ Blanche of Navarre (1424–1464)

*Queen of Castile and Leon. Name variations: (Spanish) Blanca de Navarra; Bianca. Born on June 9, 1424, in Olite; died on December 2, 1464, in Orthez; daughter of Juan also known as John II, king of Aragon (r. 1458–1479), and *Blanche of Navarre (1385–1441); sister of Charles (Carlos), prince of Viana, and *Eleanor of Navarre (1425–1479); became first wife of Enrique also known as Henry IV (b. 1425), king of Castile and Leon (r. 1454–1474), on September 15, 1440 (divorced 1453); children: none.*

Eventually, the aged King John agreed to let his daughter Eleanor take over the rule of Navarre but only under his authority, and she became more of a puppet than a true ruler. Though Eleanor's husband Gaston was killed in 1472 during one of his battles against his wife's many enemies, Eleanor refused to give up hope that she would succeed as queen regnant. At last, she achieved her dream in 1479, when her 80-year-old father died. The 53-year-old Eleanor was proclaimed queen of Navarre and no doubt looked forward to years of ruling on her own authority after so many years of struggle. But Eleanor died suddenly only 15 days after her coronation. She left her kingdom to her grandson, Francisco Febo.

SOURCES:

Echols, Anne, and Marty Williams. *An Annotated Index of Medieval Women.* NY: Markus Wiener, 1992.

Opfell, Olga. *Queens, Empresses, Grand Duchesses, and Regents: Women Rulers of Europe, 1328–1989.* Jefferson, NC: McFarland, 1989.

Laura York,
Riverside, California

Eleanor of Normandy (fl. 1000s)

*Countess of Flanders. Born before 1018; daughter of Richard II, duke of Normandy (d. 1027), and **Judith of Rennes** (c. 982–1018, daughter of Conan I, duke of Brittany); married Baldwin IV, count of Flanders; children: Baldwin V, count of Flanders.*

Eleanor of Pfalz-Neuburg (1655–1720)

Holy Roman empress. Name variations: Eleanora of Neuburg; Eleanor of Neuberg; Eleanor Magdalene of Neuburg; Eleanor Magdalene of Neuberg. Born on January 6, 1655; died on January 19, 1720; daughter of *Elizabeth Amalia of Hesse (1635–1709) and Philip William, elector Palatine; became third wife of Leopold I of Bohemia (1640–1705), Holy Roman emperor (r. 1658–1705), on December 14, 1676; children: Joseph I (1678–1711), Holy Roman emperor (r. 1705–1711); *Maria Elisabeth (1680–1741, stadholder of the Netherlands); Charles VI (1685–1740), Holy Roman emperor (r. 1711–1740); *Maria Antonia of Austria (1683–1754, who married John V, king of Portugal); *Maria Magdalena (1689–1743).

Eleanor of Portugal (1328–1348)

*Queen of Aragon. Name variations: Leonor of Portugal; Eleanor Henriques; Enriques or Enriquez. Born in 1328; died on October 29, 1348, at age 20, in Teruel, Aragon, Spain; daughter of **Beatrice of Castile and Leon** (1293–1359), queen of Portugal, and Alphonso IV, king of Portugal (r. 1325–1357); sister of Pedro or Peter I, king of Portugal (r. 1357–1367), and *Maria of Portugal (1313–1357, who married Alphonso XI of Castile); became second wife of Pedro IV also known as Peter IV the Ceremonious (b. 1319), king of Aragon (r. 1336–1387), in 1347; children: none. Peter IV's first wife was **Marie of Navarre**; his third wife was *Eleanor of Sicily (d. 1375).*

Eleanor of Portugal (1434–1467)

Portuguese princess, Holy Roman empress and queen of Germany as wife of Frederick III, and mother of Emperor Maximilian I. Name variations: Eleanora; Eleonore; Leonor. Born on September 18, 1434, in Torres Novan Vedras; died on September 3, 1467, in Wiener-Neustadt from complications of childbirth; daughter of Edward also known as Duarte I, king of Portugal (r. 1433–1438), and *Leonora of Aragon (1405–1445); married Frederick III, king of Germany and Holy Roman emperor (r. 1440–1493), on March 15, 1452; children: Christopher (b. 1455); Maxmilian I (1459–1519), Holy Roman Emperor (who married *Mary of Burgundy [1457–1482] and *Bianca Maria Sforza [1472–1510]); Johann or John (1466–1467); Helen (1460–1461); Cunegunde (1465–1520, who married Albert II of Bavaria).

Birth of Frederick III (1415); death of her uncle, Henry the Navigator (1460); accession of Frederick III as king of Germany (1440); Frederick III's coronation as Holy Roman emperor (1452); death of Frederick III (1493).

Princess Eleanor of Portugal was born on September 18, 1434, in Torres Vedras, the daughter of King Duarte I of Portugal and Queen *Leonora of Aragon. When Eleanor was 15, negotiations for her betrothal to the French crown prince failed. In 1451, her father consequently arranged her betrothal to Frederick III, king of Germany, and agreed to provide a dowry of 60,000 gold florins. Married by proxy on August 9, 1451, in Lisbon, Eleanor departed the following October by sea for Italy, where she was to meet her husband. During the voyage, pirates attacked her ten-ship fleet, but Eleanor reached Italy safely on February 2, 1452. Frederick III and his court met her in Siena, and the party then proceeded to Rome. Pope Nicholas V officiated at their wedding on March 15, 1452, and the imperial coronation four days later.

On her arrival in Germany, Eleanor probably found the country coarse and insular, compared with Portugal which was embarking on its great age. Her husband was neither handsome nor devoted. Still, from the palace-castle at Wiener-Neustadt near the Hungarian border, she faced with Frederick the nearly continuous challenge of rebellious German nobles and Turkish expansion into the Balkans. Their first child, Christopher, was born in 1455, but their joy at having a son was brief, as he died the following year. In 1459, Eleanor gave birth to Maximilian I, who succeeded his father and established in reality many of the grandiose claims Frederick made for the Habsburg dynasty. Two daughters, **Helena** (1460–1461) and *Cunegunde (1465–1520), plus another son, John (1466–1467), followed. Eleanor died on September 3, 1467, from complications of childbirth. She is buried in the Cistercian monastery of Neustadt, and in 1469 Frederick hired Niklas Gerhaert van Leyden to carve both his and Eleanor's likenesses for the tomb.

SOURCES:

Cordeiro, Luciano. *Portuguezes fôra de Portugal. Uma sobrinha do infante, imperatriz da Allemanha e rainha da Hungria.* Lisbon: Imprensa Nacional, 1894.

Fichtenau, Heinrich. *Der junge Maximilian, 1459–82.* Vienna: Verlag für Geschichte und Politik, 1959.

Heinig, Paul Joachim, ed. *Kaiser Friedrich III. (1440–1493) in seiner Zeit: Studien anlasslich des 500. Todestags am 19. August 1493/1993.* Köln: Böhlau, 1993.

Lanckmann, Nicolaus. *Historia desponsationis, benedictionis et coronationis Imp. Friderici III et coniugis ipsius Eleonorae a. 1451.* Trans. by Aires A. Nascimento. Lisbon: Edições Cosmos, 1992.

Kendall W. Brown,
Professor of History,
Brigham Young University, Provo, Utah

Eleanor of Portugal (1458–1525)

*Queen of Portugal. Name variations: Leonor of Portugal. Born on May 2, 1458, in Beja; died on November 17, 1525, in Lisbon; interred in Xabregas; daughter of *Beatrice of Beja (1430–1506) and Fernando also known as Ferdinand, duke of Beja and Viseu; sister of *Isabella of Braganza (1459–1521) and Manuel I the Fortunate (1469–1521), king of Portugal (r. 1495–1521); married Joao II also known as John II (b. 1455), king of Portugal (r. 1481–1495); children: Alfonso or Alphonso of Portugal (1475–1491); Joao (1483–1483).*

A patron of the arts, Eleanor of Portugal is best known for her patronage of Gil Vicente, a Portuguese dramatist. She also guided the publication of the Portuguese translation of *Christine de Pizan's *Livre des Trois Vertues.*

Eleanor of Portugal (1498–1558)

*Queen of Portugal and later of France. Name variations: Eléonore; Eleanor Habsburg; Eleanor of Austria; Leonor of Austria. Born in Louvain on November 15, 1498; died on February 25, 1558, near Badajoz on the Portuguese border; daughter of Philip I the Fair, king of Castile and Leon, and *Juana la Loca (1479–1555); sister of Ferdinand I and Charles V, both Holy Roman emperors, *Mary of Hungary (1505–1558), *Catherine (1507–1578), *Elisabeth of Habsburg (1501–1526); became third wife of Miguel also known as Manuel I the Fortunate (1469–1521), king of Portugal (r. 1495–1521), on November 24, 1518; became second wife of Francis I (1494–1547), king of France (r. 1515–1547), on July 4, 1530; children: (first marriage) Carlos (b. 1520); Maria de Portugal (1521–1577); (second marriage) none.*

Death of Eleanor's father, Philip the Fair (1506); accession of Charles V as king of Spain (1517); election of Charles V as Holy Roman emperor (1519); death of Manuel I (1521); defeat and capture of Francis I by Charles V at Pavia (1525); Treaty of Madrid (1526); Peace of Cambrai (Peace of the Ladies, 1529); death of Francis I (1547); death of Eleanor's mother, Juana la Loca (Joanna the Mad, 1555); abdication of Charles V (1556); death of Charles V (1558).

The eldest child of Philip I the Fair of Burgundy and *Juana la Loca (Joanna the Mad) of Spain, Eleanor of Portugal was born in Louvain on November 15, 1498. She spent her childhood in Flanders, although her parents were often in Spain where Juana stood to inherit the kingdoms of Aragon and Castile as the only surviving child of Ferdinand and *Isabella I. Eleanor's paternal grandfather was the Holy Roman Emperor Maximilian I, and her younger brother was Charles V, born in 1500. Thus, European politics inevitably dominated her life.

Charles readily sacrificed Eleanor's personal happiness on the altar of dynastic statecraft. When he discovered that she had received a love letter from Frederick, Count Palatine, Charles immediately exiled him from the Flemish court. About a year later, in 1517, she accompanied her brother to Spain, where he claimed his insane mother's throne. Charles soon wed Eleanor to the aging Manuel I of Portugal, seeking through the marital alliance to curb any attempt by rebellious Castilian nobles to obtain support from their Western neighbors. Manuel was 49 and his bride 20 when they wed on November 24, 1518. She was his third wife and gave birth to their two children (Carlos in 1520 and *Maria de

✢▶

Maria of Castile.

See Isabella I for sidebar.

Portugal in 1521) before he died on December 13, 1521. (Manuel's second wife, ◀✢ **Maria of Castile**, had died in 1517).

Returned to Spain, Eleanor soon found herself a tool in another of Charles V's political stratagems. In 1523, the emperor was at war with the French monarch Francis I. Trying to deprive Francis of one of his most valuable vassals, Charles opened negotiations with the Duke of Bourbon. Imperial emissaries promised Bourbon the hand of Eleanor, among other rewards, if he would support Charles. In 1525, Charles' forces defeated and captured Francis at the battle of Pavia. Hoping to win his freedom, Francis agreed to the Treaty of Madrid and offered to seal his compliance by marrying Eleanor. Charles feared that if he reneged on his promise to the duke of Bourbon, the duke might withdraw his support. The emperor resolved the dilemma by persuading Eleanor to announce that she did not want to marry Bourbon. To Charles' way of thinking, this freed him of his obligation to Bourbon and permitted him to betroth Eleanor to Francis, his still-captive enemy. The emperor introduced his sister to Francis in Madrid on February 13, 1526. She bowed and offered the king her hand; he grandiosely embraced and kissed her as though she were his wife, reportedly proclaiming: "It is not the hand I owe you, it is the mouth."

Eleanor's second marriage suffered a long postponement. Francis refused to abide by other provisions of the Treaty of Madrid but secured his freedom by giving his two young sons to Charles as hostages. Fearful of a Franco-Hispanic alliance, Henry VIII of England offered his daughter *Mary (I) as a wife to Francis in Eleanor's place. In the Treaty of Amiens (August 18, 1527), however, the monarchs agreed that Francis would wed Eleanor while Mary would wed the Duke of Orléans. Then to Charles and Eleanor's dismay, Francis invaded Italy. Depressed, Eleanor withdrew temporarily to a convent, knowing that the invasion meant renewed war between France and Spain. The new hostilities ended with the Treaty of Cambrai, or "Peace of the Ladies," on August 3, 1529. It stipulated that Eleanor go to France as soon as Francis complied with the terms of the pact.

On July 3, 1530, she met Francis at Roquefort-de-Marsan, and they celebrated their marriage two days later. Writes Francis' biographer Francis Hackett, "The French people welcomed the new Queen. She was a herald of peace, and they yearned for peace." But events soon showed that Charles' political strategy had sacrificed his obedient sister. Francis and Eleanor rarely lived together as husband and wife. He was enamored of his mistress, Anne d'Heilly, whom he made *Duchess d'Étampes. Eleanor had no recourse but to endure his shameful infidelities. On the rare occasions they slept together, according to Francis' sister *Margaret of Angoulême (1492–1549), Francis said, "she is very hot in bed, and desireth to be too much embraced." As Charles' sister, Eleanor dutifully led a dignified public life, sometimes appearing with Francis for official occasions such as the wedding of his son Henry (II) to *Catherine de Medici or the public execution of heretics. But in private, he accorded her neither love nor respectful affection.

Writes biographer Hackett, "Francis was wedded quite casually to the kind, good, virtuous and sensible lady whose fault was to be a chattel." After trying to win her husband's affection, Eleanor recognized that she could not overcome his passion for Madame d'Étampes. As much as possible, she tried to mediate between Francis and Charles to avoid further warfare. Otherwise, she dedicated herself to pious and charitable works. When Francis I died on March 31, 1547, his attendants had not even informed Eleanor of his fatal illness.

Her stepson Henry II invited Eleanor to remain in France, but she decided to leave the scene of so much heartache. She journeyed first to Flanders and remained there for several years. Eventually, Eleanor joined her brother in Spain. On February 25, 1558, she died near Badajoz on the Portuguese border, having gone there to visit her only surviving child, Maria de Portugal. Charles died on September 21 of the same year.

SOURCES:
Hackett, Francis. *Francis the First*. Garden City, NY: Doubleday, Doran, 1935.

Jacquart, Jean. *François Ier*. Paris: Fayard, 1981.

Knecht, R.J. *Renaissance Warrior and Patron: The Reign of Francis I*. NY: Cambridge University Press, 1994.

Kendall W. Brown,
Professor of History,
Brigham Young University, Provo, Utah

Eleanor of Provence (c. 1222–1291)

Queen of England, wife and consort of Henry III, king of England (1216–1272), mother of Edward I, king of England (1272–1306), who unjustly incurred the enmity of her nation. Name variations: Alianora; Eleanora; Elinor. Date of birth unknown but believed to be 1222, possibly in November; place of birth presumed to be Aix-en-Provence, Provence, which is now in France; died at the convent of St. Mary, Amesbury, Wiltshire, England, on June 24, 1291; her body was buried there in September 1291; her heart was interred at the church of the Friars Minors in London; daughter of Raymond Berengar or Berenger IV (some sources cite V), count of Provence and Forcalquier (1209–1245) and Beatrice of Savoy (d. 1268); sister of Margaret of Provence (1221–1295), Sancha of Provence (c. 1225–1261), and Beatrice of Provence (d. 1267); married Henry III (1206–1272), king of England (r. 1216–1272), on January 14, 1236, at Canterbury, England; children: Edward I Longshanks (1272–1307), king of England (r. 1272–1307); Margaret, Queen of Scots (1240–1275, who married Alexander III of Scotland); ✥ Beatrice (1242–1275), duchess of Brittany; Edmund Crouchback (c. 1245–1296), earl of Lancaster; and Katherine (1253–1257), Richard, John, William and Henry who all died young.

Crowned queen of England at Westminster (January 20, 1236); during Henry's absence in Gascony, named co-regent with her brother-in-law, Richard, earl of Cornwall (1253); after Henry's capture at the battle of Lewes, exiled in France (1264); returned to England when Henry regained his throne (October 1265); retired to the Convent of St. Mary, Amesbury (1276); took vows as a nun there (1286).

Eleanor of Provence was a forceful personality, strong-willed and determined with a great deal of common sense that turned this determination to practical use. Henry III clearly appreciated the strength in her character for in his will written before he left for Gascony in 1253, the king left his kingdom and his children, most particularly, his heir, in her care. He never changed this will. Their marriage was remarkable for their mutual fidelity, and their concern for the welfare of their children. Under her influence, the role of queen-consort developed in several areas, especially in the scale of income considered requisite for a queen's needs and in the manner in which it was managed. She acquired a political authority that was interpreted as interference by contemporary commentators who sowed the seeds of her unpopularity. This disaffection reached its peak in the summer of 1263 when the barge in which she was traveling on the River Thames was attacked both physically and verbally by the people of London and caused her 19th-century biographer, *Agnes Strickland, to label her "the most unpopular queen that England ever had." Fortunately, many of Eleanor's letters have survived and are today preserved in the Public Record Office in London. These show her to be diplomatic and compassionate and go far to contradict this label.

Eleanor was the second of four daughters born to Raymond Berengar IV, count of Provence

and Forcalquier, and ✥ Beatrice of Savoy. No records survive of her birth date or place but it is generally accepted that she was born in 1222. Since her father's court was constantly moving from castle to castle, it is not possible to ascertain her exact place of birth, except to say Provence. Eleanor and her sisters were renowned for their beauty, their learning and for marrying kings. *Margaret of Provence (1221–1295) became the wife of Louis IX, king of France (1226–1270); *Sancha of Provence married Richard, earl of Cornwall who was elected king of the Romans in 1257; and ✥ Beatrice of Provence (d. 1267) married Charles I d'Anjou who became king of

---

✥ **Beatrice** (1242–1275)

*English princess and duchess of Brittany. Name variations: Beatrice Plantagenet. Born on June 25, 1242, in Bordeaux, Aquitaine, France; died on March 24, 1275, in London, England; daughter of Henry III (1206–1272), king of England (r. 1216–1272) and *Eleanor of Provence (c. 1222–1291); sister of Edward I Longshanks, king of England (r. 1272–1307); married John II (1239–1305), duke of Brittany (r. 1286–1305), in 1260; children: Arthur II (d. 1312), duke of Brittany (r. 1305–1312), and six others.*

✥ **Beatrice of Savoy** (d. 1268)

*Countess of Provence. Name variations: Beatrice de Savoie. Birth date unknown; died in 1268 (some sources cite 1266); one of ten children born to Thomas I, count of Savoy, and *Margaret of Geneva; married Raymond Berengar V (1198–1245), count of Provence, in December 1220; children: *Margaret of Provence (1221–1295), queen of France; *Eleanor of Provence (c. 1222–1291); *Sancha of Provence (c. 1225–1261, who married Richard, 1st earl of Cornwall and king of the Romans); *Beatrice of Provence (d. 1267, who married Charles of Anjou, brother of Louis IX). Beatrice of Savoy and her husband Raymond Berengar were renowned for their learning and influence on the arts.*

✥ **Beatrice of Provence** (d. 1267)

*Queen of Sicily. Name variations: Countess of Provence. Died in 1267; daughter of *Beatrice of Savoy (d. 1268) and Raymond Berengar or Berenger IV (some sources cite V), count of Provence and Forcalquier; sister of *Eleanor of Provence (c. 1222–1291), *Sancha of Provence (c. 1225–1261), and *Margaret of Provence (1221–1295); married Charles I of Anjou (brother of Louis IX, king of France), king of Sicily (r. 1266–1282) and Naples (r. 1268–1285), in 1246; children: Charles II, duke of Anjou (r. 1285–1290), king of Naples (r. 1285–1309); *Beatrice of Anjou (d. 1275).*

Sicily in 1266. Since Richard of Cornwall was brother to Henry III and Charles d'Anjou was brother to Louis IX, these marriages produced an interesting combination of family relationships and loyalties.

Eleanor's mother, Beatrice of Savoy, was one of ten children born to Thomas I, count of Savoy, and *Margaret of Geneva. These eight sons and two daughters had little but birth and character yet they succeeded, mainly due to the efforts of Thomas and Beatrice, to spread the name of Savoy throughout the west of Europe. The royal court of England felt the full effect of the Savoyard invasion since, contrary to the usual practice, Henry did not dismiss those relations who accompanied Eleanor to England in 1236; instead, he lavished gifts and honors upon them which did little to endear Eleanor to her English subjects.

Eleanor's childhood in Provence gave her an appreciation of art and music, but it was dominated by poverty. As a result of early Moorish influences, Provence had become a center for literature and a source of culture and sophistication. Its troubadours and courts of love were renowned throughout the Western world; for two centuries, they had epitomized all that was most desirable in music and poetry. Her father was a skilled troubadour, and her mother a poet. Eleanor, herself, was said to have written an epic poem. Her tutor was Romeo de Villeneuve, who was also major-domo to her father, and responsible for the splendid marriages made by her and her sisters. His efforts were immortalized by Dante in his *Divina Commedia, Paradiso, Canto vi*:

> Four daughters and each one a queen
> Had Raymond Berenger: this grandeur all
> By poor Romeo had accomplished been.

The financial problems of the count were acute. In 1235, Provence was a small county between the Rhône valley and the Alps. Its mountainous terrain and lack of access to the Mediterranean Sea denied it any role in the economic structure of the West. The family had an itinerant lifestyle traveling from castle to castle to take advantage of fresh food supplies. The daughters wore clothes handed down from their mother, which were then handed down among themselves. The court officials wore patched uniforms, and minstrels did not even get food as payment for their performances. There was no money for dowries, and both Henry III and Louis IX were forced to accept their brides on the understanding that these would be paid later. There is no record that they ever were. When

Raymond Berengar died in 1246, he named Beatrice of Provence, the youngest daughter, then unmarried, as his heir. Her subsequent marriage to Charles d'Anjou made Charles the next count of Provence and Forcalquier. Since the normal practice was to divide an inheritance equally between daughters, reserving any title of dignity for the eldest, Beatrice of Provence's three sisters contested the will. Both Eleanor and Margaret continued for the rest of their lives to pursue Charles d'Anjou for restitution of their rights in Provence. Many of Eleanor's letters written in her widowhood are devoted to this subject. In May 1286, she granted her Provençal inheritance to her grandsons, Thomas, Henry, and John, sons of Edmund Crouchback, earl of Lancaster, her second son.

Escorted by Henry's envoys, Hugh, bishop of Ely, Ralph, bishop of Hereford, and the Master of the Temple in England, Eleanor arrived at Dover in January 1236 as the future bride of Henry III. She was aged about 14 years; Henry was 28 and in the 20th year of his reign. In accordance with royal tradition, the marriage was a diplomatic one. The couple had never met. Despite this, the marriage was to prove successful and happy, in direct contrast to the stormy married lives of both Henry's father, King John, and grandfather, Henry II. Henry hoped the alliance would counterbalance the effect of Louis IX's marriage with Eleanor's sister, Margaret of Provence, and would provide him with new allies on the Continent. His six earlier attempts at making such a marriage alliance had failed, although one of these, that with ◀ Joanna of Ponthieu, had reached the betrothal stage before being annulled. This was to have repercussions for Eleanor in the future, and in 1252 she was reputed to have paid the pope a large sum of money to confirm the annulment in order to safeguard both her own marriage and that proposed between her eldest son Edward I Longshanks and *Eleanor of Castile, daughter of Joanna of Ponthieu.

Eleanor was married at Canterbury by Edmund Rich, the archbishop, on January 14, 1236, and crowned queen a week later at Westminster. The coronation was a splendid occasion greeted with much rejoicing and reported in fine detail by Matthew Paris, the chronicler monk of St. Albans. The marriage lasted over 36 years, and Henry and Eleanor were remarkably faithful to each other, sharing a concern for the happiness and well-being of their children. Henry was overtly solicitous for her comfort. The Liberate Rolls which recorded the payments made

Joanna of Ponthieu. See *Eleanor of Castile* for sidebar.

from the royal coffer contain instructions for renovating and improving the royal residences, many of which were specifically for the benefit of Eleanor; for example, a covered walkway was constructed at Woodstock so that she could go to chapel "with a dry foot."

During her marriage, in her role as queen-consort, Eleanor was much maligned and verbally abused by contemporary writers, mostly monastic, who were traditionally against women in power and notably naive and uninformed about the machinations of a royal court. In truth, she was a skilled diplomat and a clever financier, who did much to hold Henry's throne for him. She fulfilled her many and varied duties with total commitment, never challenging or undermining the authority of the king but acting in his best interests and, later, in those of Edward, their son and heir.

As a mother, too, she was exemplary. Whenever possible her children traveled with her, and she kept in close contact with them after their marriages. She took an equally caring interest in her many grandchildren. It is noticeable that she suffered physical illness whenever any of her children was in trouble, for example, when ❧➤ **Margaret, Queen of Scots** was held as a prisoner during the early years of her marriage to Alexander III of Scotland, and when her youngest daughter, ❧➤ **Katherine Plantagenet**, who was born deaf, fell ill and died in 1257.

As well as settling considerable property on her as a dowry, Henry III was the first monarch to grant his queen her own wardrobe and household. In this context, the wardrobe was not merely a room where her robes and jewels were stored but an office with clerks, servants, records and accounts. In selecting its members, she showed equal favor towards those of English birth and those from Provence and Savoy. Her letters indicate her interest in and care of these members of her household.

The establishment of her own wardrobe was perhaps the most significant gesture Henry made towards the independence of his wife. Her dowry, though considerable, would not be accessible to her before Henry died, so it was his intention to direct money from his own wardrobe to pay the expenses of the queen's household. But, though she had control of her expenses, she was still largely dependent on the king for income, and his extravagant lifestyle and ambitious building plans left her regularly in debt. Eleanor, therefore, had to rely on income from taxes in order to pay her bills, and it was from

the exaction of these by the more aggressive members of her household that her unpopularity arose. No one likes paying taxes. Those open to her as queen-consort were from the queen's-gold or *aurum reginae,* which was an additional levy of ten percent paid to the queen-consort on voluntary fines made to the king, papal tenths, and the custom dues from Queenhithe, a quay on the river Thames. Another source available to her was the revenue to be gained from wardships, of which she had many. Under feudal law, if, on the death of their father, a male vassal was under the age of 21 years and a female under the age of 14 years, the king, as their feudal lord, was entitled to the wardship of both the person and their property. The right of marriage was often included too. The lord had full powers to appropriate to himself the revenues of such a minor and, by marrying a female ward to the highest bidder, the rewards could be greatly increased. Henry granted many to Eleanor, including that of **Margaret of Lincoln**, heir to William of

---

❧➤ **Margaret** (1240–1275)

Queen of Scots. Born on September 29 (some sources cite October 5), 1240, in Windsor, Berkshire, England; died at Cupar Castle, Fife, Scotland, on February 26, 1275; buried at Dunfermline, Fife, Scotland; eldest daughter of Henry III (1206–1272), king of England (r. 1216–1272), and *Eleanor of Provence (c. 1222–1291); sister of Edward I Longshanks (1239–1307), king of England (r. 1272–1307); *Beatrice (1242–1275), duchess of Brittany; Edmund Crouchback (c. 1245–1296), earl of Lancaster; and *Katherine Plantagenet (1253–1257); married Alexander III (1241–1286), king of Scotland (r. 1249–1286), on December 26, 1251; children: *Margaret of Norway (1261–1283, who married Eric II Magnusson, king of Norway); Alexander (1264–1284); David (1273–1281).

Margaret was only 11 when she married Alexander III, king of Scotland. He was ten. Fearful of English influence, Alexander's guardians confined the young bride to Edinburgh castle; she was only released by the intercession of her parents, Henry III and *Eleanor of Provence. After the death of Alexander II, Margaret and Alexander III were married on December 26, 1251.

❧➤ **Katherine Plantagenet** (1253–1257)

English princess. Born on November 25, 1253, in Westminster, London, England; died on May 3, 1257, in Windsor, Berkshire, England; buried in Westminster Abbey; daughter of Henry III (1206–1272), king of England (r. 1216–1272) and *Eleanor of Provence (c. 1222–1291). Katherine was born deaf and died at age three.

Longespée, which amounted to £2,000 annually. (It should be noted that it is not possible to equate medieval monetary values to those of the 20th century.) Despite the considerable income that these sources provided, Eleanor was forced to make large loans from, among others, the Italian bankers, to solve both her own debts and those of Edward, her son. She became so successful at managing her own finances that by the end of the reign, as **Margaret Howell** concluded, she had revolutionized the scale and style of the provision hitherto considered requisite for a queen-consort. Her expertise, however, made her few friends.

Since she derived considerable income at the expense of the Jewry, who were frequently fined, Eleanor has been accused of anti-Semitism. It is true that in 1275 she obtained Edward I's permission to order that no Jews live in any of the towns that were within her dower. And the chroniclers had no doubt that Edward I's expulsion of the Jews from England in 1289 was influenced by his mother. It would be unfair to put all the blame onto Eleanor for a practice that was not uncommon in the 13th century, but the actions do neither her nor Edward I any credit.

The reign of Henry III was a momentous one dominated by his continental ambitions and the struggle of the English nobility to assert their rights. The weak and vacillatory nature of Henry added to Eleanor's difficulties. She accompanied Henry on his journeys both in England and abroad with the exception of that of 1253 when she remained in England as co-regent together with Richard, earl of Cornwall, Henry's brother. At this time, she was appointed Lady Keeper of the Great Seal. She took her duties very seriously, remaining, as her itinerary shows, mostly in Westminster, sitting as judge in the *curia regis,* interrupted only by the birth of her third daughter, Katherine, in November 1253, and twice summoning Parliament in order to raise funds for Henry. The manner in which Parliament was summoned in February 1254 marked a landmark in parliamentary history for which Eleanor can be said to be partly responsible. For the first time, as well as the great lay and ecclesiastical lords, the lesser nobility and clergy were included. Her appeals for money, however, were unsuccessful, and she was forced to meet Henry's needs from her own resources.

Her regency was cut short in May 1254 when Eleanor left England to attend the marriage of Edward and Eleanor of Castile at the monastery of Las Huelgas in Burgos in the Pyrenees. This was followed later that year by a reunion in Paris at the French royal court of Eleanor with her mother and sisters.

A return to the English court meant facing the faction war that was developing. The Savoyards and Provençals who had arrived with Eleanor in 1236 had been joined by the Lusignans in 1247. The Lusignans were Henry's 11 half-brothers and half-sisters born to Henry's mother, *Isabella of Angoulême (1186–1246), by her second marriage to Hugh of Lusignan. Known as the "aliens" by their contemporaries, they were arrogant, violent and universally disliked except by Henry, who endeavored with limited resources to satisfy their needs. This led Henry to confiscate some of Eleanor's lands, but these were swiftly restored to her. The accounts of the queen's messengers show that though she was absent from court during much of this period she was in close communication with the king. There is no evidence to indicate whether or not she supported either faction, but she would have been very unlikely to agree to anything that could have undermined her son's future. And her absence should be seen as more of a tactical withdrawal than as evidence of a marital dispute. Baronial pressure finally forced Henry to expel the Lusignans, but it was too late to prevent the outbreak of civil war.

On May 14, 1264, Henry III was captured by Simon de Montfort, the leader of the rebel barons, at the battle of Lewes. Henry was held as prisoner by Simon until August 4, 1265, when, at the battle of Evesham, Simon was defeated and killed by a royalist army led by Prince Edward. Eleanor and her younger son, Edmund, had already crossed to France on September 23, 1263, where they remained until their return to England on October 28, 1265.

As head of a court in exile, Eleanor proved her ability to lead in what was then a man's world. Her household accounts for 1257–64 and 1264–69 show unusually high expenditure for horses and their equipment and "secret gifts and private alms." She made use of family ties on the Continent to raise money and mercenaries for the release of her husband. She successfully negotiated a considerable loan from Louis IX in exchange for three bishoprics of Limoges, Périgeux, and Cahors, which Henry had held by right of the French king through the Treaty of Paris; but failed in her appeals to Alphonse de Poitiers, Louis' younger brother, for ships. However, by the autumn of 1264, she had assembled a large army of German, Gascon, Breton, French, and Spanish mercenaries at the Flemish port of Sluys. Bad weather prevented it sailing, and as Eleanor's financial resources dwindled so did the army. Fear of it though had caused Simon de Montfort to draw up a line of defense along the south coast, and Alphonse did close the port of La Rochelle, disrupting English merchant shipping.

Edward's victory at Evesham paved the way for Eleanor's return to England. Her political role effectively ended now as Henry's declining health left Edward more and more in control. Her last official duty as queen-consort was in November 1272 when she sent messengers to Edward, who was on crusade in the Holy Land, to inform him of his father's death and his own accession to the English throne.

As queen mother, Eleanor was treated more generously by the chroniclers. Now the mother of a strong and successful king, rather than the wife of a weak one, she received praise instead of criticism. She adopted the role of family matriarch and traveled widely, both in England and abroad, visiting her children and grandchildren. Edward I clearly valued her advice and her other children were not afraid to leave their affairs in her control during their absences abroad.

In 1276, following the deaths of both her married daughters, she entered the convent of St. Mary at Amesbury in Wiltshire, a daughter-house of the great French Benedictine Abbey of Fontevrault, as a "vowess" or "veiled widow." In doing so, she followed the practice popular in the 13th and 14th centuries when widows, from royal, aristocratic and merchant families, chose to take a vow of chastity and live quietly in a religious house, accepting mantle, veil and ring, blessed by a bishop, as visible expressions of their status. Eleanor continued to travel, administer her own affairs and conduct family conferences. King Edward was a frequent visitor. Her letters show that Amesbury benefitted from her presence there. She became well known as a generous benefactor and was reported to donate £5, a considerable sum, to the poor at regular intervals. She endowed a hospital for women, St. Katherine's near the Tower at London, with lands and property. She commanded that alms be distributed there annually on the anniversary of Henry III's death.

In 1286, she took her vows as a professed nun of the order of Fontevrault, together with two of her granddaughters. She spent the remaining five years of her life in relative seclusion. A measure of the confidence her family retained in her is indicated by the fact that two important family conferences, in October 1289

and April 1290, were held in her presence at Amesbury, where both state and family business was discussed. The betrothal of Edward I's son and heir, also Edward, with *Margaret, Maid of Norway (1283–1290), heir to the throne of Scotland, was among the matters under discussion. Also the succession was agreed, since Edward I was at that time planning to go on crusade again.

Eleanor of Provence died on June 24, 1291, aged nearly 70 years. Her burial was delayed until September 10, 1291, on the orders of Edward I who was in Scotland at the time of her death and wished to participate personally in the ceremonies. She was buried in the convent of St. Mary, Amesbury. Her heart was taken to London and buried in the church of the Friars Minors. Sadly, neither the fine tomb erected at Amesbury by Edward I nor her burial place in London exist today.

Eleanor was a competent and intelligent woman with a natural ability for leadership and plenty of common sense. She came to a foreign land as a child-bride to a king and survived. As a widow, she was not too proud to exchange her crown for a veil and refer to herself as the "humble nun of the order of Fontevrault." Of her nine children, only four lived into adulthood. Her sons, Edward I and Edmund, earl of Lancaster, survived her. Her daughters, Margaret, wife of Alexander III of Scotland, and Beatrice, wife of John of Brittany, both died in 1275.

There are no portraits, statues or effigies of Eleanor of Provence. There exists only a photograph of one very weather-beaten stone boss, which was to be found, before the Dissolution of the Monasteries, on the north porch of Bridlington Priory, Yorkshire, England; it was said to commemorate her visit to York in 1251 for the marriage of her daughter, Margaret. There is nothing to compare with the crosses erected by Edward I in memory of his wife, Eleanor of Castile. The two queens are frequently confused. Not only did they share the same Christian name, but they also died within six months of each other. Only fragments of the seals of Eleanor of Provence remain today. Her most tangible memory lies in the collection of her correspondence which can be found in the Public Record Office, Chancery Lane, London.

SOURCES:

Biles, Martha. "The Indomitable Belle: Eleanor of Provence, Queen of England," in *Seven Studies In Medieval English History and other Historical Essays, Presented to Harold S. Snellgrove.* Ed. by R.H. Bowers. Jackson, Mississippi, 1983.

Calendars of the Chancery Rolls for the reigns of Henry III and Edward I published by the P.R.O. (London).

Howell, Margaret. "The Resources of Eleanor of Provence as Queen-consort," in *E.H.R.* Vol. cii, 1987, pp. 373–393.

Johnstone, H. "The Queen's Household," in *Chapters of Administrative History of Medieval England*. Edited by T.F. Tout. Vol. V. Manchester, 1920.

Paris, Matthew. *Chronica Maiora*. Ed. by H.R. Luard. Rolls Series, 1872–84.

Strickland, Agnes. *Lives of the Queens of England*. 12 vols. London, 1841.

SUGGESTED READING:

Bémont, C. *Simon de Montfort, earl of Leicester, 1208–1256.* Trans. by E.F. Jacob. Oxford, 1930.

Blaauw, W.H. *The Baron's War, including Battles of Lewes and Evesham.* London, 1844.

Cox, E.L. *The Eagles of Savoy: The House of Savoy in 13th-Century Europe.* Princeton, New Jersey, 1974.

Crawford, Anne, ed. *Letters of the Queens of England 1100–1547.* Alan Sutton, 1994.

Powicke, F.M. *King Henry III and the Lord Edward.* 2 vols. 2nd ed. Oxford, 1947.

Snellgrove, H.S. *The Lusignans in England 1247–58.* New Mexico: University New Mexico Publications in History, No. 2, 1950.

Wood, M.A.E., ed. *Letters of Royal and Illustrious Ladies of Great Britain from the beginning of 12th century to close of reign of Queen Mary.* 3 vols. London, 1846.

COLLECTIONS:

A collection of Eleanor of Provence's letters is to be found in *Ancient Correspondence* (S.C.1) in P.R.0., London.

Margaret E. Lynch, M.A.,
Lancaster, England

Eleanor of Saxe-Eisenach (1662–1696)

*Margravine of Ansbach. Born Eleanor Erdmuthe Louise on April 13, 1662; died on September 19, 1696; daughter of John George (b. 1634), duke of Saxe-Eisenach, and Johannette of Sayn-Wittgenstein (b. 1632); married John Frederick, margrave of Ansbach, on November 14, 1681; children: *Caroline of Ansbach (1683–1737, who married George II, king of England).*

Eleanor of Sicily (d. 1375)

*Queen of Aragon. Name variations: Leonor of Sicily. Died in 1375; became third wife of Pedro IV also known as Peter IV the Ceremonious (b. 1319), king of Aragon (r. 1336–1387), around 1349; children: Juan also known as John I the Hunter (b. 1350), king of Sicily and Aragon (r. 1387–1395); *Constance of Aragon (c. 1350–?); Martin I the Humane, king of Aragon (r. 1395–1410); *Eleanor of Aragon (1358–1382).*

Eleanor of Solms-Hohensolms-Lich (1871–1937)

Grand duchess of Hesse-Darmstadt. Born on September 17, 1871, in Lich, Germany; died in an airplane crash on November 16, 1937, in Steene, Belgium; married Ernest, grand duke of Hesse-Darmstadt; children: George and Louis.

Eleanor of Woodstock (1318–1355)

*English princess and duchess of Guelders. Name variations: Eleanor Plantagenet. Born on June 18, 1318, in Woodstock, Oxfordshire, England; died on April 22, 1355, in Deventer, Netherlands; daughter of *Isabella of France (1296–1358) and Edward II (1284–1327), king of England (r. 1307–1327); married Renaud also known as Rainald or Reginald II the Black Haired, duke of Guelders (also known as count of Gelderland), in May 1332 (died 1343); children: Renaud III of Guelders (b. 1334); Edward of Guelders (b. 1336). Renaud's first wife was *Sophia of Malines (d. 1329).*

Eleanor Plantagenet (1264–1297), queen of Aragon.

See Eleanor of Castile (1241–1290) for sidebar.

Eleanor Plantagenet (c. 1318–1372)

*Countess of Arundel. Name variations: Eleanor Beaumont; Eleanor Fitzalan. Born between 1311 and 1318 at Grosmont Castle, Gwent, Wales; died on November 11, 1372, at Arundel Castle, East Sussex, England; daughter of Henry Plantagenet, 3rd earl of Lancaster, and *Maud Chaworth (1282–c. 1322); married John Beaumont, 2nd baron Beaumont; married Richard Fitzalan, 8th earl of Arundel, in 1345; children: (first marriage) Henry Beaumont, 3rd baron Beaumont; (second marriage) Richard Fitzalan, 9th earl of Arundel; *Joan Fitzalan (d. 1419); John Fitzalan; *Alice Fitzalan (1352–1416); Thomas Fitzalan, archbishop of Canterbury.*

Eleanor Stewart (1427–1496).

See Joan Beaufort (c. 1410–1445) for sidebar.

Eleanor Tellez de Meneses (c. 1350–1386).

See Leonora Telles.

Eleanor Trastamara (d. 1415).

See Joanna of Navarre for sidebar.

Eleanora.

Variant of Leonora.

Eleanora Christina (1621–1698).
See Ulfeldt, Leonora Christina.

Eleanora of Reuss (1860–1917)
Queen of Bulgaria. Name variations: Eleanor Reuss. Born on August 22, 1860; died on September 12, 1917; daughter of Henry IV (b. 1821), prince Reuss of Köstritz; became second wife of Ferdinand I (1861–1948), king of Bulgaria (r. 1887–1918, abdicated), on February 28, 1908.

Electress Palatine, Elizabeth (1596–1662).
See Elizabeth of Bohemia.

Elek-Schacherer, Ilona (1907–1988).
See Mayer, Helene for sidebar on Ilona Schacherer-Elek.

Elen.
Variant of Ellen or Helen.

Elena.
Variant of Helen.

Elena (b. 1963)
Princess of Spain and duchess of Lugo. Name variations: Elena Bourbon; Helen. Born Elena Maria Isabela Dominica de los Silo on December 20, 1963, at Nuestra Señora de Loreto Clinic, Madrid, Spain; daughter of *Sophia of Greece (1938—) and Juan Carlos I (b. 1938), king of Spain (r. 1975—); married Jaime de Maricharlar y de Sáenzde, on March 18, 1995.

Elena Glinski (c. 1506–1538).
See Glinski, Elena.

Elena of Montenegro (1873–1952)
Queen of Italy. Name variations: Helena of Italy; Helen of Montenegro; Helena of Montenegro; Helen Petrovitch-Njegos or Petrovich-Njegosh. Born on January 8, 1873; died in 1952; daughter of Queen *Milena (1847–1923) and Nicholas (b. 1841), king of Montenegro (r. 1910–1918); married Victor Emmanuel III (1869–1947), king of Italy (r. 1900–1946, abdicated), on October 24, 1896; children: *Yolanda Margherita (b. 1901); Umberto II (1904–1983), king of Italy (r. 1946); *Mafalda of Hesse (1902–1944, who married Philip of Hesse); *Giovanna of Italy (b. 1907, who married Boris III, king of Bulgaria); Maria (b. 1914).

Elenora.
Variant of Eleanor.

Eleonor.
Variant of Eleanor.

Eleonora I Gonzaga (1598–1655).
See Gonzaga, Eleonora I.

Eleonora II Gonzaga (1628–1686).
See Gonzaga, Eleonora II.

Eleonora of Austria (1534–1594)
Duchess of Mantua. Name variations: Eleonora Gonzaga. Born on November 2, 1534, in Vienna; died on August 5, 1594, in Mantua; daughter of Ferdinand I, Holy Roman emperor (r. 1558–1564), and *Anna of Bohemia and Hungary (1503–1547); sister of *Elizabeth of Habsburg (d. 1545), *Catherine of Habsburg (1533–1572), and Maximilian II (1527–1576), Holy Roman emperor (r. 1564–1576); married Guglielmo Gonzaga (1538–1587), 3rd duke of Mantua (r.

Elena of Monte-negro

1550–1587), duke of Monferrato, in 1561; children: Vincenzo I (1562–1612), 4th duke of Mantua (r. 1587–1612); *Margherita Gonzaga (1564–1618); *Anna Caterina Gonzaga (1566–1621). The deeply religious Eleonora of Austria, daughter of the Holy Roman emperor, married Guglielmo Gonzaga and had three children.

Eleonora of Este.
See Este, Eleonora d'.

Eleonora of Toledo.
See Medici, Eleonora de.

Eleonore.
Variant of Eleanor or Eleanora.

Elfgifu (c. 914–?)
West Saxon princess. *Name variations: Aelfgifu or Ælfgifu. Born around 914; daughter of Edward I the Elder (c. 870–924), king of the English (r. 899–924), and *Elflaed (d. 920); possibly married Conrad, king of Burgundy (some sources cite Boleslav II the Pious, duke of Bohemia); children: (if Boleslav) possibly Boleslav III, duke of Bohemia; (if Boleslav) Jaromir Premysl, duke of Bohemia. Boleslav's second wife was *Hemma of Bohemia (c. 930–c. 1005).*

Elfgifu (d. 944)
Queen of the English. *Name variations: Aelfgifu or Ælfgifu; Saint Aelfgifu. Died in 944; became first wife of Edmund I the Magnificent (921–946), king of the English (r. 939–946), before 940; children: Edwy also known as Eadwig (c. 940–959), king of the English (r. 955–959); Edgar (944–975), king of the English (r. 959–975); and a daughter (name unknown, who married Baldwin, count of Hesdin).*

Elfgifu (d. 959)
Anglo-Saxon queen. *Name variations: Aelfgifu; Elgiva. Died in September 959 in Gloucester, Gloucestershire, England; daughter of Aethelgifu also spelled Ethelgifu; married Edwy also known as Eadwig (c. 940–959), king of the English (r. 955–959), around 955 (marriage annulled).*

Because of their blood kinship, Elfgifu was separated from her husband King Eadwig by proclamation of Archbishop Odo, a Norman prelate and noble whose half-brother was William I the Conqueror. In untrustworthy accounts of monastic legends, Elfgifu and her mother **Ethelgifu** became the brunt of cruelties imposed by Odo. Elfgifu has often been historically confused with her mother.

Elfgifu (c. 963–1002), queen of the English.
See Emma of Normandy for sidebar.

Elfgifu (c. 997–?)
West Saxon princess and countess of Northumberland. *Born around 997; daughter of *Elfgifu (c. 963–1002) and Aethelred or Ethelred II the Unready (c. 968–1016), king of the English (r. 979–1013, deposed, 1014–1016); married Uchtred, earl of Northumberland (r. around 965–1018); children: *Edith (fl. 1040, who married the brother of Duncan I, king of Scotland).*

Elfgifu of Aelfhelm (c. 1000–1044).
See Elfgifu of Northampton.

Elfgifu of Northampton (c. 1000–1044)
Regent of Norway. *Name variations: Aelfgifu, Aelgifu, Eligifu, Alfifa, Aelfgifu of Aelfhelm, Aelfgifu of Northumbria; Aelfgiva of Northampton. Born around 1000 (some sources cite 996) in Northamptonshire, England; died on December 31, 1044, in England; daughter of Earl Elfheim and Wulfrun of Northamptonshire; mistress and probably wife of Cnut II also known as Canute I the Great (c. 995/998–1035), later king of England (r. 1016–1035), Denmark (r. 1019–1035), and Norway (r. 1028–1035); children: Sven also known as Sweyn (c. 1015–1036), king of Norway (r. 1030–1035); Harald or Harold I Harefoot (c. 1015–1040), king of England (r. 1036–1039 or 1037–1040).*

Elfgifu was born into a noble Saxon family of Northamptonshire during a period of great upheaval in English history. Her parents were supporters of King Olaf Haraldson the Stout of Norway, who had invaded England with an army to try to win its crown. Olaf met the young Elfgifu and the two fell in love. Elfgifu became his mistress and reigned with Olaf until another invader, Canute I the Great of Denmark, kidnapped her in 1013, making her his mistress. Elfgifu reigned with Canute over England, Denmark, and eventually Norway, as he conquered that land as well.

Canute's marriage to Elfgifu was after the Danish custom and not one sanctioned within the Christian church; together they had two sons, Harald Harefoot and Sweyn. In July 1017, as a means of securing his claim to the English throne, Canute married *Emma of Normandy, daughter of the Saxon royal family and widow of Ethelred the Unready. A precondition for the union was that the sons of their marriage would stand in line for the English throne before Elfgifu's sons or Emma's sons by Ethelred.

But Canute apparently trusted Elfgifu politically much more than Emma; he appointed her regent of Norway around 1030 and sent her and their young son Sweyn (whom he had named Norway's future king) to enforce the laws and collect the taxes in Norway and Denmark. Elfgifu was a far from popular or benevolent ruler; she instigated harsh laws and severe punishments for lawbreakers and those disloyal to herself or Canute.

Elfgifu managed to remain in power until 1035, when word reached Norway that Canute had died. Aware that her power base was gone, Elfgifu's enemies overthrew her government and forced her to flee to England in 1036. Ironically, the leader of the overthrow was the son of her previous lover, Olaf of Norway. Elfgifu did not retire from political life in England; instead, she conducted a successful campaign to popularize her other son, Harald Harefoot, as a contender for the kingship.

SOURCES:

Garmonsway, G.N. *Canute and His Empire.* University College Press, 1964.

Larson, Laurence Marcellus. *Canute the Great, c. 995–1035, and the Rise of Danish Imperialism During the Viking Age.* Putnam, 1912.

Loyn, H.R. *The Vikings in Britain.* St. Martin's Press, 1977.

Laura York,
freelance writer in medieval and women's history,
Riverside, California

Elfgifu of Northumbria (c. 1000–1044).

See Elfgifu of Northampton.

Elflaed (d. 714)

Anglo-Saxon abbess of Whitby, the pre-eminent center of learning in Anglo-Saxon England. Name variations: Aelflaed; Aelfled; Aelfflaed; Elfleda; Elflaed; Aelfleda of Whitby; Elfleda of Whitby. Born in Northumbria, date unknown; died in 713 or 714; daughter of Oswin also known as Oswio or Oswy (612?–670), king of Northumbria, and Eanfleda

*(626–?); granddaughter of Ethelberga of Northumbria (d. 647); great-granddaughter of *Bertha of Kent.*

Elflaed was born into an early English ruling family, the daughter of *Eanfleda and Oswy, king of Northumbria, and granddaughter of Edwin and *Ethelberga of Northumbria. Eanfleda was a deeply pious Christian who worked hard to ensure that the people of Northumbria adopted Christian beliefs and practices. Her piety influenced her daughter Elflaed, who felt called to a religious life and was allowed to enter a convent instead of making a politically expedient marriage, the fate of most royal daughters. Joining the convent of Whitby, Elflaed received instruction and spiritual guidance from the venerable abbess *Hilda of Whitby, one of England's most highly educated women.

Elflaed soon became renowned as a founder of religious establishments and for her generous acts of charity. She is remembered as the founder of the first church at Canterbury, one of England's most sacred places. Honored by the nuns at Whitby when she was chosen to succeed as abbess upon Hilda's death on November 17, 680, Elflaed shared the rule with her mother Eanfleda.

A still extant letter of Elflaed's, preserved in the Boniface Correspondence, is written in Latin and addressed to **Adola**, abbess of Pfalzel, near Trier. From this, scholars observe that Elflaed wrote a very elaborate Latin. One modern scholar asserts that in the middle years of the 7th century Whitby was "the preeminent center of learning in Anglo-Saxon England."

Laura York,
freelance writer in medieval and women's history,
Riverside, California

Elflaed (d. 920)

Queen of the English. Name variations: Aelflaed; Aelflaeda; Aelfflaed; Ælfflaed; Elflaeda. Died in 920; interred at Winchester Cathedral, London; daughter of Ethelhelm, archbishop of Canterbury, and Elswitha; married Edward I the Elder (c. 870–924), king of the English (r. 899–924); children: Elfweard, king of the English (d. 924); *Edflaed* (c. 900–?, became a nun); *Edgifu* (902–951); Edwin (drowned in 933); *Elflaed* (c. 905–c. 963); *Ethelflaeda* (became a nun at Romsey); Ethelhild (son); *Edhild* (d. 946); *Edgitha* (c. 912–946); *Elfgifu* (c. 914–?).

Elflaed (c. 905–c. 963)

English princess. Born around 905; died around 963 in Winchester, England; interred at Wilton Abbey,

*Wiltshire; daughter of Edward I the Elder (c. 870–924), king of the English (r. 899–924), and *Elflaed (d. 920). Princess Elflaed became a nun at Winchester.*

Elflaed (fl. 1030)

*Queen of Scotland. Name variations: Aelflaed of Northumbria; Sybil. Flourished around 1030; daughter of Ealred, earl of Northumberland, and **Efflaed of Bernicia** (daughter of Ealdred of Bernicia, lord of Bamburgh); cousin of Siward, earl of Northumberland; married Duncan I (c. 1001–1040), king of Scots (r. 1034–1040), around 1030; children: Malcolm III Canmore (1031–1093), king of Scots (r. 1057–1093); Donalbane or Donald III (c. 1033–1099), king of Scots (r. 1093–1098); Maelmuir Dunkeld (b. around 1035).*

Elfleda.

Variant of Elflaed.

Elfleda or Elflida (869–918).

See Ethelflaed, Lady of the Mercians.

Elfrida (c. 945–c. 1000).

See Elfthrith.

Elfthrith (fl. 7th c.)

English abbess and scholar. Name variations: Aelfthrith; Aelfthryth; Aethelfryth; Elfthryth; Ethelfryth. Flourished in the 7th century.

Elfthrith was a renowned English scholar and abbess. Like the first monasteries, early convents were not only places of cloistered worship and pious contemplation, but also centers of learning and manuscript production. Elfthrith was one of many abbesses of the early Middle Ages who were highly educated and influential outside their convents. Under her direction, the Abbey of Repton became renowned for the education of its nuns and for the superior schooling given there to lay pupils.

Laura York,
freelance writer in medieval and women's history,
Riverside, California

Elfthrith (d. 929)

*Countess of Flanders. Name variations: Aelfthrith; Aelfthryth; Aethelfryth; Ælfthryth; Aefthryth; Efthryth; (Lat.) Eltrudis. Birth date unknown; died on June 7, 929, in Flanders; buried at St. Peter's Abbey, in Ghent, Flanders, Belgium; daughter of Alfred the Great (848–c. 900), king of the English (r. 871–899) and *Elswitha (d. 902); sister of *Ethelflaed*

(869–918); married Baldwin II (d. 918), count of Flanders (r. 878–918), before 900; children: Arnolph also known as Arnulf I (d. 965), count of Flanders (r. 918–950, 961–964); Adelulf, count of Boulogne; and two daughters (names unknown).

Elfthrith (c. 945–1002)

Anglo-Saxon queen. Name variations: Aelfthrith, Aelfthryth, Aethelfryth, Elfthryth, Ethelfryth, or Elfrida. Born about 945 at Lydford Castle, Devon, England; died on November 17, 1002, at Wherwell Abbey, Hampshire; interred at Wherwell Abbey; daughter of Ordgar (ealdorman of Devon); married Ethelwald (ealdorman of the East Anglians), around 962; after his death, became second wife of Eadgar or Edgar (944–975), king of the English (r. 959–975), in 965; children: (first marriage) Edmund (b. around 965); Ethelflaeda (c. 963–c. 1016, an abbess at Romsey); (second marriage) Edmund (d. 971); Aethelred or Ethelred II the Unready (968–1016), king of the English (r. 979–1016, who married Emma of Normandy).

It is said that Elfthrith caused the murder of her stepson Edward II the Martyr, king of England, at Corfe in 978, in order to secure the election of her son Ethelred II the Unready to the throne of England. Ethelred married *Emma of Normandy. Elfthrith became a nun in 986.

Elfthryth.

Variant of Elfthrith.

Elfwyn (c. 882–?).

See Ethelflaed for sidebar.

Elgar, Alice (1848–1920)

British author and wife of Sir Edward Elgar (1857–1934), who served as his inspiration, critic, literary advisor, and music scribe. Name variations: Lady Alice Roberts Elgar; Lady Caroline Alice Elgar; Caroline Alice Roberts. Born Caroline Alice Roberts on October 9, 1848, in the Residency at Bhooj (now Gujerat), India; died in London on April 7, 1920; daughter of Major-General Sir Henry Gee Roberts and Julia Maria (Raikes) Roberts; had three brothers; married Edward Elgar, in 1889; children: daughter, Carice Elgar (b. 1890).

The music of England's greatest composer, Sir Edward Elgar, was brought to light largely due to the support of his wife, Lady Alice. Born in India as the only daughter of Major-General Sir Henry Gee Roberts, Alice Roberts grew up in the English countryside after the retirement of her father, a hero of the Sepoy Mutiny and the Sikh Wars. Her mother, **Julia Raikes Roberts**, was born into a family that counted as its most distinguished member Julia's grandfather Robert Raikes, founder of Sunday Schools. By early 1880s, when the second of Alice's three brothers died (one had died in infancy), it became clear that Alice would remain with her elderly mother at the Georgian family home of Hazeldine House in Redmarley d'Abitot, southeastern Worcestershire.

Short in stature, Alice Roberts had china-blue eyes and light-brown hair. Her assured manner and quiet voice marked her as a lady of England's rural gentry, and she gave the impression of possessing considerable confidence and inner strength. Intellectually curious, she was first drawn to geology but developed other interests as well, mastering several foreign languages, particularly German. An aspiring author, she penned both a long poem (*Isabel Trevithoe*, 1879) and a novel (*Marchcroft Manor*, 1882), both of which were published in London under her full name Caroline Alice Roberts.

Alice also had a love of music, and it was this passion which would cause a woman regarded by family and friends alike as a guaranteed "spinster" to meet and eventually marry a man destined to become a great composer. Edward William Elgar was born on June 2, 1857, in Lower Broadheath near Worcester. Starting in 1863, Elgar's father William Henry ran a music shop on High Street in Worcester. By age ten, Edward was composing music. He won praise for his piano improvisations as a child, but besides violin lessons from a local teacher (and more advanced violin instruction some years later in London) he had little formal musical education. Plans for studying at the Leipzig Conservatory had to be abandoned for lack of funds. By age 16, Elgar was making his living as a freelance musician, his profession for the rest of his life.

He worked in and around Worcester as the organist at St. George's Roman Catholic Church (his mother **Ann Elgar** was Roman Catholic, and Elgar was raised in that faith) as well as playing the violin at the Worcester Philharmonic and other ensembles. He also coached and conducted the staff ensemble of the Powick County Lunatic Asylum, and in his spare hours played bassoon in a local wind quintet. Extra money was earned teaching private violin pupils. Edward was an excellent violinist and conductor, whose reputation in time spread beyond Worcester, and by 1882 he was performing in an orchestra in

Alice Elgar

Birmingham. He composed in his spare hours, and some of his orchestral compositions began to be performed locally; on one occasion, a piece of his received a public performance in London. As he approached the age of 30, however, Edward Elgar remained unknown and had accomplished nothing that could make the world at large take notice of any extraordinary talents.

In October 1886, Alice Roberts began to take violin lessons from Edward Elgar. She was almost nine years older than her teacher and appeared destined to remain unmarried. Underneath her Victorian exterior was a passionate soul, and she recognized similar feelings hidden within the reserved Elgar. After the death of her mother in 1887, Alice moved to a furnished room at Malvern Link so as to be nearer to her violin teacher. Several years earlier, Edward had fallen in love with **Helen Weaver**, an aspiring musician who was the daughter of a Worcester tradesman. Edward and Helen had briefly visited Germany together, and in 1883 they had become engaged. But soon the hopes for a permanent union evaporated, and a disappointed Edward overcame his sorrow in work. The appearance of Alice Roberts several years later changed his life.

By September 1888, Edward and Alice were engaged. His own family's disappointment that his fiancée was Anglican was more than matched by that of Alice's cousins and aunts, who were almost universally disapproving of the man she had chosen: a Roman Catholic, without financial means, often in delicate health with ailments of apparently psychosomatic origin, and with no definite prospects of success in his chosen field of music. Edward's family, being "in trade," was also regarded by Alice's as totally unsuitable for a bride-to-be from the rural gentry whose father had been a highly decorated general. Their marriage, at Brompton Oratory on May 8, 1889, was marked by a distinct lack of support from both families. Even before she married him, Alice Elgar was convinced that her husband was a potential genius, that he would soon be recognized as one of England's greatest musical creators, and that her task was to help him achieve the full potentialities of his God-given talents. Edward produced a musical setting of one of Alice's poems, "The Wind at Dawn." Whereas until now his compositions had been undistinguished, revealing little of a personal style, in the finale of this song he composed a work that revealed "an assurance that was absolutely new" in his music. That same year, 1888, Elgar composed *Salut d'amour* (*Liebesgruss*) for violin and piano, published as his Opus 12. Dedicated to Alice Roberts, this heartfelt miniature went on to become a worldwide bestseller for many decades. Most of the profits from this went to the publisher, Schott & Co., which paid its commercially naive composer a trifle in royalties.

Calling his new bride "Braut" or Alice, Elgar found in her what Michael Kennedy has called a "wife, mother, friend, mentor, and spur." It soon became apparent that Elgar's confidence, always easily bruised, was now receiving daily doses of support, and his music showed the benefits. The couple, deeply in love, artistically and personally compatible, easily ignored the gossip of the narrow-minded gentry of late Victorian Worcestershire, which regarded theirs as an unsuitable match between a patrician lady of "a certain age" who had married a mere shopkeeper's son of the lower-middle class whose social skills were suspect and who had possibly married to live off of his wife's private income.

After their wedding, Alice was determined that her husband—until now largely isolated from the fresh currents of modern musical life—should be fully exposed to the new post-Wagnerian musical scene. This would only be possible if they lived in London, to which they moved, residing in Norwood close to the Crystal Palace and its plenitude of orchestral concerts. Alice's private income was not sufficient to provide total leisure (Edward had hoped to attract a few violin students, but none appeared), but London's intellectual stimulation, and the newfound luxury of some leisure time kindled his creative energies, and he worked on several large-scale musical projects. Although the birth of a daughter, **Carice Elgar**, in August 1890 also brought joy, their stay in London was in many ways a disappointment for the Elgars. In June 1891, the family returned to the English countryside, at Malvern. Financially hard-pressed, Elgar had to resume violin teaching, which he compared to turning a grindstone with a dislocated shoulder.

Alice refused to be discouraged by a temporary setback. While in London, Edward had composed his first major orchestral work, the exuberant concert overture *Froissart,* which was accepted for publication by Novello, one of London's leading music publishers. Certain of his future, Alice prodded her husband to embark on large-scale projects, including *The Black Knight,* a choral symphony which became Elgar's first successful choral work. Other successful works, *The Light of Life, King Olaf,* and *Caractacus,* followed, all of them compositions that proved to be popular with both choral societies and audiences, and all the result of the artistic collaboration between husband and wife.

Alice contributed directly to Edward's artistic productivity on several occasions, and provided him with verse for the following works: *Scenes from the Bavarian Highlands, O Happy Eyes, Fly, Singing Bird* and *The Snow,* the latter two being excerpts from her long poem *Isabel Trevithoe.* She also provided one of the poems, *In Haven (Capri),* for Edward's orchestral song cycle, *Sea Pictures,* which received an enthusiastic reception at its 1899 premiere with *Clara Butt as the soloist. After 1900, Alice Elgar made only occasional literary contributions for her husband's compositions, as when she provided the text for a carol, *A Christmas Greeting,* which received its first performance at Hereford Cathedral on New Year's Day, 1908.

Easily discouraged, Edward sometimes found himself unable to compose while in "the slough of despond." On these occasions, when he vowed to abandon the career of musical composition, Alice provided the encouragement to strengthen his own resolve. She helped him with the arduous task of copying his manuscripts and took care of all mundane distractions to leave him to his composing. Long before he sent a manuscript off to his publishers, Alice had listened to it. Once, Edward remembered, after he had played on the piano some of his day's compositional achievement, she nodded her head appreciatively "except over one passage, at which she sat up rather grimly, I thought. However, I went to bed leaving it as it was; but I got up as soon as it was light and went down to look over what I had written. I found it as I had left it, except that there was a little piece of paper, pinned over the offending bars, on which was written 'All of it is beautiful and just right, except this ending. Don't you think, dear Edward, that this end is just a little. . . ?' Well . . . I scrapped that end." Where Alice believed the achievement of musical excellence was at stake, all else was subordinated to this ultimate goal, even if it impacted their daughter Carice, who was sent off to boarding school at an early age so as to keep the Elgar home environment calm and quiet for composing.

Realizing that her husband's composing was stimulated by the presence of others, particularly intelligent, attractive women younger than she, Alice Elgar saw to it that his friendships with such individuals flourished. Edward was a quintessential Victorian gentleman, and there is no evidence that these relationships were anything but Platonic. The most important of these friendships was with the musician **Alice Stuart-Wortley** (1862–1936, Lady Stuart of Wortley), the daughter of the noted painter Sir John Everett Millais. In his extensive correspondence of more than three decades with her, which has been published, Edward called the other Alice in his life the "Windflower," and there is little doubt that some of his most beautiful music was inspired by his relationship with her. She was closely linked with the composition of his Violin Concerto, and it was with her playing in mind (she was a pianist of considerable ability) that Elgar began sketches for a never completed Piano Concerto. Alice Elgar approved of the decades-long friendship. When she wrote to Lady Stuart Wortley, Alice Elgar invariably used the salutation "My dearest Namesake."

Another younger woman brought into Edward's world by Lady Elgar was **Dora Penny** (1874–1964), daughter of Reverend Alfred Penny, rector of Wolverhampton. Dora was employed by Lady Elgar as keeper of Edward's archives starting in the mid-1890s, and Alice encouraged the influence of Dora's youthful charm on the often moody composer, who enjoyed bicycle riding with Dora as well as listening to her piano improvisations. Naming her after a character in Mozart's opera *Così fan tutte*, Edward incorporated a character sketch of "Dorabella" in his first great orchestral score, the *Enigma Variations*.

Other women who inspired Elgar in his creative work were the sisters **Florence** and **Winifred Norbury**. The sisters, both of whom were musicians as well as ardent cyclists and tennis players, lived near the Elgar summer home in the Malvern Hills. Winifred Norbury (1861–1938), who often assisted Elgar with checking proofs of his musical manuscripts, was sketched as the "W.N." section of the *Enigma Variations*, although the composer asserted that it was not Winifred but both sisters' home, Sherridge, that had been the real subject of his work.

Lady Elgar worked tirelessly to shore up her husband's morale when it flagged, which it did on numerous occasions even after he achieved fame in 1899 with the premiere performance of the *Enigma Variations*. He often threatened to end his life, and his sense of inferiority was great. In 1897, already well-regarded in musical circles, he sent a card on the morning of a formal luncheon party, the invitation to which he had previously accepted: "You would not wish your board to be disgraced by the presence of a piano-tuner's son and his wife."

Never doubting her husband's supremacy as an artist, Alice kept a diary that remains a key source of information on her unyielding belief in his ultimate recognition. The scant material rewards of his work during the first 15 years of their marriage, pitifully tiny royalty payments, and debts incurred from the Elgars' modest savings in order to stage expensive choral works never dampened her enthusiasm. The conferring of a knighthood on Edward in 1904, transforming Alice Roberts Elgar into Lady Elgar, came after long years of struggle. Frank Schuster, one of Elgar's wealthy champions and patrons, marveled at her skills as an "indefatigable hostess and *marvelous* manager."

By the end of the First World War, the Elgars both sensed that the traditional world they had known had died in the carnage that had toppled dynasties, destroyed millions of lives and crushed the optimistic ideals of previous centuries. Edward composed a number of masterpieces during and immediately after the great conflict. These included *The Spirit of England,* a "grand and melancholy" choral composition, as well as a trio of superb chamber works (a violin sonata, a string quartet, and a piano quintet). The greatest of these autumnal works, the Cello Concerto, was composed over the period of a few months in mid-1919. Although the premiere performance was technically inadequate, critics recognized the work for the great masterpiece it is. Lady Elgar, who considered the concerto to be "a flawless work," fumed about both the conductor and his players, writing in her diary how "absolutely furious" she was with the musicians' slipshod work, including the mediocre and "shameful" quality of their rehearsals. She faithfully attended not only performances and rehearsals, but recordings of his music, which he conducted at the studios of the Gramophone Company.

By the end of 1919, Lady Elgar's health was in a visible state of decline, but she struggled to remain active. Friends noticed her fragile appearance, but in late February 1920 she summoned the energy to accompany Edward to another recording session. Fred Gaisberg, the recording manager, noted how much "motherly kindness radiated from her, and it was easy to see how much Sir Edward . . . owed to her good advice and solicitous care."

By March 26, 1920, Sir Edward himself was making notations in the diary Alice had kept for more than three decades. The entry of April 6 notes, "My darling—in great distress—cd. not understand her words—very, very painful." The next day's entry was brief and tragic: "My darling sinking . . . Sinking all day & died in my arms at 6:10 pm."

Stunned by his loss, Edward allowed his daughter Carice and close friend Frank Schuster to make the funeral arrangements. On April 10, 1920, Lady Elgar was buried in the graveyard of St. Wulstan's Catholic Church, Little Malvern, in the shadow of the hills she had known since her childhood. In the tiny church, Edward, appearing "very grey, old, and grief-stricken," listened to musician friends perform the *Piacevole* movement from one of his most recent works, the string quartet, music that Lady Elgar had instantly warmed to, describing it as "gracious and lovable." In the next months, he wrote friends: "All I have done was owing to her and I am at present a sad & broken man."

Sir Edward Elgar outlived his wife by almost 14 years, dying in February 1934, but he never again composed a musical work of great significance. Only 62 when Lady Elgar died, he enjoyed good health until the last few months of his life, but it quickly became clear that his energies were no longer focused on composing. Instead, he traveled, spent time at the races and with his dogs (Alice Elgar had been "undoggy," and her widower now reverted to the love of dogs that had marked his bachelor years), occasionally conducted, and made a series of important recordings of his major compositions. Not until the early 1930s, when close friend George Bernard Shaw prodded him to write a third symphony, did Elgar's creative spark appear to be rekindled. But it was too late, and neither the symphony nor a projected opera and other major works were ever completed.

Thanks largely to the sacrifices and interventions of his wife between 1889 and 1919, Edward Elgar created a series of great works of orchestral music that remain centerpieces of the late Romantic repertory. These would never have been composed without Alice Elgar. Without her, there might never have been the Pomp and Circumstance Marches, and the immortal tune contained within the first of the series of five, which, sung as "Land of Hope and Glory," has accompanied millions of graduates from high schools and universities in many parts of the world. One evening in 1914, she had read aloud to him passages from some of her own writings. In her diary that night Lady Elgar noted some regrets at her long-abandoned literary ambitions, but concluded her entry with the sentence: "The care of a genius is enough of a life work for any woman."

SOURCES:

Anderson, Robert. *Elgar.* NY: Schirmer Books, 1993.

"Death of Lady Elgar," in *The Times* [London]. April 8, 1920, p. 12.

Howes, Frank. *The English Musical Renaissance.* NY: Stein and Day, 1966.

Kennedy, Michael. *Portrait of Elgar.* London: Oxford University Press, 1968.

Matthew-Walker, Robert. "Elgar's Unfinished Masterpieces," in *Musical Opinion.* Vol. 120, no. 1410. Summer 1997, pp. 18–21.

Mitchell, Sally, ed. *Victorian Britain: An Encyclopedia.* New York and London: Garland, 1988.

Monk, Raymond, ed. *Elgar Studies.* Aldershot, Hants.: Scolar Press, 1990.

Moore, Jerrold Northrop. *Edward Elgar: A Creative Life.* Oxford: Oxford University Press, 1984.

———. *Edward Elgar: The Windflower Letters. Correspondence with Alice Caroline Stuart Wortley and her Family.* Oxford: Clarendon Press, 1989.

Pirie, P.J. "The Personality of Elgar," in *Music and Musicians.* Vol. 21, no. 8. April 1973, pp. 32–36.

Powell, Dora M. Penny. *Edward Elgar: Memories of a Variation.* 3rd rev. ed. London: Methuen, 1949.

Redwood, Christopher, ed. *An Elgar Companion.* Ashbourne, Derbyshire: Sequoia Publishing/ Moorland, 1982.

Roberts, Caroline Alice. *Marchcroft Manor: A Novel*. 2 vols. London: Remington, 1882.

Rushton, Julian. "Edward Elgar," in *Music and Musicians*. Vol. 21, no. 6. February 1974, pp. 18–21.

Young, Percy M. *Alice Elgar: Enigma of a Victorian Lady*. London: Dobson, 1978.

John Haag,
Assistant Professor of History,
University of Georgia, Athens, Georgia

Elgiva.

Variant of Elfgifu.

Elgiva (fl. 1020)

Queen of England. Name variations: Algiva. Married Harold I Harefoot (c. 1015–1040), king of England (r. 1036–1040); children: Elfwin, monk at St. Foi Aquitaine.

Elias, Rosalind (1930—)

American mezzo-soprano. Born on March 13, 1930, in Lowell, Massachusetts; studied at the New England Conservatory, Boston, and at the Academia di Santa Cecilia, Rome.

Debuted at the Metropolitan Opera (1954); sang the role of Erika in the premiere of Samuel Barber-Gian Carlo Menotti's Vanessa *(1958).*

American born and almost completely American trained, Rosalind Elias sang over 45 roles at the Met. She has performed widely in Europe, including appearances at Glyndebourne and in South America. Elias was a part of Leonard Bernstein's traveling casts. She also concertized widely and made many recordings for RCA. Despite a long career, Elias remained best known for her role as Erika in *Vanessa*, the Samuel Barber-Gian Carlo Menotti opera. Never a superstar, she was a reliable, hard-working artist, who was always available for roles of any size.

John Haag,
Athens, Georgia

Eligifu.

Variant of Elfgifu.

Eling Soong (1890–1973).

See Song Ailing in entry titled The Song Sisters.

Elinor.

Variant of Eleanor.

Elion, Gertrude B. (1918–1999)

American biochemist, pharmacologist, and Nobel laureate who developed drugs for treatment of leukemia and rejection of transplanted organs and laid the groundwork for the development of AZT in the fight against AIDS. Pronunciation: ELL-EE-un. Born Gertrude Belle Elion in New York, New York, on January 23, 1918; died at her home in Chapel Hill, North Carolina, on February 21, 1999; daughter of Bertha (Cohen) Elion and Robert Elion (a dentist); granted A.B., Hunter College, 1937; M.S.C., New York University, 1941; D.Sc., George Washington University, 1969; D.M.S., Brown University, 1969; never married; no children.

Awards: Garvan Medal, American Chemical Society (1968); honorary D.Sc., University of Michigan (1969); honorary D.Sc., Columbia University (1969); Judd Award, Sloan-Kettering Institute (1983); Distinguished Chemist Award (1985); Bruce F. Cain Award, American Association of Cancer Research (1985); Berther Memorial Award, M.D. Anderson (1987); Nobel Prize in Physiology and Medicine with George Hitchings and Sir James Whyte Black (1988); honorary Doctor of Medical Science, Brown University (1989); honorary D.Sc., Ohio State University (1989); honorary D.Sc., State University of North Carolina (1989); Medal of Honor, American Cancer Society (1990); honorary D.Sc., Duke University (1990); honorary D.Sc., University of North Carolina (1990); National Science Medal (1991); honorary D.Sc., McMaster University (1990); National Inventors Hall of Fame (1991); National Women's Hall of Fame (1991); Engineering and Science Hall of Fame (1992); honorary D.Sc., Utah State University (1994).

Death of grandfather (1933); enrolled Hunter College (1934); became nursing assistant, New York Hospital (1937); hired as assistant organic chemist, Denver Chemical Company (1938); became analyst in food chemistry, Quaker Maid Company (1942); worked as researcher in organic chemistry, Johnson and Johnson (1943); worked as assistant research chemist, Burroughs Wellcome (1944); U.S. Food and Drug Administration approved 6-mercaptopurine (1953); synthesized azathioprine (1957); became assistant to the director of the chemotherapy division, Burroughs Wellcome (1963); headed experimental therapy, Burroughs Wellcome (1967); served as adjunct professor of pharmacology, University of North Carolina (1973); served as adjunct professor of pharmacology, Duke University (1973); synthesized acyclovir (1975); retired from Burroughs Wellcome as emeritus scientist (1983); was president of the Association for Cancer Research (1983).

Selected publications: (with G.H. Hitchings) "Antagonists of Nucleic Acid Derivatives; Lactobacillus casei model," in Journal of Biological Chemistry

(Vol. 183, 1950); (with Hitchings and Elvira A. Falco) "Antagonists of Nucleic Acid Derivatives: Reversal Studies with Substances Structurally Related to Thymide," in Journal of Biological Chemistry (Vol. 185, 1950); (with M.E. Balis, G.B. Brown, H.C. Nathan, and Hitchings) "The Effects of 6-mercaptopurine on Lactobacillus casei," in Archives of Biochemistry and Biophysics (Vol. 71, 1957); (with S. Callahan, G. Bieber, Hitchings, and R.W. Rudles) "Experimental, Clinical, and Metabolic Studies of Thiopurines," in Cancer Chemotherapy Reports (Vol. 16, 1962); (with Hitchings) "Chemical Suppression of the Immune Response," in Pharmacological Review (Vol. 15, 1963).

In 1988, Gertrude Elion was awarded the Nobel Prize for Physiology and Medicine. Talent, ingenuity, and down-right stubbornness, account for her success.

Gertrude Elion was born in New York City on January 23, 1918, the daughter of Robert and **Bertha Cohen Elion**. Both parents were very supportive and "very anxious for me to have a career," writes Elion. The death of her grandfather from cancer in 1933 greatly influenced her decision to enter the field of chemistry. Her goal was to relieve the suffering of patients with terminal illness.

In 1937, 19-year-old Elion graduated with a bachelor's degree from Hunter College. Her choice of Hunter was fortuitous. Notes **Sue Rosser**:

> With Elion's strong determination to become a scientist, she would probably have successfully pursued her major at any college, including a coeducational institution; statistics have shown, however, that women's colleges produce proportionately more women scientists than coeducational institutions and that a higher percentage of successful women scientists attended women's colleges.

After graduating, Elion was a nursing assistant at the New York Hospital. In 1938, she joined the Denver Chemical Company as an assistant organic chemist before returning to New York University to take her master's degree in 1940. Elion was rejected by a total of 15 graduate schools when she applied for a laboratory assistantship. As *The New York Times* noted in 1988, she had to "struggle against preconceived notions of what careers were suitable for women." Unable to secure a laboratory assignment, in 1941 Elion took a position teaching chemistry in the New York public-school system, while attending New York University as a part-

time student. Following her graduation with a master's degree, she applied for several laboratory positions. Dr. Charles Frey, who interviewed her, recalled a bright young woman "who wanted to be a great research scientist." He also recalled the disappointment of Elion when all he could offer was a job washing test tubes.

The field of laboratory research had traditionally been a male preserve. With America's entry into World War II, however, a shortage of male researchers resulted. Elion found that positions were suddenly open to women. "It really was the war that gave women opportunities to get in the lab," she said. In 1942, Elion briefly held a position as an analyst in food chemistry with the Quaker Maid Company. The following year, she was hired by Johnson and Johnson as a researcher in organic chemistry. In 1944, she moved to the Burroughs Wellcome Company as a research assistant, where she worked for George Hitchings, doing research into nucleic acids. Far from treating her as an assistant, however, Hitchings considered her a colleague.

Nevertheless, her chosen career was not an easy one. "At the beginning it was a question of whether I'd get married or stay at the company," she commented. "In those days, women couldn't do both." As other professional women discovered, a stigma was attached to marriage. Employers felt that women should be in the home, taking care of their children. Thus, Elion was convinced that she could not marry and pursue a career at the same time. After a period of reflection, she decided to forsake marriage.

Elion felt that her lack of a doctorate might be an impediment to her career. Though she attempted to obtain her Ph.D. by attending night classes at Brooklyn Polytechnic, she withdrew from the program when told she must attend on a full-time basis—a proposition that would seem ludicrous years later. Thus, she achieved justifiable renown without the benefit of a doctorate.

The development of drugs prior to the Second World War had followed the well-worn path established by Paul Ehrlich, the German father of chemotherapy. Chemotherapy is the science of insinuating a poison into the body that attacks the infecting organism, without seriously harming the patient. Ehrlich advocated the unsystematic injection of a multiplicity of drugs into research animals, in order to discover the cure for specific illnesses. Others thought the animal trials were worthless. As Hitchings noted:

> The world of chemotherapy was divided sharply between the screeners and the funda-

mentalists. The screeners were dutifully poisoning infected mice with whatever came in hand or off the shelf. They hoped that if they tested enough compounds, sooner or later they would run across one that did more damage to the infecting organism than to the host. The fundamentalists disdained all this as being devoid of intellectual interest.

In their research, Elion and Hitchings wanted to develop "a middle course that would generate basic information which chemotherapy could then exploit," says Hitchings. The latitude that the research team was given by Burroughs Wellcome, he noted, was invaluable in their quest. "Our orientation was basic research and yet we turned out more drugs than people who were looking for them."

During the 1940s, knowledge of nucleic acids and purines was rudimentary at best, and the double-helical configuration of DNA had yet to be discovered by *Rosalind Franklin. Elion and Hitchings focused their efforts on the cellular synthesis of nucleotides. Bacteria cells, they discovered, do not produce nucleic acid or DNA. Therefore, bacteria cells are incapable of division, except in the presence of certain purines or proteins, and folic acid. Elion and Hitchings postulated that it might be possible to develop a drug that inhibits the rapid division of cells, such as tumors, protozoa, and bacteria. By 1951, the pair had tested over 100 purines. As a result, Elion developed antimetabolite drugs designed to block the enzymes essential for the creation of cellular DNA.

In the early 1950s, Elion's antimetabolites were tested on patients with leukemia at the Sloan-Kettering Institute. It was hoped that the new drug would prevent the growth of white blood cells sufficiently to cause remission. The clinical challenge that the new drug faced was that it might also prevent the growth of red blood cells and prove toxic to the patient. During initial trials, the drug did indeed prove to be toxic. After refinements, however, it performed effectively and safely. Noted Elion, "With 6-mercaptopurine we knew we had to be on the right track." The development of 6-mercaptopurine was one of Elion's first research successes; the drug remains one of a dozen or so used in the treatment of leukemia. In 1953, the U.S. Food and Drug Administration formally approved its use.

In 1957, Elion synthesized azathioprine, a modification of 6-mercaptopurine. The drug proved ineffective in the fight against leukemia, but colleagues at Tufts University discovered that it acted to suppress antibodies produced by

the immune system. Azathioprine proved invaluable in preventing the rejection of transplanted organs. As Paul Calabresi of Brown University noted, azathioprine "was the first immunosuppressive agent that allowed kidney and other transplants." The drug has also been used in the treatment of rheumatoid arthritis, a condition where the body believes itself to be under attack by its own tissue.

As well, Elion developed allopurinol, another modification of 6-mercaptopurine, to suppress enzymes. Her metabolic studies resulted in a new approach in the treatment of gout. The enzyme xanthine oxidase which is necessary for the body to synthesize uric acid was inhibited, and the formation of uric acid retained in the last stages of the metabolic pathway. Allopurinol is extensively used in the treatment of gout, an illness caused by an excessive build-up of uric acid in the joints. It is also employed in chemotherapy, where uric acid build-up is common in the treatment of cancer.

Gertrude B. Elion

Elion and Hitchings' research into antitumoral activity during the 1950s also laid the ground work for the development of Azidothymidine or AZT. The drug proved successful in the treatment of leukemia patients. Subsequently, it was also found to be the only effective drug in the fight against AIDS. Now, AZT is also used in the treatment of systemic lupus, chronic hepatitis, and autoimmune hemolytic anemia.

In the early 1960s, Elion began to focus her research efforts on nucleic acid synthesis in lower primates and contrasted her findings with similar tests done on humans. The research pointed to new ways of controlling infectious disease, by attacking viral DNA and bacteria. The drug pyrimethamine was developed, which is used to control the protozoa that causes malaria. As well, she developed trimethoprim, used to treat AIDS patients who develop pneumocystis carinii, a form of pneumonia which can prove fatal to those with immune-deficiency syndrome.

In 1963, Elion was appointed assistant to the director of the chemotherapy division of Burroughs Wellcome. During the next year, she and her colleagues began research into antiviral drugs. Elion was made head of experimental therapy in 1967. In 1970, Burroughs Wellcome moved their laboratories to North Carolina. Three years later, Elion was appointed adjunct professor of pharmacology at the University of North Carolina. She held the same position at Duke University.

In 1975, Elion and Hitchings synthesized the drug acyclovir, the first effective treatment for herpes. Eight years of clinical trials demonstrated its efficacy in reducing the suffering of patients with herpes encephalitis, shingles, and genital herpes. As well, the information gained from the development of acyclovir suggested new avenues of inquiry into AIDS research.

Elion retired as the head of experimental therapies at Burroughs Wellcome in 1983. She held the title of scientist emeritus and remained a consultant with the company. As well, she served as president of the Association for Cancer Research from 1983 to 1984. She also sat on the National Cancer Advisory Board until 1991.

Gertrude Elion was an acknowledged leader in the field of purine antimetabolites research for treating cancer. In 1988, she shared the Nobel Prize in Physiology and Medicine with George Hitchings, and Sir James Whyte Black. As **Marcia Meldrum** notes, the award recognized:

> Their work in developing drugs for the treatment of many critical diseases. Elion

and Hitchings, long-time collaborators at Burroughs Wellcome Research Laboratories, produced compounds that inhibit DNA synthesis and thus prevent the rapid growth of cancer cells. They then used their understanding of nucleic acid synthesis to develop immunosuppressives and antibiotics.

The Nobel committee acknowledged the multiple contributions made by Elion in the field of therapeutics. But the award was unusual in that it recognized the new drugs that she and Hitchings had created. "Only a few times in the 87-year history of the Nobel Prize has the medical award been granted to researchers who discovered drugs and worked for drug companies," noted *The New York Times*.

Gertrude Elion was only the ninth woman to be awarded the Nobel Prize in its history. Writes Meldrum: "Elion, unlike many other laureates, never expected to win the Nobel Prize. Her selection acknowledged the unheralded but important work of many women scientists whose careers, like her own, were artificially limited by their gender." In her Nobel lecture, entitled "The Purine Path to Chemotherapy," Elion outlined 40 years of research into purines and purine analogues, which led to her discovery of several drugs used in the chemotherapy treatment of various diseases.

The research done by Elion is notable not only for the development of particular drugs, but also for the insight it provided researchers into cellular DNA, and methods discovered to suppress certain pathways that form nucleic acids. Her successful development of various drugs grew out of research that created a better understanding of physiology and cell biochemistry. Her focus on sound research techniques, and her work on basic biochemical and physiological processes have been of incomparable benefit to other medical researchers. As one Nobel official said, "We are still harvesting the fruits of what they determined almost forty years ago." Indeed, as Sue Rosser wrote: "In exploring chemotherapeutic agents, she and her colleagues helped to unlock the mysteries of the interior of the cell. More significantly, she achieved her goal of finding ways to help alleviate human suffering from disease."

In 1991, Elion was honored by the Inventors Hall of Fame for her contribution to pharmacology and medicine, the first woman to be so honored. Her name now stands alongside the likes of Alexander Graham Bell and Thomas Edison. "I'm happy to be the first woman," Elion commented with a smile, "but I doubt I'll be the last." Gertrude Elion held over 40 patents, a rarity for a woman. Most of the drugs she invented are included in the World Health Organization's list of essential drugs. As well, Elion was inducted into the National Women's Hall of Fame and the Engineering and Science Hall of Fame.

Gertrude Elion was known for the care and precision she devoted to medical research. Her collaboration with George Hitchings resulted in ground-breaking advances in the treatment of disease. Upon receiving the Nobel prize, Elion commented: "The Nobel Prize is fine, but the drugs I've developed are rewards in themselves."

SOURCES:

Adcock, Edgar, ed. *American Men and Women of Science.* Vol. 2. NJ: R.R. Bowker, 1994.

"Drug Pioneers with Nobel Prize," in *New Scientist.* Vol. 20, no. 1635. London: IPC Magazines, 1988.

Marx, Jean L. "The 1988 Nobel Prize for Physiology in Medicine," in *Science.* Vol. 248, no. 4878. Washington, DC: American Association for the Advancement of Science, 1988.

Meldrum, Marcia. "Gertrude Belle Elion 1988," in *Nobel Laureates in Medicine or Physiology: A Biographical Dictionary.* Daniel M. Fox, Marcia Meldrum, and Ira Rezak, eds. NY: Garland Press, 1990.

Miller, Jane A. "Women in Chemistry," in *Women of Science.* G. Kass-Simon and Patricia Farnes, eds. Bloomington, IN: Indiana University Press, 1990.

O'Neill, Lois Decker. *The Women's Book of World Records and Achievements.* Garden City, NY: Anchor Press, 1979.

SUGGESTED READING:

Rosser, Sue V. "Gertrude Belle Elion 1988," in *The Nobel Prize Winners: Physiology and Medicine.* Vol. 3. Frank N. Magill, ed. Pasadena, CA: Salem Press, 1991.

Hugh A. Stewart, M.A.,
University of Guelph, Guelph, Ontario, Canada

Eliot, George (1819–1880).

See Evans, Mary Anne.

Eliot, Martha May (1891–1978)

American expert on child health who helped found the World Health Organization and UNICEF. Born on April 7, 1891, in Dorchester, Massachusetts; died in 1978; daughter of the Reverend Christopher Rhodes Eliot (a Unitarian cleric) and Mary Jackson (May) Eliot; attended the Winsor School, in Back Bay, Boston; graduated from Radcliffe, B.A., 1913; M.D., Johns Hopkins, 1918; lived with Ethel Collins Dunham (1883–1969, a noted pediatrician) for 55 years.

Martha May Eliot, who was born on April 7, 1891, in Dorchester, Massachusetts, would spend 30 years working for the U.S. Children's Bureau, earning an international reputation as an expert on child health. Her schooling included one year at Bryn Mawr (1910); three years at Radcliffe (1911–13); and four years in medical school at Johns Hopkins (1914–18). At Bryn Mawr, Eliot met fellow medical student **Ethel Dunham**; the two would live together, separated only occasionally by work assignments, until Dunham's death on December 13, 1969.

Following her graduation from Johns Hopkins, Eliot was house officer at the Peter Bent Brigham Hospital in Boston. She then worked as an intern at the St. Louis Children's Hospital in St. Louis (1919–20) and the Children's Clinic of the Massachusetts General Hospital in Boston (1920–21) before rejoining Dunham at Yale University School of Medicine in New Haven in 1921. Dunham was one of New Haven Hospital's first house officers, while Eliot worked in the newly established pediatric department with Dr. **Edwards A. Park**. Eliot and Dunham also took positions as instructors in pediatrics at Yale, teaching there for the next 14 years. Both advanced to assistant professorships and associate clinical professorships while Eliot did major research on the prevention and control of rickets with cod liver oil, sponsored by the U.S. Children's Bureau.

In 1924, under the urging of Bureau chief *Grace Abbott, Eliot and Dunham began to work simultaneously at Yale and the U.S. Children's Bureau—commuting between New Haven and Washington, D.C. On becoming assistant chief of the Bureau in 1935, Eliot moved with Dunham to Washington, where Dunham also took a position with the Bureau as director of the division of research in child development. Dunham would be responsible for the ground-breaking *Standards and Recommendations for the Hospital Care of Newborn Infants, Full Term and Premature* (1943).

While at the Bureau, Eliot helped found two advocacy organizations: the World Health Organization (WHO) and the United Nations International Children's Emergency Fund (UNICEF). She was also the first woman elected president of the American Public Health Association (1947).

In 1949, Eliot and Dunham moved to Geneva where Eliot was assistant-director of the World Health Organization for two years. In 1951, they returned to Washington when Eliot was made chief of the Children's Bureau. When Eliot retired in 1957, the two moved to Cambridge, Massachusetts, where Eliot served for three years on the Visiting Committee at Harvard University's School of Public Health before becoming one of the few women to join the faculty of Harvard as a full professor (Professor of Maternal and Child Health). On retirement, Eliot led the Massachusetts Committee on Children and Youth. After Dunham died at home of bronchopneumonia in 1969, Martha May Eliot retired.

SUGGESTED READING:

Rothe, Anna, ed. *Current Biography*. NY: H.W. Wilson, 1948.

RELATED MEDIA:

Papers and recorded interviews are with the Martha May Eliot Collection, Schlesinger Library, Radcliffe College.

Elisa.

Variant of Elissa.

Elisa (fl. 800 BCE?).

See Dido.

Elisabeta.

Variant of Elisabeth or Elizabeth.

Elisabeth.

Variant of Elizabeth.

Elisabeth (1894–1956)

Queen of the Hellenes. Name variations: Elisabetha; Elizabeth Hohenzollern; Elizabeth of Greece; Elizabeth of Rumania or Romania. Born Elizabeth Charlotte Josephine Alexandra Victoria on October 12, 1894, in Sinaia, Rumania; died on November 15, 1956, in Cannes, France; daughter of Ferdinand I, king of Rumania, and *Marie of Rumania (1875–1938)*; married George II (1890–1947), king of the Hellenes, on February 27, 1921 (divorced 1935); children: none.

Élisabeth, Madame (1764–1794)

French princess. Name variations: Madame Elisabeth; Elizabeth or Élisabeth de France; Elisabeth of France. Born Élisabeth Philippine Marie Hélène at Versailles, France, on May 3, 1764; guillotined on May 10, 1794; daughter and last child of Louis the Dauphin (1729–1765) and his second wife

Marie Josèphe of Saxony (1731–1767); sister of three kings of France: Louis XVI (r. 1774–1792), Louis XVIII (r. 1814–1824), and Charles X (r. 1824–1830).

Left an orphan at age three, Madame Élisabeth, shared a deep attachment with her then 13-year-old brother Louis XVI. Brought up by **Madame de Mackau**, Élisabeth often resided at Montreuil, near Paris, in a home given to her by Louis when she reached maturity. There, the princess demonstrated her generous nature, taking an interest in charitable works. She once had 60 poor young girls vaccinated at her own expense.

The pious Élisabeth refused all offers of marriage so that she might remain by the side of her brother. From the beginning of the French Revolution, she was well aware of the gravity of the situation both of them faced, but she refused to leave the king. The "eminently sensible" Élisabeth, notes Simon Schama in *Citizens,* watched Louis vacillate in his resolve as he handled the cataclysmic events. "The king is backing off," she wrote. "He is always afraid of making a mistake. Once the first impulse is passed, he is no longer tormented by anything but the fear of having done an injustice. . . . [I]t seems to me that in government as in education one should not say 'I will it' until one is sure of being right. But once having said it, never slack off from what you have ordered."

Disguised as a bonneted nurse, she accompanied Louis, his queen *Marie Antoinette, and the royal children on the June 20, 1792, flight from Versailles, and was arrested with them at Varennes. Élisabeth was present at the Legislative Assembly when Louis was stripped of his powers and imprisoned in the Temple with the royal family. But after the execution of the king and the removal of Marie Antoinette to the Conciergerie, Madame Élisabeth was left alone in the Temple prison. Before her death, Marie Antoinette wrote a last letter to her trusted Élisabeth, consigning the children into her hands.

On May 9, 1794, Élisabeth was also transferred to the Conciergerie and brought before the revolutionary tribunal. Accused of assisting the king's flight, of supplying émigrés with funds, and of encouraging the resistance of the royal troops on August 10, 1792, she was condemned to death. On May 10, 1794, while reciting *De Profundis*, Madame Élisabeth was driven to the guillotine. Twenty-five others who were to be killed that day bowed to her, one by one, as they climbed the scaffold. Then, her turn came, and she calmly walked the stairs. When her muslin shawl slipped off her shoulders, she implored the executioner, "In the name of decency, cover me up." It was reported that the generally crude and noisy crowd was subdued when her head landed in the basket.

As might be expected of a sister of Louis XVI, Madame Élisabeth was in favor of absolutist principles. But hers was one of the most touching tragedies of the Revolution; she died because she was the sister of the king. *The Mémoires de Madame-Élisabeth* (Paris, 1858), by F. de Barghon and Fort-Rion, are of questionable authenticity, as are the collection of letters and documents published in 1865 by F. Feuillet de Conches.

SUGGESTED READING:

Beauchesne, A. de. *Vie de Madame Élisabeth.* 1869.

Beaucourt, Du Fresne de. *Étude Sur Madame Élisabeth.* Paris, 1864.

d'Armaillé, La comtesse. *Madame Élisabeth.* Paris, 1886.

d'Arvor, Madame. *Madame Élisabeth.* Paris, 1898.

Ferrand, Le Comte A.F.C. *Éloge historique de Madame Élisabeth* (1814, containing 94 letters; 2nd ed., 1861, containing additional letters, but correspondence mutilated).

Maxwell-Scott, Mrs. *Madame Elizabeth of France.* 1908.

Schama, Simon. *Citizens.* NY: Knopf, 1989.

Élisabeth d'Autriche (d. 1545).

See Sforza, Bona for sidebar on Elizabeth of Habsburg.

Elisabeth of Belgium (1876–1965).

See Elizabeth of Bavaria.

Elisabeth of Habsburg (1501–1526).

See Willums, Sigbrit for sidebar.

Elisabeth of Habsburg (1554–1592)

Austrian archduchess, queen of France, and founder of the Vienna convent of Poor Clares, Our Lady of Angels, who supported reformed Catholicism (the "Counter-Reformation") in France and the Habsburg territories of Central Europe. Name variations: *Élisabeth d'Autriche; Archduchess Elizabeth; Elizabeth of Habsburg; Elizabeth of Hapsburg; Elisabeta; Isabelle d'Autriche; Isabella of Austria; Isabelle; signed her name Isabell; family name sometimes Hapsbourg, Hapsburg.* Born on July 5, 1554, in Vienna, Austria; died on January 22, 1592, in Vienna; originally interred in Our Lady of Angels Convent Church, Vienna; remains transferred to crypt of St. Stephen's Cathedral, Vienna, 1782; second daughter of Maximilian II (1527–1576), Holy Roman emperor (r. 1564–1576, son of Holy Roman Emperor Ferdinand

I) and Marie of Austria (1528–1603), Holy Roman empress; educated by private tutors; sister of Anne of Austria (c. 1550–1580), Rudolf II, Holy Roman emperor (r. 1576–1612); married Charles IX (1550–1574), king of France (crowned king of France, May 15, 1560 or 1561, on October 22, 1570 (died, May 30, 1574). children: **Marie Isabelle de France** (born on October 27, 1572; died on April 2, 1578; godchild of Queen Elizabeth I of England).

Married at 16 to the king of France in imperial ceremony (October 22, 1570) in Speyer, Germany, officiated by the Prince-Archbishop Elector of Mainz (her uncle, Archduke Ferdinand of Tyrol, served as proxy for her bridegroom); married in royal ceremony in Mezieres, France (November 26, 1570); consecrated queen of France at St. Denis (March 25, 1571), ceremony officiated by the Archbishop of Reims; made ceremonial entry into Paris (March 29, 1571); lived at French court during part of the period of the Religious Wars; eclipsed by influence of her mother-in-law Catherine de Medici; returned to Central Europe (1575) after death of her husband, leaving her daugh-

Elisabeth of Habsburg (1554–1592)

ter Marie Isabelle in France; following example of her namesake St. Elisabeth, founded a convent and supported poor and sick; acted as an important patron of the reformed Catholic cause in Central Europe, sponsoring artistic undertakings and the collection of relics; reported to have written a devotional work on the Word of God; collected an appreciable library that she bequeathed to her brother, the emperor Rudolf II.

Many have heard of the Habsburg archduchess who became queen of France in the later 18th century, the queen popularly known as *Marie Antoinette. Much of her fame is due, no doubt, to reports of her public decapitation by French revolutionaries. Approximately 200 years earlier, during a similarly tumultuous and dangerous period of French history, a period of civil war and religious violence, another young member of the Habsburg dynasty and daughter of the Holy Roman emperor and empress became queen of France. She was Elisabeth of Habsburg and called herself Isabell.

One of the best, the gentlest, the wisest, and most virtuous queens who reigned since kings and queens began to reign.

—Pierre de Bourdeille, seigneur de Brantome

Elisabeth was born in the Danubian trading city of Vienna in 1554 of doubly imperial blood: her mother and her father were children of emperors and empresses of the Holy Roman Empire. Elisabeth would also become an imperial child. Her father Maximilian was elected emperor when she was ten. This archduchess grew up in a bustling, cosmopolitan court in a bustling, cosmopolitan city. Vienna was being refurbished in the new Italian styles known later as Renaissance. The city had suffered significant damage during a siege by Ottoman forces in 1529, and, as Elisabeth grew up, Italian architects and construction workers were busy on large building projects such as the modernization of the court castle, the laying out of gardens about it, the construction of a new private court residence outside the city (simply known as the "New Construction"), and the completion of the private lodgings for Elisabeth's family across from the old castle. (This building is known today as the Stallburg.)

Elisabeth's father and grandfather were both staking out claims to the imperial title in competition with her uncle Phillip II, the king of Spain. Elisabeth would grow up in the center of these ri-

valries. Her mother, the empress **Marie of Austria**, was Phillip's sister. Some of Elisabeth's brothers and sisters were sent to Spain for training and to become familiar with the rest of the Habsburg dynasty, those Habsburgs who were using discoveries and conquests in America and Africa to buttress assertions of dynastic precedence.

The archduchess' education was marked by the linguistic diversity of the Habsburgs' holdings. It is reported that the Habsburg children in Vienna were taught German, French, Italian, Czech, Hungarian, and Latin in addition to the Spanish which seems to have been Elisabeth's primary language. Her mother spoke Spanish almost exclusively, and Elisabeth's grandfather, the emperor Ferdinand I who supervised his grandchildren's education closely, had also been born in Spain. Her father had been regent in Spain for a number of years shortly before Elisabeth's birth. A note on a German copy of Elisabeth's will implies that the will was originally written in Spanish.

Elisabeth grew up in a household with 16 children (although many of them did not survive infancy or childhood.) Her brothers and sisters would become emperors (both her brother Rudolf and her brother Matthew were elected Holy Roman emperor), heads of religious orders, kings, a queen, governors, military commanders, and so on. As one of the oldest daughters, Elisabeth was destined to play a role in the Habsburg dynasties' plans. The main way in which the Habsburgs had accumulated the vast array of titles and rights across Europe and America which they enjoyed during Elisabeth's life was via marriage. Her prospects were part of a balancing act. The Central European Habsburgs needed allies, allies versus the other Habsburgs, and allies versus the expanding Ottoman Empire which had so nearly captured Vienna a few years before. Negotiations and discussions concerning marriage plans for the archduchess began while she was quite young. It was decided that Elisabeth's older sister **Anne of Austria** would marry King Phillip of Spain (her uncle) and Elisabeth would marry her father Maximilian's godson, Charles of Valois (Charles IX), the 20-year-old king of France. These two marriages were celebrated in 1570.

Elisabeth traveled to the important administrative and trading center, the Imperial City of Speyer, for her wedding by proxy. Here in the cathedral where important imperial and Habsburg predecessors lay buried, the empire would be tied to France. The Reichstag, the empire's assembly of notables, was meeting in the city and the wedding could be used to display the rights and claims of the Habsburgs. Since 1555, an uneasy truce between battling political units in the empire was keeping further religious wars on hold, but revolts in Habsburg territories in the Low Countries called Habsburg rights and prerogatives there into question. Also, various German princes had been assisting Protestant-minded leaders both in the Netherlands and in the kingdom of France. Imperial officials questioned French appropriation of the bishoprics of Metz, Toul, and Verdun, too. When the prince-archbishop elector of Mainz, archchancellor of the Holy Roman Empire and imperial coronator, officiated at Elisabeth's wedding on October 22, 1570, in the Speyer cathedral, he did so in a contentious context, a context in which each of Elisabeth's actions would take on special significance. Would she represent the moderate policies of her father who sought to placate the religious discontents, or would she join with the advocates of a "harder line" versus religious dissidents?

At the ceremony, Elisabeth's uncle, the Archduke Ferdinand of Tyrol, served as proxy for her new husband. After celebrations and festivities that lasted a number of days, she left Speyer on November 4 accompanied by many of the most notable and prestigious courtiers and officers of the empire, including the prince-archbishop elector of Trier. With a train of a reported 1,600 riders, the young bride was escorted through the contended borderland where the empire and the kingdom met. She entered into a kingdom that was again at peace. In August, a new treaty had ended the Third War of Religion, and it seemed as if King Charles and his influential mother *Catherine de Medici might maintain this peace through a marriage alliance with the Central European Habsburgs. This alliance could conceivably split them from their Iberian dynastic rivals who played a role in the religious battles going on in the kingdom.

As Elisabeth entered the kingdom of France to meet her new spouse, she also came to fill the empty position of queen in the French constitution. Since her sister-in-law *Mary Stuart, Queen of Scots (1542–1587), consort of Charles' late brother King Francis II, had left to return to Scotland (and eventual execution at the order of Queen *Elizabeth I of England), the queen's throne had remained vacant. Now Elisabeth would have the opportunity to use the powers of this office.

The royal wedding ceremony took place in the border town of Mezieres on November 26. An account of the wedding discloses that Charles was so curious to see his bride that he slipped, disguised, into the town to get a glimpse of her before the ceremony. Reports also detail Elisabeth's finery, complete with an immensely long train on her gown. Four months after the ceremony, and the festivities that accompanied it, the process of the new queen's ceremonial integration into the French body politic continued with her consecration as queen of France by the archbishop of Reims at St. Denis on March 25, 1571. Four days later, she officially entered the city of Paris to an elaborately choreographed welcome. The decorations for Elisabeth's royal entrance procession stressed the themes of peace and underlined her imperial ties. Printed accounts of the entrance procession, together with similar ones of the wedding, served to publicize the crown's ties and prestige.

Elisabeth's stay in France was short and tragic. Within a year and a half, the peace disintegrated into the religious violence of the St. Bartholemew's Day massacres and their after-

---

➤ **Marie of Austria** (1528–1603)

*Holy Roman Empress. Name variations: Maria or Mary of Hapsburg; Marie d'Autriche. Born on June 21, 1528, in Madrid, Spain; died on February 26, 1603, in Villamonte, Spain; daughter of Holy Roman Emperor Charles V (Charles I of Spain) and *Isabella of Portugal (1503–1539); sister of Phillip II, king of Spain (r. 1556–1598), and *Joanna of Austria (1535–1573); half-sister of *Margaret of Parma (1522–1586); married Maximilian II, Holy Roman emperor (r. 1564–1576); children: *Anne of Austria (c. 1550–1580, who married Philip II of Spain); Rudolf II (1552–1612), Holy Roman emperor (r. 1576–1612); *Elisabeth of Habsburg (1554–1592, who married Charles IX); Matthew (1557–1619), king of Bohemia, also known as Matthias, Holy Roman emperor (r. 1612–1619); Archduke Ernst (governor of some Austrian duchies).*

➤ **Anne of Austria** (c. 1550–1580)

*Queen of Spain. Name variations: Anne or Anna Habsburg. Born around 1549 or 1550; died in 1580; daughter of Maximilian II, Holy Roman emperor (r. 1564–1576), and *Marie of Austria (1528–1603, daughter of Charles V, Holy Roman emperor); sister of Rudolf II (1552–1612), Holy Roman Emperor (r. 1576–1612), *Elisabeth of Habsburg (1554–1592), and Matthew (1557–1619), king of Bohemia and Holy Roman emperor as Matthias; became fourth wife of Philip II (1527–1598), king of Spain (r. 1544–1598), in 1570; children: Philip III (1578–1621), king of Spain (r. 1598–1621).*

math. Her delivery of a baby girl two months later did little to strengthen her political position at court. A female heir to the throne could not be as successfully advanced in the succession struggles that marked the last decades of the rule of the Valois dynasty. Elisabeth's daughter, the precocious Marie Isabelle, godchild of Queen Elizabeth I of England, would die in unhappy circumstances in the royal château of Amboise on April 2, 1578. King Charles preceded her. He died on May 30, 1574. Elisabeth returned to Central Europe soon after her husband's death, leaving her daughter in the care of her mother-in-law, Catherine de Medici.

As queen of France, Elisabeth received various rights and properties such as those associated with the duchies of Berry and Bourbonnais. She apparently used her position at court to advance the reformed Catholic cause associated with the canons and decrees of the Council of Trent. She helped support a Jesuit college in Bourges, a controversial move in a kingdom where the Paris Parlement had only recently (1562) even permitted the Jesuits' legal presence. (Elisabeth's grandfather Ferdinand had called the Jesuits to Vienna in the early 1550s.) Little is known of Elisabeth's other activities in France. A member of the court, the seigneur de Brantome, reports that she took her religious responsibilities very seriously. She seems to have had a particular devotion to various icons and relics. When she left France, she is reported to have taken a number of devotional objects with her. These included a finger from St. John the Baptist, a reliquary of St. **Christina "the Astonishing"**, and a copy of the famous *Mater admirabilis* painting from Maria Maggiore in Rome which had been sent to the French court by the reformed Catholic leader St. Charles Borromeo.

After her husband's death, Elisabeth chose not to remarry. She followed instead the example of her 13th-century namesake St. **Elizabeth of Hungary** (1207–1231), dedicating her life to helping the poor and sick and sponsoring other pious undertakings. The one-time imperial ambassador to the Ottoman court, Ogier-Ghislain de Busbecq, was given the task of administering her holdings in France. He was not very successful: in her will, written in 1592, Elisabeth mentions monies owed her from France. Some accounts write of how Elisabeth assigned many of her French incomes to support her sister-in-law **Margaret of Valois** (1553–1615). Others were used for the college at Bourges, for the poor, and particularly to provide dowries for underprivileged girls, enabling them to marry. Similar concerns are seen in her will: there she mentions care of the ill and indigent, poor girls, and soldiers fighting in the Hungarian wars against the Ottomans.

In her widowhood, Elisabeth was active in two of the Habsburgs' main Central European court centers: Prague and Vienna. At first, she seems to have participated in the court of her mother, Empress Marie of Austria. Marie had become a widow in 1576. The relations between the empress and her moody son, the emperor Rudolf II, led the empress to return to Spain in 1581. There, like her daughter Elisabeth and many other Habsburg widows and archduchesses, she dedicated her last years to supporting Franciscan nuns.

The 1580s were busy years for the widow Elisabeth. She actively supported the efforts of the reformed Catholic clergy. In Prague, Elisabeth sponsored the reconstruction of the All Saints Chapel in the castle hill complex. It, like much of the city's "small side," had been heavily damaged in a 1541 fire. At Elisabeth's request, the relics of the Slavic saint Prokopius were transferred to Prague from their location at the Benedictine monastery of Sazava which he had founded. Elisabeth's actions in Prague could bear some relation to the decision of Elisabeth's brother Emperor Rudolf to permanently locate his court in the city.

Another of Elisabeth's brothers, the archduke Maximilian, had become coadjutor of the Teutonic Knights and as such had gained control of the relics of St. Elizabeth of Hungary. These had been at the order's church in Marburg. One of the Middle Ages' most popular pilgrimage sites, Marburg and the relics of St. Elizabeth had been used by Lutherans to attack the type of relic veneration characteristic of Elisabeth's (and reformed Catholicism's) piety. Maximilian gave these relics of the patron of widows and orphans to his sister Elisabeth in 1588.

These relics eventually ended up in the church of the convent of Poor Clares which Elisabeth founded in Vienna in the early 1580s. Elisabeth had wanted to reopen Vienna's St. Anne's cloister, but this house—like many female houses in the empire—had been closed in the course of the 16th century. Later, their revenues were transferred to Jesuit foundations. Elisabeth had to look elsewhere for incomes to support her new house. After some investigation, the government supervisory board responsible for church property incomes (the *Klosterrat*) implemented Elisabeth's brother Archduke Ernst's (governor of some of the Austrian duchies) order to transfer rights over properties associated with the closed Benedictine house Erlakloster to support Elisabeth's foundation. These, tied with rights associated with a handful of properties scattered about the city of Vienna, would become the sources of income for the new convent Our Lady of Angels which Elisabeth had built around the corner from where she had grown up, and next door to her home at the time. In this city house, she led a modest court and kept a small chapel.

This convent, sometimes known as Queen's Cloister, St. Claire's Cloister, or (erroneously) King's Cloister, benefitted from Elisabeth's close ties and interest in the later years of her life. Most likely designed by the Italian painter and architect Pietro Ferbosco, the convent church was consecrated on August 2, 1583. After her death at age 38 on January 22, 1592, Elisabeth was buried under a simple marble slab in the choir of this church. In 1782, the church and convent were closed by Marie Antoinette's brother, the Holy Roman emperor Joseph II. Elisabeth's body was transferred to one of the crypts beneath Vienna's Cathedral of St. Stephen. Ironically for Elisabeth, a pious supporter of reformed Catholicism, a Protestant denomination later purchased the church and currently holds services there.

Elisabeth's will and a posthumous inventory of her library reveal a cultivated, religious woman tied to France and Spain as well as to Vienna and Prague. Her last testament donates money for many purposes, including the holding of Masses in the convent church for her deceased spouse, the king of France, who, the will reads, "has gone to his glory." The Jesuits of Vienna were to receive funds to support students. The pattern of donation shows a concern for the sick and the poor, as well as dedication to *Mary the Virgin, St. Michael, St. Christina the Astonishing, and the Holy Cross. (Her mother had given Elisabeth a piece of the True Cross. This she donated to the convent.)

The widowed queen's library contained books in Spanish, French, German, Latin, and Italian. The largest single number are devotional works in Spanish. A goodly number are German works by the Jesuit Georg Scherer, the court preacher at the Archduke Ernst's court in Vienna. French works dating from Elisabeth's reign in France include a book of prognostications by Nostradamus for the year 1571. Sophocles' tragedy "Antigone," as well as reports about the Indies and Japan round out the collection, which reportedly was donated to Elisabeth's older brother, the emperor Rudolf, after her death. Her wedding ring she gave to her brother Ernst.

While the seigneur de Brantome, one of the primary sources for Elisabeth's life in France, mentions that she wrote both a devotional work on the Word of God and a history of events in France during her reign, neither of these sources seems to be extant. For that reason, and because Elisabeth left almost no sources in her own hand aside from a few documents with her signature attached, this article, like all discussions of this archduchess and queen, necessarily must create Elisabeth as an object of description and interpretation.

SOURCES:

Brantome, Pierre de Bourdeille, Seigneur de. *Illustrious Dames of the Court of the Valois Kings.* Translated by Katherine Prescott Wormeley. NY: Lamb, 1912.

Czeike, Felix. *Historisches Lexikon Wien.* Vol. 3. Vienna: Kremayr & Scheriau, 1994.

Darlem, Clary. *Elisabeth d'Autriche, reine de France.* Paris: A. Franck, 1847.

Evans, R.J.W. *Rudolf II and His World: A Study in Intellectual History.* Oxford: Clarendon Press, 1984.

Graham, Victor E., and W. McAllister Johnson. *The Paris Entries of Charles IX and Elisabeth of Austria.* Toronto: University of Toronto Press, 1974.

Hamann, Brigitte. *Die Habsburger: Ein biographisches Lexikon.* Munich: Piper, 1988.

Lauzinner, Maximilian, ed. *Deutsche Reichstagakten: Reichsversammlungen 1556–1662. Der Reichstag zu Speyer 1570.* Göttingen: V & R, 1988.

Strakosch, Marianne. *Materialien zu einer Biographie Elisabeths von Österreich, Königin von Frankreich.* Unpublished doctoral dissertation, University of Vienna, 1965.

COLLECTIONS:

Some of Elisabeth's papers are to be found in the Habsburg Family Archives in the Haus-, Hof-, und Staatsarchiv, Vienna. These include lists of payment for her court officials, documents concerning the administration of the properties associated with the convent in Vienna, and the last will and testament.

Joseph F. Patrouch,
Assistant Professor of History,
Florida International University, Miami, Florida

Elisabeth of Rumania (1843–1916).

See Elizabeth of Wied.

Elisabeth of Saxe-Altenburg
(1826–1896)

*Duchess of Oldenburg. Born on March 26, 1826; died on February 2, 1896; daughter of Joseph, duke of Saxe-Altenburg, and *Amelia of Wurttemberg (1799–1848); sister of *Alexandra of Saxe-Altenburg (1830–1911); married Nicholas Frederick Peter II, duke of Oldenburg, on February 10, 1852; children:*

Frederick Augustus (b. 1852), grand duke of Oldenburg; George Ludwig (b. 1855).

Elisheba

Biblical woman. Name variations: Elizabeth. Daughter of Amminadab; married Aaron; children: Nadab, Abihu, Eleazar, and Ithamar (Ex. 6:23).

Elissa (fl. 800 BCE?).

See Dido.

Elizabeth.

Variant of Elisabeth, Isabel or Isabella.

Elizabeth (fl. 1st c.)

Biblical woman and mother of John the Baptist. Name variations: Elisabeth; Saint Elizabeth. Flourished in the 1st century; a descendant of Aaron; married Zachary also known as Zacharias (a priest); children: St. John the Baptist.

According to the Bible, though Elizabeth and her husband Zacharias "were both right-ous before God" (Luke 1:5, 13), Elizabeth was barren until late in life. Then an angel foretold to her husband about the birth of a son, and she conceived John the Baptist, who was considered the forerunner of Christ. Elizabeth was six months' pregnant when she was visited by her cousin *Mary the Virgin. In Mary's presence, Elizabeth felt the child move inside her as if to welcome the Messiah, whom Mary was carrying (Luke 1:39–63). Elizabeth's feast day is on November 5.

Elizabeth (1207–1231), saint.

See Elizabeth of Hungary.

Elizabeth (d. 1545), archduchess.

See Sforza, Bona for sidebar on Elizabeth of Habsburg.

Elizabeth (1602–1644), queen of Spain.

See Elizabeth Valois.

Elizabeth (1770–1840)

English princess, artist, and landgravine of Hesse-Homburg. Name variations: Elizabeth Guelph. Born on May 22, 1770, at Buckingham House, London, England; died on January 10, 1840, at Frankfurt-am-Main, Germany; interred in the Mausoleum of Landgraves, Homburg, Germany; daughter of Charlotte of Mecklenburg-Strelitz (1744–1818) and George III

(1738–1820), king of England (r. 1760–1820); married George Ramus (a page at the palace); married Frederick VI, landgrave of Hesse-Homburg, on April 7, 1818 (died 1829); children: (first marriage) Eliza Ramus (b. around 1786).

Princess Elizabeth, daughter of England's Queen *Charlotte of Mecklenburg-Strelitz (1744–1818) and George III, had an artistic bent; she designed a series of pictures titled *The Birth and Triumph of Cupid* in 1795. In 1808, she established a community at Windsor to provide dowries for poor girls. She moved to Germany upon her marriage to Frederick VI, landgrave of Hesse-Homburg, in 1818. Following his death 11 years later, Elizabeth set aside £6,000 per year to reduce the debts of her adopted principality. In 1834, she reissued her sketches under the title *Power and Progress of Genius* with proceeds earmarked to benefit the poor of Hanover.

Elizabeth (1831–1903)

*Archduchess of Austria. Name variations: Archduchess Elisabeth. Born on January 17, 1831; died on February 14, 1903; daughter of Archduke Joseph (b. 1776) and *Maria of Wurttemberg (1797–1855); married Ferdinand (1821–1849), archduke of Austria (r. 1835–1848, abdicated), on December 4, 1847; children: *Maria Teresa of Este (1849–1919, who married Louis III, king of Bavaria).*

Elizabeth (1837–1898), empress of Austria.

See Elizabeth of Bavaria.

Elizabeth (fl. 1850s)

*Archduchess. Flourished around 1850; married Karl Ferdinand also known as Charles Ferdinand of Austria (1818–1874); children: Friedrich Maria Albrecht (1856–1936, who married *Isabella of Croy-Dulmen); *Maria Christina of Austria (1858–1929); Karl Stefan also known as Charles Stephen (1860–1933); Eugen (1863–1954).*

Elizabeth (1864–1918), grand duchess of Russia.

See Ella.

Elizabeth I (1533–1603)

Last of the Tudor monarchs, who ruled England for 45 years, establishing that island nation as a first-rate *power in Europe. Name variations: Elizabeth Tudor, Good Queen Bess, the Virgin Queen, Gloriana. Born on September 7, 1533, at Greenwich, England; died on March 24, 1603, at Richmond upon Thames, Surrey; buried in Westminster Abbey; daughter of Henry VIII, king of England (r. 1509–1547) and his second wife, *Anne Boleyn (1507–1536); half-sister of Mary I (1516–1558), queen of England; never married.*

Inherited throne (1558); appointed William Cecil as principal secretary (1558); had coronation at Westminster Abbey (January 15, 1559); with Parliament, devised Elizabethan Settlement of Religion through Act of Supremacy and Act of Uniformity (1559); signed Treaty of Câteau-Cambrésis ending war with France (1559); supported Scottish Reformation and signed Treaty of Edinburgh with Protestant lords (1560); kept her Catholic cousin, Mary Stuart—who had assumed Scottish throne (1561) but was deposed and exiled to England—prisoner (1568–87); suppressed Northern Rebellion of English Catholic nobles (1569) and Ridolfi Plot (1571); branded a heretic and a bastard by Pope Pius V whose bull of excommunication (1570) invited English Catholics and European princes to depose her; reluctantly had Mary, Queen of Scots, executed for high treason (1587) after discovering her involvement in several plots; openly aided Dutch Revolt against Spain and licensed English privateers to prey on Spanish ships returning from the Americas (1580s); survived the major crisis of her reign when English naval forces led by Drake, Hawkins, and Howard defeated the Spanish Armada and prevented a Spanish invasion of England (1588); had latter years as queen marred by protracted and expensive war in Ireland (1595–1603), increased tension with Parliament, and betrayal by her last royal favorite, the earl of Essex, whom she had beheaded for leading a rebellion against the Crown (1601); at her death, the English throne passed peacefully to Mary Stuart's son, King James VI of Scotland.

Late in July of 1588, 130 well-armed galleons carrying 30,000 of King Philip II's seasoned veterans—the mighty Spanish Armada—was sighted off the southern coast of England. Across the Channel, a fleet of transport ships waited, ready to convey Alessandro Farnese, duke of Parma, and his army from Holland as the spearhead of a full-scale Spanish invasion of England. Two hundred smaller but highly mobile English ships sailed forth from Plymouth to meet the Spanish onslaught.

On land, Robert Dudley, earl of Leicester, assembled at Tilbury in Essex an army of largely inexperienced English soldiers, hoping to bar Parma's route to London and Spain's prime target: Queen Elizabeth I. As yet, no one knew the outcome of the great sea battle when suddenly, on August 9, there appeared in camp a woman on horseback, wearing a silver breast plate over a white velvet dress. She carried a truncheon in her hand and addressed the troops:

> I know I have the body of a weak and feeble woman, but I have the heart and stomach of a King, and a King of England too, and think foul scorn that Parma or Spain or any Prince of Europe should dare to invade the borders of my realm. . . . I myself will take up arms, I myself will be your general.

When she finished, Elizabeth's audience "all at once a mighty shout or cry did give." According to Leicester, her words "so inflamed the hearts of her good subjects [that] the weakest among them is able to match the proudest Spaniard that dares land in England."

𝒮he is only a woman, only mistress of half an island, and yet she makes herself feared by Spain, by France, by the Empire, by all.

—Pope Sixtus V

They did not have to. The English navy, and tricky winds in the North Atlantic, wreaked havoc on the *Armada Catholica*; remnants of Philip's "great enterprise" straggled home to Spain that autumn, leaving Parma's army stranded on the Dutch coast.

Born in 1533, Elizabeth Tudor grew to maturity in a dangerous and turbulent era. Her father King Henry VIII had defied the pope, divorced his first wife ❧▶ **Catherine of Aragon**, and married the Lutheran-leaning ***Anne Boleyn** in hopes of siring a male heir to the English throne. Instead, Anne Boleyn sired Elizabeth. Before Elizabeth reached age three, her mother was executed; her father married his third wife, ❧▶ **Jane Seymour**; and Elizabeth and her older half-sister Mary (1516–1558), the future ***Mary I**, were declared illegitimate. Seymour produced the much-sought-after son, Edward (the future Edward VI), but died in the process. Henry married three more times. His last wife, ❧▶ **Catherine Parr**, provided young Elizabeth with the only motherly guidance she experienced during childhood. Parr took an active interest in the education of her stepchildren, especially Elizabeth and Edward, both of whom proved to be highly intelligent, apt pupils. Tutored by some of the finest English Renaissance scholars of the age, Elizabeth acquired an exceptional grounding in

Catherine of Aragon. See Six Wives of Henry VIII.

Jane Seymour. See Six Wives of Henry VIII.

Catherine Parr. See Six Wives of Henry VIII.

Latin, Greek, French, and Italian as well as the traditional womanly arts of music, dance, and fine stitchery.

Upon the death of Henry VIII in 1547, nine-year-old Edward VI came to the throne. As usually happens when a minor inherits the crown, powerful magnates vied for control of the realm, and Elizabeth's affectionate relationship with her sickly brother did not shield her from danger.

The young king's Protestant uncle and Lord Protector, Edward Seymour, duke of Somerset, dominated the first half of the reign. Elizabeth rejected a marriage proposal from Somerset's brother, Admiral Thomas Seymour, who then promptly (and secretly) married the widow Parr with whom Elizabeth continued to live. There is evidence that the affable but vulgar Seymour may have molested Elizabeth during his brief marriage to her stepmother. Parr died in childbirth in 1548, whereupon Seymour immediately renewed his pursuit of 15-year-old Elizabeth. The Council arrested him, and Elizabeth had difficulty extricating herself from complicity in the affair. When Seymour went to the block for treason a few months later, Elizabeth remarked coldly: "This day died a man of much wit and very little judgment."

In 1550, Lord Protector Somerset lost his power struggle with the Duke of Northumberland, and in 1552 was likewise beheaded for treason. Radical Protestantism and naked ambition characterized Northumberland's government; none of Henry VIII's three children was free from danger while this greedy duke controlled the Council. In 1553, King Edward died of consumption. In an effort to exclude both Catholic Mary and Protestant Elizabeth from the throne, Northumberland proclaimed Lady *Jane Grey, their cousin and his daughter-in-law, as queen. The plot failed and Mary was crowned, leaving Elizabeth at the mercy of a bitter half-sister who despised and distrusted her.

Mary Tudor, daughter of Catherine of Aragon, was a fervent Catholic, determined to return England to the papal fold. Elizabeth conformed, attended mass, and tried to reassure the queen of her steadfast loyalty. But throughout "Bloody Mary's" tragic reign, Elizabeth faced constant peril. Most of England's Protestant leaders either escaped to the Continent or were burned at the stake for heresy. When Mary's unpopular marriage to King Philip II of Spain sparked Wyatt's Rebellion in 1555, Elizabeth found herself imprisoned in the Tower of London. Always under suspicion for both heresy

and sedition, she kept a low profile and bided her time. Mary died childless in November of 1558, and 25-year-old Elizabeth Tudor became queen of England.

The kingdom Elizabeth inherited needed all her considerable talents—plus those of others—to establish external security and internal tranquillity. Thanks to her brother-in-law, Philip, England was in a losing war with his rival, France; trouble brewed on the Scottish border; the exchequer (treasury) was bankrupt; and religious divisions threatened to split the nation apart. In her first official act, she appointed Cambridge-educated Sir William Cecil (later Lord Burghley) as principal secretary of state. "This judgement I have of you," she told him, "that you will not be corrupted by any manner of gift and that you will be faithful to the state; and that without respect of my private gain will you give me that counsel which you think best." Thus began a 40-year political partnership—perhaps the most successful one in English history. Other Privy Council members also reflected Elizabeth's uncanny instinct for, in the words of Francis Bacon, "reading men as well as books"; like Cecil, they were intelligent, hard-working men, devoted to their new queen. The brilliance of her advisors has led some historians to underestimate the queen's role in creating policy. Most modern authorities now concede, however, that throughout her reign, Elizabeth I made most of the important policy decisions herself.

Unlike other female monarchs of the age, Elizabeth frequently acted as her own foreign minister. Her facility with languages, her astute grasp of European politics, and her insistence upon controlling her own government, all enabled her to deal directly with foreign princes and their ambassadors. Three countries—France, Spain, and Scotland—needed to be watched carefully, as each represented a danger to England's security as well as Elizabeth's hold on her throne.

In March of 1559, she signed the Treaty of Câteau-Cambrésis, ending a costly war with France. She preserved a nominal friendship with Spain, temporarily, via sisterly correspondence with Philip II, who even proposed marriage to her. But the real key lay in Scotland, whose absent queen, *Mary Stuart, Queen of Scots (1542–1587), was married to Francis II, heir to the French throne. As Elizabeth's cousin, Mary Stuart stood first in line to the English throne; as a Catholic, she already claimed to be England's rightful queen. When Protestant Scottish lords revolted against an unpopular French Catholic re-

Elizabeth I

gency in 1560, Elizabeth prevented French reinforcements from landing in Scotland and signed the Treaty of Edinburgh recognizing the new Protestant government. In so doing, she secured England's northern border and broke up the long-standing alliance between Scotland and France.

In solving England's most urgent internal problem—that of religion—Elizabeth sought Parliament's help but designed a settlement suited to her own principles. Parliament moved quickly to restore the Henrician Act of Supremacy, ending papal authority and naming the queen as "supreme governor" of the Church of England in 1559. At the same time, the Act of Uniformity established a somewhat ambiguous English liturgy based on the 1552 Book of Common Prayer. Elizabeth then appointed the moderate and conciliatory Matthew Parker as archbishop of Canterbury. The Elizabethan Compromise combined Catholic ritual and episcopal governance with Protestant theology; it produced Anglicanism as the basis of a national church. Hardcore Papists and Puritans resisted throughout her reign, but the majority of English subjects—weary of both extreme Protestantism and Catholic persecutions—accepted the settlement. England was thus spared the divisive religious warfare that racked many other European countries in the late 16th century.

Elizabeth's heir until 1587 was her cousin, Mary Stuart. Widowed in 1560, Mary returned from France to Scotland where, as a Catholic, she quarreled bitterly with the Presbyterian Council of Lords. Marriage to her foppish Stuart cousin, Lord Darnley, provided Scotland with a male heir but ended disastrously when Mary, implicated in her husband's murder, was deposed in 1568. She fled to England where, though kept virtually prisoner for 20 years, she became the focus of numerous plots to depose Elizabeth and take the throne as queen of England. Elizabeth and Cecil quickly suppressed two early conspiracies, the Northern Rebellion in 1569 and the Ridolfi Plot of 1571. Meanwhile, Pope Pius V belatedly issued a Bull of Excommunication (1570) branding Elizabeth a heretic and a bastard, absolving English Catholics of their allegiance to her, and inviting European princes to invade England. Until Mary Stuart's trial and inevitable execution in February of 1587, Elizabeth had good reason to fear her Scottish rival.

For Parliament, the Privy Council, and the average English subject, the most perplexing question regarding their queen was her marriage. After Elizabeth contracted smallpox and nearly died in 1562, Parliament regularly petitioned her to marry and provide a Protestant heir to the throne. Instead, she used her eligibility as a tool in foreign policy, dangling marriage prospects before a dozen princely suitors for over 20 years. The Duke of Parma likened her marriage diplomacy to "the weaving of Penelope, undoing every night what was done before and then reweaving anew." Most biographers agree that she loved, and in 1559–60, really wanted to marry her court favorite, Robert Dudley (later earl of Leicester). Marriage to any Englishman, however, might sow the seeds of civil war; marriage to a foreigner risked having England dominated by another nation's interests, something the queen was determined to avoid. In the end, she rejected all proposals—the last one in 1581 from a much younger duke of Anjou—preferring to remain the Virgin Queen.

During the late 1560s and 1570s, Elizabeth used religious conflicts on the Continent to weaken England's two principal enemies, France and Spain. Both countries had Protestant rebel factions: the Huguenots in France and the Dutch Calvinists in Spanish-held Netherlands. She gave these Protestant causes just enough covert assistance to keep them viable, but not enough to drag England into war. Pressured by her Council to intervene directly, Elizabeth refused. War would interrupt England's thriving trade, force the queen to rely on Parliament for subsidies, and ultimately burden her subjects with unpopular taxes. Elizabeth's goal was the safety and prosperity of England, not the salvation of Continental Protestantism. By the 1580s, however, England's expanding sea ventures and Spain's emergence as Europe's Catholic superpower forced her into open conflict with Philip II.

For several years Francis Drake, John Hawkins, and other English privateers had been preying on Spanish treasure ships returning from the New World. As a prime investor in these acts of piracy, Elizabeth realized a handsome profit— as much as 4,700% on one voyage alone—a fact that infuriated King Philip. When she sent to the Netherlands an English army commanded by Leicester to prop up the failing Dutch revolt in 1585, all pretext of peace with Spain evaporated. Philip began in earnest to plan an all-out assault on England.

The long-dreaded Spanish Armada set sail in July of 1588 with orders to rendezvous with Spanish troops in Holland and support their invasion of England. Elizabeth now faced the supreme crisis of her reign—the 16th-century equivalent of the Battle of Britain. On the eve of the anticipated invasion, Elizabeth delivered to Leicester's troops at Tilbury one of the finest speeches in the English language.

> My loving people, we have been persuaded by some that are careful of our safety to take heed how we commit ourselves to armed multitudes for fear of treachery. Let tyrants fear. I have always behaved myself that, under God, I have placed my chiefest strength and safeguard in the loyal hearts and goodwill of my subjects. And therefore I am come amongst you . . . not for my recreation and disport, but being resolved, in the

Elizabeth I as a young princess.

midst and heat of the battle, to live or die amongst you all; to lay down for my God and for my kingdom and for my people my honour and my blood. . . . I know I have the body of a weak and feeble woman, but I have the heart and stomach of a King, and a King of England too.

Her performance at the Tilbury encampment was a public-relations triumph. Meanwhile, English ships built by Hawkins and led by Drake and Lord Howard out-sailed and out-gunned the Armada in a nine-day running battle up the English Channel. Those English mariners left unscathed encountered a "Protestant wind" off the Scottish coast; barely half the Spanish Armada survived to limp home in defeat. The English navy had come of age.

The defeat of the Spanish Armada in 1588 represented the zenith of Elizabeth's power and fame. The remainder of her reign was fraught with internal struggles with Parliament and the Puritans, and costly external warfare in Holland, France, and Ireland. Elizabeth quarreled regularly with Puritans whose demands for revisions in her 1559 religious settlement she angrily rejected; several Puritan MP's—including the outspoken free speech advocate, Peter Wentworth—ended up in the Tower in 1593 for their "insolence" to the Crown. In 1601, she gave in to rancorous parliamentary demands to end monopolies, but rising food prices, high taxes, and declining trade all combined to erode the aging queen's popularity.

Nothing drained royal coffers and disrupted Elizabeth's domestic tranquillity more than the Irish Rebellion of 1595 to 1603. Only nominally under English rule since Norman times, Ireland became fertile ground for Jesuit missionaries and Spanish intrigues late in the 16th century. In 1599, Elizabeth sent Robert Devereaux, earl of Essex, to crush the uprising. Instead, Essex negotiated a deal with rebel leader, the Earl of Tyrone, which he then haughtily demanded his queen accept. Banished from court for his disobedience, in 1601 Essex tried to raise a revolt against Elizabeth in London. Despite deep personal affection for her last royal favorite, Elizabeth did not hesitate to "teach him better manners" by way of the headsman's axe. Meanwhile, under new leadership—and at great cost—an English army finally harried and starved the Irish into submission.

As Elizabeth lay dying in March of 1603, Robert Cecil—Lord Burghley's son and successor as her principal secretary—quietly arranged for James VI of Scotland to become king of England. Following her death on March 24, Elizabeth I was interred in Westminster Abbey, in the crypt beside her grandfather, Henry VII.

Elizabeth Tudor ruled England by force of her own personality and by the tradition of absolute monarchy she inherited from her father. It is true that she was vain, fond of opulent displays of royal splendor, and possessed of a fiery and sometimes violent temper. It is equally true, however, that she put duty and patriotism ahead of private wants and desires. Her superb diplomacy, wily political sense, and regal bearing

earned Elizabeth the respect of her enemies and the love of her subjects. She inspired poets, playwrights, composers and explorers and succeeded in identifying herself so completely with her times that historians still call the second half of the 16th century the "Elizabethan Age."

SOURCES:

Neale, J.E. *Queen Elizabeth*. London: Jonathan Cape, 1934.

Read, Conyers. *Mr. Secretary Cecil and Queen Elizabeth*. NY: Alfred Knopf, 1960.

Ridley, Jasper. *Elizabeth I: The Shrewdness of Virtue*. NY: Viking Press, 1987.

Routh, C.R. *Who's Who in Tudor England*. London: Shepheard-Walwyn, 1990.

Somerset, Ann. *Elizabeth I*. NY: St. Martin's Press, 1991.

SUGGESTED READING:

MacCaffrey, Wallace. *Elizabeth I*. Routledge, 1993.

Mattingly, Garrett. *The Armada*. Boston, MA: Houghton Mifflin, 1959.

McGrath, Patrick. *Papists and Puritans under Elizabeth I*. NY: Walker, 1967.

Neale, J.E. *Elizabeth and Her Parliaments*. 2 vols. NY: St. Martin's Press, 1958.

Plowden, Alison. *Tudor Women: Queens and Commoners*. NY: Atheneum, 1979.

Rowse, A.L. *The Expansion of Elizabethan England*. NY: St. Martin's Press, 1955.

COLLECTIONS:

Calendar of State Papers (Domestic Series) of the Reigns of Edward VI, Mary, Elizabeth (1547–1603) (ed. R. Lemon, Mary Everett Green, *et al.*). London, 1856–70; *Calendar of State Papers (Foreign Series) of the Reign of Elizabeth (1558–1589)* (ed. J. Stevenson, R. B. Wernham, *et al.*). London, 1863–1950.

RELATED MEDIA:

"Elizabeth R" (540 min.), historically faithful six-part mini-series starring *Glenda Jackson, BBC-TV and Time-Life Multimedia, 1976.

"The Private Lives of Elizabeth and Essex" (VHS; 1 hr. 46 min.), fictionalized account starring *Bette Davis and Errol Flynn, Warner Bros., 1939.

"The Virgin Queen" (VHS; 1 hr. 32 min.), fictionalized account starring Bette Davis, Richard Todd, and Joan Collins, Twentieth Century-Fox, 1955.

Constance B. Rynder,
Professor of History,
University of Tampa, Tampa, Florida

Elizabeth I of Russia (1709–1762).

See Elizabeth Petrovna.

Elizabeth I Petrovna (1709–1762).

See Elizabeth Petrovna.

Elizabeth II (1926—)

Queen of the United Kingdom of Great Britain and Northern Ireland. Name variations: Elizabeth Windsor. Born Elizabeth Alexandra Mary Windsor on April 21, 1926, at the home of her maternal grandparents, in London's West End; elder daughter of Albert Fred-

Elizabeth II

erick Arthur George, 13th duke of York, also known as George VI, king of England (r. 1936–1952), and Elizabeth Bowes-Lyon (b. 1900); sister of Princess Margaret Rose (b. 1930); educated privately by governesses and at a small school at Windsor Castle; married Lieutenant Philip Mountbatten, R.N., duke of Edinburgh (son of the late Prince Andrew of Greece and Princess *Alice of Battenberg), on November 20, 1947; children: Charles, prince of Wales (b. November 14, 1948); Princess *Anne (b. August 15, 1950); Prince Andrew, duke of York (b. February 19, 1960); Prince Edward (b. March 10, 1964).

Named Heir Presumptive in 1936, after the abdication of Edward VIII brought her father to the throne as George VI, Elizabeth II acceded to the throne in 1952 following the death of the king. She is the 42nd sovereign of England since William I the Conqueror, yet only the sixth woman to occupy the English throne in her own right. Her predecessors were *Mary I, *Elizabeth I, *Mary II, *Anne, and *Victoria.

Elizabeth, nicknamed "Lilibet," enjoyed an idyllic childhood spent at the family town house in London and at the Royal Lodge at Windsor Castle. Winston Churchill, who first encountered Elizabeth at Balmoral when she was two, dubbed her a "character." In a letter to his wife, he wrote, "She has an air of authority and reflectiveness astonishing in an infant." Elizabeth and her younger sister *Margaret Rose had a series of governesses and tutors, including Marion Crawford ("Crawfie"), who was hired in 1933. When Elizabeth became Heir Presumptive (the title Heir Apparent being withheld in favor of a possible male heir), her education became more specialized, but her doting parents insisted that school continue to be a place of enjoyment for her. From age 12, she was tutored by Sir Henry Marten, a famous history teacher and later provost of Eton, while her grandmother, Queen *Mary of Teck, schooled her in the mysteries of royal behavior. Country life was a family tradition, and Elizabeth is reported to have said that had she not been heir to the throne she would have wanted "to be a lady living in the country, with lots of horses and dogs."

Following the outbreak of World War II, the princesses lived at Windsor during the blitz while their parents, King George and Queen *Elizabeth Bowes-Lyon, spent most of their time in London. During this time, Elizabeth began to take on some official duties and to enter fully into public life. On October 13, 1940, she made her first radio broadcast, assuring the children of the empire in a clear and precise voice, "We know, every one of us, that in the end all will be well." At age 16, after months of lobbying her father to let her undertake National Service, she was allowed to join the Auxiliary Transport Service, where she was trained in motor transport and maintenance. A short time later, on May 8, 1945, Elizabeth, dressed in her ATS uniform, joined her family on the balcony of Buckingham Palace to celebrate V-E (Victory in Europe) Day. That afternoon, she was allowed to leave the palace and join the celebration on The Mall; it was the last occasion that she would enjoy as "one of the people."

On the occasion of her 21st birthday, while on a goodwill tour of South Africa with the royal family, Elizabeth made a radio broadcast to the Commonwealth that would come to symbolize the spirit of her reign. "I declare before you all," she said, "that my whole life, whether it be long or short, shall be devoted to your service and the service of the great imperial family to which we all belong." Upon Elizabeth's return from South Africa, the king and queen announced her engagement to Lieutenant Philip Mountbatten, described by Crawfie as "a fair-haired boy, rather like a Viking, with a sharp face and piercing blue eyes." Elizabeth first met Philip on a family visit to the Royal Naval College at Dartmouth when she was 13. Although she rarely saw him for the next six years, there was never another man in her life.

The wedding, which was the first great State occasion after the war, was celebrated at Westminster Abbey on November 20, 1947. The couple spent their first five years of marriage at Clarence House, where Elizabeth gave birth to her first two children, Prince Charles and Princess *Anne. (They were followed later by Prince Andrew and Prince Edward.) Philip resumed his naval career, and Elizabeth often left the children with their nurses and grandparents to join her husband in Malta, where he was posted. Although she occasionally returned to Britain to represent her ailing father in official duties, Elizabeth's early years of marriage were the most carefree and happy of her life.

On February 6, 1952, while in Kenya on an extended Commonwealth Tour, Elizabeth received the news of her father's death and immediately returned to England where she was proclaimed queen two days later. The coronation took place of June 2, 1953, at Westminster Abbey. Despite the rain, thousands lined the route from Buckingham Palace to the Abbey, and an estimated 20 million British viewers watched the ceremony on television. The coronation caused as much sensation in the United States, where film of the ceremony was airlifted across the ocean for prompt telecasting. The broadcast, the first of its kind, ushered in the age of mass media and significantly changed the way the British monarchy was presented to the public.

Once settled, the new queen embarked on a half-year of nonstop travel, making visits to as many countries of the Commonwealth as possible. Her round-the-world itinerary ranks as the longest royal tour ever, encompassing 14 countries and covering 50,000 miles. Elizabeth has become by far the most traveled monarch in Britain's history, even touring extensively in Canada during her third pregnancy. In her 1977 Silver Jubilee year, she visited 36 countries in the United Kingdom over a period of three months. In addition to her widespread tours and her ceremonial functions, the queen dedicates a good deal of time to her constitutional role as Head of State. Her daily "boxes" (leather-covered despatch boxes from the prime minister's office, the Foreign Office, and other government departments) follow her when she is traveling or on vacation. All nine of her prime ministers, whether Conservative or Labour, have praised her for her professionalism and dedication.

Hoping to modernize the monarchy, Elizabeth made herself more accessible to the public as early as 1956. That year, she began holding informal lunches at Buckingham Palace so that she could meet those who had achieved distinction in a wide range of fields. Throughout the years, she has invited 40,000 a year to attend garden parties, and her informal "walkabouts," reminiscent of those initiated by her mother and father, have put her in touch with common citizens whom she might not otherwise encounter. Although intensely private about her family life, during the 1960s Elizabeth agreed to several television documentaries designed to further humanize the monarchy. The first production, *Royal Palaces,* was followed in 1969 by *Royal Family,* which provided a sanitized view of the royals at work and play and attracted an audience of 40 million in the United Kingdom alone.

With her life increasingly lived in the glare of the public spotlight, Elizabeth remains a private and self-contained person. Her biographer **Sarah Bradford** explains: "She does not give of herself easily, in public or in private, performing her role with dignity and an economy of emotion which has made it possible for her to carry the burden that she does." Many who are close to the queen find her more at ease with her horses and Corgi dogs than with people. Her passion for breeding and racing thoroughbred horses seems to provide therapy for the stresses of her daily life. Elizabeth's central relationship is with her husband Philip, whom she adores and defers to, despite the fact that he has been described as a brusque, short-tempered, and self-willed man. In the few years immediately following the queen's accession to the throne, the marriage suffered what Graham and **Heather Fisher** term "a succession of marital hiccups," while Philip adjusted to his lack of involvement in the monarchy. Eventually establishing his own career, Philip assumed the position as head of the family and has had a dominant role in raising the children.

Elizabeth has had her detractors from the beginning. As early as 1955, there was a public outcry when she did not sanction the marriage of Princess Margaret Rose to Peter Townsend, a hero of the Battle of Britain, who had been recently divorced. (Margaret later married Anthony Armstrong-Jones with disastrous results.) In 1956, the press was harsh over Elizabeth's treatment of the Suez crisis and the subsequent resignation of Prime Minister Anthony Eden. The following year, Lord Altrincham, writing in the *National Review,* criticized her public speaking, calling her voice that of a "priggish schoolgirl." He also accused her of being out of touch, surrounded by "a tweedy entourage who know nothing of life outside the restricted circle of the Establishment." Beginning in 1969, the royal finances came under fire, and, bowing to pressure, the queen began paying taxes in the 1990s. Most damaging to the monarchy, however, has been the conduct of the young royals and the breakdown of three of their marriages. In 1992, Andrew's separation from ❧➤ **Sarah Ferguson,** duchess of York, the ongoing troubles between Charles and *Diana, princess of Wales, and a fire that destroyed part of Windsor Castle so demoralized Elizabeth that she declared the year, "an *annus horribilis.*" With an equally heavy heart, she wrote to Charles and Diana in 1995 advising divorce.

As the millennium approached, the survival of the monarchy after Elizabeth was in question. Diana's sudden death in 1997 and the half-hearted response from the monarchy as the world mourned exacerbated the issue. However, the queen still held the heart of most Britishers. In 1998, as the anniversary of Diana's death approached, Buckingham Palace announced that the royal family would be marking the day quietly and privately at Balmoral, where no specific mention of Diana was made during chapel services. The Palace also avoided mentioning the results of a Gallup poll it had commissioned just two months after Diana's death, which showed that 71% of the British public thought the

❧➤ **Ferguson, Sarah** (1959—)
Duchess of York. Name variations: Fergie. Born Sarah Margaret Ferguson on October 15, 1959, in London, England; daughter of Ronald Ferguson (polo manager for the queen) and Susan Wright Ferguson Barrantes (died in an auto accident in September 1998); married Andrew, duke of York, on July 23, 1986 (divorced 1996); children: Beatrice (b. August 8, 1988); Eugenie (b. March 23, 1990).

monarchy should "definitely continue." It had been the most positive response ever recorded.

Standing on the balcony of Buckingham Palace during the World War II anniversary celebration in 1995, Elizabeth, along with her sister Margaret and the Queen Mother, had evoked a sense of continuity and tradition that is at the core of the monarchy. As Bradford points out, the queen also represents "values which most people still recognize even if they don't either practice them or aspire to them themselves—courage, decency, and a sense of duty."

SOURCES:

Allison, Ronald, and Sarah Riddell, eds. *The Royal Encyclopedia.* NY: Macmillan, 1991.

Bradford, Sarah. *Elizabeth: A Biography of Britain's Queen.* NY: Farrar, Straus and Giroux, 1996.

Fisher, Graham, and Heather Fisher. *Monarch: A Biography of Elizabeth II.* Salem, NH: Salem House, 1985.

Fraser, Antonia, ed. *The Lives of the Kings and Queens of England.* London: Weidenfeld and Nicolson, 1975.

Harris, Kenneth. *The Queen.* NY: St. Martin's Press, 1994.

Barbara Morgan,
Melrose, Massachusetts

Elizabeth Alexandra of Saxe-Altenburg (1830–1911).

See Alexandra of Saxe-Altenburg.

Elizabeth Amalia of Hesse

(1635–1709)

*Electress of the Palatinate. Name variations: Elizabeth Amalie von Hesse-Darmstadt. Born on March 20, 1635; died on August 4, 1709; married Philip Wilhelm or Philip William, Elector Palatine of the Rhine, on September 3, 1653; children: John William (b. 1658), elector of the Palatinate; Charles III Philip (b. 1661), elector of the Palatinate; *Maria Sophia of Neuberg (1666–1699); *Maria Anna of Neuberg (1667–1740); *Eleanor of Pfalz-Neuberg (1655–1720). Philip William's first wife was *Anna Constancia (1619–1651).*

Elizabeth Bowes-Lyon (1900—)

Queen-consort of England and mother of Elizabeth II. Name variations: Queen Elizabeth; Queen Mum; Duchess of York. Born Lady Elizabeth Angela Marguerite Bowes-Lyon on August 4, 1900, in London, England; youngest daughter and 9th of 10 children of Claude Bowes-Lyon, 14th earl of Strathmore and Kinghorne, and ❧▶ Nina Cavendish-Bentinck, Lady Strathmore; descendent of Robert Bruce, king of Scotland; married Albert (d. 1952), duke of York, also known as George VI, king of England (r. 1936–1952), on April 26, 1923; children: Elizabeth Alexandra Mary (future queen of England as Elizabeth II, b. April 21, 1926); Princess Margaret Rose (b. 1930).

Queen Elizabeth Bowes-Lyon did not follow the usual path to the throne but arrived there by default in 1936, when her husband Albert, duke of York, became King George VI following the abdication of his brother Edward VIII (who then married ***Wallis Warfield, duchess of Windsor**). Often described as a reluctant queen, Elizabeth Bowes-Lyon helped her husband, a shy, sensitive man with a debilitating stutter, rise to become a national figurehead, and she also became the most popular queen-consort in British history.

A commoner, Elizabeth Bowes-Lyon was born into Scottish aristocracy, the ninth of ten children in a close-knit family that divided their days between Glamis Castle, north of Dundee, and St. Paul's Walden Bury, 30 miles from London. She was an adventuresome child who spent many hours outdoors, romping with a menagerie of family pets and riding her Shetland pony, Bobs. Indoors, she delighted in dragging period costumes from the attic and presenting herself as a "princess" at family gatherings. Having an early fondness for tea cakes and conversation, Elizabeth was described by a governess as being mature beyond her years, with a natural talent for making others feel at ease. Schooled mostly at home (she attended a nursery class in London and two terms at a girls' day school), by the age of 21 she had blossomed into a wistfully pretty girl, confident and witty, with a number of hopeful young men in tow. In February 1922, reportedly while serving as a bridesmaid at the wedding of Princess ***Mary** (1897–1965) and Viscount Lascelles, she met Albert, the young duke of York, known to all as Bertie. Although Elizabeth turned down Albert's first two proposals, they became the next royals to be wed at Westminster Abbey.

Elizabeth had a calming, reassuring influence on her new husband and brought fresh air to the somewhat stuffy House of Windsor, providing laughter and good humor to a family not famed for either. Even King George V, with his reputation for gruffness, adored his new daughter-in-law, as evidenced by a letter he sent to Albert shortly after the marriage. "The better I know and the more I see of your dear little wife," he wrote, "the more charming I think she is."

With Elizabeth's encouragement, Albert undertook a long and exhausting treatment for his stuttering, and she remained at his side throughout the regimen of breathing and speech exercises as he gradually began to improve. The couple's first child, *Elizabeth (II), was born in London on April 21, 1926; *Margaret Rose followed in 1930. Princess Elizabeth was only seven months old when her mother was forced to leave her to accompany the duke on a state visit to Australia and New Zealand. Bowes-Lyon was so distraught at parting with her baby daughter that the royal car had to make an additional circle around Grosvenor Gardens on the way to Victoria Station, to give her enough time to compose herself before facing the crowds gathered on the platform to see them off.

The coronation of Albert as King George VI and Elizabeth as queen-consort was held on May 12, 1937, just five months after Edward's abdication, which weighed heavily on Britishers who were still mourning the death of King George V. During the first years of their reign, the new royals suffered profound insecurity, which was not helped by the growing threat of war. In the spring of 1939, they undertook one of the first Royal tours in North America—including a visit with the prime minister of Canada and a weekend visit with Franklin and *Eleanor Roosevelt at their Hyde Park home. Elizabeth and Albert soon endeared themselves to the public with their refreshing informality, including "walkabouts" and chats, a common touch that would become the hallmark of their reign. The Roosevelts were disarmed when the king and queen joined them for a picnic of hot dogs and beer. The stunning success of the royals across the Atlantic prompted new confidence at home. Their return to London was greeted by a celebratory mood that rivaled that of the coronation. Harold Nicolson recorded the event in his diary entry of June 23, 1939: "We lost all our dignity and yelled and yelled. The King wore a happy schoolboy grin; the Queen was superb. She really does manage to convey to each individual in the crowd that he or she has had a personal greeting. It is due, I think, to the brilliance of her eyes. . . . She is in truth one of the most amazing Queens since *Cleopatra [VII]."

During the war, the king and queen confirmed their position in the hearts of the people. Braving personal danger, they refused to leave London and remained highly visible throughout the Blitz. They were often seen visiting raid victims, "he in a naval uniform," wrote **Elizabeth Longford**, "she in flowery hat and pretty shoes stepping over the debris of splintered wood and glass." After the bombing of Buckingham Palace

Elizabeth Bowes-Lyon, 1922

in 1940, Elizabeth remarked, "I'm glad we've been bombed. It makes me feel I can look the East End in the face." So adept was she in boosting morale that Adolf Hitler often referred to her as the most dangerous woman in Europe.

The king was already ill in 1947, when he and Elizabeth Bowes-Lyon shared the happy occasion of their eldest daughter's marriage to Prince Philip. When the king died in February 1952, Elizabeth Bowes-Lyon was overcome with grief but determined to rebuild her life. Adopting the title of the Queen Mother, while her daughter ascended the throne as Elizabeth II, Bowes-Lyon took refuge in Scotland, where she found solace in restoring a 16th-century castle. (The Castle of Mey has since become her private hideaway, and the only home she personally owns.) Although it was suggested that she be dispatched for a two- or three-year tour of duty

&➤ **Cavendish-Bentinck, Nina** (c. 1860–?)
Countess of Strathmore. Name variations: Lady Strathmore. Born Nina Cecilia Cavendish-Bentinck around 1860; daughter of a Mrs. Scott and Charles Cavendish-Bentinck; married Claude Bowes-Lyon, 14th earl of Strathmore and Kinghorne, in 1881; children: **Violet Bowes-Lyon** *(1882–1893);* **Mary Bowes-Lyon** *(b. 1883); Patrick (b. 1884); John (1886–1930); Alexander (1887–1911); Fergus (1889–1915);* **Rose Bowes-Lyon** *(b. 1890); Michael (b. 1893);* ***Elizabeth Bowes-Lyon** *(b. 1900); David (b. 1902).*

to Canada or Australia, her daughter Elizabeth II would not hear of it. ("Oh no, we could not possibly do without Mummy," was the queen's often quoted reaction.) Instead, Elizabeth Bowes-Lyon continued the royal tours so popular in the late 1930s and, through the years, became a kind of roving ambassador for Britain.

Considered the matriarch of the entire royal clan since the death of Queen *Mary of Teck in 1953, Elizabeth Bowes-Lyon spread good will throughout the world and tended to an overwhelming schedule of official duties at home. Ann Morrow, in her biography *The Queen Mother,* described the queen's workload as so heavy at times that there were frequent changeovers of the ladies-in-waiting, most of whom had difficulty keeping up the pace. Possessed with a remarkable stamina and good health, which she has retained through the practice of homeopathy, the queen mother has always loved the outdoors, which she also attributes to keeping her in the pink. "A good strong wind," she remarked, "blows the germs away." She has also avidly pursued the sport of horse racing and has owned more than 50 horses.

Always a devoted grandmother, the queen mother supported her six grandchildren through difficult passages. In 1978, her grandson Prince Charles wrote of their relationship: "Ever since I can remember, my grandmother has been the most wonderful example of fun, laughter, warmth, infinite security and above all else exquisite taste. . . . For me she has always been one of those extraordinarily rare people whose touch can turn everything to gold."

In May 1995, resplendent in head-to-toe canary yellow, the queen mother appeared with her two daughters on the balcony of Buckingham Palace to celebrate the 50th anniversary of the end of World War II. Her appearance elicited the same outpouring of affection as it had in 1945, when she, the king, and the two princesses appeared on the same balcony for the first victory observance. As Daniel Pedersen pointed out in an article for *Newsweek,* the 1995 celebration provided a respite from the cynicism that pervaded the monarchy throughout the 1990s. Amid the failed marriages and scandals of the younger royals, the queen mother remains, in Pedersen's words, as "a living link to an age of national unity and greatness."

SOURCES:
Fellowes-Gordon, Ian. *Famous Scottish Lives.* Middlesex: Odhams, 1967.
Lacey, Robert. *Queen Mother.* Boston, MA: Little, Brown, 1987.

Longford, Elizabeth. *The Royal House of Windsor.* NY: Alfred A. Knopf, 1974.
Morrow, Ann. *The Queen Mother.* NY: Stein and Day, 1984.
Pedersen, Daniel. "Queen Mum: What Royalty Is Good For," in *Newsweek.* May 22, 1995.

SUGGESTED READING:
Forbes, Grania. *My Darling Buffy: The Early Life of the Queen Mother.* London: Richard Cohen Books, 1997.
Whitmore, Richard. *Hertfordshire's Queen.* London: Countryside Books, 1997.

Barbara Morgan,
Melrose, Massachusetts.

Elizabeth Caroline (1740–1759)

*English princess. Name variations: Elizabeth Guelph; Elizabeth Caroline Hanover. Born on December 30, 1740, at Norfolk House, London, England; died on September 4, 1759, in Kew Palace, Richmond, Surrey, England; buried at Westminster Abbey; daughter of Frederick Louis, prince of Wales, and *Augusta of Saxe-Gotha (1719–1772); sister of George III, king of England.*

Elizabeth-Charlotte (1676–1744)

*Duchess of Lorraine. Name variations: Elizabeth-Charlotte Bourbon-Orleans; Elizabeth Charlotte d'Orleans. Born on September 13, 1676; died on December 23, 1744; daughter of *Charlotte Elizabeth of Bavaria (1652–1722) and Philip, duke of Orléans (brother of Louis XIV of France); married Leopold, duke of Lorraine, on October 25, 1698; children: Leopold; Francis III (b. 1708), duke of Lorraine and Bar, also known as Francis I, Holy Roman emperor; Charles (b. 1712); *Elizabeth of Lorraine (1711–1741); Anna Charlotte of Lorraine (1714–1774).*

Elizabeth-Charlotte of Bavaria (1652–1722).

See Charlotte Elizabeth of Bavaria.

Elizabeth Charlotte of the Palatinate (fl. 1620)

Electress of Brandenburg and duchess of Cleves. Flourished around 1620; married George William (1595–1640), elector of Brandenburg (r. 1619–1640), duke of Cleves and Prussia; children: Frederick William (1620–1688), the Great Elector of Brandenburg (r. 1640–1688).

Elizabeth-Charlotte of the Palatinate (1652–1722).

See Charlotte Elizabeth of Bavaria.

Elizabeth Christina of Brunswick-Wolfenbuttel (1691–1750), Holy Roman empress.

See Maria Theresa of Austria for sidebar.

Elizabeth Christina of Brunswick-Wolfenbuttel (1715–1797)

Queen of Prussia. Name variations: Elizabeth Christina of Brunswick-Wolfenbüttel; Elizabeth Christine. Born on November 8, 1715; died on January 13, 1797; daughter of Antoinetta Amelia (1696–1762) and Ferdinand Albert II, duke of Brunswick-Wolfenbüttel; married Frederick II the Great, king of Prussia (1712–1786, r. 1740–1786), on June 12, 1733; children: none.

In 1733, at his father's insistence, Frederick II the Great married the German princess Elizabeth Christina of Brunswick-Wolfenbuttel, though he never loved her. Once he became king in 1740, Frederick had nothing more to do with her. He would later die childless, with a nephew to succeed him.

Elizabeth Christine.

See Elizabeth Christina of Brunswick-Wolfenbuttel (1691–1750) or (1715–1797).

Elizabeth de Burgh (d. 1327)

*Queen of Scots. Name variations: Ellen; Elizabeth of Ulster. Died on October 26, 1327, in Cullen, Grampian, Scotland; buried in Dunfermline Abbey, Fife, Scotland; daughter of Richard de Burgh (known as The Red Earl), 2nd earl of Ulster, and *Margaret de Burgh (d. 1303); became second wife of Robert I the Bruce, king of Scots (r. 1306–1329), in 1302; children: *Matilda Bruce (d. 1353); *Margaret Bruce (d. 1346); David II (1323–1370), king of Scotland (r. 1329–1370); John Bruce (b. around 1325).*

Elizabeth de Burgh, the second wife of Robert the Bruce, king of the Scots, was the daughter of Richard de Burgh, the powerful earl of Ulster, one of King Edward I of England's staunchest supporters.

Elizabeth de Burgh (1332–1363)

*Countess of Ulster. Born on July 6, 1332, in Carrickfergus Castle, Northern Ireland; died on April 25, 1363, in Dublin, Ireland; buried in Clare Priory, Suffolk, England; daughter of William de Burgh, 3rd earl of Ulster, and Maud Plantagenet (c. 1310–c. 1377); granddaughter of *Elizabeth de Clare who was also known as Elizabeth de Burgh (1295–1360); married Lionel of Antwerp (1338–1368), duke of Clarence, on September 9, 1352; children: *Philippa Mortimer (1355–1382), countess of Ulster and March.*

Elizabeth de Burgh was the sole heir to the earldom of Ulster, when her father William de Burgh, the "Brown Earl," was murdered by order of his cousins. While still a child, Elizabeth was taken to England by her mother *Maud Plantagenet. In 1352, the 20-year-old Elizabeth married Lionel of Antwerp, duke of Clarence, the son of King Edward III. Because of the marriage, Lionel, as the 5th earl of Ulster, could lay claim to the extensive de Burgh estates in Ireland but was unable to enforce those rights during his lifetime. In the era of the Tudors, the English monarchy once again laid claim. Following the death of Elizabeth de Burgh in 1363, Lionel of Antwerp married *Violet Visconti (c. 1353–1386).

Elizabeth de Farnese (1692–1766).
See Farnese, Elizabeth.

Elizabeth de France (1764–1794).
See Elizabeth, Madame.

Elizabeth de la Pole (1444–1503).
See Pole, Elizabeth de la.

Elizabeth Farnese (1692–1766).
See Farnese, Elizabeth.

Elizabeth Feodorovna (1864–1918).
See Ella.

Elizabeth Ferrers (1392–1434).
See Joan Beaufort (1379–1440) for sidebar.

Elizabeth Frederike of Bayreuth (fl. 1750)

Duchess of Wurttemberg. Flourished around 1750; first wife of Karl Eugene also known as Charles Eugene (1728–1793), duke of Wurttemberg (r. 1737–1793).

Elizabeth Henrietta of Hesse-Cassel (1661–1683)

German noblewoman. Born on November 8, 1661, in Cassel; died on June 27, 1683, in Coln au Der, Spree; daughter of William VI the Just (b. 1629), landgrave of Hesse-Cassel; became first wife of Frederick III (1657–1713), elector of Brandenburg (r. 1688–1701), *later Frederick I, king of Prussia (r. 1701–1713), on August 23, 1679; children: *Louise Dorothea of Brandenburg (1680–1705). Frederick's second wife was *Sophie Charlotte of Hanover (1668–1705).*

Elizabeth Hohenzollern

(1815–1885)

Grand duchess of Hesse. Name variations: Elizabeth of Prussia; princess of Prussia. Born Mary Elizabeth Caroline Victoria on June 18, 1815; died on March 21, 1885; daughter of William Hohenzollern and **Mary of Hesse-Homburg (1785–1846); married Charles of Hesse-Darmstadt, on October 22, 1836; children: Louis IV (1837–1892), grand duke of Hesse-Darmstadt; Henry (b. 1838); Anna of Hesse (1843–1865, who married Francis II Frederick, grand duke of Mecklenburg); William (b. 1845).*

Elizabeth Hohenzollern (1894–1956).
See Elizabeth, queen of the Hellenes.

Elizabeth Howard (1494–1558).
See Howard, Elizabeth.

Elizabeth Howard (d. 1534).
See Howard, Elizabeth.

Elizabeth Howard (d. 1538).
See Boleyn, Anne for sidebar.

Elizabeth Maria of Thurn and Taxis (1860–1881)

Duchess of Braganza. Born on May 28, 1860, in Dresden; died on February 7, 1881, in Odenburg; daughter of Maximilian Anton Lamoral, prince of Thurn and Taxis, and **Helene of Bavaria (1834–1890); married Miguel, duke of Braganza, on October 17, 1877; children: Miguel Maximiliano (b. 1878), duke of Vizeu; Francisco José Gerado (b. 1879); Maria Teresa Carolina (1881–1945, who married Charles Louis, prince of Thurn and Taxis).*

Elizabeth Muir or Mure (d. before 1355).
See Muir, Elizabeth.

Elizabeth of Anhalt (1563–1607)

Electress of Brandenburg. Born on September 25, 1563; died on September 28, 1607; daughter of Joachim Ernst (b. 1536), prince of Anhalt, and Agnes of Barby (1540–1569); became third wife of John George (1525–1598), elector of Brandenburg (r. 1571–1598), on October 6, 1577; children: **Magda-*

lene of Brandenburg (1582–1616); Joachim Ernst (1583–1625), margrave of Ansbach.

Elizabeth of Anhalt-Dessau

(1857–1933)

Grand duchess of Mecklenburg-Strelitz. Born Elizabeth Mary Fredericka Amelia Agnes on September 7, 1857; died on July 20, 1933; daughter of Leopold Frederick I, duke of Anhalt-Dessau; married Adolphus Frederick V, grand duke of Mecklenburg-Strelitz, on April 17, 1877; children: **Victoria of Mecklenburg-Strelitz (1878–1948); *Jutta of Mecklenburg-Strelitz (1880–1946); Adolphus Frederick VI, grand duke of Mecklenburg-Strelitz (1882–1918).*

Elizabeth of Austria (c. 1430–1505).
See Elizabeth of Hungary.

Elizabeth of Austria (1743–1808)

Habsburg princess and abbess. Name variations: Maria Elisabeth. Born Maria Elisabeth on August 13, 1743, in Vienna; died on September 22, 1808, in Linz; daughter of **Maria Theresa of Austria (1717–1780) and Frances I, emperor of Austria (r. 1804–1835), also known as Francis II, Holy Roman emperor (r. 1792–1806); sister of *Marie Antoinette (1755–1793), *Maria Carolina (1752–1814), and Joseph II, Holy Roman emperor (r. 1765–1790). Elizabeth of Austria was an abbess in Innsbruck.*

Elizabeth of Austria (1837–1898).
See Elizabeth of Bavaria.

Elizabeth of Baden (1779–1826)

German princess and empress of All the Russias. Name variations: Elizabeth Louise; Luisa of Baden; Louise of Baden; Tsarina Elizaveta; Yelizaveta Alekseyevna von Baden. Born Luisa of Baden around 1777 in the Rhine Valley of Germany; daughter of Charles Louis of Padua (b. 1755), prince of Padua and Baden, and **Amalie of Hesse-Darmstadt (1754–1832); married Alexander I (1777–1825), tsar of Russia (r. 1801–1825), on October 9, 1793; children: Marie (1799–1800); Elizabeth (1806–1808).*

In 1793, when Alexander I was 16, in 1793, his grandmother *Catherine II the Great arranged his marriage to the German princess Luisa of Baden. (Luisa then appropriated the Russian name Elizaveta or Elizabeth.) In 1796, Catherine died unexpectedly, and Alexander's father Paul I then began his short and turbulent rule as tsar (1796–1801). A change in the law of succession was one of Paul's first acts (1797). No longer could nobles and courtiers conspire to determine the next tsar; the first-born male would now automatically become heir apparent. Thus, Alexander I would inherit a position that he longed to forsake. His preference would have been retirement to one of the royal estates with his new wife or life abroad in the German Rhine valley (Elizabeth of Baden's homeland) where he could continue his studies as an amateur naturalist.

Following a successful reign, wherein he defeated Napoleon and attempted to bring constitutional reforms to his country, Alexander died of gastric fever in 1825 while visiting his wife, who was also ill, in remote Taganrob on the Sea of Azov. Since the marriage of Elizabeth of Baden and Alexander produced only two daughters who had died in infancy, by the law of succession Alexander's eldest brother Constantine was next in line for the throne. Constantine, however, abdicated his responsibilities to the next brother in line, Nicholas I.

Elizabeth of Bavaria (fl. 1200s)

*Princess Palatine. Flourished in the 1200s; daughter of Otto II, count Palatine (r. 1231–1253) and *Agnes of Saxony; first wife of Conrad IV (1228–1254), Holy Roman emperor (r. 1250–1254, not crowned) and king of Jerusalem (r. 1250–1254), king of Naples and Sicily (r. 1250–1254); married Meinhard IV of Gorizia; children: (first marriage) Conradin, king of Naples and Sicily (r. 1254–1268) and king of Jerusalem (r. 1254–1268).*

Elizabeth of Bavaria (1371–1435).

See Isabeau of Bavaria.

Elizabeth of Bavaria (1801–1873)

*Bavarian princess. Born on November 13, 1801; died on December 14, 1873; daughter of Maximilian I Joseph, elector of Bavaria (r. 1799–1805), king of Bavaria (r. 1805–1825), and *Caroline of Baden (1776–1841); twin sister of *Amalia of Bavaria (1801–1877); married Frederick William IV (1795–1861), king of Prussia (r. 1840–1861), on November 29, 1823.*

Elizabeth of Bavaria (1837–1898)

*Empress of Austria and Hungary. Name variations: Elizabeth of Austria; Elisabeth von Habsburg or Hapsburg; Elisabeth of Austria-Hungary; (nickname) Empress Sisi or Sissi. Born Elizabeth Amélie Eugénie on December 24, 1837, at the castle of Possenhofen on Lake Starnberg; died of stab wounds on September 10, 1898, in Geneva; daughter of Maximilian Joseph, duke of Bavaria, and *Ludovica (1808–1892); married her cousin Francis Joseph (Franz Joseph I), emperor of Austria (r. 1848–1916), on April 24, 1854; children: eldest daughter died in infancy; Gisela (1856–1932); Marie Valerie (1868–1924); crown prince Rudolf (1858–1889, who died at Mayerling).*

Elizabeth of Bavaria inherited the lively intelligence and artistic taste of the Wittelsbach royal house. Her education was unconventional, and she became an adroit rider and climber while accompanying her father, Maximilian Joseph, duke of Bavaria, on his hunting expeditions. She called on the peasants in their cottages and enjoyed bucolic pleasures.

In August 1853, when the emperor of Austria, Franz Joseph, met the Bavarian ducal family at Ischl, he immediately fell in love with 16-year-old Elizabeth who was reputedly the most beautiful princess in Europe. The marriage took place in Vienna on April 24, 1854. Elizabeth's attempts to modify court etiquette, and her extreme love of horses and frequent visits to the imperial riding school, scandalized Austrian society, and in the early days of her marriage, she frequently encountered Viennese prejudice.

Her predilection for Hungary and for all things Hungarian also cut into her popularity. She had first visited Hungary in 1857. Ten years later, she and Franz Joseph were crowned its queen and king with the advent of the Dual Monarchy which created the kingdom of Hungary, east of the river Leith, and the kingdom of Austria, west of the river Leith. Each kingdom had its own constitution and parliament, but they shared rule and a common ministry for finance and foreign affairs. Elizabeth's appeal for the Hungarians remained unchanged throughout her life, and the castle of Gödöllö, presented as a coronation gift, was one of her favorite residences.

Intellectually independent and freedom-loving, Elizabeth was thought to be much brighter than her plodding husband, the emperor. She did not believe in the monarchical form of government, regarding it as "a ruin" that had become obsolete in her own time. Outside of Hungarian affairs, she took little interest in politics, but she was one of the most charitable queens. In the Seven Weeks' War with Prussia in 1866, Elizabeth's popularity with her Austrian subjects was more than restored by her diligent care of the

Elizabeth of Bavaria (1837–1898)

wounded after the defeat at Königgrätz. Besides her public altruism, she was also privately charitable.

Her eldest daughter died in infancy; her daughter *Gisela (b. 1856) married Prince Leopold of Bavaria; and her youngest daughter *Marie Valerie (1868–1924) married the Archduke Francis Salvator. The tragic death of her only son, the crown prince Rudolf, in 1889, was a shock from which Elizabeth never truly recovered. Rudolf, the heir apparent, killed his lover *Marie Vetsera and committed suicide at a hunting lodge outside of Vienna at Mayerling. Elizabeth was also deeply affected by the suicide of

her cousin Louis II of Bavaria and by the death of her sister *Sophie of Bayern, who perished in the fire of the Paris charity bazaar in 1897. Events, it seems, conspired against the house of Habsburg. Elizabeth's brother-in-law, Archduke Karl Ludwig, also known as Charles Louis (1883–1896), drank from the river Jordan while on a pilgrimage and died from an intestinal infection; her other brother-in-law Maximilian, emperor of Mexico, was shot by a firing squad (1867); and her sister-in-law *Carlota was driven mad.

Experiencing symptoms of lung disease in 1861, Elizabeth spent some months recuperating in Madeira, but she was soon able to resume her outdoor sports and, for some years before 1882, when she had to give up riding, was a frequent visitor on English and Irish hunting fields. In her later years, her dislike of publicity increased. Much of her time was spent in travel or at the Achilleion, the palace she had built in the Greek style in Corfu.

On September 10, 1898, as she walked from her hotel to the steamer at Geneva, she was stabbed by the anarchist Luigi Luccheni and died within a few hours. The random, senseless assassination completed the list of misfortunes of the Austrian house and aroused intense anger throughout Europe. On learning of his beloved wife's death, Franz Joseph remarked, "Nothing has been spared me in this world."

SOURCES

de Burgh, A. *Elizabeth, Empress of Austria: A Memoir.* London, 1898.

Friedmann, E., and J. Paves. *Kaiserin Elisabeth.* Berlin, 1898.

Murad, Anatol. *Franz Joseph I of Austria and his Empire.* Twayne, 1968.

Redlich, Joseph. *Emperor Francis Joseph of Austria: A Biography.* Macmillan, 1929.

RELATED MEDIA:

*Gabrielle Dorziat appeared as Elizabeth in the film *Mayerling*, 1936.

"Sisi," a 26-segment work for Hungarian television by *Márta Mészáros, 1992.

Elizabeth of Bavaria (1876–1965)

*German-born queen of the Belgians, patron of music, and humanitarian who was one of the most admired European sovereigns of the 20th century. Name variations: Elisabeth, Dowager Queen of·Belgium; Elisabeth of Belgium; Elizabeth von Wittelsbach, duchess in Bavaria. Born Elisabeth Valerie Gabrielle Marie von Wittelsbach at Possenhofen Castle, Bavaria, on July 25, 1876; died at Château de Stuyvenberg, near Brussels, on November 23, 1965; buried at Laeken, Brussels, Belgium; daughter of *Maria Josepha of Portugal (1857–1943) and Karl Theodor "Gackl" also known as Karl Theodor von Wittelsbach, duke in Bavaria [sic]; earned a medical degree from the University of Leipzig; married Albert I (1875–1934), king of the Belgians (r. 1909–1934), on October 2, 1900; children: Leopold III (b. 1901), king of the Belgians; Charles Theodore (b. 1903); Marie José of Belgium (b. 1906, who married Umberto II of Italy).*

One of the most beloved royals of the modern age, Belgium's Queen Elizabeth of Bavaria was born in Germany, making her by birth a citizen of a nation few if any modern Belgians had reason to respect or admire. She was born in Bavaria as Elisabeth Valerie Gabrielle Marie von Wittelsbach, daughter of *Maria Josepha of Portugal and Karl Theodor, duke *in* Bavaria, which meant that he did not have a claim to the Bavarian throne as would a duke *of* Bavaria. Karl Theodor was the brother of the empress of Austria-Hungary, *Elizabeth of Bavaria (1837–1898), who would be assassinated by an anarchist in Geneva in 1898. His cousin, King Ludwig II, was the "Mad King of Bavaria" who had provided vast sums of money to the composer Richard Wagner and decreed the construction of extravagant neo-medieval castles at Neuschwanstein and elsewhere in his kingdom.

The eccentric and often self-destructive strain evident for generations in the Wittelsbach family manifested itself in a more benign fashion in Karl Theodor, who ignored his aristocratic calling, insisting instead on studying medicine in Munich and Vienna. A formative event in his life was his participation as an officer in the Franco-Prussian War of 1870–1871. Having witnessed the cruelties and suffering endured by wounded soldiers, he resolved to dedicate himself to humane ideals and the alleviation of disease and pain. Once he had earned his medical degree, the duke went on to practice his specialty of diseases of the eye. He founded three eye hospitals, the chief of which was situated at the Royal Schloss at Tegernsee. Here the "Oculist Duke" performed his surgeries, often operating free of cost on indigent patients. Those who could afford to pay were expected to contribute to the hospital's collection box, which was periodically emptied for distribution to the poor people of the region.

Along with her brothers and sisters, Elizabeth of Bavaria was raised in an environment of the utmost simplicity. Their father, considered a model husband, respected the personalities and potentialities of his children. He impressed upon them the need for a strong sense of duty toward the poorer and weaker members of society, and he insisted that this duty must be expressed in a practical, never patronizing, fashion. One of Elizabeth's brothers took Holy Orders, working as a curate in one of Bavaria's poorest parishes. Elizabeth was particularly close to her father, who personally supervised her education and encouraged her musical interests which included piano and violin, on both of which she achieved considerable skill. She often assisted him in his hospital and chose to accompany him on his rounds with peasant patients. To prepare for a life of giving to the less fortunate, Elizabeth studied nursing, earning a medical degree from the University of Leipzig. From her earliest years, she showed a strong affinity for nature and enjoyed a mountain-climbing expedition in the Bavarian alps with her brothers.

Elizabeth first caught the eye of Belgium's Prince Albert (1875–1934) in Paris during May 1897 when both attended the funeral of *Sophie of Bayern, duchess of Alençon. They met again the next year in Vienna to attend another funeral, that of Elizabeth's paternal aunt, the Empress Elizabeth of Bavaria. Albert and Elizabeth fell in love and announced their betrothal in Paris in 1900. Although German Kaiser Wilhelm II viewed the marriage of a Bavarian princess to the heir of the throne of neighboring Belgium as an important geopolitical victory, the marriage of Albert and Elizabeth in Munich on October 2, 1900, was in fact born of love, not a mere dynastic arrangement.

The couple arrived in Brussels a few days later and almost instantly won over the hearts of millions of Belgians. Albert was heir to a throne still occupied by King Leopold II, who was little loved by most of his subjects both because of an autocratic personality and colossal greed. Leopold had amassed an immense private fortune through exploitation of Africa's Congo region, which he ruled as a personal possession. In contrast, the young Prince Albert and his Bavarian-born bride soon provided convincing evidence of their strong sense of duty.

Albert busied himself with numerous philanthropies, and Elizabeth dedicated her energies to learning about the sick and needy citizens of Belgium. Before long, she became a familiar sight in Brussels hospitals and orphanages. Years before Albert became king, both he and Elizabeth became immensely popular in all social strata, but particularly among the poor and dispossessed. Both royals showed a dislike of excessive formality, behaving in a manner that was considered to be extremely egalitarian for the age. From the time Albert became king of the Belgians in 1909, his reign was characterized by a strong social conscience on the part of the entire royal family. Elizabeth fully shared the sentiments King Albert I had expressed in December 1909, during his first speech from the throne: "Our prosperity depends upon the prosperity of the masses."

Both Elizabeth and her husband were interested in the arts, and even before 1909 their home in Brussels' Place de l'Industrie had often been the site of gatherings of Belgium's most brilliant artists, writers, and musicians. The queen's interest in the arts and her medical training crossed paths when she secured the best possible medical treatment for the celebrated painter Laermans who was threatened with the loss of his eyesight.

The bourgeois probity exhibited by the couple—particularly after the birth of their three children, Leopold, Charles and *Marie José of Belgium—was much admired by a Belgian public that had long ago become disillusioned by the scandalous private life of King Leopold II. Albert and Elizabeth greatly enjoyed their family life, which was simple and unadorned by the royal standards of the day, and their people responded to them with ever-growing respect. The elevation of Albert to kingship in 1909 had elated the entire Belgian nation, and most people anticipated a long, prosperous and peaceful reign. These hopes, however, were not to be realized.

World War I began on the Western front with Germany's violation of Belgian neutrality. This was part of the secret Schlieffen Plan which called for a war on two fronts in which France would be defeated in a *blitzkrieg* via Belgium that would enable German forces to fight Russia in the east as soon as Paris capitulated. Stubborn Belgian resistance in the first weeks of the campaign frustrated Berlin's grand strategy, but at a very high cost to tiny Belgium. During these first weeks, Queen Elizabeth helped to transform the Royal Palace into an emergency hospital for wounded Belgian soldiers. The queen waited until the last possible moment, with German troops already in the Brussels suburbs, before she joined retreating Belgian forces.

Elizabeth and Albert decided to send their three young children to the safety of England, but both were determined to remain with their people. Thanks to the bravery of Belgian troops, as well as King Albert's decision to flood the Yser valley in October 1914, it was possible to keep a small patch of Belgian soil, measuring no more than 20 square miles, from falling into the hands of German occupying forces. Belgian blood and decisiveness had allowed the French to retain possession of their Channel ports and very likely changed the course of not only the great conflict but also of world history.

The German invasion of Belgium that began World War I was a national catastrophe for millions of Belgians as well as a personal tragedy for Queen Elizabeth. German-born, she now had to break all relations with her family in Bavaria. She did so without hesitation, recalling an incident before the war when Germany's Kaiser Wilhelm II had tried to pressure King Albert toward a more pro-German course. On that occasion, her succinct reply to the ruler of Belgium's powerful neighbor made clear her loyalties: "My husband and I are one, I abide by his decisions." Elizabeth dealt with the issue of her relations with her family, now living in an enemy nation, in the simplest terms possible, noting, "It is finished between me and them; henceforth an iron curtain has descended between us which will never be raised."

On the Channel coast, the royal couple spent the next four years in a modest house in the small fishing village of La Panne, located in sand dunes near Furnes. There was hardly an undestroyed house in La Panne, which was less than eight miles from the front and well within the range of German artillery. "As long as one square foot of Belgian soil is left," said Elizabeth, "I will stay on it." The years of nursing experience in her father's hospitals in Bavaria now proved valuable to the queen, who for the next four years spent countless hours with the wounded soldiers in the La Panne military hospital. Over the course of the war, more than 200,000 wounded were treated there, and, because of the excellent quality of care they received, a relatively low number of 10,000 died, some of them literally in her arms.

To many Belgians suffering the horrors of war, Queen Elizabeth was the embodiment of the spirit of a small nation's will to resist oppression and foreign tyranny. She received many unofficial titles including "Heroine of the Yser," "Belgium's Soul," and "The Angel of the Field Hospitals." Occasionally, she would receive visitors at La Panne to remind her of better days. These included the violinist Eugene Ysaye, the composer Saint-Saëns, and the poet Verhaeren. Another famous visitor to La Panne, French President Raymond Poincaré, described Elizabeth, who received him dressed in white: "Delicate and frail, it seems as if she should have been broken by the storm; but she has an indomitable soul; she has given herself wholly to her husband, her children and Belgium."

After four years at La Panne, during which Elizabeth made visits to the trenches along with King Albert, the war finally ended in November 1918. With her children, she accompanied Albert on triumphal visits to Dunkirk, Bruges, and Antwerp. At long last, on November 22, 1918, the king and queen of the Belgians, accompanied by their sons Prince Leopold and Prince Charles, entered the liberated city of Brussels in triumph. Albert and his sons smiled at the crowds, but it was Queen Elizabeth, mounted on a huge white

charger and wearing a faded grey riding habit, who presented the most moving sight. An eyewitness recalled how an obviously overwhelmed queen of the Belgians "sat erect and motionless on her white horse, her face piteously grave in the midst of so much rejoicing, and her eyes stonily fixed on the road ahead, as though she dare not glance to right or left for fear of breaking down."

The postwar years were busy ones for Elizabeth and Albert. Accompanied by their son Crown Prince Leopold, they made a triumphant tour of the United States in 1919, which included a visit with President Woodrow Wilson at the White House. Freed of her wartime duties, the queen was now able to enjoy some leisure time, which included an hour or more of violin practice almost daily. Although she was modest about her musical abilities, Elizabeth was in fact a more than competent violinist, having taken lessons from such masters as Ysaye, Jacques Thibaud, and Georges Enesco. On at least one occasion, she played a violin duo with the American violin prodigy Yehudi Menuhin. The incomparable Catalan cellist Pablo Casals became one of her closest friends. Elizabeth also sculpted and was an enthusiastic amateur painter.

Elizabeth of Bavaria (1876–1965)

The bulk of her time, however, was allocated to an ever-expanding number of philanthropic and cultural activities, as well as to her three children and a growing number of grandchildren. Although Europe's great war had ended, it left in its wake permanently disabled soldiers, as well as widows and orphans who needed care. Elizabeth provided both material support and emotional sustenance for these victims of war. She also busied herself with other projects. Intrigued by the mysteries of ancient Egypt since a visit to Egypt in her youth, Elizabeth traveled there in February 1923 and witnessed the ongoing excavation of the tomb of the young Pharaoh Tutankhamen. Her visit was responsible for the creation of a Queen Elizabeth Egyptological Foundation.

Elizabeth chartered other foundations dealing with blindness, polio, cancer, and tuberculosis. Various aspects of child welfare were of high concern to her, and in 1958 she was patron of the World Child Welfare Congress that was held in conjunction with the Brussels World Fair. In the 1950s, these organizations were combined into one large charitable entity under the queen's auspices, the *Front Blanc de la Santé.*

Sensitive to the needs of the indigenous peoples living under Belgian rule in the Congo colony, in the late 1920s Elizabeth took steps to establish a medical foundation specializing in the study, treatment, and prevention of the tropical diseases found in the Congo and other regions of equatorial Africa. She also kept current with the newest discoveries in science and technology. Both she and King Albert visited factories and laboratories to see firsthand the latest technological breakthroughs. When visiting laboratories and universities, she insisted on meeting the most celebrated scientific innovators of her day, including *Marie Curie, Niels Bohr, Paul Langevin, Lord Rutherford, and, of course, Albert Einstein.

The 1930s, which started with a world economic depression and ended with the onset of a second World War, was a tragic decade for the royal family. Economic hardship exacerbated existing tensions between the French-speaking and Flemish-speaking sectors of the country, which greatly distressed the queen. A more personal blow took place on February 17, 1934, when Albert fell to his death while climbing a cliff near Namur. Elizabeth went into a deep depression and was just starting to find a new equilibrium in her life when in August 1935 her daughter-in-law Queen *Astrid of Sweden, wife of her son, the new King Leopold III, was killed in an automobile accident in Switzerland.

Although this second family tragedy was almost more than Elizabeth could bear, she began to slowly revive during an extended stay in Naples, where her daughter Marie José lived as crown princess of Italy, having married Crown Prince Umberto in 1930. On Elizabeth's return to Brussels, one of her ladies-in-waiting coaxed her back into a regimen of violin practice. In 1937, she presided over an international music contest for violinists, the *Concours Ysaye.* Known in later years as the *Concours Musical International Reine Elizabeth,* this contest came to include pianists as well as violinists in one of the musical world's most important festivals. Conscientious to a fault as the patron of the event, Elizabeth attended all of the elimination rounds in 1937 and would do so in later years as well. She was present at the special gala performance at which the first winner, the Soviet violinist David Oistrakh, performed brilliantly. In 1938, the first piano competition was won by another talented young Soviet musician, Emil Gilels.

With her daughter-in-law Astrid's death in Switzerland, Dowager Queen Elizabeth had effectively become Belgium's only queen. More burdens were soon to be thrust upon her and her adopted nation. In May 1940, Nazi Germany invaded Belgium. For the second time in a generation, German troops marched through the streets of Brussels and other cities and towns in Belgium. If the first German occupation was at times harsh, this occupation was infinitely worse in its inhumanity. Members of the Belgian resistance were tortured before their executions, and starting in 1942 Belgian Jews were rounded up to be sent to the East for "special treatment," i.e., systematic murder.

Unlike the Dutch royal family which fled to London and set up an anti-Nazi Government in Exile, the Belgian king remained in Brussels. Leopold III's British and French allies, and many Belgians as well, were critical of their king for having surrendered to Nazi Germany after only a few days' fighting. To many, Leopold seemed to show an insufficient spirit of resistance to the Nazis now occupying his nation, and he seemed incapable of halting the collaborationist tendencies that flourished among many of his subjects. His wartime marriage to *Liliane Baels served to further infuriate and alienate his subjects. Like her son, Queen Elizabeth also chose to remain in Belgium, living in seclusion at Laeken Castle near Brussels.

Being German-born, Elizabeth could communicate more easily than most Belgians with high officials of the occupying forces. Some of the leading occupation officials hoped that despite her reputation as a Belgian patriot she might still harbor at least some vague lingering sympathies for Germany. In these beliefs, they were totally mistaken. Elizabeth submerged as best she could her profound hatred for Nazism, using her position to ameliorate the lives of many Belgians. Once it was clear that the country's Jews were targeted for annihilation, she made special efforts to save as many of them as possible. She had always admired Jews both as individuals and as a people, and now she signalled her solidarity with them by wearing in public a five-pointed brooch that resembled the Star of David that Jews were ordered to wear whenever they appeared in public. Her interventions on behalf of Jews took many forms. Sometimes a visit to a threatened household kept German authorities from arresting those individuals for at least a period of time sufficient for them to attempt to go into hiding. On at least one occasion, she contacted one of her son's German guards, knowing that this officer was not sympathetic to Nazism. The officer was able to get a positive response from the top German general, von Falkenhausen. In other instances, her intervention made it possible to save the lives of Jewish children, who found refuge in convents, orphanages and with farm families who willingly risked their own lives to save the life of a child.

Belgium was liberated by Allied forces in the spring of 1945, but the nation could not fully enjoy its freedom for long. Divisions quickly surfaced between those factions that forgave King Leopold III for his wartime behavior and were willing to move ahead in a spirit of national reconciliation, and those Belgians who demanded that the king abdicate because of what they considered a weak performance during a time that had called for a strong example of courage. From the moment of its birth in 1830, Belgium had always been deeply divided along linguistic and cultural lines, and many observers felt that the country was in grave danger of national disintegration. Leopold III abdicated his throne in 1951. During the following years, Elizabeth remained above partisan strife, becoming a unifying element and a universally admired symbol of the Belgian national spirit at its best. Tireless in her charitable and cultural activities, the dowager queen continued to be the embodiment of charm, tenacity, and human compassion.

Queen Elizabeth did not fear the Nazi occupiers of her nation during the darkest days of World War II. Neither did she succumb to the hysteria that seemed to grip the West at the height of the Cold War. She was considerably ahead of her time in her awareness of the dangers raised by the expanding nuclear arsenals of the United States and the Soviet Union. Since the late 1930s when Soviet musicians had won prizes during the first years of her music festival, Elizabeth had felt a kinship to the Soviet Union. During the war, she had kept informed of the sacrifices made by the Soviets in their war against Hitler. Although many in the West branded the Stockholm Peace Appeal of 1950 as little more than Communist-inspired propaganda because it unequivocally called for the banning of all nuclear weapons, Queen Elizabeth gave it her enthusiastic support.

Many of her fellow Belgians disagreed with Elizabeth's determination to challenge Cold War orthodoxies, but she refused to change either her views or public actions. Every year, she welcomed musicians who came to Brussels from behind the Iron Curtain to participate in her music festival. Always an enthusiastic traveler, she made few concessions to her age, visiting in her later years the United States, Israel, Italy, Poland, Yugoslavia, the Soviet Union and the People's Republic of China. Her trips to the two largest and most powerful Communist nations left her open to charges from conservatives and anti-Communists that she was politically naive and that her actions were harming her nation. Some hostile newspaper accounts dubbed her the "Red Queen."

She infuriated some Belgians by sponsoring the Belgo-Soviet Friendship Society and was once even photographed carrying a copy of *Le Drapeau Rouge*, the official newspaper of the Belgian Communist Party. The paranoia, so characteristic of the Cold War era, never stopped Elizabeth from speaking out candidly on those issues, particularly the theme of world peace, that she believed to be of major importance to humanity. Not without a touch of imperiousness, the queen would simply state, "I always do what I wish."

Never in robust health, Elizabeth gave many the impression of being physically fragile. This was, however, misleading. Enjoying her role as the much-beloved dowager queen of the Belgians, Elizabeth remained healthy and active into her late 80s. Many of her subjects found it hard to look forward to a time when she would no longer be with them. During her last decades, she did yoga exercises and took long walks, as well as engaging in a continuing regimen of swimming, sunbathing and ice-cold baths. When she suffered a heart attack on November 4, 1965, she initially astonished her physicians by appearing to make a rapid recovery. But a second, more severe attack on the evening of November 23 resulted in her death at Stuyvenberg Palace. Three days of national mourning were declared.

The queen's funeral in Brussels attracted not only royalty from throughout Europe but countless thousands of her loyal subjects. Through the new technology of television, millions of Belgians watched from their homes. After three days of rain and storm, the day of her funeral was cold and sunny. Her simple mahogany coffin was borne on a flag-decked hearse and drawn by 70 Grenadiers, the regiment of her late husband Albert. At the requiem mass in St. Michael's Roman Catholic Cathedral, Cardinal Léon-Joseph Suenens eulogized Elizabeth as "simultaneously the Queen of the scholars and the unfortunate, the Queen of artists and writers, the Queen with an unlimited heart." The German-born sovereign who had displayed her fierce love for her adopted homeland during two devastating wars of German aggression was buried at Laeken Castle. She was honored on a number of occasions by being depicted on Belgian postage stamps, including two stamps that were issued in May 1976 to honor her memory on the centenary of her birth.

SOURCES:

Aronson, Theo. *Defiant Dynasty: The Coburgs of Belgium.* Indianapolis, IN: Bobbs-Merrill, 1968.

Larson, Wanda Z. *Elisabeth: A Biography. From Bavarian Princess to Queen of the Belgians.* San Francisco, CA: International Scholars, 1997.

Laurent, Lea. *Our Lady of Belgium (Notre Dame de Belgique).* Translated by Elisabeth M. Lockwood. London: Iris, 1916.

Mallinson, Vernon. *Belgium.* NY: Praeger, 1970.

Mender, Mona. *Extraordinary Women in Support of Music.* Lanham, MD: Scarecrow Press, 1997.

Nicholas, Alison. *Elisabeth, Queen of the Belgians: Her Life and Times.* Bognor Regis, England: New Horizon, 1982.

"Queen and Humanist: Elisabeth of Belgium," in *Memo from Belgium.* No. 72. January 1966, pp. 1–24.

"Queen Elisabeth, 89, of Belgium, Is Dead," in *The New York Times.* November 24, 1965, pp. 1 and 39.

"Queen Elisabeth of Belgium," in *The Times* [London]. November 24, 1965, p. 14.

John Haag,
Assistant Professor of History,
University of Georgia, Athens, Georgia

Elizabeth of Bavaria-Landshut
(1383–1442)

Electress of Brandenburg. Born in 1383; died on November 13, 1442; daughter of Frederick, duke of Bavaria-Landshut; married Frederick I of Nuremberg (1371–1440), elector of Brandenburg (r. 1417–1440), on September 18, 1401; children: John the Alchemist III (b. 1406), margrave of Brandenburg; Frederick II (1413–1471), elector of Brandenburg (r. 1440–1470); Albert Achilles (1414–1486), elector of Brandenburg as Albert III (r. 1470–1486); Frederick the Fat (1424–1463), margrave of Brandenburg.*

Elizabeth of Belgium (1876–1965).
See Elizabeth of Bavaria.

Elizabeth of Bohemia (1292–1339)

Countess of Luxemburg and queen of Bohemia. Born in 1292; died on September 28, 1339; daughter of Wenceslas II (1271–1305), king of Bohemia (r. 1278–1305), and *Elizabeth of Poland (fl. 1298–1305); sister of Wenceslas III, king of Bohemia; married John Limburg also known as John of Luxemburg (1296–1346), count of Luxemburg and king of Bohemia (r. 1310–1346), on August 31, 1310; children: *Bona of Bohemia (1315–1349, who married John II, king of France); Wenceslas I (b. 1337), duke of Luxemburg and Brabant; Charles IV Luxemburg (b. 1316), Holy Roman Emperor (r. 1347–1378), and John Henry (1322–1375), margrave of Moravia (who married *Margaret Maultasch). Elizabeth of Bohemia's husband John of Luxemburg was the son of Henry VII of Luxemburg, Holy Roman emperor.

Elizabeth of Bohemia (1358–1373)

Duchess of Austria. Born on March 19, 1358, in Prague; died on September 19, 1373, in Vienna; first wife of Albrecht also known as Albert III (c. 1349–1395), duke of Austria (r. 1365–1395). Albert's second wife was *Beatrice of Brandenburg (1360–1414).

Elizabeth of Bohemia (1596–1662)

Electress Palatine and queen of Bohemia. Name variations: Elisabeth of Bohemia; Elizabeth of England; Elizabeth, Electress Palatine; Elizabeth Stuart, the Winter Queen. Born at Falkland Castle in Fifeshire, Scotland, on August 15 or 19, 1596; died at Leicester House in Leicester Fields, England, on February 13, 1662; interred at Westminster Abbey, London; eldest daughter of Anne of Denmark (1574–1619) and James VI (1566–1625), king of Scotland (r. 1567–1625), later king of England as James I (r. 1603–1625); sister of Charles I, king of England (r. 1625–1649); married Frederick V (d. 1632), Elector Palatine and titular king of Bohemia, on February 14, 1613; children: 13, including Frederick Henry (1614–1629, who drowned in *the Haarlem Meer); Charles I Louis also known as Karl Ludwig, Elector Palatine (1617–1680, whose daughter *Charlotte Elizabeth of Bavaria married Philippe I, duke of Orléans, and became the ancestor of the elder, and Roman Catholic, branch of the royal family of England); *Elizabeth of Bohemia (1618–1680, princess of Palatine, German philosopher, disciple of Descartes); Rupert (1619–1682), duke of Cumberland; Maurice (1620–1654); ❧▶ Louisa (1622–1709), abbess; Edward Simmern (1624–1663, who married *Anne Simmern, "princesse palatine"); *Henrietta Maria (1626–1651, who married Count Sigismund Ragotzki and died childless); Charlotte (1628–1631); Philip (1629–1650); *Sophia, electress of Hanover (1630–1714, who married Ernst August, elector of Hanover, and was mother of George I of England); Gustav (1632–1641).*

As was typical for royal daughters, Princess Elizabeth, the eldest daughter of *Anne of Denmark and King James VI of Scotland, was reared away from her parents, in the homes of various English nobles who had proven their loyalty to the crown. She was entrusted to the care of the Earl of Linlithgow during her infancy. Following the 1603 departure of the royal family to England, where her father was crowned James I, Elizabeth was entrusted to the care of the Countess of Kildare. When she was nine years old and under the care of Lord and Lady Harington at Combe Abbey in Warwickshire, a conspiracy against the king, now known as the Gunpowder Plot, was formed. The conspirators were Catholic extremists determined to assassinate the Protestant King James and bring England back to the Catholic Church. Their plan included kidnapping Elizabeth and making her queen after killing her parents and older brother Henry, heir to the throne. The plot failed, and for her own safety Lord Harington removed Elizabeth from Warwickshire to Coventry.

Three years later, the 12-year-old Elizabeth appeared at court, primarily so her parents could find her a proper suitor. Her beauty soon attracted admiration and became the inspiration for poets. Her suitors included France's dauphin, Maurice, prince of Orange, Gustavus Adolphus, Philip III of Spain, and Frederick V, the elector Palatine. Despite the opposition of her mother Anne of Denmark, a union with Frederick was finally arranged to strengthen the alliance with the Protestant powers in Germany. The marriage took place at Whitehall on February 14, 1613, with great feasting, jousting, fireworks, and masques, while Elizabeth's mother reportedly entertained her new son-in-law "with a fixed countenance." On June 17, the 16-year-old new-

lyweds moved to Heidelberg where Elizabeth, who had developed extravagant taste and a high-spirited personality in her early years, enjoyed five years of leisure and merrymaking with funds from an English annuity. The small German court was totally unaccustomed to such activities, and Elizabeth found that her new subjects did not approve of her behavior.

The country Elizabeth had inherited was on the brink of eruption. When Matthias, king of Bohemia and Hungary, died in 1619 after the start of the Thirty Years' War, the electors of the empire met in Frankfort to choose his successor.

Elizabeth of Bohemia (1596–1662)

❧▶ **Louisa** (1622–1709)

Princess Palatine and abbess of Maubisson. Name variations: Louise Hollandine; Louise Simmern. Born Louisa Hollandine on April 17 or 18, 1622, at The Hague, Netherlands; died on February 11, 1709, in Maubuisson; daughter of *Elizabeth of Bohemia (1596–1662) and Frederick V, Elector Palatine and titular king of Bohemia; sister of *Elizabeth of Bohemia (1618–1680) and *Sophia (1630–1714), electress of Hanover; became abbess of Maubuisson.

Emperors were elected by the Seven Electors, key figures in the constitution. Although the electors reluctantly chose Matthias' nephew Ferdinand II, the election was hardly concluded when news reached Frankfort that the Bohemians had deposed Ferdinand and elected as their new king Elizabeth's husband, the inexperienced Frederick V, Elector Palatine, leader of the German Calvinists.

There is no evidence to show that Frederick's acceptance was instigated by Elizabeth or that she had any influence in her husband's political career, though she did declare that she would rather eat sauerkraut as the wife of a king than dine off gold plates as the wife of an elector; she also offered to sell all her jewels for the cause. Elizabeth accompanied Frederick to Prague in October 1619 and was crowned queen on November 7. As in Germany, Elizabeth's vivaciousness and ostentatious spending, as well as her immaturity, caused concern and dislike among the Bohemians. Frederick was only to hold onto his crown for one year.

Ferdinand quickly amassed a coalition army in response. In October 1619, he struck a deal with his brother-in-law Maximilian, duke of Bavaria. As head of the Catholic League (an alliance of Catholic princes in whose name he maintained an army), Maximilian agreed to attack the rebels if Ferdinand would give him Frederick V's lands and electoral rank. Ferdinand and Maximilian were not the only ones who desired Frederick's ruin. John George, the Lutheran Elector of Saxony, was willing to attack Frederick in exchange for the Bohemian province of Lusatia. Spain offered money and cooperation if they were allowed to conquer Frederick and Elizabeth's richest possession, the Lower Palatinate, which lay along the Rhine River and blocked Spanish access to the Netherlands. Although the northern half of the Netherlands had rebelled against Spain and established its independence, a truce with this Protestant Dutch Republic was about to expire.

In August 1620, the army of Maximilian's Catholic League, led by Count Tilly, crossed into Bohemia while the Saxons invaded Lusatia. On November 8, at White Mountain just outside Prague, Tilly destroyed the rebel forces, and Frederick fled Bohemia while his remaining territory, the Upper Palatinate, also fell to Maximilian. Though Elizabeth's high spirits and gaiety had offended the citizens of Prague, in time of trouble she showed courage and grit. Driven out of Prague on November 8, 1620, after her husband's defeat, Elizabeth traveled to Berlin and Wolfen-

büttel; finally, she and Frederick took refuge at The Hague with Prince Maurice of Orange.

As Elizabeth and Frederick were stripped of their lands and titles, all or part of the estates of 658 families and 50 towns in Bohemia were confiscated, and the lands were sold to loyal, Catholic purchasers at nearly a third of their value. A new, largely foreign aristocracy took advantage of the bargains to amass enormous wealth. Eventually, in 1627, the remaining Protestants were given the choice between conversion and exile. The kingdom of Bohemia was now Catholic.

Help sought from Elizabeth's father James I came only in the form of useless emissaries and negotiations. The assistance of her chivalrous cousin Duke Christian of Brunswick, and other young men who were inspired by the beauty and grace of the Queen of Hearts, as Elizabeth was now called, did not improve their situation.

Elizabeth's new residence was at Rhenen near Arnheim, where she received many English visitors and endeavored to maintain her strength and spirit, despite frequent disappointments, including the drowning death of her first born in 1629.

The Dutch, unable to accept permanent Spanish control of the Rhine, signed a treaty to help Frederick V regain his lands. King Christian IV of Denmark prepared to rescue Protestantism by invading the empire. But Count Tilly and his army of the Catholic League defeated King Christian at the Battle of Lutter in 1626, and Denmark eventually made peace at Lübeck in 1629. Meanwhile, Gustavus Adolphus, the Lutheran king of Sweden, had come to the aid of Frederick and the Protestants. Landing on the Baltic coast, he quickly occupied the northeastern quarter of the empire. He then summoned all the Protestant princes to Leipzig where they declared war against Ferdinand unless he withdrew the Edict of Restitution. By the fall and winter of 1631, Gustavus had conquered all of western Germany. Then, at the battle of Lützen on November 16, 1632, Gustavus Adolphus lay dead on the field, though he had won the battle.

Gustavus Adolphus' victories secured no permanent advantage for the Protestants, and his death at Lützen was followed by that of Frederick's on November 29, 1632. Elizabeth wrote her brother Charles I of England saying that this was "the first time she was frighted:" for it struck her "so cold as ice and she could neither cry nor speak nor eat nor drink nor sleep for three days." Subsequent attempts by Elizabeth to reinstate her son Charles Louis to their lost lands were unsuccessful. Not until the Peace of Westphalia in 1648, which ended the Thirty Years' War, did her son regain a portion of them, the Rhenish Palatinate. Although Charles Louis regained part of his father's lands, disputes with his mother led Charles to refuse to receive her in the Palatine, and so she remained in exile.

Meanwhile, Elizabeth's position in Holland grew more and more unsatisfactory. The payment of her English annuity of £12,000 stopped after the outbreak of England's Civil War; the death of her brother Charles in 1649 put an end to all hopes from that quarter; and the pension allowed her by the house of Orange ceased in 1650.

Because of dissension, her children abandoned her. Her nephew Charles II, at the restoration of his English crown, showed no desire to receive her in England. Parliament voted her £20,000 in 1660 for the payment of her debts, but Elizabeth did not receive the money. On May 19, 1661, despite Charles II's attempts to block her journey, Elizabeth, now 65, left The Hague and returned to England for the first time since she had left as a child of 16. She received no official welcome on her arrival in London and stayed at Lord Craven's house in Drury Lane. Her son Charles, however, had a change of heart and subsequently granted her a pension and treated her with kindness. On February 8, 1662, she moved to Leicester House in Leicester Fields; she died shortly afterwards on the 13th and was buried in Westminster Abbey.

Elizabeth's beauty, grace and vivacity charmed her contemporaries, but her incredible popularity was probably enhanced by her string of misfortunes and by the fact that these misfortunes were incurred in defense of the Protestant cause. Later, as the ancestor of the Protestant Hanoverian dynasty, she secured a prominent place in English history. She has long been regarded as a martyr to Protestantism.

Elizabeth of Bohemia (1618–1680)

German philosopher, Princess Palatine, and abbess of Hervorden. Name variations: Elisabeth; Elizabeth of Hervorden; Elizabeth of the Palatinate; Elizabeth Simmern; "La Greque." Born on December 26, 1618, in Heidelberg, Baden-Wurttemberg, Germany; died on February 8, 1680 (some sources cite February 11, 1681), in Herford, North Rhine-Westphalia, Germany; daughter of Frederic V, king of Bohemia (Elector Palatine, also known as The Winter King) and *Elizabeth of Bohemia (1596–1662); 13 brothers and sisters, including Sophia, electress of Hanover (1630–1714); educated by tutors. Was abbess of Hervorden Convent in Herford, Westphalia, Germany.

Selected works: Die Briefe der Kinder des Winterkönigs. Hrsg. und mit einer Einleitung versehen von Karl Hauck *(1908);* Descartes, la princesse Elisabeth, et la reine Christine, d'apres des lettres inédites, par le comte Foucher de Careil *(1909);* Lettres sur la morale: correspondance avec la princess Elisabeth, Chanut et la reine Christine *(1935).*

Elizabeth of Bohemia's parents, Frederic V and Elizabeth Stuart (also known as *Elizabeth of Bohemia [1596–1662]), were deposed as king and queen of Bohemia while she was still a child. In exile, Elizabeth was raised by her grandmother *Louisa Juliana and an aunt in Silesia until the age of nine, when she joined her parents in Holland at the Hague Court. At the age of 20, she was offered the Bohemian throne but chose to remain at court in the Hague.

Elizabeth learned music, dancing, art, Latin, as well as sciences, and she took to Greek so well that she received the family nickname of "La Greque." In Holland, she met and became the disciple of the philosopher René Descartes, who is considered the father of modern philosophy for his move away from religious contemplation to a concentration on the way in which we experience the world. Of her 13 brothers and sisters, her sister *Sophia, electress of Hanover, also became a philosophical disciple, following Gottfried Wilhelm Leibniz.

As the disciple of Descartes, Elizabeth became known as a *femme philosophe.* But she was more than his pupil. Their long friendship and extensive correspondence, which was the primary medium of philosophical discourse at the time, influenced him greatly. In his introduction to *Principles of Philosophy* (1644), Descartes commends the intelligence of Elizabeth, whom he believed understood his writings better than anyone else, and who had an ease of understanding in both mathematics and philosophy that was like his own. He dedicated this, his largest work, to her. Her questions and criticisms were so provoking that his letters back to her became part of the content of his book *Passions of the Soul* (1646).

Elizabeth, a sufferer of recurring depression, was a single woman who spent most of her early adult life at the homes of various relatives. Around 1661, she joined the Protestant Convent at Hervorden, in Herford, Westphalia, as a coadjutor. In 1661, she acquired the important position of abbess at Hervorden, which provided her both independence and stature. *Anna Maria van Schurmann, a disciple of Descartes with whom Elizabeth had corresponded, took refuge in the Convent from religious persecution. During this time, they became good friends. Elizabeth retained her position as abbess until her death in 1680 after a long illness.

SOURCES:

Atherton, Margaret. *Women Philosophers of the Early Modern Period.* Indianapolis: Hackett, 1994.

Kersey, Ethel M. *Women Philosophers: a Bio-critical Source Book.* NY: Greenwood Press, 1989.

Waithe, Mary Ellen, ed. *A History of Women Philosophers.* Boston: Martinus Nijhoff Publications, 1987–1995.

Catherine Hundleby, M.A.
Philosophy, University of Guelph

Elizabeth of Bosnia (c. 1345–1387), queen of Hungary.

See Jadwiga for sidebar.

Elizabeth of Bosnia (d. 1339)

*Queen of Poland. Name variations: Elzbieta of Bosnia; some sources cite her as Jadwiga of Wielpolska. Died in 1339; possibly daughter of Anna of Plock and Henry V of Zagan; married Vladislav IV also known as Wladyslaw I the Short or Ladislas I Lokietek (1260–1333), king of Poland (r. 1306–1333); children: *Cunigunde (d. after 1370); *Elizabeth of Poland (1305–1380); Casimir III (1309–1370), king of Poland (r. 1333–1370).*

Elizabeth of Brabant (1243–1261)

*Princess of Brabant. Born in 1243; died on October 9, 1261; daughter of *Sophia of Thuringia (1224–1284) and Henry II (1207–1248), duke of Brabant (r. 1235–1248); married Albert I, duke of Brunswick-Luneburg, on July 13, 1254. Two years after the death of Elizabeth of Brabant, Albert I married Adelheid of Montferrat (d. 1285), daughter of Boniface III, marquess of Montferrat; Albert and Adelheid had seven children.*

Elizabeth of Brandenburg (1485–1555).

See Elizabeth of Denmark.

Elizabeth of Brandenburg (1510–1558)

*Duchess of Brunswick. Born on August 24, 1510; died on May 25, 1558; daughter of *Elizabeth of Denmark (1485–1555) and Joachim I Nestor*

(1484–1535), elector of Brandenburg (r. 1499–1535); married Erik I the Elder (1470–1540), duke of Brunswick (r. 1495–1540), on March 12, 1525; children: Erik II the Younger (b. 1528), duke of Brunswick; *Anne Marie of Brunswick (1532–1568).*

Elizabeth of Brunswick (1691–1750).

See Maria Theresa of Austria for sidebar on Elizabeth Christina of Brunswick-Wolfenbuttel.

Elizabeth of Brunswick (1746–1840)

*Prussian royal. Name variations: Eleonore Christina Ulrica. Born Elizabeth Christine Ulrica on November 8, 1746, in Wolfenbüttel, Germany; died on February 18, 1840, in Stettin; daughter of Charles (b. 1713), duke of Brunswick-Wolfenbüttel, and *Philippine Charlotte (1716–1801); became first wife of Frederick William II (1744–1797), king of Prussia (r. 1786–1797), on August 14, 1765 (divorced 1769); children: *Frederica of Prussia (1767–1820).*

Elizabeth of Brunswick-Wolfenbuttel (1593–1650)

*Duchess of Saxe-Altenburg. Born on June 23, 1593; died on March 25, 1650; daughter of *Elizabeth of Denmark (1573–1626) and Henry Julius, duke of Brunswick; married John Philipp, duke of Saxe-Altenburg, on October 25, 1618; children: *Elizabeth Sophie of Saxe-Altenburg (1619–1680).*

Elizabeth of Carinthia (c. 1262–1313).

See Agnes of Austria for sidebar on Elizabeth of Tyrol.

Elizabeth of Courtenay (d. 1205)

*French royal. Died in 1205; daughter of Reinald, lord of Courtenay, and Hawise de Donjon; married Peter I de Courtenay (c. 1126–1180), after 1150; children: Peter or Pierre II de Courtenay (d. 1218), emperor of Constantinople (r. 1216–1217); *Alice de Courtenay (d. 1211).*

Elizabeth of Denmark (1485–1555)

*Electress of Brandenburg. Name variations: Elizabeth of Brandenburg; Elizabeth Oldenburg. Born in 1485; died on June 10, 1555; daughter of *Christina of Saxony (1461–1521) and John I, also known as Hans (1455–1513), king of Norway and Denmark (r.*

1483–1513); married Joachim I Nestor (1484–1535), elector of Brandenburg (r. 1499–1535), on April 10, 1502; children: Joachim II Hektor (1513–1571), elector of Brandenburg (r. 1535–1571); *Anna of Brandenburg (1507–1567); *Elizabeth of Brandenburg (1510–1558); John of Brandenburg (1513–1571), landgrave of Brandenburg.

Elizabeth of Denmark (1524–1586)

Duchess of Mecklenburg-Güstrow. Name variations: Elizabeth Oldenburg. Born on October 14, 1524; died on October 15, 1586; daughter of *Sophia of Pomerania (1498–1568) and Frederick I (1471–1533), king of Denmark and Norway (r. 1523–1533); married Magnus of Mecklenburg-Schwerin, on August 26, 1543; married Ulrich III, duke of Mecklenburg-Güstrow, on February 16, 1556; children: *Sophia of Mecklenburg (1557–1631).

Elizabeth of Denmark (1573–1626)

Duchess of Brunswick. Name variations: Elizabeth Oldenburg. Born on August 25, 1573; died on June 19, 1626; daughter of Frederick II, king of Denmark and Norway (r. 1559–1588), and *Sophia of Mecklenburg (1557–1631); sister of *Anne of Denmark (1574–1619); married Heinrich Julius also known as Henry Julius (1564–1613), duke of Brunswick (r. 1589–1613), on April 19, 1590; children: Frederick Ulrich (b. 1591), duke of Brunswick; *Elizabeth of Brunswick-Wolfenbuttel (1593–1650, who married John Philipp, duke of Saxe-Altenburg). Henry Julius' first wife was *Dorothea of Saxony (1563–1587).

Elizabeth of England (1596–1662).

See Elizabeth of Bohemia.

Elizabeth of Farnese (1692–1766).

See Farnese, Elizabeth.

Elizabeth of Gorlitz (c. 1380–c. 1444)

Duchess of Luxemburg. Name variations: Elizabeth of Görlitz; Elizabeth of Luxembourg, Luxemburg, or Limbourg. Born around 1380 in Luxemburg; died around 1444 in Luxemburg; daughter of John of Burgundy and Richarde of Mekelburg; second wife of Antoine or Anthony, duke of Brabant (died 1415); married John of Bavaria, around 1419; children: (first marriage) John IV, duke of Brabant (r. 1415–1427, who married *Jacqueline of Hainault); Philip, duke of Brabant (r. 1427–1430).

Daughter of the ruling house of Luxemburg, Elizabeth of Gorlitz married Duke Antoine of Brabant about 1400 and had two children, John and Philip. She seems to have been an ambitious, shrewd woman, qualities she shared with her husband. When the Holy Roman emperor Wenceslas IV, who was also ruler of Luxemburg, was imprisoned by his German vassals after years of a chaotic reign, Elizabeth and Antoine claimed the throne of Luxemburg for themselves in 1412, on the grounds that it adjoined their legitimate holdings in Brabant and Limburg. The couple held the duchy together, co-ruling, for three years, until Antoine's death in 1415 at the battle of Agincourt. The imprisoned Wenceslas also died in 1415, paving the way for Elizabeth to retain Luxemburg. She ruled alone until around 1419, when she married Duke John of Bavaria, who assumed the rule of Luxemburg with her. He died only six years later, and Elizabeth again ruled alone. She outlived both of her sons and thus was forced to cede the duchy to Philip the Good when she retired from governing in 1443. Elizabeth is believed to have died the following year.

Laura York,
Riverside, California

Elizabeth of Greece (1894–1956).

See Elisabeth, Queen of the Hellenes.

Elizabeth of Hainault (1170–1190).

See Isabella of Hainault.

Elizabeth of Habsburg (1293–1352)

Duchess of Lorraine. Born around 1293 in Vienna; died on May 19, 1352, in Nancy; daughter of *Elizabeth of Tyrol (c. 1262–1313) and Albrecht also spelled Albert I of Habsburg (1255–1308), king of Germany (r. 1298–1308), Holy Roman emperor (r. 1298–1308, but not crowned); married Ferry IV also known as Frédéric or Frederick IV (1282–1328), duke of Lorraine (r. 1312–1328); children: Rodolphe also known as Rudolf (1318–1346), duke of Lorraine (r. 1328–1346); Margareta of Lorraine (who married John de Chalon and died after 1376).

Elizabeth of Habsburg (1501–1526).

See Willums, Sigbrit for sidebar.

Elizabeth of Habsburg (d. 1545), queen of Poland.

See Sforza, Bona for sidebar.

Elizabeth of Habsburg (1554–1592).

See Elisabeth of Habsburg.

Elizabeth of Habsburg (1883–1963).

See Elizabeth von Habsburg.

Elizabeth of Hardwick (1518–1608).

See Talbot, Elizabeth.

Elizabeth of Hervorden (1618–1680).

See Elizabeth of Bohemia.

Elizabeth of Hesse-Darmstadt (1864–1918).

See Ella.

Elizabeth of Holstein (fl. 1329)

Queen of Denmark. Name variations: Elizabeth von Holstein. Flourished around 1329; daughter of Henry I (b. 1258), count of Holstein, and Heilwig of Bronkhorst (d. after July 15, 1310); married Eric, king of Denmark (r. 1321–1326, 1330–1332), in 1329 (divorced 1331).

Elizabeth of Hungary (1207–1231)

Hungarian saint and princess who defied the customs of her age and class by her tireless efforts to care for the sick and poor. Name variations: Saint Elizabeth of Hungary; St. Elizabeth of Thuringia. Born on June 7, 1207, in Pressburg (Bratislava); died of exhaustion and malnourishment on November 19, 1231, at Marburg; daughter of King Andrew II, king of Hungary (r. 1202–1235), and Gertrude of Andrechs-Meran (c. 1185–1213); married Louis IV also known as Ludwig IV, landgrave of Thuringia, in 1221; children: Hermann (1222); Sophia of Thuringia (1224–1284, some sources note another daughter Sophia born in 1225); Gertrude of Thuringia (b. 1227).

Betrothed to Ludwig IV, future landgrave of Thuringia (1211); widowed when Ludwig died on crusade (1227); canonized by Pope Gregory IX (1235).

In many ways, the life of Elizabeth of Hungary illustrates important trends in 13th-century religious sensibilities. Her brief existence—she died at age 24—was dramatically packed with the ordinary events commonly experienced by women of her class and era: marriage and childbearing. Yet the young princess found ingenious ways to enrich these activities by suffusing them with deeper religious meaning. The great thrust of the newer religious orders of the period, especially the Franciscans, was to highlight the poverty of Christ and to stress the cultivation of spiritual riches regardless of material conditions. Elizabeth found ways to fervently embrace these ideals and live them in her daily life. In a period

when women only rarely dared to pursue activity in the secular world, Elizabeth's rather flamboyant acts of charity and self-abnegation earned her both personal satisfaction and public recognition of her sanctity.

Elizabeth's many charitable acts and disregard for her personal comfort won her great admiration and resulted in her canonization only four years after her death. It is difficult, therefore, to evaluate the sources that chronicle her life and death, as legend is mixed so inextricably with biographical details. Material concerning Elizabeth's life was gathered almost immediately upon her death, as the canonization process was undertaken soon after 1231. The sources include a letter written by her spiritual director, Conrad of Marburg, to Pope Gregory IX, as well as statements made by two of her ladies-in-waiting and other servants who had assisted Elizabeth's work at the hospital she founded.

Elizabeth's father Andrew (II) became king of Hungary in 1205. Since the Hungarians were one of the last European peoples to become Christianized (King Stephen I officially converted in 1000), they were one of the newest members of the international Catholic community. As "new" Christians, they were anxious to conform to current standards of ecclesiastical discipline, and the royal family maintained close ties with the papacy. Marriage alliances were utilized to ensure healthy diplomatic relations with both the Holy Roman Empire and smaller German political entities.

Since medieval women were largely shaped by their family context, it is helpful to examine the circumstances in her immediate family that may have contributed to Elizabeth's religious attitudes. Her mother *Gertrude of Andrechs-Meran was the daughter of Bertold, duke of Meran. Gertrude's family was not only extremely devout, but it produced several female saints and male bishops. Elizabeth's maternal aunt, *Hedwig of Silesia (1174–1243), the patron saint of Silesia, is an interesting example of pious models available to Elizabeth within her family. Hedwig married Henry, duke of Silesia, and gave birth to seven children before she convinced him to live chastely with her. She had an extraordinary love for female lepers and imposed many voluntary hardships on herself in order to identify more fully with the poor. Elizabeth's maternal uncle, Eckembert, was the bishop of Bamberg. The longstanding piety of her maternal family, combined with the fervent convert attitude of her paternal family, help to advance the deep religious impulses that shaped young Elizabeth:

she was inordinately exposed to spiritual concerns, even by the standards of her day.

In 1211, Hermann, landgrave of Thuringia, arranged for the betrothal of his son Ludwig (IV) to Elizabeth. The four-year old princess was taken to the Thuringian royal castle at Wartburg, where she was raised by ❧➤ **Sophia, landgravine of Thuringia,** her future mother-in-law. This arrangement was common among the nobility of medieval Europe, for it allowed minor girls to acquire a deeper familiarity with the cultural nuances they were expected to operate within upon their marriages. In Elizabeth's case, the early exposure to her intended groom resulted in a solid friendship between her and Ludwig; indeed, their marriage was an extremely happy one by all accounts.

However, Sophia did not develop a friendly relationship with her future daughter-in-law. Accounts of Elizabeth's life refer to strained relations between the two, apparently stemming from Sophia's disappointment that a more prestigious match could not have been found for her son. On an important feast day, the entire family attended church in their finest attire. When Elizabeth encountered the enormous crucifix on the door of the church at Eisenach, she removed her crown and prostrated herself before the cross. Sophia rebuked her with the taunt that perhaps the royal crown was too heavy for her head, suggesting her unsuitability as a wife for Ludwig. Elizabeth responded that it seemed inappropriate to wear jewels and pearls on her head when Christ himself wore only thorns.

Although charitable activities of Sophia are recorded, it appears that a "contest" was entered into early by the mother and daughter-in-law. Ludwig seems to have supported his fiancée in her struggle against Sophia's disapproval: according to the testimony of one of Elizabeth's servants who lived with the princess from her early childhood until after 1221:

> [S]he endured heavy and open persecution from the relatives, and vassals, and counselors of her betrothed; they were always trying to induce [Ludwig], by every means in their power, to repudiate her, and send her back to the king, her father. . . . But, in spite of all, and contrary to all anticipation, she had in her betrothed a secret consoler in all her sorrow and affliction.

It is interesting that the sources collected after Elizabeth's death all stress the theme of her single-minded devotion to piety within the context of her love for Ludwig. Contemporary historians note that the model of sanctity for earlier periods involved female celibacy in the monastic milieu; but by the early 13th century, a woman who exemplified both religious fervor and devotion to her husband became an acceptable model.

ℰlizabeth was perfect in body, handsome, brown complexioned, earnest in her conduct, modest in all her ways, kindly in speech, fervent in her prayers, and overflowing in her charity to poor people, . . . and full of virtues and godly love at all times.
—Adam Baring von Molberg, 16th-century chronicler

When Hermann died in 1216, 16-year-old Ludwig became the new landgrave of Thuringia, and his marriage to Elizabeth was celebrated in 1221 when she was 14 years old. The wedding was a lavish ceremony, but Elizabeth immediately afterward began to openly practice extreme acts of charity and personal renunciation of food and comfort. Many of the sources mention her antipathy towards court finery, and her secret feeding of poor beggars, often with food intended for her own consumption. One account of her devotion to the poor and sick involves her mother-in-law Sophia's continual efforts to undermine Elizabeth's activities: the young wife allowed a leper to occupy Ludwig's bed while her husband was away from home. It was easier for Elizabeth to nurse the dying man in this way. But when Sophia learned of her son's imminent arrival, she immediately warned him that his bed had been infected by his wife's preference for poor lepers over her own husband. She took Ludwig to his bed chamber to show him the wretched leper, but her son saw instead Jesus himself cared for in the bed.

In 1222, the year after her marriage, Elizabeth produced an heir, named Hermann, to the landgraviate of Thuringia, though the boy's succession was later threatened by Elizabeth's brother-in-law, Henry Raspe IV. Elizabeth named her first daughter *Sophia of Thuringia (b. 1224); some sources indicate that she gave

---

❧➤ **Sophia** (fl. 1211)

*Landgravine of Thuringia. Name variations: Sophie; Sophia of Thuringia or Thüringia. Flourished around 1211; married Hermann I, landgrave of Thuringia (died 1216); children: Louis IV also known as Ludwig IV, landgrave of Thuringia; Agnes of Thuringia (mother of *Jutta of Saxony).*

birth to another daughter the following year whom she also named Sophia, in an apparent effort to impress her mother-in-law. However, most of the evidence indicates that she and Ludwig produced three children rather than four. Her last child, **Gertrude of Thuringia**, was born in 1227, shortly after Ludwig's death.

During the course of their marriage, Ludwig was frequently away from their home at Wartburg castle because his position as landgrave involved frequent military expeditions. Whenever he was away, Ludwig allowed Elizabeth to oversee the financial affairs of Thuringia, and she was thus able to indulge her concern for the poor—much to the chagrin of Sophia and Elizabeth's brothers-in-law. Elizabeth established a hospital for lepers near the castle at Wartburg, and in 1226, a year of severe famine, she distributed food from the public granary and ordered all churches and chapels to house the poor. She also sold most of her personal jewels in order to distribute money to the poor. Rather surprisingly, Ludwig supported his wife's extreme generosity. Still, one of the most popular legends about Elizabeth contradicts this image of Ludwig as the magnanimous champion of his wife's compulsive giving: one night Elizabeth stole outside the castle with royal loaves of bread in her apron to distribute to the poor. When Ludwig apprehended her and inquired what she was doing outside at that hour, she opened her apron and—instead of bread—roses were revealed. This enduring tale, celebrated in artistic motifs depicting Elizabeth's life, indicates that perhaps her unstinting generosity at times alarmed Ludwig and his family.

Elizabeth's relationship with her spiritual director, a fanatical Franciscan named Conrad of Marburg, dominated the last part of her life. It is unclear whether her husband wished her to be subject to Conrad's influence, or whether Pope Gregory IX appointed Conrad as Elizabeth's protector after Ludwig's death on crusade. It is certain, however, that the association was not a beneficent one for Elizabeth. Conrad was an extremely severe and demanding presence in her life: if Ludwig was impressed by such inquisitorial zeal that he allowed his wife to be spiritually ruled by such a tyrant, he would have been appalled at the deleterious effects this ultimately had on Elizabeth's health.

Conrad was Pope Gregory IX's agent in Thuringia. His primary obligation was to find and punish heretics, and also to monitor the moral behavior of priests, monks, and nuns throughout the German-speaking lands. As the spiritual director of Elizabeth, his harsh brand of

discipline and insistence on blind obedience were exercised. Once, Elizabeth disregarded Conrad's demand that she attend his sermon at Eisenach: she instead felt obligated to welcome one of her husband's relatives in person at Wartburg. Enraged at her failure to appear at his sermon, Conrad announced his resignation as her spiritual director. Since Elizabeth had pledged to take Conrad as her perpetual religious advisor, she immediately implored him to continue in this capacity. Conrad agreed but demanded that she and her ladies submit to a scourging—which they did.

In 1227, Ludwig made arrangements to join Holy Roman Emperor Frederick II on the sixth crusade. But Elizabeth's young husband died of plague in Italy before his contingent left for the Holy Land. Devastated by Ludwig's death, Elizabeth's problems were compounded by her brother-in-law's plan to usurp her four-year-old son's position as heir to the Thuringian throne. (In 1240, 18-year-old Hermann was poisoned by his uncle.) Henry Raspe ordered Elizabeth to leave Wartburg castle, and she was forced to rely on local charity for shelter for her family.

Elizabeth of Hungary endured a winter of extreme hardship in 1227–28. She was forced to sell her dower jewels in order to purchase food for her young family, and accounts of her life detail her attempts to secure lodging. Often, she had to sleep in cold parish churches. One of her servants, Isentrude von Horselgau, testified that, despite such privation, Elizabeth maintained an unshaken faith that her suffering was pleasing to God. Finally, **Matilda, abbess of Kitzingen**, a Franconian Benedictine monastic establishment, offered shelter to Elizabeth and her family. Soon after, her uncle, Bishop Eckembert, offered her the temporary use of his castle at Pottenstein. Elizabeth left one of her daughters with the abbess of Kitzingen—it was a common practice to present young children to monastic institutions, where they were raised to become monks or nuns—and traveled with her other children to Pottenstein in 1228.

When Ludwig IV's body was returned to Thuringia for burial, Bishop Eckembert included Elizabeth in his entourage so that her brother-in-law's hostility would not exclude her from the funeral rites. Elizabeth appealed to the Thuringian nobles who had supported Ludwig to uphold her son Hermann's position as heir to the landgraviate. Under enormous pressure, Henry Raspe agreed to grant Elizabeth the town of Marburg and maintenance at Wartburg castle, but this arrangement did not work for long. Soon her late husband's family pressured her to

Opposite page

*E*lizabeth of

*H*ungary

(1207–1231)

abandon Wartburg and occupy a smaller castle at Marburg, and a cash settlement was granted to Elizabeth in order to facilitate this move. Elizabeth's immediate impulse was to distribute this money to the poor of Marburg, but her spiritual director forbade her to do so. Conrad named himself Elizabeth's treasurer and closely monitored her charitable donations. If she gave more than he considered appropriate, he physically abused Elizabeth by beating her with a stick. In addition, he would not allow her to beg for her food—a custom she longed to follow since it was practiced by the Friars Minor whom she greatly admired. Conrad also refused to allow Elizabeth to nurse the most desperately ill lepers, although she was permitted to assist the less sick patients in the hospital she founded in Marburg.

Late in 1228, Elizabeth provided for the future of her children and became a Franciscan tertiary, but she remained under Conrad's supervision for the rest of her life. She continued to nurse the sick in her small hospital but also supported herself by spinning, and she expanded her charitable practices by cleaning the houses of the poor. Elizabeth's dietary restrictions had been an important element of her piety even during her marriage; she had appeared at banquets, but according to statements made by her servants, she refused to eat food purchased by unjust taxes on the poor—which meant, in effect, that she ate very little. In the last years of her life, her food avoidance became even more extreme. It is certain that her enthusiastic acceptance of voluntary poverty and charitable practices, along with Conrad's frequent beatings, ultimately affected the young landgravine's health. She died on November 19, 1231, at the age of 24. Elizabeth was buried in the hospital church she had founded, and immediately afterward many healings were reported at her tomb. Pope Gregory IX authorized an investigation of these claims, and materials concerning her life were collected. In 1235, she was canonized, and her body was transferred to an elaborate church built in her honor at Marburg.

SOURCES:

Analecta Bollandiana. Vol. XXVII. Brussels: Societe des Bollandistes, 1908.

Huyskens, Albert, ed. *Der sog. Libellus de dictis quatuor ancillarum s. Elisabeth confectus.* Munich, 1911.

SUGGESTED READING:

Bell, Rudolph M., and Donald Weinstein. *Saints and Society: The Two Worlds of Western Christendom, 1000–1700.* Chicago, IL: University of Chicago Press, 1982.

Blumenfeld-Kosinski, Renate, and Timea Szell, eds. *Images of Sainthood in Medieval Europe.* Ithaca: Cornell University Press, 1991.

Bynum, Caroline Walker. *Holy Feast and Holy Fast: The Religious Significance of Food to Medieval Women.* Berkeley, CA: University of California Press, 1987.

Shahar, Shulamith, *The Fourth Estate: A History of Women in the Middle Ages.* NY: Routledge, 1984.

Uminski, Sigmund H. *The Royal Beggar: A Story of Saint Elizabeth of Hungary.* NY: The Polish Publication Society of America, 1971.

White, Kristin E. *A Guide to the Saints.* NY: Ivy Books, 1991.

Cathy Jorgensen Itnyre,
Professor of History, Copper Mountain College
(College of the Desert), Joshua Tree, California

Elizabeth of Hungary (fl. 1250s)

*Duchess of Lower Bavaria. Flourished around the 1250s; daughter of Bela IV, king of Hungary (r. 1235–1270), and *Salome of Hungary (1201–c. 1270); niece of *Elizabeth of Hungary (1207–1231); married Henry XIII also known as Henry I, duke of Lower Bavaria (r. 1255–1290); children: Otho of Bavaria also known as Otto III, duke of Lower Bavaria (r. 1290–1312), king of Hungary (r. 1305–1308); Louis III of Lower Bavaria (r. 1290–1296); Stephen I of Lower Bavaria (r. 1290–1310).*

Elizabeth of Hungary (1305–1380).

See Elizabeth of Poland.

Elizabeth of Hungary

(c. 1430–1505)

*Queen of Poland. Name variations: Elizabeth of Austria. Born around 1429 or 1430 (some sources cite 1436 or 1437); died on August 30, 1505, in Krakow; daughter of Albert V, king of Hungary (1437) and Bohemia (1438) and Holy Roman emperor as Albert II (r. 1438–1439), and *Elizabeth of Luxemburg (1409–1442, daughter of Sigismund); married Kazimierz also known as Casimir IV Jagiellon (1427–1492), grand duke of Lithuania (r. 1440–1492), king of Poland (r. 1446–1492); children: Ladislas II of Bohemia (1456–1516), king of Bohemia (r. 1471–1516), king of Hungary (r. 1490–1516); John I Albert (1459–1501), king of Poland (r. 1492–1501); *Sophie of Poland (1464–1512); Alexander, king of Poland (r. 1501–1506); Sigismund I (1467–1548), king of Poland (r. 1506–1548); Frederick, bishop of Cracow; *Barbara of Poland (1478–1534); Jadwiga also known as Hedwig (who married George, duke of Bavaria); Saint Casimir.*

Elizabeth of Kiev (fl. 1045)

Queen of Norway. Name variations: Ellisef or Ellisif; Ellisif Jaroslavna. Born around 1032; daughter of Jaroslav also known as Yaroslav I the Wise (978–1054), grand prince of Kiev (r. 1019–1054), and Ingigerd Olafsdottir (c. 1001–1050); married Harald III Hardraade also known as Harald III Haardrada, king of Norway (1015–1066), in 1045; possibly married Svend II Estridsen (d. 1076), king of Denmark (r. 1047–1074), in 1067; children: (first marriage, two daughters) Maria Haraldsdottir (who was killed on September 25, 1066); Ingigerd Haraldsdottir.*

One of the last of the Viking kings, Harald III Hardraade of Norway became attracted to Elizabeth of Kiev, the daughter of *Ingigerd Olafsdottir** and Yaroslav, grand prince of Kiev, while he was campaigning in Russia in 1044. Elizabeth scorned Harald's love; even so, she was given in marriage to him on his return from Greece. In 1045, he and Elizabeth set out on their voyage to Norway, fortified by the dowry from Yaroslav and the considerable wealth amassed during Harald's Byzantine campaigns. In addition to his wife, Harald had a concubine *Thora, with whom he had two sons, Magnus and Olaf.

Determined to topple the newly crowned English king Harold II Godwineson in 1066, Harald Hardraade prepared for what would turn out to be his final campaign. He proclaimed his illegitimate son Magnus as king and named him regent of Norway. On his way to England, Harald was accompanied by Elizabeth and their two daughters, as well as by Olaf, his other son with Thora. En route, Harald received reinforcements from Shetland and Orkney, where Elizabeth and her daughter *Ingigerd Haraldsdottir** were left to await the result of the invasion. The Norwegian force sailed to the vicinity of York. In the decisive clash between Harald Hardraade and Harold II Godwineson, Harald Hardraade was killed by an arrow in his throat at Stamford Bridge. Elizabeth, left behind in the Orkneys, returned to Norway with her stepson Olaf and her daughter Ingigerd. Elizabeth's other daughter, **Maria Haraldsdottir**, was killed at Stamford Bridge.

Elizabeth of Kumania (c. 1242–?)

*Queen of Hungary. Name variations: Elizabeth of Kumanien. Born around 1242; died after 1290; married Stephen V, king of Hungary (r. 1270–1272); children: *Anna of Hungary (who married Andronicus II Paleologus, emperor of Nicaea); Ladislas IV (1262–1290), king of Hungary (r. 1272–1290); *Marie of Hungary (d. 1323, who married Charles II of Anjou).*

Elizabeth of Lancaster (1364–1425)

Duchess of Exeter. Name variations: Elizabeth Hastings; Elizabeth Holland; Elizabeth Cornwall. Born in 1364; died in 1425 (some sources cite 1426); daughter of John of Gaunt, 1st duke of Lancaster, and *Blanche of Lancaster (1341–1369); sister of *Philippa of Lancaster (c. 1359–1415, who married John I, king of Portugal); sister of Henry IV (r. 1399–1413), king of England (r. 1399–1413); married John Hastings (1372–1389), 3rd earl of Pembroke, on June 24, 1380 (divorced); married John Holland, duke of Exeter, in 1386 (died 1400); married John Cornwall, 1st baron Fanhope; children: (second marriage) five, including John Holland (1395–1447), duke of Exeter; *Constance Holland.

In 1386, 22-year-old Elizabeth of Lancaster married John Holland, duke of Exeter. Fourteen years later, on February 9, 1400, John was beheaded at Pleshey at the command of Henry IV, king of England. Elizabeth then married Sir John Cornwall, who was created Baron Fanhope.

Elizabeth of Lorraine (1711–1741)

French royal. Born in 1711; died in 1741; daughter of *Elizabeth-Charlotte (1676–1744) and Leopold, duke of Lorraine; married Charles Emmanuel III (1701–1773), king of Sardinia (r. 1730–1773). Charles Emmanuel was also married to *Louisa Christina of Bavaria.

Elizabeth of Luxemburg (1409–1442)

Queen of Hungary and duchess of Austria. Name variations: Elizabeth of Bohemia; Elizabeth of Luxembourg. Born on November 27, 1409, in Luxemburg; died on December 19 or 25, 1442, in Ofen (Buda), Hungary; daughter of Sigismund I of Luxemburg (d. 1368), king of Hungary and Poland, also Holy Roman emperor, and Barbara of Cilli; married Albert V (1404–1439), duke of Austria (r. 1404–1439), king of Germany (r. 1404–1439), Hungary (r. 1437), and Bohemia (r. 1438), also Holy Roman emperor as Albert II (r. 1438–1439), on November 28, 1421; children: *Anne of Austria (1432–1462, who married William III of Saxony); *Elizabeth of Hungary (c. 1430–1505, who married Casimir IV, king of Poland); Ladislas, later Ladislas V Posthumus, king of Hungary (r. 1444–1457), king of Bohemia (r. 1452).

Elizabeth of Luxemburg was the daughter and heiress of ***Barbara of Cilli** and Holy Roman Emperor Sigismund I, who was also king of Hungary, Germany, and Bohemia. She married Duke Albert V Habsburg of Austria in 1421. Through her, Albert was elected Holy Roman emperor (as Albert II) and king of Hungary upon Sigismund's death in 1437. Although the couple claimed many titles and regions as their own, Elizabeth is most remembered for her career as queen of Hungary. Albert, who showed remarkable leadership ability and promised to be an able ruler, died in battle only two years after becoming emperor. Soon after, Elizabeth gave birth to a son, but not until King Ladislas III of Poland was chosen as Albert's successor. The birth of Albert's son, also called Ladislas, jeopardized the Polish king's claim, and many Hungarians switched their allegiance from the Polish foreigner to the infant boy.

With the help of her lady-in-waiting ***Helene Kottanner**, Elizabeth managed to have her son crowned king in an effort to secure the throne. She also had several powerful foreign allies in her quest as well as the support of the Hungarian people. However, Ladislas III commanded a large armed force, and he was as determined to remain king of Hungary as Elizabeth was to depose him. Elizabeth died in 1442 with the outcome of the war very much undecided and left her son in the care of her cousin Frederick V of Styria, later Emperor Frederick II. The two forces continued to fight in a stalemate for some years, until Ladislas III of Poland's death in 1452 allowed Elizabeth's son, now 12 years old, to succeed to the Hungarian throne as Ladislas V.

Laura York,
Riverside, California

Elizabeth of Nevers (fl. 1460)

Duchess of Cleves. Flourished around 1460; married John I, duke of Cleves (r. 1448–1481); children: John II, duke of Cleves (r. 1481–1521); Engelbert, duke of Nevers.

Elizabeth of Poland (1288–1335).

See Ryksa of Poland.

Elizabeth of Poland (fl. 1298–1305)

Queen of Bohemia. Flourished between 1298 and 1305; third wife of Wenceslas II (1271–1305), king of Bohemia (r. 1278–1305); children: Wenceslas III (1289–1306), king of Bohemia (r. 1305–1306); *Anna of Bohemia (who married Henry of Carinthia, king of Bohemia, r. 1306–1310); *Elizabeth of Bohemia (1292–1339). Wenceslas II's first wife was *Judith

(1271–1297); his second was *Ryksa of Poland (d. 1335).

Elizabeth of Poland (1305–1380)

Queen of Hungary. Name variations: Elizabeth Loki-etek; Elizabeth of Hungary. Born in 1305 in Poland; died in 1380 in Hungary (some sources cite 1386); daughter of *Elizabeth of Bosnia (d. 1339) and Ladislas I Lokietek (1260–1333), king of Poland (r. 1306–1333); married Charles Robert of Anjou (1288–1342) also known as Charles I, king of Hungary (r. 1307–1342), in 1320; children: Louis I (b. 1326), king of Hungary (r. 1342–1382), king of Poland (r. 1370–1382); Andrew of Hungary (d. 1345, who married Joanna I of Naples).

A princess of the Polish royal house, Elizabeth of Poland was married as a child to Charles Robert of Anjou (who was also known as Charles I, king of Hungary) in 1320. The marriage was intended to forge a political alliance between her father, Ladislas I Lokietek, and Hungary. Elizabeth, who gave birth to two children, Louis and Andrew, had great hopes for her elder son Louis. Among other schemes, she petitioned the pope unsuccessfully to award Louis the crown of Naples. She did manage, however, to wed her younger son Andrew to the ruler whom the pope supported, *Joanna I of Naples.

Besides her political aspirations for her family, the Hungarian queen became well-known for her charity and deep piety; she was also very interested in science and medicine. When Elizabeth's brother Casimir (III), who had succeeded their father as king of Poland, died in 1370, he left the throne to Elizabeth's son Louis. Not interested in ruling it himself, Louis appointed his mother regent of Poland. Elizabeth retained the regency until her death. She was also influential in the upbringing of her powerful granddaughter, *Jadwiga (1374–1399), queen of Poland.

Laura York,
Riverside, California

Elizabeth of Poland (d. 1361)

Duchess of Pomerania. Name variations: Elzbieta. Died in 1361; daughter of Casimir III the Great, king of Poland (r. 1333–1370) and one of his four wives, *Aldona of Lithuania (d. 1339), Adelaide of Hesse, Krystryna Rokizanska, or *Jadwiga of Glogow; married Boguslav also known as Boleslav V of Slupsk, duke of Pomerania; children: *Elizabeth of Pomerania (1347–1393).

Elizabeth of Pomerania (1347–1393).

See Anne of Bohemia for sidebar.

Elizabeth of Portugal (1271–1336)

Saint and queen of Portugal. Name variations: Isabel or Isabella of Aragon; Isabella of Portugal. Born in 1271 in Aragon; died on July 4, 1336, in Estremos, Portugal; interred in Coimbra; daughter of Pedro also known as Peter III, king of Aragon, and Constance of Sicily (r. 1282–1302); grandniece of *Elizabeth of Hungary (1207–1231); married Diniz also spelled Dinis or Denis (1261–1325), king of Portugal (r. 1279–1325), in 1280 or 1282; children: Alphonso IV (1291–1357), king of Portugal (r. 1325–1357); *Constance of Portugal (1290–1313), later queen of Castile.

Elizabeth of Portugal was an Aragonese princess, the daughter of King Peter III and *Constance of Sicily. She married King Denis of Portugal in 1280. Her diplomatic skills and pious nature led her to act as a mediator to various political factions within both the Aragonese and Portuguese royal families, earning her the sobriquet "the Peacemaker." Despite her mediating role, Elizabeth never played a central part in the actual administration of the kingdom. Extremely unhappy in her marriage, she sought activities that could be pursued away from her husband and that would fulfill her pious inclinations. She became increasingly involved in charitable works and acts of personal piety, including extreme fasting. Elizabeth was celebrated throughout Portugal for her generous donations to public works such as hospitals and orphanages, and she founded a college designed to prepare young women to be farmers.

In 1325, when King Denis died, Elizabeth's eldest son succeeded as Alphonso IV. Freed from the constraints of marriage and queenship at age 54, Elizabeth joined the monastic order of the Poor Clares and embarked on pilgrimages. Over time, she developed a following of those who believed she was exceptionally gifted and could perform miracles; one legend claims that she restored sight to a blind child. After her death in 1336, a shrine was built for Elizabeth in Coimbra. Despite the popularity of the queen during her life, and of the shrine after her death, Elizabeth of Portugal was not canonized until 1625.

Laura York,
Riverside, California

Élizabeth of Ranfaing.

See French "Witches."

Elizabeth of Rumania (1843–1916).

See Elizabeth of Wied.

Elizabeth of Rumania (1894–1956).

See Elisabeth, Queen of the Hellenes.

Elizabeth of Savoy-Carignan (1800–1856)

Archduchess of Austria. Name variations: *Marie Elizabeth Francesca. Born in 1800; died in 1856; possibly sister of Charles Albert, king of Sardinia; married Ranieri also known as Rainer, archduke of Austria; children: *Marie Adelaide of Austria (1822–1855).*

Elizabeth of Saxe-Hildburghausen (1713–1761)

Duchess of Mecklenburg-Strelitz. Name variations: *Elisabeth Albertine, Princess of Saxony-Hildburghausen. Born Elisabeth Albertine on August 3, 1713; died on June 29, 1761; married Duke Charles I of Mecklenburg-Strelitz (1708–1752); children: Prince Charles II Louis Frederick of Mecklenburg-Strelitz (father of Louise of Prussia); *Charlotte of Mecklenburg-Strelitz (1744–1818, queen to George III).*

Elizabeth of Saxony (1830–1912)

Duchess of Genoa. Born in 1830; died in 1912; married Ferdinando or Ferdinand of Savoy (1822–1855), duke of Genoa.*

Elizabeth of Schönau (c. 1129–1164)

German mystic. Name variations: *Elisabeth von Schönau; Schonau or Schoenau. Born around 1129; died in 1164.*

A celebrated German mystic, Elizabeth of Schönau was a nun at the abbey of Schönau in Silesia. She told of her visions in her *Book of the Ways of God* which she dedicated to her brother, the canon Egbert. Her feast day is June 18.

Elizabeth of Sicily (fl. 1200s)

Queen of Hungary. Flourished in the 1200s; married Ladislas IV, king of Hungary (r. 1272–1290).*

Elizabeth of Sicily (d. 1349)

Duchess of Bavaria. Died on March 31, possibly 1349; daughter of *Lenore of Sicily (1289–1341) and Frederick II, king of Sicily (r. 1271–1296); sister of Peter II, king of Sicily; married Stephen II*

(1317–1375), duke of Bavaria (r. 1363–1375), on June 27, 1328; children: Stephen III (b. 1337), duke of Bavaria (r. 1375–1413); Frederick (b. 1339), duke of Bavaria (r. 1375–1393); John II (b. 1341), duke of Bavaria (r. 1375–1397). After 1347, Bavaria was divided into several parts.

Elizabeth of Silesia (fl. 1257)

Silesian princess. Flourished around 1257; daughter of Henry II the Pious of Silesia and *Anna of Bohemia; married Przemyslav or Przemysl I of Wielkopolska (1220–1257), king of Poland; children: Przemysl II (1257–1296), king of Poland (r. 1290–1296); Constancia.*

Elizabeth of the Netherlands (1501–1526).

See Willums, Sigbrit for sidebar on Elisabeth of Habsburg.

Elizabeth of the Palatinate (1618–1680).

See Elizabeth of Bohemia.

Elizabeth of Thuringia (1207–1231).

See Elizabeth of Hungary.

Elizabeth of Thurn and Taxis

Saxon royal. Married Frederick Christian (b. 1893, son of *Louisa Toselli and Frederick Augustus III, king of Saxony); children: Emanuel (b. 1926); Albert (b. 1934).*

Elizabeth of Tyrol (c. 1262–1313), queen of Germany.

See Agnes of Austria (1281–1364) for sidebar.

Elizabeth of Ulster (d. 1327).

See Elizabeth de Burgh.

Elizabeth of Valois (1545–1568)

Queen of Spain. Name variations: *Elisabeth or Élizabeth de France; Princess Elizabeth of France; Elizabeth of the Peace; Isabel or Isabella of France. Born at Fontainbleau, France, on April 2 (some sources cite April 13), 1545; died in childbirth at age 23 in Madrid, Spain, on October 3, 1568; daughter of Henry II of Valois (1519–1559), king of France (r. 1547–1559), and Catherine de Medici (1519–1589); sister of *Claude de France (1547–1575), and *Margaret of Valois (1553–1615), as well as Francis II, Charles IX, and Henry III, all kings of France; became third wife of Philip II (1527–1598), king of Spain (r.*

Elizabeth of Valois

younger daughter, Elizabeth's sister *Margaret of Valois, but Philip was determined to take his French connection no further, even though Elizabeth's death was mourned in Spain. "Her figure was very fine, taller than that of her sisters, which made her much admired in Spain, where such tall women are rare, and for that the more esteemed," wrote Saint-Beuve. "And with this figure she had a bearing, a majesty, a gesture, a gait, and grace that intermingled the Frenchwoman with the Spaniard in sweetness and gravity; so that, as I myself saw, when she passed through her Court, or went out to certain places, whether churches, or monasteries, or gardens, there was such great press to see her, and the crowd of persons was so thick, there was no turning round in the mob." Elizabeth's subjects called her *la reyna de la paz y de la bondad* (the queen of peace and kindness).

SOURCES:

Saint-Beuve, C.A., and Pierre de Bourdeille. *Illustrious Dames of the Court of The Valois Kings*. Translated by Katharine Prescott Wormeley. NY: Lamb Publishing, 1912.

Elizabeth of Wied (1843–1916)

Queen of Rumania, painter, musician, writer, poet, and translator. Name variations: Elisabeth of Rumania or Romania; Elizabeth, Queen of Rumania; Elisabeth zu Wied; (pseudonyms) Carmen Sylva and Dito Und Idem. Born Pauline Elizabeth Ottilie Louise (or Luise) in Neuwied, Prussia, on December 29, 1843; died on March 3, 1916, in Curtea de Arges, Rumania; daughter of Prince Hermann of Neuwied; married Prince Karl von Hohenzollern also known as Carol I (1839–1914), king of Rumania (r. 1881–1914), on November 15, 1869; children: Marie (1870–1874).

Elizabeth of Wied, widely known for her cultural interests and voluminous writings, was the daughter of Prince Hermann of Neuwied. She met Prince Karl von Hohenzollern in Berlin and married him in 1869; 12 years later, in 1881, she became queen of Rumania and he became king as Carol I. During the Russo-Turkish War of 1877–78, Elizabeth tended the wounded, establishing the Order of Elizabeth (a gold cross on a blue ribbon), to reward others for similar service. She founded other charitable societies as well and helped foster the higher education of women in Rumania.

A talented musician and painter, as well as a writer, Elizabeth produced poems, plays, novels, short stories, essays, collections of adages, and

1544–1598), in 1559 or 1560, in Toledo, Spain; children: twin daughters born in 1564 (died at birth); *Isabella Clara Eugenia of Austria (1566–1633); *Catherine of Spain (1567–1597, duchesse of Savoy); another daughter (b. 1568) died at birth.

At a time of religious conflict throughout Europe, Philip II of Spain married a sweetheart of the French court, Elizabeth of Valois, after the death of his second wife *Mary I of England. The Catholic monarchs of France and Spain had just made peace at Câteau-Cambrésis in 1559, both because they were bankrupt and in order to unite their forces against Protestantism. The Treaty was sealed by the marriage of Philip II to Elizabeth, the teenaged and favorite daughter of *Catherine de Medici and Henry II, king of France. At the joust held to mark the wedding celebrations, however, Henry II was fatally injured by a lance wielded by a Calvinist noble, the Comte de Montgomery. The lance shattered Henry's helmet, pierced his eye, and entered his brain. Henry's death a few days later brought his oldest son and Elizabeth's brother, 16-year-old Francis II, to the throne.

When Elizabeth died in childbirth in 1568, Catherine hoped King Philip II might marry her

Elizabeth of
Wied

translations. In addition to her original works, many of which were written under the pen name of "Carmen Sylva," she also put into literary form much of the folklore of the Rumanian peasantry. Two of her earliest poetry collections, *Sappho* (1880) and *Stuerme* (1882), are notable, and

in 1888, she received the Prix Botta, a prize awarded triennially by the French Academy, for her volume of prose aphorisms, *Les Pensées d'une reine* (1882), a German version of which is entitled *Vom Amboss* (1890). A volume of religious meditations in Rumanian, *Cuvinte Su-*

fletesci (1888), was also translated into German in 1890 under the title of *Seelen-Gespracke*. Elizabeth also used the pseudonym "Dito Und Idem" to indicate the joint authorship of several works on which she collaborated with her lady-in-waiting ◀⍟ **Marie Kremnitz**. They include *Aus zwei Welten* (1884), a novel, *Anna Boleyn* (1886), a tragedy, *Inderlrre* (1888), a collection of short stories, *Edleen Vaughan; or Paths of Peril* (1894), another novel, and *Sweet Hours* (1904), a collection of poems written in English. Among her translations are German versions of Pierre Loti's romance *Pêcheur d'Islande*, and Paul de St. Victor's dramatic criticisms *Les Deux Masques*. Particularly notable is *The Bard of the Dimbovitza*, an English version of **Helene Vacarescu**'s collection of Rumanian folksongs entitled *Lieder aus dem Dimbovitzathal* (1889), done in collaboration with **Alma Strettell**.

Elizabeth of York

Elizabeth of Wittelsbach
(1540–1594)

*Electress of Saxony. Born on June 30, 1540; died on February 8, 1594; daughter of *Marie of Brandenburg-Kulmbach (1519–1567) and Frederick III the Pious, elector of the Palatinate; married John Frederick II, elector of Saxony, on June 12, 1558. John Frederick's first wife was *Agnes of Hesse (1527–1555).*

Elizabeth of Wurttemberg
(1767–1790)

Princess of Wurttemberg. Name variations: Elizabeth Wilhelmine. Born Elizabeth Wilhelmine von Wurt-

*temberg on April 21, 1767; died on February 18, 1790; daughter of *Sophia Dorothea of Brandenburg (1736–1798) and Frederick II Eugene, duke of Wurttemberg (r. 1795–1797); became first wife of Francis I (1768–1835) emperor of Austria (r. 1804–1835), also known as Francis II, Holy Roman emperor (r. 1792–1806), on January 6, 1788; children: Ludovika (1790–1791).*

Holy Roman emperor Francis II had four wives: Elizabeth of Wurttemberg (1767–1790), *Maria Teresa of Naples (1772–1807), *Maria Ludovica of Modena (1787–1816), and *Caroline Augusta of Bavaria (1792–1873).

Elizabeth of Wurttemberg
(1802–1864)

*Princess of Baden. Born on February 27, 1802; died on December 5, 1864; daughter of Louis of Wurttemberg and *Henrietta of Nassau-Weilburg (1780–1857); niece of Frederick I, king of Prussia; married William, prince of Baden, October 16, 1830; children: four, including *Leopoldine (1837–1903).*

Elizabeth of York (1466–1503)

*Queen of England. Name variations: Elizabeth Plantagenet. Born on February 11, 1466 (some sources cite 1465), in Westminster, London, England; died in childbirth on February 11, 1503 (some sources cite 1502), in the Tower of London, England; buried in Westminster Abbey; oldest daughter of Edward IV, king of England, and Elizabeth Woodville; married Henry VII, king of England (r. 1485–1509), on January 18, 1486; children: Arthur Tudor (1486–1502), prince of Wales; *Margaret Tudor (1489–1541); Henry VIII (1491–1547), king of England (r. 1509–1547); Elizabeth Tudor (1492–1495); *Mary Tudor (1496–1533, who married Louis XII, king of France); Edmund Tudor, duke of Somerset (1499–1500); Edward Tudor (died in infancy); Katherine Tudor (1503–1503).*

Following the murder of her two younger brothers in the Tower of London, the gentle Elizabeth of York—daughter of Edward IV, king of England, and *Elizabeth Woodville—became heir to the throne. In 1486, Elizabeth united the white rose of the Yorks with the red roses of the Lancastrians when she married Henry Tudor (Henry VII), the victorious Lancastrian in the Wars of the Roses. Though Henry married Elizabeth for political reasons, he was genuinely fond of her and grieved when she died in childbirth, the day of her 37th birthday, in 1503.

Elizabeth Oldenburg (1904–1955)

Greek princess. Born on May 24, 1904; died on January 11, 1955; daughter of *Helena of Russia (1882–1957) and Prince Nicholas (Oldenburg) of Greece (uncle of England's Prince Philip); sister of *Marina of Greece (1906–1968) and *Olga Oldenburg (1903–1981).

Elizabeth Petrovna (1709–1762)

Russian empress who ruled from 1741 to 1761 in a reign marked by Russia's continued development as a major power and an acceleration of Westernization. Name variations: Elizabeth I of Russia; Elizaveta; Yelizaveta. Pronunciation: Pa-TROV-na. Born Elizabeth Petrovna on December 7, 1709 (dates are according to the Julian calendar, in use in Imperial Russia, which was 12 days behind the Georgian calendar) in Kolomenskoye near Moscow, Russia; died in St. Petersburg, Russia, on December 25, 1762; daughter of Peter I the Great (1672–1725), tsar of Russia (r. 1682–1725), and Marta Skovoronski or Skavronska (later Empress Catherine I, 1684–1727); educated by tutors, but only superficially and informally; probably secretly married Aleksei Razumovsky, in 1742 or 1744; no children.

Lived in Moscow and St. Petersburg during her early years; consigned to care and upbringing of the Dowager Empress of Ivan V; named to the Supreme Privy Council in the will of Catherine I (1727); passed over for the throne, retired to the self-exile of her estate (1729); led a coup d'état against Regent Anna Leopoldovna (1741); defeated Sweden (1743); founded Moscow University (1755); opposed Prussia in the Seven Years' War (1756).

"Time to get up, sister," whispered Elizabeth Petrovna as she shook regent ❧➤ **Anna Leopoldovna** awake from her sleep on the night of November 24–25, 1741. With those words and the help of Russian boyars and members of the military dissatisfied with the German domination at the court of the infant Tsar Ivan VI, Elizabeth Petrovna carried out a bloodless coup d'état and installed herself as empress of Russia.

Elizabeth Petrovna, daughter of Peter I the Great and his common-law wife Marta Skovoronski (later Empress *Catherine I), was born in Kolomenskoye, near Moscow, on December 7, 1709. But Marta was Peter's second wife, and he did not marry her until three years after their daughter's arrival. Although Peter recognized Elizabeth immediately, and she was later legitimized, her illegitimate birth haunted both her marriage prospects and her claims to the Russian throne. Elizabeth grew up with security and love from her parents who also provided her with religious guidance. She had nurses from Karelia and Russia and a governess from France which gave her an early appreciation of both Western culture and Russian traditions. Blue-eyed and fair-haired, the girl was cheerful, energetic, graceful, and attractive.

Elizabeth was declared of age by her father on January 28, 1722. At 15, she was a beautiful young woman and many minor princes of Europe were interested in marriage with her. Her father wanted to marry her to young Louis XV of France and even journeyed to Paris in 1717 without success. Despite her remarkable beauty, grace, and fluent French and German, Elizabeth's illegitimacy created a sensitivity at all the major courts of Europe. After Peter's death in 1725, her mother, now Empress Catherine, failed in a second effort to secure the marriage agreement with the French king. Elizabeth's marriage prospects reached such a desperation that an engagement was finally arranged with Karl, prince-bishop of Lübeck. Both Elizabeth and her mother approved of Karl, but he died of smallpox before the wedding day. There were no further efforts to secure an acceptable marriage for the 17-year-old. Elizabeth consoled herself by having affairs outside the bounds of matrimony.

Catherine's brief reign was characterized by her disinterest in the business of absolutist government and her reliance on the ambitious Prince Alexander Menshikov's domination of the newly created Supreme Privy Council. Catherine was kind and took an interest in Elizabeth and her only other surviving child, ❧➤ **Anne Petrovna**. Before Catherine died in 1727, she instructed in the will that Elizabeth and Anne receive equal divisions of her personal estate and both were to be appointed primary members of the Council which was the regency for her successor, the youthful Tsar Peter II (r. 1727–1730), grandson of Peter the Great. Menshikov and the other members of the Council ignored the will and ignored the two sisters' positions as heirs of Peter should he die intestate. Anne married Charles Frederick, duke of Holstein, and went to live at his estate in Schleswig-Holstein-Gottorp, where she would soon die shortly after giving birth in 1728 to the future Peter III (r. 1761–1762). Elizabeth, who had inherited two country estates and the house at Tsarskoe Seloe, retreated to hunting and hawking on her rural estate. On her meager income,

Anna Leopoldovna.
See Anna Ivanovna for sidebar.

See sidebar on the following page

❧▶ **Anne Petrovna** (1708–1728)

Princess of Russia and duchess of Holstein. *Name variations: Anna Petrovna. Born on March 9, 1708; died on June 1, 1728; daughter of* ***Catherine I*** *(1684–1727), empress of Russia (r. 1725–1727) and Peter I the Great, tsar of Russia (r. 1682–1725); sister of* ***Elizabeth Petrovna*** *(1709–1762); married Charles Frederick (1700–1739), duke of Holstein-Gottorp (r. 1702–1739), on June 1, 1725; children: Peter III (b. 1728), tsar of Russia (1728–1762, who married* ***Catherine II the Great***).

she maintained a household staff but devoted her time to the pursuit of pleasure. She danced and sang folk songs with local peasants and became involved with pages or local young men.

The Council, now dominated by the Dolgoruky family, no longer saw Elizabeth as a threat and invited her back to court. Known as a fashion leader, she continued her carefree life by attending balls and bear-baiting events; she also often hunted with her nephew, the young tsar. She behaved scandalously, bragged openly of her contentment with love, turned down an opportunity to marry Ivan Dolgoruky because it would limit her freedom and choice of lovers, and was seen as a person of no political importance.

Like Moses, Elizabeth had come to release Russia from the night of Egyptian servitude; like Noah, she had saved Russia from an alien flood.

—Mikhail V. Lomonosov

In early 1730, Peter II died shortly before his coronation. According to Catherine's will, Elizabeth should have been declared empress of Russia. When she was passed over for her cousin, Anna of Courland, who became Empress **Anna Ivanovna** (1693–1740), Elizabeth refused to demand her rightful claim, partly out of fear and partly out of her distaste for power, protocol, and responsibility. At the time, Elizabeth was deeply attached to her lover, Alexei Shubin, and she remained absent from the court. Jealous of her beautiful and popular cousin, Anna Ivanovna had Shubin arrested and exiled and actually considered ordering Elizabeth to a nunnery. Elizabeth was followed by Anna's spies and forced to be politically discreet. Lonely and disillusioned, Elizabeth fell in love with a member of the court chapel choir, Alexei Razumovsky. Anna Ivanovna eventually required Elizabeth to take an oath

of loyalty and welcomed her to court. Satisfied that Elizabeth and Razumovsky were no threat, she finally left them alone. Though it seemed that Elizabeth wasted her life during the 1730s, she made friendships and established contacts between nobles and soldiers that would be useful to her future political ambitions.

Anna Ivanovna's court was dominated by several German nobles who were either leftovers from the court of Peter the Great or accompanied her from her Duchy of Courland. The major figures in her regime were Count Ernst Johann Biron, Count Burkhard Christoph von Münnich and Count Andrei I. Ostermann. She disliked the idea of Elizabeth as her possible successor, preferring the son of her niece Anna Leopoldovna who had married Prince Anton Ulrich of Brunswick; their marriage had produced Ivan in 1740. Anna Ivanovna designated Ivan as her successor with Anna Leopoldovna as regent. Before her death, however, the empress changed the regency from Anna to her longtime favorite, Ernst Biron, her secretary and lover, who had emerged as the notable individual at her court. Elizabeth maintained her distance and retained an appearance of disinterest in the palace intrigues.

Thus, on the death of Anna Ivanovna, the infant Ivan VI became tsar, the last of the farcical successors to Peter the Great. Three weeks into the regency, Biron, who was on the worst terms with Münnich, Ostermann, Ulrich, and Anna Leopoldovna, was overthrown and exiled to Siberia. Anna Leopoldovna became regent and the German faction continued their internal struggles for wealth and power. Dissension among the Germans weakened the regency and created a discontent among the Russian Guards, particularly after the outbreak of an unpopular war with Sweden. Russian hopes for change centered on Peter the Great's daughter, Elizabeth Petrovna. The French and Swedish ambassadors, unhappy with the regency's ties to Prussia, began to intrigue with Elizabeth through her close friend, Dr. Armand Lestocq. Although she was still reluctant to lead a coup d'état, Elizabeth finally was persuaded by her intimate friends and officers in the guards to lead the uprising.

In the early hours of November 25, 1741, Elizabeth, carrying a cross and wearing a cuirass (armor), appeared at the barracks of the Preobrazhensky Guards. At the head of several hundred guards and her small group of conspirators, she advanced to the Winter Palace, where the sentries were bloodlessly captured or joined the conspirators. Elizabeth led her insurgents into the bedchamber of Anna Leopoldovna where she

Elizabeth
Petrovna

found the regent sleeping with her German lover, **Julia Mengden**. With snow dripping from her cape, Elizabeth shook Anna by the shoulder and whispered her wakeup call. Ivan VI, Ulrich, Ostermann, Münnich, and other high officials were arrested in other parts of the palace. Ostermann and Münnich were exiled to Siberia, Anna Leopoldovna and Ulrich were exiled to the provinces, and the young tsar was sent to a dungeon, where he grew to adulthood only to be murdered to prevent opportunistic plots for his restoration to power.

Elizabeth Petrovna was a 32-year-old woman when she assumed the throne. Her sub-

jects accepted her with a sigh of relief because it ended the despised period of German domination. Elizabeth was ill-educated and poorly trained to govern, but her fervent patriotism and abhorrence of war endeared her to the people. The Swedish war was ended in 1743 with Russia gaining some territory in southern Finland. Elizabeth quickly abolished the Supreme Privy Council system of government that had been begun by her predecessors and formally restored the Senate to the same role created by her father. This was only a nominal reform because she actually ruled the country through her private chancery. Although her reign has been generally characterized as a return to the traditions and principles of Peter the Great, she, in fact, abolished many of his major reforms. For example, the opportunity for lower classes to achieve noble ranks by state service was terminated by Elizabeth, and she regularly met with "Her Majesty's Chancery" which managed the government administration and financial matters.

The events of November 1741 not only produced a new ruler but also a new group of Russian leaders. Elizabeth promoted many of her friends and elevated other capable men to leadership positions. Important figures during Elizabeth's reign included Count Michael Voronstov and Count Alexis Bestuzhev-Ryumin, who were excellent in foreign policy; Alexander Shuvalov, chair of the Secret Chancery; Peter Shuvalov, chief of the secret police; Ivan Shuvalov, head of the Academy of Arts; and her closest advisor Alexei Razumovsky, who may have earlier been morganatically married to the empress. Cyril Razumovsky, younger brother of Alexei, held several high offices, including that of field marshal. The Dolgoruky and Golitsyn families, persecuted during the German era, were restored to their former status and eminence in the Russian nobility.

During Elizabeth's reign, there was a slight increase in French influence. This was partly in response to France's support of Elizabeth's accession to the throne but was mostly a reaction to German rigidity at the court. Elizabeth placed a greater emphasis on art, philosophy, and literature, especially French culture, instead of the technology and trades emphasized during the Westernization of Peter the Great. She took a great interest in cultural matters. In 1755, at the behest of Ivan Shuvalov, Elizabeth founded the University of Moscow. Because she and Shuvalov ardently loved opera, ballet, and theater, they established the Imperial Academy of Fine Arts in 1757. Fedor Volkov opened a theater in St. Petersburg which, under Elizabeth's patronage, became a national institution. During her reign, St. Petersburg became a center of architectural splendor. French and Italian architects, particularly Bartolomeo Rastrelli, constructed and improved for the empress the beautiful palaces of Peterhof, Tsarskoe Seloe, and the Winter Palace. Rastrelli also designed the graceful Smolnyi Convent and many lesser palaces for prominent boyar (noble) families.

Literature also made great advances during the reign of Elizabeth. When Cyril Razumovsky returned to Russia from his studies in Western Europe, Elizabeth appointed him president of the Academy of Sciences. He placed more emphasis upon the arts, which had previously been offered only to students unfit for the sciences, and initiated the first monthly periodical printed in Russia. Razumovsky was also the patron of Vasili Adadurov who authored the first Russian grammar book, and historian Vasily Tatischev's *Russian History from Earliest Times* was posthumously published in St. Petersburg. The greatest talent to emerge from Elizabeth's literary patronage was Mikhail Lomonosov, a fisher's son who came to St. Petersburg in the reign of Anna Ivanovna and grew, during Elizabeth's rule, to be one of the greatest scholars in Russian history. He produced a new vernacular poetry style and mastered such diverse studies as geology, meteorology, and physics. Vasily Trediakovsky, in 1766, translated Fenelon's *Télémaque* which introduced the hexameter for the first time into Russian poetry. Alexander Sumarokov was the first Russian professional author who chose national subjects for his plays. He introduced Shakespeare to the Russian people with his adaptation of *Hamlet,* and it was as a spectator at his play *Khorev* that Elizabeth fell in love with Nikita Beketov who played the leading role.

When Elizabeth came to the throne, she had immediately realized that Russia's legal code, last revised in 1644 by Tsar Alexis I (r. 1645–1676), needed extensive changes. She gave this responsibility to Michael Voronstov and Peter Shuvalov who endeavored to reform the judicial system. Though the work of Shuvalov's Commission on the Law Code made excellent progress, the codes were not completed until the reign of *Catherine II the Great. Under Elizabeth's reign, the serfs and peasants continued to lose their few remaining rights. Serfs could no longer marry a person from another estate without his owner's permission, and in 1760 Elizabeth issued an edict giving boyars the power to deport peasants to Siberia. This led to massive numbers of peasants and serfs fleeing to the frontiers. The policies also resulted in serious peasant uprisings that were violently suppressed in the Ural or Bashkir regions. Elizabeth tried to humanize the penal codes; and, to the displeasure of her ministers, she commuted every death sentence issued by the courts.

During the first 15 years of Elizabeth's reign, Russia was at peace. Simultaneously, Russia's prestige as a European power grew under the direction of Bestuzhev-Ryumin, who enjoyed Elizabeth's total confidence and guided Russia along a pro-Austrian and anti-Prussian foreign policy. But in 1756, Elizabeth reluctantly honored the Austro-Russian alliance of 1746 by joining the European coalition against the Prussia of Frederick II the Great. Russian troops invaded East Prussia in 1757, won the decisive battle of Kunersdorf in 1759, and reached Berlin in 1760. Prussia would be saved by political divisions among Elizabeth's allies as well as her death, which would result in her successor withdrawing Russia from the war.

Elizabeth's reign was marked by an exciting and splendid court, with Western culture, fashion, styles and secular values. While she took a sincere interest in all aspects of the state, she usually left the details and the administration of her policies to highly capable ministers and advisors. Continuing to enjoy the company of common soldiers and peasant women, she loved the promenades at court and spent astounding sums on her wardrobe that contained over 15,000 dresses. She was devoted to the Russian Orthodox Church and never missed Sunday masses. The empress took pilgrimages to her favorite monasteries and supported a vigorous missionary program into all areas of her empire. Though she endeavored to improve the distribution of church wealth and to improve the literary levels of the clergy, she had very limited success in those areas.

Elizabeth had no children and, shortly after her accession to the throne, had designated her nephew Peter as her successor. He was the son of Elizabeth's older sister Anne Petrovna and the duke of Holstein. Shortly after his birth and the death of his parents, the young boy, who was regarded as an heir to the Swedish throne, was taught Swedish and brought up as a Lutheran. In 1742, Elizabeth brought him to Russia, crowned him as grand duke, and required his conversion to the Russian Orthodox Church. In agreement with her advisors, Elizabeth married the 17-year-old Peter to Sophia Augusta Frederika, later baptized Catherine (later known as Catherine the Great), in 1745. Peter resented this entire process and for nearly two decades sullenly accepted Elizabeth's decisions while virtually worshiping her rival, Frederick the Great.

With her beauty and youth behind her, Elizabeth Petrovna entered a period of depression. She gained weight, rarely exercised, and began to doubt her own accomplishments as empress. After 1749, she suffered from asthma, colic, dropsy, and constipation. Strokes in 1756 and 1759 left her barely able to walk. On December 12, 1761, she took a fever and began to hemorrhage from the mouth. She recovered enough to sign decrees five days later reducing salt taxes and granting amnesties for tax offenders. On December 22, she suffered a relapse, exhibiting fainting spells, impaired speech, and thought. She died at the age of 52 on December 25, 1761.

SOURCES:

Bain, R. Nisbet. *The Daughter of Peter the Great.* Westminster: Constable, 1899.

Coughlan, Robert. *Elizabeth and Catherine: Empresses of All the Russias.* NY: Putnam, 1974.

Longworth, Philip. *The Three Empresses: Catherine I, Anne and Elizabeth of Russia.* NY: Holt, Rinehart and Winston, 1972.

Rice, Tamara Talbot. *Elizabeth: Empress of Russia.* NY: Praeger, 1970.

Wieczynski, Joseph L., ed. *The Modern Encyclopedia of Russian and Soviet History.* Gulf Breeze, FL: Academic International Press, 1976.

SUGGESTED READING:

Bain, Nisbet. *Peter III: Emperor of Russia.* Westminster: Constable, 1902.

———. *The Pupils of Peter the Great: A History of the Russian Court and Empire from 1697 to 1740.* London: Constable, 1897.

Kaus, Gina. *Catherine: The Portrait of an Empress.* Translated by June Head. NY: Viking, 1935.

Kluyuchevsky, V.O. *A History of Russia.* Vol. 4. Translated by C.J. Hogarth. NY: Russell & Russell, 1960.

Marsden, Christopher. *Palmyra of the North: The First Days of St. Petersburg.* London: Faber, 1942.

Miliukov, Paul, C. Seignobos, and L. Eisenmann. *History of Russia.* Vol. 2: *The Successors of Peter the Great.* Translated by C.L. Markmann. NY: Funk & Wagnalls, 1968.

Morfill, W.R. *A History of Russia from the Birth of Peter the Great to the Death of Alexander II.* London: Methuen, 1902.

COLLECTIONS:

Orders of Empress Elizabeth, Iazykov Collection, 1613–1936, Department of Special Collections, University of California, Davis.

Phillip E. Koerper,
Professor of History, Jacksonville State University,
Jacksonville, Alabama

Elizabeth Plantagenet (1282–1316).

See Eleanor of Castile (1241–1290) for sidebar.

Elizabeth-Ryksa (1288–1335).

See Ryksa of Poland.

Elizabeth Sophie of Saxe-Altenburg (1619–1680)

Duchess of Saxe-Gotha. Born on October 10, 1619; died on December 20, 1680; daughter of *Elizabeth of Brunswick-Wolfenbuttel (1593–1650) and John Philipp, duke of Saxe-Altenburg; married Ernst I, duke of Saxe-Gotha, on October 24, 1636; children: Frederick I (b. 1646), duke of Saxe-Gotha; Berharnd I (b. 1649), duke of Saxe-Meiningen; John Ernst (b.

1658), duke of Saxe-Coburg-Saalfeld; Ernst (b. 1655), duke of Saxe-Hilburghausen.

Elizabeth Stuart (1596–1662).
See Elizabeth of Bohemia.

Elizabeth Stuart (1635–1650)

English princess. *Name variations: Princess Elizabeth. Born on December 29 (some sources cite the 28th), 1635, at St. James's Palace in London, England; died it is said of grief over her father's execution at age 15 on September 8, 1650, at Carisbrooke Castle, Isle of Wight, England; buried at Newport, Isle of Wight; second daughter of *Henrietta Maria (1609–1669) and Charles I, king of England; sister of James II and Charles II, kings of England; *Mary of Orange (1631–1660); Henry (1640–1660), duke of Gloucester; and *Henrietta Anne (1644–1670), duchess of Orléans; said to have been considerably proficient in Greek, Hebrew, and Latin, as well as in Italian and French.*

At the outbreak of England's Civil War in 1642, with their mother *Henrietta Maria in Holland and their father, King Charles I, out of London, Princess Elizabeth and her infant brother Henry, duke of Gloucester, were left under the care of Parliament. That October, Elizabeth, a serious and intelligent child, sent a letter to the House of Lords begging that her old attendants be allowed to remain with her. In July 1644, the royal children were sent to Sir John Danvers at Chelsea, and in 1645 to Algernon and *Elizabeth Percy, earl and countess of Northumberland. After the final defeat of the king in 1646, the children were joined by their brother James (later James II), and during 1647 paid several visits to the king at Caversham, near Reading, and Hampton Court, but were again separated by Charles' imprisonment at Carisbrooke Castle. On April 21, 1648, Elizabeth persuaded James to escape, boasting that if she were a boy she would not be confined for much longer.

The last meeting between Charles I and his two children, at which 13-year-old Elizabeth was overcome with grief, took place on January 20, 1640, the day before his execution. In tears, she promised her father she would "write down the particulars" of the meeting and later produced a short account in which Charles had instructed Henry: "Sweetheart, now they will Cut Off thy Father's Head; mark, child, what I say; they will Cut Off my Head and perhaps make thee a king; but—mark what I say—you must

not be a king so long as your brothers Charles and James do live, for they will cut off your Brother's Heads (when they can catch them) And Cut thy Head off too at last."

In June, Elizabeth was entrusted to the care of the earl and countess of Leicester at Penshurst. But in 1650, when her brother Charles II landed in Scotland, intent on reclaiming the throne of England, the Parliament ordered the royal children to be taken for security to Carisbrooke Castle. By then, the princess' health was precarious. Almost immediately upon her arrival, she fell ill and died of fever on September 8. She was buried in St. Thomas' church at Newport, Isle of Wight, where only the initials "E.S." marked her grave. In 1856, a monument was erected to her memory by Queen *Victoria. Elizabeth Stuart's sad life and early death have made her a popular subject. Her restrained demeanor and manners while in the hands of her father's enemies earned her the name of "Temperance."

Elizabeth the Good (1386–1420)

Saint. *Born in 1386; died in 1420.*

Blessed Elizabeth the Good was a nun of the Franciscan third order who was celebrated for the demonic persecutions she endured. She lived and died at Reute near the Waldsee (Swabia). Her feast day is on November 25.

Elizabeth Tudor (1533–1603).
See Elizabeth I.

Elizabeth Valois (1602–1644)

Queen of Spain. *Name variations: Elizabeth of France; Elizabeth of Valois; Isabella. Born in 1602; died in 1644; daughter of Henry IV, king of France (r. 1589–1610), and *Marie de Medici (1573?–1642); sister of *Henrietta Maria (1609–1669, who married Charles I, king of England), Christine of France (1606–1663), and Louis XIII, king of France (r. 1610–1643); became first wife of Philip IV (1605–1665), king of Spain (r. 1621–1665), in 1615 (some sources cite 1621); children: *Maria Teresa of Spain (1638–1683, first wife of Louis XIV of France). Philip IV's second wife was *Maria Anna of Austria (1634–1696).*

Elizabeth von Habsburg (1837–1898).
See Elizabeth of Bavaria.

Elizabeth von Habsburg

(1883–1963)

Austrian aristocrat, orphaned by the suicide of her father Crown Prince Rudolf, who displayed a spirit of intellectual independence by joining the Social Democratic Party and becoming renowned as the "Red Archduchess." Name variations: Archduchess Elisabeth Marie; Elisabeth Marie von Habsburg; Erzsi; the Red Archduchess. Born Elizabeth Marie von Habsburg in Laxenburg near Vienna, on September 2, 1883; died in Vienna on March 16, 1963; daughter of Crown Prince Rudolph or Rudolf (1858–1889) of Austria-Hungary and Stephanie of Belgium (1864–1945); married Otto zu Windischgraetz also known as Otto Windisch-Graetz, prince of Windischgrätz, on January 23, 1902; married Leopold Petznek (1881–1956, a militant Marxist leader and president of the Parliament of Lower Austria); children: Ernst Ferdinand; Franz Joseph; Rudolf; Stefanie.

Born in 1883 into the imperial family of Austria-Hungary, Elizabeth von Habsburg was the daughter of a Belgian mother and Austrian father whose marriage was emotionally dead. She was baptized Elizabeth in honor of Saint *Elizabeth of Hungary (1207–1231) as well as her beautiful grandmother, *Elizabeth of Bavaria (1837–1898), who was known as Empress Sisi. At the age of five, Elizabeth von Habs-

burg became an orphan when her father, the highly intelligent but emotionally unstable Crown Prince Rudolf took his own life and that of his 17-year-old mistress, Baroness *Marie Vetsera, in a suicide pact in January 1889. Never close to her mother *Stephanie of Belgium, young Elizabeth early showed signs of the same intellectual independence that had often made life difficult for her father, who yearned to reform the decrepit monarchy of his reactionary father, Emperor Franz Joseph (or Francis Joseph). Rudolf had engaged in secret journalistic assignments for Austria's leading liberal newspaper, the *Neue Freie Presse*. Many of Rudolf's friends were progressive Jewish intellectuals, and this fact, as well as his critical attitudes toward the Roman Catholic Church, the aristocracy, and Pan-Nationalist extremists, made his name anathema in anti-Semitic, reactionary and racist circles. Rudolf's only child, who would be known throughout her life as "Erzsi" (the Hungarian diminutive for Elizabeth), also developed into a "Royal Rebel."

Although loved and pampered by her grandfather Franz Joseph, the emperor of Austria-Hungary, Elizabeth rejected the socially rigid, conservative values of his ancient clan. Instead, in January 1902, "Erzsi" became a Court rebel by marrying Prince Otto Windisch-Graetz, a man regarded in Court circles as being considerably beneath her in social rank. Although it

Elizabeth von Habsburg (1883–1963)

produced four children, the marriage turned out to be a disaster, with both partners engaging in numerous affairs that soon became the talk of Viennese society. Although Elizabeth longed for a divorce, this was impossible because of her aristocratic status. When she legally became a commoner with the demise of the Habsburg monarchy in November 1918, she could then file for divorce from Windisch-Graetz. Bureaucratic delays and a bitterly contested struggle with her husband over custody of their children, however, resulted in sensationalistic press coverage of domestic animosities that included attempts to kidnap the children and several desperate calls for police intervention. The divorce would not become final until 1924.

During her extended battles with her husband, Elizabeth found strong support from the Social Democratic Party, which had long advocated women's rights, including the right to divorce and to retain custody of their children. On one dramatic occasion, Elizabeth von Habsburg, aristocrat and child of privilege, found herself receiving protection from a contingent of ordinary workers who arrived at her palace to shield her from toughs hired by her husband. Now moving more and more in Viennese Social Democratic circles, she met and soon fell in love with one of the leaders of "Red Vienna," Leopold Petznek, a militant Marxist for whom politics and struggle was simply part of daily life. A schoolteacher of working class origins, Petznek was one of the best-known personalities in the Republican Protective League (*Republikanischer Schutzbund*), a highly trained formation of workers who provided security for Social Democratic meetings and met the challenge of armed Nazis and Fascists on Vienna's streets and neighborhoods. Highly respected by Vienna's workers, Leopold Petznek served for many years in the Parliament of Lower Austria and was elected its president in 1927.

Despite having grown up in a radically different world, Elizabeth von Habsburg was thrilled by the energy and idealism of Vienna's organized working class, and she chose to become a card-carrying member of the Social Democratic Party. As one of the very few ex-aristocrats in the Marxist movement that governed Vienna from 1920 through 1934, Elizabeth would always be the center of attention at party meetings and rallies, which she attended faithfully until the end of her long life. She also marched in May Day celebrations, adding a touch of class to the thousands of her militantly class-conscious colleagues who turned out for the hallowed proletarian holiday.

Austria became a Fascist dictatorship in 1934, and Elizabeth von Habsburg's beloved Vienna was destroyed. The Anschluss which absorbed Austria into the Third Reich in March 1938 was another profound blow to her and to her companion Leopold Petznek, who served five months in prison in 1934 because of his political militancy. No longer young, both Elizabeth and Leopold survived the Nazi occupation and the war years (Petznek was briefly incarcerated in a Nazi concentration camp in 1945). Until they finally moved to a family castle after the war, they lived for many years in an extremely modest apartment. In 1948, their relationship was formalized by marriage. As an anti-Nazi veteran, Petznek was chosen to serve in several important posts after 1945 (he retired as president of the Highest Court of Audits) and died in 1956. After the death of her beloved husband, Elizabeth von Habsburg increasingly withdrew into seclusion, at least in part because of a severe case of gout that now confined her to a wheelchair. But the older generation of Viennese continued to remember her as the strong-willed daughter of Crown Prince Rudolf, as a woman who had been able to fashion a life uniquely her own. Elizabeth von Habsburg died in Vienna on March 16, 1963, and is buried in Vienna's Hütteldorf cemetery.

SOURCES:

Hamann, Brigitte, ed. *Die Habsburger: Ein biographisches Lexikon*. Munich: Piper Verlag, 1988.

———. *Rudolf, Kronprinz und Rebell*. Vienna: Amalthea Verlag, 1978.

Listowel, Judith Marffy-Mantuano Hare, Countess of. *A Habsburg Tragedy: Crown Prince Rudolf*. London: Ascent Books, 1978.

Nabl, Franz. *Schichtwechsel* (play), 1929.

Planer, Franz. *Das Jahrbuch der Wiener Gesellschaft: Biographische Beiträge zur Wiener Zeitgeschichte*. Vienna: Verlag Franz Planer, 1929.

Salburg, Edith Gräfin. *Das Enkelkind der Majestäten*. Dresden: M. Seyfert Verlag, 1929.

———. *Liesl und ihre Kinder: Roman*. Dresden: M. Seyfert Verlag, 1930.

Salvendy, John T. *Royal Rebel: A Psychological Portrait of Crown Prince Rudolf of Austria-Hungary*. Lanham, MD: University Press of America, 1988.

Weissensteiner, Friedrich. *Die rote Erzherzogin: Das ungewöhnliche Leben der Tochter des Kronprinzen Rudolf*. Vienna: Österreichischer Bundesverlag, 1984.

RELATED MEDIA:

"The Hapsburgs: A European Family History" (4 videocassettes), Princeton, NJ: Films for the Humanities, 1998.

John Haag,
Assistant Professor of History,
University of Georgia, Athens, Georgia

Elizabeth von Pommern (1347–1393).

See Anne of Bohemia for sidebar on Elizabeth of Pomerania.

Elizabeth Woodville (1437–1492).

See Woodville, Elizabeth.

Elizaveta.

Variant of Elizabeth.

Ella (1864–1918)

Princess of Hesse-Darmstadt and grand duchess of Russia. Name variations: after her marriage, became known as Elizabeth Feodorovna; Grand Duchess Elizabeth; Elizabeth or Ella Saxe-Coburg. Born Elizabeth Alexandra Louise on November 1, 1864, in the city of Darmstadt in the German principality of Hesse-Darmstadt; murdered by the Bolsheviks around July 17, 1918, and thrown down a mine pit in Alapaievsk, Russia, the day after her brother-in-law Tsar Nicholas II, her sister Empress *Alexandra Feodorovna, and her nephew and nieces were slaughtered; second daughter of Prince Louis of Hesse-Darmstadt and Princess *Alice Maud Mary (1843–1878) of Great Britain; granddaughter of Queen *Victoria, queen of England (r. 1837–1901); educated by private tutors; married Grand Duke Serge of Russia (Sergius Alexandrovitch, son of Tsar Alexander II), on June 15, 1884.

SUGGESTED READING:

Mager, Hugo. *Elizabeth, Grand Duchess of Russia.* Carroll & Graf, 1998.

Ellen.

Variant of Eleanor or Helena.

Ellen of Wales (d. 1253)

Countess of Huntingdon and Chester. Name variations: Elen; Helena. Died in 1253; daughter of Llywelyn II the Great (1173–1240), ruler of All Wales, and his mistress *Tangwystl (some sources cite *Joan of England); married John of Chester (1207–1237), earl of Chester (r. 1232–1237), in 1220 or 1222; married Robert de Quinci, in 1237; children: (second marriage) *Joan de Quinci (d. 1283, who married Humphrey Bohun); Hawise de Quinci (c. 1250–c. 1295, who married Baldwin Wake).

Ellenborough, Countess or Lady (1807–1881).

See Digby el Mesrab, Jane.

Ellerman, Winifred (1894–1983)

English novelist and benefactor. Name variations: Bryher; Winifred Bryher; Annie Winifred Ellerman. Born Annie Winifred Ellerman in 1894; died in 1983; daughter of Sir John Ellerman (a shipping magnate) and Hannah Glover; attended Queenwood, a girls' boarding school; married Robert McAlmon, in February 1921; married Kenneth Macpherson.

Selected writings: Region of Lutany *(poems, Chapman & Hall, 1914);* Amy Lowell: A Critical Appreciation *(London: Eyre & Spottiswoode, 1918);* Development *(London: Constable, 1920);* Film Problems of Soviet Russia *(1929); (autobiography)* The Heart to Artemis *(1962);* The Coin of Carthage *(1963);* The Days of Mars, 1940–46 *(1972).*

Annie Winifred Ellerman was born in 1894, though her parents did not marry until 1908, in time for the birth of her younger brother John. Throughout her life, she preferred to be known as Bryher. Her father John Ellerman was a shipping magnate, a self-made man whose wife **Hannah Glover** had been born into the middle class; thus, though the Ellermans lived in a large house on South Audley Street in London and John Ellerman had made a fortune, the family was not

Winifred Ellerman

a part of London's high society. John, who would later receive a knighthood, was deeply involved in world affairs and traveled with his family throughout Europe, Africa, and the Near East.

At 15, Bryher was enrolled in a girls' boarding school known as Queenwood. She would subsequently write in her autobiography, *The Heart to Artemis:* "Though as age has chilled the emotions I can accept Queenwood as a necessary part of my experience, the impact was a shattering one and it was hell while it lasted." She so hated the school that her first novel, the highly critical *Development* (1920), would be based on her school years. While at Queenwood, she spent a holiday at a friend's home on the Scilly Islands, off Cornwall's coast, and fell in love with the area. She would legally borrow the name Bryher from one of the islands. With a passion for the sea, Bryher longed to be a boy and stow away on an outbound ship. She wrote in her autobiography:

> What a disappointment I was to my parents! All their friends had liked me as a child but here I was with the raw aggressiveness of a boy, clamoring to be loosed upon a world that had no use for me. . . . It must have been disconcerting when a guest, meaning to be kind, asked me what my hobbies were and got the answer, "I want to find out how people think." Once in an unguarded moment I said something about writing. There was a roar of laughter and a visitor answered, "Oh no, Miss Winifred, I'm afraid that is a little out of your range but I'm sure you'll run the garden splendidly in a year or two."

Though the Ellermans regarded writing as a selfish occupation, Bryher persuaded her father to allow her to have some poems published as *Region of Lutany* (1914). Frequenting bookstores, she devoured the little magazines that contained the latest poetry and, at 19, fell in love with the Imagists. But with the advent of World War I, she found herself trapped in her parents' household with no avenue of escape. Her only happiness seemed to be in discovering the Imagist anthologies of *Amy Lowell, which were sent by an American friend. Lowell and Bryher began corresponding regularly, and before long Bryher was sending Lowell poems for criticism while Lowell introduced her to the work of *Hilda Doolittle (H.D.) and *Dorothy Richardson. In 1918, Bryher published *Amy Lowell: A Critical Appreciation.* Bryher was fascinated by H.D. and soon knew all the poems in Doolittle's *Sea Garden.* On learning that H.D. lived in England, Bryher set out to meet her. The engagement, she wrote Lowell, was a success, as she and Doolittle became instant friends.

Bryher planned trips with her to Greece and America, while H.D. encouraged Bryher's writing and helped her move out of her parents' house into a London flat. During H.D.'s pregnancy, Bryher was a support for the poet, and when H.D. came down with a deadly flu virus it was Bryher who put her into a nursing home for the birth. For the next few years, they lived together and traveled together—Greece, Paris, Switzerland, Egypt, New York and California. A devoted Bryher was to aid H.D. both mentally and materially for the rest of her life. Without Bryher, it is questionable if Doolittle would have had the means to write.

While in New York in 1920, Bryher met Robert McAlmon, a 25-year-old writer from America's midwest. McAlmon had the same dream as Bryher: he longed to board a ship and sail to exotic places. He was also intent on moving to Paris to meet James Joyce. Since McAlmon and Bryher enjoyed each other's company, Bryher proposed a marriage of convenience in which both would benefit: she would back his adventures, while, as a married woman, she would finally be free of her parents and could continue living with H.D. The pact was set, and McAlmon and Bryher were married at City Hall in New York in February of 1921.

Delighted with the marriage, the Ellermans greeted their son-in-law with open arms. Bryher and H.D. moved to Territet, near Montreux, Switzerland, where they would live for the next few years. McAlmon often visited. With Bryher's support, he formed the Contact Publishing Company in Paris, publishing the work of *Mina Loy, Bryher, H.D., *Djuna Barnes, *Mary Butts, *Gertrude Stein, Ernest Hemingway, and Marsden Hartley between the years 1922 to 1928. When McAlmon finally met James Joyce, he and Bryher agreed to pay Joyce $150 a month until *Ulysses* found a publisher. Throughout her life, Bryher would heed the words of her father: "Always buy a painting by a living man, Miggy, what use is money to him when he is dead?" Belonging to the influential women's network of writers in Paris of the 1920s, Bryher often journeyed to that city. She also contributed generously to *Sylvia Beach's bookstore and funded many publications for *Harriet Weaver's Egoist Press in London.

With McAlmon chafing under the marital arrangement, the couple divorced in 1927. Sir John, Bryher's father, gave her husband a divorce settlement of reportedly £14,000, earning McAlmon the nickname of McAlimony.

Soon after, Bryher met Kenneth Macpherson, a Brit who had fallen in love with Doolittle. Since H.D. was by then legally married, Bryher hit on another idea whereby *she* would marry Macpherson to regain her British citizenship and maintain her protected married status. All agreed to the arrangement, and they remained a happy threesome even after the passion went out of Macpherson's relationship with Doolittle.

Together, Bryher and Macpherson started the first film magazine, *Close-up*. Sold in Sylvia Beach's Shakespeare and Company, its contributors were H.D., Dorothy Richardson and Gertrude Stein. In 1929, Bryher published *Film Problems of Soviet Russia*, and the following year she and Macpherson built Kenwin, a lakeside villa near Montreux, which they shared as a base. Bryher would live out her life there. With Kenneth's enthusiasm, the Macphersons became more actively involved in filmmaking, their efforts culminating in the 1930 silent *Borderline*, starring Doolittle and Paul Robeson. By now, though still friends, H.D. and Bryher were seeing less of each other. Eventually, Bryher and Macpherson would adopt H.D.'s daughter **Perdita**.

In 1935, Bryher took over the literary journal *Life and Letters To-day*; she also abetted the founding of the *Psychoanalytic Review*. During World War II, she helped Jewish refugees escape from Germany, then joined H.D. in London and worked on her first historical novel *Beowulf* while Macpherson stayed in New York. In 1947, Bryher and Macpherson amicably separated. Bryher and H.D., however, remained friends for 42 years, a relationship described by Bryher in her *Days of Mars, 1940–46* (1972). Bryher was with H.D when she died on September 27, 1961. Informed of Doolittle's death, *****Alice B. Toklas** commented: "It is impossible to believe in Bryher without H.D."

SOURCES:

Bryher. *The Heart to Artemis*. NY: Harcourt, Brace, 1962.

———. *Two Selves*. Paris: Contact Publishing, 1923.

Hanscombe, Gillian, and Virginia L. Smyers. *Writing for Their Lives: The Modernist Women, 1910–1940*. Boston, MA: Northeastern University Press, 1987.

Ellet, Elizabeth (c. 1812–1877)

American author and historian. Name variations: Elizabeth Lummis. Born Elizabeth Fries Lummis in Sodus, New York, probably in 1812 (some sources cite 1818); died in New York on June 3, 1877; daughter of William N. Lummis (a physician) and Sarah (Maxwell) Lummis; attended Female Seminary, Aurora, New York; married William H. Ellet (a doctor and chemistry professor), around 1835.

Selected writings: Poems, Translated and Original (1835); Characters of Schiller (1839); Scenes in the Life of Joanna of Sicily (1840); Rambles about the Country (1840); Women of the American Revolution (1848); Domestic History of the American Revolution (1850); Evenings at Woodlawn (1849); Family Pictures from the Bible (1849); Watching Spirits (1951); Novelettes of the Musicians (1852); Pioneer Women of the West (1853); Summer Rambles in the West (1853); The Practical Housekeeper (1857); Women Artists in All Ages and Countries (1859); Queens of American Society (1867); (with Mrs. R.E. Mack) Court Circles of the Republic (1869).

Elizabeth Ellet

The author of 15 books, a volume of poetry, and numerous magazine articles, Elizabeth Lummis Ellet was one of the first female writers to identify the role of women in the early history of the United States. Fluent in French, Italian, and German, Ellet began writing at age 15 and published her first original work, *Poems, Translated and Original*, in 1835. After her marriage to William H. Ellet, a doctor and professor of chemistry at Columbia College, New York, she moved with him to Columbia, South Carolina. They returned to New York in 1848, where Ellet remained a figure of the New York literary society until her death in 1877.

Notable among Ellet's books is *Women of the American Revolution* (1848), a three-volume work sketching the lives of 160 women who played a part in, witnessed, or merely commented on the events of the Revolution. A pioneering effort, the book remained a major source through several editions. A subsequent work, *Domestic History of the American Revolution* (1850), drew from related material. Similar in format to her work on the Revolution was *Pioneer Women of the West* (1953), and *Queens of American Society* (1867).

Elliot, Cass (1941–1974)

American ensemble and solo singer who played a crucial role in generating the phenomenal success enjoyed by The Mamas and the Papas. Name variations: Mama Cass. Born Ellen Naomi Cohen in Baltimore, Maryland, on September 19, 1941; died of a heart attack in London, England, on July 29, 1974; daughter of Philip Cohen and Beth (Levine) Cohen; married James R. Hendricks; married Donald von Weidenman; children: daughter, Owen Vanessa Elliot-Kugell (b. 1967).

Largely thanks to the crystalline contralto voice of "Mama" Cass Elliot, the American vocal quartet The Mamas and the Papas enjoyed huge success during the mid-1960s. Elliot was the most popular member of this group probably because of her down-to-earth persona, which included her frequent references to her struggles with being overweight. Born Ellen Naomi Cohen, she grew up in the 1940s and 1950s in a Jewish-American, middle-class home. Her parents were in the restaurant business and had a strong affinity for music. Her father Philip was an opera buff, her mother Beth a piano player. Attracted to music from her earliest years, Ellen found favorite singers in *Ella Fitzgerald, *Judy Garland, and **Blossom Dearie**. She took piano lessons in grade school and later learned to play the guitar because of her growing interest in folk music. Comfortable performing, she sang in her high school choir and acted in high school theater productions.

By the time she was 17, Ellen Naomi Cohen had chosen a stage name, Cassandra Elliot. Nicknamed Cass by her father for the prophetess Cassandra of Greek mythology, she included "Elliot" in honor of a friend who had died in a car accident. Cass Elliot dropped out of Baltimore's Forest Park High School shortly before graduation and never received her diploma. Instead, she moved to New York City to embark on a stage career. In Manhattan, she landed a few Off-Broadway parts as well as a role in the touring company of *The Music Man*. Elliot also paid her rent by directing at *Ellen Stewart's Café La Mama.

During her first years in New York, she became involved in the richly creative folk music scene of that era. Her marriage in 1963 to James R. Hendricks resulted in her singing along with Hendricks and Tim Rose in the Big Three, a short-lived but pivotal folk group. The Big Three recorded two albums for the FM label, *The Big Three* and *Live at the Recording Studio*, but neither achieved hit status. By summer 1964, the Big Three had evolved into a new group called The Mugwumps. Besides Elliot and Hendricks, The Mugwumps included two Canadian-born musicians, Dennis (Denny) Doherty and Zalman Yanovsky. The Mugwumps, who went electric, had an original sound and received decent reviews, but there was little response from the public. An album tape they made for Warner Bros. Records would not be released until Elliot and Doherty had both become superstars as members of another group.

By 1964, Cass Elliot's musical talents had been spotted by a number of musicians, including John Phillips. Six years older than Elliot, South Carolina-born Phillips had a recording career that dated back to 1960. As a member of the folk trio The Journeymen, he had recorded three albums for Capitol Records. In 1964, John and his wife ***Michelle Phillips** moved to the Virgin Islands and along with ex-Mugwump Denny Doherty were in the process of forming a new vocal group. Cass Elliot joined the trio in the islands, where for five months Elliot and her new musical partners worked to perfect the sound of their ensemble. Financially down-and-out but artistically inspired, the group received free accommodations in exchange for singing at a local nightclub.

Confident of their future, Elliot and the others flew to Los Angeles to try to launch their new group with a record deal. They were soon discovered by Lou Adler, a dynamic producer who had just formed the Dunhill Records label and was searching for fresh faces and new talent. He was impressed by the group's distinctive personality and sound, which was a seductive blend of Elliot's soaring contralto, Michelle Phillips' soprano, and Denny Doherty's tenor, along with the tenor voice and strong guitar work of John Phillips who effectively led the group. Convinced that they had created a unique sound and had a future, Adler offered to both record the quartet and serve as their manager. He also gave his approval to the group's catchy name, The Mamas and the Papas.

The March 1966 Dunhill release of a song co-written by John and Michelle Phillips, "California Dreamin'," caught the mood of generational change of the mid-1960s. With its faintly melancholy evocation of an earthly Utopia within reach, "California Dreamin'" shot to #4 on the charts and sold more than one-million copies; it also did well in the United Kingdom, reaching #23 on the British charts. "Monday Monday" was released two months later, and it

Cass Elliot, with Michelle Phillips, John Phillips, and Denny Doherty of The Mamas and the Papas.

too soared on the charts, becoming #1 in the United States and achieving #3 in the United Kingdom.

In May 1966, when the first Mamas and Papas album, *If You Can Believe Your Eyes and Ears,* which contained both "California Dreamin'" and "Monday Monday," was released, it soon climbed to the top of the charts, remaining there for more than two years and selling more than one-million copies. Four other Mamas and Papas singles became Top Five hits in 1966 and 1967: "I Saw Her Again," "Words of Love," "Dedicated to the One I Love" (a reworking of the **Shirelles** classic), and "Creeque Alley," a humorous chronicling of the group's rise to fame and fortune. By the end of 1966, their second album, *The Mamas and the Papas,* had also sold a million copies. In March 1967, the group received a Grammy Award for "Monday Monday."

By 1967, The Mamas and the Papas had become a musical sensation, one of America's most popular folk-pop groups. They had also become

a statement of cultural revolution. Their folk-pop songs, although a sophisticated commercial production, gave the appearance of simplicity and innocence at the dawn of the era of flower power and "power-to-the-people." Outlandishly "psychedelic" with their fur hats and other oddities, the group outfitted themselves in a manner that identified them with the youthful allure of San Francisco's counter-culture. They were an emerging but essentially sanitized and unthreatening image of the "hip" subculture that was starting to transform the world of rock music.

Critic Geoffrey Stokes has attributed the success of these talented professionals to the "controlled, elaborate, cool" harmonies that made for "an extraordinarily beautiful pop sound." Songs like "California Dreamin'," "Monday Monday" and other Mamas and Papas hits delivered a sound that was as sophisticated as that which the best Hollywood studios of the day could conjure up, and the group's intelligently crafted combinations of folk, rock and just plain pop were presented in the form of fine melodies and complex but effective harmonies that have been described as "some of the finest in all of rock."

One of the group's most important achievements took place in June 1967, when John Phillips and Lou Adler organized the three-day International Pop Festival that took place in Monterey, California. Possibly the first, and certainly one of the most successful, rock music festivals of the late 1960s, this extravaganza launched the careers of *Janis Joplin, Jimi Hendrix, and The Who. The Mamas and the Papas performed as the closing act of the third and final evening of the festival. Although they did not know it, this would be the last time they would perform together in a live concert.

Cass Elliot, with a soaring voice that some critics have described as being simply "stupendous," made a major contribution to the popular success of The Mamas and the Papas. Although she was called "Mama" for her warm, brassy personality and her physical amplitude, she always strongly disliked this label, describing it as "a stigma." In an October 1968 Rolling Stone interview, she emphasized her attempts to stop people from calling her Mama for "all my folksinging life." With the appearance of The Mamas and the Papas, the name Mama Cass became even more strongly linked with Elliot despite her continuing distaste for it. With the birth of her daughter Owen Vanessa (Elliot-Kugell) in March 1967, she would find it virtually impossible to prevent people from calling her "Mama."

Elliot struggled with obesity throughout her life. Overweight since her earliest years, the 5'5" brunette at times weighed as much as 300 pounds. She attempted a number of crash diets, once claiming to have lost 120 pounds. But her attempts to be slim like Michelle Phillips always failed and quite possibly impacted negatively on her general state of health. She asserted that her weight had been, if anything, an advantage in her career, setting her apart from the others. "After all, you'd never mistake me for Jane Fonda, would you?" Elliot insisted that her sense of humor had not developed as a defense mechanism because of her weight. She remarked of her lifelong weight problem, "I simply learned that's the way I am and so I live with it."

In addition to health concerns as a result of her obesity, Elliot abused drugs and alcohol which may have contributed to her occasionally erratic behavior. In October 1967, she was arrested after docking in Southampton, charged with stealing blankets and keys from a hotel on an earlier visit to London. After she spent a night in jail, the charges were dropped, but the ruckus caused a series of Mamas and Papas concerts scheduled for the Royal Albert Hall to be cancelled. By this time, there were rumors of the group's imminent breakup. Largely because of the collapse of John and Michelle Phillips' marriage, The Mamas and the Papas officially disbanded as a group in July 1968. Cass Elliot immediately embarked on an ambitious solo career, signing a $40,000 a week contract to perform in Las Vegas' Caesar's Palace starting in October 1968. After the first night, her act was cancelled, and Cass checked into a hospital for eight weeks. Following her release, the star announced that she had given up her dependency on both drugs and alcohol.

Billing herself as Mama Cass, Elliot now became the most successful solo performer of the individual members of the former Mamas and Papas, each of whom was now concentrating on a solo singing career. Her first solo album, Dream a Little Dream (1968), made it to #87 on the American charts while her second solo single, California Earthquake, did considerably better by advancing to #67. In August 1969, her It's Getting Better reached #30 on the American charts and became a hit in the United Kingdom, reaching #8 there. In 1970, her songs New World Coming and A Song That Never Comes were in the American Top Hundred at #42 and #99 respectively. Her 1969 solo album Make Your Own Kind of Music was no more than a modest success, peaking at #169 on the U.S. charts.

Elliot would keep busy the next several years making albums and singles as well as working a live performance schedule by appearing in nightclubs. She was often seen on television specials and variety shows such as the "Red Skelton Show." Continuing to experiment, she made some never-released tapes with the group Electric Flag as well as a critically acclaimed but commercially disappointing album with British rock star Dave Mason, with whom she also performed at Fillmore East. Elliot's 1971 compilation Mama's Big Ones peaked at a disappointing #194 on the American charts. Her three final solo LPs, for RCA Records, Cass Elliot (1972), The Road Is No Place for a Lady (1972), and Don't Call Me Mama Anymore (1973), were unable to produce any more hits.

As the era of the flower children began to fade and a "big chill" mood of disillusionment began to grip the world, Cass Elliot still remained optimistic about both her career and life. In 1971, she married a German Baron, Donald von Weidenman, but the marriage soon resulted in an annulment. Cass Elliot died suddenly in London on July 29, 1974. Early news stories reported that she had choked to death while eating a sandwich. This apocryphal tale of the star's demise quickly became a word-of-mouth legend, often embellished into the myth that she had died on stage, choking on a ham sandwich. The official coroner's report put these rumors to rest, finding the cause of death to be a massive heart attack due to obesity and stress. Although she had died abroad, Elliot's ashes were scattered over the Pacific Ocean.

Elliot's musical partner Michelle Phillips was emotionally shaken by Mama Cass's sudden death and made special efforts to maintain her own health. Phillips retained an interest in Cass's daughter Owen, who had been born out of wedlock and did not know her father's name. After Phillips placed notices in magazines to discover the father's identity, Owen received a call from Michelle in 1987 saying, "I found your dad. Here's a plane ticket. Go meet him." Leaving behind a rich musical legacy, Cass Elliot had shared a voice with countless fans that became a part of her nation's cultural history. In January 1998, The Mamas and the Papas were inducted into the Rock-and-Roll Hall of Fame.

SOURCES:

Amende, Coral. *Legends in Their Own Time.* NY: Prentice Hall, 1994.

Geitner, Paul. "Elliot, Cass ("Mama")," in Kenneth T. Jackson et al., eds. *Dictionary of American Biography.* Supplement, Vol. 9. NY: Scribner, 1994, pp. 261–262.

Helander, Brock. *The Rock Who's Who.* NY: Schirmer, 1982.

Johnson, Jon. *Make Your Own Kind of Music: A Career Retrospective of Cass Elliot.* Detroit, MI: Music Archives Press, 1987.

McConnell, Stacy A. *Contemporary Musicians: Profiles of the People in Music.* Vol. 21. Detroit, MI: Gale Research, 1998.

Phillips, John, with Jim Jerome. *Papa John: An Autobiography.* Garden City, NY: Doubleday, 1986.

Phillips, Michelle. *California Dreamin': The True Story of the Mamas and the Papas.* NY: Warner, 1986.

Rees, Dafydd, and Luke Crampton. *DK Encyclopedia of Rock Stars.* NY: DK Publishing, 1996.

Rockwell, John. "Cass Elliot, Pop Singer, Dies; Star of the Mamas and Papas," in *The New York Times Biographical Edition.* July 1974, p. 947.

"The Rolling Stone Interview: Cass Elliot," in *Rolling Stone.* No. 20. October 26, 1968, pp. 19–20 and 22–24.

Romanowski, Patricia, and Holly George-Warren, eds. *The New Rolling Stone Encyclopedia of Rock & Roll.* NY: Fireside/Rolling Stone Press, 1995.

Schindehette, Susan, *et al.* "The Mamas and The Papas' Kids," in *People Weekly.* Vol. 45. No. 24. June 17, 1996, pp. 144–148.

Selvin, Joel. *Monterey Pop: June 16–18, 1967.* San Francisco, CA: Chronicle Books, 1992.

Sumrall, Harry. *Pioneers of Rock and Roll: 100 Artists Who Changed the Face of Rock.* NY: Billboard Books, 1994.

Ward, Ed, Geoffrey Stokes, and Ken Tucker. *Rock of Ages: The Rolling Stone History of Rock and Roll.* NY: Rolling Stone Press/Summit Books, 1986.

Wenning, Elizabeth. "Cass Elliot," in Michael L. LaBlanc, ed., *Contemporary Musicians: Profiles of the People in Music.* Detroit, MI: Gale Research, 1991, Vol. 5, pp. 48–49.

York, William. *Who's Who in Rock Music.* Rev. ed. NY: Scribner, 1982.

RELATED MEDIA:

"Historic Performances at the Monterey Pop Festival: The Mamas and the Papas" (compact disc), MCA Special Products (MCAD–22033).

The Mamas & the Papas: Straight Shooter, ABC Video, Stamford, CT, 1994.

Monterey Pop, film by D.A. Pennebaker, Janus Films, Santa Monica, CA, 1988.

Straight Shooter: The Story of John Phillips and the Mamas & the Papas, Rhino Home Video, Santa Monica, CA, 1989.

John Haag,
Assistant Professor of History,
University of Georgia, Athens, Georgia

Elliott, Gertrude (1874–1950)

American actress and sister of Maxine Elliott. Born in Rockland, Maine, in 1874; died in 1950; daughter of Thomas (a sea captain) and Adelaide (Hall) Dermot; younger sister of actress Maxine Elliott (1868–1940); married Sir Johnston Forbes-Robertson (an English actor-manager), in 1900; children: several, including **Diana Forbes-Robertson** *(author of* My Aunt Maxine: The Story of Maxine Elliott*) and* **Jean Forbes-Robertson** *(an actress).*

Gertrude Elliott was born in Rockland, Maine, in 1874, the daughter of Thomas and Adelaide Hall Dermot. Encouraged in her stage career by her older sister *Maxine Elliott, Gertrude Elliott made her New York debut in 1894. From 1897 to 1899, she appeared with Nathaniel Goodwin (whom her sister married in 1898, then later divorced) in *In Missoura, The Rivals,* and *Nathan Hale.* Gertrude made her London debut in 1899 as Midge in *The Cowboy and the Lady* and later appeared with Johnston Forbes-Robertson, playing Ophelia to his Hamlet. The two were married in 1900 and often returned to America, where Gertrude created the role of Cleopatra in Shaw's *Caesar and Cleopatra,* among others. Praised as much for her humor and eloquent speech as her beauty, she performed with her husband until his retirement in 1913, after which she toured under her own management. In one of her last performances in New York in 1936, she played Gertrude in *Hamlet* opposite Leslie Howard. From 1911, Gertrude and her family resided with her sister Maxine at Hartsbourne Manor, in England. Her daughter **Jean Forbes-Robertson**, one of several children, was also on the stage.

Elliott, Maud Howe (1854–1948)

*American novelist and historian. Name variations: Maud Howe. Born Maud Howe at the Perkins Institute in Boston, Massachusetts, on November 9, 1854; died at her summer home in Newport, Rhode Island, on March 19, 1948; daughter of Samuel Gridley Howe (founder of the Perkins Institute for the Blind) and *Julia Ward Howe (1819–1910); sister of Laura E. Richards (1850–1943); attended the pioneer Kindergarten of America, established and taught by Elizabeth Peabody; married John Elliott (an artist), on February 7, 1887.*

Maud Elliott and her sister *Laura E. Richards** received the first Pulitzer Prize for Biography (1917) for a 2-volume work on their mother, *Julia Ward Howe, 1819–1910* (Boston: Houghton Mifflin, 1916). In her autobiography *Three Generations*, published by Little, Brown, in 1923, Elliott describes her childhood: "Looking back upon the first six or seven years of my life, I find myself in a dim enchanted land, which I have come to think of as 'The Twilight of the Gods,' for the figures that peopled it were, indeed, heroes and demigods. They drop easily apart into two groups, Mama's friends and

Papa's friends. Mama's friends—we called them 'The Owls'—were poets, philosophers, and theologians, speculative men who sat long and discussed abstract things. Papa's friends were statesmen, soldiers, militant philanthropists, men of action whose time was too precious for long visits." Her mother's friends included Henry James the elder (while Maud grew up with the "James boys," Henry and Willie), *Elizabeth Peabody, Ralph Waldo Emerson, Thomas Carlyle, *Margaret Fuller, *Maria Edgeworth, *Florence Nightingale and "a host of others."

Maud Elliott was a correspondent for several newspapers and also wrote *A Newport Aquarelle* (1883), *The San Rosario Ranch* (1884), *Atalanta in the South* (1886), *Mammon* (1888), *Two in Italy* (Little Brown, 1905), *Honor,* and *Phyllida.* An inveterate traveler, she and her husband lived in Newport, Boston, Chicago, Rome, and Santo Domingo, while visiting Algeria and Greece. Her travels inform many of her books. Maud Howe Elliott was given an honorary degree of Doctor of Letters from Brown University in 1940.

SOURCES:
Elliott, Maud Howe. *Three Generations.* Boston, MA: Little, Brown, 1923.

Elliott, Maxine (1868–1940)

American actress. Born Jessie Carolyn Dermot in Rockland, Maine, on February 5, 1868 (some sources cite 1871 or 1875); died in Cannes, France, on March 5, 1940; daughter of Thomas (a sea captain) and Adelaide (Hall) Dermot; older sister of actress Gertrude Elliott (1874–1950); attended Notre Dame Academy, Roxbury, Massachusetts; married George A. McDermott (a lawyer and marshal to New York Mayor William R. Grace), around 1884 (divorced 1896); married Nathaniel C. Goodwin (an actor and comedian), on February 20, 1898 (divorced 1908).

Although never acclaimed a great actress, Maxine Elliott was a significant figure in the American theater. A breathtaking brunette with a statuesque figure, she captured the attention of American and English theatergoers and became the toast of British society. Upon seeing her for the first time, *Ethel Barrymore called her "the Venus de Milo with arms." Elliott opened her own theater in 1908, thus becoming the first woman manager and theater owner in New York. At age 52 (49 by her count), she left the theater for "a peaceful life" as a society matron.

The daughter of a New England sea captain, Maxine Elliott appeared in a number of school

---

❧ **Coghlan, Rose** (1852–1932)

English-American actress. Born on March 18, 1852 (some sources cite 1853) in Peterborough, England; died in 1932; sister of actor Charles Coghlan; naturalized U.S. citizen, 1902; married and divorced twice; no children.

Famous for her mellow voice, Rose Coghlan made her debut in Scotland at age 13 and went on to star on the London stage. In 1872, she arrived in New York, where she would later appear as Countess Zicka in the American premiere of *Diplomacy* (1878). In 1880, Coghlan was a great success as Stephanie in *Forget-Me-Not.* From 1880 to 1889, she worked with Wallack's company. Her career declined in later years, when the over-dramatic style of acting to which she belonged became outmoded. Coghlan spent her last five years at St. Vincent's Retreat for Nervous and Mental Disorders in Harrison, New York, having thrice declared bankruptcy.

---

theatricals while attending Notre Dame Academy in Massachusetts. While still in her teens, she made her way to New York to study acting with famed playwright-actor-manager Dion Boucicault. Elliott made her first stage appearance at Palmer's Theater in 1890, in *The Middleman,* then did a season each with ◄❧ **Rose Coghlan**'s and Augustin Daly's companies (1894 and 1895), making her London debut at Daly's Theater as Sylvia in *Two Gentlemen of Verona* (1895).

Early in her career, she had married George McDermott, a lawyer twice her age. The marriage ended in 1896, and two years later she married Nathaniel C. Goodwin, a well-established actor and notorious womanizer whom she toured with in Australia. For the next several years, Elliott worked exclusively with her husband, playing small parts to his leading ones. The couple enjoyed a string of successful hits, including *Nathan Hale, A Gilded Fool,* and *The Cowboy and the Lady.* During this period, Elliott's sister *Gertrude Elliott, also an actress, appeared in Goodwin's company.

True to his reputation, Goodwin left Elliott in 1902, and the couple divorced in 1908. The actress then established herself as a star in *Her Own Way,* written by playwright Clyde Fitch expressly for her. Nearly every review of the play opened with the identical line: "Maxine Elliott had *Her Own Way* at the Garrick Theater last night," and most went on to praise her acting as well as her striking appearance. Elliott, long tired of being heralded for her looks, was thankful for credit as an actress. She told a reviewer for *Theater Magazine* that being termed a stage beauty was a hindrance to a budding career. It draws "attention," she explained, "and one's poor beginnings as an artist stand out more glaringly because of the prominence one would so gladly escape during those first two or three years."

In 1905, after a long run in New York, Elliott took *Her Own Way* to London, where she attracted the attention of Edward VII, who requested an introduction and thereafter remained a warm admirer. In 1908, with help from the Shubert brothers (and reputedly financed by J.P. Morgan), Elliott opened the Maxine Elliott Theater in New York, which was considered a model of elegance and decor for its time. After appearing in the theater's opening production of *The Chaperon,* she began devoting more time to her theatrical enterprises than to acting. In 1911, she purchased a large estate known as Hartsbourne Manor in England for herself and for Gertrude and her family. Her London appearance in *Joseph and His Brethren* in 1913 marked

Maxine Elliott

the end of her theatrical career, except for brief engagements on the American stage in *Lord and Lady Algy* (1918) and *Trimmed in Scarlet* (1920). In 1916, she made a few silent films, notably the *Eternal Magdalen* and *Fighting Odds.*

During World War I, Elliott immersed herself in relief work. She enlisted as a Red Cross nurse and had her automobile transformed into an ambulance. Using her own money, she outfitted a fleet of barges to carry relief supplies to civilians along the canals of Belgium. For her effort, she received the Belgian Order of the Crown as well as decorations from the French and British governments.

From 1925, Elliott spent most of her time on the Riviera, where her estate Villa de l'Horizon, near Cannes, was a gathering place of the international social set. She refused even the suggestion of a comeback and was quoted in a 1937 interview as saying: "I never did like playing—never did really. All I care about are my friends and peace." The actress was 72 when she died at her villa. Though generous to her friends and family throughout her life (she reportedly gave her niece $500,000 as a wedding present in 1924), she left an estate in excess of one million dollars.

SUGGESTED READING:

Forbes-Robertson, Diana. *My Aunt Maxine: The Story of Maxine Elliott.* NY: Viking, 1964.

Barbara Morgan,
Melrose, Massachusetts.

Elliott, Sumner Locke (1881–1917).

See Locke, Sumner.

Ellis, Florence Hawley (1906–1991)

American archaeologist, anthropologist and ethnohistorian who was a leading authority on the Pueblo Indians of the American Southwest. Name variations: Florence M. Hawley; Florence H. Senter. Born Florence M. Hawley in Cananea, Sonora, Mexico, on September 17, 1906; died in Albuquerque, New Mexico, on April 6, 1991; daughter of Fred Graham Hawley and Amy (Roach) Hawley; married Donovan Senter (divorced 1947); married Bruce T. Ellis (curator of collections at Albuquerque's Museum of New Mexico); children: (first marriage) daughter, Andrea Senter.

In 1906, Florence Hawley was born to American parents in the Mexican copper-mining town of Cananea. Soon after Mexico's revolutionary turbulence made life too precarious for foreigners, the family moved back to the United States, and her father, a mining chemist, settled

them in Miami, Arizona. There, the young Florence began her formal education. From both of her parents, she learned to rely on herself from an early age, later remarking that she had been "raised simply to be independent" which was "just part of my family's philosophy." An excellent student, she entered the University of Arizona at the age of 16. Her interests were literary, and she decided on English as her major. She also had a strong interest in history, but was soon floored by a course in American history, which from her perspective simply demanded "too many dates to remember." A family friend, anthropology professor Byron Cummings, suggested that she might find archaeology a more congenial subject to study. His suggestion was on target, and before long Florence had become fascinated by the prehistory of the American Southwest, artifacts of which were available to her literally down the nearest road.

By 1928, she had written a path-breaking master's thesis on ceramics fragments that had been excavated in sites near Miami, Arizona. She was able to distinguish three closely successive stages of pottery, separating three sequential types (Early, Middle and Late Gila Polychrome) and making a strong case for the relationships of these artifacts to certain Mexican Indian pottery types. These insights from the young scholar represented significant contributions to the development of what was at the time still an embryonic field of expertise, Southwestern prehistory.

At the same time that she was working on her master's thesis, Hawley collaborated with her father, whose expertise in chemical analysis enabled her to describe in precise terms the pigments of black pottery (carbon, carbon-mineral, and manganese). Here too her research represented pioneering work in the methodology of Southwestern American archaeology, establishing methods and criteria that would enable later researchers to effectively use chemical distinctions in their ceramic analyses as well as in their cultural hypotheses and interpretations. Her insights were communicated to the profession in an important series of papers published in the journals *American Anthropologist* and the *Journal of Chemical Education.*

After receiving her master's degree in 1928, Hawley began teaching as a member of the anthropology department of the University of Arizona. Although her salary, $1,350 per annum, was hardly munificent, she was enthusiastic. Her responsibilities, which included not only teaching classes but also museum and field work with analysis of ceramics and tree-ring specimens, provided Hawley with many opportunities to further her understanding of a vast and rapidly expanding field of knowledge. Among the most important skills she mastered during this period was a detailed knowledge of tree-ring dating (dendrochronology), which she learned from one of the pioneers of this archaeological technique, A.E. Douglass.

Starting in 1929, Hawley began to spend several months each summer in New Mexico, where she concentrated on field work at the archaeological site of Chetro Ketl. This site was situated in Chaco Canyon, which had been established as a National Monument in 1907 by President Theodore Roosevelt and was a treasure trove of archaeological artifacts from many centuries of American Southwestern Indian life and culture. The key figure in this research program was Edgar L. Hewett, a scholar who headed the University of New Mexico's anthropology department. Not only a brilliant theorist and indefatigable field investigator, Hewett was a man ahead of his time in his attitudes toward the role of women in this male-dominated field. He was highly unusual in his acceptance of women as field school students and encouraged them to work on significant research projects from the beginning of their careers. Aware of the glaring salary discrepancies between male and female faculty, Hewett made serious efforts to bring about meaningful increases in the pay of the female members of his department, including newly hired faculty like Hawley. The sources of Hewett's progressive attitudes toward the role of women in anthropological and archaeological research have not been definitively traced, but some sources suggest that his respect for the intellectual talents of women was fostered by his mother, as well as by the years he spent working on his doctorate in Switzerland, a nation with advanced attitudes toward women's education in the decades before World War I.

In 1928, Hewett had begun an archaeological field school in Chaco Canyon that operated under the joint auspices of the University of New Mexico and the School of American Research. Imparting her knowledge to the select group of 20 graduate and advanced undergraduate students permitted to register for the field school, Hawley worked in the meticulous excavation of the canyon's trash mound. As shards of ceramics and various tree-ring specimens saw the light of day, she began the painstaking process of identifying and cataloguing them.

In Chaco Canyon, Florence Hawley and the other young diggers were enthusiastic "boys and girls of summer" who learned immensely from the direct confrontation with thousands of years of Native American history. Conditions in the canyon were rudimentary at best. When torrential rains came, she and the others had to push the expedition's supply truck through the rapidly flooding arroyo to safer grounds. Communications with the outside world were erratic and often interrupted when a cow leaned too hard against any of the 40 miles of fencing which carried the sole telephone line to Chaco Canyon. Each member of the group was allotted a single gallon of water a day, which was delivered to her or his tent in a canvas bag. This precious gallon was for brushing one's teeth, for washing clothing, and for personal hygiene. Those who felt they needed more water had to go to considerable effort to fetch an additional supply. On weekends, Hawley and the others each took their baths in a bucket, using the leftover water to temporarily tame the dust on their tent floors. The few hours of leisure were spent at the trading post looking for snacks or attending a ceremonial at the nearby Navajo settlement. Evenings were often spent in front of a campfire listening to a talk on archaeological theory and practice by Professor Hewett, or occasionally hearing one of the Zuni workers' songs and traditional stories.

In 1933, in the depth of the Great Depression, Hawley and several other young University of Arizona faculty members were informed that due to a budgetary crisis they would have to be laid off for one academic year. Viewing the situation as much as an opportunity as a catastrophe, Florence Hawley signed up for the doctoral program at the University of Chicago and went north with her modest savings and a substantial amount of data from her years of work at Chetro Ketl. Aware that Chicago scholars demanded mathematical skills, Hawley took a course prior to her trip north. This decision would be of great value for her doctoral research, for it enabled her to scientifically establish the significance of the stratified variations in ceramics she had observed in the Chetro Ketl East Dump. The result of her investigation was one of the earliest uses of form statistics (Chi square) in American archaeology. Hawley's dissertation, and the published monograph based on it, combined this solid data with dendrochronologic (tree-ring dating) studies from nine Chacoan sites to explain human occupation and desertion of the region in terms of ecologic change. The scientific community came to consider this publication as the first of several research milestones in the development of Southwestern archaeology.

Upon her graduation from the University of Chicago, Hawley was offered a position with an academic institution she had come to know well in recent years, the University of New Mexico's anthropology department. She had for some time regarded its longtime chair, Edgar Hewett, as a giant in the field of Southwestern anthropological research, and she had an equally strong personal respect for him. Arriving in Albuquerque in 1934 with little beyond her prestigious doctoral degree from the University of Chicago, Hawley was rich in hopes but poor in finances. In fact, her impoverished state compelled her to pawn her wristwatch and take a lien on her battered old Ford. Nevertheless, she quickly felt at home in Albuquerque and would serve with great distinction as a member of her department for almost four decades, retiring in 1971.

In her early 30s, Hawley was already nationally recognized as a pioneering scholar. Her specialized knowledge of American Southwestern archaeology led to an arrangement between her own institution and the University of Chicago which allowed her to share her knowledge and talents. From 1937 to 1941, she was on loan half-time to Chicago to teach dendrochronology and added to her knowledge by developing a dendrochronological sequence for the Midwestern American states. The publications that resulted from her years in Chicago remain classics in the field.

In 1936, within two years of taking the job in Albuquerque, she published a classic typological study of Southwestern ceramics, the *Field Manual of Southwestern Pottery Types*. This highly detailed volume remains after more than two generations the standard reference work for the prehistoric pottery of the New Mexico region. In 1936, Hawley married Donovan Senter, and had a daughter, **Andrea Senter**. From her earliest years, Andrea accompanied her mother on her field work, growing deeply attached to the Indian lore of New Mexico. For a while, Hawley and her husband collaborated on several ethnological projects related to New Mexico's Spanish American population. In time, however, cooperation led to perceptions of competition, and the marriage was terminated in 1947. Several years later, she married Bruce Ellis, who became curator of collections at Albuquerque's Museum of New Mexico.

For nearly four decades, Florence Hawley Ellis was one of the academic luminaries of the

University of New Mexico. By the 1940s, her name and the field of Southwestern archaeology were virtually indistinguishable. Possessing extraordinary energy, she would often complete one research project to commence on another one before the raw data from the earlier work had been prepared for publication. A number of projects that had not progressed beyond the initial write-up stage remained in her personal files at the time of her retirement, which was a long and active one. By the end of her writing career, she had produced over 150 separate publications, an enormous body of writings universally regarded as foundational works in the literature of the field.

Florence Hawley Ellis' scholarly productivity was fueled in large part by the catholicity of her research interests, which revealed the interaction of ethnographical and ethnological approaches to data. Her unusual sensitivity toward the cultural values and moral insights of the Pueblo began from her first contacts with them in 1929. A decade later, the relationship had matured to one of mutual respect. Accompanied by her daughter Andrea, Ellis spent countless hours with members of the Pueblo and Navajo tribes, sharing work, food and confidences with them, thus coming in time to be regarded not as an interloper but rather as a trusted friend.

She became a strong defender of Indian rights and in 1983 testified on behalf of the San Ildefonso, Nambe, Tesuque and Pojoaque Pueblos in a water rights case that had dragged on for 17 years. With a profound knowledge of Pueblo culture, she argued persuasively that, even though Pojoaque Pueblo had been abandoned between 1912 and 1932, its people had never ceased being members of the social unit, and thus their moving into houses near their fields "would have nothing to do with the extinguishing of membership" in the Pueblo.

Florence Hawley Ellis spent her final years working on many projects including a museum of anthropology named in her honor. Located in breathtaking "*Georgia O'Keefe country," 60 miles north of Santa Fe, New Mexico, her museum is situated in Abiquiu, site of the Ghost Ranch Conference Center of the Presbyterian Church, USA. Here both the Florence Hawley Ellis Museum of Anthropology and the associated Ruth Hall Museum of Paleontology serve scientists and amateurs alike by organizing excavations of native artifacts, fossils and dinosaur remains. The museum has mounted a number of regionally oriented exhibits representing successive cultures in the northern Rio Grande, from

Opposite page

Miranda Richardson as Ruth Ellis, in Dance with a Stranger.

Paleo-Indian through Archaic, Pueblo, and finally the Spanish and the Anglo. Active to the very end of her long career as a scholar and teacher and highly respected by her colleagues, Florence Hawley Ellis died in Albuquerque, New Mexico, on April 6, 1991.

SOURCES:

Aveni, Anthony F., ed. *Archaeoastronomy in Pre-Columbian America.* Austin, TX: University of Texas Press, 1975.

Babcock, Barbara A., and Nancy J. Parezo. *Daughters of the Desert: Women Anthropologists and the Native American Southwest, 1880–1980: An Illustrated Catalogue.* Albuquerque, NM: University of New Mexico Press, 1988.

Bailey, Martha J. *American Women in Science: A Biographical Dictionary.* Santa Barbara, CA: ABC-CLIO, 1994.

Ellis, Florence Hawley. *An Anthropological Study of the Navajo Indians.* NY: Garland, 1974.

Frisbie, Theodore R., ed. *Collected Papers in Honor of Florence Hawley Ellis.* Norman, OK: Archaeological Society of New Mexico/Hooper Publishing, 1975.

Irwin-Williams, Cynthia. "Women in the Field: The Role of Women in Anthropology before 1960," in Gabriele Kass-Simon and Patricia Farnes, eds., *Women of Science: Righting the Record.* Bloomington, IN: Indiana University Press, 1990, pp. 1–41.

Joiner, Carol. "The Boys and Girls of Summer: The University of New Mexico Archaeological Field School in Chaco Canyon," in *Journal of Anthropological Research.* Vol. 48. No. 1. Spring 1992, pp. 49–66.

Parezo, Nancy J., ed. *Hidden Scholars: Women Anthropologists and the Native American Southwest.* Albuquerque, NM: University of New Mexico Press, 1993.

John Haag,
Assistant Professor of History,
University of Georgia, Athens, Georgia

Ellis, Mina A.

Canadian explorer and author. Born in Bewdly, Ontario, Canada; graduated from the Brooklyn (New York) Training School for Nurses; married Leonidas Hubbard (a journalist and explorer), in 1901.

Superintendent of the Virginia Hospital in Richmond, Mina Ellis married Leonidas Hubbard, a journalist and explorer, in 1901; he perished in Labrador two years later. Intent on completing her husband's work, Ellis organized an expedition which in 1905 successfully crossed the northeastern part of the Labrador Peninsula; in doing so, she became the first white person to cross the Great Divide between the Naskaupi and George Rivers. On her return home, Ellis provided an account of the expedition to the American Geographical Society. *A Woman's Way through Unknown Labrador* was published in 1908.

Ellis, Ruth (1927–1955)

British murderer and last woman to be hanged in England. Born in the Welsh town of Rhyl in 1927; executed by hanging in North London's Holloway Women's Prison on July 13, 1955; raised in Manchester, England; married a dentist, in 1950 (divorced); children: a stepson by marriage; a daughter, born out of wedlock.

Ruth Ellis had survived a love affair with an American soldier, who was killed in 1944, and a failed marriage to a dentist before she began a tempestuous affair with racetrack driver David Blakely in 1953. Uneducated, with two children to support, she was employed in a London night-club when she met Blakely. A year into their relationship, Ellis also became intimately involved with Blakely's friend Desmond Cussen. After Blakely became aware of her affair with Cussen, his anger often erupted into violent and abusive outbursts. The romantic triangle endured for over a year, during which time Ellis tried unsuccessfully to terminate her seemingly obsessive relationship with Blakely. After Blakely began seeing another woman, she reportedly said: "I had a peculiar idea that I wanted to kill him." On April 10, 1955, she took a cab to a local pub, waited for him to emerge, and shot him dead.

Ellis immediately confessed to the police and at her trial admitted that she had fully intended to kill Blakely. After a short deliberation, the jury found her guilty of murder, and she was sentenced to death by hanging. The sentence, however, brought a storm of protest in England from those opposed to capital punishment. A petition, with more than 2,000 signatures, was filed on her behalf but turned down. On July 13, 1955, Ellis became the last woman to be hanged in Great Britain. A year later, in 1956, the House of Commons voted to abolish the practice of capital punishment. The acclaimed 1985 movie *Dance with a Stranger* (starring **Miranda Richardson** and Rupert Everett, with screenplay by ❧ **Shelagh Delaney**) was based on the Ellis story.

Barbara Morgan,
Melrose, Massachusetts

Ellisif.

See Elizabeth of Kiev (fl. 1045).

El Moutawakel, Nawal (1962—)

Moroccan runner. Name variations: Moutawakil. Born in Casablanca on April 15, 1962; married; children: two.

Convinced she would come in last, Nawal el Moutawakel, a converted sprinter, beat out **Judi Brown** (b. 1961) of the United States and **Christina Cojocaru** of Rumania in the women's first-ever 400-meter hurdles in Los Angeles in 1984, setting an Olympic record of 54.61. El Moutawakel was the first Moroccan, the first African woman, and the first Islamic woman to ever win a gold medal. There was rejoicing in the streets of Casablanca.

"It is very hard for Arab women to do sports," said el Moutawakel; they are discouraged from competing. Her father, who believed that she would be a champion some day, had to accompany her whenever she trained as it would have gone against Islamic tradition for her to be alone.

By winning African and Arab meets as a teenager, el Moutawakel had attracted the attention of the international track-and-field community and had been offered a scholarship to study in America at Iowa State. At Iowa, she was captain of her team and won the national collegiate championship in 1984. But two events spanning her freshman and sophomore years would send her back to Casablanca, shaken. The first was her father's death soon after her arrival. The second was a plane crash that killed all of her college teammates; el Moutawakel would have been on the plane as well had her coach not insisted she remain behind to study.

Deciding to try one last competition before retiring, she set her sights on the Los Angeles Olympics. During the race, the image of her father spurred her on in the last few hurdles, and upon winning she sobbed into the Moroccan flag. El Moutawakel continues to live in Casablanca, where she is director of a new training center for female athletes and coaches the Moroccan Olympic track team. She also writes for Morocco's *La Gazette du Sport.*

Elmy, Elizabeth Wolstenholme (1834–1913).

See Wolstenholme-Elmy, Elizabeth.

Elphide (c. 654–c. 714).

See Alphaida.

Elphinstone, Eupheme

Mistress of a Scottish king. Mistress of James V (1512–1542), king of Scotland (r. 1513–1542); children: (with James V) Robert Stewart (b. 1533), earl of Orkney.

❧▶
Delaney, Shelagh. See Littlewood, Joan for sidebar.

Elphinstone, Hester Maria

(1764–1857)

*Viscountess Keith. Born in 1764; died in 1857; daughter of Henry and *Hester Lynch Piozzi (1741–1821); education directed by Dr. Samuel Johnson; studied Hebrew and mathematics; married George Keith Elphinstone, Viscount Keith (1746–1823, an admiral).*

Elphinstone, Margaret Mercer

(1788–1867)

*Viscountess Keith, comtesse de Flahault, and Baroness Nairne. Born in 1788; died in 1867; daughter of George Keith Elphinstone, Viscount Keith (1746–1823, an admiral), and *Hester Maria Elphinstone (1764–1857); granddaughter of *Hester Lynch Piozzi (1741–1821); married the comte de Flahault, in 1817. Margaret Mercer Elphinstone was a confidante of Princess *Charlotte Augusta (1796–1817).*

El Saadawi, Nawal (1931—)

*Leading radical Egyptian feminist, physician, journalist and novelist, forceful and outspoken critic of women's oppression in the Middle East and globally, whose writings address the impact of misogynist social structures on Egyptian women, especially the sexual abuse Egyptian women undergo, such as the practice of female genital mutilation. Name variations: el Sad'adawi, el-Saadawi, al-Saadawi. Pronunciation: Na-WAA-l el SA-a-da-we. Born in Kafr Tahla, Egypt, in 1931 (some sources cite 1930); her father graduated from Cairo University in 1937 and worked as a civil servant in one of the provinces; her mother was educated in French schools; graduated from School of Medicine, Cairo University, M.D., 1955; married three times; her third husband is Sherif Hetata (a physician); children: daughter **Mona Helmi** (a writer); son Atef Hetata (a film director).*

Practiced medicine in rural and urban areas; promoted to director of Health Education and editor-in-chief of the magazine Health; *dismissed from her positions (August 1971) and blacklisted by the Egyptian government because of her controversial book,* Women and Sex *(1972); practiced medicine part-time and wrote novels depicting the universe of Egyptian women; researched women's neuroses while on the Faculty of Medicine at Ain Shams University (1973–76); served as United Nations' advisor for the Women's Program in Africa (ECA) and the Middle East (ECWA, 1979–80); imprisoned for three months (1981) by President Sadat; established the Arab Women's Solidarity Association (AWSA, 1982);* fought the banning of AWSA (early 1990s); accepted a visiting professorship at Duke University (1993); currently resides in Egypt. President of the Arab Women's Solidarity Association.

Selected nonfiction works (translated): The Hidden Face of Eve: Women in the Arab World *(trans. by Sherif Hetata, London: Zed, 1980);* Memoirs from the Women's Prison *(trans. by Marilyn Booth, 1983, London: The Women's Press, 1991);* My Travels Around the World *(trans. by Shirley Eber, London: Methuen, 1991). Selected fiction (translated):* The Circling Song *(London: Zed, 1989);* Death of an Ex-Minister *(trans. by Shirley Eber, London: Methuen, 1987);* The Fall of the Imam *(trans. by Sherif Hetata, Minerva, 1989);* God Dies by the Nile *(trans. by Hetata, Zed, 1985);* The Innocence of the Devil *(trans. by Hetata, Berkeley: University of California Press, 1994);* Memoirs of a Woman Doctor: A Novel *(trans. by Catherine Cobham, San Francisco: City Lights Books, 1989);* Searching *(trans. by Shirley Eber, London: Zed, 1991);* She Has No Place in Paradise *(trans. by Shirley Eber, 1987, London: Minerva, 1989);* Two Women in One *(trans. by Osman Nusairi and Jana Gough, 1975; Seattle: The Seal Press, 1986);* The Well of Life *(trans. by Hetata, London: Lime Tree, 1993);* Woman at Point Zero *(trans. by Hetata, London: Zed, 1983).*

Nawal el Saadawi, a leading contemporary Egyptian feminist who came of age as an activist after Egypt wrested its independence from Great Britain in 1952, began her work as a doctor and writer within an already existing tradition of Egyptian women struggling for national independence and gender justice. The Egyptian women's movement began in the early 20th century and was intimately linked with the Egyptian nationalist movement for independence. Great Britain occupied Egypt in 1882 and in the next seven decades an unequal economic and political relationship characterized the link between the two nations. One of the earliest Egyptian women to become active in the political arena was *Huda Shaarawi (1879–1947), who galvanized other upper-class Egyptian women to combat both British colonialism and national social and legal structures oppressive to women. Few people outside the Middle East are aware that veiled Egyptian women left their homes to demonstrate on the streets in Cairo in the 1919 uprising against the British. The activities of these women established a respected tradition of women's activism which focused on changing women's unequal legal status as well as women's welfare in the areas of health, work, political participation, and education.

Nawal el Saadawi is one of many women actively engaged in working to improve women's rights and lives. No other Egyptian feminist has spoken out so forcefully and critically about the impact of misogynist social structures on Egyptian women, the specific nature of sexual oppression, and its links to capitalism and imperialism. Partially because of the topics she broaches, el Saadawi occupies a contentious place within the Egyptian women's movement. Her voice is heard by a number of audiences in the Middle East and globally, and she is well-connected with the international women's movement. She is the best-known Egyptian feminist in the West, with many of her works available in English.

Born in 1931, el Saadawi grew up in a loving household. She recalls with great affection the soft voice of her father who sacrificed his needs for those of his children. Her parents had what she considered an ideal relationship, characterized by tenderness and civility, and el Saadawi points to their relationship as being a critical factor in giving her an ability to recognize and terminate her first two marriages which were less than ideal. Her childhood also allowed her to understand the lack of personal and political freedom she encountered as an adult Egyptian woman. She notes in an essay published in *Woman Against Her Sex* that her childhood freedom "sparked off the rebellion against my first husband, against the head of state and against any dictator at work who failed to provide me with the freedom to which I had been accustomed by my mother and father." Notwithstanding this freedom, el Saadawi and her sister were subjected to female genital mutilation, a practice that she was to fight against as an adult. She describes her experiences in her book *The Hidden Face of Eve*:

> I was six years old that night when I lay in my bed, warm and peaceful in that pleasurable state which lies half way between wakefulness and sleep, with the rosy dreams of childhood flitting by . . . .
>
> They carried me to the bathroom. . . . All I remember is that I was frightened and that there were many of them, and that something like an iron grasp caught hold of my hand and my arms and my thighs, so that I became unable to resist or even to move. . . .
>
> I realized that my thighs had been pulled wide apart, and that each of my lower limbs was being held as far away from the other as possible, gripped by steel fingers that never relinquished their pressure. I felt that the rasping knife or blade was heading straight down towards my throat. Then suddenly the sharp metallic edge seemed to drop between my thighs and there cut off a piece of flesh from my body.

> I screamed with pain despite the tight hand held over my mouth, for the pain was not just a pain, it was like a searing flame that went through my whole body. After a few moments, I saw a red pool of blood around my hips.
>
> I did not know what they had cut off from my body, and I did not try to find out. I just wept, and called out to my mother for help. But the worst shock of all was when I looked around and found her standing by my side. Yes, it was her, I could not be mistaken, in flesh and blood, right in the midst of these strangers, talking to them and smiling at them, as though they had not participated in slaughtering her daughter just a few moments ago.

El Saadawi had many other opportunities to notice how girls and women within her family were treated differently from boys and men. Growing up in a large family of six daughters and three sons, she proved to be more intelligent and successful than her brothers, and yet had to work harder at domestic chores. In response to pressure from her mother, her father agreed to delay her marriage, and el Saadawi attended medical school where she participated briefly in student demonstrations against the British occupation of Egypt. She married her first husband, a physician, against the wishes of her family and soon realized that she could not continue in the relationship when he asked her to stop practicing medicine. Her marriage and subsequent divorce led her to ask more questions about the social system established for women. El Saadawi left her second husband, a lawyer, because he insisted she stop writing. Thus, el Saadawi's philosophy of women's liberation is deeply rooted in her experiences in the home and in her activities as a nationalist, committed to Egyptian independence and welfare.

Her career as a doctor received a set-back when she was dismissed as the director-general of the Ministry of Health in 1972. At that time, she was also editor of a magazine *Health* and had founded the Health Association. She had used the magazine and association to promote her idea that women's health and sexuality were harmed by female genital mutilation. Furthermore, el Saadawi proposed that politics and health were intimately linked to one another. As a result of her beliefs, el Saadawi lost her positions, and her books were censored for the next 11 years. She continued to write novels and to publish her fiction in Lebanon. El Saadawi characterizes this part of her life as a conflict any creative woman faces as she challenges her society's entrenched values. She notes in an essay in *Ergo!*

The Bumbershoot Literary Magazine: "I could feel the silent struggle going on between me and these forces, a struggle which increased in intensity as time passed, and I became more mature as my activities grew in extent and depth, whether in the medical or the literary field. Now it was no longer hidden or silent but open and declared, characterized by the variety of weapons used, which ranged from neglect to a complete lack of attention, disapproval, criticism and vilification, to different warnings and threats."

El Saadawi accepted a position in the United Nations, working as an advisor on Women's Programs for Africa, and then as a Senior Program Officer in charge of the Women's Voluntary Fund. After two years, she realized that the structure of the United Nations was no different from the bureaucracy she had left in Egypt: it was another organization run by a patriarchy, this time of Western, upper-class men who cared more for their material comforts than in allowing for creative work to be done in the area of development. She resigned from her UN position in 1980.

On September 6, 1981, el Saadawi was alone in her Cairo apartment when she was arrested for her criticisms of President Anwar Sadat and his Open Door Policy, which aimed at dismantling the socialist policies of his predecessor, Gamal Abdel Nasser. To quell the voices of his critics, Sadat issued a decree that allowed him to incarcerate over 1,000 Egyptian women activists and intellectuals, including el Saadawi. She describes her arrest in her autobiography *Memoirs from the Women's Prison*:

> I heard a knock at the door. . . . I ignored the knock. Perhaps it was the concierge. . . . The fourth rapping, and the fifth, and the knocking on the door went on and on. . . . I heard the sound—like an explosion—of the door breaking. Their metallic boots pounded the floor in quick rhythm like army troops bursting forth in the direction of battle. They attacked the flat like savage locusts, their open mouths panting and their rifles pointed. . . . For a moment, they stood fixed, as if pinned to the ground before me. I must have appeared frightening to them, and I spoke in a voice which was also terrifying, 'You broke down the door. This is a crime.'
>
> I don't know what happened then; perhaps my voice confirmed to them that I was a woman and not a devil. Maybe they were surprised that I was still in the flat and had not escaped.

El Saadawi was to remain in prison for three months, and while there, secretly wrote a book about her prison experiences on toilet paper. She

and the other political prisoners were released only when Sadat was assassinated. One year after her release, in 1982, she founded and presided over the Tadamun al-Ma'at al 'Arabiyya, the Arab Women's Solidarity Association (AWSA). The AWSA and its magazine *Noon* were banned in 1991, and her activities and house were monitored by government security guards, ostensibly for her security. She was informed death threats had been made against her person. Feeling increasingly insecure, she left Egypt in 1993 with her husband to take a position as visiting professor at Duke University in North Carolina. Her third husband Sherif Hetata, also a physician and novelist, had spent 13 years in Egyptian prisons. He has translated many of el Saadawi's novels into English.

> Half of our society is women. They should start to speak for themselves, to write for themselves, to think for themselves, and to correct laws that oppress them. . . . We also need to create union among women, to create political power. We have two slogans: UNVEILING OF THE MIND, creating awareness among women, and UNION AND SOLIDARITY to bring political power for women.
>
> —Nawal el Saadawi

El Saadawi has had a greater impact through her fiction and nonfiction writings than by her organizing activities. Her works have been translated into a number of languages and are read in many Muslim communities around the world. Her philosophy on politics, religion, and sexual justice is unique in that she combines a socialist, materialist view of the world that draws heavily on her personal experiences, as well as on the history of women in the Middle East and in Islam. She calls herself a "historical socialist feminist," and while she acknowledges her debt to Western feminist writings on the topic of patriarchy, she is quick to state that her feminism is indigenous to the Third World. El Saadawi points to the fact that she began writing about women's oppression before she could read English. As el Saadawi notes in an interview "A Feminist in the Arab World":

> We call ourselves historical socialist feminists. We depend on our history in our analysis of our ideas. We are inspired by those great women in our history. We say we are socialist because we are against class oppression and colonialism. We call ourselves feminists because we are against patriarchy

and male oppression. . . . And we believe and say that we have a feminism that is original and not copied from the West.

El Saadawi's writings are concerned with the impact of poverty and powerlessness on women in their daily lives; with how religion and cultures perpetuate women's powerlessness in a variety of subtle and overt ways; and with how men and women, suffering from a lack of political and economic strength, are compelled to subordinate themselves to local, national and international elites. In a vivid and dramatic way, she demonstrates how the universal institution of patriarchy which oppresses women is linked to the economic and political forces of capitalism, colonialism, imperialism, and Zionism. Her solution to these devastating social problems lies in women becoming aware of these interconnections, and in women uniting and creating a universal philosophy which allows them to free themselves as individuals and build bases of power in their countries. Ultimately, she hopes women will organize internationally and wrest political and economic power for themselves and use it to end the exploitation of women. El Saadawi's works are an important step in this struggle to end exploitation and bring about sexual justice. As she writes in her short essay "Toward Women's Power, Nationally and Internationally": "I think that we women are ourselves responsible for war, for massacres, if we ourselves do not fight for our rights. We should fight. We should not compromise with our rights. We should not turn away from our own power."

SOURCES:

el Saadawi, Nawal. *The Hidden Face of Eve: Women in the Arab World*. Translated and edited by Sherif Hetata. London: Zed: 1980.

————. "Creative Women in Changing Societies, an excerpt," in *Ergo! The Bumbershoot Literary Magazine*. (City of Seattle, 1993), pp. 18–26.

————. "A Feminist in the Arab World," in *Feminist Foremothers in Women's Studies, Psychology, and Mental Health*. Interview by Mary E. Willmuth. Edited by Phyllis Chester, Esther D. Rothblum, and Ellen Cole. The Haworth Press, 1995, pp. 435–42.

————. *Memoirs from the Women's Prison*. Translated by Marilyn Booth. London: The Women's Press, 1991.

————. "Toward Women's Power, Nationally and Internationally," in *Speaking of Faith: Global Perspectives on Women, Religion and Social Change*. Edited by Diana L. Eck and Devaki Jain. Philadelphia, PA: New Society Publishers, 1987, pp. 266–74.

Tarabishi, Georges. "Nawal el-Saadawi's Reply," in *Woman Against Her Sex: A Critique of Nawal el-Saadawi with a Reply by Nawal el-Saadawi*. Translated by Basil Hatim and Elisabeth Orsini. London: Saqi Books, 1988, pp. 189–211.

SUGGESTED READING:

Badran, Margot, and Miriam Cooke, eds. "Reflections of a Feminist, 1986," in *Opening the Gates: A Century of Arab Feminist Writing*. Interview with Fedwa Malti-Douglas and Allen Douglas (Cairo, August 15, 1986). Bloomington: Indiana University Press, 1990, pp. 394–404.

el Saadawi, Nawal. "The Political Challenges Facing Arab Women at the End of the 20th Century," in *Women of the Arab World: The Coming Challenge. Papers of the Arab Women's Solidarity Association Conference*. Translated by Marilyn Booth. Edited by Nahid Tubia and translated by Nahed El Gamal. London: Zed, 1988, pp. 8–26.

Hatem, Mervat. "Economic and Political Liberation in Egypt and the Demise of State Feminism," in *International Journal of Middle East Studies*. Vol. 24, 1992, pp. 231–51.

Lerner, George. "The Progressive Interview: Nawal el-Saadawi," in *The Progressive*. April 1992, pp. 32–5.

Malti-Douglas, Fedwa. *Men, Women, and God(s): Nawal El Saadawi and Arab Feminist Poetics*. Berkeley: University of California Press, 1996.

Hoda M. Zaki,
Associate Professor of Political Science,
Hood College, Frederick, Maryland

Elssler, Fanny (1810–1884)

*Austrian dancer. Born in Vienna, Austria, on June 23, 1810; died of cancer in Vienna on November 27, 1884; father was a professional musician and copyist; sister of **Thérèse Elssler** (1808–1878); cousin of Hermine Elssler (a dancer); studied ballet under Jean Aumer and Philippe Taglioni; never married; children: (with Leopold, prince of Salerno) Franz (b. 1827); (with Anton Stuhlmüller) **Theresa von Webenau** (b. 1833).*

Fanny Elssler was trained for the ballet from her earliest years and made her appearance at the Kärnthner-Thor theater in Vienna before she was seven. She almost invariably danced with her sister Thérèse, who was two years her senior. They were born into a family of musicians: their father, two uncles, and one brother were all professionals. Before Fanny and Thérèse were born, Herr Elssler had been a copyist and valet to Haydn, and the family lived in comfort, but after the composer's death in 1808, the family fell on hard times. They lived over a public laundry where Frau Elssler did laundry to help feed her five children; all the children were launched into early careers in hopes they would soon become self-supporting.

After some years' experience together in Vienna, in 1827 the sisters accompanied Domenico Barbaja, manager of the Kärnthner-Thor, to Naples. Their success there—due more to Fanny than the less-gifted Thérèse (who tended to restrain herself in order to heighten the effect of Fanny's more brilliant powers)—led to an engagement in Berlin in 1830. This was the beginning of a series of triumphs for Fanny's pre-Raphaelite beauty and lively dancing.

Fanny
Elssler

While in Naples, *Maria Carolina and Ferdinand IV's son Leopold, prince of Salerno, sought her favors. Fat, self-indulgent, 20 years Fanny's senior and married to his own niece, Leopold had little to offer, but it is conjectured that, after the misery of her childhood, his opulence might have held some attraction. Whatever the case, the 17-year-old Fanny became his mistress, was soon pregnant, and had to return to Vienna. Since the Kärnthner-Thor had a strict rule that mothers could not perform there, the birth of Franz on June 4, 1827, was hushed up, and the boy was placed in a foster home.

Fanny then incurred the passion of the aged and brilliant statesman Friedrich von Gentz, councillor to Metternich. An intellectual, Gentz was determined to educate his paramour, perfecting her German and teaching her French; he also provided her with advantageous introductions to further her career. Elssler, still shy and unspoiled, was devoted to him. But when the Berlin Opera offered the sisters a contract in Autumn of 1830 and Gentz proposed, Elssler preferred to dance in the Prussian capital. Gentz died in June 1832; Fanny was at his bedside.

Though they had captivated the hearts of Berlin and Vienna, the sisters still lived humbly. Alphonse Royer remembers watching them trudge home through the snow after a performance, carrying a basket. Having grown very tall by 19th-century standards, and having earned the sobriquet *la maestosa*, Thérèse had her last great triumph as a dancer in Berlin. The Germans prized statuesque dancers. When Thérèse became the male half of an Elssler *pas de deux* called *adagio*, Fanny's future rival, *Maria Taglioni, bristled: "We owe the beginning of this bad taste to the Elssler sisters. The elder, Thérèse, who was big, too big, wore male costume. She was extremely deft at turning her sister Fanny. The ensemble produced a great effect; but no one could have called it art." Thérèse would go on to choreograph and restage *La Fée et le Chevalier* (July 1833) and *Armide*.

Fanny, however, had turned her attentions to dancer and fellow student Anton Stuhlmüller who was now *premier danseur* in Berlin, and she was soon pregnant again. In February 1833, she paid a visit to London, where she was taken in by George and *Harriet Grote; three months after her arrival, Fanny gave birth to a daughter Theresa. At a time when "ladies" did not associate with "theatricals," Harriet Grote, a historian and friend of Gentz's, ignored such prejudices and took in Fanny and her baby. George Grote was a banker and Member of Parliament. Except for 18 months in Paris with her mother, Theresa lived with the Grotes until she was nine.

In September 1834, with much trepidation, Fanny Elssler appeared at the Opéra in Paris, very aware of Maria Taglioni's supremacy on that stage. The result of her appearance was another triumph and the temporary eclipse of Taglioni, who, although the finer artist of the two, could not compete with the newcomer's ability to enchant. Mlle Taglioni was a "Christian dancer," while Fanny was "quite pagan," said Théophile Gautier.

By this time, Fanny had developed her staccato, or *taqueté*, style, in contrast with Taglioni's floating, *ballonné* method. In Elssler's performance of the Spanish *cachucha*, while in the role of Florinda in *Le Diable boiteux* (June 1936), she outshone all rivals. She was the German girl who became Spanish, and she caused a sensation. In her pink-and-black lace costume, Fanny Elssler graced snuffboxes, fans, prints and statuettes. Maria Taglioni accepted an engagement in St. Petersburg.

The Marquis de La Valette, who seemed to prefer dancers, having fathered children with **Pauline Guichard** and **Pauline Duvernay**, entered Elssler's life for a short while. From him, Elssler moved on to Henry Wikoff, an American diplomat who was a little too Philadelphia for Europe's taste. Wikoff arranged for Fanny to tour America, though Thérèse decided to forgo the chance to meet wild Indians.

In March 1840, when Fanny sailed for New York, her retinue included Wikoff and her companion **Kathi Prinster**. Upon arrival, she was greeted by "Elssler mania," received at the White House, and enjoyed two years of unblemished success. Then the press began to question her private life with impresario Wikoff, especially after a long shared holiday from Louisiana to the Canadian border, but her fans could have cared less. In July 1842, with the tour over, along with her relationship with Wikoff, Elssler sailed for England. During the following five years, she appeared in Germany, Austria, Italy, England and Russia. In France, however, *Carlotta Grisi had replaced her in the hearts of a fickle public.

In 1845, having amassed a fortune, Fanny Elssler retired from the stage after her farewell performance with Perrot in his *Faust* at La Scala. In 1848, she traveled to St. Petersburg and appeared as an actress in *Giselle*; the play ran over two years. She then settled near Hamburg for three years, before spending her last days in Vienna with her son Franz and her companion Prinster. Her son Franz committed suicide in 1873, at age 47. Theresa, who remained devoted to her mother, married Baron Victor Weber von Webenau and named her daughter Fanny (she also continued to visit Harriet Grote).

Fanny's sister Thérèse contracted a morganatic marriage with Prince Adalbert of Prussia and was ennobled under the title of Baroness von Barnim. When Thérèse was left a widow in 1873, she moved in with her niece Theresa where she died on November 19, 1878. Six years later, Fanny Elssler died in Vienna of cancer on November 27, 1884. The sisters Elssler share with Haydn a small museum at Eisenstadt near Vienna.

SOURCES:

Migel, Parmenia. *The Ballerinas: From the Court of Louis XIV to Pavlova.* NY: Macmillan, 1972.

Elstob, Elizabeth (1683–1756)

English Anglo-Saxon scholar. Born in Newcastle, England, in 1683; died in 1756.

Renowned as one of the few women scholars of her day, Elizabeth Elstob received her early education from her mother who died when she was eight. She then went to live with her uncle, the Reverend C. Elstob, in Canterbury, where she continued her language studies despite her uncle's disapproval. From 1702 to 1715, Elstob resided in London with her brother William, a cleric and also an Anglo-Saxon scholar. There, she undertook the translation of *Madeleine de Scudéry's *Essay on Glory* and the *Anglo-Saxon Homily on the Nativity of St. Gregory* (1709), in which she used the preface to defend the right of women to obtain an education and to engage in theological discussions about the Old English Church. In 1715, she produced a grammar book, *Rudiments of Grammar for the English-Saxon Tongue, first given in English; with an Apology for the Study of Northern Antiquities.* A proposed edition of Aelfric's *Homilies,* for which she obtained several eminent patrons, including Queen *Caroline of Ansbach and Lord Oxford, was never completed.

After her brother's death, Elstob encountered financial difficulties that ended her scholarly pursuits. In 1718, to escape her debts, she left London and opened a small school in Evensham, Worcestershire, which provided a modest income. In 1738, she became the governess to the children of **Margaret Bentinck**, the duchess of Portland and daughter of Lord Oxford, remaining there until her death in 1756.

Elswitha (d. 902)

*Queen of the English. Name variations: Alwitha; Ealhswith; Ealhswyth; Elswith; Ealhswith of the Gaini. Died on December 5, 902 (some sources cite 905), at St. Mary's Abbey, Winchester, Dorset; interred at Winchester Cathedral, London; daughter of Ethelred the Great, ealdorman of the Gainis, and *Eadburh; married Alfred the Great (848–c. 900), king of the English (r. 871–899), in 868; children: Edmund (died young); Edward I the Elder (c. 870–924), king of the English (r. 899–924); Ethelweard (880–922); and three daughters, *Ethelflaed (869–918), *Ethelgeofu (d. around 896), and *Elfthrith (d. 929).*

A member of the Mercian royal family, Elswitha was the daughter of Ethelred the Great, ealdorman of the Gainis, and *Eadburh. She married Alfred the Great, king of the English, in 868. Following the death of her husband around 900, Elswitha became a nun. She was reputed to be a saint.

Elthelthrith (630–679)

*Queen of Northumbria and abbess of Ely. Name variations: Aelthelthrith; Aethelthrith; Aethelthryth; Saint Audrey; Ethelreda; Etheldreda; Ethelthrith or Ethelthryth. Born in 630 in East Anglia, England; died in 679 at convent of Ely; daughter of Saewara and probably Anna (635–654), king of East Anglia; sister of Saint *Sexburga (d. 699?) and *Withburga and half-sister of Saint *Ethelburga (d. 665); married Tondberht of South Gyrwas, ealdorman of South Gyrwas, also known as Prince Tonbert (died three years later); married Ecgfrith or Egfrid, king of Northumbria, around 671 (died 685).*

Elthelthrith was probably the daughter of Anna, king of East Anglia, although she may have come from a royal Saxon house. Like most young noblewomen, her marriage was arranged by her parents for their financial and political benefit. Elthelthrith, however, was committed from childhood to a religious life and persuaded her new husband, Prince Tonbert, to agree not to consummate their union and to give up all claims on her as his wife. Following his death three years later, Elthelthrith retired to a life of prayer until political considerations compelled her to marry Ecgfrith in 671, shortly after his accession to the throne as king of Northumbria.

Their nuptials, performed in the presence of their spiritual father, St. Wilfrid, archbishop of York, included a vow to live together as brother and sister. When Ecgfrith began to tire of the arrangement, St. Wilfrid advised Elthelthrith to abandon the marriage and take up her religious pursuits once again. By 678, Ecgfrith would take a second wife **Eormenburg**.

Around 672, using her personal fortune, Elthelthrith founded two abbeys on the island of Ely, one for men and one for women, which she supervised until her death. (According to one source, she established only the abbey for women.) Those entering the abbeys received an excellent education, as well as spiritual guidance, and were trained in the arts of calligraphy and illumination. Ely eventually became renowned for its scriptorium and for the beauty of the manuscripts produced there.

Elthelthrith's personal life was one of great austerity. Except for official feasts, she ate but once a day and frequently prayed through the night. Toward the end of her life, she suffered from an abscess of the throat; she would be deemed the patron of those suffering similar afflictions following her death of the plague in 679. Her feast day is June 23.

Etherington, Marie Susan.
See Tempest, Marie.

Eluard, Nusch (1906–1946).
See Agar, Eileen for sidebar.

Elvira (1038–1101)
Princess of Castile. Born in 1038; died on November 15, 1101; daughter of *Sancha of Leon (1013–1067) and Ferdinand I (c. 1017–1065), king of Castile and Leon (r. 1038–1065).

Elvira (fl. 1080s)
Countess of Toulouse. Flourished in the 1080s; married Raymond IV, count of Toulouse (r. 1088–1105); children: Bertrand de Rouergue, count of Toulouse (r. 1105–1112); Alphonso de Rouergue, count of Toulouse (r. 1112–1114).

Elvira (d. 1135)
Duchess of Apulia and queen of Sicily. Died on February 8, 1135; illegitimate daughter of *Zaida (d. 1107) and Alphonso VI, king of Castile and Leon; married Roger II, king of Sicily (r. 1103–1154), duke

of Apulia (r. 1128–1154). Robert II was also married to *Beatrice of Rethel and *Sibylle of Burgundy.

Elvira Gonzalez of Galicia
(d. 1022)
Queen of Leon and Asturias. Name variations: Geloria. Died on December 2, 1022; daughter of Menendo, count Gonzalez; married Alphonso or Alphonso V, king of Leon and Asturias (r. 999–1027), in 1015; children: Vermudo III (b. 1010), king of Leon; *Sancha of Leon (1013–1067).

Elzbieta.
Variant of Elizabeth.

Emerald, Connie (1891–1959).
See Lupino, Ida for sidebar.

Emerson, Gladys Anderson
(1903–1984)
American biochemist and nutritionist who conducted important research on vitamin E, amino acids, and the B-vitamin complex. Born in Caldwell, Kansas, on July 1, 1903; died in Santa Monica, California, on January 18, 1984; daughter of Otis Anderson and Louise (Williams) Anderson; bachelor's degree in English and chemistry from Oklahoma College for Women, 1925; M.A. in history from Stanford University; Ph.D. in biochemistry from University of Berkeley, 1932; married Oliver Emerson, a biochemist (divorced 1940).

One of the outstanding American biochemists of her generation, Gladys Anderson was born an only child in Kansas, but she grew up in Texas and Oklahoma. As a multitalented student who excelled in mathematics, music, languages and public debating, Gladys graduated from high school in El Reno, Oklahoma, going on to Oklahoma College for Women, which in 1925 awarded her bachelor's degrees in both English and chemistry. With a strong interest in both history and chemistry, she accepted an offer of an assistantship from Stanford University. After earning a master's degree in history from Stanford, she taught for several years at a junior high school in Oklahoma City, Oklahoma, soon advancing to the position of head of its history, geography and citizenship department.

Despite her considerable professional achievements in Oklahoma City, she continued to be interested in the sciences. A graduate fellowship in chemistry offered by the University of California, Berkeley, was too much to resist, and she moved west to pursue the advanced degree. At Berkeley, Anderson concentrated on biochemistry, particularly the area of nutrition. In 1932, she received her Ph.D. in the fields of biochemistry and animal nutrition. At that time, Germany was still a world leader in research in all areas of chemistry, so Gladys, now married to fellow biochemist Oliver Emerson, signed up for a year of postgraduate study at the University of Göttingen.

At Göttingen, the couple worked closely with two illustrious researchers, Adolf Windaus and Adolf Butenandt. Windaus had already won a Nobel Prize by 1932. (Butenandt's research on hormones would also earn him a Nobel Prize which he would be forced to decline because by then a Nazi decree banned all German citizens from accepting the award.) In the first weeks of 1933, after barely having settled into the academic routine of Göttingen, Gladys Emerson and her husband found themselves in the middle of the *Machtergreifung*, the Nazi seizure of power.

A swift succession of decrees and hastily drafted laws led to the purging of Jews, liberals, and other members of the Göttingen faculty deemed to be "un-German" in their racial backgrounds or political views. In the streets of Göttingen, Nazi students and brownshirted toughs marched, intimidating ordinary citizens into submission to the new fascist order. As American citizens, the Emersons were not directly affected by the Nazi terror, but Gladys would never forget the atmosphere of uncertainty and fear that within a few short weeks had suffocated the spirit of free inquiry in a once-great center of learning. After the collapse of Nazi Germany, Gladys would renew her professional relationships with many of the scientists she met in the supremely dramatic year of 1932.

Returning to the United States in 1933, Emerson went back to Berkeley as a research associate in the University of California's Institute of Experimental Biology. It was here that she was part of a brilliant research team that included her husband Oliver and H.M. Evans. Working long hours in the laboratory over the next years, Emerson and her colleagues were able to isolate vitamin E. Painstaking work enabled her team to discover three different forms of the vitamin, designated as alpha, beta and gamma tocopherols. One of Emerson's significant contributions to the team's investigative strategy was her choice of wheat-germ oil as a source for vitamin E.

Extensive further investigations of the vitamin revealed its chemical structure, which enabled it to be created synthetically in the laboratory. At this point, additional research proved that natural and synthetic vitamin E had both the same effects and potency. Laboratory research on rats indicated how essential this vitamin was for successful reproduction; one of Emerson's landmark animal studies showed how a diet low in vitamin E resulted in the appearance of muscular dystrophy in baby rats.

After almost a decade of research on vitamin E at Berkeley, a number of major changes took place in Gladys Emerson's life in the early 1940s. In 1940, she and her husband divorced. Two years later, in 1942, she accepted the position of head of the department of animal nutrition at the Merck Institute for Therapeutic Research in Rahway, New Jersey. Because of her reputation as a pioneering contributor to the discovery of vitamin E, Emerson was entrusted with major research projects at Merck which included investigations of vitamins B-6 and B-12 as well as amino acids. Some of her research at Merck, including investigations of 5,6-Dimethylbenizmidazole, a component of the molecule of vitamin B-12, would significantly contribute to the momentum of later research on the chemotherapy of viral infections.

Working at Merck with both rats and rhesus monkeys (which she characterized as being "wild, ferocious little beasts"), Gladys Emerson discovered that when the monkeys' diet was lacking in vitamin B-6, they developed lesions closely resembling arteriosclerosis in human beings. Additional research on dogs yielded similar results. Other animal investigations, centering largely on the B-complex family of vitamins, yielded important findings, including the fact that vitamin deficiencies could lead to abnormal growth as well as abnormalities of the liver, kidney, eye, skin, and posture.

As one of the leading nutritional researchers in the United States, Emerson was called on to lecture at most of the nation's major universities. Internationally recognized as well, she lectured in foreign countries including Japan. From 1950 through 1953, she was a research associate with the Sloan-Kettering Institute for Cancer Research in New York City, where her research concentrated on the effects of diet and hormones on the growth of tumors. In 1957, she left Merck to return to California, accepting a position as professor and chair of the department of home economics at the University of California, Los Angeles (UCLA). In 1962, she became head of the nutrition division at the UCLA School of Public Health, a post she occupied until her retirement in

1970. From 1959 through 1964, Gladys Emerson was a member of the food and nutrition board of the National Research Council. As a pioneering woman scientist in her field, she was honored with the Garvan Medal in 1952.

An impressive lecturer, Emerson enjoyed teaching and working with countless students over the decades. Fully aware of the many aspects of discrimination against women in the sciences, she was nevertheless a conservative whose essential philosophy was one of hard work; said Emerson to her female students: "Work and don't gripe." She usually owned a dog, noting, "it was nice to return home and be enthusiastically welcomed." One of her favorite canines was named "Chemie," the German word for chemistry. Her pleasures in life included singing songs with students and old friends and loyally attending UCLA football games. She was also an enthusiastic amateur photographer who won numerous awards. Gladys Emerson died at her home in Santa Monica, California, on January 18, 1984, and was buried next to her parents in El Reno, Oklahoma.

SOURCES:

Bailey, Martha J. *American Women in Science: A Biographical Dictionary*. Santa Barbara, CA: ABC-Clio, 1994.

Evans, Herbert M. "The Pioneer History of Vitamin E," in *Vitamins and Hormones: Advances in Research and Applications*. Vol. 20. NY: Academic Press, 1962, pp. 379–387.

Folkers, Karl. "Gladys Anderson Emerson (1903–1984): A Biographical Sketch," in *Journal of Nutrition*. Vol. 115. No. 7. July 1985, pp. 837–841.

Yost, Edna. *Women of Modern Science*. Reprint ed. Westport, CT: Greenwood Press, 1984.

John Haag,
Assistant Professor of History,
University of Georgia, Athens, Georgia

Emerson, Mary Moody

(1774–1863)

American essayist, diarist, and thinker, who played a crucial role in the intellectual development of her nephew Ralph Waldo Emerson as a Transcendentalist thinker. Born on August 25, 1774, in Concord, Massachusetts; died in Brooklyn, New York, on May 1, 1863; daughter of William Emerson and Phebe (Bliss) Emerson; had four brothers and sisters.

Mary Moody Emerson's birth coincided with the birth of the United States as a free nation. When she was one year old, the battle of Concord took place literally outside the windows of her home, the Old Manse, which still stands as a spacious two-story clapboard house near the North Bridge on Monument Street in Concord,

Massachusetts. The death of her cleric father in 1776 and her mother's remarriage in 1780 left Mary to be reared by her aunt and uncle on a farm in Malden, Massachusetts. The elderly couple was desperately poor, and young Mary, expected to get by on a legacy of ten dollars a year "for clothes and charity," grew up in an atmosphere of solitude and material scarcity. But her restless young mind had been stimulated by reading the Bible, several volumes of sermons, and a battered book lacking covers and title page that she would only years later discover to have been John Milton's classic *Paradise Lost*.

Mary Emerson's youth was austere and even bleak, since the prevailing theology of New England in her day was one of unrelenting, unforgiving Calvinism. Except for a few years' attendance at the local school, she was completely self-taught. She remained a fiercely devout Calvinist, while she was intellectually stimulated by the ideas of Plato, Plotinus, Locke, Coleridge and Byron. Her eccentric behavior—her self-described "oddities"—can likely be traced to these years, when she "was driven to find Nature her companion and solace," writes Ralph Waldo Emerson.

After the deaths of her aunt and uncle, she inherited their farm and sold it in order to live off the proceeds the rest of her life in a state of penurious independence. Although she had an offer of marriage, Mary turned it down. From this point on, she was a traveler, living in many places in New England. For years, she lived with her sister **Rebecca Emerson** at her farm, "Elm Vale," in South Waterford, Maine, enjoying the stunning countryside of that region. Mary Emerson would spend much of her life boarding with friends and relatives, seeking places to live where she would have minimal responsibilities, thus being free to carry on her "vocation" of reading, writing and engaging in lively conversations and debates.

Mary Moody Emerson supervised with inexorable zeal the education and intellectual development of her four nephews, the sons of her deceased brother William Emerson (1769–1811). Convinced that "they were born to be educated," she saw to it that major obstacles in the way of their education were removed. She believed that, through vigorous debate and challenges to the intellect, their minds and personalities would grow up to become strong and independent. Particularly attached to young Ralph Waldo Emerson, she made every effort to influence his intellectual growth. An indefatigable conversationalist and letter writer, Mary Emerson had gifts of eloquence, sharp wit and original metaphors which played a significant role in helping her nephew form his own unique literary style.

Throughout his long life (1803–1882), Ralph Waldo Emerson revealed his deep respect for his aunt, seeing her as a living bond between himself and his ancestors. From his earliest years, he recognized and appreciated her religious impulses. Although she chose to break with Ralph Waldo over his increasingly radical theological views (even refusing to live in the same town with him), in time she did reconcile with him, and was in fact secretly proud of her nephew for the fame he had achieved through his lectures and writings. As late as the early 1870s, years after her death, he continued to read and draw intellectual enrichment from her papers, and many of his celebrated essays were indebted to her, both stylistically and thematically.

Although loved and appreciated by her family and a few close friends who included Henry David Thoreau, Mary Emerson defended and prized her independence. In 1817, she wrote of her commitment to a life of freedom: "give me that oh God—it is holy independence—it is honor & immortality—dearer than friends, wealth & influence . . . I bless thee for giving me to see the advantage of loneliness." Both a passion for introspection and an appetite for intellectual stimulation and lively debate characterized her personality.

A large selection of Emerson's letters to her family was recently published, and **Nancy Craig Simmons** makes a persuasive argument that Mary Moody Emerson's letters served to "transform the minor genre of letter writing into a major vehicle for free discussion." Unlike traditional family letters which might include trivial news and gossip, Emerson's letters dealt with moral debates, metaphysical controversy, and issues of world importance. She could at times combine Transcendental concerns with practical philosophizing, as when she informed the recently married **Ann Sargent Gage**, "Beware, my young friend, how you go to keeping house on this ball of dust so as to lay up treasure in Heaven. However we theorise contemptuously of earth, it gets dominion & the grandure of the soul lies beneath rubbish, Pardon the caution."

While she was flinty and intellectually irrepressible within the circles of her friends and family, Emerson's eccentric appearance and comments in public appalled most strangers and conservative New England townsfolk. Her "macabre humors" as well as her "brutal, sardonic candor" in most matters did not endear her to the conventionally

minded of her contemporaries. In his classic pen portrait of Mary Moody Emerson, "The Cassandra of New England," Van Wyck Brooks provided many examples of her outrageous verbal assaults on both friends and strangers. She stood out among others due to her height (4'3"), her predilection for dressing in a shroud of her own making, and her customary brooding on death ("O dear worms! Most valuable companions!"). Although Emerson rhetorically invited death, confiding to her diary how she yearned for a "tedious indisposition" to take a fatal turn that "would open the cool sweet grave," in reality she remained a woman tenaciously attached to life.

Underneath the bizarre exterior she had created, Emerson was a woman of great intellectual and personal integrity. Having once defined herself as a "puny pilgrim whose sole talent was sympathy," she remained on course throughout her long life, searching for God and the myriad truths that help explain both the divine and human aspects of the universe. Those who knew her well chose to ignore her eccentricities, as did Henry David Thoreau, who recognized that she was "really and perseveringly interested to know what thinkers think." Toward the end of her life, Mary Moody Emerson mellowed, becoming kinder and happier. But she never lost her mystic sense of wonder, writing that to be "Alive with God is enough—'tis rapture."

The last four years of Emerson's life were spent in Williamsburg, now part of the Borough of Brooklyn, New York City, where she was cared for by her devoted niece **Hannah Haskins Parsons**. After her death on May 1, 1863, her remains were taken to her hometown of Concord, where she was buried in the Emerson family plot in Sleepy Hollow Cemetery.

SOURCES:

Allen, Gay Wilson. *Waldo Emerson: A Biography.* NY: Penguin, 1982.

Brooks, Van Wyck. "The Cassandra of New England," in *Scribner's Magazine.* Vol. 81. No. 10. February 1927, pp. 125–129.

Chambers-Schiller, Lee Virginia. *Liberty, A Better Husband: Single Women in America, the Generations of 1780–1840.* New Haven, CT: Yale University Press, 1984.

Christopherson, Johan Arthur. "The Post-Christian Turn: A Study of Ralph Waldo Emerson's Sermons" (Ph.D. dissertation, University of Minnesota, 1998).

Cole, Phyllis. "The Advantage of Loneliness: Mary Moody Emerson's Almanacks, 1802–1855," in *Harvard English Studies.* Vol. 10, 1982, pp. 1–32.

———. "The Divinity School Address of Mary Moody Emerson: Women's Silence and Women's Speech in the American Puritan Tradition," in *Harvard Divinity Bulletin.* Vol. 16. No. 2. December 1985–January, 1986, pp. 4–6.

———. *Mary Moody Emerson and the Origins of Transcendentalism: A Family History.* NY: Oxford University Press, 1998.

Feltenstein, Rosalie. "Mary Moody Emerson: The Gadfly of Concord," in *American Quarterly.* Vol. 5. No. 3. Fall 1953, pp. 231–246.

Mott, Wesley T., ed. *Biographical Dictionary of Transcendentalism.* Westport, CT: Greenwood Press, 1996.

———, ed. *Encyclopedia of Transcendentalism.* Westport, CT: Greenwood Press, 1996.

Myerson, Joel, ed. *Studies in the American Renaissance.* Charlottesville: University Press of Virginia, 1986.

Simmons, Nancy Craig, ed. *The Selected Letters of Mary Moody Emerson.* Athens: University of Georgia Press, 1993.

Williams, David Ross. "Wilderness Lost: New England in the Jaws of an Angry God" (Ph.D. dissertation, Brown University, 1982).

John Haag,
Assistant Professor of History,
University of Georgia, Athens, Georgia

Emhart, Maria (1901–1981)

Austrian Socialist activist and leader of the anti-Fascist underground, 1934–1938, who was honored as one of the most respected veteran survivors of a heroic period of Austrian Social Democracy. Name variations: name while in the anti-Fascist underground, 1934–1936: Gretl Meyer. Born in Pyhra, Lower Austria, on May 27, 1901; died in Bischofshofen, Austria, on October 9, 1981; daughter of Johann Raps and Maria Kreutzer Raps; married Karl Emhart.

A militant Social Democrat from earliest years, embodied the militant beliefs of the Austrian working class (1920s and 1930s); became internationally celebrated during the trial of captured leaders of the underground Social Democratic movement (March 1936).

Born among an exploited working class in the 1880s in the multinational Habsburg monarchy, Austrian Socialism came of age in the model social experiment of "Red Vienna" during a tumultuous 1920s and 1930s. After 1945, it served as a major participant in the process that has made the contemporary Republic of Austria one of the most stable and prosperous nations in Europe. The well-known careers of the leaders of the Austrian Social Democratic Party, almost exclusively male professional politicians like Otto Bauer, Karl Renner, and Bruno Kreisky, have obscured the lives and achievements of a large number of women without whose dedication the movement would not have succeeded in changing the course of Central European history. Maria Emhart is one such woman.

She was born Maria Raps in the village of Pyhra near the city St. Pölten, Lower Austria, three months before her mother **Maria Kreutzer**

married Johann Raps. After their marriage, Maria and Johann lived in St. Pölten where he worked for the railroad, and Maria, who had been a poor agricultural laborer, began to raise a family that in time included four daughters and a son. Typical for working-class households of the day, the large family lived in a cramped apartment consisting of one room and a kitchen. Later, when the Raps family took in two additional children whom Johann's sister was unable to raise, the family was squeezed into a slightly larger apartment which was totally inadequate for its nine inhabitants.

Life for her family in St. Pölten was often stressful, in part because of the constant specter of malnutrition and also because father Johann took out his frustrations through violent outbursts against his wife and children. Maria's mother suffered greatly under these constant pressures, which likely contributed to her premature death at age 49. Maria became pregnant at age 18 by her future husband, Karl Emhart. Forced to sell a watch and a revolver to help pay for an illegal abortion in Vienna, Maria came to believe that this procedure had made it impossible for her and her husband to have children in later years. Countless Austrian working-class women died as a result of illegal abortions performed under medically inadequate conditions.

At age 14, Maria had begun working in one of St. Pölten's textile mills to help support her family, increasingly impoverished by World War I which was disproportionately burdening the poor and working classes of Austria. She was expected to place her entire wage packet at her father's disposal. At work, the lack of laws protecting the rights of workers (and nonenforcement of those on the books) meant that Maria often performed physically demanding tasks meant for adult males, who were now at the front. She often worked night shifts for the same low wages. By late 1917, a revolutionary spirit had taken hold of many of the workers of St. Pölten, who had heard stories about a workers' state being created in Russia, and of strikes in Vienna, Berlin, and elsewhere. A revulsion toward the war and a burning desire for social justice, expressed in the phrase "bread and peace," became a slogan that Maria and her fellow workers repeated as they went on strike. She became a militant trade unionist and developed a vision of a world free of both war and the kind of economic injustices she and her fellow workers were forced to experience.

In 1918, a rebellious and politically aware Maria joined the Austrian Social Democratic

Party. She would remain a loyal Social Democrat to the end of her life, believing strongly in democratic Socialism rather than in the dictatorial version of Marxism that began to emerge in Soviet Russia after 1917. Staying in St. Pölten as a textile worker, in 1921 she married Karl Emhart, who like her father worked for the railroad. Even with a combined income, the newlyweds remained impoverished, living in a modest apartment in one of St. Pölten's proletarian neighborhoods. St. Pölten grew dramatically in population after World War I, registering an increase from 23,000 inhabitants in 1920 to 37,000 in 1932. The city's militant working class guaranteed that the Social Democrats always won the great majority of votes in both local and national elections. Despite Austria's grinding poverty after its military defeat and its dissolution as a multinational state in 1918, in St. Pölten the new political climate resulted in impressive social improvements, including improved working conditions and more assistance to mothers and children, as well as pensioners, and major educational reforms.

Maria Emhart invested virtually every spare minute in the 1920s in her activities for the Social Democrats of St. Pölten. Chosen by her fellow workers in her factory to represent them, she was a conscientious works councillor (*Betriebsrätin*) who took every opportunity to try to improve labor conditions for both men and women. Aware of the inadequacies of her formal education, Emhart took the train twice a week to Vienna for classes at the Social Democratic Workers' University (Arbeiterhochschule) where night students, most of them from deprived working-class backgrounds, absorbed new ideas and insights from such prominent members of the Social Democratic leadership as Otto Bauer, *Emmy Freundlich, *Adelheid Popp, and Karl Renner. A close friendship developed during these years between Emhart and *Rosa Jochmann, one of the party's most energetic and idealistic young women.

Astute party leaders could see in women like Emhart and Jochmann the leadership qualities that an increasingly beleaguered working class would need as the promise of Central European democracy disintegrated in the late 1920s. Nonetheless, the full potential of women was never to be realized within Austrian Socialism despite its theoretical ideological commitment to gender equality. Party inner circles remained male-dominated. In provincial towns like St. Pölten, Socialist stalwarts including Maria Emhart often despaired about the future. The mass appeals of Austrian-born Adolf Hitler's Nazi movement in Germany now spilled over into his native land, and mass unemployment in industrial areas including St. Pölten demoralized workers, making some susceptible to National Socialist propaganda.

In 1932, Emhart was elected to the St. Pölten city council, where she served as one of three women among the total of 43 representatives. Trusted by her constituents, many of whom had become unemployed because of the world economic depression, she worked tirelessly on their behalf. Not only local but national and world issues concerned Emhart during these years. In January 1933, Adolf Hitler became German chancellor, quickly transforming the Reich into a brutal dictatorship. Led by its own anti-democratic chancellor, Engelbert Dollfuss, Austria too abandoned democracy in 1933, albeit first at a slower pace and with somewhat less bloody methods. As the Austrian Socialist movement found itself being inexorably strangled throughout 1933 and early 1934, Emhart and her colleagues planned for the inevitable suppression of the Social Democratic Party and with it the organized working class. A stirring orator, she spoke not only at city council sessions but at public rallies of the Republican Guard, the armed workers' formation which hoped to defend democracy and the achievements of Austria's proletariat.

But hopes alone did not save Austrian Socialism, which was crushed in a bloody civil war in February 1934. Most workers were caught off guard. Although there was bitter fighting in Vienna and elsewhere, given the immense advantages possessed by the Dollfuss regime the ultimate outcome of the conflict was never in doubt. In St. Pölten, many leaders excused themselves from the conflict, but Emhart convinced some militants of the need to fight. She oversaw countless details of the battle with government forces including the recruitment of women who were able to transport ammunition in baby carriages across enemy-held territory to the workers' strongpoints where it was desperately needed.

While many men had fought bravely, some of the most remarkable deeds of the doomed workers' struggle in St. Pölten were carried out by women. For her fearless and uncompromising leadership, Emhart quickly became a legend throughout Socialist circles both within Austria and among exiles. She was known simply as the St. Pölten's Flintenweib (Musket Moll) as well as its Schutzbund-Mizzi (Workers' Militia Mizzi). Other women, including local militant youth leader **Herma Paschinger**, saved many Socialists from future arrest and imprisonment. Paschinger nonchalantly spirited away from under the noses of forces already occupying Socialist party headquarters the complete local membership list, which she then proceeded to burn.

With the suppression of the conflict, Maria Emhart and many others were arrested. The police dressed her in a Schutzbund uniform before she was photographed. Although she showed no fear to her captors, Emhart later admitted that while in her cell secret tears were shed, in the belief that she would be shot under the regime of martial law still in force. At the time of her arrest, she had overheard a conversation of some pro-regime militia in which one had voiced his satisfaction that as "a dangerous Red," Maria Emhart would most likely be the first woman to be hanged in Austria in many years. She expected to receive a sentence of at least 10 to 15 years in prison for high treason. As it turned out, she was in fact released after a relatively brief incarceration of 17 weeks. A cheering crowd met Emhart on her release from prison, and they accompanied her to her home. Annoyed local authorities did not want to turn her into more of a popular heroine, but they did decide to fine her a relatively modest 70 schillings for being the leader of a banned demonstration.

Ostensibly the reason given for her release was one of "insufficient evidence," but in reality the unpopular Dollfuss government found itself under domestic pressure from both Right and Left, as well as under sharp international scrutiny. Political observers of the time noted that a beleaguered Vienna Fascist regime, hated by both Austrian Nazis and Social Democrats, hoped that by initiating a policy of relatively mild treatment toward the rebels of the Left (some men were in fact executed) it might perhaps be able to initiate a process of national reconciliation and thus more effectively strengthen Austria against the threat of Adolf Hitler's Reich.

In February 1934, virtually all of the Social Democratic leadership had fled to nearby Czechoslovakia. Calling themselves "Revolutionary Socialists" to distinguish themselves from the old, crushed and discredited party, an underground organization was built up in the next months in both Vienna and the Austrian provinces. After her release from prison, Emhart remained as dedicated as before to the ideals of Socialism and democracy. She now became a leading personality of the underground Revolutionary Socialists in Lower Austria, living at times in Vienna illegally under the alias "Gretl Meyer."

Despite her poor health—she had to spend some time in a Swiss sanitarium during this period because of an active case of tuberculosis—Emhart worked to build up the Revolutionary Socialist organization in Vienna and Lower Austria. She was one of the few women in the underground leadership and attended many important illegal conferences, each time taking considerable risks. On January 26, 1935, she was arrested along with her sister **Anna Emhart**. Anna was soon released for lack of evidence, but Maria was interrogated for many weeks, deprived of sleep and denied changes of clothing in order to break her down both physically and psychologically. As a result, her latent tuberculosis became active again and her health deteriorated rapidly. Soon after her arrest, she discovered that her husband Karl had been arrested after she was.

The Fascist Austrian regime, which claimed to be Christian in inspiration and had promulgated a constitution in which state power was defined as deriving from God rather than the people, carried on a relentless war against the majority of its population. While many in the impoverished middle class sympathized with Nazi Germany, and the peasantry passively supported the authoritarian government in Vienna, the majority of the working classes remained loyal to the ideals of democratic Socialism, as did Emhart. In the police's attempt to break her spirit, they threatened her husband with the loss of his railway job unless he agreed to divorce his wife. Bowing to economic necessity and vowing to remain faithful to each other, Karl Emhart divorced his wife of 14 years on April 3, 1936. An even more dramatic event, however, had taken place before this.

Determined to break the organization of the underground Revolutionary Socialist movement, Austrian authorities decided in January 1936 to mount a massive political trial against captured leaders of the Leftist opposition. Among the 27 accused, of which 25 were Revolutionary Socialists and two Communists, there were four women. Of these, Maria Emhart was soon to emerge as not only the most courageous and eloquent among the women defendants, but indeed also among the entire group of political prisoners. The trial, which began in Vienna on March 16, 1936, quickly became a news story not only in Austria (where it was reported in a heavily censored press) but throughout much of the world. The confidence and defiance of the defendants made it clear that Austrian Socialism, which had ruled the city of Vienna as a model of social progress from 1920 through 1933, was down but by no means out. A number of the prisoners made eloquent speeches in court. One of these was a young law student, Bruno Kreisky, who four decades later would serve as Austria's chancellor.

Emhart's speech to the court was powerful and moving in its unadorned sincerity. She began by declining the judge's offer to sit while she spoke, noting that her tuberculosis had not been taken into account during her 14 months of incarceration and would not now play any role in her decisions. She began the body of her address by declaring, "Yes, I am an enthusiastic Socialist!" Emhart then went on to recount the impact of a harsh and poverty-stricken childhood and adolescence on the emergence of her later political ideals. "As a child I came to know all about the poverty, misery and deprivations, as well as the humiliations, that one can expect to experience if one comes into the world on the bottom rungs of the social system." She went on to explain that early in her life she had learned from daily experiences that "as an individual one is powerless" but that as a member of a trade union, or a powerfully organized working-class political party such as the Austrian Social Democrats, many individuals working in concert could in fact seek to banish from the world such ancient evils as poverty, exploitation, injustice, and war.

Emhart ended her address to the court with an eloquent defense of her faith in the ideals of Socialism, a faith she felt as deeply as possible and which, she said, "unites me with millions in the world." Showing no fear of a court that she fully expected would sentence her to a long prison term, she went on to defend her Socialist ideals, which for her represented the only global prescription for widespread poverty and misery that troubled the world of 1936. For Emhart, only a new social system would be able to build the justice and permanent peace that would banish the universal fear of Fascism and imminent war that now gripped the world.

The court rendered its judgments and pronounced its sentences on March 24, 1936. Clearly bowing to the pressures of international public opinion and the unstable domestic political environment, it was extraordinarily lenient in its sentencing. Thirteen defendants were found not guilty. Of those found guilty, the longest jail sentence, 20 months, was for Karl Hans Sailer. Maria Emhart received a sentence of 18 months, with the other remaining defendants receiving sentences of from 16 months to only six weeks. For all those sentenced to prison, the time already served in jail would be counted as part of their incarceration.

As the result of a general political amnesty issued in July 1936, Emhart was released from prison. Although she was legally now divorced, she returned immediately to St. Pölten to continue to live with Karl Emhart. Among the petty harassments she had to endure was a requirement to appear personally at the police station on a daily basis. This form of bureaucratic humiliation, however, was not sufficient punishment as far as some officials were concerned. Determined to continue their campaign against a woman who showed no sign of fear or compromise in her political views, local railroad officials—doubtless authorized to do so by their Viennese superiors—transferred Karl Emhart to the small town of Bischofshofen in Salzburg province. It is likely that the idea behind this was to isolate Maria Emhart, who was allowed to follow Karl to this remote place, thus eliminating once and for all the political influence she had continued to enjoy in St. Pölten.

In December 1937, Austrian police managed to arrest the top leadership of the Revolutionary Socialists. By this time, Maria Emhart was resigned to her new role as a party member, rather than a leader. Life in Bischofshofen was often tense and difficult for her; she and Karl lived in a small apartment with a Nazi as their landlord, and they had to be extremely cautious in their political activities. With the Nazi annexation of Austria in March 1938, Maria Emhart hated Fascism more than ever now that she was forced to live in Hitler's Third Reich. Through the anti-Nazi grapevine, she heard that some of her old comrades had escaped into foreign exile, while others—many of them Jewish—were taken to death camps where they were murdered. During World War II, Maria regularly sent food packages to comrades imprisoned in concentration camps, including her good friend Rosa Jochmann in Ravensbrück.

In 1943, Emhart was accused of listening to enemy radio broadcasts. A visit to her home by the Gestapo followed, but fortunately a case against her was never made. When another member of the underground was arrested, the name "Emmy" came up during an interrogation but this was not connected with Maria's last name and there were no further investigations.

In early May 1945, she and several other veteran anti-Nazis took over the municipal government of Bischofshofen even though it would be several days before American troops arrived in the town. Emhart feared that, as had taken place elsewhere, she and the others might be killed at the last minute by Nazi fanatics. But

Emhart lived and began to busy herself with the immediate tasks of reconstruction. She was somewhat shocked when early in the occupation an American officer found her working in the mayor's office and said, "Can you cook, are you married? Then go home and cook, this work of local politics is a man's business."

By the end of 1945, Emhart had reestablished her political career. She made countless speeches on behalf of the newly founded Socialist Party of Austria, helping to build up its organization in Salzburg province. In November 1945, she was elected as the only woman to serve in the Provincial Diet of Salzburg. She also spent many periods in Vienna as a member of the Socialist Party's women's committee. Much of her time went into finding creative ways of providing Austrians of all ages with at least a minimum of food, clothing and shelter during a difficult period of physical and moral reconstruction.

In April 1946, Emhart was elected vice-mayor of Bischofshofen, the first woman in the history of Austria to be elected to such a high municipal office. She held this post for a full two decades, retiring in August 1966. In 1953, while still serving in her Bischofshofen post, she was elected to the Austrian National Assembly, where her speeches were generally regarded as of a very high caliber. On issues relating to women's welfare, few could argue that her opinions were based not only on a conscientious study of facts but also on long and painful personal experiences.

Because of her husband's declining health, Emhart chose to not stand for re-election to her National Assembly seat in 1964. Both her withdrawal from national political life and her husband's death were painful and difficult for her to accept. For a time, she was so depressed that she thought of suicide as a way out of her suffering. But friendships and her continuing interest in the larger issues of the world reawakened her zest for living, and she came to enjoy her final years as one of Austrian Socialism's most respected veterans. At times, she wondered whether or not her generation's sacrifices would be remembered by young men and women more interested in personal happiness and consumption than memories of war and Fascism.

In her final decades, Maria Emhart was often concerned by what she saw to be a lack of idealism in her party, noting that one "can only hope that above all else young Socialist functionaries get the picture of a time when what mattered most to people was not jobs and promotions but instead only the attainment of democracy and freedom." In her unpublished memoirs, she asks with concern if "Our descendants will one day be pleased by the fact that we went to the bastions on their behalf?" Maria Emhart died in Bischofshofen on October 9, 1981.

SOURCES:

Arbeitsgemeinschaft "Biografisches Lexikon der österreichischen Frau," Institut für Wissenschaft und Kunst, Vienna.

Emhart, Maria. "Erinnerungen" (unpublished memoirs, Dokumentationsarchiv des österreichischen Widerstandes, Vienna, Akte Nr. 14694).

Fischer, Lisa. "Maria Emhart," in Edith Prost, ed., *"Die Partei hat mich nie enttäuscht—": Österreichische Sozialdemokratinnen*. Vienna: Verlag für Gesellschaftskritik, 1989, pp. 255–287.

"Gedenken an Maria Emhart," in *Der sozialistische Kämpfer*. No. 9/10. September–October, 1981, p. 9.

Holtmann, Everhard. *Zwischen Unterdrückung und Befriedung: sozialistische Arbeiterbewegung und autoritäres Regime in Österreich 1933–1938*. Munich: R. Oldenbourg Verlag, 1978.

Kreisky, Bruno. "50 Jahre Sozialistenprozess 1936: 'Wie es kam . . .'," in *Der sozialistische Kämpfer*. No. 1/2. January–February, 1986, pp. 1–2.

Kykal, Inez. "Der Sozialistenprozess 1936" (Ph.D. dissertation, University of Vienna, 1968).

"Maria Emhart 75 Jahre," in *Der sozialistische Kämpfer*. No. 7/8. July–August, 1976, pp. 27–28.

"Maria Emhart 80 Jahre," *Der sozialistische Kämpfer*, No. 4/6. April–June, 1981, p. 11.

Marschalek, Manfred. "Der Wiener Sozialistenprozess 1936," in Karl L. Stadler, ed., *Sozialistenprozesse: Politische Justiz in Österreich 1870–1936*. Vienna: Europaverlag, 1986, pp. 429–490.

Nasko, Siegfried. *Empor aus dumpfen Träumen: Arbeiterbewegung und Sozialdemokratie im St. Pöltener Raum*. Vienna and St. Pölten: SPÖ-Bezirksorganisation St. Pölten, 1986.

Österreichisches Institut für Zeitgeschichte, Vienna, Microfilm A/34.

Sporrer, Maria, and Herbert Steiner, eds. *Rosa Jochmann: Zeitzeugin*. 3rd ed. Vienna: Europaverlag, 1987.

Weinzierl, Erika. *Emanzipation? Österreichische Frauen im 20. Jahrhundert*. Vienna: Verlag Jugend & Volk, 1975.

Wisshaupt, Walter. *Wir kommen wieder! Eine Geschichte der Revolutionären Sozialisten Österreichs 1934–1938*. Vienna: Verlag der Wiener Volksbuchhandlung, 1967.

John Haag,
Assistant Professor of History,
University of Georgia, Athens, Georgia

Emilia of Orange (1569–1629)

Princess of Orange. Born on April 10, 1569, in Cologne, Germany; died on March 16, 1629, in Geneva; daughter of *Anna of Saxony (1544–1577) and William I the Silent (1533–1584), prince of Orange, count of Nassau, stadholder of Holland, Zealand, and

Utrecht (r. 1572–1584); married Manuel of Portugal, on November 17, 1597; children: Manuel II (b. 1600), prince of Portugal; Louis William (b. 1601), prince of Portugal; **Maria Belgica** *(1599–1647, who married Johan Theodor de Croll);* **Anna Frisia Luisa** *(1606–1669);* **Juliane Katherina** *(1603–1680);* **Emilia Luise** *(1605–1670);* **Mauritia Eleanora** *(1609–1674, who married Georg Friedrich, prince of Nassau-Siegen);* **Sabine Dorothea** *(1610–1670).*

Emma (fl. 600s)

Queen, possibly of Mercia. *Flourished in the 600s; children: sons St. Ethered, St. Ethelbright, and St. Ermenbert; daughter* ****Ermenburga*** *(fl. late 600s); grandmother of saints* ****Milburg*** *(d. 722?) and* ****Mildred*** *(d. 700?).*

Emma (fl. 1080s)

Marquise. *Flourished in the 1080s; daughter of Robert Guiscard (d. 1085), a Frankish noble, duke of Apulia and Calabria, count of Sicily (r. 1057–1085), and* ****Sichelgaita of Salerno*** *(1040–1090); married Odo the marquis; children: possibly Tancred, prince of Antioch (d. 1112). Some scholars believe that Tancred's mother was the sister, not the daughter, of Robert Guiscard.*

Emma (1836–1885)

Queen of Hawaii and consort to King Kamehameha IV. *Name variations: Emma Rooke; Kaleleokalani or Kaleleonalani. Born on January 2, 1836, either in Honolulu or at Kawaihae on the Kohala coast of the island of Hawaii (then called the Sandwich Islands); died on April 25, 1885, in Honolulu; daughter and only child of George Naea and* **Fanny Kekelaokalani Young***; given at birth to her childless aunt, Grace Kamaukui Young Rooke and her husband Thomas C.B. Rooke (a physician), who gave her the name of Emma Rooke; attended Royal School in Honolulu; later tutored privately in French, geography, and history; married King Kamehameha IV (Alexander Liholiho), on June 19, 1856 (died, November 30, 1863); children: Prince Albert Edward Kauikeaouli Leiopapa a Kamehameha (1858–1862).*

Emma was born in 1836 of Hawaiian and English ancestry. According to the Hawaiian tradition of the time, she was given at birth to her childless aunt **Grace Kamaukui Rooke**, who, with her husband Thomas C.B. Rooke, named the child Emma Rooke and legally adopted her. Emma attended a school established by American Congregational missionaries for the children of native chiefs. Her English attitudes and tastes were largely influenced by her adoptive father Thomas, a physician who owned one of the finest collections of books on the island. Her later education was tended to by a cultured Englishwoman hired by her father.

Emma's marriage to newly enthroned King Kamehameha IV stemmed partly from dynastic considerations, but her intelligence and refinement also prompted the match. The 20-year-old Emma was married on June 19, 1856, in Kawaiahao Church, and the wedding was officiated by a Congregational missionary. The king and queen presided over a stylish, cultured, and elegant royal court. Emma was a spirited hostess and oversaw the establishment of an impressive library filled with the English classics she so adored. (The collection was later bequeathed to the Honolulu Library, now part of the Library of Hawaii.) The birth of a son in 1858, Prince Albert Edward, inspired much celebration and appeared to strengthen an already harmonious marriage. In 1859, however, the king became involved in a scandal that he would later refer to as "the great false act of my life." Suspicious of Emma's fidelity, in a drunken rage he shot and severely wound-

$\mathcal{E}$mma
(1836–1885)

ed his young American secretary and close friend, Henry A. Neilson. Although a period of difficult uncertainty followed the incident, during which the king seriously considered abdication, Emma remained steadfast in her loyalty.

The king's remorse ultimately strengthened his commitment to humanitarian and religious aims. At Emma's request, he personally solicited funds for the construction of Queen's Hospital, the first public hospital in Hawaii. Opened in 1860, it is now called Queen's Medical Center and is one of the largest and best-equipped medical facilities in Hawaii. In 1863, Queen Emma organized the District Visiting Society, a group of women who acted as an early hospital auxiliary. Members of the society visited the poor, encouraging the sick to enter the Queen's Hospital, and instructed families with members who had contracted leprosy in the proper care and safe segregation of the afflicted. In 1865, a segregation law was passed that demanded that leprosy victims present themselves for treatment in public facilities.

Emma, who had her young prince baptized by an Anglican cleric, was also instrumental in establishing the Anglican church in Hawaii, although it was designated as the "Hawaiian Reformed Catholic Church." The church would provide great solace for the queen, whose beloved son died in 1862, at age four. A little over a year later, King Kamehameha IV died, and his brother, Kamehameha V, became the new king. After the death of her son, Queen Emma called herself Kaleleokalani ("The flight of the heavenly chief") and took the name Kaleleonalani ("The flight of the heavenly chiefs") after the death of her husband. With these names, she believed she would embody the two vanished chieftains.

In 1865, the widowed queen left for England to regain her health and to stimulate interest in the Anglican mission in Hawaii. In London, her fundraising appearances were widely publicized and brought her international prominence. In addition to raising $16,000 for the mission, she toured Europe and the eastern United States and was presented to President Andrew Johnson at the White House as well as several crowned heads of Europe including Queen *Victoria, Emperor Napoleon III and Empress *Eugénie. She returned to Honolulu in 1866 and concentrated her efforts on education, particularly St. Andrew's Priory, an Episcopal school for Hawaiian girls, and a boarding school for boys established by her husband in 1862.

In 1874, Emma became a candidate for the throne when Lunalilo, who had become king after Kamehameha V's death in 1872, died without naming a successor. Under Hawaiian law, the succession fell to the legislature. Emma campaigned vigorously but lost to her rival Kalakaua by a vote of 39 to 6. After Emma's defeat, her supporters (the "Queenites") rioted, storming the courthouse and destroying valuable records and legal volumes, as well as some of the furniture. The next day, King Kalakaua called Queen Emma, who had not sanctioned the riot, and formal relations were reestablished.

For the next 11 years, Emma occupied herself with politics, social functions, and her philanthropies. She died in 1885, at age 49, after a series of cerebral hemorrhages. Emma left most of her estate in trust for the Queen's Hospital, St. Andrew's Priory, and St. Andrew's Cathedral, all of which are located in what is now Queen Emma Square in Honolulu.

SOURCES:
Peterson, Barbara Bennett, ed. *Notable Women of Hawaii*. Honolulu: University of Hawaii Press, 1984.

Barbara Morgan,
Melrose, Massachusetts

Emma de Gatinais (fl. 1150–1170).

See Marie de Champagne (1145–1198) for sidebar.

Emma of Bavaria (d. 876)

Queen of the Germans. Died in 876; daughter of Welf of Bavaria and Heilwig; sister of *Judith of Bavaria (802–843); married Louis II the German (804–876), king of the Germans (r. 843–876); children: Carloman of Bavaria (c. 828–880); Louis the Young (b. around 835), king of the East Franks, king of Saxony (r. 876–882); Charles III the Fat (839–887), king of the France (r. 884–887), king of Germany (r. 876–887), Holy Roman emperor as Charles II (r. 881–887); *Hildegarde of Bavaria (c. 840–?).

Emma of Burgundy (d. 939)

Queen of France. Died in 939 (some sources cite 935); daughter of Robert, count of Paris, also known as Robert I (c. 865–923), king of France (r. 922–923), and *Beatrice of Vermandois (880–931); sister of Hugh the Great (or Hugh the White), count of Paris and duke of Burgundy (d. 956); married Raoul also known as Ralph or Rudolf (son of Richard, duke of Burgundy and Aquitaine), duke of Burgundy, king of France (r. 923–936).

Emma of Burgundy, queen of France, was an important military figure. In addition to political skills such as negotiation, she organized the defense of Laon in the early 10th century. She led forces that captured Avalon in 931, and in 933 conducted a siege against Château Thierry; **Pauline Stafford** notes that the castle was surrendered directly to Emma and not to her husband Rudolf. Leagued with her father Robert, count of Paris, Rudolf had driven Charles III the Simple, king of France, from his throne. Rudolf and Emma supported Robert on his throne until his death in 923; then Rudolf became king and ruled from 923 to 936.

SUGGESTED READING:

Stafford, Pauline. *Queens, Concubines, and Dowagers: The King's Wife in the Early Middle Ages.* Athens, GA: University of Georgia Press, 1983.

Emma of Hereford (d. 1100).

See Emma of Norfolk.

Emma of Italy (948–after 990)

Queen of France. Name variations: Emma of France; Emme. Born in 948 in Italy; died after 990 in France; daughter of Adelaide of Burgundy (931–999) and Lothair (Lothar), king of Italy; stepdaughter of Otto I the Great, king of Germany (r. 936–973), Holy Roman emperor (r. 962–973); married Lothair or Lothaire (941–986), king of France (r. 954–986), around 966; children: at least two sons, Louis V (c. 967–987), king of France (r. 986–987); Otto, cleric at Rheims.

Mother of the last of the Carolingians, Emma was born into the royal house of Italy, the daughter of *Adelaide of Burgundy and King Lothair of Italy. Around 966, she married Lothair, king of the West Franks, who had begun an aggressive policy of expansion in 956. Emma was an active participant in the administration of the Frankish realm and seemed to play an especially important role in Lothair's military campaigns. She accompanied him on various missions and took charge of the defense of Verdun after they had conquered it. Lothair's effort to gain Lorraine in 978 led to an invasion by Emperor Otto II who made it to the walls of Paris. When Hugh Capet took the side of Otto, the two successfully wiped away Lothair's rule at Laon.

Named regent for her young son Louis V after Lothair's death, Emma encountered considerable threat to her power from her husband's brother Charles of Lorraine, who wanted to rule. Among other schemes, Charles accused Emma of committing adultery with a bishop in order to cast doubt on Louis' legitimacy. Louis died young in 987, the last Carolingian ruler of France. He was succeeded by Hugh Capet, and Emma retired from political activism.

Laura York,
Riverside, California

Emma of Norfolk (d. 1100)

Countess of Norfolk. Name variations: Emma FitzOsbern; Emma Guader; Emma of Hereford. Born in England; died in 1100 in Brittany; daughter of William FitzOsbern and Adeliza of Tosny; married Ralph Guader, earl of Norfolk, in 1075; children: Alan, later earl of Norfolk; Ralph, later lord of Gael and Montfort; Amicia de Waer, countess of Leicester.

Emma, the 11th-century countess of Norfolk, England, was the formidable defender of the town and castle of Norwich. She married Ralph Guader, earl of Norfolk, in 1075. That same year, the earl revolted against the king of England, William I the Conqueror, which resulted in a siege of Norwich by the king's troops. The earl was forced to flee to France for safety and left Emma to defend Norwich. Despite the odds against her, Emma refused to yield to the king's men. She orchestrated the defense of the town for so long that the king eventually had to compromise with Emma to restore peace. Part of the settlement included a safe conduct for Emma to leave England and join her husband in Brittany. In 1096, the couple joined the First Crusade, accompanied by their son, Alan. After the Crusade, Emma returned to Brittany, where she died in 1100.

Laura York,
Riverside, California

Emma of Normandy (c. 985–1052)

Norman queen who married two English kings, gave birth to two English kings, and remained firmly in the center of the diplomatic and martial activities that rocked the Anglo-Saxon state. Name variations: Imme or Imma; Aelfgifu, Ælfgifu, or Elfgifu; Ælfgifu-Emma; Lady of Winchester. Born around 985 in Normandy; died on March 6, 1052, in Winchester, Hampshire, England; buried at Winchester Cathedral, Hampshire; daughter of Duke Richard I of Normandy and Gunnor of Denmark (d. 1031); married Aethelred or Ethelred II the Unready, king of England (r. 979–1016), in 1002 (died 1016); married Cnut or Canute I the Great, king of England (r. 1016–1035), Denmark (r. 1019–1035), Norway (r. 1028–1035), in

1017 (died 1035); children: (first marriage) Edward III the Confessor (c. 1005–1066), king of the English (r. 1042–1066); Alfred (d. 1037); Godgifu (c. 1010–c. 1049); (second marriage) Harthacanute also spelled Hardacnut or Hardicanute (c. 1020–1042), king of Denmark (r. 1039–1042); Gunhild (c. 1020–1038).

Lived in Normandy (1013–17); was in exile in Bruges (1037–40); returned with son Hardicanute to England, where Hardicanute was crowned king (1040); following death of Hardicanute and accession of Edward (1042), deprived of properties and wealth by her son Edward (1043).

𝒢aul, I say, rejoiced to have brought forth so great a lady, and one worthy of so great a King, the country of the English indeed rejoiced to have received such a one into its towns.

—*Encomium Emmae Reginae*, c. 1041

The events of 1066 in England attract the attention of professional and amateur historians to such an extent that the preceding decades are often deemed as inevitable stepping stones to William the Conqueror's great invasion. This view minimizes the significance of the life-or-death decisions that England's rulers faced at every juncture in the first half of the tumultuous 11th century. One woman's career as wife and mother of England's kings illustrates not only the competing powers that made the Anglo-Saxon kingdom fall, but displays the human consequences of policies that did not always attain their intended goals. Emma of Normandy—great-aunt of William the Conqueror—married King Ethelred the Unready of England in 1002, and until her death 50 years later, she remained firmly in the center of the diplomatic and martial activities that rocked the Anglo-Saxon state. Ethelred's choice of Emma as wife was intended to stabilize his kingdom against the terrible violence the Vikings were inflicting on England, but in the long run, the marriage provided an opportunity for the rising Norman power to acquire new territory in the north.

The Anglo-Saxon, Norman, and Scandinavian peoples shared similar interests and outlooks by the late 10th century. Indeed, the Normans themselves were the products of early 10th-century Viking raids in northern France: Rolf (Rollo) was a Viking leader who was granted the territory later known as Normandy by the weak French king Charles III the Simple in 911. During this time, there were also extensive contacts between other Viking bands with Anglo-Saxon England; the *Anglo-Saxon Chronicle* reports attacks beginning in 793, and the intensity of the raids accelerated dramatically throughout the 9th and 10th centuries. By Ethelred's time (979–1016), Vikings wintered in Norman ports to facilitate their harrying campaigns in England, demonstrating both the amiable relations that arose from their common ancestry, and the good business sense of the Normans. Many Danish Vikings established permanent settlements in England, particularly in the north. Thus, these three northern peoples traded, raided, and occupied each others' territories with great regularity prior to the 11th century.

Religion divided the Scandinavians from their Norman cousins and the Anglo-Saxons, for Christianity had been introduced to England centuries earlier, and the Normans themselves accepted the religion of the area they won from Charles in the early 10th century. But the Vikings retained their pagan outlook until the late 10th century, when with the assistance of kings like Ethelred, they discerned that the new religion was both inevitable and practical if they wished to consolidate their states and enter into relations with the rest of Europe. Although German bishops played a large role in the conversion of the Scandinavians, it is clear that English kings such as Ethelstan and Ethelred also acted as catalysts for Christianity's acceptance, especially since it afforded the English monarchs opportunities to establish spiritual kinship ties with aggressive and dangerous Viking leaders. Ethelred, for example, served as the Norwegian Olaf Tryggvason's confirmation sponsor.

Emma, daughter of Richard I of Normandy and great granddaughter of Rolf, the original duke, lived in all three worlds—Norman, English, and Scandinavian—by virtue of her marital and maternal exploits. The *Anglo-Saxon Chronicle* gives the significant events of Emma's career in its characteristically brief fashion, although its main attraction as a source is the political backdrop it provides for Emma's period. Many 11th-century chroniclers, such as William of Poitiers, William of Jumièges, and William of Malmesbury, and the 12th-century Florence of Worcester, add further details concerning Emma, although all of these chroniclers demonstrate clear biases in their points of view. Emma is also represented in Old Norse historical writing, because her position as the wife of King Canute I of Norway, Denmark and England (r. 1016–1035), as well as her role as mother of Hardicanute (r. 1040–1042), had intrinsic interest for Scandinavian authors.

Perhaps the most interesting source for Emma's role as English queen is one that she solicited from a northern French cleric: the *Encomium Emmae Reginae*. This work, written when Emma was queen mother to her son Hardicanute, portrays Emma in an extremely favorable light and so must be treated cautiously. As one recent biographer of Emma warns:

> [T]he encomiast used omission and ambiguous wording when he wanted to conceal the truth: for example, when he had to portray a favorable evaluation of Emma in instances which did not lend themselves to such an impression of her.

Still, the *Encomium* sheds valuable light on a particularly successful period in Emma's life when she was twice-widowed but exerted enormous influence on her sons Hardicanute and Edward.

Of the many sources that record Emma's activities, none are concerned with her childhood years prior to her marriage to Ethelred in 1002. We cannot be certain even of her birth year, although most scholars believe that she was relatively young when she arrived in England to marry Ethelred. Her parents, Duke Richard I of Normandy (ruled 943–996) and *Gunnor of Denmark, had many children both before and after their marriage. Emma and her brother, Richard II, who succeeded Richard I in 996, were most likely born after their parents' wedding.

Prior to Ethelred's marriage to Emma, English kings typically married English women. This suggests that the betrothal had some diplomatic significance, and it is likely that the union was an attempt to reinforce friendly Norman-English relations initiated in a treaty between Richard I and Ethelred in 991. Further, the *Anglo-Saxon Chronicle* records many serious Viking attacks on England in the 990s, and Ethelred's wedding in 1002, with the sister of the powerful duke of Normandy, may have been an attempt to further induce the Normans to close their ports to raiders.

Emma was Ethelred's second wife. He had been married earlier to ✥▶ **Elfgifu** (c. 963–1002), daughter of earl Ethelbert, and they had at least ten children together. Since all of their sons were viewed by contemporaries as legitimate potential successors to Ethelred, Elfgifu must have died some time prior to 1002; the legitimacy of the children indicates that there was likely a formal marriage (as opposed to concubinage) between Elfgifu and Ethelred.

Soon after her wedding in the spring of 1002, Emma adopted the name "Elfgifu" as her official name; this was used when she witnessed royal documents, although she retained "Emma" or "Imme" in her private life. The main reason for her name change was that Emma's foreign Norman name did not lend itself to the mnemonic device employed by the kings of Ethelred's line to assist the memorization of royal names. Some chronicles use both "Elfgifu" and "Emma" in referring to Ethelred's wife.

Very early in her marriage to Ethelred, Emma was given the title of queen. The title's significance was that it was one indicator of status—and therefore influence—that a queen-mother could use to position her own offspring more advantageously in the line of succession. The custom in which the eldest son inherits the throne (primogeniture) was not yet in practice, so all legitimate sons had a claim to the throne in the early 11th century. Her title of queen would help Emma secure favorable positions for any offspring she might have. Indeed, by 1005 her childbearing career began with the birth of Edward the Confessor. Two other children followed, Alfred and a daughter, *Godgifu.

Both medieval and modern writers have suggested that Emma did not love Ethelred and her children by him. For example, the Worcester version of the *Anglo-Saxon Chronicle* notes for the year of Edward's accession:

> [T]he king was advised to ride from Gloucester, and [with] earl Leofric and earl Godwine and earl Siward and their band came to Winchester and took the Lady unawares, and deprived her of all the treasures which she possessed which were innumer-

---

✥▶ **Elfgifu** (c. 963–1002)

*Queen of the English. Name variations: Aelfgifu or Ælfgifu; Elfled, Elfreda, Elgifu. Born around 963; died in February 1002, in Winchester, England; daughter of Thored, sometimes referred to as Ethelbert, and Hilda; became first wife of Aethelred or Ethelred II the Unready (c. 968–1016), king of the English (r. 979–1013, deposed, 1014–1016), in 985; children: Athelstan or Ethelstan the Atheling (d. 1015); Egbert (d. around 1005); Edmund II Ironside (c. 989–1016), king of the English (r. 1016); Edred (d. around 1012); Eadwig (or Edwy, d. in 1017); Edgar (d. around 1012); *Edith (who m. Edric Streona and Thurkil the Tall); *Elfgifu (c. 997–?, who m. Uchtred, earl of Northumberland); *Wulfhild (who m. Ulfcytel), and two others. Ethelred II's second wife was *Emma of Normandy (c. 985–1052).*

able, because she had been too strict with the King, her son, in that she had done less for him than he wished, both before his accession and afterwards.

However, there is no clear evidence of Emma's private feelings—or lack of them—for her first family; indeed, Ethelred's bestowal of towns, goods, and estates on her throughout their marriage indicate that the union contained some affection. For example, Emma was given Winchester and Exeter, as well as other properties, up to the end of Ethelred's reign.

The Viking threat to Anglo-Saxon England intensified in the time after 1002. By 1013, the situation was so dangerous that Emma fled to her brother's court in Normandy, and Ethelred sent their children soon after to join her. Although none of the sources detail her activities during the period 1013–1017, she perhaps strove to use her position as Duke Richard II's sister to enlist assistance for her husband and sons. However, the powerful forces of the Danish king Sweyn Forkbeard and, after the latter's death in 1013, his son Canute, resulted in a dangerously chaotic atmosphere in England. From 1014 to 1016, Ethelred and Edmund II Ironside, a son by his first marriage, disagreed as to what actions should be taken against Canute's Danes. When Ethelred died on April 23, 1016, his oldest surviving son Edmund Ironside came to the throne. The *Anglo-Saxon Chronicle* records that Edmund reached an agreement with Canute that divided England between them. However, by late 1016, Edmund died, and shortly after, in 1017, Canute was proclaimed king of England.

Emma faced a predicament: her son Edward was far too young to mount an effective campaign against the Danish king of England, and she herself was still in Normandy. Canute's proposal of marriage in the summer of 1017, then, must have seemed not at all preposterous to the widowed queen mother: rather than viewing Canute as her late husband's mortal enemy, she saw him as a vehicle to re-establish her own position as the leading lady of England. Presumably, she could either create a new dynasty with her new husband, or remain in a position to press the claims of her sons by Ethelred. Several contemporary views of her marriage to Canute are provided by the various chroniclers. The *Encomium* puts a favorable face on the marriage:

> In view of her distinguished qualities . . . she was much desired by the king, and especially because she derived her origin from a victorious people, who had appropriated for themselves part of Gaul, in despite of the French and their prince.

Although the encomiast does not dwell on the more practical aspects of such a proposal, it is important to consider that Canute must have been well aware that Emma's sons by Ethelred, Edward and Albert, were potential recipients of assistance from their powerful Norman uncle, Richard II; by marrying the boys' mother, Canute might expect Richard II to withhold such support from his nephews.

Before Emma agreed to marry Canute, however, she insisted on a mutual agreement that their children by previous unions would be set aside in the line of succession in favor of any offspring they might have together. The *Encomium* relates that:

> [S]he refused ever to become the bride of Knútr, unless he would affirm to her by oath, that he would never set up the son of any other wife than herself to rule after him, if it happened that God should give her a son by him. For she had information that the king had had sons by some other woman; so she, wisely providing for her offspring, knew in her wisdom how to make arrangements in advance, which were to be to their advantage.

The "other woman" who had borne sons to Canute was *Elfgifu of Northampton (c. 1000–c. 1040), an English woman who apparently was Canute's concubine rather than wife. Despite the questionable legitimacy of Elfgifu's sons Sweyn and Harald Harefoot, Canute seems to have considered them credible candidates for the throne, even though he agreed to Emma's stipulation that their own children should have precedence.

Emma and Canute were married in July or August of 1017, and within a few years their son Hardicanute was born. The *Encomium* records that they sent away their other children (from their previous unions), "while keeping this one with themselves, inasmuch as he was to be the heir to the kingdom." They had another child, a daughter named *Gunhild, who married the German emperor Henry III in 1036.

By examining the position of Emma's name on official documents, it is possible to speculate on the degree of her influence. For example, the most recent editor of the *Encomium* suggests that the low placement of her name on royal documents early in her marriage to Canute signifies her initial uninfluential status at the court, but the more prominent position of her signature after 1020 reflects her enhanced standing as the mother of Hardicanute, the new heir. Emma's position as queen and queen-mother also allowed her to make many charitable donations to churches throughout England during her second husband's reign.

When Canute unexpectedly died in 1035, Emma faced an extremely challenging situation. Her sons with Ethelred, Edward and Albert, had remained in Normandy since 1017; all of her ambitions for the throne of England were centered on her son with Canute, Hardicanute. Despite his young age, Hardicanute was ruling in Denmark at the time of his father's death. His half-brother, Harald Harefoot, was the only one of Canute's three sons who was present in England at the time of his father's death, since Elfgifu of Northampton had accompanied her elder son Sweyn to Norway, where he was trying to maintain order. Emma immediately claimed England for Hardicanute, but her claim was ineffectual without the actual presence of her son. Hardicanute faced political difficulties in Denmark: he needed to remain there to prevent a Norwegian attack, for the Norwegians under their king Magnus had expelled Elfgifu and Sweyn, and these two took refuge with Hardicanute late in 1035. When Sweyn died at Hardicanute's court shortly thereafter, the field of competition for Canute's kingdoms narrowed: Elfgifu of Northampton's son Harald Harefoot considered himself his father's heir in England; and Hardicanute, unable to join his mother, was forced to rely on Emma's on-the-spot efforts on his behalf.

The Peterborough version of the *Anglo-Saxon Chronicle* records that the English nobles acted quickly to secure stable government in England after Canute's death, and notes that factions soon developed around the two royal candidates. The northern English supported Harald Harefoot as regent for himself and his half-brother, but:

> Godwine and all the most prominent men in Wessex remained in opposition as long as ever they could, but they could put no obstacle in the way. Then it was decided that [Emma], Harthacnut's mother, should reside in Winchester with the housecarles of the king her son, and hold all Wessex in trust for him, and earl Godwine was her most trusted supporter.

The powerful earl Godwine (father of Harald Godwineson, the English king who was defeated by William the Conqueror in 1066) proved to be a treacherous ally to Emma, for the following year, as Harald Harefoot's power steadily grew, Godwine switched his allegiance. Emma in 1036 appealed to her sons in Normandy to come to her assistance. Alfred arrived in England to join his mother in Winchester, but Godwine captured and blinded the young

prince, and Alfred died of his injuries soon afterward. Godwine's betrayal reflects the increasing strength of Harald Harefoot; the latter was the beneficiary of his half-brother Hardicanute's preoccupation with Danish affairs.

When in 1037 the English recognized Harald Harefoot as their king, Emma was driven out of the country and sought refuge in Flanders with her relative, Count Baldwin V. Her exile in Bruges lasted from the late autumn of 1037 until 1040. During this time, according to the *Encomium,* Emma contacted her son Edward in Normandy and invited him to join her at Baldwin V's court. When she suggested that he take action in England, "the son declared that he pitied his mother's misfortunes, but that he was in no way able to help, since the English nobles had sworn no oath to him." The implication was that only Hardicanute had the potential support to unseat Harald Harefoot. By 1039, Hardicanute was able to join Emma in Flanders, and the two planned an invasion of England. But Harald Harefoot's death in March of 1040 eliminated the need for an invasion, and in June of 1040 Hardicanute and Emma landed at Sandwich. Emma and Canute's son was at last recognized as king of England.

The *Encomium,* written during Hardicanute's brief reign of 1040–1042, holds that after his accession to the throne, he sent for his half-brother Edward to join him in ruling England; the encomiast ends his work with the optimistic observation that:

> the mother and both sons, having no disagreement between them, enjoy the ready amenities of the kingdom. Here there *is* loyalty among sharers of rule, here the bond of motherly and brotherly love is of strength indestructible.

The briefness of Hardicanute's reign did not allow for fraternal rivalry; in June of 1042, according to the *Anglo-Saxon Chronicle,* Hardicanute died "as he stood at his drink."

Thus, Emma's son with Ethelred, Edward the Confessor, was chosen king in 1042. Emma's status as queen-mother took a dramatic turn for the worse: months after his coronation in 1043, Edward deprived his mother of her properties and wealth. Although the sources do not clearly specify the reason for Edward's action against his mother, two versions of the *Anglo-Saxon Chronicle* hold that the despoliation occurred "because she had been too tight-fisted with him." In addition, Edward may have resented Emma's previous actions favoring Hardicanute over his and Alfred's interests resulting from Emma's 1017 marital agreement with Canute.

However, Emma and Edward were reconciled shortly afterward, for in 1044 and 1045 she witnessed royal documents. But in 1045, when Edward married *Edith (c. 1025–1075), Godwine's daughter—the same Godwine who had been responsible for the blinding and death of Emma's son Alfred—Emma's influence over Edward ended. Her name does not appear on any other royal documents, and she lived quietly at Winchester until her death on March 6, 1052.

It is rather ironic that Emma, who worked so hard throughout her life to exert her royal influence through her husbands and sons, produced sons who were dynastic dead-ends: Alfred and Hardicanute were unmarried and fairly young when they died, and Edward, who ruled until his death in January of 1066, remained childless despite his marriage to Edith. Emma's 50-year career as queen and queen-mother produced, in the long run, a Norman conqueror on the throne.

SOURCES:

Campbell, Alistair, ed. *Encomium Emmae Reginae.* London: Offices of the Royal Historical Society, 1949.

Garmonsway, G.N., trans. *The Anglo-Saxon Chronicle.* NY: Dutton, 1965.

SUGGESTED READING:

Andersson, Theodore M. "The Viking Policy of Ethelred the Unready," in *Anglo-Scandinavian England: Norse-English Relations in the Period Before the Conquest.* Edited by John D. Niles and Mark Amodio. NY: University Press of America, 1989, pp. 1–11.

Barlow, Frank. *Edward the Confessor.* Berkeley, CA: University of California Press, 1970.

Blair, Peter Hunter. *An Introduction to Anglo-Saxon England.* 2nd ed. Cambridge: Cambridge University Press, 1977.

Brown, R. Allen. *The Normans and the Norman Conquest.* 2nd ed. NY: The Boydell Press, 1969.

Campbell, Miles W. "Queen Emma and Ælfgifu of Northampton: Canute the Great's Women," in *Medieval Scandinavia.* Vol. 4, 1971, pp. 66–79.

Jones, Gwyn. *A History of the Vikings.* London: Oxford University Press, 1973.

Larson, Laurence M. *Canute the Great and the Rise of Danish Imperialism during the Viking Age.* NY: Putnam, 1912 (rep. ed. NY: AMS Press, 1970).

Stribling, Susan Teresa. *An Evaluation of Emma, Lady of England (1002–1052).* MA thesis, American University, 1983.

Cathy Jorgensen Itnyre,
Professor of History, Copper Mountain College
(College of the Desert), Joshua Tree, California

Emma of Paris (d. 968)

Duchess of Normandy. Died on March 19, 968; daughter of Hedwig (c. 915–965), and Hugh the Great also known as Hugh the White (c. 895–956), count of Paris and duke of Burgundy; sister of Hugh Capet (939–996), duke of France (r. 956–996), king of France (r. 987–996), first of the Capetian kings, who

*married *Adelaide of Poitou (c. 950–c. 1004); married Richard I the Fearless (d. 996), duke of Normandy (r. 942–996). Richard the Fearless' second wife was *Gunnor of Denmark (d. 1031), mother of *Emma of Normandy (c. 985–1052).*

Emma of Waldeck (1858–1934), queen of the Netherlands.

See Wilhelmina for sidebar.

Emma of Werden (d. around 1050)

Saint. Died around 1050; daughter of Adela and an unknown father; sister of Meinwerk, bishop of Paderborn; married Count Ludger (d. around 1010); children: son, Imad (also bishop of Paderborn).

Emma of Werden is reported to have been temperamental and violent in her early years. She was descended from Widukind, whose defeat and subsequent baptism were celebrated by the order of Pope Hadrian I (r. 772–795). After her husband Count Ludger died around 1010, Emma spent the next 40 years doing good works. She used her enormous fortune to improve the lives of the poor and to construct churches in the diocese of Bremen. She died around 1050. When her tomb was opened in later years, Emma's body was found to be reduced to dust except for her right hand which was intact. It was taken to the church of the abbey of St. Ludger at Werden to be kept there. Her feast day is April 19.

Emme.

Variant of Emma.

Emmelia of Cappadocia (fl. 300s)

*Christian woman. Married Basil (a distinguished lawyer and professor of rhetoric in Cappadocia); children: ten, including *Macrina (327–379); Peter (bishop of Sebaste); Basil the Great (329–379), bishop of Caesarea (whose authority extended over 11 provinces of Asia Minor); Gregory of Nyssa (335–387, one of the fathers of the Eastern Church); Naucratius (who died young).*

Emmerich, Anna Katharina (1774–1824)

German Augustinian nun and mystic. Name variations: Emmerick. Born in Westphalia in 1774; died in 1824.

Following an extremely pious youth, Anna Katharina Emmerich became celebrated for her visions of the Passion of Christ, for her revelations, and for bearing the stigmata (the wounds of Christ). When the poet Clemens Brentano came to the monastery of Dülmen to record her visions in 1818, she declared that his coming was a fulfillment of the will of God as it had been revealed to her in a vision. The following year, her gifts were investigated by an episcopal commission as well as by a commission appointed by the government, and they were attested as genuine. Her life and supernatural experiences were subsequently described in a biography by Brentano (Munich, 1852) and in another by Abbé Cazales (Paris, 1870).

Emmett, Dorothy Mary (b. 1904)

British philosopher. Born September 29, 1904; Oxford University, Lady Margaret Hall, B.A., 1927, M.A. 1931; Radcliffe College, M.A., 1930.

Lecturer in Philosophy, University of Durham, King's College (1931–38); Lecturer in Philosophy of Religion, University of Manchester (1938–45); Sir Samuel Hall Professor of Philosophy, University of Manchester (1946–66). Honorary D.Litt., University of Glasgow; Honorary D.Litt., University of Leicester; Professor Emeritus, University of Glasgow, 1966—; lived in Cambridge, England.

Selected works: Whitehead's Philosophy of Organism *(1932);* Philosophy and Faith *(1936);* The Nature of Metaphysical Thinking *(1945);* Alfred North Whitehead, 1861–1947 *(1949);* Presuppositions and Finite Truths *(1949);* Function, Purpose and Powers: Some Concepts in the Study of Individuals and Societies *(1958);* Sociological Theory and Philosophical Analysis *(1970);* The Moral Prism *(1979);* The Effectiveness of Causes *(1984).*

After studying philosophy at Oxford University and Radcliffe College, Dorothy Emmett was hired as a lecturer at the University of Durham. During her time there (1931 to 1938), she published her first two books in which Emmett's study with the eminent philosopher Alfred North Whitehead was reflected. In *Whitehead's Philosophy of Organism,* published in 1932, she sides with Whitehead against philosophers who argue the pointlessness of metaphysical speculation (reflection on the nature of reality), such as Ludwig Wittgenstein. Her second book, *Philosophy and Faith* (1936), concerns philosophy of religion, the subject for which Whitehead is best known.

From 1931 to 1945, Emmett was at the University of Manchester, initially as a lecturer, then as Sir Samuel Hall Professor of Philosophy. The rest of her career was spent at the University of Glasgow, where she became professor emeritus and published many books and papers in philosophical journals. Although Emmett's interest in metaphysics and religion continued, she became more interested in ethics as her career progressed.

SOURCES:

Kersey, Ethel M. *Women Philosophers: a Bio-critical Source Book*. NY: Greenwood Press, 1989.

Catherine Hundleby, M.A.
Philosophy, University of Guelph

Emmons, Chansonetta Stanley
(1858–1937)

American photographer and painter. Born Chansonetta Stanley in Kingfield, Maine, on December 30, 1858; died in Newton, Massachusetts, on March 18, 1937; one of eight children and only daughter of Liberty Solomon (a farmer and teacher) and Apphia (French) Stanley; sister of twins F.E. and F.O. Stanley, who created the Stanley Steamer automobile and the Stanley photographic dry plate; attended District No. I School, Kingfield, Maine; attended Western State Normal School, Farmington, Maine; studied painting with J.J. Enneking, William Preston Phelps, and J.G. Brown; married James Nathaniel Whitman Emmons (a businessman), on February 2, 1887; children: Dorothy Emmons (1891–1960, also a painter and photographer).

Modestly recognized during her time and nearly forgotten by the close of the 20th century, Chansonetta Stanley Emmons was one of the few people in the first 30 years of the century to photograph the "domestic vernacular," especially in northern New England. Beginning in the 1890s in her native village of Kingfield, Maine, she photographed the farmyards, barns, gristmills, kitchens, and parlors of her neighbors and friends, thus preserving for posterity the haunting images of a seemingly innocent and long-forgotten world. She also lugged her cumbersome box-type camera into the countrysides of Massachusetts, New Hampshire, and Vermont and took some of her most forceful pictures during two trips to the South. In his book on Emmons, Marius Péladeau writes: "Not since the great genre artists of 19th-century America has the rural scene been so accurately and sympathetically preserved."

Emmons, the only girl in a family of seven boys, developed an early interest in art. She entered Western State Normal School intending to become an instructor and left wanting to become an artist. After teaching drawing and sketching in the New Portland and Kingfield schools, she later joined her brother F.E. Stanley in the more metropolitan area of Lewiston, where Emmons first became interested in photography. F.E. was a photographer and crayon artist who was working with his twin brother F.O. to perfect what would later become the successful dry-plate photographic process. (The brothers would also produce the Stanley Steamer automobile and become millionaires.) Around 1885, Chansonetta moved to Boston where she taught art and used her income to finance her own painting lessons. There, she met and married James Emmons, a businessman, and settled into life as a housewife and mother. The marriage was apparently a happy one, although James' borderline business skills kept the family constantly on the move. In 1895, F.O., thinking his sister needed more stability in her life, bought the couple a house in the New Dorchester section of Boston. Among Emmons' early

photographs are 45 prints in a family album documenting the years between 1897 and 1899, and including pictures of home life in Dorchester. After the sudden death of her husband in 1898, she began to work more steadily at photography and continued to paint. Neither endeavor, however, brought in enough income to support her and her daughter **Dorothy Emmons**. Throughout the remainder of Emmons' life, her brother F.O. provided for her larger expenses.

After giving up her Dorchester home for a more modest duplex in Newton, Massachusetts, Emmons returned to Kingfield, Maine, to recover from her husband's death. She began a series of penetrating and incisive portrait photographs of relatives and old family friends, who considered her a bit odd and "citified" but were honored to pose for her nonetheless. A side excursion to New Hampshire in 1900 to take lessons in oil painting from the popular genre and landscape artist William Preston Phelps produced some of her most engaging photographs of children. By 1901, Emmons' work had reached professional quality,

Photo by Chansonetta Emmons.

and she had amassed a large enough body of prints to begin exhibiting her work.

Accompanied by her daughter Dorothy, Emmons continued to spend most of her summers in Kingfield, although she also made occasional excursions in other directions. Her trips to the Carolinas in 1897 and 1926 produced a variety of sensitive photographs portraying the beauty of the land as well as the dignity and poverty of many rural blacks and whites of the region. Péladeau theorizes that Emmons may have been fascinated by the area because it was so far removed from her own life: "It was as if old stereotypes of the South, which Chansonetta had been taught as a child—of a land of magnolia blossoms and ladies in hoop skirts—were immediately shattered and replaced by a harsh reality, with the result that Mrs. Emmons felt she had to go about feverishly photographing the South which she had discovered was not the one of her dreams."

From 1904 until her death, Emmons used a 5x7-inch Century camera and developed, printed, and matted all her photographs herself. For her interior shots, she relied only on a natural light source which she employed to create form and space. She never had an official darkroom and used the kitchen in Newton or an empty room or closet when she stayed on the road. The Kingfield residents remembered her as a perfectionist in everything, from the meticulous manner of her dress to the posing and composition of her photographs. One subject who modeled for her as a child remembered the endless hours spent in posing for her photographs and the countless exposures of the same scene with minute variations.

After Emmons' daughter Dorothy graduated from Wellesley, she became her mother's companion and chauffeur, almost a necessity due to Emmons' increasing deafness. Emmons never cultivated a wide circle of friends outside of those in Kingfield and Newton, and she limited her professional affiliations to the Guild of Photographers of the Society of Arts and Crafts in Boston and the American Artists' Professional League. She exhibited with the Guild for many years in the 1920s, including at the large Tricentennial Exhibit at the Museum of Fine Arts in 1927. In 1913, her South Carolina photographs were shown at the South Carolina Art Association in Charleston and at Wellesley College's Farnsworth Museum of Art.

To augment her income in the mid-1920s, Emmons had her best photographs made into glass-lantern slides, and she presented slide shows to women's groups and other social and civic organizations throughout eastern Massachusetts and the Franklin County area of Maine. All of the 103 lantern slides that comprised the show were hand-tinted by her daughter, who also narrated the presentation.

Emmons remained active through her later years, making money painting miniatures on ivory and experimenting with wood-block engraving. Her daughter's illness and long recuperation in 1935, however, sapped Emmons' strength, and a trip to Kingfield in 1936 was her last. In early March 1937, at age 79, she suffered a heart attack from which she never recovered. Chansonetta Emmons died in her sleep on March 18. After a private funeral, she was buried at Riverside Cemetery, overlooking the Carrabasset River, in Kingfield.

SOURCES:

"The Face of Maine," in *American Heritage.* Vol. XIII, no. 2. February 1962, p. 45.

Péladeau, Marius B. *Chansonetta: The Life and Photographs of Chansonetta Stanley Emmons, 1858–1937.* Waldoboro, ME: Maine Antique Digest, 1977.

Barbara Morgan,
Melrose, Massachusetts

Emnilde (fl. 986)

Third wife of Boleslaw I the Brave. Name variations: Heminilde von Meissen. Flourished around 986; daughter of Rigdag, margrave of Meissen; became third wife of Boleslav Chrobry also known as Boleslaw I the Brave (c. 967–1025), duke of Bohemia (r. 1003–1004), king of Poland (r. 992–1025), in 986 (divorced).

Ena (1887–1969)

*Queen of Spain. Name variations: Victoria Eugenie of Battenberg; Victoria Eugenia; Victoria of Battenberg. Born Victoria Eugenia Julia Ena on October 24, 1887, at Balmoral Castle, Grampian, Scotland; died on April 15, 1969, in Lausanne, Switzerland; daughter of Prince Henry Maurice of Battenberg and Princess Beatrice of England (1857–1944, daughter of Queen Victoria); married Alphonso XIII (1886–1941), king of Spain (r. 1886–1931), in May 1906; children: Alfonso or Alphonso (1907–1938, whose hemophilia forced his abdication and resulted in his death in a motor accident); Jaime, duke of Segovia (1908–1933); *Beatriz of Spain (b. 1909); son (1910–1910); *Maria Cristina (1911–1996); John Bourbon (b. 1913), count of Barcelona (father of Juan Carlos I, king of Spain);*

Gonzalo (1914–1934, who also suffered from hemophilia and also died as the result of a motor accident).

There was a bomb threat in May 1906 when Princess Ena, granddaughter of Queen *Victoria, prepared to marry King Alphonso XIII of Spain. Even so, the marriage took place in Madrid as scheduled. But as the wedding procession wound through the streets on the way to the palace following the service, an anarchist tossed an explosive from above onto the street. Twenty people were killed, 60 wounded. The newlyweds were littered with broken glass, while Ena's gown was covered in the blood of the entourage's horses and footmen.

The devastating public tragedy was a portent of private tragedies to come. Two of Princess Ena's sons were born with hemophilia, a disease that had been passed on by their maternal grandmother, Princess *Beatrice of England. Another of Ena's sons was seriously deaf and a fourth was stillborn. (Another famous granddaughter of Victoria, *Alexandra Feodorovna, the Empress of Russia, passed on the disease of hemophilia to her son.) Both Alexandra and Ena shared another fate: dethronement by insurrection. In Spain, a republican revolution drove Ena and Alphonso out of the country into a life of exile, and the couple eventually separated. Ena died in 1969.

Ender, Kornelia (1958—)

East German swimmer. Born on October 25, 1958, in what was then the German Democratic Republic of East Germany; married Roland Matthes (a swimmer), in 1988 (divorced); remarried; children: (first marriage) one daughter; (second marriage) one daughter.

Selected championships and honors—individual: silver medal in the 200-meter medley in Olympics (1972); silver medal in the 200-meter individual medley, World championships (1973); gold medals in the 100-meter freestyle, World championships (1963 and 1976); silver medal, 200-meter freestyle, World championships (1975); gold medals in the 100-meter butterfly, World championships (1973 and 1975); gold medals in the 100-meter freestyle, 200-meter freestyle, and 100-meter butterfly, Olympic Games (1976); gold medal in the 100-meter butterfly in the Olympic Games (1976); named World Swimmer of the Year (1973, 1975, and 1976).

Selected championships and honors—team: silver medals in the 4x100 freestyle relay and 4x100-meter medley relay in Olympics (1972); gold medal in 4x100-meter medley relay and silver in the 4x100-

meter freestyle relay in Olympics (1976); World championships in the 4x100-meter medley relay (1973 and 1975); World championships in the 4x100-meter freestyle relay (1973 and 1975); inducted into International Swimming Hall of Fame (1981).

The first woman to win four gold medals at a single Olympics, Kornelia Ender was a member of the East German swimming team that dominated the 1976 Olympics in Montreal, taking gold medals in 11 out of 13 events and shattering eight world records. The success of the East German swimmers, however, was clouded with charges of drug use among some of the athletes. Particularly outspoken in her accusations was *Shirley Babashoff, who was Ender's most daunting challenger. Babashoff was branded as a poor sport at the time, although with the fall of the Berlin Wall in 1991, 20 former East German coaches admitted that they had given steroids to selected athletes as a matter of government policy. Ender was never implicated in connection with steroid use and denies having ever used performance-enhancing drugs. "I don't think I was the type who needed something," she told a reporter for *Sports Illustrated*. "I didn't lift weights much. I was agile, naturally strong. I did drills. I had a naturally perfect freestyle stroke. I was used as an example to others."

The daughter of an army officer and a nurse, Ender was a robust child who was an outstanding swimmer by the age of six. Her talent was such that age 11 she left home to enter the Chemie Club training center in Halle. There, in a program that controlled her activities around the clock, she was rigorously trained under the supervision of a coach and a team physician, swimming six or seven miles a day. "After every workout I got a 'cocktail' with vitamins," Ender recalled, although she was quick to add that no one ever mentioned drugs. "Sports officials never talked to us about anything. . . . I wish I could ask Coach Langheim, but he died of cancer in 1982."

At the 1972 Olympic games, Ender, then 13, anchored two silver medal-swimming relay teams and placed second in the 200-meter medley. In the four years that followed she became so proficient in the butterfly and freestyle sprints that she was virtually unbeatable. She was World Swimmer of the Year in 1973 and 1975, winning four gold medals in both World championships. A *Sports Illustrated* reporter once described her as "propelling herself into the water with such authority as to give the impression that she was pulling the pool toward her."

At the 1976 Olympics in Montreal, the 5'8", 155-pound swimmer played a crucial role in East Germany's success, winning the 100-meter and 200-meter freestyle sprints, the 100-meter butterfly, and anchoring the 400-meter medley relay team that took the gold. She not only broke a world record in each event but swam two of the individual events—the 100-meter butterfly and the 200-meter freestyle—back-to-back, substituting for **Barbara Krause** in the freestyle. *Time* magazine described her as exploding out of the starting block with such force that she picked up a three-foot lead before she even started to swim. "She dives shallow and planes high like a speedboat, with much of her body out of the water. Her motion is so efficient—though not stylish—that she is able to set world records while taking substantially fewer strokes per minute than the women she leaves in her wake." In addition to her four golds, Ender also took home a fifth medal—a silver—in the 4x100-meter freestyle relay. Thus, she and Babashoff share the distinction of being the only women to win five medals in swimming in a single Olympic Games.

Against the wishes of her coaches, Ender retired from swimming after the 1976 Olympics, a decision that ended her chance for a hero's life in East Germany. Her marriage to fellow swimmer Roland Matthes, with whom she had a child, ended in divorce, and plans to become a doctor were dashed when a medical school professor did not promote her. In 1984, Ender married once more and had a second daughter, after which she and her second husband tried unsuccessfully to apply for an emigration visa. Finally, in 1989, she and her family were able to settle in West Germany, where she currently practices physiotherapy.

SOURCES:
"The Games: Up in the Air," in *Time*. August 2, 1976.
Grace & Glory: A Century of Women in the Olympics. Chicago, IL: Triumph Books, 1996.
Johnson, Anne Janette. *Great Women in Sports.* Detroit, MI: Visible Ink Press, 1998.
Markel, Robert, ed. *The Women's Sports Encyclopedia.* NY: Henry Holt, 1997.
Whitten, Phillip. "The Glory that Never Was," in *Swimming World and Junior Swimmer.* Vol. 37, issue 7. July 1996, p. 37.
————. "The Way Things Should Have Been," in *Swimming World and Junior Swimmer.* Vol. 38, issue 8. August 1997, p 13.

Barbara Morgan,
Melrose, Massachusetts

Engeberge.

See Engelberga.

❧▶
See photograph of Kornelia Ender on following page

Opposite page

Ena

Kornelia
Ender

Engel-Kramer, Ingrid (1943—)

East German diver. Name variations: Ingrid Kramer. Born on July 29, 1943.

In 1960, Ingrid Engel-Kramer won two gold medals in the Rome Olympics for platform and springboard diving. In 1964, she repeated her triumph in springboard while winning a silver in platform diving.

Engelberga (c. 840–890)

*Holy Roman empress. Name variations: Angelberga; Engelbertha; Engeberge; Ingelberg. Born around 840 in Germany; died around 890 at convent of Placenza, Italy; married Louis II le Jeune also known as Louis II the Child (c. 822–875), king of Italy (r. 844), king of Lorraine (r. 872–875), Holy Roman emperor (r. 855–875); children: *Ermengarde of Provence; Gisela.*

Daughter of a Frankish noble, Engelberga married Emperor Louis II the Child in her teens and was one of the first medieval queen-consorts to co-rule openly with her husband. Administrative documents bore both their names, as did coins minted during their reign. Engelberga proved to be a capable leader of armies as well as an effective administrator. She and Louis led troops into battle together in central and southern Italy, and he also appointed her regent in northern Italy. However, Engelberga apparently overstepped her bounds and alienated many Italians with her aggressive policies. She and Louis divorced around 872. Though he remarried, his second union was less successful than his first, and Engelberga was reinstated as empress a few years before Louis' death in 875. His successor, Charles III the Fat, feared Engelberga's continuing political influence over the Italians and had her banished to Switzerland where she remained for some years. But by 888 Engelberga was in Italy again, this time interested in more pious activities than war and governing. In her days as empress, she had founded a monastery at Placenza, and it was to this convent she retired to live out the last few years of her life.

Laura York,
Riverside, California

Engelberga of Aquitaine (877–917)

*Duchess of Aquitaine. Born in 877; died in 917; daughter of *Ermengarde of Provence and Boso, king of Provence (r. 879–887); married William I the Pious, duke of Aquitaine.*

Engelbretsdatter, Dorothe
(1634–1716)

Norwegian poet, known as the first great female writer of hymns in Denmark-Norway. Name variations: Dorothe Engelbrechtsdatter. Born in Bergen, Norway, on June 16, 1634; died in Bergen on February 19, 1716; daughter of Engelbrecht Jörgensen (originally rector of the high school in that city and afterwards dean of the cathedral); apparently received no education other than that supplied by her father; married Ambrosius Hardenbeck or Hardenbech (a theological writer famous for his flowery funeral sermons who succeeded her father at the cathedral in 1659), in 1652 (died 1683); children: five sons and four daughters.

Dorothe Engelbretsdatter was born into a pious and highly educated family of Bergen, Norway. Her father was Engelbrecht Jorgensen, a professor of theology, and Dorothe received an excellent education, strong in theology. (The name she is known by means "daughter of Engelbrecht.") As a young girl, she spent the years 1647 to 1650 in Copenhagen, capital of the Dano-Norwegian kingdom. At 18, however, she was back in Norway and married Ambrosius Hardenbeck, another professor of theology, who took over her father's vicarage at the cathedral of Bergen. They lived together for 31 years in an apparently harmonious marriage, and had nine children, seven of whom died early. Dorothe's grief at her children's deaths was one source of inspiration for her early writings, which she published in Copenhagen as *Själens Sangoffer* (*The Soul's Song Offering*) in 1678. It is a collection of morning and evening prayers as well as hymns to be sung on special days and holidays. The underlying question of these pieces is how a man's—or a woman's—soul may prepare for its encounter with God. Her books sold well, especially *Själens Sangoffer* which over the years has been published in 30 editions. She thus established herself as a full-time professional writer in an era when such was an unusual occupation for men as well as women.

In addition to religious works, Dorothe Engelbretsdatter's poetry includes occasional, sometimes satirical, verses of a secular nature. Written in simple language and metaphors borrowed from everyday life, her poems are indigenous to the religious and local traditions of the day. Her hymns and prayers were composed in the context of 30 years of war, plague, fires, and famine—disasters beyond human control—and the strong element of penance in her poetry is underscored by a voice of sincerity, intensity, and eroticism.

The writer of these hymns was a controversial figure in her day. Male students especially refused to believe she had written them herself, alleging that her minister husband Ambrosious Hardenbeck was the real author. Dorothe defended herself, arguing: "God wills the birds to sing because that is the way He had created them. Likewise, women are a part of God's nature and to be included in God's culture."

After her husband's death in 1683, she became more lonely and financially straitened, so to give vent to her grief and to supplement her meager widow's pension, she wrote a second volume of hymns, published in 1685 as *Taare Offer* (*Offering of Tears*) and dedicated to Queen *Charlotte Amalia of Hesse. This work portrays the sinful woman along the lines of *Mary Magdalene who through repentance and service works her way to a meeting with the divine for her subsequent salvation. Engelbretsdatter traveled to Copenhagen to initiate publication of her husband's funeral oration and *Taare Offer,* the latter of which was published in 1685. Her journey prompted rumors of romantic liaisons which infuriated the virtuous hymn writer and occasioned several satires from her hand. Self-assured and well aware of the status and position granted her by the learned societies of both Norway and Denmark, she managed to acquire the rights to decide who would publish her writings, a significant privilege after she had suffered the humiliation of seeing her work printed incorrectly and carelessly for the sake of "insatiable people's worldly profit." Henceforth a fee was levied against pirated versions, which caused a drastic reduction in their circulation.

During her stay in Copenhagen in 1684–85, Engelbretsdatter also obtained exemption from taxation, granted by the king of Denmark. The "poet's stipend," as it might be called, enabled her to continue her life as minister's widow and writer without having to remarry for financial reasons. She lived a quiet and relatively uneventful life at least until 1692 when the great fire in Bergen robbed her of her house and possessions. She made a second appeal to the king for help but did not live under her own roof again until 1712.

Popular during the 1600s, her poetry came under attack during the following two centuries. Critics alleged that her poems lacked originality and that her success was owed to her male admirers being more interested in her sex than her output. Her use of irony was considered vulgar, her satire coarse. Her poems showed too much emotion. She used too many words; she was too "mystical," too severe, too sincere, and too womanly.

Norwegians still sing her hymns, however, and to her undiminished credit she was among the first to demonstrate publicly that use of the pen as a tool is no male prerogative. Nor has anyone disputed her claim to be "the first she-poet in the Dano-Norwegian kingdom." Dorothe Engelbretsdatter died on February 19, 1716, confident in God and with expectations of being reunited with her family in the hereafter.

SOURCES:
Danske kvindelige forfattere. Edited by Stig Dalager and Anne-Marie Mai. Copenhagen: Gyldendal, 1981.
Nordisk kvindelitteraturhistorie. Edited by Elisabeth Moller Jensen. Copenhagen: Rosinante/ Munksgaard, 1993.

Inga Wiehl,
Yakima Valley Community College, Yakima, Washington

England, queen of.

English, queen of the.

Engracia.

Variant of Grace.

Enheduanna (fl. 2300 BCE)

Sumerian poet. Born around 2300 BCE; daughter of King Sargon I of Agade (2334–2279 BCE); became a high priestess of the moon goddess Inanna, in whose honor she wrote The Exaltation of Inanna.

Enheduanna, the daughter of King Sargon I of Agade (the world's first empire, extending from the Mediterranean to Persia), was a high priestess of the moon goddess Inanna, for whom she wrote her famous *The Exhaltation of Inanna.* Enheduanna is the first writer in history whose name and work have been preserved. Over 40 poems, recorded on cuneiform tablets, have survived the ages. In her verses to Inanna, she addresses the moon goddess as a friend who has descended to the earth to help her in her need. The poems have been likened to *Sappho's poems to Aphrodite in their sensuality and intimacy. Enheduanna was revered for generations and her religious poems influenced many later writers.

SUGGESTED READING:

Gioiseffi, Daniela, ed. *Women on War: Essential Voices for the Nuclear Age.* NY: Touchstone Books/Simon & Schuster, 1988.

Enke, Karin (b. 1961).

See Kania-Enke, Karin.

Enright, Elizabeth (1909–1968)

American writer for young people. Born on September 17, 1909, in Oak Park, Illinois; died on June 8, 1968; daughter of Walter J. Enright (a political cartoonist) and **Maginel Wright***; studied at Edgewood School, Greenwich, Connecticut, at Art Students League of New York, 1927-28, in Paris, 1928, and at Parsons School of Design; married Robert Marty Gillham (an advertising man and television executive), on April 24, 1930; children: Nicholas Wright; Robert II; Oliver.*

Began as magazine illustrator but started writing the stories to accompany her drawings and eventually stopped illustrating; was author of books for children and of short stories for adults, appearing in The New Yorker *and other national magazines and published as collections; was lecturer in creative writing at Barnard College (1960–62), and at writing seminars at Indiana University, University of Connecticut, and University of Utah.*

Awards, honors: John Newbery Medal of American Library Association, 1939, for Thimble Summer; *New York Herald Tribune* Children's Spring Book Festival Award (1957), *runner-up for Newbery Award (1958), both for* Gone-Away Lake; *named by American Library Association as U.S. nominee for International Hans Christian Andersen Award (1963), for outstanding literary quality of complete works;* Tatsinda *was an Honor Book in* New York Herald Tribune Children's Spring Book Festival, *1963; LL.D., Nasson College, 1966.*

Elizabeth
Enright

Selected writings—juvenile: Kintu: A Cargo Adventure *(Farrar, 1935);* Thimble Summer *(Farrar, 1938);* The Sea Is All Around *(Farrar, 1940);* The Saturdays *(Farrar, 1941);* The Four-Story Mistake *(Farrar, 1942);* Then There Were Five *(Farrar, 1944);* The Melendy Family *(Rinehart, 1947);* Christmas Tree for Lydia *(Rinehart, 1951);* Spiderweb for Two: A Melendy Maze *(Rinehart, 1951);* Gone-Away Lake *(Harcourt, 1957);* Return to Gone-Away *(Harcourt, 1961);* Tatsinda *(Harcourt 1963);* Zee *(Harcourt 1965).*

Selected writings—adult: Borrowed Summer and Other Stories *(Rinehart, 1946);* The Moment Before the Rain *(Harcourt, 1955);* The Riddle of the Fly and Other Stories *(Harcourt, 1959);* Doublefields: Memories and Stories *(autobiographical sketches, short stories, and one novella, Harcourt, 1966).*

Bulk of short stories first published in The New Yorker, *but others appeared in* Ladies' Home Journal, Cosmopolitan, Mademoiselle, Redbook, Yale Review, Harper's, McCall's, *and* Saturday Evening Post. *Her stories were included in* Prize Stories: The O. Henry Awards *(1946, 1949, 1951, 1955, 1958, 1960) and* Best American Short Stories *(1950, 1952, 1954). Contributed reviews of children's books to* The New York Times.

Elizabeth Enright, author and illustrator of fiction for children, critic, and short-story writer for adults, was recognized as an outstanding contributor to the genres of realistic fiction and fantasy for children.

Although born in Illinois, she grew up in New York City, where from an early age she was surrounded by artists. Her parents were magazine illustrator *Maginel Wright and political cartoonist Walter J. Enright. Enright studied at the Art Students League in New York from 1927 to 1928 and in Paris during 1928. She began her career as a magazine illustrator until she illustrated Marian King's book *Kees* in 1930. In 1935, she wrote and illustrated her first book *Kintu: A Congo Adventure.*

Enright was successful in creating imaginative and realistic works. "Things come back and we know them again and use them," she wrote, "and if we use them well the book seems real because in essence, if not in fact, what happens in the book has roots in what was real." Episodes, characters and locales from Enright's own childhood as well as her son's recur in her children's books. Her characters have inquiring minds and come from families where relationships are based on love and mutual support. Although her work is not devoid of the pain and conflicts of childhood, Enright stresses the joys in life. "What I think to be the means of creating believable characters in a believable story [is]: first our own experience remembered; then the observation of children themselves and respect for their vision of life, still not smudged or overlaid with the dust of repetition. Then the inward view: the deeper remembering."

In her work, Enright dealt with realism and fantasy with striking success. Critics praised her books for having "been lifted above the superficial, the ephemeral—in which one hangs on from page to page simply to find out what happens next."

Although she included elements of fantasy in her earlier fiction, Enright did not complete a book in this genre until the end of her career. Her last two works, *Tatsinda* and *Zee*, are successful combinations of fairytale tradition and original invention.

Enright, Maginel Wright (1881–1916).

See Wright, Maginel.

Entenmann, Martha (1906–1996)

American entrepreneur who ran one of the nation's largest bakeries. Born Martha Schneider in Hoboken, New Jersey, in 1906; died on September 29, 1996, in West Islip, New York; married William Entenmann, Jr., in 1925 (died 1951); children: Robert, Charles, and William.

When 19-year-old Martha Schneider signed on as a saleswoman for Entenmann's (founded in

1898) in Bay Shore, Long Island, the small bakery was managed by William Entenmann, Jr., son of the founder. She married William in 1925. Martha took an active part in managing the home-delivery of donuts, rolls, cakes, cookies, and bread in white boxes with a blue-scripted label; she kept the books and ran the office. Following her husband's death in 1951, she and her three sons continued running the 14-acre Bay Shore plant. In 1976, the firm ended home delivery and went public, expanding their sales reach from Long Island to a large section of the East Coast, including Miami, New York, and Chicago. Stock certificates bore her likeness. For more than 50 years, Martha Entenmann, known as Mrs. E to hundreds of employees, ran the prosperous bakery with her sons. In 1978, the bakery was sold to Warner-Lambert for $233 million.

Enters, Angna (1907–1989)

American dancer, painter, and author who was the foremost mime of her day. Born in New York City on April 28, 1907; died in Tenafly, New Jersey, on February 25, 1989; grew up in Milwaukee, Wisconsin; daughter of Edward and Henriette (Gasseur-Styleau) Enters; art study, she wrote, consisted of "an intermittent elementary school course, some work (chiefly swimming) during an adolescent summer month in a camp, and one unfinished evening semester at the New York Art Students League" under John Sloan.

After touring with Japanese dancer Michio Itow, Angna Enters borrowed money to rent the Greenwich Village theater, sent out handbills, chose costumes from her own closet, and made her New York City debut in a solo mime recital in 1926; the theater soon became known as the Theater of Angna Enters, in which she portrayed over 300 characters. She followed this with appearances in London and Paris and a European tour. Because Enters created novel combinations of dance, pantomime, and music, presented with original scenic and lighting effects, the critics did not know how to cast her. Louis Untermeyer wrote in *The Nation* (December 5, 1928), that she was a "dancer who does not dance; an actress who does not speak; a dramatist who makes the audience supply the drama." He then went on to rave of her work.

In *The Queen of Heaven*, for example, she would sit in a stained-glass window, wearing a richly brocaded, vestment-like robe, holding a red heart that was clearly intended to represent the Christ child, all the while moving gracefully from one pose to another, recreating the various

Angna
Enters

depictions of the Madonna and Child as found in medieval art. In another skit, at the opposite end of the thematic spectrum, she humorously portrayed a Parisian prostitute eyeing potential customers from her seat at a sidewalk cafe, every gesture and glance perfectly on target.

After 1933, Enters began to exhibit over 1,000 of her paintings in American galleries and gave individual exhibitions in 71 leading American and European museums and galleries; she was awarded two Guggenheim fellowships. Some of her paintings are in the Metropolitan Museum of Art, New York City. She wrote many books, often self-illustrated. Among her works are the volumes of personal reminiscences *First Person Plural* (1937) and *Silly Girl* (1944), the play *Love Possessed Juana* (1939), the screenplays *Lost Angel* (1944) and *Tenth Avenue Angel* (1948), and nearly 150 dance compositions set to her own music. Her story "Mama's Angel" was filmed by MGM as *Lost Angel* with *Margaret O'Brien in the lead. In the 1960s, Enters served artistic residencies at the Dallas Theater Center and Baylor University.

SOURCES:
Current Biography. NY: H.W. Wilson, 1940 and 1952.

SUGGESTED READING:
Enters, Angna. *Silly Girl.* NY: Houghton, 1944.

Entragues, Catherine Henriette de Balzac d' (1579–1633).

See Medici, Marie de for sidebar on Henriette d'Entragues.

Épinay, Louise-Florence-Pétronille, Madame la Live d'

(1726–1783)

French literary and social figure, friend of Voltaire, Rousseau, and Diderot, who wrote on education and an autobiographical novel depicting life in the upper classes during the Enlightenment. Name variations: Madame d'Epinay; Louise d'Épinay. Pronunciation: LOO-ees flo-RONS pay-tro-NEEL tar-DEEUR DESS-cla-VELL, mah-DAHM la LEEV DAY-pee-nay. Born Louise-Florence-Pétronille Tardieu d'Esclavelles on March 11, 1726, in Valenciennes (Nord); died in Paris of nephritis and influenza on April 15, 1783; buried in the family tomb at the church in Épinay; daughter of Louis-Gabriel Tardieu, Baron d'Esclavelles (1665–1736, an army officer) and Florence-Angélique Prouveur de Preux (1696–1762); educated at home and in Paris at a convent school, 1737–39; sister-in-law and cousin of Sophie d'Houdetot (1730–1813); married Denis-Joseph La Live (Lalive) de Bellegarde, later d'Épinay (1724–1782), on December 24, 1745; children: (with husband) a son, Louis-Joseph (1746–1807) and a daughter, Suzanne-Françoise-Thérèse (1747–1748); (with Claude-Louis Dupin de Francueil) a daughter, Angélique-Louise-Charlotte de Belzunce also seen as Belsunce (1749–1807); a son, Jean-Claude Le Blanc de Beaulieu (1753–1825).

Began a liaison with Dupin de Francueil (1748); obtained a separation of property from her husband (1749); through Francueil and Rousseau, met Friedrich Melchior Grimm (1751); ended the liaison with Francueil (1752); began a lifelong liaison with Grimm (1755); Rousseau lived at The Hermitage on her estate and left after a quarrel (1756–67); resided in Geneva and published Mes Moments heureux *and* Lettres à mon fils *(1757–79); became a close friend of Diderot (1760); husband lost his post as a* fermier-général *(1762); began a long correspondence with Abbé Galiani (1769); published the first edition of* Conversations d'Émilie *(1774); published the second edition of the* Conversations *(1781), which received the Montyon Prize of the Académie Française (1783); publication of an abridged version of her novel, which the editor entitled* Mémoires et correspondence de Madame d'Épinay *(1818).*

Writings (original editions): Mes Moments heureux *(privately printed, Geneva, 1758, 2nd ed., 1759);* Lettres à mon fils *(Geneva, 1759);* Les Conversations d'Émilie *(Leipzig: Crusius, 1774, and Paris: Pissot, 1775, 2nd ed., 2 vols., Paris: Belin, 1781); a novel published posthumously as* Mémoires et correspondance de Madame d'Épinay *(3 vols., ed. J.-C. Brunet, Paris: Brunet, 1818, 2nd ed., enlarged, Paris: Volland le Jeune, 1819); abridged contributions to Friedrich Grimm and Denis Diderot,* Correspondance littéraire, philosophique, et critique *(16 vols., Maurice Tourneux, ed., Paris: Garnier, 1877–82);* L'Amitié de deux jolies femmes *and* Une Rêve de Madamoiselle Clairon *(Maurice Tourneux, ed., Paris: Librairie des bibliophiles, 1885);* La Signora d'Epinay e l'abate Galiani: Lettere inedite (1762–1772) *(Fausto Nicolini, ed., Bari: Laterze, 1929);* Gli ultimi anni della signora d'Epinay: Lettere inedite (1773–1782) *(Fausto Nicolini, ed., Bari: Laterza, 1933). The definitive edition of her novel is Georges Roth, ed.,* Les Pseudo-Mémoires de Madame d'Épinay: Histoire de Madame Montbrillant *(3 vols., Paris: Gallimard, 1951).* Mes Moments heureux *and* Lettres à mon fils *were published together as* Oeuvres de Madame d'Épinay *(P.-A. Challemel-Lacour, ed., 2 vols., Paris: Sauton, 1869) and also in* Lettres à mon fils . . . et morceaux choisis *(Ruth Plaut Weinreb, ed., Concord, MA: Wayside Publications, 1984).*

Two deaths haunted the childhood of Louise Tardieu d'Esclavelles, the future Madame d'Épinay. Her maternal grandfather died only hours after she was born, and her father died suddenly at 71 when she was 10 and moving to Paris with her parents. These events engendered feelings of grief, anger, and guilt, which her mother only abetted, maintains her biographer **Evelyn Simha**. Louise blamed herself and longed for protection, love, and paternal guidance. She felt a deep need to justify her very existence. This need in turn fostered ambition, a drive that was fueled by a conviction she never lost despite her childhood conflicts, namely, a belief in her own natural superiority.

Her parents were from the petty provincial nobility. Louis-Gabriel Tardieu, Baron d'Esclavelles, was 58 when he married her much younger mother, **Florence-Angélique Prouveur de Preux**. He was a retired (1723) soldier, whose career was rewarded with the *charge d'honneur* of the governorship of the fortress at Valenciennes (Nord). Louise, an only child, was born there on March 11, 1726. He was a "grandfatherly" father who indulged her and encouraged her to learn, a sharp contrast to her mother, who was unloving, rigid, and ferociously pious. This parental inconsistency made her constantly concerned about others' opinions of her, a trait that marked her for life. Even so, as a child she was self-assured and lively, writes Simha, not melancholic and self-contained as biographers have tended to portray her because of the impression she often left on others as an adult.

She was put to the test after her father's death when her mother moved in with her sister **Madame de Bellegarde**, whose husband was Louis-Denis La Live de Bellegarde, an immensely rich *fermier-général*. (The members of the General Farm, a state tax-collecting consortium, were among the wealthiest men in France.) They owned a mansion on the fashionable rue Saint-Honoré and a fine estate, La Chevrette, just north of Paris at Épinay-sur-Siene. Among their six children was a daughter, ✍➤ **Sophie d'Houdetot**, with whom Rousseau would fall madly in love (unrequited) and make the heroine of his famous novel *Julie, ou La Nouvelle Héloïse*. Louise's uncle was a generous, kindly man, but her aunt was ill-tempered and took a dislike to Louise, whose brains showed up her daughters' lesser endowments. Madame de Bellegarde even forbade her a tutor, so Louise took to listening to the lessons taught to her cousins. She also spent two years (1737–39) as a scholarship student in a convent school, which she despised. She learned religious and social duties, some drawing and music, and smatterings of history and geography: "Above all, we were never taught to think; and any study of science was scrupulously avoided as being inappropriate to our sex."

To the consternation of her mother and aunt, Louise fell in love with her cousin, the Bellegarde heir, Denis-Joseph. Their teenage romance was interrupted by his military schooling and his long stint in Brittany as the inheritor (1744) of his father's *fermier-général* position. (These posts were owned.) Denis also received the *seigneurie* of Épinay and henceforth took his name from it. Meanwhile, Madame de Bellegarde died (1743), and Louise's mother became manager of the Bellegarde household. Louise nearly decided to break off with Denis when he returned from Brittany with a venereal disease. He assured her he was "cured," and after her mother dropped her objections, Louise married him a few minutes after midnight on December 24, 1745, at the church of Saint-Roch in Paris.

The honeymoon lasted three months, after which Denis careened into a lifelong dissipation, chasing women and piling up debts which even by the standards of a profligate upper class made him notorious. Louise, heartbroken and humiliated, disliking his ostentatious spending and her overbearing mother, who resented her son-in-law's authority over her, tried to remain the dutiful wife. She gave birth to a son, Louis-Joseph (1746–1807) and a daughter, Suzanne-Françoise-Thérèse in 1747 who would die the following year. Louise discovered, however, that

✍➤ **Houdetot, Sophie, Comtesse d'** (1730–1813)

French poet and subject of Rousseau's Confessions. *Name variations: Countess d'Houdetot; Mme Houdetot. Name variations: Sophie de Bellegarde. Born Élisabeth Françoise Sophie de la Livé de Bellegardé in Paris, France, in 1730; died on January 22, 1813; daughter of Louis-Denis de la Livé de Bellegardé (a rich fermier-général) and Madame de Bellegarde (d. 1743, sister of Florence-Angelique Prouveur de Preux who was the mother of Madame d'Épinay); sister-in-law and cousin of Mme d'Epinay (1726–1783); married the comte de Houdetot, in 1748; children: son César Louis Marie François Ange (b. 1749) was governor of Martinique.*

Sophie, comtesse de Houdetot, a sometime poet known more for her charm than her beauty, was born in 1730. She married the comte de Houdetot in 1748, but the couple separated amicably five years later. In 1753, she began a relationship with the Marquis de Saint Lambert which lasted until his death. She then met Jean-Jacques Rousseau while staying with her cousin/sister-in-law *Mme d'Épinay at Montmorency. In his *Confessions,* Rousseau describes his unrequited passion for Sophie. Questioned on the subject, she replied that he had greatly exaggerated; nevertheless it brought her a great deal of notoriety even though she remained faithful to Saint Lambert. A quite different view from that of Rousseau's is to be found in the *Mémoires of Mme d'Epinay.* Houdetot's poetry was included in a volume of the work of Saint-John Crèvecour in 1833.

Denis had infected her with a venereal disease, so she demanded an end to sexual relations. A final break came when Denis, drunk, came home with a drunken friend and offered her to him. In May 1749, she obtained a *séparation des biens,* which restored her 30,000-livre dowry. (One could live very comfortably in Paris on 5–6,000 livres per year; laborers earned less than 300.) For fear of scandal, she was persuaded not to seek a full *séparation des corps.* Her father-in-law, disgusted with his son, saw to it she was paid part of his subsidy and ensured that the arrangement continued after his death.

An eagle in a gossamer cage.
—**Voltaire on Madame d'Épinay, c. 1758**

Her role as a wife in ruins, Louise turned to motherhood, with mixed results. She had wanted to breastfeed her son, a most uncommon practice in her class, but Denis forbade it. She also wanted to undertake his education—again, almost unheard of—but governesses and tutors moved in. Still, she never lost her interest in education. In the meantime, she had been urged by a new friend, **Marie-Louise d'Ette**, to banish her depression by finding a lover. She rejected the idea, but in October 1746 one Charles-Louis Dupin de Francueil, a friend of Denis, appeared. He was a rich Treasury official—his family owned the magnificent Château de Chenonceaux—and was married but never seen with his wife. In the words of *George Sand, his granddaughter by a second wife, he was "handsome, elegant, always faultlessly turned out, graceful, jovial, courteous, affectionate, even-tempered to the day of his death."

It was Francueil who introduced Louise to the intelligentsia of the Enlightenment, which aroused in her a thirst to educate herself and become more than a mute presence at the dinners given by **Mlle Quinault** and the Comte de Caylus. He introduced her to (the still obscure) Jean-Jacques Rousseau in 1747 and to the novelist Crébillon *fils*, the dramatist Merivaux, and the novelist-historian Charles Duclos. She loved the theater, was a good actress herself, and staged plays at La Chevrette, including Rousseau's *L' Engagement téméraire* on September 14, 1748. In the spring of that year, she had finally surrendered to Francueil, and on August 1, 1749, she gave birth to their daughter, Angélique-Louise-Charlotte (d. 1807).

Francueil's ardor cooled by the summer of 1751, and in the fall of 1752 the liaison ended. Unfortunately, Louise found herself again pregnant by him and on May 29, 1753, gave birth to a son, Jean-Claude Le Blanc de Beaulieu (d. 1825). She ignored the child, not even mentioning him in her "memoirs"; he was raised by foster parents in the provinces and became bishop of Soissons. It is uncertain why the liaison ended, but probably her discovery that Francueil was being unfaithful to her in company with her husband proved fatal. Francueil nevertheless continued to be a guest at La Chevrette.

Madame d'Épinay, no longer a naive young woman, was growing intellectually. She ceased living with her mother after her uncle's death (1751), but she still felt under her spell and still looked for a protector and mentor. Duclos tried to fill the role, but it was not until March 1755 that she formed a new liaison, with Friedrich Melchior Grimm (1723–1807). For her it proved to be a lifelong love; for him something less, although he remained her intimate friend until her death. Born in Ratisbon, he had come to Paris with traveling German nobles as a secretary-companion. Rousseau (suddenly famous now) introduced him to Parisian intellectual so-

ciety in 1750 and to Louise in 1751. He became a close friend of Diderot and Baron d'Holbach and began publishing pieces on Germany and music. In 1753, Abbé Raynal left to him the editorship of the *Correspondance littéraire, philosophique, et critique*, a high-toned newsletter on Parisian affairs, published in Germany to avoid censorship and circulated every two to four weeks to some 20 royal and princely subscribers, including Frederick the Great and *Catherine II the Great.

Grimm, a polymath, was active, authoritarian, moralistic, ambitious, and self-absorbed, but perhaps less cold in temperament than simply stoic. Her attraction to him warmed when (as her "memoirs" relate, anyhow) she learned he had defended her good name in a duel in the winter of 1752–53. He became her mentor on all matters—she at last broke free of her mother—and after March 1755 they were lovers. She had already started to write; now she began to blossom as a woman of letters. Grimm encouraged her, but he always seemed ambivalent about the quality of her work and probably bore some responsibility (with Diderot) for persuading her not to publish her novel during her lifetime.

About this time she described herself in terms unusually nuanced for that era, when the custom was to portray women as either beautiful or homely: "I am not at all pretty, but I am not ugly. I am petite, thin, with a good figure. I have a youthful look, but without freshness, noble, gentle, lively, and interesting." Voltaire noted her large black eyes, "eyes so beautiful," an admirer wrote, "so tender, so eloquent of her soul that one is scarcely aware of the rest." In short, she was no great beauty but undeniably attractive.

In September 1755, Mme d'Épinay invited Rousseau to live at The Hermitage (L'Ermitage), a building in the *parc* at La Chevrette which she renovated for the purpose: "My bear," she coyly wrote, "there is your hideway." After his usual churlish protests, he (as usually happened) accepted the favor and lived at The Hermitage from April 1756 to December 1757, during which time he wrote *La Nouvelle Héloïse* and started *Émile* and *Le Contrat social*, save for the *Confessions*, his most famous works. Why she invited him is not certain. She found him attractive in an odd way, but it is impossible to believe she wanted anything more than a close friendship—his conversation and attention and probably comments on her writings. He was also good at arranging musical entertainments. And it is quite likely she saw that this new celebrity, being

Mme d'Épinay

chased after by Parisian society precisely because he ostentatiously snubbed it, would be a "catch."

This idyll soured at the edges when Rousseau complained, probably with some justification, that his patron was demanding too much of his time. Finally, from late August 1757 until Mme d'Épinay left on October 30 for a long stay in Geneva to consult Voltaire's physician, Dr. Théodore Tronchin, one of the most famous quarrels in the history of literature erupted. The Hermitage affair, Rousseau wrote in his *Confessions,* divided his life in half; it sealed the rejection of him by the philosophes, led by his erstwhile friend Diderot. The principals were Rousseau, hypersensitive, in the early stages of paranoia; Diderot, who barged in offering unwanted advice; Mme d'Épinay, her feelings hurt by Rousseau's suspicions and piqued that his raging passion for her cousin, Sophie d'Houdetot (in whom he saw his "Julie" in the flesh) was causing him to neglect her; the Marquis de Saint-Lambert, Sophie's true love; Grimm, Saint-Lambert's friend, who had probably opposed inviting Rousseau to The Hermitage because he knew him well enough to expect trouble would follow; **Thérèse La Vasseur**, Rousseau's longtime lower-class mistress, jealous of these fancy ladies and ready to spread gossip about them; and Thérèse's old mother, an accomplished mischief-maker. Moliére could not have invented a finer cast for a farce. This one, however, ended with unhappiness and recriminations all around.

It would be pointless here to wade into this swamp to find the truth. The evidence lies in well-doctored, self-serving accounts by clever, all-too-articulate *littéraires,* which makes it impossible to separate with much confidence fact from artful fiction. Suffice it to say, the imbroglio centered on two overlapping quarrels, one involving the threatened embarrassing revelation of Rousseau's passion for Sophie, the other around Mme d'Épinay's invitation to him, which he spurned, to accompany her on the journey to Geneva, perhaps as a way to get him away from Sophie. Rousseau, who surely had to sense by now that he was outstaying his welcome, became sincerely convinced that Diderot, Grimm, and Mme d'Épinay were plotting against him: "You have sought to reduce me to servitude, or to use me for your secret ends," he wrote to her near the end of October. Probably she *had* written to Grimm, but not to Saint-Lambert, as Rousseau believed, about his love for Sophie, and Grimm likely had said something to Saint-Lambert. (Both were with the army at the time.) But evidence of a true "plot" against him is highly circumstantial at best. Mme d'Épinay, seething over a spiteful letter he had written to Grimm asserting that *he* had done *her* a favor by living at The Hermitage, wrote to him from Geneva that she "pitied" him. He replied saying that on advice of friends he was staying on until spring. She replied icily that she did not consult her friends about her duty. He took the hint and left on December 18.

As will appear, the affair was not entirely over. Meanwhile, Mme d'Épinay stayed in Geneva until October 5, 1759, benefiting from Dr. Tronchin's care. She was ailing most of her life. Venereal disease (syphilis?) doubtless contributed to her ills, which included migraine, vertigo, stones, and stomach, bowel, and kidney pain hinting at Bright's disease or cancer. She longed desperately for Grimm's presence: he finally came down in February 1759 for an eight-month honeymoon (the happiest months of her life, she wrote) until she reluctantly returned with him to Paris. To occupy herself in Geneva, she began to write steadily, privately publishing *Mes Moments heureux* (My Happy Moments) in 1758 (revised in 1759) and *Lettres à mon fils* (Letters to My Son) in 1759, and finishing much of a huge autobiographical epistolary novel, *Histoire de*

Madame Montbrillant. Protestant Geneva's enlightened, moral society stimulated her, and she made friends, including Voltaire (living nearby at Ferney), who wrote of her, "She is no scatter-brain: she is a philosophe, with a very clear, strong mind." Noting her physical fragility, he called her "an eagle in a gossamer cage."

Moments, a miscellany of stories, light verse, and essays, was published anonymously in 25 copies for friends but soon was circulating in pirated editions. (It survives only in an 1869 edition of the 1759 revision.) She felt she had discovered her true self and hence was bold (or vain) enough to dedicate it to her own guiding spirit ("a reparation I owe you"), with a preface expressing hope she would become a "woman of distinction." Most of the pieces were written in 1756, but some dated back to 1747; as with the *Lettres,* some had appeared in Grimm's *Correspondance littéraire.* The *Lettres* contained 12 essays, "letters" ostensibly to her 13-year-old son on education in the broadest sense of the word—society, philosophy, morality. These together with an essay-letter to her daughter's governess in *Moments,* presented ideas she had discussed with Rousseau (whose *Émile* appeared in 1762) but which probably owed less to him than is usually said, notes **Ruth Weinreb**. She advocated involvement of parents, especially mothers, in their children's education, closely collaborating with their tutor—a novelty for that time; virtually the same education for girls as for boys; and a curriculum to include foreign languages, philosophy, and respect for the great natural world. A didactic, strongly conscience-based moral tone pervaded the *Lettres,* where she condemned defects in her son's knowledge and conduct. Predictably, the poor pre-adolescent boy, who moreover hated Grimm's presence, soon followed his father's dreadful example, to his mother's sorrow. Not surprisingly, too, her books earned her criticism for her pretensions to literary eminence and her too candid, even callous, airing of her son's faults.

Back now in Paris, Mme d'Épinay suffered a severe blow when the Treasury revoked her husband as a *fermier-général* on January 1, 1762, because of his habitually huge debt problem. A complicated settlement resulted in her receiving a share of his successor's income, and when her mother died on November 1 she inherited 90,000 livres. Still, she was forced to cut back; La Chevrette and part of the rue Saint-Honoré mansion were rented out, she moved to a place in the faubourg Monceau, and used a smaller, cozier château, La Briche (in Épinay) as her summer residence. In 1760, she and Diderot had become close friends—that she contributed anonymously to his great *Encyclopédie* (Vol. 8—) is probable but unprovable—and during the 1760s she and Grimm entertained him, Baron d'Holbach, the abbés Raynal and Galiani, Dr. Tronchin, and a passel of lesser Enlightenment notables at La Briche. She conducted no formal salon, with set hours and guest list, but let people come when they chose.

She helped some with Grimm's *Correspondance,* but his frequent, lengthening absences and her poor health left her often depressed. She finished her novel, but the last chapters lacked verve. And there were her children. In 1764, panicked for the future of her talented 15-year-old daughter, Angélique, because of her husband's crash, she hastily married her off to Vicomte Dominique de Belzunce, a 36-year-old wounded officer. She watched Angélique shrivel in a cold château near the Pyrenees. Meanwhile, her gadabout son was falling heavily into debt. As a mother, this woman who preached the virtues of motherhood, stared at stark failure.

The 1770s proved both highly active and stressful for Mme d'Épinay. Financial pressures forced her to rent out La Briche (1769) and move from place to place in Paris. Making an excruciating decision, she and Denis had son Louis imprisoned for two years on a *lettre de cachet* (a king's order) to prevent him from gambling away the family's fortune. (Upper-class families sometimes resorted to this procedure to protect inheritances.) He had lost his post with the Parlement of Pau, now lost his army commission, was jailed again briefly in 1773, and finally was sent off to Switzerland, where he married in 1775. "One is not a mother with impunity," she wrote to Abbé Galiani in 1770. "Nothing makes a person more idiotic. Take my advice, my friend, never become a mother." Furthermore, pain from her ailments, enough to cause her to roll on the floor sometimes, forced her to take opium in large quantities as time wore on. And Grimm's absences, notably on diplomatic missions for German states, grew longer still. On the positive side, in 1778 Voltaire honored her with a visit shortly before his death, and Mozart, penniless, gratefully stayed with her for two months after the sudden death of his mother.

As a result of Grimm's travels—"my German butterfly," she dubbed him—she, Diderot and a Swiss, Jacques-Henri Meister, were left with most of the work of the *Correspondance.* In September 1774, Grimm formally ceded the paper to Meister, who continued it to 1793. Mme d'Épinay was most active on it from late 1768 to 1775, managing business, editing, writing theater and book reviews, and discussing politics, economics, and philosophy—a veritable female *philosophe*. From July 1771 to January 1772, she published it almost alone, but after 1775, with Grimm out and her health crumbling, she gave up the grind.

Besides the *Correspondance* work, she edited Abbé Galiani's famous *Dialogues sur le commerce des blés* (Dialogues on the Grain Trade, 1770) and carried on one of the most noteworthy correspondences of the century with him after he was recalled to Naples in 1769. She also published, anonymously in Leipzig doubtless with Grimm's help, the first version of *Conversations d'Émilie* (1774), a book on education inspired by her granddaughter **Émilie de Belzunce**, whom she began raising in 1769 and who revived her maternal hopes. The book, containing 12 dialogues, met success in France, Germany, and Italy, so she revised and expanded it to 20 dialogues and in 1781 republished it in Paris in two volumes under her own name. The labor, pushed on despite her son's disasters and her illnesses, helped her overcome "the terrors of death," she wrote in the preface.

While many ideas in the *Conversations* repeated or resembled those in the *Moments* and *Lettres,* she emerged at last as a fully confident, independent woman. Like Rousseau, whom she did not mention by name, she believed in allowing the child to discover the truth, hence avoiding long, complicated expositions, and in attending to physical education. But thereafter she parted ways with him. She gave the essential role to the mother, not the tutor, in supervising the child's education—a word, incidentally, connoting "upbringing" more than simply "instruction." Only the mother has the time to do this. Moral education should be given from a very early age, not postponed (as with Rousseau). Above all, unlike Rousseau's "Sophie," raised merely to please and serve "Émile," Émilie would be educated the same as any boy, for women are the intellectual equals of men and learning is important to their happiness. Mme d'Épinay had been raised as a "Sophie" and hated it: Émilie would be what she herself had wanted to be—happy, intelligent, and independent—notes **Elisabeth Badinter**. Moreover, unlike most contemporary theorists, she opposed class distinctions in education, calling instead for a general "republican" education, at least as an ideal. Worth is achieved by effort, not conferred by inheritance. Reversing her position in the *Lettres,* she also preferred boarding school to strictly private tutoring, for children need companionship. In all cases, the inculcation of virtue and social usefulness should drive the whole process.

Yearning for recognition and immortality, with death approaching, she offered her work to the Académie Française for the first Prix Monty-on, "the book published in the current year that might be of greatest benefit to society." Despite the intrigues of *Mme de Genlis, whose *Adèle et Théodore* was a strong candidate, Mme d'Épinay was awarded the prize on January 13, 1783.

But what of the novel, which would be her best-known work? It was not published until 1818 and only in abridged form under a totally misleading title: *Mémoires et correspondance de Madame d'Épinay.* She had willed the manuscript to Grimm, who left it in Paris (thinking he would return) when he fled the Terror during the Revolution. The government carelessly divided it and stored it in the National and Arsenal libraries; the parts were discovered and published in sundry deformed editions during the 19th century. The unabridged, authoritative version, edited by Georges Roth in three volumes, appeared at last in 1951 under the title *Les Pseu-do-Mémoires de Madame d'Épinay, Histoire de Madame de Montbrillant.*

This sprawling work—the Roth edition fills 2,000 pages but does include extensive notes—was "the longest, most ambitious novel authored by a French woman in the eighteenth century," claims Weinreb. An autobiographically based novel with a story similar to her life from 1736 to 1763 but recast as fiction, it is, with Rousseau's *Nouvelle Héloïse,* a *roman personal,* an innovation which broke ground for *Germaine de Staël, *Charlotte Brontë, Flaubert, Proust, et al. It is also a *roman de moeurs* whose portrayal of 18th-century society the eminent 19th-century critic Saint-Beuve praised as unsurpassed: "The *Mémoires* [sic] of Mme d'Épinay are not a book, they are an epoch."

In form it is predominately epistolary, but also with diary and third-person narrative elements. The earliest ideas stemmed from her reading of Duclos's *Confessions du comte de *** around 1746, and perhaps by 1750 she had started to write. She was most active from 1756 through her stay in Geneva; work on the first draft then trailed on through the 1760s, after which revisions began. Her purpose seems most clearly to have been a desire to search for her true self by tracing her transformation, writes Weinreb, from "a timid, rather ignorant girl, an oppressed daughter and wife, to a devoted mother and liberated, well-educated woman." The book, notes Simha, was "the fruit of her self-discovery at the same time that it is the record of her voyage." It must be emphasized, however, that this is a novel, a fiction, in which dates, events, documents, and persons have been altered at the author's whim. Readers and historians too often have tended to forget this simple fact about this complicated work.

The main complication was revealed by a Rousseau scholar, **Frederika MacDonald**, who in 1906 published an exposé of extensive revisions in the work undertaken after 1770. In that year, Rousseau finished his *Confessions* and in 1771 began to read it in salons, creating a public scandal. He had reached the Hermitage affair when Mme d'Épinay asked a friend, chief of police Sartine, to politely but firmly tell him to desist—which Rousseau did, being unhappy anyhow with the readings' reception. He died in 1778, the first six books of the *Confessions* (up to the Hermitage affair) were published in 1782, the rest in 1789. He obviously had wanted to justify himself to posterity. So did Mme d'Épinay—and Diderot and Grimm, who were in mortal fear their reputations and the *encyclopédiste* party would be wrecked by Rousseau's revelations. Hence, from 1770 until her death in 1783 she willingly accepted (besides extensive editorial suggestions) changes that would blacken Rousseau's reputation and make him appear to be a lying ingrate. At the same time, it is only fair to note, she said or wrote nothing in public disparaging to Rousseau while she lived even though she could easily have done so, for example, in the *Correspondance littéraire.* She had even tried to help him anonymously from Geneva. To the end, despite everything, she felt a lingering attraction, it seems, to this genius from another planet.

Whether she intended to publish her novel is an open question; but it was clear, especially to Diderot, that it should not be published until all the principals were dead. She, Diderot, and Grimm thus would have the last word. Yet, after Diderot's death in 1784, Grimm prudently decided not to publish the novel. Why didn't he then destroy the manuscript copy and the incriminating notes? As it was, until MacDonald's revelations, Mme d'Épinay's "memoirs" were taken as the true account of the Hermitage affair and Rousseau's version—which itself is falsified—dismissed. The irony here is that Mme d'Épinay did write a novel, but she conspired to alter it in hopes her fiction would be read as thinly veiled fact. As a result, after MacDonald's work her reputation sank—unduly so. As for the true story of the Hermitage affair, it obviously can never be fully recovered.

Mme d'Épinay spent her last 20 years in physical and financial distress. Catherine the Great, appealed to by Grimm, whom she knew well, bought her diamonds in 1779 to bail her son out of debt; but in 1780 she was writing to Dr. Tronchin to intercede with Controller-General Necker to prevent creditors from seizing her furniture. And in 1781 she turned to Catherine again, dedicating the second edition of the *Conversations* to her. Catherine liked it and helped out once more, with 16,000 livres plus a diamond brooch for Émilie.

Denis d'Épinay, husband in name only, died of venereal disease on February 16, 1782. He richly deserved Diderot's scathing epitaph: "So ended a man who wasted two million without ever saying a witty word or doing a good thing." A year later, Mme d'Épinay followed. On April 15, 1783, two months after receiving the Prix Montyon, she died, aged 57, from stomach disease, nephritis, and influenza at her home on the Chausée d'Antin. On the 17th, she was interred in the family vault in the church at Épinay.

Mme d'Épinay has been called, writes Lester Crocker, "one of the most brilliant women of a century prolific in brilliant women." Brilliant probably; complex certainly. She was naturally graceful, carefully groomed, and attractive owing to her beautiful eyes, self-mocking humor, good sense, warmth, intelligence, and lack of arrogance or artificiality—besetting sins of her social class. More sentimental than passionate, she was no famous wit and in large gatherings preferred to listen, being skilled in getting others to talk. In small groups, she was agreeable, lively, and to the point. She was more at ease and eloquent on paper than in speech. She wrote in a light, elegant style, in expression simple and apt.

Beneath this agreeable exterior, however, surged powerful contrary feelings. Her novel is revealing. The underlying theme is that of trust rewarded by abandonment. Pain, despair, isolation predominate; there is no joy, nothing sweet or lyrical. Her heroine dies for having defied convention—a conventional theme. Yet, in real life Mme d'Épinay herself struggled on heroically despite deep despair over her husband's humiliation of her, her children's failures, Fran-

cueil's betrayal, Grimm's long absences and obvious cooling, grave financial worries, and near ceaseless physical pain.

With every reason simply to bask in the opulent life of *fermier-général* society, she chose instead to educate herself in order to join the intelligentsia. Interestingly, almost all her friends were men. Had she been a man she could have been counted among the philosophes instead of being all but hidden in the shade cast by Voltaire, Rousseau, Diderot, d'Holbach, and the rest. Her own smiling dismissals of her writings as mere "amusements" for her friends masked a powerful ambition to be considered a serious *littéraire*. Instead, the conventions of a male-dominated society frustrated her. She deplored the restrictions it placed upon women's ability to develop their full powers: "I say that a woman, because she is a woman," she wrote to Abbé Galiani in 1771, "is not in a position to acquire a fund of knowledge sufficient to make her useful to society; and it seems to me that the ability to be useful is the only thing one can be proud of. . . . We are excluded from so many things! Everything that touches on the science of administration, on politics, on commerce, is alien to us and forbidden." In no way (save in the most obvious biological sense) did she find any *natural* difference between men and women. In these matters, she formed independent judgments and acted with the courage of her convictions. In time, she learned to count on herself alone, certainly not on any man.

Mme d'Épinay's interest in education, especially for girls, flowed from these concerns. She also came to the subject from her concentration on motherhood, a compensation for her failures as a wife (as far as she thought herself responsible) and her bad conscience over her adulteries. Suffice it to say, she was one of the earliest advocates of the roles women assumed in the 19th and much of the 20th centuries, namely, as intensively involved mothers and the primary educators of children. Ironically, she was prevented from or failed in fulfilling these roles with her own children, and in a serious sense the roles ran contrary to her desire to open to women all those permitted to men. She was a complicated person indeed.

SOURCES:

Badinter, Elisabeth. *Émilie, Émilie: L'Ambition féminine au XVIIIᵉ siècle*. Paris Flammarion, 1983 (a study of Émilie du Châtelet and Louise d'Épinay).

Blanchard, William H. *Rousseau and the Spirit of Revolt: A Psychological Study*. Ann Arbor, MI: University of Michigan Press, 1967.

Crocker, Lester G. *The Embattled Philosopher: A Biography of Denis Diderot.* Lansing, MI: Michigan State College Press, 1954.

————. *Jean-Jacques Rousseau.* 2 vols. NY: Macmillan, 1968–73.

Green, F.C. *Jean-Jacques Rousseau: A Critical Study of His Life and Writings.* Cambridge: Cambridge University Press, 1955.

Gribble, Francis. *Rousseau and the Women He Loved.* NY: Scribner, 1908.

Hulliung, Mark. *The Autocritique of the Enlightenment: Rousseau and the Philosophes.* Cambridge, MA: Harvard University Press, 1994.

MacDonald, Frederika. *Jean-Jacques Rousseau: A New Criticism.* 2 vols. NY: Putnam, 1906.

Simha, Evelyn Singer. "An Eagle in a Cage of Gauze: Mme d'Épinay's *Histoire de Madame de Montbrillant.*" Yale University diss., 1968. Ann Arbor, MI: University Microfilms, 1968.

Steegmuller, Francis. *A Woman, a Man, and Two Kingdoms: The Story of Madame d'Épinay and the Abbé Galiani.* NY: Alfred A. Knopf, 1991.

Weinreb, Ruth Plaut. *Eagle in a Gauze Cage: Louise d'Épinay, femme de lettres.* NY: AMS Press, 1993.

SUGGESTED READING:

Cazes, André. *Grimm et les encyclopédistes.* Paris: Presses Universitaires de France, 1933.

Diderot, Denis. *Correspondance.* G. Roth and J. Varloost, eds. 16 vols. Paris: Minuit, 1955–70 (frequent mentions of Mme d'Épinay).

Guilleman, Henri. "Les Affaires de l'Ermitage," in *Annales de la Société Jean-Jacques Rousseau.* Vol. 19, 1941–42, pp. 58–258 (the basic account).

Hageman, Jeanne Kathryn. "Les Conversations d'Émilie: The Education of Women by Women in Eighteenth-Century France." Univ. of Wisconsin diss., 1991.

Legros, A. *Madame d'Épinay, Valenciennoise.* Valenciennes, 1920 (a valuable account).

Magetti, Daniel, and Georges Dulac, eds. *Correspondance de l' abbé Galiani et de Mme d'Épinay.* Paris: Desjonquières, 1992—.

Rey, Auguste. *Le Château de La Chevrette et Madame d'Épinay.* Paris: Plon, 1904.

Rousseau, Jean-Jacques. *The Confessions of Jean-Jacques Rousseau.* J.M. Cohen, tr. Baltimore: Penguin Books, 1954.

————. *Correspondance complète.* R.A. Leigh, ed. 14 vols. Geneva: Institut et Musée Voltaire, 1966–67 (esp. vols. 3, 4).

Scherer, Edmond. *Melchior Grimm.* Paris: Calmann-Lévy, 1887.

Smiley, Joseph Royall. *Diderot's Relations with Grimm.* Urbana, IL: University of Illinois Press, 1950.

Spencer, Samia, ed. *French Women and the Age of Enlightenment.* Bloomington, IN: Indiana University Press, 1984.

Trouille, Mary. "Sexual/Textual Politics in the Enlightenment: Diderot and d'Epinay Respond to Thomas's Essay on Women," in *Romantic Review.* Vol. 85, 1994, pp. 191–210.

Weinreb, Ruth Plaut. "Émilie ou Émile? Madame d'Épinay and the Education of Girls in Eighteenth-Century France," in *Eighteenth-Century Women and the Arts.* CT: Greenwood Press, 1988, pp. 57–66.

————. "Madame d'Épinay's Contribution to the Correspondance littéraire," in *Studies in Eighteenth-Century Culture.* Vol. 18, 1988, pp. 389–403.

Wilson, Arthur M. *Diderot.* NY: Oxford University Press, 1972.

COLLECTIONS:

Paris: Archives nationales; Bibliothèque de l'Arsenal; Bibliothèque de la Ville de Paris (articles in the Correspondance littéraire).

Naples: *Biblioteca di Storia Patria* (letters to Galiani).

David S. Newhall,
Pottinger Distinguished Professor of History Emeritus,
Centre College, Danville, Kentucky

Eponina (40–78 CE)

Heroine of conjugal affection. Wife of Julius Sabinus.

Eponina, who lived between 40 and 78 CE, captured the sympathies of the Roman people with heroic fidelity to her husband, even choosing to die with him when her efforts to save his life failed.

Eponina's husband Julius Sabinus, maintaining he was a descendant of Julius Caesar, laid claim to the throne and was defeated, putting his life in danger. To escape capture, he staged his own death by burning his house down, and taking refuge in a cave beneath the ruins. Eponina, away at the time of the fire, was so overcome with grief at the loss of her husband that she refused to eat, endangering her own life. When she was told that her husband was not dead, but hidden in the cave, she began visiting him at night, all the while keeping up the appearance of grief. She carried on her conjugal visits for nine long years before Sabinus was finally discovered and brought before the emperor Vespasian. When Sabinus was sentenced to die, Eponina pleaded with the emperor to spare her husband's life but failed to win a reprieve. She then chose to share her husband's fate. As the two were led to execution, Eponina faced death stoically. "Learn, Vespasian," she said to the emperor, "that I have enjoyed more happiness in the performance of my duties and in prolonging the life of your victim, though but in the rude recesses of an obscure cavern, than you will henceforth ever enjoy amidst the splendors that surround your throne."

Eppes, Maria Jefferson (1778–1804).

See Jefferson, Martha for sidebar.

Epstein, Charlotte (1884–1938)

American swimmer, founder of the Women's Swimming Association (WSA), who was largely responsible for gathering the first team of American women swimmers to participate in the Antwerp Olympic Games in 1920. Name variations: Eppy Epstein. Born in New York City in September 1884; died on August 27, 1938.

At the beginning of the 20th century, social custom was biased against female participation in sports. Swimming was a particularly difficult milieu for women mainly due to the costumes they were required to wear. In 1903, a male swimming instructor donned a woman's swimsuit in order to determine its liabilities:

> Just to satisfy myself upon this point of costume, I once wore a close imitation of the usual suit for women. Not until then did I rightly understand what a serious matter a few feet of superfluous cloth might become in water. The suit was amply large, yet pounds of apparently dead weight seemed to be pulling at me in every direction. In that gear a swim of one hundred yards was as serious a task as a mile in my own suit. After that experience I no longer wondered why so few women swim really well, but rather that they are able to swim at all.

Although Charlotte Epstein was not a particularly talented athlete, she believed that athletic competition was as important for women as for men. She became especially interested in equal participation after women's swimming was introduced in the 1912 Stockholm Olympics (*Fanny Durack of Australia won the gold medal in the 100-meter freestyle). In 1914, Epstein founded the National Women's Life Saving League, offering a place for women to swim as well as take lessons. That same year, giving up on the programs of the colleges and universities, she convinced the Amateur Athletic Union (AAU) to permit women to register with their organization for the first time and to sponsor meets. Until then, the president of the AAU had been James Sullivan, who was adamantly opposed to women participating in competitive sports.

In 1919, with the help of a tiny group of businesswomen, Epstein founded the New York Women's Swimming Association (WSA). While working on the national front, she also pushed on an international level to have women's swimming included in the 1920 Antwerp Olympics. American women had participated as archers and golfers in previous Olympics, but the permanent inclusion of women's swimming was an important step because the International Olympic Committee considered swimming a major sport rather than a minor one like golf and archery.

Epstein's WSA played a crucial role in the development of women's swimming as a competitive sport. American domination of swimming in the 1920 Antwerp Olympics was such that Americans took the gold in all three events to which women were limited: the 100-meter freestyle, the 300-meter freestyle, and the 4x100-meter freestyle relay. *Ethelda Bleibtrey, ✥▶ Margaret Woodbridge, and ✥▶ Frances Schroth took the gold, silver, and bronze, respectively, in the 300-meter freestyle. Bleibtrey, ✥▶Irene Guest, and Schroth won the gold, silver, and bronze, respectively, in the 100-meter freestyle, and Woodbridge, Bleibtrey, Schroth, and Guest won the gold in the 4x100-meter freestyle relay. Some of these athletes were Epstein's swimmers.

Though Epstein was an administrator rather than a coach, her efforts made competitive swimming possible for countless women. In 1924, 1928, and 1932, American women continued to dominate Olympic swimming. Among Epstein's protégés were *Eleanor Holm, *Aileen Riggin, and *Gertrude Ederle, "who might have disappeared into anonymity," writes Allen Guttmann, "but for the intervention of Charlotte Epstein. . . . Epstein was a remarkable woman." Charlotte Epstein worked as a legal secretary and court stenographer while she promoted women's competitive swimming. During Epstein's 22 years with the Women's Swimming Association, her swimmers held 51 world records and put together 30 national-champion relay teams.

SOURCES:

Guttmann, Allen. *Women's Sports: A History.* NY: Columbia University Press, 1991.

Howell, Reet, ed. *Her Story in Sport: A Historical Anthology of Women in Sports.* West Point, NY: Leisure Press, 1982.

Slater, Robert. *Great Jews in Sports.* Middle Village, NY: Jonathan David Publishers, 1983.

Wallechinsky, David. *The Complete Book of the Olympics.* NY: Viking, 1988.

Karin Loewen Haag,
Athens, Georgia

Epstein, Eppy (1884–1938).

See Epstein, Charlotte.

Epstein, Marie (c. 1899–1995)

French screenwriter and director. Born Marie-Antoine Epstein in Warsaw, Poland, around 1899; died in Paris, France, in 1995; sister and partner of Jean Epstein; partner of Jean Benoit-Lévy.

Filmography: L'Affiche *(1924);* Le Double de Amour *(1925);* Six et Demi-onze *(1927);* Ames d'en-

***Woodbridge, Margaret.** See* Bleibtrey, Ethelda *for sidebar.*

***Schroth, Frances.** See* Bleibtrey, Ethelda *for sidebar.*

***Guest, Irene.** See* Bleibtrey, Ethelda *for sidebar.*

fants *(1928)*; Peau de péche *(1929)*; Maternité *(1929)*; Le Coeur de Paris *(1931)*; La Maternelle *(1933)*; Itto *(1934)*; Helene *(1936)*; La Mort du cygne *(1937)*; Ballerina *(1937)*; Altitude 3200 *(1938)*; Le Feu de paille *(1939)*; Le Grande esperance *(1953)*.

Although Marie Epstein was one of the most important screenwriter-directors in the early avant-garde cinema in France, she is often ignored or overshadowed by her two collaborators, her brother, Jean Epstein (c. 1897–1953), and director, Jean Benoit-Lévy (1888–1959). The disregard of Epstein from film histories "necessitates a kind of foregrounding of her activity to redress the balance and involves a work of reconstruction as well," writes film historian **Sally Flitterman-Lewis**. Epstein apparently was born in Warsaw to a Jewish-French father and a Polish mother. The family immigrated to France while the children were in their teens. Marie began her career in film as an assistant director and actress in her brother's *Coeur fidele* in 1923. Subsequently, she wrote several screenplays he directed which are considered among his best work. But Epstein's most important collaboration was with Jean Benoit-Lévy, with whom she shared a director credit on several films, including *Ames d'enfants* (1928), *Peau de péche* (1929), *Maternité* (1929) and *La Maternelle* (1933). Adapted from a novel by Leon Frapie, *La Maternelle* is considered one of the best early French sound films.

Her work is best known for combining social issues with poetic imagery and creative cinematic techniques. In particular, she was concerned with the plight of poor children and disadvantaged women. The poignant *La Maternelle* is told from the point of view of an impoverished woman who is about to commit suicide. During the climactic scene, the character looks directly into the camera, as if to implicate the audience in her plight. This was one of the earliest uses of the technique known as "breaking the fourth wall."

During the Nazi occupation of France, Jean Epstein was barred from the studios by the Vichy regime. Apparently both brother and sister were arrested by the Gestapo but were saved from deportation or worse through the efforts of friends and the intervention of the Red Cross.

Following World War II, Marie Epstein made a documentary on atomic energy called *La Grande esperance* (1953). Until her retirement in 1977, she worked as a film preservationist at Cinémathèque Française where she painstakingly restored some of her brother's silent films as well as the renowned *Napoleon* by director Abel Gance. One of her last appearances was in a documentary released in 1995 called *Citizen Langlois*. Directed by Edgardo Cozarinsky, the film is about the founding of the Cinémathèque Française by director Henri Langlois (1914–1977).

SOURCES:

Flitterman-Lewis, Sandy. *To Desire Differently: Feminism and the French Cinema.* Urbana, IL: University of Illinois Press, 1990.

Foster, Gwendolyn. *Women Film Directors: An International Bio-critical Dictionary.* Westport, CT: Greenwood Press, 1995.

Kuhn, Annette, and Susannah Radstone, eds. *The Women's Companion To International Film.* Berkeley, CA: University of California Press, 1990.

Deborah Jones,
Studio City, California

Epstein, Selma (1927—)

American pianist, internationally known for her performances of 20th-century composers. Born in Brooklyn, New York, on August 14, 1927; daughter of Tillie (Schneider) Schectman and Samuel Schectman; studied at Juilliard with Rosina Lhevinne and at the Philadelphia Conservatory of Music with Edward Steuermann; married Joseph Epstein (a concert pianist).

Selma Epstein began her long concert career with a performance at Carnegie Hall when she was 15. She continued her studies at Juilliard where she was ***Rosina Lhevinne**'s youngest student, then received the D. Hendrick Ezerman Foundation Scholarship at the Philadelphia Conservatory of Music where she studied with Edward Steuermann. After beginning her concert career, Epstein began to realize that few modern composers' works appeared in concert halls. Contemporary composers did not always face great obstacles to having their works performed. At one time, performers wanted only works "hot off the press," but, as the repertoire became increasingly set in the 19th century, contemporary composers suffered. Epstein decided to pioneer contemporary music, a decision that was not motivated by a desire to enhance her career, because the obstacles women face as performers are increased for those who dedicate their efforts to contemporary music.

Epstein concertized in Europe and America, but her tours of Australia were to have a profound effect on her professional life. On a second tour, she was invited to teach at the New South Wales Conservatorium, the first American ever offered a major teaching post there. From 1972 to 1975, Epstein became a resident recording artist for the Australian Broadcasting Company. During this time, **Ella Grainger** asked Epstein to record some of the unpublished music of her husband Percy Grainger, the first native Australian to achieve worldwide fame as a conductor and composer. Epstein not only recorded and performed his music, but she founded the American Grainger Society to promote the composer's works at a series of international festivals and began to perform all-Grainger concerts. Eventually, her efforts helped to establish his work in international concert halls. Epstein also devoted her energies to promoting other 20th-century composers. Her determination to introduce contemporary composers to music audiences gained her international acclaim.

SOURCES:

"Selma Epstein. Concert Pianist, Teacher" in Le Page, Jane Wiener. *Women Composers, Conductors, and Musicians of the Twentieth Century: Selected Biographies.* Vol. II. Metuchen, NJ: Scarecrow Press, 1988, pp. 104–114.

John Haag,
Athens, Georgia

Erauso, Catalina de (1592–1635)

Spanish woman who fled a convent and, disguised as a man, rose to the rank of lieutenant in the Spanish colonial army in South America, then returned to Spain where her exploits were immortalized. Name variations: Erauzo; Erauzú; Francisco de Erauso; Francisco de Loyola; Alfonso Díaz Ramírez de Guzmán; called La Monja Alférez ("the Nun Ensign"). Pronunciation: Eh-RAU-so. Born Catalina de Erauso on February 10, 1592 (some sources cite 1585), in San Sebastián, in northern Spain; disappeared and assumed dead in Mexico at Veracruz, 1635 (some sources cite her survival in Mexico until 1650); daughter of Miguel de Erauso and María Pérez de Galarraga y Arce; attended the Dominican Convent of San Sebastián el Antiguo, to age 15; never married; no children.

Escaped the convent, dressed as a man, and worked as an accountant and page (1607); fled to America as a "cabin boy" and became soldier of fortune in Perú, Bolivia, Chile, and Argentina (beginning 1608); revealed in confession that she was a woman (c. 1623); returned to Spain, where she was received by the king and awarded lifelong military pension, then visited the Pope (1625); collaborated with Juan Pérez de Montalván in penning drama based on her adventures (c. 1626–27); returned to Mexico (1630).

Disguised as a man, Catalina de Erauso, the legendary "nun-ensign," knifed rivals, killed sol-diers, and swashbuckled her way towards acceptance and even popularity in the intolerant Spanish society of the 1600s. What we know of the adventurous life of this runaway novice comes to us filtered through the prejudices of her century. Even so, Erauso emerges as one of the most rebellious Spanish women of all time. In the story of her life, it is difficult to separate fact from myth, truth from fiction; even the volume that appeared as her autobiography, 200 years after it was alleged to have been written, may be apocryphal, and her death is shrouded in mystery. Many of the adventures attributed to her may well be a composite of the lives of several historic personages. But there was a real Catalina de Erauso, and the heart of her story is true.

The fate of Catalina de Erauso was decided, to some extent, long before her birth. Her father was a soldier, serving in Flanders, when he was gravely wounded in battle and made a vow to the Virgin of Atocha. He promised to marry, should he survive his wounds, and all his sons would serve in the army, while all his daughters would become nuns. Some years later, in 1592, Catalina was born in the coastal town of San Sebastián, in the northern Basque region of Spain, and spent most of her childhood, along with her three older sisters, interned in the Dominican Convent of San Sebastián el Antiguo. Some sources indicate that her cloistered life may have begun by the time she was four years old.

From the beginning, Catalina rebelled against the restrictions of convent life. At age 15, following a violent quarrel with an older nun, she climbed the convent wall and escaped, taking some of the convent money with her. She lived off the countryside, eating roots and wild berries for three days before approaching a peasant to plead for a pair of pants. Then, according to her autobiography, "I cut off my hair and threw it away, and the third night I started off I knew not where, scurrying over roads and skirting villages so as to get far away."

Approaching the town of Vitoria, Erauso introduced herself as Francisco de Loyola, the name she would use for the next several years. She found employment as a messenger, then as an accountant for a merchant in Vitoria, saving her money. After two years, she set off in search of adventure, wandering throughout northern Spain until she sought work again in the town of Valladolid, as a page in the mansion of Juan Idiáguez, secretary to Spain's king, Philip III. Idiáguez was so impressed by the manners and intelligence of the "young boy" that he made Catalina a special page to receive visitors. She wore the gold-braided and buttoned uniform happily, until the day she had to announce a new guest, her father, who had come to ask his old friend Idiáguez for help in locating his escaped daughter. Still unrecognized, Erauso wrapped her few possessions in a bundle and stole away that night.

Returning to San Sebastián, the town of her birth, Erauso hid out in the home of an aunt who protected her secret while the girl decided whether to make herself known to her parents. After several months, her need for freedom won out, and she headed south to the Andalusian coastal town of Cádiz, where she enrolled as a "cabin boy" in the Spanish navy. At age 19, she embarked for Mexico, dreaming of the conquest and conversion of "heathen" Indians to Christianity by means of the sword.

His Holiness [Pope Urban VIII] was clearly amazed at my story and graciously gave me leave to go on wearing men's clothes, urging me to live upright in the future, to avoid injuring my neighbor, and to fear God's vengeance respecting His commandment— Thou shalt not kill.

—Catalina de Erauso

The ship landed at Veracruz, where Erauso, true to her nature, deserted the navy in favor of joining the Spanish army, which promised more challenges and more risks. Spain's colonial enterprise was then in full swing, with armies spread throughout Mexico and Central and South America. In addition to expanding colonial territories, soldiers imposed the political and religious will of the Spanish monarchy on the various Indian nations. As the soldier "Francisco," Erauso traveled the length of South America, gaining a reputation both for courage and skill in battle. She also gained a reputation as somewhat of a playboy, courting various women and not infrequently finding herself in duels with her rivals.

Apparently prone to violence and nearly unbeatable at swordplay, on one occasion Erauso was sentenced to life in prison for the killing of two young men. As the story goes, she quickly escaped, caught a ship south to Perú and again found employment with a merchant. There, in one of her frequent visits to the theater, she took exception to the attitude of a certain Señor Reyes, and the knife fight that ensued sent him to the hospital and Erauso again to jail. Released with the help of her employer, she left Perú to enlist with the troops involved in the conquest of

Charcas, a region that corresponds approximately to modern-day Bolivia.

In Charcas, Erauso became military aide to Captain Recio de León and gained a reputation as a skillful and ferocious Indian fighter. At the end of the military campaign, she again found employment with a wealthy merchant, but her aggressive nature led once more to her involvement in a series of violent, but possibly apocryphal, incidents. Some narratives insist that at this point she killed one of her own brothers in a duel before realizing who he was. In another story, after threatening the mayor of a small town in a card game, she fled to La Paz, where she challenged a local official and reportedly killed him in a duel. Normally this would have brought death by hanging, but Erauso was given a life sentence because of her youth.

In prison, we are told, "Francisco" was paid visits by a rich widow, who supplied her with a dagger, a deck of cards, and a bottle of local liquor that she used to bribe her jailer and escape. Shortly after, in July of 1615, she was on board a battleship of the Spanish Armada off the coast of Perú, fighting under the name of Alfonso Díaz Ramírez de Guzmán, against the Dutch fleet. According to the Peruvian author Ricardo Palma, she was the only Spanish survivor of the battle.

Reaching Lima, Erauso joined troops headed for southern Chile to take part in one of the most perilous campaigns of the Spanish conquest, known as the War of the Araucania. The Araucanian Indians were renowned warriors who lived at the southern tip of Latin America. Spain never really conquered them. Erauso was stationed at Fort Paincaví, in the frigid southern Chilean region of Purén, and the autobiography ascribed to her contains a description of her role in a key battle, which won her the rank of lieutenant:

[I]n the last engagement their reinforcements came up, things took a bad turn for us, and they killed many of our men and some captains . . . and they captured our flag. Seeing it carried off, I and two mounted men galloped after it into the midst of the throng, trampling, killing and receiving hard knocks. One of the three soon fell dead; the two of us pressed on and reached the flag, when my comrade was laid low by a lance thrust; I received a nasty wound in the leg, killed a cacique, who was carrying the standard, recaptured it from him, and set spurs to my horse, trampling, killing and wounding no end, but was badly wounded myself, pierced by three arrows.

In the writings attributed to her, Erauso describes many hours spent wandering alone through the southern Chilean forests. Here as elsewhere, she was a solitary soul, as well as a fierce patriot and soldier, and during this period she was seemingly quite happy. But in a typical incident, playing cards with other soldiers, she thrust the same dagger given her by the Bolivian widow through the hand of a cheating companion.

While still on Chile's southern frontier, Erauso suffered a wound in her shoulder which failed to heal and was sent to the city of Concepción. After recuperating, she was assigned to lead a force of 25 men back to Fort Paincaví, where the war with the Araucanians had reached a critical point. In one battle, Catalina is purported to have turned the tide by capturing a chief named Guipihuanche, dragging him back to the fort and hanging him.

Once the Spanish made peace with the indomitable Araucanians, Erauso had no command and saw herself destined for a demotion and outpost duty at Fort Arauco. She preferred to desert her post. With two others, she traveled north and apparently crossed the Andes mountains into Argentina. Her companions died from the conditions of hunger, thirst, and the frigid temperatures, but Erauso reached Tucumán. Soon, she returned to Perú where she again enlisted in the army but was struck down by a terrible fever. Convinced that she was on her death bed, she called for a priest to make her confession and revealed her true identity for the first time since leaving Spain.

To the priest, Erauso declared that she had always felt "a special inclination to take up arms in defense of the Catholic faith, and to be employed in his majesty's service." She believed that her destiny was to become a soldier, no matter what social norms might dictate, and also insisted that she had remained a virgin. After two matrons had certified that she was "a maid entire, as on the day I was born," she was embraced by the priest, who pronounced her a remarkable person, and then made her promise that if she recovered, she would return to her family in Spain.

Recover she did, and, while still in Peru, she was received by the archbishop, who praised her valor and loyalty to the Spanish crown. On the day of Corpus Christi, in response to the public enthusiasm at learning that the notorious Alfonso Ramírez was in fact a young nun escaped from a convent, Erauso accompanied the archbishop in the procession, dressed as a Clarissan nun with her sword at her side.

The nun-ensign had spent two years in a convent in Lima when word arrived from the mother superior in San Sebastián that Catalina de Erauso had never actually taken her religious vows. Advised by the local church authorities to return to Spain, Erauso departed as a celebrity. Once back in Europe, however, somewhat worried about the state of her soul, she determined to travel to Rome in search of religious guidance. She was arrested in Italy, accused of being a Spanish spy, her official papers were stolen, and she was held in jail for 50 days before being released. Barefoot and without funds, she made her way to Toulouse, France, where a friend, the Count of Gramont, supplied her with money and a horse to reach Spain. In Madrid, now probably 33 years old, Erauso gained an audience with King Philip IV, who was so impressed by her adventures that in August 1625 she was awarded a lifelong military pension in honor of her services.

Ever restless, Erauso again traveled to Italy and, accompanied by several cardinals of the Catholic Church, had an audience with Pope Urbano VIII. Her past adventures were given the blessing of the Vatican, and she received the pope's authorization to dress in men's clothing whenever she wished. According to her biographical account, "My case became notorious in Rome, and I saw myself surrounded by a remarkable crowd of great personages—princes, bishops, and cardinals—and every door was thrown open to me." When a cardinal once declared that Erauso's only defect was that she was a Spaniard, she replied, "Your Eminence, I think that is the only good thing about me."

Erauso may have settled for a while in Naples, where she wrote the autobiography entitled *The Story of the Nun-Ensign*. According to tradition, the manuscript was left in Italy. Many years after her death, a wealthy and cultured Spaniard, Joaquín María Ferrer, said he had discovered the original copy of her memoirs. Ferrer published the autobiography in Paris in 1829. Most scholars believe that this book is not Erauso's original version but one based on firsthand knowledge of the original manuscript or tales that had been circulating in Spain for many years.

Upon returning to Spain, the nun-ensign settled in La Coruña, where she met the author Juan Pérez de Montalván, a disciple of the renowned Spanish playwright Lope de Vega. Montalván wrote a drama based on stories told to him by Erauso, and the play became popular throughout the Iberian Peninsula. About this time, the Spanish painter Pacheco made a portrait of Erauso, which shows her to be tall and slim, dark-complexioned, with animated black eyes and a certain martial elegance in her stance. The painting hangs at the Schepeler Gallery in Aix-la-Chapelle, France.

Catalina de Erauso chose never to return to visit her parents and other relatives. Instead, eventually tiring of the sedentary life in La Coruña, she asked the king for permission to return to the Americas to enter into business in one of the many cities she knew well. The king agreed and Catalina, now adopting the name of Francisco de Erauso, sailed for Mexico in 1635. The voyage was a rough one, and the vessel arrived in the Mexican port city of Veracruz in the middle of a terrible storm. A group of officials decided to disembark despite the dangers, and Erauso asked to accompany them. Fighting the torrent, the small landing boat finally reached shore, but when the captain called the roll it was discovered that Francisco de Erauso had disappeared.

The ship's crew, assuming Erauso drowned, prayed for her soul. From this point on, all trace of Catalina de Erauso vanished from official Spanish records. Some have thought she committed suicide; there is certainly the possibility that she again fled in order to establish a new identity, since much of her life had been a struggle to maintain autonomy and anonymity.

It is also worth noting that many details of the life of Catalina de Erauso mirror the picaresque tradition so important in Spanish literature. In the picaresque genre, a male or female protagonist travels through his country, or the world, experiencing humorous, fantastic or scandalous adventures. The *pícaro* is a kind of antihero who lives by his or her wits, serves many masters, and usually ends up prosperous and respected after a period of youthful difficulties and rebellion. It is also true that the picaresque evolved out of the real adventures of people who revolted against the social strictures of a highly structured society and survived by their wits and agility. The stories of the nun-ensign fit both aspects of the literary tradition.

There is little doubt that her story has been enhanced, and that the "nun-ensign" is now the stuff of legend. In 1635, befitting a legend, she disappeared into the murk of a tempestuous night. According to some accounts, she lived another 15 years in the small Mexican village of Cotaxtla, where she died in 1650 at the age of 58. The bishop of Puebla, Monsignor Palafox, believed that the woman he buried there was the nun-ensign, and on her tombstone were engraved these words: "Here lies a brave and Christian woman." Whatever her end, Catalina de Erauso stands as an example of a Spanish woman who seemed destined by birth and society to spend her life in a convent, but who chose her own path to military glory and adventures that spanned two continents.

SOURCES:

Brandon, William. *Quivira*. Athens, OH: Ohio University Press, 1990.

Fitzpatrick-Kelly, James, ed. and trans. *The Nun Ensign*. London: T. Fisher Unwin, 1908 (included are the English translation of Erauso's autobiography, and Juan Pérez de Montalbán's play *La monja alférez* in the original Spanish, with introduction and notes).

Jarpa Gana de Laso, Sara. *La monja alférez*. Santiago, Chile: Editorial del Pacífico, 1960.

SUGGESTED READING:

Erauso, Catalina de. *Lieutenant Nun: Memoir of a Basque Transvestite in the New World*. Translated by Michele and Gabriel Stepto. Beacon, 1995.

Henderson, Linda Roddy, and James D. *Ten Notable Women of Latin America*. Chicago, IL: Nelson-Hall, 1978.

Virginia Gibbs,
Assistant Professor of Spanish Language and Literature,
Luther College, Decorah, Iowa

Erikson, Joan (c. 1902–1997)

Canadian-born collaborator and wife of Erik Erikson. Born Joan Mowat in Canada, around 1902; died on August 3, 1997, in Brewster, Massachusetts; graduated from Barnard College; master's degree from Columbia University Teachers College; married Erik Erikson (a psychologist), in 1930 (died 1994); children: two sons and a daughter.

The daughter of an Anglican priest, Canadian-born Joan Erikson was in Vienna doing research on her doctoral dissertation on dance, when she met Erik Erikson, a young psychologist who was there to help set up a progressive school with *Anna Freud and to study with Anna's father, Sigmund Freud. Joan was so smitten with Erik that she gave up her own research and took a job with him at the school. The couple married in 1930, and two years and two children later they moved to the United States, living first at Harvard University, then at Yale (where they had a third child), while Erik finished his studies. They eventually settled at the University of California at Berkeley, where Erik taught until 1951. (He resigned rather than sign a loyalty oath imposed during the hysteria of the McCarthy Era.)

It was while the couple was at Berkeley that the eight-cycle theory of human development was formulated. Although it has been credited solely to Erik, the concept was in fact a collaborative effort with Joan. She helped formulate some of the language of the theory, including the term "basic trust," to describe the relationship an infant gains from the mother. Joan also had input into the formulation of an additional cycle, the child-bearing years, to what Erik had initially conceived as a seven-cycle theory. After her husband's death in 1994, Joan Erikson continued their work, adding yet a ninth stage of development which appears in a recent reissue of the book *Life Cycle Completed.*

Joan also had an ongoing passion for weaving and jewelry making, and wrote a book on beading in 1969, *The Universal Bead.* In 1951, when her husband took a job treating severely disturbed children and young adults at the Riggs Center in Stockbridge, Massachusetts, Joan helped expand the facility's occupational therapy program by bringing in painters, sculptors, weavers, potters, and dancers to help provide a wider range of therapeutic outlets. Her work resulted in the 1976 publication *Activity, Recovery and Growth.*

The Eriksons spent the 1960s at Harvard, and in the 1980s conducted joint classes at the Joan and Erik Erikson Center. As a couple, they were the ideal embodiment of their own theories, reaching a graceful and productive old age. They also remained lovers throughout their long relationship, walking hand-in-hand and unabashedly kissing in public even in their later years.

SOURCES:

Thomas, Robert McG., Jr. "Obituaries," in *The New York Times.* August 8, 1997.

Erinna (fl. 7th c. BCE)

Ancient Greek composer and poet. Name variations: Lesbia; Erina. Born at Rhodes or Telos around 600 BCE; died at age 19, by which time her poems and compositions were widely admired.

Sometimes known as Lesbia because she came from the island of Lesbos, Erinna was said to love singing so much that her mother, determined that her daughter spin rather than sing, chained her to a spinning wheel. A celebrated Greek poet, Erinna studied at the art school in Mytilene founded by her friend *Sappho and was said to have been her most gifted student. Her talent was quickly demonstrated, especially in poetry, and some regarded her gifts to be greater than Sappho's. The only remaining fragment of Erinna's work is a lyric about a female singer named **Baucis.** Later titled "The Distaff" or "The Spindle," this work was a lament with recurring cries of sorrow.

Eristavi-Xostaria, Anastasia

(1868–1951)

Georgian novelist, generally regarded as the most distinguished female novelist in Georgian literary history. Name variations: Anast'asia Eristav-Khosht'aria or Khoshtaria. Born in 1868; died in 1951.

As a result of the demise of the Soviet Union in 1991, the independent nation of Georgia can once again boast of ancient cultural traditions more than 2,000 years old. The country was converted to Christianity by St. Nino early in the 4th century CE and developed a rich literary tradition. One of the greatest works of medieval Georgia, Shota Rustaveli's *The Man in the Panther's Skin,* written during the reign of Queen *Tamara (r. 1184–1212), has been judged to be one of the great works of world literature (copies of this epic poem are traditionally included in every Georgian bride's dowry). The loss of Georgian independence to tsarist Russia in 1801 led to a period of political and cultural oppression that in turn sparked a spirit of intellectual resistance. By the 1870s, a national renaissance was in full bloom, led by the immensely popular lyric poet Akaki Tsereteli (1840–1915).

Swept along by the national enthusiasm of the Georgian intelligentsia, Anastasia Eristavi-Xostaria grew up in the 1870s and 1880s with the dream of one day becoming a famous writer. To earn her daily bread, she worked as a schoolteacher, but she used her spare time to write or engage in passionate debates over the fine points of literary theory and practice. In the 1890s, Akaki Tsereteli recognized her talent and encouraged her to write a major work. Her first novel *Molip'ul gzaze* (*On the Slippery Path*) was published in 1897 to positive reviews. Four years later, in 1901, came *Be'lis t'riali* (*The Wheel of Fate*).

Over the next two decades, Eristavi-Xostaria published more novels and short stories that were well received by the Georgian reading public. Her writings follow a general pattern in which a noblewoman must face the turmoil brought on by the collapse of the old economic and moral order in Georgia in the second half of the 19th century. Her protagonists defend their ideals of love and decency in a world that is corrupt and in which few of the male characters exhibit strength of character or basic honor. The heroine of *On the Slippery*

Path, the artist Ketino, decides against marrying a man she does not love, travels abroad in search of new artistic insights, and finally returns to Georgia mortally ill to be united with Paliko, the man she has always truly loved.

In *The Wheel of Fate,* the idealistic Sidonia is disillusioned by her marriage to Geno, a brute who bullies his peasants and seduces his servants. This novel ends dramatically with the death of Geno, who is lynched by peasants who can bear no more of his acts of humiliation. Despite some stylistic weaknesses that have been noted by literary critics, Eristavi-Xostaria's novels and short stories have been popular in Georgia for over a century. They exhibit, in the judgment of Professor Robert B. Pynsent, the qualities of "narrative drive" and "noble aims."

Although she was a member of the "national bourgeoisie," Anastasia Eristavi-Xostaria remained a major figure in Georgian literary circles after the assumption of power by the Bolshevik Party in 1921. She spent the final decades of her long life as an honored "living classic" of the nation's literary renaissance. While not following a Marxist line, her "social novels" were nevertheless regarded as important documents of a changing national culture. Although Eristavi-Xostaria wrote no major works after the 1920s, she did pen ideologically corrective introductions to the reprint editions of her writings that were regularly published during the Soviet period.

SOURCES:
Abuladze, M.S., *et al. Istoriia gruzinskoi literatury.* Moscow: Nauka, 1977.

Baramize, Aleksandre Giorgis ze, *et al. Istoriia gruzinskoi literatury: kratky ocherk.* Tbilisi: Zaria vostoka, 1958.

Eristavi-Xostaria, Anastasia. *Txzulebani.* 2 vols. Tbilisi: Saxelmcipo gamomcemloba, 1952–1958.

Jiblaze, Giorgi. *Romantiki i realisty v gruzinskoi literature XIX veka.* Tbilisi: Lit-ra i iskusstvo, 1963.

Lang, David Marshall. *A Modern History of Soviet Georgia.* Westport, CT: Greenwood Press, 1975.

———, ed. "Armenian and Georgian Literature," in *A Guide to Eastern Literatures.* London: Weidenfeld and Nicolson, 1971, pp. 179–194.

Pynsent, Robert B., and S.I. Kanikova, eds. *Reader's Encyclopedia of Eastern European Literature.* NY: HarperCollins. 1993.

Rayfield, Donald. "Beria and the Policing of Literature," in *Scottish Slavonic Review.* Vol. 18. Spring 1992, pp. 7–24.

John Haag,
Assistant Professor of History,
University of Georgia, Athens, Georgia

Ermenburga (fl. late 600s)

Queen of Mercia. Name variations: Eormenburga. Daughter of Queen *Emma *(fl. 600s); married* *Merowald or Merwald, king of Mercia; sister of saints Ethered, Ethelbright, and Ermenbert; children: daughters Milburg (d. 722?); Mildred (d. 700?); Mildgyth or Mildgithe; son Mervin or Mervyn.*

Ermenburga, queen of Mercia, had three daughters and one son. All of her daughters became nuns, and two—***Mildred** and ***Milburg**—were canonized saints.

Ermenburga, who flourished in the late 600s, was born into a pious family. But her uncle Egbert, king of the English, caused her two brothers, Ethelred and Ethelbright, to be secretly murdered, employing a Count Thunor as his agent. Count Thunor then buried the bodies of the murdered princes beneath the king's throne in the royal palace of Estria. Thereafter, the king, whose guilty conscience made him see everything with a distorted vision, was terrified one day when he beheld a ray of light that he was certain darted direct from heaven to the graves. (It was probably no more than an ordinary sunbeam.)

Urged to restitution by his terror, Egbert sent for Ermenburga and gave her "48 ploughs of land" as *weregild,* the fine imposed by the laws of England to be paid by a murderer to the relatives of the murdered. Queen Ermenburga devoted the 48 ploughs of land to the founding of a monastery, called Menstrey or Minstre, situated in the Isle of Thanet, where the village of Minster near Ramsgate resides. Therein, the repose of the souls of the murdered princes was to be prayed for. The king aided in the foundation of the monastery, hoping no doubt to further ease his guilt.

Ermenburga sent her daughter Mildred over to France, to the Abbey of Chelles, where Mildred took the veil and was duly trained in all religious exercises. Upon her return to England, Mildred was appointed first abbess of her mother's newly founded Monastery of Minstre.

Ermengarde.

Variant of Irmengarde.

Ermengarde (d. 773).

See Desiderata.

Ermengarde (c. 778–818)

Queen of France and Holy Roman empress. Name variations: Ermingarde; Irmengard of Hesbain. Born around 778; died in 818; daughter of Count Ingram; became first wife of Louis I the Pious (778–840), king of Aquitaine (r. 781–814), king of France (r.

814–840), and Holy Roman Emperor (r. 814–840), in 798; children: Lothair I, Holy Roman emperor (r. 840–855); Pepin or Pippin (d. 838), king of Aquitaine (r. 814–838); *Adelaide (c. 794–after 852); Louis II the German (804–876), king of the Germans (r. 843–876); *Rotrud (800–841); *Hildegard (c. 802–841). Louis I the Pious' second wife was *Judith of Bavaria (802–843).

Ermengarde de Gatinais (d. 1147).

See Ermengarde of Anjou.

Ermengarde Melusina von der Schulenburg, baroness Schulenburg (1667–1743).

See Schulenburg, Ehrengard Melusina von der.

Ermengarde of Anjou (1018–1076)

Duchess of Burgundy. Name variations: Ermengard d'Anjou. Born in 1018; died on March 18, 1076, in Fleury-sur-Ouche; daughter of Fulk III the Black, count of Anjou; married Geoffrey, count of Gastinois; married Robert I (1011–1076), duke of Burgundy (r. 1031–1076), around 1048; children: (first marriage) Geoffrey III the Bearded, count of Anjou; Fulk IV the Rude, count of Anjou; (second marriage) *Hildegard of Burgundy (1050–after 1104). Robert I was also married to *Helia de Semur.

Ermengarde of Anjou (d. 1147)

Duchess of Brittany. Name variations: Ermengarde of Brittany; Ermengarde de Gatinais. Died in 1147 (some sources cite 1146) in Brittany; daughter of Fulk IV, count of Anjou, and **Audearde de Beaugency**; married William IX, duke of Aquitaine, in 1088 (divorced 1091); married Alan IV, duke of Brittany, in 1091 or 1092 (died 1119); children: (second marriage) Conan III, duke of Brittany (d. 1148). Became a nun.

Ermengarde was born into the ruling house of Anjou. Around 1088, she married Duke William IX of Poitiers, a renowned warrior and troubadour and duke of Aquitaine. Their marriage lasted only three years; Ermengarde's rather quiet, conventional character contrasted too sharply with William's irreverent behavior (he was even excommunicated), and both agreed they should separate. Ermengarde married again in 1091 or 1092, becoming the wife of Count Alan IV of Brittany. They seem to have had a happy marriage, although Alan was absent much of the time, on crusade as well as for other military exploits. During his long absences (1096–1101, 1112–1119), he appointed Ermengarde to act as his regent. She was a successful ruler and gained the approval of many Bretons for her even-tempered sense of justice and her attempts to improve their living conditions.

Alan died in 1119, and their son succeeded as duke of Brittany. Ermengarde continued her work as regent for him, as he was not yet of an age to rule. She also began a campaign to regain her title as duchess of Aquitaine, which she had long since given up after her separation from Duke William. Determined, she even petitioned the pope on the matter, but her claims were too weak and the pope refused to comply. Ermengarde then turned her energies to more attainable goals closer to home; one of her most successful projects was the rewriting of the law code of Brittany. Under her direction, laws were made more fair and less burdensome on poor Bretons.

Around 1131, with her son old enough to reign alone, Ermengarde left Brittany for a pilgrimage to Jerusalem. This journey, and perhaps also her advancing age, altered her perspectives and values; she returned to Brittany several years later with a more devout religiosity, intent on serving God and helping others do the same. She used her wealth to found at least one monastery and donated generously to several local religious houses. Duchess Ermengarde earned widespread respect for these efforts and was well-remembered by the Bretons for many years after her death in 1147.

Laura York,
Riverside, California

Ermengarde of Beaumont (d. 1234)

Queen of Scotland. Name variations: Ermengarde Beaumont; Ermengarde de Beaumont. Died on February 11, 1234 (some sources cite 1233); buried at Balmerino Abbey, Fife, Scotland; daughter of Richard Beaumont, Viscount Beaumont, and *Constance (daughter of *Sybilla Corbert and Henry I, king of England); married William I the Lion (1143–1214), king of the Scots (r. 1165–1214), on September 5, 1186; children: Alexander II (1198–1249), king of Scotland (r. 1214–1249); *Margaret de Burgh (c. 1193–1259); *Isabel (who married Robert Bigod, 3rd earl of Norfolk); Marjory (d. 1244). William I the Lion had children with two other women.

Ermengarde of Brittany (d. 1147).

See Ermengarde of Anjou.

Ermengarde of Carcassonne
(d. 1070)

Countess of Carcassonne. Died in 1070 in Carcassonne. Daughter of Roger II, count of Carcassonne; married Raimond Bernard (a French noble); children: unknown.

Ermengarde was the well-educated daughter of Count Roger II of Carcassonne. Carcassonne was a small but prosperous county in what is now southwestern France. She married Raimond Bernard, a petty noble. Her brother succeeded their father in 1060 as Roger III, but he died young in 1067, leaving no heirs. Ermengarde thus succeeded as countess in her own name. She ruled alone for the next three years, until her death in 1070.

Laura York,
Riverside, California

Ermengarde of Narbonne
(c. 1120–c. 1194)

Viscountess of Narbonne. Born around 1120 in Narbonne; died around 1194 in Narbonne; daughter of Aimery II, viscount of Narbonne; married at least three times, although husbands' identities are uncertain; children: none.

Ermengarde was the eldest daughter and heiress of Viscount Aimery II of Narbonne, a county located in what is now southeast France. Her father died when she was still young, and thus she faced the dangers encountered by all medieval women left with a sizeable inheritance—the possibilities of invasion, rebellion, or kidnapping and forced marriage. Ermengarde proved herself capable of handling her affairs well despite her youth. She used her troops to put down incipient rebellions by her vassals, and repelled Count Alphonse of Toulouse's attempts to take over Narbonne while ostensibly protecting its young heiress. Ermengarde married several times, although sources do not clearly identify her husbands, and they did not play a major role in her government. She was fiercely loyal to the pious King Louis VII of France and led her troops to help Louis put down rebellions by his vassals in southern France. During her reign of more than 60 years, Ermengarde became famous as a benevolent and balanced judge in feudal court cases under her jurisdiction. The viscountess was also renowned as a patron of troubadours, the singer-poets who composed themes on various aspects of love. She died around 1194.

Laura York,
Riverside, California

Ermengarde of Provence (fl. 876)

*Queen of Provence. Name variations: Ermingarde. Flourished around 876; daughter of Louis II le Jeune also known as Louis II the Child (c. 822–875), king of Italy (r. 844), king of Lorraine (r. 872–875), Holy Roman Emperor (r. 855–875), and *Engelberga (c. 840–890); married Boso, king of Provence (r. 879–887), in 876; children: Louis III the Blind of Provence, Holy Roman emperor (r. 901–905); *Engelberga of Aquitaine (877–917).*

Ermenilda (d. around 700)

*Queen of Mercia. Name variations: Eormengild of Kent. Died around 700; daughter of Earconbert also known as Ercombert, king of Kent, and Saint *Sexburga (d. 699?); married Wulfhere, king of Mercia (r. 657–675); children: Saint *Werburga (d. 700?, who was also abbess of Sheppey and Ely); Coenred, king of Mercia; Behrtwald.*

After being widowed, Ermenilda served as abbess of Sheppey, then of Ely. Her feast day is February 13.

Ermensinde (d. 1247).

See Ermesinde of Luxemburg.

Ermentrude (d. 869)

*Queen of France. Died in 869; daughter of Vodon, earl of Orléans, and Engeltrude; became first wife of Charles I the Bald, king of France (r. 840–877), known also as Charles II, Holy Roman emperor (r. 875–877), in 842; children: Louis II the Stammerer (846–879), king of France (r. 877–879); *Judith Martel (c. 844–?); Carloman (d. 874); Charles (c. 847–865), king of Aquitaine; Ermentrude of Hasnon, abbess of Hasnon; Hildegard; Gisele; Rotrude of Poitiers, abbess of St. Radegund; Drogo; Pippin; Lothar. Charles I the Bald's second wife was *Richilde of Autun.*

Ermentrude (d. 1126)

*Countess of Maine. Name variations: Aremburg or Heremburge; Ermengarde du Maine. Died in 1126; daughter of Elias I, count of Maine, and Matilda of Château du Loir; married Fulk V (b. 1092), count of Anjou and king of Jerusalem, on July 11, 1110; children: five, including *Matilda of Anjou (1107–1154); *Sybilla of Anjou (1112–1165); Geoffrey IV, count of Anjou; and Elias II, count of Maine.*

Ermentrude de Roucy (d. 1005)

*Countess of Burgundy. Name variations: Ermentrude de Rouci; Ermentrude Rheims; Irmtrude. Died on March 5, 1005; daughter of Renaud or Rainald de Roucy and Alberade of Lorraine (930–973); married Othon-Guillaume also known as Otto William, count of Burgundy, around 982 (died 1026); children: *Agnes of Aquitaine (c. 995–1068); Gerberga of Burgundy (who married William II, count of Provence); Matilda of Burgundy (who married Landeric, count of Nevers); Renaud I (990–1057), 1st count of Burgundy.*

Ermesind of Luxemburg (fl. 1200)

Countess of Namur. Name variations: Ermensinde; Ermesinde. Flourished around 1200; daughter of Conrad I, count of Luxemburg (r. 1059–1086); sister of Gilbert, Henry III, and William (all counts of Luxemburg); married Godfrey, count of Namur; children: Henry IV the Blond also known as Henry IV the Blind, count of Luxemburg (r. 1136–1196).

Ermesind of Luxemburg (d. 1247)

*Countess and ruler of Luxemburg. Name variations: Ermensinde; Ermesinde; countess of Namur. Reigned from 1196 to 1247; died in 1247; daughter of Henry IV the Blind also known as Henry IV the Blond, count of Luxemburg (son of Godfrey, count of Namur, and *Ermesind of Luxemburg [fl. 1200]); married Walram III, duke of Limburg; children: Henry V the Blind also known as Henry V the Blond (1217–1281), count of Luxemburg (r. 1247–1281).*

Born into the House of Namur, Ermesind became ruler of the principality of Luxemburg in 1196, following the death of her father Count Henry IV. When she died in 1247, her son Henry V became count of Luxemburg.

Ermingarde.

Variant of Ermengarde.

Ermoleva, Zinaida (1898–1974)

Russian microbiologist, "bacteriochemist," and cholera expert of the Soviet era who is known as "the Mother of Soviet Antibiotics." Name variations: Zinaida Vissarionovna Ermol'eva; Zinaida Yermolyeva or Yermoleva. Born on October 24, 1898, in Frolovo; died in 1974.

Obtained the first Soviet samples of penicillin (1942); obtained laboratory samples of streptomycin (1947); developed a number of Soviet antibiotic agents including interferon, ekmonovicillin, Bicillins, ekmolin, and dipasfen; received the highest scientific honors the Soviet Union bestowed.

One of the few women to rise to the top of the Soviet scientific pyramid, Zinaida Ermoleva began her career in 1921 during the infancy of the Soviet state, when its very survival appeared questionable to most observers. As a researcher working at the Northern Caucasus Bacteriological Institute, she coped with frustrating shortages of laboratory equipment and funds, as well as constant political pressures to create near miracles of public-health reform. Her work was brought to the attention of her superiors, and in 1925 she began working as a researcher at the A.N. Bakh Biochemical Institute of the People's Commissariat for Public Health of the USSR. By the late 1930s, she had also become a leading researcher in the All-Union Institute of Experimental Medicine of the USSR, where she concentrated on discovering, and preparing for clinical use, new therapies for infectious diseases. She became a noted expert on cholera and, as early as 1931, was able to create a new treatment for infectious diseases, lysozyme.

During World War II, Ermoleva's two decades of intensive research in the area of infectious diseases was harnessed to the immediate strategic needs of a Soviet Union fighting for its existence against a brutal Nazi foe. She was assigned to the city of Stalingrad during its heroic battle against Hitler's Sixth Army. As an authority on human intestinal infections, she directed the efforts to provide germ-free water—from the Volga river—for the city's Soviet defenders. Her efforts helped to maintain the health of the soldiers who eventually destroyed a previously undefeated Nazi juggernaut. Ermoleva's ampules of bacteriophage, which helped restore to health Red Army soldiers who had become infected with cholera, were flown into besieged Stalingrad along with cases of cartridges and hand grenades. Soviet military leaders regarded the medical supplies approved by Ermoleva to be as important a weapon for achieving victory as the guns, tanks and rocket launchers that were also delivered to the Stalingrad and other fronts.

Because of the immense loss of life and permanent injuries resulting from war-related wounds and infections, Ermoleva felt immense pressure during World War II to quickly develop new and more effective treatments for the septic wounds and gangrene that were all too common at Soviet front-line hospitals and first-aid stations. She had heard about the work of Sir Alexander Fleming in Great Britain, whose discovery of penicillin had saved lives in what had been before considered hopeless cases of advanced infection. Using the traditional method of trial and error, Ermoleva and her assistant **Tamara Balezina** analyzed many hundreds of mold cultures, working to find one that was effective against infectious bacteria. She hoped to quickly find and isolate a culture that would be effective in ordinary medical practice.

Their spirits flagging, Ermoleva and Balezina one day found themselves in a dank air-raid shelter and noticed some mold growing in a crack of the shelter's wall. They took a sample to their laboratory and almost miraculously discovered that this variety of mold exhibited the effect that they had so long hoped for. This tiny piece of mold became the source of the first sample of Soviet-produced penicillin. Success in the laboratory by no means guaranteed mass production of what appeared to be a promising new medicine, so Ermoleva embarked on another facet of her career, as manager of a major industrial enterprise. She took charge of the facility that manufactured Soviet penicillin on a mass-produced basis. Her success in this work made it possible for the Soviet military to be less dependent on an unreliable flow of medical supplies from its Western Allies. As a result, thousands of lives of Soviet fighting men and women were saved after they had been wounded in battle.

After World War II, Ermoleva's fame continued to increase, and from 1947 to 1954 she worked at the Institute of Antibiotics of the USSR Ministry of Public Health. In 1947, she obtained the first samples of Soviet-produced streptomycin. Over the next decades, she led research teams that produced other antibiotic agents, including interferon, ekmonovicillin, Bicillins, ekmolin, and dipasfen. She developed a reputation for immense energy and superb organization, prompting one of her colleagues, N.F. Gamaleya, to note: "What distinguishes her as a researcher is her readiness to tackle the problems which are most urgent at the moment . . . and her ability to supply speedy and productive answers to questions posed by life."

A loyal Soviet citizen of the Stalin regime, Ermoleva never questioned the nature or human costs of the Soviet state. In 1943, she received the State Prize of the USSR and over the years received many other awards including two Orders of Lenin as well as numerous medals and commendations. She served for many years as chair of the USSR Ministry of Health Committee on Antibiotics. Her other assignments included that of editor-in-chief of the journal *Antibiotiki* and Soviet representative to the World Health Organization. Many of her students and co-workers could be found applying their knowledge in universities, research institutes and hospitals throughout the Soviet Union.

Elected a corresponding member of the USSR Academy of Medical Sciences in 1945, she became a full Academician of that prestigious body in 1965. In 1970, Ermoleva was named an Honored Scientific Worker of the Russian Soviet Federated Socialist Republic. Her accomplishments were often reported in the Soviet press and scientific literature. Following her death in 1974, the high quality of her scientific work in cholera control and prevention, as well as her contributions to the development of antibiotic agents, continued to be cited in scientific journals in the post-Soviet era (most recently in 1998 on the occasion of the centenary of her birth, despite the demise of the Soviet regime in 1991). Memories of Zinaida Ermoleva's powerful and tenacious personality also continued to resonate in the literature of the history of Soviet medical research.

SOURCES:

Ermoleva Centenary Commemorative Articles, *Antibiotiki i Khimioterapia* [Moscow]. Vol. 43, no. 5. May 1998, pp. 1–46.

Maximov, Leonid. "Mother of Soviet Antibiotics," in *Culture and Life* [Moscow]. No. 3, 1973, pp. 8–9.

Soviet Antibiotics Research. Washington, D.C.: Joint Publications Research Service, 1968.

John Haag,
Assistant Professor of History,
University of Georgia, Athens, Georgia

Ermolova, Mariia (1853–1928)

Russian actress whose powerful interpretations set a new standard for acting on the Moscow stage. Name variations: Maria Nikolaijevna Yermolova; Maria M. Ermolova. Born Mariia Nikolaevna Ermolova in Moscow, Russia, on July 15, 1853; died in Moscow on March 12, 1928; daughter of Nikolai Ermolov.

Mariia Ermolova, one of the greatest stars of the Russian stage for five decades, was born into the theater. Her father, Nikolai Ermolov, was a prompter at one of Moscow's leading theaters, the Malyi, and in her youth Mariia spent countless hours in the company of actors and actresses. In 1870, while she was still a student, her talents were revealed when she made her debut at the Malyi Theater in the starring role of Lessing's *Emilia Galotti*. She began her professional acting career in 1871 by joining the Malyi ensemble, quickly becoming a mainstay of the Malyi.

Ermolova came to maturity during a period of great intellectual and political ferment in Russia. Tsarist attempts at reform only whetted the appetites for greater freedom of a younger generation of intellectuals who were determined to bring their nation into the mainstream of civilization as it was evolving in the West.

This exclusive group, Russia's intelligentsia, dreamed of a nation free of oppression, injustice and poverty in what was for them a repressive police state, often as petty as it was brutal. In their efforts to break down the walls of repression, Russian intellectuals relied on novels, poetry and plays to voice their opposition to tsarism, despite the press and theater censorship which weighed heavily on their attempts.

The lead characters Mariia Ermolova chose to portray were women who embodied the ideals of freedom, truth and beauty about which her audiences felt so passionately. Her stirring portrayals of Katerina in Ostrovsky's *The Thunderstorm* and Laurencia in Lope de Vega's *Fuente Ovejuna* brought audiences to a state of moral exaltation, reflecting the expectant mood of the times. Ermolova's discovery of a contemporary message in *Fuente Ovejuna,* in which an ordinary girl emerges as the leader of a popular uprising, did not escape the notice of police agents. After witnessing several wildly acclaimed performances that ended with political demon-

strations, the officials banned any further performances of the play because its message was deemed subversive of established authority.

With her extraordinary acting abilities, Mariia Ermolova discovered new depths in her characterizations in plays that had not been regarded as political. She both expanded her artistic range and came to embody the ideals of social activists. After her success in creating the role of Katerina in *The Thunderstorm,* she went on to portray several more characters in other Ostrovsky plays. Probing the emotional structures of strongly independent women, Ermolova gave soulful performances as Iuliia Tugina in *The Last Victim,* Evlaliia in *Slaves,* Kruchnina in *Guilty Though Guiltless,* and Negina in *Talents and Suitors.* In the last role, first performed in 1881, she created one of her most memorable personas, that of a socially engaged woman who chooses to sacrifice personal happiness for her artistic vocation. Other star roles in which she instantly won over audiences included Phaedra, *Sappho, and Clärchen in Goethe's *Egmont,* as well as several Shakespearean women, including Lady Macbeth (*Gruoch).

Repression of Russia's intellectual life intensified after the assassination of Tsar Alexander II in 1881. Despite this, resourceful artists like Ermolova challenged the regime more than ever before through their portrayals. The Malyi The-

*Mariia
Ermolova*

ater was at the heart of this clandestine resistance to tsarist tyranny and was dubbed Moscow's "second university." Students who attended plays claimed that they learned as much from Malyi performances as from professorial lectures. Youthful intellectuals made a ritual of preparing themselves for an evening at the Malyi Theater, reading the play and the critical literature about it, and meeting beforehand to discuss its fine points, even at times inviting an expert to lecture their group and then supervise the ensuing debate. Later in the evening, her fans were not disappointed when Ermolova appeared in beloved classic Russian plays by playwrights Pushkin, Turgeniev, Ostrovsky and others.

Mariia Ermolova was known to be extremely modest, kindly and even timid in private life. She could be easily embarrassed by compliments, seeming hardly aware of her talents. Once on stage, however, she revealed a passionate temperament, the capacity to project nuances of mood and emotion, and a profound sensitivity to a vast range of human behaviors. One evening her portrayal of a woman in the throes of death who has drunk a vial of poison was done so realistically that her colleagues in the wings and even the veteran stage director Chernevsky became concerned about what sort of liquid she had actually consumed, and several in the audience rushed to the foyer to summon a physician.

With her handsome, mobile face and sparkling eyes, she was also noted for the expressive warmth of her low voice, her beautiful figure and flawless complexion. Ermolova enchanted not only audiences but her theater colleagues as well. Constantin Stanislavski recalled in his memoirs the warmth and plasticity of her voice, which retained its harmony and rhythm even in a state of exaltation. He was enthralled by what he saw as her unique ability to coordinate the inner apparatus (perception of feelings) and the outer manifestations of emotions (gesture and voice), as well as by the astonishing variations of human emotions she created. A true virtuoso, she could alternate with ease between whispers, tenderness, and savage outbursts of rage.

For decades, legions of Mariia Ermolova's admirers packed the house at the Malyi. Although they were stirred by virtually all of her performances, she reached the peak of her career in the plays of Friedrich von Schiller, whose noble, elevated style was in harmony with her talent and beliefs. Ermolova performed five roles in his major dramas, achieving her greatest success as Johanna (*Joan of Arc) in *Die Jungfrau von Orleans*. As the heroic Johanna, Ermolova became the undisputed queen of Moscow in the final years of the 19th century. She first performed this role in 1884. In 1902, she made her last appearance as Johanna, the Maid of Orleans, realizing that as an aging actress she could only do a disservice to the role of a young woman as depicted in Schiller's great tragedy and that she must move on. Other Schiller roles that Ermolova made her own were the title role in *Maria Stuart* and Elizabeth de Valois in *Don Carlos*. By the end of the 1890s, she was enjoying universal acclaim as "the Joan of Arc of the Russian theater."

Rich in years and honors, Mariia Ermolova retired from the stage in 1921, her last role being that of Mamelfa Dmitrievna in Alexei Tolstoy's *Viceroy*. The previous year, on the 50th anniversary of the beginning of her career, she had become the first person to receive the fledgling Soviet state's award of People's Artist of the Republic. To celebrate her anniversary, the revered actress chose to perform the third act of Schiller's *Maria Stuart*. In 1924, she was honored with the title of Hero of Labor. Ermolova died in Moscow on March 12, 1928. Her name lived on after her death, first in an actors' studio named for her, and in 1937 with the creation of the Moscow Ermolova Theater. On December 28, 1957, Soviet postal authorities issued a 40 kopeck postage stamp in her honor. In 1970, her former residence in Moscow on Tverskoy Boulevard was opened as a branch of the A.A. Bakhrushin State Central Theater Museum.

SOURCES:

Benedetti, Jean. *Stanislavski*. London: Methuen, 1988.

Durylin, Sergei Nikolaevich. *Mariia Nikolaevna Ermolova, 1853–1928: Ocherki zhizni i tvorchestva*. Moscow: Izd-vo Akademii nauk SSSR, 1953.

Ermolova, Mariia Nikolaevna. *Pisma, iz literaturnogo naslediia, vospominaniia sovremennikov*. Edited by Sergei Nikolaevich Durylin. Moscow: Iskusstvo, 1955.

Evreinov, Nikolai Bikolaevich. *History of the Russian Theater, from Its Origins to 1917*. NY: Chekhov Publishing House of the East European Fund, 1955.

Pushkareva, Natalia. *Women in Russian History from the Tenth to the Twentieth Century*. Translated and edited by Eve Levin. Armonk, NY: M.E. Sharpe, 1997.

Rayfield, Donald. *Anton Chekhov: A Life*. NY: Henry Holt, 1998.

Revutsky, Valerian. "Schiller and Ermolova," in *Germano-Slavica*. Vol. 5. Spring 1975, pp. 47–58.

Rudnitsky, Konstantin. *Russian and Soviet Theater 1905–1932*. Edited by Lesley Milne, translated by Roxane Permar. NY: Harry N. Abrams, 1988.

Shchepkina-Kupernik, Tatiana Lvovna. *Ermolova*. 3rd ed. Moscow: Iskusstvo, 1983.

Slonim, Marc. *Russian Theater, from the Empire to the Soviets*. Cleveland, OH: World, 1961.

Trilse, Christoph, Klaus Hammer and Rolf Kabel. *Theater Lexikon*. Berlin: Henschelverlag Kunst und Gesellschaft, 1977.

Tynianova, Lidiia Nikolaevna. *Povest o velikoi aktrise*. Moscow: "Detskaia lit-ra," 1966.

John Haag,
Assistant Professor of History,
University of Georgia, Athens, Georgia

Erskine, Margaret.

See Mary Stuart, Queen of Scots, for sidebar.

Ertmann, Dorothea von (1781–1849).

See Von Ertmann, Dorothea.

Erxleben, Dorothea (1715–1762)

German physician who was the first woman in Germany to be awarded an M.D. degree. Name variations: Dorothea von Erxleben; Dorothea Leporin-Erxleben. Born Dorothea Christiane Leporin in Quedlinburg, on November 13, 1715; died in Quedlinburg on June 13, 1762; daughter of Christian Polycarp Leporin (1689–1747, a physician) and Anna Sophia (Meinecke) Leporin; sister of Christian Polycarp Leporin; received her medical degree in 1754 and successfully practiced medicine in Quedlinburg until her death; married Johann Christian Erxleben; children: two daughters and two sons, including the noted physician Johann Christian Polycarp Erxleben (1744–1777), as well as five stepchildren.

Born in 1715 in the city of Quedlinburg, Dorothea Christiane Leporin grew up in a middle-class domestic environment that was remarkably liberal for its time and place. Her father, the physician Christian Polycarp Leporin (1689–1747), was open to the new ideas of the Enlightenment that were then sweeping through Europe's educated classes. The Leporin family embodied the virtues of Germany's *Bürgertum*, whose bourgeois ideals emphasized hard work, personal responsibility, thrift and education. Dorothea's mother, **Anna Sophia Leporin** (1680–1757), was descended from one of Quedlinburg's most respected families, with her father being the city's leading Lutheran pastor. Dorothea's father believed strongly that both his daughter and his son Christian Polycarp Leporin should be exposed to the best possible education available in Quedlinburg. Both children took Latin lessons from the local Lutheran pastor, and at home they were instructed by their father in the medical arts, both theoretical and practical.

Dorothea Leporin showed great intellectual gifts and systematically studied medicine along with her brother Christian, who planned to enter the newly founded University of Halle/Saale. The siblings were strongly encouraged in their career plans by a liberal father who saw no reason why his daughter, or indeed any talented young woman, could not choose medicine as a calling. Her plans were delayed but not stopped when Christian had to report for military service. Upon his return in 1740, Christian prepared to enter the University of Halle/Saale, and thereupon Dorothea petitioned Prussia's king, Frederick II, for permission to accompany him and study for a degree. The young sovereign, eventually to be known as Frederick the Great and already regarding himself as an enlightened ruler, approved the April 1741 positive recommendation of the Royal Department for Intellectual Affairs that both Christian and Dorothea Leporin be permitted to enroll for university studies in Halle/Saale.

Dorothea's admission to the university was met with a mixture of angry indignation and warm support. Critics of her admission to the portals of an institution of higher education included one Johann Rhetius, who argued that women were forbidden by law to practice medicine and thus there was no point in their earning university degrees even if one individual might in

$\mathcal{D}$orothea
$\mathcal{E}$rxleben

fact be able to do so. Dorothea followed the debate on women's education carefully and assembled notes on the issue for her own use, but apparently had no intention of entering into the controversy personally. When her father discovered her notes, he was so impressed by her arguments that he insisted that the work be completed and marketed. Published in 1742, her book, *A Thorough Inquiry into the Causes Preventing the Female Sex from Studying*, advanced a strong case for a nation to take advantage of the talents of its women, who represented a great untapped source of energy and experience. Dorothea Leporin's father wrote a long introduction to the *Inquiry*, arguing that Germany's universities were greatly in need of reform, and that the admittance of a pool of talented women to study at them would accelerate that long-overdue change.

Many were surprised in 1742 when Dorothea Leporin decided not to immediately enroll for university studies but instead get married. That year, she wed Johann Christian Erxleben (1697–1759), a respected Quedlinburg Lutheran deacon. A widower, Johann Erxleben brought five children into his marriage with his bride of 26. Over the next years, Dorothea gave birth to two daughters and two sons. One of her sons, Johann Christian Polycarp Erxleben (1744–1777), became a highly respected professor at the University of Göttingen where he taught physics and wrote a number of textbooks that were popular in Central Europe for many decades. Dorothea's marriage was a happy one, and she was kept busy at home raising not only her own four children but the five her husband had brought with him into their union. She never abandoned her goal of becoming a physician and was able to ration her time sufficiently to continue her medical studies, albeit at a reduced pace.

Unforeseen problems, however, slowed her progress toward a medical degree. In 1747, her father died, leaving the Leporin family with considerable debts. Her husband's health also deteriorated, and the bulk of responsibilities for her large family now fell on her shoulders. Refusing to become discouraged, she regularly practiced medicine in Quedlinburg without a degree, highly respected by her patients and the great majority of the town's citizens. Her popularity, however, angered some of the local physicians who looked upon her success not only in legal but economic terms, threatening their medical monopoly.

In 1753, three local doctors filed a law suit against Erxleben, charging her with medical quackery (*medicinischen Pfuscherey*). Showing great self-confidence, she responded to the legal challenge by answering to the several charges made against her. These included charges that 1) she allowed herself to be called "Frau Doctorin", 2) she often visited patients, and 3) she sometimes accepted money for her services. She responded to these accusations by asserting that 1) her accusers had "never brought forward anyone who called me [Frau Doctorin], or heard someone call me that, without being severely reprimanded," 2) she did not deny that she often visited patients, but she did not go to them in secret, and 3) she admitted to sometimes accepting payment for her services but also stated that "with God's help I cured people who gave me nothing but their best wishes. Would my gentlemen adversaries have me deny help to the poor?" Refusing to be cowed by the medical establishment of her city, Erxleben fought back in a 16-page letter, calling their accusations "gross insults to truth" and concluding her defense by offering to take a qualifying examination—on condition that her accusers also take the same examination.

The outraged physicians refused to take any examination and raised the ante in the ongoing controversy by calling on officials to try her for malpractice (one of her many patients had died), throwing more fuel on the fire by accusing Erxleben of being a witch because she had treated a patient she had not met face to face. She was also described as "a dear lady [who] considers herself a doctor, only by virtue of the fact that she can toss around some broken Latin and French." Not surprising was the emphasis on her sex. Not only was she a woman lacking in sufficient intelligence for the practice of medicine, but her many pregnancies (she was again pregnant at the time) also should be regarded as an impediment to a successful practice of the medical arts.

Her pregnancy brought about a delay in the case, but in January 1754 the matter came before Frederick the Great. The sympathetic king gave his nod of approval to the solution of the matter, namely that Erxleben would have to take an examination and submit a dissertation at the University of Halle/Saale. Fortunately the university's rector, Dr. Johann Junker, believed in the value of higher education for women and was able to advance sufficiently strong historical and legal arguments in favor of allowing Dorothea Erxleben to sit for a medical degree. The rector believed strongly that in respect to academic degrees, no legal distinction was to be made between the sexes, and that any exclusions in this field represented "an inexcusable injustice." Rector Junker was doubtless also aware of the fact that his own institution had already seen fit to award honorary degrees to women poets, and he probably had heard that Erxleben's hometown of Quedlinburg already boasted of one of Germany's very few woman lawyers, a **Dr. Siegelin.**

With Rector Junker's full support, Dorothea Erxleben requested to sit for final examinations and submitted her "medical inaugural dissertation," entitled *Concerning the Swift and Pleasant but for that Reason less than Full Cure of Illnesses.* In this thought-provoking work, she argued that doctors too often were responsible for undertaking unnecessary cures, partly because some physicians intervened too quickly and some patients as well were too eager for immediate relief of minor problems that could be treated with less (or more appropriate) medications. She made a number of suggestions including proper use of purgatives, the best interventions to promote urination or menstruation, and the correct usage of opiates. Word of the usefulness of Erxleben's dissertation quickly spread throughout Germany, particularly among women with health problems, and she eventually would translate it from Latin into German to make it more accessible to the afflicted.

Dorothea Erxleben's doctoral examination took place on May 6, 1754. Answering her examiners in Latin, she responded with both accuracy and eloquence, more than satisfying the committee. Rector Junker commented on her performance by noting, *"sich männlich erwiesen,"* that she "proved herself a man."

After many years of study, Erxleben finally was awarded the M.D. degree on June 12, 1754, by the dean of the medical faculty of the University of Halle/Saale, thus becoming the first woman in Germany to receive a medical degree and to have the right to practice as a physician. A public celebration took place in Halle/Saale that day, and in her speech marking her final triumph she affected the modesty deemed proper for women of the day: "My powers are limited, and I lack the art of well-turned phrases, even on this unusual occasion. . . . I feel all of my weaknesses, not only those which affect all people, but especially those to which the weaker sex is accustomed." At the same time, however, she also gave at least a glimpse of her other, perhaps even more authentic side, namely her confidence in her own talents and skills as a physician, enumerating her accomplishments as a healer "without arrogance but also without fear."

The remainder of Dorothea Erxleben's life and medical career was both uneventful and successful. Enjoying support from her large family and great respect from the townspeople of Quedlinburg, she practiced medicine there until her death on June 13, 1762. The life of Dorothea Erxleben is well known in Germany, where on September 17, 1987, the German Federal Post Office issued a 60 pfennig postage stamp honoring her as part of its ongoing definitive stamp series "The Women of German History."

SOURCES:

Beaucamp, Gerta. *Johann Christian Polycarp Erxleben: Versuch einer Biographie und Bibliographie.* Göttingen: Wallstein, 1994.

Böhm, Heinz. *Dorothea Christiane Erxleben: Ihr Leben und Wirken.* Quedlinburg: Städtische Museen, 1985.

———. *Zum 250. Geburtstag von Frau Dr. Dorothea Christiane Erxleben.* Halle/Saale: Martin-Luther-Universität, 1965.

Brencken, Julia von. *Doktorhut und Weibermütze: Dorothea Erxleben, die erste Ärztin/Biographischer Roman.* 2nd ed. Heilbronn: Salzer, 1992.

Feyl, Renate. *Der lautlose Aufbruch: Frauen in der Wissenschaft.* Cologne: Kiepenheuer & Witsch, 1994.

Fischer-Defoy, Werner. "Die Promotion der ersten deutschen Ärztin, Dorothea Christiane Erxleben, und ihre Vorgeschichte," in *Archiv für Geschichte der Medizin.* Vol. 4, 1911, pp. 440–461.

Knabe, Ludwig. "Die erste Promotion einer Frau in Deutschland zur Dr. med. an der Universität Halle 1754," in *450 Jahre Martin-Luther-Universität Halle-Wittenberg.* 3 vols. Halle/Saale: Martin-Luther-Universität Halle-Wittenberg, 1952, Vol. II, pp. 109–124.

Kraetke-Rumpf, Emmy. *Die Quedlinburger Doktorin: Lebensroman der ersten Deutschen Ärztin.* Leipzig: Hase & Koehler Verlag, 1939.

Langer, Thurid, ed. *Über die Gelehrsamkeit eines Frauenzimmers: Texte von und über Frauenzimmer.* Halle/Saale: Hallescher Verlag, 1996.

Lebensbeschreibungen einiger gelehrten Frauenzimmer. Vienna: Im Verlage der Albertischen Buchdruckerey, 1794.

Renker, Karlheinz. *Dr. med. Dorothea Erxleben: Festvortrag aus Anlass der Feierlichkeiten zur 250. Wiederkehr ihres Geburtstages am 13, November 1965.* Halle-Wittenberg: Martin-Luther-Universität Halle-Wittenberg, 1966.

Schelenz, Hermann. *Frauen im Reiche Aeskulaps: Ein Versuch zur Geschichte der Frau in der Medizin unter Bezugnahme auf die Zukunft der modernen Ärztinnen und Apothekerinnen.* Leipzig: Ernst Günther's Verlag, 1900.

Schiebinger, Londa. *The Mind Has No Sex? Women in the Origins of Modern Science.* Cambridge, MA: Harvard University Press, 1989.

Schönfeld, Walther H.P. *Frauen in der abendländischen Heilkunde vom klassischen Altertum bis zum Ausgang des 19. Jahrhunderts.* Stuttgart: Ferdinand Enke Verlag, 1947.

John Haag,
Assistant Professor of History,
University of Georgia, Athens, Georgia

Erythro (c. 778–after 839).

See Irene of Athens for sidebar on Rotrude.

Erzsi von Habsburg (1883–1963).

See Elizabeth von Habsburg.

Esato (fl. 10th c. CE).

See Judith.

Esau, Katherine (1898–1997)

Russian-born American botanist, internationally recognized for her work in the field of plant anatomy and plant viral diseases. Born in Ekaterinoslav, Russia (now Dnepropetrovsk, Ukraine), on April 3, 1898; died in Santa Barbara, California, on June 4, 1997; daughter of John Esau and Margarethe (Toews) Esau; never married.

Katherine Esau was born in 1898 in the city of Ekaterinoslav, located in tsarist Russia's agriculturally productive province of Ukraine. Her parents John and **Margarethe Esau** were Mennonites, a religious minority from Germany who had sought refuge and land in imperial Russia in the 18th century. Empress *Catherine II the Great granted the Mennonites tracts of land on which they could farm and flourish. As religious pacifists, they declined en masse to participate in wars, and the Russian empress took these convictions into account when she granted the group an exemption from military service for a full century. The Mennonites prospered in their agricultural colonies, maintaining a separate cultural, religious and linguistic identity, which by the late 19th century began to expose them collectively to Russian and Ukrainian accusations that they constituted alien islands of arrogant and inassimilable Germans in a Slavic sea.

Katherine's father John had an unusual background that helped shield against such charges from his Ukrainian and Russian neighbors. As one of the very few Mennonites who had attended Russian schools, he spoke perfect Russian and Ukrainian, had earned a degree as a mechanical engineer in Riga, and by the time Katherine was born in 1898 as his last child (son Nicolai and daughter Marie had died in infancy, and Paul, born in 1894, survived) the Esau family had become prosperous. A successful businessman, John Esau served first as a city councillor and then as mayor of Ekaterinoslav.

World War I proved difficult for the Russian empire as the backwardness of the state and the inefficiency and corruption of the tsarist system brought about increasing chaos. War-weary Russians overthrew the Romanov dynasty in early 1917 and by the end of that year Vladimir Lenin's Bolshevik Party had seized power so as to end the war and embark on creating a Marxist Utopia. Imperial Germany took advantage of the disintegration to conquer grain-rich Ukrainian lands, and with Ekaterinoslav now under German military rule John Esau once again sat in the mayor's seat. This time, however, events were highly unstable and, with the defeat of Germany in November 1918, the situation in Ekaterinoslav became anarchic.

Regarded by the local Bolshevik revolutionaries as a quintessential German alien, as well as the embodiment of a now-despised world of bourgeois capitalism, John Esau found himself declared a counterrevolutionary and an "enemy of the people." No longer able to guarantee his own or his family's safety, John Esau decided on the spot to quickly liquidate his assets as best he could. Packing essential possessions including food in suitcases for a long rail journey, the Esau family departed for Germany with once-proud but now demoralized German troops on December 20, 1918. The evening of their departure, an armed horde seized virtually all of the family's baggage including their food and clothing. The trip to their destination, Berlin, normally took two days, but in the utter chaos of revolutionary Ukraine it took two exhausting and dangerous weeks. Only the payment of large sums of money as bribes made it possible for the train to receive permission to pass safely through various areas that were controlled by motley revolutionary committees and local bandits.

Katherine Esau and her family arrived in Berlin on January 5, 1919, tired but safe. Berlin was itself suffering from bloody disorders at this time which climaxed in mid-January with the violent suppression of the Spartacist uprising that had intended to create a Leninist Soviet republic in Germany. Determined to find stability, the Esau family quickly settled down in Berlin. Their ability to speak German like natives facilitated their rapid acculturation to a new country despite the fact that the country sometimes teetered on the brink of anarchy. John Esau became active in Mennonite relief work while Paul continued his studies.

Soon after her arrival in Berlin, Katherine Esau had to decide what kind of academic program in which to enroll. In Ekaterinoslav, she had been an excellent student at the local gymnasium, showing a strong interest in the sciences. Graduating in 1916, she continued her studies in the fall of that year by enrolling at

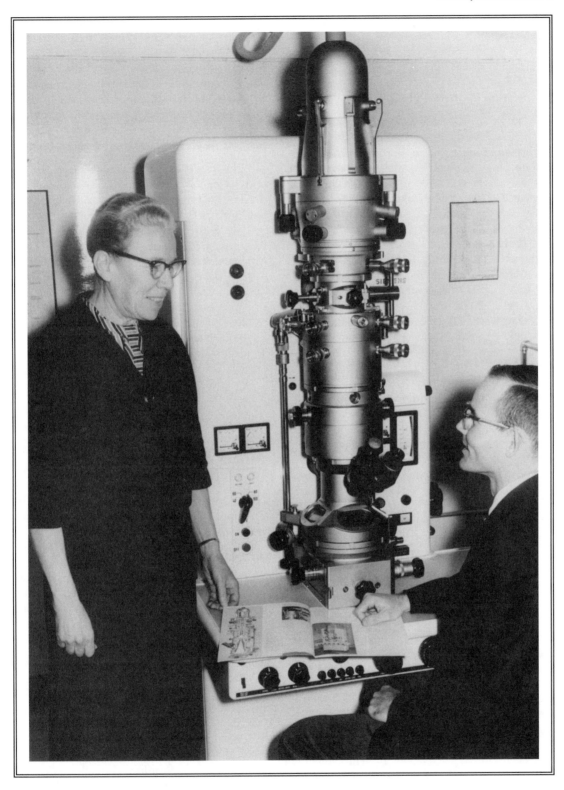

Katherine Esau, with her assistant Robert Gill.

Moscow's Golitsin Women's College of Agriculture. She excelled in her first year, taking courses in natural sciences, physics, chemistry and geology. At this stage in her life, she chose agriculture over botany, because she was convinced that botany was a sterile discipline that did little more than name and classify plants. She saw agriculture as an area full of new ideas that also could lead to practical results, including increased food production in a time of shortages and near-famine conditions. Katherine's formal education in Russia had ended with the Bolshevik Revolution, but during her final year in that ravaged nation she had continued her studies by learning English, taking piano lessons, attending a gardening school, and accumulating a collection of plant specimens that she planned to present as a completed project when more settled conditions made it possible to resume her interrupted formal studies.

Determined to achieve her educational goals despite her family's painful displacement, Katherine Esau registered in Berlin's highly regarded College of Agriculture. Unlike many refugees in that period, she was able to present her education credentials to the school's registrar, including not only the necessary documentation of her completed course work but even the gold medal that the Ekaterinoslav gymnasium had awarded her for academic excellence. She excelled in her studies and, during her second year, spent two semesters taking specialized agricultural courses in the Swabian town of Hohenheim near Stuttgart. Returning to Berlin to complete her course work, she graduated with the title of agricultural instructor (*Landwirtschaftslehrerin*). Additional courses with the noted geneticist Erwin Baur led to her certification as an expert in plant breeding. The politically naive Baur suggested to Esau that she should consider returning to Russia because, despite her youth, she now possessed skills that would enable her to make major contributions to that devastated nation's agricultural sector. Esau knew that as a hated bourgeois and member of a German Christian pacifist sect, she stood little chance of doing any effective work in Lenin's Soviet state. By this time, in fact, she and her family had already decided to immigrate to the United States.

Katherine Esau, with her parents and her brother Paul, arrived in the United States, settling immediately in Reedley, California, in which a large number of Mennonites lived as farmers. Katherine took a series of jobs including one in the town of Oxnard with a struggling seed company. The work was often hard but always challenging as she oversaw the planting of seed and learned Spanish in order to better communicate with Mexican laborers. Through no fault of her own, the company failed, and she soon found another job, this time with a sugar company in Spreckels, a California settlement near Salinas.

Esau's solid European education in plant genetics would serve her well on this assignment, which included developing a sugar beet that was resistant to curly top disease, a condition known to be caused by a virus transmitted by an insect, the beet leafhopper. A disease-resistant strain of sugar beet had already been developed, but it was of little economic value since it had a poorly shaped root and low sugar content. At Spreckels, Esau's job was to improve this beet's strain by hybridization. Ignoring primitive conditions and long hours, she spent the next few years developing the sought-after strain of sugar beet.

The quality of her work with sugar-beet hybrids eventually came to the attention of the chair of the botany division of the University of California at Davis (UC-Davis), and in the spring of 1928 Esau began full-time graduate work at the university's College of Agriculture at Davis. Although the bulk of her graduate work took place at Davis, she was officially enrolled at University of California at Berkeley, where she took a number of advanced courses in botany. An excellent student who was elected to Phi Beta Kappa, Katherine Esau was awarded her Ph.D. degree in botany in December 1931, officially receiving it at the 1932 Berkeley commencement.

The question of how Esau would support herself in an economically depressed country was quickly resolved when she was offered a dual position at the Davis branch of the University of California. Half of her time would be spent teaching, the rest carrying out research projects at the College of Agriculture's experiment station. At first, Esau was concerned that she would not meet the challenges of teaching, but once she began her instructional tasks, which included teaching plant anatomy, systematic botany, morphology of plant crops and microtechnique, she discovered that she enjoyed teaching. Her classes, which were popular with students, were conducted in a relaxed manner and enlivened by her keen sense of humor.

From the start of her academic career at Davis, Esau worked on an ambitious research agenda. She was particularly interested in the phloem tissue of plants, which conducted food through the organism. Her research findings over the next decades made important contributions to the understanding of how viruses are able to bring about the destruction of plant structures by spreading through a plant's phloem system. Her carefully executed and systematic investigations of infected and noninfected sugar beets clarified previously little-understood mechanisms of viral infection and degeneration in plants. Working with tobacco plants, she discovered that, in the case of the curly top virus, it was clear that the virus depended on the phloem for both initiating the infection and spreading it throughout the plant. With this work, she made a major contribution to an understanding of plant pathology, establishing the concept of a "phloem-limited virus."

Katherine Esau's work was her life. She continued to live with her parents in a house near the Davis campus, and it was here that she spent many hours in a darkroom working on microphotographs. There was a darkroom in the university botany division, but it lacked air conditioning and was miserably hot many months of the year. At home in the evenings, Esau could work at her own pace, meticulously developing photographs of plant structures. These would eventually appear in her classic textbook *Plant Anatomy*. First published in 1953, this text quickly became a standard work in its field, popularly known among students as "Aunt Kitty's Bible."

During World War II, Esau became involved in a project to find more productive rubber-yielding strains of the guayule plant. Researchers had not been able to explain why certain guayule strains had failed to yield hybrids when crossed with other strains, producing instead an unwanted type of progeny. Painstaking work on her part explained the mystery, namely that the problem was due to fact that the plant had been able to reproduce without sexual union taking place. The next years were extremely busy ones for Esau, who carried out consequential investigations of diseases of grapevines, beets and celery. Collaborating over many decades with another distinguished botantist, V.I. Cheadle, she published many important papers relating to the evolutionary specialization of phloem tissue as it relates to plant functions.

In 1960, when Esau was in her early 60s, an age when other scientists often started planning for retirement, she began a new and even more productive phase of her scientific career when she began working with the electron microscope at UC-Davis. By this stage of her work, she had become world famous, with honors that included membership in the National Academy of Science.

In 1963, Esau moved to the University of California at Santa Barbara, where she continued her investigations of plant viral diseases. Collaborating with Lynn Hoefert, she made discoveries regarding the virus causing western yellows disease in beets. These insights were of great value for botanists worldwide who were trying to find a deeper understanding of the mechanisms of plant diseases, particularly in crops that played a significant role in the human food supply.

Throughout the 1960s and 1970s, Esau's productivity continued, although she had officially "retired" from her teaching duties in Santa Barbara in 1965. She continued to be involved in important experimental work while at the same time publishing a significant number of scientific papers. Her many reviews of the current botanical literature, which she had begun to publish early in her career, were a model of clarity and completeness, and they provided a vast sum of information for structural botanists. Her linguistic gifts (besides English, German and Russian, she could read books and journals written in French, Spanish and Portuguese) allowed her to transverse virtually the entire globe of botanical research.

Enjoying robust good health, Esau carried out research work into her late 80s. Unintimidated by the new, she mastered a personal computer in the mid-1980s when working on the revision of her standard textbook *Plant Anatomy*. She was the recipient of many honors in the final decades of her long and productive life. A building on the UC-Santa Barbara was named in her honor. The Botanical Society of America, which elected her to its presidency, created the Katherine Esau Award for the single most outstanding paper in developmental and structural botany. In October 1989, President George Bush awarded Esau the National Medal of Science: she was cited for the excellence of her work, "which has spanned more than six decades; for her superlative performance as an educator, in the classroom and through her books; for the encouragement and inspiration she has given to a legion of young, aspiring plant biologists; and for providing a special role model for women in science."

Katherine Esau died at her home in Santa Barbara, California, on June 4, 1997. She was praised by Dr. Peter S. Raven, director of the Missouri Botanical Garden, as one of the most influential botanists of the 20th century, an investigator who had "absolutely dominated the field of plant anatomy and morphology for several decades," and whose lasting achievement was to have "set the stage for all kinds of modern advances in plant physiology and molecular biology."

SOURCES:

Abir-Am, P. G., and Dorinda Outram, eds., *Uneasy Careers and Intimate Lives: Women in Science 1789–1979*. New Brunswick, NJ: Rutgers University Press, 1987.

Esau, Katherine. *Anatomy of Plant Seeds*. 2nd ed. New York: John Wiley, 1977.

———. *Plant Anatomy*. NY: John Wiley, 1953, 2nd ed., 1965.

———. *Plants, Viruses, and Insects*. Cambridge, MA: Harvard University Press, 1961.

———. *Vascular Differentiation in Plants*. NY: Holt, Rinehart and Winston, 1965.

Evert, Ray F. "Katherine Esau," in *Plant Science Bulletin*. Vol. 31, no. 5. October 1985, pp. 33–37.

———, and Susan E. Eichhorn. "Katherine Esau (1898—)," in Louise S. Grinstein et al., eds., *Women in the Biological Sciences: A Biobibliographic Sourcebook*. Westport, CT: Greenwood Press, 1997, pp. 150–162.

Freeman, Karen. "Katherine Esau Is Dead At 99: A World Authority on Botany," in *The New York Times*. June 18, 1997, p. D23.

International Journal of Plant Sciences. Vol. 153, no. 3. Part 2, 1992, Katherine Esau Symposium Special Issue: Plant Structure—Concepts, Connection, and Challenges, University of California, Davis, March 28–31, 1992.

McDavid, Lee. "Katherine Esau (1898—)," in Benjamin F. Shearer and Barbara S. Shearer, eds. *Notable Women in the Life Sciences: A Biographical Dictionary*. Westport, CT: Greenwood Press, 1996, pp. 113–117.

O'Hern, Elizabeth Moot. "Profiles of Pioneer Women Scientists: Katherine Esau," in *Botanical Review*. Vol. 62, no. 3. July 1996, pp. 209–271.

Russell, David E. "Life in Czarist Russia: A Conversation with Katherine Esau," in *Soundings*. Vol. 23, no. 29, 1992, pp. 5–32.

John Haag,
Assistant Professor of History,
University of Georgia, Athens, Georgia

Eschenbach, Marie Ebner (1830–1916).

See Ebner-Eschenbach, Marie.

Eschiva of Ibelin (fl. late 1100s)

*Mother of the king of Cyprus. Flourished in the late 1100s; first wife of Aimery de Lusignan (brother of Guy de Lusignan [d. 1194]) also known as Amalric II, king of Jerusalem (r. 1197–1205), king of Cyprus; children: Hugh I, king of Cyprus (r. 1205–1218). Amalric's second wife was *Isabella I of Jerusalem* (d. 1205).*

Eschiva of Ibelin (r. 1282–c. 1284)

*Queen of Beirut. Reigned from 1282 to around 1284; younger daughter of John II of Beirut and **Alice de la Roche** of Athens; younger sister of Isabella (d. 1282), queen of Beirut; married Humphrey of Montfort, younger son of Philip of Montfort, lord of Toron and Tyre (died around 1284); married Guy de Lusignan (d. 1308, youngest son of Hugh XII); children: (first marriage) one son, Roupen.*

Eschiva of Ibelin became queen of Beirut in 1282, upon the death of her sister Queen *Isabella. Eschiva's first husband Humphrey of Montfort inherited Tyre (in southern Lebanon) in 1283, when his brother John died. When Humphrey died around 1284, Tyre then went to his brother John's widow, Margaret. Eschiva later married Guy de Lusignan, the son of King Hugh XII.

Eschiva is known for her intervention with the Mameluk sultan Qalawun, which resulted in a truce that prevented the Mameluks (former slaves from Russia and Central Asia who founded a dynasty in Egypt and Syria in 1250) from attacking Beirut. In 1291, however, the truce was broken under the leader Shujai, who tore down the walls of Beirut and the Castle of the Ibelins and turned the cathedral into a mosque.

Escobar, Marisol (b. 1930).

See Marisol.

Escot, Pozzi (1933—)

Peruvian-born composer whose work was performed by the New York Philharmonic in 1975. Born in Lima, Peru, on October 1, 1933; fifth of six children of M. Pozzi-Escot (a French bacteriologist and diplomat) and a Moroccan mother; studied at Reed College, Juilliard, and the Hochschule für Musik with Philipp Jarnach.

Pozzi Escot was raised speaking French, English, and Spanish. Her father wanted all six of his children to contribute to the benefit of humanity. One of the many tutors who came to her home was André Sas, the well-known Belgian composer, who helped Escot develop her musical skills. In 1953, she came to the United States where she studied at Reed College and Juilliard, followed by several years of study in Germany. By 1964, she had been appointed to the New England Conservatory of Music to teach theory and composition. In the meantime, several of her compositions had become widely known. Virgil Thomson admired Escot's work, considering her "the most interesting and original woman composer now functioning."

By 1960, she was so much in demand that she wrote music only on commission. Although Escot quickly received great acclaim in the musical world, she refused to sacrifice her standards in order to have her works performed. For example, when she was commissioned by the government of Venezuela to write an orchestral composition for the 400th anniversary of the city of Caracas, she did not score for the instrumentation generally associated with a symphony orchestra. "As a 20th-century composer I feel that orchestras are obsolete," she said, "for they represent the culture of a hundred years ago and they do not fulfill the needs of our own culture today." *Sands*, the work written for this celebration, was scored for saxophones, electrical guitar, bass drums, violins, and basses. A true musical genius, Escot has received many grants and awards to support her compositions. She has worked especially hard on behalf of American performers and composers whom she felt were often overlooked in favor of Europeans.

John Haag,
Athens, Georgia

Eskenazi, Roza (c. 1900–1980)

Greek popular singer, who performed in the cafe amán *style, whose many recordings brought her as much fame abroad among the Greek diaspora as within Greece itself. Name variations: Rosa Eskenazy; Roza Eskenaze. Born in the Ottoman Empire around 1900; died in 1980.*

Roza Eskenazi was born into a Jewish family in the Ottoman Empire at the beginning of the 20th century and grew up in a society that was stimulating in its religious, cultural, linguistic and musical diversity. At a very young age, she began her career as a *defi* player in what was then rapidly evolving into a lively new world of popular entertainment, the Greek cafe music scene. In the *cafe amáns* of Constantinople where she performed (in Turkish, the exclamation *amàn* means "mercy" or "pity"), Eskenazi quickly became one of the most celebrated singers in the Smyrnaic-Rebetic tradition of song and dance that was taking shape at that time. The *cafe amàn* style of musical performance developed in the last decades of the 19th century in cities of the Aegean Sea such as Athens, Constantinople and particularly Smyrna, from which the term Smyrnaic-Rebetic is derived.

Roza Eskenazi grew up in the complex multiethnic world of the late Ottoman Empire in which Armenian, Greek, Roma (Gypsy), Jewish and Turkish musicians worked together. Artists within each group were able to enlarge and enrich their own artistic vision because of constant interactions with various cultural styles. Eskenazi's skills as a vocalist—with her sweet but reedy soprano voice, as expressive as it was pure—were complemented on her hundreds of recordings by the brilliance of the instrumentalists with whom she chose to work. These included the violinist Dhimitris Sémsis as well as the celebrated oud player Agápios Tomboúlis, whose performances on her classic recordings helped to frame her unique vocal art in a superb

fashion. She was also fortunate in receiving enthusiastic support from directors of major record firms, including Smyrna-born Spiros Peristéris of the Odeon-Parlophone firm, as well as from Dhimitris Sémsis of His Master's Voice records who successfully balanced his career as instrumentalist with the demands of a busy recording executive.

By the early 1930s, Roza Eskenazi was a superstar in the world of Greek popular entertainment, already surpassing the fame of **Marika Papagika**, the reigning vocal queen of the previous decade. Many of Eskenazi's recordings were highly successful in the Greek diaspora, particularly in the United States where her 78s sold well despite the Great Depression. Her recordings reminded listeners of the world they had left behind while providing an aural portrait of the Ottoman culture that had been destroyed by World War I and its bloody aftermath. Eskenazi reflected this complex world in her singing, which was done not only in Greek, but also in Turkish,

Roza Eskenazi

Kurdish, and Ladino (the Spanish-derived language of the Sephardic Jewish diaspora of the Mediterranean).

Roza Eskenazi escaped from Greece before Nazi Germany occupied the country in the spring of 1941. During the war years, she lived in the United States, where she performed before enthusiastic audiences. While there, she also made recordings but returned to Greece soon after the end of World War II. Just when it appeared that she would end her days a forgotten star of yesteryear, in the 1970s a new interest in her life and art brought about a revival of Eskenazi's career. Her classic recordings were reissued, and through the efforts of Tassos Schorellis and other enthusiasts, her achievements became known once again to a younger generation of Greek music lovers. By the late 1990s, compact disc reissues had preserved her recorded legacy.

SOURCES:

Archives of Traditional Music, Indiana University, Bloomington.

Eskenazi, Roza, as told to Kostas Hatzidoulis. *Auta Pou Thymamai* [That Which I Remember]. Athens: Kaktos, 1982.

Frangos, Steve. "Portraits in Modern Greek Music: Roza Eskenazi," in *Resound: A Quarterly of the Archives of Traditional Music.* Vol. 12, no. 1–2. January–April, 1993, pp. 5–8.

RELATED MEDIA:

Rembetica: Historic Urban Folk Songs from Greece. Rounder Records C–1079.

Roza Eskenazi: Rembétissa. Rounder Records CD-1080.

Schwartz, Martin, and Chris Strachwitz. *Greek-Oriental Rebetica: Songs and Dances in the Asia Minor Style.* Arhoolie/Folklyric CD-7005.

Women of the Rebetiko Song. HM Records CD-632: Hellenikos Phonographos/The Greek Archives, Vol. 6.

John Haag,
Assistant Professor of History,
University of Georgia, Athens, Georgia

Esmond, Jill (1908–1990).

See Leigh, Vivien for sidebar.

Espanca, Florbela (1894–1930)

Portuguese poet and short-story writer who is generally regarded as Portugal's foremost woman poet. Name variations: Florbela de Alma da Conceição Espanca. Born in December 1894 in Vila Viçosa, Portugal; died in Matosinhos, Portugal, on December 7, 1930; married three times.

Born out of wedlock in 1894 into the provincial world of the town of Vila Viçosa in Portugal's Alto Alentejo province, Florbela Espanca lived life with an intensity that many of her contemporaries regarded as flagrantly reckless. Already divorced from the first of her three husbands at age 18, Espanca poured her emotions into lyric verse and short stories strongly influenced by the decadent symbolist literature popular at that time; these early works would be published posthumously in 1931. By 1917, she was in Lisbon, where she studied law and married a second time. In 1919, Espanca's first book of poems, *Livro de mágoas* (*Book of Woes*), was published and was little noticed by critics. Although they revealed Espanca's considerable talent, these poems also showed the influence of her mentor, Antonio Nobre. Her second marriage was as troubled as the first, and despite her personal unhappiness she marked her 1923 divorce with the publication of a second book of verse. This volume, *Livro de Sóror Saudade* (*Book of Sister Saudade*), has as its title the name given Espanca by a friend and fellow poet, Américo Durão.

Like her first book, *Livro de Sóror Saudade* received minimal attention from literary critics. This time, however, it was because the volume boldly challenged the puritanism and patriarchy of a deeply conservative society. In her verse, she chose to reveal many aspects of her sexuality and her desire for personal freedom, subjects considered profoundly "improper" by the literary powers of Portugal and its social, economic and ecclesiastical oligarchs. By challenging the assumptions of patriarchy and machismo in the strongest terms, Espanca declared war on a world that expected women to live in their own limited spheres of home, family and church. Her erotic poetry as well as a private life seen by many as immoral marked her as a sworn enemy of the conservative values of traditional Portugal.

Considered decadent in her works and life, Espanca shocked the bourgeoisie of the city of Porto and the small town of Matosinhos, where she lived after returning from Lisbon. Many who neither read her books nor met her in person came to regard Espanca as a threat to public decency and as a terrifying example of a younger generation's lack of restraint. Poets and connoisseurs of contemporary literature, however, began to read and admire her books and looked upon her erotic poetry as opening new insights into human experience. Some of Portugal's small contingent of feminists were impressed by the intensity and clarity of Florbela Espanca's writings, seeing her as a writer determined to grapple directly with the problems of being a woman and an artist in a society unsympathetic to both women's rights and the idea of artistic freedom.

Still seeking happiness and stability in her personal life, Espanca had married for a third time in 1930 and was busy preparing two manuscripts of poetry and short stories for publication when she died in Matosinhos on December 7, 1930. She succumbed to an overdose of barbiturates on the eve of her 36th birthday. At the time, she was still known more for her reputation as a "scandalous woman" than for her work as a writer. Yet within a year of her death, the publication of the two books she had been editing, *Charneca em Flor* (*Flowering Heath*) and *Reliquiae* (*Relics*), brought her passionate voice to a growing number of readers and admirers not only in Portugal, but also in Lusophone, Brazil, and (through the work of her translator and confidant Professor Guido Battelli) in Italy as well.

By the 1950s, Florbela Espanca had achieved a towering reputation as not only modern Portugal's greatest female poet, but also as one of that nation's most eloquent artistic advocates of the right of all women to seek personal freedom and happiness. She was honored by the Portuguese postal system on February 21, 1994, with the issuance of a 100 escudos postage stamp bearing her portrait.

SOURCES:

Alonso, Claudia Pazos, and Gloria Fernandes, eds. *Women, Literature, and Culture in the Portuguese-Speaking World.* Lewiston, NY: Edwin Mellen Press, 1996.

Barge, Thomas J. "Florbela Espanca: The Limbs of a Passion," in *Hispania.* Vol. 73, no. 4. December 1990, pp. 978–982.

Barros, Thereza Leitao de. *Escritoras de Portugal: genio feminino revelado na literatura portuguesa.* 2 vols. Lisbon: [Tip. de A. O. Artur], 1924–1927.

Delgado Corral, Concepcion. "A Obra de Florbela Espanca" (Ph.D. dissertation, Universidade de Santiago de Compostela, 1994).

Guedes, Rui. *Florbela Espanca: Fotobiografia.* Lisbon: Dom Quixote, 1985.

Hines, Samantha L. "Twentieth-Century Portuguese Women Writers: An Annotated Bibliography and Bibliometric Study of Literature" (M.A. thesis, University of Rhode Island, 1994).

Klobucka, Anna. "O Formato Mulher: As Poeticas do Feminino na Obra de Florbela Espanca, Sophia de Mello Breyner Andresen, Maria Teresa Horta e Luiza Neto Jorge" (Ph.D. dissertation, Harvard University, 1993).

Luis, Agustina Bessa. *Florbela Espanca.* Lisbon: Guimaraes Editores, 1984.

———. *A Vida e a Obra de Florbela Espanca.* Lisbon: Arcádia, 1979.

Maciunas, Billie. "Reading Florbela Espanca: The Imaginary of the Mother" (M.A. thesis, University of North Carolina at Chapel Hill, 1988).

Moises, Massaud. *Literatura portuguesa moderna: guia biografico, critico e bibliografico.* Sao Paulo: Editora de Universidade de Sao Paulo, 1973.

Régio, José. *Ensaios de interpretaçao critica.* 2nd ed. Porto: Brasilia editora, 1980.

Sena, Jorge de. *Da poesia portuguesa.* Lisbon: Edicoes Atica, 1959.

———. *Florbela Espanca ou a Expressão do Feminino na Poesia Portuguesa.* Porto: Fenianos, 1947.

The Story of Fado (Hemisphere CD 7243 8 55647 2 7).

John Haag,
Assistant Professor of History,
University of Georgia, Athens, Georgia

Florbela
Espanca

Espaze, Martiale.

See French "Witches."

Espín de Castro, Vilma (1934—)

Cuban revolutionary and women's activist who was the long-time president of the Federación de Mujeres Cubanas (Federation of Cuban Women). Name variations: Vilma Espín Guillois; Vilma Espín or Espin; Deborah. Pronunciation: VEEL-mah Ess-PEEN dav KAH-strow. Born Vilma Espín Guillois in 1934 in Santiago de Cuba; daughter of a lawyer for the Bacardi Rum Company and a mother of French extraction; spent two years in a secular school and two years in a religious school; earned a degree in chemical engineering at the Universidad de Oriente; attended the Massachusetts Institute of Technology and studied architecture; married Raúl Castro, on January 26, 1959; children: four sons.

Was a founding member and leader of the 26th of July Movement in Oriente Province, Cuba (1955–59); was a founder and president of the Federación de Mujeres Cubanas (Federation of Cuban Women, 1960); made an alternate member of the Politburo of the Cuban Communist Party (1980) and a full member (1986); retired from the Politburo (1991).

The Cuban middle class produced most of the leaders of the revolutionary movement that toppled President Fulgencio Batista from power in 1959. Students were especially prominent. In this respect, Vilma Espín seems a "typical" revolutionary. Born to an upper-middle-class family in the eastern city of Santiago de Cuba in 1934, she enjoyed the comfortable lifestyle of her class. According to John Dorschner and Roberto Fabricio, she grew up "in the liberal Rotarian-Lions Club milieu that permeated the city's upper class." And even though her father had essentially traditional ideas, he saw "no harm in giving his daughter an education as good as man received." Two years of secular instruction were followed by two years in a religious school, although Vilma later insisted that "naturally I had no religious beliefs." All her primary and secondary education took place in Santiago. It was also here that she earned a degree in chemical engineering at the Universidad de Oriente. Her knowledge of chemistry would be put to use in the coming struggle against the dictatorship of Fulgencio Batista.

If we use the term "help" we are accepting that [child care and household duties] are women's responsibilities and such is not the case: we say "share" because they are a family responsibility.

—Vilma Espín de Castro

On March 10, 1952, Cubans who tuned in their radios to confirm the rumors of a coup heard only the same uninterrupted music up and down the dial. Fulgencio Batista had not only ousted the corrupt and discredited Auténtico government of President Prío but he also ended constitutional rule in Cuba. The little opposition to Batista was not well organized and was, for the most part, outside of normal political channels. Vilma Espín, at the time a university student, began her political education with the coup. An anti-Batista movement at the University of Havana led by Rafael García Bárcenas, a philosophy professor, journalist, and founder of the ousted Auténtico Party, captured the imaginations of professors and students at the University of Oriente.

Espín remembered that she and others grew concerned with Cuba's social problems. As she told interviewer **Margaret Randall**: "Why are there beggars in the streets? How could this be resolved? There were no answers." The questions raised for Vilma could not be answered in a Marxist context, as would be the case later in her life, because she had not read Marx, and Marxism was not taught in the schools. But the strong presence of the United States in Cuba did impress her, and in her own mind she began to link "yankee imperialism" with the Batista dictatorship. The fundamental problem for Espín was how to free Cuba from the twin tyranny of Batista and imperialism: she drew inspiration from the late-19th-century struggle for independence led by José Marti.

A professor at Oriente radicalized the romantic. He spoke of the need for a political uprising against Batista, and, in Espin's words, "we felt very enthusiastic about the idea of rebellion." While Vilma entertained idealistic notions, her younger sister **Nilsa** was already working with political activist Frank País who would establish an anti-Batista movement in Santiago. Shortly, Vilma herself joined an action group, and "we set up an organization like the one that would become the 26th of July Movement (Fidel Castro's organization)." She told diarist Carlos Franqui: "I was working on finances, collecting money. Can you imagine, they gave us five cents only now and then. It was awful in the beginning." For the rest of 1952, the rebellion in Santiago consisted of protests, manifestos, proclamations, marches, and confrontations with the police.

Violence exploded in Santiago on July 26, 1953, when Fidel Castro led an attack on the Moncada military barracks. Espín and her friends were caught unawares: "We knew nothing of what had happened. Castro was little known in Santiago—only as the young leader of the Ortodoxos (a political party). But his actions in Santiago won him the sympathy and admiration of many." The attack was disastrous, and those rebels who were not killed outright were tortured to death or jailed. "When they attacked Moncada," Espín told Franqui, "I wanted to go to the hospital to see who was there. . . . [We] were very worried, because we could hear shots, which meant they were still killing our men." What amounted to a slaughter in essence radicalized Santiago, whose population became protective of young rebels like Espín. As the revolution against Batista deepened in the mid-and-late 1950s, a fairly effective network of "watchers" and safe-houses was established. "The people were really fantastic," Espín remembered.

At his trial, Fidel Castro delivered an electric defense of the Moncada attack, entitled "History Will Absolve Me." Espín noted that Castro's impassioned speech redirected the youth of Santiago. "We began to see things differently and Fidel took over his position as leader of all who took up the struggle all over the island." But Castro was jailed, and Batista was confident that rebellion had been stilled. Perhaps, in the wake of these events, Espín was unsure of her career as an activist. At any rate, she enrolled in graduate work at the Massachusetts Institute of Technology where she studied architecture. She told Randall that it was in the United States that she learned about the oppression of the poor and of blacks; at the MIT library, she dabbled in Marx. Espín felt "asphyxiated" in the United States, isolated; no one would speak to her about politics. It was also the era of McCarthyism.

In the meantime in Cuba, when Batista in 1955 granted an amnesty to Castro and the survivors of the Moncada attack, Castro fled to Mexico where he established the 26th of July Movement and plotted the overthrow of the Cuban dictator. Espín, frustrated by her experiences in the United States, made contact with the 26th of July people in Mexico. When she returned home to Cuba, she did so via Mexico "in case Fidel's people wanted me to carry something into the country." She was given an oral message that she delivered to Frank País in Santiago—from that point, she was wholly engaged in the struggle.

In Santiago, Espín began to build an infrastructure for the 26th of July Movement. Medical facilities and personnel were in place when Castro's forces landed near Santiago in November 1956. The invasion was a disaster, and Castro and a handful of survivors barely escaped into the Sierra Maestre of Oriente Province. País was killed, and Espín narrowly evaded capture. She continued to work in Santiago in 1957. Her parents, whom she did not see, were sympathetic to the struggle, and her father probably played a role in the Civic Resistance. When the underground in Santiago needed rest, they were sent into the Sierra to carry messages to Castro. On one occasion, in April 1957, she used her education as a chemical engineer to construct a napalm bomb for mission A-001 of the Rebel Air Force, which consisted of a single plane. It was in the mountains that she first met Fidel and later his brother, Raúl. There was an immediate, mutual attraction between Raúl and Vilma.

Raúl had established a "second front," the Segundo Frente 'Frank Pais,' in the Sierra Cristal of northern Oriente Province. During that period, Espín was convinced after one of her visits that it would be "absurd" for her to return to Santiago, "where they were actively searching

Vilma Espín
de Castro

for me." She remained in the Sierra with the second front until the triumph of the revolution. Espín worked hard to create, among other duties, an administrative network responsible for the maintenance of 11 hospitals and dispensaries, and 100 schools staffed by 26th of July Movement personnel.

Even in the Sierra, Espín clung to what some might call vestiges of her middle-class roots. According to Dorschner and Fabricio, Vilma "never abandoned the fastidiousness of her girls' school upbringing. She kept her long black hair clean and pulled back in a ponytail. Her rebel uniform was tailor-made and she managed, even during bombing attacks, to brush her teeth and put on lipstick each morning."

Ideologically, Vilma was still largely uninformed and ambivalent. Undoubtedly, she wanted the destruction of Batista and wanted to avoid the failures of previous governments. "She was not certain what kind of government that meant, but whatever it was, it had to herald a new era, something that would wipe out the past and eliminate completely the American dominance of Cuban affairs." While in the Sierra, she was most likely not a Marxist. Marxism was a theory that at best was ancillary to Cuban nationalism. When Raúl asked her to teach a course on Communist principles at the rebel political school, she objected. In Dorschner and Fabricio's account, she said: "I don't know anything about Marxism." Raúl reportedly assured her that it was a logical extension of what they were fighting for. Be that as it may, she eventually focused her teaching on the sayings of José Martí into which she injected a little Marx. In the Sierra, however, political theory was always subordinate to the day-to-day struggle.

During 1958, Vilma became Raúl's secretary and served as a translator, following the capture of American and Canadian citizens and some U.S. Marines who had been on leave in Guantánamo City. The hostages were taken to protect Raúl Castro's forces from persistent strafing and bombing attacks by Batista's planes. It was also in 1958 that many journalists made their way into the Sierra to interview the rebels. One, a Spaniard named Enrique Meneses, spoke with Espín at length about religion. She stated that she was a "passionate atheist." Said Meneses, "I'd met very few people with so much faith, but this made her furious, because faith reminded her of religion, and her only religion was unbelief." Not surprisingly, her marriage to Raúl Castro on January 26, 1959, just after Batista fled and Fidel came to power, was a civil affair at the Rancho Country Club in Santiago.

Espín found an important niche in the new revolutionary government. In November 1959, she planned to lead a Cuban delegation to the Chilean Congress on the Rights of Women and Children. As Vilma prepared for the task, she quickly became aware of the "limited organized opportunities that existed for women in Cuba." She told Randall that there were small groups of women whose focus was politics while others were devoted to social action. For the most part, these small organizations were found among upper-class women or within the Catholic Church. But there was no strong feminist organization in Cuba. Preparation for the Congress laid the groundwork for the creation of the Federación de Mujeres Cubanas (FMC; Federation of Cuban Women) which occurred on August 26, 1960.

The FMC combined the various women's affiliates of the 26th of July Movement, groups associated with the Socialist, later Communist, Party, and a Catholic organization known as *Con la cruz y con la patria* (With the Cross and the Homeland). Marifeli Pérez-Stable noted that the FMC was largely free of conflict, in part because of the secondary role ascribed to it by the leaders of Cuba's revolution. They "did not consider gender to be central to the revolution, as class was . . . . Born with and for the revolution, the FMC gave many women their first opportunity to have a life outside the home." Vilma Espín de Castro was appointed the FMC's first and to date only president.

Cuban women were mobilized for the revolution under the auspices of the FMC. As noted by Pérez-Stable, household servants were retrained for meaningful jobs, thousands of rural women were trained as seamstresses, women received first-aid instruction and were provided with day-care centers. The FMC worked through the Public Health Ministry to promote a greater awareness of personal hygiene and pre- and postnatal care. As Espín stated in 1962: "The ideal new woman is a healthy woman, mother of the future generations who will grow up under communism." In 1963, the FMC reached out to women workers in Cuba's factories.

In addition to her duties as president of the FMC, Vilma also worked as chemical engineer for the Ministerio de la Industria Alimenticia (Food Industry Ministry), met with visiting delegations of foreign women, and gave birth to four sons. On occasion, she participated in international congresses devoted to women.

Cuban women suffered a blow in 1976 when the Labor Ministry passed a resolution that prohibited women from nearly 300 job categories. Pérez-Stable notes that while health hazards were claimed as the issue, male unemployment was the root cause for the decision. Espín fought hard to undercut the resolution, and by the mid-1980s the original 1976 list of 300 had been cut to 25. Even though a blow had been struck to end job discrimination on the basis of gender, the 1976 legislation, with its implied discrimination, remained on the books. Espín's position on employment for women was clear: "The establishment of prohibitions for women in general is indeed negative, because they constitute a violation of the principle of equality." The battle for equality was hard fought in other areas. Although a Family Code enacted in 1975 spelled out equality of the sexes at home and at work, in 1984 Espín still had to insist that child care and household duties were to be shared: "If we use the term 'help' we are accepting that these are women's responsibilities and such is not the case: we say 'share' because they are a family responsibility." Similar complaints were heard from the FMC as late as 1990.

In the highest ranks of the revolutionary government, women were conspicuous for their absence. Espín was promoted to an alternate in the Politburo in 1980 and was made a full Politburo member at the Party Congress in 1986. At that time, two other women were named as alternates. Though women have made inroads, the pace has been slow.

In October 1991, at the Fourth Congress of the Cuban Communist Party, some "old-time" Politburo members retired. Included on the list was Vilma Espín de Castro. Mirroring Espín's retirement was the increasing marginalization of the FMC. At its height in the mid-1980s, by 1994 it appeared increasingly as a relic of the revolutionary past. But Vilma Espín had left her mark on the revolution and had struck several blows for women's rights in Cuba and in the world.

SOURCES:

Dorschner, John, and Roberto Fabricio. *The Winds of December.* NY: Coward, McCann and Geohagen, 1980.

Franqui, Carlos. *Diary of the Cuban Revolution.* NY: Viking, 1976.

Meneses, Enrique. *Fidel Castro.* NY: Taplinger, 1966.

Oppenheimer, Andrés. *Castro's Final Hour: The Secret Story Behind the Coming Downfall of Communist Cuba.* NY: Simon and Schuster, 1992.

Pérez-Stable, Marifeli. *The Cuban Revolution: Origins, Course, and Legacy.* NY: Oxford, 1993.

Quirk, Robert E. *Fidel Castro.* NY: W.W. Norton, 1993.

Randall, Margaret. *Mujeres en la Revolución: conversa con mujeres cubanas.* 4th ed. Mexico City: Siglo XXI, 1978.

Szulc, Tad. *Fidel: A Critical Portrait.* NY: William Morrow, 1986.

SUGGESTED READING:

Pérez, Louis A., Jr. *Cuba: Between Reform and Revolution.* New York; Oxford, 1988.

Paul B. Goodwin, Jr.,
Professor of History,
the University of Connecticut, Storrs, Connecticut

Espina, Concha (1869–1955)

Spanish writer. Name variations: Concha Espina de Serna. Born Concepción Jesusa Basilisa Tagle y Espina in Santander, Spain, in 1869; died in 1955; seventh child of Víctor Espina and Ascensión Tagle; married Ramón de la Serna, in 1892 (separated 1908); children: Ramón; Víctor; José; **Josefina de la Maza;** *Luis.*

Concha Espina was born in Santander, Spain, in 1869, the seventh child of Víctor Espina and **Ascensión Tagle**. Raised in a solidly middle-class home and educated in convent schools and by private tutors, she married Ramón de la Serna in 1892. Shortly thereafter, they moved to Chile where he represented family business interests. Neither the business nor the marriage prospered, although Espina eventually had five children. During the three years before they returned to Europe, she began earning a small income by writing and publishing poetry. Back in Spain, her husband resented her independence, and they eventually separated in 1908.

Espina moved to Madrid and became a full-time author, the first Spanish woman to support

herself from her writing. Among Espina's best works were the novel *La esfinge maragata* (*Mariflor,* 1914) and a play entitled *El jayón* (*The Foundling*). *El metal de los muertos* (*Metal of the Dead*), an epic novel that depicts social conditions among miners in the Río Tinto district, brought her a nomination for the Nobel Prize. Although many of her works are mediocre, some parts are first-rate. Curious and observant, Espina traveled and lectured widely through the Americas and Europe. She served as a Spanish cultural emissary to the Caribbean and as vice-president of the Hispanic Society of New York City in 1943 and received many awards in Spain, including the great cross of Alphonso the Wise. King Alphonso XIII presided at the unveiling of Espina's statue in her native land. Despite her achievements, some Spanish male authors and literary critics belittled her. She suffered from blindness in old age and died in 1955.

SOURCES:

Bretz, Mary Lee. *Concha Espina.* Boston: Twayne Publishers, 1980.

Maza, Josefina de la. *Vida de mi madre, Concha Espina.* Madrid: Magisterio Español, 1969.

Kendall W. Brown,
Professor of History,
Brigham Young University, Provo, Utah

Espinasse, Mademoiselle de l'
(1732–1776).

See Salonnières for sidebar on Julie de Lespinasse.

Essex, countess of.

See Maud of Mandeville (d. 1236).
See Bohun, Maud (fl. 1275).
See Eleanor of Castile (1241–1290) for sidebar on Elizabeth Plantagenet (1282–1316).
See Maud of Lusignan (d. 1241).
See Joan de Quinci (d. 1283).
See Bohun, Alianore (d. 1313).
See Fitzalan, Joan (fl. 1325).
See Fitzalan, Joan (d. 1419).
See Isabel (1409–1484).
See Bourchier, Anne (1512–1571).
See Knollys, Lettice (c. 1541–1634).
See Walsingham, Frances (d. 1631).
See Stephens, Catherine (1794–1882).

Essipova, Annette (1851–1914)

Russian pianist who, after establishing a concert career, taught at the St. Petersburg Conservatory and was one of Europe's preeminent teachers. Name variations: Annette Essipoff. Born in St. Petersburg, Russia, on February 13, 1851; died in St. Petersburg on

August 18, 1914; married Theodor Leschetizky, in 1880 (divorced 1892).

Annette Essipova studied with Theodor Leschetizky in Vienna; the two would eventually marry in 1880 and divorce in 1892. Regarded by her contemporaries as a pianist of the highest caliber, Essipova played throughout Europe and in America. She helped Ignace Paderewski early in his career and premiered several of his compositions, including the Concerto and the now ubiquitous Minuet in G. After her tours, she returned to Russia, where from 1893 to 1908 she was the most sought after teacher at the St. Petersburg Conservatory. Her high level of technique and beauty of tone were keenly appreciated in Russian pianism. Her students included Sergei Prokofiev, *Isabelle Vengerova, Simon Barere, Lev Pouishnov, Ignace Hilsberg, Thomas de Hartmann and others. "Her playing in many ways was perfect," Paderewski wrote in his memoirs, "except when it came to strong, effective pieces—then she was lacking in real force."

John Haag,
Athens, Georgia

Este, Alda d'

Ferrarese noblewoman. Name variations: Alda Rangoni. Born Alda Rangoni; married Aldobrandino II, lord of Ferrara (d. 1326); children: Rinaldo, lord of Ferrara (r. 1317–1335); Niccolo I (d. 1344); Obizzo III (1294–1352); *Elisa d'Este (d. 1329).

Este, Alda d' (1333–1381)

Noblewoman of Mantua. Name variations: Alda Gonzaga. Born in 1333; died in 1381; legitimated daughter of *Lippa d'Este and Obizzo III d'Este (1294–1352), lord of Ferrara; married Louis also known as Lodovico or Ludovico II Gonzaga (1334–1382), 3rd captain general of Mantua (r. 1369–1382); children: Francesco Gonzaga (1366–1407), 4th captain general of Mantua (r. 1382–1407, who married *Agnes Visconti and *Margherita Gonzaga).

Este, Anna d' (1473–1497).

See Sforza, Anna.

Este, Anna d' (1531-1607), duchess of Guise.

See Morata, Fulvia for sidebar on Anne of Ferrara.

Este, Beata Beatrice I d' (d. 1226)

Ferrarese noblewoman. Died in 1226; daughter of Azo also known as Azzo VI d'Este (1170–1212), first lord of Ferrara (r. 1208–1212), and *Leonora of Savoy.

Este, Beata Beatrice II d' (d. 1262)

Ferrarese noblewoman. Died in 1262; daughter of Azzo VII Novello d'Este, lord of Ferrara (d. 1264) and *Giovanna d'Este.

Este, Beatrice d' (d. 1245)

Queen of Hungary. Name variations: Beatrix of Este. Died in 1245; daughter of Aldobrandino I d'Este (d. 1215), podesta of Ferrara; became third wife of Andrew II, king of Hungary (r. 1205–1235), on May 14, 1234; children: Istvan also known as Stephen (b. 1235), duke of Slavonia.

Este, Beatrice d' (fl. 1290s)

Ferrarese noblewoman. Name variations: Beatrice d'Anjou. Second wife of Azzo VIII d'Este, lord of Ferrara (r. 1293–1308).

Este, Beatrice d' (d. 1334)

Milanese noblewoman. Name variations: Beatrice Visconti. Died in 1334; daughter of *Giacoma d'Este and Obizzo II d'Este (1247–1293), lord of Ferrara; married Nino Visconti; married Galeazzo I Visconti (c. 1277–1328), lord of Milan (r. 1322–1328); children: Azzo Visconti (1302–1339), lord of Milan (r. 1328–1339).

Este, Beatrice d' (fl. 1300s)

Ferrarese noblewoman. Name variations: Beatrice Gonzaga. Born Beatrice Gonzaga; married Nicholas also known as Niccolo I d'Este, lord of Ferrara (r. 1317–1344).

Este, Beatrice d' (fl. 1350s)

Ferrarese noblewoman. Born Beatrice da Camino; married Aldobrandino III d'Este (1335–1361), lord of Ferrara; children: Obizzo (1356–1388).

Este, Beatrice d' (1427–1497)

Ferrarese noblewoman. Name variations: Beatrice da Corregio or Correggio; Beatrice Sforza. Born in 1427; died in 1497; illegitimate daughter of Nicholas also known as Niccolo III d'Este (1383–1441), 12th marquis of Ferrara; married Niccolo da Coreggio; married

Tristano Sforza (d. 1477); children: Niccolo da Corregio (1450–1508, who married Cassandra Colleoni).

Este, Beatrice d' and Isabella d'

Este, Beatrice d' (1475–1497). Duchess of Milan who became famous for her patronage of artists during the Italian Renaissance. Name variations: Bianca or Beatrice Sforza; Beatriz; Bice; Duchess of Bari. Pronunciation: bee-uh-TREES DEHS-tuh. Born on June 29, 1475, in Ferrara, Italy; died in childbirth on January 2, 1497, in Milan, Italy; daughter of Ercole I d'Este (1431–1505), 2nd duke of Ferrara and Modena, and Leonora of Aragon (1450–1493); sister of Alfonso I (1476–1534), 3rd duke of Ferrara, who married *Lucrezia Borgia; married Louis also known as Ludovico or Lodovico il Moro Sforza (1451–1508), duke of Milan (r. 1479–1500), on January 17, 1491; daughter-in-law of *Bianca Maria Visconti (1423–1470); children: Ercole, duke of Milan (b. 1493, called Maximilian); Francesco Maria (b. 1495), duke of Milan (r. 1521–1535).*

Moved to Naples (1477); betrothed (1480); returned to Ferrara (1485); established court at Milan (1491); became duchess of Milan (1494); began artistic patronage (1495).

Este, Isabella d' (1474–1539). Marchioness of Mantua and important leader of the Italian Renaissance as patron of the arts, as well as a politician who worked to advance her family's power and prestige. Name variations: Isabel, Isabeau; Isabella Gonzaga; Marchioness or Marchesa of Mantua. Pronunciation: eez-uh-BELL-uh DEHS-tuh. Born on May 18, 1474, in Ferrara, Italy; died on February 13, 1539, in Mantua, Italy; daughter of Ercole I d'Este (1431–1505), 2nd duke of Ferrara and Modena, and Leonora of Aragon (1450–1493); sister of Alfonso I (1476–1534), 3rd duke of Ferrara, who married *Lucrezia Borgia; married Francesco also known as Gianfrancesco Gonzaga (1466–1519), 4th marquis of Mantua (r. 1484–1519), February 11, 1490; children: Eleonora Gonzaga (1493–1543); Margherita (1496–1496); Frederigo also known as Federico (1500–1540), 5th marquis of Mantua (r. 1519–1540); Ippolita Gonzaga (1503–1570, became a nun); Ercole (1505–1563, a cardinal); Ferrante (1507–1557, prince of Guastalla); Paola Gonzaga (1508–1569, became a nun). Francesco Gonzaga also had two illegitimate daughters.*

Betrothed (1480); established court at Mantua (1490); began artistic patronage (1495); commissioned Leonardo da Vinci to sketch portrait (1499); arranged for husband's release from prison (1509).

Isabella d'Este and her younger sister Beatrice were two of the most famous women of the Renaissance period in Europe (about 1450–1550). Despite their fame, until 1976 only one obscure full-length biography had been written on each in the 400 years since their deaths. Each woman was a politically active, wealthy noblewoman who contributed immensely to the Italian Renaissance by her patronage of many of its greatest artists, including Leonardo da Vinci.

Beatrice and Isabella were the first and second children born to the powerful duke and duchess of Ferrara. Ferrara was only a small state in northern Italy, but it had been raised to prominence by the shrewd political leadership of the Este family, including their father, Ercole I of Ferrara. Duke Ercole was well-loved by his subjects, for he kept Ferrara safe from invasion during the turbulent late-15th century, when Italian politics was a massive tangle of civil wars between city-states. Their mother, *Leonora of

Beatrice d'Este (1475–1497)

Aragon, was the daughter of King Ferrante of Naples; thus, Isabella and Beatrice had both noble and royal family heritages.

In the later Middle Ages and Renaissance, power, titles, and property were usually passed down through the male line of a family. Most families attributed little importance to the birth of a daughter, whose marriage could make a political alliance but who traditionally could not inherit her parents' estates. Consequently, it is not surprising that neither Isabella nor Beatrice received much of a welcome into the world at birth. As **Julia Cartwright** wrote, a chronicler recorded in 1475 that "a daughter was born this day to Duke Ercole, and received the name of Beatrice, being the child of Madonna Leonora, his wife. And there were no rejoicings, because everyone wished for a boy." This cold, factual report can be contrasted to the celebrations held the following year, when shops were closed, banquets held, and concerts given in honor of her brother.

Isabella d'Este (1474–1539)

Two years after Beatrice's birth, Duchess Leonora took her two daughters to visit their grandfather, Ferrante of Naples. Several months later, she returned to Ferrara but left Beatrice behind, for Ferrante had grown attached to the small child and refused to allow her to leave. Beatrice remained in Naples under her grandfather's watchful eye for the next eight years, while Isabella was raised in Ferrara. Thus, the two girls spent most of their childhood apart, although this did not seem to diminish their affection for one another in later years. Then in May 1480, Ercole and Leonora announced that betrothal agreements had been made for both girls—Isabella was to marry Francesco Gonzaga, son of the Marquis Federico of Mantua, while Beatrice's betrothed was the powerful regent of Milan, Ludovico Sforza. These alliances represented the union of Italy's most powerful and prominent families.

Beatrice returned to her father's court in 1485 at age ten, where she and Isabella continued their schooling together. Both received a classical education, which, though uncommon for daughters in the Middle Ages, was becoming more popular during the early years of the Italian Renaissance. They studied French and Latin language and literature, the ancient Greek authors in translation, as well as some of the sciences, mathematics, and geometry. Unlike male students, Isabella and Beatrice were also taught those accomplishments considered necessary for noblewomen: dancing, embroidery, playing an instrument, and singing. Both were described as intelligent, quick learners by their tutors. In addition, the princesses learned from their parents about the importance and beauty of the arts—music, painting, architecture, and sculpture—and of the tangled alliances and enmities between the various Italian states.

When Isabella reached her 16th year, she married her betrothed Francesco Gonzaga, who had succeeded as marquis of Mantua on his father's death in 1484 and was now about 24 years old. The young princess was described at the time of her wedding as being of moderate height, with pale skin, fine blonde hair, and black eyes. The elaborate wedding was held at Ferrara on February 11, 1490. Preparations for the ceremony and its accompanying celebrations had begun more than a year before and employed hundreds of artists and artisans to create every object and piece of furniture to be used during the event. The time and money invested in the details of the wedding reveal the significance of the ritual for all the people of both city-states, since a wedding between two nobles was not just a personal commitment but a political alliance made by two families and sealed with both a dowry and a dower (gifts of money and land exchanged by the two families).

Thus, the ceremonies involved in the actual wedding were political events involving many speeches, banquets in honor of various family members, and a grand display of wealth. As an example of the ostentatious show, Isabella rode through Ferrara after the ceremony in a new chariot draped with a cloth of pure gold, and her hundreds of guests ate off crystal and gold plates at her wedding feast. The day after the wedding, Isabella and Francesco sailed up the Po River to Mantua, Isabella's new home. There she was met by the people of Mantua, who welcomed her warmly, and the new marchioness attended even more banquets and pageants in her honor.

Isabella had met her husband only once before their wedding but had been corresponding with him ever since their betrothal was announced. Despite the eight years between them, they seemed to be quite happy together and grew very affectionate with one another. Isabella's devotion to her new husband spread to his family as well. She became especially fond of Francesco's sister, *Elisabetta Montefeltro, who later became duchess of Urbino. They remained intimate friends for the rest of their lives, often corresponding after Elisabetta left Mantua for Urbino. In one letter, Isabella tells her friend that "there is no one I love like you, excepting my only sister." In addition, Isabella shared her love of music and singing with many in Mantua, and quickly became the well-loved center of the Mantuan court.

In the November after her wedding, Isabella returned to Ferrara to participate in the preparations for Beatrice's upcoming wedding. The sisters had become very close during their teen years, and Isabella wrote that she could not bear to be left out of such an important occasion in Beatrice's life. She traveled with her mother and Beatrice to Pavia for the ceremonies and only after several months returned to Mantua. The wedding of Ludovico Sforza and Beatrice d'Este, held in January 1491, was as elaborate and costly as that of Isabella, and the festivities lasted for about a week. The bride, at age 16, was described by court ambassadors as tall, with olive skin, black hair, and dark eyes.

The man Beatrice married had already led a long, adventurous life in the 40 years before his marriage. He was a politically savvy member of one of Italy's most prominent houses, whose intrigues and military exploits led him to be ban-

ished for several years. In 1479, Ludovico, always known as "Il Moro," returned to Milan and was named duke of Bari by the king of Naples. Later that year, he led a successful invasion of Milan which resulted in his being named regent of Milan for his nephew, Gian Galeazzo. He retained the regency for 15 years, acting as duke in all but name.

Both Beatrice, now duchess of Bari, and Isabella became the trusted companions and political associates of their husbands. Since ruling a state in the 15th century entailed almost constant travel for the regent of Milan and the marquis of Mantua, their wives played important roles in administering the government in their absences. Unlike Beatrice, Isabella took to her political duties eagerly; she had a keen ability to master the endless diplomacies and intrigues which made up Italian politics and seemed to enjoy the responsibilities and burdens of rule. She had a strong concern for the public good and spent much of her time corresponding with Ludovico Sforza, her father, and her husband, consulting with them on how to meet the needs of the people of Mantua.

Yet her duties to the state did not occupy all of the marchioness' time. Isabella spent hours consulting with the many jewelry designers, artisans, wardrobe designers, tailors, and furriers whom she employed. She had a great love of, and appreciation for, jewels and luxurious dresses and was continuously involved in the design and execution of new pieces of jewelry and gowns for her collections.

Beatrice, on the other hand, did not share Isabella's political bent. She took on the responsibilities of a duchess—from managing her household to taking care of state matters—but did not derive the pleasure from it that her sister did. She quickly filled her more serious obligations and then occupied herself with what were called "the joys of living," i.e., dancing, singing, hunting, having poems and stories read to her, bringing those people to court who were reputed to have the best artistic and musical talents. She did, however, share with Isabella her love of fine clothing and expensive gems and spent a considerable amount each month on new gowns and other luxuries.

It seems part of Beatrice's motivation to look her best was spurred on by her jealousy of the princess ❧➤ **Isabella of Naples**, bride of Gian Galeazzo, the young duke of Milan. It was no secret that the wife of the regent and the wife of the duke were engaged in a serious rivalry for domi-

See sidebar on the following page ❧➤

❧ Isabella of Naples (1470–1524)

*Duchess of Milan. Name variations: Isabella of Aragon; Isabella Sforza; Isabella di Bari; duchesa di Bari. Born on October 2, 1470; died in Naples in 1524; daughter of Alphonso II (b. 1448), king of Naples, and *Ippolita (1446–1484); married Giangaleazzo or Gian Galeazzo Sforza (1469–1494), 6th duke of Milan (r. 1476–1479); sister-in-law of *Caterina Sforza (c. 1462–1509); children: Francesco (d. 1511); *Bona Sforza (1493–1557, who married Sigismund, king of Poland).*

nance at the Milanese court; it was unclear which lady should have precedence and which should pay homage to the other, since Ludovico ruled Milan in fact, whereas Duke Gian Galeazzo ruled in name. It created a palpable tension at court which was felt by all courtiers who, trained in the intricacies of protocol and paying homage based on fine differences of rank, could not be sure which "Lady" to treat with the greater obeisance. Both Beatrice and Isabella of Naples tried to outdo one another by showing the most wealth in terms of costume and adornment.

Beatrice and her sister Isabella corresponded regularly, each writing at least once a week. In 1492, their much-beloved mother Leonora died, and the bereaved sisters wrote to one another long letters of consolation and sympathy. Later that year, Isabella gave birth to her first child, a daughter, whom she named *Eleonora (Gonzaga) in honor of her departed mother. The next year witnessed the birth of Beatrice's son, baptized Ercole after their father. In 1494, Beatrice triumphed in her rivalry with Isabella of Naples, for the young Duke Gian Galeazzo died suddenly and Ludovico Sforza was proclaimed his successor, forcing Isabella of Naples to retire to her dower estates.

The year 1495 proved to be important for the two princesses of Ferrara. In January, Isabella traveled to Milan to be present for the birth of Beatrice's second child, Francesco. The sisters spent much of their time consulting with the various artists who surrounded the Milanese court, for Beatrice had developed a keen interest in the patronage of up-and-coming painters, sculptors, and poets, who were rewarded handsomely if their work pleased the young duchess. This generous patronage made the beneficent duchess one of Europe's most admired women. But Isabella's visit was cut short by news that France had invaded and conquered Naples; an international league including Milan and Mantua was

formed to fight against the French, and Francesco Gonzaga was named captain of the new armies. Isabella was forced to return home in March to govern Mantua in Francesco's place; although they could not have known, she and Beatrice had parted for the last time.

Isabella spent almost the next year and a half involved heavily in the day-to-day administration of a wartime state and sold many of the precious jewels and other ornaments to raise money for her husband to pay his soldiers. In July 1496, she gave birth to another daughter, Margherita, who lived for only a few months. More tragedy struck when the marchioness received word that Francesco was gravely ill with a fever; Isabella immediately ordered an entourage to accompany her to her husband, who lay ill at Ancona, and brought him home to Mantua, where he eventually recovered.

A few months later, news came to Mantua which caused deep mourning throughout the city. It was announced that Beatrice, duchess of Milan, had died on January 2, 1497, at age 21, having given birth that evening to a still-born son. The duchess' courtiers told how the young woman had seemed to be in a profound depression for the preceding months, although she would not explain the cause of her sadness, and spent much of her time in prayer. Her husband Ludovico reacted with shock and sorrow, refusing for several days to see anyone except his secretary, to whom he dictated letters bearing the news of Beatrice's death to her family. To Francesco Gonzaga, he wrote of his suffering:

> This cruel and premature end has filled me with bitter and indescribable anguish, so much so that I would rather have died myself than lose the dearest and most precious thing that I had in this world. . . . And I beg you not to send anyone to condole with me, as that would only renew my sorrow. I would not write to Madonna Marchesana [Isabella], and leave you to break the news to her as you think best, knowing well how inexpressible her sorrow will be.

Indeed, Isabella was inconsolable when Francesco conveyed Ludovico's message. She wrote to her father of her grief on January 5: "When I think what a loving, honored, and only sister I have lost, I am so much oppressed with the burden of this sudden loss that I know not how I can ever find comfort."

The war against France had spread until many of Italy's city-states were also warring against one another, and in this chaotic climate, Isabella could scarcely afford the luxury of a long mourning period. She soon had to turn her attention back to matters of state, for in June 1497 Francesco was dismissed from his post as army captain because of internal conflicts with other leaders of the anti-French league. Her brother-in-law Ludovico saw his downfall soon after, when a treaty between Venice and France led to his deposition as duke of Milan; he fled the state, and Beatrice's children were sent into exile.

Isabella cared deeply about Ludovico's well-being, but her overriding concern was for her own safety and for peace in Milan; thus, she began the difficult task of negotiating with the French in the interests of Milan. In 1499, she learned that Ludovico had been taken captive by the French. The man whose fortunes had risen so steadily in his early years and had spent his middle years as one of Italy's most powerful men died a prisoner in Touraine, France, in 1508. Beatrice's son Ercole was restored to his father's duchy in 1512, and one chronicler writes that during Ercole's reign, Ludovico's body was removed to Milan and buried next to Beatrice.

Isabella continued to give birth to children at regular intervals, seven in total. In 1500, her first son Federico was born, to the joy of Francesco and the Milanese, who had longed for an heir to the marquis. *Ippolita Gonzaga (born 1503), Ercole (1505), who would become a cardinal, Ferrante (1507), and *Paola Gonzaga (1508) were her last four children.

In her treatment of children, Isabella was a typical mother for her time. She paid the most attention to her eldest son Federico, writing to Francesco almost daily about the child's growth and progress with tutors; in contrast, she virtually ignored her daughters, scarcely mentioning them in any of her correspondence. She closely supervised the education of all her children, however, making sure each was well-taught in the classics as she had been; she also planned for their marriages with an eye toward political and financial gain. But she did not reveal in her letters true affection or maternal love for any of them. This was not uncommon in the 15th century, when the value of children was sometimes equated with their potential to increase their family's wealth and prestige.

In the years following Beatrice's death, Isabella became famed across Europe for her patronage of the Renaissance's greatest artists. She commissioned hundreds of portraits and other paintings, giving the finished works as gifts or keeping them in one of her many studios and galleries. At the end of 1499, the famous master Leonardo da Vinci made a long visit to the court of Mantua. It was during this time that he executed a portrait of Isabella in red chalk; it is one of the few existing pictures of the marchioness and now hangs in the Louvre Museum in Paris.

Isabella paid enormous sums of money for the works she ordered, and she was very difficult to satisfy. For instance, she penned more than 50 letters to Perugino, the artist from whom she had commissioned a single picture, criticizing the work and requesting improvement before she paid for it. She would return books to their printers, demanding more careful revision, and send back musical instruments to their makers if their tones were not sweet enough.

Yet, as Julia Cartwright noted in *Isabella D'Este:* "If Isabella was a fastidious and sometimes severe critic, she was also a generous and kindly patron, prompt to recognize true merit and stimulate creative effort, and ever ready to befriend struggling artists." Castiglione, Niccolo da Correggio, Bembo, Bellini, Michelangelo, and Titian, indeed many of the most well-known names of the Italian Renaissance, counted Isabella as one of their most generous and supportive patrons and sponsors. In return for her financial rewards and the publicity she gave them, all these artists paid tribute to the marchioness in their paintings, in their poems extolling her virtues, in their verses written for her, and in their songs in Italian and Latin and French dedicated to her.

Meanwhile, the war against the French continued off and on. Francesco obtained a new commission to lead troops against the enemies of Mantua and spent the better part of ten years away from home, returning only briefly every few months. In July 1509, Isabella learned that Francesco had been taken captive by the Venetians and was being held in Venice. She immediately set to work trying to effect his release, sending envoys asking for help to the pope, the French king, the Holy Roman Emperor Maximilian, and others. A year later, the marquis was freed, but only after Isabella pawned much of her jewelry for ransom and persuaded the pope to assist her by pressuring the Venetians on her behalf.

Isabella continued acting as the chief administrator of Mantua when Francesco again returned to war. In 1519, more tragedy struck. In January, her friend the Emperor Maximilian passed away, as well as her longtime personal secretary. While she was recovering from her grief, the Marquis Francesco fell ill while staying at Mantua. He died on March 29 with Isabella, his children, and his sisters at his bedside. Isabella's son Federico was proclaimed the new marquis and looked to his mother for her guidance and the value of her experience.

Despite the fact that a mourning Isabella officially ceased to hold the title of marchioness with Francesco's death, she continued to act in her former capacity for some time. She spent the next few years actively involved in the administration of her son's reign but gradually began to tire of the constant demands such a position made on her. She began to free herself from the constraints of ruling and indulged more and more in her favorite activities. This included nearly constant traveling across Italy, visiting her relatives and the many friends whom she had made in her youth and early adult life. Of course, she remained somewhat politically active, including successfully pressuring the pope to put her son Ercole on the college of cardinals. But in these later years of widowhood, Isabella turned her attention to playing the role of artistic patron and serious art collector, a role she had been forced to neglect during the last few years of Francesco's life. She created one of the finest libraries in Europe, filled her palaces with Greek and Roman antiques, and turned back to the intellectual pursuits of learning which she had not engaged in since her youth.

In late 1538, Isabella's health began to fail. She was 64 years old, an advanced age for that period. She made out her last will, providing for the future security of her children and grandchildren as well as for the ladies-in-waiting and other servants who had been in her service for many years. She made one last trip to Venice in September, to visit her son Ercole, and returned to Mantua in November. Her children were summoned to their mother's bedside in early February when it became clear her health would not improve. She said goodbye to her grieving children and grandchildren, and died peacefully on February 13, 1539. She was buried beside her husband in the Church of San Francesco in Mantua.

SOURCES:

Cartwright, Julia. *Beatrice D'Este, Duchess of Milan: A Study of the Renaissance.* London: J.M. Dent, 1899.

———. *Isabella D'Este: Marchioness of Mantua (1474–1539): A Study of the Renaissance in Two Volumes.* London: J.M. Dent, 1903.

SUGGESTED READING:

King, Margaret. *Women of the Renaissance.* Chicago, IL: University of Chicago Press, 1991.

Marek, George R. *The Bed and the Throne: The life of Isabella D'Este.* NY: Harper, 1976.

Laura York,
freelance writer in medieval history and women's history,
Riverside, California

Este, Bianca Maria d' (1440–1506)

Ferrarese noblewoman. Born in 1440; died in 1506; illegitimate daughter of Nicholas also known as Niccolo III d'Este (1383–1441), 12th marquis of Ferrara; married Galeotto Pico della Mirandola.

Este, Catherine d'

Duchess of Savoy-Carignan. Married Emmanuel Philibert, duke of Savoy-Carignan (d. 1709); children: Victor Amadeus (d. 1741) and possibly *Anna Victoria of Savoy.*

Este, Costanza d'

Ferrarese noblewoman. Name variations: Costanza Aldobrandeschi. Daughter of *Mambilia d'Este and Azzo VII Novello d'Este, lord of Ferrara (d. 1264); married Umberto Aldobrandeschi.

Este, Costanza d'

Ferrarese noblewoman. Name variations: Costanza della Scala. Born Costanza della Scala; second wife of Obizzo II d'Este (1247–1293), lord of Ferrara and Modena (r. 1264–1293).

Este, Cunegunda d' (c. 1012–1055)

Marquise of Este. Born around 1012; died in 1055; daughter of Guelph also known as Welf of Altdorf and *Imagi of Luxemburg (c. 1000–1057); married Azo also known as Azzo II, marquis of Este; children: Guelph also known as Welf IV, duke of Bavaria.

Este, Eleanora d' (1450–1493).

See Leonora of Aragon.

Este, Eleonora d' (1515–1575)

Abbess. Name variations: Leonora; Leonor d'Este. Born in 1515; died in 1575; daughter of *Lucrezia Borgia (1480–1519) and Alfonso I d'Este, 3rd duke of Ferrara and Modena; niece of *Isabella d'Este (1474–1539). Abbess of the monastery of Corpus Domini in Ferrara.

Este, Eleonora d' (1537–1581)

Ferrarese princess who was beloved by Tasso. Name variations: Leonora d'Este; Eleonora of Este. Born on June 19, 1537; died on February 10, 1581; daughter of Renée of France (1510–1575) and Hercules II also known as Ercole II (1508–1559), 4th duke of

Eleonora
d'Este
(1537–1581)

Ferrara and Modena; sister of Alfonso II
(1533–1597), 5th duke of Ferraro and Modena; never
married; no children.

An Italian princess, Eleonora d'Este was
born in 1537, the daughter of *Renée of France
and Ercole II, 4th duke of Ferrara and Modena.
She was also the sister of Alfonso II, 5th duke of
Ferraro and Modena, and came under his sway
in 1559 on the death of her father. Eleonora
d'Este is best known as the beloved of Italian
poet Torquato Tasso (1544–1595).

In 1565, Tasso was 21 when he first met the beautiful 28-year-old Eleonora at the court of Alfonso, and he was quickly infatuated. An indiscreet remark made by one of the courtiers regarding the poet's veneration of the princess caused Tasso to challenge the offender. The courtier, along with his three brothers, attacked Tasso, but others put an end to the duel. Alphonso, incensed by this outburst, sent Tasso away from the court, where he remained subject to the duke's call.

According to legend, Tasso wrote verses to his beloved Eleonora that touched her heart. A few years later, at the wedding of one of the Gonzaga family, celebrated at the court of Este, Tasso kissed the princess Eleonora on the cheek. Furious, Alphonso turned coolly to his courtiers and remarked, "What a great pity that the finest genius of the age has become suddenly mad!" The duke had Tasso shut up in the hospital of St. Anna in Ferrara. (In actuality, Tasso had been beset by delusional fears of persecution starting in 1575 and began a series of mad wanderings around 1577.)

Tasso's long years of imprisonment (1579–86), his sufferings, his laments, are well known. Obliged to witness the cruel punishment of her lover and knowing the inflexible character of her brother, Eleonora fell into a slow fever and died in 1581, about a year after Tasso's imprisonment. Thus, when the doors of Tasso's prison were at length opened, Eleonora was dead. Youth, love, fortune, all had vanished; only fame remained. For his epic poetry, the laurel wreath was placed on Tasso's head in Rome during a splendid festival. Wrote Goethe in his *Torquato Tasso*:

> "Of you alone I thought while I composed;
> You to delight, was still my highest wish,
> You to enrapture, was my final aim."

Este, Elisa d' (d. 1329)

*Ferrarese noblewoman. Name variations: Elisa Bonacolsi. Died in 1329; daughter of *Alda d'Este and Aldobrandino II, lord of Ferrara (d. 1326); married Passarino Bonacolsi.*

Este, Elisabetta d'

Ferrarese noblewoman. Name variations: Elisabetta Pio. Illegitimate daughter of Ippolito I d'Este (1479–1520, a cardinal); married Giberto Pio.

Este, Giacoma d'

Ferrarese noblewoman. Name variations: Giacoma de' Fieschi. First wife of Obizzo II d'Este (1247–1293),

lord of Ferrara (r. 1264–1293); children: Azzo VIII, lord of Ferrara (r. 1293–1308); Aldobrandino II (d. 1326); Francesco (murdered in 1312); *Beatrice d'Este (d. 1334). Obizzo's second wife was *Costanza d'Este.*

Este, Giacoma d'

Ferrarese noblewoman. Name variations: Giacoma de' Pepoli. First wife of Obizzo III d'Este (1294–1352), lord of Ferrara.

Este, Gigliola d'

Marquesa of Ferrara. Name variations: Gigliola da Carrara. Married Nicholas also known as Niccolo III d'Este (1383–1441), 12th marquis of Ferrara, in 1397.

Este, Ginevra d' (1414–1440)

*Ferrarese noblewoman. Name variations: Ginevra Malatesta. Born in 1414 (some sources cite 1419); died in 1440; daughter of *Parisina (Malatesta) d'Este and Nicholas also known as Niccolo III d'Este (1383–1441), 12th marquis of Ferrara; married Sigismondo Pandolfo Malatesta (1417–1486); children: Roberto Malatesta (d. 1484). Sigismondo's second wife was Polissena Sforza; his 3rd wife was Isotta degli Atti.*

Este, Giovanna d' (fl. 1240s)

*Ferrarese noblewoman. Name variations: Joanna. First wife of Azzo VII Novello d'Este, lord of Ferrara (d. 1264); children: Rinaldo d'Este (d. 1251); *Beata Beatrice II d'Este (d. 1262). Azzo's second wife was *Mambilia d'Este.*

Este, Giovanna d' (fl. 1280s)

*Ferrarese noblewoman. Name variations: Joanna. Born Giovanna Orsini; first wife of Azzo VIII d'Este, lord of Ferrara (r. 1293–1308). Azzo's second wife was *Beatrice d'Este (fl. 1290s).*

Este, Giovanna d' (fl. 1300s)

*Ferrarese noblewoman. Name variations: Giovanna de' Roberti; first wife of Alberto (1347–1393), lord of Ferrara. Alberto's second wife was *Isotta d'Este (fl. 1300s).*

Este, Giulia d'.

See Rovere, Giulia della.

Este, Isabella d' (1474–1539).

See Este, Beatrice d' and Isabella d'.

Este, Isotta d' (fl. 1300s)

*Ferrarese noblewoman. Name variations: Isotta Albaresani. Second wife of Alberto (1347–1393), lord of Ferrara; children: Nicholas also known as Niccolo III d'Este, lord of Ferrara. Alberto's first wife was *Giovanna d'Este (fl. 1300s).*

Este, Isotta d' (1425–1456)

Ferrarese noblewoman. Name variations: Isotta da Montefeltro; Isotta Frangipani. Born in 1425; died in 1456; illegitimate daughter of Nicholas also known as Niccolo III d'Este (1383–1441), 12th marquis of Ferrara; married Oddo Antonio da Montefeltro; married Stefano Frangipani.

Este, Lippa d'

*Ferrarese noblewoman. Name variations: Lippa degli Ariosti. Second wife of Obizzo III d'Este (1294–1352), lord of Ferrara; children: *Alda d'Este (1333–1381); Aldobrandino III (1335–1361); Niccolo II Zoppo (1338–1388); Ugo (1344–1370); Alberto (1347–1393).*

Este, Lucia d' (1419–1437)

*Ferrarese noblewoman. Name variations: Lucia Gonzaga. Born in 1419; died in 1437; daughter of *Parisina d'Este and Nicholas also known as Niccolo III d'Este (1383–1441), 12th marquis of Ferrara; married Carlo Gonzaga.*

Este, Lucrezia d'

Ferrarese noblewoman. Name variations: Lucrezia of Montferrat; Lucrecia. Married Rinaldo d'Este (illegimate son of Nicholas also known as Niccolo III d'Este [1383–1441], 12th marquis of Ferrara).

Este, Lucrezia d' (d. 1516/18)

*Ferrarese princess. Name variations: Lucrezia d'Este Bentivoglio. Born before 1473 and died in 1516/18; illegitimate daughter of Hercules I also known as Ercole I (1431–1505), 2nd duke of Ferrara and Modena; half-sister of *Isabella d'Este (1474–1539) and *Beatrice d'Este (1475–1497); married Annibale Bentivoglio.*

Este, Lucrezia d' (1535–1598)

*Duchess of Urbino. Name variations: Lucrezia della Rovere. Born in 1535; died in 1598; daughter of Hercules II also known as Ercole II (1508–1559), 4th duke of Ferrara and Modena, and *Renée of France (1510–1575); sister of *Eleonora d'Este (1515–1575); married Francesco Maria II della Rovere, duke of Urbino.*

Este, Mambilia d'

*Ferrarese noblewoman. Name variations: Mambilia Pelavicino. Second wife of Azzo VII Novello d'Este, lord of Ferrara (d. 1264); children: *Costanza d'Este (who married Umberto Aldobrandeschi). Azzo's first wife was *Giovanna d'Este (fl. 1240s).*

Este, Margherita d' (1418–1439).

See Gonzaga, Margherita.

Este, Margherita d' (d. 1452)

Ferrarese noblewoman. Name variations: Margherita Pio. Died in 1452; illegitimate daughter of Nicholas also known as Niccolo III d'Este (1383–1441), 12th marquis of Ferrara; married Galasso Pio.

Este, Margherita d' (1564–1618).

See Gonzaga, Margherita.

Este, Maria Beatrice d' (1750–1829).

See Maria Beatrice of Modena.

Este, Mary Beatrice d' (1658–1718).

See Mary of Modena.

Este, Parisina d'

*Marquesa of Ferrara. Name variations: Parisina Malatesta. Married Nicholas also known as Niccolo III d'Este (1383–1441), 12th marquis of Ferrara, in 1418; children: *Ginevra d'Este (1414–1440); *Lucia d'Este (1419–1437).*

Niccolo III was also married to *Ricciarda d'Este and had many illegitimate children: Ugo Aldobrandino (1405–1425); Meliaduse (1406–1452); Leonello (1407–1450, who was eventually legitimated and became the 13th marquis of Ferrara); Borso (1413–1471, 1st duke of Modena and Ferrara); Alberto (1415–1502); Gurone Maria (d. 1484); *Isotta d'Este (1425–1456); *Beatrice d'Este (1427–1497); Rinaldo (d. 1503); *Margherita d'Este (d. 1452); *Bianca Maria d'Este (1440–1506); Baldassare; and others.

Este, Pizzocara d'

Ferrarese noblewoman. Married Sigismondo d'Este (1433–1507); children: Ercole di Sigismondo d'Este (who married *Angela Sforza); Bianca d'Este (who married Alberigo da San Severino); Diana d'Este (who married Uguccione di Ambrogio de' Contrari).

Este, Ricciarda d'

Marquesa of Ferrara. Name variations: Ricciarda da Saluzzo. Married Nicholas also known as Niccolo III d'Este (1383–1441), 12th marquis of Ferrara, in 1431; children: Ercole I (1431–1505), 2nd duke of Ferrara and Modena (who married *Leonora of Aragon [1450–1493]); Sigismondo (1433–1507).

Niccolo III was also married to *Parisina d'Este and had many illegitimate children: Ugo Aldobrandino (1405–1425); Meliaduse (1406–1452); Leonello (1407–1450, who was eventually legitimated and became the 13th marquis of Ferrara); Borso (1413–1471, 1st duke of Modena and Ferrara); Alberto (1415–1502); Gurone Maria (d. 1484); *Isotta d'Este (1425–1456); *Beatrice d'Este (1427–1497); Rinaldo (d. 1503); *Margherita d'Este (d. 1452); *Bianca Maria d'Este (1440–1506); Baldassare; and others.

Este, Taddea d' (1365–1404)

Ferrarese noblewoman. Name variations: Thaddaea. Born in 1365; died in 1404; daughter of *Verde d'Este and Nicholas also known as Niccolo II Zoppo (1338–1388), lord of Ferrara; married Francesco Novello da Carrara.

Este, Verde d'

Ferrarese noblewoman. Name variations: Verde della Scala; Virida. Possibly the daughter of Mastino II della Scala, count of Verona; possibly sister of *Beatrice della Scala (1340–1384); married Nicholas also known as Niccolo II Zoppo (1338–1388), lord of Ferrara; children: *Taddea d'Este (1365–1404, who married Francesco Novello da Carrara).

Este, Virginia d' (b. 1573?)

Duchess of Modena. Name variations: Virginia de Medici. Born around 1573; daughter of *Camilla Martelli and Cosimo I de Medici (1519–1574), grand duke of Tuscany (r. 1569–1574); married Cesare d'Este (1562–1628), duke of Ferrara (r. 1597), duke of Modena (r. 1597–1628).

Estefania of Barcelona (fl. 1038)

Queen of Navarre. Name variations: Etienette of Barcelona; Estefania of Foix. Flourished around 1038; daughter of Bernard I, count of Foix, and *Gersenda, countess of Bigorre; married Garcia III, king of Navarre, in 1038; children: Sancho IV (1039–1076), king of Navarre (r. 1054–1076); Fernando (who married Nuna de Biscaya); Raimundo also known as Ramon of Navarre (d. 1084); Cameros; Hermesinda (who married Fortun Sanchez de Yarnoz); Mayor of Navarre (who married Guy II, count of Beaune and Mascon); Urraca (who married Garcia, count of Najera and Granon); Jimena.

Esther (fl. 475 BCE)

Hebrew queen. Name variations: Edissa. Flourished around 475 BCE; daughter of Abihail; niece of Mordecai; married Xerxes I (c. 518–465, known in the Biblical text as Ahasuerus or Assuerus), king of Persia (r. 486–465); children: Darius, Hystaspes, and Artaxerxes.

In the ahistorical Old Testament *Book of Esther* (written 2nd century BCE?), Esther is portrayed as an Israelite beauty who became the wife of the Persian king, Xerxes (Ahasuerus in the Biblical text), despite her religious background which was kept hidden from Ahasuerus for a time. Esther's rise is credited to the fall of Ahasuerus' previous wife, *Vashti, whose disobedience toward the king led to her rejection—a rejection that angered some of her supporters at court. Discarding one wife, Ahasuerus ordered that the most beautiful virgins of the Persian Empire be brought to his harem at Susa, so that he might choose another. Among these was Esther, said to have been the daughter of one Abihail but raised by her uncle Mordecai—a prominent Israelite living in Susa as a result of the diaspora brought on by the Babylonian king, Nebuchadnezzar (whose realm had subsequently been incorporated into the Persian Empire). Fearing that her Jewishness might cause his niece harm, Mordecai advised Esther to conceal her religion, and Esther took his advice. It is said that Ahasuerus was so taken by Esther's beauty and demeanor that he made her his new wife.

Thereafter Esther is said to have been the savior of her husband, her uncle, and her people. She protected her husband against a plot organized by Vashti's partisans—a conspiracy discovered by Mordecai and revealed to Ahasuerus through Esther. She saved Mordecai and the Israelites from Haman, one of Ahasuerus' officials, who conceived a great hatred toward both Mordecai and all of his people because the Israelite would not kneel before Haman's imperial authority. Beset by hubris and angered by Mordecai's defiance, Haman supposedly retali-

ated by plotting the extermination of all Persian Jews. Incited by Haman to act against the Israelites, Ahasuerus, unaware of his wife's religion, ordered their extermination. However, Mordecai, acting upon inside information, besought Esther's aid. Putting her faith in God, Esther approached her husband, revealed her background, and convinced Ahasuerus to reward Mordecai's past services (including his part in uncovering the earlier assassination attempt), which had been previously overlooked. After Haman later agreed, without knowing who was involved, that a loyal servant should be rewarded by the king, and, after Ahasuerus caught Haman in an attempt to seduce Esther, Ahasuerus executed Haman and replaced him with Mordecai. Therefore, Haman's extermination of the Persian Jews was averted, leading to a general celebration recreated in the feast of Purim.

The Book of Esther renders testimony for the religious toleration that was a hallmark of Persian dominion throughout the reign of the Achaemenid Dynasty (c. 550–331 BCE). More a historical novella than a historical record from Xerxes' reign, the story offers an explanation for the origin of the festival of Purim, but cannot be held to detail accurately the career of a historical Persian queen.

SUGGESTED READING:
The Book of Esther (in the Old Testament).

William Greenwalt,
Associate Professor of Classical History,
Santa Clara University, Santa Clara, California

Esther before Ahasuerus, *by Artemisia Gentileschi.*

Estraigues, Henriette d' (1579–1633).

See Medici, Marie de for sidebar on Entragues, Henriette d'.

Estrées, Angélique, d'.

See Estrées, Gabrielle d' for sidebar.

Estrées, Diane, d' (b. 1572).

See Estrées, Gabrielle d' for sidebar.

Estrées, Françoise Babou de la Bourdaisière, Dame d'.

See Estrées, Gabrielle d' for sidebar.

Estrées, Gabrielle d' (1573–1599)

*French mistress of Henry IV of France who, in her 26 years of life, became queen of the realm in all but name. Name variations: Gabrielle d'Estrees; Duchess of Beaufort or Duchess de Beaufort; Duchess d'Etampes or Duchess d'Étampes; Marquise de Monceaux or Marchioness of Monceaux; Dame de Liencourt; Dame de Vandeuil. Born on December 23, 1573, at Coeuvres, in Picardy (some sources erroneously cite 1565 in the château at la Bourdaisière); died on April 10, 1599, in Paris, France; daughter of Antoine d'Estrées, marquis of Coeuvres, and Françoise Babou de la Bourdaisière; sister of François-Annibal d'Estrées, bishop of Noyon and constable of France; married Nicolas d'Amerval, Sieur de Liencourt (Baron de Benais), in June 1592 (divorced 1594); mistress Henry of Navarre also known as Henry IV (1553–1610), king of France (r. 1589–1610); children: (with Henry IV) Caesar, duke of Vendôme; **Catherine Henriette de Vendôme**, duchess of Elbeuf; Alexander, Chevalier de Vendôme.*

Gabrielle d'Estrées

Though Gabrielle d'Estrées was only one of 56 documented mistresses of Henry IV, king of France, she was the only woman to whom he remained faithful. Together, they had three children, all legitimized by royal decree, and it was only the sudden death of d'Estrées at age 26 that thwarted their probable marriage. Though 20 years younger than the king, d'Estrées possessed a keen intellect, irresistible charm, and an inborn political savvy, all of which she used to advance Henry's cause of a united France. Historians credit her with promulgating the Edict of Nantes (1598), a decree guaranteeing religious freedom to the Protestants of France, which ended the Wars of the Faith. "It was she," writes Noel Gerson, "acting as a self-appointed agent, who brought about a reconciliation between Henry and the great nobles who had bled France dry to prevent him from acquiring the crown that was rightfully his. It was Gabrielle, acting decisively in a moment of national peril, who supplied the funds that enabled Henry's army to defeat the most persistent of his foes, the legions of Philip II of Spain."

The daughter of Antoine d'Estrées, marquis of Coeuvres, Gabrielle grew up a castle in the town of Coeuvres, a few miles southeast of Soissons, France. She had two brothers, François-Annibal d'Estrées, who wrote extensively about Gabrielle in his *Memoirs* (1666), and François-Louis d'Estrées, and five sisters, including **Françoise d'Estrées**, ❧▶ **Angélique d'Estrées**, Julienne d'Estrées, and ❧▶ **Diane d'Estrées**, who later wrote the book *Memorial to Gabrielle, Duchess de Beaufort* (1615). (The fifth sister is not named in the available sources.) Absent from the household was Gabrielle's mother ❧▶ **Françoise Babou de la Bourdaisière d'Estrées**, who had run off with a neighbor, taking her youngest daughter with her. She would later give birth to an illegitimate daughter, compounding the scandal that surrounded her. (In June 1592, Françoise and her lover were murdered, although nothing is known about the circumstances of the crime.) Gabrielle was raised by her mother's sister ❧▶ **Isabelle de Sourdis**, wife of the former governor of Chartres and mistress of Armand de Chiverny, Henry IV's legal advisor. From age ten on, Gabrielle never saw her mother again; it was Isabelle who exercised any maternal influence.

Antoine d'Estrées was a strict father, intent on keeping his daughters from their mother's legacy. A somewhat enlightened man, however, he insisted that all of his children learn to read and write, and to that end employed a tutor. Gabrielle was a reluctant scholar at best, preferring to be out in the fields riding her pony.

Estrées, Angélique d'

French abbess. Name variations: Abbess of Maubisson. Daughter and one of eight children of Antoine d'Estrées, marquis of Coeuvres, and **Françoise Babou de la Bourdaisière d'Estrées**; *sister of François-Annibal d'Estrées, bishop of Noyon and constable of France, and* **Gabrielle d'Estrées** *(1573–1599).*

Quite nearly as corrupt as her mother, Angélique d'Estrées had numerous affairs, then joined the Convent of Maubisson, where she rose to become abbess. She not only continued to take lovers, but encouraged the young nuns in her charge to do the same, outraging even the lenient church hierarchy of the time. She was eventually banished to the Renaissance equivalent of a home for delinquents, where she lived out the remainder of her life under close observation.

Estrées, Diane d' (b. 1572)

French author. Name variations: Dame de Balagny. Born in 1572; daughter and one of eight children of Antoine d'Estrées, marquis of Coeuvres, and **Françoise Babou de la Bourdaisière d'Estrées**; *sister of François-Annibal d'Estrées, bishop of Noyon and constable of France, and* **Gabrielle d'Estrées** *(1573–1599); second wife of Louis de Balagny, Prince de Cambrai; children: several.*

Just a year older than Gabrielle and very close to her sister, Diane d'Estrées provided much of what is known about Gabrielle in her book *Memorial to Gabrielle, Duchess de Beaufort.* Diane married Louis de Balagny and had several children.

Estrées, Françoise Babou de la Bourdaisière, Dame d' (d. 1592)

Notorious French woman. Born Françoise Babou de la Bourdaisière at the chateau La Bourdaisière near Tours; one of seven daughters of Jean Babou (a prominent soldier, politician, and diplomat in the reign of Henry II); married Antoine d'Estrées, marquis of Coeuvres; eloped with Antoine, Marquis de Tourzel-Alègre, in 1583; children: (with Antoine d'Estrées) eight, including François-Annibal d'Estrées; François-Louis d'Estrées; Françoise d'Estrées; Julienne d'Estrées; *Diane d'Estrées (b. 1572); Gabrielle d'Estrées (1573–1599); *Angélique d'Estrées; (with Antoine Tourzel-Alègre) one daughter.*

"The sisters Babou were the seven deadly sins," wrote Voltaire, and it would seem that Françoise may have been the most beautiful and the most dissolute. Soon after her marriage to Antoine d'Estrées, she embarked on a number of casual affairs but then took herself out of circulation to give birth to eight children in as many years, including *Gabrielle d'Estrées. In 1583, at age 40, she tired of marriage and eloped with Antoine, Marquis de Tourzel-Alègre, a much younger man. She lived openly with him in Picardy, bearing an illegitimate daughter and becoming a symbol of sin for her country neighbors. The murder of Françoise and her lover, in June 1592, occurred in the very week of Gabrielle's wedding to Nicolas d'Amerval. By that time, however, Gabrielle, as well as her siblings, had long since ceased to think much about their mother, and they mourned her passing only as duty dictated.

Sourdis, Isabelle de

Aunt of Gabrielle d'Estrées. Name variations: Isabelle Babou de Sourdis. Born Isabelle Babou; one of seven daughters of Jean Babou (a prominent soldier, politician, and diplomat in the reign of Henry II) sister of *Françoise Babou de la Bourdaisière d'Estrées; married M. de Sourdis (governor of Chartre).*

Married to the governor of Chartre and mistress of Armand de Chiverny, Henry IV's legal advisor, Isabelle de Sourdis rescued the household of Antoine d'Estrées after her sister Françoise deserted the family. She unabashedly promoted Gabrielle's relationship with Henry primarily to achieve her own ambitions to join the royal court. Following Gabrielle's death, Isabelle purportedly begged the king for custody of Gabrielle's children, probably less out of concern for them than her desire to maintain her influence at court. Henry eventually rejected the idea, and Isabelle quickly faded into obscurity.

As teenagers, the sisters spent two years in Paris (1587–89), in their father's townhouse, Hôtel d'Estrées, located on the Rue des Bons-Enfants. With the eruption of France's civil war, the girls were forced to return to Coeuvres for their safety. There, they led privileged though confined and boring lives, seldom rising before the afternoon meal. "Gabrielle, in those days, would have slept until dusk if allowed to rest undisturbed," wrote Diane. Though she fought the tendency in her nature, Gabrielle's indolence became her most outstanding trait. Her brother, François-Annibal, attributed his sister's laziness to her remarkable beauty. "My father's knights fawned upon Gabrielle from the time she was scarcely out of swaddling clothes," he wrote in his *Memoirs*, "and even the most ferocious visiting warriors thawed when she smiled at them. . . . With that smile she gained the ability to set armies in motion, and not until she began to return the love of the King did she know that it is simpler to begin a war than to halt one."

Gabrielle's father, despite his Catholicism, was loyal to the future Huguenot king Henry IV, but he protected his large landholdings by receiving the commanders of any troops who were operating in the area. In summer 1589, upon hearing that King Henry III had been murdered, Antoine had members of his family sign a pledge of loyalty to Henry IV. "Gabrielle would sign no paper and cried that she wanted peace so she could taste the joys of Paris which were being denied her," writes Diane. "For two days she sulked in our rooms, and in vain our father begged her to join us at table. When she would not, he directed that no viands be served to her in her chamber. . . . I comment on these events, long past, not to hold up my sister to ridicule nor to parade her ignorance, but to show how marked is the contrast between her thinking in those days and in the times that followed. It is scarcely credible that she who cared nothing of the world populated by kings should have become the most powerful woman in France, showing a strength of purpose exceeded only by that of the King, and a subtlety in political maneuvers equaled by none."

Earlier in Paris, Gabrielle had fallen in love with Roger de Saint-Larry, duke of Bellegarde, a handsome man about 11 years her senior. (Biographer Adrien Desclozeaux maintains that Roger was Gabrielle's only lover before Henry IV, but others claim there were several intimates before the king.) Roger, who served as chief equerry to Henry IV in his struggle against the Catholic League (15,000 Spanish, Austrian, and Papal State troops), often boasted to the king of his conquest of Gabrielle, and Henry, long separated from his wife *Margaret of Valois (1553–1615) and an avowed womanizer, grew increasingly curious about the "glorious Venus" Roger described. On November 8 or 10, 1589, Henry accompanied his aide to Coeuvres to meet Gabrielle, who in the course of the visit made it quite clear that her heart belonged to Roger. Henry made a strategic withdrawal, although Gabrielle's beauty and charm did not go unnoticed. Sometime around December 1590, as the forces of the League were occupying the town of Coeuvres, Henry made a second attempt to see Gabrielle, risking his life to do so. Reappearing at the castle gates disguised as a woodcutter, he

looked so bedraggled that the sentries would not let him in until Gabrielle's brother arrived at the gate and identified him. Gabrielle, for her part, had to be coaxed away from her beauty regimen to spend time with Henry. Polite and charming during his two-day visit, she was nonetheless unimpressed with the man, whose intelligence and wit were no substitute for Roger's good looks. Henry, however, left the castle besotted and firmly suggested to his chief equerry that he look elsewhere for love. "There are many hundreds of young ladies of quality in France," he purportedly told Roger. "Disport yourself with one of them. I believe that the lovely d'Estrées has learned to care only for me." Roger, confident in Gabrielle's feelings for him, paid little heed and continued to meet his love in secret, though he was more discreet around the king. (The circumstances of their courtship would be detailed in *Aventures de la Cour de Perse*, written by Gabrielle's close friend **Louise de Guise**, later the Princess de Conti, a year after Henry's death.)

By January 1591, Henry's army had laid siege to the city of Chartres, which was in the hands of the League, and he had set up headquarters in a small castle outside the city of Bonneval. Having just dismissed his then mistress **Corisande d'Audoins**, countess of Guiche, Henry was no doubt delighted when Mme de Sourdis appeared at his headquarters with her nieces Diane and Gabrielle in tow. Sourdis had arrived ostensibly to join her husband, who having been governor of Chartres under Henry III, had attached himself to Henry IV. However, the de Sourdises were embarrassed over the fact that Isabelle's brother was the commandant of the League forces holding the city, and she therefore was particularly anxious to demonstrate her loyalty to the king. Henry, taking full advantage of the situation, whiled away siege time by courting Gabrielle: "The King showed valor in the siege of Chartres that he conducted by day, and my sister showed equal courage in the siege of Gabrielle that he conducted by night," writes Diane in her *Memorial*. "She spurned his advances gently, but with such frequency that our aunt and uncle feared that their future was ruined." Following the siege and their uncle's return to his post as governor of Chartres, Gabrielle and Diane returned to Coeuvres and a year passed before Gabrielle and Henry met again.

The common notion that Gabrielle became Henry's mistress during the siege of Chartres has not been remotely substantiated. In fact, she was still in love with Roger and might have been hoping to see him in Bonneval. In one of the few communications still extant by Gabrielle in her own handwriting, she wrote to her father: "I have seen Roger at a distance, but he is afraid to speak to me. I fear that my hopes of becoming the Duchess of Bellegarde will not be realized."

In June 1592, aware that the king was not interested in marrying his daughter and hoping to save her reputation, Antoine d'Estrées arranged for Gabrielle to marry Nicolas d'Amerval, Sieur de Liencour, a widower whose late wife was Antoine's cousin. Although a wealthy member of the minor nobility in Picardy, Nicolas was short and plump, and the father of two teenage daughters. On first hearing of the marriage arrangement, Gabrielle was shocked and spoke to no one for four days. However, custom dictated that she obey her father, and so she dutifully wed Nicolas and moved into his house, Liencourt. The early days of the marriage, difficult to be sure, were further darkened by news of the murder of Gabrielle's mother and her lover.

Surprised by the nuptials, Henry impulsively arrived at Liencourt a few day after the ceremony with gifts for the bride: an estate and manor at Assy and a château at Saint-Lambert, each of which would assure her an independent income. The king spent only one night at Liencourt before making a hasty retreat, but the gifts drove a wedge between husband and wife. For the next three months, they did not sleep together, and Gabrielle was reported as continually weeping. (In her later divorce proceedings, Gabrielle would claim that her husband was impotent.)

Soon after his visit, Henry wrote Gabrielle an impassioned plea to join him before he set off to fight Alexander Farnese, duke of Parma, who had organized a new army in the Low Countries. On September 4, 1592, chaperoned by her aunt, Gabrielle left Liencourt and joined Henry at Chartres the following day. Diane maintained that her aunt, anxious to become part of court life, persuaded Gabrielle to abandon her husband, and that Gabrielle only consented in hopes of being reunited with Roger, with whom she had continued to correspond. Upon reaching Henry's headquarters at Chartres, Gabrielle remained with him as he traveled from town to town, struggling to unify his kingdom. It was a nomadic existence, with long hours spent on horseback and little of the luxury that Gabrielle so cherished. Under Isabelle's careful scrutiny, however, she voiced no complaints. Occasionally, an increased pace forced Henry to leave the women behind, at which times he wrote Gabrielle at least once every day. As might be imagined, Gabrielle was an indifferent letter writer.

On her own for the first time and heady with freedom, Gabrielle continued her relationship with Roger, much to the displeasure of her father and of Henry, who suffered fits of jealousy and poured out his pain in his letters. Though he eventually dismissed Roger as his equerry, Henry was careful not to force the duke into siding with his enemies. By April 1593, however, Gabrielle had given up her affair with Roger, having fallen in love with Henry. "My sister told me that she loved the King with her heart and soul," writes Diane, "and was so sincere in her protestations of that love that our father forgave her transgressions." All who knew Gabrielle remarked on the dramatic changes in her behavior. Well-known for her habit of inconsiderate tardiness, by July she began to pick up the trait of her paramour who was famous for his punctuality. From then on, Gabrielle matured quickly, growing increasingly fascinated with the world around her and taking great interest in the affairs of state and Henry's position in them.

In 1593, Gabrielle, more pragmatic than religious, talked Henry into converting to Catholicism, reasoning that as a Catholic, he would be welcomed in every city in France, including Paris and Rouen which remained in the hands of the League. His conversion might also pave the way for a papal divorce decree, ending his marriage to Margaret of Valois and opening the door for her. In masterminding Henry's conversion, Gabrielle enlisted the aid of the king's sister *Catherine of Bourbon, who, early in 1593, made a journey to France and decided to stay. As devout a Protestant as Henry but desirous of marrying a Catholic of whom her brother disapproved, Catherine had much to gain by supporting Gabrielle's plan. While Henry's conversion was of personal concern to Gabrielle, it carried enormous political implications that were debated endlessly by the royal Council. In the end, however, Gabrielle was the deciding factor, much to the dismay of those opposing conversion. Maximilien de Béthune, duke of Sully, begrudgingly credits Gabrielle with accomplishing what no royal advisor had been able to do. "She, and she alone, was responsible for the King's failure to remain true to the faith for which so many of his friends had suffered and died," he declared in his *Memoirs*. "She alone flattered and bemused him, until he scarce knew what to think, and when his brain became addled by her seductive temptations, she used her sly wiles to speak of the benefits that he would reap if he became a papist."

Following the conversion ceremony, which was held on July 25, 1593, Henry sent letters to the parliaments of every province in the country asking for support, and dispatched a mission to Rome to lay the groundwork for conciliation with Pope Clement VIII. He also met with angry Huguenot leaders to mollify and reassure them, enlisting Gabrielle to reinforce his efforts. "Each of us who had sworn to uphold the King of Navarre, a faithful member of the Reformed Church, was now required to visit the salon of the d'Estrées, mistress of the Catholic King of France" recorded Maximilien in a biased account. "She played her role with pretty gestures, sweet exclamations, and fervent protestations that all would be as it had been in former years." Despite the duke's lingering disapproval, Gabrielle succeeded in assuring the Huguenots that they would be safe and the king would not betray them.

With domestic opposition to Henry virtually over, Paris opened its gates, and on March 22, 1594, he and Gabrielle made a triumphant entry into the city. A few months later, on June 7, 1594, Gabrielle gave birth to her first child, a son named Caesar. That same year, Henry used his prestige and power to obtain a divorce for Gabrielle, although he had not yet decided to marry her. After her divorce was granted, Gabrielle adopted the title Madame the Marquise de Monceaux and was appointed a miniature court. At the same time, her son Caesar was pronounced legitimate under the law of the realm. (Henry would pronounce each of their subsequent children legitimate in the same manner.) After clarifying Gabrielle's status, Henry put her in charge of the delicate negotiation with the pope to readmit France to the Church, a tribute to his faith in her skill as a diplomat.

While Henry tended to an erupting conflict with Spain, Gabrielle attempted to open the lines of communication with the Vatican, which she eventually did through correspondence with Cardinal Arnaud d'Ossat, bishop of Rennes, who relayed her documents to the pope. Her appeal, set forth in two letters (March 19 and March 30, 1595) and probably reviewed by Henry and several French cardinals, was a straightforward plea from a concerned wife and mother. "My position is not that of an ordinary woman, though ordinary I be, save that I enjoy the confidence of him who is King of France," she wrote in the first letter. "His son is my son, and together we must strive to make for him, and for others, a community in France, as in all other lands, safe from the rages of war." Her second letter, sent long before she could have received a reply to the first, retained a delicate tone but ended on a strongly po-

litical note. "I pray that His Holiness will open his ears when Your Grace goes before him, and that France will soon be accepted within the Church, a prayer in which all women in this realm do most fervently join." Though there is no way of judging the impact of Gabrielle's letters, the outcome was overwhelmingly favorable. In letters to all the religious houses and orders in France, dated April 15, 16, and 17, Pope Clement directed them to pray for Henry IV's prosperity, health, and well-being.

Flush with the victory of his admission to the Church, Henry gave his mistress carte blanche to negotiate on his behalf, although she held no official government post and was not entitled to attend Council meetings. In March 1596, in a precedent-setting declaration, Henry gave Gabrielle the guardianship of Caesar and the right to administer all of his property. Soon afterward, he made Gabrielle and his sister Catherine of Bourbon official members of the royal Council, presenting each of them with the symbolic set of golden keys. (The keys were among several items stolen from Gabrielle on her deathbed; Henry would conduct a painstaking search for them, but they would never be found.) By the autumn of 1596, Gabrielle was attending Council meetings regularly, and in October she traveled to Rouen, where Henry presided over "an assembly of notables." In November, she gave birth to a daughter Catherine named after Henry's sister, who became the child's godmother. Shortly thereafter, Gabrielle returned to the Council which had convened to discuss the invasion of Spanish troops into a number of towns, including Calais. (Luckily, given Henry's depleted war chest, *Elizabeth I of England sent British troops to Calais, thus relieving the king of some of the military burden.) That winter, departing briefly from her official duties, Gabrielle played matchmaker, arranging the marriage of one of her younger sisters, Julienne, to Georges de Villars Brancas, Chevalier d'Oyse, an event that was celebrated splendidly at the palace.

In 1597, during the lively celebration preceding Lent, Henry received word that Spain had launched a surprise attack on Amiens, signifying that Philip II was initiating a campaign to destroy Henry. While the king immediately rallied his troops for battle, Gabrielle, aware that the royal treasury was depleted, gathered all her ready cash and gave it to Henry. That same evening, she visited the town houses of the greatest nobles to solicit further contributions, and even roused the banker from a sound sleep in order to sell her jewelry. In a final gesture of support, she rode out of Paris with the army's vanguard, meeting up with Henry at the fortress at Beauvais and remaining with him at the front throughout the campaign. Given Gabrielle's behavior, there could no longer be any doubt about her loyalty to Henry, for she put her very security in jeopardy. If Henry were killed in battle, she and her children would be left unprotected. If France was defeated, it would be impossible for Henry to repay her the cash she had given him or redeem her jewelry. In the act of joining Henry on the battlefront, she not only faced the hardships of traveling with the army but risked losing her life.

It was not until September that Henry was finally victorious over the Spaniards, and he and an exhausted Gabrielle returned to Paris. Thankful for Gabrielle's loyalty, the king repaid her the thousands of écus she had given him and redeemed all of her jewels. He also made her a gift of several properties that he had purchased at a bargain price from the debt-ridden Duchess de Guise. In addition, Henry issued letters patent, raising Gabrielle's properties to a dukedom for her. A gala ball was planned in honor of the new duchess but was canceled at Gabrielle's request. She was pregnant again and needed time to regain her strength.

Gabrielle d'Estrées continued to play an important role in affairs of state, particularly in the touchy negotiation surrounding Henry's reclamation of Brittany, then under control of *Marie of Luxemburg and her husband Philippe-Emmanuel, duc de Mercoeur, the brother of dowager queen *Louise of Lorraine, widow of Henry III. (As part of the peace agreement, Gabrielle contracted a marriage between her four-year-old son Caesar and the daughter of Philippe-Emmanuel and Marie, who was older than the prospective bridegroom by six months.) Though advanced in her pregnancy, Gabrielle remained involved in the most important project of Henry's reign, the reconciliation of Catholics and Protestants. She participated in all the discussions for a final treaty of peace with Spain, many of which were held at a château at Nantes. The Edict of Nantes, which ultimately reunited Protestants and Catholics for the first time since the Reformation had divided them, was issued on April 13, 1598, just four days before Gabrielle gave birth to a third child, a son named Alexander. Gabrielle took a month-long rest after the birth. "The door of my sister's chamber was barred to those gentlemen who wanted His Majesty to modify the Edict granting religious freedom to the Huguenots," writes François-Annibal, "and to those who believed that they had received too little liberty."

There is only speculation as to when Henry decided to marry Gabrielle, but in the spring of 1598, he broached the matter of divorce with Margaret of Valois (ensconced in a château outside Usson in the Auvergne) and sent his ecclesiastical diplomat Cardinal d'Ossat on a mission to Rome to sound out the Pope on the matter. So certain was Henry that the response from Rome would be favorable that, on March 2, he publicly announced that the wedding would take place on Easter Sunday. (Later, when hope for the Papal decree dimmed, he secretly made arrangements that would compel a member of the French ecclesiastical hierarchy to dissolve his marriage and perform the ceremony that would make Gabrielle queen.) While waiting for official word from Rome, Gabrielle rehearsed for her royal role. She moved all her belongings into the palace and ordered new furniture and a closet full of new gowns. On November 17, 1598—Henry's birthday—she moved into the official Louvre bedchamber, after which she virtually became queen of the realm in all but name. "My sister was more powerful than the King at this time," writes François-Annibal, "His Majesty's faith in her being so great that he left in her hands many matters that otherwise would have required his personal attention."

What Gabrielle and Henry did not know as they planned their Easter wedding was that the Vatican was opposed to their marriage on political grounds, the pope having decided that Henry's marriage to *Marie de Medici would better serve the interest of peace. Meanwhile, Gabrielle became pregnant with her fourth child. As word from Rome was further delayed, her normally robust health declined, and she began to experience premonitions of disaster. She became depressed and weepy and was awakened from her sleep frequently by nightmares. A short time before Easter, 1599, at the suggestion of Father René Benoit, the king's confessor, Gabrielle was sent from the palace at Fontainebleau to Paris to offer prayers in her own parish church. (Benoit believed this would set a good example and atone for the questionable behavior of her past.) By this time, Gabrielle was exhausted from her wedding preparations, and six months along in her pregnancy. When she left the palace on April 5, 1599, her physicians felt it unwise for her to ride in a coach, so she was carried in a litter for the two-day journey to the bank of the Seine where a boat was waiting to take her across the narrow river to Paris. While saying her good-byes to Henry on the riverbank, she broke down in tears, telling the king she was sure that they would not see each other again. At one point, she purportedly became so hysterical that Henry offered to take her back to Fontainebleau, but she eventually decided to complete the journey.

Upon arriving in Paris, she had dinner at the home of Louis Zamet, a wealthy Swiss financier who kept a house in the city, and then retired to the apartment of her aunt Isabelle de Sourdis. The next morning, she traveled to the church of Petit Saint-Antoine by litter, waving to the friendly crowds that lined the street. During the church service, Gabrielle complained about the heat and afterwards immediately returned to her aunt's house. Now bothered by a terrible headache, she lost consciousness, but recovered within an hour and appeared better. She canceled two dinner engagements for that evening, but slept peacefully through the night and the next day was given permission by her attending physicians to keep her normal schedule. At two o'clock in the afternoon, however, she went into premature labor, which lasted until Friday morning, when the child was stillborn. Throughout the day, she was in increasing pain, and died of puerperal convulsions at five o'clock on Saturday morning, April 10, 1599.

For the week following Gabrielle's death, Henry wore black, an unprecedented act that established a new custom. Returning to Paris with his now motherless children, he ordered a state funeral to be held on Saturday, April 17. Since Henry had not married Gabrielle, her funeral service could not be held at Notre Dame, so it took place at the church of Saint-Germain-l'Auxerrois. (No funeral services were held at Notre Dame for persons of lower rank than a king or queen.) In the days following the funeral, handbills were circulated in Paris suggesting that Gabrielle had been purposely poisoned, but after a short period of speculation, it was determined that she had eaten a "corrupt" bit of fruit at the home of Louis Zamet.

About six months after Gabrielle's death, Henry took a new mistress, ◄❀ Henriette d'Entragues, Marquise de Verneuil, a difficult woman who was later implicated in his assassination (1610). It was Marie de Medici, however, who finally won the king's hand in marriage and became queen of France. She had five children, the eldest of whom became Louis XIII, but Henry continued to love and protect Gabrielle's two sons and daughters who lived with the royal

❀►
Henriette d'Entragues.
See Medici, Marie d' for sidebar.

family. Caesar de Vendôme grew up to lead a quiet life, marrying a noblewoman of no particular distinction. Alexander, Chevalier de Vendôme, likewise, had an undistinguished career in the military, and never married. **Catherine Henriette de Vendôme**, Henry's favorite, was distinguished by her brilliant marriage to Charles of Lorraine, duc d'Elbeuf, a prominent member of the Guise family. In the middle of the 17th century, she and her brother Caesar became involved in an ugly legal dispute over their mother's property. For a brief time, the old scandals were revisited, and Gabrielle's reputation was called into question, just as it had been earlier with the publication of Maximilien's widely read *Memoirs*. Although curiosity about Gabrielle d'Estrées flared from time to time after that, her remarkable story has been, for the most part, lost to modern history.

SOURCES:
Desclozeaux, Adrien. "Gabrielle d'Estrées" (monograph). Paris, 1887.
Lewis, Paul [Noel B. Gerson]. *Lady of France*. NY: Funk & Wagnalls, 1963.

Estrid.

Variant of Estrith.

Estrith (fl. 1017–1032)

*Danish princess. Name variations: Astrid; Astrith; Estrid; Margaret of Denmark. Daughter of Sven or Sweyn I Forkbeard, king of Denmark (r. 985–1014), king of England, and *Sigrid the Haughty; married Ulf also known as Wolf (c. 967–1027), jarl of Denmark, around 1018; second wife of Richard II, duke of Normandy (divorced); children: (first marriage) Beorn, earl of England; Asbjorn; Sweyn Ulfson also known as Sweyn Estridson or Svend II (b. around 1019), king of Denmark (r. 1047–1074).*

Étampes, Anne de Pisseleu d'Heilly, Duchesse d' (1508–c. 1580)

Duchess and mistress of Francis I. Name variations: Anne d'Heilly; duchess of Etampes. Born Anne de Pisseleu d'Heilly in 1508; died around 1580; daughter of Guillaume de Pisseleu, sieur d'Heilly (a noble of Picardy); married Jean de Brosse, eventually the duc d'Étampes; mistress of Francis I, king of France (r. 1515–1547).

Anne de Pisseleu d'Heilly, duchesse d'Étampes, came to the French court before 1522 as one of the maids of honor of *Louise of Savoy. Francis I made her his mistress, probably on his return from his captivity at Madrid in 1526, and soon gave up *Comtesse de Châteaubriant for her. Known as sprightly, pretty, witty and cultured, Anne would succeed in keeping the favor of the king until his death. The liaison received some official recognition. When *Eleanor of Portugal (1498–1558) entered Paris to marry Francis in 1530, Francis and Anne viewed her arrival from the same window.

In 1533, Francis gave Anne in marriage to Jean de Brosse, whom he created duc d'Étampes. The influence of the duchesse d'Étampes, especially in the last years of the reign, was considerable. She upheld Admiral Chabot against the constable de Montmorency, who was supported by her rival, *Diane de Poitiers, the dauphin's (Henry II's) mistress. Anne also co-operated with the king's sister, *Margaret of Angoulême (1492–1549), and used her influence to elevate and enrich her family, with the result that her uncle, Antoine Sanguin (d. 1559), was made bishop of Orléans in 1535 and a cardinal in 1539. Although accusations were made against her of allowing herself to be won over by Emperor Charles V and of playing the traitor in 1544, they rest on no serious proof. After the death of Francis I in 1547, Anne d'Heilly was dismissed from the court by her rival Diane de Poitiers and humiliated in every way. She died in obscurity around 1580, during the reign of Henry III.

Étampes, countess of.
See Margaret of Orleans.

Étampes, duchess of.
See Estrées, Gabrielle d' (1573–1599).

Eteye of Azeb (fl. 10th c. BCE).
See Sheba, queen of.

Ethelberga.
Variant of Ethelburga.

Ethelberga of Northumbria (d. 647)
*Queen of Northumbria. Name variations: Aethelburh; Aethelburg; Ethelburga. Died in 647; daughter of *Bertha of Kent (c. 565–c. 616) and Aethelbert or Ethelbert, king of Kent; sister of Eadbald, king of Kent; married Edwin (Eadwine) of Northumbria (c. 585–633), in 625; children: Ethelhun; Wuscfrea; Ethelthryth; Eanfleda (wife of Oswy, king of Northumbria); grandmother of Elflaed (fl. 640–714), abbess of Whitby.*

When Ethelberga married Edwin, king of Northumbria, she brought a monk named Paulinus along to her new kingdom and was instrumental in converting her husband and family members to Christianity. In a wooden church at York on Easter Eve, in 627, Paulinus baptized the king and many of his relatives, including his great-niece *Hilda of Whitby, who would later become the abbess of Whitby. Ethelberga then reared Hilda as a Christian. Six years later, when Edwin was killed in battle, Ethelberga took Hilda and found sanctuary with relatives at Kent. Edwin's successor, King Oswy (Oswio), and his queen, Ethelberga's daughter *Eanfleda, continued to champion Christianity; they placed their one-year-old daughter *Elflaed under the tutelage of Hilda. On Hilda's death, Elflaed, Ethelberga's granddaughter, became abbess of Whitby in 680.

Ethelburg (fl. 722)
Saxon queen.

The political dynamics of early English society offered many opportunities for royal women to exert power, both in making laws and on the battlefield. Ethelburg was one of many Saxon queens who did so, though we know little about her life. Ruler of the Ine tribe, she led armies, successfully planned battle strategies, and added territories to her kingdom through her military prowess.

Laura York,
freelance writer in medieval and women's history,
Riverside, California

Ethelburga (d. 665)
*Saint and abbess. Name variations: Ethelberga; St. Aubierge. Died in 665 at Faremoutier, Brie, France; interred at St. Stephen the Martyr Church; daughter of Hereswitha (d. c. 690) and Anna (635–654), king of East Anglia; half-sister of *Sexburga (d. 699?) and *Elthelthrith (630–679); niece of *Hilda of Whitby.*

Ethelburga, the daughter of *Hereswitha, eventually became abbess of Faremoutier in Brie, France. Her feast day is July 7.

Ethelburga (d. 676?)
Saxon saint and abbess of Barking. Name variations: Aethelburh; Ethelburh; Ethelberga. Died around 676; sister of Saint Erkonwald.

When Saint Erkonwald founded the monastery of Chertsey for himself, he founded a convent at Barking, Essex, for his sister Ethelburga; he then sent to France for *Hildeletha and committed his sister to her care. When Ethelburga died as abbess of Barking, Hildeletha succeeded her. Ethelburga is commemorated on Oct. 11.

Ethelburh (d. 676?).

See Ethelburga.

Etheldreda (d. around 840)

*Saint. Name variations: Alfrida. Died around 840; possibly daughter of Offa II, king of Mercia, and Cynethryth (fl. 736–796); possibly sister of *Eadburgh (c. 773–after 802).*

Etheldreda, the daughter of *Cynethryth and Offa, king of Mercia, lived for some 40 years as a recluse on the island of Croyland. Her feast day is August 2.

Ethelflaed (869–918)

*Ruler of Mercia who constructed a national system of fortifications in partnership with Edward the Elder and contributed to the defeat of the Vikings in England. Name variations: Lady of the Mercians. Originally the Teutonic (Germanic) Æ was used, Aethelflaed or Aethelfleda; this had the value of a short sound before the 11th century, but in some citations was later dropped from common usage, becoming Ethelflaed or Ethelfleda; also Elfleda or Elflida. Pronunciation: Eth-EL-fled. Born in Wessex in 869; died on June 12, 918 (some sources cite 919), in Tamworth, Mercia; buried in St. Peter's monastery, Gloucester, Mercia; eldest daughter of Elswitha (d. 902) and Alfred the Great (848–c. 900), king of the English (r. 871–899); sister of *Elfthrith (d. 929); married Ethelred II, ealdorman of Mercia (r. 879–911), in 886 or 887; children: Elfwyn (c. 882–?).*

Conference held between Alfred, Ethelflaed, and Ethelred II on the subject of the defense of London (898); death of Alfred the Great (899 or 900); Edward the Elder crowned king of Wessex (899); Ethelflaed inherited a portion of the Wiltshire estate of Damerham (899); town of Worcester leased land to Ethelflaed and her husband (901); Ethelflaed founded monastery of St. Peter and moved the bones of St. Oswald from Northumbria to Gloucester (909); Battle of Tettenhal (909); Ethelflaed began building fortresses for the defense of Mercia and built fortress at Bremesburh (910); death of Ethelred II (911); Edward the Elder reclaimed London (911); Ethelflaed built fortresses of Scargate and Bridgenorth (912) and forti-

fied Tamworth and Stafford (913); first Battle of Corbridge (914); Ethelflaed fortified Eddisbury and Warwick (914), erected fortresses at Chirbury, Weardburh, and Runcorn (915), and launched expedition against Wales (916); conquest of Derby (917); northern alliance (918); second Battle of Corbridge (918); surrender of Leicester (918); Ethelflaed negotiated with Northumbrian Vikings (918).

Characteristic of so many women, the life and death of Ethelflaed, Lady of the Mercians, was obscured by her contemporaries. This oversight, as F.T. Wainwright explains, has as much to do with the political intrigues of 10th-century England as to the haphazard documentation of women throughout history:

> There is no word of her victories, no word of her share in the national program of fortress-building, no word of her high reputation in the north, and no word of her loyal and successful co-operation with [her brother] Edward. It is clear that the blanket of official policy has kept her achievements out of the national record.

During the late-9th and early-10th centuries, England experienced a period of extreme political instability. Viking raids, begun as plundering expeditions, evolved into campaigns of conquest—wholesale immigration soon followed. By 865, conquest and settlement had displaced Anglo-Saxon authority on much of the island. In the north, only the isolated kingdom of Northumbria still stood, while in the south, the existence of Wessex and Mercia hung by a slim thread. Much of Mercia had been overrun in the previous four decades. Large sections of central and eastern Mercia, known as the Five Boroughs, had been lost during protracted hostilities with the Danes. Mercia lived a perilous existence, politically unstable and under constant threat of attack.

In an age of almost continual warfare, skilled military leadership was essential. Alfred the Great proved to be the focal point of a national military effort. In 886, after prolonged campaigning, Alfred recaptured London and Oxford. In that year, he also entered into a treaty with the Danish chieftain Guthrum, which freed large parts of Mercia from Viking control. Alfred was recognized as sovereign of all England. In the once powerful kingdom of Mercia, he installed an ealdorman or subking named Ethelred II and also entrusted him with the defense of London. The allegiance of Mercia, now a dependency of Wessex, was further safeguarded by the marriage of Alfred's daughter, Ethelflaed, to the Mercian ealdorman.

The *De Rebus Gestis Aelfredis* informs us that Ethelflaed, the first child of Alfred the Great and *Elswitha, was born "as the time for matrimony approached." Little is known of Ethelflaed's early life. It is recorded that her father was a diligent reader who began the first court schools in England. His own children, girls as well as boys, attended, along with the children of the local nobility, and the cost was borne by Alfred. He intended that all "freeborn youth" should have the opportunity to learn to read and write English, and that those who had the talent to go further ought to be taught Latin as well. In her later years, Ethelflaed showed herself to be her father's daughter; she was a woman of formidable character, endowed with remarkable political, diplomatic, and military talents.

Ethelflaed's half-Mercian parentage guaranteed her acceptance among the Mercians. The kingdom of Mercia, to which she went as a bride in 877, was one that was beginning to prosper again, after the incompetent reigns of Burgred and Ceolwulf II. It seems likely that Ethelred was much older than his bride, but despite the difference in age Ethelflaed proved to be more than a mere pawn on the diplomatic chess board.

In approximately 882, Ethelflaed gave birth to a daughter, ⚭▶ **Elfwyn**. However, as the medieval English chronicler, William of Malmesbury, noted, "from the difficulty of her first labour, ever after [Ethelflaed] refused the embraces of her husband; protesting that it was unbecoming of the daughter of a king to give way to a delight which, after a time, produced such painful consequences."

In 898, a conference was held in Chelsea, at which Alfred, Ethelflaed, and Ethelred discussed provisions for the defense of London. Shortly thereafter, the venerable Alfred died. It is not known for certain how he died, only that death came on October 26, probably in the year 900, when Alfred was 52 years old. In his will, he bequeathed part of his Wiltshire estate in Damerham to his daughter. His son, Edward, known as the Elder, mounted the throne of Wessex, then sent his son Ethelstan to be educated at the Mercian court. This arrangement continued Alfred's policy of forging political links between the two nations.

War was an expensive undertaking, and a 901 charter from Worcester illustrates how revenues were raised to finance its prosecution. In the charter, the town of Worcester agreed to lease part of its lands to Ethelflaed and her husband in order to compensate them for the expenses incurred in defending the borough. Similar arrangements must have been common, and the later establishment of fortresses, which served as the nucleus for emerging towns, provided a comfortable marriage between commerce and defense.

Mighty Ethelflaed! Maiden, thou should'st bear the name of man—though nature cast thy frame in woman's softer mould—yet fear thy matchless might!

—**Henry of Huntingdon**

Ethelflaed's interests were not merely confined to matters military. In 909, she founded the monastery of St. Peter in Gloucester, and insured that the bones of St. Oswald were safely transported from Northumbria to this peaceful resting place. In the same year, Ethelflaed also laid out a new street plan for Gloucester, as well as repairing the Roman walls, and at least one of the Roman gateways. In later years, the ill-health of Ethelred forced Ethelflaed increasingly into the forefront of public affairs. In the last years of her husband's life, she acted as regent and commander the Mercian army. During the Battle of Tettenhal in 909, fought between the Danes, the Mercians, and their Wessex allies, it is probable that Ethelflaed commanded the Mercian contingent.

Upon the death of her husband in 911, Ethelflaed became the ruler of Mercia. She took the title of "Lady of the Mercians," just as her husband had been styled "Lord of the Mercians." In the same year, her brother Edward the Elder demanded the return of London, demonstrating a desire to maintain a firmer grip on the internal politics of Mercia. Nevertheless, Ethelflaed continued to cooperate with Edward, and together they developed a joint military policy, the cornerstone of which was the construction of a chain of bulwarks. Ethelflaed's fortifi-

⚭▶ **Elfwyn** (c. 882–?)

*Queen of Mercia. Name variations: Aelfwyn; Ælfwyn; Elfwynn. Born around 882; daughter of *Ethelflaed (869–918), Lady of the Mercians, and Ethelred II, ealdorman of Mercia; married a West Saxon noble.*

On the death of her mother, Elfwyn briefly ruled Mercia from June 918 to December of that year. Her reign was cut short by her uncle Edward the Elder, who removed her to Wessex.

cations formed part of a national system. Her policy owed much to her father's emphasis on their construction. These forts served both as a defensive bulwark against Danish attacks and a jumping off point for offensive military operations against the enemy. Each fortress was built within 30 miles of the nearest Viking base.

Ethelflaed clearly understood the importance of well-sited fortresses. The locations of her strongholds illustrate a keen strategic eye and an acute ability to forecast the movements of her enemies. In 910, she built the first of these fortresses at Bremesburh. Bremesburh dominated a ford on the Severn river, which the Danes had twice in living memory used to invade Mercia. Two years later, the fortresses of Scargate and Bridgenorth were erected. These bulwarks established Ethelflaed on the flank of the Danelaw and controlled access to Mercia via Walting Street, Roman Britain's most important line of communications.

Ethelflaed was often in the field. *The Mercian Register* records that in 913 "by the grace of God, Ethelflaed, Lady of the Mercians, went with all the Mercians to Tamworth, and built the fortress there in early summer." Tamworth was the site of an old Mercian palace and commanded a ford on the Trent river. On this site Ethelflaed built up a mound of earth and crowned it with a brickwork palisade. At Stafford in the same year, she erected another fortress which controlled access to the upper Trent valley. The fortress of Stafford proved to be the single most important strategic point in the English Midlands.

Each of Ethelflaed's fortresses controlled the surrounding countryside and provided permanent protection against sudden Viking raids. The lightly armed Vikings were incapable of mounting prolonged sieges of fortified bases. Nor were they capable of keeping large forces in the field for long periods of time. In 914, Ethelflaed repaired the pre-Roman camp on Eddisbury Hill. From there, her troops intercepted Viking raiders descending from Northumbria. Warwick was also fortified.

Traditional antagonism was strong between the Welsh and the Mercians. Although the fortresses at Scargate and Bridgenorth were designed to intercept Viking raiders traveling through Wales, they nevertheless presented a hostile façade to the Welsh. The murder of the Mercian abbot Ecgbeorht in 916 provoked a Mercian expedition against the king of the Brycheiniog. During the attack, Ethelflaed's troops captured the king's wife and 33 others.

By 916, Edward the Elder had already scored numerous victories against the Danes. Ethelflaed concentrated her energies on recapturing the Five Boroughs. In July 917, the first of these fell. She captured the town of Derby while Edward was occupied in heavy fighting around Towcester and Bedford. *The Anglo-Saxon Chronicle* records that:

> In this year . . . Ethelflaed, the Lady of the Mercians, won the borough called Derby with God's help, together with the region that it controlled. Four of her thanes, who were dear to her, were slain there within the gate.

The fall of Derby illustrates the level of military coordination that existed between Ethelflaed and her brother. She attacked the town while its defenders were fighting against Edward, and many have suggested that her attack was either designed to relieve pressure on Edward's forces or that his attack was designed to draw the defenders of Derby away from the town.

Ethelflaed and Edward did not always act in concert, however. In 918, she took independent action when confronted with an invasion by the Norwegian chieftain Ragnald. Four years earlier, Ragnald had conquered southern Northumbria in the first Battle of Corbridge. Ethelflaed reacted by erecting the fortresses of Eddisbury and Runcorn and launching punitive attacks against his forces.

The threat that Ragnald posed to the north was so great that the Picts, Scots, and the men of Strathclyde entered into an alliance with Mercia. Ethelflaed became leader of the northern coalition. In the second Battle of Corbridge, Ragnald and his army was soundly defeated by Ethelflaed and her allies. As a result *The Ulster Annals* record that Ethelflaed's "fame spread abroad in every direction."

By the end of the 917 campaigning season, Danish opposition had all but collapsed in East Anglia, Cambridge, Bedford, and Northampton. Four centers of resistance remained—Nottingham, Stamford, Leicester, and Lincoln. By June of 918, Edward the Elder captured Stamford. Leicester, the second of the Five Boroughs, submitted to Ethelflaed in the summer of 918 without a fight. The surrender of Leicester was probably influenced by the approach of Ragnald's army. Ethelflaed also entered into negotiations with a dissenting faction at York. She was on the verge of making peace with the Norwegians of

Northumbria when she died on June 12, 918. Curiously, while the Ulster annals record her death, they make no mention of the death of her illustrious father Alfred the Great.

Ethelflaed missed the collapse of Danish opposition in the English Midlands by six months. Edward the Elder, however, did not continue negotiations with the Norwegians at York, suggesting that he was not held in as high esteem as his sister. The opportunity for the peaceful annexation of Northumbria never again materialized, and no army of Wessex intervened to prevent the consolidation of a Viking kingdom in the north.

Ethelflaed intended that her daughter Elfwyn should rule as her successor. But as soon as Edward the Elder learned of Ethelflaed's death, he hastened to occupy Tamworth. Though he allowed Ethelflaed's daughter to rule for six months, in December 918, as *The Anglo-Saxon Chronicle* notes, Elfwyn was "deprived of all authority in Mercia" and taken into Wessex "by her uncle Edward the Elder."

The peaceful annexation of Mercia was probably an eventuality that Ethelflaed had anticipated but was powerless to prevent. In various documents relating to her rule, Ethelflaed is styled as *Rex Regina*. Since she belonged to the Mercian royal family, she could have declared herself queen had she wished and become the focus of a Mercian national movement. But instead her loyalties remained with Wessex.

Indeed, Ethelflaed's marriage to Ethelred in 887 provided the pretext for the formal annexation of Mercia. Edward the Elder, citing King Alfred's will, claimed that any male kinsman had the right to claim the property of a female relative. This provision fits in well with Alfred's own territorial ambitions, and may have been inserted into the will in recognition of the fact that Ethelred's poor health could prove politically advantageous.

The fact that Edward the Elder feared nationalist dissent in Mercia accounts for much of the official silence in *The Anglo-Saxon Chronicle* surrounding Ethelflaed's achievements. As **Christine Fell** noted, "We all need to watch *The Anglo-Saxon Chronicle* for its West-Saxon propaganda, and it is important to remember that the suppression of information about female achievement is not necessarily anti-feminist."

And yet, despite the best efforts of the Wessex chroniclers, the accomplishments of Ethelflaed have not been entirely obscured. She initiated a national program of fortress building. As well, the cooperation that had been so close between her father and her husband was continued with her brother. Their collaboration during the campaigns of 917–918 led to the liberation of most of the English Midlands after 40 years of Danish occupation. In addition, her independent actions in the north effectively held at bay a substantial portion of the Viking force in England, and exploited the disunity of the Viking military leadership.

Indeed, the legacy that Ethelflaed, Lady of the Mercians, left over a period of seven short years is nothing short of breathtaking. While protecting the Mercian population at home, she waged war against an intractable invader that had controlled much of England for a generation. Her fortress-building program created new towns and commercial centers throughout the land, and her understanding of the dangers of an England divided and vulnerable to invasion have influenced the political geography of Britain to this day.

SOURCES:

Fell, Christine E. *Women in Anglo-Saxon England*. NY: Blackwell, 1987.

Garmonsway, G.N., trans. *The Anglo-Saxon Chronicle*. London: J.M. Dent and sons, 1953.

Hooke, Della. *The Anglo-Saxon Landscape*. Manchester: Manchester University Press, 1985.

Jones, Gwyn. *A History of the Vikings*. Oxford: Oxford University Press, 1968.

Lees, Beatrice Adelaide. *Alfred the Great*. NY: Knickerbocker, 1915.

Malmesbury, William of. *The History of the Kings of England*. London: Longmans, 1815.

Stenton, Doris Mary. *The English Woman in History*. London: George Allen and Unwin, 1957.

SUGGESTED READING:

Wainwright, F.T. "Aethelflaed Lady of the Mercians," in *The Anglo-Saxons: Studies in Some Aspects of Their History and Culture*. Edited by Peter Clemoes. London: Bowes and Bowes, 1959.

Hugh A. Stewart, M.A.,
Guelph, Ontario, Canada

Ethelflaed (d. 962)

Queen of the English. Name variations: Aethelflaeda the Fair; Ethelfled; the White Duck. Died in childbirth in 962 (some sources cite 965) in Wessex, England; interred at Wilton Abbey, Wiltshire; daughter of Ordmaer, an ealdorman, and Ealda; became first wife of Edgar the Peaceful (944–975), king of the English (r. 959–975), in 959; children: Edward II the Martyr (962–978), king of the English (r. 975–978).

Ethelflaed (d. after 975)

Queen of the English. Name variations: Aethelflaed of Domerham. Died after 975; daughter of Elfgar, eal-

dorman of Wiltshire; second wife of Edmund I the Magnificent (921–946), king of the English (r. 939–946). Edmund's first wife was *Elfgifu (d. 944).

Ethelflaeda (fl. 900s)

*Abbess of Romsey. Name variations: Aethelflaeda. Flourished in the 900s; interred at Romsey Abbey, Hampshire, England; daughter of Edward I the Elder (c. 870–924), king of the English (r. 899–924), and *Elflaed (d. 920). Ethelflaeda was a nun at Romsey.*

Ethelflaeda (c. 963–c. 1016)

*Abbess at Romsey. Name variations: Aethelflaeda; Ethelfleda. Born around 963; died around 1016; daughter of *Elfthrith (c. 945–1002) and Edgar (944–975), king of the English (r. 959–975).*

Ethelfled.

Variant of Ethelflaed.

Ethelfleda.

Variant of Ethelfaeda.

Ethelgeofu (d. around 896)

*Saxon princess. Name variations: Aethelgeofu; Ethelgiva. Died around 896 at Shaftesbury Abbey, Dorset; daughter of Alfred the Great (848–c. 900), king of the English (r. 871–899); and *Elswitha (d. 902); sister of *Ethelflaed (869–918); never married. Sometimes referred to as abbess of Shaftesbury.*

Ethelreda (fl. 1090)

Queen of Scots. Name variations: Aethelreda. Buried at Dunfermline Abbey, Fife, Scotland; daughter of Gospatric, earl of Northumberland, and Ethelreda; married Duncan II (c. 1060–1094), king of the Scots (r. 1094), around 1090; children: William the Noble Dunkeld, earl of Moray.

Ethelreda (630–679).

See Elthelthrith.

Ethelswyth (c. 843–889)

*Queen of Mercia. Name variations: Aethelswyth or Æthelswyth. Born around 843; died in Paris while on a journey to Rome in 889; buried at Pavia or Ticino, Italy; daughter of Ethelwulf, king of the English, and *Osburga (?–c. 855); sister of Alfred the Great, king of the English (r. 871–899); married Burghred, king of Mercia, after April 2, 853.*

Ethelswyth became a nun on widowhood; she died on pilgrimage to Rome and is buried at either Pavia or Ticino.

Ethelthrith or Ethelthryth (630–679).

See Elthelthrith.

Etienette of Barcelona (fl. 1038).

See Estefania of Barcelona.

Etruria (1782–1824), queen of.

See Maria Luisa of Etruria.

Etting, Ruth (1896–1978)

American singer known as "the radio canary" during the golden age of network radio in the 1920s and 1930s. Born on November 23, 1896, in David City, Nebraska; died on September 24, 1978, in Colorado Springs, Colorado; only child of Winifred and Alfred Etting; educated in local schools and attended Chicago Academy of Fine Arts; married Martin "Moe" Snyder, in 1922 (divorced 1937); married Myrl Alderman, in 1938 (died 1966); children: none.

Began her singing career shortly after World War I as a chorus girl in a Chicago nightclub; went on the vaudeville circuit (1924); made her New York debut (1927); appeared for five consecutive years in The Ziegfeld Follies, where she established her reputation as a so-called "torch singer"; appeared in Broadway musical revues and short films and made her national network radio debut (1930); retired from show business after public scandal involving her ex-husband (1937), but briefly revived her career ten years later; her life formed the basis of the 1955 film Love Me or Leave Me.

Filmography: Roman Scandals (1933); The Gift of Gab (1935); Hips, Hips, Hooray (1939); plus some 30 musical shorts.

A visitor to the sedate retirement home tucked away in a quiet neighborhood of Colorado Springs in the late 1970s would barely have noticed the slim, well-dressed woman crocheting sweaters or watching sports on television, no different than any of the other elderly residents with whom she engaged in easy conversation. It would have been difficult to imagine that some 40 years earlier, this same woman had been as familiar to millions of Americans as a sister; had had lines of clothing, hosiery, and even ice-cream sundaes named after her; had been voted the most popular woman in America; had been at the center of one of the most notorious scandals to hit the gossip columns of the

Ruth
Etting

time, one that would have destroyed the reputation of a less level-headed celebrity; and had even had a movie made of her life.

There was nothing in Ruth Etting's childhood to indicate such an exalted future. She had been born in November of 1896 in David City, Nebraska, and, except for the occasional trip to Omaha, never left her parents' farm until doctors recommended that her ailing mother seek a cure in the more moderate climate of San Diego. **Winifred Etting** took her five-year-old daughter west with her, but died shortly after they arrived. Ruth returned to Nebraska, where her father—Alfred Etting, a bank teller—left her with his parents while he sought work elsewhere. Ruth would see little of him from then on, even when Alfred later remarried.

It was her grandfather, George Etting, who taught her what would turn out to be the most important lesson of her life. "Any fool can make money," he told her, "but only somebody smart knows enough to save it." The son of German immigrants who had arrived in Nebraska in covered wagons, George Etting practiced his own advice, for he owned David City's major industry, a textile mill, and was able to give Ruth a comfortable childhood. Etting would also remember going to the opera house her grandfather had built for the town, where circus acts and traveling tent shows would perform every summer.

Nor would her singing in the church choir have suggested what lay ahead. "I sang in a high, squeaky soprano," Etting said later. "It sounded terrible, but I didn't know I could sing in any other range." Ruth gave up the idea of college after graduating from high school with only mediocre grades and, following her grandfather's advice, took a job in an Omaha department store. Fascinated by the ladies' fashions she had never seen in David City, she managed to talk George Etting into letting her travel further north to attend the Chicago Academy of Fine Arts, where she studied fashion design.

There, one of her professors offered her an interesting assignment. The owner of the Marigold Gardens, a Chicago nightclub, needed someone to draw the costume designs his wife had suggested for the chorus girls, the eponymous Marigolds. Sent to the club and invited to catch the show, Etting was immediately stagestruck—so much so that she asked for a job there and then. At first, she used her chorus girl's $25-a-week salary to pay her school expenses, but show business soon eclipsed the fashion world. She quit school without telling her grandparents and was soon immersed in Chicago's vaudeville life, working with such stars as *Sophie Tucker and Bill "Bojangles" Robinson. What was more surprising to her was the discovery that despite her experience with the church choir, she could sing when not required to be a soprano. The club's management was quick to make the same discovery and gave Etting her first solo number, "Hats Off to the Polo Girl," which she sang dressed as a man.

In later years, Etting would always claim ignorance of the world she was entering in the Chicago of the early 1920s. It was the world of shady figures in fedoras, toting "pieces"; of mobsters, molls, and drive-by shootings; of political corruption, cops on the take, and Eliot Ness. "All the Chicago clubs were run by mobsters," she told a reporter for a show-business newspaper in 1977. "Working them could be dangerous." A case in point was the fate of comedian Joe E. Brown, who discovered that switching his act from one club to another, which really meant switching allegiance from one mob to another, was a risky decision. Brown had his throat slashed in an alleyway and was left for dead, spending several weeks in a hospital recuperating. Even more at risk was a naive farm girl from Nebraska who couldn't turn for advice to a family ignorant of her decision to quit school, and, worse yet, her entry into show business. Instead, Etting turned to Moe "The Gimp" Snyder.

Also known as "Colonel Gimp," Snyder was a low-level gangster, little more than a bodyguard for mid-level bosses, and, for extra cash, some of the top names on Chicago's nightclub circuit—Jimmy Durante, Al Jolson, and Eddie Cantor. His limp was said to be due to the 14 lead slugs lodged in his right leg. One of his favorite hangouts was the Marigolds Gardens, and his favorite chorus girl was Ruth Etting. Despite his crude manners and volatile temper, Snyder developed a protective affection for "the little lady," as he took to calling her, and Etting was only too happy to accept the advice of someone who seemed to know his way around the murky world in which she now found herself. On July 12, 1922, Ruth became Mrs. Martin Snyder.

As it turned out, Moe was also something of a promoter. Before long, Ruth moved—without incident, thanks to Moe—to The Rainbow Gardens, a larger club paying larger salaries. She was hired as one of the headliners for a cabaret act in which she co-starred with *Helen Morgan, whose career would parallel Etting's own. The act ran for an unprecedented seven months, with Moe glowing proudly every night from the wings and boasting to his cronies about his "little lady." After the cabaret closed, Etting opened at Big Jim Colosimo's, one of the most popular hangouts for the mob, where she stepped off the stage and sauntered from table to table, singing requests and becoming what was known as a "ceiling singer"—so called because of the demure upward gaze some female singers affected while an audience member slipped a tip into their décolletage. "I did my work, minded my own business, and went home," Etting later said, relying on Moe to keep her away from trouble, apparently so smoothly that Ruth was shocked to find that the man she knew as "Mr. Brown," the one who was known for his especially generous tips, was actually Al Capone. Moe always avoided pointing him out, and it was only when Capone's picture appeared in the newspapers that she made the connection.

By 1925, Etting had signed her first recording contract with Columbia Records and was on the vaudeville circuit—first the Orpheum circuit through the Midwest, and later the Pantages circuit on the West Coast. Reviewers were invariably impressed with her sultry renditions of standard love songs, like the captivated columnist in San Diego who wrote: "Does she have IT? Well, dearie, she positively exudes IT! She makes you think of orchids in the moonlight and other things that leave you absolutely breathless!" By now, it was impossible to hide her career from her grandparents, and she took Moe home to David City to meet them. Apparently, with the help of her growing fame, she convinced George Etting she had made the right decision.

Under Moe's watchful, and increasingly jealous, eye, Etting arrived in New York in 1927, where she sang with Paul Whiteman's band and got a call from Broadway's reigning producer of musical entertainment, Florenz Ziegfeld, creator of the legendary *Ziegfeld Follies*. Her audition for him was not what she expected. After some small talk, Ziegfeld asked her to walk around his office. "He looked at my ankles, and that was it," she once recalled. "That was my audition. He wouldn't hire anyone, no matter how talented, with thick ankles."

Having passed the ankle test, Etting opened in Ziegfeld's 1927 *Follies* at $400 a week—nearly 20 times what she had been paid at the Marigold Gardens just a few years earlier. *Variety* noted that her delivery "leaves a likeable impression right away," but *Mae West, who was backstage for Etting's *Follies* debut, was more to the point. "She had a sex quality that seemed to mesmerize the audience," she said. "And when she finished

singing, they kind of went crazy." Ziegfeld would claim that Ruth Etting was the greatest singer he had ever managed, although after seeing her attempts at the tap dance she was to perform after her first number, "Shakin' the Blues," he casually suggested she just finish singing and leave the stage. "I got the message," Ruth said, admitting that she was a "lousy" dancer.

> *Ruth, when you get through singing, just walk off the stage.*
>
> **—Florenz Ziegfeld to Ruth Etting, after her attempt to end on a dance step**

By 1930, Etting had become the darling of the national radio audience, appearing on Rudy Vallee's weekly show and, later, Chesterfield's twice-weekly "Music That Satisfies." She became known as "the radio canary" and "America's radio sweetheart." Moe, as usual, looked out for her in unexpected, and unwelcome, ways. While the Chesterfield show was on the air, he would scan the audience for anyone not smoking the sponsor's product, grab the offending cigarette out of his victim's mouth, and offer a Chesterfield "compliments of the little lady." She appeared on Broadway with Ed Wynn in *Simple Simon,* in which she introduced one of her signature "torch songs," "Ten Cents a Dance," written by Richard Rogers and Lorenz Hart. In the 1931 *Follies,* she sang for the first time what became her trademark number, "Shine On, Harvest Moon," an old vaudeville tune from 1911 to which she gave a new, wistful interpretation. "Every song must be studied separately to find a way to make the audience hear, see, and feel the story it tells," she told a reporter, and her care with her material paid off. By the early 1930s, she was selling an average of 40,000 records for each song she recorded, an immense sales volume for the time. "Miss Etting," said Walter Winchell, "is alone in her field, far outdistancing any of her competitors." An Etting mania seized the country, with perfumes and lines of clothing named after her. A letter addressed to "Ruth Etting, Studio, New York" found its way to her without the least delay.

While Etting was never known for her dancing or her acting, Hollywood was quick to use her as box-office "bait" for some of its most lavish musicals. Sam Goldwyn was the first to add her name on the list of stars for MGM's *Roman Scandals* of 1933, with audiences piling in to theaters only to see Ruth sing one brief number, "No More Love," before she disappeared from the story altogether. Likewise, she appeared for a few brief minutes in Universal's *Gift of Gab* with

*Ethel Waters, and her role in RKO's *Hips, Hips, Hooray* was so ephemeral that one reviewer complained of "another of those enigmas frequently confronting the picture goer."

But the musicals, in addition to some 30 "shorts," paid Etting up to $15,000 per appearance, often for less than a day's work. Even so, she avoided the spendthrift movie-star lifestyle, partly because of her grandfather's advice of years before and partly because of Moe's rough manners and crude treatment of others. "It was easier not to mingle with picture people," she said. "So I either saw non-professionals or New Yorkers, who knew how to take Moe." But even a veteran New Yorker like Flo Ziegfeld refused to put up with Snyder, who accused Ziegfeld of giving Ruth's rival, Helen Morgan, preferential treatment during the 1931 *Follies*. "You ain't gonna shove the little lady around," he threateningly told Ziegfeld, who promptly had him banned from the theater.

In 1935, Etting shocked everyone by announcing her retirement from show business. "I have been planning it for fifteen years," she told New York's *World Telegram* in April of that year, complaining that radio was "nervous work," that the glamour had gone out of the legitimate stage with the death of Flo Ziegfeld, and that her film work always ended up on the cutting-room floor. She looked forward to retiring to the home she had bought in Beverly Hills, she said, where she could learn to swim in her new pool and "do so many things I haven't been able to do since I was a kid in Nebraska." *Variety* claimed that Etting was one of the wealthiest stars in the country, investing her money wisely during the 1920s, cashing out of the market before the crash of 1929, and using the proceeds of some $400,000 to buy land in California and in her home state. Though Etting never did officially retire that year, close friends took it as a sign that she was under a great deal of stress and worried about her acceptance of a role in a London musical, *Transatlantic Rhythm,* which opened in the West End in 1936. Shortly after, Moe happened upon Ruth and the production's costume designer in the middle of an argument over one of her outfits for the show. Although Etting later claimed it was strictly a professional dispute, Moe took it as another attack on her and beat the costume designer severely enough to require hospitalization. When another argument broke out with the show's producer over delayed salaries, Etting left the show and came home.

In November of 1937, she was granted an uncontested divorce from Moe Snyder, claiming the last straw had been in London when, she said, he beat her legs with a cane. Moe later claimed he didn't contest the divorce because he always thought Ruth would come back to him; but no doubt the large sum of money that Etting settled on him helped ease the separation. His cronies were only too glad to relieve him of the cash when he embarked on a round of heavy gambling in New York, where he claimed that when the money ran out, he'd head for the Hudson River "and keep on walking until my hat floats." Once the divorce became public, Etting destroyed all her sheet music, her press clippings, her wardrobe, gave up the reported $200,000 a year she had been earning, and finally did retire from show business once and for all, moving permanently into her Beverly Hills home with Moe's daughter **Edith Snyder**, from his first marriage. Edith, too, had grown tired of her father's bullying and gladly accepted Etting's offer to take her on as a secretary. But both women would see Moe Snyder once more, with disastrous consequences.

About three years before the divorce, Moe had hired a new accompanist for Etting, a genial pianist named Myrl Alderman. Though Ruth would later claim that she and Myrl never became lovers until after her divorce from Moe, the two were married in December of 1938, barely a month after the divorce became final. When a gossip columnist leaked the rumor to Moe Snyder, he swore he'd find out the truth. His method was to abduct Myrl at gunpoint from a Beverly Hills parking lot, force him to drive home, and confront a terrified Ruth and Edith, demanding to know if it was true that Etting and Alderman had been married. Before anyone could answer, Moe fired first, or Myrl fired first, or Ruth ran for her own gun. What happened depended on who was doing the explaining, as the police found out when they arrived. The only certainty was that Myrl had suffered a serious gunshot wound to the abdomen, bleeding so profusely when he fell to the floor that both Ruth and Edith were convinced he was dead. It also appeared that Etting had, indeed, attempted to shoot Snyder with her own gun and was prevented from doing so by Edith's intervention. "I would gladly have killed Moe Snyder if I could have held the gun steady enough," she told the reporters outside the Los Angeles courtroom where Moe went on trial, "and I could kill him now if I had a gun."

While he was waiting for his trial to begin, Moe told young Hollywood columnist Ed Sullivan that he was lost without Ruth. "When my money runs out, I'll hit myself in the topper with a couple of slugs and call it a day," he said, and claimed that, without him, Etting's career would have fizzled long ago. Found guilty of kidnapping, attempted murder, and violating California gun laws, Moe was sentenced to up to 20 years in prison. His lawyer managed to land a new trial on a technicality, but by then neither Ruth nor Edith would testify against him. "Love is a funny thing to define," Etting told the court at the first trial, and in the end Moe served only a year of his sentence. He and Etting never saw each other again.

Myrl's first wife sued Ruth for $150,000, claiming Etting had broken up her marriage, but lost the case several months later. Once the decision was handed down, Ruth Etting disappeared from show business, selling the Beverly Hills house and moving to Colorado Springs to be with Myrl and his family. (Edith died of complications of rheumatic fever in 1939.) During the next seven years, Etting made only one appearance, at a World War II rally for war bonds in New York.

Shortly after the war's end, listeners to Rudy Vallee's weekly radio show were surprised to hear a familiar voice. Etting had decided to return to the business, but only because doctors had suggested that Myrl go back to writing and playing music as part of his recovery from wartime injuries. In 1947, she opened at the Copacabana in New York, and *Time* featured her in an article which reminded readers that Ruth Etting had once been "the nation's leading torch singer, rivalled only by Helen Morgan." The reviews of her Copa act were respectful, with *Variety* reporting that "her figure is still svelte and her song-selling effective if, betimes, she wisely skirts the top notes." But after trying out the business again for two years, Etting knew she'd been right to leave it in 1937 and returned to a quiet life in Colorado Springs. After the film *Love Me or Leave Me,* based on her years with Moe Snyder, was released in 1955, Etting refused a five-figure contract to return to singing and even decided not to sue the producers of the film, though unhappy with *Doris Day's portrayal of her, to avoid any further publicity. After Myrl's death in 1966, she made only one public appearance, returning to David City, Nebraska, in 1973 for the town's centennial celebrations. Shortly after, she moved into a retirement home.

"My sad story," she told a reporter who visited her there a year before her death in 1978, "is that my first marriage wasn't a marriage at all. It was a mistake." After reminiscing briefly about the old days, she seemed tired and the reporter turned to go. But she had one final thought for him. "If I had my life to do over again," she said, "I wouldn't go into show business."

SOURCES:

Eells, George. *Ginger, Loretta and Irene Who?* NY: Putnam, 1976.

RELATED MEDIA:

Love Me or Leave Me, starring Doris Day as Ruth Etting and James Cagney as Martin Snyder, directed by Charles Vidor, screenplay by *Isobel Lennart and Daniel Fuchs, costumes by *Helen Rose, MGM, 1955.

Norman Powers,
writer/producer, Chelsea Lane Productions,
New York, New York

Eu, Comtesse d' or Condessa de
(1846–1921).

See Isabel of Brazil.

Eudocia (c. 400–460)

East Roman empress of Athenian origin who, though baptized a Christian upon her marriage to Theodosius II, is said to have admired classical culture and to have harbored sympathies for learned pagans throughout her life. Name variations: Aelia Eudocia; Aelia Licinia Eudocia; Athenais; Athenaïs; Athenaïs-Eudokia of Athens; Eudocia Augusta; Eudociae. Pronunciation: AYE-lee-ah Yoo-dock-EE-ah; Ath-ayn-AH-is. Born Athenaïs in Athens or Antioch c. 400; died peacefully in Jerusalem on October 20, 460; daughter of Leontius (an Athenian sophist); educated in Athens by her father, and by the grammarians Hyperechius and Orion in Constantinople and Jerusalem; married Theodosius II, East Roman emperor (r. 408–450), on June 7, 421; children: Licinia Eudoxia (b. 422); Flaccilla (d. 431); Arcadius (d. before 450).

After death of father Leontius, left Athens for Constantinople; was baptized there and betrothed to Theodosius II (421); proclaimed Augusta (423); was thought to have influenced the foundation of the University of Constantinople (425); saw marriage of daughter Licinia Eudoxia to West Roman Emperor Valentinian III (437); made pilgrimage to Jerusalem and visited Antioch, where she addressed the senate (438); fell from favor at court and withdrew to Jerusalem (443).

Literary works: verses on Roman victories over Persia; verse paraphrase of portions of the Old Testament in eight books; oration in praise of the city of Antioch (all extant only in sparse fragments); poem on *the martyrdom of St. Cyprian and* Homerocentones *(both extant in large fragments). Fragments collected in* Eudociae Augustae, Procli Lycii, Claudiani: carminum graecorum reliquiae, *Teubner (1897).*

Philanthropy: built walls around Antioch (438); in Jerusalem restored walls and built fortifications, an episcopal palace, and the church of St. Stephen, in addition to many churches and shelters for pilgrims, the poor, and the elderly.

At his death in 395, Theodosius I left the Roman Empire divided between his two sons as emperors ("Augusti") of the West and East. Despite the almost complete entrenchment of Christianity during his reign, the old Roman Empire was no longer unified or resilient enough to withstand the external pressures exerted by barbarian hordes through the 5th century. The division of power resulted in what Theodosius I had not planned for: the de facto creation of two new political entities. The year 395 thus marks the clear bifurcation of the legacy of Rome in East and West. The Latin West would last scarcely a century more before the last Augustus, Romulus, was overthrown by the German Odoacer in 476. The Greek East, however, would survive as the Byzantine Empire in the Aegean and Asia Minor for another millennium. The period between 395 and 476 into which Eudocia was born describes an important transitional period in the history of social, political, and religious life.

One of the most interesting aspects of change in this era is the phenomenon of female *basileía,* the officially sanctioned partnership of women in imperial power. Beginning with *Flaccilla (c. 355-386), empress and wife of Theodosius I, is a line of imperial women who wielded public power in a way that the Roman world had never before seen. Eudocia, wife of Theodosius II from 421, has been considered by many as one of the most appealing of these women both because of the romantic stories of her origin and downfall, and for the intrinsic characteristics of intelligence and dignity that she manifested through a long and difficult career.

The Empress Eudocia was born in 400 as Athenaïs; it is safe to say that her family had no inkling of what she would become. We have no record of her mother's name, but her father Leontius was a Greek sophist (a philosopher-rhetorician). Her place of birth is traditionally thought to be Athens, though it has been recently suggested that it was actually Antioch (present-day Antakya, in southern Turkey). It does seems certain that she spent a large portion of her youth in Athens, which was a preeminent center of classical learning, and the place where her father held an important professorship from around 415 to his death a few years later. Though we cannot be certain as to what extent Leontius and his family adhered to official Christianity, the fact that he held the position he did in Athens suggests that Eudocia was heavily exposed to, if not taught in the ways of, classical systems of philosophy and literature in this city of many schools. In addition to this indication of a pagan upbringing, there is the matter of her birth name Athenaïs, which is obviously derived from that of the Olympian protectress of Athens, the goddess Athena, and which had to be changed to Eudocia upon her baptism immediately before marriage.

There is much uncertainty in the ancient accounts of Eudocia's life. She is mentioned by several Church historians and chronographers dating from the generation preceding her death until well into the Byzantine era, but the fullest and most lively account is that of John Malalas, who lived between 491 and 578; it is with him that the romantic tradition of Eudocia's discovery in Constantinople begins. Although we must suspect the rhetorical embellishment of his account, and supply dates to the events as we know them from other sources, Malalas provides us with the most comprehensive story of Eudocia.

Leontius died probably in 420, and legend has it that he left the lion's share of his estate to his two sons, Valerius and Gesius, setting aside only one hundred coins to his daughter, "because her good fortune, which surpasses that of all other women, will be enough." Valerius and Gesius refused to override their father's will and make a more equitable division of the estate with their sister, and so Eudocia traveled to Constantinople, where she hoped that she could arrange an audience with the Empress *Pulcheria Augusta.

Pulcheria, another of the impressive imperial women of the period, is a character who figures prominently in the life history of Eudocia. She had been regent for her younger brother Theodosius II when he was a boy, and for most of his reign she continued to exert a considerable influence at court. Eudocia's visit to Constantinople coincided with Pulcheria's search for Theodosius' bride. When the young Athenian appeared before the empress to make her inheritance case, Pulcheria saw a woman of such learning and beauty that she immediately arranged for Theodosius, a studious and passionate young man, to view Eudocia secretly. We are then told that he and his boyhood friend Paulinus observed her from behind a curtain in his private apartments. He fell immediately in love, and plans were set straightaway for marriage.

After catechism and baptism by the patriarch of Constantinople, Eudocia dropped the name Athenaïs, took the name Aelia Eudocia ("the benevolent will of God"), and married Theodosius II on June 7, 421. The next year the imperial couple had a daughter, *Licinia Eudoxia, later to be Augusta in the West. On January 2, 423, Eudocia was herself proclaimed Augusta, which made her a theoretical equal with the redoubtable Pulcheria, the other woman in Theodosius' life.

Pulcheria was of a rather severe religious cast, and this, in combination with a remarkable political adeptness and a thirst for wielding power, made some sort of confrontation between the Augustae inevitable. Theodosius, though intelligent and benevolent, was a weak and complacent ruler whose long reign can be plotted in terms of which courtier or relation exerted the most influence over him at any given time. By the time Eudocia was brought into the palace, Pulcheria had made the court into a sort of cloister: she had elevated theological concerns to high importance in imperial politics and had dedicated herself—and her two sisters, Arcadia and Marina—to perpetual chastity. Her zeal is evident in a constitution signed by Theodosius in 415 forbidding the construction of new synagogues and ordering the destruction of old ones, and in another of the same year excluding pagans from positions in the army or administration. In the two years following Eudocia's elevation, however, a new influence seems to be evident in Theodosius' appointments and policies.

On the day before Eudocia's investiture as Augusta, a man called Asclepiodotus was named to the highest civil position in government, the praetorian prefecture. He was Eudocia's maternal uncle. On April 6, 423, Theodosius presented a new law to Asclepiodotus reaffirming harsh penalties against various Christian heresies as well as against pagans and Jews. Asclepiodotus was able to mollify the emperor's harshness by bringing before him evidence of Christian outrages against Jews, and by apparently convincing him that there were really no pagans left in the Roman world to suppress. Theodosius appended provisions to his law to protect peaceful pagans and Jews from attack. Asclepiodotus made every effort to enforce the emperor's new rulings, but they were eventually repealed after St. Simeon the Stylite threatened the timorous

Theodosius with divine punishment. Nevertheless, this outcome only emphasizes the independence of outlook that dared to discourage the violent Christian piety popular in Roman society at the time. It is very unlikely that Pulcheria, so intense in her love of the Church and her hatred of those outside of it, would have appealed for clemency. It is a far more likely conjecture that the new Augusta Eudocia was ultimately responsible for the concessions: despite her recent conversion to Christianity, her upbringing is likely to have given her some sympathy for the position of loyal pagan citizens in the empire.

> The story of a fair and virtuous maiden, exalted from a private condition to the Imperial throne, might be deemed an incredible romance, if such a romance had not been verified in the marriage of Theodosius.
>
> —Edward Gibbon

Another key event in the reign of Theodosius often associated with the influence of Eudocia is the foundation of the University of Constantinople on February 7, 425. It was established to compete with the traditional places of classical education in Antioch, Alexandria, and Athens as an institution with an emphasis on Christian learning within the classical disciplines of grammar, rhetoric, philosophy, and jurisprudence. Again the involvement of the new empress in this endeavor seems plausible because of the conjectured status of traditional education in her upbringing. It is worth noting that Christianity did not require of its adherents the wholesale rejection of pagan culture. Many learned bishops and saints of the time cultivated their understanding of the past to further their Christian goals; to say that the baptized Eudocia understood and appreciated pagans is not to suggest that she was behaving hypocritically.

On October 29, 437, Eudocia and Theodosius' first child Licinia Eudoxia was married to her cousin Valentinian III, Augustus in the West. After the departure of her daughter, Eudocia decided to make a pilgrimage to Jerusalem in order to render thanks for the successful marriage. In the spring of the same year, she made her way to the holy city with a stop in Antioch, the occasion of a famous display of her learned eloquence. There, before the local senate, she delivered an oration in praise of the city, the final line of which—a quotation from Homer—brought down the house: "I boast that I am of your race and blood." The senators responded to the compliment by erecting two statues to the empress, and she persuaded Theodosius to undertake several public works to improve the city.

Eudocia's itinerary in Jerusalem included visits with the pious and wealthy Roman widow *Melania the Younger (who had established a religious house there), prayers and devotions at the holy sites in the city, and the collection of some important relics, including those of St. Stephen the Protomartyr, which Eudocia triumphantly brought back with her to Constantinople in 439. In these details, her journey recalled that of *Helena, the mother of Constantine the Great, some 100 years earlier. This recollection only served to increase her renown—and perhaps Pulcheria's jealousy.

At her arrival back in the imperial city, Eudocia's influence was still strong, but whatever disharmony had existed between herself and Pulcheria came quickly to a head. One likely point of contention was a theological dispute that was raging throughout the East at the time: the controversy between the Orthodox party, to which Pulcheria adhered, and the Monophysite heresy, to which Eudocia inclined. But it took more than an argument about the nature of Christ to bring full-fledged dissension to the palace. The real author of the dispute that led to Pulcheria's withdrawal from court soon after 441 seems to have been one Chrysaphius Tzumas, a court eunuch who had been gaining steady influence over the weak-willed emperor since 440. Chrysaphius pointed out to Eudocia that Pulcheria had enjoyed for some time the service of a chamberlain in her household, and suggested that she demand of Theodosius a chamberlain for herself. When Theodosius refused, Chrysaphius suggested that Eudocia urge the emperor to have his sister ordained a deaconess—ostensible flattery for the purity of her life, but actually a ploy to break her power, since the ordination would place her in subservience to the archbishop of Constantinople. Pulcheria sensed the object of these machinations and withdrew from the palace to bide her time, having sent her chamberlain over to Eudocia.

Chrysaphius' complete domination of the emperor was now obstructed by only Eudocia, and he is probably behind the rumors that soon reached Theodosius about adulterous liaisons between Eudocia and his old friend Paulinus, now a high official in the palace. Just as John Malalas provides us with the most vivid account of Eudocia's rise to prosperity, he gives a fabulous account of her fall from grace. At the feast of Epiphany, Malalas tells us, a poor man brought Theodosius an apple of prodigious size, which the emperor bought and presented to Eudocia. The empress in turn gave the apple to Paulinus, who was ill. He, unaware of its origin, then made a gift of it to Theodosius. When the emperor questioned Eudocia as to what she had done with his present to her, she swore that she had eaten it. This made Theodosius believe that his old friend and his wife had indeed been engaged in an illicit romance, and he had Paulinus killed. The folk-tale elements of this account do not permit us to fully credit its details, but we do know from an independent source that Paulinus was executed in 444, and that in 443 Eudocia secured Theodosius' permission to go for a second time to Jerusalem; she would never return.

Though the move to Jerusalem was a diminishment of her former power at court, Eudocia was allowed initially to maintain the tokens of her Augustan dignity, which included not only her title, but also a large retinue and revenue. In fact, she was so active in building and charity in the city that Theodosius apparently felt threatened and, at some point, sent the commander of his guards, Saturninus, to chastise her. His first act was to execute her two most trusted confidantes, the clerics Severus and John. We have it on good authority that the enraged Eudocia then killed the imperial emissary with her own hands. At this point, Theodosius deprived her of her imperial staff and ceased to include her image on coins struck at the government mints. Nevertheless, we have no evidence that she ever lost her imperial title. The last we know of the empress in Jerusalem is her involvement in strife between the partisans of the Monophysite and Orthodox causes in the Holy Land. She at first supported the usurpant Monophysite bishop of Jerusalem in his violent measures against the Orthodox, but after he was suppressed by imperial intercession she had a change of heart, and in 460 died peacefully in the Orthodox communion. She was entombed in the Church of St. Stephen, which she had helped to build with her patronage.

The most accessible remains of Eudocia (at least to readers of Ancient Greek) are the fragments of her writings that have survived the ravages of time. Of her encomium on Antioch, J.B. Bury suggests that she posed "rather as one trained in Greek rhetoric and devoted to Hellenic traditions and proud of her Athenian descent, than as a pilgrim on her way to the great Christian shrine." The two faces of Eudocia's soul, pagan and Christian, also seem to be evident in the two works that have come down to us relatively intact. Her *Life of St. Cyprian* is an account of the martyrdom of an Antiochene bishop cast into arduous Homeric hexameters. Eudocia's *Homerocentones*, or "Homeric Stitchings," is a work on which she collaborated with a number of other scholars. It comprises paraphrases of Bible stories constructed by lifting complete lines from the *Iliad* and *Odyssey* and "stitching" them together in a new order. Eudocia's literary undertakings beg the question: do they demonstrate the desire of a nominal Christian to satisfy her love for pagan literature, or the desire of a sincere Christian to present her religion in a manner acceptable to cultivated pagans? In either case, as Alan Cameron remarks, "it is safe to say that no-one would ever have heard of so minor a poet as Eudocia if she had not become empress." It is perhaps best to see her poetic efforts as an analogous representation of the woman herself: enigmatic in her passions, noble in her endeavors, but ultimately frustrated in her quest for pure greatness.

SOURCES:

Bury, J.B. *History of the Later Roman Empire.* Vol. I. London: St. Martin's Press, 1923 (reprint, NY: Dover Publications, 1958).

Cameron, Alan. "The Empress and the Poet: Paganism and Politics at the Court of Theodosius II," in *Yale Classical Studies.* Vol. 27, 1981, pp. 217–89.

Gibbon, Edward. *The History of the Decline and Fall of the Roman Empire.* Edited by J.B. Bury. Volume 3. London: Methuen, 1901.

Holum, Kenneth G. *Theodosian Empresses: Women and Imperial Dominion in Late Antiquity.* Berkeley, CA: University of California Press, 1982.

Ioannis Malalae Chronographia. Edited by L. Dindorf. Bonn: Weber, 1831.

SUGGESTED READING:

Tsatsos, Ioanna. *Empress Athenais-Eudocia: A Fifth Century Byzantine Humanist.* Translated by Jean Demos. Brookline, MA: Holy Cross Orthodox Press, 1977.

COLLECTIONS:

Eudociae Augustae, Procli Lycii, Claudiani carminum graecorum reliquae. Edited by A. Ludwich. Leipzig: Teubner, 1897.

Peter O'Brien, Department of Classical Studies, Boston University, Boston, Massachusetts

Eudocia (b. 422).

See Licinia Eudoxia.

Eudocia (fl. 600s CE).

See Fabia-Eudocia.

Eudocia (fl. 700s)

Wife of Justinian II. Flourished in the 700s; first wife of Justinian II Rhinotmetos, Byzantine emperor (r. 685–695 and 705–711).

Eudocia was the first wife of Byzantine emperor, Justinian II Rhinotmetos. Her fate is unknown. His second wife was *Theodora of the Khazars.

Eudocia (fl. 700s)

Byzantine empress. Name variations: Eudokia. Third wife of Constantine V, Byzantine emperor (r. 741–775); children: Nicephorus; Christopher; Nicetas; Anthimus; Eudocimus.

Constantine V married three times. His first wife was *Irene of the Khazars, his second *Maria (fl. 700s). His third marriage to Eudocia defied the Orthodox tradition that prohibited more than two marriages. Eudocia had many children, including a set of twins.

Eudocia (b. 978).

See Zoë Porphyrogenita for sidebar.

Eudocia (c. 1260–?)

Byzantine princess. Born around 1260; daughter of Theodora Ducas and Michael VIII Paleologus (1224–1282), emperor of Nicaea (r. 1261–1282); married John of Trebizond.

Eudocia Angelina (fl. 1204)

*Byzantine empress. Flourished in 1204; daughter of Alexius III Angelus, Byzantine emperor (r. 1195–1203) and *Euphrosyne (d. 1203); married Stephen of Serbia; married Alexius V Ducas, Nicaean emperor (r. 1204); sister of *Anna Angelina (d. 1210?, who married Theodore I Lascaris).*

Eudocia Baiane (d. 902).

See Zöe Carbopsina for sidebar.

Eudocia Comnena (fl. 1100)

*Byzantine princess and sister of Anna Comnena. Flourished in 1100; daughter of Irene Ducas (c. 1066–1133) and Alexius I Comnenus, emperor of Byzantium (r. 1081–1118); sister of *Anna Comnena (1083–1153/55).*

Eudocia Decapolita (fl. 800s)

Byzantine empress. Name variations: Euxokia Dekapolitissa (meaning "10 cities"). Married Michael III the Drunkard (c. 836–867), Byzantine emperor (r. 842–867), in 855.

When 15-year-old Michael III the Drunkard, the future Byzantine emperor, fell in love with, and took as his mistress, *Eudocia Ingerina, his mother *Theodora the Blessed as regent had other plans. She compelled him to marry the aristocratic Eudocia Decapolita in 855. Michael acquiesced, then proceeded to neglect his wife while openly inundating his mistress with favors.

Eudocia Ingerina (fl. 800s)

*Byzantine empress. Name variations: Eudokia Ingerina; Ingerina. Flourished in the late 800s; daughter of Inger; probably of Scandinavian descent; became second wife of Basil I the Macedonian, Byzantine emperor (r. 867–886), around 865; also mistress of Michael III the Drunkard, Byzantine emperor (r. 842–867); children: Leo VI the Wise (b. 866), Byzantine emperor (r. 886–912); Alexander (b. 870), Byzantine emperor (r. 912–913); Stephen (born around 871). Basil's first wife was *Maria of Macedonia.*

From the little that has been written about her, it would appear that Eudocia Ingerina was the unwitting pawn in several royal power struggles during the Golden Age of the Byzantine Empire (843–1025). Lowly-born, probably of Scandinavian descent, she became the mistress of **Michael III**, the pleasure-loving, teen-age son of the empress-regent *Theodora the Blessed. (Michael's wild ways, particularly his love of drink, led Byzantine chroniclers to dub him "Michael the Drunkard," although modern scholars believe that his behavior may have been exaggerated by his detractors.) Theodora, a strong-willed woman, had set her sights on a more aristocratic mate for her son and forced Michael into marriage with *Eudocia Decapolita in 855. While outwardly obeying his mother's wishes, Michael continued his relationship with Eudocia Ingerina, openly favoring her over his wife. Eudocia Ingerina remained Michael's mistress for the next ten years or so, during which time Theodora was coerced into a convent, and Michael came to serve as emperor under the rule of his uncle **Caesar Bardas**.

Further complications arose for Eudocia Ingerina with the arrival in Constantinople of **Basil I**, an unscrupulous, ambitious young man who would befriend Michael in order to advance himself. Illiterate but strong and muscular, Basil attracted Michael's attention when he won a wrestling match at the imperial palace; shortly thereafter, he was hired as the emperor's horse trainer. Over the next few years, Basil and Michael became friends, then co-conspirators,

eventually plotting the assassination of Caesar Bardas, whom Basil viewed as his major political foe. Following the death of his uncle, Michael made Basil his co-emperor and gave him Eudocia Ingerina as his wife. (The wedding ceremony took place around 865.) But Michael also kept Eudocia Ingerina as his mistress, an unusual arrangement that lasted for a year, until Michael abruptly turned against Basil and conspired to have him killed. Warned in advance, however, Basil set into motion his own plan of revenge. On the night of September 23, 867, after Michael had drunk himself into a stupor at an "arranged" banquet, Basil had his henchmen murder him. Basil I then embarked on his solo rule as emperor, with Eudocia Ingerina at his side as empress.

Unfortunately, there is no way of knowing Eudocia Ingerina's reactions to all these events, most of them seemingly out of her control. An account by **Constance Head** does imply that her marriage to Basil never advanced much beyond the "perennial spirit of distrust between them." Even the couple's three sons—Leo, Alexander, and Stephen—were never popular with their father, who doted instead on Constantine, his son with his first wife *Maria of Macedonia and heir to the throne. (Basil was never certain whether Leo, born in 866, was his legitimate son or Michael's, and developed such a dislike for the frail and bookish boy that he reputedly once threw him around by his hair.) When Constantine died prematurely in 879, and Leo became next in line to the throne, Basil slipped into a deep depression from which he never recovered. He died in a hunting accident on August 29, 886, after which Leo, dubbed "Leo the Wise" because of his scholarly manner and ability to predict the future, served as emperor until 912. (Quite recently, it was determined that Leo was indeed the legitimate son of Basil I.) Nothing further is known of Eudocia Ingerina, not even the date of her death.

SOURCES:

Head, Constance. *Imperial Byzantine Portraits: A Verbal and Graphic Gallery.* New Rochelle, NY: Caratzas Brothers, 1982.

Ostrogorsky, George. *History of the Byzantine State.* Translated by Joan Hussey. New Brunswick, NJ: Rutgers University Press, 1969.

Eudocia Macrembolitissa (1021–1096)

Byzantine empress. Name variations: Eudoxia, Eudokia Makrembolitissa. Born in 1021; died in 1096 in Constantinople; daughter of John Macrembolites; married Constantine X Ducas (d. 1067), Byzantine emperor (r. 1059–1067); married Romanus IV Dio-

genes, Byzantine emperor (r. 1068–1071), in 1068; children: (first marriage) Michael VII Ducas, Byzantine emperor (r. 1071–1078); Andronicus I, Byzantine emperor; Constantine XII, Byzantine emperor; *Zoe Ducas; *Theodora Ducas; (with Romanus) two sons.

A Byzantine noblewoman, Eudocia Macrembolitissa was the wife of Constantine X Ducas, emperor of Byzantium. She had five children with Constantine before his death in 1067. It is believed that Constantine himself ordered on his deathbed that Eudocia take over the government, and she assumed the regency for her young son, who would succeed his father as Michael VII Ducas. "When the empress Eudokia, in accordance with the wishes of her husband, succeeded him as supreme ruler, she did not hand over the government to others," writes Psellus. "She assumed control of the whole administration in person. . . . Her pronouncements had the note of authority which one associates with an emperor. Nor was this surprising, for she was in fact an exceedingly clever woman. On either side of her were her two sons, both of whom stood almost rooted to the spot, quite overcome with awe and reverence for their mother."

Eudocia Macrembolitissa had sworn to Constantine as his dying wish never to remarry, and she had even imprisoned and exiled the military leader Romanus IV Diogenes, who was suspected of aspiring to the throne. (He marched around in imperial garb, red shoes and all.) Perceiving, however, that she was incapable of averting the invasions that threatened the eastern frontier of the empire unaided, she revoked her oath and married Romanus on New Year's Day, 1068. Together, they dispelled the impending danger.

In a very different version of the story, Eudocia set her cap for the handsome Romanus and convinced the patriarch of Constantinople, John Xiphilin, to relinquish the copy of her vow of non-marriage that had been filed with him, by hinting that she wanted to marry the patriarch's brother. When the patriarch gave her back the contract, she married Romanus Diogenes and proclaimed him emperor, much to the dismay of her teenaged son Michael. The patriarch, Eudocia's brother-in-law Caesar John Ducas, and ex-minister Michael Psellus (who was now tutor to Michael VII) were furious over the deceit. The accession of Romanus literally meant the accession of the army and the end of the reign of the Ducae.

Eudocia did not live happily with her new husband, who was warlike and self-willed. Romanus was also disliked by the people of Byzan-

tium, who did not grieve when he was taken prisoner by a Turkish army in 1071. A conflict ensued in Constantinople, as citizens took sides over who should rule: Eudocia alone or her son Michael. When news arrived that Romanus had been freed, Michael, fearing his mother would restore Romanus to his previous position as co-regent, reluctantly issued a decree that his mother must be sent to a convent. Eudocia was forced to comply. On his return in 1072, Romanus was attacked and killed by Michael's supporters. Eudocia remained at her convent until her death in 1096, but it is unlikely that she became a nun. Hoping to become empress again, she once proposed marriage to the widowed emperor Nicephorus III Botaneiates; he did not accept.

Christ Crowning Romanus IV Diogenes and Eudocia Macrembolitissa.

Eudocia of Byzantium (d. 404)

Empress of Byzantium. Name variations: Eudocia Augusta; Eudokia; Eudoxia; Eudoxia the Frank. Died in 404 in Constantinople; daughter of Bauto, a Frankish military official; married Arcadius, emperor of

*Byzantium (r. 395–408), in 395; mother-in-law of *Eudocia (c. 400–460); children: Theodocius also known as Theodosius II, East Roman emperor (r. 408–450); and stepdaughters *Pulcheria (c. 398–453), Arcadia, and Marina.*

Eudocia of Byzantium was the daughter of a Frankish mercenary general. In 395, she married Emperor Arcadius of Byzantium, a union arranged as part of a scheme by the court official Eutropius to further his own interests. Arcadius proved to be an incompetent ruler and weak-willed man who was easily dominated by his advisors, including Eutropius. Eudocia used her position to help Eutropius' enemies banish Eutropius from the empire in 399. Possessed of powerful character and intelligence, she exerted enormous power over the imperial government. Eudocia became so important to the administration that in 400 she was given the title "Augusta," which was usually reserved for a woman ruling in her own name. She continued to act as the real ruler of Byzantium until her death from a miscarriage in 404.

Laura York,
Riverside, California

Eudocia of Byzantium (fl. 1181)

*Lady of Montpellier. Name variations: Eudoxia of Byzantium. Flourished around 1180. Granddaughter of John II Comnenus, Byzantine emperor (r. 1118–1143), and *Priska-Irene of Hungary (c. 1085–1133); niece of Manuel I Comnenus, emperor of Byzantium (r. 1143–1180); married Guillem also known as William VIII, lord of Montpellier; children: *Maria of Montpellier (1181–1213).*

Eudoxia Lopukhina

Eudokia.

Variant of Eudocia.

Eudoxia.

Variant of Eudocia.

Eudoxia Gorbarty or Gorbaty (1534–1581)

See Eudoxia Jaroslavovna.

Eudoxia Jaroslavovna (1534–1581)

Matriarch of the House of Romanov. Name variations: Eudoxia Yaroslavovna; Eudoxia Gor-

*barty or Gorbaty. Born in 1534; died on April 4, 1581; possibly daughter of Alexander Gorbaty; married Nikita Romanov (1530–1586), in 1553; children: Fedor also known as Theodore, the Monk Philaret (1558–1633); Alexander (d. 1602); Michael (d. 1602); Vassili (d. 1602); Ivan; *Martha Romanov (who married Boris Tscherkaski); *Irina Romanov (who married Ivan Godunov in 1601); *Euphamia Romanov (who married Ivan Sitzki); Marpha; Anastasia; *Anna Romanov (who married Ivan Troiekurow).*

Eudoxia Lopukhina (1669–1731)

Empress of Russia. Name variations: Eudoxia Lopukhin; Lapuchin; (nickname) Dunka. Born in 1669 (some sources cite 1672); died on September 7, 1731, in Moscow; daughter of Theodore Lopukhin, a boyar; married Peter I the Great (1672–1725), tsar of Russia (r. 1682–1725), on January 27, 1689 (marriage repudiated in 1703; divorced 1718); children: Alexis (1690–1718, who married Charlotte of Brunswick-Wolfenbuttel); Alexander (1691–1692).

In 1669, Eudoxia Lopukhina was born in Moscow into a *boyarin* family; *boyars* were the equivalent of the Russian aristocracy. She received a poor education, as was then typical for Russian women, but grew up extremely devoted to the Russian Orthodox Church. Eudoxia was chosen among many candidates to become the bride of the Tsar Peter I, then a youth of 17, in 1689, the same year he succeeded to his father's (Tsar Alexis') throne. The marriage came at the command of Peter's mother *Natalya Narishkina who hoped that Eudoxia, a woman as pious as she was beautiful, would wean him from Moscow's wicked ways. But the couple were poorly matched. Peter was anything but traditional in his education; worldly, he had studied much and believed in the superiority of Western European culture over his own "backward" Russian culture. Eudoxia had been raised in the traditional Russian *terem*, or women's quarters, rooms of total seclusion from the outside world. The tsar and tsarina had almost nothing in common, and they separated after Eudoxia gave birth to their second son, Alexander, who did not survive long.

When Peter demanded a divorce so that he could remarry, Eudoxia staunchly refused, because divorce was a great sin in the Orthodox Church. In 1698, her obstinacy led Peter to order her removed from Moscow and taken to a monastery at Suzdal. She found more happiness at the convent than she ever had in Peter's untraditional, Westernized court; she was given the respect her position as tsarina demanded and found the convent environment more suited to her retiring, introverted nature. However, her solitude was shattered in 1718 when Peter, who had not given up his plan to divorce Eudoxia and remarry, accused her of adultery. She was forced to travel back to Moscow to answer the charges, which were almost certainly trumped up to force her to agree to a divorce. Peter's plan worked. She was compelled to make a public confession and was divorced in 1718. Eudoxia was then allowed to enter another monastery at Ladoga.

Her elder son Alexis was Peter's original heir, but Alexis was ignored by Peter until he was old enough to be of use, by which time he had become a weakling. Under Peter's direct tutelage, Alexis came to manifest all of his father's vices and none of his virtues. A drunkard and a wastrel, he became the locus around whom general opposition to Peter began to coalesce. When Peter discovered his son at the center of a plot, Peter subjected him to torture, which led to Alexis' death.

Upon Peter's demise in 1725, his second wife *Catherine I was named his successor. When Catherine died in 1727, Eudoxia's grandson (son of Alexis and *Charlotte of Brunswick-Wolfenbuttel) succeeded as Peter II. Conservative forces in the Russian government, who had opposed Peter the Great's many reforms, sought out Eudoxia and convinced her to return to Moscow to act as her grandson's regent. Escorted with great ceremony to Moscow, she did return in 1728 and was presented to the people attired in the splendid, old-fashioned robes of a tsaritsa. However, a life spent mainly in conventual isolation had little prepared her for the demands of regency. Her closest friends determined that she was more suited to convent than throne. Provided an allowance of 60,000 rubles a year, she gave up her new title and once again retired from the world into a monastery at Moscow, where she died in 1731.

Laura York,
Riverside, California

Eudoxia of Moscow (1483–1513)

*Russian princess. Name variations: Evdokhiia. Born in 1483 (some sources cite 1492); died in 1513; daughter of *Sophia of Byzantium (1448–1503) and Ivan III the Great (1440–1505), grand prince of Moscow (r. 1462–1505); married Peter Ibragimovich, prince of Khazan.*

Eudoxia Streshnev

Eudoxia Streshnev (1608–1645)

*Empress of Russia. Name variations: Streshneva; Streshniev. Born in 1608; died on August 18, 1645; daughter of Lucas Streshnev and Anne Volkonska; became second wife of Mikhail also known as Michael III (1596–1645), tsar of Russia (r. 1613–1645), on February 5, 1626; children: *Irina Romanov (1627–1679); Pelagia (1628–1629); Alexis I (1629–1676), tsar of Russia (r. 1645–1676); Ivan (1631–1639); *Anna Romanov (1632–1692, who married Boris Morozov); Vassili (1633–1645); Sophie Romanov (1634–1676); Tatiana Romanov; Eudoxia Romanov; Marpha Romanov. Michael's first wife was *Marie Dolgorukova (d. 1625).*

Eufemia.

Variant of Euphemia.

Eufrozyna.

Variant of Euphrosyne.

Eugenia (d. around 258)

Saint. Died around 258; daughter of Philip, governor of Egypt.

Eugenia, the beautiful and well-educated daughter of Philip, the governor of Egypt, lived during the reign of Roman Emperor Valerian (r. 253–259) who at the end of his rule faced severe economic difficulties. Believing that any riches accrued by the Church meant less for the State, he issued an edict demanding that Christians be stripped of their riches and made to abjure their faith under penalty of death.

According to legend, Eugenia was converted to Christianity one day when passing a monastery with her servants, Hyacinth and Protus, and hearing a psalm being sung: "The gods of the gentiles are demons; He whom we adore is the true God, creator of heaven on earth." Upon her conversion, Eugenia was given permission by the bishop of Heliopolis to pose as a man and to become a monk with Hyacinth and Protus. Purportedly, all three lived at the monastery of Heliopolis for a period of time without being discovered. After leaving the monastery, Eugenia converted her entire family and founded a convent of Christian virgins in Africa. She later returned to Rome, where, under Valerian's edict, she was beheaded. Her feast day is December 25.

Eugénie (1826–1920)

Empress of the French and wife of Napoleon III who, by her elegance and charm, contributed largely to the brilliancy of the imperial regime and showed calmness and courage in the face of the rising tide of revolution. Name variations: Eugenie de Montijo; Eugénie-Marie, Countess of Teba. Pronunciation: ou-JHAY-knee. Born Marie Eugénie Ignace Augustine de Montijo on May 5, 1826, in Grenada, Spain; died on July 11, 1920, in Madrid, Spain; daughter of Cipriano Guzman y Porto Carrero, count of Teba (subsequently count of Montijo and grandee of Spain) and Manuela Kirkpatrick (1794–1879, daughter of William Kirkpatrick, U.S. consul at Malaga, a Scot by birth and an American by nationality); sister of Paca (1825–1860), duchess of Alba; educated at the convent of the Sacré Coeur and the Gymnase Normal, Civil et Orthosomatique; briefly attended an exclusive girls' boarding school, in Clifton, England; married Louis Napoleon (Napoleon III), emperor of France (r. 1852–1870), on January 30, 1853 (died, January 1873); children: son Napoleon Louis ("Lou-Lou," 1856–1879, known during the empire as prince imperial).

$\mathcal{D}$on't dramatize life. It is quite dramatic enough as it is.

—Empress Eugénie

In 1853, Eugénie de Montijo, a Spanish noblewoman of partially Scottish descent, married Napoleon III, emperor of France; for the next 17 years, she reigned as empress of that glittering epoch in French history known as the "Circus Empire." Although praised for her beauty and

credited with transforming the Tuileries Palace into a mecca for European society, Eugénie was more than an arbiter of style; she was one of the most courageous and influential women of her age. She endured three wars, a scandalous private life, and deep-rooted prejudice against her background. As Napoleon's health failed and his politics floundered, Eugénie grew stronger and more resolute in her attempt to protect the throne. Historians, however, have been less than kind to the empress, often citing her frigidity and her erratic judgment in politics and diplomacy as the cause of the fall of the empire. Biographer John Bierman attempts a slightly more balanced view, factoring in Napoleon's own shortcomings and calling Eugénie merely a contributor to the downfall. "For all her faults," he writes, "she was never quite the vindictive, self-centered, priest-ridden reactionary of republican legend. . . . [F]or all her virtues, she was never quite the strong, loyal, long-suffering, and misunderstood heroine portrayed by revisionist historians."

Eugénie's birth on May 5, 1826, coincided with an earthquake, an ill omen by all accounts, though she came to believe it might have meant that she was destined to "convulse the world." Given her ambitious mother and her Bonapartist father, her place in history seems preordained. Her father was the one-eyed Cipriano Guzman y Porto Carrero, the younger son and eventual heir of the count of Montijo, an impoverished noble who was one of the grandees of Spain. An enthusiastic admirer of Napoleon I Bonaparte, Cipriano joined with the French in 1808, fighting in the Bonapartist army and remaining loyal until the final battle at Waterloo in 1815. Owing to his part in the wars of the empire, he was prosecuted and imprisoned by order of Ferdinand VII, king of Spain, after Napoleon's fall. Released from prison after a year and a half, he remained under what might be considered house arrest until 1830.

Eugénie's mother, **Manuela Kirkpatrick de Montijo,** was the daughter of expatriate Scot William Kirkpatrick, the U.S. consul in Malaga and an exporter of Spanish fruit and wines. Manuela, whose mother **Françoise Kirkpatrick** was Belgian, profited greatly from her diverse background, combining, as one observer noted, "Andalusian grace, English genuineness and French facility." She was also a fiercely determined woman, intent on having the best life had to offer. Cipriano and Manuela, who first met in Paris in 1813, were married late in 1817, although, as David Duff points out, their opposing views on practically everything doomed the union from the start:

She loved entertaining—he could not abide people about the house. He was mean with money—she was open handed and generous. He believed in the benefits of privation and hardship—she revelled in luxury. He took politics in deadly earnest—she was prepared to shift her ground to suit her convenience. He lived much in the past—she walked in the present and dreamed of the future.

Given their differences, the marriage endured long separations, until the couple no longer saw each other at all.

It was not until 1825 that their first daughter ❧▶ **Paca** was born, followed a little less than a year later by the arrival of Eugénie. The sisters were opposites in appearance as well as temperament. Paca, a dark-eyed brunette, was passive and much her mother's girl. Eugénie, volatile in nature, not only inherited her father's red hair and blue eyes but also his passion for outdoor pursuits, especially riding. As might be expected, Cipriano and Manuela had separate notions regarding child rearing. Manuela wanted the girls schooled in the social graces to prepare them for brilliant careers in society. Cipriano favored serious education, simple clothes, and a plain diet, hoping his daughters would grow up to be rugged and independent. As children, both girls were placed in the convent of the Sacré Coeur in Paris, where their parents moved to avoid the revolutionary disturbances and cholera epidemics that were rampant in Spain. After two years, Cipriano, who as a nominal Catholic was unhappy about having his daughters under the influence of the nuns, enrolled them in the Gymnase Normal, an avant-garde co-educational institution specializing in physical training. Eugénie flourished in the freer environment but never lost her preoccupation with the outward forms of the Catholic faith.

Manuela and Cipriano's disagreements continued to weaken their marriage, and in 1835 Cipriano returned to Madrid, leaving his wife in Paris. During this time, Manuela resumed her friendship with author Prosper Mérimée, who took a grandfatherly interest in Paca and Eugénie. (He would later dictate Eugénie's love letters to Napoleon during their courtship.) Mérimée also introduced the family to then unknown author Henri Beyle ("Stendhal"), who, like Cipriano, was a fervent admirer of the Great Emperor and entertained the girls with the same Napoleonic legends first heard from their father. In 1837, Manuela placed her daughters in an exclusive English boarding school near Bristol and returned to Paris (supposedly to continue an ongoing affair with English diplomat George Villi-

er). Teased and called "Carrots" because of her red hair, Eugénie hated the school and complained to her father that the place was dull and she wanted to come home. As a result, the girls were returned to Paris in the care of a new governess, Miss Flowers, who remained in the service of the family until the 1880s.

Eugénie, who missed her father terribly during his long separations from the family, was greatly affected by his death in 1840, and by her mother's subsequent lapse into what David Duff terms "middle-aged lechery." Now residing in Spain with a healthy inheritance, Manuela indulged herself. Eugénie, idealistic and devoted to her father's memory, did not approve of her mother's behavior, nor indeed of the lax morals of Spanish society at the time. Duff speculates that Manuela's conspicuous carnality may have had much to do with Eugénie's later aversion to sex and her deep contempt for men.

When not attending to her paramours, Manuela set her sights on finding husbands for her beautiful and marriageable daughters. Eugénie, now 16, obliged by falling in love with one of the greatest of Spanish nobles, the Duke of Alba and Berwick, her enormously rich 21-year-old distant cousin. Unfortunately, Manuela arranged for the duke to take Paca's hand instead, a decision that threw Eugénie into teenage despair, during which she threatened suicide or retreat to a convent. But Paca's marriage provided Eugénie with frequent respites from her mother, and she began to spend as much time with her sister and brother-in-law at the Palacio de Liria as she did at home. Eugénie turned her affections toward her sister with whom she remained close until Paca's death from breast cancer in 1860.

After her first amorous disappointment, Eugénie perfected the art of the coquette—flirtatious and inviting, but eventually dismissive of

---

❧▶ **Paca** (1825–1860)

Duchess of Alba. Name variations: Francisca Teresa; Paquita. Born Maria Francisca in 1825; died of breast cancer in 1860; daughter of Cipriano Guzman y Porto Carrero, count of Teba (subsequently count of Montijo and grandee of Spain) and Manuela Kirkpatrick, countess of Montijo (daughter of William Kirkpatrick, U.S. consul at Malaga); sister of *Eugénie (1826–1920), empress of France; married the duke of Alba and Berwick.

any young admirer. One of her disappointed suitors was Louis Napoleon's cousin, Joseph Napoleon ("Plon-Plon"), who became enamored with her on a visit to Madrid in 1844. Now in her late teens, Eugénie was a dazzling beauty, but also something of a paradox. In contrast to the coldness she displayed to the young men of her acquaintance, she frequented bullfights and gypsy (Roma) camps, where she abandoned herself to the wild rhythms of the Flamenco. By some accounts, she was occasionally seen riding through the streets of Madrid with her hair flowing behind her and a cigarette clamped between her teeth. Her behavior, writes Duff, was both fascinating and repellent. "Her temper was quick and violent . . . and her voice was hard. She was often *difficile* and made clear her independence. She set high standards and was cruel in her censure if those standards were not met."

Shortly before her encounter with Napoleon III, Eugénie fell in love for a second time. The object of her affections was the worldly and wealthy Marques Pepe de Alcanizes, who was actually in love with Paca and used Eugénie to gain access to the Liria Palace. When Eugénie realized the situation, she was so humiliated that she attempted to kill herself by swallowing a home-brewed concoction of match heads and milk. It was only after Pepe further mortified her by visiting her bedside and requesting the return of his letters before she died, that Eugénie agreed to take an antidote. After this unfortunate affair, Manuela knew that, in order to marry off her difficult second daughter, she must leave Spain. Writes Bierman: "It was the start of a four-year Grand Tour in which an increasingly desperate mother vainly paraded a resolutely intransigent daughter around the marriage markets of Europe and the British Isles." While Manuela became known as the most energetic matchmaker in Europe, Eugénie rebuffed a trail of suitors.

During the early 1850s, Eugénie frequently appeared with her mother at the balls at the Élysée given by Prince Louis Napoleon, president of the Republic, nephew of the great French emperor, and soon to be Emperor Napoleon III; it was apparently at one of these affairs that Louis first noticed his future wife. Louis Napoleon, often referred to as "the sphinx of the Tuileries," was as much of an enigma as Eugénie. He was "compellingly likable," writes Bierman, but strange; "a dictator with democratic leanings, an imperialist who championed self-determination, a capitalist with socialist tendencies, a militarist who retched at the sight of a battlefield on the morning after."

At the time of his first encounter with Eugénie, Louis Napoleon, whose amatory exploits scandalized even the French, was romancing a mistress, *Elizabeth Ann Howard, and secretly conspiring to pull off a royal marriage to Princess *Adelaide of Hohenlohe-Langenburg, niece of Queen *Victoria. In November 1852, Manuela and Eugénie were invited to a hunt at Fontainebleau, and it was in that picturesque setting that Eugénie, beautifully turned out on one of the stable's finest thoroughbreds, captured Louis Napoleon's heart. One contemporary, obviously dazzled, described her attire:

> Her dainty figure was well-defined by a closely-buttoned habit; the skirt was long and wide, over grey breeches. With one of her tiny gloved hands she held the reins, while she used the other to urge on her excited horse with the help of a little riding-whip, the handle of which was set with pearls. She wore patent leather boots with high heels and spurs. She sat her horse like a knight, and despised the saddle ordinarily used by ladies.

That evening, Louis Napoleon gifted her with flowers, followed the next day by the horse she was riding. Dazzled by his attention and entertaining thoughts of the imperial crown, Eugénie nonetheless made it clear to him that the only path to her bedroom was through the wedding chapel. For the remainder of the festivities at Fontainebleau, tongues wagged. "That devil of a horse," Eugénie would later say.

In 1852, Louis Napoleon was proclaimed Napoleon III, emperor of the French, heightening the mission to marry and sire a son. Though there was no doubt about his allegiances, Napoleon waited for Adelaide's reply to his proposal before pursuing Eugénie, who now endured the intense scrutiny of ministers and royal watchers. Some of the most bitter opposition to Eugénie came from the beleaguered imperial family. Princess *Mathilde (1820–1904), Napoleon III's cousin, feared losing her position as the emperor's official hostess; Mathilde's brother Plon-Plon, once infatuated with Eugénie, faced the realization that with the birth of a male heir, he would have no hope of succeeding to the throne. Eventually, Princess Adelaide, heeding the advice of her family, refused Napoleon, stating in a dictated note that she did not feel capable of undertaking the job of empress. The emperor's long-time mistress Elizabeth Howard was subsequently dismissed with a settlement and a title.

On January 22, 1853, Napoleon III, appearing pale and drawn from strain, announced his engagement to Eugénie and justified what some

Eugénie

people considered a misalliance. "I have preferred," he said, "a woman whom I love and respect to an unknown one, an alliance with whom might with its advantages have brought the necessity for sacrifices. Without disrespect to anyone, I yield to my inclinations." On that same day, after moving into the Élysée Palace with Manuela (whom the emperor detested and bought off after the marriage), Eugénie wrote a melancholy letter to her sister, who would be unable to attend the nuptials because of the rushed wedding plans.

> This is a sad time. I am saying farewell to my family and my country in order to devote myself exclusively to the man who has loved me sufficiently to raise me up to his throne. . . . I fear the responsibilities that will weigh upon me, yet I am fulfilling my destiny. . . . On the eve of mounting one of the greatest thrones of Europe, I cannot help feeling somewhat terrified.

On January 30, 1853, after a civil ceremony at the Tuileries Palace on the preceding evening, Eugénie and Napoleon were married against the backdrop of the imposing Notre Dame Cathedral, which held some 2,800 spectators. By all accounts, the bride stole the day, appearing, wrote one historian, beside the sallow and paunchy emperor like "a captive fairy queen, her hair trimmed with orange blossoms, a diadem on her head." For the next few months, the couple appeared very much in love, although it is well documented that Eugénie barely endured her new husband's enamored advances, which were possibly less than sensitive to her inexperience. Her attitude toward sex was evident in a remark she made to a confidante: "But really, why do men never think of anything but *that*?" Napoleon was patient with his bride for six weeks before seeking the company of his former mistress, Elizabeth Howard.

In addition to the difficulties of the bedchamber, Eugénie found the day-to-day formalities of court stultifying, though compared to the courts of the old monarchies of Europe, it was brash, glittery, and nouveau riche. "I have gained a crown," she lamented to her sister, "but what does that mean, other than the fact that I am the leading slave of my kingdom?" In another letter to Paca, Eugénie complained of the constant round of balls and ceremonies and her lack of privacy. When the formality and tedium became too much, she would occasionally insist on an after-dinner game which she called "potting the candles," whereby guests would kick rubber balls in the direction of the candles until they had put them out. After six months, however, even these outbreaks of girlish energy subsided. Baron Josef von Hübner, the Austrian envoy wrote:

> She is no longer the young bride, the improvised sovereign. . . . She is the mistress of the house who is conscious of her position and asserts it by her manner, by her gestures, by the orders she gives to the ladies, by the glance—a little disdainful, a little blasé, but penetrating—with which she scans the hall allowing no detail to escape her.

Although intelligent, quick-witted, and forceful in manner, Eugénie lacked formal education and experience. Ignorant of history, politics, science, economics, and the arts, she appeared incapable of prolonged intellectual pursuits. Her ideas on religion were considered incongruous at best. While devoutly Catholic in practice, she followed the occult (fashionable at the time) and often held seances at court. According to Bierman, Eugénie also quickly lost any romantic illusions about her husband as a bold man of action. Having achieved his goal of supreme power, other facets of his personality came into play. "He was altogether too complex and cautious, too torn by the often contradictory elements in his political agenda, to conduct the affairs of France with the dash and decisiveness she had expected."

Although fully aware that her first priority as empress was to produce an heir, Eugénie was apparently not built to bear children easily. During the first year of her marriage, she suffered a miscarriage, apparently brought on by an overly hot bath taken to alleviate the pain of an accidental fall. The ordeal sidelined her for weeks and provoked a deep depression. "What might have been the sad fate of my child?" she asked Paca. "A thousand times I would prefer that a son of mine should wear a less brilliant but more secure crown." Napoleon, while voicing concern for Eugénie's welfare, satisfied his needs elsewhere. "I need my little amusements," he told his cousin, "but I always return to her with pleasure."

Three years into the marriage, after a second miscarriage, Eugénie produced an heir. Prince Napoleon Louis ("Lou-Lou") was born March 16, 1866. Both the pregnancy and delivery were difficult, and Eugénie was left so weak by the ordeal that it was not until May that she could walk without support. The doctor reported that another pregnancy might cost her her life. There would be no more children and no further physical relationship between husband and wife. Napoleon, suffering his own health problems, lost no time in adding to his growing list of amorous liaisons, which eventually included the Countess *Virginie de Castiglione (an Italian spy who was called "the most beautiful woman in Europe"), **Marianne Walewska** (the wife of the minister of Foreign Affairs), and **Marguerite Bellanger** (a circus stunt rider and would-be actress).

Accounts vary regarding Eugénie's reaction to her husband's philandering. Her detractors depict a vindictive woman, deprived of a conjugal role and dallying in affairs of state as consolation. Others saw her as maturing, realizing her limitations, and accepting a more enlightened view of her duties as empress. She was, after all, facing a less-than-predictable future. Her husband's rapidly declining health no doubt gave rise to concerns about preserving the French throne for her infant son. Another event, in 1858, cast an even more ominous shadow. On the evening of January 14, she and the emperor were the targets of an assassination attempt carried out by Felice Orsini and a small group of Italian terrorists who viewed Napoleon's regime as the keystone of European imperialism and suppression. As the royal carriage was pulling up to the steps of the Opera House on the Rue Lepelletier, an explosion rocked the street, followed by another and then a third. By a miracle, neither Eugénie nor the emperor were seriously hurt, although 12 were killed and many were wounded by the bombs. Though badly shaken and cut near the eye by a glass splinter, Eugénie displayed remarkable aplomb. "Let us show the assassins that we have more courage than them," she is quoted as saying. She then led her dazed husband into the theater to the front of the imperial box to show the audience they had escaped harm.

Whatever her motivation, Eugénie became increasingly more involved in the affairs of state, and Napoleon, physically weakened and perhaps remorseful over his own behavior, often let her have her way. Thrice, she acted as regent during the absence of the emperor (1859, 1865, and 1870), and she was generally consulted on significant issues. Against the wishes of the ministers, she often sat in on Ministerial Councils, where she slowly began to assert herself.

By about 1860, the emperor's approval rating among his subjects had fallen dramatically, and although Eugénie had certainly gained respect, she was still too Spanish and too reactionary to be totally embraced by the French. She believed that radicalism was a threat to the throne and should be forcefully repressed, a point of view increasingly at variance with that of her husband, who argued that reform was necessary to shore up the sagging popularity of his regime. On that point the emperor won, introducing a series of reforms in the 1860s that proved, however, to be neither effective nor popular.

Eugénie's influence in diplomacy proved more dominant and may have resulted in France's isolation from the other powers. By the end of the 1860s, there was speculation that the empire was approaching collapse. Eugénie felt an intense attachment to Pope Pius IX, who was so unpopular with his fellow Italians that he faced constant protest. The empress persuaded her husband to maintain a French army in Rome to protect the pontiff, a presence that was greatly resented by the Italian government. Eugénie was also involved in Napoleon's endorsement of the suicidal attempt by France to establish a puppet state in Mexico, under the rule of the Austrian Archduke Maximilian and *Carlota (1840–1927). To Eugénie, this would demolish the Mexican republican movement and serve as a counterweight to the United States, for which the conservative empress had little use. The French monarchs persuaded the reluctant archduke to accept the Mexican crown, convinced he would rule with wisdom and clemency under tutorial direction from Paris, and outfitted the army that would place this prize in his hands.

The expedition succeeded in establishing Maximilian on the throne in Mexico City, but he was even more unpopular among his subjects than Napoleon and Eugénie were with the French. He would soon become engaged in a civil war which would end in 1867 with his capture and execution. This would do much to satisfy the Americans and a number of European powers, who considered the entire Mexican adventure an example of Bonapartist hubris. Maximilian's death would be a mortifying blow to Eugénie and Napoleon and one that would soon be followed by an even more alarming development.

Of all of their neighbors, France had watched Prussia with the greatest suspicion, for it was wealthy, ambitious, and in possession of a large, well-trained army. From 1862, the king of Prussia had as his minister-president the most remarkable, and most ruthless, diplomat in Europe, Otto von Bismarck. Bismarck was determined that all of Germany was to be united under Prussia, an accomplishment that he knew would be strenuously opposed by Austria. In 1866, Bismarck had concocted a war with Austria which the Prussians won with a spectacular show of force. On the brink of victory, in 1867 Bismarck had proclaimed the union of northern Germany under Prussia, obviously a prelude to the acquisition of the southern states. Napoleon had declared that he would go to war with Prussia rather than see Germany united. To prepare, he ordered the French army in Mexico to come home, thus insuring Maximilian's defeat at the hands of the Mexican revolutionaries. Bismarck was a man who could not be intimidated by threats, and it seemed likely that when he believed Prussia was ready to take on France he would go to war.

Eugénie was now seriously alarmed. The failure to win popular support through domestic reforms, as well as the diplomatic disasters in Italy and Germany, had further eroded Napoleon's popularity, as well as her own. It could be restored, and the imperial crown secured for her son, only by a policy of fortitude and determination. When, in the summer of 1870, a crisis broke out between Prussia and France over the candidacy of a German prince for the crown of Spain, Eugénie relentlessly insisted that it was an issue that called for war unless Bismarck gave in. She believed that France would win and resisted those who argued that it would be more prudent to deal with the matter diplomatically. Bismarck matched Eugénie in determination and was equally as focused on war. He therefore refused any compromise, and, on July 1870, a reluctant Napoleon declared war on Prussia.

By the end of six weeks, Napoleon had been defeated at Sedan, had surrendered his army, and had been transported to Germany as a prisoner. Eugénie, worn down by her duties as regent (which included daily visits to the hospital units she had set up in the Tuileries) and anguished over the lack of information from the front, broke down upon hearing the news. "No, the Emperor has not surrendered!" she screamed at her acting secretaries. "A Napoleon never surrenders! . . . I tell you he is dead and they're trying to hide it from me." She then contradicted herself: "Why didn't he kill himself? Why didn't he have himself buried under the walls of Sedan? Could he not feel he was disgracing himself? What a name to leave to his son!" As was always the case with Eugénie, her fury was short-lived, and she soon resumed her duties as regent.

On the following day, September 4, with a mob storming the Tuileries, the dethroned empress and her 14-year-old son Lou-Lou, the prince imperial, fled for their lives from a side door in the palace and sought refuge with the emperor's American dentist, Dr. Evans. He arranged for them to proceed incognito to England, where Eugénie took up residence in a rented house in Camden Place, Chislehurst, which ironically belonged to an executor of the late Elizabeth Howard. It was two weeks before Eugénie was once again in contact with Napoleon. Her rage diminished, she was now moved by his outpouring of love, as well as his dignity in defeat. (It did not hurt that tales of his bravery in battle had enhanced his international reputation.) Quite alarming to her, however, was the state of his health, which had deteriorated even further. Bismarck eventually permitted Napoleon to join his family at Chislehurst, and the deposed emperor relished the quiet life of exile, although Eugénie found it necessary to break up the boredom with holidays in the West Country and a trip to Spain to visit her mother. Although the tide in France was turning and for a time it appeared that Napoleon might be returned to power, his health remained an obstacle. After surviving several operations to remove a kidney stone, he died unexpectedly on January 10, 1873, the morning of what was to be the final surgery.

While she had lost a husband, Eugénie gained a friend in Queen Victoria, who was also widowed by the death of Albert in 1861. Victoria not only supported Eugénie against the revenge of Plon-Plon, who was furious over being completely ignored in Napoleon's will, but also helped fill the gap left in the life of the prince imperial by the death of his father. Welcomed by Victoria on visits to Osborne and Windsor, the prince felt more at home with royalty than at his dreary house at Woolrich, where he was enrolled as a cadet. Although the queen joined Eugénie in efforts to stir up interest in France in a Bonapartist restoration for the prince, a wave of enthusiasm that had been envisaged in 1874, did not materialize. The young prince, who eventually became an officer in the British army, perished in a war against the Zulus in South Africa in 1879. Upon news of his death, Eugénie was inconsolable. "I am left alone," she wrote, "the sole remnant of a shipwreck; which proves how vain are the grandeurs of this world. . . . I cannot even die; and God, in his infinite mercy, will give me a hundred years of life." Eugénie later visited the spot of his death and brought back his body to be interred beside his father.

Now 54, Eugénie did not dwell upon her grief. After seeing to it that the memory of her husband and son were suitably enshrined in a mausoleum at her new property at Farnborough Hill, she led a full and active life up until a few days before her death. She divided her time between England and a villa she had built at Cape Martin on the Riviera. She traveled extensively by train and yacht and surrounded herself with the young and beautiful. She visited Queen Victoria each summer at Osborne Cottage on the Isle of Wight and in the autumn at Abergeldie Castle on Deeside, where she rode and fished. The death of Queen Victoria in 1901 left Eugénie the senior member of the sovereign class of Europe. Her dignity in exile won her great respect, and as war with Germany loomed again, diplomats sought her advice. Amazingly young for her age, even at 80, Eugénie continued to travel in Europe and the Mediterranean, and in 1906, she climbed Vesuvius. In July 1914, she attracted the attention of the press when, during a trip to Paris, she made a pilgrimage to her former homes: Fontainebleau, the ruins of St. Cloud, Compiègne, and Malmaison.

When England went to war (World War I), Eugénie opened a wing of Farnborough Hill as a hospital for wounded officers, just as she had at the Tuileries in 1870. She purchased medical equipment with her own money and hired young and attractive nurses, believing that the soldiers would recuperate faster if allowed a bit of flirting. "It will do them good to fall in love," she said. In 1920, Eugénie made a last visit to Madrid where she stayed with her relatives at the Palacio de Liria. While there, she underwent a successful cataract operation, which allowed her to see clearly for the first time in years. However, on June 10, she suddenly became ill and slipped away quietly the following day. "I am tired," the 94-year-old Eugénie whispered to a relative not long before the end, "and it is time for me to go away."

SOURCES:

Aronson, Theo. *The Fall of the Third Napoleon.* Indianapolis, IN: The Bobbs-Merrill, 1970.

Baker, Nancy N. *Distaff Diplomacy: The Empress Eugénie and the Foreign Policy of the Second Empires.* Austin, 1967.

Bierman, John. *Napoleon III and his Carnival Empire.* NY: St. Martin's Press, 1988.

De Soissons, Count. *The True Story of the Empress Eugénie.* London: Bodley Head.

Duff, David. *Eugenie and Napoleon III.* NY: William Morrow, 1978.

Fleury, Comte. *Memoirs of the Empress Eugenie.* Vols. I and II. NY: D. Appleton, 1920.

Kurtz, Harold. *The Empress Eugénie, 1826–1920.* Boston, 1964.

Ridley, Jasper. *Napoleon III and Eugénie.* New York, 1980.

Stacton, David. *The Bonapartes.* NY: Simon and Schuster, 1966.

Barbara Morgan,
Melrose, Massachusetts

Eugenie (1830–1889)

Swedish princess and composer. Name variations: Eugenie Bernadotte. Born Eugenie Charlotte Augusta Amalia Albertina on April 24, 1830; died on April 23, 1889; daughter of Queen *Josephine Beauharnais (1807–1876, granddaughter of *Joséphine and Napoleon), and Oscar I (1799–1859), king of Sweden (r. 1844–1859); sister of kings Charles XV and Oscar II.

Princess Eugenie was born in 1830, the daughter of Queen *Josephine Beauharnais and Sweden's king Oscar I, a man of considerable musical talent. Eugenie's own early interest in music and composing was seen as quite normal in the family. Her brother, Gustaf, also musically inclined, became known as the "singing prince." Princess Eugenie's compositions were largely for the piano and voice, but many were not heard outside Sweden because they were written in Swedish. Eugenie was one of the first members of the Royal Academy of Music, an organization in which her participation was important since women were only then beginning to be admitted to the ranks of musicians (until the mid-19th century, Sweden had a law prohibiting women from playing the organ). In addition to composing, Eugenie devoted her life to the arts and to charitable works.

John Haag,
Athens, Georgia

Eugénie Hortense (1808–1847)

Princess of Hohenzollern-Hechingen. Name variations: Eugenie Hortense de Beauharnais. Born on December 23, 1808; died on September 1, 1847; daughter of *Amalie Auguste (1788–1851) and Eugene de Beauharnais, duke of Leuchtenburg (d. 1824); married Frederick-William, a prince of Hohenzollern-Hechingen, on May 22, 1826.

Eulalia (290–304)

Roman Christian martyr and saint. Name variations: Eulalia of Barcelona. Born in 290; died in 304.

Born of Christian parents, Eulalia was a 14-year-old Roman virgin who was tortured then burned alive in 304 during the persecution of Diocletian. She had been determined to be a martyr for her faith. There is some confusion as to whether there were two Eulalias who died under similar circumstances—Eulalia of Barcelona and Eulalia of Mérida—or if this is one and the same girl. Highly honored in Spain, Saint Eulalia of Barcelona's feast day is on February 12. Eulalia of Mérida is celebrated on December 10.

Eulalia (b. 1864)

Spanish princess and duchess of Galliera. Name variations: Eulalia de Asis de la Piedad, infanta of Spain. Born Mary Eulalia Francesca di Assisi Margaret Roberta Isabel Francesca de Paola Christine Maria de la Piedad in 1864; daughter of *Isabella II (1830–1904), queen of Spain, and Francisco de Asiz; married Anthony or Antoine Bourbon, 4th duke of Galliera; children: Alphonso Bourbon, 5th duke of Galliera (b. 1886).

Eulogia Paleologina (fl. 1200s)

Byzantine of the Paleologi family. Name variations: Eulogia (Irene) of Byzantium; Irene Paleologina or Palaeologina. Daughter of Andronicus Paleologus and *Theodora Paleologina; sister of Michael VIII Paleologus, emperor of Nicaea (r. 1261–1282); children: Maria Paleologina (fl. 1278–1279, who married Constantine Tich and Ivajlo, both tsars of Bulgaria); *Anna Paleologina-Cantacuzene (fl. 1270–1313).

Eumetis (fl. 570 BCE).

See Cleobulina of Rhodes.

Eunice

Biblical woman. Daughter of Lois; children: Timothy.

Eunice, a Jew married to a Gentile, was distinguished by her "unfeigned faith." She was the mother of Timothy, and the apostle Paul credited Eunice and her mother **Lois** with training Timothy in the Scriptures (2 Tim. 3:15).

Euphemia (fl. 1100s)

Lady Annandale. Name variations: Lady Annandale; Euphemia Bruce. Married Robert Bruce, 2nd Lord of Annandale; children: Robert Bruce, 3rd Lord of Annandale, and William Bruce, 4th Lord of Annandale.

Euphemia (1317–after 1336)

*Duchess of Mecklenburg. Name variations: Euphemia Eriksdottir or Ericsdottir. Born in 1317; died after April 10, 1336; daughter of *Ingeborg (c. 1300–c. 1360) and Eric Magnusson, duke of Südermannland; sister of Magnus VII Eriksson, king of Norway and Sweden; married Albert II (1318–1379), duke of Mecklenburg, on April 10, 1336; children: Albert (1340?–1412), duke of Mecklenburg and king of Sweden (r. 1365–1388); Henry of Mecklenburg (who married *Ingeborg [1347–1370]);* **Ingeburg of Mecklenburg** *(who married Henry II, duke of Holstein).*

Euphemia of Kiev (d. 1139)

Queen of Hungary. Died on April 4, 1139; daughter of Vladimir II (b. 1053), grand duke of Kiev; married Koloman also known as Coloman (b. around 1070), king of Hungary (r. 1095–1114), in 1104 (divorced in 1113); children: one daughter (name unknown).

Euphemia of Pomerania (d. 1330)

Queen of Denmark. Name variations: Eufemia; Euphamia of Pommerania. Died on July 26, 1330; married Christopher II (1276–1332), king of Denmark (r. 1319–26, 1330–1332); children: Eric, king of Denmark (r. 1321–1326, 1330–1332); Waldemar IV Atterdag, king of Denmark (r. 1340–1375); Otto, duke of Loland and Estland; Agnes Christofsdottir (d. 1312); **Heilwig Christofsdottir;** *Margaret Christofsdottir (c. 1305–1340).*

Euphemia of Rugen (d. 1312)

*Queen of Norway. Name variations: Euphamia von Rügen. Died on May 1, 1312; daughter of Wizlaw II, prince of Rügen; married Haakon V Longlegs (1270–1319), king of Norway (r. 1299–1319), in 1299; children: *Ingeborg (c. 1300–c. 1360);* **Agnes Haakonsdottir** *(who married Hafthor Jonson).*

Euphemia Ross (d. 1387).

See Ross, Euphemia.

Euphrasia of Constantinople

(d. around 412)

Saint. Died around 412; daughter of Antigonus; mother's name unknown.

Having lost her father when she was only a year old, Euphrasia of Constantinople became the ward of a relative, Emperor Theodosius I the Great. When Euphrasia was just five, Theodosius promised her in marriage to the son of a wealthy senator, but her mother managed to have the nuptials put off until the child reached marriageable age. Her mother then fled with Euphrasia to Egypt, settling near a convent where the child was received as a nun at the age of seven. Following her mother's death a short time later, Euphrasia was called upon to honor the marriage promise. In a letter to the emperor, the young nun begged to be released from the betrothal. "Knowing, invincible emperor, that I have promised Jesus Christ to live in continual continence, would you have me violate my promise by marrying a mortal man, destined to become the prey of worms?" Euphrasia further asked that any possessions left to her by her parents be disposed of among the orphans, the poor, and the churches. She also requested that her slaves be freed and her farmers released from their debts, "so that it may be possible for me to serve God in future without any cares." The emperor communicated Euphrasia's message to the senate, where it was deemed that her religious commitment superseded the marriage agreement. Euphrasia remained in the convent until her death at the age of 30. Her feast day is on March 13.

Euphrosine.

Variant of Euphrosyne.

Euphrosine (d. 1102)

Countess and ruler of Vendôme (r. 1085–1102). Reigned from 1085 to 1102; died in 1102; sister of Count Bouchard III, ruler of Vendôme (1066–1085); married Geoffroi Jourdain, sire de Previlly.

Euphrosine became countess and ruler of Vendôme upon the death of her brother, Count Bouchard III. She was succeeded by Count Geoffroi Grisegonella.

Euphrosyne (c. 790–840)

Byzantine empress and supporter of Iconophiles. Pronunciation: YOU-fro-SOON-ey. Born in Constantinople around 790; died in 840; daughter of Maria of Amnia and Constantine VI Porphyrogenitus, Byzantine emperor (r. 780–797); second wife of Michael II of Amorion, Byzantine emperor (r. 820–829); children: (stepchild) Theophilus.

Euphrosyne was the daughter of the Byzantine emperor Constantine VI and the granddaughter of the empress *Irene of Athens (c. 752–802). Reportedly beautiful, she had little interest in participating in public life and entered the convent on the island of Prinkipo where she lived with her mother *Maria of Amnia. She was later married to the emperor Michael II (820–29) after the death of his first wife *Thecla. Michael chose Euphrosyne because of her ties to the imperial family, but, since she was also a nun, the marriage was considered unseemly and brought condemnation from leading Byzantine churchmen. Euphrosyne did not have children but became stepmother to the future emperor Theophilus (r. 829–842). For her stepson, she arranged a "bride-show" whereby a group of women deemed worthy to become the future empress were selected from different regions of the empire and brought to Constantinople to be interviewed by Theophilus. He chose the future empress and regent *Theodora the Blessed (r. 842–856) to be his wife.

At this time, the Byzantine emperors were promoting the religious policy of iconoclasm whereby the use of the icon in religious worship was forbidden, and they ordered the destruction of any artwork that depicted religious figures. Theodora and Euphrosyne, however, both favored the restoration of the icons in Orthodox worship. After Theophilus succeeded to the throne, Euphrosyne returned to the convent at Prinkipo. Theophilus later learned that she was secretly venerating the icons in her convent with his daughters, including St. *Thecla and *Anastasia. He then prohibited his daughters from ever visiting their stepmother again. Euphrosyne died in 840. Theophilus' wife Theodora would later bring about the formal restoration of the icons after her husband's death.

SOURCES:

Bekker, I., ed. *Theophanes Continuatus.* Bonn: Corpus Scriptorum Historiae Byzantinae, 1838.

Bury, J.B. *A History of the Eastern Roman Empire.* London, 1912.

SUGGESTED READING:

Ostrogorsky, George. *History of the Byzantine State.* 2nd ed. New Brunswick, NJ: Rutgers University Press, 1968.

Treadgold, Warren. *A History of the Byzantine State and Society.* Stanford, CA: Stanford University Press, 1997.

Vasiliev, A.A. *History of the Byzantine Empire, 324–1453.* Madison, WI: University of Wisconsin Press, 1952.

Dr. John F. Shean,
Visiting Assistant Professor,
Clarion University of Pennsylvania

Euphrosyne (fl. 1200s)

Byzantine princess. Flourished in the 1200s; illegitimate daughter of Michael VIII, Byzantine emperor (r. 1259–1282); married Nogaj.

Euphrosyne (d. 1203)

*Empress of Byzantium. Name variations: Euphrosyne Doukaina Kamatera or Docaina Kamatera; Euphrosine. Died in 1203 in Constantinople; married Alexius III Angelus, emperor of Byzantium (r. 1195–1203); children: *Irene (who married Alexius Paleologus); ❧ Anna Angelina (d. 1210?, who married Theodore I Lascaris, Nicaean emperor); *Eudocia Angelina.*

Little is known about Euphrosyne's family or early years. She married the future emperor of Byzantium, Alexius III Angelus, a greedy man whose ambition led him to mutilate and depose his own brother in order to ascend the throne in 1095. He then adopted the surname Comnenus to associate himself in the minds of the Byzantine people with the great Comneni emperors of the past. Alexius allowed Euphrosyne to co-rule with him, giving her authority over many domestic affairs while he concentrated on foreign policy issues. An unpopular empress, Euphrosyne was disliked by her subjects for her corrupt politics and lavish lifestyle.

Laura York,
Riverside, California

Euphrosyne of Kiev (fl. 1130–1180)

Queen of Hungary. Name variations: Euphrosine. Daughter of Mstislav, prince of Kiev, and Ljubava Saviditsch (d. 1167); married Geza II (1130–1161), king of Hungary (r. 1141–1161), in 1146; children: Stephen III (c. 1147–1173), king of Hungary (r. 1161–1173); Bela III (1148–1196), king of Hungary (r. 1173–1196).

Euphrosyne of Opole (d. 1293)

Mother of Ladislas I, king of Poland. Died in 1293; married Casimir of Kujawy; children: Leszek II the Black, duke of Cracow; Wladyslaw I the Short also

◀❧

Anna Angelina.
See Irene Lascaris for sidebar.

known as Ladislas I Lokietek, king of Poland (r. 1306–1333); Siemowit of Dobrzyn.

Eurydice (c. 410–350s BCE)

Macedonian who saved the throne for her two living sons against royal pretenders and whose most famous son, Philip II, made Macedonia a world power and united the Greek world under his authority. Born around 410 BCE; died in the 350s BCE; daughter of Sirrhas, king of Lyncus in northwestern Macedonia; married Amyntas III of lower Macedonia, around 393; married Ptolemy of Alorus; children: (first marriage) daughter Eurynoe; sons Alexander II, Perdiccas III, and Philip II, all of whom ruled Macedonia.

Eurydice was born around 410 into the royal family of Lyncus in northwestern Macedonia. This strategic realm lay between Illyria (to the north and west) and lowland Macedonia (to the east); through it ran the best east-west land route in northern Greece. Her family had intermarried with the Illyrian aristocracy in the 5th century, which explains the Illyrian origin of her father's name, Sirrhas. At the beginning of the 4th century, a powerful Illyrian state began to coalesce to the northwest of Lyncus, and this power threatened both Lyncus and the other regions of Macedonia which lay to the east of Eurydice's native canton.

In 393, after seven years of civil war had devastated his realm, and with the Illyrians supporting an alternative candidate for the Argead throne of lower Macedonia, Amyntas III both assumed the Macedonian throne and married Eurydice in an attempt to shore up his northwestern frontier. In this Amyntas was only partially successful, for in the 380s yet another in a series of devastating raids from Illyria swept across Macedonia. Nevertheless, the support that Eurydice brought to Amyntas from her natal family helped him to weather this and other crises, and as a result he enjoyed a long—if hardly prosperous—reign.

Argead kings were polygamous. Amyntas' first wife was a fellow kinswoman named **Gygaea**, whom he had married in order to fortify his initial claim to the Argead throne. So important was Eurydice and the support she brought to Amyntas' battered reign, however, that she came to replace Gygaea as Amyntas' principal wife within only a brief time of their marriage. Indeed, Eurydice's prestige was so high in Macedonia that her three sons (Alexander II, Perdiccas III, and Philip II) came to replace the three sons of Gygaea in the line of royal succession. As a result, when Amyntas III died in 370, his oldest son, Alexander II succeeded without difficulty.

Alexander, however, was reform minded (he hoped to augment the military might of his aristocracy by the development of an equally powerful middle class, from which he wanted to draft an infantry for the better defense of his realm), and many within his kingdom feared a loss of influence if conditions in Macedonia substantially changed. As a result, after a reign of less than two years, Alexander was assassinated. Probably involved in the plot was another Argead, Ptolemy of Alorus. Since Alexander's two younger brothers were too young to rule for themselves, Ptolemy claimed the regency of Macedonia after Alexander's death. This Ptolemy (once the husband of Eurydice's daughter **Eurynoe**) also displayed his royal ambitions by marrying Eurydice. Undoubtedly, Eurydice agreed to marry her one-time son-in-law and the probable conspirator in her son's murder because she thereby hoped to protect her two youngest sons from death. Indeed, both survived into adulthood.

The throne of Macedonia thus thrown open, between 368 and 365 other royal pretenders attempted to seize royal authority. One, a Pausanias, was close to succeeding until Eurydice, in a personal appeal to the Athenian mercenary general Iphicrates, convinced him to save the throne for her sons. Her appeal was successful, and when Perdiccas came of age in 365 he celebrated his accession with the murder of Ptolemy, thus avenging the death of his brother. Perdiccas ruled for five years, and fathered one son (an Amyntas), while overseeing the reconstruction of Macedonian society which had been hard hit by war over the last generation. So successful was he that the Illyrians began to see him as a threat to their regional hegemony, resulting in yet another massive invasion of Macedonia in 360. When this occurred, Perdiccas was killed with most of his army, and Macedonia was thrown back into a state of chaos. Perdiccas' heir, Amyntas, was too young to assume royal duties in 360, and thus after a short time he was replaced as king by his uncle Philip II, the youngest of Eurydice's sons.

Philip II would go on to become famous for his restoration of Macedonian security, for his extension of Macedonian power throughout the north (the first major power to feel his wrath were the Illyrians), for his subjection of the Greeks of southern Greece, and perhaps mostly for his being the father of Alexander the Great.

Despite his greatness, however, Philip never forgot the debt he owed to Eurydice. Late in life, he began the construction of a dynastic monument at the famous religious sanctuary of Zeus at Olympia in which he prominently placed a statue of his mother. In another indication of Philip's affection for Eurydice, when Athenian diplomats were attempting to win favors for Athens from Philip after he had proven his power, at least one of their number realized that one way to get into Philip's good graces was by evoking the memory of his mother, who in the mid-360s had employed an Athenian to save the kingdom of Macedonia for her line. When Eurydice died is unknown, but it is doubtful that she lived long into her third son's reign.

SUGGESTED READING:

Justin. *Epitome of the Philippic History*. Scholars Press, 1994 (especially Book Seven).

Macurdy, Grace. *Hellenistic Queens*. Johns Hopkins Press, 1932.

William Greenwalt, Associate Professor of Classical History, Santa Clara University

Eurydice (c. 337–317 BCE)

Granddaughter of two Macedonian kings who met Olympias in a decisive battle. Name variations: Adea Eurydice. Born Adea shortly before the accession of Alexander III the Great, her second cousin-uncle-stepbrother-in-law, around 337 BCE; died in 317 BCE; daughter of Cynnane (who was the daughter of Philip II of Macedonia and his Illyrian wife, Audata) and Amyntas (son of Perdiccas III); granddaughter of *Eurydice (c. 410–350s BCE); married Arrhidaeus (Philip III).

Eurydice's mother *Cynnane was the daughter of **Audata**, an Illyrian, and Philip II of Macedonia. Eurydice's father Amyntas was the son of Perdiccas III, who was Philip II's older brother and royal predecessor (r. 365–360). When Perdiccas lost his life trying to defend his realm from a massive Illyrian invasion, Amyntas was very young. Although he seems to have been acknowledged as Macedonia's monarch for a brief period, the intensity of the crisis brought on by Illyrian devastation forced the Macedonians to replace Amyntas with Philip II, who was a militarily adept adult. Philip quickly proved himself worthy of his elevation by defeating the Illyrians and others who attempted to take advantage of Macedonia's temporary collapse. As part of the treaty which won for Macedonia at least a temporary peace along its northwestern Illyrian frontier, Philip married Audata—the daughter of Bardylis, Philip's now defeated Illyrian adversary. This was Philip's first of seven marriages, and it produced a daughter, Cynnane.

After his accession to the throne, Philip proved more compassionate than most other Macedonian kings. Those newly elevated to the Argead throne of Macedonia usually disposed of all potential royal rivals, but Philip did not execute his nephew Amyntas. Instead, Amyntas was raised at Philip's court, perhaps originally as his heir. Whatever might have been Philip's intention, even after 356 when his wife *Olympias gave birth to Alexander III (who would become the "Great")—thus even after Philip had begun to father sons of his own—Amyntas remained close to Philip, eventually marrying his oldest daughter, Cynnane, when both were of an appropriate age (c. 338). This union produced their daughter Adea (who would later be known as Eurydice or Adea Eurydice) in either 337 or 336.

Soon after her birth, disaster struck Eurydice's immediate family, beginning in October 336 with the shocking assassination of King Philip (by a disgruntled, dishonored Macedonian aristocrat) just days before the great man was to embark on an invasion of Asia (18 months later, this invasion would be pursued by Alexander III). Philip's murder brought Alexander III to the Macedonian throne and completely reconfigured the existing relationships with the Argead royal house. By proving himself worthy of Macedonia's throne by expelling enemies from its land, Philip had been able to consolidate his hold on the throne before Amyntas was old enough to put forth any royal claim of his own. Older now, Amyntas threatened his cousin's accession as he never had Philip's. Not only was Amyntas the senior of Alexander III, but also, as a youth Amyntas had probably actually been recognized, albeit for a brief period, as the Macedonian king. In addition, although Alexander had held important positions under Philip, he had yet to prove his competence as an independent leader. Already insecure about his accession because of a number of problems he had had with Philip before the latter's murder, Alexander III acted decisively to seize the kingship. Among the steps quickly taken in the wake of Philip's death was the execution of Amyntas, Eurydice's father, at Alexander's command.

Alexander III gave some thought to Eurydice's mother Cynnane immediately after the death of Amyntas, when he sought to marry her to a minor prince named Langarus from Paeonia to the northeast of Macedonia. Alexander's interests in the union were self-serving, for not only would he tie Langarus more closely to himself with the gift of a half-sister, but also, by marrying Cynnane to a figure everyone (except the Paeonians) thought beneath her status, he would eliminate the possibility of her marrying a greater threat to his interests. (This was a time when marriages were arranged by the head of a family. Now that Alexander III had succeeded his father as the head of the Argead house, he controlled the marriages of all of those closely related to him—even those numbered among his victims.) Nevertheless, when Langarus died before the marriage occurred, Alexander gave up on seeing Cynnane remarried, probably thinking that most prospective grooms had the capacity to do him more harm than good.

Cynnane thereafter seems to have abandoned the Macedonian court for the refuge of a country estate, where she reared Eurydice (as Cynnane had been reared by Audata) in the fashion of Illyrian aristocratic women—in a military manner. We know little about this pair as long as Alexander III lived, but it is clear from subsequent events that Eurydice was also trained to loathe Alexander and all connected with his dynastic line. Doubtless the murder of Amyntas was not only emotionally traumatic, but a sharp blow to the hope that future Argead kings would be produced from Cynnane and Amyntas' marriage. As a result, Eurydice was raised as the son Amyntas never had. She was cautioned to bide her time against the moment when the opportunity for vengeance might present itself.

Most of Alexander's reign was spent in his conquest of Persia (334–323). While Alexander III was away, Macedonia was left under the joint control of Antipater (an established figure who held the position of general for European Affairs), his mother Olympias, and full sister, ◄ Cleopatra (354 BCE–?). The precise roles intended for the women of Alexander's family were never clearly defined, but they did function in an official capacity. It is likely that their authorities were established so that persons with identical interests to Alexander's would look after those interests in his absence.

Alexander's premature death (he was not yet 33) at Babylon in June of 323 BCE, however, precipitated a crisis that provided Cynnane and Eurydice with the opportunity for which they had long prayed in their political exile. Although Alexander III had three official wives (the last two only lately acquired), none had given birth to any children before he died. *Roxane (his first official wife), however, was five months pregnant during the fateful month of Alexander's

Cleopatra (354 BCE–?). See Olympias for sidebar.

death. (It should be noted that Alexander probably had been the father of a son, Heracles, by an earlier sexual liaison with a woman named *Statira. Yet, since the boy had never officially been acknowledged by Alexander, Heracles played only a peripheral role in the successional crisis stimulated by Alexander's death.)

The situation at Babylon in 323 was unprecedented in the history of the Argead dynasty going back more than 300 years: with the sudden removal of Alexander III, there was no Argead who could reasonably assume the Macedonian throne. Since about 650 BCE, Macedonia had been ruled by the scion of the Argead house; since kingship in the dynasty occasionally skipped from one collateral branch of the family to another, the only absolute essential for a would-be Macedonian king was that he be a male of the royal house. The duties of Argead kingship involved many religious obligations on a daily basis, and, for whatever reason, it was generally believed that only a member of the Argead family could fulfill the necessary religious responsibilities on behalf of the entire realm.

At the time of Alexander's death, there was one living male of the Argead house, Alexander's half-brother, Arrhidaeus. This Arrhidaeus was the son of Philip II by his wife **Philinna** and almost as old as Alexander. Arrhidaeus, however, was mentally incompetent and not up to the rigorous demands placed upon Macedonian kings. When the most important officers at Babylon at the time of Alexander's death got together under another Perdiccas (a general to whom Alexander had given his signet ring of state just before he had breathed his last) to discuss the succession, they overlooked Arrhidaeus as a suitable candidate for the kingship. Their solution was that an interim regency composed of themselves would rule until Roxane gave birth, at which time, if the child were male, he would be acclaimed the king, again to be guided by these regents for years until he came of age.

Fraught with difficulties, this arrangement was immediately unpopular with the army's rank and file, who smelled conspiracy. This latter group, having seen Arrhidaeus recently associating with Alexander in important religious ceremonies, was unaware of his mental incompetency (after all, most royalties do not broadcast their family's infirmities). They demanded that Arrhidaeus be hailed as king immediately. The stage was thereby set for a split between most of the Macedonian officer corps at Babylon and their men—a split which threatened to break out into open violence (which no one wanted, since the army was hundreds of miles from home, without an acknowledged leader, amidst an empire which was not yet wholly pacified) until the compromise of the dual monarchy was established.

By this arrangement, Arrhidaeus was promoted to the throne at once (where he could officiate over the essential religious rituals and satisfy the rank and file that an Argead was still in control). It was also agreed that if Roxane had a son, he would share the throne with his uncle. When Roxane gave birth to Alexander IV in the fall of 323 BCE, Macedonia had its first ever dual monarchy, albeit one in which neither king was competent to act in his, or the realm's, best interests. When Arrhidaeus was elevated, he received the throne name Philip III. Throne names were not common in Macedonia, but since Arrhidaeus had lived a fairly private life and was thus unfamiliar to most of his subjects, and since names were used within the Argead family to indicate blood descent (and thus political affiliation), it was thought best to insure, through the new name, that everybody understood Arrhidaeus to have been the legitimate son of Philip II.

Almost immediately, the fragile nature of the dual monarchy made itself manifest. Perdiccas began to assume a larger role for himself than many of his peers thought had been warranted by his relative position under Alexander the Great. Perdiccas had been fortunate that Alexander had died when he did, for, although he was among the highest ranking of the generals at Babylon at that time, Alexander had shown him no exceptional honor that might be interpreted as empowering him to arrange the royal succession. No Macedonian respected Perdiccas as much as they respected Antipater (still in Macedonia) or Craterus (the general recently dispatched by Alexander from Babylon to Macedonia with a force of older Macedonians returning to their homes and retirement). Thus, when Perdiccas began to manipulate his position as the guardian of the two kings by issuing all sorts of orders in their names—orders that looked to many to have been more in Perdiccas' interest than in the interests of the kings or their empire—many of those who considered themselves to be Perdiccas' colleagues, not his subordinates, began first to grumble and then to fortify themselves against his unwarranted exploitation of current circumstances.

Since the very unity of Alexander's empire was at stake, some sought to reinforce the relationships among the most important Macedonian generals. In particular, Antipater began to

forge an alliance by marrying his daughters— ❧▸ Nicaea and ❧▸ Eurydice (fl. 321 BCE)—to the foremost of his contemporaries, including Perdiccas. Antipater did everything he could to quiet potential rivalries within the royal house, knowing full well that two kings meant two potentially volatile factions, each of which could develop strong reasons for eliminating its opposition. Initially, Antipater was particularly concerned with Olympias, for he had long hated this grandmother of Alexander IV for what he considered to be her meddling in his European affairs while Alexander III had been in Asia. But Antipater was soon threatened from another royal source as well. When Cynnane learned that the unmarried, incompetent, Philip III had been proclaimed king, and that Perdiccas had brought him to Anatolia (where Perdiccas was campaigning both to conquer areas not previously approached by Alexander and to consolidate his personal power over the royal administration), she plotted to see her daughter Eurydice and Philip III married.

◂❧
Nicaea. See
*Arsinoe II
Philadelphus* for
sidebar.

◂❧
**Eurydice (fl. 321
BCE).** See
Berenice I for
sidebar.

After marrying and soon losing Amyntas, the son of Perdiccas, [Cynnane] did not venture to take a chance on a second husband, but she trained her only daughter [Eurydice] for war.

—Polyaenus *Stratagems* 8.61

Cynnane and Eurydice fled Macedonia against the will of both Antipater and Olympias, escaping only after they routed the military force sent to retain them. In Asia, Perdiccas, equally anxious to prevent Eurydice's marriage to Philip, sent his brother, Alcetas, to arrest the two Argead women. In the fracas which arose when neither Cynnane nor Eurydice recognized the authority of Alcetas, Cynnane was slain. When Perdiccas' army learned of Cynnane's fate, they were horrified that a daughter of Philip II had been killed by a Macedonian seeking to intrude into the politics of royal succession. Rebelling against Perdiccas' opposition to the proposed match, the army forced him to allow the marriage. Thus Eurydice—probably not yet 15 and on her own—married her uncle Philip and foiled the will of many powerful adversaries. Upon her marriage to Philip III, Eurydice, still known as Adea, assumed the throne name Eurydice, as a clear indication of her own ambition. The last Argead *Eurydice (c. 410–350s BCE) had been the mother of Philip II, who in the mid-360s BCE had saved the throne of Macedonia against a pretender from a collateral branch of the royal family. The younger Eurydice now planned to do the same for hers, hoping to have children by Philip III who would displace the line of Alexander III as Macedonia's future monarchs. The name Eurydice was also important in another sense, for Olympias had become the most important woman of the Argead court by replacing Philip's mother Philinna in that capacity. Such transitions of influence are never accomplished without some ill will, and it can be assumed that the elder Eurydice had resented the rise of Olympias. Thus, by becoming a new Eurydice, Adea was laying down the gauntlet: a new Eurydice (and her dynastic interests) would replace the queen who had "usurped" the status of the old Eurydice. The genius of this name adoption came in the new Eurydice's ability to claim to be the true successor of the old Eurydice, being twice her descendent through Perdiccas III and Philip II. Olympias, on the other hand, may have had a noteworthy son, but his seed had yet to take root, and it represented a parallel descent which may have been legitimated through Philip, but which did not combine—as the new Eurydice's line would—the claims of both Perdiccas' and Philip's lines.

Although the general Perdiccas kept Eurydice in check for a time, other circumstances conspired to ruin him. One of the biggest mistakes he made occurred while he was in Anatolia, where he was approached with two offers of marriages. The first came from Antipater, who offered his daughter Nicaea to Perdiccas as a token of his willingness to work together with the guardian of the kings. Although Perdiccas diplomatically accepted, when a second offer came from Olympias, offering the hand of her now widowed daughter, Cleopatra, he hesitated, knowing that a marriage to Alexander the Great's sister would elevate him above his aristocratic colleagues in the eyes of common Macedonians. Aware, however, that a marriage to Cleopatra would alienate Antipater and lead other generals to suspect his ambitions, Perdiccas declined Olympias' offer. But he did not decline in time, for he delayed just long enough to worry his rivals. One Antigonus, already at odds with Perdiccas over the latter's Anatolian policy, fled Asia Minor for Europe where he revealed to Antipater and Craterus Olympias' offer and—more important—Perdiccas' temptation. Taken into consideration with other factors—including the growing hostility between Perdiccas and Ptolemy (the satrap of Egypt), made all the more explosive by Ptolemy's hijacking of Alexander the Great's corpse to Egypt—Perdiccas' reflection on a marriage with Cleopatra stimulated a war between Antipater, Craterus, and Ptolemy on the one hand, and the faction of Perdiccas on the other. This war led to Perdiccas' assassination (321) at the hands of his own officers, when his attempt to invade Egypt proved a miserable failure.

Shortly after Perdiccas' death, the kings and Eurydice fell under the control of Antipater, who, however, only took possession of the royal pawns after Eurydice staged a nearly successful mutiny intended to give her sole control of her childlike husband. On the Palestinian coast, before Antipater had made his peace with Perdiccas' army and claimed the kings, Eurydice professed that she and her husband had no need for an aristocratic guardian, since Philip, with her help, was capable of ruling on his own behalf. (The status of Alexander IV was ominously left out of the discussion.) Using the army's unrest over not being paid for some time, Eurydice was able to rouse the Macedonians on hand against those who would "use" the troops against the interests of the established royal dynasty (as represented by herself and her husband). A talented speaker, Eurydice almost incited a full-scale riot as Antipater approached their camp. Just in the nick of time, however, Antipater and Antigonus were able to cow the army and gain control of the situation. The two asserted their status as established generals, while convincing the army that this young queen, however noble, was but a novice in the complicated game of politics. Antipater railed against Eurydice as a new Olympias and declared to his men that they had better beware of political women. Military reputations dominated the day, Eurydice's effort was aborted, and Antipater saw to it that she would be given no such second chance. Hurriedly, Antipater made his way back to Macedonia where he remained with the kings under strict control until he died in 319. During these last two years of Antipater's life, Olympias lived in her native Epirus, which was fine with Antipater, who may have hated Olympias but saw the future of the Argead dynasty in Alexander IV, whom the old general hoped to school against his grandmother.

Although Antipater intended to provide the steady hand which would allow the Argead dynasty to survive its hiatus of incompetence, he did not live long enough to resolve the dynastic crisis. Clearly, Antipater saw little promise in Philip III and was certainly pleased that whatever ailed Philip's mind seemed to have prevented him from fathering a dynastic complication by Eurydice. Yet Antipater made a critical error in choosing his own successor as guardian of the kings, Philip and the young Alexander. He chose not his own son, Cassander, but a trusted friend named

Polyperchon. Why Antipater overlooked Cassander is unknown, but his choice of Polyperchon split his party and caused Cassander to rebel, not against the kings, but against Polyperchon. In an attempt to stabilize his personal authority, Polyperchon recalled Olympias to Macedonia, hoping the fame of her son would break Cassander's rebellion. However, Eurydice, rightly fearing that Olympias' return would mean the deaths of herself and Philip III, fled with her husband from Polyperchon's camp (Alexander IV remained with Polyperchon, beyond Eurydice's reach). Thereafter, Eurydice announced on behalf of her husband the demotion of Polyperchon, her own assumption of Philip's guardianship, and her promotion of Cassander as the general who would insure the final enthronement of Philip as Macedonia's true king.

The Argead house was now openly split into two factions, each led by the chief woman proponent of a royal heir. The Macedonian nation was itself split in two behind the two royal parties. In the climactic moment of the subsequent conflict, Olympias (Polyperchon being otherwise involved) invaded Macedonia from the west with an army she collected from Epirus. Eurydice (Cassander also being otherwise involved) raised an army of her own in defense. As the two armies approached each other, Olympias—having a better feel for what the soldiers present considered appropriate behavior for a woman—attired herself in the robes of a devotee of Dionysus. Eurydice, in the manner of *Joan of Arc, went to battle dressed as a man.

But before battle was engaged (the first ever in Greece to be commanded by two opposing women), the Macedonians proved unable to follow an Illyrian-like queen into battle against the great Alexander's mother. As a result, they surrendered to Olympias and betrayed both Philip III and Eurydice (317 BCE). Within weeks, Philip had been starved to death, and Eurydice forced to commit suicide, as a triumphant Olympias removed the obstacle to the acceptance of her grandson as Macedonia's sole monarch. Of course, Alexander IV was still young, and Olympias expected to rule in his stead for at least a decade.

Olympias' rule, however, was harsh, especially against the family and supporters of Antipater's and Cassander's family. When her brutality (made all the more harsh after having fought for so long for the status she thought she innately deserved) became too much for Macedonia to bear, the disenchanted realm turned ironically to Cassander in enough numbers that

he captured Olympias and saw to her death (316). Although Alexander IV would stay alive for a few years under Cassander's house arrest (or as Cassander put it, Alexander's "protection"), the time eventually came when the young king was anonymously assassinated (310), thereby exterminating the Argead house. What followed was an age dominated by Alexander the Great's one-time marshals desperately seeking a way to legitimize their respective authorities carved, by force, from the carcass of a rapidly decaying empire.

SOURCES:

Diodorus. *Universal History.* Vol. IX. Cambridge, MA: Harvard University Press, 1947.

Polyaenus. *Stratagems of War.* 2 vols. Ares Press, 1994.

SUGGESTED READING:

Macurdy, Grace H. *Hellenistic Queens.* MD: Johns Hopkins University Press, 1932.

William Greenwalt,
Associate Professor of Classical History,
Santa Clara University, Santa Clara, California

Eurydice (fl. 321 BCE).

See Berenice I for sidebar.

Euryleonis (fl. 368 BCE).

See Bilistiche for sidebar.

Eusebia of Bergamo (fl. 3rd c.)

Saint and martyr. Died the end of the 3rd century; niece of St. Domnius. Her feast day is on October 29.

Eusebia of Macedonia (fl. 300 CE)

Byzantine empress. Flourished around 300 CE; second wife of Constantius II, Eastern Roman emperor (r. 337–361).

Eustis, Dorothy (1886–1946)

American philanthropist who introduced "Seeing Eye" dogs to America. Born Dorothy Leib Harrison on May 30, 1886, in Philadelphia, Pennsylvania; died on September 8, 1946, in New York City; the youngest of six children, three boys and three girls, of Charles Custis Harrison (owner of a sugar refinery and provost of the University of Pennsylvania) and Ellen Nixon (Waln) Harrison; attended the Agnes Irwin School, Philadelphia, Pennsylvania, and Rathgowrie School, Eastbourne, England; married Walter Abbott Wood (a businessman and a New York state senator), on October 6, 1906 (died 1915); married George Morris Eustis, on June 23, 1923 (divorced); children: (first marriage) two sons.

Born Dorothy Leib Harrison on May 30, 1886, in Philadelphia, Pennsylvania, Dorothy Eustis was the youngest of six children of Charles Custis Harrison, provost of the University of Pennsylvania, and **Ellen Waln Harrison**. She was raised in a well-off environment and ed-ucated at private schools in her home city and in England. Married at the age of 20, she settled near Hoosick Falls, New York, where she and her husband Walter Wood operated an experimental dairy farm under the aegis of the Department of Agriculture. It was on the farm that Eustis first recognized the innate intelligence, gentleness, and loyalty of her German shepherd dog, Hans, and began to consider the possibilities of selectively breeding German shepherds in order to develop these qualities more widely.

After the death of her husband in 1915, Eustis continued the work of the dairy farm for two years, then moved to Radnor, Pennsylvania. In 1921, she relocated to Vevey, Switzerland, where she established an experimental breeding kennel. With her second husband, George Morris Eustis, whom she married in 1923, and an American horse breeder and trainer, Elliott S. ("Jack") Humphrey, she began a research and experimental program that ultimately developed a superior strain of German shepherds. The dogs were exceptionally intelligent, alert, obedient, and gentle, and were initially trained for police and army duty in Switzerland.

In 1927, George Eustis discovered a training center in Pottsdam, Germany, that was successfully training dogs to serve as guides for blind veterans. Intrigued by the program, Dorothy wrote an article about it called "The Seeing Eye," which was published in the *Saturday Evening Post*. The piece brought an inquiry from Morris S. Frank, a blind insurance salesman from Tennessee, who was interested in obtaining a dog for himself. In response to his request, Eustis reoriented her work and began training guide dogs to assist the blind. Her first trained dog, Buddy, was given to Frank, who traveled to Switzerland to pick up the dog and learn how to use him. The publicity surrounding his return to Tennessee with a guide dog sparked further inquiries from the blind community in the United States.

In 1929, divorced from her husband, Eustis left Switzerland to solicit funds and sponsors for a training center in the United States. Incorporated as The Seeing Eye, she founded the first facility in Morristown, New Jersey, then, in 1932, moved to a more permanent location on a 56-acre estate she purchased in Whippany, New Jersey. She served as president of the school until 1940, training many of the dogs herself and donating much of her personal fortune to the project. From 1929 to 1933, she also headed up L'Oeil qui Voit, a Swiss school that trained guide dogs as well as instructors.

In recognition of her work, Eustis was awarded an honorary degree from the University of Pennsylvania in 1933, and a gold medal from the National Institute of Social Sciences in 1936. At the time of her death in 1946, The Seeing Eye had provided over 1,300 guide dogs to the blind.

SOURCES:
James, Edward T., ed. *Notable American Women 1607–1950.* Cambridge, MA: The Belknap Press of Harvard University Press, 1971.
McHenry, Robert, ed. *Famous American Women.* NY: Dover, 1983.

Barbara Morgan,
Melrose, Massachusetts

Eutropia (fl. 270–300 CE)

Roman empress. Flourished around 270–300 CE; married Afranius Hannibalianus; married Maximian, Western emperor of Rome (r. 285/86–305 CE); children: (first marriage) *Theodora (fl. 290s); *Fausta (d. 324, who married Constantine I the Great); Maxentius (Western Roman usurper, r. 306–312 CE).

Eutropia (fl. 330s)

Roman noblewoman. Flourished in the 330s CE; daughter of *Theodora (fl. 290s) and Constantius I, Roman emperor (r. 305–306); married Nepotianus; children: Nepotianus (usurper, r. 350).

Evans, Augusta Jane (1835–1909).

See Wilson, Augusta Evans.

Evans, Betty (1925–1979).

See Grayson, Betty Evans.

Evans, Dale (b. 1912).

See Rogers, Dale Evans.

Evans, Edith (1888–1976)

English actress, one of the greatest in the 20th century, who was adept at Shakespeare and Shaw and famed for her interpretation of Restoration comedy and her performance as Lady Bracknell in **The Importance of Being Earnest.** *Name variations: Dame Edith Evans. Born Mary Edith Evans in the Belgravia neighborhood of Westminster, London, on February 8, 1888; died at her country home in Goudhurst, Kent, on October 14, 1976; daughter of Edward Evans and Caroline Ellen (Foster) Evans; attended local London schools; early apprenticed as a milliner; married George Booth (a petroleum engineer), in 1925 (died 1935); no children.*

Awards: Dame Commander of the Order of the British Empire (1946); honorary doctorates in letters from The University of London (1950), Cambridge (1951) and Oxford (1954).

Made first appearance as Gautami in William Poel's amateur production of Sakuntala and as Cressida in his professional production of Shakespeare's Troilus and Cressida at the Haymarket Theater (De-

cember 12, 1912); appeared as Martin in Elizabeth Cooper *(1913), as Gertrude in* Hamlet, *as Isota in* The Ladies' Comedy, *as Mrs. Taylor in* Acid Drops, *as Moeder Kaatje and as Miss Sylvia in* My Lady's Dress *(all 1914); appeared as Lady Frances Ponsonby in* The Conference, *as Miss Myrtle in* The Man Who Stayed Home *(1916), as the nurse in* The Dead City *(1918); toured in variety theaters with Dame Ellen Terry in scenes from Shakespeare (1918); appeared as The Witch of the Alps and as Destiny in* Manfred *(1918), as Nina in* The Player Queen *and as Nerissa in* The Merchant of Venice *(1919), as Moeder Kaatje and Lady Appleby in* My Lady's Dress, *as Mrs. Hunter in* Wedding Bells *(1920), as Madame Girard in* Daniel, *as Mrs. Van Zile in* Polly with a Past, *as Anne Radcliffe in* The Witch of Edmonton, *as Mrs. Barraclough in* Out to Win, *and as Lady Utterword in the first production of George Bernard Shaw's* Heartbreak House *(1921); appeared as Mrs. Faraker in* At The Wheel, *as Cleopatra in Dryden's* All for Love, *as Kate Harding in* I Serve, *as Cynthia Dell in* The Laughing Lady, *as Ruby in* Rumour *(1922); appeared as Marged in* Taffy, *as Mistress Page in* The Merry Wives of Windsor, *and originated the parts of the Oracle, the Serpent and the She-Ancient in Shaw's* Back to Methusalah *at the Birmingham Repertory Company (1923); appeared as Mrs. Millamant in* The Way of the World, *as Daisy in* The Adding Machine, *as Suzanne in* Tiger Cats, *as Mrs. Collins in Shaw's* Getting Married, *as Helena in* A Midsummer Night's Dream *(1924); appeared in* Everyman, *as Ann in* The Painted Swan, *as Evadne in* The Maid's Tragedy *(1925); worked with the Old Vic Company appearing as Portia in* The Merchant of Venice, *as Queen Margaret in* Richard III, *as Katherine in* The Taming of the Shrew, *as Mariana in* Measure for Measure, *as Cleopatra in* Antony and Cleopatra, *as Mistress Page in* The Merry Wives of Windsor, *as Kate Hardcastle in* She Stoops to Conquer, *as Beatrice in* Much Ado About Nothing, *as Rosalind in* As You Like It, *as Dame Margery Eyre in* The Shoemaker's Holiday, *as the Nurse in* Romeo and Juliet, *as Rosalind in* As You Like It *(September 1925–May 1926); appeared as Maude Fulton in* Caroline, *as Rebecca West in* Rosmersholm *(1926), as Mrs. Sullen in* The Beaux' Stratagem, *as Maitre Bolbec in* The Lady and the Law, *as Mrs. Millamant in* The Way of the World *(1927), as Miriam Rooth in* The Tragic Muse, *as Josephine in* Napoleon's Josephine *(1928), as Florence Nightingale in* The Lady with the Lamp, *as Orinthia in* The Apple Cart *(1929), as Mrs. Carruthers in* O.H.M.S., *as Suzanne in* Tiger Cats, *as Laetitia in* The Old Bachelor *(1931), as Irela in* Evensong *(1932), as Irma Peterson in* Bulldog Drummond

(New York, 1933), as May Daniels in Once in a Lifetime, *as Gwenny in* The Late Christopher Bean *(1933), as Sarah, Duchess of Marlborough, in* The Viceroy Sarah *(1934), as the Nurse in* Romeo and Juliet *(New York, 1934); appeared as Agatha Payne in* The Old Ladies *(1935), as Irina Arkadina in* The Seagull, *as Lady Fidget in Farquar's* The Country Wife *(1936), as Mother Savage in* The Witch of Edmonton, *as Katharina in* The Taming of the Shrew *(1937), as Sanchia Carson in* Robert's Wife *(1937–39), as Lady Bracknell in* The Importance of Being Earnest *(1939), as Muriel Meihac in* Cousin Muriel *(1940), as Katherine Markham in* Old Acquaintance *(1941), as Hesione Hushaby in* Heartbreak House *(1943); entertained British troops overseas (1943–45); appeared as Mrs. Malaprop in* The Rivals *(London, 1946), as Katerina Ivanovna in* Crime and Punishment, *as Lady Wishfort in* The Way of the World, *and as Madame Ranevsky in Chekhov's* The Cherry Orchard *(1948); appeared as Lady Pitts in* Daphne Laureola *(1949), as Helen Lancaster in* Waters of the Moon *(1951–52); appeared in* The Consul *(1952); appeared as the Countess Rosmarin in Christopher Fry's* The Dark is Light Enough *(1954), as Mrs. St. Maugham in Enid Bagnold's* The Chalk Garden *(1956), as Queen Catherine in* Henry VIII *(in London, Paris, Antwerp and Brussels, 1958), as the Countess of Rousillon in* All's Well That Ends Well *and as Volumnia in* Coriolanus *(1959), as Queen Margaret in* Richard III *(1961), as Violet Lazara in* Gentle Jack *(1963), as Judith Bliss in Coward's* Hay Fever *(1964), as Mrs. Forest in Enid Bagnold's* The Chinese Prime Minister *(1965), as the female narrator in* The Adventures of the Black Girl in her Search for God *(at the Edinburgh Festival, 1968), as Queen Margaret in* Richard III; *toured in the recital* Edith Evans . . . and Friends *(1973-74); appeared as the comical dowager queen in a television production of "The Slipper and the Rose: The Story of Cinderella."*

Films: The Queen of Spades *(1948);* The Last Days of Dolwyn *(1948); as Lady Bracknell in* The Importance of Being Earnest *(1951);* Look Back in Anger *(1959);* The Nun's Story *(1959);* Tom Jones *(1963);* The Chalk Garden *(1964);* Young Cassidy *(1965);* The Whisperers *(1966).*

Television: "Waters of the Moon," "The Importance of Being Earnest" (in Canada), "Crooks and Coronets," "Scrooge," "Craze," "Hay Fever," and "The Slipper and the Rose."

Edith Evans was born Edith Mary Evans in the Belgravia neighborhood of Westminster, London, on February 8, 1888, the only daughter of Edward and **Caroline Evans**. Her only broth-

Edith
Evans

er died at the age of four. Despite her surname, she was not of Welsh descent as often supposed, both of her parents' families having deep roots in Surrey. Like many of the great actresses of her generation (*Gladys Cooper, *Peggy Ashcroft, etc.), Edith Evans came from a modestly comfortable middle-class family, her father having been a civil servant exercising an administrative function in the postal service, and her mother having run her home as a boarding house. As a child, Edith Evans attended St. Michael's School in nearby Chester Square in the Pimlico district

Fogerty, Elsie.
See Ashcroft,
Peggy for
sidebar.

but, again, as was usual with girls of her generation, she left school at age 15 to become an apprentice, in her case to a milliner because, as she said, "I wanted to make beautiful things." This was a goal that she would pursue throughout her life.

Edith Evans, so great an actress, spent the first ten years of her working life making hats. There was no theater in her background, she rarely attended plays, and she evinced no interest in a theatrical career, until, at age 16, for social reasons, she joined an elocution class. There, encouraged by her teacher, she began to appear in amateur performances, though she did not set foot on a stage until 1910, at age 22. Then, in 1911, quite by chance, she was seen performing as Beatrice in Shakespeare's *Much Ado About Nothing,* directed by William Poel, at that time head of the Elizabethan Stage Society. The following year, he invited her to appear in Cambridge in the role of Gautami in his amateur production of the classic Hindu drama *Sakuntala;* she made her London debut the same year in his Elizabethan Stage Society production of Shakespeare's baffling and difficult *Troilus and Cressida,* for which she received both a standing ovation from an audience largely made up of Shakespearean experts, and good reviews in the press. This experience was enough to decide the 24-year-old milliner to turn professional which she did before the year was out. She then played three more roles under Poel's direction: Knowledge in the medieval morality play, *Everyman,* a bishop in *The Trial of Joan of Arc,* and, in 1914, Queen Gertrude in *Hamlet.*

Thereafter, Edith Evans appeared regularly on the London stage throughout World War I but left it briefly in 1917 to tour the provincial variety theaters with Dame *Ellen Terry, the greatest English actress of the late 19th and early 20th centuries, playing Mistress Ford in the basket scene from *The Merry Wives of Windsor* and Nerissa to Terry's Portia in *The Merchant of Venice.* Terry took Evans under her wing. In later years, Evans gave much credit to her first teachers, asserting that she learned more from Poel than from any of her later directors, and more from Terry than from any other actress with whom she played. Ellen Terry's daughter, **Edith Craig,** said at the time: "Edith Evans is the only one of our younger actresses who has enough personality to play up to mother." Evans gave tribute to Terry for her speaking ability, claiming that she had merely followed the great artist's instructions to "speak up" and continued to do so for the rest of her career. She also stud-

ied voice under ◄ **Elsie Fogerty,** founder of the Central School, and on other occasions gave Fogerty full credit for teaching her to make the best use of her rich vocal talents.

At the end of her provincial tour, Evans left for France to perform with the *Lena Ashwell Troupe, entertaining British soldiers at the front, a personal and professional obligation that she would fulfill during World War II as well. After the war, Evans returned to the London theater appearing in a variety of contemporary plays such as in the dual roles of The Witch of the Alps and Destiny in *Manfred* (1918); as Nina in *The Player Queen* (1919); in the dual roles of Moeder Kaatje and Lady Appleby in *My Lady's Dress,* as Mrs. Hunter in *Wedding Bells* (1920); as Madame Girard in *Daniel* and as Mrs. Van Zile in *Polly with a Past.* In these immediate postwar years, however, Evans continued to appear in classic plays as well as modern. In a few years, she began to show great promise as a classical actress, appearing as Nerissa in *The Merchant of Venice* (1919), as Aquilina in Otway's Restoration drama, *Venice Preserv'd* (1920) and in the Jacobean tragedy *The Witch of Edmonton* (1921).

It was in October 1921 that Evans first made her appearance in a work by George Bernard Shaw, playing Lady Utterword in the London debut of his *Heartbreak House.* Thereafter, she became well known as an interpreter of Shavian parts and in October 1923 created the roles of the Oracle, the Serpent, and the She-Ancient in his *Back to Methuselah* at the Birmingham Repertory Theater.

But it was in Restoration comedy that Evans was first to make her name. The overthrow of England's king Charles I in 1649 had led to the closing of the theaters and the flight of many of its best writers and performers to France. With the fall of the Cromwellian regime in 1660, however, and the restoration of the monarchy, the theaters not only reopened but did so with a bawdiness and wit that reflected a backlash against the suppression of native British earthiness. For nearly 50 years thereafter, a succession of gifted playwrights gave forth with a dazzling series of witty and saucy "Restoration comedies" that never cease to be produced on the English-speaking stage. It was as Mrs. Millamant—"she of the thousand lovers"—in Congreve's *The Way of the World* (1924) that Edith Evans, now 36, achieved her first critical triumph, receiving rave reviews from the leading critics. From this time on, she was not only a star but was considered to be one of the outstanding actresses on the English stage. At the time, James Agate, critic for the *London Times,* wrote that, in the part of Millamant, Evans possessed "the very genius of humour," while, in his biography of her published in 1954, J.C. Trewin wrote: "Other players have explored the Restoration. One feels that Edith Evans has always been there before them. . . . She can let a sentence stream out upon the air, a silken scarf unfurling in a light wind. She can let the voice crackle through an intricate pattern; a mazy damascene or else flash a speech home with a thrust and a twist."

Edith Evans' triumph in *The Way of the World* was immediately followed by her appearance in a modern play, *The Tiger Cat,* another critical and public success. Thereafter, however, she astonished the London theater world by abandoning the West End stage to work for an entire season (1925–26) at the struggling Old Vic Company across the river in the then unfashionable county of Surrey. Asked why she buried herself in a small theater surrounded by tenements and selling seats at a shilling a ticket, Evans said that she "wanted to stretch her lungs a bit in Shakespeare." In her months at the Old Vic, she played over a dozen roles, from Cleopatra (a failure) to Queen Margaret in *Richard III* (a triumph) to the Nurse in *Romeo and Juliet* (which later in her career she would turn into another triumph).

Shortly after leaving the Old Vic in 1926, Evans appeared as Rebecca West in *Rosmersholm,* her sole attempt as an Ibsen heroine. She returned to Restoration comedy in the role of Mrs. Sullen in *The Beaux' Stratagem* (1927 and 1930). In between, she teamed with Leon M. Lion as co-manager of Wyndham's Theater. Here, she appeared as Maitre Bolbec in *The Lady and the Law* and then successfully revived *The Way of the World* followed by the poor and poorly received *The Old Bachelor* (1931). This last play was not Evans' sole failure, however, for, like any actress, her career was by no means an unbroken string of triumphs. She was not well received in the role of Viola in *Twelfth Night* (1932), which some critics held that she played as if it were a Restoration part, nor as the heroine in *The Taming of the Shrew* (1937).

Unlike Peggy Ashcroft, whose rare appearances in New York led to her being almost unknown in America until the end of her career, Evans was no stranger to Broadway audiences. Highly regarded by American critics, even when her plays were not commercially successful, her appearance on the New York stage was always

considered one of the high points of the season. Her first emergence there was as *Florence Nightingale in *The Lady with the Lamp* by Reginald Berkeley, at the *Maxine Elliott Theater (1931), and then in *Evensong* (1933) in both of which she was warmly applauded by the critics though neither play did well. True success in New York came to Evans only when she played Juliet's Nurse, which came as a result of her having come into the orbit of John Gielgud in 1932. A gifted actor, Gielgud was also a gifted director, and under his guidance, Evans had returned to the role of the Nurse in his production of *Romeo and Juliet* at the Oxford University Dramatic Society, with Peggy Ashcroft as Juliet. There, Evans gave what was considered by the critics to have been a virtually definitive performance. In 1934, she repeated the role in New York in the *Katharine Cornell production of *Romeo and Juliet,* with Basil Rathbone as Romeo and Brian Aherne as Mercutio.

> [Edith Evans] can bring tears to your eyes by the sheer splendour of her voice . . . ; the beauty of each vowel just hangs in the air, lingering a moment . . . , assuming a crystalline shape in the mind and then melting away.
>
> —**Kenneth Tynan**

Once more under the direction of Gielgud, Evans appeared in *The Old Ladies* (1935), a macabre melodrama in which she was required to play a malevolent old woman. It was under Gielgud's direction that Evans reached new heights in her career, performing for the first time in a Chekhov play as Irina in *The Seagull* with Gielgud in the role of Trigorin and Ashcroft as Nina, and then in the Gielgud revival of Oscar Wilde's most famous comedy, *The Importance of Being Earnest.* While enthusiastically received in the Russian play, her success as Chekhov's Irina was completely overshadowed by her triumph as Wilde's Lady Bracknell, one of the great comic performances on the English stage. So well did she interpret this otherwise totally unrealistic caricature, that, thereafter, the role was considered to be virtually her personal property, and thankfully it was later preserved on film. In the scene where the hero confesses to Lady Bracknell that he has no idea who his real parents are as he was found in a handbag abandoned in a railway station, the aristocratic dowager utters the horrified cry "In . . . a . . . HAND . . . bag!," which in the mouth of Edith Evans became one of the classic lines in English comedy.

As she grew older, Evans returned to some of the comedies in which she had appeared in her youth, not hesitating to take the part of the older character in plays in which she had once triumphed in the younger role. Thus, to her successes as Lady Utterword in *Heartbreak House,* and as Millamant in *The Way of the World,* she added the role of Hesione Hushaby in the former (on tour during World War II), and that of Lady Wishfort in the latter (1948). Like many other British theatrical stars, Evans spent most of the war years entertaining the troops (going to Gibraltar, for example, with a company that included Gielgud and *Beatrice Lillie), so much so that, after the war was over, she was awarded the coveted title of Dame Commander of the Order of the British Empire, an honor only rarely accorded to a theatrical personage before that time.

After the war, Evans returned to Shakespeare playing Cleopatra for the second time but, unfortunately, with even less success than before; she was now simply too old for the part. She then took a two-year leave from work but in 1948 returned to the Old Vic company which, bombed out of its own venue during the wartime blitz, was still performing at the New Theater. It was here, in 1948, that she played Lady Wishfort in *The Way of the World* followed by an outstanding portrayal of Madame Ranevsky in Chekhov's *The Cherry Orchard.* The following year, she scored another triumph in James Bridie's play *Daphne Laureola,* a modern drama, in a performance that T.C. Worsley described as Evans "at the height of her powers." When the Old Vic Theater was reopened in 1950, Dame Edith Evans was invited to present the prologue at the opening-night gala program. The same year, she again "made the jump," as she termed her expeditions to New York, recreating her role as Lady Pitts in *Daphne Laureola* on Broadway to critical and public acclaim.

It was not until she was 60 that Evans consented to appear in motion pictures, but once she did so, she took to the medium and made several films that have preserved an invaluable record of her artistry. Her first film was a screen version of Alexander Pushkin's famous tale of gambling, *The Queen of Spades,* in which she appeared opposite Anton Walbrook. This was followed by her role as an old Welsh woman in Emlyn Williams' *The Last Days of Dolwyn* (1951), after which she immediately set to work filming *The Importance of Being Earnest.* Later, she also appeared as the Ghost of Christmas Past in *Scrooge,* a dramatization of Dickens' *A Christmas Carol,* and as the poverty-stricken landlady in the film version of John Osborne's play, *Look Back in Anger.* But her most successful film role was in *The Whisperers* for which she was nominated for an Academy Award as Best Supporting Actress of the year.

The location of the British film studios in the outskirts of London facilitated an actor's appearing in films and stage plays simultaneously, and throughout the 1950s Evans continued to work in the theater, appearing as Helen Lancaster in N.C. Hunter's comedy *Waters of the Moon* (1951); as the Countess Rosmarin in Christopher Fry's *The Dark is Light Enough* (1954); and performing brilliantly in *Enid Bagnold*'s *The Chalk Garden* (1956). Returning to the Old Vic in 1958, she gave another outstanding performance as Queen Catherine in Shakespeare's *Henry VIII.* These years saw the flowering of a veritable Golden Age in the British theater. Dame *Sybil Thorndike and Gladys Cooper were still performing; Peggy Ashcroft, Laurence Olivier, and John Gielgud were at the heights of their careers; Michael Redgrave and Paul Scofield were appearing regularly; The Old Vic and the National Theater were flourishing; revivals of Shakespeare, the Restoration playwrights, Chekhov, Ibsen, Strindberg, and Shaw were regular occurrences, and new playwrights, such as Christopher Fry, John Osborne, and Enid Bagnold, were enriching the English theatrical repertoire. It was in this glittering age that Dame Edith Evans, still only in her 60s, together with Thorndike, with whom she co-starred in *Waters of the Moon,* presided as two queens.

In March 1964, Evans was invited to appear in the program *Homage to Shakespeare* at the Philharmonic Hall in New York in commemoration of the 400th anniversary of the Bard's birth. Now 76, this was her last visit to the United States, and the same year she made her last appearance at the Old Vic in a revival of Noel Coward's comedy *Hay Fever,* which had had its first staging in 1925. A shallow piece of froth, it nevertheless offered a marvelous role as a vain and aging actress, and Evans made the most of it, giving a performance that Richard Findlater described as one of "comic genius."

As an actress, her artistry consisted in her ability to cut a part down to its bare essentials and then build it up again piece by piece in such a way as to present an original interpretation while remaining completely true to the character as written. There was never any artificiality in her acting or her interpretation of a role, and she never warped or twisted a part to suit her own purposes. Evans had a magnificent voice and her timing was flawless; without being a particularly funny person, she had an enormous sense of fun that she conveyed through the comic characters she so often portrayed. For all that, she was adept at serious roles and even at tragedy and could convey a sense of humanity through even the most shallowly written characters of the Restoration plays.

Evans was a private person; there were few actresses of her generation who so succeeded in keeping their lives separate from their public personas as she did. She lived with her parents until she was 37 but then, in 1925, suddenly married George Booth, a petroleum engineer who was resident manager of British-controlled oil interests in Venezuela, managing to keep this a secret for several months. The couple were often separated when Booth's business took him to South America, and they had no children, but they were apparently devoted to one another, and, when Booth died in 1935, Edith Evans did not remarry. Relationships with others existed over the years, but she kept them out of the public eye, mentioning them in her biography only obliquely as "heartbreaks." In 1967, she said in an interview with Rex Reed:

> I have a secluded little flat right near Piccadilly Circus in London, which is very much like living near your Times Square in New York, and I am alone much of the time. But there is a difference between loneliness and aloneness. You can be alone like I am but not lonely. Thirty years ago I lost my mother and my husband in the same year. I was inconsolable. I think of them often especially my mother. I had so little conscious appreciation of the security and warmth they gave me. Now if I could only have them again. I want to say things to them. Share little triumphs with them. . . . But I had to press on.

Although Evans lived alone, both in her flat at the Albany in Piccadilly and at her Tudor country home, and had a reputation for being a poor interview, she was anything but stand-off-ish and had a heartiness and directness about her that reminded some observers of the Restoration characters that she so excelled in playing. A religious woman who devoutly adhered to the Christian Science faith, she repudiated prejudices against people because of the groups to which they belonged, considering people to be essentially the same the world over and all children of God.

Concerning her art, Evans could be ambivalent. In 1967, she told Reed: "People always ask me the most ridiculous questions. They want to know 'How do you approach a role?' Well, I don't know. I approach it by first saying 'yes,' then getting on with the bloody thing." Yet, on another occasion, she said, "An actress must learn to dig out of a part the character in the mind of the playwright and make it live from her own consciousness. I place myself in the role, study over it, dig down to its foundations until I actually feel that I am the character and then— the rest is easy."

Despite her advancing years, Evans refused to retire and was reluctant to look backwards. "I'm no good talking about the past," she once said, "I live for now. I'm much better now than ever before and my best days are still to come." In 1971, she appeared in Jean Anouilh's *Dear Antoine* at the Chichester Festival; in 1974, at age 86, no longer able to carry a full play, she appeared at the Haymarket Theater in a recital entitled *Edith Evans . . . and Friends,* in which she had been touring since the year before and in which she read poems and recited passages from her great roles, interspersed with musical selections by the "friends." Frail and sadly aged but still gifted with her magnificent voice, she was making her last appearance on any stage. In early 1976, she appeared as the comical dowager queen in a television production of "The Slipper and the Rose: The Story of Cinderella." It was the last role of her career. Later the same year, she gave a performance of her solo show before a select audience after which she announced that, having already suffered a heart attack, she was closing her life on the stage. Dame Edith Evans died at her country home in Goudhurst, Kent, some 40 miles southeast of London, England, on October 14, 1976, at age 88, from respiratory complications following a head cold. She had been an actress for over 60 years. Her death occurred a few weeks after that of her great contemporary, Dame Sybil Thorndike; together, they were widely considered the greatest English actresses of the 20th century.

SOURCES:

Beaton, C.W.H., and Kenneth Tynan. *Persona Grata.* London, 1952.

Current Biography. NY: H.W. Wilson, 1966.

Findlater, R. *The Player Queens.* NY: Taplinger, 1977.

Herbert, Ian, ed. *Who's Who in the Theater.* 16th ed. NY: Pitman, 1977.

Oxford Companion to the Theater. NY: Oxford U. Press, 1993.

Philadelphia Free Library, Theater Collection.

SUGGESTED READING:

Trewin, J.C. *Edith Evans.* London, 1954.

Robert H. Hewsen,
Professor of History, Rowan University,
Glassboro, New Jersey

Evans, Elizabeth Glendower

(1856–1937)

American social and labor reformer. Born Elizabeth Gardiner in New Rochelle, New York, on February 28, 1856; died of pneumonia in Brookline, Massachusetts, on December 12, 1937; fourth of five children born to Edward and Sophia (Mifflin) Gardiner; privately educated; married Glendower Evans, on May 18, 1882 (died 1886); no children.

Served as trustee, Massachusetts State Reform Schools (1886–1914); was a member of the Massachusetts Consumers' League and the Women's Educational and Industrial Union of Boston (1890s); was a member and officer, Boston Women's Trade Union League (1904–12); was a member of the Massachusetts Minimum Wage Commission (1911–12); was active in the campaign for women's suffrage (1912–14); sent as a delegate to the International Congress of Women at the Hague (1915); was a national director, American Civil Liberties Union (1920–37); was on the Sacco-Vanzetti defense committee (1920–27); awarded the first annual Ford Hall Forum medal (1933). *Publications: several articles in* LaFollette's Weekly, The Progressive, *and other periodicals.*

Elizabeth Glendower Evans (center)

Born in New Rochelle, New York in 1856, Elizabeth Glendower Evans was connected by blood and marriage to several prominent Boston families. When her father died in 1859, her mother moved the young family into the Boston home of her father-in-law, William Howard Gardiner. There, Evans grew up, attending the best private schools with her wealthy cousins, yet often feeling like the "poor relation." Despite her inheritance at age 26 of a sizable fortune upon the death of her grandfather, Evans retained a sensitivity to class issues the rest of her life. At 26, she also married Glendower Evans, a young Harvard Law School graduate who had just entered into practice with Oliver Wendell Holmes, Jr. When her husband died suddenly in 1886, the devastated widow took her husband's name as her own. She would be known as Elizabeth Glendower Evans and devote her wealth to a variety of social and labor reforms.

As a State Reform school trustee, Evans was a leading spokesperson for the case-work approach and vocational training for juveniles in need. During the 1890s, she became an active member of the Women's Educational and Industrial Union in Boston as well as the Massachusetts Consumers League. In 1904, Evans joined the Women's Trade Union League (WTUL), holding office on both the Boston executive board and on the national level. She resigned from the WTUL in 1912 along with her good friend *Mary Kenney O'Sullivan, in protest over the WTUL's refusal to support the striking textile workers in Lawrence, Massachusetts, during that year. In addition to serving on committees and constantly donating money to various causes, Evans used her social position to aid in reform. As a member of the Massachusetts Child Labor Committee, she gained entry in 1907 to a number of southern textile mills by displaying a letter on corporate stationary identifying herself as a major stockholder.

Known as "Auntie Bee" to the children of her good friends *Florence Kelley (1859–1932), Louis Brandeis and Felix Frankfurter, Evans shared with these leading Progressive reformers a concern for human dignity in a more orderly industrial society. At Kelley's urging, Evans led the fight for the establishment of a minimum wage for Massachusetts women industrial workers. When the minimum wage became law in 1912, it was the first in the nation and served as a model for the dozen other states that passed similar laws in the next few years. Evans was also active in the campaign for woman suffrage and, during World War I, was a devoted pacifist.

After a trip to England in 1908, she became a Fabian Socialist, interested in reforming society through law. She was a co-founder and 17-year board member of the American Civil Liberties Union. During the 1920s, Evans devoted her time and financial resources to Nicola Sacco and Bartolomeo Vanzetti, two Italian anarchists famously accused of robbery and murder. After their execution in 1927, she remained interested in prison reform. During the 1930s, as her health declined and her fortune dwindled, Evans spent her last few years quietly until her death in 1937. Yet, she would be long remembered as an unselfish advocate of human justice. While awaiting appeal of his death sentence, Nicola Sacco wrote Evans: "I will never forget the generous heart that fights without rest for the liberty of humanity oppressed."

SOURCES:

Frankfurter, Marion Denman, and Gardner Jackson, eds., *The Letters of Sacco and Vanzetti.* NY: The Viking Press, 1928.

James, Edward T., ed. *Notable American Women, 1607–1950.* Cambridge, MA: Belknap Press of Harvard University Press, 1971, pp. 588–589.

COLLECTIONS:

Elizabeth Glendower Evans Papers, Schlesinger Library, Radcliffe College.

Kathleen Banks Nutter,
Manuscripts Processor at the Sophia Smith Collection,
Smith College, Northampton, Massachusetts

Evans, Janet (1971—)

American swimmer. Born on August 28, 1971, in Placentia, California; daughter of Paul Evans (a veterinarian) and Barbara Evans.

Finished 3rd in the 800-meter and 1,500-meter freestyles at the Goodwill Games (1986); won Olympic gold medals in the 400-meter freestyle, the 800-meter freestyle, and the 400-meter individual medley in Seoul, Korea (1988); won an Olympic silver medal in the 400-meter freestyle and a gold medal in the 800-meter freestyle in Barcelona, Spain (1992); won World championship gold medals in the 800-meter freestyle (1993–1994).

Born in Placentia, California, in 1971, daughter of Paul, a veterinarian, and **Barbara Evans**, Janet Evans learned to swim shortly after learning to walk. By 15, she had a national ranking, winning the Phillips Performance Award at the U.S. Open Swim Meet. As a high school junior, she set national high school records in the 200-yard individual medley and the 500-yard freestyle. Evans swam with an odd, windmill-like, stiff-arm stroke. "It's not one you would teach," said her future coach Mark Schubert, "but only an idiot would have tried to change it."

In the 1988 Summer Games in Seoul, Korea, 17-year-old Evans became a tremendous media story, winning three gold medals in the Olympic pool. The 5'5½" swimmer who weighed in at 105 pounds was remarkable for her endurance. She won the Olympic gold medal in the 400-meter freestyle, beating the powerful **Heike Friedrich** of East Germany, with an astounding world record of 4:03.85. "That's not a world record," said team manager Frank Keefe, "that's a universe record."

As the Games progressed, the high school senior from El Dorado High School in Placentia, became America's sweetheart, wrote *Charlotte Observer* staff writer Joe Posnanski, with a "poster-perfect smile, and the best freestyle stroke in women's swimming." Teasingly called the Princess because of her occasionally imperious complaints (she was amazed at Seoul that they had to *walk* to practice), Evans took the 800-meter freestyle, beating **Astrid Strauss** of East Germany with an Olympic record of 8:20.20. She also won the 400-meter individual medley (backstroke, butterfly, breaststroke, and free) at 4:37.76, beating **Noemi Ildiko Lung** of Rumania.

Though American television viewers were only aware of Evans, *****Kristin Otto** of East Germany took home more medals than Evans, winning the 50- and 100-meter freestyle, the 100-meter backstroke, and the 100-meter medley. Except for Evans, Eastern European women swimmers captured all the other gold medals. In fact, East Germany's women's swim team, now said to have been notoriously aided by drugs, walked off with 27 medals, while other Eastern European countries took home an additional eight.

Besieged by commercial offers after the Games, Evans instead enrolled in Stanford University, known for its swim program, and continued training. Not totally satisfied with her progress, she left Stanford after two years and joined the Texas Aquatics, coached by Schubert, the U.S. Olympic team coach. She won the 1989 Sullivan Award as the nation's top amateur athlete.

Evans trained hard, six hours a day for four years, to return to the 1992 Olympics in Barcelona. "Seventeen is too young to quit," she said. When she took a silver in the 400-meter freestyle behind Germany's **Dagmar Hase**, an event she was expected to win, she quipped, "The sun will come up tomorrow." But a few moments later, when reporters caught a tear, she was more solemn: "You don't understand the pressure that's placed on athletes here. I gave it everything I had." Two days later, she won a gold in the 800-meter freestyle with an uninspiring time. Even so, she was then the only American woman to win four gold medals in swimming.

A depressed and disappointed Evans quit swimming and entered the University of Southern California. She came out of retirement three months later, however, and regrouped with Schubert who convinced her that it was not a disgrace to be one of the two or three best distance swimmers in the world. In 1996, taller by two inches, heavier by nearly 20 muscular pounds, Evans qualified for the Olympics in Atlanta. Three months earlier, she had torn ligaments in her left foot in a jogging accident and had to train in the pool with only her arms. But in Atlanta, *****Amy Van Dyken** became the media darling of the swimming events, while Evans failed to qualify for the 400 freestyle final and was left out of the medals. At the end of the Games, she announced her retirement. "I'm going to miss the sport," she said. "It's fun to come to the Olympics and win a gold medal, but I think now I know what the Olympics is really about. . . . I can say I had a complete Olympic experience. I felt the highs and the *lows*." As she spoke, her world records set in the 1980s had yet to be surpassed.

SOURCES:

Skow, John. "One Last Splash," in *Time*. Special Edition. Summer 1996, p. 60–61.

Time. August 10, 1992, p. 54–55, October 3, 1988, p. 58–59.

Evans, Mary Anne (1819–1880)

Major English writer of the 19th century who, under the pseudonym George Eliot, wrote seven novels, including Silas Marner, Middlemarch, Adam Bede, *and* The Mill on the Floss. *Name variations: Mary Ann Evans; Marian Evans; Marian Evans Lewes; Mary Ann Cross; Mrs. John W. Cross; (nicknames) Polly, Pollian; (pseudonym) George Eliot. Pronunciation: Lewes pronounced Lewis. Born Mary Anne Evans on November 22, 1819, in Warwickshire, England; died on December 22, 1880, in London; daughter of Robert Evans (a carpenter turned estate agent) and Christiana (Pearson) Evans; attended village dame school, then boarding schools in Attleborough, Nuneaton, and Coventry; lived as the wife of George Henry Lewes from 1854 until his death on November 30, 1878; married John Walter Cross, on May 6, 1880; no children.*

Born on the Arbury estate in Warwickshire; grew up at Chilvers Coton, near Nuneaton; under the influence of evangelical teachers, had a conversion experience at about age 15; left school (1835) during mother's terminal illness; kept house for her father after mother's death (1836); though religion dominated her life until age 22, moved with her father to Coventry and rejected orthodox religion; translated Strauss' Das Leben Jesu, published (1846); wrote for the Coventry Herald and cared for her father until his death (1849); went abroad with friends (1849); returned to England (1850); settled in London (1851) where she wrote for

and served as de facto managing editor of the West-minster Review; established friendships with Herbert Spencer and George Henry Lewes; intimacy with Lewes began (1853); translated Feuerbach's Essence of Christianity, published (1854); left England with Lewes for Germany (1854); lived with him as Marian Lewes after their return (1855); liaison caused break with family and scandal to conventional society; wrote her first fiction and assumed George Eliot as pseudonym (1857); subsequently wrote seven novels, a verse drama, a collection of poetry, and a collection of essays; honored as major novelist and sage in later

Mary Anne Evans

years; visited by distinguished figures from England, America, and Europe.

Selected publications: Scenes of Clerical Life *(1858);* Adam Bede *(1859);* The Mill on the Floss *(1860);* Silas Marner *(1861);* Romola *(1863);* Felix Holt, the Radical *(1866);* Middlemarch *(1871–72);* Daniel Deronda *(1876).*

In her last novel, *Daniel Deronda,* George Eliot wrote: "A human life should be well rooted in some spot of a native land, where it may get the love of tender kinship for the face of the earth, for the labours men go forth to, for the sounds and accents that haunt it, . . . a spot where the definiteness of early memories may be inwrought with affection." Mary Anne Evans' deep emotional life was rooted in the heart of England, in the rich farm fields, golden meadowlands, and flowering hedgerows of the Midlands. The writer George Eliot's destiny, however, lay in the intellectual and artistic milieu of London, where she could escape the constraints imposed on her sex by provincial mores and fulfill her ambition to share in and contribute to the life of the mind. This tension between the sensuous, affectionate woman and the rigorously self-disciplined thinker and writer was further complicated by a religious temperament that led her, after great emotional and intellectual turmoil, to reject orthodox religion in young adulthood, but never allowed her to escape the moral earnestness of her early evangelical views.

Her need for love and affection is manifested in the many complicated personal relationships with men and women that marked her life from her childhood until her death at 61. This emotional dimension of her personality, with its strong links to the people, scenes, and events of her childhood, accounts for those aspects of her art which have proved the most universally admired and enduring: her ability to portray sympathetically, through her aesthetic of realism, commonplace characters whose psychological needs conflict with social conditions and conventions and with both external and internal moral imperatives.

Mary Anne Evans was born on November 22, 1819, at South Farm on the 7,000-acre Arbury estate in Warwickshire, which her father Robert Evans managed for the Newdigate family. Her mother **Christiana Pearson Evans** came from a family of well-established and prosperous yeoman farmers. Christiana was Robert Evans' second wife, his first having died in 1809 after the birth of a third child. Mary Anne Evans, her name as it appears on her baptismal record, grew up with her stepbrother Robert (b. 1802), her stepsister **Fanny Evans** (b. 1805), her sister **Chrissey Evans** (b. 1814), and her brother Issac Evans (b. 1816). The family lived at Griff House, a comfortable Georgian-style farmhouse on the edge of the Arbury estate, near Nuneaton on the Coventry Road, where she and her brother Issac, on whom she lavished her first intense love, were inseparable playmates. Never very close to her mother, Mary Anne glowed in the light of her father's attention as the baby of the family, delighting in standing in the wagon between his knees when he drove about the great estate as his business took him to fields and woods, to cottages and stables, to Astley Castle and Arbury Hall.

She and Issac attended a dame's school across the road from their house until 1824, when she was five; then Issac was sent to school near Coventry and she joined Chrissey at Miss Latham's, three miles from home. Evans was never able to reestablish the intimate bond with Issac broken by their separation, but the theme of childhood love between sister and brother persists in her writing, most markedly in *The Mill on the Floss* and the "Brother and Sister" sonnets of the late 1860s. In 1828, she was sent to Mrs. Wallington's Boarding School in Nuneaton, where the benevolent evangelical earnestness and special attention of the principal governess, **Maria Lewis**, was to have an important effect on the unprepossessing, self-conscious, introspective child. Under Lewis' influence, Mary Anne gained a thorough knowledge of the Bible and a reputation for seriousness and piety.

By the time she was 13, Evans had mastered the school's curriculum, and her father was advised to send her to the Miss Franklins' School in Coventry, where she excelled in English composition, French, and music. Although the religious tone at the school was Calvinistic, the Franklins were liberal in encouraging their students to read extensively, and Evans became familiar with the works of contemporary writers such as Scott and Byron as well as the classic works of Shakespeare, Milton, and Pope. Here, at about 15, she had a conversion experience that intensified the comparatively gentle evangelical bent she had developed under the influence of Miss Lewis to a gloomy and ascetic Calvinism. Until Evans was 22, this experience dominated her life, and she lived with a conviction that human sinfulness could be redeemed only by the atonement of Christ. She practiced renunciation and humility in an attempt to repress her desire for recognition, approval, and love.

In 1835, Mary Anne returned home to help her sister keep house for her father and brother when it became clear that her mother was dying of cancer. Christiana Evans died after great suffering in 1836, and in 1837, Chrissey married and left home. At this time, Mary Anne's religious zeal was at its most intense. Devoting her life to duty and self-sacrifice, she tended to her father's needs, visited the poor and sick in the neighborhood, and showed her disapproval of her brother's lack of religious enthusiasm. Her father engaged a tutor from Coventry to teach her Italian and German and soon she was studying Latin on her own. She became immersed in readings on religious history and theology.

In 1841, Robert Evans retired and Issac married and took over his father's estate management and the house at Griff. Mary Ann (as she began to write her name in 1837) and her father moved to Foleshill, Coventry, where she continued her private study and reading. For some time, she had been reading books on geology and astronomy that attempted to reconcile the claims of science with those of religious revelation. Gradually, these readings, as well as Charles Hennell's *An Inquiry concerning the Origins of Christianity,* Thomas Carlyle's *Sartor Resartus,* and works of the Romantic poets, especially William Wordsworth— her favorite poet and a major influence on her novels—loosened the hold of evangelicalism on her mind and emotions.

In addition to her wide-ranging reading, at Coventry Evans made the acquaintance of **Caroline Bray** (1814–1905), known as Cara, and her husband Charles. Both were free-thinking intellectuals under whose influence Evans' rejection of orthodox Christianity crystallized. Having lost the empathy of her brother Issac as a result of her dour religious views, she fractured her relationship with her father by refusing to attend church with him in January of 1842, explaining to him in a letter (because he would not speak to her about her religious doubts) that she "could not without vile hypocrisy and a miserable truckling to the smile of the world for the sake of my supposed interests, profess to join in worship which I wholly disapprove. This and this alone I will not do even for your sake—anything else however painful I would cheerfully brave to give you a moment's joy."

Her action precipitated a family crisis: her father, feeling his authority and respectability challenged by her disobedience and rebellion, threatened to have nothing more to do with her, put the house up for lease, and arranged to move alone to his cottage at Packington. Issac, Fanny, and Chrissey tried to mediate the conflict, but father and daughter were well matched in stubbornness. Mary Anne was sent to Issac's at Griff to wait until the situation cooled down. Eventually a truce was reached: Evans would accompany her father to church, but she could think what she liked during the service. She moved back to Foleshill at the end of April. Robert Evans was satisfied that appearances were kept up, and Mary Anne felt she had asserted her intellectual independence.

Friendship with the Brays widened Evans' world. Through them, she met Cara's sister, **Sara Hennell** (1812–1899), and her brother, Charles Hennell, the author of *An Inquiry concerning the Origins of Christianity.* She also took several trips with her new friends, visiting London, Manchester, Windemere, Wales, and Scotland. As a result of the connections to the intellectual world made through her new acquaintances, she was asked to translate Strauss' *Das Leben Jesu.* For two years, she worked on a translation of the book that would have a profound influence on religious thought in 19th-century England. In 1846, *The Life of Jesus, Critically Examined* by David Friedrich Strauss was published by Chapman Brothers in three volumes. Mary Anne Evans' name did not appear in the volumes; she was paid £20 for her labor.

*M*y artistic bent is directed not at all to the presentation of eminently irreproachable characters, but to the presentation of mixed human beings in such a way as to call forth tolerant judgment, pity, and sympathy.

—**Mary Anne Evans**

In 1846 and 1847, Evans wrote pieces for the Coventry *Herald* while her father's declining health demanded more and more of her time and attention. She nursed him through his final illness and was at a loss when he died in May of 1849. On the night before his death, she wrote, "What shall I be without my Father? It will seem as if a part of my moral nature were gone." Five days after the funeral, she set off with the Brays on a continental tour. When the Brays returned to England after a month, Mary Anne remained alone in Geneva to ponder her future. She would soon be 30, a woman with a reputation for strong-minded unconventionality and with little prospect of marriage. The income from her inheritance would allow her a bare independent living, with no money for books, lessons, or travel. She dreaded the prospect of living as a dependent with her brother, or of surrendering her freedom and leisure to earn a paltry living as a teacher or governess. She wondered if it were possible for her to earn a living as a writer.

Upon returning to England in 1850, she stayed with the Brays. John Chapman, who had published her translation of Strauss, visited Coventry and asked her to write a review of R.W. Mackay's *The Progress of the Intellect* for the *Westminster Review.* She delivered the article personally to Chapman in London and stayed for two weeks at his large house in the Strand, where he had his publishing and book-selling offices and where his wife lodged literary people visiting London. Encouraged by the success of her article, Evans decided that if she lived in London, she could make a living by writing. She took lodgings in Chapman's house in January of 1851.

She had hardly settled in London, where she met some of the city's leading intellectual lights at Chapman's soirees, when the peculiar living arrangements and relationships at the Chapmans' created problems. In a short time, both Chapman's wife and his mistress, who lived in the household as the Chapmans' children's governess, made no secret of their jealousy of his attentions to the new boarder and their disapproval of her lack of discretion in allowing him to spend hours in her room listening to her play Mozart and being tutored in German. Although she enjoyed such attention, it was clear that she could not in her present circumstances sustain both her aspirations to establish herself as a professional writer and a flirtation with Chapman. When Chapman told her that although he had a great affection for her, he loved his wife and mistress too, Marian Evans, as she now spelled her name, returned to Coventry.

Soon after her departure, Chapman bought the *Westminster Review.* He needed an editor who could return the magazine to the high standard set by its founder, John Stuart Mill. Recognizing that Evans could fulfill this role admirably, he went to Coventry to discuss his plans for the magazine with her. She agreed to an arrangement in which he would be the nominal editor and she would write for the magazine and serve as his anonymous assistant. He persuaded his wife and mistress to allow her to return to the house on this professional footing. It is generally agreed that the great success of the *Westminster Review* during the next two years can be attributed to Evans, who earned fees for the anonymous articles she wrote but was unpaid and largely unrecognized for her brilliant editorial work on ten numbers of the journal.

She enjoyed the challenge of her new career, however, and the interesting people she met in London. She established lasting friendships with ✠▶ **Bessie Parkes**, later editor of the *English Women's Journal,* which advocated education and employment for women, and with Barbara Leigh Smith (later *Barbara Bodichon), activist and organizer of many feminist causes, including the suffrage movement and the founding of Girton College for women at Cambridge in 1869. As her infatuation with Chapman cooled, Evans made other friends, among them Herbert Spencer, who worked across the street from Chapman's as an editor of *The Economist.* In 1851, he often escorted her to plays and operas, and it was rumored that they were engaged. Evans apparently offered more than the intellectual friendship that for Spencer defined their relationship, and once more found her love rejected because, as Spencer later wrote in his *Autobiography,* "the lack of physical attraction was fatal" to a more intimate relationship.

In 1852, Evans began to see George Henry Lewes, dramatist, novelist, and journalist, a writer for the *Westminster Review* since 1840, as well as writer and editor for the *Leader,* a radical weekly that he and Thornton Hunt had founded in 1850. Lewes was a quick and amiable conversationalist and an animated storyteller with interests in philosophy, literature, and science. He was married and the father of three sons when Evans met him. His wife **Agnes** had had a child with Hunt in 1850, but Lewes had overlooked her infidelity and given the child his name. When in 1852 she gave birth to the second of four children she was to have with Hunt, however, Lewes ceased to regard her as his wife. A divorce was out of the question because Lewes had previously condoned her adultery. Lewes supported Agnes and her children for the rest of his life.

Evans at first disliked Lewes because of what she regarded as his lack of seriousness, but in her loneliness after her relationship with Spencer had failed, she grew to value Lewes' companionship. In 1853, she moved from Chapman's house to lodgings near Hyde Park, where she could receive visitors privately, and where, according to her biographer Gordon Haight, her sexual relationship with Lewes began. Her chief project at this time was a translation of Feuerbach's *The Origins of Christianity,* published in 1854, the only published work on which the name Marian Evans appears. In summer of 1854, she left for Germany with Lewes, commencing a union that would bring her great personal happiness and nurture her creative life for 24 years.

In Germany, Lewes worked on a biography of Goethe and wrote articles for the *Leader* while Evans wrote for the *Westminster Review* and began a translation of Spinoza's *Ethics*. On their return to England in 1855, Evans stayed in Dover while Lewes settled his separation from Agnes. Gossip that reached London from abroad had already stigmatized Evans, and when she took up residence openly with Lewes, she did so knowing full well that she had put herself beyond the pale of respectable society. She requested that the few friends who did write or visit her call her Marian Lewes.

In 1856, at Lewes' suggestion that she try her hand at fiction, Evans began to write "The Sad Fortunes of the Reverend Amos Barton," which would usher in her career as a novelist. The story was published in *Blackwood's Magazine* in January of 1857, where Lewes had sent it as the work of a friend who wished to remain anonymous. When pressed by the publishers, Evans offered "George Eliot" as the name under which the author wished to be known. She retained the pseudonym throughout her career. This first story was soon followed in *Blackwood's* by "Mr. Gilfil's Love Story" and "Janet's Repentance."

When the stories were reprinted in 1858 as *Scenes of Clerical Life,* they were enthusiastically reviewed and widely read. Readers from Warwickshire recognized characters and events from their own past, and there was much speculation and controversy about the identity of the author so well acquainted with the history of the region. In the midst of the stir, Evans, fearing that her authorship would be discovered, wrote her family to inform them that she had "changed [her] name, and [had] someone to take care of [her] in this world." When Issac learned that her relationship with Lewes was not a legal marriage, although, as Evans wrote, it was "regarded by us both as a sacred bond," he broke off communication with her and forbade Fanny and Chrissey to communicate with the infidel who had brought disgrace upon the family.

Alienated from her family and the scenes of her early life, Evans returned to them in her memory and transformed them through her imagination in her greatest fiction. Her first novel, *Adam Bede,* purported to be set in Derbyshire and Staffordshire rather than in her native Warwickshire, but the character of Adam Bede is based on her father's early life, and the incident of the Methodist woman preacher visiting the young woman in prison accused of child murder was based on a personal reminiscence Evans had heard from her Methodist aunt, **Mrs.**

❧▶ Parkes, Bessie Rayner (1829–1925)

English feminist, poet, and essayist. Name variations: Bessie Belloc. Born in 1829; died in 1925; daughter of Joseph Parkes (a Birmingham solicitor) and Elizabeth (Priestley) Parkes (daughter of Unitarian scientist Joseph Priestley); married Louis Belloc (Irish-French writer), in 1867 (died 1872); children: Hilaire Belloc (1870–1953); Marie Belloc-Lowndes (1868–1947).

Bessie Rayner Parkes grew up surrounded by a circle of reforming activists, including Jeremy Bentham and John Stuart Mill, who were friends of her father Joseph Parkes. In 1946, she met feminist *Barbara Bodichon; since both were intent on reforming women's education, they became lifelong friends and established the *English Woman's Journal* (1858). Edited by Parkes, the journal served as a magnet to a circle of women known as the Langham Place Group.

In the 1860s, Parkes converted to Roman Catholicism, influenced by the Irish Sisters of Mercy and the death of her friend *Adelaide Procter. She then met Louis Belloc and their five-year marriage produced two more writers, her son Hilaire Belloc and her daughter *Marie Belloc-Lowndes. Louis Belloc's sudden death left Parkes distraught and destitute, and she moved with her children to Slindon, Sussex. In time, her daughter distanced herself from the women's movement while her son was rabidly anti-feminist. Bessie Parkes' writings include *Remarks Upon the Education of Girls* (1854), *Essays on Women's Work* (1865), and *In a Walled Garden* (1895).

SUGGESTED READING:

Belloc-Lowndes, Marie. *I Too Have Lived in Arcadia.*

Samuel Evans. Published in installments in *Blackwood's,* then as a three-volume novel in February of 1859, *Adam Bede* was a sensational success, both with critics and the reading public. The *Times* review is typical: "It's a first rate novel, and its author takes rank at once among the masters of the art." By October, 14,000 copies had been sold. Queen *Victoria so much enjoyed *Adam Bede* that she commissioned watercolors based on scenes from the novel.

The Mill on the Floss, published in 1860, imaginatively revisited Evans' childhood in the sister-brother relationship of Maggie and Tom Tulliver as it traced the tragic consequences of Maggie's need to love and be loved. By the time this most autobiographical of her novels was published, Issac Evans, who had recognized in *Adam Bede* "things . . . about my father," was no longer deceived by his sister's pseudonym and was annoyed by the novel's caricatures of his Pearson aunts as the "emmet-like Dodsons." In fact, Evans had seen the futility of trying to preserve the incognito since June of 1859, when Lewes wrote to Barbara Bodichon that "we have come to the resolution of no longer concealing the authorship. It makes me angry to think that people should say that the secret was kept because there was any fear of the effect of the author's name. . . . The object of anonymity was to get the book judged on its own merits, and not prejudged as the work of a woman, or of a particular woman." After the success of *The Mill on the Floss,* it was difficult for people to withdraw praise when it became widely known that the author of the best-selling and critically acclaimed books was George Lewes' mistress. As her fame grew, so did her fortune. Through Lewes' shrewd management as her literary agent, Evans commanded the highest fees of any living novelist, and her only rival in popularity was Charles Dickens.

While on a trip to Italy in 1860, Lewes suggested that Evans try a historical novel based on the life of Savonarola, the 15th-century Florentine hero. She immersed herself in reading and research for this ambitious project, her first attempt at fiction not grounded in her own memory and experiences. The work proved difficult, and at several points she felt blocked and lost confidence in her ability to write a novel so remote from her own experience in time and place. She set aside her work on this project to write *Silas Marner,* published in 1861, a novel set among the familiar English pastoral scenes of humble life at the beginning of the century and based on a "recollection of having once, in early childhood, seen a linen weaver with a bag on his back." Once again, this novel won accolades for the author.

With her confidence restored by the success of *Silas Marner,* Evans returned to work on her historical novel, *Romola.* Smith and Elder, the publishing company that had recently introduced the *Cornhill Magazine,* offered to pay an unprecedented £10,000 for George Eliot's new work, to be published in 16 installments. Because she felt that *Romola* was not suited to publication in short segments, she agreed to fewer but longer installments for £7,000. Unfortunately, *Romola* did not bolster the circulation of the *Cornhill* or sell as well as expected when it was issued in three volumes in 1863.

Eager to demonstrate her versatility as a writer, Evans began a verse drama, *The Spanish Gypsy,* with Lewes' encouragement. Again, she had difficulty with unfamiliar subject matter and an unfamiliar form. She interrupted work on her poem to write *Felix Holt, the Radical,* a novel

Opposite page

Juliet Aubrey as Dorothea Brooke in George Eliot's Middlemarch *on "Masterpiece Theatre,"* PBS.

based on her memories of the hardships of the unemployed weavers and miners of Coventry and the election riots that took place in Nuneaton after the passage of the Great Reform Bill of 1832. The novel's publication was especially timely in 1866 during the debate that preceded the passage of the Second Reform Bill of 1867; it was well received critically although sales lagged somewhat behind expectations. After a trip to Spain in 1867, Evans completed *The Spanish Gypsy,* published in 1868.

Evans' earnings had made the Leweses wealthy enough to take a 49-year lease on the Priory, the stately London home where she was to live from 1863 until the last year of her life. With George Eliot's literary fame at its peak in the 60s, Lewes cautiously set about the rehabilitation of Marian Evans Lewes' social reputation. During years of ostracism, Evans had maintained social ties with only a few close friends. To avoid the pain of rejection, she neither expected nor extended invitations. After the move to the Priory, however, the Leweses let it be known that though they never visited, they received visitors on Sunday afternoons. Lewes began by issuing invitations to friends in scientific and literary circles. In time, the Priory became a salon where the intellectual elite of England gathered to pay tribute to the person and accomplishments of George Eliot.

With the stunning success of *Middlemarch,* generally acknowledged as her masterpiece, in 1871–72 Evans' fame reached its zenith. She was dubbed "the Madonna" by Lewes, and Dickens captured the tone of idolatry that developed as the Sunday afternoons attracted ardent admirers in his remark that "On Sunday I hope to attend service at the Priory." In 1872, Lewes wrote, "Lords and Ladies, poets and cabinet ministers, artists and men of science crowd upon us" to meet the celebrated writer described by one visitor as "a plain woman who talked of Homer as simply as she would of flat-irons." By 1876, when *Daniel Deronda* appeared, polite society had apparently either forgotten or overlooked the irregularity of Evans' marital situation: after all, in addition to being known as the greatest living English novelist, she had been received by three of Queen Victoria's daughters.

The novels that mark the final phase of George Eliot's career as a novelist, *Middlemarch* (1871–72) and *Daniel Deronda* (1876) mark a shift from the sympathetic treatment of commonplace characters in pastoral settings that dominates her early work to a more analytic and critical view of the ways in which human potential, aspiration, and happiness are circumscribed by social conditions and self-delusion. *Middlemarch,* her deep and elaborate analysis of the intricate web of personal and social relationships that defined provincial life in her native Midlands around the time of the passage of the Great Reform Bill, criticizes a society dominated by the pursuit of wealth and social status, analyzes the false expectations that people bring to marriage, and reveals the waste of lives spent in pursuit of illusions. *Daniel Deronda,* her only novel with a contemporary setting, exposes the effects of the double standard of sexual morality in polite society, the consequences of arranged marriages, and the prejudice against Jews.

By the 1870s, Evans, given her secure role at the center of the elite intellectual and social salon at the Priory, could allow George Eliot's critical intelligence, irony, and skepticism free play. She had weathered years of ostracism and had earned the right to participate with the nation's leading intellectuals in the great discussions of her day. Since Dickens' death, she was regarded as the greatest living novelist. Her income in 1874 exceeded £5,000. Her views on contemporary issues were sought and quoted. Although her essential conservatism prevented her giving full support to the growing women's movement, she contributed to causes that advanced education for women. She had become an idol to a generation of young women like **Elma Stuart** and *Edith Simcox, whose ardent and demonstrative affection she encouraged but sometimes found embarrassing. She had found happiness in her union with Lewes and, by the summer of 1878, had realized her dream of having a house in the country.

This happiness was shattered when Lewes, whose health had been deteriorating for some time, became seriously ill in the fall of 1878. When he died on November 30, she secluded herself in grief for months. She came to terms with her loss by fulfilling her promise to complete the work on psychology Lewes had left unfinished and by establishing a scholarship in his name for a qualified and needy young man or woman at Cambridge. When her friends felt confident that she had reorganized her life, she surprised them by announcing her marriage, in May of 1880, to John Walter Cross, a friend of the family who had served as the Leweses' financial advisor for several years. As he assisted her in arrangements regarding Lewes' estate, Evans transferred her emotional dependence to Johnny, 20 years her junior, who had lost his mother shortly after George Lewes' death. After their

marriage in an Anglican ceremony, she was deeply touched when her brother Issac wrote for the first time since 1857 to send his good wishes.

The Crosses left for a honeymoon in Europe. While they were in Venice, Johnny, in an apparently temporary mental derangement, threw himself from the balcony of their hotel into the Grand Canal. Mary Ann Cross, as she now signed her name, nursed him back to health and, with the help of his family, got him safely back to England. Johnny had bought a house in Chelsea, which he and Evans moved into at the beginning of December. Later in the month, she became ill with a sore throat. Her condition rapidly declined, and she died on December 22, 1880.

John tried to arrange for burial in the poet's corner of Westminster Abbey, but in the light of expressed concerns about Evans' past "antagonism to Christian practice in regard to marriage and Christian theory in regard to dogma," he did not press the issue. She was buried in an unconsecrated plot in Highgate Cemetery near the grave of George Henry Lewes.

SOURCES:
Haight, Gordon S. *George Eliot: A Biography*. Oxford: Oxford University Press, 1968.
——, ed. *Selections From George Eliot's Letters*. New Haven, CT: Yale University Press, 1985.
McSweeney, Kerry. *George Eliot (Marian Evans): A Literary Life*. NY: St. Martin's Press, 1991.
Redinger, Ruby V. *George Eliot: The Emergent Self*. NY: Alfred Knopf, 1976.
Taylor, Ina. *A Woman of Contradictions: The Life of George Eliot*. NY: William Morrow, 1989.

SUGGESTED READING:
Ashton, Rosemary. *George Eliot: A Life*. Penguin, 1997.
Dodd, Valerie A. *George Eliot: An Intellectual Life*. NY: St. Martin's Press, 1990.
Gilbert, Sandra M., and Susan Gubar. *The Madwoman in the Attic: The Woman Writer and the Nineteenth-Century Literary Imagination*. New Haven, CT: Yale University Press, 1979.
Hardy, Barbara. *The Novels of George Eliot: A Study in Form*. NY: Oxford University Press, 1959.
Karl, Frederick R. *George Eliot: Voice of a Century*. Norton, 1995.
Showalter, Elaine. "The Greening of Sister George," in *Nineteenth-Century Fiction*. Vol. 35, December 1980, pp. 292–311.

Patricia B. Heaman,
Professor of English, Wilkes University,
Wilkes-Barre, Pennsylvania

Evans, Matilda Arabella

(1872–1935)

African-American physician, humanitarian, and child advocate. Born Matilda Arabella Evans on May 13, 1872, in Aiken, South Carolina; died on November 17, 1935, in Columbia, South Carolina; daughter of Anderson Evans and Harriet Evans; attended Schofield Industrial School, Aiken, South Carolina; Oberlin College, B.A., 1891; Woman's Medical College of Pennsylvania, M.D., 1897; never married; children: adopted seven who bear her surname.

The 19th-century physician and child advocate Matilda Arabella Evans was a pioneer in the battle for health care across the nation and, in particular, for impoverished African-Americans in Columbia, South Carolina. Born in Aiken, South Carolina, she was one of the first students to enroll in the Schofield Industrial School, which was established in 1868 to educate all black children in South Carolina, by *Martha Schofield of Philadelphia, Pennsylvania, under the auspices of the Pennsylvania Freedmen's Relief Association. After graduating, Evans won a tuition scholarship to Oberlin College, where she worked in the dining hall and canned fruit during the summers to provide for her other expenses. After graduating in 1891, she returned to Schofield to teach. In 1893, using her meager salary, a $100 grant, and some money from Martha Schofield, she entered the Woman's Medical College of Pennsylvania with hopes of becoming a medical missionary.

After earning her M.D. in 1897, Evans returned to Columbia, South Carolina, the first black woman to practice medicine in that city. She ran a busy practice, for white as well as black patients, and opened her home to serve as a hospital. She gradually gave up her dream of becoming a missionary, focusing instead on improving the inadequate health facilities in Columbia. With the goal of establishing a clinic, she created a planning board and visited the cities of Durham, Philadelphia, and New York to gather ideas for setting up a community facility. Initially, her Columbia Clinic Association operated out of a church basement but soon moved to permanent quarters. Offering free health service and education to the public, her clinic was equipped to provide vaccinations for children and was staffed with a dentist, and an eye, ear, nose, and throat specialist. Evans, who was particularly concerned with the poorer children of the area, also obtained permission from the authorities to examine African-American children within the public schools at her own expense. Finding many medical problems due to neglect, she convinced the school system to implement a permanent program to provide students with regular examinations.

Evans also founded the Negro Health Care Association of South Carolina and the Taylor

Lane Hospital and Training School for Nurses (later Saint Luke Hospital), in Columbia. Taylor Lane was the only hospital in the area for black patients, and Evans gave up her private practice in order to become its superintendent. She also wrote articles and several larger works, including a biography of her mentor, *Martha Schofield: Pioneer Negro Educator* (1916).

Evans' love of children and generosity of spirit was also manifested in her personal life. Although she never married, she adopted seven children, whom she raised as a single mother. Evans died at the age of 63, after a brief illness.

Barbara Morgan,
Melrose, Massachusetts

Evans, Nancy (1915—)

British mezzo-soprano, one of the major British singers of her generation, who was closely linked with the music of Benjamin Britten. Born in Liverpool, England, on March 19, 1915; married Walter Legge; married Eric Crozier, in 1949.

Born in Liverpool during World War I, Nancy Evans studied vocal music there with John Tobin, later studying in London with **Eva de Reusz** and the acclaimed *Maggie Teyte. After singing as a member of the chorus at the Glyndebourne Festival in 1938, Evans made her London stage debut that same year in Sir Arthur Sullivan's comic opera *The Rose of Persia*. For the next several years, she was occupied singing small roles at the Royal Albert Hall and at the Royal Opera House, Covent Garden. The first opera in which she sang was Wagner's *Parsifal*, in the roles of a Flower Maiden and the Voice from on High. During these years, she met musicians at the very end of their careers who represented living links with a brilliant era of 19th-century musical history. One of her conductors, Felix Weingartner, had personally known Johannes Brahms. At Covent Garden, she sang the role of a Valkyrie, the conductor in this instance being the illustrious Sir Thomas Beecham.

As a young singer, Evans represented the future of music as the older generation retired and left the stage. Some of her professional relationships evolved into warm friendships that enriched her both artistically and personally. During World War II, Evans sang on several occasions with the revered Irish singer John McCormack. World renowned and honored by the pope with the title of count, McCormack performed with Evans on several occasions at fundraising concerts for the Red Cross. After one of

these events, he played some of his old recordings for his protegé. No doubt moved by memories of his own youth, he held Evans's arm, saying to her, "Listen to that child. I don't know how I did that. How did I do that?" His stories of singing with legendary artists like *Luisa Tetrazzini inspired a youthful Evans who had yet to become a star herself.

The end of World War II found Great Britain in a perilous economic situation and geopolitically on the decline. In its musical life, however, the victory over the Fascist powers in 1945 signaled the start of a glorious musical renaissance. The key personality in this burst of creative energy was the composer Benjamin Britten (1913–1976). The wildly successful 1945 premiere of Britten's opera *Peter Grimes* marked the start of a series of innovative Britten stage works. Still relatively unknown after the war, Evans answered the phone one day and heard words that would change her life: "My name's Benjamin Britten. I'm writing an opera, and I'd like you to sing in it." The opera Britten had composed was *The Rape of Lucretia*. Alternating with the great singer *Kathleen Ferrier, Evans created the role of Lucretia with Ferrier in the highly acclaimed 1946 premiere performances at the Glyndebourne Festival. Evans alone sang this role in 1947 at Covent Garden's first presentation of *The Rape to Lucretia*, garnering excellent reviews. In June 1947, she created the role of Nancy in Britten's next opera, *Albert Herring*.

Over the next two decades, Evans was one of the leading ensemble members of the English Opera Group, starring in performances not only of Britten's stage works but those of other contemporary composers. Tours took her abroad to Belgium, The Netherlands, Scandinavia and Switzerland. Back in England, she performed not only in operas but in oratorios and recitals.

Nancy Evans' reputation brought her to the attention of several leading composers including the venerable Ralph Vaughan Williams as well as Lennox Berkeley and Malcolm Williamson. Vaughan Williams composed the solo part in his Nativity composition *Hodie (This Day)* with Evans in mind; she sang this at its world premiere performance, with the composer conducting, at Worcester Cathedral on September 8, 1954. That year, Vaughan Williams chose Evans to give the world premiere performance of his revised version of his 1927 composition for solo female voice and violin, *Along the Field*, based on settings of A.E. Housman poems. This work was first presented to the public at Benjamin

Britten's Aldeburgh Festival, and Evans also recorded it.

In 1968, she took the starring role in the world premiere performance of Malcolm Williamson's opera *The Growing Castle*. Based on a play by August Strindberg, the work was made up of many short scenes. Only four singers were called for by the composer, with two male and two female parts. In a feat that was possibly unique in the history of opera, Evans created eight separate characters, the Poet and seven others. Years later, reminiscing about her performance, she noted that her demanding but exciting role called for "a lot of quick changes, both of costume and character."

Thoroughly satisfied with her warm-toned singing and convincing acting style, Benjamin Britten quickly began to view Evans as one of his closest artistic collaborators, choosing her to sing the key role of Polly Peachum in his version of the 18th-century classic *The Beggar's Opera*. An acclaimed operatic star by her early 30s, she starred as ***Dido** in Purcell's *Dido and Aeneas*, as well as in the role of Lucinda Woodcock in *Love in a Village*. In 1947, Britten provided tangible evidence of his high esteem for Evans' artistry when he composed for her his song cycle "A Charm of Lullabies," Opus 41. This work hinted of an emerging new style in his musical evolution. One of the high points of this composition of five linked lullabies is a charming Scottish air, "Highland Balou," said to have been inspired by the composer's memories of Scottish herring girls singing during his childhood in the town of Lowestoft. Though she performed the work, unfortunately Evans never recorded it.

In 1949, Nancy Evans married Eric Crozier after her first marriage (to record producer Walter Legge) had ended in divorce. Her marriage to Crozier was a happy one, and she and her husband would work together for many years in the musical world. Crozier too was closely linked to the career of Britten, having been the producer of the 1945 Sadler's Wells premiere of Britten's first great opera success *Peter Grimes*. However, by the 1960s both Crozier and Evans had become estranged from Britten, who could at times be harshly insensitive to those closest to him. Fortunately for all involved, ill feelings evaporated by the final years of the great composer's life. Evans and Crozier would be provided for by Britten in his will, written less than a year before his death on December 4, 1976. Nancy Evans, by now retired from the stage, would continue her close links to Britten's musical legacy by remaining at Aldeburgh's Britten-Pears School for Advanced Musical Studies, teaching vocal master classes to a new generation of aspiring singers.

SOURCES:
Carpenter, Humphrey. *Benjamin Britten: A Biography*. NY: Scribner, 1992.
Herbert, David, ed. *The Operas of Benjamin Britten*. London: Hamish Hamilton, 1979.
Johnson, Graham. "Voice and Piano," in Christopher Palmer, ed. *The Britten Companion*. Cambridge, U.K.: Cambridge University Press, 1984, pp. 286–307.
Law, Joe K. "Linking the Past with the Present: A Conversation with Nancy Evans and Eric Crozier," in *Opera Quarterly*. Vol. 3, no. 1. Spring 1985, pp. 72–79.
Mitchell, Donald, *et al.*, *Letters From a Life: The Selected Letters and Diaries of Benjamin Britten 1913–1976*. 2 vols. Berkeley, CA: University of California Press, 1991.
Nicolai, Annette. "Benjamin Britten's 'A Charm of Lullabies': Historical Survey, Analysis and Performance" (Master of Music Thesis, California State University, Long Beach, 1992).

John Haag,
Assistant Professor of History,
University of Georgia, Athens, Georgia

Evarts, Esther (1900–1972).

See Benson, Sally.

Evdokhiia.

Variant of Eudoxia.

Eve

Biblical woman, written as the first woman, wife of Adam, and the ancestor of the human race. Name variations: (Hebrew) hawwâ (life). Created by God from Adam to be his companion in the Garden of Eden (Book of Genesis); children: Cain, Abel, and Seth, among others.

The Book of Genesis (Chapters 2 and 3) relates the story of the creation of Adam from "the dust of the ground," and Eve from the rib of Adam, so that they might live together in closeness and permanency forever. ("Therefore shall a man leave his father and his mother and shall cleave unto his wife; and they shall be one flesh.") Placed in the Garden of Eden, the first couple were sanctioned by God to eat of the fruit from any trees in the garden except that from the Tree of Knowledge of Good and Evil. The couple lived in innocent contentment until Eve was lured by the serpent (Satan) to partake of the forbidden fruit, which she ate, then tempted Adam to do the same. Immediately upon this transgression, they became aware and ashamed of their nakedness. For their disobedience, God expelled them from the Garden of Eden; Eve was

Fragment of Temptation and Expulsion from Eden, by Michelangelo.

made to suffer the pain of childbirth and her husband's dominion over her, and Adam was made to toil for a living by the sweat of his brow. Their greatest punishment was eventual death.

After the expulsion, Adam and Eve lived many years and gave birth to both sons and daughters, although the Bible calls only three by name: sons Cain, Abel, and Seth. There are only hints about Eve's life after leaving Eden. It is written that her first son Cain grew into "a sullen, self-willed, haughty, vindictive man" (Genesis 4), who, in an act of jealously, murdered his brother Abel. For his crime, God exiled Cain to a life of wandering and placed upon him "the mark of Cain." Eve named her third son Seth, meaning *appointed* or a *substitute,* saying "for God hath appointed me another seed instead of Abel, whom Cain slew" (Genesis 4:25; 5:3).

Biblical scholars now view the story of Genesis as an expression of the sacred authors' beliefs concerning the relationship of humans with God and the universe, and the human journey is foreshadowed in the experience of Adam and Eve.

Everleigh, Aida (1864–1960) and Minna (1866–1948)

American madams. Name variations: for professional purposes, the name Everleigh was taken from their grandmother's letter closings, "Everly Yours"; for legitimate business, they used the name Lester; also known as The Scarlet Sisters. Born Aida (1864) and Minna (1866) Simms in Stanardsville, a small town in Greene County, Virginia (because the sisters concealed their origins, biographers have continued to mistakenly place their birth in Kentucky); Minna died on September 16, 1948; Aida died on January 3, 1960; daughters of George Montgomery Simms (a widower and successful lawyer); attended private schools; in her early 20s, Minna married an older man named Lester; Aida married his brother; both marriages ended in divorce the following year.

Two sisters ran the Everleigh Club, the most successful and most expensive bordello in American history. Attractive daughters of George Montgomery Simms, a successful lawyer, Minna and Aida Simms grew up in southern gentility; they were tutored in dancing and elocution and attended private schools. While in their early 20s, they both endured arranged marriages to brothers who were "suspicious and jealous," complained Minna, "brutes with unbearable characters." A year later, both sisters divorced. Since acting and schoolteaching were the primary careers open to women, they joined an acting troupe during the early 1890s. In 1898, they found themselves stranded in Omaha, Nebraska. With the $35,000 inherited from their father, the sisters cast about for a less risky occupation.

Omaha was then host to the Trans-Mississippi Exposition, which made for an excess of tourists and cowboys in town. Savvy in business and seeing an unfilled need, the sisters opened a posh boardinghouse. They soon learned, however, that most other boardinghouses in their district were actually bordellos, fulfilling other needs. Since the Everleigh sisters did not want to lose their investment, "it was simply a matter of doing the right thing," said Aida. So they lined up attractive women, some of them actresses from the road show, and expanded the services and decor of their house. But posh remained. There was a Tiffany stained-glass ceiling in the foyer, gilt-edged mirrors, expensive wine and champagne, and a $15,000 gold-plated piano played by a music professor in full-evening dress.

Aida Everleigh

Aida was considered a business genius, the brains of the operation; Minna, with her charm and wit, was good press copy. By the end of the Exposition, they had parlayed their inheritance into $75,000, but the population of the town thinned and the Everleigh sisters decided to move on. In 1899, they went on a business tour of bordellos, canvassing New York, New Orleans and San Francisco. On the advice of Washington D.C. madam **Cleo Maitland**, the Everleighs settled in the red-light district in the Levee in Chicago. When they heard that the opulent house at 2131–33 South Dearborn Street —once run by Chicago's then most famous madam, the recently deceased **Lizzie Allen**—was available, the sis-

Minna Everleigh

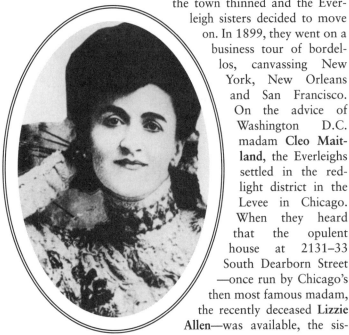

ters plunked down a deposit of $70,000 for a lifetime lease. The two three-story buildings, containing 50 rooms, had been run in the interim by **Effie Hankins**, who was thought to be a little too lowlife for the high-class house.

Like incoming presidents, the sisters immediately redecorated and replaced the staff. Aida, who considered the previous occupants "unschooled strumpets," set about holding interviews for new personnel, promising that they would retire rich. Choosing the prettiest and classiest—no amateurs need apply—the sisters soon had a waiting list of potential employees. Impeccably dressed and swathed in "house" jewels, the 30 chosen were among America's finest: beautiful, intelligent, and classy. Four hundred women would eventually find employment in the house, and many, as Aida predicted, retired with a great deal of money or married millionaires.

The Everleigh Club ("ask the operator for Calumet 412") opened with a press conference on February 1, 1900, followed by a tour. The sisters had not held back. Two-thirds of their capital had been spent on furnishings for the dining rooms, the large salons, and the 14 special reception rooms which included the Persian Room, the Japanese Room, the Rose Parlor, the Hall of a Thousand Mirrors, the Turkish Ballroom complete with fountain, and the Gold Room, featuring gold cuspidors, gold-rimmed fishbowls, and a $15,000 gold piano. There was plush velvet everywhere, along with tuxedoed orchestras, canaries chirping in gold cages, and a 1,000-book library. Most popular was the excellent food served at the buffet, a room decked out like a plush Pullman dining car. *Polly Adler, no slouch herself in the receiving department, gushed: "In every corner of the house there were always fresh roses, and on special nights Minna would have live butterflies fluttering about."

The captains of industry poured in, as did European royalty, as did celebrated athletes and actors, including John Barrymore and Gentleman Jim Corbett. An entrance fee was $50, an overnight fee $500. Tabs for an evening of comfort ran closer to $1,000. The sisters were admitted snobs, letting in only the elite; they wanted "no clerks on holiday." The less-than-affluent were not allowed, except for reporters who were pampered at reduced rates. Well aware that free advertising enhanced their business, Minna Everleigh also published an expensive brochure complete with half-tones, discreetly placed with the uppercrust; it advertised "steam heat in winter, fans in summer," along with valet service and 30 beautiful "girls" in any season. By 1902, Chicago boasted two tourist attractions: the Union stockyards and the Everleigh Club.

The sisters, said to net $120,000 a year, were always fashionably dressed and did their banking in a green velvet livery, generally accompanied by one of their beauties who sat up front like a bus ad. But there were hidden costs: $10,000 a year in bribes and protection. Chicago's notorious Big Jim Colosimo, who was married to another whorehouse madam **Victoria Moresco**, served as their middleman.

All this ended in 1911 when evangelists began a crusade to close the Levee. A bust-popping, attention-getting ride down Chicago's sacrosanct Michigan Avenue by **Vicki Shaw** (another madam, whom Minna felt had no class) didn't help the situation. When one of Minna's tasteful brochures landed by mistake, or by setup, on the mayor's desk, a special commission on vice was convened. The mayor ordered the closing of the house on October 24, 1911. Getting wind of the impending raid, the Everleigh sisters embarked on a six-month tour of Europe, having laid off their staff with six-months' severance pay. Upon their return, the sisters retired. The twosome bought a brownstone on West 70th Street in Manhattan near Central Park, furnished it with the finest from the Everleigh Club, began using the name Lester, and lived the life of respectable club women; they also formed a poetry circle. "They was more like a pair of female professors than madams," said Vicki Shaw. "They was interested in all them long-hair things." The shrewd Aida managed to steer their earnings through the Great Depression intact. The growing worth of the "house" jewels was estimated at anywhere from $200,000 to $1 million. "The Everleigh sisters made the logical retort to a business economy that discriminated against them on the basis of their sex," writes **Caroline Bird** in *Enterprising Women*; "they found a way to capitalize on the very fact that excluded them from the business world."

Just before 82-year-old Minna died on September 16, 1948, she reputedly said to a reporter: "We never hurt anybody, did we? We never robbed widows and we made no false representations, did we?" After shipping her sister's body to Roanoke, Virginia, for burial, Aida moved into a small cottage nearby; there she lived to be 95, dying on January 3, 1960. The tombstones for both are marked Lester.

SOURCES:

Adler, Polly. *A House is Not a Home.* NY: Rinehart, 1953.

Bird, Caroline. *Enterprising Women.* NY: W.W. Norton, 1976.

Nash, Jay Robert. *Look for the Woman.* NY: M. Evans. 1981.

Evert, Chris (1954—)

American tennis player, winner of six U.S Open and three Wimbledon titles, who, at the time of retirement, had won more singles titles and matches than any other player in the history of tennis. Name variations: Chris Evert Lloyd; Chris Evert Mill. Born Christine Marie Evert on December 21, 1954, in Fort Lauderdale, Florida; one of five children of James and Collette Evert; educated in local public schools; married John Lloyd, in 1979 (divorced 1987); married Andrew Mill, in 1988; children: (second marriage) Alexander (b. 1991); Nicholas (b. 1993); Colton Jack (b. 1995).

Began playing tennis seriously at six under her father's coaching (1960); played her first U.S. Open (1971); won the first of three titles at Wimbledon (1974); won the first of six women's singles titles in the U.S. Open (1975); became world's top-seeded female tennis player (1980) and remained among the top five on the women's tour until 1985, when personal problems affected her game; retired from the professional tour (1989), but has since appeared in various celebrity tours, and as a network TV commentator; also active in charity fund-raising.

Won the women's singles championship at Wimbledon (1974, 1976, 1981); won the women's singles U.S. Open championships (1975–1978, 1980, 1982); won the Australian Open (1982, 1984); won the French Open (1974, 1975, 1979, 1980, 1983, 1985, 1986); won 18 "Grand Slam" singles titles during her career.

The crowd at the women's semifinals match at Wimbledon in 1989 stood and cheered when **Steffi Graf defeated her opponent, but even Graf knew the cheers weren't as much for her as for the trim blonde facing her across the net. The thundering applause and shouts of support were the public's sendoff for its beloved "Chris America," Christine Marie Evert, who had just played her last set at Wimbledon after an 18-year tour on the women's professional circuit in which she had won nearly 90% of some 1,300 career matches, and had ranked among the top three women players in the world for 14 of those years. Now 34, Evert had announced her retirement earlier in the year, but few knew the personal journey that had led to such a difficult decision.

Tennis had been Evert's entire life. When she was barely six years old, she began her first lessons with her father James Evert, a tennis pro and coach in Fort Lauderdale, Florida, where Chris was born in 1954. Despite the early start, Chris would always credit her family background for giving her the strength to survive 18 years in a sport highly competitive in both an athletic and social sense. "I had great parents," she says. "Yes, my father was my coach when I started out, but he never travelled the tour, never pushed or prodded me in public." It was, in fact, her mother **Collette Evert** who did the chaperoning. Both parents emphasized court etiquette over winning, the basis for Evert's later reputation for grace and calm, no matter if she'd just won or lost. At home, she says, she was treated just like the other four Evert children and, like them, had to take out the trash and do the dishes. "I stayed within the rules," she says. "I was not a risk taker and I didn't have a rebellious nature."

The truth is, my life began the day my career ended.

—Chris Evert

It was her father who taught her the trademarks for which her game would be known. By nature a serious, publicly undemonstrative man, Jim Evert taught Chris to never show emotion on court. "That way," he would tell her, "your opponent never knows what you're thinking." So carefully did Chris put this advice into practice that she would come to be called "The Ice Maiden" for her poker-faced demeanor. Jim Evert also developed Chris' signature, two-fisted backhand and her uncanny ability to lob a ball to the exact spot that would be most unreachable for her opponent. He helped her develop the overall strategy that would characterize her game—outwaiting her opposition rather than taking a chance or going for a quick win. Looking back at her career from seven years' distance, Evert says, "I can see how tough I was, the killer instinct, the single-mindedness, playing like a machine. I was a tough cookie, but then the cookie crumbled."

Evert entered her first major match at the age of 16, in Charlotte, North Carolina, where she bested *Margaret Court, who had just won tennis' coveted Grand Slam—the U.S. Open, the French Open, Wimbledon, and the Australian Open. The next year, 1971, Evert made it to the semifinals of the U.S. Open by saving six match points to beat **Mary Ann Eisel** in the second round—a remarkable feat for a 16-year-old barely out of high school. Just four years later, she took her first Open title, beating Australian *Evonne Goolagong 6–2 in the third round. It

would be followed by five more Open titles in 18 visits to Forest Hills.

Always shy and uncertain in social situations, Evert soon discovered that tennis was about more than court strategy and keeping cool. "Winning made me feel like I was somebody," she told journalist Alan Ebert in 1990. "It made me feel pretty. It was like being hooked on a drug. I needed the wins, the applause, in order to have an identity." But it was only in retrospect that Evert would realize the mental and emotional agony to which she subjected herself for the game and find the support to discover a new identity far removed from the cheering and attention.

The tennis world of the early 1970s was dominated by *Billie Jean King, Margaret Court, *Rosie Casals, and *Virginia Wade, all of whom served as mentors for Evert and for whom she maintains a deep respect. But by the mid-1970s, Chris' generation had come into its own on the courts, as she was joined by **Pam Shriver** and the woman with whom she would form the closest friendship and most intense rivalry of her playing years, *Martina Navratilova. Following Martina's defection from the then Soviet-dominated Czechoslovakia in the early 1970s, it was Evert who helped her adjust to life in the West.

The two had met in 1973 in Fort Lauderdale and were close professionally and socially by 1975. They became doubles partners at the French Open (Evert beat Navratilova in the singles competition), and Navratilova won her first Wimbledon title the following year when she and Evert won the doubles competition. "We had a ball together," Navratilova recalls, "hitting the great restaurants, having picnics in our hotel rooms." But the relationship nearly foundered in the face of professional pressure, especially when Navratilova began training under coach *Nancy Lieberman-Cline. "As I became more competitive," Martina once said diplomatically, "Chris pulled back a little." Chris is more direct. "Nancy taught Martina to hate me," she says. "And it worked." While Evert swept 14 of her first 16 singles matches with Navratilova from 1973 to 1976, Lieberman-Cline's intense psychological program, coupled with bodybuilding and running, pushed Navratilova to number one by 1983, elbowing Evert firmly out of the way for the next three years. Evert retaliated by embarking on a rigorous weight training and aerobics regimen. At the semifinals of the Australian Open in 1987, the two women faced off. "I thought, Whoa! Wait a minute," Navratilova remembers. "Where is my friend? This woman across the net is trying to kill me!" Evert soundly

Chris
Evert

trounced Navratilova in straight sets, but both of them learned a lesson in priorities. Their friendship has never faltered since.

For Evert, the 1970s brought more than a changing of the guard and a consolidation of her position as one of the world's best tennis players. Despite the public image of the quintessential good sport, Evert was becoming increasingly troubled. "I hated being a role model," she once confessed, "hated being placed on a pedestal. I was never the girl next door and I certainly was no angel." As if rebelling against her strict upbringing and carefully controlled court persona, she embarked on a series of less-than-private affairs, including her well-publicized but short-lived engagement to Jimmy Connors. It was quickly followed by brief affairs with Burt Reynolds, former President Gerald Ford's son, Jack Ford, and British rock star Adam Faith. On tour nearly constantly and gathering a sizeable entourage around her, she was unable to separate real friends from those who sought her company merely as a celebrity tennis star. In the locker room, Evert became known for an earthy, and often bitingly sarcastic, wit sharply at odds with her public image.

Despite the adulation and attention she daily received, Evert had never been lonelier. She particularly remembers one year when, after winning Wimbledon, she returned to her hotel room with an overwhelming sense of emptiness. "I had just won tennis' biggest tournament," she said, "and was feeling awful. It was then I knew there had to be something more to life."

Her "something more," at first, was her marriage to Britain's second-ranked tennis player, John Lloyd, in 1979. The two had met at Wimbledon the year before. "He was kind and a real gentleman," Evert told an interviewer shortly after the marriage. "He never complains when people push him aside or pay more attention to me." Nonetheless, the couple had separated by 1984, and Evert put the blame for the breakup squarely on her own shoulders. "Because tennis requires that you be totally self-involved," she said some years later, "I never learned how to be there for another person. I put all my emotions into my game and had little left over to give John what he needed." John's own game and rankings had plummeted precipitously during their time together, and he admitted to the press that he didn't react very well when "all of a sudden I'd gone from being just a tennis player to Evert's husband. I was just sitting around and watching television." Although the two would remain good friends, their separation became permanent and was followed by a divorce in 1987. Chris was the first Evert to seek a divorce, and her parents, both devout Catholics, strongly objected. Nevertheless, there were positive reverberations for her. "Divorcing John marked the first time I took sole responsibility for me and my happiness," she recalls. "It was a turning point."

Her separation from John marked the beginning of what Evert calls her "blue period," two introspective years in which she dealt with her feelings of guilt for her unsuccessful marriage and tried to find the direction she wanted her life to take. It was during this time that it became apparent to her that the future would have to be built on something more solid than a clay tennis court. In 1986, she told *Life* that she had been a "little robot" for the past ten years; "Wind her up and she plays tennis," she said. "Now I can't wait for my rest weeks so that I can do normal things. I've had enormous success, but you have to find your own happiness and peace." A knee injury forced her off the court for several months that same year—not beneficial to her game, by any means, but slowing her down enough to give her time to think.

Part of this self-enforced downtime was spent with Navratilova in Aspen, Colorado, where Martina spent most of her own off-court time. The friendship had survived their professional rivalry, to the extent that Navratilova tried to help Evert get back on a solid emotional footing. In 1986, Navratilova dragged Evert to a New Year's Eve party in Aspen and introduced her to Andy Mill, a former Olympic skier. Although it wasn't exactly love at first sight, the two discovered in the next few weeks that they had more in common than either had at first suspected. Mill was himself in the middle of a troublesome divorce proceeding; but more important, he had undergone the same transformation five years earlier that Evert was now seeking, when a catastrophic skiing accident had left him with a fractured neck, back, and leg and scotched any future plans for a professional career. Forced to create a new life, Mill had begun by coaching children on the slopes with such success that he soon had a loyal following of adult students, and he had convinced a Denver television station to carry a five-minute "ski tips" series he had written. By the time he met Evert, the show had been nationally syndicated, and Mill had a profitable television contract with NBC Sports as a guest commentator for the network's coverage of World Cup skiing.

Mill's success suggested to Evert that there could be life after tennis. "For many years," she said, "I won matches for my father. Later, I won for John. Andy told me to win only for me, or not to play at all if that was my wish, because in his mind I was a winner no matter what." In May of 1988, Chris and Andy were married. Shortly afterward, with her knee injury healed, Evert went back on tour.

But Mill's advice stuck with her. As 1988 wore on, Evert came to realize it would be her last year. She knew she wasn't playing in top form anymore, and she found it difficult matching the intensity of the younger opponents she met on the court; and while she maintained her ranking among the top four players in the world, Steffi Graf and other younger players like *Gabriela Sabatini and Monica Seles, to all of whom she was now losing, were closing in. Evert had always publicly maintained that the only way an athlete can mark the prime of her career is to play past it. By mid-1988, she knew her own peak was behind her. In May, after losing a match in Geneva to Barbara Paulus, she came off the court, walked up to Mill, and told him she wanted to go home. Her plans to play the upcoming French Open were canceled, and she formally announced her retirement from the women's tour that summer. Just as an older generation had made room for her, Evert told reporters that it was time for the younger women to have their day. "Each time I watch them," she said, "I remember how it felt to be young and fresh and keen. The fact is, I'm not going to get any better, and they are."

The lamentations and regrets were many, but Evert handled them with her usual calm demeanor. Her father was the most difficult to convince, but even he eventually realized the inevitability of her decision. Navratilova wrote that Evert's retirement would leave "an aching hollow in women's tennis and, indeed, in all of sport. Her legacy . . . is dignity." Equally as important, Evert helped redefine the woman athlete in a traditionally male-dominated sport. She was quick to come to Martina's defense when Navratilova announced she was gay, costing Martina professional and public censure, especially from parents who had held Navratilova up to their children as a role model. "I would tell my children," Evert told *Sports Illustrated*, "to look at the way she conducts herself on the court. Look at how she fights for every point. And look how honest she is with people. I guess a lot of parents aren't ready for that yet."

Evert left the tour after 18 years with a record of winning more singles titles and matches (157 and 1,300, respectively) than any other player in the history of tennis. Her earnings from the game totaled nearly $9 million, second only to Navratilova. Since her retirement, Evert has played numerous celebrity tournaments, notably the "Legends Tour" with Navratilova, Billie Jean King, and *Tracy Austin; has joined Mill as a commentator for NBC Sports; and has raised close to a million dollars for Florida's Ounce of Prevention Fund, an outreach program for drug-addicted pregnant women for which she is an advocate. She has served several terms as president of the Women's International Tennis Association and, in July of 1995, was inducted into the International Tennis Hall of Fame.

Today, however, she considers her major achievements to be more personal in nature; namely her marriage to Mill and the birth of their three sons—Alexander (b. 1991), Nicholas (b. 1993), and Colton Jack (b. 1995). There are no plans for any of the boys to take up tennis seriously. "I don't want any child of mine to come away from what is only a game feeling he's either a winner or a loser," Evert says. "I'd rather see a smile on his face than a trophy in his hand." Chris Evert has been lucky enough to have both.

SOURCES:

Ebert, Alan. "Chris Evert: My Love Match with Andy," in *Good Housekeeping*. Vol. 211, no. 4. October 1990.

———. "Chris Evert: Always a Winner," in *Good Housekeeping*. Vol. 221, no. 1. July 1995.

Evert, Chris, with Curry Kirkpatrick. "Tennis Was My Showcase," in *Sports Illustrated*. Vol. 71, no. 9. August 28, 1989.

Henry, William A., III. "I Can See How Tough I Was," in *Time*. Vol. 134, no. 11. September 11, 1989.

Jenkins, Sally. "I've Lived a Charmed Life," in *Sports Illustrated*. Vol. 76, no. 20. May 25, 1992.

Johnson, Bonny, and Meg Grant. "Special Delivery (Chris Evert Had a Baby Boy)," in *People Weekly*. Vol. 36, no. 20. November 25, 1991.

Navratilova, Martina. "A Great Friend and Foe; No One Will Miss Chris Evert More Than Her Chief Rival," in *Sports Illustrated*. Vol. 71, no. 9. August 28, 1989.

Whipple, Christopher. "Chrissie: With a Handsome Husband and Millions of Bucks, What's the Matter with Evert Lloyd?," in *Life*. Vol. 9. June 1986.

Norman Powers,
writer/producer, Chelsea Lane Productions,
New York, New York

Ewing, Juliana Horatia

(1841–1885)

British writer who produced a number of children's books with a simple, unaffected style, including Jackanapes *and* Lob-Lie-by-the-Fire. *Born Juliana Horatia Gatty on August 3, 1841; died on May 13, 1885; second of the eight surviving children of Dr. Alfred Gatty, vicar of Ecclesfield, and Margaret (Scott) Gatty (1809–1873, a writer); married Major Alexander "Rex" Ewing (a soldier in the commissariat), on June 1, 1867.*

Writings—books: Melchior's Dream and Other Tales *(London: Bell & Daldy, 1862);* Mrs. Overtheway's Remembrances *(London: Bell & Daldy, 1869);* The Brownies and Other Tales *(London: Bell & Daldy, 1870);* A Flat Iron for a Farthing *(London:*

Bell, 1872); Lob Lie-by-the-fire, or The Luck of Lingborough, and Other Tales (London: Bell, 1874); Six to Sixteen (London: Bell, 1875); Jan of the Windmill; A Story of the Plains (London: Bell, 1876); A Great Emergency and Other Tales (London: Bell, 1877); We and the World (London: Bell, 1880); Old-Fashioned Fairy Tales (London: Bell, 1882); Brothers of Pity and Other Tales of Beasts and Men (London: Society for Promoting Christian Knowledge, 1882); Blue and Red, or The Discontented Lobster (London: S.P.C.K., 1883); The Dolls' Wash; Rhymes (London: S.P.C.K., 1883); A Week Spent in the Glass Pond by the Great Water Beetle (London: Wells, Darton, 1883); Master Fritz; Rhymes (London: S.P.C.K., 1883); Jackanapes (London: S.P.C.K., 1883); Our Garden; Rhymes (London: S.P.C.K., 1883); A Soldier's Children; Rhymes (London: S.P.C.K., 1883); A Sweet Little Dear; Rhymes (London: S.P.C.K., 1883); Three Little Nest-Birds; Rhymes (London: S.P.C.K., 1883); The Blue Bells on the Lea (London: S.P.C.K., 1884); Daddy Darwin's Dovecote (London: S.P.C.K., 1884); Dolls' Housekeeping; Rhymes (London: S.P.C.K., 1884); Little Boys and Wooden Horses; Rhymes (London: S.P.C.K., 1884); Papa Poodle and Other Pets; Rhymes (London: S.P.C.K., 1884); Tongues in Trees; Rhymes (London: S.P.C.K., 1884); "Touch Him If You Dare": A Tale of the Hedge; Rhymes (London: S.P.C.K., 1884); Poems of Child Life and Country Life (London: S.P.C.K., 1885); The Story of a Short Life (London: S.P.C.K., 1885); Mary's Meadow and Other Tales (London: S.P.C.K., 1886); Dandelion Clocks and Other Tales (London: S.P.C.K., 1887); The Peace Egg and A Christmas Mumming Play (London: S.P.C.K., 1887); Snap-Dragons, and Old Father Christmas (London: S.P.C.K., 1888); Verses for Children, 3 vols. (London: S.P.C.K., 1888); Works, 18 vols. (London: S.P.C.K., 1894–96).

Letters: Elizabeth S. Tucker, Leaves from Juliana Horatia Ewing's "Canada Home" (Boston: Roberts Brothers, 1896); Margaret Howard Blom and Thomas E. Blom, eds., Canada Home: Juliana Ewing's Fredericton Letters 1867–1869 (Vancouver: University of British Columbia Press, 1983).

Juliana Horatia Ewing was a storyteller par excellence. Writing only for children and concentrating on the experiences of youngsters in either the nursery or the schoolroom, Ewing showed a natural sympathy and grace reminiscent of Hans Christian Andersen, an exquisite and careful attention to the details of family life, and a deep identification with her characters. No aspect of a child's experience was too small or insignificant for Ewing; she tended to favor

pensive, aesthetically inclined, tractable, but high-spirited central characters who enjoy gardening, animals, and adventure. Ewing's upbringing in a staunch Church of England circle and her unquestioned fidelity to Anglicanism never translated into wearying didacticism in her tales, verse, and full-length novels. As a cleric's daughter who became a soldier's wife, Ewing also wrote with firsthand knowledge and real affection about the military; life in a camp bungalow, the frequency of moves from one station to another, and the continuing efforts to beautify new surroundings and create a garden were elements of her experience reflected in her writing.

There is a delicacy about Ewing's tales, as there was about the author, who because of a childhood susceptibility to quinsy (inflamed tonsils) was dubbed by her mother the "Countess of Homeopathy." She believed firmly in the law of reticence; aware of "the blunder of throwing away powder and shot," she insisted that "a real artist needs strong warrants of Conscience when he dips into . . . the highest hopes, the deepest sufferings of humanity." However, although Ewing did not shy away from these heights and depths in criticizing authoritarian or negligent adults and inadequate educational systems in her family stories, she was no joyless crusader. Sparkling wit, geniality, and an unshakeable belief in human goodness mark all her work.

She won a loyal following among contemporary writers and artists for the young and those of the next generation influenced by her; John Ruskin was a regular subscriber to Aunt Judy's Magazine, the periodical started by Ewing's mother, in which most of Ewing's tales first appeared; *Charlotte Mary Yonge was an admirer and an early supporter of her work; and Randolph Caldecott, who agreed to illustrate some of her work, observed that Ewing possessed "a larger bump of imagination than falls to the skulls of most critics." Rudyard Kipling admitted having almost memorized whole stories by Ewing, while Arnold Bennett was convinced that Kipling's portraits of military life owed a great deal to his having read Ewing as a child.

Born on August 3, 1841, the second of the eight surviving children of Dr. Alfred Gatty, vicar of Ecclesfield, and *Margaret Gatty, Juliana Horatia Gatty was a true child of the manse. The life of the Ecclesfield vicarage, with its High Church principles, family loyalties, and middle-class prejudices, was the first influence on her work and would be one of the most prevailing. Juliana and her sisters were educated at home by their mother; the boys were sent to public schools (Eton, Winchester, Marlborough, and Charterhouse). "Julie," as her siblings called her, was a natural leader. Her sister **Horatia Eden** pictured Julie as "at once the projector and manager of all our nursery doings."

As reflections of what she knew best, the responsibilities of family life loom large in Ewing's first stories. Throughout her writing career she stressed the importance of family and friendly mentors and the transformational potential of special or instructive experiences. She was also fond of the device of nesting a story within a story, a technique at which she became expert. Thanks to her mother's reputation, Ewing gained an entrée to Yonge's magazine, *Monthly Packet,* where her first stories, "A Bit of Green," "The Blackbird's Nest," and "Melchior's Dream," were published (in July, August, and December 1861).

From the beginning, amid the solemn moral trappings of these tales, Ewing was distinguished as a fine storyteller who developed fully the emotional life of her characters. The doctor's son in "A Bit of Green," whose plans for a vacation in the country have been thwarted by his father's busy schedule, learns a valuable lesson by visiting one of his father's patients in the slums. Bill, a consumptive cripple who has never been outside the city, lives in a stark and ugly room; "but through the glass panes that were left, in full glory streamed the sun, and in the midst of the blaze stood a pot of musk in full bloom." The flowers and fragrance of this bit of green leave the once ill-humored narrator "lost in admiration." Ewing likely assimilated the paradigm of the privileged child learning from the experience of helping the less fortunate from the sentimental evangelical novels of **Mary Louisa Charlesworth,** especially *Ministering Children* (1854). Although Ewing presents the moral about "the grace of Thankfulness," especially after Bill "was transplanted into a heavenly garden," without much subtlety, she succeeds in creating a believable child narrator.

The girl narrator of "The Blackbird's Nest" is similarly credible: she finds three birds and imagines that she will "walk about with them on [her] shoulders like Goody Twoshoes, and be admired by everybody." The curate tries to dissuade her, and when she discovers her pets "cold and dead," he helps to console her by relating an incident of his own youthful presumptuousness. Ewing succeeds in meshing fancy with noninsistent mentoring.

An adult friend and a story within a story both figure in "Melchior's Dream," but this nar-

Juliana
Horatia
Ewing

rative—the most refined of the early trio—is expansive and nuanced, allowing a young boy fed up with his siblings to journey into the future and preview their various torments. The lad quickly feels the point of the story about his alter ego, admitting, "it hit me rather hard" and confessing, "I want to say that though I didn't mean all I said about being an only son (when a fellow gets put out he doesn't know what he means), yet I know I was quite wrong, and the story is quite right." Christian moralizing, unobtrusive yet scripturally sound and therefore appealing to both High Church and chapel tastes, concludes "Melchior's Dream," which alludes to "a better Home than any earthly one, and a Family that shall never be divided."

Yonge's *Monthly Packet* published two more stories by Ewing: "The Yew Lane Ghosts" (1865) and "The Brownies" (1865). The former displays a terrific capacity for creating suspense, a feature Ewing chose not to develop in her later work. Although she offered no explanation for not continuing in this vein, speculations include her possible discomfort with stage-managing the supernatural and with almost unregenerate malevolence. When the friends of a lad who is being terrorized by a village bully rally round to help him, they manage, with the help of chemicals, to produce their own "scenic effects." They succeed in frightening Bully Tom into penitence by creating a grotesque, headless apparition.

Confining its effects to the domestic sphere, "The Brownies," dedicated to "my very dear and honoured Mother," is not nearly as horrific. A poor tailor's idle sons become true helpers and are mistaken for Brownies, "a race of tiny beings who . . . take up their abode with some worthy couple . . . and take little troubles out of hands full of great anxieties."

Two major sources of power and agency in Ewing's literary life were her mother and her husband. As a bookish young woman, Margaret Gatty had made presents to friends of her own illuminated and translated versions of Dante. Even as the mother of a large family, she pursued her scientific interest in varieties of seaweed. Her parables, allegories, and tales do not hesitate to instruct and moralize. Quickly realizing the superior literary ability of her daughter, she encouraged Julie from the outset. *Aunt Judy's Magazine,* so called after the family nickname for Juliana, was the main outlet for most of Julie's stories. It was also a needed source of income for the Gatty menage, which could not exist on the vicar's scanty salary. Ewing eventually shared her mother's pecuniary anxieties too, since both women ended up paying the debts incurred by their husbands.

Besides being influenced by her mother's tastes and talents for writing and translating and understanding the need of these activities to pay for her brothers' school fees, Julie followed another family tradition in facing and surmounting opposition to her marriage plans. Just as the suitors of Margaret Gatty had been rejected initially, so too Major Alexander "Rex" Ewing, a soldier in the commissariat and ten years her senior, was not immediately welcomed by the Gattys. Julie, by contrast, was rhapsodic about her fiancé, confiding to a correspondent in December 1866: "A beautiful musician-good linguist-well read, etc.—a dab at meteorology, photography, awfully fond of dogs, good rider, finally a high free mason (a knight Templar) and . . . a . . . *mesmerist!* He suits me to a shade." They were married on June 1, 1867, and sailed for Canada, Rex's new assignment, on June 8.

Marriage was a form of liberation for Ewing, who was freed from duties around the vicarage and from the need to contribute to the family purse; she was also freed to start a life of adventure as a military wife. As **Christabel Maxwell** relates, Ewing wrote to her family that she had "found a double of [her]self and that it feels like the addition of a few new faculties—a large accession of strength—and a sort of mental companion, footman, courier, lady's maid, lover, and attendant geni rolled into one."

Ironies surround this liberation, however. Ewing ended up facing greater financial anxieties than those she had left behind; the separation from her family and especially from her mother led to serious bouts of homesickness. Yet her clear enjoyment of the life of a military camp, the friendships with other military families, and the spirited theatrical entertainments to which she often contributed also meant that Ewing was a much more productive writer, publishing 11 short stories before her marriage and more than twice that amount plus three novels in her first six years as an army wife.

Gatty's editorship of *Aunt Judy's Magazine*—which she launched in 1866 and continued until her death in 1873, after which her daughters took over the enterprise and continued publication until 1885—supplied a stable venue for Ewing's stories. The five interrelated stories comprising *Mrs. Overtheway's Remembrances* (1869)—"Ida," "Mrs. Moss," "The Snoring Ghost," "Reka Dom," and "Kerguelen's Land"—first appeared serially in *Aunt Judy's Magazine* from 1866 to 1868.

The Ewings arrived in Fredericton during the celebrations for Confederation, "a very gay week" according to the young bride's letter home; they left two years later as the last British troops withdrew from New Brunswick. Thomas and **Margaret Blom** have edited a portion of Ewing's letters and sketches from Canada, and these documents reveal a largely idyllic period, during which the newlyweds discovered snowshoeing and canoeing, benefited from the warm and protective hospitality of the Anglican community who were familiar with both Ewing's and Gatty's works, and learned of basic domestic needs, such as the thawing of meat for 24 hours before cooking and the necessity of wool blankets. Rex studied Hebrew with the bishop of Fredericton, and Julie was so enchanted by the autumn foliage that she sent a box of scarlet maple leaves to her sisters in Yorkshire as decorations for the harvest home festivities at the Ecclesfield church. They called their first home in

Fredericton, rented from the president of the University of New Brunswick, Reka Dom, Russian for "River House" and the title of a story that Ewing wrote while in Canada.

In England the most settled posting for Major Ewing was Aldershot, where the couple stayed until 1877. In Julie Ewing's stories details of military and family life mingled more noticeably. One of her finest early portraits of this blending is "The Peace Egg" (1871), the account of a Christmas change of heart brought about not by Dickensian ghosts but by ebullient children. A crusty old widower has disinherited his daughter because she went against his wishes and married a soldier. After years of foreign postings the Captain and his wife and family are at last back in England and living close to the cantankerous gentleman who is, unknown to the children, their own grandfather. Ewing conveys this information in the opening pages and then lets the emotional pilgrimage begin. Her loyalties as a narrator clearly lie with the young couple and their military life. In contrast to the misanthropy of the old

man's existence, their marriage is a secure partnership, built on uncomplaining thoughtfulness and handiness on both sides. The children, whose performance of the nursery mumming play melts the obduracy of their neighbor and effects the reconciliation of their parents and newly discovered grandfather, are precocious and self-possessed. Class differences also work to favor and promote the mummers. When the old man's "timid-looking" maid opens the door to the Christmas troupe and tries to shoo them away, the poor woman's employer thunders in support of the mummers. The transformation of this authoritarian employer into a fond grandpapa and the hatching of "happy peacemaking" and "general rejoicing" from "The Peace Egg" may, in fact, be a little hard to believe, but Ewing's attraction to harmony determines the sort of resolution for which she always strives.

An increasingly remarkable feature of Ewing's work is her skill in observing the patterns of family life, an aptitude that came into prominence in stories without the normal com-

Ecclesfield Vicarage. (From Juliana Horatia Ewing and Her Books, by Horatia K.F. Eden. Drawing by Juliana Horatia Ewing.)

plement of natural parents: *Lob Lie-by-the-Fire, or The Luck of Lingborough* (1874), *Six to Sixteen* (1875), and *Jan of the Windmill; A Story of the Plains* (1876; originally published as "The Miller's Thumb" in *Aunt Judy's Magazine* from November 1872 to October 1873). The kind ministrations of generous women propel the narrative in these stories. When two spinster sisters from Lingborough Hall find a male baby beneath a broom bush, the reactions of Miss Betty and Miss Kitty point to the practical common sense of their Christian philanthropy. The first major decision the ladies must make concerns the name of the lad. Countering Miss Kitty's wish for a "pretty" and "romantic" name, Miss Betty opts for simple functionality; as she reasons, "The boy is to be brought up in that station in life for which one syllable is ample. . . . I propose to call him Broom. He was found under a bush of broom, and it goes very well with John, and sounds plain and respectable."

Concepts of plainness and respectability trigger most of the episodes of this extended tale, which relates how young John runs away from the abusive bailiff to whom he is apprenticed and how he finally finds his way back to Lingborough thanks to the intervention of a dying Highland soldier. It is a long homeward journey for John Broom, one that brings good luck to Lingborough. Although Broom settles as a respected citizen and raises a family in the area, "it is doubtful if John Broom was ever looked upon by the rustics as quite 'like other folk.' The favourite version of his history is that he was Lob under the guise of a child."

The realism is not magical but decidedly down-to-earth in *Six to Sixteen*, the diarylike entries of the orphaned Margaret Vandaleur, who comes to live with the Arkwrights and finds a sisterly companion in Eleanor Arkwright. One winter these teenaged girls decide to follow the "fad" of writing autobiographies, "merely to be lives of our own selves, for nobody but us two to read when we are both old maids." Although Margaret, coming upon her story a year later, regards it as but "a dusty relic of an old fad," Ewing's "sketch of domestic life" chronicles the eventful life of a Victorian orphan—from her childhood spent at a military camp in India to her private schooling at the home of her guardian, a Yorkshire vicar. With accurate strokes Ewing pictures the self-appointed director of all army wives, Mrs. Minchin, a notorious gossip; Margaret's Aunt Theresa, whose foolish gadding as Minchin's protegé leads to the neglect of her own daughter; the housekeeper Kezi-

ah, whose refreshing common sense sets the tone for the welcoming Arkwright home; and the knowledgeable mistress of this home, who unconventionally performs her maternal duties while also pursuing her interests as an amateur zoologist. Clearly this digressive account of the journey from girlhood to adolescence draws on many of Ewing's experiences and memories as an older sister who was likely part Eleanor and part Keziah.

Jan of the Windmill, one of Ewing's most successful novels, outlines the rewards, both monetary and aesthetic, that the foster child Jan brings to the family of an industrious miller, Abel Lake. Ewing concentrates not only on the minutiae of family life but also on the generally acknowledged superiority of the young boy with an artistic temperament over his adoptive and working-class parents. It is really a novel of cloaked identities, a juvenile Samuel Richardson or Henry Fielding novel, with Jan's aristocratic lineage being revealed at the end and an appropriate daughter of a squire being chosen as his wife. Ewing's deference to the gentry in matters of taste and morals, sometimes problematic for late-20th-century readers, is not veiled in any way, and the racist slurs that went unquestioned in her mid-Victorian Anglican milieu crop up too. When describing the appearance of the mysterious infant as the nurse delivers him to the Abel home, Ewing writes, "The contrast between the natural red of the baby's complexion and its snowy finery was ludicrously suggestive of an over-dressed nigger to begin with."

The death of her mother on October 4, 1873, was a severe blow to Ewing, who was deprived of her earliest and most intuitive mentor. As she admitted in a letter to her husband shortly after, "I have a feeling as if she were an ever-present conscience to me . . . which I hope by God's grace may never leave me." Her elegy, "In Memoriam, Margaret Gatty" (1873), clarifies how her mother had fostered many of Ewing's interests. Gatty's pencil drawings of trees and her determination to "attack bits of waste or neglected ground from which every body else shrank" promoted her daughter's love of gardens and beautification. Gatty loved animals; "the household pets were about her to the end." Despite the lingering effects of the stroke that gradually robbed her of the use of limbs and voice, Gatty maintained "a strong sense of humour" and "a child's pure delight in little things."

Ewing's ideas on literary models were certain and deliberate. Walter Scott had her vote over George Eliot (*Mary Anne Evans*) because of his control of tone, his "artlessness and roughness." She liked the narrative sweep, the sense of historical saga, and the layered social scene in Scott as opposed to the intense character studies of Eliot. In a letter of 16 March 1880, she disclosed what she considered the "two qualifications for a writer of fiction" that Scott possessed in abundance: "Dramatism and individuality amongst his characters." Although she deemed Eliot's writing "glorious," she concluded pointedly: "Imagination limited—Dramatism—nil!" Her assessment of Eliot seems uncharacteristically extreme and limited; perhaps Ewing, as a writer for the young, learned the most from Scott's control of narrative incident.

John Ruskin was an admired contemporary who treated "Aunt Judy" with great respect and attentiveness on her visits to Herne Hill. Ewing confided in a letter to her family (October 11, 1879) that she found Ruskin "far more personally lovable than . . . expected." "We are so utterly at one on some points," she declared. "I mean it is uncommonly pleasant to hear things one has long thought very vehemently, put to one by a Master! . . . And then to my delight I found him soldier—mad!!"

One of Ewing's best-known soldier stories, *Jackanapes* (1883; first published in *Aunt Judy's Magazine,* October 1879), combines dramatism and individuality to touching effect. It was prompted by the news of the death of the French prince imperial during the Zulu War in June 1879 and the need Ewing felt to offer some explanation of military honor to skeptical civilians. Her control of a narrative stretching from infancy to adulthood reflects the lessons learned about panoramic design from Scott. Jackanapes (whose real but unused name is Theodore), the orphan son of a soldier killed at the battle of Waterloo, is raised by his great-aunt, Miss Jessamine.

The novel's emphasis is on the wholeness and balance of experience. While it is true that the hero has a lion's share of virtue, he has been brought up to appreciate both manly and womanly traits. Ewing indulges in observations about Jackanapes's education that sound like a philosophical aside from Eliot herself:

> In good sooth, a young maid is all the better for learning some robuster virtues than maidenliness and not to move the antimacassars. And the robuster virtues require some fresh air and freedom. As, on the other hand, Jackanapes (who had a boy's full share of the little beast and the young monkey in his natural composition) was none the worse, at his tender years, for learning some maidenliness—so far as maidenliness

means decency, pity, unselfishness, and pretty behaviour.

In adult life Jackanapes dies on the battlefield while saving his childhood friend Tony Johnson. Selfless to the end, he expires defending and explaining his friend to the Major. It is thanks to Tony and his filial ministrations to the frail Miss Jessamine that the blow of her nephew's loss is cushioned. The praise that Jackanapes receives from all quarters echoes in Ewing's closing remarks about eternal verities, "things such as Love, and Honour, and the Soul of Man, which cannot be bought with a price, and which do not die with death." This credal statement constitutes Ewing's formulation of true military honor.

The ways in which the incorporation of a child within a community reflects on the group's specific values, openness, aspirations, and restrictions are the underlying concerns of all Ewing's final books. The "country tale" of *Daddy Darwin's Dovecote* (1884; first published in *Aunt Judy's Magazine,* November 1881) deserves to be compared with Eliot's *Silas Marner* (1861). As Eppie brightened the miserly Silas' life, so too Daddy Darwin's adoption of the workhouse lad Jack March brings prosperity to the dovecote and happiness to many in the region. Ewing shows an acute awareness of the social rounds of both working and middle classes in this Yorkshire country setting. The precise details of the schedule of the parson's well-meaning daughter show how much Ewing was drawing on her own memories of the Ecclesfield vicarage and the accounts of her younger sisters who continued to run it and look after their father. Within the overwhelmingly Christian norms of this country community, it is fitting that Jack's faithful, honest commitment to Daddy Darwin extends and continues the church-centered rhythms of their simple lives.

In *The Story of a Short Life* (1885; first published in *Aunt Judy's Magazine,* May-October 1882) involvement in the life of the nearby barracks transforms the spoiled and peevish Leonard into a saintly sufferer. Ewing's love of military life, despite the exhaustion entailed in its constant uprootings, shines through; she enjoyed the camaraderie of the barracks, the display of parades, the good fellowship of army theatricals, and the overall discipline of a camp. Ironically, Ewing proved to be a stronger advocate of the military life than her husband, who often pined to return to musical studies.

The frequent moves, however, did take their toll on Ewing. After Aldershot, shorter assignments at Bowdon, York, and Fulford followed. Poor health prevented her from joining Rex in Malta in 1879. She also stayed behind while he took up his next position in Ceylon in 1881. Rex was likely not aware of the depth of his wife's loneliness and sense of isolation; in her own way Julie soldiered on, although she had confided to her mother from Fredericton in 1869 that "the natural terrors of an untravelled and not herculean woman about the ups and downs of a wandering, homeless sort of life like ours are not so comprehensible by him, he having travelled so much, never felt a qualm of sea-sickness, and less than the average of home-sickness, from circumstances." In May 1883, the Ewings were finally together when they moved outside Taunton in a home they named Villa Ponente, named, as Horatia Eden explains, for "its aspect towards the setting sun." Despite her precarious health, Ewing—as always—threw herself into the digging of the garden.

Along with a love of animals, another common trait of the children in Ewing's stories is their passion for flowers. In one of her final works, "Letters from a Little Garden" (1884–1885), Ewing admitted that "harmony and gradation of colour always give me more pleasure than contrast." Hers was an earthbound botanism that delighted in growing, picking, and arranging flowers.

Flowers fulfill several roles in Ewing's work. More than a mere scenic backdrop, they are often reflectors of personality and initiators of action. The childhood custom of blowing dandelion clocks ("you blow till the seed is all blown away, and you count each of the puffs—an hour to a puff") to tell the time accounts for the difference between Peter Paul, the young Dutch boy in "Dandelion Clocks" (1876), and his two sisters. Ewing relates, "it was Peter Paul's peculiarity that he always did want to know more about everything; a habit whose first and foremost inconvenience is that one can so seldom get people to answer one's questions." Even when he returns years later, after a life of wandering and adventure, Peter Paul realizes how far his own restlessness keeps him from his sisters' matronly contentment. "But he did not now ask why dandelion clocks go differently with different people."

An earlier story, "The Blind Hermit and the Trinity Flower" (1871), often compared to "Dandelion Clocks," makes the three-petaled flower an emblem of the dying man's faith and perseverance. Ewing noted in a letter dated October 25, 1871, that "this is one of my greatest favourites amongst my efforts." Charlotte Yonge, she added, "prefers it to anything I have ever done." The "mystic Three" controls the growth of the Trillium erythrocarpum (trinity flower). As the Hermit explains to his young apprentice, "Every part was threefold. The leaves were three, the petals three, the sepals three. The flower was snow-white, but on each of the three parts it was stained with crimson stripes, like white garments dyed in blood." In this moving legend, the trillium's form forecasts the hermit's prayer of resignation: "If THOU wilt. When THOU wilt. As THOU wilt!"

"Mary's Meadow" (1883–1884) is another poignant flower story. Its late appearance makes it an almost final credal statement from Ewing. The child who plants flowers to beautify wayside places brings about reconciliation between her father and the squire and also inherits a once-contested plot of land. Taking a cue from her chosen epigraph from George Herbert's "The Garden" (1633), with its acknowledgment that "we are but flowers that glide," Ewing imbues the aesthetic vision of the young heroine with a truly creative potential: Mary not only makes flowers grow, but she also unites feuding parties. Taking their cue from this character, readers of *Aunt Judy's Magazine* formed a "Parkinson Society," with the aim of cultivating older species of flowers and disseminating information on gardens "to try and prevent the extermination of rare wild flowers as well as of garden treasures." Ewing was the first president of this society.

Finally, as her strength deteriorated, even the salubrious air of Bath did not help Ewing. After two unsuccessful and mysterious operations (either blood poisoning or cancer is a plausible speculation), she died there on May 13, 1885. She was buried with a military funeral in her parish churchyard of Trull, near Taunton, "in a grave," Eden relates, "literally lined with moss and flowers."

Juliana Horatia Ewing was, in many respects, the product of an era and of a specific community. Her friendships with Yonge and Ruskin and associations with the illustrators Randolph Caldecott (who illustrated *Lob Lie-by-the-Fire*, *Jackanapes*, and *Daddy Darwin's Dovecote*) and Gordon Browne all had a distinctive establishment cast. Kipling loved her work and learned from her warm characterizations of family life, as did *Edith Nesbit and *Mary Louisa Molesworth.

In her monograph on Ewing, Gillian Avery distinguishes between mother and daughter by suggesting that, unlike Mrs. Gatty, Ewing, "blessed with far more leisure and fewer responsibilities, wrote because she loved it." Ewing was a gifted and enchanting storyteller, even in childhood. Her writing seems to have supplied emotional and intellectual companionship throughout her life, particularly during periods of homesickness, loneliness, and depression. Writing not only permitted Ewing to participate in a rich imaginative universe, but also kept her close and sympathetically attuned to the feelings and perceptions of a generally happy childhood.

Some critics complain about the thinness of her plots and how they depend on stock devices. Ewing's stories are usually bulging with action—within the conventions of the Victorian maternal voice, blending entertainment and instruction to promote the goal of family unity and concord. But she definitely wanted to captivate young readers with more than the conventional. Whether animating toys or insects, whether detailing the routines of the barracks (which, thanks to Rex's tuition, she represented with great accuracy), or whether vivifying the yearnings of children as different as Ida, Jackanapes, Leonard, Jack March, and John Broom, Ewing makes an investment in characters and places. She is determined to tell a story, but she is prepared to linger, comment, and digress en route.

As a major contributor to the expansion of Victorian children's literature, which was releasing itself from an explicitly religious mission, Ewing helped to create a wider horizon for Society for Promoting Christian Knowledge publications. Writing for and appealing to both boys and girls, she made the detailed realism of her setting and the compassionate examination of the child character's emotional life the salient devices of her narrative art. Although F.J. Harvey Darton notes that with Ewing "literary qualities outweighed didactic excrescences," he concludes that her appeal to later generations is "limited." In Lance Salway's estimate her work now seems "excessively sentimental." Today Ewing may only be known to students of Victorian culture and historical children's literature, but the delicate nuance of her finest stories will always be enjoyed by a select readership.

SOURCES AND SUGGESTED READING:

Biographies:

Eden, Horatia Katherine Frances. *Juliana Horatia Ewing and Her Books.* London: Society for Promoting Christian Knowledge, 1896.

Laski, Marghanita. *Mrs. Ewing, Mrs. Molesworth and Mrs. Hodgson Burnett.* London: Arthur Barker, 1958.

Maxwell, Christabel. *Mrs. Gatty and Mrs. Ewing.* London: Constable, 1949.

REFERENCES:

Avery, Gillian. *Mrs. Ewing.* London: Bodley Head, 1961.

Bratton, Jacqueline. *The Impact of Victorian Children's Fiction.* London: Croom Helm, 1981.

Darton, F.J. Harvey. *Children's Books in England; Five Centuries of Social Life.* 3rd ed. Revised by Brian Alderson. Cambridge: Cambridge University Press, 1982, pp. 276-292.

McDonald, Donna. *Illustrated News: Juliana Horatia Ewing's Canadian Pictures 1867–1869.* Toronto & London: Dundurn Press, 1985.

Molesworth, Louisa. "Juliana Horatia Ewing," in *Contemporary Review.* Vol. 49. May 1886, pp. 675–686.

Plotz, Judith A. "A Victorian Comfort Book: Juliana Ewing's The Story of a Short Life," in *Romanticism and Children's Literature in Nineteenth-Century England.* Edited by J.H. McGavran Jr. Athens: University of Georgia Press, 1991, pp. 168–189.

Salway, Lance. *A Peculiar Gift: Nineteenth Century Writings on Books for Children.* Harmondsworth, Middlesex: Kestrel Books, 1976.

Wolff, Robert Lee. *Nineteenth-Century Fiction: A Bibliographical Catalogue.* NY: Garland, 1982.

Patricia Demers,
University of Alberta, for *Dictionary of Literary Biography,*
Volume 163: *British Children's Writers, 1800-1880.*
A Bruccoli Clark Layman Book. Edited by Meena Khorana,
Morgan State University. Gale Research, 1996, pp. 91–99

Exeter, duchess of.

See Elizabeth of Lancaster (1364–1425).
See Anne Plantagenet (1439–1476).
See Montacute, Anne (d. 1457).
See Neville, Margaret (c. 1377–c. 1424).
See Stafford, Anne (d. 1432).

Exter, Alexandra (1882–1949)

Russian abstract artist who was influential in bringing Western trends to her native country and went on to become a noted stage designer. Name variations: Ekster. Pronunciation: X-ter. Born Alexandra Alexandrovna Grigorovich on January 19, 1882, in the Russian town of Belostok, Grodno Province; died at Fontenay-aux-Roses, near Paris, on March 17, 1949; daughter of Alexander Abramovich Grigorovich (a tax official); attended Kiev Girls' Gymnasium (secondary school), 1892–99; Kiev Art School, 1901–06; married Nikolai Evgenievich Exter, sometime around 1903 (died 1918;) married Georgi Georgievich (George) Nekrasov, on October 25, 1920 (died 1945); no children.

Moved with family to Kiev (1886); studied in Paris, had first meeting with Cubists, participated in "The Link" exhibition in Kiev (1908); began work as theater designer, returned to Russia from Paris (1914); worked under influence of Malevich and Tatlin (1915–16); set up teaching studio in Kiev (1918);

began work as puppet designer (1918–19); joined Vkhutemas, participated in Constructivist 5x5=25 exhibit in Moscow (1921); worked as movie scene designer (1923–24); left Russia for Western Europe (1924); held one-woman exhibit in Berlin, settled in suburbs of Paris (1930); held one-woman exhibit in Prague (1937).

Paintings: The Bridge *(Sèvres),* Museum of Ukrainian Visual Art, Kiev *(1912);* Grapes in a Vase, *Leonard Hutton Galleries, New York (1913);* Composition, *Trekiakov Gallery, Moscow (1914);* Firenze (Florence), *Trekiakov Gallery, Moscow (1914–15). Designs: "Costume for the Protozanov film* Aelita," *Luis Mestre Fine Arts, New York (1924).*

In the Russian art world of the early 20th century, the country's artists often experienced a rapid process of professional development. In many cases, the outstanding stimulus for their changing styles came from abroad. Russian artists went to the West, notably to Paris, to study and work, while such leading artists as Henri Matisse and Filippo Marinetti visited Russia. Extensive exhibitions of Western art became available in Russia's leading cities, while increasingly prominent Russian artists found it possible to show their work in such venues as Paris, Rome, and Budapest. The theoretical writing of Western artists was quickly translated into Russian; for example, Marinetti's article "Founding and Future Manifesto of Futurism" reached Russia and was made available to a Russian-language audience almost immediately after it was first published in Paris in 1909. Finally, Russian artists with extensive contact with the West presented formal lectures to audiences at art schools. A further notable feature of the Russian art world was the part that women played in the most important and novel developments. As John Bowlt has put it, "The brilliant constellation of Exter, [*Natalia] Goncharova, [*Olga] Rozanova, [*Varvara] Stepanova and [*Nadezhda] Udaltsova gave modern Russian art much of its creative power."

The young Alexandra Exter stands at the center of Russia's artistic evolution. In less than two decades, she moved from an early interest in the French impressionists to work in such diverse styles as Cubism, Futurism, Supremacism, and finally the politically charged style of Constructivism. Although a devotee of such distinguished mentors as Picasso, Exter at the peak of her career added a substantial element of originality to the models they set for her. Her work in Cubism and other styles, for example, was distinguished by a vivid sense of color that added a heightened emotional content to many of her paintings. She also did memorable work as a stage designer in the 1920s.

Exter, like all members of the Russian population, found herself living through a series of dramatic and disrupting changes as her country entered the 20th century. While she was in her early 20s, Russia went to war in the Far East against Japan. The conflict was a military catastrophe as both the Russian army and navy found themselves outfought by the forces of an island nation with only one-fourth of Russia's population. The strains of early industrialization and a rapidly rising rural population created deep discontents. Fused with the stress of the war and its resulting military calamities, popular unrest came to a head in the Revolution of 1905. Although the monarchy of Tsar Nicholas II was able to maintain its existence, Russia soon plunged into the even greater crisis of World War I. Once again, the country was rocked by a series of military humiliations, and once again they brought to a head the simmering resentment of both Russian factory workers and Russian peasants working the land. An initial, spontaneous revolution in March 1917 brought down the monarchy. A second, deliberately conducted revolution in November brought to power the radical Marxist faction known as the Bolsheviks with a determined leader in the person of V.I. Lenin as the revolution's guiding personality. Even someone like Exter, who had not been visibly political in the past, and many of her contemporaries in the world of the arts found the Bolshevik Revolution of November 1917 an attractive shift in their country's fortunes. She joined other artists such as *Liubov Popova in devoting much of her work in the years following to an art that would be consistent with the ideals of the revolution.

Although she was a well-known member of Russia's artistic community, Exter left little information about her personal affairs. Students of her career are uncertain about the circumstances and even the date of her marriage to her cousin, Nikolai Exter. Similarly, the reason for her decision to leave Soviet Russia, along with her second husband George Nekrasov, remains uncertain. But Exter left a clear artistic legacy during the second and third decades of the century. Distinguished as a painter, she also, like her contemporaries Popova and Natalia Goncharova, developed a strong reputation as a set designer for the Russian stage in the 1920s. But, after settling in France in 1924, her most productive years were over. The final portion of her life saw

Salome, *by Alexandra Exter, 1917.*

Exter working without distinction in the modes where she had already made her reputation.

Alexandra Exter was born in the Russian town of Belostok in Grodno province, a region which is now a part of Poland, on January 19, 1882. She was the daughter of a tax official, and she and the rest of her family followed him to his new assignment in Kiev in the mid-1880s. She received her basic education at the Kiev Girls' Gymnasium, an elite secondary school designed to prepare students for further schooling. She married her cousin, the attorney Nikolai Exter, sometime around 1903. Her art education she obtained between 1901 and 1906 at the Kiev Art School, but like many Russian and other European artists of the time, she made her way to Paris, the cultural capital, to further her training. During the years from 1908 to 1914, she divided her days between her Russian home and Paris. Meanwhile, she had her first exhibits in St. Petersburg and Kiev in 1908. The exhibition at Kiev, organized by David Burliuk, was a milestone in the development of modern Russian art. It showed the new trends, put forth a manifesto condemning a public of "complacent bourgeois," and shocked critics who still saw the standards of art defined by the academic realism of the 19th century. One stunned critic was appalled by the painting of an artist he mistakenly identified as "Mr. Exter."

$\mathcal{E}$xter was a crucial figure in the dialogue between Russia and the West, both before and after the Revolution. She made bold contributions in every field of artistic practice.

—M.N. Yablonskaya

During the years from 1909 to the outbreak of World War I, Exter traveled widely and worked primarily in Western Europe. After setting up a studio in Paris in 1909, she became acquainted with proponents of the artistic currents that were dominating the scene in France and Italy. Pablo Picasso and Georges Braque, pioneers of Cubism, were two of the artists who influenced her; so too were the young Italians, Filippo Marinetti and Giovanni Papini, who were developing the dynamic artistic style known as Futurism. As M.N. Yablonskaya notes: "Exter was not an artist to be rigidly bound to a specific ideology or group." Thus, the prewar period saw her "associated with many different factions of the Russian avant-garde." Her close ties to the Western world of art made her a source of information on developments there for her more homebound Russian colleagues. Meanwhile, she added to her international reputation by exhibiting her work regularly in Paris, often side by side with the leading Cubists.

Exter did some of her most impressive work before World War I in the Cubist tradition. The Cubist approach to art involved showing reality through the use of geometric forms such as cones, and viewing an object from a number of different angles simultaneously. She departed from the work done by Picasso and Braque by her desire to experiment in adding bright colors to her paintings, and she sometimes found her-

self the object of their criticism for such a departure. Examples of Exter's achievements in this style were her *Still Life* of 1913 and her painting entitled *Wine* finished in 1914. As Bowlt wrote in 1974, "Exter's sensitivity to color" gave her painting "a synthetic, emotive quality lacking in the more cerebral, analytical work of Braque and Picasso." In the last months before Europe plunged into war, after a trip to Italy in April and May 1914, she incorporated Futurist influences into her painting. Futurist artists broke up reality in ways similar to the Cubists, but they sought as well to give the sensation of motion to the objects they painted; Futurists also incorporated such devices as placing written words in their paintings. Exter the Futurist can be seen most vividly in paintings like *Florence* and *The Dynamic City,* both finished in 1915.

Back in Russia, during the prewar years, she had exhibited in Riga, St. Petersburg, and Kiev. With the outbreak of World War I, travel to Western Europe became difficult, and Exter spent the period starting in 1914 in her homeland. Her painting now departed even more emphatically from direct representation as she came under the influence of Kasimir Malevich. Malevich influenced a number of young Russian artists during these years, his work stressing nonobjective painting that employed planes. This led Exter to produce such non-objective works as *Venice* in 1916, which some art historians see as a turning point in her work, and the subsequent *Abstract Composition* of 1917. Despite her willingness to accept Malevich's technique of constructing a painting around a number of planes, Exter continued to put her own stamp on what her mentors suggested, as she had done with the Cubists. Specifically, her sense of color drove her painting in a different direction from that of Malevich. The surface of her work, writes Yablonskaya, "moves and pulsates, evoking precise emotional equivalents such as disturbance, agitation, rebellion, and inspiration."

In 1914, Exter took up stage design while continuing to work as a painter. She became affiliated with the Moscow Chamber Theater of Alexandre Taitov, with whom she shared a devotion to a modernist and abstract style for theatrical productions. Here she expressed another facet of her artistic personality: her interest in ancient mythology. She designed the sets for Taitov's production of *Famira Kifared,* a play based upon ancient Greek mythology. Her set designs drew upon the dual traditions in ancient Greek art of the restraint of Apollonianism and the wild abandon of the Dionysian. Her costumes for the satyrs in the play, for example, showed the absence of restraint in the satyrs' personalities by decking them out with false breasts and wigs. Drawing upon the techniques of the ancient Greek vase painters, Exter used paint on the muscles of the actors' legs in order to emphasize their physical forms. This was a device the Futurists had used in order to shock bourgeois society, but Exter made it a part of her theatrical vocabulary. As always, her work in the theater showed her dramatic attraction to brilliant coloring. She followed up her debut as a stage designer in 1917 with an equally imaginative and successful set of designs for the play *Salome* by English author Oscar Wilde. The work she did in *Salome* is attributed by some art historians to the continuing influence of Kasimir Malevich and his doctrine of Supremacism. Supremacism stressed the need for the artist to rely on pure geometric elements such as the square and triangle, and these Exter incorporated in daring fashion. The death of the title figure in the play, for example, was represented by the fall of five red triangles onto the stage.

The outbreak of revolution in 1917 found her at home. When the moderate revolutionaries of March 1917 were ousted by Lenin and his Bolsheviks, Exter participated in this radical turn in Russian life. Establishing her own studio in Kiev, she and her students worked to further the cause of revolution. In a direct political effort, she helped plan and decorate the propaganda trains that Lenin's Bolsheviks (now renamed the Communists) used in the civil war of 1918–21 in defeating the coalition of opponents called the Whites. The trains contained propaganda literature as well as movie projectors. But Exter the artist remained present along with Exter the devotee of Russia's new political direction. Thus, some of the trains she and her students painted were decorated with clear and striking propaganda pictures. Others carried the non-objective artistic tradition of Supremacism.

She participated in the new cultural academies called *Vkhutemas,* a cyrillic abbreviation of "Higher State Artistic and Technical Workshops." These bodies were to train artists for the practical work of building a new socialist society, thus turning art usefully toward the goals of the revolution. In her studio at Kiev, she adopted a technique common to the *Vkhutemas* movement; this was to teach all the leading artistic trends from 19th-century Realism to the latest developments in Cubism and Futurism. Employing such a teaching style, which drew on her own eclectic interests, she asked her students to draw the same object using the style of the French Impressionists and the Cubists as well as imitating the work of Cezanne.

These same years of turmoil and civil war also saw her take up work as a puppet designer. In 1918 and 1919, she produced original marionettes for the puppeteer *Nina Simonovich-Efimova. Meanwhile, she continued her work for the stage and her collaboration with Taitov. In 1920, she designed sets and costumes for both dramatic and ballet productions. The following year, she completed her work for the Chamber Theater with designs for the production of *Romeo and Juliet*. The abstract and modernist tendency of her work appealed to advanced artistic circles of Moscow but, as Donald Oenslager points out, not to "those who viewed it from the Kremlin."

Although Exter's continuing ties to modernist art remained evident, she compensated for them by her vehement support for the revolution and in following the politically acceptable art trend known as Constructivism, which was now firmly established in the Soviet Union. This called for the artist's talent to be put to practical uses. Exter turned her efforts to such fields as clothing design. In her theoretical writing, she noted how clothes designed for mass production should "be suitable for the workers and the kind of work which will be done in it." But, once again Exter's unwillingness or inability to be confined by an existing style became evident. Notes **Christina Lodder**: Exter "never adopted a rigorously Constructivist position in either theory or practice." Thus, even her designs for mass production included "considerations of elegance and beauty." She used many decorative devices in her popular clothing designs, which can be found in the costumes she put on display when she turned to the world of Soviet filmmaking. In 1923, she designed costumes, as well as scenery, for the film *Aelita*. Produced by Yakov Protazanov and based on the novel by Alexis Tolstoy, *Aelita* included scenes set on Mars, and Exter did some of her most exciting work designing the costumes and stage sets in this exotic locale.

In 1923, Exter again expressed her links to the new world of Soviet art by a collaboration with Soviet architects. In that year's All Union Agricultural Exhibition, Exter and other artists painted the decorations for the pavilion. Working in a number of styles, she produced one memorable work for this ephemeral project in the panel she painted, in a Realist style, for the Forestry Pavilion (the Exhibition was completely dismantled afterward). In 1924, Exter applied her daring modernism in stage design one last time in her native country. She designed the costumes and sets for the Moscow Art Theater's production of Calderon's *La Dama duende*.

In 1918, Exter's first husband died, and in 1920 she married an actor named George Nekrasov. According to a friend of the family, Nekrasov was so impressed with his wife's reputation that he introduced himself as "George Exter." In 1924 (some authorities say in late 1923), for reasons that remain uncertain, the two of them left their native country, settling in France. There she spent the remainder of her life and her artistic career. Like many Russian exiles, Exter and her new husband had to scramble to maintain even a modest standard of living. She became an instructor in stage design, decorated private homes, and, as she had before 1914, joined the lively artistic circles of the French capital. Sometime in 1929 or 1930, she and her husband moved permanently to the town of Fontenay-aux-Roses, outside Paris.

Exter continued to work designing marionettes. To this miniature form—the marionettes were only two feet high—she brought her range of experience in the Cubist, Suprematist, and Constructivist traditions. She also occupied herself doing the illustrations for original decorative books, produced in limited editions, in collaboration with friends who were calligraphers. But she no longer occupied a central and energetic role in the larger fields of easel painting and stage design. She produced no work of note after 1933.

The World War II years were especially difficult for Exter and her husband. She suffered increasingly from heart disease, and the two of them lived in harsh poverty. During the last years of her life, in the hungry circumstances of postwar France, she subsisted in part on CARE packages that arrived from the United States. In a final act of artistic will, she sculpted an angel to be placed above the joint grave she expected to occupy with George, her husband of three decades, who had died in 1945. Exter soon followed, passing away at Fontenay-aux-Roses on March 17, 1949.

Exter's reputation languished in obscurity for many years. As a self-exile from the Soviet Union, according to Andrei Nakov, "her name was deliberately forgotten during the years of triumphant socialist realism." But her reputation revived in her own country in the 1970s, and she received even more attention abroad. In 1974, for example, her theatrical designs were the subject of an exhibition at the Vincent Astor Gallery in New York City. Her works were also included in exhibitions of Russian avant-garde painting and design at New York's Museum of Modern Art in 1978 and the Los Angeles County Museum in 1980. An exhibition devoted to Exter's marionettes and theater designs was held at the Hirschhorn Museum and Sculpture Garden, Washington, D.C., in 1980.

SOURCES:
Artist of the Theater: Alexandra Exter: Four Essays on Exhibit at Vincent Astor Gallery. Spring–Summer 1974. NY: New York Public Library, 1974.
Bowlt, John E. "Aleksandra Exter: A Veritable Amazon of the Avant-garde," in *Art News.* Vol. 73, April 1974.
Lodder, Christina. *Russian Constructivism.* New Haven, CT: Yale University Press, 1983.
Parton, Anthony. *Mikhail Larionov and the Russian Avant-Garde.* Princeton, NJ: Princeton University Press, 1993.
Rudenstine, Angelica Zander. *Russian Avant-Garde Art: The George Costakis Collection.* NY: Harry N. Abrams, 1981.
Yablonskaya, M.N. *Women Artists of Russia's New Age. 1900–1935.* Edited by Anthony Parton. London: Thames and Hudson, 1990.

SUGGESTED READING:
Bowlt, John E., ed. and trans. *Russian Art of the Avant-Garde: Theory and Criticism. 1902–1924.* London: Thames and Hudson, 1988.
Compton, Susan P. "Alexandra Exter and the Dynamic Stage," in *Art in America.* September–October 1974.
Harris, Anne Sutherland, and Linda Nochlin. *Women Artists: 1550–1950.* NY: Alfred A. Knopf, 1976.

Neil M. Heyman,
Professor of History, San Diego State University,
San Diego, California

Eyck, Margaretha van (fl. 1420s–1430s)

Flemish painter. Name variations: Margarete van Eyck. Born at Maeseyck, around 1370, and flourished between 1420 and 1430; sister of artists Hubert (c. 1366–1426), Jan (c. 1370–c. 1440) and Lambert van Eyck.

Sister of artists Hubert, Jan, and Lambert van Eyck, founders of the Flemish school of painting, Margaretha van Eyck is said to have been a skillful painter, though no picture is known that can be positively ascribed to her. She and her brothers reputedly originated the process of oil painting with a drying varnish. She was buried in the Cathedral of Ghent, along with her brother Hubert.

Eymery, Marguerite (c. 1860–1953).

See Vallette, Marguerite.

Ezekiel, Denise Tourover

(1903–1980)

American Hadassah leader who saw the "Teheran Children" to safety and whose outraged voice demanded action from diplomats and presidents on behalf of disenfranchised and oppressed people around the world. Name variations: Denise Tourover. Pronunciation: TOUR-over. Born Denise Levy in New Orleans, Louisiana, on May 16, 1903; died of congestive heart failure in Washington, D.C., on January 16, 1980; daughter of Leopold (a New Iberia, Louisiana, dry goods merchant) and Blanche (Cogenheim) Levy; graduated from George Washington University School of Law, LL.B., 1924; married Raphael Tourover, on November 14, 1926 (died, November 2, 1961); married Walter N. Ezekiel, on September 27, 1972; children: (first marriage) one daughter, **Mendelle Tourover.**

Moved to Washington, D.C. (1920); admitted to the Bar of the District of Columbia (1924); began more than 50 years of service through Hadassah as member of Washington, D.C., section (1925); elected section president (1936); elected to National Board and chosen as Washington representative (1939); during World War II, served as Hadassah's liaison to diplomats, Congress and the White House to ensure safe passage of European refugees to Palestine; through Hadassah, coordinated food distribution to Israel from the U.S. Agency for International Development (1950–74) and Operation Reindeer (1953); represented Hadassah on State Department's American Food for Peace Council (1960–64); was a member of Actions Committee, World Zionist Organization (1956–76).

Presidents, diplomats and leaders of international organizations struggled to win freedom for 700 refugee children stranded in Persia (present-day Iran) during World War II, but Denise Tourover saved them. Known by many as the "Teheran Children," the 2-to-17-year-old refugees had been orphaned by Hitler's invasion of Poland and wandered across Eastern Europe for three years. Temporarily housed in a refugee camp, the children had been given papers allowing their immigration to Palestine. Without transportation and a safe route, however, no document would take them to the emerging Jewish State. During the war, Persia endured shortages of food and housing and strict limitations on air traffic. Opposed to Jewish settlement, the Iraqi government refused to allow the children to travel through their territory. Struggling to remain neutral, Turkey also refused to help.

In Washington, Denise Tourover worked tirelessly to find a solution. As a representative of Hadassah, the Women's Zionist Organization of America, she met with *Eleanor Roosevelt, the president of Standard Oil Company, ambassadors from Iraq and Turkey, State Department officials, the Red Cross and the heads of various wartime agencies. Although her efforts put the children on President Franklin Roosevelt's agenda, the United States was unsuccessful in negotiations with Iraq. Frustrated, Tourover wrote in October 1942, "I am truly incensed that a 2 by 4 government like Iraq should set up its will against such a humanitarian effort when all the governments of the world have refugee committees concerned with the fate of helpless people." That December, she convinced Lord Halifax, the British ambassador to the United States, to intervene with the British War Ministry, and the children were taken to Palestine by British transport ship in January 1943.

> *W*hen all the diplomats and others may have failed, I still feel that the voice of the outraged women of Hadassah can make itself heard by one means or another.
>
> —Denise Ezekiel

The rescue of the Teheran children was the most dramatic example of Tourover's lifelong work on behalf of oppressed and disenfranchised people around the world. Born in 1903 in New Orleans, Louisiana, she moved with her father to Washington, D.C., after her mother's death in 1920. In 1924, she completed a law degree, won admission to the Bar of the District of Columbia and went to work on Capitol Hill. While she worked on the *Congressional Record* and committees set up to establish the Tennessee Valley Authority and examine the Teapot Dome Scandal, she made important political and media contacts. During an interview with Marlin Levin, she recalled, "When it became necessary to use some of these contacts for Hadassah, I reestablished those contacts. Friends made it possible for me to meet other people and doors were opened to me by many friends."

Although her paid employment ended sometime after her marriage to Raphael Tourover in 1926, her work continued. As early as 1925, she was on the board of directors of the Washington, D.C., section of Hadassah. Founded by *Henrietta Szold in 1912, Hadassah funded hospitals, training schools and homes for Jewish settlers in Palestine and continues to support projects in Israel. In 1926, Tourover served as publicity chair of the Washington Section,

Denise
Tourover
Ezekiel

and she accepted increasing amounts of responsibility over the next ten years. She was elected president of the section in 1936.

Hadassah's work gained urgency as Nazi influence spread across Europe, and the national

board, headquartered in New York, recognized the need for a strong voice in the U.S. capital. In 1939, Hadassah named Tourover their first Washington representative. Throughout World War II, her close friendship with **Elinor Morgenthau**, wife of the secretary of the treasury, helped her to win access to key diplomats, top government officials and the president. In addition to assisting thousands like the Teheran children who were fleeing Europe for Palestine, Tourover worked through the State Department and wartime agencies like the Combined Agency for Middle East Supply to obtain export licenses for sorely needed medical supplies and food.

Her work did not end with the war. After Israel declared its independence in May 1948, war erupted in the Middle East and the new state suffered many shortages. As a member of the President's Advisory Committee on Voluntary Foreign Aid, Hadassah was eligible to receive government surplus foods for free distribution. Tourover went to work ensuring that food from U.S. government warehouses reached families in Israel. Between 1950 and 1974, Tourover coordinated food distribution to Israel through Hadassah by serving on numerous government committees and projects including Operation Reindeer (1953), the State Department's American Food for Peace Council (1960–64) and food distribution projects of the U.S. Agency for International Development (USAID, 1950–74). Food and supplies were distributed to Jews, Christians and Muslims alike, in bags stamped with insignias of both the United States and Hadassah.

In 1976, Denise Tourover retired from her position as Hadassah's Washington representative. Gradually, her failing health forced her to cut back on her work. She died of congestive heart failure in Washington, D.C., in 1980.

SOURCES:

Geller, L.D. *The Papers of Denise Tourover Ezekiel, 1936–1981, in the Hadassah Archives*. NY: Hadassah, The Women's Zionist Organization of America, 1984.

Levin, Marlin. *Balm in Gilead: The Story of Hadassah*. NY: Schocken, 1973.

SUGGESTED READING:

Sochen, June. *Consecrate Every Day: The Public Lives of Jewish American Women, 1880–1981*. Albany, NY: State University of New York Press, 1981.

Sommers, David. *Women in Organizations: An Analysis of the Role and Status of Women in American Voluntary Organizations*. Washington, DC: B'nai B'rith International, 1983.

COLLECTIONS:

Correspondence, interviews, papers and photographs located in the Hadassah Archives, National Offices of Hadassah, New York; newspaper clippings and reference materials located in the Washingtoniana Division, Washington, D.C., Public Library, Martin Luther King Memorial Branch; Women's History Collection, Jewish Historical Society of Greater Washington, Lillian and Albert Small Museum, Washington, D.C.

RELATED MEDIA:

Meringolo, Denise Danielle, curator. *Tzedakah: Jewish Women Creating a Capital Community, 1895–1948*. Exhibit at the Jewish Historical Society of Greater Washington, May 12, 1996 to December 1997.

Denise D. Meringolo, Ph.D. candidate,
George Washington University, Washington, D.C.

Faber, Cecilia Böhl de (1796–1877).

See Böhl von Faber, Cecilia.

Fabia-Eudocia (fl. 600s CE)

Byzantine empress. Name variations: Fabia-Eudocia or Eudokia. Born in Carthage; first wife of Herakleos also known as Heraclius I of Carthage, Byzantine emperor (r. 610–641); children: Heraclonas-Constantine, emperor of Byzantium (r. 641). Heraclius I's second wife was *Martina.

Fabia-Eudocia was a young Carthaginian woman whom Emperor Heraclius I married shortly after he ascended the throne. She died young; her son Heraclonas-Constantine succeeded his father on the throne at age 30, but died shortly thereafter of tuberculosis.

Fabian, Dora (1901–1935)

German anti-Nazi activist, writer and journalist who, along with fellow political emigré Mathilde Wurm, was found dead in her London flat on April 4, 1935, raising questions that remain unsolved to this day. Born Dora Heinemann in Berlin, Germany, on May 28, 1901; along with Mathilde Wurm, died under mysterious circumstances during the night of March 31–April 1, 1935; daughter of Hugo Heinemann and Else (Levy) Heinemann; no siblings; married Walter Fabian.

Described by the British Socialist leader Fenner Brockway as "one of the most courageous persons I have ever met," Dora Fabian was born into an assimilated German-Jewish family that was strongly committed to the ideals of Socialism. Her mother was **Else Levy Heinemann**; her father, the lawyer Hugo Heinemann, enjoyed an international reputation as a defender of political radicals and trade unionists. Deeply interested in political affairs from her earliest years, Dora signaled her opposition to Germany's imperialist policies during World War I by becoming an active member of the Independent Social Democratic Party while still a schoolgirl. She was intellectually precocious as well as politically militant; friends of her family commented approvingly at the time that "she certainly has her father's head." A gift for foreign languages enabled her to fully master English, which would prove to be of considerable value years later when Nazism forced her to flee Germany to seek refuge in Great Britain. In 1928, the academically gifted Dora received a doctorate in economics and political science from the University of Giessen. During her student years she became politically active, on at least one occasion annoying the university administration when she participated in a student demonstration to protest the assassination by Nazis of Germany's Jewish foreign minister, Walther Rathenau.

In 1924, Dora married Walter Fabian, a young Social Democratic activist who like his bride hoped to create a new Germany based on the ideals of social justice and international cooperation. Both were active as journalists and educators, particularly within the Socialist youth movement. Both Dora and Walter Fabian pinned their hopes for the permanent triumph of democracy in Germany on the younger generation of the Social Democratic Party, the Jungsozialisten. Tragically, the top party leadership of a bureaucratically top-heavy Social Democrat Party (SPD) was insensitive to the necessity of finding ways to appeal to politically idealistic young men and women. This neglect was to prove catastrophic in the years after 1929 when an aggressive National Socialist movement won over millions of young Germans for the creation of a dictatorial regime that promised a clean break with the past and the restoration of national honor.

By the late 1920s, Dora Fabian was finding fault with many aspects of the SPD youth organization. In particular, she believed that it had missed countless opportunities to spread Socialist ideals among women, many of whom remained stubbornly attached to conservative, even reactionary, social values and who now were becoming a significant source of political support for Hitler's explosively expanding Nazi movement. As an alternative way of recruiting women of all ages for organized Socialism, Fabian pointed to the successful female organization of the British Labour Party, which she observed firsthand during two visits to the United Kingdom. A gifted public speaker as well as a skilled journalist and writer, Fabian had by the end of the 1920s become a thorn in the side of a Social Democratic leadership.

The early 1930s were difficult years for all Germans, and Dora Fabian too found herself buffeted by both personal and political turmoil. In 1930, she divorced Walter Fabian, although in the next years their relationship would remain strong, both as friends and political colleagues in the struggle against Hitlerism. In the fall of 1931, after both Walter and Dora were finally expelled from the Social Democratic Party for what amounted to acts of insubordination, they and several like-minded militant socialists immediately announced the formation of a new party, the Socialist Workers' Party (Sozialistische Arbeiterpartei; SAP). Although Dora and members of the new party were strongly committed to democracy and critical of the dictatorial methods of the German Communist Party (KPD), they were convinced that only a united German labor movement would be able to stand up against the Nazis. An anti-Nazi united front, they believed, could be forged by a new party like the SAP, which took a position between the SPD and the KPD.

During the final years of German democracy before the Nazi takeover of 1933, Dora Fabian worked tirelessly to alert her fellow Germans to the dangers posed by Adolf Hitler and his followers. She was particularly alert to the loss of rights that women would suffer under a Nazi dictatorship, warning them in an April 1932 article on "Hitler and Women" in the SAP newspaper of how they were simply being used by a Nazi Party that regarded them contemptuously as little more than "voting beasts" (*Stimmvieh*) who could be lied to again and again with impunity. Fabian on more than one instance chose to attend Nazi rallies in order to personally study the mass psychology of Fascism. On one occasion, at a mass rally at Berlin's Lustgarten, a helpful SS man lifted her into the air ("Party Comrade, I'm certain that you would like to see our Führer better!") without realizing that she was in fact a militant socialist and Jewish as well.

Always regarding herself as a political realist, in the first weeks of 1933 Fabian chose to resign from the Socialist Workers' Party, looking upon its efforts to halt the march of Nazism as a failure. Unfortunately, her grim assessment of the situation was all too accurate, for on January 30, 1933, Hitler was appointed chancellor of a near-prostrate German Reich. Although she had become disillusioned by the interminable bickering and leadership feuds of the SAP and never again would join a political party, Fabian was at this point more than ever before a believer in democratic socialism and a bitter foe of the Nazis who were now poised to impose their totalitarian ideals on all Germans.

As a militant anti-Nazi, Fabian had long been regarded as an enemy to be eliminated, and in March 1933, soon after the elections in Germany, she was arrested in Berlin. Among the most incriminating aspects of her situation was the fact that she had once worked as secretary to Ernst Toller, a Jewish writer and radical who was one of the most hated intellectual enemies of National Socialism. After a few days, she was released from prison and fled Germany as quickly as possible (a prudent move since storm troopers planned to re-arrest her); she also took with her into exile a large trunk filled with several of Toller's unpublished manuscripts which would doubtless have been destroyed by the Nazis.

Fabian first spent a short time in Prague, then found herself in another nation of refuge, Switzerland. After a short stay in Zurich, she went to Geneva, where she hoped to find employment with the League of Nations which was situated in that city. When these hopes were dashed, she arrived in Great Britain in early September 1933. She was able to prove to British immigration officials that she could support herself financially and was given permission to remain temporarily in the country until May 31, 1935. Because of her two earlier visits and the fact that she was able to speak the language, she rapidly integrated into British political life. With her knowledge of both German and English, and her extensive experience in the struggle against National Socialism, Fabian was more likely than most refugees to find immediate uses for her skills. She soon found employment working as an editor and translator for another refugee from Nazism, the noted pacifist activist and writer Otto Lehmann-Russbüldt.

Once settled in London, Fabian continued to work for the cause of anti-Nazism. Because of her years of political activism and her undisputed knowledge of German affairs, she soon became an important source of information on Nazi Germany for the politically alert leaders of the British Left. Fabian could rely on numerous sources of information on the situation in Hitler's Reich, including her former husband Walter Fabian, who had chosen to remain in Berlin as a member of an ever-diminishing anti-Nazi underground until he was compelled to flee to Paris. Determined to bring the facts about Nazi barbarism to the attention of the world, Fabian worked in London as a researcher and translator and also helped to co-author a publication on the situation of women in both Nazi Germany and the Soviet Union. She was encouraged in her work by her roommate **Mathilde Wurm** (1874–1935), a fellow refugee from Nazism who could look back on a distinguished career in Germany's Social Democratic movement.

By 1935, Dora Fabian had become acclimated to her new life in London, writing to a political friend in Prague: "I no longer feel like a stranger here." Starting in March 1935 several events took up most of her time. One was preparing the details for the International Congress of Writers for the Defense of Culture scheduled to take place in Paris in July of that year. The other event, which took place in Switzerland in March, was of a much more ominous nature, namely the kidnapping by Nazi agents of the noted anti-Nazi journalist Berthold Jacob. Both Dora Fabian and Berthold Jacob were regarded by the Nazi regime as being among the most dangerous Germans in exile because of their contacts with anti-Nazis within the Third Reich. Fabian's informants within military circles enabled her to collect documentation on the rapid rearmament that was then taking place inside Nazi Germany. Her work was known to the German Embassy in London, and in 1934 two highly suspicious "burglaries" took place in the flat she shared with Mathilde Wurm. One of Fabian's neighbors, the Labour Party activist *Ellen Wilkinson, recalled later that the flat "had been ransacked . . . [and] . . . every scrap of paper had been looked at." Even after the break-ins, Fabian received a number of threatening letters and was convinced that she was under Nazi surveillance.

The bodies of Dora Fabian and Mathilde Wurm were discovered in their Great Ormond Street flat on April 4, 1935. Their bedroom door was locked, their apartment appeared to be in good order, and the inquest declared that they died of veronal poisoning, most likely as a double suicide. Yet from the very start, there were doubts as to whether or not Dora Fabian and Mathilde Wurm had taken their own lives. There was some evidence that Fabian had become depressed because her planned marriage to Karl Korsch, a German exile in London, had been cancelled. Furthermore, it appeared that Fabian was in serious financial straits, having fallen into debt and having written a number of checks on Mathilde Wurm's account. Lack of funds would have endangered both Fabian's and Wurm's right to remain in Great Britain. A few in the German exile community went beyond accusing Dora Fabian of embezzlement, even accusing her of being a spy for the Nazis. These facts in the case convinced some, but by no means all, that the two political exiles had taken their own lives.

There was, however, evidence on the other side. Neither woman had acted suspiciously during the final days of their lives. Both had been active in assisting a British anti-Nazi, Roy Ganz, in his inquiries into Nazi activities in the United Kingdom. It was well known that the Nazi regime feared and hated the German exiles, many of whom were busy exposing its atrocities, rearmament programs and general inhumanity. The Nazis were known to strike out at their foes abroad, not only kidnapping some like the journalist Berthold Jacob, but also eliminating several of the most vociferous of the anti-Nazi exiles, including Professor Theodor Lessing, who had been dramatically murdered in Czechoslovakia in 1933.

In retrospect, it became clear that the British authorities were less interested in solving the case of the deaths of Dora Fabian and Mathilde Wurm than they were in depoliticizing it, so as to render it harmless on both national and international levels. In 1935, the British government was simply not ready to antagonize Nazi Germany, hoping instead that Hitler could be appeased. The deaths of two anti-Nazi women were inconvenient at best, and to emphasize the unanswered aspects of the case would only serve to inflame diplomatic relations between the two nations. After a week or two of intense press coverage of the case, the British public was eager to move on to a more pleasant subject, namely preparations for the celebrations of the 25th anniversary of the start of the reign of King George V. To this day, despite intensive research by scholars, the cause of the deaths of Dora Fabian and Mathilde Wurm remains a mystery.

SOURCES:

Brinson, Charmian. *The Strange Case of Dora Fabian and Mathilde Wurm: A Study of German Political Exiles in London during the 1930's*. Berne: Peter Lang, 1997.

———. "The Strange Case of Dora Fabian and Mathilde Wurm," in *German Life and Letters*. Vol. 45, no. 4. October 1992, pp. 323–344.

Brockway, Fenner. *Indien*. Translated by Dora Fabian. Dresden: Kaden & Co. [1931].

[Browning, Hilda, and Dora Fabian]. *Women under Fascism and Communism*. London: M. Lawrence Ltd. [1934].

Fabian, Dora. *Arbeiterschaft und Kolonialpolitik*. Berlin: E. Laubsche Verlagsbuchhandlung, 1928.

Hertz, Paul. "Frauentragödie: Zum Tode von Mathilde Wurm und Dora Fabian," in *Neuer Vorwärts*. April 14, 1935, p. 2.

Kantorowicz, Alfred. *Politik und Literatur im Exil: Deutschsprachige Schriftsteller im Kampf gegen den Nationalsozialismus*. Munich: Deutscher Taschenbuch Verlag, 1978.

Lehmann-Russbüldt, Otto. *Germany's Air Force*. London: G. Allen & Unwin, 1935.

Schröder, Wilhelm Heinz. *Sozialdemokratische Parlamentarier in den Deutschen Reichs- und Landtagen 1867–1933: Biographien, Chronik, Wahldokumentation*. Düsseldorf: Droste Verlag, 1995.

John Haag,
Assistant Professor of History,
University of Georgia, Athens, Georgia

Fabiola (d. 399 CE)

Early Christian saint and founder of the first public hospital in Rome. Name variations: Saint Fabiola. Pronunciation: Fab-ee-OH-la; date of birth unknown; died in 399 CE; married twice to men unnamed in sources.

Made public recantation of sins after the death of her second husband; donated large sums of money to the poor and religious institutions and founded a house for the sick in Rome; traveled to Jerusalem (395) and studied Scripture with St. Jerome; returned to Rome at onset of Huns; founded a house for pilgrims in Portus.

Fabiola lived in the first century of legal, state-sanctioned Christianity in the Roman Empire. This period, in which Christianity was fused with traditional Roman and pre-Roman customs and beliefs, was one of great social change in habits and viewpoints of all classes in the empire. Fabiola appears as one of a number of aristocratic women who personified this transition in the renunciation of the traditional (as far as our sources let us see) wifely role of the Roman woman.

Details of the life of Fabiola come to us from a letter (77) of St. Jerome's written in 399 to Oceanus, a relative of hers, and a few incidental remarks in other letters (55, 66). Jerome also wrote two letters on theological subjects to Fabiola herself (64, 78). In his letter to Oceanus, Jerome gives Fabiola an appropriate aristocratic

pedigree as descended from the *gens Fabia* that produced notable heroes during the period of the Roman republic. It is unlikely that this family had survived in lineal descent over six centuries to Fabiola's time from the time of Fabius Cunctator, the general of the Second Punic War. Nevertheless, it is clear that Fabiola belonged to a wealthy and well-thought-of family.

Jerome dwells on the fact that Fabiola was married twice. This appears to have been cause for scandal even later in her life. Her first husband troubled Fabiola deeply. Jerome tells us that he "possessed such vices that not even a prostitute or a low slave could endure them" (77.3). She separated from him, an act somewhat risqué for a proper Roman matron, but laudable according to Jerome's Christian morality since men were required to divorce unfaithful wives. In one of the more egalitarian pronouncements of early Christianity, Jerome says: "Whatever is ordained for men consequently also applies to women" (77.3). Although her husband's behavior was cause for public discussion, Fabiola remained silent on the subject.

> *With her own hand she would offer food and give water to a living corpse.*
>
> —Jerome

Because she was still quite young at the time, she took another husband, a fact that Jerome does not excuse but justifies on the ground that this was better than adultery. "She saw another law in her members fighting against the law of her mind and saw herself a chained captive dragged into sexual intercourse" (77.3). Jerome also remarks that at this time she was ignorant of the Christian teaching that precluded a woman from marrying again while her first husband lived. This prompts a question as to whether or not Fabiola had yet converted to Christianity. If she had already done so, then her attachment to the religion as a young woman must have been nominal or untutored. In any case, this period of her life seems to have been luxurious, and she held parties and sought out upper-crust society.

After the death of her second husband, Fabiola appeared in the Lateran basilica in Rome and confessed her sins publicly and with great humility. Jerome praises her honesty and lack of shame in announcing her relations with men. Fabiola began the life of a penitent Christian. She dressed in pauper's clothing, sold some of her estates and donated the money to the poor. With these funds she also opened a *noso-*

comeion, a house for the sick, apparently the first of its kind in Rome. Although the Romans had hospital facilities in military camps, most health care was performed at home. It was the Christians of this period, starting in the provinces of the Eastern Empire, who tended to the sick among the poor and built special structures for this purpose. Jerome details how Fabiola took an active role in cleansing the wounds of the sick, as well as in transporting them and in feeding them. She supplied clothing and gave money to the indigent. Jerome emphasizes the extent to which this behavior was unusual, even among faithful donors to the church. So industrious was she that the healthy were said to envy the sick. Fabiola also traveled to parts of Italy and endowed monasteries both directly and through intermediaries.

In 395, somewhat surprisingly, she left her work in Italy and traveled to Jerusalem in the province of Palaestina. Fabiola's reputation had preceded her, and a large crowd welcomed her. Jerome himself hosted her, possibly at his residence in Bethlehem, and oversaw her study of sacred Scripture. He relates the fervor and extent of her investigations, which included asking him questions that he could not answer. Around this time he may have written his Letter 54 to her, explaining the meaning of holy vestments in the Old Testament. A second Letter, 78, to her published after her death, discussed the places passed by the Israelites on their journey from Egypt. Jerome also mentions her interest during this period in visiting any place that *Mary the Virgin, the mother of Christ, had stopped.

When an invasion of the Eurasian Huns threatened the eastern provinces, many of Jerome's circle prepared to leave Judea, though Jerome remained. Fabiola returned to Rome, but she did not stay long, complaining that the walls of the city shut her in. She continued her charitable work, making a point of distributing alms to the poor in person. In Portus, a community neighboring Ostia, the harbor of Rome, she and St. Pammachius founded a xenodochium (as Jerome calls it in Letters 66.11 and 77.10) or house for strangers. This is the regular Late Antique word for hospital (in Letter 77.10 Jerome also uses the Latin hospitium) although Jerome indicates that it served to house pilgrims as well as the destitute.

Shortly after this, Fabiola, believing that her remaining time on earth was limited, gathered together monks to continue her work. She died in her sleep in 399. Many people attended her funeral at Rome; at a later date in the early history of the Church, she was canonized. Her feast day is December 27.

SUGGESTED READING:

Gask, George E., and Todd John, "The Origin of Hospitals," in E. Ashworth Underwood, ed., *Science, Medicine, and History. Essays on the Evolution of Scientific Thought and Medical Practice Written in honor of Charles Singer.* Vol. 1. London: Oxford University Press, 1953.

Jerome, Letters 66, 77.

Alexander Ingle,
Lecturer in the Department of Classical Studies,
University of Michigan, Ann Arbor, Michigan

Fabiola (1928—)

Queen of the Belgians. Name variations: Fabiola de Mora y Aragón; Fabiola of Aragon. Born Fabiola Fernanda Maria de las Victori Antonia Adelaide on June 11, 1928, in Madrid, Spain; daughter of Gonzalo Mora y Fernandez (d. 1954), count of Mora; married Boudewijn also known as Baudouin I (1930–1993), king of the Belgians (r. 1951–1993), on December 15, 1960 (died, July 31, 1993); no children.

When the engagement of Belgium's King Baudouin I to the 34-year-old Spanish aristocrat Fabiola de Mora y Aragón was announced in September 1960, the country breathed a collective sigh of relief, for it was only through marriage that the king would be released from the overwhelming influence of his father Leopold III, who abdicated in 1951 but continued to occupy the palace and advise his son. The young King Baudouin, who had once aspired to be a Trappist monk, took years to grow into a figure of authority and as much time to choose a wife. The bride-to-be was even more conservative than her fiancé. One of seven children of the Spanish count of Mora, she grew up in an orderly and disciplined household, which, following the count's death in 1954, took on the additional somberness of mourning. Fabiola, who at the time of her engagement was still living at home with her mother, was employed as a surgical nurse at a military hospital in Madrid and also shared her mother's interest in charitable work. Extremely religious, Fabiola attended daily mass and alternated with her mother in leading the 17-member household staff in evening prayers.

After some initial shock that the king was marrying a Spanish woman about whom nothing was known, the Belgians welcomed Fabiola warmly into their midst. (For a time, there was concern over Fabiola's colorful brother Jaime, marquis of Casasiera, a Latin American playboy with a flamboyant wardrobe and a "showgirl" wife, but neither he nor any other member of the

Mora clan had much to do with the royal family.) Following the couple's wedding on December 15, 1960 (officiated by Cardinal de Malines, who had married Baudouin's father 30 years earlier), Queen Fabiola graciously embraced the people of her adopted country. "From now on my heart and my life are shared not only with my husband but with all of you," she said in a speech delivered after the nuptials.

Fabiola's reign was distinguished by her charitable work, which began immediately following her honeymoon when a series of crippling strikes brought the country to a standstill. Often traveling alone and driving her own small car, Fabiola visited destitute families, bringing hope and winning admiration. On the heels of the strikes came a landslide that buried one village and a flood that destroyed another. The queen was one of the first on the scene at both disasters, organizing first aid and giving solace to the victims. In addition to official duties that she tended to in well-ordered fashion, the queen frequently went out of her way to visit those who wrote to the palace with special requests. It was also rumored that she sometimes dipped into her own substantial fortune to assist her subjects. "It is customary to say that queens are good," write **Laure Boulay** and **Françoise Jaudel**, "but with Fabiola it's more than simple goodness; a royal and fraternal devotion to the whole of her people seem to govern her entire life."

Queen Fabiola also oversaw the palace with grace and ease, having been accustomed to a large home and staff since childhood. Breaking with tradition, she kept no official ladies-in-waiting, and her daily life very much revolved around the king. They breakfasted and lunched together daily and attended mass three times a week in the chapel of Laeken Palace. When not presiding over official functions, the couple enjoyed informal dinners with friends or going to a restaurant or the theater. (A popular late-night haunt was a self-service bookstore in Brussels.)

Since the king and queen had no children (Queen Fabiola suffered a miscarriage during her only pregnancy), the king's brother Albert (II) was next in line to the throne. Because Albert was only four years younger than Baudouin, it was assumed that the role of king would fall to Albert's oldest son, Philippe. Baudouin and Fabiola were said to have had a soft spot for Albert's children. When Albert's daughter **Astrid** (b. 1962) turned 18, they broke from their usual reserve and threw an extravagant party for her in the greenhouse of the palace.

King Baudouin, however, did die before his brother, succumbing to a heart attack in 1993, while vacationing in Spain. Though Albert was expected to stand aside for Philippe to rule, it was decided that his years of diplomatic and economic experience made him the better choice as king. His wife, European aristocrat *Paola, known for her charitable activities as much as her beauty, succeeded Fabiola as queen.

SOURCES:

Boulay, Laure, and Françoise Jaudel. *There Are Still Kings: The Ten Royal Families of Europe.* Translated by Linda Dannenberg. NY: Crown, 1981.
Europe. Issue 329. September 1993, pp. 26–28.
Graham, Judith, ed. *Current Biography Yearbook 1993.* NY: H.W. Wilson, 1993.

Barbara Morgan,
Melrose, Massachusetts

Fabricius, Sara (1880–1874).

See Sandel, Cora.

Fabula (fl. 9th, 8th, or 7th c. BCE).

See Larentia, Acca.

Faccio, Rina (1876–1960).

See Pierangeli, Rina Faccio.

Fadilla (b. 159).

See Faustina II for sidebar.

Fadl (d. around 870)

Arabian singer and poet who was much beloved as a performer. Born in Basra (now Iraq), date unknown; died in Baghdad, probably in 870 CE; performed in the court of Caliph al-Mutawakki and caliphs al-Muntasir and al-Mutamid.

Different versions are told of Fadl's childhood. In one account, she was the daughter of a slave woman, who originally came from Yamama, and was brought up by the slave woman's master before being sold when she reached adulthood. Fadl and her mother, however, maintained that Fadl's father was the master and that when he died, his son sold her. In yet another version, the master recognized Fadl as a legitimate heir. When he died, one of Fadl's half-brothers sold her in order to prevent her from receiving her fair share of the inheritance due under Islamic law.

No matter what her beginnings, Fadl changed owners several times as a slave before coming to the court of Caliph al-Mutawakki (r. 847–861) of Baghdad. The caliph was enchanted by her talents as a composer and singer as well as her wit and beauty, and Fadl became his favorite.

An excellent poet, she often set her poetry to music. In addition, some of her verses were musically arranged by other Arab singers, among them *Oraib, who was also famous. The caliph eventually gave Fadl her freedom. Many of her poems were dedicated to the poet Sa'id Ibn Humaid. Later she left him for Bunan Ibn Amr, another favored court singer. When Caliph al-Mutawakki died, Fadl's gifts were equally prized by his successors, al-Muntasir (r. 861–862) and al-Mutamid (r. 870–892).

John Haag,
Athens, Georgia

Faggs, Mae (1932—)

African-American sprinter. Name variations: Mae Faggs Starr. Born Aeriwentha Mae Faggs in Mays Landing, New York, on April 10, 1932; married Eddie Starr (a high school principal).

First American woman to participate in three Olympics (1948, 1952, and 1956); winner of the AAU 200-meters (1954, 1955, and 1956); won the silver in the 200-meter and the gold in the 4x100-meter relay at the Pan Am Games (1955); won the gold medal in the 4x100-meter relay with a 45.9 time in the Olympics in Helsinki (1952), and the bronze medal in the 4x100-meter relay with a time of 44.9 in the Melbourne Olympics (1956).

Mae Faggs' track career began thanks to her alliance with a New York policeman. When she was in elementary school, Patrolman Dykes came to recruit members for the Police Athletic League (PAL). "Naturally, I was interested," said Mae. "I was nothing but a tomboy, anyhow." As the boys were running, Faggs looked up at him and said: "Patrolman Dykes, I can beat everyone of those boys running out there." He said, "Let's see." "So he lined up some boys with me," said Faggs, "and we took off down the school court and I beat 'em." Dykes put her on the girls' team from the 111th Precinct. Then, Sergeant John Brennan started an AAU team with young athletes from the city (1947). Soon, Brennan was predicting that she would make the Olympic team.

Brennan became her mentor. In 1948, he entered Faggs in the trials for the U.S. Olympic Team in Providence, Rhode Island. He was certain she would win; she was less so. Faggs recounts:

> I was digging my holes—I didn't bother with starting blocks then—and I took off my sweats and the starter said, "OK let's make our marks." All of a sudden I just stood up and I walked to Mr. Brennan and I said,

> "Mr. Brennan, I can't do it." He said, "Wait a minute; you come here," and he just talked to me for a few minutes. . . . I walked back out on the track and I was ready. All the way back home I kept asking Mr. Brennan, "Have I really made the Olympic Team?" and he said, "Yes, you've made it."

Faggs had finished third behind two more experienced runners, 🐾➤ **Audrey Patterson** of Tennessee State and *Nell Jackson of Tuskegee. As the team's youngest member, Faggs was soon on board the *SS America* bound for London and the 1948 Olympics. The enormous city, 100,000 spectators, and 5,000 athletes from 58 countries did not intimidate her. She ran the 200-meter trial heat with *Fanny Blankers-Koen, the 30-year-old Dutch housewife who went on to win four Olympic gold medals. Though Faggs was defeated in the trials, *Alice Coachman, the African-American track star who won 26 national championships, consoled her: "Young as you are, you can be in two or three Olympic Games."

Mae Faggs was 15 when she ran in her first AAU national indoor meet in 1949. Her competitors were Patterson and *Stella Walsh, both well-known champions. "Well, Toots, you ought to be very good in this meet," said Brennan, who was always at her side. "As a matter of fact I am expecting you to take first place in the 220." Faggs beat Walsh and Patterson with a new American record of 25.8. In 1952, Faggs anchored the Police Athletic League to win the 440-yard relay and the 220-yard dash and tied the indoor record in the 100-yard dash. In the Olympic trials, she was first in the 100 meters and second in the 200. For some time, Faggs had been competing against Nell Jackson as well as **Jean Patterson** and **Mary McNabb**. Faggs expected these African-American runners to be members of the U.S. Olympic team, but Nell Jackson dropped out of the trials; Mary McNabb pulled a leg muscle and was unable to compete; and Jean Patterson was also injured, leaving Faggs to head for Helsinki without them.

A veteran at the Helsinki Olympics in 1952, Faggs was determined to medal, but prospects were not good. This was the beginning of the Cold War and of a sports rivalry between the U.S. and USSR that would last for four decades. "The United States is not expected to do much in women's track, in which the Russians are very strong," predicted *The New York Times*. As the Helsinki Games progressed, these words proved prophetic. **Mabel Landry**, America's best broad jumper, broke an Olympic record with one jump in the qualifying trials only to come in 7th in the finals. America's 🐾➤ **Catherine Hardy** was eliminated in the 100-meter qualifying rounds. Mae Faggs came in 6th in the 100-meter finals. The weather was wet and cold; spirits were low.

All that remained was the 4x100 meter relay, and the Americans' chances looked dismal. ❧ **Janet Moreau** from Providence, Rhode Island, Catherine Hardy from Fort Valley, Georgia, *Barbara Jones from Chicago, and Mae Faggs from New York made up the relay team. Jones, only 15, was too discouraged to practice and the other two runners were almost indifferent. Only Faggs felt a medal was within reach. The key to winning a relay is passing the baton. Races have been lost when the baton is dropped or when runners waste precious seconds looking back as the baton is passed. Faggs wanted to avoid these costly mistakes and urged the team to practice for split-second accuracy. When the teenage Jones balked, Faggs threatened: "If you can't come out and train with us and get this stick passing right, then I am not going to set your hair." Jones showed up for practice.

Led by *Marjorie Jackson, a two-time gold-medal winner, the Australians were slated to win the 4x100-meter relay. But by the time Faggs ran the first lap and passed the baton to Jones, the U.S. was out front by almost two yards. Jones added another yard but Moreau lost ground. When Hardy took the baton for the 4th and final leg of the race, Australia was in the lead, followed by England and Germany. Then Marjorie Jackson dropped the baton, putting the Australians out of contention. Hardy passed the German runner 30 yards from the finish, then passed the English runner two yards from the tape. The Americans, coming from behind, set a new world record of 45.9 seconds and won an Olympic gold medal.

When Mae Faggs returned to America, she began college at Tennessee State University where friends had arranged a work scholarship. Home of the famous Tennessee Tigerbelles, TSU would one day be known for its women track stars, including *Wilma Rudolph and *Wyomia Tyus. But Faggs arrived before the glory days and was bitterly disappointed by the status of women's track at Tennessee. She was the lone star on the women's track team. There was no money to travel to track meets, nor funds to pay Faggs' way to the AAU national meet so she could defend her title in the 220-yard dash which she had held since 1949. In retaliation, Faggs decided to win every sprint she could.

Two years later, the TSU women's track team began to whip itself into competitive

❧▶ **Patterson, Audrey** (1926—)
American track-and-field champion. Born on September 27, 1926.

Audrey Patterson, of Tennessee State, won a bronze medal in the 200 meters in London in the 1948 Olympics.

❧▶ **Hardy, Catherine** (1932—)
African-American track-and-field champion. Born on February 8, 1932 (some sources cite 1930), in Carrollton, Georgia.

As a member of the U.S. team, Catherine Hardy won the gold medal in the 4x100-meter relay in the Helsinki Olympics in 1952. Hardy had also won the AAU indoor 50 yards in 1951 and the AAU outdoor double in 1952.

❧▶ **Moreau, Janet** (1927—)
American track-and-field champion. Born on October 26, 1927; lived in Providence, Rhode Island.

As a member of the U.S. team, Janet Moreau won the gold medal in the 4x100-meter relay in the Helsinki Olympics in 1952.

shape. **Isabelle Daniels** of Jakin, Georgia, and *Lucinda Williams of Bloomingdale, Georgia, joined the team. Faggs, Daniels, Williams, and **Cynthia Thompson**, a 31-year-old who had been a member of the Jamaican Olympic track teams (1948 and 1952), formed the Tennessee State 800-meter relay team which set a new American record at the AAU outdoor nationals in Harrisburg, Pennsylvania, in 1954. Faggs also won the 220-yard run that same year.

In 1955, the AAU indoor nationals were held in Chicago, where the TSU Tigerbelles struggled against the Chicago Comets, a Catholic Youth Organization (CYO) team. The CYO's Mabel Landry, the broad jumper, and Barbara Jones, the sprinter on the 1952 Olympic team, competed against the runners from Tennessee, winning the 440-yard relay, the 440-yard medley, the 110-yard dash, and the 220-yard dash. Several of the Comets came to Tennessee in 1956, adding new talent to the team. At the Pan American Games held in Mexico City in March 1956, Faggs beat **Bertha Diaz** of Cuba in the first heat of the 60-meter dash, but Diaz came back to win in the finals. In the 400-meter relay, Landry, Jones, Daniels, and Faggs won the event.

As the women's track program developed at Tennessee State University, Faggs remained the central athlete and her leadership was vital.

Promising athletes continued to stream into the women's track program. Wilma Rudolph and *Martha Hudson were two of the rookies. Inevitably, some of these younger runners beat Faggs, and she encouraged them. But Faggs never stayed beaten for long. She preferred being in first place, and in the outdoor nationals in Philadelphia (1956) Faggs won the gold in the 100-yard dash, the 220-yard dash, and the 440-yard relay.

She was the only woman chosen, along with six outstanding male athletes, to make a goodwill tour of Monrovia, Liberia, Accra, the Gold Coast (now Ghana), Lagos, and Ibada in Nigeria for the U.S. State Department. When a Nashville merchant heard that Faggs could not afford a coat for the tour, she was offered one at half price.

In the 1956 Olympics trials, the third for Faggs, she was determined to calm the nervous "Skeeter," as Wilma Rudolph was known by friends. Though Faggs and Rudolph tied the American record of 24.1, Faggs crossed the tape first. "As we came off the turn," said Faggs, "Skeeter was in front of me. But she turned to look back, and when she did, I beat her to the tape by just inches." Faggs later told Rudolph: "'As long as you live, don't you ever look back in a race again.' And she never did."

The Tennessee State women's track program had come a long way. Six of its athletes made the Olympic team in 1956. For the first time in the history of the women's Olympic track-and-field program, the Americans had a black woman coach: Nell Jackson of Tuskegee. The 1956 Melbourne games were not easy. Faggs was eliminated in the first heat of the 100 meter, and *Betty Cuthbert took the gold. In the 200, Rudolph was ousted in the trial heat. The relay team was also having a miserable time. "After qualifying heats in the morning," said Faggs, "Skeeter was upset. She thought she had run out of the passing zone. Margaret and Isabel were down in the dumps because of our slow time. So I took all of them to the warm-up track in the back of the stadium, and I said some terrible words to them. I told them I didn't know what they were going to do, but I was going to have me a medal." Though Australia took the relay with the fastest Olympic time ever recorded, the all-Tennessee State team came in third, capturing the bronze. Faggs had another medal.

The 1956 Olympics ended Mae Faggs' career, but she left a powerful legacy. She had arrived at Tennessee State University as the sole track star in a woefully underfunded program; by the time she left, she had poured the foundation for one of the most successful women's track teams in collegiate history. She was instrumental in the stellar career of Wilma Rudolph and those of many others. Faggs continued her education after graduating from Tennessee State, studying toward a master's degree in special education at the University of Cincinnati. She became a school teacher, married Eddie Starr, a high school principal, and became well known in Cincinnati for promoting youth programs. In 1996, Mae Faggs was inducted into the Women's Sports Hall of Fame.

SOURCES:
Davis, Michael D. *Black American Women in Olympic Track and Field*. Jefferson, NC: McFarland, 1992.
Page, James A. *Black Olympian Medalists*. Englewood, CO: Libraries Unlimited, 1991.

Karin Loewen Haag,
freelance writer, Athens, Georgia

Faileuba (fl. 586–587)

Queen of Austrasia and queen of Burgundy. Flourished around 586 and 587; married Childebert II, king of Austrasia (r. 575–595), king of Burgundy (r. 593–595); children: Thibert also known as Theudebert II (586–612), king of Austrasia (r. 595–612); Thierry also known as Theuderic or Theodoric II (587–613), king of Burgundy (r. 595–613), king of Austrasia (r. 612–613).

Fairclough, Ellen (b. 1905)

Canadian secretary of state and businesswoman. Name variations: The Right Honourable Ellen Fairclough. Born Ellen Louks Cook in Hamilton, Ontario, on January 28, 1905; daughter of Norman Ellsworth (a farmer) and Nellie Bell (Louks) Cook; attended Hamilton public schools until age 16; married David Henry Gordon Fairclough (owner of a printing business), on January 28, 1931; children: David Fairclough.

Ellen Fairclough, the first woman in Canada to hold a Cabinet position, was born and raised in Hamilton, Ontario. She quit school at age 16, following the failure of her father's farm, and worked at a variety of jobs before becoming an accountant with a brokerage firm. When her employer went out of business in 1935, she opened her own accounting and tax service business.

Fairclough's husband David Fairclough led her into politics. She became vice president of the Young Conservative Association (Ontario) and in 1946 was elected to the Hamilton city council as an alderman. In 1950, after an unsuccessful run for federal Parliament, she was elected controller for the city of Hamilton. Receiving more votes than any other candidate in the municipal polling, she automatically became deputy mayor. In May 1950, she became a candidate in a by-election to fill a vacant seat in the House of Commons. Campaigning with the slogan "Canada needs a woman's voice," she easily won over her opponent. At the opening session of Parliament, Fairclough was appointed chair of the labor committee of the official Opposition caucus; as such, she became the "voice" of the opposition on labor matters. She remained a member of the opposition party for seven years, then spent six years in the Cabinet. Colleagues remember her as eloquent and persistent in pushing through legislation, particularly that which benefited working women.

In 1957, under the Progressive Conservative Party of Prime Minister John G. Diefenbaker, Fairclough was appointed secretary of state, becoming the first woman Cabinet minister in Canadian history. Her department served "as the official channel of communications between the federal government and the British Crown, and between Ottawa and the provincial governments," noted *The New York Times* (June 22, 1957). After a year, Fairclough became minister of citizenship and immigration, and in 1962 was named postmaster general. Defeated in the 1963 election, she once again picked up her business career, eventually becoming vice president, director, and secretary-treasurer of the Hamilton Trust and Savings Corporation, an institution that she helped build from scratch.

Fairclough, who never considered herself much of a feminist, called equality "a chance to prove oneself." Acknowledging that family ties seem to tether women more than men, she credited an understanding husband and a full-time housekeeper with making her path a bit easier.

SOURCES:
Current Biography 1957. NY: H.W. Wilson, 1957.
Harakas, Margo. "Ellen Fairclough," in *Fort Lauderdale* [Florida] *Sun-Sentinel.* September 26, 1975.

Barbara Morgan,
Melrose, Massachusetts

Fairfax Somerville, Mary (1780–1872).
See Somerville, Mary Fairfax.

Fairfield, Cicely (1892–1983).
See West, Rebecca.

Fairfield, Flora (1832–1888).
See Alcott, Louisa May.

Fair Geraldine, The (c. 1528–1589).
See Fitzgerald, Elizabeth.

Fair Maid of Brabant (c. 1102–1151).
See Adelicia of Louvain.

Fair Maid of Kent (1328–1385).
See Joan of Kent.

Fair Maid of Norway (c. 1283–1290).
See Margaret, Maid of Norway.

Fair Rosamond or Rosamund (c. 1145–1176).
See Clifford, Rosamund.

Faithfull, Emily (1835–1895)

English feminist, philanthropist, and businesswoman. Name variations: Faithful. Born at Headley Rectory in Surrey, England, in 1835; died in Manchester, England, on May 31, 1895; youngest daughter of Ferdinand Faithfull (rector of Headley, near Epsom, England); attended boarding school in Kensington and was presented at court.

Emily Faithfull, aware of the lack of opportunities for women in industry, set up her own printing firm in Edinburgh in 1857, employing women only. Moving to London the following year, she became secretary of the first Society for Promoting the Employment of Women. Two years later, she founded the Victoria Press in Great Coram Street. But because she employed women along with men, the company was received with hostility from the printer's unions; presumably because it encouraged immorality. Even so, it soon acquired a reputation for excellent work, and in 1862 Faithfull was appointed printer and publisher-in-ordinary to Queen *Victoria. In 1863, she started the *Victoria Magazine*, a monthly that for 18 years advocated a woman's right to hold monetary employment. Faithfull also became involved with publications that her firm printed, including *The Englishwoman's Journal*, and published a novel in 1868, *Change Upon Change: A Love Story*.

In 1864, her reputation was permanently tarnished when she became involved in a highly publicized divorce suit between Henry Codrington (later admiral) and **Helen Codrington**. Faithfull resigned from the Victoria Press, but after joining the Women's Trade Union League she founded the *West London Express* in 1877, again staffed by women compositors. She also lectured widely and successfully on women's issues both in England and the United States, which she had visited in 1872 and would again in 1882. In 1888, Faithfull was awarded a civil list pension of £50.

Renée Falconetti

pressly for her. Describing her voice, a contemporary wrote that it was "an incomparable metal, a timbre like nothing that has ever been heard." Despite this fact, she had problems in the upper register. Six years after her debut, in 1838, Falcon's voice gave out in the middle of a performance. She went to Italy for a holiday and further vocal training. In 1840, she returned to the stage in Paris where she was greeted with great enthusiasm. Unfortunately, her voice was never able to recover, and she retired from the opera stage.

John Haag,
Athens, Georgia

Falconetti, Renée (1892–1946)

French actress and producer. Name variations: Renee Falconetti; Maria Falconetti. Born Renée Maria Falconetti in Sermano, Corsica, in 1892; died in Buenos Aires, Argentina, in 1946.

Renée Falconetti, a celebrated French stage actress and producer, made a single film appearance in Carl Dreyer's silent masterpiece *La Passion de Jeanne D'Arc* (*The Passion of *Joan of Arc*) in 1927. Her performance was so outstanding that it earned her a place in the annals of film history. Dreyer's film, which condenses the trial, torture, and execution of the French saint into an intense 24-hour period, was based on actual trial records and shot in extreme close-ups against stark white backgrounds in order to enhance its psychological realism. To further increase the real-life effect, all of the actors performed without make-up. Falconetti, known for comedy roles, was a powerful Joan, revealing much of the character's anguish through her beautiful and expressive face. It was said that Dreyer bullied her unmercifully to draw out her performance. The actress died in Buenos Aires, where she had immigrated just before the outbreak of World War II.

Barbara Morgan,
Melrose, Massachusetts

Falco, Joao (1892–1958).

See Lisboa, Irene.

Falcon, Marie Cornélie (1814–1897)

French soprano and mezzo-soprano. Name variations: Marie Cornelie Falcon. Born on January 28, 1814, in Paris; died on February 25, 1897, in Paris; studied with Bordogni and A. Nourrit at the Paris Conservatory.

Debuted at the Paris Opéra (1832); lost her voice during a performance (1838) and was forced to retire (1840).

Roles that demand a combination of dramatic soprano and dramatic mezzo-soprano are referred to as "falcon," a term borrowed from Marie Cornélie Falcon because she sang so many roles that overlapped between the soprano and mezzo-soprano voice. Marie Falcon entered the Paris Conservatory at age 13. Four years later, she won first prize in singing and soon made her debut at the Paris Opéra. The roles of Valentine in Meyerbeer's *Les huguenots* (1836) and Rachel in Halévy's *La Juive* (1835) were created ex-

Falconieri, Juliana (1270–1341)

Italian saint and religious founder. Name variations: Guiliana. Born in 1270 in Florence; died in 1341 in Florence; niece of St. Alexis; never married; no children.

Little is known of Juliana Falconieri's childhood, except that she was born in Florence, dedicated her life to holy work at a young age, and felt a special connection to *Mary the Virgin. Around 1285, the teenager established a new religious community, called the Mantellate Sisters.

Its members were all female, and the primary purpose of the order was to pray and worship the Virgin and serve among the poor in her name. Juliana's unusual commitment and deep devotion earned her many supporters, even among the upper classes, who patronized the Mantellate order and helped Juliana's reputation spread across Italy. After her death at about age 71, Juliana's followers campaigned successfully for her canonization. Her feast day is on June 19.

Laura York,
Riverside, California

Falkestein, Beatrice von

(c. 1253–1277)

*Queen of the Romans. Name variations: Beatrix of Falkenburg; queen of Germany. Born around 1253 at Falkenburg Castle, Germany; died on October 17, 1277; buried at Church of Franciscan Friars Minor, Oxford, Oxfordshire, England; daughter of Theodore von Falkestein, count of Falkenburg, or William de Fauquemont, count of Falkenburg, and Joan van Loon; niece of Conrad, archbishop of Cologne; married Richard of Cornwall (1209–1272), 1st earl of Cornwall, king of the Romans (r. 1227–1272), on June 16, 1269. Richard of Cornwall's first wife was *Isabel Marshall (1200–1240); his second was *Sancha of Provence (c. 1225–1261).*

Fältskog, Agnetha (b. 1950).

See ABBA.

Fannia (fl. mid–1st c.)

Roman noblewoman. Flourished mid–1st century CE; daughter of Thrasea Paetus and Arria Minor; granddaughter of Caecina Paetus (a Roman senator) and Arria Major (d. 42 CE); married Helvidius Priscus the Elder (praetor 70 CE); children: (stepson) Helvidius Priscus the Younger.

As the daughter of Thrasea Paetus and **Arria Minor** and the granddaughter of Caecina Paetus and *Arria Major (d. 42 CE), Fannia was a dissenter to the manor born; she sided with her husband Helvidius Priscus the Elder in his provocative attitude toward the emperor Vespasian (r. 69–79), causing her repeated exile; her stepson continued the cause. Like Arria Minor, Fannia returned to Rome after the death of Domitian (r. 81–96), in 96 CE.

Fanny.

Variant of Frances.

Fanny, Aunt (1808–1884).

See Gage, Frances D.

Fanshawe, Anne (1625–1680)

English Royalist and memoirist. Name variations: Lady Anne Fanshawe. Born Anne Harrison in London, England, on March 25, 1625; died at Ware Park, Hertfordshire, England, on January 30, 1680; elder daughter and fourth child of Sir John Harrison (a prominent Royalist) and Margaret (Fanshawe) Harrison; married Sir Richard Fanshawe (1608–1666, a diplomat, author, and relative of her mother), in 1644; children: 14, of whom only five survived to adulthood.

The daughter of **Margaret Fanshawe Harrison** and Sir John Harrison, a Royalist and friend of Charles I, Anne Fanshawe was characterized as "a hoyting girl," who loved physical activity and the outdoors. Her education, probably at home, included French, music, needlework, and dancing, as was the custom of the day. At 19, she married Sir Richard Fanshawe, a poet and translator, who was 12 years her senior and her mother's first cousin. Like Anne's father, Richard was also an eminent Royalist who, after his marriage to Anne, embarked on an extensive diplomatic career that would take the couple to France, Ireland, The Hague, Portugal, and Spain. Anne, a devoted and loving wife, supported her husband through imprisonment, debt, shipwreck, and even an attack by pirates, all the while mothering the couple's 14 children (of whom only five survived to adulthood). Following the restoration of Charles II to the British throne in 1660, Richard was posted in Portugal, and then in Spain, where life settled into a more normal routine. Richard's sudden death in Madrid in 1666, however, shortly after he had been ordered to return home by the British government, left Anne burdened with his debts. By one account, *Maria Anna of Austria (1634–1696), the queen-regent of Spain, was so moved by Anne's desolation that she offered her a handsome pension if she would embrace the Catholic faith, but Fanshawe, though grateful, could not accept the favor with such conditions attached. Through the assistance of *Anne of Austria, who also died in 1666, Fanshawe was able to have her husband's remains shipped to England for burial, and she later had a monument erected in his memory.

The *Memoirs* for which Fanshawe is known were completed in 1676 but would not be published until 1829, almost 150 years after her death. The work, which includes a partial narrative of her adventures during the Commonwealth (1649–1660), was probably quite dated by the time it came out, for the reviews were less than favorable. Her contemporary, *Mary de la Rivière, writing for *New Atlantis,* described Fanshawe as a woman with "affected learning, eternal tattle, insipid gaiety and a false sense of wit," and another of her critics, Horace Walpole, thought her work focused too much on "private domestic distresses." The book was reprinted in 1979, together with the memoirs of another 17th-century aristocrat, Lady *Anne Halkett, as *The Memoirs of Anne, Lady Halkett and Anne, Lady Fanshawe.*

Barbara Morgan,
Melrose, Massachusetts

Fanshawe, Catherine Maria

(1765–1834)

English poet. Born in Chipstead, Surrey, England, on July 6, 1765; died at Putney Heath, England, on April 17, 1834; second daughter and one of five children of John Fanshawe of Shabden, a Surrey squire, and Penelope (Dredge) Fanshawe; never married; no children.

Catherine Maria Fanshawe was born in Surrey in 1765 and would be a semi-invalid throughout her life. On the death of her parents and two brothers, she moved with her two sisters to a house in Berkeley Square, London, and later Midhurst House, Richmond. Known for her charm and wit, Fanshawe was admired in her own circle and her home was often frequented by the literati of her day, but she rarely agreed to have her worked included in publications. Her best-known poem, a riddle on the letter H which began "'Twas whispered in heaven, 'twas muttered in Hell," was often attributed to Lord Byron. Limited editions of her *Memorials,* which contained most of her poems, and of her *Literary Remains* appeared in 1865 and 1876, respectively. Several of her poems were included in *Joanna Baillie's collection, *Poetic Miscellanies,* published in 1823. Fanshawe often visited Italy for her health. A gifted watercolorist, she also made many sketches of Italian scenes.

Fara (d. 667)

Frankish saint and religious founder. Name variations: Burgundofara; Saint Fara or Fare. Born in the neighborhood of Meaux; birth date unknown; died at Evoriac, France, in 667; sister of St. Chagnoaldus (monk of Luxeuil) and St. Faro (bishop of Meaux for 46 years and chancellor for King Clotaire II); never married; no children.

Born into a noble Frankish family, Saint Fara refused to marry and founded a double monastery at Evoriac, later called Faremoutiers, after spending her youth in a convent. As was common in such situations, Fara was elected abbess of her new establishment and served in that capacity for 40 years. The 7th century saw many such nobles creating religious institutions. Many of these were women who took for themselves the authority otherwise reserved for male religious. Fara, for instance, saw no reason why she could not act as a priest when she was the spiritual head of both nuns and monks. She administered the sacraments, heard confessions, and even excommunicated disobedient or criminal members. Fara ruled with a strong sense of discipline and order; her leadership qualities and great devotion led the Church to declare her a saint some years after her death. Her feast day is April 3.

Laura York,
Riverside, California

Fare (d. 667).
See Fara.

Farida (c. 830–?)

Arabian singer. Born around 830 CE; death date unknown; flourished in the court of Caliph al-Watiq (r. 842–847) and his brother Caliph al-Mutawakki (r. 847–861); married al-Mutawakki; children: at least one son.

Like many Arabian singers, Farida was a slave whose musical career depended not only on her own talents but also on the whims of her master. Farida was purchased, brought up, and educated by the singer Amr Ibn Bana before she was presented as a gift to Caliph al-Watiq. At his court, she studied with *Shariyya, another singer, but rivalry began to distance the two. Their musical preferences may have caused dissent between them as Shariyya belonged to the romantic school of Arabic music while Farida preferred classical performers like Ishaq al-Mausili.

A member of Caliph al-Watiq's harem, Farida was his favorite and exerted considerable influence at court. But al-Watiq's obsession with her caused problems. As Farida played for him one day, he was seized with jealousy, perceiving that in the event of his death she would play as sweetly for his brother and heir. He kicked her from her seat and also broke her lute. When al-Watiq died, Farida did, indeed, come to belong to his brother, al-Mutawakki. Cut from the same cloth, al-Mutawakki became enraged whenever she sang mournful songs in memory of his late brother. Nonetheless, al-Mutawakki married Farida, and they had a son.

John Haag,
Athens, Georgia

Farjeon, Eleanor (1881–1965)

English children's writer whose Little Bookroom *won the Hans Andersen and Carnegie medals. Name variations: (pseudonyms) Tomfool and Chimaera. Born on February 13, 1881, in London, England; died on June 5, 1965, in Hampstead, London; third of five children of Benjamin Leopold (a novelist) and Margaret Jane (Jefferson) Farjeon (an actress); no formal schooling; never married; no children.*

Awards, honors: First recipient of International Hans Christian Andersen Award (1956) for The Little Bookroom *(the medal is presented biennially by the International Board on Books for Young People, in cooperation with UNESCO, for the best book of fiction for children); Carnegie Medal of Library Association in England (1956) for* The Little Bookroom; *first Regina Medal of Catholic Library Association (1959).*

Selected writings: (based on a story by Heinrich Zschoekke) Floretta: Opera in Two Acts *(Henderson and Spaulding, 1899);* The Registry Office: An Original Comic Opera in One Act *(Henderson and Spaulding, 1900); (poems)* Pan-Worship *(Elkin Matthews, 1908);* Dream-Songs for the Beloved *(Orpheus Press, 1911);* Trees *(Fellowship Books, 1913, Batsford, 1918);* Nursery Rhymes of London Town *(Duckworth, 1916);* All the Way to Alfriston *(Morland Press, 1918);* Singing Games for Children *(Dent, 1918);* Poems and Sonnets *(Blackwell, 1918);* Gypsy and Ginger *(Dutton, 1920);* Martin Pippin in the Apple Orchard *(Collins, 1921);* Songs for Music and Lyrical Poems *(Selwyn and Blount, 1922);* Tunes of a Penny Piper *(Selwyn and Blount, 1922);* The Soul of Kol Nikon *(Stokes, 1923); (verse)* All the Year Round *(Collins, 1923);* The Town Child's Alphabet *(Poetry Bookshop, London, 1924);* The Country Child's Alphabet *(Poetry Bookshop, 1924);* Mighty Men, *Book 1,* From Achilles to Julius Caesar *(Basil Blackwell, 1924), Book 2,* From Beowulf to William the Conqueror *(Basil Blackwell, 1924);* Young Folk and Old *(High House Press, 1925);* Tom Cobble *(Basil Blackwell, 1925);* Faithful Jenny Dove, and Other Tales *(Collins, 1925, reissued as* Faithful Jenny Dove, and Other Illusions, *M. Joseph, 1963);* Joan's Door *(Collins, 1926);* Nuts and May, a Medley for Children *(Collins, 1926);* Italian Peepshow and Other Tales *(Stokes, 1926);* Come Christmas *(Collins, 1927);* The Mill of Dreams; or, Jennifer's Tale *(Collins, 1927);* The King's Barn; or, Joan's Tale *(Collins, 1927);* The Wonderful Knight *(Basil Blackwell, 1927);* Young Gerard; or, Joyce's Tale *(Collins, 1927);* Open Winkins; or, Jessica's Tale *(Collins, 1928);* Kaleidoscope *(Collins, 1928); (verse)* The A.B.C. of the B.B.C. *(Collins, 1928);* An Alphabet of Magic *(Medici Society, London, 1928);* A Bad Day for Martha *(Basil Blackwell, 1928);* First Chap-Book of Rounds *(Dutton, c. 1928);* Second Chap-Book of Rounds *(Dutton, c. 1928);* The Perfect Zoo *(McKay, 1929);* A Collection of Poems *(Collins, 1929);* The King's Daughter Cries for the Moon *(Basil Blackwell, 1929);* The Tale of Tom Tiddler *(Collins, 1929, published as* Tale of Tom Tiddler; with Rhymes of London Town, *Stokes, 1930);* Proud Rosalind and the Hart-Royal *(Collins, 1930);* King's Barn *(Collins, 1930);* Westwood *(Basil Blackwell, 1930);* Tales from Chaucer; The Canterbury Tales Done into Prose *(R. Hale, 1930, reissued as* Tales from Chaucer, ReTold, *Oxford University Press, 1960);* Ladybrook *(Stokes, 1931);* The Old Nurse's Stocking-Basket *(Stokes, 1931);* Perkin the Pedlar *(Faber, 1932);* The Fair of St. James *(Stokes, 1932, published in England as* The Fair of St. James; a Fantasia, *Faber, 1932);* Katy Kruse at the Seaside; or, The Deserted Islanders *(McKay, 1932);* Pannychys *(High*

Eleanor Farjeon

House Press, 1933); Ameliaranne and the Magic Ring *(McKay, 1933); (poems for children)* Over the Garden Wall *(Stokes, 1933);* Ameliaranne's Prize Packet *(Harrap, 1933);* Jim at the Corner and Other Stories *(Basil Blackwell, 1934);* The Old Sailor's Yarn Box *(Stokes, 1934);* Ameliaranne's Washing Day *(McKay, 1934);* The Clumber Pup *(Basil Blackwell, 1934);* The Children's Bells; a Selection of Poems *(Basil Blackwell, 1934); (autobiographical)* A Nursery in the Nineties *(Gollancz, 1935, published as* Portrait of a Family, *Stokes, 1936, reprinted, Oxford University Press, 1960);* And I Dance Mine Own Child *(Basil Blackwell, 1935);* Ten Saints *(Oxford University Press, 1936);* Jim and the Pirates *(Basil Blackwell, 1936); (novel),* Humming Bird *(M. Joseph, 1936);* Paladins in Spain *(Nelson, 1937);* The Wonders of Herodotus *(Nelson, 1937);* Martin Pippin in the Daisy Field *(M. Joseph, 1937);* Love Affair *(M. Joseph, 1937); (verse for children)* Sing For Your Supper *(Stokes, 1938);* One Foot in Fairyland *(Stokes, 1938); (children's plays and games; illustrated by Joan Jefferson Farjeon)* Grannie Gray *(Dent, 1939);* A Sussex Alphabet *(Pear Tree Press, 1939);* Miss Granby's Secret; or The Bastard of Pinsk *(M. Joseph, 1940);* Brave Old Woman *(M. Joseph, 1941);* Magic Casements *(Allen and Unwin, 1941);* The New Book of Days *(Oxford University Press, 1941);* Songs from Punch; Set to Music *(Saville, c. 1941); (poems for children)* Cherrystones *(M. Joseph, 1942);* The Fair Venetian *(M. Joseph, 1943);* Golden Coney *(M. Joseph, 1943);* Dark World of Animals *(Sylvan Press, 1945); (verse)* A Prayer for Little Things *(Houghton, 1945);* Ariadne and the Bull *(M. Joseph, 1945);* The Mulberry Bush *(M. Joseph, 1945);* First and Second Love: Sonnets *(M. Joseph, 1947); (verses)* The Starry Floor *(M. Joseph, 1949); (narrative poem)* Mrs. Malone *(M. Joseph, 1950);* Poems for Children *(Lippincott, 1951);* Silver-Sand and Snow *(M. Joseph, 1951); (play for children)* The Silver Curlew *(produced in England, 1948, illustrated by Ernest Shepard, Oxford University Press, 1953); (short stories for children)* The Little Bookroom *(Oxford University Press, 1955);* Elizabeth Myers *(St. Albert's Press, 1957);* Then There Were Three: Being Cherrystones, The Mulberry Bush, The Starry Floor *(M. Joseph, 1953);* Memoirs: *Book I (of a projected 4),* Edward Thomas: The Last Four Years *(Oxford University Press, 1958); (ed. by Eleanor Graham)* Eleanor Farjeon's Book *(Penguin, 1960); (ed. with William James Carter Mayne)* The Hamish Hamilton Book of Kings *(Hamish Hamilton, 1964, published as* A Cavalcade of Kings, *Walck, 1965); (ed. and author of introduction)* Edward Thomas, The Green Roads: Poems *(Holt, 1965); (ed. with Mayne)* A Cavalcade of

Queens *(Walck, 1965);* Mr. Garden *(Walck, 1966); (poems)* Around the Seasons *(Walck, 1969).*

Topical and nonsense poet of Daily Herald *(London) under pseudonym Tomfool (1919–32). Contributor to* Time and Tide *under pseudonym Chimaera, and to* Punch *and other periodicals. Two selections of Nonsense Poems, "Tomfooleries" and "Moonshine," were published by Labour Press (1920, 1921).*

"I was a dreamy, timid, sickly, lachrymose, painfully shy, sensitive, greedy, ill-regulated little girl," wrote Eleanor Farjeon, one of England's most distinguished writers for children. She was the third of five children of Benjamin Farjeon, a prolific writer of mysteries and novels, and **Margaret Jefferson**, an actress and daughter of the renowned American actor Joseph Jefferson. The Farjeon household was dominated by Benjamin, a brilliant and volatile man whose temperament vacillated between tremendous highs, during which the house was crammed with artistic and theatrical friends, and abysmal lows, at which time the family lived in enforced silence. In order to deal with the tensions, Eleanor Farjeon wrapped herself in fantasy, playing imaginative games with her eldest brother Harry and losing herself among the 8,000 books that comprised the family library. Since her father did not believe in a formal education for his daughter, the library became her schoolroom as well as her escape. "It would have been more natural to live without clothes than without books," she later said. Her father did, however, recognize his children's prodigious talents and encouraged Farjeon and her brothers in their literary and artistic pursuits. He presented each of them with a book in which they could write stories, plays, and poems, and when he felt that something was particularly good he allowed them to copy it into a large volume that he kept on his desk. Farjeon often collaborated with her brother Harry who was a brilliant musician. Their light operetta, *Floretta,* was performed by the Royal Academy of Music, where Harry was a student, in 1898. Harry would later serve as a professor at the Royal Academy, until his death in 1948.

When Ben Farjeon died in 1903 after a short illness, he left little money. The family was forced to move to a smaller house, and the boys had to quit school and find work. Eleanor Farjeon, now 22, remained at home with her mother and in 1908 paid to have her first book of poetry, *Pan-Worship and Other Poems,* published. She still had no real sense of self. "I was nearly 30 before I gave life a chance to grab me," she later remarked. "I ran away and hid when I might have been falling in love, and could have been bearing children. I was ignorant of my human longings, and among people was unconscious of having any individuality beyond my acutely painful shyness." The turning point in her life was her introduction to poet Edward Thomas (1878–1917), author of highly regarded books about southern England's countryside, in 1912. The two were immediately drawn together by their mutual interest in writing, and, though Thomas was married, Farjeon fell deeply in love with him. His death in France while fighting at the Battle of Arras in 1917 was a terrible blow but ultimately matured her as a writer. She recorded their relationship in her later work, *Edward Thomas: The Last Four Years* (1958). Farjeon subsequently entered into a 30-year liaison with George Earle, a scholar, who was also married.

After Thomas' death, Farjeon moved to a cottage in Sussex and immersed herself in writing. During this time, she produced *Martin Pippin in the Apple Orchard* (1921), a romantic fantasy combining verse, prose, and folklore. Although it was originally intended for adult readers, the book's tremendous appeal to youngsters through the years led to its re-release in 1952 as a children's story. In the early 1920s, Farjeon returned to Hampstead, London, where she released a steady stream of children's books, poems, games, and folktales. In eight years, she produced 22 works and also penned daily verses for the *Daily Herald*, using the name Tomfool, as well as a weekly poem for the feminist *Time and Tide*, written under the pseudonym Chimaera.

Following her mother's death in 1933, Farjeon embarked on a family memoir, *A Nursery in the Nineties*, which was published in 1935 and presents a compelling study of bohemian family life. She collaborated with her younger brother Herbert on many works, including the operetta *The Two Bouquets* (1936), which was produced in London and America, and a children's play, *The Glass Slipper* (1944). During the 1930s and 1940s, Farjeon also wrote a number of adult books: *Ladybrook* (1931), *Humming Bird* (1936), *Miss Granby's Secret* (1940), and *Ariadne and the Bull* (1945).

In her later years, Farjeon created what are considered her best children's books, some of them reworked from earlier publications. Notable from this period are *Silver-Sand and Snow* (1951) and *The Children's Bells* (1957) as well as *The Little Bookroom* (1955), a collection of stories that won the Carnegie and the Hans Andersen medals for children's literature. Farjeon's best work followed the resolution of her spiritual beliefs. Raised in a Jewish-Christian household, she had never been instructed in a particular religion and only late in life began to understand her own convictions. In 1951, calling herself "a very old baby," she was received into the Roman Catholic Church.

Despite cataracts and bouts of bronchitis, Farjeon continued to write until the end of her life. She was in the midst of what were to be four volumes of her memoirs (the first of which was *Edward Thomas*) when she died on June 5, 1965, at age 84. Upon her death, the Eleanor Farjeon annual award for children's writing was established in her honor. Although revered for her children's books, the author is also known for the hymn "Morning has broken," which she wrote in the early 1920s, and which soared to the Top Ten when recorded in the early 1970s by singer Cat Stevens.

SOURCES:

Beaty, Susan. "Eleanor Farjeon," in *This England*. Spring 1989.

Commire, Anne. *Something about the Author*. Vol. 2. Detroit, MI: Gale Research.

Shattock, Joanne. *The Oxford Guide to British Women Writers*. Oxford and NY: Oxford University Press, 1993.

SUGGESTED READING:

Farjeon, Annabel. *Morning Has Broken*. Julia MacRae Books, 1986.

Farjeon, Eleanor. *Edward Thomas: The Last Four Years*. Oxford University Press, 1958.

Barbara Morgan,
Melrose, Massachusetts

Farley, Harriet (c. 1813–1907)

American writer and editor. Born on February 18, 1813 (some sources cite 1815 or 1817), in Claremont, New Hampshire; died on November 12, 1907, in New York City; daughter and the sixth of ten children of Stephen Farley (a Congregational minister and school administrator) and Lucy (Sanders) Farley; attended Atkinson Academy in Atkinson, New Hampshire (where her father was the principal); married John Intaglio Donlevy (an engraver and inventor), in 1854 (died 1880); children: one daughter, Inez Donlevy; (stepdaughter) Alice Heighes Donlevy.

Major works: Shells from the Strand of the Sea of Genius *(1847);* Operatives Reply to . . . Jere Clemens *(1850);* Happy Nights at Hazel Nook; or, Cottage Stories *(1954);* Fancy's Frolics; or, Christmas Stories Told in a Happy Home of New England *(1880).*

Harriet Farley was born around 1813, the bookish daughter of Stephen Farley, a Congregational minister, and **Lucy Sanders Farley,** the mother of ten, who was described as becoming "harmlessly insane." Harriet spent much of her childhood in Atkinson, New Hampshire, where her father had a parish and also served as principal of the Atkinson Academy. Although she was able to attend her father's school, she was also called upon to contribute to the family's income and from the age of 14 engaged in plaiting straw for hats, binding shoes, and various other home manufacturing jobs. In 1837, after a short, unfulfilling interval as a teacher, Farley left Atkinson to take a job in one of the textile mills in Lowell, Massachusetts. Despite 13-hour days and the cramped dormitory housing provided by her employer, Farley felt liberated and spent what free time she had writing, reading, and participating in an improvement circle.

In 1840, Farley received some notoriety when the *Lowell Offering,* a journal published by and for the "mill girls," printed her reply to Orestes Brownson, who, in an attack upon the textile mill owners, referred to the mill women as suffering in "health, spirits, and morals." Answering Brownson's charges, Farley upheld the workers as intelligent and principled, and also pointed out that any restraints placed on the operatives by the mill owners were "voluntarily assumed." In 1842, when the *Offering* was purchased by a local newspaper, Farley left her job and took over the editorship. A year later, another mill woman, **Harriot Curtis,** became co-editor.

As an editor, Farley produced a conventional literary publication devoted to inspirational and principled pieces and avoiding the larger issues of wages, hours, and working conditions that were sparking heated debate all around her. **Susan Sutton Smith** points out that Farley's goal was simply to provide a little "cheer" for the operatives. Indeed, she virtually ignored any controversy. "With wages and board, etc., we have nothing to do," proclaimed the *Offering.* "These depend on circumstances over which we have no control." Needless to say, the more militant factions within the mills, including the Lowell Female Labor Reform Association, took Farley to task, accusing her of pandering to the mill owners. (Farley firmly denied that her publication received corporate funding, but her father and brother were known to have received financial help from mill-owner Amos Lawrence from time to time.) The best of Farley's essays and stories, most of which were criticized as "tiresomely inspirational," provided some insights into the lives of the young women who toiled in Lowell's mills. Smith points to "Letters from Susan,"

which was serialized in the 1844 issues of the *Offering,* as enlightening. Based on Farley's own experiences, the fictitious Susan relates her impressions of Lowell, describing the crowded, noisy working conditions but also rejoicing over new-found independence. Other stories, including "The Sister" and "Evening before Pay-Day," use a factory or boardinghouse setting to relate what Smith calls "sentimental homilies of self-sacrificing sisters or daughters."

The rise of the ten-hour movement in the mid-1840s, together with the emergence of the labor paper the *Voice of Industry* in 1845, signaled the end of the *Lowell Offering,* although it made a brief comeback in 1847 after the failure of the ten-hour movement. That same year, Farley published *Shells from the Strand of the Sea of Genius,* a collection of homilies, many of which had appeared in the *Offering.* By 1850, the *Offering* was defunct again, and Farley went to New York City to pursue her literary career. She contributed to *Godey's Lady's Book,* which was edited by a friend, and in 1853 published a children's book, *Happy Nights at Hazel Nook.* However, after her marriage to John Donlevy in 1854, Farley gave up her career, preferring obscurity over her husband's scorn. In 1880, seven years after her husband's death, Farley published her last book, *Fancy's Frolics,* a collection of Christmas stories. Harriet Farley died in 1907, at the Home for Incurables in New York City.

SOURCES:

James, Edward T., ed. *Notable American Women 1607–1950.* Cambridge, MA: The Belknap Press of Harvard University Press, 1971.

Mainiero, Lina, ed. *American Women Writers.* NY: Frederick Ungar, 1980.

McHenry, Robert. *Famous American Women.* NY: Dover, 1983.

Barbara Morgan,
Melrose, Massachusetts

Farmborough, Florence

(1887–1978)

British nurse whose extensive diary of her World War I experiences as a nurse with the Russian Army became a major source on the breakdown of the tsarist system during the eve of revolution. Born in Buckinghamshire, England, on April 15, 1887; died in Marple, England, on August 18, 1978; had five brothers and sisters; never married; no children.

At the end of her long life, 91-year-old Florence Farmborough could look back on countless adventures as well as many solid accomplishments. As a frontline nurse with the

Russian Army during World War I, she compiled an extraordinary diary of 400,000 words that chronicled in great detail the progressive collapse of morale in the tsar's armed forces, a catastrophe that made all but inevitable the two revolutions of 1917 and radically transformed both Russian and world history. This important historical document remained unknown until 1974, when it was published in London to enthusiastic reviews. Thus Florence Farmborough became somewhat of a celebrity in her old age, but she took it all in stride as a dignified lady without ever abandoning her natural British reserve and composure.

Florence Farmborough grew up in a large family as the fourth of six children. Wanting to see the world, she received her parents' approval in 1908 when she moved to Kiev to teach. After two years, she moved to Moscow, where she was hired by Dr. Pavel Sergeyevich, a pioneering heart surgeon, to teach English to his daughters **Asya** and **Nadya Sergeyevich**. This pleasant life was shattered in the summer of 1914 when Farmborough, just returned from a trip home to England, found herself in a Russia engulfed in war with Germany and Austria-Hungary. Determined to remain in Russia and be of help to the war effort, Farmborough volunteered to work for the Russian Red Cross along with Asya and Nadya as nursing volunteers in a hospital operating under the patronage of **Princess Golitsin**.

After some months of this work, Farmborough determined that she would be of greater value if she could work as a nurse in a frontline unit. By January 1915, she was busily preparing to leave for the Galician front. Among other things, she bought war clothing: a flannel-lined, black leather jacket and a thick sheepskin waistcoat called a *dushgreychka* ("soul-warmer)." At the moment of her departure, Farmborough was requested by **Anna Ivanovna Sergeyevich**, her Russian "mother," to kneel before her. Thereupon Ivanovna fastened a chain with an icon and cross that had been blessed by an Orthodox priest around Florence's neck, kissed her three times, and solemnly blessed her and wished her Godspeed. The young Englishwoman was now a soldier in the tsar's army departing to the front.

On Saturday, April 11, 1915, Farmborough and her medical unit arrived at the frontline town of Gorlice in Galicia. Gorlice was "a poor, tormented town under constant fire from the Austrian guns," she wrote in her diary. "For over five months, its inhabitants have been obliged to lead the existence of night birds. Their days are spent in the cellars, for the slightest movement in the streets could bring a shower of bullets. After dusk, they come creeping out, begging sympathy and food from each other and from the soldiers—the Russian soldiers." Farmborough spent the next two years at the front with a field surgical unit, saving lives and watching countless young men die in agony far from home. Besides keeping her extensive diary, she also took many photographs with a plate camera and tripod, developing the plates in improvised darkrooms under makeshift conditions.

By early 1917, Farmborough had survived innumerable bombardments, advances, and retreats in her sector of the front. Morale was increasingly eroded as tales of corruption on the home front reached her unit. Constant shortages of food and munitions sapped the soldiers' will to fight on, and a profound sense of war-weariness permeated all elements of the tsarist army. Another sign of social decay caused by the war was an increase in anti-Semitism, the Jews now being seen by some as the cause of Russia's woes.

The abdication of the tsar in early 1917 did little to arrest the general decline in morale, and the Bolshevik Party led by Vladimir Lenin took full advantage of the situation to call for an end to the war and a new social order based on "Bread, Land and Peace." In her voluminous diary, Farmborough chronicled these events. When her unit disintegrated as a viable fighting force, it was ordered to return to Moscow by whatever means available. Farmborough managed to save not only herself but her diary and photographs. She sold her camera to pay for a ticket on the Trans-Siberian Railroad to the Pacific port of Vladivostok and from there sailed for the United States.

Farmborough's adventures in wartorn Russia did not slake her wanderlust; some years later, she went to Spain and took a job teaching English at the University of Valencia. Her years in Russia had made her an implacable foe of Bolshevism, making it easy for her to support the anti-Marxist crusade of the Spanish conservative and fascist forces during that country's civil war of 1936–1939. Farmborough supported General Francisco Franco by reading daily news bulletins on the Spanish National Radio. In 1938, she also published a book enthusiastically supporting Franco's rebel forces, which she regarded as upholders of Western and Christian ideals in an age of intellectual and moral error. Although she never changed her views on Communism, Farmborough did revisit Russia—this time in peacetime—in 1962.

Florence Farmborough was enjoying her retirement when in April 1971, at age 84, she arranged an exhibition of her photographs and memorabilia at Heswall, Cheshire. Her remarkable collection soon came to the attention of journalists and publishers, and in 1974 her memoirs were published simultaneously in London and New York. Reviews of her book, which had been edited down by Farmborough from over 400,000 words to a more publishable manuscript about half that length, were enthusiastic. She was named a life member of the British Red Cross, among other honors. In 1979, a selection from her series of war photographs, entitled *Russian Album,* was published. Florence Farmborough spent her last years at the home of her nephew J.L. Farmborough, the vicar of Marple. She died there on August 18, 1978, leaving behind an important body of historical documentation of some of the most crucial events of the 20th century.

SOURCES:

Blodgett, Harriet, ed. *Capacious Hold-All: An Anthology of Englishwomen's Diary Writings.* Charlottesville, VA: University Press of Virginia, 1991.

Crankshaw, Edward. *Putting Up With the Russians.* NY: Elisabeth Sifton/Penguin Books, 1985.

Farmborough, Florence. *Life and People in National Spain.* London: Sheed & Ward, 1938.

———. *Russian Album 1908–1918.* Edited by John Jolliffe. Salisbury: Michael Russell, 1979.

———. "Three Weeks in a Coal Siding in Vladivostok," in *The Times* [London]. September 11, 1918.

———. *With the Armies of the Tsar: A Nurse on the Russian Front, 1914–18.* NY: Stein and Day, 1974.

Glover, Jon, and Jon Silkin, eds. *The Penguin Book of First World War Prose.* London: Viking, 1989.

"Miss Florence Farmborough," in *The Times* [London]. August 21, 1978, p. 12.

John Haag,
Assistant Professor of History,
University of Georgia, Athens,
Georgia

Fannie Merritt Farmer

Farmer, Fannie Merritt

(1857–1915)

American authority on cooking. Born on March 23, 1857, in Boston, Massachusetts; died on January 15, 1915, in Boston; eldest of four daughters of John Franklin (a printer) and Mary Watson (Merritt) Farmer; attended public school in Medford, Massachusetts, until age 16; graduated from the Boston Cooking School, 1889; never married; no children.

Born on March 23, 1857, eldest daughter of John Franklin Farmer and **Mary Merritt Farmer,** Fannie Farmer grew up in Boston and Medford, Massachusetts, where she received her early education. Paralysis in her left leg (possibly the result of polio) when she was 16 ended her education and left her with a permanent limp. In 1880, to help with the family income, she took a job as a mother's helper in the home of a family friend. It was there that she discovered her aptitude for cooking and meal planning. Encouraged by her employer and her family, Farmer enrolled in the relatively new Boston Cooking School, which had been established in 1879 by the Woman's Education Association of Boston. After graduating in 1889, she stayed on as assistant director and in 1894 became head of the school.

Farmer gained national recognition with her *Boston Cooking School Cook Book.* First published in 1896, the cookbook was considered such a risky venture that Farmer had to pay for the first edition with her own funds. *Boston Cooking,* one of the most profitable books ever for its Boston publisher, has been revised numerous times and is still a bestseller in a modernized version, *The Fannie Farmer Cookbook.* Along with personally tested recipes, the book included menus and sections on formal entertaining, kitchen management, and etiquette. Farmer was revolutionary in her use of explicit descriptions ("to bake is to cook in an oven"), clear step-by-step directions, and standardized level measurements, which replaced the ill-defined "handful," "pinch," or "heaping teaspoon" used by other authors. With Farmer's "kitchen bible" at hand, anyone who could read could cook, and each recipe came out the same every time. Farmer went on to produce a number of other popular cookbooks including *Chafing Dish Possibilities* (1898), *What to Have for Dinner* (1905), *Catering for Special Occasions, with Menus and Recipes* (1911), and *A New Book of Cookery* (1912). For ten years, with her sister **Cora Farmer,** Fannie also contributed monthly to *The Woman's Home Companion.*

In 1902, Farmer left the Boston Cooking School to open her own Miss Farmer's School of Cookery, with the purpose of instructing housewives and nurses rather than institutional cooks, servants, and prospective domestic-science teachers. Although she was extremely shy by nature, her weekly lecture-demonstrations proved so lively and popular that reports of them were carried in the *Boston Transcript* and other newspapers across the country. Farmer's true interest, however, was in improving health through diet. "The time is not far distant," she wrote, "when a knowledge of the principles of diet will be an essential part of one's education. Then mankind will eat to live, will be able to do better mental and physical work, and disease will be less frequent." She drew great satisfaction from teaching nutrition for the sick to nurses, hospital dietitians, and students of the Harvard Medical School. Dr. Elliott P. Joslin, who did pioneering work on diabetes, credited Farmer with stimulating him to pursue his research on the origins of the disease. In 1904, Farmer published *Food and Cookery for the Sick and Convalescent,* which she considered her most important work.

Farmer continued to lecture even after two strokes confined her to a wheelchair. She died in Boston on January 15, 1915, ten days after giving her last talk. Her legacy lived on through her sister Cora, and a niece, **Wilma Lord Perkins**, who co-authored a cookbook for children, *The Fannie Farmer Junior Cookbook,* in 1937. The book sold more than 250,000 copies over the years and was revised in 1957. It was updated in the early 1990s, to reflect contemporary preferences and attitudes about food and diet. A chain of candy stores also bears Fannie Farmer's name.

SOURCES:

Bird, Caroline. *Enterprising Women.* NY: W.W. Norton, 1976.

James, Edward T., ed. *Notable American Women.* Cambridge, MA: The Belknap Press of Harvard University Press, 1971.

McHenry, Robert, ed. *Famous American Women.* NY: Dover, 1983.

Roback, Diane, ed., "Children's Books," *Publishers Weekly.* September 6, 1993, p. 27.

Uglow, Jennifer S., comp. and ed. *The International Dictionary of Women's Biography.* NY: Continuum, 1985.

Weatherford, Doris. *American Women's History.* NY: Prentice Hall, 1994.

Barbara Morgan,
Melrose, Massachusetts

Farmer, Frances (1913–1970)

American actress whose tragic life became the subject of the movie Frances. *Born September 19, 1913, in Seattle, Washington; died of cancer on August 1, 1970, in Indianapolis, Indiana; daughter of Lillian (Van Ornum) Farmer and Ernest Farmer; sister of* **Edith Farmer Elliot**; *married Leif Erickson (an actor), in 1936 (divorced 1942); married Alfred Lobley, in 1954 (divorced 1957); married Leland Mikesell, in 1958 (divorced the same year); no children.*

After studying drama at the University of Washington, made her screen debut (1936) amid expectations of future stardom; dislike of the studio system and criticism for her involvement in left-wing causes during the so-called "Red Scare" (1930s–1940s) exacerbated alcohol and drug addictions and led to several rebellious incidents well-covered in the tabloid press; eventually declared "mentally incompetent" by court order, spent 11 years in a series of institutions, often under horrific conditions, and was exposed to a number of unproven, experimental treatments before being declared "cured" and released in the early 1950s; appeared in only one film after her release, worked at a series of odd jobs, and hosted a local television show in Indianapolis, Indiana, before the effects of her previous psychiatric treatments and the return of her alcoholism permanently ended her working years.

Filmography: Too Many Parents *(1936);* Come and Get It *(1936);* Border Flight *(1936);* Rhythm on the Range *(1936);* Exclusive *(1937);* Ebb Tide *(1937);* The Toast of New York *(1937);* Ride a Crooked Mile *(1938);* South of Pago Pago *(1940);* Flowing Gold *(1940);* World Premiere *(1941);* Badlands of Dakota *(1941);* Among the Living *(1941);* Son of Fury *(1942);* The Party Crashers *(1958).*

On the evening of January 27, 1958, millions of Americans watched as one of the nation's most popular television shows, "This Is Your Life," prepared to examine the personal triumphs of another guest. But there was something odd about the elegant, well-dressed woman who was that evening's subject, something disturbing. Twenty years previous, Frances Farmer had been a familiar face on movie screens across the country, promoted as a formidable rival to *Carole Lombard. But now, as she stared blankly at host Ralph Edwards and answered his questions in an expressionless monotone, and as the usual parade of high school teachers and old college chums produced no discernible effect on her, it seemed that the vivacious, intelligent actress of two decades before had become as flat as the TV screens on which her blurry image now appeared. Something was missing, but it would be years before the story of what had been stolen from her, and how it had been taken, would be known.

Unlike the ghostly presence of 1958, the Frances of childhood could hardly help attracting attention. She was an exceptionally beautiful child; but almost as striking were her outspoken opinions and her penchant for sometimes brutal honesty. It was a trait she had inherited from her mother, **Lillian Van Ornum Farmer**, well known around town for, among other things, demanding the closing of bakeries whose products Lillian did not deem nutritionally adequate and condemning the Seattle school board for allowing Communism to be taught in the classroom. Lillian was, in fact, as ardent in her anti-Communism as she was in her jingoistic enthusiasm for America. She had even produced a strain of chicken she had bred from a Rhode Island Red, a White Leghorn, and an Andalusian Blue, which she called the "Bird Americana," and which she very seriously proposed should replace the eagle as the new national emblem. It was no wonder, Seattle gossiped, that Lillian's first husband had left her.

Equally unusual was Lillian's choice for her second husband, a lawyer from Minnesota who came to stay at the boarding house she ran to support herself and a daughter after her divorce. Ernest Farmer was a left-leaning liberal who took to defending in court the labor organizers of the International Workers of the World, the Communist-inspired "Wobblies" intent on unionizing the shops and factories owned by Seattle's wealthy and conservative upper class. Lillian and Ernest managed their political differences well enough to produce a son and their first daughter, Edith, before Frances arrived on September 19, 1913. But the marriage was already in trouble by then and foundered completely when Frances was seven. Ernest moved out of the Farmers' West Seattle house in 1920, visiting on weekends and remaining very much in the background of Frances' life.

My future is very vague as yet—
I don't have anything definite in mind.
—**Frances Farmer, after her release, 1944**

Frances Farmer became nationally famous years before she ever stepped in front of a camera, when she was a junior at West Seattle High School and wrote an essay in which she baldly asserted that "God was gone." Relating how her prayer to recover a lost hat had been answered while Providence failed to save a friend from dying in a car accident, Frances wrote that "God was such a useless thing. It seemed such a waste of time to have Him." The essay won a writing contest and set off a storm of protest. "Seattle Girl Denies God and Wins Prize!" reported a shocked *Seattle Star and Times*, a story the national press found too good to pass by. Within weeks, Frances Farmer had been dubbed the "Bad Girl of West Seattle" and was being denounced from pulpits across the

country. "If the young people of this city are going to hell," fulminated one Baptist minister in Seattle, "Frances Farmer is surely leading them there." At 18, Farmer was already an outsider and under intense scrutiny.

It seemed she had found a safe haven when she arrived at the University of Washington in 1932, the same year her parents were officially divorced. Her sanctuary was the school's drama department where, she learned, acting allowed one to say the most shocking things with impunity. The excited talk among the school's drama department, as it was for optimistic young actors across the county, was of New York's daring Group Theater, an experimental company formed in reaction to more commercial theater companies like the Theater Guild. Fascinated by the difficult social themes tackled by the Group Theater in plays like Clifford Odets' *Waiting For Lefty*, Farmer vowed that she would not be happy until she could act with The Group. One of her professors had no doubt she'd make it to New York after directing her in one of the school's student offerings. "Whatever it is that makes a star, she had it," he later said, "and you knew it the minute you looked at her." Her work even attracted the attention of Seattle's professional theater critics, one of whom wrote of the "divine, intangible maturity of her acting that is destined for the lights of Broadway."

But it was the clash of ideologies, rather than the theater, that brought her to New York in 1934, in the midst of the infamous "Red Scare" of the 1930s. Washington State's long history of labor unrest provided a fertile ground for the burgeoning American Communist Party, the successor to the "Wobblies," idealistic in its fervent belief that Communism was the economic savior of the lower classes and that the workers' paradise being created in the Soviet Union should be duplicated in the United States. College campuses were the logical starting point for the cause, and college arts and drama departments seemed particularly suited to the effort. Farmer's drama coach, **Sophie Rosenstein**, was in fact an enthusiastic party member. It was Rosenstein who convinced Frances to allow her name to be used in a subscription drive by *The Voice of Action*, the Seattle Communist newspaper. When the paper's gratitude for aiding the cause took the form of a free trip to Russia, the ranks of conservative authority closed ever tighter against Frances, her own mother among them. Lillian told a Seattle newspaper that although she couldn't prevent her daughter from going to Moscow, "the dagger of Communism has struck deep into America. If I must sacrifice my daughter to Communism," she said, "I hope other mothers save their daughters before they are turned into radicals in our schools." The same newspaper that had been outraged by Frances' atheism three years earlier now trumpeted "Coed Determined to Act for Reds!" Farmer published a disclaimer stating that her trip to the Soviet Union was strictly to study the acting techniques that formed the basis for much of the new work being done in American theater. "The chance to view first hand one of the ten most important theatrical centers is the best thing that could happen to me," she wrote, promising to give America an "unbiased report" on the state of affairs in Russia when she returned.

One of the few fortunate aspects of the trip was that Farmer was able to visit the Group Theater on a stopover in New York in April of 1935, during which she met founders Harold Clurman, *Cheryl Crawford and Lee Strasberg, as well as Odets himself. Dogged by reporters, Frances finally set sail for Russia, was much photographed marching in Moscow's May Day parade, and returned to New York in late May to report that she had found Russia fascinating

Frances
Farmer

and that it was a "marvelous place for art." Although she emphasized that she had gone to Moscow because of her interest in the theater, there was no outright denouncement of Communism. Indeed, Farmer said, her sympathies were with the Russian people, another frank statement she was forced to defend.

Perhaps judging it unwise to return to the critical atmosphere of conservative Seattle, Frances chose to stay in New York on her return from Russia and began making the rounds of agents and advertising agencies, which resulted in a few modeling jobs before she was signed by Shepard Traube, an agent with close ties to Hollywood. Traube got her a screentest for Paramount. "You couldn't take your eyes off her," reported Paramount's. New York talent chief after watching the test, predicting that Frances Farmer had the potential to become a very big star indeed. By October of 1935, Farmer was on the Paramount lot in Hollywood as part of its stable of hopeful young actresses. But she immediately formed a strong dislike for the humbug and fakery of the Hollywood dream machine and complained that film acting was not serious acting. Paramount, however, was willing to put up with the outspoken behavior of a young woman with such remarkable screen potential. Less than six months after signing her, the studio cast her in the ingenue role in *Too Many Parents,* a 1936 comedy set at a military school which performed well at the box office precisely because of Farmer's reputation. Even Frances' surprise marriage in Yuma, Arizona, in February of 1936, to one of the studio's matinee idols, Wycliffe Anderson, failed to permanently damp Paramount's enthusiasm. (Anderson would later change his name to Leif Erickson, pursue a mediocre career in films, and finally make his mark with television audiences in the 1960's series "High Chaparral.")

But Farmer's frustration with the film business was apparent and detrimental. After playing opposite Bing Crosby in *Rhythm on the Range,* she told an interviewer that she had no idea what the film was about while she was shooting it. "I was just the tall, skinny dame," she said. "It was a long, sweet nightmare for me." Even her breakthrough film, *Come and Get It,* failed to elicit much respect from its leading lady. While the film's original director, Howard Hawks, recognized Farmer's talent, his replacement found her pugnacious attitude difficult to control. "The nicest thing I can say about Frances Farmer is that she's unbearable," William Wyler complained when the picture was

completed, while Frances told a friend that "acting with Wyler is the nearest thing to slavery." Nor would Frances buckle down to the platitudes and artificial smiles at the film's premiere in her home town. "Remember me? I'm the freak from West Seattle High," she said icily to one of the Baptist ministers who had spoken out against her five years earlier over her controversial high school essay, but was now eager to be photographed with her; and when a conservative Congressman who had criticized her publicly for her Communist sympathies strode onto the stage with hand extended, she called him a hypocrite and walked away. "She talked directly, frankly, and at times, with a touch of sarcasm," one reporter noted tactfully.

By the time she completed work on *Exclusive,* a drama set at a big city newspaper, her future as Hollywood's next female superstar seemed assured. But the more secure her position became, the more puzzling was her behavior to Hollywood insiders. She lived unglamorously with her husband in a small, unpretentious cottage in the canyons above more fashionable Bel Air, drove an old rattletrap of a car around town, dressed as she pleased, and had no compunctions about using in public the vulgarisms for which she was notorious in private. "She . . . thinks movie gossip is blah, and will give up all salary boosts ever heard of if they'll give her a decent picture to play in," one journalist wrote after being granted a rare interview. The studio bristled again when Farmer talked freely with *Collier's* magazine about her admiration for the Soviet Union, the deplorable conditions under which California's migrant farm workers labored, and her sympathies for the Loyalist cause in the Spanish Civil War. By the end of 1936, Paramount thought it wise to grant Frances' demand to spend the summer on the legitimate stage back East.

Her natural talent for the stage brought her good reviews in two summer stock productions in suburban New York and, more important, an invitation from Harold Clurman to star in the Group Theater's premiere of a new play by Clifford Odets, *Golden Boy.* Her performance was universally praised, giving a much-needed boost to the financially strapped Group, and Farmer found herself the toast of Manhattan during that fall of 1937, even as resentment against her in Hollywood grew. There, she was seen as a traitor by the more conservative elements in the film industry who were deeply suspicious of her attachment to a theater company that counted several Communists among its membership. Some film historians have suggested that a right-wing alliance of industry and political conservatives undertook a subversive campaign to topple her, an assertion that has never been more than an elusive theory, but it is true that Frances' triumph in New York was the beginning of the end.

At the very least, it certainly seemed as if Paramount wanted to punish her for her desertion. The studio recalled her to appear in a B-picture that was far below her former status. Worse yet, *Walk a Crooked Mile,* a western with leaden dialogue and cardboard characters, starred Leif Erickson, from whom Farmer was now estranged. (A divorce would be finalized in 1952.) A return to the safety of the stage failed to improve the situation: her next two productions with the Group closed after just a few performances each. A disastrous affair with Clifford Odets left Farmer so depressed that she failed to appear for rehearsals for a Theater Guild production of *Fifth Column,* adapted from an Ernest Hemingway story. The show had to be canceled because of her absence, earning her the enmity of the only group of professionals who had accepted her.

"The highbrow Frances Farmer, who found Hollywood so beneath her a few years ago, is playing, of all things, Calamity Jane," sniffed gossip queen *Louella Parsons, referring to Farmer's appearance in *Badlands of Dakota,* her next assignment from Paramount. Parsons refrained, however, from mentioning the rumors of Frances' increasingly odd behavior. She dropped completely out of sight for a month in mid-1941, for example, telling a reporter when she re-emerged that she had taken time off at an isolated cabin in Washington State to recuperate from a heavy work load. The word on the Hollywood grapevine, however, was that Frances had suffered a severe breakdown and had actually spent the time at her mother's house. Her deep depression after the bombing of Pearl Harbor at the end of 1941 added further credence to the reports that Frances Farmer had "gone crazy." Although Farmer's alcoholism was by now common knowledge, most people were unaware of her addiction to the Benzedrine the studio had given her to control her weight, an amphetamine which, taken in sufficient quantities, can induce schizophrenia-like behavior.

She seemed to recover her balance while filming what would soon become her best-known film after *Come and Get It,* a historical drama called *Son of Fury* in which she played opposite Tyrone Power. But on the night of October 9, 1942, after finishing work on the pic-

ture, Farmer was arrested in Santa Monica on charges of drunken driving. Although she had been stopped for driving in a wartime "dim-out" zone with her headlights on, the arresting officer reported she was intoxicated, was driving without a license, and was extremely abusive toward him. She was never given a breath test, either at the scene or at the police station, was never allowed to call an attorney, and was found guilty at a hearing which issued a six-month suspended jail term. Louella Parsons led the press charge in reporting the incident, provoking Farmer to leave town by accepting an offer of work in a Mexican film.

It was an unfortunate decision. In her haste, Frances had failed to read the script and discovered on her arrival in Mexico City that the film was little more than an amateur production. Trying desperately to free herself from the picture and suffering from dysentery, she was spirited to the border by American Embassy officials and left in a motel just inside the United States.

Frances Farmer after her arrest in Los Angeles.

Parsons now reported that not only had Frances Farmer been deported from Mexico but that she had been committed to a "sanitarium." Farmer publicly repudiated the story and tried to tell the Hollywood press what had really happened, but by now it was too late. "You have to realize that they were out to get Frances, and she knew it," scriptwriter Dalton Trumbo said many years later, after he himself had been forced out of the business during the McCarthy era. Trumbo identified "they" as "the cops," and the reason for their pursuit of Frances as "the political thing, the migrant worker thing. You name it."

The end came when Farmer attacked a hairdresser on the set of a low-budget picture and dislocated the woman's jaw, behavior consistent with the effects of high doses of amphetamines. Charged with assault, Farmer was taken to jail after the police who came to arrest her had to forcibly subdue her in the face of flying fists and kicking legs. In court the next morning, Frances was captured on film by the press with her hair hanging loosely around her face and her clothes torn and rumpled; her sarcastic replies to the judge's questions were also widely reported. Again denied a lawyer, Frances' sudden sprint across the courtroom toward a pay phone and the subsequent image of burly policemen dragging her from the room were prominently featured on the front pages of the next day's newspapers, as were photographs of her strait-jacketed in a jail cell as she began a six-month sentence.

But the jail term was cut short. Instead, Farmer was placed without her consent in a sanitarium after a psychiatrist received permission to interview her. Dr. Thomas Leonard had followed her case in the newspapers, he said, and might be able to help her. Leonard later reported to the court that Frances had been "hostile and uncooperative" during his meeting with her, and showed signs of what he called "manic depressive psychosis, probably the forerunner of a definite dementia praecox"—a diagnosis that would be meaningless by today's standards. Leonard declared that, in his opinion, Frances Farmer was insane, while Lillian told a court hearing that her daughter was "unbalanced from her past years' experience of frustration in her career." At the end of January 1943, Farmer was taken to the Screen Actors' Guild sanitarium, La Crescenta, just outside Los Angeles. The only protest lodged against her confinement came, not from Hollywood, but from New York, where actors from the Group Theater and the Theater Guild signed a petition demanding her release. It was ignored by the court.

Farmer's great misfortune was to enter the psychiatric care system at a time of experimentation in new treatment therapies and few safeguards against patient abuse. One of the new therapies being tested was insulin shock, in which massive amounts of injected insulin were thought to overwhelm the brain's circuitry and somehow re-order it into more "normal" patterns. Insulin shock is much discredited today, but in Farmer's time it was seen as a promising new treatment that she was given up to three times a week, with her parents' consent. By the fall of 1943, she had lost the ability to concentrate or to remember recent events, common side effects of such therapies. But she was clear-headed enough to successfully escape from La Crescenta by scaling a wall and making her way to her half-sister's home nearby, where she called her mother and tearfully pleaded to come home. Lillian, who professed alarm at her daughter's condition, demanded her release from the sanitarium on the grounds that Frances had never been legally declared insane and could not be held against her parents' wishes.

Ernest Farmer later wrote that Frances appeared "pale, gaunt, and weak . . . obviously distraught" when she arrived home in Seattle. She seemed to recover during the winter of 1943–44, however, while Lillian, without Frances' knowledge, contacted studios in Hollywood and told them her daughter was looking for work. While Frances' refusal to return to the environment which had affected her so severely can be seen as a sign of her recovered mental health, her mother was shocked when Frances turned down the offer of a small film role. Arguments between them grew increasingly violent, sometimes physically so, and by the spring of 1944 Lillian became convinced that the doctors were right and that Frances had fooled them all with her apparent return to sanity. On the morning of March 21, 1944, as Frances was eating her breakfast, three orderlies arrived at the house and spirited her off to Seattle's Harborview Hospital. The day before, Lillian had sworn out a complaint in which she said she could no longer handle her daughter's physically abusive behavior. She recounted one incident in which Frances refused Lillian's request to turn down the radio by grabbing her mother's wrists and pushing her into a chair. "My arms became black and blue," Lillian testified. "I realized at once that she needs institutional care, as I am entirely unable to control her at home." This time, the court legally declared Frances insane, identifying her in documents by her married name of "Mrs. F.E. Anderson."

Conspiracy theorists point out that the judge who presided over the hearing had been an ultra-conservative Seattle politician before moving to the bench and had spoken out against "the Bad Girl from West Seattle" for her notorious high school essay, for her trip to Russia, and for her left-wing sympathies. He was also said to be an important figure in a shadowy group called "The American Vigilantes," which staged violent union-busting raids during the 1930s and spied on groups suspected of being Communist fronts. Equally odd was the behavior of the attorney appointed by the court to represent Farmer, who signed a document waiving Farmer's right to a jury trial as Frances was interviewed by the psychiatrist appointed by the court, Donald Nicholson. Frances, Nicholson wrote in his report to the bench, was "excited, arrogant and inclined to be resistive" during their meeting and became "exceedingly vulgar and profane" as the interview progressed. Nicholson declared her insane and recommended the court commit her to the Washington State Hospital for the Insane at Steilacoom, a forbidding, turreted institution perched on a cliff overlooking Puget Sound. It had been built a century earlier and had never been renovated.

Except for a ten-month period from July of 1944 to May of 1945, Farmer spent the next six years at Steilacoom under conditions so hideous that her story seems drawn from some 19th-century horror tale. She was repeatedly subjected without her consent to electroconvulsive therapy, commonly called "shock treatment"; to hydrotherapy, in which she was forced to spend hours immersed to the neck in ice cold water; and to a variety of experimental drug therapies which may have included LSD treatments. She lived in a filthy common room reserved for the violently insane, infested with rats and reeking with the stench of vomit and excrement. Even more horrifying was the fact that Steilacoom served as, in the words of one former orderly, "the whorehouse for Fort Lewis," a nearby military base for whose soldiers the hospital's guards would procure women from among the inmates. Her ten-month hiatus from Steilacoom, much of it spent under close observation at the rural ranch of an aunt in Nevada, ended with her escape and subsequent arrest as a vagrant. Nicholson, who had hailed her release as "a significant victory for the mental hygiene movement in Washington State," promptly convinced her parents to commit her once again. There were some who were not convinced Farmer was mentally ill. One was a nurse assigned to Frances' ward, who came to believe after numerous conversa-

From the movie Frances, *starring Jessica Lange as Farmer.*

tions that Frances' bravery in the face of such disaster was proof of her sanity. "Pictures just didn't do justice to her," the nurse said many years later. "You don't know how beautiful she was unless you saw her in person." But the nurse's protest filed with hospital authorities only led to a reprimand and reassignment to another facility.

It is likely that during this second phase of her institutionalization Farmer became one of hundreds of patients given what was known as a "transorbital lobotomy." The procedure had been developed by Walter Freeman as a refinement on the even more drastic frontal lobotomy which had been in use for a decade. Freeman claimed that by inserting a surgical instrument, not unlike an ice pick, between a patient's eyeball and eye-socket and directly into the brain, thus severing several nerves in the frontal lobes, miraculous results could be achieved in patients whose behavior had become dangerously uncontrollable. The operation took just a few minutes, and Freeman was known to perform it on as many as 60 patients at a time. By the late 1940s, Freeman was much respected by the psychiatric establishment and had virtual carte blanche at any institution in the country. Sometime in late 1948 or early 1949, Freeman arrived at Steilacoom and asked to see Frances Farmer. After interviewing her in the company of several staff members, he administered shock treatments to her until she was unconscious and then asked to be left alone with the patient. What happened while the two were alone will never be known for sure, but it is likely that Freeman performed his operation.

The most telling indication that Farmer had become one of Freeman's victims was the almost immediate change in her behavior. She became quiet and obedient, and began to cooperate with her doctors instead of fighting them. She listened meekly as they described her previous behavior and became convinced that she had been a "sinner." She became, as she described it with some difficulty years later, "like a bowl of jelly, agreeable and pliable." In March of 1950, when Lillian suffered a stroke and had no one at home to look after her, doctors pronounced Frances Farmer cured and released her.

By 1953, after her mental competency had been confirmed by the courts and her civil rights restored, Frances got a job in the laundry of a Seattle hotel, began to date, and eventually married a civil engineer named Alfred Lobley in April of 1954. But Lobley had not counted on Frances' strange, erratic behavior and her continued fondness for alcohol. She disappeared after six months, turning up in northern California, where she took a job as secretary at a photography studio. Lobley knew nothing of her whereabouts until both her parents died—Lillian of a stroke in 1955, and Ernest the next year—and Social Security officials finally tracked Frances down. Lobley divorced her in 1957, but by then Frances had met a young entrepreneur named Lee Mikesell. It was Mikesell who stage-managed a peculiar, sad comeback for Frances, taking advantage of a growing popular interest in psychology and the interest in *Lillian Roth's account of her own recovery from depression, *I'll Cry Tomorrow*.

Farmer's first public appearance in nearly 15 years was on the "Ed Sullivan Show" in June of 1957, during which she sang two folk songs. Although the shock and drug treatments had seriously affected her ability to memorize lines, she managed to earn respectful reviews in a production of "The Chalk Garden" at the Bucks County Playhouse in Pennsylvania and for an appearance on "Playhouse 90," a weekly network presentation of original drama. Then came the uncomfortable and embarrassing appearance on "This Is Your Life," followed by a small part in a teenage B-film amid complaints from the picture's director that she was drunk most of the time. In a series of confessional interviews in national magazines, Frances talked of divine punishment for her earlier behavior. "I shall always thank Him," she said. "I am very much in love and think that, from now on, life is going to be wonderful." But Mikesell, whom she had married early in 1958, divorced her later that year and sued her for $250,000 in management fees. After a summer stock production of "The Chalk Garden" closed unexpectedly early in Indianapolis, Farmer found herself stranded and broke in a strange city.

She spent her final years under the careful eye of a woman she befriended named **Jeanira Ratcliffe** and found a job introducing movies on the local television station in a weekly program called "Frances Farmer Presents." The show was canceled after six years because, some said, of Frances' drinking. Plagued by high blood pressure and ulcers, and nearly penniless after a scheme to start a cosmetics company with Ratcliffe failed, Farmer agreed to tape several hours of interviews with a writer who proposed writing her biography. But the project had barely got underway when she was diagnosed with cancer of the esophagus in April of 1970. Four months later, on August 1, Frances Farmer died and was buried in a simple grave in a small cemetery just outside Indianapolis.

There was a short flurry of interest in her career following her death. Films that Hollywood had withheld from circulation since the 1940s briefly resurfaced. A purported autobiography, *Will There Really Be a Morning?*, published the year after her death was actually written by Ratcliffe, based on the interviews Frances had recorded and what Ratcliffe could remember Frances telling her in their years together. It is floridly written and unreliable in its facts, but at least the horrors that Farmer endured during her incarceration finally reached a wide readership: the book was a bestseller. Frances' older sister Edith, who had been living in Hawaii during Frances' most troubled years and could speak of none of it firsthand, privately printed a rebuttal to Ratcliffe's book, in which she wrote she wanted to "set the record straight, to correct the salacious lies, half truths, defamation of character dealt our family members." Despite her geographical distance during those tortuous years, Edith claimed Frances had not undergone surgery of any kind and, like Lillian, blamed her sister's illness on Communists in general and on The Group in particular.

The fact was that Frances Farmer was a non-conformist at a time when American society, beset by social upheaval and moral challenges, ostracized anyone who strayed too far from the path and when Hollywood was in the throes of a conservative backlash against its freewheeling past. Whether or not some sort of conspiracy against her existed, there is no doubt the film community, as well as her own family, turned its back on her when she refused to come to heel. "They wanted to bust that kid wide open," as Dalton Trumbo put it. The great tragedy was that after Frances Farmer ventured too far into unknown territory, there was no one to lead her home again.

SOURCES:

Arnold, William. *Shadowland.* NY: McGraw Hill, 1978.

Elliot, Edith Farmer. *Look Back In Love.* Sequim, WA: Gemaia Press, 1978.

Farmer, Frances. *Will There Really Be a Morning?* NY: Putnam, 1972.

RELATED MEDIA:

Frances (film), starring **Jessica Lange**, directed by Graeme Clifford. Brooksfilms, 1982.

Norman Powers,
writer-producer, Chelsea Lane Productions, New York

Farnadi, Edith (1921–1973)

Hungarian pianist who made extensive recordings reinterpreting Liszt. Born in Budapest, Hungary, on September 25, 1921; died in Graz, Austria, on December 14, 1973.

Edith Farnadi was born in Budapest on September 25, 1921, and studied at the Budapest Academy. Her debut took place in Budapest in 1933 with her performing Beethoven's C major Piano Concerto, which she conducted from the keyboard. After graduation from the academy at age 16, she became a faculty member there, and engaged in extensive concert tours in Europe. She was a noted chamber-music performer and made many recordings, including a large number of works by Liszt. Farnadi's interpretations of Liszt were marked by a careful, restrained intelligence and avoided the explosive rhetoric of the traditional Romantic style with which his music had long been associated.

John Haag,
Athens, Georgia

Farnese, Elizabeth (1692–1766)

Queen of Spain who wielded wide political power during her husband Philip V's prolonged periods of insanity and inertia. Name variations: Elizabeth of Farnese or Elizabeth de Farnese, Princess of Parma; Isabel Farnese or Isabella of Parma; Isabella Elizabeth Farnese; (Ital.) Isabel de Farnesio. Born on October 25, 1692, in Parma, Italy; died on July 10, 1766; daughter of Dorothea Sophia of Neuburg and Odoardo also known as Edward Farnese of Parma (eldest son of Ranucci II, duke of Parma); married Philip V (1683–1746), king of Spain (r. 1700–1724, 1724–1746), on December 24, 1714; children: Charles IV (1716–1788), king of Naples and Sicily (r. 1735–1759), also known as Charles III, king of Spain (r. 1759–1788); Francisco (b. 1717); Maria Ana Victoria (1718–1781); Philip (1720–1765); *Maria Theresa of Spain (1726–1746, who married Louis le dauphin); Louis or Luis Antonio (b. 1727); *Maria Antonia of Spain (1729–1785).

Daughter of **Dorothea Sophia of Neuburg** and Edward Farnese, eldest son of Ranucci II, duke of Parma, Elizabeth Farnese was born on October 25, 1692. The girl's father died the following year, "suffocated by his extraordinary fatness," according to court historian Poggiali. Unwilling to submit to a widow's life, Dorothea Sophia persuaded Edward's younger brother Antonio Farnese to marry her. It soon became obvious, however, that the couple would have no children and that young Elizabeth would inherit the duchy of Parma after her uncle. Thereupon, Dorothea Sophia closely limited Elizabeth's education, apparently hoping to break the girl's spirit and ensure that the mother would continue to wield power. Although Elizabeth learned to speak German, French, Latin, and Spanish and studied history, geography, philosophy, rhetoric, and religion, she never developed a hunger for intellectual matters. As an adult, she read nothing but sermons and other pious works. Her interest in politics was rudimentary. Of more concern to her was the smallpox, which scarred her face.

Fate thrust Elizabeth on the international stage shortly after the death on February 14, 1714, of Queen ***Marie Louise of Savoy**, wife of Philip V of Spain. His wife's body was barely cold when Philip began casting about for a replacement. The second grandson of Louis XIV, France's Philip had succeeded to the Spanish throne upon the death in 1700 of the last Spanish Habsburg, Charles II. Though the Castilians optimistically supported Philip during the War of the Spanish Succession (1701–13), anticipating that he would resurrect the monarchy, Philip baffled them. Louis XIV had raised and educated Philip to be submissive so as to pose no threat to his older brother's claim to the French throne. Philip was thus poorly suited to rule Spain when the childless Charles II named him heir. Once he arrived in Spain, his subjects found Philip's personal behavior bizarre. "Driven by two compulsions, sex and religion," wrote one historian, "he spent his nights, and much of his days, in constant transit between his wife and his confessor, torn between desire and guilt, a comic figure easily subject to conjugal blackmail."

Within a week of Marie Louise of Savoy's death, Giulio Alberoni, the Parmesan envoy, reportedly approached the Spanish court with the suggestion that Philip marry Elizabeth Farnese. Rather than dealing with Philip directly, he discussed Elizabeth with *Marie-Anne de la Trémouille, princess of the Ursins. Louis XIV had sent the princess to Madrid ostensibly as head of Marie Louise's household but more important to bend Spanish policy to French aims through her dominance of Marie Louise and thus her indirect influence over Philip. According to some malicious tongues, the power-hungry Ursins attempted to persuade Philip to marry her. But Philip's sensuality found little appetite for a woman 40 years his senior. Ursins then listened more carefully to Alberoni's sly enticements: Philip would find Elizabeth robust and charming, and as she had little interest in politics, Ursins would be able to dominate her. Taking Alberoni's bait, Ursins persuaded Philip and Louis XIV to approve the Italian marriage. In Parma on September 16, 1714, Elizabeth wed Philip by proxy.

Her trip to meet Philip turned out to be one of the decisive events of her life, although it did not begin with much promise. Embarking by sea to meet her husband at Alicante, Elizabeth fell seasick and ordered a landing in Monaco. She then proceeded overland, making prolonged visits along the way. The slow pace frustrated Philip, waiting ardently for the woman who would, in the words of the king's confessor, enable him to "satisfy his masculinity." As she made a wintry crossing through the mountains of Navarre, Alberoni met Elizabeth and advised her how to deal with Philip and Ursins. On December 22, 1714, the king awaited in Guadalajara, while Ursins, as head of the queen's household, went to the nearby village of Jadraque to meet Elizabeth. Taking the young queen aside, Ursins imperiously upbraided Elizabeth for her delayed arrival and her unsuitable clothing. Ursins evi-

dently hoped thereby to intimidate the young woman, but exactly the opposite happened, due to Alberoni's planning and Elizabeth's own volatile temperament. The angry queen dismissed Ursins and commanded her to leave Spain. A guard placed Ursins in a carriage, which delivered her posthaste into France. When a surprised Philip learned what had transpired, he made no attempt to help Ursins. As the king had jocularly announced, he was intent upon spending a *Noche Buena* (Christmas Eve; literally "good night") with his new wife. She indeed arrived at Guadalajara on December 24, whereupon Philip immediately ordered performance of the necessary religious ceremonies. Elizabeth's triumph at Jadraque not only eliminated her chief rival but put her in a position to dominate Philip.

The king found his new bride enchanting. She proved energetic, up early to go hunting with him and receptive to his sensual urges. Courtiers even praised her sharpshooting. She approached meals with equal zeal, requisitioning supplies from Italy to overcome her disappointment with Spanish cuisine. On January 20, 1716, she gave birth to the royal couple's first child, the future Charles III. Meanwhile, Philip showed slight interest in anything except the hunt and his wife, providing ample opportunity for her to influence royal policy. But Elizabeth had little inclination to shoulder the burden of government, to the consternation of Alberoni who hoped to direct the king through his wife.

In fact, Elizabeth confronted a difficult political and cultural dilemma as queen. Her subjects had grown restive over Philip's dependence on France and his reliance on French advisors. Ambitious Spaniards hoped that the death of Louis XIV and Elizabeth's arrival would eliminate such heavy foreign influence over the king. Elizabeth's dismissal of Ursins heightened their hopes. But the queen remained Italian and condescending to things Spanish. Italian influence increased. Despite being the duke of Parma's envoy, Alberoni emerged as the unofficial chief minister of Spain from 1714 until his fall in 1719, and other Italians found influential posts. With Elizabeth and Alberoni guiding Spanish policy, Italian considerations received undue weight. This especially frustrated Spanish aristocrats, among whom the queen was unpopular. Tensions grew in 1717 when Philip showed clear signs of mental instability. As his illness worsened, the king declared that in the event of his death, his wife and Alberoni should govern as regents until Philip's eldest son from his first marriage, Louis (I), came of age to rule. Disgruntled nobles plotted with the French to oust the two Italians in Louis' name, but the conspirators only managed to discredit themselves.

From Spain, Elizabeth maneuvered to protect her claims to Parma so they might be passed on to her own sons. The Treaty of Utrecht (1713), which ended the War of the Spanish Succession, hindered those efforts. Under its terms, the Spanish monarchy surrendered its Italian possessions, including Milan, to the Austrian Habsburgs and Sicily to the duke of Savoy. Thus, Spain had few geopolitical reasons to intervene on Elizabeth's behalf in Italy. But she proved willing to expend Spanish resources and manpower if necessary to obtain Italian territories for her sons to govern.

Meanwhile, Elizabeth gave the government what little direction it received from the throne. The queen possessed no real understanding of statecraft or of the true interests of her subjects. But within a few months of her arrival in Spain, the Council began holding its meetings in her rooms. Her biographer, José Calvo Poyato, writes: "She was a strong personality, in contrast with the indecisive and irresolute character of her husband. In this circumstance Philip V had someone on whom he could let fall the responsibilities of the government." She made little effort to win the approval of Spaniards, who resented her reliance on Italian advisers. Alberoni lamented her "invincible indolence and dislike of business" and remarked that he could not bring her to "talk seriously for a quarter of an hour." Yet except in time of war, which somehow seemed to energize him, Philip refused to rule at all. This created the opportunity for Elizabeth to satisfy her ambitions for her children.

Nonetheless, Philip's mental state made the monarchy fragile. For one thing, the Treaty of Utrecht had forced him to renounce all claims to the French throne, but he longed to return and rule his native land. Furthermore, he began to suffer recurring episodes of hysteria and melancholy. In 1717, for example, he became convinced that the royal couple's undergarments and bedclothing were radiating light because they had not paid to have sufficient masses said for his deceased first wife. Two years later, mentally unbalanced and longing for France, Philip confided to Elizabeth and his confessor that he intended to abdicate. Over the following years, he occasionally renewed his secret pledge. Rumors about it spread, however, and some concluded that he wanted to give up the Spanish throne to make himself available to rule France should Louis XV die without an heir.

Elizabeth Farnese

To Elizabeth's dismay, on January 10, 1724, Philip abdicated in favor of Louis, his 16-year-old son with his first wife, Marie Louise of Savoy. Out of power, Elizabeth could not satisfy her ambitions for her sons. Thus, when Louis died of smallpox on August 31, 1724, Elizabeth must have experienced relief, because Philip decided to reclaim the throne rather than allow the accession of Ferdinand (VI), his second son with Marie Louise. Back in the seat of power, Elizabeth removed Philip's confessor, Father Bermúdez, whom she hated for having tried to convince Philip not to retake the crown. Then she tried to negotiate the marriage of her son Charles to *Maria Teresa (1717–1780), heir of Charles VI, the Austrian emperor and Philip's rival during the War of the Spanish Succession. As Parma was subject to Austria, this alliance would have guaranteed Elizabeth's hold. But the Austrians rejected the marriage, preferring a crown prince to one of the second rank.

In Philip's deteriorated mental state, the queen feared he might try to abdicate again. He recovered somewhat in 1726, when a gravely ill Louis XV appeared likely to die without an heir. But Louis' recovery dashed Philip's hope of returning to rule France and plunged him into a severe depression. By 1727, the king absolutely refused to conduct or even discuss any matters of state. He and chief minister José Patiño made out a political testament, naming Elizabeth regent for the duration of his illness. The situation undoubtedly distressed her, for she truly loved Philip. But his bizarre actions, abusive and violent behavior, and constant demands exacted an emotional and physical toll on her. Because he refused association with almost everyone at court, she personally had to supervise him closely. On one occasion, in 1728, while the exhausted queen was taking a nap, he surreptitiously sent a note to the Council of Castile, ordering it to convene for the purpose of accepting his abdication. Elizabeth managed to thwart this new attempt.

To lessen the likelihood of further communication with the Council and hopeful that a change of scenery might improve his outlook, she then moved the court south to Andalusia. The ostensible motive for their departure was to attend the double marriage between the Spanish and Portuguese royal families on January 20, 1729, near Badajoz, on the Portuguese frontier. Philip's eldest surviving son Ferdinand wed Princess *Maria Barbara of Braganza and Elizabeth's daughter ◄ Maria Ana Victoria wed Joseph I Emanuel (José Manuel), who would inherit the Portuguese crown in 1750. Maria Ana's marriage was especially satisfying to Elizabeth. Engaged as a young child to Philip's young nephew, Louis XV, the girl had gone to Versailles to be raised in the French court. But two years later, before the children were married, a shift in French policy sent her packing back to Spain.

Following the royal marriages, Philip and Elizabeth proceeded on to Seville and took up residence there for four years. Madrid suffered from its loss of the court, and popular opinion turned against the monarchs. Growing numbers wanted to depose Philip and give the crown to Ferdinand, although the latter did little to encourage such talk. Philip's state improved but not for long. For 19 months, he refused to change his clothes, shave, or cut his hair. He stayed up all night and slept during the day, which forced Elizabeth and the court to do the same. Elizabeth could do little but humor him. When they finally returned to Madrid in May 1733, she looked, according to a British observer, "fat and dull."

In terms of her children, however, the situation had begun to improve. The duke of Parma died in 1731, and Charles inherited the duchy, despite opposition from the Austrian emperor. In late 1733, Charles assumed the government

Maria Ana Victoria. *See Maria I Braganza for sidebar.*

and almost immediately seized Naples and Sicily, with Spanish and French backing. Some Spaniards argued that the Two Sicilies should not pass to Charles but to Ferdinand, Philip's heir. After all, they argued, the Two Sicilies had belonged to Spain and had only been stripped away by the Treaty of Utrecht. As Spanish arms had now reconquered them, they should revert to the Spanish crown. But Elizabeth and Charles carried the day. On July 3, 1734, Charles was proclaimed king of the Two Sicilies, and Elizabeth abandoned her maneuvers to have him named king of Poland. Austria only recognized Charles, however, on the condition that he give up title to Parma and Tuscany.

Elizabeth then turned her energy to her son Philip de Bourbon's ambitions. She secured his marriage in 1739 to *Louise Elizabeth, eldest daughter of Louis XV. When the Austrian emperor died in 1740 and the War of the Austrian Succession erupted, Philip and Elizabeth exploited the international chaos to seize Parma, Tuscany, Plasencia, and Milan. During the peace negotiations, however, their French allies betrayed the duo, and in the end Philip was unable to keep Milan.

Early on the morning of July 9, 1746, Philip V suffered an apoplectic seizure and died minutes later in Elizabeth's arms. This placed her in a precarious situation. The Spanish people disliked her, and she had not treated her stepson, Ferdinand VI, with warmth. Yet he allowed her to remain in Madrid, contrary to custom, and attended to her with considerable kindness. Italian influence waned at court, and Ferdinand ordered the Spanish troops home from Italy. This cost Philip some reversals in Parma, and he returned to Spain also. But son and mother meddled and plotted so much that Ferdinand VI sent the army back, in part to remove his half-brother from Spain. Eventually, in July 1747, Ferdinand's wife, Maria Barbara of Braganza, prevailed upon her husband to exile Elizabeth from Madrid. He offered Valladolid, Burgos, or Segovia as the site of her residence but in the end permitted her to live at the palace San Ildefonso, which she and Philip had enlarged and beautified.

She remained isolated there, outside Segovia, until 1759, when Ferdinand died on August 10. He left no children and his wife had passed away the year before. That made Elizabeth's son Charles next in line to the throne and temporarily brought about the old queen's political resurrection. Ferdinand's will named her regent until Charles could arrive from Italy. The whole situation caused anxiety among the political elite, who had rejoiced at Elizabeth's eclipse, spurned her during her years at San Ildefonso, but now faced her as mother of the new monarch. Charles III abdicated the throne of the Two Sicilies in favor of his third son Ferdinand and then returned to Spain, arriving in Madrid on December 9, 1759. Elizabeth acted as regent during the intervening months.

Charles III treated his mother kindly but refused to give her political influence. He allowed her to remain at court but would not meet with her alone, to avoid giving the impression that he consulted with her. By this time, she was infirm and nearly blind. Although she continued to grant audiences, two retainers had to hold her up because she was unable to stand for long. Even then, however, she possessed continued ambitions for her children and regretted her failure to provide for Louis as she had for his two older brothers. One observer remarked that he expected her last words to be: "Remember Tuscany for Don Louis!" Elizabeth died July 11, 1766, and in accordance with her desires, was buried at San Ildefonso, next to her husband, rather than in the royal mausoleum at El Escorial.

Elizabeth Farnese was, according to Alberoni, "indolent, but yet ambitious, resolute at a crisis, negligent in everyday life." She remained first and foremost a wife, a mother, and an Italian. Despite Philip's derangement, "she sincerely loved this tyrant that she tyrannized." Hungry for popularity and grandeur, she lacked the discipline and understanding of state affairs to achieve them. To the British, French, and Austrians, she was a meddlesome, misguided woman, a "termagant." But Elizabeth provided more energy and direction to the Spanish government than it received from her husband. Edward Armstrong, her biographer, asserted of Philip: "No man has ever given such an example of the misuse of marriage, allowing himself to be ruled by his wife, who ruled him badly." Yet she achieved her objectives for her family and Parma, and during her reign, Spain began to recover some of its earlier prosperity and glory. Those successes compensated to some degree for her failure to assimilate the interests of Spain and make them her own.

SOURCES:

Armstrong, Edward. *Elisabeth Farnese: "The Termagant of Spain."* London: Longman, Green, 1892.

Calvo Poyato, José. *Felipe V, el primer Borbón.* Colección Memoria de la Historia/69. Barcelona: Editorial Planeta, 1992.

Coxe, William. *Memoirs of the Kings of Spain of the House of Bourbon, from the Accession of Philip V, to the Death of Charles III: 1700 to 1788.* 2nd ed. 5 vols. London: Longman, Hurst, Rees, Orem, and Brown, 1815.

Erlanger, Philippe. *Philippe V d'Espagne: Un roi baroque esclave des femmes.* Paris: Librairie Académique Perrin, 1978.

Lynch, John. *Bourbon Spain, 1700–1808.* Oxford: Basil Blackwell, 1989.

SUGGESTED READING:

Memoirs of Elizabeth Farnesio, the Present Queen Dowager of Spain. London: T. Gardner, 1746.

Moore, George. *Lives of Cardinal Alberoni, the Duke of Ripperda, and Marquis of Pombal, Three Distinguished Political Adventurers of the Last Century, Exhibiting a view of the Kingdoms of Spain and Portugal, During a Considerable Portion of That Period.* 2nd ed. London: Rodwell, 1814.

Taxonera, Luciano de. *Isabel de Farnesio: retrato de una reina y perfil de una mujer (1692–1766).* Barcelona: Editorial Juventud, 1943.

Kendall W. Brown,
Professor of History, Brigham Young University,
Provo, Utah

Farnese, Giulia (1474–1518?).

See Borgia, Lucrezia for sidebar.

Farnese, Isabel (1692–1766).

See Farnese, Elizabeth.

Farnese, Julia (1474–1518?).

See Borgia, Lucrezia for sidebar on Giulia Farnese.

Farnham, Eliza W. (1815–1864)

American philanthropist and writer. Born Eliza Woodson Burhans at Rensselaerville, Albany County, New York, on November 17, 1815, of an old Dutch family; died in New York City, on December 15, 1864; married Thomas J. Farnham (a lawyer and travel writer), in 1836 (died 1849); married a second time; children: four.

Born near Albany in 1815, Eliza Farnham was six when her Quaker mother died. Eliza then went to live with an uncle in Maple Springs, in western New York, rather than stay with a stepmother. Her uncle's wife was abusive, and Eliza was treated like a charity child and denied schooling. Farnham read everything in the household from Congressional debates, Masonic tracts, and Voltaire, to Paine, *Zoonomia* by Erasmus Darwin, and a biography of *Elizabeth Fry. She felt, said Farnham, "an intense curiosity to penetrate the innermost centre of the stained soul."

At 17, she was finally reunited with her sisters and brothers in Palmyra and began attending a Friends' boarding school. Soon, she qualified to teach and took a job at an Eastern academy where she met a friend of her brother's, Vermont lawyer Thomas J. Farnham. For health reasons, Thomas was leaving for Illinois to partake of the climate. In 1835, at age 19, Eliza journeyed to Illinois to marry him. They had a son who died of yellow fever while still an infant.

Thomas Farnham was a rover. On May 30, 1839, he set out on an expedition to Oregon; upon his return, he wrote the popular *Travels in the Great Western Prairies*. The couple moved back to New York in 1841, where Eliza began to visit prisons and lecture to women. Sometime in the mid-1840s, Thomas headed for California. To support herself, Eliza took a job in Sing Sing (then called Mt. Pleasant) where for four years (1844–48) she was matron of the women's division of the New York State Prison. Learning that many of the women had turned to crime only after they had "lost their self-respect through prostitution," Farnham sought to govern by "Kindness alone." At this time, she edited Sampson's *Criminal Jurisprudence* and published *Life in Prairie Land* about her experiences in the wilderness of Illinois.

In 1848, Farnham moved to Boston, where she was connected with the management for the Institution for the Blind. When Thomas Farnham died unexpectedly in 1849, she sailed for the Pacific Coast to settle his estate. In San Francisco, a boomtown where men outnumbered women ten to one, the 34-year-old Farnham found walking on the street an uncomfortable experience: "Doorways filled instantly, and little islands in the streets were thronged with men who seemed to gather in a moment, and who remained immovable . . . incredulous." Farnham attributed most of the evils of the Gold Rush to the lack of females and believed that the presence of women, whom she regarded as the great civilizer, would lend some stability to western expansion. Returning East, she organized a society to aid and protect destitute women, and encouraged the unmarried to emigrate. She often escorted these women to the Western states. On her return to New York in 1856, Farnham published a bestseller, *California, Indoors and Out*. For the next two years, she studied medicine, and in 1859 she published *My Early Days*.

Emboldened by the implications of the unisexual barnacle of Charles Darwin, grandson of Erasmus, Eliza Farnham produced her most important work, *Women and her Era,* in two volumes that were begun in 1856 and published in 1864, the last year of her life. In this treatise on the position and rights of women, Farnham adamantly disputed the claim of the women's movement that women were equal to men; she maintained, instead, that they were better—much, much better. Since Farnham's premise was not in accord with that of the women's movement, the movement tended to shy away from her work.

Written in a style that was sweet, spiritual, and extremely non-Victorian, Farnham's book dealt fearlessly with reproduction and anatomy. She saw women, whose role was as matron and guardian of the race, as responsible for the advancement of the species, because men were certainly incapable. Although both women and men had bosoms, Farnham remarked that women's were not only decorative but useful. Woman's sphere was procreation and maternity, and her place was in the home, a striking assertion given that Farnham wrote, worked in a prison, trekked back and forth to California, built her own home, plowed, planted, and rode horseback in a Bloomer dress. Farnham, however, had a ready reply for this contradiction: only a few Women, with a capital W, could be trusted with this kind of freedom; such independence would prevent many from facing up to their gender's responsibilities.

Farnham pleaded the superiority of women based on biology, art, literature, history, religion, and philosophy. She saw women's power to reproduce as "a creative power second only to God." "The purpose of these unique volumes," wrote a reviewer in the New York *Tribune,* "is to present a scientific exposition and proof of the time-honored adage, that 'woman is the better half of creation.'"

"Mrs. Farnham accepts this proposition not only as an undeniable truth, founded upon a deep and wide basis in the mental and physical constitution of the female sex, but as a truth of vital importance to the true order of society and the eternal interests of humanity," wrote the brothers Duyckinck in their 1875 edition of the *Cyclopædia of American Literature.* "She would redeem this cardinal idea, as she regards it, from the province of romantic sentiment, trace it to a more profound source in human nature than the enthusiasm of the affections, present it in the light of accurate analysis and philosophical argument, and exhibit its practical applications to domestic and social life."

"No one can give a candid perusal to her work without being deeply impressed with the sincerity of her convictions and the purity of her motives," continued the brothers, "whatever view may be entertained of the validity of her reasoning and the soundness of her conclusions. With glaring, and almost odious faults of execution, the transparent earnestness of her book, the lofty standard of womanly excellence which it sets forth, and the faith in God and humanity with which it is inspired, atone, in a great degree, for its perpetual violation of good taste, and stamp it as an original and remarkable production."

Eliza Farnham died prematurely at 49, possibly from an illness contracted the preceding year while doing volunteer nursing at Gettysburg. Her novel, *The Ideal Attained,* was printed posthumously in 1865.

SOURCES:

Duyckinck, Evert A. and George. *Cyclopædia of American Literature.* Vol. II. Philadelphia, PA: Wm. Rutter, 1875.

Woodward, Helen Beal. *The Bold Women.* NY: Farrar, Straus, 1953.

Farningham, Marianne

(1834–1909)

English Victorian Baptist who was an educationalist, journalist, and lecturer at a time when women were not expected to enter public life. Name variations: Mary Ann Hearn; Marianne Farningham Hearn; (pseudonym) Eva Hope. Pronunciation: FAR-ning-am. Born Mary Ann Hearn on December 17, 1834, in Farningham, Kent, England (Marianne Farningham is a pseudonym); died on March 16, 1909, in Barmouth, Wales; first child of Joseph (a merchant) and Rebecca (Bowers) Hearn (both members of Eynsford Particular Baptist Church); attended sporadically Eynsford British School between 1844 and 1850?; few weeks attendance at Home and Colonial College, London, around 1852; never married; no children.

Mother died (1846); was baptized and accepted into membership of Eynsford Particular Baptist Church (June 1848 or 1849); took first teaching post in Bristol (1852); sister Rebecca died (1853); contributed poem to the first issue of The Christian World *(1857); moved to Northampton as head of the Infant Department of the British School (1859); contributed to the first issue of* The Sunday School Times and Home Educator *(1860); left teaching to become a salaried member of staff on* The Christian World *(1867); first addressed the annual meeting of the Sunday School Union (1874); gave first public lecture in Daventry, Northamptonshire (1877); became editor of* The Sunday School Times *(1885); became member of Northampton school board (1886); resigned post on Northampton school board (1891); received presentation by the people of Northampton "on the com-*

pletion of half a century of noble work in the cause of religion and education" (1907).

Selected publications: almost 50 books of poetry and prose, mainly collections of contributions to The Christian World *and* The Sunday School Times *(e.g. Lays and Lyrics of the Blessed Life, 1860, Girlhood, 1869, Women and their Saviour, 1904) but also novels (e.g. A Window in Paris, 1898) and an autobiography, A Working Woman's Life, 1907. Also, under the pseudonym of Eva Hope, biographies (e.g. Grace Darling, the Heroine of the Farne Islands, 1875; New World Heroes, 1893) and some introductions to the Canterbury Poets edition of poetic works (e.g. John Greenleaf Whittier, 1885).*

Though Mary Ann Hearn, who wrote under the pseudonym Marianne Farningham, was a teacher, lecturer, and journalist, her base was always clearly the family. During her long life, she managed to step firmly outside the "private sphere" allotted to Victorian women and enter the hurly-burly of the masculine "public sphere" while retaining virtually all those qualities that were required of Victorian femininity.

The town of Farningham in Kent, S.E. England, was a village of some 700 inhabitants when Mary Ann Hearn was born there on December 17, 1834. The town's importance, compared to the surrounding villages, hung on the fact that it lay halfway along the busy main road between London and Maidstone. It was a convenient stopping-place for the horse-drawn traffic of the day, and the Hearns' house was opposite one of the chief coaching inns, the Bull. Despite this, it was not until Mary Ann was about 10 or 11 that she went to London, to accompany her sick mother who needed to consult a specialist.

Farningham's early days revolved around Eynsford Calvinistic Particular Baptist Church. "The life of the chapel was their life," she said of her parents, "and it became mine." Taken to her first service at a month old, she recalled attending regularly as soon as she could walk the mile between Farningham and Eynsford. Most of Sunday was spent at chapel, both dinner and tea being eaten there between services. From an early age, she had a simple but fervent faith that never deserted her. In her autobiography, she tells how, after tearing her pinafore, she prayed to God to mend it for her. Having got out of bed several times to examine the hole in hopes of its having disappeared, she burst into tears until an aunt came into the room and mended it for her. "I have many times since imagined the smiles of the little family group downstairs," she commented, "but I think it was very sweet of them not to laugh my faith away." At about 14 or 15, Farningham became a member of Eynsford Particular Baptist Church after having been baptized. Although Calvinistic Baptists preached redemption for only particular believers and laid much stress on sin and repentance, it was their seeming joyousness that appealed to the young girl and continued to do so throughout her life.

> On the evidence of her poetry alone . . . Marianne Farningham was a woman whose working life merits better than oblivion.
>
> —Shirley Burgoyne Black

In her autobiography, Farningham lays stress on the paucity of her formal education yet, considering her social class, her sex and her circumstances, she seems to have fared far better than many at this time. It is probable that her parents and all four grandparents could both read and write. She was taught to read by her paternal grandmother who died when Farningham was still only five years old. She was taught to write some time later by a cousin. Although there was a local National School, Farningham was not allowed to attend. Her autobiography implies that her father was complying with the dictates of his fellow worshippers in this, rather than acting on his own conviction. National Schools were run by the Church of England and were boycotted by Nonconformist parents as all pupils were taught the Church catechism. However, when Farningham was about ten, already beyond the age when many Victorian working-class children attended school, the Nonconformist British and Foreign School Society opened a school in Eynsford. Until her mother died in 1846, Farningham attended regularly and even after that sporadically, despite the fact that she was needed at home to care for her younger siblings and keep house for her father. After she nearly set her bedroom on fire trying to learn by candlelight while the rest of the family was asleep, her father allowed her to go back to school in return for her help with his shoemaking business. She tells how she took his work to school with her to do in her dinner hour.

We do not know how long Farningham remained a pupil at Eynsford British School, but in 1852 she went to Bristol, about 160 miles away, as a teacher. Teaching was one of the few professions considered respectable for women at this time; as it also met the Christian ethic of service, it was not entirely unusual for Nonconformist working-class girls, with aspirations, to become teachers. The distance is explained by the fact that she went as assistant to Miss Barnford who had lodged at the home of her maternal grandfather while teaching at Eynsford. Her only training was a few weeks at the Home and Colonial College in London where **Elizabeth Mayo** (1793–1865) and her brother Dr. Charles Mayo ran a course that normally lasted six months.

A year later, Farningham was called back home to nurse her dying sister, but in 1859, after a short spell in Gravesend only 20 miles away, she went to the British School in Northampton. This was a far more decisive move, but once again she went as part of a teacher friend's team, this time as headmistress of the Infants' Department. At first, she lived in lodgings with a teacher friend and two other young women, but before long her sister **Hephzibah** and her family moved to Northampton; for many years, Farningham had a large room in her sister's house.

However, it was not only teaching that interested Farningham. From an early age, she composed poems. Her first attempt at rhyming, before she could write, was "an epitaph on a dead toad" found in the garden. But she seems to have begun to write poetry more seriously during the period of her sister's illness, and she occasionally sent copies to magazines, which were always accepted. Her breakthrough came in 1857. At this time, the pastor at Eynsford was the Reverend Jonathan Whittemore who combined his religious duties with his other great interest—publishing.

After editing several papers, Whittemore perceived a gap in the market catering to tolerantly minded Nonconformists; on April 9, 1857, he began to produce *The Christian World*. This first edition contained a poem by Marianne Farningham, and she continued to write for the paper weekly. When, at the end of 1858, American writer *Fanny Fern* became extremely popular in England, Farningham began to contribute short prose pieces to *The Christian World* in emulation of her. From Whittemore, the budding writer received much encouragement. According to her, it was he who suggested the Farningham pen-name and it was he who suggested that her contributions be brought out in book form as soon as there were enough. So, in 1860, a book of poems entitled *Lays and Lyrics of the Blessed Life* was published. However, this was her second book. In 1858, her father had helped to finance a book of poetry and prose published under the name, Marianne Hearn.

It was in 1860 also that Whittemore embarked on *The Sunday School Times and Home Educator*. He wanted to cater to the ready market for periodicals with the rapidly expanding Sunday School movement and the increased interest in the family which was evident as *Victoria*'s reign progressed. Marianne Farningham was closely involved from the beginning, and she continued to contribute to both papers, though by now she was living in Northampton.

In the beginning, Farningham seems to have enjoyed her new teaching post, but, after the marriage of her friend and the arrival of a new headteacher, life was harder and less congenial. She was not really sufficiently educated or experienced for such duties as training pupil teachers. So it was with a measure of relief that she retired from teaching in 1867 to become a fully salaried member of *The Christian World*.

Farningham probably first became a Sunday School teacher shortly after being baptized. She was certainly the Girls' Bible Class teacher at Eynsford Baptist Chapel in 1853 even though "no older than the other girls" as she says in her autobiography. So when asked to take over College Street Baptist Chapel Girls' Bible Class at Northampton in 1867 she felt well up to the task. But her first week there was a salutary one. The majority of the Northampton girls were better educated than those in Eynsford and at least "one of the girls knew far more about the lesson" than Farningham did. Yet, it was for her Bible Class that Marianne Farningham became particularly celebrated in Northampton. In its heyday, it boasted over 100 members of various denominations. They held additional weekly meetings in her own home, made weekend excursions into the surrounding countryside, and took summer holidays in various parts of Britain. Farningham notes that she remained in Northampton after she had determined to leave because "the spell which drew me into its heart, and kept me there, was its Bible Class."

She only relinquished her post with great regret in 1901 when she "began to realize, as I had never done before, that my way home was all uphill." Following her death in 1909, she would be memorialized in an article in the Northamptonshire Sunday School Union Year Book.

Marianne Farningham's involvement with the Sunday School Union was gradual. She wrote hymns for special occasions, particularly the annual anniversary service, the most famous of these being "Just as I am" which was for many years sung at every Anglican Confirmation Service. Then in 1874, she was asked to

Marianne
Farningham

read a paper on the future of the Sunday School (in 1871, she had published a book entitled *Sunday Schools of the Future*). From then on, she was in great demand as a speaker at Sunday School Union meetings both locally and nationally. In 1904, she addressed the National Autumn Sunday School Convention along with 17 others: 14 of these were men, one of the women was **Jessie Ackerman** of the United States.

It was this experience of public speaking which gave Farningham the confidence to enter the lecturing circuit in 1877 on the hot topic of women's rights. In 1876, the Royal Commission on Factories and Workshops had inquired into women's working conditions. In September 1877, the Trades Union Congress debated the question of women and paid labor. In the same year, *Annie Besant* published *The Law of Population* advocating birth control. Women were steadily being given the chance to take a more active part in local government and women's suffrage was on everybody's lips.

Farningham's lecture would hardly have set the Victorian feminist world aflame, but she clearly did have some leanings in their direction. According to a report in the *Western Daily Press,* "She did not appear as a 'women's rights' advocate, though not altogether because she had no sympathy with the matter." She considered that there were "some wrongs that needed to be righted" and advocated the parliamentary vote for women who already had a Municipal vote—that is, for those who, like herself, were householders. For the next six or seven years, she traveled about the country giving a new lecture each winter in about 100 venues annually. Partly, she lectured for charity; nevertheless, with the proceeds, she was able to buy herself a house in Northampton.

All this time, Farningham continued to write at the rate of about two books a year, contributing her poems, articles, and stories regularly to *The Christian World* and *The Sunday School Times.* Starting in 1875, she also undertook a series of biographies for another firm of publishers, under the pseudonym Eva Hope. To this, she added, during 1884 and 1885, some of the introductions to a series of books entitled *The Canterbury Poets,* using the same pen-name. In 1885, she reached the pinnacle of her journalistic career when she was made editor of *The Sunday School Times.* She retained this appointment for many years, sometimes writing virtually the entire periodical herself.

In January 1886, Farningham once again entered the world of education by becoming a member of the Northampton school board. The Education Act of 1870 caused school boards to be set up in areas where existing school provision was insufficient to provide for the potential number of pupils. Women were permitted to vote for school-board members and also to sit on the boards themselves. However, in practice, few seem to have done so. School-board work was time consuming: as well as the general meetings, there were also subcommittees to attend and the schools themselves to be visited. Furthermore, the work, although dealing with children and therefore ostensibly within the feminine ambit, was of a very public nature and required women to work on equal terms with men. For many Victorian women, this was asking too much. Farningham, however, served two terms of office before resigning in December 1891, pleading "the exigencies of my literary work."

Marianne Farningham suffered one serious setback in 1889 when she had a nervous breakdown. Along with her punishing workload, she was actively involved in the life of her family. In the previous two years, she had coped with the death of her brother and subsequent caring for his wife and children, the absence of her beloved sister who was in South Africa, the illness with typhoid fever of her absent sister's son, and finally the death of her father who had been living with her "more or less ill all the time." She recuperated with a trip to Italy, as traveling both in Britain and abroad had always been one of her great pleasures. She was once invited to go to America where "they assured me that I should receive a hearty welcome . . . and promised to pass me on from city to city and from home to home, and give me 'a real good time'" but her doctor would not let her go.

Throughout her life, Farningham championed children. From the beginning, she encouraged The Young People's Society of Christian Endeavor as it struggled to gain a foothold in England from America. She supported the Temperance Bands of Hope, the Boys' Life Saving Brigade, the Girls' Life Brigade, and the Society for the Prevention of Cruelty to Children. "I am thankful to have watched a wonderful growth of respect for the child," she wrote. "Children are among the chief assets of the nation."

Some time in the 1880s, Marianne Farningham rented a cottage in Barmouth, a small seaside town in North Wales. She spent an ever-increasing amount of time there and became friendly with **Mrs. C.T. Talbot**, a very early benefactor of the National Trust, and with *Frances Power Cobbe, the famous journalist, feminist and founder of the Anti-Vivisection Society. When Cobbe died, Farningham was one of the directors entrusted with housing her library for the use of the people of Barmouth. It was here that she died in 1909.

Towards the end of her life, Marianne Farningham received several honors. In 1909, she was the first Sunday School teacher ever to be presented with a testimonial for prolonged service by the Sunday School Union. The Golden Jubilee of *The Christian World* was also celebrated as her Jubilee, and she received many gifts and tributes. Presentation ceremonies were held both by the people of Northampton and the people of Barmouth. When she died on March 16, her obituary notice in *The Times* was 30 lines long and that in the *Northampton-Independent* covered eight columns and was headed "Death of Northampton's Most Notable Woman."

SOURCES AND SUGGESTED READING:
Black, Shirley Burgoyne, ed. *A Farningham Childhood: Chapters from the Life of Marianne Farningham.* Sevenoaks: Darenth Valley Publication, 1988.

Farningham, Marianne. *A Working Woman's Life*. London: James Clarke, 1907.

Glandwr-Morgan, Rev. W. *Marianne Farningham in her Welsh Home*. Birmingham: Ellesmere Press, 1909 (reprinted 1923).

Barbara Evans,
Research Associate in Women's Studies at Nene College,
Northampton, England

Farnsworth, Emma J. (1860–1952)

American photographer, known for her allegorical and narrative studies. Born Emma Justine Farnsworth in Albany, New York, in 1860; died in Albany, New York, in 1952.

Trained as an artist, Emma Farnsworth turned to photography in 1890, after receiving a camera as a Christmas present. The following decade was her most active period, during which time she joined the Camera Club of New York. In 1892, fellow club member George M. Allen published a book of her figure studies accompanied by classical verse, entitled *In Arcadia*. Her characteristic bold figure studies, classically draped, were shown at the Chicago World's Columbian Exposition in 1893 and were part of *Frances Benjamin Johnston's exhibition of 1900–1901. Farnsworth was also one of seven women Johnston wrote about in "The Foremost Women Photographers of America," a series she did for *Ladies' Home Journal* (1901–02). Farnsworth won close to 30 medals in exhibitions abroad and was the subject of the Camera Club's second solo exhibition (1898).

Barbara Morgan,
Melrose, Massachusetts

Farquharson, Martha (1828–1909).

See Finley, Martha Farquharson.

Farr, Wanda K. (1895–1983)

American cytologist who pioneered X-ray diffraction techniques for plant cell research and discovered the mechanism for cellulose manufacture in plant cells. Name variations: Wanda Kirkbride; Mrs. R.C. Faulwetter. Pronunciation: FAR. Born Wanda Marguerite Kirkbride on January 9, 1895, at New Matamoras, Ohio; died in April 1983, possibly in New York City; daughter of Frederick and Clara Nikolaus Kirkbride; attended Ohio University, B.S., 1915; Columbia University, M.S., 1918; married Clifford Harrison Farr, on May 28, 1917 (died 1928); married Roy Christopher Faulwetter, date unknown (divorced); children: (first marriage) Robert Nicklaus Farr (b. July 3, 1920).

Worked as researcher on plant cells, University of Iowa (1919–24); was research associate, Barnard Skin and Cancer Hospital, St. Louis, Missouri (1925–28); instructed classes at Henry Shaw School of Botany, Washington University, St. Louis (1928); carried on studies on root-hair growth financed by National Academy of Sciences' Bache Fund (1928); was plant physiologist, Boyce Thompson Institute for Plant Research, Inc. (1928–29); served as associate cotton technologist for U.S. Department of Agriculture (1929–36); served as director, Cellulose Laboratory, Boyce Thompson Institute (1936–40); announced discovery of origins of cellulose manufacture in plant cells (1939); was research microchemist, American Cyanamid Company (1940–43); was research associate, Celanese Corporation of America (1943–54); worked as research consultant (1954–67); was associate professor of botany, University of Maine (1957–68); worked as researcher, Farr Cytochemical Labs (1960s–70s).

Selected writings: "Cell-Division of the Pollen-Mother-Cell of Coboea scandens alba," in Bulletin of the Torrey Botanical Club (Vol. 47, 1920, pp. 325–338); "Studies on the Growth of Root Hairs in Solutions: the pH Molar-Rate Relation for Brassica oleracea in Calcium Sulphate," in Proceedings of the National Academy of Sciences (Vol. 15, 1929, pp. 464–470); "Cotton Fibers. I. Origin and Early Stages of Elongation," in Contributions from Boyce Thompson Institute (CBTI, Vol. 3, 1931, pp. 441–458); (with George L. Clark) "Cotton Fibers. II. Structural Features of the Wall Suggested by X-ray Diffraction Analyses and Observations in Ordinary and Plane-Polarized Light," in CBTI (Vol. 4, 1932, pp. 273–295); "Cotton Fibers. III. Cell Divisions in the Epidermal Layer of the Ovule Subsequent to Fertilization," in CBTI (Vol. 6, 1933, pp. 167–172); "Cotton Fibers. IV. Fiber Abnormalities and Density of the Fiber Mass Within the Boll," in CBTI (Vol. 6, 1934, pp. 471–478); (with Sophia H. Eckerson) "Formation of Cellulose Membranes by Microscopic Particles of Uniform Size in Linear Arrangement," in CBTI (Vol. 6, 1934, pp. 189–203); (with Eckerson) "Separation of Cellulose Particles in Membranes of Cotton Fibers by Treatment with Hydrochloric Acid," in CBTI (Vol. 6, 1934, pp. 309–313); (with Wayne A. Sisson) "X-ray Diffraction Patterns of Cellulose Particles and Interpretations of Cellulose Diffraction Data," in CBTI (Vol. 6, 1934, pp. 315–321); "The Membrane Structure of Valonia," in Proceedings of American Chemical Society, Division of Cellulose Chemistry (93rd meeting, Chapel Hill, North Carolina, April 1937, p. C2); "Certain Colloidal Reactions of Cellulose Membranes," in Journal of Physical Chemistry *(Vol. 41, 1937, pp. 987–995); "Behavior of the Cell Membrane of the Cotton Fiber in Cuprammonium Hydroxide Solution," in* CBTI *(Vol. 10, 1938, pp. 71–112); "The Microscopic Structure of Plant Cell Membranes in Relation to the Micellar Hypothesis," in* Journal of Physical Chemistry *(Vol. 42, 1938, pp. 1113–1147); (with Sisson) "Observations on the Membranes of Epidermal Cells of the Avena coleoptile," in* CBTI *(Vol. 10, 1939, pp. 127–137); "Formation of Microscopic Cellulose Particles in Colorless Plastids of the Cotton Fiber," in* CBTI *(Vol. 12, 1941, pp. 181–194); "Plant Cell Membranes," in* Jerome Alexander, Colloid Chemistry *(Vol. 5, NY: Reinhold Publishing, 1944, pp. 610, 667);* Cytochemical Studies of Fungi Which Contaminate Aircraft Fuels and Deteriorate Materials *(Camden, ME: Farr Cytochemical Laboratories, 1962);* Research on the Cytochemistry of Cell Walls of Microorganisms *(Camden, ME: Farr Cytochemical Laboratories, 1964).*

While her schoolmates were enjoying recess, young Wanda Kirkbride was likely to be found gazing into the sole microscope of her high school laboratory, her pockets bulging with leaves and plants she had gathered to examine. This early inquisitiveness about the structure of native flora was to culminate in a lifelong career in plant physiology, particularly cytology, the study of cells. In her plant-cell investigations Kirkbride was to pioneer X-ray diffraction techniques for analyzing natural fibers, and her discovery of the origin of cellulose answered century-old questions about plant structure.

A credulous student hardly ever makes a successful scientist.

—Wanda Kirkbride Farr

Wanda Marguerite Kirkbride was born on January 9, 1895, near the river town of New Matamoras, Ohio. Following the death of her father Frederick of tuberculosis when she was four, Wanda moved with her mother **Clara Nikolaus Kirkbride** into the home of her grandparents, where the household also included her great-grandfather, Dr. Samuel Richardson. A country physician who served for a while as a state senator, Richardson was fluent in French and German and maintained a library of current medical and science journals, both American and foreign. He encouraged Wanda toward a liberal education, introducing her to his technical periodicals, debating international issues with her, criticizing her poetry, and teaching her about natural histo-

ry, especially indigenous Ohio plant life. The curiosity and independence of mind instilled by her great-grandfather led her to refuse to accept incomplete explanations from her science teacher, a Professor Barr, and to be less gullible than her schoolmates in her pursuit of a full understanding of basic scientific processes.

Wanda also wanted to follow in her great-grandfather's footsteps by becoming a physician. She planned to attend medical school at Ohio State University, but because of her family's worries that the stresses encountered by doctors might cause her to succumb to tuberculosis like her father, she opted for the healthier lifestyle of a research scientist and elected to attend Ohio University at Athens.

Participating in the Science Club, YWCA, and Tennis Association, Wanda majored in botany and chemistry. She completed her requirements for a bachelor's degree in three years, graduating Phi Beta Kappa in 1915. Botany was still a young science, not fully professionalized until the late 19th century, and offered few career-enhancing positions for qualified women, but Wanda's work as a laboratory assistant in the botany department led to an invitation to spend her fourth collegiate year pursuing advanced studies at Columbia University.

Soon after arriving at Columbia, Wanda met Clifford Harrison Farr, a graduate of the University of Iowa who had conducted botanical explorations on the island of Jamaica and was completing his Ph.D. in botany. Clifford was impressed with the engaging young woman, who showed considerable skill at preparing microscope slides, and was ardently courting her when he was offered a position as assistant professor of plant physiology at Texas Agricultural and Mechanical College. To be near Clifford, Wanda soon took a position as an instructor in botany at Kansas State Agricultural College, and the couple married on May 28, 1917, establishing a collaboration that was to be scientific as well as personal.

World War I was underway, and when Clifford was assigned wartime research in Washington, D.C., for the U.S. Bureau of Plant Industry, Farr procured a microscope to finish her thesis. After receiving her master's degree from Columbia in 1918, she taught in the botany department of Texas A&M. In the autumn of 1919, Clifford transferred to his alma mater in Iowa City, and the two began to conduct joint research on plant cells. After the birth of their only child, Robert Farr, on July 3, 1920, Farr stopped teaching, but she continued her independent research on living plant cells in Clifford's laboratory. The couple cultivated grapevines, bottling their own grape juice, and their interest in plant physiology dominated their home. As a child, Robert would complain to house guests that he could not find any books to read at home because he preferred "anything that doesn't have plants in it." In later years, Robert Farr was a science writer and war correspondent for Scripps-Howard and CBS.

In 1925, Clifford accepted a position as associate professor in the Henry Shaw School of Botany at Washington University in St. Louis, Missouri, where Farr worked as a botany instructor and continued with their research. Here they began to develop new methods for the microscopic investigation of plant growth, particularly the growth of root hairs in solutions and cell division in pollen mother cells.

Clifford's interest in root hairs grew out of his observations that these hairs, unlike other cells that enlarged along numerous paths, grew from one cell of the root's surface, in one direction. He initiated further research to uncover a uniform means of understanding cell growth. Farr meanwhile went to work as a research associate for Dr. Montrose Burrows, who had perfected techniques of removing living cells from animal organisms and transferring them to grow in petri dishes, at the Barnard Skin and Cancer Hospital. Farr adapted Burrows' methodology to her research on plant cells and took up the study of advanced mathematics to improve her research procedures.

From 1925 to 1927, the Farrs spent their summers at the Marine Biological Laboratory at Woods Hole, Massachusetts, where they measured the elongation of aquatic root hairs through micrometer eye-pieces every ten minutes in a dark basement room. Clifford published the results of their root-hair growth studies in a two-year series in the *American Journal of Botany* and presented their data to the Society of Experimental Biology and Medicine and the first international congress on soil science, while also producing popular articles about plant growth for the *Atlantic Monthly*.

Aware of a chronic heart ailment, Clifford tried to prepare Wanda for his early demise. He saved funds for her to earn a Ph.D. so that she could financially support their son and urged her to begin such studies. Farr, who only wanted to attend Columbia, delayed the studies because she did not wish to be separated from her family at this time; in fact, she was never to earn a Ph.D.

When Clifford died on February 10, 1928, in St. Louis, Washington University administrators asked Farr to teach his courses. She was lecturing and perpetuating his laboratory research within a week. Later that year, the National Academy of Sciences agreed to finance her studies on root-hair growth through the Bache Fund.

On her own, Farr's botanical work moved into a highly productive new phase, focusing on plant fibers for academia, government, and industry. In late 1928, she entered the industrial sector when she accepted a yearlong position as investigator of plant physiology for the Boyce Thompson Institute for Plant Research, Inc., at Yonkers, New York. Founded by Colonel William Boyce Thompson in 1924, the institute operated on a $10 million endowment created through mining investments, and its declared mission was the study of fundamental life processes through basic plant physiology research in order to increase crop yields that could lead to the general improvement of society. Farr bought a white-frame, colonial house near the institute, hired an English housekeeper to look after her son, and set up further root-hair studies. The following year, her reputation as a researcher led to her appointment as associate cotton technologist for the Division of Cotton Marketing in the U.S. Department of Agriculture's Bureau of Agricultural Economics, to assist the cotton industry in grading the quality of field cotton.

In the 1920s, cotton was a vital agricultural crop in the U.S. Its growth is similar to that of root hairs, extending from a single cell on the seed. For a decade during the 1930s, Farr carried out her research in a Washington, D.C., laboratory, studying cell differentiation, especially in the formation and structure of the cell walls of cotton fibers, and examining field samples provided by Clemson College in South Carolina, showing cotton at different stages of maturity.

In 1930, Farr returned to her laboratory at Boyce Thompson Institute. In addition to the cotton fibers she received from the South, she cultivated plants in greenhouses at Yonkers in order to study their maturation firsthand. This close proximity to the maturing cotton plants enabled her to observe cotton-fiber development. Through an arrangement with the Department of Chemistry at the University of Illinois, she utilized its X-ray laboratory to learn microscopic and chemical techniques, particularly X-ray diffraction, for the analysis of her cell samples.

Working with microchemist Dr. **Sophia H. Eckerson**, Farr considered the structural problems in developing cotton. At first, the two scientists made microscopic observations of cellulose-forming bacterium, especially their membranes. In 1936, they were able to increase their facilities and staff through funds provided by the Chemical Foundation, Inc. Designated director of the new cellulose laboratory, Farr welcomed such skilled scientists as Drs. **Florence L. Barrows** and Wayne A. Sisson and supervised specialists that included organic chemists, bacteriologists, microscopists, X-ray chemists, and a photographer, on a carefully utilized budget of $40,000.

In the laboratory's detailed dissection and analysis of plant life, experiments with cotton fibers concentrated on cell enlargement in root hairs as they developed from the seed's epidermal cells. Use of polarized light and X-ray diffraction revealed new information about root hairs that originated from cells that divided before fertilization, root-hair structure, and how the root hairs received nutrition from the seed. By 1940, when a lack of funding brought the project to an end, Farr's cell membrane analyses had clarified basic formational and structural problems.

During this ten-year period, Farr's research provided one of the major underpinnings of modern botany through its analysis of the fundamental plant material, cellulose. Plants, unlike animals (including humans), which rely on the consumption of animal and vegetable matter for basic nutrients, are self-sustaining, utilizing only soil and air for the manufacture of nourishment within their own cells. Cellulose, the basic material providing the structural framework of plants, had long intrigued the scientific community. To understand how the plant cells produce their own food, scientists examined cell structures and discovered that microscopic plastids, floating in cellular protoplasm, process hydrogen, carbon, and oxygen from sunlight, carbon dioxide, and water to produce starches, which are held within the plant as food reserves. The conversion of these starches into sugars fuels plant growth.

Plant cells, unlike animal cells, are surrounded by a rigid cell wall formed of cellulose. This tissue material provides support for the plant and insures that its leaves are exposed to sunlight. Using microscopes, scientists before Farr had been able to observe the manufacture of starches and sugars within plants, but the process of cellulose production eluded them. Cellulose particles would appear in cellular protoplasm suddenly and fully-formed, already aligned and attached to cell walls. For almost a century before Farr began her work, botanists had sought to observe the origin of cellulose particles.

The walls of cotton fibers consist of almost 90% cellulose. At the Boyce Thompson Institute, Farr and her researchers determined that each cotton fiber contained a mass of cellulose fibrils cemented together to form a single strong fiber. Although they pinpointed information valuable to the cotton industry about the structure, growth, chemical content, and strengths and weaknesses of the cotton fibers, they were unable to detect cellulose formation.

In the late 1930s, Farr began to examine a single-celled green algae, Halicystis, sent to her from Bermuda. Using high-powered microscopes to magnify and photograph the algae, she observed the manufacture of cellulose in the same plastids of the Halicystis that manufactured starch, and realized that plastids in cotton fibers might be invisible in the cell because they shared similar refractive indexes with the cell's protoplasm.

Up to this point, the cellulose-manufacturing plastids were water-mounted on slides for viewing under the microscope. By mounting the cotton fibers in their own juices, Farr rendered the plastids visible. She was then able to view the manufacture of cellulose, and the explosion of the plastid that released visible cellulose particles into the cell's protoplasm. Farr discovered that plastids in the cotton-fiber cells were miniature cellulose factories, processing carbon, hydrogen, and oxygen into a compound for the manufacture of cellulose, much as plastids in leaf cells produced starch. She also revealed that cellulose could be produced without chlorophyll, the photosynthetic material that provides plants with their green color.

In December 1939, Farr presented her discoveries in a session of the annual meeting of the American Association for the Advancement of Science in Ohio. The work earned her laurels as a national authority in plant physiology and as the most prominent woman in contemporary science. *The New York Times,* however, repeatedly used masculine pronouns in referring to the discoveries of "Dr. Farr" (who may have held an honorary title by then), while other publications described her as a "dark and slender woman" who was "versatile, chic, vivacious, as modern as tomorrow."

Although some scientists had been skeptical about aspects of her previously published exploratory work, her new conclusions quickly gained acceptance and respect among the majority of the scientific community. Scientists anticipated their application in the artificial creation of infinite food and fuel supplies, while industry, hoping to duplicate the natural process, yearned to produce synthetic materials that were structural imitations of fiber, cloth, paper, and wood.

When scientists were unable to duplicate her findings, Farr was able to demonstrate how the problem lay in their methodology. In preparing their specimens for microscopic slides, these scientists used techniques that included softening the specimens in a blender to a slush, which altered their basic structure and rendered them incapable of being compared with her living plant cell samples.

Farr was named a fellow of the Royal Microscope Society and of the American Association for the Advancement of Science. She was active in the New York Academy of Sciences and the Society for the Study of Development and Growth, and contributed scholarly articles to journals including the *Bulletin of the Torrey Botanical Club*, *Contributions from Boyce Thompson Institute*, and the *Journal of Physical Chemistry*. As the professional honors mounted, she was also asked to lend her expertise to the analysis of fiber samples from the mummy of Queen *Hatshepsut for the Metropolitan Museum to determine if they were cotton or linen. Meanwhile, she monitored the education of her son (who studied scientific journalism), collected botanical specimens near Yonkers, and gardened in her backyard.

In 1940, she became involved in the Allied effort of World War II as a research microchemist for the American Cyanamid Company in Stamford, Connecticut. By 1943, she had transferred to the research division of the Celanese Corporation of America in Summit, New Jersey, where she analyzed natural and synthetic materials.

In 1954, Farr left Celanese to initiate a career as a research consultant. She served as Curie lecturer at Pennsylvania State University and established a laboratory in St. Clairsville, Ohio, in 1955. Continuing to focus on living cells, she began research with fungi and the derivation of antibiotics, and worked on the manuscript for a book, tentatively titled "Plant Histochemistry and Cytochemistry," but its publication has not been confirmed. In 1957, she consulted for the Brown & Williamson Tobacco Corporation and for the British American Tobacco Company the following year.

In 1957, Farr also returned to academia as an associate professor of botany at the University of Maine, where she cooperated with the college's Agricultural Experiment Station, participated in a research project on poultry fungal infections funded by the National Institute of Health, and gave occasional lectures up to 1968. Utilizing her special knowledge of the chemical composition of plant cell walls, she explored how to prevent fungi from destroying tissue in both plants and animals. The New York Academy of Sciences honored her for her accomplishments in this area of research, and the E.I. DuPont Company featured her as one of six famous American women scientists in its January–February 1960 issue of *Better Living*. During this period, Farr also established the Farr Cytochemical Laboratory, first in her home at Camden, Maine, then in Nyack, New York, where she moved in 1969. She continued consulting with the Celanese Corporation based in Cumberland, Maryland. Under government contracts, she conducted food and waste research for NASA and General Foods, Inc., in her home laboratories into the early 1970s, when she was past 75.

Little is known of Farr's personal life in her latter years. After Clifford's death, she married Roy Christopher Faulwetter, who was also a scientist; Boyce Thompson records indicate the change of surname on her personnel papers in December 1930, and newspaper indexes in 1940, citing her discovery of the origin of cellulose, list her by her second husband's surname. Farr and Faulwetter divorced sometime during the 1940s, and he died in Detroit, Michigan, in 1967. Since Farr guarded her privacy carefully, much of what is known about her is taken from the biographical profiles of her first husband's career.

Details of Farr's death are similarly elusive. According to the Social Security death index, she died in April 1983. The place of her death is unknown; her last Social Security check was sent to Rockland, Maine, possibly her son's place of residence at that time, but no death certificate was filed in her name in that state. It is known that she suffered a stroke in April 1971, but recovered slightly and was able to spend about two hours daily in her laboratory. As her condition worsened, she was unable to write, and relied on a nurse to communicate for her. She sought newspaper publicity only because she was desperate to donate her vast laboratory equipment, estimated to be worth $60,000, to scientists when the lease on her Nyack apartment expired. In the mid-1970s, this was her last published address. Neither *The New York Times* nor the major professional scientific journals carried an obituary notice to mark her passing.

Described as a woman whose "world revolves around her microscopes, her test tubes, her cameras," Wanda Farr practiced the deliberative scientific methodology that she endorsed, expounding her motto, "A credulous student hardly ever makes a successful scientist," to students who visited her laboratory. Her research for government and industry resulted in significant scientific achievements through the synthesis of basic materials that add to comfort in daily life through stronger, more affordable, and readily abundant consumer goods. More important, her unquenchable curiosity, lack of gullibility, and challenging attitudes led to the resolution of the scientific mystery surrounding the fundamental component of plant life, cellulose, that had befuddled multitudes of scientists for decades.

SOURCES:

"Cellulose Scientist," in *The New York Times*. December 31, 1939, section IV, p. 2.

Farr, Wanda K. "Plant Cell Membranes," in *Growth of Plants: Twenty Years' Research at Boyce Thompson Institute*. Chapt. 8. Edited by William Crocker. NY: Reinhold Publishing, 1948.

Laurence, William L. "Cellulose Factory Located in Plants: Dr. W.K. Farr Tells Scientists Mystery of Place of Origin is Solved," in *The New York Times*. December 27, 1939, p. 22.

McLaughlin, Kathleen. "Challenging Approach to Study Brings Rewards to Scientist: Dr. Wanda Farr, Head of Cellulose Laboratories in Yonkers, Is Noted for Researches," in *The New York Times*. January 14, 1940, section II, p. 8.

"No Takers for $60,000 Lab," in *Nyack Journal News*. March 8, 1972.

"Woman Scientist Discovers How Plants Make Cellulose," in *Science News Letter*. Vol. 37, January 6, 1940, pp. 6–7.

Yost, Edna. *American Women of Science*. Rev. ed. Philadelphia, PA: J.B. Lippincott, 1955.

SUGGESTED READING:

McCallan, S.E.A. *A Personalized History of Boyce Thompson Institute*. Yonkers: Boyce Thompson Institute, 1975.

Morton, Alan G. *History of Botanical Science: An Account of the Development of Botany From Ancient Times to the Present Day*. London: Academic Press, 1981.

Reed, Howard S. *A Short History of the Plant Sciences*. Waltham, MA: Chronica Botanica, 1942.

Rossiter, Margaret W. *Women Scientists in America: Struggles and Strategies to 1940*. Baltimore, MD: Johns Hopkins University Press, 1982.

Slack, Nancy G. "Nineteenth-Century American Women Botanists: Wives, Widows, and Work," in *Uneasy Careers and Intimate Lives: Women in Science 1789–1979*. Edited by Pnina G. Abir-Am and Dorinda Outram. Foreword by Margaret W. Rossiter. New Brunswick, NJ: Rutgers University Press, 1987, pp. 77–103.

Elizabeth D. Schafer, Ph.D.,
freelance writer in history of technology and science,
Loachapoka, Alabama

Farrand, Beatrix Jones (1872–1959)

One of the finest landscape architects of her time, internationally known for her knowledge of plants and her keen sense of design, who was the only woman founder of the American Society of Landscape Architects. Name variations: Beatrix Jones. Born Beatrix Cadwalader Jones on June 19, 1872, in New York City; died in Bar Harbor, Maine, on February 27, 1959; daughter of Frederic Rhinelander Jones and Mary Cadwalader Rawle Jones; paternal niece of Edith Wharton; tutored at home; married Max Farrand, on December 17, 1913; no children.

Apprenticed at Arnold Arboretum under Charles Sprague Sargent (1892); opened first office (1895); given first important commission (1896); was the only woman to help co-found the American Society of Landscape Architects (1899); discharged last commission, a guesthouse for David Rockefeller at Seal Harbor, Maine (1949).

Major commissions: Princeton University, Princeton New Jersey (1913–41); Grove Point, the estate of S. Vernon Mann in Great Neck, New York (1918–30); Eolia, estate of Edward S. Harkness, in New London, Connecticut (1919–32, now Harkness Memorial State Park); Dumbarton Oaks, residence of Mildred and Robert Bliss, Washington, D.C. (1921–47); Yale University, New Haven, Connecticut (1922–45); The Haven, estate of Gerrish H. Milliken in Northeast Harbor, Maine (1925–45); The Eyrie, garden of Mrs. John D. Rockefeller, Jr. (Abby Aldrich Rockefeller), in Seal Harbor, Maine (1926–50); Dartington Hall, Ltd., Totnes, Devonshire, England (1933–38).

In the words of her aunt, ***Edith Wharton**, Beatrix Jones Farrand was born into "a life of leisure and amiable hospitality," in the highly structured environment of polite society of New York City in 1870s. Farrand described herself as having descended from five generations of garden lovers, and remembered one of the first espaliered fruit gardens in Newport, which was owned by her paternal grandmother **Lucretia Rhinelander Jones**, as well as the laying out of the roads and gardens at her family's summer place at Bar Harbor, Maine, when she was young.

Farrand came from a family of strong-willed women: she was very close to her mother **Mary Cadwalader Jones**, known as "Minnie" to her close friends, and her aunt, the well-known author Edith Wharton. She was also close to her mother's brother, John Cadwalader, with whom she frequently enjoyed shooting trips in Scotland. Cadwalader recognized her determination and her keen powers of observation, and predicted that whatever she did would be done well.

Beatrix's mother has been described as quick and energetic with an eager curiosity. Her father Frederic Rhinelander Jones was Wharton's older brother, but the Joneses' marriage ended before Beatrix was 12. To help support herself after the divorce, Minnie acted as part-time literary agent for Wharton. She also managed the New York Assembly Ball for a number of years, organized the Charity Hospital on Blackwell's (now Roosevelt) Island, and became social director of the New York 400 Club. Minnie's house was described by her friend ✥➤ **Margaret Chanler** as combining "all creature comforts with a sense of civilized tradition and intellectual resource," and she was said to have kept one of the liveliest salons in New York City. Some of the best literary and artistic minds of the period—John La Farge, Marion Crawford, and Henry and Brooks Adams—were frequent guests; Henry James corresponded with Minnie and stayed in her home on his visits to New York. Beatrix described her mother as "the best companion, wise, kindly, brave, witty and distinguished."

Farrand was tutored at home, as was common among women of her class; the boundaries imposed on women in the Victorian era caused many born to such privilege to lead primarily unproductive and self-indulgent lives, but Beatrix was encouraged to reach beyond. She had studied music and had a fine voice, but at 18, she decided against a career in that field. In her early 20s, she had the good fortune to be invited to the home of **Mary Allen Sargent**, in Brookline, Massachusetts, where she met the husband of her hostess, Professor Charles Sargent, who was the founder and first director of the Arnold Arboretum, then being established in Boston. When Charles Sargent suggested that she study landscape gardening, Farrand agreed to become his student in Boston.

The year was 1893, and Sargent was the dean of American horticulture, in the process of laying out the grounds of the Arnold Arboretum with perhaps America's most famous landscape artist, Frederick Law Olmsted. Beatrix lived with the Sargents for many months, studying botany, learning how to survey and stake out a plot of land, and other basic principles of her profession. Sargent advised her to study the tastes of the owner and to "make the plan fit the ground and not twist the ground to fit a plan." He also encouraged her to travel and view the great gardens of Europe, analyze natural beauty, and see the best of landscape paintings, endowing her with a sense that all the great arts are interrelated.

✥➤ **Chanler, Margaret** (b. 1862)

American author. Name variations: Mrs. Winthrop Chanler; Daisy Chanler or Daisy Terry. Born Margaret Terry in Rome, Italy, on August 6, 1862; daughter of Luther Terry and Louisa Cutler (Ward) Terry; privately educated; awarded diploma in music from St. Cecilia Conservatory, Rome; awarded D.Litt from Nazareth College, Rochester, New York; married Winthrop Chanler, on December 16, 1886; children: Laura Astor (Mrs. Lawrence Grant White); John Winthrop; Beatrice (Mrs. Pierre Francis Allegaert); Hester Marion (Mrs. Edward Motley Pickman); Marion Winthrop; Gabrielle (Mrs. Porter Ralph Chandler); Hubert Winthrop; Theodore Ward.

Born in Rome, Margaret Terry, known as Daisy, arrived in the United States in 1886; that December, she married socialite Winthrop "Winty" Chanler. The Chanlers, who had an estate in Newport, were great friends with Theodore Roosevelt and *Edith Wharton; Margaret often went on sojourns with Wharton, cruising the Aegean, following the abandoned trail of medieval pilgrims across the Pyrenees to the shrine of Compostela. "She was a striking rather than a beautiful woman; her strong features glinted intelligence and humor, and a readiness for affection," writes R.W.B. Lewis in *Edith Wharton: A Biography* (Harper and Row, 1975). Margaret Chanler's memoirs, *Roman Spring* (1934) and *Autumn in the Valley* (1936), contain observations on Wharton; Chanler also translated *Gertrud von Le Fort's *Hymns to the Church* (1937).

SUGGESTED READING:

Auchincloss, Louis. *Love Without Wings: Some Friendships in Literature and Politics* (includes a chapter on Chanler and her friendship with Edith Wharton). Boston: Houghton Mifflin, 1991.

Under Sargent's guidance, Beatrix studied the works of Joseph Paxton, John and **Jane Loudon**, Jacob Bigelow, and Asa Gray. Through her studies, she grew to respect and understand the importance of botany and plants in creating beauty and improving public health. Learning horticulture first hand, she kept journals of her observations, making a study of plants that continued throughout her life.

*W*ith this grand art of mine I do not envy the greatest painter, or sculptor or poet that lived. It seems to me that all arts are combined in this.

—Beatrix Jones Farrand

In October 1893, Beatrix attended the Columbian Exposition in Chicago, whose monumental design marked the triumph of the Beaux Arts and the end of an era of Romantic design. In the spring of 1895, following Sargent's advice, she went abroad, sailing to Gibraltar and then proceeding to Italy to visit many popular villas and gardens. That summer, she journeyed to England, where she made several visits to the Royal Botanic Gardens at Kew, as well as to Hampton Court, Hyde Park, Kensington Gardens, and Penshurst, a Tudor garden that had been recently rejuvenated.

In July, Beatrix visited the home of *Gertrude Jekyll, the leading proponent of the cottage garden in England and known for her use of wild and native materials as well as her harmonious and subtle use of color in garden plantings. Jekyll's approach had a large impact on Beatrix, and several features seen at Penshurst, as well as the use of plants in an architectural manner learned from European gardens, were later incorporated in her work.

Beatrix
Jones
Farrand

In September 1895, Beatrix returned to New York, where she opened a small office in the top floor of her mother's house at 21 East 11th Street. Beginning with small residential garden designs for close friends, she built a reputation as one of the top landscape architects in the country, opening an office with a small staff at 124 East 40th Street within three years. In the 1920s, her employees were graduates of the Cambridge and Lowthrope schools of landscape architecture, which provided an education for women in the field, still denied at the time at all-male Harvard.

By 1899, landscape architects had become successful enough to recognize the need for a professional organization. On January 4, at age 27, Beatrix Jones met with Samuel Parsons Jr., John C. Olmsted and eight others in New York to found the American Society of Landscape Architects (ASLA), the first professional landscape architecture association in America.

On December 17, 1913, at age 41, Beatrix Jones married Max Farrand, a distinguished constitutional historian and chair of the history department at Yale. From then on, she divided her time between New Haven, her office in New York, and Reef Point, the couple's summer residence in

Bar Harbor, Maine. After 1927, when Max was appointed director of the Henry E. Huntington Library and Art Gallery in San Marino, California, the couple's move to the West Coast led Beatrix Farrand to adapt a number of her ideas to the California climate, topography, and plants. That same year, she began her work as a consulting landscape gardener at Princeton, which continued for many years. She later performed similar duties at Yale, the University of Chicago, Oberlin, and other colleges and universities, while also developing a number of private estates.

At a time when women who were professionals generally worked for others, or alone if they had their own business, Farrand maintained offices employing from four to six people. She primarily hired women, several of whom went on to form their own practices; her three principle assistants were **Anne Baker**, **Margaret Bailie**, and after 1929, **Ruth Havey**. Farrand traveled constantly between her offices and visits to clients, working many hours on trains and in hotel rooms. Commuting became a way of life, and she used her travel time efficiently. Ruth Havey, who took over one of Farrand's largest commissions after she retired, the landscaping of Dumbarton Oaks, has recalled how they worked:

> I would bring the drawings being developed at the office and get on the train in New York and meet her on the train. She was usually on her way to do field work in one of the jobs. We would review the plans, she would make suggestions and critiques or changes. As soon as the review was finished, I would get off at the next station, wherever that may be, and take a train back to New York.

In late spring, Farrand would move her practice to Bar Harbor, where her family had a summer home, and return to New York in the fall. The summer office in Bar Harbor handled all the commissions for gardens located in Maine, which was an important resort area in the 1920s. After the move to California, where she spent the winters, she set up a small practice there, but never enough to justify a full-fledged office, which she continued to maintain in New York.

Around the turn of the century, as a woman pioneering in a profession dominated by males, Farrand had found the large-scale public projects available to her well-known male contemporaries, such as Frederick Law Olmsted, unavailable to her. Another obstacle was her upper-class background, which caused some not to take her seriously as a professional; to avoid classification as an amateur or volunteer, she was always careful to bill according to her professional status.

Eolia, estate of Edward S. Harkness, New London, Connecticut, garden designed by Beatrix Farrand.

Farrand had phenomenal energy and thoroughness, and inspired others to push themselves. She had a long list of private clients, many of whom were quite well known. She did not discuss her work often, but she did once admit that there was a time in her professional life when a garden done by her was "believed to open certain social doors to its owner." She preferred to attribute her success to demand exceeding supply, but acknowledged that it did enable her to choose the work she preferred. Among the many large private estates on Long Island that were part of her work was one owned by Dorothy (*Dorothy Payne Whitney) and Willard Straight, who were her clients from 1914 to 1932. In 1925, several years after the death of Willard, Dorothy remarried Leonard Elmhirst and the couple acquired Dartington Hall, in England, which became Farrand's only overseas commission. Work there lasted until the outbreak of World War II.

In 1926, Beatrix was asked by *Abby Aldrich Rockefeller and her husband John D.

Eolia, now Harkness State Park.

Rockefeller, Jr., to design a garden at The Eyrie, their summer home at Seal Harbor on Mt. Desert Island, Maine. This remains the most famous of her many works on the island, and is rare in that it remains essentially intact and maintained according to her plans (as does Eolia, the estate of Edward S. Harkness, in New London, Connecticut, now Harkness Memorial State Park).

The gardens of Beatrix Farrand all required a high level of maintenance; without proper attention, the design concept could be lost. She was a perfectionist, who wrote extensive maintenance notes, and she or a member of her staff would supervise gardeners over a period of years to guarantee the implementation of her designs. In some cases, the hiring of gardeners, and payroll and maintenance costs of a project, were handled through her office.

Farrand felt that a landscaped garden should be a place of both beauty and restfulness where people are comfortable. She also strove to convince her clients that it could evolve into a work of art if constantly refined. This required the active intervention of the designer over an extended period of time. Her approach took into account the fact that plants are living organisms each involved in a unique cycle of seed, vegetative growth, and reproduction. Even in her most formal designs, if the plants were not properly maintained, the effect after a while would no longer be true to her original composition, like a painting modified by a lesser hand.

The works that Farrand found most satisfying were those in which long-term maintenance was possible. At Dumbarton Oaks, she worked intensively over a 26-year period; her work on Eyrie, the Rockefeller estate in Seal Harbor, Maine, lasted from 1926 to 1950; and she was involved with The Haven, the Milliken estate in Northeast Harbor, Maine, from 1925 to 1945. Her work on college campuses included 31 years at Princeton, from 1912 to 1943, and 23 at Yale, from 1922 to 1945.

In the 1890s, campus landscaping received much more attention than in later years, and college campuses became an integral part of her work at an early stage. It was during this time that many of the most established American colleges and universities took on the gracious look we now associate with them. Sadly, lowered standards of maintenance over the ensuing decades have also resulted in the deterioration of some campuses.

Few of Farrand's private gardens, designed between 1896 and 1913, have survived to the present day, but drawings, plans and photographs give some indication of the nature and quality of these early works. These show a tendency toward classical lines in her designs, the use of architectural and sculptural details derived from classical models, and a strong sense of appropriateness in scale and materials.

Farrand's lifetime honors include the achievement medal of the Garden Club of America, the Gold Medal of the Massachusetts Horti-

culture Society, the Distinguished Service Award of the New York Botanic Garden, an honorary Doctorate of Letters from Smith College, and the rank of professor and an honorary Master of Arts from Yale. She believed that the professions of architecture and landscape architecture should function hand-in-hand from the beginning of a project to avoid working at odds with each other, and late in life her achievements in this area were recognized when she was made an honorary member of the American Institute of Architects.

The best example of Farrand's work intact to this day can be seen in Georgetown, Washington, D.C., at Dumbarton Oaks, an estate bought in the early 1920s by Robert and *Mildred Barnes Bliss. Because of the rather dominating house that existed on the property and the very steep grades surrounding it, as well as the strong personal preferences of the owners, the landscaping offered Farrand one of her most difficult challenges. Farrand worked closely with Mildred Bliss, who was herself an imaginative designer, and over two decades the former farm land was transformed into one of the finest gardens in the country. The estate is now a research center for Byzantine art owned by Harvard University, the grounds receive the same meticulous care they did as a private estate, and they are open to the public.

Dumbarton Oaks and her own home, Reef Point, in Bar Harbor, were Farrand's favorite works. In addition to the designs she was able to bring to fruition there, she was free from society's bias against women in the professional realm. This expression is not always evident in her campus work, particularly at Princeton and Yale, where she was referred to by some as the "bush woman."

Dedicated to their separate lines of work, the Farrands appear to have had a happy and constructive marriage. During the last years of her life, Farrand became even more devoted to her project at Reef Point. The Bar Harbor home, which had been designed for her parents by Arthur Rotch, a Boston architect, had been left to her by her mother, and on seven acres resting against the rocky Atlantic coast, she pursued her horticultural interests with a passion. She planted an enormous variety of flowers, shrubs and ground cover interwoven with secluded paths and protected conifers; through particular attention to microclimate, she was able to grow plants that were native from Newfoundland to North Carolina. She and Max, who in 1940 was elected president of the American Historical Association, hoped to leave it behind as an institution for scholarly and experimental purposes. After his death in 1945, she continued her work there. The grounds ultimately included a test garden of native flora, a collection of single roses thought to be the most complete in the U.S., a herbarium, and a working library containing, among other things, the original garden plans of Gertrude Jekyll.

The difficulty of assuring that the estate would be competently maintained over the years eventually proved too big an obstacle, however. In 1955, at age 82, Farrand had the house torn down, sold the property, and moved many of the plants to a new home she had built several miles away. The contents of her library, the herbarium, her invaluable collection of Gertrude Jekyll's notes and papers, her office correspondence and garden plans were all donated to the landscape architecture department at the University of California at Berkeley, where they are preserved today. Beatrix Farrand lived at Bar Harbor until her death, on February 27, 1959.

Geraldine Farrar

SOURCES:

Balmori, Diana, Diane Kostial McGuire, and Eleanor M. McPeck. *Beatrix Farrand's American Landscapes.* Sagaponack, NY: Sagapress, 1985.

McGuire, Diane Kostial, and Lois Fern. *Beatrix Jones Farrand (1872-1959): Fifty Years of American Landscape Architecture.* Washington, DC: Dumbarton Oaks, Trustees for Harvard University, 1982.

Patterson, Robert W., Lanning Roper, and Mildred Bliss. *Beatrix Jones Farrand, 1872-1959: An Appreciation of a Great Landscape Gardener.* Mrs. Robert Woods Bliss, 1960.

Sicherman, Barbara, and Carol Hurd Green, ed. *Notable American Women.* Cambridge, MA: Belknap Press of Harvard University Press, 1980.

Whitehill, Walter Muir. *Dumbarton Oaks.* Cambridge, MA: Belknap Press of Harvard University Press, 1967.

Blake Harper,
graduate student, Department of Landscape Architecture,
University of Massachusetts, Amherst, Massachusetts

Farrar, Geraldine (1882–1967)

*American soprano. Born on February 28, 1882, in Melrose, Massachusetts; died March 11, 1967, in Ridgefield, Connecticut; only daughter of Sidney Farrar (a businessman and outstanding baseball player) and Henrietta (Barnes) Farrar; studied voice with Mrs. John H. Long, Emma Thursby, Trabadello, Francesco Graziani, and *Lilli Lehmann; married Lou Tellegen (an actor), around 1915 (divorced).*

Debuted at the Berlin Royal Opera as Marguerite in Faust *(1901); debuted at the Metropolitan Opera as Juliette in* Roméo et Juliette; *created the roles of the Goose Girl in Humperdinck's* Königskinder *(1910) and Louise in Charpentier's* Julien; *sang 29 roles at the Met, frequently with Enrico Caruso (1906–22); retired from the stage in 1922.*

Born in the small New England town of Melrose, Massachusetts, Geraldine Farrar was the only daughter of musically gifted parents, and from an early age she was drawn into the fantasy of a singing career. Able to pick out tunes on the piano as a toddler, Farrar sang her first solo in Sunday school at the age of three and soon after began voice lessons. At ten, she sang at a church social; at twelve, she captivated the audience at the Town Hall with her impersonation of *Jenny Lind. As a teenager, Farrar saw her first opera, *Carmen*, starring *Emma Calvé, after which she dedicated herself to becoming an opera singer.

Following her first recital in Boston, Farrar successfully auditioned to study with the famous voice teacher ✥➤ Luisa Cappiani and was accepted, but she turned down the offer in order to go to New York, where she took both acting and voice lessons. Farrar was invited to sing minor roles with the Metropolitan Opera which she also turned down, wanting nothing less than a lead, and opted instead to study in Paris. On October 15, 1901, at age 20, Farrar made her operatic debut as Marguerite in a production of *Faust* at the Berlin Royal Opera. For the next three years, she remained the Royal Opera's leading soprano, singing roles that included Gounod's Juliette in *Roméo et Juliette*, Violetta in *La Traviata*, Zerlina in *Don Giovanni*, Gilda in *Rigoletto*, and Leonora in *Il Trovatore*. A string of successful performances followed in Munich, Warsaw, Monte Carlo, and Paris. She made her New York debut at the Metropolitan on November 26, 1906, as Gounod's Juliette, and for the next 16 years reigned as the opera house's leading diva.

Farrar had an extensive vocal range; her upper register was brilliant and her middle and lower ranges were rich. Her tonal coloration was almost limitless. Her vocal technique was considered exceptional, although some critics felt that she forced the upper register of her voice at times. In addition to her magnificent voice, she was also known as a charismatic dramatic actress and was meticulous in the preparation for her roles. For her most famous role as Cio-Cio-San in Puccini's *Madame Butterfly*, she spent time with the Japanese actress **Fu-ji Ko**, learning how to portray the perfect Japanese lady. (Puccini apparently had different ideas about how the role should be played, and the composer and singer often clashed.) When approaching the role of Tosca, she consulted with *Sarah Bernhardt** for whom Victorien Sardou had written the play on which the opera was based. Farrar's acting was considered realistic and convincing, in large part due to her careful preparation. She also introduced new staging and costuming in her portrayals and many of her innovations became standard practice.

Although Farrar's petite stature and refined features were ideally suited to the romantic heroines of her early career, she later undertook more flamboyant roles, winning acclaim for her Carmen and Zazà. The tenor Enrico Caruso was her frequent partner and a sold-out house was guaranteed if both singers performed. Caruso and Farrar were never surpassed as the Metropolitan Opera's most dynamic vocal duo.

Farrar also enjoyed a second minor career in films, beginning with *Carmen* in 1915, and including *Joan the Woman* (1917), among others. In April 1922, at age 40, she made her 493rd and last appearance at the Met, but she contin-

❧▶ Cappiani, Luisa (b. 1835)

Austrian musician. Name variations: *Louisa Kapp-Young. Born Luisa Young in Austria in 1835; daughter of a tenor and a musically gifted mother; educated in Vienna; married a Mr. Kapp (an Austrian counselor), in 1847 (died 1850); children: two.*

By age six, it was evident that Luisa Young was a musical prodigy, and she was given thorough musical training. She married an Austrian counselor by the name of Kapp at age 17, but her husband died three years later, leaving her with two children. To provide for her family, Luisa began a music career under the name of Kapp-Young. Later, to satisfy the 19th-century preference for Italian musicians, she fused her name into Cappiani. She became a renowned voice teacher.

ued to appear in solo concerts until 1931. After her retirement, she served on the Board of the Metropolitan Opera and was a radio commentator for one season. She wrote two autobiographies, *Geraldine Farrar: The Story of an American Singer by Herself* (1916) and *Such Sweet Compulsion* (1938). Geraldine Farrar died on March 11, 1967, at her home in Ridgefield, Connecticut.

SUGGESTED READING:

Farrar, Geraldine. *Such Sweet Compulsion.* NY: Greystone Press, 1938.

Farrar, Margaret (1897–1984)

American crossword-puzzle editor for the New York Times. *Born Margaret Petherbridge on March 23, 1897, in Brooklyn, New York; died on June 11, 1984, in New York, New York; daughter and one of three children of Henry Wade (an executive with the National Licorice Company) and Margaret Elizabeth (Furey) Petherbridge; graduated from Berkeley Institute, Brooklyn, New York, 1916; B.A. from Smith College, Northampton, Massachusetts, 1919; married John Chipman Farrar (a publisher, co-founder of Farrar, Straus, and author), on May 28, 1926; children: John Farrar; Alison Farrar; Janice Farrar.*

Once called the "world's supreme authority on crosswords," Margaret Farrar was the first editor of the much-revered crossword puzzles of *The New York Times* and also collaborated on the first *Cross Word Puzzle Book*. Before her retirement in 1968, she had edited over 130 collections of puzzles.

A history major at Smith College, Farrar worked in a bank before finding a position with the *New York World*, where, as secretary to the Sunday editor, she was placed in charge of the weekly crossword puzzle, a feature the *World* pioneered in 1913. By 1924, crosswords had become a national pastime, and Farrar and two colleagues from the paper, F. Gregory Hartswick and Prosper Buranelli, edited the *Cross Word Puzzle Book*, the first of its kind. Publisher Simon and Schuster was so dubious about its success that they issued it under another imprint. The book sold nearly 400,000 copies the first year, and Farrar continued to edit puzzle books for Simon and Schuster at the rate of about two a year. Later, she also produced similar books for Pocket Books as well as a *Crossword Puzzle Omnibus* series. In 1942, *The New York Times*, the only major American newspaper to hold out against the crossword-puzzle craze, called on Farrar to edit a puzzle for the *Times Sunday Magazine*. In 1950, under Farrar's editorship, the newspaper introduced a daily crossword puzzle, and over the years also produced 18 collections of puzzles.

Although Farrar constructed many puzzles herself, she usually edited the work of other constructors. She began by working out the puzzle to make sure it was interesting and of sufficient difficulty. In final editing, she would check again for errors and to make sure that words and definition were not being repeated from puzzle to puzzle. Farrar admitted that she made enough mistakes to prove she was human. "During the war we had the Russians taking an important objective two weeks before they really got there," she once related. "I suppose they're still marvelling about the prophetic insight of *Times* reporters and the queer places they hide their news." Farrar was credited with modernizing the numbering system and using more lively definitions based on current events, including the titles of movies, books, and plays. She also introduced topical puzzles that centered on a single theme, like Christmas, food, animals, or sports.

Farrar also edited a mystery book for Farrar, Straus, the publishing company cofounded by her husband. The mother of three children, she was a member of the Children's Book Committee of the Child Study Association (1935–1942) and was active on various school committees. During World War II, she worked for the Red Cross and the War Council in Ossining, New York.

SOURCES:

Current Biography 1955. NY: H.W. Wilson, 1955.

McHenry, Robert, ed. *Famous American Women.* NY: Dover, 1983.

Read, Phyllis J., and Bernard L. Witlieb. *The Book of Women's Firsts.* NY: Random House, 1992.

Farrell, Eileen (1920—)

American soprano. Born on February 13, 1920, in Willimantic, Connecticut; daughter of Michael John Farrell and Catherine (Kennedy) Farrell (erstwhile vaudeville performers, known as "The Singing O'Farrells," and music teachers); studied with Merle Alcock and Eleanor McLellan; married Robert V. Reagan, in 1946; children: Robert V. Reagan; Kathleen Reagan.

Made debut as singer on CBS (1941); sang with the San Carlo Opera in Tampa, Florida (1956); made San Francisco debut in Il Trovatore (1957); made Metropolitan Opera debut (1960); was Distinguished Professor of Music at Indiana University's School of Music (1971–80); was Distinguished Professor of Music at the University of Maine (1984).

As the daughter of ex-vaudeville performers ("The Singing O'Farrells") turned music teachers, Eileen Farrell received musical training at an early age, especially from her mother **Catherine Kennedy Farrell**. After graduating from high school in 1939, Eileen enrolled in art school, but her passion for music eventually led her to New York, where she began vocal instruction with the former Metropolitan Opera contralto **Merle Alcock**, who remained her vocal coach until 1944. After failing an audition for the "Major Bowes' Original Amateur Hour," in 1940, she successfully auditioned for the CBS radio choruses and ensembles. Her impression of the renowned soprano *Rosa Ponselle on a "March of Time" broadcast eventually led to her own weekly half-hour show, "Eileen Farrell Sings," which lasted for six years.

In 1944, Farrell began studying under **Eleanor McLellan**, to whom she attributed much of her success. She transferred to concert work in 1947, making her first extensive U.S. tour during the 1947–48 season and performing in South America two years later. During the 1950–51 season, Farrell made 61 appearances with the New York Philharmonic, establishing a record and beginning a long association with that organization. She remained on the concert circuit for a number of years, also making recordings and guest appearances on popular television shows. In 1955, Farrell sang the role of Medea in a concert performance of the Italian opera on the stage of New York's Town Hall. She subsequently added several additional operatic roles to her repertoire, although her official debut as a member of a major operatic company did not occur until 1957, when she performed in *Il Trovatore* with the San Francisco Opera. On November 9, 1959, Farrell again performed *Il*

Trovatore, with the Richmond Opera Company of Staten Island, where she also made her home. Her neighbors cheered, and Ross Parmenter of *The New York Times* (November 10, 1959) observed: "She was a handsome, appealing, dignified and natural figure on the stage, and she did the greatest part of her acting in the place where it counted most—her voice."

Farrell initiated her professional career in Europe in 1959, with a performance at Gian-Carlo Menotti's Festival of Two Worlds (Spoleto, Italy), where she gave a recital of French and German art songs, and also sang in Verdi's *Requiem.* One exacting Italian critic observed: "We find ourselves witnessing a miracle." Her long-overdue debut with the Metropolitan Opera occurred in December 1960, some 15 years after Edward Johnson, the managing director, had invited her to sing. Her performance in Gluck's *Alcestis* firmly established her as one of America's leading dramatic sopranos, although critics found the overall production disappointing, and a few noted that she had some strain in her upper register. Her recordings, which embraced an eclectic variety of music from opera to the blues, added to her popularity. In 1960, Columbia released three separate Farrell recordings: Puccini arias, French and German art songs, and American popular songs.

Eileen Farrell married a policeman in 1946 and had two children. Choosing to put family concerns before her career development, she explored other media for public performance. Radio and recording better suited her personal needs. Later, she combined singing with teaching, serving as a distinguished professor of music at Indiana University (1971–80) and the University of Maine (1984).

Farrell, M.J. (1904–1996)

See Keane, Molly.

Farrell, Suzanne (1945—)

American ballerina and leading interpreter of the work of choreographer George Balanchine. Name variations: Suzanne Ficker. Born Roberta Sue Ficker on August 16, 1945, in Cincinnati, Ohio; one of three daughters of Robert and Donna Ficker; attended Assumption School, Holy Name School, and the Ursuline Academy, all in Cincinnati; attended Professional Children's School and the Rhodes School, New York; studied ballet at the University of Cincinnati College Conservatory of Music and the School of American

Eileen
Farrell

Ballet; married Paul Mejia (a dancer), on February 21, 1969 (divorced 1997).

Danced with the New York City Ballet (1961–69 and 1975–87); danced with Ballet of the 20th Century (1970–75); became a master teacher at the Kennedy Center (1993); teaches and stages Balanchine ballets for companies in the U.S. and abroad.

Filmography: A Midsummer Night's Dream (1966), Elusive Muse (1996); television: "Dance in America: Choreography by Balanchine" (1977–79), "Sesame Street" (1983), "Love, Sidney" (1983).

Suzanne Farrell, one of America's most celebrated ballerinas, began studying ballet at the age of eight as a cure for "tomboyishness." "I didn't like it much," she told Walter Terry of the *New York World Journal Tribune* (November 20, 1966). "I was so tall that in school recitals, I always had to play the boys' parts, and that didn't make me very enthusiastic." At age 12, Farrell finally got to play her first female role, and, despite picking up a splinter in her foot from the stage floor, dancing became her passion. In 1959, she auditioned for the School of American Ballet, the official school of the New York City Ballet, headed by George Balanchine. She was admitted on a Ford Foundation scholarship, thus beginning her long-time professional and personal association with the renowned choreographer.

In 1960, Farrell made her first New York appearance, as an angel in the American Ballet's annual Christmas production of *The Nutcracker*. Following a short stint in the New York City Ballet's corps de ballet, she became a featured dancer, performing in *Serenade* during a 1962 summer tour. Her first solo performance was that of a young girl in the premiere of John Taras' *Arcade* on March 28, 1963, followed by the leading role opposite Jacques d'Amboise in the new Balanchine-Stravinsky ballet *Movements for Piano and Orchestra*. Farrell continued to add to her repertoire, dancing roles in *La Valse, Concerto Barocco, Liebeslieder Walzer, Donizetti Variations, A Midsummer Night's Dream, Invesiana, Glinka-iana, Stars and Stripes, Prodigal Son*, and *Symphony in C*. She also danced in a trio of new ballets that Balanchine created for her, the romantic *Meditation*, the abstract *Agon*, and *Clarinade*, a jazz ballet featuring Benny Goodman in a clarinet solo. The critics were enthralled by the young dancer. In his review of *Clarinade*, Louis Biancolli wrote in the *New York World-Telegram and Sun* (April 30, 1964): "This lady has everything—the pliant body, the face and figure, the sense of legato, and a unique way of making a cushion of empty space."

Farrell attained overnight stardom with her performance of the full-length ballet *Don Quixote*, which premiered on May 28, 1965. Not only did Balanchine create the ballet for Farrell, but he danced the leading role of Don Quixote himself. As Dulcinea—Quixote's ideal woman—Farrell was called "ravishingly lovely," in both her appearance and her dancing. "Suzanne Farrell was absolutely flawless . . . technically impeccable, light as a soap bubble, perfect in line and style," wrote **Rosalyn Krokover** of *High Fidelity* (August 1965). "This was an exhibition of artistry which put her into the top echelon of world ballerinas." Following her triumph, Farrell was appointed a principal dancer and joined the company in a summer tour of Europe and the Middle East, returning in the fall to roles in *La Sonnambula* and *Raymonda Variations*. In assessing her progress as a dancer, Clive Barnes wrote in *The New York Times* (November 3, 1965): "Miss Farrell, riding in on the surf of her marvelous role in *Don Quixote*, has a lithe, lissome quality to her dancing, and a cool edge to her personality. She is the embodiment of music, and already has a freely expansive dance style. It is . . . experience alone, that should add the flavor of temperament to an already fascinating dancer."

Farrell had a complex relationship with Balanchine, who was notorious for his Pygmalion-Galatea relationships with his young ballerinas. In her 1990 autobiography, she claimed he was "as much a part of my life and my soul as my own self." It may be that Balanchine was deeply in love with his young protégé, despite the fact that he was 40 years her senior and a married man. (He obtained a Mexican divorce from his fifth wife just 17 days before Farrell married Paul Mejia, a lesser dancer in the company, in 1969.) Farrell's professional allegiance to Balanchine, consistently burdened with the weight of his romantic overtures, was torturous, especially given her youth and her strong Catholic beliefs. The relationship was particularly strained by Farrell's marriage and

Suzanne Farrell

reached a point of crisis in May 1969 after both she and her new husband were scratched from the roster of dancers for an evening performance without explanation. Feeling confused and betrayed, Farrell resigned from the company, even though she feared for her professional survival without Balanchine as her guide.

In 1970, Farrell became the principal dancer in the controversial Maurice Béjart Ballet of the 20th Century (Brussels), a company as divergent as possible from Balanchine's. Avant-garde rather than classical, Béjart's male-dominated company used electronic and oriental music as well as classical (including Wagner, a composer Balanchine thought was entirely inappropriate for dance). "Balanchine experimented in extending the human body in space," writes Farrell in her autobiography, "while Béjart, who also used enormous amounts of space, filled it with props, dramatic gestures, voices, elaborate scenery and costumes, and choruses of glamorous, half-naked young men." Although disoriented at the onset, Farrell created many new roles in her years with Béjart, including parts in *Sonate, Les Fleurs du mal, Nijinsky, Clown de Dieu, Golestan, Farah,* and *Erotica,* which Farrell performed during one of the company's first tours in New York. The critics dismissed the work as "expressionistic pop art," although audiences, curious about the unusual new company, flocked to performances.

In 1975, after several letters to Balanchine suggesting a reconciliation, Farrell had a cordial reunion with him and returned to the New York City Ballet amid great speculation about how her reappearance might affect the company. As it turned out, her return ushered in several years of artistic success and financial stability for the enterprise. She performed in the premieres of three major Balanchine ballets, each radically different from the other: *Chaconne, Union Jack,* and *Vienna Waltzes,* a richly romantic work that was perhaps the single most successful ballet in the company's history. In 1978, after suffering a minor heart attack, Balanchine began to show more affection toward Farrell and apologized for his past behavior. In the years that followed, even while battling declining health, Balanchine remained incredibly productive. He created two important ballets for Farrell, *Davidsbündlertänze* and *Mozartiana,* a ballet that had tremendous meaning for the dancer. "Having danced it, I felt that I had just begun to dance," she wrote, "just been borne into life itself. In *Mozartiana* George and I were at peace with each other, and the pervasive calm and corre-

sponding strength I felt while performing it were truly transcendent." Farrell believes that because of this ballet she was able to survive Balanchine's death in 1982. In his will, Balanchine left Farrell two ballets, *Tzigane* and *Don Quixote.*

In February 1979, shortly after her husband had accepted the directorship of the Ballet Guatemala, ushering a period of geographical separation for the couple (Paul was later associated with the Chicago Lyric Ballet), Farrell, who had been unaware that she was pregnant, suffered a miscarriage. After joining Paul in Guatemala for her convalescence, she returned to the company, and despite arthritis in her right hip continued to perform in a number of Balanchine revivals as well as a new ballet by Jerome Robbins, *In Memory of . . . .* In 1986, after announcing her retirement at the end of the season, Farrell underwent successful hip-replacement surgery. With a great deal of hard work, she returned to perform a year later in a revival of *Vienna Waltzes.* In 1988, she traveled to Leningrad (now St. Petersburg) to stage *Scotch Symphony* for the Kirov Ballet, and the ballet was later performed in Leningrad as part of "An Evening of Balanchine." Only after returning from Russia did Farrell feel ready to retire from dancing and move on. On November 26, 1989, the dancer made an emotional farewell appearance in the performance of two ballets, *Vienna Waltzes* and *Sophisticated Lady.* At her curtain call, she was showered with over 5,000 white roses, from which volunteers of the New York City ballet had painstakingly removed every thorn. Farrell likened the experience to being Cinderella at the ball. "I did, of course, think of Mr. B, the little push, the absent partner, the silver rose under my gown. As I said at the time, my last bow will always be to him."

SOURCES:
Farrell, Suzanne, with Toni Bentley. *Holding on to the Air.* NY: Summit Books, 1990.
Moritz, Charles, ed. *Current Biography 1967.* NY: H.W. Wilson, 1967.

RELATED MEDIA:
"Suzanne Farrell Elusive Muse," (90 min.) documentary film (nominated for an Academy Award) by **Anne Belle** and **Deborah Dickson**, 1996; aired on PBS' "Great Performances' Dance in America" series, June 1997.

Barbara Morgan,
Melrose, Massachusetts

Farren, Elizabeth (c. 1759–1829)

English actress and the countess of Derby. Name variations: Eliza Farren. Born around 1759 in Cork, Ireland; died at Knowsley Park, Lancashire, on April 29, 1829;

daughter of George Farren (an apothecary and sur-geon) and an actress mother; married Edward Stanley, 12th earl of Derby, on May 1, 1797; children: three.

Following the death of her husband, the mother of Elizabeth Farren toured the English provinces as an actress to support her three children. In 1777, Elizabeth made her first London appearance at the Haymarket as Miss Hardcastle in *She Stoops to Conquer*. Subsequent successes established her reputation. She was the original Nancy Lovel in George Colman's *Suicide* and appeared at the Drury Lane, both 1778. Tall and slim, elegant and refined, Farren was popular with London's upper crust, and her character was considered beyond reproach, except by jealous rivals. She retired from the stage on April 8, 1797, following her marriage to the earl of Derby. She was a rival of *Frances Abington.

Farren, Ellen (1848–1904).

See Farren, Nellie.

Farren, Nellie (1848–1904)

English actress. Name variations: Ellen Farren; Nelly Farren. Born Ellen Farren in 1848; died in 1904; daughter of Henry Farren (1826–1860, an actor); great-grand-daughter of actor William Farren (1725–1795); grand-daughter of actor William Farren (1786–1861).

Descending from a long line of actors, Nellie Farren was the great-granddaughter of William Farren (1725–1795), who appeared in the first productions of Richard Sheridan's *The School for Scandal* (1777), and *The Critic* (1779), and the granddaughter of the second William Farren (1786–1861), who was known for his portrayal of Sir Peter Teazle in *The School for Scandal*, as well as many Shakespearean roles. Her father Henry Farren was a well-known London actor before going to America where he managed a theater in St. Louis, Missouri. Nellie, whose real name was Ellen, began her career at the Olympic Theater (1864–1868), then was associated with John Hollingshead's company at the Gaiety Theater until her retirement in 1891. Short and slight of frame, she specialized in playing young boys, notably Smike in Charles Dickens' *Nicholas Nickleby*, and Sam Willoughby in Tom Taylor's *Ticket-of-Leave Man*. Her female roles included Lydia Languish in *The Rivals* (1874) and Maria in *Twelfth Night* (1876). Characterized as spirited, humorous, and droll, Farren was quite popular in her day.

Farrenc, Louise (1804–1875)

French concert pianist, composer, teacher, and scholar. Born Jean-Louise Dumont in Paris, France, on May 31, 1804; died in Paris, on September 15, 1875; married Aristide Farrenc (a music publisher).

Louise Farrenc studied with the noted composer Anton Reicha. For over 30 years (1842–73), she was the only woman piano teacher at the Paris Conservatoire and the only woman to hold a post of this rank in the 19th century. Her husband Aristide Farrenc was a music publisher whose compilation of piano music, *Trésor des Pianistes*, was a valuable source of information for performers. After his death in 1865, she continued this project. Her editions of keyboard music from the 16th to the 19th century were of high quality. Farrenc's compositions include three symphonies and a piano concerto. Her piano compositions were praised by Robert Schumann, and modern commentators find her etudes to be full of imaginative touches.

SUGGESTED READING:
Friedland, Bea. "Louise Farrenc (1804–1875): Composer, Performer, Scholar," in *Musical Quarterly*. Vol. 60, no. 2. April 1974, pp. 257–274.
Timbrell, Charles. *French Pianism: An Historical Perspective*. White Plains, NY: Pro/Am Music Resources, 1992.

John Haag,
Athens, Georgia

Farrington, Sara Willis (1811–1872).

See Fern, Fanny.

Farrokhzad, Forugh (1935–1967)

Major Iranian poet who was an early feminist and one of her country's first important female writers. Name variations: Farrough, Foroogh, Furogh, or Furugh Farrukhzad or Farrokhzaad or Farrokhzād. Pronunciation: Four-UGH Farroch-ZHAHD. Born Forugh Farrokhzad in Tehran, Iran, on January 5, 1935; died of injuries sustained in an automobile accident in Tehran, on February 14, 1967; daughter of Mohammed Farrokhzad (a colonel in the Iranian Army) and Turan Vaziri Tabar Farrokhzad; attended a coeducational secondary school and a girls' high school as far as the ninth grade in Tehran; attended the Kamalolmolk Technical School; married Parviz Shapur, in 1951 (divorced 1954); children: one son.

First poems published in Tehran newspapers and magazines (1953); had nervous breakdown (1954); had love affair with Nader Naderpur (1954–56); made first trip abroad (1956); became assistant at

Ebrahim Golestan's film studio and began love affair with Golestan (1958); went to England to study film production (1959); began work as documentary filmmaker (1960); completed documentary film on Iranian lepers (1962); acted in stage production of Six Characters in Search of an Author *(1963); was the subject of UNESCO film (1965).*

Selected works: The Captive *(1955);* The Wall *(1956);* Rebellion *(1958);* Another Birth *(1964);* Let Us Believe in the Beginning of the Cold Season *(1974).*

Forugh Farrokhzad was a prominent Iranian poet and filmmaker during the middle decades of the 20th century. Dying young, she produced only 127 poems, presented to the public in five collections, plus a small number of verses that appeared in various Iranian magazines. Nonetheless, many critics believe she is the greatest female poet in the history of the Persian language and one of the luminaries of Persian literature. In the modern Iranian tradition, her readers often refer to her by her first name alone.

Farrokhzad rebelled against the strictures of her conservative homeland both in her writing and her lifestyle and, as a consequence, faced widespread condemnation. Even in her early years, she explored her identity as a woman and lover in ways that shocked her contemporaries. Maturing as a poet, she went into still more dangerous areas in criticizing aspects of Iranian society and in examining the role of women in general. She was drawn to filmmaking during the last years of her life, and the topics that she took up, such as the treatment of lepers, again showed her critical temperament. The young writer's zest for exploring the world through her poetry was expressed in a letter she wrote to her last lover, Ebrahim Golestan: "I want to pierce everything and as much as possible to penetrate into all things. I want to reach the depths of the earth." For critic Farzaneh Milani, "Forugh's entire canon of work might be considered the first *Bildungsroman* written by and about a woman in Iran."

Forugh Farrokhzad was born in 1935, the third child of an upper-middle-class Iranian family. Her mother was **Turan Vaziri Tabar Farrokhzad**; her father, Mohammed Farrokhzad, was an army colonel who presided over four sons and three daughters. His superior officer, **Reza Shah Pahlavi**, had seized control of the country by means of a coup in 1921 and had begun a process of Westernization. Thus, the Farrokhzads were members of a new urban elite firmly established in a modernizing society.

Forugh, whose name means "brilliance, radiance" in Iranian, grew up in a comfortable house in central Tehran.

The Farrokhzads valued education, and all four of Forugh's brothers attended universities in Germany. But even the three girls in the family obtained some of the benefits of their father's personal library and his educational aspirations: he personally taught them to read. Forugh attended a local coeducational grammar school and, at age 13, entered an all-girl secondary school, the Khosrow Khavar High School. By this time, she was writing poetry in the classic forms of the Persian tradition, and she continued with her literary efforts when she dropped out of ninth grade to enter the Kamalolmolk Technical School to be trained in dressmaking and painting. At this institution, she studied with some of Iran's most prominent artists, including the female painter **Behjat Sadr**.

$\mathcal{S}$he was a lonely woman, an intriguingly unyielding rebel; an adventuress of both body and mind. . . . Relentlessly, she trespassed boundaries and explored new domains.

—**Farzaneh Milani**

Farrokhzad married Parvis Shapur in 1951. He was an Iranian civil servant and amateur writer whom the Farrokhzads reluctantly gave their daughter permission to marry at the age of 16. She had by this time already caused her parents concern as a result of her unwillingness to observe the restrictions on females in traditional Iranian society. Unable to control this wayward daughter and anxious to secure the family honor by protecting her virginity, Farrokhzad's parents were willing to allow her to pursue her desires. She may have felt that Parvis, with his contacts in the Iranian literary world, offered her a degree of cultural stimulation and opportunity she could not get at home.

Within a year, Farrokhzad gave birth to a son Kamyar (meaning "desired friend"), but even as a young mother her mode of dress, with its tight-fitting clothes and short skirts, caused comment among the neighbors. With her husband's encouragement, she continued her writing and began to publish her verse in Tehran's newspapers and magazines. Even these early works contained a feminine viewpoint that impressed many readers in a society in which women's ideas were seldom heard in public.

Her first collection of poetry, *The Captive*, appeared in the summer of 1955, when she was only 20, and caused an immediate stir. A woman poet was a rarity in the Iranian literary world. Although sexual themes had played a large role in the country's literature since World War II, this writer's verses were unique in featuring a candid expression of a female's personal thoughts and feelings. For example, she compared her life to that of a caged bird. Her lines caused an even greater uproar as the young woman narrator described her own love affairs. The most famous poem in the collection, "The Sin," is a forceful description of love-making. In it Farrokhzad wrote: "I sinned, a sin full of pleasure." A second poem contained in the volume, "The Wedding Band," gives the reader a bitter view of marriage as a mechanism for reducing women to a lifetime of servitude. Some Iranian readers and critics believed that the contents of *The Captive* could undermine the moral basis of the society. Certainly the poet drew upon her own experiences in a constricting marriage as an inspiration for such verses.

Forugh Farrokhzad later wrote that she did not believe she was accomplishing "anything extraordinary" with such writing but "this commotion has arisen around me" due to the fact that "no woman before me took steps toward loosening these chains of constraints that have bound women's hands and feet." In the view of her biographer, Michael Hillmann, her accomplishment was all the greater since Farrokhzad was writing "without benefit of models or the psychological or personal support of other women writers." Moreover since she had no facility with foreign languages at this time, she could hardly draw on role models from Western literature. She was, in short, "more on her own in the mid-1950s than almost any other woman writers from Europe or North America during the last two centuries."

In the view of some critics, even in this early collection, the young poet presented a second challenge to Iranian tradition: she showed signs of rejecting the established forms of traditional Persian poetry and began to reflect the influence of Nima Yushif, the country's pioneer of literary "modernism." For example, *The Captive* reflected Yushif's ideas by its use of an identifiable poetic speaker, and thus Farrokhzad joined other young poets who were moving away from traditional forms by the middle years of the 1950s. Nonetheless, her shift in style was only a small literary rebellion compared to the inflammatory content of her works. In fact, at this time, she retained important features of the Persian tradition in writing verse, e.g. in using rhyming couplets and lines of equal length. By Milani's count, only 12 of Forugh's first 86 poems depart from the classical forms of Persian poetry.

In 1954, Forugh divorced Shapur. In doing so, she lost custody of her son, since both Iranian law and the fact that she was known to have committed adultery dictated that the child go to his father. In Hillmann's view, the young poet was troubled by the loss of her child but understood her inability to be either a housewife or mother "because her personal and professional commitment to poetry meant an independent life-style and a renunciation of such conventional feminine roles." Nonetheless, she apparently remained on cordial terms with her former husband. In 1956, she dedicated *The Wall* to him "in memory of our shared past" and with thanks for "his innumerable kindnesses."

Even supposedly worldly and Westernized members of Tehran society gossiped viciously about this young woman, who now published candid poetry in newspapers and magazines about her sexual adventures. In Milani's telling description, in the absence of any women's movement in Iran in the '50s and '60s Forugh Farrokhzad "was a leading lady without a supporting cast, without the unity of community," and her isolation and loneliness were "both brutal and devastating." Combined with the strain resulting from the collapse of her marriage, these pressures led Farrokhzad to a nervous collapse in the fall of 1954. In the aftermath of this episode, both her lifestyle and her rhetoric became more flamboyant. She began a two-year love affair with Nader Naderpur, a prominent Iranian poet. In a new edition of *The Captive*, she declared her intention to free "the hands and feet of art from the chains of rotten conditions" and to help women "to describe what is in their heart without fear and concern for the criticism of others." She lamented the fact that men had been able to describe their experiences of love in poetry without evoking criticism, and she insisted on her right to do the same from a feminine perspective.

Farrokhzad published a second volume of poetry, *The Wall*, containing 25 of her works in 1956. As in *The Captive*, she combined a personal voice and themes drawn from a woman's love life with relatively conventional verse patterns. In this volume, her celebration of physical love was even more candid—and shocking to her Iranian readers—than in her first collection. Shortly afterward, she took her first trip abroad. In a nine-month stay in Europe, she reveled in the freer intellectual and social environment she found there. Traveling in Germany and Italy, she began a new set of poems. Upon her return to Iran, she found work on a local literary magazine and apparently engaged in a new series of love affairs.

Her latest works, from her trip abroad and from her first months back home, appeared in *Rebellion,* a collection of 17 poems published in 1958. *Rebellion* introduced new elements into her work, notably a critical posture toward religious belief. Her style remained largely traditional, however, and she herself remarked about the naive level of her craftsmanship.

Hillmann, Milani, and other critics find a fundamental change in Forugh's work after 1958. From that point until her death less than a decade later, she produced her finest work, which embodied an emphatic acceptance of literary modernism. Moving forward from her first three volumes, in which she had explored her own feelings and identity as a woman in a traditional society, her final two books of poetry show her examining society as a whole. The years after 1958 were also marked by her longstanding relationship with the writer and filmmaker Ebrahim Golestan. As one of Iran's most prominent intellectuals, Golestan offered Farrokhzad both financial and emotional support for her work. Nonetheless, the reaction of acquaintances in Iranian society to her open affair with this married man caused the poet deep anguish. On one occasion, she reportedly tried to commit suicide.

The last two volumes of her work also show a new stylistic daring as Farrokhzad followed the example of Nima Yushif into more flexible rhyming patterns and even into free verse. She became more sophisticated in her use of metaphor, and she developed a new precision in choosing words and in the internal structure of her poems. As Milani put it, Farrokhzad now "allowed the inner landscape of each poem to reveal itself of its own accord and to determine the particular form the poem would assume." She was no longer merely an adventurer in subject matter but "an adventurer in language and poetic forms as well."

Following a trip to England in 1959 to study English and filmmaking, Farrokhzad returned to Iran to take up work as a filmmaker. For the remainder of her life, she was active as a producer, editor, and actress in various filmmaking projects. Her most prominent production was a documentary on the Iranian leper colony at Tabriz, *The House is Black,* which she filmed in 1962.

By the early 1960s, Iran was in increasing turmoil as fundamentalist Islamic religious opposition grew against the government's program of Westernization. Farrokhzad remained apart from these dramatic political developments. Her most notable achievement in these years was to begin work as a stage actress with a successful role in a production of Luigi Pirandello's *Six Characters in Search of an Author* in 1963.

Another Birth, the collection of 35 poems she published in 1964, saw Forugh Farrokhzad recognized as a major figure on the Iranian literary scene. Some critics in her country disregarded any mention of her gender and simply hailed Farrokhzad as a major poet. Forugh herself considered *Another Birth* as a sign of her maturation as a writer. It reflected a wider set of themes than had concerned her before and expressed them with a deepened set of images than those of her previous works. Her poetic voice, writes Hillmann, "no longer seems to represent merely her autobiographical self in the expression of feelings and views, but rather all Iranians with similar feelings."

The social commentary and satirical thrust of *Another Birth* was embodied in "O Jewel-Studied Land," in which the poem's narrator criticizes a society that has lost its bearings in a frenzy of technological advances and superficial Westernization. The poem's title is drawn from a popular patriotic song of the time. On social occasions in which she encountered members of the Shah's family, Farrokhzad was equally frank in expressing her criticism of contemporary Iranian life. By 1965, she had become enough of a figure on the international scene for her life to become the subject of a film produced by UNESCO.

In a final trip to Europe in the spring of 1966, Farrokhzad visited England and Italy. She reportedly encountered a Rom (Gypsy) fortuneteller at this time who warned her of a serious accident in her future. Shortly after her return to Tehran, she and Golestan were in fact injured in an automobile accident in the Iranian countryside. Nevertheless, she continued to live her life at a frantic pace, devoting much of her energy toward learning English. Her immediate plans for the future included a role on the stage playing the title character in an Iranian production of George Bernard Shaw's *Saint Joan.* Before she could realize this ambition, however, Farrokhzad was involved in a second, and this time fatal, accident on February 14, 1967. While traveling by car through Tehran to pick up a reel of film for Golestan, she swerved to avoid a vehicle approaching from the opposite direction and crashed into a wall. She was thrown from her car and died of the resulting injuries to her head.

Forugh Farrokhzad remains a singular figure in the history of modern Iranian literature. Writes Hillmann: "[N]o feminine voice in the 1970s emerged in the arts with Farrokhzad's intensity and audacity, in part because no equally talented woman proved willing to take the risks Farrokhzad took or pay the price that she paid." Although her total literary output could be held in a single, relatively small volume, she left a vivid memory of a talented woman who had challenged the mores of her conservative society in both her work and the way she lived her life.

A final volume of her work, *Let Us Believe in the Beginning of the Cold Season*, appeared in print in 1972. This posthumous collection introduced new, darker themes into Farrokhzad's writing: loneliness and death. She now spoke of herself, although still in her early 30s, as "a lonely woman on the threshold of a cold season," and she explored the themes of death with terrible images of deformed babies and vicious knife-wielding murderers. Paradoxically, this same volume also contain poems of profound lyrical beauty.

For critics like Milani, Farrokhzad's tragic death was doubly sad because "she had just, in her last six or seven years, reached her poetic maturity and had finally found her own voice," and the brilliant young woman poet thus "left much of her life's work undone." For John Zubizarreta, she was "a daring, innovative writer" who had refused the limits of a society that traditionally inhibited the growth of females. She had produced "a poetry that addresses poignantly and forcefully the sensuality and grace of love, the sweetness and grace of love, the sweetness of personal and social freedom."

SOURCES:

Hillmann, Michael C. *A Lonely Woman: Forugh Farrokhzad and Her Poetry*. Washington, DC: Three Continents Press and Mage Publishers, 1987.

———. *Iranian Culture: A Persianist View*. Lanham, MD: University Press of America, 1990.

Klein, Leonard S., general ed. *Encyclopedia of World Literature in the 20th Century*. Rev. ed. Vol. 2. NY: Frederick Ungar, 1981.

Mahdavi, Shireen. "Captivity, Rebellion, and Rebirth," in *Parnassus: Poetry in Review*. 12–13, 1985, pp. 303–400.

Milani, Farzaneh. "Furogh Farrokhzad," in *Persian Literature*. Edited by Ehsan Yarshater. Albany, NY: Biblioteca Persica, 1988.

Uglow, Jennifer S., ed. *The Continuum Dictionary of Women's Biography*. Rev. ed. NY: Continuum, 1989.

Zubizarreta, John. "The Woman Who Sings No, No, No: Love, Freedom, and Rebellion in the Poetry of Forugh Farrokhzad," in *World Literature Today*. Vol. 66. Summer 1992, pp. 421–26.

SUGGESTED READING:

Najmabadi, Afsaneh, ed. *Women's Autobiographies in Contemporary Iran*. Cambridge, MA: Harvard University Press, 1990.

Neil M. Heyman,
Professor of History, San Diego State University,
San Diego, California

Fassbaender, Brigitte (1939—)

German mezzo-soprano. Name variations: Fassbander or Fassbänder. Born on July 3, 1939, in Berlin, Germany; studied with her father, baritone Willi Domgraf-Fassbaender, at Nuremberg Conservatory (1957–61).

Debut at the Bayerische Staatsoper in Munich (1961); debuted at Covent Garden (1971), Salzburg (1973), Metropolitan Opera (1974); made a Bavarian Kammersängerin, a title awarded a singer of outstanding merit (1970).

Brigitte Fassbaender's fame grew slowly—in part, because her voice had a lean, reedy sound and was not conventionally beautiful; in part, because she preferred to dedicate her time to concertizing rather than to the opera. Nonetheless, in the latter half of her career she focused on Wagner and has been associated with many operatic roles. Though her vocal abilities were somewhat flawed, her interpretive ability was matchless. Her career continued to thrive as she addressed her weaknesses and used her strengths. When Fassbaender reached 50, she was considered one of the finest female lieder singers on the concert stage. She appeared less frequently in opera but each appearance was greeted with enthusiasm by critics and fans alike. Fassbaender made many recordings that document her great talent.

SUGGESTED READING:

Current Biography. NY: H.W. Wilson, 1994.

John Haag,
Athens, Georgia

Fassett, Cornelia (1831–1898)

American portrait painter. Born Cornelia Adele Strong in Owasco, New York, on November 9, 1831; died in Washington, D.C., on January 4, 1898; daughter of Captain Walter Strong and Elizabeth (Gonsales) Strong; married Samuel Montague Fassett (an artist and photographer); children: seven.

Cornelia Fassett, one of the most successful portrait painters of the mid-19th century, is best known for her *Electoral Commission in Open*

Session, which hangs in the U.S. Capitol. She was born Cornelia Adele Strong in Owasco, New York, on November 9, 1831, the daughter of Captain Walter Strong and **Elizabeth Gonsales Strong.** She studied watercolor in New York City with the English painter J.B. Wandesforde and reportedly studied abroad for three years after her marriage in 1851, at age 20, to the artist and photographer Samuel Fassett.

In Chicago, to which the couple moved in 1855, she tended to her growing family (they would have seven children) and painted, while her husband ran a photographic studio. Her portraits, which included a number of prominent Chicago citizens, established her reputation, and in 1874 she was elected an associate member of the Chicago Academy of Design.

In 1875, the family moved to Washington, D.C., where Samuel took a job as a photographer to the Supervising Architect of the Treasury Department. In a studio located atop a music store on Pennsylvania Avenue, Fassett painted such luminaries as presidents Ulysses S. Grant, Rutherford B. Hayes, and James A. Garfield, and Vice President Henry Wilson. She was elected to the Washington Art Club and became part of the city's lively social scene.

In February 1877, Fassett was inspired to memorialize the historical meeting of the Electoral Commission, which convened in the Supreme Court chamber to settle disputed ballots in four states in the Hayes-Tilden presidential election. The large canvas depicting the prominent Washington figures who attended the hearing took two years to complete and includes more than 200 individual portraits both from life and from photographs taken by her husband. "Each face is so turned that the features can easily be studied," wrote *Pearson's Magazine* (1903), "and the likeness of nearly all are so faithful as to be a source of constant wonder and delight." **Charlotte Rubinstein** notes that although the painting might appear naive by modern-day standards it was then "a *tour de force* of realism, very much in tune with the nineteenth century predilection for 'casts of thousands.'" After the painting was completed in 1879, there was some controversy over whether the government should buy it. The work was eventually purchased in 1886 for $7,500 (some sources quote a purchase price as high as $15,000) and hung in the Senate wing of the Capitol.

Fassett continued to win acclaim for her individual portraits. Her 1878 portrait of New York historian *****Martha J.R. Lamb** was de-scribed as capturing "the quintessence of upper-class American life. . . . The portrait of an energetic New York lady is like an illustration of an *****Edith Wharton** novel." In her later years, Fassett concentrated on miniature painting. While rushing from one Washington party to get to another, the artist was stricken with a fatal heart attack and died at the age of 58.

SOURCES:

McHenry, Robert, ed. *Famous American Women.* NY: Dover, 1983.

Rubinstein, Charlotte Streifer. *American Women Artists.* Boston, MA: G.K. Hall, 1982.

Barbara Morgan,
Melrose, Massachusetts

Fastrada (d. 794)

*Queen of the Franks. Name variations: Fastrade. Died on August 10, 794; daughter of Count Rudolph and Luitgarde; became fourth wife of Charles I also known as Charlemagne (742–814), king of the Franks (r. 768–814), Holy Roman emperor (r. 800–814), in 783; children: *Theodrada, abbess of Argenteuil; *Hiltrude. Fastrada was married to Charlemagne for 11 years.*

Fatima.

Variant of Fatimah.

Fatimah (605/11–632/33 CE)

Most famous and controversial woman from early Islamic history who, though honored by all Muslims as a participant in the first two formative decades of Islam, is especially significant to Shi'is of various sects since they trace their legitimacy to Muhammad through her and her descendants. Name variations: Fatima. Namesake of the Fatimid dynasty. Born in Mecca between 605 and 611 CE; died in 632 or 633 CE; daughter of the Prophet Muhammad and Khadijah; sister of Zaynab, Umm Kulthum, and Ruqaiyah; married `Ali b. Abi Talib, the fourth caliph of Islam; children: two daughters, Zaynab and Umm Kulthum; two sons, Hasan and Husain (the Shi'ite martyr, al-Husain b. `Ali), and possibly a third son named Muhassin who died in infancy.

Fatimah is more powerful as a timeless abstraction than as a historical person. She is noted more for her offspring than for her accomplishments. Although voluminous biographical literature about this holy woman exists, concrete historical facts are scarce. She is not mentioned in the *Qur'an,* and the poetry of the first century A.H. (*Anno Hegirae,* the year of the emigration from

Mecca in 622) omits her altogether. The *Tabakat* of the historian Ibn Sa'd gives a full account of `Ali without ever naming his wife. The principle source of information about Fatimah is the *hadiths,* or "reports." The *hadiths* preserve details of the *sunna*—a reference to the "way of the Prophet" or the collective habits and sayings of Muhammad. The *hadiths* augment the *Qur'an* in providing further information on how to lead a worthy life; for the Prophet and his family are held by Muslims to be models of virtue. Although it is through the *hadith* literature that we have the clearest picture of Fatimah, even this source preserves only random details about her life.

Fatimah was the daughter of Muhammad and his first wife *Khadijah. She was born in the sacred city of Mecca, which, even in pre-Islamic Arabia, was a site of pilgrimage where warring tribes suspended animosities and came together during months of truce to worship at the ancient shrine of the Ka`aba. Scholars have not reached consensus on exactly when Fatimah was born or what position she held in the family. Her importance to subsequent history has led some to assume that she had the distinguished position of the eldest of four daughters, although there is no solid evidence for this claim. It is partially motivated by the aversion of some Muslim biographers to the suggestion that Fatimah was born to Khadijah when she was an old woman.

The most loved of women to the prophet of God is Fatimah.

—Syed Ameer Ali

We know Fatimah was wed shortly after 622, and if she had been the oldest of the daughters she would have been between fifteen and twenty when she married. It was a matter of prestige for girls to marry between the ages of nine and twelve. For this reason, some scholars, predominantly Shi'ite, claim that Fatimah was not the eldest, but the youngest daughter because they reject the possibility that a woman of such holiness could have remained single past the ordinary period of celibacy—a condition abhorred by Arab women of the time. For Muhammad to permit Fatimah to remain unmarried when she was first nubile would constitute callous indifference on the part of the Prophet towards his daughter. Further, many scholars argue that Muhammad's daughters would undoubtedly have been ardently sought after as marriage partners, so Fatimah, the most excellent of the children, would certainly have been betrothed at a young age. The best guess is that Fatimah was born shortly before Muhammad's

first revelation in 610. She was raised in a household with her sisters (two brothers died in infancy) and `Ali, her kinsman and future husband. One of the few glimpses we get of her childhood comes in 619 at Khadijah's death as Muhammad comforts his weeping daughter.

The message of Islam that Muhammad delivered to the people of Mecca was initially unpopular among the powerful elite of the city. The Prophet and his earliest converts suffered ostracization and active persecution. At one point during this period, Muhammad was praying at the Ka`aba when his detractors pelted him with refuse consisting of goat entrails used in pagan sacrifice. Enraged, Fatimah rushed to her father's defense, shouted at the offenders, and cleaned the filth from him. In 622, the Prophet and his followers, including Fatimah, left Mecca for the nearby city of Medina where they could practice their religion unmolested.

Shortly after the small group of Muslims arrived in Medina, Fatimah was married. She seems to have had a melancholy temperament, was physically frail, often ill, and is seldom described as beautiful. Fatimah had no dowry, despite the wealth her mother acquired through trading ventures. These disadvantages aside, the Prophet's daughter had many suitors of very high quality. By divine inspiration, Muhammad settled on his cousin, `Ali.

Fatimah and her husband lived in close proximity to Muhammad and shared his hardships; the newly established community was tight-knit and poor. Fatimah's biographers paint a picture of a young housewife, working hard to support her family under strained circumstances. She was a devoted daughter, loyal to her father and committed to the message he preached. All the *hadith* collections refer to the assistance Fatimah gave Muhammad in the struggle for the survival of Islam. When the Muslims returned defeated from the Battle of Uhud, Fatimah tended Muhammad's wounds and washed his sword. She accompanied her father on the military mission in which Mecca surrendered and was present at the farewell pilgrimage when Muhammad solidified the rites of the *hajj* (pilgrimage) and left Mecca for the last time. The *Sahih* and the *Musnad* indicate that Muhammad stopped each day at this daughter's door to announce that it was time for the early morning prayer. She preached the precepts of Islam to her friends and children and modeled the importance, particularly, of fasting and almsgiving by going without food in order to feed the poor, even when food was scarce.

According to Muslim tradition, there have been only four perfect women; Fatimah and her mother were two of them. Both of these women were perfect, in part because they performed their functions admirably. Modern distinctions between public and private life did not exist in 7th-century Medina, yet primary roles and expectations for women in early Islamic culture were distinct from those of men. After her duty to submit to Allah, the essential obligations of a woman were to produce children and provide a healthy environment in which they could grow. Fatimah did this. She had two sons, Hasan and Husain, and two daughters, **Zaynab** and **Umm Kulthum** who was born in the last year of her mother's life. Shi'ite tradition claims that Fatimah and `Ali had a third son named Muhassin who died in infancy.

Although idealized as a loving daughter and devoted mother, Fatimah found her role as wife difficult. She remained loyal to `Ali, but their relationship was stormy. When Muhammad first offered his daughter to `Ali, he declined the match on the grounds that he was too poor. Muhammad won his acquiescence by giving him booty acquired at the Battle of Badr. Fatimah was no more eager than `Ali. `Ali was a brave soldier but was indeed penurious and, according to some reports, lacked intelligence. The couple argued frequently and loudly, so much so that Muhammad often was forced to play the role of peacemaker. Tradition has it that Fatimah was compelled to take on chores too taxing for her. She ground corn and carried water, doing much of the work that in a family of her social status would normally have been left to servants, but `Ali was not able, or perhaps willing, to procure assistance for his wife. Fatimah was even physically abused by `Ali to the extent that she sought the protection of her father. `Ali became so exasperated with his wife that he neglected the conjugal bed and slept in the mosque. Fatimah objected when `Ali wanted a second wife and successfully sought her father's support against her husband. "She is," said Muhammad, "a portion of my flesh. Whoever hurts her, has hurt me, and whoever hurts me has hurt God." `Ali refrained from remarrying while Fatimah was alive, but after she died he took nine more wives.

Muhammad finally felt compelled to seal off the door between his and Fatimah's apartments. This was only partially because of the rows between his daughter and son-in-law. Fatimah was also at odds with *A'ishah, Muhammad's favorite wife and the daughter of Abu Bakr, Muhammad's successor. A'ishah was very

resourceful and frequently exercised more sway over the Prophet than Fatimah did. Two spheres of influence developed around Muhammad: one represented by A'ishah and Abu Bakr, one by Fatimah and `Ali. Envy, disappointment, scarce resources, and competition for Muhammad's attention strained relations among the Prophet's wives and daughter.

Muhammad died in 632. Despite A'ishah's jealous supervision of the sickbed, Fatimah was able to make her way to her dying father in time to hear him predict that she would be the first member of the family to follow him to Paradise. Muhammad left no provision for a successor to lead the growing Muslim community. Some felt that `Ali was the logical choice because of his relationship to the Prophet, because he had been the first male convert to Islam, and because, according to many, Muhammad had, in fact, designated that `Ali follow him. However, Abu Bakr, who was older than `Ali and commanded more respect in the community, led the public prayers in Muhammad's stead, and by general agreement, became the first caliph (successor). A rift developed between `Ali's party (called Alids) and the supporters of Abu Bakr, and Fatimah suffered in this conflict. After Muhammad's death, Abu Bakr refused Fatimah lands at Fadak and Khaybar which she felt were rightly hers because they had been her father's personal property. When Fatimah contested the disposition of the properties, Abu Bakr responded, "Prophets do not leave heirs." At one point in this tumultuous year of the Prophet's death, `Umar (a partisan of Abu Bakr) and his men arrived at `Ali's house to coerce him and his supporters to recognize the leadership of Abu Bakr. Fatimah came into the street threatening to uncover her hair—a sign of great distress. When she became ill a few months later, she shunned A'ishah and refused even to see Abu Bakr. Because of this enmity, `Ali delayed pledging allegiance to the first caliph until after Fatimah's death.

Fatimah died of consumption in the same year as her father. Her funeral was prepared in haste and carried out at night. `Ali would finally become caliph years later. As Abu Bakr lay dying, he designated `Umar his successor. When `Umar died in 644, `Uthman followed him. `Ali became the fourth caliph in 656, but by that time the *umma* (community of believers) was rent by factional conflict. The division between Sunni and Shi'ite Muslims can be traced to the friction over leadership which followed the death of the Prophet. A Shi'i is one who belongs to the Shi'ah or party of `Ali. Shi'is hold that `Ali was the rightful successor to Muhammad and view Abu Bakr, `Umar, and `Uthman as interlopers. `Ali was murdered in 661 by a disgruntled supporter.

`Ali's eldest son by Fatimah, Husan, relinquished leadership to Mu'awiya, a member of a powerful Meccan clan and governor of Syria. Mu'awiya was not a part of the Prophet's family; in fact, his clan had persecuted Muhammad and was late to adopt Islam. The Alids rejected Mu'awiya insisting that the charisma required for guidance of the *umma* inheres only in descendants of the Prophet. As Fatimah was the only child of Muhammad who survived him, it is through her, they claimed, that the spiritual authority to guide Islam is transferred. For Shi'ite Muslim, `Ali was the first Imam (rightful leader of Islam invested with infallible guidance by God). Hasan was the second Imam and Fatimah's second son, Husain, was the third.

By the time Mu'awiya died and his son, Yazid, succeeded him, there was enough opposition to this new Umayyad dynasty that Husain was successful in rallying the support, especially in Iraq, to attempt a coup. In 680, as Husain and a small group of his supporters were advancing through Iraq, they were ambushed by Yazid's troops near Karbala. The entire company was massacred, except the women and children. Fatimah's daughter, Zaynab, was with her brother at Karbala. She saved one of Husain's sons, although two of her own were slaughtered. Zaynab shepherded the prisoners from Karbala to Damascus where they were held captive. She persuaded the caliph to spare Husain's son, `Ali Zain al-Abidin, who was eventually rescued and assumed the title of Imam. Although the position carried no political power, in him the lineage of Muhammad through Fatimah was preserved.

After the murder of Husain, factionalism associated with the Alids became permanent. Although the Shi'is have always been a minority in Islam—often persecuted and driven underground—they have continued to argue that leadership of the *umma* rightly inheres in the house of the Prophet through his daughter Fatimah, her husband, `Ali, and their son, Husain. Some later extremists even believed that the revelation of Islam had been intended for `Ali and that the angel Gabriel gave it to Muhammad by mistake. From 909 to 1171, a Shi'ite regime came to power in North Africa and then Egypt. To underscore their legitimacy, they called themselves Fatimids because of their leader's descent from the woman through whom the charisma of the Prophet was transferred.

`Ali and Husain are honored at their tombs in Najaf and Karbala, both in Iraq, and venerated by Shi'is in annual ceremonies. Since Fatimah's place of burial is unknown, she is principally remembered through her name. Generations of Muslims have called their girls Fatimah after the holy daughter of the Prophet. One of these women, **Fatimah al-Ma'sumah**, achieved fame during the reign of al-Ma'mun (r. 813–833) for piety and her defense of the rights of `Ali's progeny. She is buried in the sacred city of Qum and her golden-domed shrine is a principle site of pilgrimage for Shi'ite Muslims.

Although Fatimah led an unremarkable life, stories about her seemingly prosaic activities are charged with political significance. Because Fatimah is the linchpin between Muhammad and the Shi'ite sects and because she is the conduit through which the Shi'is have claimed political and spiritual power, a "correct" presentation of her in the literature is critical to them. Discussions about Fatimah's date of birth and age at marriage, for instance, are not dispassionate. In fact, there is little that is neutral about the life of Fatimah. For example, some Sunni writers have claimed that when Fatimah was too weak to breast-feed her sons, one of the wives of Abbas nursed them for her. This claim insinuates Abbas, the uncle of Muhammad, into the immediate family of the prophet. It was through the lineage of Abbas that the Abbasids claimed the caliphate in 750 when they successfully overthrew the existing Umayyad dynasty. Connections to Muhammad, especially through his most famous child, Fatimah, have provided powerful propagandistic leverage throughout the history of Islam.

A seemingly inconsequential passage in the *Qur'an* (iii. 59–60) sets the framework for an anecdote that has assumed great significance, especially to Shi'is. Muhammad had an important meeting with Christian envoys from Nadjran, and he pointedly chose to bring Fatimah and her family with him. This scene lends support to another more powerful story wherein, on one occasion, Muhammad wrapped Fatimah, `Ali, and their two sons in his cloak and said, "These are the members of my family." This group of five persons has since been known as the *Ashab al-Kisa* (privileged ones of the cloak). *Sura* (chapter) 33 of the *Qur'an* states, "Allah will cleanse you, people of the house, and purify you." Shi'is have asserted that the "people of the house" is a reference to Fatimah and her family, and on this basis have claimed a special purity for their sect.

The early collections of *hadiths* tend to portray Fatimah as very human, with foibles and failings, but later collections of the tradition, especially Shi'ite works, ascribe to this woman—the person closest to Muhammad—increasingly elevated virtues and privileges. She is "the queen of the women of Paradise." Similar to *Mary the Virgin, mother of Jesus, many Muslims consider Fatimah *batul,* or virgin. On the day of resurrection, she will be on a level with her father, and as she passes an angel will demand, "Lower your eyes, ye mortals." The Shi'ite *mahdi* (savior) will be born from her line. In much of the literature, Fatimah is pitted against A'ishah in a fierce competition for the ideal of female perfection.

The obscurity of Fatimah's life has lent itself to manipulation by generations of Muslim historians and hagiographers. Those who endow Fatimah with all physical graces and mental gifts have embellished her biography with stories of prophecies, miracles, and her pivotal role in early Islam. Sunnis, who tend to view the spiritual inheritance of Muhammad as diffused throughout the *umma* and not the special property of the Prophet's family, although they honor Fatimah, portray her less the saint and more a model of womanhood.

As is generally the case in revolutionary movements, women played a significant role in the early development of Islam. The wives and daughters of Muhammad were trusted and respected councilors. Khadijah was Muhammad's first convert, and A'ishah played a particularly active political and military role in the early Medinese community. Many of the sayings of the Prophet that comprise the *hadith* literature were transmitted by women. Fatimah's recognition is well deserved because she was a player in this drama. However much her role in history may have been thrust upon her, or her legend embroidered to suit later political advocacies, Fatimah was a courageous woman. Coping with loneliness, poverty, ill-health, and cataclysmic social change, she was dutiful to her family and devoted to Islam.

SOURCES:

Denny, Frederick Mathewson. *An Introduction to Islam.* 2nd ed. New York, 1994.

Encyclopaedia of Islam. New ed. Leiden, 1954.

Haykal, Muhammad Husayn. *The Life of Muhammad.* 8th ed. Translated by Isma'il Ragi A. al Faruqi. Indianapolis, 1976.

Keddie, N., and B. Baron, eds. *Women in Middle Eastern History: Skirting Boundaries in Sex and Gender.* 1991.

Lammens, Henri. *Fatima et les filles de Mahomet.* Rome, 1912.

Stern, Gertrude. "The First Women Converts in Early Islam," in *Islamic Cultures.* Vol. 13, 1939.

Waddy, Charis. *Women in Muslim History.* London, 1980.

Watt, W. Montgomery. *Muhammad at Medina.* Oxford, 1956.

SUGGESTED READING:

Abbot, Nabia. *A'isha, The Beloved of Muhammad.* Chicago, 1941.

Ahmed, Leila. *Women and Gender in Islam: Roots of a Modern Debate.* New Haven, 1992.

Muir, William. *The Life of Muhammad from Original Sources.* Edinburgh, 1923.

Watt, W. Montgomery. *Muhammad at Mecca.* Oxford, 1953.

Martha Rampton,
Assistant Professor of History,
Pacific University, Forest Grove, Oregon

Faucit, Helena Saville (1817–1898)

English actress. Name variations: Helen Faucit; Lady Martin, or Mrs. Theodore Martin. Born Helena Saville Faucit in London, England, in 1817; died at her home near Llangollen, Wales, on October 31, 1898; daughter of John Saville Faucit (an actor); married Sir Theodore Martin (a British poet, translator, and essayist), in 1851.

An eminent actress of the 19th-century British stage, Helena Faucit was part of a large theatrical family; her mother and father, as well as all of her five siblings, were associated with the theater in one way or another. She received her early training from Percival Farren, the great-uncle of *Nellie Farren, and made her debut at a theater near London in 1833, playing Juliet in Shakespeare's *Romeo and Juliet.* Although she was received "kindly" by the public, the critics felt that she was too much of a novice to succeed in such a difficult role. (At the time, actresses usually did not attempt Juliet until they were near 50, although the role as written is that of a 14-year-old girl.) During her London debut in January 1836, playing Julia in Sheridan Knowles' *The Hunchback,* Faucit was nearly overcome by stage fright but managed to save her performance by focusing on a friend who was in the audience. From that time on, she apparently gained confidence, for over the next 15 years her career flourished. She played opposite William Charles Macready in roles that included Desdemona, Cordelia, Portia, Lady Macbeth, Rosalind, and, of course, Juliet, which she grew into quite nicely. She also portrayed the leading female roles in Robert Bulwer-Lytton's *The Lady of Lyons* (1838), *Richelieu* (1839), and *Money* (1840), as well as Robert Browning's *Strafford* (1842), and *Blot on the Scutcheon* (1843). Among her successful tours was a visit to Paris in 1844–45, where she acted with Macready in several Shakespearean plays.

A word-portrait of the actress, written during her time, describes "a tall, elegant figure; a frank, sweet, expressive, good face; large dark-brown eyes, full of eager intelligence; and a stately head, finely poised upon a swan-like neck, and crowned with luxuriant dark hair that falls in abundant curls on her snowy, sloping shoulders." Mrs. S.C. Hall (*Anna Maria Hall), a critic who saw Faucit play numerous characters, reviewed her signature role of Pauline in *The Lady of Lyons*, calling it "a perfect performance," that appeared seamless and natural. "[I]t is also the perfection of art where art is never, even for a moment, seen; the result of careful and continuous study, but with the ease and force of nature in every word, look, and motion." Detractors of the actress frequently accused her of imitating her famous co-star, calling her "Macready in white muslin." Evidently, it was not unusual for actors who played with Macready to pick up a few of his mannerisms.

In 1851, Faucit married Theodore Martin (afterward Sir), after which she acted only occasionally for charity. One of her last appearances was as Beatrice, on the opening of the Shakespeare Memorial at Stratford-on-Avon, on April 23, 1879. In 1881, *Blackwood's Magazine* carried the first of her *Letters on some of Shakespeare's Heroines,* which were later published in book form as *On Some of Shakespeare's Female Characters* (1885).

Helena Faucit died at her home near Llangollen, in Wales, on October 31, 1898. There is a portrait figure of Faucit in the Shakespeare Memorial, and the marble pulpit in the Shakespeare church—with her portrait as Saint *Helena (c. 255–329)—was given in her memory by her husband.

Barbara Morgan,
Melrose, Massachusetts

Fauconberg, Mary (1636–1712).

See Cromwell, Mary.

Faulwetter, Mrs. R.C. (1895–1983).

See Farr, Wanda K.

Fauset, Crystal Bird (1893–1965)

First African-American woman to be elected to a state legislature. Born Crystal Dreda Bird on June 27, 1893, in Princess Anne, Maryland; died on March 28, 1965, in Philadelphia, Pennsylvania; youngest of nine children of Benjamin (a school principal) and Portia E. (Lovett) Bird; attended public school in Boston; graduated from Boston Normal School, 1914; B.A. from Columbia University's Teachers College, New York, 1931; married Arthur Huff Fauset (an educator), in June 1931 (divorced 1944).

Born in Pennsylvania in 1893, Crystal Fauset grew up in Boston, where she lived with her aunt following the death of her parents. After graduating from Normal School in 1914, she taught school for three years. Fauset began to speak out about the concerns of the black American community and race relations in general, through her association with the Young Women's Christian Association (YWCA) and the American Friends Service Committee. In 1931, she received her bachelor's degree from Columbia University and also married Arthur Fauset, the principal of Philadelphia's Singerley School. They would divorce in 1944. During the early 1930s, thinking she could reach more people through political action, Fauset joined the administrative staff of the Works Progress Administration (WPA) of Philadelphia and organized the Philadelphia Democratic Women's League. In 1936, she became the director of black women's activities for the National Democratic Committee and, as reported in the *Philadelphia Record,* started "selling Roosevelt humanitarianism to Negro housewives."

In 1938, with the backing of party leaders, Fauset ran for Democratic representative in the Pennsylvania legislature. Believing that low economic status was the largest problem in the black community, she vowed to fight for "more relief, more WPA and better housing." Conducting her campaign mainly by telephone, she beat her opponent by 7,000 votes, in a district that was predominately white, and took her place as the only woman among six black members in the Pennsylvania legislature at the time. Her legislative tenure was marked by a number of impassioned speeches, during which she encouraged all citizens, especially black women, to become actively involved in community activities and to use the power of the ballot to alter the course of history.

Late in 1939, after less than a year in her legislative post, Fauset resigned to join the WPA as assistant state director of the Education and Recreation Program, hoping that it would give her a broader opportunity to improve race relations. In 1941, as a result of her leadership in Roosevelt's election campaigns and her friendship with *Eleanor Roosevelt, Fauset was named special consultant to the director of the Office of Civilian Defense. In 1944, she resigned that post to take part in the Democratic election campaign, but she subsequently withdrew from the

Democratic National Committee over a dispute with party leadership and switched her support to the Republican candidate for president, Governor Thomas E. Dewey. Fauset helped establish the United Nations Council of Philadelphia in 1945 and served as an officer until 1950, the year she attended the founding of the United Nations in San Francisco. She later embarked on speaking tours in India, the Middle East and Nigeria, and also pursued a diplomatic post in Africa.

By 1955, when Fauset was awarded a second Meritorious Service Medal from the Commonwealth of Pennsylvania (her first was awarded in 1939), she was becoming disenchanted with politics. Despite her disappointments, she remained active in political and educational concerns until her death on March 28, 1965.

SOURCES:
Smith, Jessie Carney, ed. *Notable Black American Women.* Detroit, MI: Gale Research, 1992.

Barbara Morgan,
Melrose, Massachusetts

Fauset, Jessie Redmon (1882–1961).

See Women of the Harlem Renaissance.

Fausta (d. 324).

See Helena (c. 255–329) for sidebar.

Fausta (fl. 600s)

Byzantine empress. Flourished in the 600s CE; married Constantine III (also known as Constans II), Byzantine emperor (r. 641–668); children: Constantine IV (r. 668–685); Heraclius; and Tiberius.

Fausta, Cornelia (b. 88 BCE)

Roman noblewoman. Born about 88 BCE; daughter of Lucius Cornelius Sulla (consul, 88–80 BCE, and Roman dictator, 82–79) and his fourth wife Caecilia Metella; married the praetor C. Memmius (divorced); married Titus Annius Milo (praetor), in 55 BCE.

A daughter of the Roman dictator Sulla and his fourth wife **Caecilia Metella**, Cornelia Fausta married at an early age to praetor C. Memmius. Divorced from Memmius, she then married the praetor T. Annius Milo in 55 BCE. Fausta was notorious for her marital infidelity but may not have had an unbiased appraisal. Historian Sallust is said to have been one of her paramours.

Faustina, Anna or Annia Galeria
(c. 90–141 CE).

See Faustina I.

Faustina I (c. 90–141 CE)

Roman empress and wife of Antoninus Pius. Name variations: Anna or Annia Galeria Faustina; Faustina Maior; Faustina Mater (Faustina the Mother); Faustina the Elder; titled Augusta (Revered), Pia (Pious), and, after her death, Diva (Deified). Pronunciation: Fow-STEEN-ah. Born around 90 CE; died in 141 CE; daughter of *Rupilia Faustina and M. Annius Verus; married T. Aurelius Fulvus Boionus Antoninus, later the Roman emperor Antoninus Pius (r. 138–161), around 110; children: M. Aurelius Fulvus Antoninus; M. Galerius Aurelius Antoninus; ❧➤ Aurelia Fadilla (date of birth unknown); Faustina II (130–175).

Given the title Augusta by the Senate (138); died and was deified by the Senate (141); commemorated on surviving coins issued (138–141).

Only a few lines from less than reliable sources survive from antiquity to provide a view of the life of Faustina I. We know that she married the future emperor Antoninus Pius and that she therefore must have come from a wealthy aristocratic family, whose origins appear to have been in one of the provinces of what is now modern Spain. Exact dates and any sense of her early personal life, however, are almost entirely lacking. We know that she gave birth to four children, two of whom (the boys) died in infancy and the third sometime after marriage. Of her children, only details of her youngest daughter and namesake, *Faustina II (who later married the elder Faustina I's nephew, the future emperor Marcus Aurelius) are available.

The anonymous author of the *Augustan History* alludes to Faustina I's excessive license and loose living (*Life of Antoninus Pius* 3. 7). When she reproached her husband for extreme frugality with the household, possibly with the slaves, he is said to have addressed her as "Stupid" and reminded her that they had passed to a new way of life by acquiring the empire (4. 8). Yet Faustina does appear to have been close to her husband, who wrote to Marcus Aurelius' tutor M. Cornelius Fronto: "By Hercules I would rather live on Gyaris with her than on the Palatium without her." (Fronto, *Correspondence with Antoninus Pius.* 2.) By Gyaris, Pius referred to a forsaken island in the Aegean; the Palatium was the hill in Rome on which was located the imperial residence. Perhaps the spurious letter of 174 attributed to her daughter Faustina II, in which the younger relates that the elder Faustina urged Pius to attend to the needs of the family before all others during a rebellion (*Augustan History, Life of Avidius Cassius* 10. 1), preserves

➤❧
Aurelia Fadilla.
See Faustina II for sidebar.

a tradition of an empress with political savvy who may have earned her husband's gratitude.

At Faustina I's death in 141, only three years after she had become empress, the Senate deified her and consecrated a temple to her with priestess, as well as gold and silver, statues (*Augustan History, Life of Antoninus Pius* 6. 7). The same passage also tells us that the emperor allowed her image to be placed in circuses. This information and her surviving images on the coins of the empire should remind us that although we can say very little about her today Faustina was a public figure in her time and known to millions throughout the Roman Empire.

SOURCES:

Augustan History, Life of Antoninus Pius. 1. 7; 3. 7; 4. 8; 5. 2; 6. 7.

Augustan History, Life of Avidius Cassius. 10. 1.

Marcus Cornelius Fronto. *Correspondence with Antoninus Pius*. 2.

SUGGESTED READING:

A. Geissen, "Die ältere Faustina auf alexandrischen Tetradrachmen," in *Zeitschrift für Papyrologie und Epigraphik*. Vol. 9, 1992, p. 177–78.

Alexander Ingle,
Lecturer in the Department of Classical Studies, University of Michigan, Ann Arbor, Michigan

Faustina II (130–175 CE)

*Roman empress and wife of Marcus Aurelius. Name variations: Annia Galeria Faustina; Faustina Minor; Faustina the Younger; (Greek) Faustina Nea (Faustina the Younger); titled Augusta (Revered), Pia (Pious), Mater Castrorum (Mother of the Camp), and, after her death, Diva (Deified). Pronunciation: Fow-STEEN-ah. Born in 130 CE; died in 175 CE in Halala, later renamed Faustinopolis, in Asia Minor; daughter of the Roman emperor Antoninus Pius (r. 138–161) and Faustina I (c. 90–141 CE); married her cousin Marcus Annius Verus, later the emperor Marcus Aurelius (r. 161–180), in 145; children—14: ❦▸ Domitia Faustina (b. 147); the twins T. Aurelius Antoninus and T. Aelius Aurelius (b. 149); Lucilla (Annia Aurelia Galeria Lucilla, b. 150); *Faustina III (Annia Aurelia Galeria Faustina, b. 151), T. Aelius Antoninus (b. 152); Fadilla (Arria Fadilla, b. 159); ❦▸ Cornificia (b. 160); her second set of twins T. Aurelius Fulvus (also called Antoninus) and the future emperor L. Aurelius Commodus (b. August 31, 161); M. Annius Verus (b. 162); Hadrianus (date of birth unknown); ❦▸ Vibia Aurelia Sabina (b. 166); and an unnamed son (date of birth unknown).*

Reared in the imperial household (138–145 CE); betrothed in childhood to Lucius Aurelius Commodus (later the co-emperor Verus) but married Marcus Aure-lius (April 145); given the title Augusta by the Senate (147); gave birth to 14 children (147–166); accompanied Marcus to war (174); implicated in the revolt of Avidius Cassius (174); died in Halala, later renamed Faustinopolis, in Asia Minor while accompanying Marcus on campaign, and deified by the Senate (175); commemorated on scores of surviving inscriptions, coin-issues, and statues throughout the Roman Empire (147–176).

Faustina II was born in 130 CE to *Faustina I and T. Aurelius Fulvus Boionus Antoninus, the future emperor Antoninus Pius, during the reign of Hadrian. She had two older brothers who died in infancy and an older sister, ❦▸ Aurelia Fadilla, who married but died sometime before 138.

Faustina II lived during a historical moment of stability in the political superstructure of the Roman Empire. Civil wars and the ravages of so-called bad emperors had taught the upper classes in Roman society to look for a smooth and orderly succession to the throne. There was a concerted attempt by ruling circles in Rome in the late 1st and early 2nd centuries to peacefully manage the transfer of imperial power. As part of this effort, the emperor Hadrian first adopted Aelius Verus as his co-ruler, presumably with the intention that he would succeed him as effortlessly as Hadrian had succeeded his predecessor Trajan. After Aelius Verus' inconvenient death Hadrian adopted Faustina's father, Antoninus Pius, who simultaneously adopted Marcus Aurelius. As a result, the young Faustina was destined to play a part in the dynastic plans of Hadrian. Hadrian betrothed her to Aelius Verus' son, Lucius Verus, under the assumption that the younger Verus would eventually govern the empire. After Hadrian's death, her father betrothed her to Marcus, "because," as the anonymous Augustan History (Life of Verus 2. 3) says, ". . . Verus seemed too young."

All we can hazard about her childhood is that she was raised from her earliest years to be an empress; she must have been aware of the role for which Hadrian and Pius had cast her. At age 15, Faustina married the 24-year-old Marcus in what the *Augustan History* describes as a "most famous celeberrimas" (wedding celebration), complete with a bonus to the army (*Life of Antoninus Pius* 10. 3).

We can also assume without difficulty that the presence of children in this woman's life must have been outstanding: she had 14 in at least 21 years. The birth of her first child impelled the Senate to grant to her the title of Augusta in 147 (even before her husband was Augustus, i. e., the ruling emperor), the highest formal designation that a woman could obtain in Roman society. Her role as mother was celebrated publicly on coins and inscriptions: in 159, at the birth of her daughter ❧▸ Fadilla, coins issued depict her as Juno Lucina, the goddess of childbirth, and in 160 coins with her image bear the title "Fertility of the Augusta" (*Fecunditas Augustae*).

The premature deaths of at least six of her children were undoubtedly a source of pain, although it should be remembered that infant mortality was much higher in ancient Rome (even among the wealthy land-owning classes) than in modern society, and that a Roman woman might well have expected to lose such a high proportion of her children. Her husband writes in his letters to Fronto of his need to contain his sadness at the sickness and death of his children, and there are no indications in surviving documents that Faustina was more distant from family life.

But there are few written sources with which to reconstruct with certainty her life or character. In a letter to Fronto in 147 (*Correspondence with Marcus Aurelius Caesar 5. 26*) the future emperor remarked that he was disturbed by a fever of Faustina's but that she appeared content in his presence and conducted herself "*obtemperanter*" (obediently). Some two or three decades later in his famous Meditations, her husband called her "obedient, affectionate, and simple." (1. 17. 18). In 162, a great-aunt of Faustina's died and left a large fortune to hangers-on and not to the empress, her legitimate heir. This put the imperial family in the position of seeming avaricious if it pressed its claims. Marcus and, it is clear, Faustina decided not to do so. Faustina even refused to buy a famous string of pearls from the estate should it come to auction (Fronto, *Correspondence with Marcus Aurelius Imperator 2. 1.*).

The less dependable *Augustan History* (*Life of Commodus Antoninus 1. 3*) records that in 161 when she was pregnant with the twins Commodus and Fulvus, Faustina dreamed that she had given birth to two serpents, one of which was stronger than the other. Commodus did indeed outlive Fulvus to become one of the more sociopathic emperors. According to the *Augustan History* (7-9), Commodus was abusive and violent from boyhood. Romans would naturally have attributed this to innate qualities inherited from his parents and therefore blame Faustina and allege that she had affairs with gladiators. Commodus' conduct, such as ordering a slave

❧▸ **Domitia Faustina** (b. 147)
*Roman noblewoman. Born November 30, 147; daughter of *Faustina II (130–175 CE) and Marcus Aurelius, Roman emperor (r. 161–180).*

❧▸ **Cornificia** (b. 160)
*Roman noblewoman. Born in 160 CE; daughter of *Faustina II (130–175 CE) and Marcus Aurelius, Roman emperor (r. 161–180).*

❧▸ **Vibia Aurelia Sabina** (b. 166)
*Roman noblewoman. Born in 166 CE; daughter of *Faustina II (130–175 CE) and Marcus Aurelius, Roman emperor (r. 161–180).*

❧▸ **Aurelia Fadilla** (d. before 138)
*Roman noblewoman. Died before 138; daughter of *Faustina I (c. 90–141 CE) and Antoninus Pius (r. 138–161); sister of *Faustina II (130–175 CE); married.*

❧▸ **Fadilla** (b. 159)
*Roman noblewoman. Name variations: Arria Fadilla. Born in 159; daughter of *Faustina II (130–175 CE) and Marcus Aurelius, Roman emperor (r. 161–180).*

who had drawn his bath too cool to be burned alive, might reflect badly on Faustina and her husband as far as the behavior of children in the imperial household went. Her son's behavior indicates the potentially violent nature of imperial power in which Faustina herself had been raised and lived.

An important change occurred in Faustina's life when her father died and her husband assumed full control of the empire in 161. She was now the reigning Augusta. In addition, her father left her an enormous fortune but willed the revenue from this to the state. Inscriptions on several surviving bricks attest to the existence of landed estates that belonged to Faustina and to both Faustina and Marcus. We also hear of time spent on the paternal estate at Lanuvium, south of Rome.

At this time, the empire was going through enormous changes, the implications of which are not fully clear today and were probably even less apparent to Faustina and her contemporaries. Her husband Marcus Aurelius was the last of the five so-called good emperors, universally praised by extant Greek and Roman writers as temperate, modest, and merciful. But the Pax Romana

(Roman Peace) that had allowed the upper classes to plunder neighboring peoples and exploit their slaves and the free poor undisturbed (and relatively free from depredations by emperors) was coming to an end even during the lifetime of Faustina. The empire was passing from what elite writers regarded as a golden age to one of "iron and rust" (Cassius Dio, *Roman History* 71. 36. 4). After 164, the western provinces of the empire were stricken with a plague that thinned the population and may have had ramifications on the labor force. The Germanic tribes of the Quadi and Macromanni approached Italy in 169. The emperor then began a war that was to last for the next six years. Greece was invaded and Egypt was shaken by a rebellion. During all of this, Marcus' health seems to have been poor: he may have had an ulcer and appears to have become addicted to opium as a pain reliever.

*L*eaders and soldiers are accustomed to crush others if they themselves are not crushed.

—Faustina II

Exactly how these conditions affected Faustina we cannot tell. Her husband was absent from Rome now for long periods. She surely had huge responsibilities there as mother of the imperial family, but we have only incidental glimpses of her. She opposed the marriage of her daughter ◄❧ Lucilla, the widow of the co-emperor Verus and an Augusta, to Claudius Pompeianus, whose father had not even been a senator, although the marriage took place since Marcus wished it. We also know that Faustina accompanied Marcus to the northern front, probably in what is now modern Hungary, at least by 174 when she is titled Mater Castrorum (Mother of the Camp).

In 174, one of Marcus' leading generals in the eastern provinces, Avidius Cassius, revolted. Faustina's role in this revolt and her relationship to Cassius has been debated since ancient times. The *Augustan History* cites some writers as saying that she saluted Avidius Cassius as emperor but quickly seeks to deny this charge by reproducing excerpts of correspondence between Faustina and Marcus that clear her of compliance in the revolt and, in fact, show her stridently demanding punishment for Cassius and his accomplices (*Life of Avidius Cassius* 9. 5–11). These letters are regarded as spurious today, but even so they have contributed to an image in antiquity of Faustina as a political player, one more determined and less humane than her husband.

Despite these forgeries, we should note that the Greco-Roman writer Cassius Dio (*Roman History* 71. 22. 3–23. 1) admits the possibility that Faustina, frightened at her husband's failing health and wishing to avoid the dangers that his death might bring to her and her children, saw in Avidius Cassius a potential savior. In any case, the revolt was quickly crushed. Faustina died the next year on campaign with Marcus in the village of Halala at the foot of the Taurus mountain in the south of modern Turkey. The cause was natural, although Cassius Dio avers to the possibility of suicide. In her memory Marcus erected a temple in the area, founded the town of colonia Faustiniana, also called Faustinopolis, and established a charitable organization for girls called the puellae Faustinianae (Faustianian girls). The Senate deified her in 175, and she was laid to rest in the mausoleum of Hadrian in Rome.

Faustina seems to have been followed in her life and after by persistent rumors of infidelity to Marcus. The *Augustan History* reports that she was involved with her son-in-law and Marcus' colleague Lucius Verus (to whom she was originally betrothed) and that she poisoned him because he had betrayed the affair to Lucilla, who was her daughter and his wife (*Life of Lucius Verus* 10. 1–5). The history tells us that she labored heavily under a reputation for lewdness (*Life of Marcus Antoninus* 26. 5). In its assessment of Marcus, the history notes that it was held against this good emperor that he advanced his wife's lovers to high political offices, even after catching her breakfasting with one of them, and that he endured public ridicule in the theater where the name of one of Faustina's lovers was punned in his presence. Faustina and Marcus' son Commodus also promoted one her lovers (*Life of Commodus Antoninus* 8. 1.).

Even if there is some fact behind these stories of which Marcus may have been aware, there was little he could do. The *Augustan History* reports that she was inflamed by love for a gladiator, and that when the emperor reported this to his astrologers, they advised her to bathe in gladiator's blood and then sleep with her husband. This did not satisfy her appetite, so the work claims, and she continued to seek out glad-

❧► Lucilla (b. 150)

*Roman noblewoman. Born Annia or Anna Aurelia Galeria Lucilla on February 7, 150; daughter of *Faustina II (130–175 CE) and Marcus Aurelius, Roman emperor (r. 161–180); married Lucius Verus; married Ti. Claudius Pompeianus.*

iators and sailors as lovers. When this was reported to Marcus in order that he might murder or divorce her, he said, "If I send away my wife, I must also repudiate her dowry." Her dowry, of course, was the Roman Empire (*Life of Marcus Antoninus* 19. 2–4).

Little appears to have been written concerning Faustina in the Middle Ages or the Renaissance, although Antonio de Guevara mentions her in Book II of his 1528 *Golden Book of Marcus Aurelius*. Faustina has occasionally appeared as a character in historical fiction as well, most recently in a detective story by Wallace Nichols, "The Case of the Empress's Jewels," in *The Mammoth Book of Historical Whodunnits*, edited by Mike Ashley (NY: Carroll and Graf, 1993).

In the absence of rich or dependable sources on her life, Faustina's permanent legacy must rest with the material representations of her. Many images of her on coins and in stone remain. These have been collected and analyzed by Klaus Fittschen in his *Die Bildnistypen der Faustina minor und die Fecunditas Augustae*.

SOURCES:
Augustan History. *Life of Antoninus Pius* 10. 3.
Augustan History. *Life of Avidius Cassius* 9. 5–11.
Augustan History. *Life of Commodus Antoninus* 8. 1.
Augustan History. *Life of Lucius Verus* 2. 3; 10. 1–5.
Augustan History. *Life of Marcus Antoninus* 19. 2–4; 26. 5.
Cassius Dio, *Roman History* 71. 22. 3–23. 1.
Marcus Aurelius, *Meditations* 1. 17. 18.
Marcus Cornelius Fronto. *Correspondence with Marcus Aurelius Caesar* 5. 26, 60.
Marcus Cornelius Fronto. *Correspondence with Marcus Aurelius Imperator* 2. 1.

SUGGESTED READING:
Fittschen, Klaus. *Die Bildnistypen der Faustina minor und die Fecunditas Augustae: Abhandlungen der Akademie der Wissenschaften in Göttingen.* Philologisch-historische Klasse dritte Folge Nr. 126, Göttingen: Vandenhoek and Ruprecht, 1982.

Alexander Ingle,
Lecturer in the Department of Classical Studies,
University of Michigan, Ann Arbor, Michigan

Faustina III (b. 151)

*Roman noblewoman. Name variations: Anna Aurelia Galeria Faustina. Born Annia Aurelia Galeria Faustina in 151; daughter of *Faustina II (130–175 CE) and Marcus Aurelius, Roman emperor (r. 161–180); possibly married Cn. Julius Severus.*

Faustina Maior or Major (c. 90–141 CE).

See Faustina I.

Faustina of Antioch (fl. 300s)

*Byzantine empress. Flourished in the 300s; was the third wife of Constantius II, Eastern Roman emperor and Byzantine emperor (r. 337–361); children: Constantia Postuma. Constantius II's first wife was the daughter of *Galla (fl. 320); his second was *Eusebia of Macedonia.*

Faustina the Elder (c. 90–141 CE).

See Faustina I.

Faut, Jean (1925—)

American baseball player who pitched two perfect games in 1951 and 1953 for the South Bend Blue Sox. Born January 17, 1925, in East Greenville, Pennsylvania; married Karl Winsch (a baseball player, later manager of South Bend Blue Sox), in 1947; children: at least one.

Jean Faut of the South Bend Blue Sox distinguished herself by pitching two perfect games in the All-American Girls Baseball League (1943–54), the first and only women's professional baseball organization. Playing during the seven-year period of overhand pitching, Faut was known for the control and variety of her pitches. "She put them all just where she wanted," said the league's leading hitter, ***Dottie Kamenshek**, of the Rockford Peaches. "Pitching overhand was never foreign to the Blue Sox ace. She grew up playing hardball, and when the league switched to overhand, Jean was like a fish in water, moving effortlessly through the environment."

Born in East Greenville, Pennsylvania, the young Jean Faut lived a few blocks from the practice field of a semipro baseball team and learned how to pitch from some of the players. While still in high school, she pitched several exhibition games for the semipro Buck-Montgomery League. In 1946, she was spotted by a scout and offered a chance to attend the All-American Girls Baseball League's sprint training camp in Pascagoula, Mississippi, where she was picked up by the South Bend Blue Sox. Because of her strong arm, she started at third base but did some pitching late in her rookie season. Faut did not like sidearm pitching and was relieved when the league switched to overhand in 1948. At the end of her first year, she married Karl Winsch, a player who left his pitching position with the Philadelphia Phillies due to injury. In her second year, pregnant with her first child, Faut pitched 44 games to post a 19–13 record. After the baby's birth in March

1948, she regained her strength and matured as a player. In 1949, she started 34 games and finished the season with a 24–8 record and a 1.10 ERA.

In addition to a remarkable repertoire of pitches, Faut also had phenomenal mental control. "Part of my success was that in my mind I could record the pitches and the order of pitches I threw to each girl, so they never saw the same thing twice," she recalled. "I was a mathematical whiz in school. They'd never know what was coming, so they'd start guessing. When batters start guessing, they're never right."

On July 21, 1951, Faut made history by pitching a perfect game against the Rockford Peaches, retiring 27 batters in a row. Kamenshek struck out twice. "It was the best game I've ever seen pitched," she said later. "It was just perfect. Overpowering." The next morning's *South Bend Tribune* reported: "Jean Faut, a sturdy gal with a lot of heart, a fast ball that hops, and a curve that breaks off like a country road, pitched a perfect no-hit, no run game to subdue the Rockford Peaches 2–0." Faut ended the season with a 15–7 pitching record and was chosen Player of the Year. Her second perfect game was played in 1953, against the Kalamazoo Lassies. Again elected Player of the Year, she was only the second person in league history to receive the award twice (the other was *Doris Sams).

Marriage and motherhood made Faut something of a loner; she didn't room with other players or take part in pregame and postgame activities. In 1951, when her husband became manager of the South Bend Blue Sox, it created problems for the hurler, who found that neither her teammates nor her husband would openly communicate with her. She retired from baseball at the end of the 1953 season, citing that it was just too difficult being married to the manager. She left with impressive career statistics—140 wins and 64 losses, and a 1.23 ERA, of which she is most proud because "that's the most important statistic of a pitcher." Miserable because she wasn't playing, Faut took up bowling and became so skilled at the sport that she turned pro in 1960, retaining that status until 1988. Her highest game was a 299, just short of perfect.

SOURCES:

Gregorich, Barbara. *Women at Play: The Story of Women in Baseball.* NY: Harcourt Brace, 1993.

Macy, Sue. *A Whole New Game.* NY: Henry Holt, 1993.

Barbara Morgan,
Melrose, Massachusetts

Favart, Marie (1727–1772)

French soprano, actress, and dramatist. Name variations: Madame Favart. Born Marie Justine Benoîte du Ronceray at Avignon, France, on June 15, 1727; died in Paris on May 12, 1772; married Charles Simon Favart (a French playwright and librettist), in 1745 (died 1792); children: Charles Nicolas Justin Favart (1749–1806).

Born in Avignon in 1727, Marie Justine Benoîte du Ronceray made her debut in 1745 at the Opéra-Comiqueas as Mme Chantilly in *Les fêtes publiques* by Charles Simon Favart. She married Favart, a French playwright known as the creator of the musical comedy or comic opera, that same year. The couple organized a theater for the troops in Flanders and appeared in Brussels for the next two years, until their patron Maréchal de Saxe forced them to leave because Marie refused to be his mistress. From then on, Marie Favart sang in Paris at the Comédie-Italienne until her death in 1772. She appeared in the title role of *La serva padrona* as well as many works with librettos by her husband. A gifted actress if an indifferent singer, she also collaborated with her husband on several librettos. Marie Favart was the subject of Offenbach's 1878 opera *Mme Favart.*

SUGGESTED READING:

Pougin, A. *Madame Favart.* Paris, 1912.

Favart, Marie (b. 1833)

French actress. Born Marie Pierette Ignace Pingaud Favart at Beaune, France, on February 16, 1833.

A noted French actress, Marie Favart made her debut in 1848 at the Comédie Française. She became a member of the Comédie in 1854 and resigned in 1881. In 1883, she toured Russia with Coquelin and played in classic comedy, notably in *Tartuffe.* Favart created many original parts and was especially successful in contemporary drama.

Favre, Julie Velten (1834–1896)

French educator and philosopher who was the director of École Normale Superieure de Sevres (1881–96). Name variations: Mme. Jules Favre. Born Julie Velten in Wissembourg, France, on November 5, 1834; died in January 1896; daughter of a Lutheran pastor and official; had two brothers and three sisters; obtained teacher's degree from Wissembourg; married Gabriel Claude Jules Favre (1809–1880, French lawyer and diplomat), in 1870.

Selected works: La Morale des Stoïciens (The Morality of the Stoics, *1887);* La Morale de Socrate (The Morality of Socrates, *1887);* Montaigne moraliste et pédagogue (Montaigne as a moralist and a pedagog, *1887);* La Morale d'Aristotle (The Morality of Aristotle, *1888);* La Morale de Ciceron (The Morality of Cicero, *1889);* La Morale de Plutarque (The Morality of Plutarch*).*

Julie Favre rebelled against her strict Lutheran upbringing even in childhood. Although her work reflected a belief that morality, the main subject of her writings, was related to spirituality, she argued that it could be learned without religious enforcement. Favre believed wholeheartedly in the importance of freedom and choice, and she aligned herself with the French Republicans, who resisted monarchy.

She was trained as a teacher in Wissembourg, the town in which she had grown up. In Paris, she started as the head assistant of a boarding school for girls run by **Mme Frère-jean.** They became close friends and would remain so until Frère-jean's death in 1860, at which time Favre took over as director. Both practiced liberal education, emphasizing the health, well-being, and freedom of the students, while trying to build their students' moral education and personal strengths.

In 1870, Julie married Jules Favre, also a Republican, who had been leader of the opposition to the Second Empire (1863–68), and would be minister of foreign affairs and vice-president of the Government of National Defense (1870–71), as well as a member of the Senate (1876–80). After Frère-jean's death, Julie ran the school and translated German and Swiss books into French. Her husband died in 1880, and during her long mourning Favre compiled his writing, which was published in several multivolume sets.

In 1881, she began the directorship of the new École Normale Superieure de Sevres, which allowed young women to receive a broad secondary education. In a move unusual for a European nation at the time, the French government, which had instituted the school, emphasized the importance of having women instructors. Favre's program stressed student freedom, and the strong devotion she earned from her students was attributed to her commitment to following her convictions. The school was very popular, attracting pupils from all over France, but was resented by members of the local community, who were sometimes at odds with the ideas of student independence fostered by Favre.

SOURCES:

Allen, Jeffner. "Julie Velten Favre," in Mary Ellen Waithe, ed., *A History of Women Philosophers.* Boston: Martinus Nijhoff, 1987–1995.

Catherine Hundleby, M.A.
Philosophy, University of Guelph, Guelph, Ontario, Canada

Fawcett, Joy.

See Soccer: Women's World Cup, 1999.

Fawcett, Millicent Garrett
(1847–1929)

British feminist author, speaker, and political leader who witnessed the formal initiation of the women's suffrage campaign in 1867, led the moderate movement for women's enfranchisement, and lived to see the extension of suffrage to women on equal terms with men in 1928. Name variations: Millicent Garrett. Born Millicent Garrett in Aldeburgh, England, on June 11, 1847; died on August 5, 1929, in London, England; daughter of Newson (a well-to-do merchant) and Louisa (Dunnell) Garrett; sister of Elizabeth Garrett Anderson; married Henry Fawcett, in 1867; children: daughter Philippa Fawcett (b. 1868).

Elected to executive committee of London National Society for Women's Suffrage (1867); gave first public speech on women's suffrage (1869); became president of National Union of Women's Suffrage Societies (1907–19); awarded honorary degree from the University of St. Andrew's, Scotland (1899); awarded Dame Grand Cross of the British Empire (1925).

Selected publications on women's suffrage and related topics: Women's Suffrage: A Short History of a Great Movement *(1912);* The Women's Victory—and After: Personal Reminiscences, 1911–1918 *(1920); (autobiography)* What I Remember *(1924);* Some Eminent Women of our Times *(1889);* Life of Her Majesty Queen Victoria *(1895);* Five Famous French Women *(1905); numerous pamphlets and articles published in periodicals such as* Common Cause, The Englishwoman, Woman's Leader, Contemporary Review, Nineteenth Century.

When Millicent Garrett was a very young girl, according to a tale recounted by her biographer and close friend, *Ray Strachey,** she spent an evening raptly listening to a discussion of the important women's issues of the day between her older sister *Elizabeth Garrett** (**Anderson**) and her sister's good friend, *Emily Davies.** At the end of the night, Davies supposedly allocated tasks among the three in the upcoming struggle for female emancipation. Davies herself would secure women's equal access to higher education,

Elizabeth Garrett would open up the medical profession to women, and little Millicent, as the youngest, would undertake the long fight to obtain the vote for British women on equal terms with men. That quiet evening discussion among three determined girls bore impressive fruit, for Davies founded Girton College at Cambridge University, which allowed women to study for the first time at one of the great British universities, Elizabeth Garrett became the first British woman doctor and a leader in the medical profession, and young Millicent Garrett grew up to become, through her articles and public speaking, the most well-known figure in the British women's suffrage movement, the president of the largest women's suffrage organization in Britain, the National Union of Women's Suffrage Societies, and one of the most important figures in securing the vote for women.

I believe it will one day be considered almost incredible that there ever was a time when the idea of giving votes to women who fulfill the conditions which enable men to vote was regarded as dangerous and revolutionary.

—**Millicent Garrett Fawcett**

In her long life, Millicent Fawcett witnessed unprecedented changes in women's position in British society. At her birth in 1847, women were barred from most educational opportunities and entrance into the professions. For middle-class women especially, their aspirations and endeavors were limited to the realm of home and family. Born into this restrictive environment, Millicent Fawcett nonetheless claimed that she "was a woman suffragist . . . from my cradle." Indeed, the Garrett family proved to be a veritable breeding ground for future champions of women's emancipation. In addition to the accomplishments of Millicent and Elizabeth, the eldest girl, **Louisa Garrett**, was actively involved in the early campaign for suffrage reform, another sister, **Agnes Garrett**, became one of the first female interior decorators and still another sister, **Alice Garrett**, was a pioneer in local government by women, while their younger brother, Sam, was an attorney who assisted Millicent in her suffrage work and campaigned to open the legal profession to women.

Aldeburgh, where Newson and **Louisa Dunnell Garrett** raised their extraordinary family of six daughters and four sons, was a quiet town on the coast of Suffolk, England. Louisa was a devoutly Christian woman, who believed in strict observance of the Sabbath. Her strong religious views were not shared by her husband nor, it appears, by her children. Yet, her steadfast devotion may have influenced Millicent's dedication to the cause of female suffrage. Long after Louisa's death, Millicent's sister Alice wrote to her, "I felt . . . that the cause is to you what religion was to dear mother." Newson was a successful businessman, prominent in local politics, who relished the rapid technological changes such as the spread of the railways which characterized industrializing Britain at mid-century. Apparently, he also enjoyed a rousing fight for a good cause, although this led to a reputation for being quarrelsome. He willingly took on the British medical establishment (and incurred his wife's censure) in assisting Elizabeth Garrett to become a doctor. Millicent, too, never shied away from fighting for her beliefs. She proved to be one of the most able and tenacious debaters in the women's suffrage movement.

Millicent's education was similar in many ways to that of most upper-middle-class Victorian girls. She and her sisters were educated at home by a governess until their early teen years. Millicent then attended a school for girls in London that was unusual in its emphasis on intellectual attainments rather than such traditionally "feminine" accomplishments as needlework and sketching. Millicent's eldest sister, Louisa, who was then married and living in London, introduced the adolescent schoolgirl to the exciting world of mid-century radical politics, bringing her to hear speeches by the reforming cleric F.D. Maurice and the great liberal philosopher and economist, John Stuart Mill.

It was at one of these political gatherings that Millicent Garrett met Henry Fawcett, a Liberal member of Parliament and professor of economics at Cambridge University who was 14 years her senior. Although blinded in a hunting accident, Henry Fawcett remained unbowed by his handicap. In addition to his significant academic and political successes, he maintained an active lifestyle, riding, hiking, and fishing as any sighted person would. In October 1866, Henry and Millicent became engaged, after overcoming some initial reluctance by her family (which may have arisen from the fact that Henry had proposed to Elizabeth Garrett a scant one year earlier), and were married in April of the following year.

For several years, Millicent Fawcett served as her husband's secretary. She read parliamentary blue books aloud to him, culled the newspapers and periodicals for articles of political inter-

est which she then summarized, and escorted him to Parliament where she often watched the debates from the ladies' gallery. These activities, which fit in well with the Victorian ideal of wife as self-sacrificing helpmate, actually contributed greatly to Millicent Fawcett's theoretical and practical political education, knowledge which she would subsequently put to good use in the struggle for the enfranchisement of women. Indeed, Fawcett was present on the historic occasion when J.S. Mill initiated the first of many legislative attempts to secure the vote for women.

Like Mill, Fawcett and her husband were both liberals. In the political terminology of 19th-century Britain, this meant that they favored a policy of laissez-faire economics, with minimal government interference in the workings of the marketplace. The Fawcetts advocated a "fair field and no favor" for women, as the slogan of the day expressed it; that is, they believed in strict equality of men and women, with no governmental advantages to aid one sex over the other. Thus, Millicent Fawcett's goal was not to obtain suffrage for all women. Rather, she argued that women should simply be enfranchised on the same basis as men. In 19th-century Britain, the right to vote was conditioned on the ownership of property. Thus, many Victorian men, as well as all women, were not permitted to exercise the franchise. However, Parliament gradually extended the suffrage to more men with the Reform Acts of 1832, 1867, and 1884. Millicent Fawcett saw the enfranchisement of women as a logical sequel to these voting reforms. In 1883, she wrote, "The movement for the representation of women is nothing more nor less than a simple outgrowth of the democracy which has been the gradual product of this century."

In addition to her hands-on political experience working with her husband, Fawcett was an unusual Victorian woman in other respects. At a time when most women authors confined themselves to fiction, Millicent Fawcett, with the support and encouragement of her husband, wrote extensively on the political and economic issues of her day. Her *Political Economy for Beginners,* published in 1870, set forth liberal economic theory in an accessible fashion. The book became a bestseller and was reissued in several editions. Millicent and Henry Fawcett also published a collection of political essays containing selections by each of them.

More important for Fawcett's future role as the leader of the women's suffrage movement, she began to speak in public. In the mid-19th century, many people felt that it was not quite respectable for women to lecture in public. Thus, it was with much trepidation that Fawcett delivered her first speech on women's suffrage at a public meeting in July 1869. With Henry Fawcett's backing, Millicent Fawcett also addressed his Brighton constituency at a political rally. From then on, Fawcett spoke at numerous Liberal Party meetings and other political occasions and was generally lauded for her clear speaking style and intellectual acumen. Those public appearances counteracted two of the stereotypes commonly employed to attack female advocates of women's rights. On the one hand, it was often asserted that such women were unattractive and mannish in their appearance. Millicent Fawcett, however, was petite and attractive, a devoted wife and, after 1868, the mother of a little girl, **Philippa Fawcett**. In short, Fawcett epitomized Victorian womanhood while ardently advocating women's rights. On the other hand, detractors of the women's movement argued that women should be barred from the exercise of public rights such as voting because they were irrational and overly emotional. In her public appearances, Fawcett also belied this negative depiction. Her speeches relied on rigorous logic to argue her own position and negate objections raised by opponents of women's suffrage. When speaking publicly, Fawcett steadfastly hid her own strong emotions on the topic of women's enfranchisement. Indeed, she was so successful in her endeavor to appear strictly rational and unemotional that later in life even some close friends believed her to be a rather cold and unfeeling person.

Finally, Fawcett was also one of the pioneers in establishing the organizational basis for the women's suffrage movement. She was elected to the executive committee of the London National Society for Women's Suffrage, founded in 1867. Her leadership position in that Society allowed Fawcett to develop and exercise her abilities as an organizer and, most important, as a conciliator. She possessed the rare talent of framing positions on tactics and issues that could garner widespread acceptance across the spectrum of the society's membership.

Like many other Victorian feminists, Fawcett believed that the struggle to ensure equality for women was not merely a matter of obtaining the vote. It was expected, of course, that female enfranchisement would lead to more equitable governmental regulation in areas of special concern to women such as social welfare, education, access to the professions for men and women, and standards of public morality. While vigorously pursuing the campaign for women's suffrage, however, Fawcett lent both active and moral support to the struggle for equality in several other areas.

At their home in Cambridge, the Fawcetts hosted a series of lectures for women by professors from the university. These lectures served as the precursor of Newnham College which, with Girton, was one of the first two colleges for women affiliated with Cambridge University. Fawcett later reaped great personal satisfaction and political vindication from this early support of higher education. In 1890, her daughter Philippa Fawcett, an undergraduate at Newnham College, placed above the highest-scoring man on the university's most prestigious mathematics examination. Philippa's ranking "above the senior wrangler" garnered worldwide acclaim and seemed to provide an irrefutable argument that women could succeed academically, even in such traditionally "masculine" subjects as mathematics and the sciences.

Fawcett also opposed the sexual double standard commonly accepted in Victorian Britain that dictated different morality for men and women. She privately supported *Josephine Butler's successful campaign for the repeal of the Contagious Diseases Acts which mandated registration of known or suspected female prostitutes. However, because Fawcett always gave priority to the struggle for the enfranchisement of women, she refrained from public involvement in this controversial campaign, fearing that a linkage of the two issues in the public's mind would damage the suffrage cause. Like many Victorian feminists, Fawcett believed that women would benefit most from greater sexual restraint and higher standards of moral behavior for both men and women, rather than from increased sexual freedom for women. As a member of the National Vigilance Association, Fawcett worked to prevent girls and young women from being enticed into prostitution and to "rescue" those who were already working as prostitutes. She actively supported the newspaper editor W.T. Stead in his 1885 campaign against the white slave trade chronicled in his famous series of articles, "The Maiden Tribute of Modern Babylon." From 1887 to 1889, Fawcett worked to remove children from the stages of London theaters, where she felt young people were vulnerable to sexual exploitation. She also participated in the campaign to raise the minimum marriage age in British India. Fawcett's almost puritanical morality extended to her colleagues in the women's suffrage movement. She upbraided *Elizabeth Wolstenholme-Elmy, who flaunted Victorian morality by living with a man before marriage, asserting that she had done "a great injury to the cause of women."

After her husband Henry died unexpectedly in 1884, Millicent Fawcett found solace in her suffrage work and pursued her writing and speaking with redoubled vigor. Fawcett and other suffragists used personal contacts with MPs to influence parliamentary opinion. In addition, Fawcett's speeches and articles attempted to sway educated public opinion in their favor and to rebut the arguments of the increasingly vocal anti-suffragist faction.

In 1897, the London National Society for Women's Suffrage, of which Fawcett was the leader, and 16 other local women's suffrage organizations, joined together to form the National Union for Women's Suffrage Societies (NUWSS), an umbrella organization of various groups supporting women's enfranchisement. The NUWSS would eventually become the largest women's suffrage organization in Britain, with over 305 affiliated organizations by 1911. In 1907, when the NUWSS adopted a strategy of centralized direction for its member organizations, Fawcett was elected president, a position she held until her resignation in 1919.

In 1901, Fawcett took a short hiatus from her suffrage work to head up the first governmental commission of inquiry composed solely of women. During the Boer War in South Africa (1899–1902), the British army rounded up civilians, including women and children, and placed them in concentration camps to ensure that they would not provide aid to Boer soldiers. Conditions in the camps, including a high mortality rate among children, led to criticism of the British government and the war effort in the British press. Fawcett, an avid patriot who supported the British effort in South Africa, had written a well-publicized article rebutting some of these charges. The War Office appointed Fawcett and five other women to investigate conditions in the camps and issue a report, much to the chagrin of *Emily Hobhouse who was angling for quick reforms. Fawcett and her committee spent several months in South Africa, visiting the camps and talking with the inmates as well as the supervising army personnel. Although many had anticipated a whitewash from the commission, given Fawcett's pro-government stance, her final report recommended sweeping sanitary and administrative reforms in the camps, although still sanctioning the general government policy.

Britain was not the only nation in which women were working for enfranchisement. In 1902, the International Woman Suffrage Alliance was established in Washington, D.C., to unite partisans of the women's suffrage movement around the world. As the most prominent leader of the British movement, Fawcett was naturally involved with this new women's organization. She served as both second and first vice-president and established contacts with leaders of the many women's rights organizations around the world.

However, Fawcett's main focus continued to be the struggle for voting rights in Britain. In 1903, the founding of the Women's Social and Political Union (WSPU) drastically altered the situation of the women's suffrage movement in England. *Emmeline Pankhurst and her daughter *Christabel Pankhurst, leaders of the WSPU suffragettes, as they were called, advocated more militant methods to secure the suffrage. The suffragettes interrupted Liberal Party meetings with embarrassing questions for the speakers, were forcibly ejected from political gatherings, and staged mass demonstrations of angry women in front of Parliament. Initially, Fawcett sanctioned the more militant tactics of the WSPU, hoping that their radicalism would succeed where the strictly parliamentary strategy of the NUWSS had so far failed. However, as the WSPU became more violent, destroying property, engaging in massive window-smashing demonstrations in London and arson in the countryside, Fawcett withdrew her support. She later wrote, "I had no doubt whatever that what was right for me and the NUWSS was to keep strictly to our principle of supporting our movement only by argument, based on common sense and experience and not by personal violence or lawbreaking of any kind."

However, the WSPU's militancy affected Fawcett and the NUWSS in two ways. First, Fawcett's more conservative organization, fearful of losing members, adopted some of the mass mobilization techniques pioneered by the Pankhursts. In February 1907, Fawcett was the principal speaker at the "Mud March" (so called because of the effects of inclement weather), a huge suffrage demonstration by women of all political persuasions. The NUWSS also organized the 1913 "Pilgrimage," a march by non-militant suffragists from all regions of England to a massive rally in London. Second, the radical tactics of the WSPU attracted public attention to the question of women's enfranchisement. Fawcett and the moderate suffragists had concentrated on quietly influencing members of Parliament to support women's suffrage and to initiate legislative reform. With the issue of "Votes for Women" being discussed throughout Britain, Fawcett and her colleagues tried to seize the moment of heightened public interest to push a suffrage reform bill through Parliament.

In the years before World War I, however, Fawcett's parliamentary tactics were blocked by Prime Minister Herbert Asquith who staunchly opposed women's suffrage. Fawcett christened him, "our greatest enemy in the Liberal Party." In frustration, Fawcett and the NUWSS aban-doned their long-standing policy of providing electoral support to parliamentary candidates who advocated women's enfranchisement and instead vowed to support only candidates of the fledgling Labour Party, the sole political party in Britain to adopt a female suffrage plank as part of its platform.

It was World War I that finally turned the tide for women's suffrage. Fawcett urged women to participate actively in war work, as nurses or doctors at the front, as workers in the wartime munitions industries at home, or simply as replacements in offices and factories for the millions of men who had gone to fight. Her immediate and wholehearted support for the war was motivated by her strong patriotism, her belief that the war was part of the struggle for democracy which alone could secure women's equality, and the idea that women could best justify their claim to the vote by behaving as responsible citizens. But many of her compatriots in the NUWSS were pacifists opposed to British participation in World War I. They strongly believed that women should refrain from assisting the war effort, but instead should work for peace and understanding. In 1915, these opposing views created a rift within the NUWSS. Fawcett survived a challenge to her leadership from the pacifist faction, but many dedicated suffragists left the organization rather than endorse its prowar position.

Even so, women's work during World War I convinced many diehard opponents of female suffrage that women deserved the full rights of citizenship. In 1918, Parliament granted the vote to most women over the age of 30 and simultaneously enacted universal male suffrage. (British women aged 21 and over received the vote ten years later, in 1928.) Millicent Fawcett triumphantly watched the debates and the vote in the House of Commons from the same spot in which she had witnessed the initial parliamentary bid for female suffrage made by Mill more than 50 years earlier. In 1919, the NUWSS became the National Union of Societies for Equal Citizenship (NUSEC). Her primary task accomplished, Fawcett resigned the presidency, citing her age as the decisive factor. However, she also disagreed with the NUSEC's plan immediately to request votes for women on the same terms as men.

Fawcett spent the remaining decade of her life writing her memoirs and traveling with her sister Agnes who had been her constant companion since Henry's death in 1884. She received several honors from the British government. Fawcett was appointed a magistrate in 1920 and in 1925 she became a Dame Grand Cross of the British Empire. She died after a brief illness on August 5, 1929.

SOURCES:

Fawcett, Millicent Garrett. *What I Remember*. NY: Putnam, 1925.

Hume, Leslie Parker. *The National Union of Women's Suffrage Societies 1897–1914*. NY: Garland, 1982.

Rubinstein, David. *A Different World for Women: The Life of Millicent Garrett Fawcett*. Columbus, OH: Ohio State University Press, 1991.

Strachey, Ray. *"The Cause": A Short History of the Women's Movement in Great Britain*. London: G. Bell and Sons.

———. *Millicent Garrett Fawcett*. London: John Murray, 1931.

SUGGESTED READING:

Caine, Barbara. *Victorian Feminists*. Oxford: Oxford University Press, 1992.

Lewis, Jane, ed. *Before the Vote was Won: Arguments For and Against Women's Suffrage*. London: Routledge & Kegan Paul, 1987.

Morgan, David. *Suffragists and Liberals*. Totowa, NJ: Rowman and Littlefield, 1975.

Pugh, Martin. *Women's Suffrage in Britain*. London: The Historical Association, 1980.

COLLECTIONS:

The Fawcett Library, London, England.

Mary A. Procida,
Visiting Assistant Professor of History,
Temple University, Philadelphia, Pennsylvania

Fay, Amy (1844–1928)

American pianist who wrote the popular Music-Study in Germany, *managed the New York Women's Philharmonic Society, and enjoyed a major concert career. Born Amelia Muller Fay in Bayou Goula, Mississippi, on May 21, 1844; died in Watertown, Massachusetts, on February 28, 1928; fifth of nine children of Charles Fay (a scholar) and* Charlotte Emily (Hopkins) Fay *(1817–1856, a visual artist and pianist); sister of Melusina "Zina" Fay Peirce (1836–1923); never married.*

Amy Fay studied in Berlin with Carl Tausig, Ludwig Deppe, and Theodor Kullak, and was accepted in Franz Liszt's master class. She returned to the United States in 1875, settled in Boston, and quickly achieved a major career as a concert artist. Her letters home from Berlin were published as *Music-Study in Germany* (Chicago: Jansen, McClurg), a volume of sharp observations on cultural stresses endured by a young American student in Germany. First published in 1880, the book went through 25 editions and was published in Great Britain and France as well as in the United States. *Music-Study in Germany* was reprinted by Dover with an introduction by **Frances Dillon** in 1965 and has been translated into French and German. Fay's biographical details of Liszt the man and artist are especially revealing and continue to be of value.

After living in Chicago for several decades, she moved to New York, where she and her energetic sister **Melusina Fay Peirce** managed the New York Women's Philharmonic Society (1899–1914), an organization that vigorously promoted the cause of women in the world of classical music. In an article for *Music* magazine in October 1900, Fay argued that women were too preoccupied with encouraging men in composition, with the result of neglecting their own talents. In a letter to the Music Teachers Association in 1903 regarding its forthcoming convention, she lamented the lack of women on the performing platform and noted that women seemed to be used only as social props and for fund-raising. Her personal friends included Ignace Paderewski and other noted musicians as well as literary giants, including the poet Henry Wadsworth Longfellow.

SOURCES:

McCarthy, S. Margaret William. "Fay, Amy [Amelia Muller]," in *New Grove Dictionary of American Music*. Vol. 2, p. 105.

SUGGESTED READING:

James, Edward T., Janet W. James, and Paul S. Boyer. *Notable American Women, 1607–1950*. Belknap, 1971.

McCarthy, S. Margaret William, ed. *Amy Fay: The American Years, 1879–1916*. Detroit, MI: Information Coordinators, 1986.

———. *Amy Fay: America's Notable Woman of Music*. Warren, MI: Harmonie Park Press, 1995.

Shaffer, Karen A., and Robert Dumm. "Amy Fay, American Pianist: Something to Write Home About," in *The Maud Powell Signature*. Vol. 1, no. 2. Fall 1995.

COLLECTIONS:

Some of Amy Fay's correspondence can be found in the Boston Public Library, Music Division, Department of Rare Books and Manuscripts; correspondence can also be found in Boston's Isabella Stewart Gardner Museum and New England Conservatory of Music (concert programs).

John Haag,
Athens, Georgia

Faye, Alice (1912–1998)

American actress. Born Alice Jeanne Leppert on May 5, 1912, in New York, New York; died in Rancho Mirage, California, on May 9, 1998; only daughter and one of three children of Charles (a police officer) and Alice (Moffat) Leppert; attended public school until age 13; married Tony Martin (a singer), on September 3, 1937 (divorced 1940); married Phil Harris (a bandleader-actor), on May 12, 1941; children: two daughters, Alice Harris Regan *(b. 1942);* Phyllis Harris *(b. 1944).*

Filmography: George White's Scandals *(1934);* She Learned About Sailors *(1934);* Now I'll Tell *(When New York Sleeps, 1934);* 365 Nights in Hollywood *(1934);* George White's 1935 Scandals *(1935);* Music is Magic *(1935);* Every Night at Eight *(1935);* Poor Little Rich Girl *(1936);* Sing, Baby, Sing *(1936);* King of Burlesque *(1936);* Stowaway *(1936);* On the Avenue *(1937);* Wake Up and Live *(1937);* You Can't Have Everything *(1937);* You're a Sweetheart *(1937);* In Old Chicago *(1938);* Sally, Irene and Mary *(1938);* Alexander's Ragtime Band *(1938);* Tail Spin *(1939);* Hollywood Cavalcade *(1939);* Rose of Washington Square *(1939);* Barricade *(1939);* Lillian Russell *(1940);* Little Old New York *(1940);* Tin Pan Alley *(1940);* That Night in Rio *(1941);* The Great American Broadcast *(1941);* Weekend in Havana *(1941);* Hello, Frisco, Hello *(1943);* The Gang's All Here *(The Girls He Left Behind, 1943);* Four Jills in a Jeep *(1944);* Fallen Angel *(1945);* State Fair *(1962);* Won Ton Ton, The Dog Who Saved Hollywood *(1976);* The Magic of Lassie *(1978);* Every Girl Should Have One *(1979).*

Plays: George White's Scandals of 1931 *(1931);* Good News *(revival, 1973).*

Alice Faye

Radio series: "The Fleischmann's Hour" (1931–34); "Music from Hollywood" (1937); "The Phil Harris-Alice Faye Show" (1946–54).

Alice Faye was born on Tenth Avenue, in the Hell's Kitchen section of New York City, which she jokingly referred to as "Double Fifth Avenue." Intent on an acting career from an early age, she left school at 13 to audition for the Ziegfeld Follies but was turned down. At 14, she began singing and dancing professionally and, in 1931, landed a job in the chorus of *George White's Scandals,* where she was spotted by Rudy Vallee, who signed her up for his weekly radio show and later as a singer with his band. Vallee was also responsible for her role as his co-star in the Fox film *George White's Scandals* (1934). When his original co-star, *Lillian Harvey, walked off the set in a dispute over the size of her role, Vallee convinced the studio to give Faye the part. The film opened to good reviews for the young newcomer, including one from Richard Watts, Jr., of the *New York Herald Tribune*: "A Cute Broadway blonde of the *Jean Harlow school, Miss Faye reveals, in addition to considerable personal allure, a talent for projecting a hot song number that is extremely helpful to the work." The studio, impressed with her debut, offered Faye a long-term contract.

For the first few years, Fox exploited Faye's Harlow-type image in such vehicles as *Now I'll Tell* (1934), with Spencer Tracy, and two comedy-musicals showcasing the comedy team of Jack Durant and Frank Mitchell, *She Learned about Sailors* and *365 Nights in Hollywood* (both 1934). Perhaps the best to be said of these early efforts was that Faye's warm contralto emerged, which helped turn her movie songs into popular recordings. In 1935, Darryl F. Zanuck, head of the new 20th Century-Fox Films, decided to soften Faye's brassy screen image. Adopting a more natural blonde hair color and altering her pencil-thin eyebrows, the remodeled Alice Faye first appeared in *Poor Little Rich Girl* (1936), with the new moppet star *Shirley Temple (Black). With her toned-down looks and signature husky voice, Faye found her niche as the sweet and vulnerable girl-next-door. In her tenth film, *Sing, Baby, Sing* (1936), she received her first star billing and also met her future husband, singer Tony Martin, whom she married in 1937. In *Stowaway* (1936), again with Shirley Temple, Faye sang one of her most memorable screen songs, "Goodnight, My Love," which she recorded for Brunswick. Unfortunately, around this time, Zanuck decided to save the talents of his musical stars for the cam-

era and banned all of his studio stars from the recording studio. As a result, Faye did not make another recording for a decade.

Faye hit her stride at Fox with two big-budget 1938 musicals, *In Old Chicago* and *Alexander's Ragtime Band,* both co-starring Tyrone Power and Don Ameche. However, it was the eight films that she made between 1940 and 1943 that are commonly believed to be the most memorable of her career. Among them was *Lillian Russell* (1940), in which she portrayed the entertainer in a less than factual account of her numerous romances. Faye was paired with *Betty Grable in *Tin Pan Alley* (1940) and also worked for the first time with *Carmen Miranda in *That Night in Rio* (1941), which was her sixth and last picture with Don Ameche.

After divorcing Tony Martin in 1940, Faye married the bandleader-actor Phil Harris, whom she had met while singing with Vallee. "My career for the first time in my life doesn't mean a thing to me," she pronounced after the nuptials. Soon after her marriage, she was once again paired with Miranda in the very successful *Weekend in Havana* (1941), proving that she still had box-office appeal. Faye gave birth to her first child, Alice, in 1942, losing starring roles in two pictures due to her pregnancy. She returned for two films before giving birth to a second daughter, Phyllis, in the spring of 1944.

During 1945, in a surprising bit of casting, Faye was announced for a dramatic role in Otto Preminger's *Fallen Angel,* playing a sedate rural girl who marries Dana Andrews, only to find out that he wants to leave her for the town "trollop" played by *Linda Darnell. "I became tired of playing those big musicals," she told columnist *Hedda Hopper, who questioned her about the role. "But I felt if I could make pictures I'd be proud to show my kids some day, that would be different. . . . I wear simple dresses and tailored knits and, above all, I'm a real person—a human being—a woman with a heart. Not just a painted, doll-like dummy." But Faye was not up to the heavily dramatic part and much of her performance, including her only song, "Slowly," landed on the cutting-room floor. Parting with Fox and blaming Zanuck for what she believed to be a "betrayal," Faye withdrew from films, even though the studio continued to offer her decent roles.

From 1946 to 1954, she co-starred with her husband on the hugely popular Sunday-night radio program "The Phil Harris-Alice Faye Show." Her first experience with television was in 1959, when she appeared with Harris on a

Timex Hour special, singing songs from her various movie roles. In 1962, she returned to films as Pat Boone's mother in a forgettable remake of *State Fair*. This was followed by a series of guest spots on several popular television variety shows, including "The Red Skelton Show" and "The Hollywood Palace." "I feel as though I'm starting all over again, slow but sure," she told an interviewer in 1962. "I'm doing a little dance routine with Perry [Como] and I feel as though I've got two left feet. . . . I can't just sit and rot. I've got to do something." She appeared on stage in a revival of *Good News* (1973) and was one of many former stars who did a cameo in Paramount's *Won Ton Ton, The Dog Who Saved Hollywood* (1976). During the 1980s, Faye was an occasional guest on "The Love Boat" and became the spokesperson for Pfizer's "Help Yourself to Good Health," a fitness program for seniors.

Faye reminisced nostalgically about her past movie career. "They were beautiful days," she told the *London Evening Standard*. "Everything was first class. . . . Not any more." Aside from turning down producer David Merrick's offer to play the lead in the Broadway hit *Hello, Dolly!*, she appears to have had few regrets.

SOURCES:

Katz, Ephraim. *The Film Encyclopedia*. NY: HarperCollins, 1994.

Parish, James Robert. *The Fox Girls*. Arlington House, 1974.

—— and Michael R. Pitts. *Hollywood Songsters*. NY: Garland, 1991.

Shipman, David. *The Great Movie Stars*. Boston, MA: Little, Brown, 1970.

Barbara Morgan,
Melrose, Massachusetts

Fayette, Madame de La (1634–1693).

See La Fayette, Marie-Madeleine de.

Fedele, Cassandra Fidelis

(1465–1558)

Italian scholar. Born Cassandra Fidelis Fedele in Venice, Italy, in 1465; daughter of Angelo Fedele and Barbara Leoni; educated at home by her father and by Gasparino Borro; married Giovan Maria Mapelli.

Works: (still extant) some letters and the following three orations—(1) "In Praise of Literature," (2) "Welcome to Bona Sforza, Queen of Poland," (3) "Oration for Bertuccio Lamberti, Receiving Honors of the Liberal Arts"; (lost) "De Scietiarum ordine" ("On the Order of the Sciences)," "Degressioni

morali" ("Moral Digressions"), "Elogi degli uomini illustri" ("Praises of Illustrious Men"), and poetry.

Until the age of 12, Cassandra Fedele was educated in Latin at home by her father, who longed for the social status a woman scholar could give to his family. She was then tutored in theology and sciences by Gasparino Borro. Until the age of 22, she pursued rhetoric, philosophy, and languages on her own—including Greek with which she had difficulty.

By this age, Fedele, who did not wish to marry, was already well-known for her erudition, and she became a local celebrity. The doge of Venice was particularly fond of her as a public "decoration" and forbade her to leave the city to accept the invitations to the courts of *Isabella I (1451–1504), queen of Spain, and Louis XII, king of France. Fedele wrote poetry but was particularly known for her public orations. One, on morality, was given in 1487 at the convocation of a relative at the University of Padua: "Oration for Bertuccio Lamberti, Receiving Honors of the Liberal Arts." Fedele was also asked to give the public welcome to *Bona Sforza, queen of Poland, when the queen arrived in Venice.

Despite her popularity, Fedele's lifestyle was not grand, and she was forced to marry when the novelty of her public presence faded with her beauty. In 1520, while returning on a ship from several years in Crete with her husband, Giovan Maria Mapelli (a doctor from Vicenza), most of her property was lost in a severe storm. Mapelli died the same year, widowing Fidele at a young age, and she often had to beg for financial assistance from others. At age 80, in 1547, she requested help from Pope Paul III who granted her a position as prioress of the girls' orphanage associated with the Church of S. Domenico di Castello in Venice. She remained there for 11 years before her death in 1558.

SOURCES:

Kersey, Ethel M. *Women Philosophers: a Bio-critical Source Book*. NY: Greenwood Press, 1989.

Russell, Rinaldina. "Cassandra Fedele," in Katharina Wilson, ed., *Encyclopedia of Continental Women Writers*. NY: Garland, 1991.

Catherine Hundleby, M.A.
Philosophy, University of Guelph,
Guelph, Ontario, Canada

Feigner, Vera (1852–1942).

See Figner, Vera.

Feist, Margot (b. 1927).

See Honecker, Margot.

Fel, Marie (1713–1794)

French soprano. Born in Bordeaux, France, on October 24, 1713; died in Chailot, France, on February 9, 1794; sister of Antoine Fel (1694–1771).

A student of Italian singer **Mme Van Loo**, Marie Fel made her debut at the Paris Opera in 1734, as Vénus in the prologue of *Philomèle*. She was a regular at the Opera until 1758, performing in over 100 premieres and revivals, including major roles in most of the works of Jean-Phillippe Rameau (1683–1764). Fel also appeared in works by Lully, Campra, Mouret, and Boismortier and was particularly known for her portrayal of Colette in Rousseau's *Le devin du village*. Praised for her clear and supple voice, her precise articulation, and her intelligence and grace, she was called "*séduisante*" by Voltaire, while the critic Friedrich Melchior Grimm quite literally fell in love with her. Apparently, Fel's romantic liaisons were as newsworthy as her performances; she was known to have been the mistress of the librettist Jean-Louis Cahusac and the painter Quentin La Tour. Upon her retirement from the Opera, she was replaced by her pupil, *Sophie Arnould. Fel's brother Antoine Fel was also a singer as well as a composer.

Felicia.

Variant of Felicitas.

Felicie, Jacoba or Jacqueline (fl. 1322).

See de Almania, Jacqueline Felicie.

Felicitas or Felicitas of Carthage (d. 203 CE).

See joint entry on Perpetua and Felicitas.

Felicitas of Rome (d. 162?)

Saint and Christian martyr. Name variations: (French) Félicités. Died in Rome around 162; may have been a widow with seven sons: Januarius, Felix, Philip, Silvanus, Alexander, Vitalis, and Martial.

One of two Christian martyrs named Felicitas, Felicitas of Rome lived during the 2nd century and was, according to the ancient *Passions*, tortured and killed with her seven sons at the hands of the Romans under the rule of Emperor Marcus Aurelius.

A pious widow who was well-known in Rome, Felicitas was called upon to renounce her Christian faith in order to venerate the gods. When she refused, she was tried in the forum of Mars along with her seven sons whom she inspired with her steadfast faith. "Lift your eyes to heaven; look up, my children," she instructed them, "there Christ awaits you; fight for your souls; stay firm in His love." Remaining resolute in their faith, all were condemned to die horrible deaths. Felicitas was forced to watch while her seven sons were tortured, then flung over a rock, and later beheaded. By one account, Felicitas was then boiled in oil and beheaded. In another account, she was just beheaded. There are those historians who disclaim this story completely, believing that the author of the *Passions* may indeed have combined it with the story of the Machabee brothers. In fact, the seven lads purported to be the sons of Felicitas may not have been related to her or to each other.

Felicity.

Variant of Felicitas.

Félix, Elizabeth (1821–1858).

See Rachel.

Félix, Lia (b. 1830).

See Rachel for sidebar.

Marie Fel

Felix, Maria (1915—)

Mexican actress. Born Maria de Los Angeles Felix
Guereña in Alamos, Sonoras, Mexico, in 1915.

Selected films: El Peñon de las Animas *(1942);*
Doña Barbara *(1943);* Amok *(1944);* Le Mujer de todos
(1946); Rio Escondido *(*Hidden River, *1947);* Vertigo
(1947); Enamorada *(1948);* Mare Nostrum *(Sp., 1948);*
Doña Diabla *(1949);* La Corona negra *(Sp., 1951);* Mes-
salina *(It., 1951);* La Pasión desnuda *(Arg., 1952);*
Camelia *(1953);* La Belle Otéro *(Fr., 1954);* French Cancan *(Fr., 1955);* Les Héros sont fatigués *(*Heroes and Sinners, *Fr., 1955);* La Escondida *(1956);* Faustina *(1956);*
Flor de Mayo *(*Beyond All Limits, *1957);* La Cucaracha
(1958); La Fièvre monte à El Pao *(*Los Ambiciosos *or*
Republic of Sin, *Fr./Mex., 1959);* Sonatas *(1959);* La Es-
trella vacia *(*The Empty Star, *1960);* Juana Gallo *(1961);*
La Bandida *(1962);* Amor y Sexo *(1963);* La Valentina
(1965); Le Generala *(1970).*

A strikingly beautiful, forceful actress,
Maria Felix was the leading box-office attraction in the Spanish-speaking world from the
early 1940s. In addition to Mexico, she worked
in Spain, Italy, and France where she played La
Belle Abbesse in Jean Renoir's *French Cancan*
(1955). Her later films included *La Fièvre mont
à El Pao* (1959), in which she starred with
Gérard Philipe, France's most popular star of his
generation. (Philipe became ill while making the
picture and died of a heart attack before his 37th
birthday.) Widowed by her fifth husband, Felix
retired to Mexico in the 1970s.

Félix, Rachel (1821–1858).

See Rachel.

Fell, Margaret (1614–1702)

*Religious leader and one of the founders of Quakerism,
an English movement that survived heavy persecution
to become a powerful influence in Anglo-American history.* Name variations: Margaret Fox. Born Margaret
Askew in 1614 at Marsh Grange, near Dalton, England;
died on April 23, 1702, at Swarthmoor Hall in Furness;
daughter of John Askew (a gentry landowner); mother's
name unknown; married Judge Thomas Fell, in 1632
(died 1658); married George Fox, in October 1669
(died 1691); children: (first marriage) Margaret Fell, Jr.
(b. 1633?); Bridget Fell (b. 1635?); Isabel Fell (b.
1637?); George Fell (b. 1638?); Sarah Fell (b. 1642);
Mary Fell (b. 1647); Susannah Fell (b. 1650); Rachel
Fell (b. October 1653); and one child lost in infancy.

*Converted to Quakerism and began holding
Quaker meetings in her home (1652); wrote letters to*
Cromwell and made ten visits to kings in London describing persecution of Quakers; imprisoned many
times after Judge Fell's death for her connection with
Quakerism (beginning 1664); wrote several Quaker
monographs; founded Swarthmoor Women's Monthly
Meeting (1671); traveled throughout England facilitating Quaker meetings.

Selected writings: To Manasseth-ben-Israel
(1656); A loving salutation to the seed of Abraham
(1656); The Citie of London Reproved *(1660);* A Call
to the Universall Seed of God *(1665);* Women's Speaking Justified *(1666, 2nd ed., 1667);* Epistle to Charles
II *(1666);* A Touch-stone, or a perfect tryal *(1666);*
The Standard of the Lord Revealed *(1667);* A Call to
the Seed of Israel *(1668);* A Relation of Margaret Fell,
Her Birth, Life, Testimony and Sufferings for the
Lord's Everlasting Truth in her Generation *(1690);*
"The Testimony of Margaret Fox concerning her late
husband, George Fox; together with a brief account of
some of his Travels, Sufferings, and Hardships endured for the Truth's Sake" *(1694);* Epistle to Friends
Concerning Oaths *(1698). In 1712, Margaret Fell's*
Works *were published by her family as* A Brief Collection of Remarkable Passages and Occurrences Relating to the Birth, Education, Life, Conversion, Travels,
Services, and Deep Sufferings of that ancient Eminent
and Faithful Servant of the Lord, Margaret Fell, but
by her Second Marriage, M. Fox.

In 1652, Margaret Fell was attending an
Anglican church service at St. Mary's, Ulverston,
when George Fox made a dramatic entrance and
asked the congregation for permission to speak.
The traveling preacher, credited as a founder of
Quakerism, then discoursed amid hubbub, asserting that priests and other "hireling" clergy
were not aware of the Inner Light (Truth). Margaret Fell rose to her feet, speechless and
amazed: the idea that everyone has the Inner
Light already within them directly contradicted
traditional Church teaching which claimed
everyone was sinful and only some would be
saved. She later recorded her strong reaction:

> This opened me so, that it cut me to the
> heart. Then I saw clearly, we were all wrong.
> So I sat me down in my pew again, and cried
> bitterly. I cried in my spirit to the Lord, "We
> are all thieves, we are all thieves. We have
> taken the scriptures in words, and know
> nothing of them in ourselves."

Describing herself as "one that sought after the
best things, being desirous to serve God," and
who often attended lectures of visiting ministers,
Fell was convinced that she had found the spiritual truth she sought.

The rise of Quakerism, or the Society of Friends, during the Interregnum period in England illustrates shifts in religious and social attitudes during a time of turbulent history. The early Quaker movement grew amid considerable instability of political leadership, bringing many concepts to surface: social equality and de-emphasis upon class structure, ministry of laypersons versus paid clergy, pacifism and spiritual equality among men and women. Margaret Fell, known traditionally as the "nursing mother of Quakerism," represents one of many early Friends whose role is being reconsidered in light of 17th-century English nonconformity. Her words and acts, when read in context of prevailing social attitudes of the time, testify to an articulate and determined woman who used her means and talent to further the Quaker cause, whatever the cost.

Margaret Fell was born in 1614 at Marsh Grange, a home owned by her father, John Askew, and located near the parish of Dalton, England. Little detail of Fell's childhood is known, including the name of her mother. Margaret's writings and skilled management of her husband's estate attest to an education consistent with her father's gentry status. Her only sibling was a sister, whose name is also unknown. Each daughter inherited a large legacy after John Askew's death; Fell inherited Marsh Grange.

Margaret married Judge Thomas Fell in 1632. She was 17 or 18, he was 34. In her short autobiography *A Relation of Margaret Fell: Her Birth, Life, Testimony, and Sufferings for the Lord's Everlasting Truth in Her Generation* (1690), Fell lists the accomplishments of her husband: barrister at law of Gray's Inn, member of Parliament, circuit judge, and more. The Fells resided at Swarthmoor Hall, manor house for the nearby town of Ulverston in Furness, where they raised eight children. Their middle daughter kept a detailed account book (*The Household Account Book of Sarah Fell*), which sketches the Fells' gentry lifestyle and how the large household was managed.

In the days following her "convincement" in 1652, Fell listened intently to Fox's call to a life of the Inner Light, to know the spiritual presence of Christ within. Judge Fell was away from Swarthmoor at the time, and Margaret Fell encouraged her entire household, children and servants, to embrace Quakerism. When Judge Fell returned home, several neighbors met him on the last leg of his journey to "inform" him that his family no longer attended service at St. Mary's. That evening, Margaret shared her religious experience with her husband. Fell notes in her *Testimony*: "When he came home and found us the most part of the family changed from our former principle and persuasion which he left us in when he went from home, he was much surprised at our sudden change." The judge listened to the testimony of his wife, then to that of George Fox, and finally to the protest of Lampitt, St. Mary's priest.

Though Thomas Fell continued to attend Anglican services and never officially joined the Quaker movement, he was sympathetic to the convictions of his wife and family. During the remaining six years of his life, Judge Fell's position protected Margaret, George Fox, and other Friends from imprisonment and persecution. He offered Swarthmoor as a Meeting house for the Friends, a tradition that continued until 1690, nearly 50 years.

> *I* told them that I should not deny my faith and principles for any thing they could do against me, and while it pleased the Lord to let me have a house, I would endeavor to worship Him in it.
>
> —Margaret Fell

Swarthmoor Hall became a center of communication as preachers like George Fox and other "Publishers of Truth" traveled throughout England with their message. Margaret Fell fulfilled many roles in the nascent Quaker movement. She coordinated Meetings, hosted traveling Quakers, organized charity projects, and established a fund to aid traveling ministers and their families. Later, she wrote extensively and helped establish Women's Meetings, organizations run strictly by female Quakers. Fell's extensive correspondence with other Friends spreading Quakerism in England, Europe, and America, documents early efforts of traveling Friends. Swarthmoor Hall provided a stable hub for early Quaker activity.

Judge Fell died in 1658. As a widow of independent means, Margaret Fell used her social position and wealth to expand her circle of influence for Quakerism beyond Swarthmoor and its surrounding community. She continued her role as administrator of Swarthmoor (though traditionally her only son might have assumed this role) and managed the estate with the help of her six daughters.

Fell used the written word to spread the Quaker gospel. A prolific letter writer, she maintained correspondence as a network among traveling Quakers and as a vehicle of Quaker apologetics penned for England's rulers. As early as 1655, Fell wrote two letters to Oliver Cromwell regarding Quakerism. Two weeks after Charles II's arrival at court, Margaret felt "moved of the Lord" to go to London and present papers regarding Quaker beliefs and to plead on behalf of hundreds of Friends imprisoned in England, Scotland, and Ireland for those beliefs. Throughout her life, Fell defended Quakerism against increasing persecution with letters and papers addressed to kings (Charles II, James II, William III) and political leaders of the Interregnum period.

Fell began writing books and papers to address issues central to Quaker principles. Topics included conversion of the Jews, nonviolence, and women's right to preach. She wrote "fervent millenialist messages" for officers of the army to follow peaceable policies (including just treatment of Quakers) and to consider the coming judgment against those who embraced violence. Scholar **Bonnelyn Young Kunze** names Margaret Fell as the first Quaker to write a "declaration against the persecution of peaceful Quakers and against war and violence for any purpose." Pacifism remains an important issue for modern Quakers.

Fell's work in the area of Quaker apologetics included efforts to explain the Friends' opposition to "hat honor" (doffing one's hat in deference to a superior), oath-taking, or enforced tithing to Charles II. (See *A Declaration and an Information from the People of God Called Quakers to the Present Governors, the King and both Houses of Parliament and all whom it may concern.*) Fell is perhaps best known for her book *Women's Speaking Justified*, which addresses the issue of women's preaching and role in the faith.

Her first book (1656), *To Manasseth-ben-Israel; The Call of the Jews Out of Babylon*, as well as several other subsequent works, appealed to Jews to turn to the Light of God. Fell and George Fox both expressed interest in the Jews, believing conversion of Jews helped usher the Second Coming of Christ. Fell's book was taken by millenarian Quakers to Holland, a center of European Jewish culture, where it was translated into Hebrew. Some biographers and scholars suggest that Baruch de Spinoza may have served as translator of Fell's work into Hebrew.

Margaret Fell traveled widely on behalf of the Quakers, organizing Meetings and visiting imprisoned disciples. When she traveled to London for an audience with Charles II in 1660 "concerning the truth and the sufferers for it," she remained there for more than a year. She spoke often with the king, provided papers and letters to each member of the royal family, and visited local Friends Meetings. Though it was unusual for a woman of 17th-century England to be absent from home for so long, Fell placed Swarthmoor Hall and its activities in the hands of her capable daughters and set to work. Endowed with a strong sense of purpose and the means to pursue it, Fell was in a unique position to leave her home for months on end to advance Quakerism. After returning home from her first London visit, Fell remained at Swarthmoor only nine months before she journeyed back to London for another four-month stay. By this time, she was describing beatings of Quakers by soldiers, as well as other persecutions.

Beginning in 1663, Fell began to travel through various counties to visit Friends, logging nearly 1,000 miles on her journey. On this circuit, George Fox met her party and returned with them to Swarthmoor; he was arrested immediately and imprisoned in Lancaster Castle. Shortly thereafter, Fox's prosecutors summoned Fell and required her to answer the "Oath of Allegiance," knowing that a devout Quaker would refuse to take any oath before God and therefore could be imprisoned.

The justices told Fell they would not tender her the Oath if she promised not to hold Meetings at Swarthmoor. She refused to compromise, kept silent when read the Oath, and after receiving indictment, answered the judge, "I rather choose a prison for obeying of God, than my liberty for obeying of men contrary to my conscience." While she was confined in prison at Lancaster from 1664 to 1668, Fell turned again to the written word to continue her work. She wrote epistles to other Friends, maintained correspondence with her family, and wrote an appeal to Charles II which went unanswered; she also wrote four books. The first, *A Call to the Universal Seed of God*, exhorted Jews and Gentiles to recognize the inward religion of Christ. *The Standard of the Lord Revealed* was written for Friends and traced the history of God's work through the Bible. *A Touch-Stone, or a perfect Tryal* addressed clergy, whether Roman Catholic or Protestant, and outlined her protest against "outward sacraments." Fell's 1666 work, *Women's Speaking Justified*, cites multiple biblical precedents for the spiritual equality of women and their role as preachers of the Gospel. As soon as she was released from prison in 1668, Fell resumed her full schedule of activity, traveling to northern and western England and visiting London for a third time that winter.

In the fall of 1669, Margaret Fell married George Fox. Fox had approached Fell's children before the marriage to assure himself that they were "satisfied" with the match and understood he was not interested in their mother's estate. Indeed, the marriage of Fox and Fell was unusual in many respects. Both partners continued to travel extensively and were separated by various prison sentences. During their 11-year marriage, they lived under the same roof for only a few years. Fox's lack of intervention in the management of Swarthmoor or other Fell holdings was also considered unusual, since a man who married a wealthy wife would be expected to assume administration of her property. Fell remained firmly in control of her family estate. Over the years, speculation on the nature of the Fell-Fox marriage has ranged from the idea of a "spiritual" union to a rather businesslike agreement to join forces for the sake of Quakerism.

Margaret Fell wrote a short tribute to George Fox after his death in 1691. She spent her remaining 11 years at Swarthmoor. By 1690, the Friends Meeting begun at her estate had been moved to a Meeting house nearby, and persecution of Quakerism had been greatly reduced. An Act passed by Parliament in 1696 allowed for "easement" in oath-taking, requiring Friends to "declare and affirm" rather than "declare in the presence of the Almighty God." The Society of Friends had been resisting the old oath for nearly 50 years.

In her final years, Fell reminded Quakers of the founding principles. After a half century or more, the movement had become more institutionalized, with Friends interested in building new Meeting houses and defining their faith. Inevitable differences of opinion arose, and Fell quickly rebutted issues she felt were not central to Quaker identity, such as the growing support for "outward ceremonies" of gray dress and the trend towards quietism. Alarmed by emphasis upon outward appearance, Fell reminded Friends of principles of inward purity. She wrote in an epistle, "It's a dangerous thing to lead young Friends much into observation of outward things, for that will be easily done. . . . But this will not make them true Christians: it's the Spirit that gives life." She regretted the increasing tendency towards separatism and repeatedly called Friends back to the idea of inward spiritual religion.

After more than 50 years of vigorous service to the cause she supported, Margaret Fell died on April 23, 1702, at Swarthmoor Hall. In Quaker hagiography, Fell is remembered as the "nursing mother of Quakerism," an epithet coined by the first Publishers of Truth, or founding Quaker leaders. Recent reevaluation of Fell's contributions, especially by feminist scholarship, recognizes the unique position Fell carved for herself as she labored for the early Quaker movement. Kunze, for example, suggests that instead of "nursing mother" of Quakerism, Fell might be more accurately considered "mother superior." By any assessment, Margaret Fell remains an excellent example of the capable ingenuity displayed by Quaker women who worked to establish and spread their faith. Fell's considerable legacy of writings allows an unusually detailed examination of her theology and accomplishments, providing rare insight into the personality and unconventionality of the author.

SOURCES:

Crosfield, Helen. *Margaret Fox of Swarthmoor Hall.* London: Headley Bros., 1913.

Fell, Margaret. *A call to the Universall seed of God.* London: 1665.

———. *The Citie of London Reproved.* London: Robert Wilson, 1660.

———. *A loving salutation to the seed of Abraham.* London: Th. Simmons, 1656.

———. *A Relation of Margaret Fell, Her Birth, Life, Testimony and Sufferings for the Lord's Everlasting Truth in her Generation,* 1690.

———. *Women's Speaking Justified.* London, 1666, 2nd ed., 1667.

Fox, Margaret Fell. "The Testimony of Margaret Fox concerning her late husband, George Fox; together with a brief account of some of his Travels, Sufferings, and Hardships endured for the Truth's Sake."

Kunze, Bonnelyn Young. *Margaret Fell and the Rise of Quakerism.* London: Macmillan, 1994.

Ross, Ishbel. *Margaret Fell: Mother of Quakerism.* London: Longman, 1949 (reprint, 1984).

SUGGESTED READING:

Fell, Margaret. *A Brief Collection of Remarkable Passages and Occurrences Relating to the Birth, Education, Life, Conversion, Travels, Services and Deep Sufferings of that ancient Eminent and Faithful Servant of the Lord, Margaret Fell, but by her Second Marriage, M. Fox.* London: J. Sowle, 1712.

COLLECTIONS:

Correspondence and manuscripts located in Friends House Library, London; the Friends Historical Library, Swarthmoor College, Swarthmoor, Pennsylvania; and the Quaker collection, Haverford College, Haverford, Pennsylvania.

Sherry Nanninga Walker, M.A.,
freelance writer in religion,
Colorado Springs, Colorado

Felton, Rebecca Latimer

(1835–1930)

American reformer and journalist who was the first woman seated in the U.S. Senate. Born Rebecca Ann Latimer on June 10, 1835, in DeKalb County, near Decatur, Georgia; died on June 24, 1930, in Atlanta, Georgia; oldest of three children of Charles (a farmer and businessman) and Eleanor (Swift) Latimer; at-

*tended private schools in Oxford and Decatur; gradu-
ated from Madison Female College, Madison, Georgia, in 1852; married William Harrell Felton (a physician and Methodist cleric), on October 11, 1853 (died
1909); children: four sons (three of whom died before
adulthood) and one daughter (who died in infancy).*

Independent and competitive as a child, Rebecca Ann Felton grew up in a liberal household
and received the best education then available to
girls in her home state of Georgia. After graduating from Madison Female College at the head of
her class, she married William Harrell Felton, a
physician and Methodist cleric who later aspired
to a political career. Because of poor health,
William took up farming near Cartersville in
northwest Georgia, where Rebecca, within a six-
year period, gave birth to two sons and to a
daughter who died in infancy. During the Civil
War, the Feltons embraced the Confederate
cause and were subjected to horrors that would
color their outlook forever. Forced to flee their
farm when Sherman invaded Georgia, they

*Rebecca
Latimer
Felton*

sought refuge in a run-down farmhouse near
Macon, where they were terrorized by Federal
raiders, Confederate deserters, and freed slaves.
One son died of measles in 1864 and the other
of malaria a year later. Two more sons were
born after the war, but only one survived to
adulthood.

During the Reconstruction years, while rebuilding the family farm in Cartersville and
helping her husband run a school, Felton became active in the local temperance club and the
ladies' society to aid Confederate widows and
orphans. She then moved on to assist her husband's political career, which included service as
a congressional representative and later in the
Georgia legislature. Felton served as his campaign manager and press secretary during his
three successful runs for Congress (1874, 1876,
and 1878), and she proved to be a formidable
opponent when under political attack. She
served as his secretary in Washington, and, when
he was defeated in 1880 and they returned to
Cartersville, she helped found and edit a local
newspaper. From 1884 to 1890, when William
served in the Georgia legislature, Rebecca again
ran his election campaigns, drafted bills and
speeches, and served as a general adviser. By the
time her husband retired from politics, she had
become a public figure in her own right.

For several decades, well into her 80s, Felton was a leader of several reform movements,
notably those for prison reform, particularly the
battle against convict leasing which allowed
women and child convicts to be housed with
men. She also supported women's rights and was
active in Georgia's suffrage movement, which
for many years was led by her sister **Mary Latimer McLendon** (1840–1921). With her husband, Felton defended the state university from
attacks by denominational colleges and campaigned for the admission of women. It was
largely through her efforts that the Georgia
Training School for Girls, which provided vocational training for the state's poor white girls,
was founded in Atlanta in 1915. Felton served
on the board of lady managers of the World's
Columbian Exposition in Chicago (1893) and
also chaired the women's executive board of the
Cotton States and International Exposition in
Atlanta (1894–95).

In 1899, the *Atlanta Journal,* in an effort to
boost circulation of its rural semi-weekly edition, hired Felton as a columnist. In a regular
feature entitled "Mrs. Felton's Timely Talks,"
she offered advice on farming, household management, child labor laws, and the doctrine of

evolution, while her views reflected the predominant bias of the region against blacks, Catholics, and Jews. Felton's writing during this period also involved several autobiographical books, including *My Memoirs of Georgia Politics* (1911) and *Country Life in Georgia in the Days of My Youth* (1919). She retired from the *Journal* in 1927, having won the respect and admiration of farm families throughout Georgia and the southeast.

In 1920, at age 85, Felton entered the political arena again, campaigning to elect Thomas E. Watson as U.S. senator and his fellow isolationist Thomas Hardwick as governor. When Watson died in office, Hardwick appointed Felton to fill the unexpired term, a mere gesture, since a successor would be elected before Congress reconvened. Felton, however, persuaded the elected successor, Walter F. George, to delay his appearance in the reconvened Senate, and on November 21, 1922, opening day, she took her seat on the Senate floor, the first woman ever to do so. The next day, after a brief speech, she relinquished the seat to George. Felton returned to Cartersville, where she continued to chide the press when events or people displeased her, and also worked on her final autobiography, *The Romantic Story of Georgia Women* (1930), a chronicle (and elaboration) of her achievements. She died at the age of 95, in Atlanta, where she had gone to attend a trustees' meeting of the Georgia Training School for Girls. She was buried in Cartersville, in a marble mausoleum she had erected near the grave of her husband.

SOURCES:

James, Edward T., ed., *Notable American Women*. Cambridge, MA: The Belknap Press of Harvard University Press, 1971.

McHenry, Robert, ed. *Famous American Women*. NY: Dover, 1983.

SUGGESTED READING:

Talmadge, John E. *Rebecca Latimer Felton: Nine Stormy Decades*, 1980.

COLLECTIONS:

An extensive collection of Rebecca Felton's papers are located in the University of Georgia Library.

Barbara Morgan,
Melrose, Massachusetts

Fénelon, Fania (1918–1983)

French singer and activist in the French resistance, whose experiences in Auschwitz chronicle the mixture of suffering and solidarity that made up her daily routine as a death-camp prisoner. Name variations: Fanny Goldstein; Fania Fenelon. Pronunciation: FAHN-ya FAY-ne-lawn. Born Fanny Goldstein in Paris, France, on September 2, 1918; died in Paris on December 19, 1983; daughter of Jules Goldstein (an engineer and a Jew) and Marie (Bernier) Goldstein (a Catholic); graduated from the Paris Conservatoire with a first in piano, 1934; never married; no children.

Became a music-hall singer following graduation from the Paris Conservatoire (1934); joined the French underground after Germany occupied France (1940); arrested as a member of the resistance (1943); sent to the Auschwitz-Birkenau concentration camp and became a member of the orchestra led by Alma Rosé (January 1944); liberated from Bergen-Belsen (April 15, 1945); published Playing for Time, *about her camp experiences (1977), which was dramatized by playwright Arthur Miller for television (1980) and produced on stage in England (1985).*

Fania Fénelon's life in a German Nazi death camp during World War II embodied the juxtaposition of one of humanity's most noble intellectual creations, music, with the almost inconceivable horrors of the Holocaust. She experienced this bizarre incongruity of beauty and evil every day, as a prisoner whose very existence depended on her continuing to perform as a musician and thus keep her captors entertained. Late in her life, the singer finally chose to tell her extraordinary story of a small group of women within the dreaded Auschwitz-Birkenau concentration camp. Millions now know it through her memoir, *Playing for Time,* and the play and television drama based on her work.

Fanny Goldstein was born into a Parisian bourgeois family, the daughter of Jules Goldstein, an engineer, and **Marie Bernier Goldstein**, a gifted singer. The child's talent for music was evident early, and by age ten she was enrolled at the Paris Conservatoire. In 1934, she graduated, with a first prize in piano. At age 16, she had a pleasant soprano voice and considerable stage presence, when she adopted Fania Fénelon as her *nom de théâtre* and set out to become a music-hall chanteuse. By the late 1930s, she was barely into her 20s and enjoying a successful career.

But Fénelon became increasingly aware of the pro-Fascist and anti-Semitic attitudes that gradually became accepted in France. The Nazi occupation which began in the late spring of 1940 radically changed her life. She found herself classified as a "non-Aryan" because her father was a Jew. In June 1940, when she witnessed a triumphant and gloating Adolf Hitler on his brief tour of a prostrate Paris, the humane values learned from her parents made Fénelon eager to "destroy this plague."

Before the end of 1940, Fénelon had secretly taken up arms against the German occupiers by joining the French resistance movement. As a singer in cabarets frequented by German officers, she found many opportunities to spy on the enemy. While German soldiers were drunk or occupied with a woman, she would photograph the contents of their briefcases and pass the film on to her associates in the underground. On two occasions, she was arrested and interrogated but released for lack of evidence.

In early 1943, betrayed to the Gestapo by a Russian member of her resistance cell, 25-year-old Fénelon was arrested. Though all of her compatriots were executed, she alone was kept alive in order to be interrogated and tortured for a period of months. She was then transferred to Drancy, a house of detention outside Paris.

We weren't saints. We did what we had to to stay alive.

—Fania Fénelon

On January 20, 1944, in the dead of winter, Fénelon was loaded along with 120 others into an overcrowded railroad car, where there was insufficient ventilation and no room to lie down. As sanitary conditions deteriorated, the prisoners were left filthy and further humiliated, and some of the weaker deportees died standing up during the journey. After almost three days, the train arrived at its unannounced destination, where many of the prisoners were relieved to see vehicles marked with red crosses. In the dark, some entered them with relief that they would not have to walk to the nearby camp, while others, exhausted by the horrendous journey, were now marched a distance of about two miles through the bitterly cold night to a gate bearing the slogan "Arbeit macht frei." Their destination was in fact Auschwitz-Birkenau and the "fortunate" prisoners chosen to ride in the Red Cross vehicles had actually been selected to be taken immediately to the camp's gas chambers from which their bodies would be removed and burned in the nearby crematorium.

Fénelon spent 48 hours in the quarantine section of the camp, where she and her fellow deportees were stripped, shaved, and tattooed on their arms; her number was 74862, with a tiny inverted triangle in blue ink. Soon afterward, she found herself addressed in Polish by a well-dressed woman, obviously a prisoner-trustee. All Fénelon could make out were the words for "Madame Butterfly." The thought that sprang to her mind was that all indeed must be lost, to find talk of music in such a hellish place as Auschwitz. Then a girl appeared and translated the woman's request: a musician was wanted who could play the piano and sing Puccini's *Madame Butterfly*.

Intrigued, but unsure what the request might signify, Fania soon found herself in a surprisingly warm and well-lit room in Auschwitz's Camp No. 2, complete with a Bechstein grand piano. Also in the barracks was a group of rather well-clothed women, all with musical instruments. Fénelon performed before the conductor of the ensemble, an attractive young woman with a slight Viennese accent, who proved to be none other than the young Viennese musician, *Alma Rosé, a niece of the great composer-conductor Gustav Mahler, and daughter of Arnold Rosé, a brilliant violinist who was for many decades concertmaster of the Vienna Philharmonic Orchestra. Frightened but ready to take advantage of the situation, Fénelon sang arias from Puccini's beloved opera as well as a popular hit song by Peter Kreuder, "When Spring Arrives" (*Wenn es Frühling wird*), and passed the audition with flying colors.

The origin of the Auschwitz-Birkenau women's orchestra was in many ways typical of the appalling fusion of culture and brutality that was the norm in the National Socialist German Reich. The commandant of the women's division, **Maria Mandel**, and the commandant of Auschwitz-Birkenau, Josef Kramer, were enthusiastic music lovers, who wanted personal orchestras for themselves. They believed such ensembles would entertain both the prisoners and the SS guards of the various camps within the vast Auschwitz complex. Once it existed, the orchestra performed almost without interruption. Alma Rosé and her musicians practiced and performed from morning through night—17 hours in an average day. The 47 women in the group were a veritable League of Nations, from ten different countries. Another vocalist besides Fénelon was from Hungary, and another was the German singer **Lotte Lebeda**, who had been a successful singer at the Prague Opera House. The orchestra performed under varying conditions and for many different kinds of audiences; sometimes they played for as few as three or four SS men gathered for the concert.

When Alma Rosé conducted her musicians in the women's block, the performance was almost invariably a grim occasion, for the audiences who listened to a concert in the morning were customarily marched off to the gas chambers that same afternoon. Some mornings, the orchestra played charming waltzes of Franz Lehar for infirm prisoners, knowing the fate awaiting them a few hours later. They were also required to play for visiting dignitaries, including Reichsführer-SS Heinrich Himmler, the commander-in-chief of the vast empire of death in the Nazi camps. The response of the listeners to these performances varied greatly. Some sang along with the music and even smiled, obviously moved; others, worn down by starvation, torture and knowledge of their impending deaths, appeared utterly indifferent. Some were doubtless envious of the musicians who seemed to have discovered the secret of indefinitely prolonging their existence in the world of suffering and extinction.

For virtually all camp prisoners, the highest priority was not comfort or abstract dignity, but pure and simple physical survival. Against this standard, members of the Auschwitz women's orchestra were in fact a truly privileged group. Whether it reflected their cultural respect for music, or their awareness that the ensemble required some degree of self-respect in order to perform up to a competent musical standard, the Nazi commandants saw to it that the musicians benefited in ways denied their fellow prisoners. Although Fénelon and her fellow performers suffered from the near-starvation food rations common among the inmates, they enjoyed daily showers (others prisoners could shower every three weeks) and better toilet facilities. They were also relatively well-clothed compared to those who endured the frigid air in thin and inadequate garments. The musicians' barracks boasted individual beds, a stove, and an adequate supply of wood.

To calm his nerves, Josef Kramer insisted on hearing the orchestra's rendition of Robert Schumann's "Träumerei" from the Romantic composer's beloved and tender "Scenes of Childhood." Decades later, in a 1980 interview for a German newspaper, Fénelon noted the grotesque contrast between the murderous daily activities of the camp commandant, in which he oversaw the gassing of tens of thousands of prisoners he viewed as inferior life forms deserving to be extinguished, and his ardent desire for spiritual release by listening to the great compositions from the German musical pantheon. Listening to some particularly beautiful composition by a Teutonic master performed by this ensemble of "racially undesirable" and "sub-human" women, Kramer and other SS men were sometimes moved to tears. Faced with the question of fellow prisoners, who could never understand how the women

Fania
Fénelon

performed for such an audience, Fénelon's answer, decades after the war, was simply: "What could we do? Should we have simply refused to perform, thus telling our captors, all right, now you can send us to the gas chambers?"

Alma Rosé did not live to see the day of liberation, dying in 1944; accounts differ as to the cause of her death. While Fania Fénelon was among those who did survive, there were several occasions when her life hung by a thread. On September 2, 1944, her 36th birthday, she was extremely ill and feared that the SS would use her weakness as a pretext—as it often did—to send her to the gas chambers. To keep Fénelon from being sent to the infirmary, which was often a prelude to extermination, her fellow musicians gave up precious pieces of their own bread to help her recover her health. At one point, clad in their nightshirts, they surrounded her bed and quietly sang the resistance songs she had often performed for them late at night when only a few guards were in the watchtowers.

Fénelon never forgot this unique and moving act of human compassion.

During the last months in Auschwitz, the members of the orchestra, numb with grief after Rosé's death, struggled to keep intact her legacy of musical excellence and fierce determination to survive the camp. When Rosé's designated successor, a Russian pianist named Sonia, proved incapable of keeping the ensemble musically coherent, Fénelon would conduct secretly behind her back. As the quality of their music deteriorated, the musicians' fear for their survival increased with each passing day. Adding to the tension was the fact that, in the fall of 1944, Soviet forces were rapidly advancing on the camp. As she was about to enter the shower on November 1, 1944, Fénelon was told by a guard that the musicians were not to return to their barracks but to prepare instead for immediate evacuation. Marched to a waiting train, they boarded for three days of travel, without food and with no idea of their destination. They disembarked in an anonymous location where they were forced to stand in the freezing rain for nine hours before they realized their transfer had been to the notorious Bergen-Belsen camp. The facility was in no way equipped to handle the many new prisoners. Not surprisingly, Fénelon and many of her fellow-musicians became desperately ill.

Suffering from typhus and close to death, she nevertheless witnessed the liberation of Bergen-Belsen by British forces on April 15, 1945. The musicians, scheduled for execution at 3 PM that day, instead saw the arrival of the British at 10 AM. On the only available piano, which was badly out of tune, Fénelon sang at the insistence of her comrades, improvising on "God Save the King" for at least half an hour, croaking out France's "La Marseillaise" and the Russian's adopted communist anthem, the "Internationale." When a British soldier brought her a microphone, her weakened voice was transmitted to London and broadcast by the BBC, and a recording of this incredibly moving concert of liberation survives in the BBC Recorded Sound Archives.

Fania Fénelon arrived back in Paris on May 17, 1945, still in fragile health. Eager to entertain the Allied troops that had smashed the Fascist system, she joined some American entertainers touring G.I. bases in occupied Germany. After she had recovered physically, it took many years before Fania Fénelon found the courage to tell her story. Sublimating her emotions in her work, she performed in recitals throughout Europe, always singing one song that she told her audiences she had learned at Auschwitz. For many years, she taught in music conservatories of the war-torn cities of Dresden, Leipzig, and East Berlin. Fearful that West Germany had been too quick in burying and hiding its bloody past, she lived and worked for decades in the German Democratic Republic, under East German rule, finally believing that the lessons of the Nazi evil had been truly learned and a new generation was free of anti-Semitism and militarism.

In the 1960s and 1970s, when signs of a rising tide of neo-Nazism threatened a generation of young people in West Germany who had little or no knowledge of the horrors of Nazi genocide, Fénelon was finally motivated to write her autobiography as a warning to the younger generation. Her book *Playing for Time* was published in several countries, including the U.S. and England, was adapted by American playwright Arthur Miller into a powerful teleplay, and became a key part of the personal record of the Holocaust. Having spent time at the edge of the 20th-century's moral abyss, Fénelon had no illusions, but she still held hope for a better future for a sorely tested human race.

SOURCES:

Anderson, Susan Heller. "Fania Fénelon: Musical Gift Meant Survival," in *The New York Times Biographical Service*. January 1978, pp. 42–43.

Die Zeit. Nr. 41, October 3, 1980, p. 64, cited in Kuhn, Annette and Valentine Rothe, *Frauen im deutschen Faschismus*. 2nd ed. 2 vols. Düsseldorf: Verlag Schwann, 1983, vol. II, pp. 200–204.

"Fania Fénelon," in *The Times* [London]. December 23, 1983, p. 12.

"Fania Fénelon, 74 [sic]; In Inmate Orchestra While at Auschwitz," in *The New York Times Biographical Service*. December 1983, p. 1439.

Fénelon, Fania. *Playing for Time*. NY: Atheneum, 1977.

Miller, Arthur. *Arthur Miller's Playing for Time*. Chicago, IL: Dramatic Publishing, 1985.

Wadler, Joyce. "Singing for Her Life at Auschwitz: Memoirs of a Survivor Who Has Always Been a Fighter," in *The Washington Post*. March 3, 1978, pp. D1, D3.

RELATED MEDIA:

Playing for Time (148 min.), television drama, adapted by Arthur Miller, starring **Vanessa Redgrave**, **Melanie Mayron**, and **Jane Alexander** (1980), directed by Daniel Mann.

John Haag,
Associate Professor, University of Georgia,
Athens, Georgia

Feng, Amy (1969—)

Chinese-born table tennis champion. Born on April 9, 1969, in Tianjin, China, near Beijing; moved to

Wheaton, Maryland, then Augusta, Georgia; married; children: one.

Born in Tianjin, China, near the city of Beijing, on April 9, 1969, Amy Feng began playing table tennis at the age of nine. In March 1992, she moved to the United States and has since been the number-one ranked woman in American table tennis. Internationally, she won the women's singles in table tennis at the Polish Open (1985), the Chinese World College championships (1987), the Canadian National Exhibition (1992), as well as the North American championship series, Women's Allstar Singles, and the Chinese New Year tournament (all 1994). In the United States, Feng placed first at the Southern Open, the Pacific Rim Open in Portland, Oregon, and the Sun TV Open (all 1992) and was North American champion (1993). Known for her quick serve and explosive attack, Feng was the U.S. Table Tennis National champion in women's singles in 1992, 1993, 1994, and 1995, and came in second at the U.S. Olympic trials in 1996. But Feng failed to medal in the Atlanta Olympics. **Liu Wei** of China defeated her 16–21, 21–8, 21–15, taking advantage of forehand errors in the final two sets.

Fenning, Elizabeth (1792–1815)

English criminal. Name variations: Eliza Fenning. Born in 1792; hanged on June 26, 1815.

In March 1815, 21-year-old Elizabeth Fenning stood accused of attempting to poison the family of her employer, Orlibar Turner, by mixing arsenic in the dumplings. Fenning, who had been in domestic service since she was 14, strongly protested her innocence and proved that she too had been made ill by the dumplings. But there were those who were convinced that she had only sampled the poisoned food to deflect blame. Convicted, she was sentenced to hang. Because of public sympathy and her protestations, however, the verdict was twice reconsidered by the Home Office. Fenning was hanged nonetheless on June 26, 1815.

Fenton, Faith (1857–1936).

See Freeman, Alice.

Fenton, Lavinia (1708–1760)

English actress. Name variations: Duchess of Bolton. Born in 1708; died on January 24, 1760; probably the daughter of a naval lieutenant named Beswick; married Charles Paulet, 3rd duke of Bolton, in 1751; children: three (all died young).

Lavinia Fenton was probably the daughter of a naval lieutenant named Beswick, but she took the name of her mother's second husband, a man named Fenton. Her first appearance on stage was as Monimia in Otway's *Orphans* (1726) at the Haymarket. She then joined the company of players at the theater in Lincoln's Inn Fields, where her success and beauty made her the toast of the town. It was in Gay's *Beggar's Opera*, as Polly Peachum, that Fenton made her greatest success in 1728. That same year, she appeared as Ophelia in *Hamlet*. She was the rage in London: her pictures were in great demand, verses were written to her, and books were published about her. William Hogarth portrayed her in a scene from *Hamlet*, with Charles Paulet, 3rd duke of Bolton, in a theater box-seat (she had lived with the duke for many years). After appearing in several comedies, and then in numerous productions of the *Beggar's Opera*, she ran away with her lover Paulet, a man much older than herself. After the death of his wife in 1751, Paulet married Fenton who then left the stage.

Fenwick, Ethel Gordon
(1857–1947)

English pioneer of nursing reform. Born Ethel Gordon Manson in England in 1857; died in 1947; married Bedford Fenwick (a physician), in 1887.

Following nursing positions at Nottingham children's hospital and the London Hospital, Ethel Fenwick was appointed matron of St. Bartholemew's Hospital, a post she held for six years, until her marriage in 1887. That year, she led a group of nurses in the formation of the British Nurses' Association (BNA), of which she was president. The association sought to raise the standards of the profession by accepting nursing candidates exclusively from the higher social classes. After the BNA was granted a Royal Charter in 1893, Fenwick was deposed as president. In opposition, she and her husband would form the British College of Nurses in 1926.

Fenwick also started the Matrons' Council of Great Britain and Ireland, a group that lobbied Parliament for state registration of matrons (obtained in 1919). To aid her campaign efforts, Fenwick and her husband purchased *The Nursing Record*, later called *The British Journal of Nursing*. At the International Council of

Women, which met in London in 1899, Fenwick and the Matron's Council organized the International Council of Nurses, the very first organization for health professionals.

Fenwick, Millicent (1910–1992)

U.S. Republican Congresswoman who was celebrated for her political independence. Name variations: Millicent Hammond Fenwick. Born Millicent Vernon Hammond in New York City on February 25, 1910; died on September 16, 1992, of heart failure at her home in Bernardsville, New Jersey; second of three children of Ogden Haggerty Hammond (a financier and state representative) and Mary Picton Stevens Hammond (an heiress and humanitarian); attended Foxcroft School, Middleburg, Virginia; studied philosophy under Bertrand Russell at the New School for Social Research; attended classes at Columbia University's extension school in 1933; married Hugh Fenwick, in 1934 (divorced 1945); children: Hugh H. Fenwick; Mary Fenwick Reckford.

Elected councilwoman for Bernardsville, N.J. (1958–64); elected New Jersey State Assemblywoman (1969–72); appointed New Jersey director of consumer affairs (1972); elected U.S. Congresswoman (1974–83); served as U.S. envoy to the United Nations Food and Agriculture Organization (1983–87).

Selected publications: Vogue Book of Etiquette *(1948);* Speaking Up *(1982).*

Millicent Fenwick spoke with the cultivated accent that is acquired only in the most select finishing schools; yet in her 60s, when she sat back after delivering a political speech, she would reach into her handbag, take out a pipe, and light it. Fenwick gave two reasons for this particular eccentricity: her doctor told her to give up cigarettes, and, after the birth of her seventh grandchild, she felt she had the right to do as she pleased.

One of three siblings born early in the 20th century to a wealthy, well-established family, Fenwick used her connections to further her aims at the same time she chafed against convention. Her father Ogden Hammond was a businessman in New York and New Jersey and served two terms as a Republican member of the New Jersey House of Representatives. Her mother **Mary Stevens Hammond**, active in humanitarian work, was a descendant of John Stevens, a colonel in the American Revolutionary Army who became an inventor and builder; he established the family fortune by buying 500 acres of land across the Hudson River from New

York City. The Stevens home is the site of the Stevens Institute of Technology in Hoboken, New Jersey.

As a tiny child standing on the porch of the family home, Millicent Hammond watched her parents don goggles, gloves, and driving coats to take spins in their first Packard. At age five, in May 1915, she learned that her mother had drowned when a German submarine sank the *Lusitania* off the coast of Ireland. Mary Stevens Hammond had been traveling with her husband to Paris to set up a hospital for war victims. "Daddy was never the same," Fenwick told **Elisabeth Bumiller** of the *Washington Post*. "Before that, he loved riding the hounds. He was gay, dark, quite a handsome man. When he came back, he was taciturn and different." A few years later, he married **Marguerite McClure Howland**, with whom Millicent Hammond constantly clashed. Millicent attended Foxcroft in Virginia, until Calvin Coolidge appointed her father ambassador to Spain. Her formal education ended when she joined the family in Madrid, but she did become fluent in Spanish, French, and Italian as a result of her European stay. Living a privileged, pampered life, Millicent and her sister had at their disposal a car and chauffeur. "Whenever we went out to play golf, a maid would go along with us. And if we wanted to play golf with a man, a married woman had to be present. There was a lot of drama to life—every man was dangerous dynamite," Fenwick recalled.

The family returned to New Jersey when Millicent was 19. She took some courses at Columbia University and studied philosophy with Bertrand Russell at the New School for Social Research. They struck up a friendship, and Fenwick dined with Russell and his wife ◄❧ **Alys Berenson** on a weekly basis, but they grew apart, reportedly because Fenwick objected to his negative attitude toward the United States. The social side of her life continued to claim her attention. At a lawn party in New Jersey, Millicent became spellbound by a married man named Hugh Fenwick, who was five years her senior. While his wife spent the summer on Long Island, a scandalous romance ensued. "There was a terrible row. It was rather seamy," Fenwick said of her courtship. "The family, of course, was furious. But I was determined." Millicent's cousin **Mary Baird** described his appeal to *People Weekly*: "Hugh Fenwick was heavy, and he never had much hair, but he was full of charm. I remember sitting with him on a screened porch one night and a moth was circling the light. Instead of getting up and turning off the switch, Hugh pulled a

❧►
Berenson, Alys.
See Berenson, Mary for sidebar on Alys Smith Russell.

Millicent Fenwick

pistol from his belt and shot out the bulb."

Millicent and Hugh were married after his divorce, but the ceremony was overshadowed by the scandal, and her stepmother unplugged the lights so a photographer could not properly record the event. The marriage produced two children and lasted less than a decade, during which time Millicent occasionally modeled for *Harper's Bazaar*. The Fenwick fortunes were battered in the Wall Street crash of 1929, but when her marriage ended, Millicent paid off his debts by going to work for *Vogue* in 1938. Her first assignment was to interview *Mary Martin. "I was so scared. I didn't want to be rude, but I also wanted to get everything for my story. As it turned out, it was also the first time anyone had interviewed her," said Fenwick.

After Pearl Harbor, Millicent became war editor for the magazine, assigning features on the conflict abroad and on the home front. "Actually, it was Hitler that got me into politics. I was pushed into [joining] the National Conference of Christians and Jews by hearing him," she told **Louise Sweeney** of *The Christian Science Monitor*. Fenwick banned flattering photos and stories about those who were collaborating with the Nazis from the magazine. Notably, she refused to run a picture of J.P. Morgan's daughter

*Anne Morgan in *Vogue* because Anne gave a party for the Vichy ambassador. Although *Vogue* had to scramble for fashion coverage, when Fenwick learned that a Swiss man, who was selling fashion sketches, was actually representing a designer working in German-held Paris, she announced, "I would rather publish *Vogue* with blank pages than send one cent to support the Nazis." Meanwhile, her economic difficulties continued. Friday evenings, when she returned home to New Jersey, she was regularly greeted by a process server and presented with a fresh suit for non-payment of her former husband's debts.

The whole point of government is justice.

—Millicent Fenwick

After the war, in 1948, Fenwick compiled *Vogue's Book of Etiquette,* which sold a million copies. While she was reportedly embarrassed to be writing on the placement of dessert spoons, she enjoyed promoting the book, traveling by train to regions of the country she had not seen before. In 1952, a belated inheritance from her mother and the growth of the family real-estate interests enabled her to retire from *Vogue.* To economize, she tore down two-thirds of the family's 38-room mansion and lived mainly, and elegantly, in what had been the library. She volunteered for local New Jersey causes like legal aid and prison reform and worked for Republican candidates. She would later disdain her volunteer work as "the typical female pattern." "I always wanted things in the most foolish, over-modest, hesitant way. I finally learned that when a man wants more he says, 'Listen, George. I want a bit of the action.' Well, we've been taught: 'you have to wait to be invited to dance.'" In 1958, she ran for the borough council in Bernardsville and was twice re-elected. She left office in 1964, suffering from a nervous disorder.

In 1969, Fenwick was elected to the New Jersey General Assembly, where she earned the nickname "Outhouse Millie" because she lobbied for better working conditions for migrant workers, including portable toilets. In 1972, she resigned to become the state's director of consumer affairs. There she battled deceptive auto advertising and required funeral homes to itemize their bills in advance. In 1974, she won election on the Republican ticket to the 94th Congress. She was 64 years old and her victory was described as "a geriatric triumph." At a dinner of the Washington Press Club soon afterward, she told the story of her exchange with a male delegate to the New Jersey assembly when they were debating the Equal Rights Amendment. He said, "I just don't like this amendment. I always thought women were meant to be kissable, cuddly and sweet-smelling." Fenwick retorted, "That's what I thought of men—and I hope, for your sake, you haven't been disappointed as many times as I've been." The remark became famous and made her a Washington celebrity. She captured the imagination of the cartoonist Garry Trudeau who caricatured her as Lacey Davenport in his *Doonesbury* comic strip. (Beholding a group of striking workers, Lacey exclaimed, "You poor dears!") Fenwick had an affinity for Lacey, "She's useful, unpretentious and kindly," and the popular strip honed her image as the *Katharine Hepburn of politics. Fenwick was in fact tall, patrician, and idiosyncratic. Frugality was a hallmark. She wore 40-year-old designer suits that flattered her model-thin frame, drove a Chevrolet when she could have afforded a Cadillac, and carefully counted change due her from the office coffee fund.

One of her closest allies in the House of Representatives was *Bella Abzug, a New York liberal, who had begun life as the daughter of a butcher. In March 1975, they traveled together to Vietnam and Cambodia with a Congressional delegation to investigate Gerald Ford's request to increase funds for South Vietnam. During a heated discussion while driving though Saigon, Fenwick sided with those who feared a bloodbath if funds were cut off. Abzug said a bloodbath was already in progress and that the corrupt government in Saigon was selling off the arms the United States provided. A congressman traveling with them was upset when the two women began shouting, but they told him to let them continue their debate and when they were done, recalled Fenwick, "Bella said, 'Wasn't that fun?'" Soon after, Fenwick joined Abzug in opposing increased funding for Vietnam. She wrote in a *New York Times* piece, "I think we must face the fact that military aid sent from America will not succeed. It will only delay the development of the kind of stable situation—whatever form that takes—that will at least stop the horrible suffering of war." She supported humanitarian assistance, however, saying, "We oughtn't to worry who's in the palace when people are hungry; we should just send food."

Working 12- and 14-hour days, often arriving at her office at seven in the morning, Fenwick espoused a number of causes, including civil rights, peace in Vietnam, aid for asbestos victims, help for the poor, prison reforms, strip-mining controls, urban renewal, gun control, reduction of military programs, and restrictions on capital punishment. She also voted in favor of most of Ronald Reagan's budget cuts. She came from a long line of Republicans, but said that her party allegiance was philosophical: "It is because I don't trust government that I am a Republican," she wrote in her book *Speaking Up.* "Democrats don't mind mandatory laws, regulations and ordinances. . . . Republicans tend to ask 'Why? Is the situation such that we must order people around?'"

Fenwick was a lead sponsor of the resolution creating the commission to monitor the 1975 Helsinki accords on human rights. She was re-elected to Congress three times by increasing margins—in 1980, she received 78% of the vote. In 1982, at the end of her Congressional term, she refused political-action committee (PAC) money and ran for the U.S. Senate but was narrowly defeated by Frank R. Lautenberg, a Democrat and millionaire who portrayed her as an aging eccentric. Ronald Reagan appointed her the first American envoy to the United Nations Food and Agriculture Organization in Rome, where her fluent Italian charmed her hosts. Millicent Fenwick retired in 1987 and died at her family home in Bernardsville on September 16, 1992.

SOURCES:

Bumiller, Elisabeth. "The Wit and Grit of Millicent Fenwick," in *The Washington Post.* January 20, 1982, p. C1.

Current Biography. NY: H.W. Wilson, 1977.

Diliberto, Gioia. "Millicent Fenwick," in *People Weekly.* September 13, 1982.

Fenwick, Millicent. *Speaking Up.* NY: Harper & Row, 1982.

The New York Times. March 3, 1976, p. 33; September 17, 1992 p. 25.

Sweeney, Louise. *The Christian Science Monitor.* June 25, 1975.

SUGGESTED READING:

Seebohm, Carolyn. *The Man Who Was Vogue.* NY: Viking Press, 1982.

Kathleen Brady,
author of *Lucille: The Life of Lucille Ball* (Hyperion)
and *Ida Tarbell: Portrait of A Muckraker*
(University of Pittsburgh Press)

Feodore of Hohenlohe-Langenburg (1866–1932)

Princess of Leiningen. Born Feodore Victoria Alberta on July 23, 1866; died on November 1, 1932; daughter of Hermann, 6th prince of Hohenlohe-Langenburg, and *Leopoldine (1837–1903); married Emich, 5th prince of Leiningen, on July 12, 1894; children: five, including Charles, 6th prince of Leiningen.

Feodore of Leiningen (1807–1872)

*Princess of Hohenlohe-Langenburg and half-sister of Queen Victoria. Name variations: Feodora of Hohenlohe-Langenburg. Born Anne Feodorovna Augusta Charlotte Wilhelmina on December 7, 1807, in Amorbach, Germany; died on September 23, 1872, in Baden-Baden, Germany; daughter of *Victoria of Coburg (1786–1861) and Emich, 2nd prince of Leiningen; half-sister of Queen *Victoria (1819–1901); married Ernest, 4th prince of Hohenlohe-Langenburg; children: *Adelaide of Hohenlohe-Langenburg (1835–1900); Hermann, 6th prince of Hohenlohe-Langenburg (1832–1913).*

Feodorovna, Alexandra (1798–1860).
See Charlotte of Prussia.

Feodorovna, Alexandra (1872–1918).
See Alexandra Feodorovna.

Feodorovna, Elizabeth (1864–1918).
See Ella, Princess of Hesse-Darmstadt.

Feodorovna, Marie (1759–1828).
See Sophia Dorothea of Wurttemberg.

Feodorovna, Marie (1847–1928).
See Marie Feodorovna.

Feodorovna, Marie (1876–1936).
See Victoria Melita of Saxe-Coburg.

Feodorovna, Olga (1839–1891).
See Cecilia of Baden.

Feodosia.
Variant of Theodosia.

Ferber, Edna (1885–1968)

Pulitzer Prize-winning American author of Showboat, So Big, and Giant, whose novels examine American values and culture, especially their impact on women. Born on August 15, 1885, in Kalamazoo, Michigan; died on April 17, 1968, in New York City, of cancer; daughter of Jacob and Julia (Foster) Ferber; had one sister, Fanny; never married; no children.

After graduation from high school, became the first female reporter for a small Wisconsin newspaper and, later, the Milwaukee Journal; *published her first short story (1910) and her first novel (1911); awarded the Pulitzer Prize for* So Big *(1925), published the previous year; remained one of America's most popular authors with works such as* Show Boat *(the basis for the groundbreaking musical of the same name),* Cimarron, *and* Giant, *in addition to a collection of short stories and nine plays (1920–60).*

Selected writings: Dawn O'Hara, the Girl Who Laughed *(Stokes, 1911);* Fanny Herself *(Stokes, 1917);* The Girls *(Doubleday, 1921);* So Big *(Doubleday, 1924);* Show Boat *(Doubleday, 1925);* Cimarron *(Doubleday, 1930);* American Beauty *(Doubleday, 1931);* Come and Get It *(Doubleday, 1935); (two novellas)* Nobody's in Town *(Doubleday, 1938); (autobiography)* A Peculiar Treasure *(Doubleday, 1939);* Saratoga Trunk *(Doubleday, 1941);* Great Son *(Doubleday, 1945);* Giant *(Doubleday, 1952);* Ice Palace *(Doubleday, 1958); (autobiography)* A Kind of Magic *(Doubleday, 1963); also wrote short stories and plays, including* The Royal Family, Dinner at Eight, *and* Stage Door *(all with George S. Kaufman).*

Shortly after America's entry into World War II, playwright George S. Kaufman received a phone call from his frequent collaborator, Edna Ferber. Ferber wanted his suggestions as to what she might do to help the war effort, and Kaufman recommended that she merely wait until she was asked to contribute. Yes, but what should she *do?*, Ferber impatiently insisted. "Well, Edna," Kaufman ventured, "you could be a tank."

Kaufman may have been joking, but Ferber's dogged determination had already brought her a Pulitzer Prize for fiction 20 years earlier, as well as her position as one of the country's most popular and well-recompensed authors, known for her sweeping sagas dissecting Americans and their national culture. She was an early and vociferous exponent of women's rights, almost all of her female characters being strong, adventurous, and practical-minded while many of her male creations were frequently brought low by a swaggering, hollow machismo. Among her many friends, Ferber's quixotic temper, likely to flare at unexpected and inconvenient times, was much respected. "I walked on eggs with Edna because you never knew what was going to offend her at what moment, but I loved her," **Dorothy Rodgers** once said of her, and her husband Richard's, long friendship with Ferber. "She was worth all the trouble, you know, she really was. She was just a great woman."

Edna Ferber had been a fighter from the time of her childhood when, she once noted, she had been "too little and too ugly" to be shown any favoritism. The eldest daughter of immigrant parents, Ferber had lived a peripatetic childhood after her birth in Kalamazoo, Michigan, on August 15, 1885. (Although the generally reported year of her birth is 1887, her mother **Julia Foster Ferber**'s meticulously kept diary places it two years earlier.) Her father Jacob Ferber had emigrated from Hungary some years earlier with hopes of opening a dry goods store in America's Midwest, where many of his fellow Eastern European Jews had settled. Arriving in Kalamazoo, Jacob met and married Julia Foster and settled down to await the birth of what the couple expected to be a son, to be named Edward. With his wife and new daughter Edna, Jacob embarked on a search for the perfect location for his store, traveling from Kalamazoo to Iowa and on to Chicago before finally setting up shop in Appleton, Wisconsin, not far from Milwaukee. Along the way, another daughter, **Fanny Ferber**, was born.

Although the dry goods store provided a steady income for the Ferbers, Jacob's poor health forced Julia and her eldest daughter to help out financially as best they could. Julia became increasingly involved in running the store, while Edna found a job as the *Appleton Daily Crescent*'s first female news reporter after her graduation from high school. The two women's struggles—Julia's, to save the store from collapse as Jacob's health deteriorated; Edna's, to try and turn her talent for writing into a career that would support her family—forged a lasting bond between the two older women and drove a wedge between Edna and her younger sister Fanny, allowed to remain at home and look after her invalid father. At the time of Julia's death in 1949, Edna noted that her mother "married a man she did not love, a decent, dull, rather handsome man, because her mother said she must. Her life . . . was a tragic thing. How she emerged from it fun-loving and high-spirited, I cannot imagine." But Ferber could, indeed, imagine. She used her pen to decry the conditions under which American women lived and to free herself from her mother's plight.

With her father's death in September of 1909, money became even more of a problem. Julia tried to keep the dry goods store afloat while Edna managed to find a higher-paying job at the *Milwaukee Journal*, living away from Julia for the first time in her life. The pressure to produce an income proved considerable, although it would become the catalyst that launched Ferber's long and productive career. One morning in 1910, she collapsed in a faint on her way to work and was forced to quit her job and return to Appleton to recover. During her convalescence, she managed to publish her first short story in *Everybody's Magazine,* for which she was paid precisely $50.60. This was followed by the first in a series of stories featuring "Mrs. McChesney." Ferber drew on her own precarious experience to

create Emma McChesney, a woman forced by a painful divorce to support herself and her young son by becoming a traveling salesperson hawking women's underwear. Published between 1911 and 1915 in *American Magazine* and *Cosmopolitan*, the Mrs. McChesney stories were

wildly popular and were America's first introduction to the name Ferber. Even Theodore Roosevelt was a fan, although he once wrote to Ferber begging that for propriety's sake, Emma McChesney be allowed to re-marry and revert to being a housewife—a suggestion Edna rejected out of hand. "The idea that anyone ever questioned the propriety of a woman's going into business . . . will be obsolete as millstones," she predicted. The series eventually formed the basis for Ferber's first work for the stage, *Our Mrs. McChesney,* which she co-wrote with George Hobart and which opened on Broadway in 1905, starring *Ethel Barrymore in the title role. Ferber soon became a national symbol for the "modern woman," a role she would incorporate into her future novels.

$\mathcal{S}$he told the story of America.
—Herbert Mayes

Encouraged by the sale of her first Mrs. McChesney story, Edna sent the manuscript of a novel to New York literary agent **Flora May Holly.** *Dawn O'Hara: The Girl Who Laughed* appeared in 1911, followed by two more over the next ten years—*The Girls* and *Fanny Herself,* an autobiographical novel about a Jewish girl growing up in Wisconsin. All the while, Ferber kept up her journalistic work, traveling to the 1912 Democratic Convention in Kansas City to report the nomination of Teddy Roosevelt. There, she met William Allen White, a well-respected newspaper publisher and man of letters. The two struck up a close friendship that would prove invaluable in the coming years.

By the time *Our Mrs. McChesney* opened on Broadway, Ferber had made enough money from her writing to take her mother on the first of many tours of Europe in 1914, from which they returned just as war broke out in August of that year. By the end of World War I, Ferber had published her first collection of short stories and was living in New York, at the stately Majestic Hotel on Central Park West. She wrote for all the leading magazines of the day and plunged enthusiastically into the city's heady social and literary life. "Sometimes I wish I was back on the Appleton, Wisconsin, *Daily Crescent,*" she wrote to Julia, now living in Chicago; then added quickly, "No, I don't, either." Among her acquaintances was the drama editor for *The New York Times,* George S. Kaufman, who suggested that one of her short stories, *Old Man Minick,* might form the basis for a play. *Minick,* the first collaboration in a partnership that would stretch over the next 20 years, opened in 1924 to lukewarm reviews. "There is no love interest, no sex, not even rough language," complained the drama critic for *The Herald Examiner.* "It is as natural as a pain in the back." Although it may not have been an auspicious beginning, *Minick* would prove the exception to a string of popular plays co-written by Ferber and Kaufman, among them *Dinner at Eight, Stage Door,* and *The Royal Family,* all of which eventually were made into films. Through Kaufman, Ferber met drama critic Alexander Woolcott, to whom she wrote a pleading note in 1921 asking, "Could I maybe lunch at the Round Table once?" Although Ferber's association with the Algonquin Round Table was not a long one, she formed some of her most rewarding friendships among this fluid group of wits and cynical arbiters of New York's artistic life, learning to trade sharp-edged ripostes with the best of them. Noel Coward, once noting Edna's severely cut, double-breasted jacket, cattily remarked, "Why, Edna, you almost look like a man." To which Edna famously replied, "Why, Noel, so do you!"

A year after *Minick* began its brief Broadway run, Ferber's name became a household word when it was announced she had won the Pulitzer Prize for fiction for her novel *So Big.* Her story of the Wisconsin farm widow-turned-schoolteacher Selina and her troublesome son Dirk, with its strong sense of place and a heroine who seemed to embody America's primal strength in an era of flappers and bathtub gin, had been suggested to the Pulitzer selection committee by none other than William Allen White. White had recognized Ferber's talent from their first meeting in Kansas City 15 years earlier and had spoken warmly of her work to several friends close to the Pulitzer committee. But even as the accolades were pouring in, Edna was preparing the book that would do even more for her stature than the Pulitzer.

During the tedious and sometimes difficult rehearsals for *Minick,* the show's producer had jokingly suggested that the company give up and run away to join a show boat. "What's a show boat?," Edna inquired. She spent much of the next year finding out, tracking down one Charles Hunter on the coast of North Carolina. Hunter was one of the last surviving captains of the stately old Mississippi paddle-wheelers that brought entertainment to the river towns during the late 19th and early 20th centuries. Hunter's show boat, "The James Adams Floating Palace Theater," was still docked not far from his home. "He knew show boats from stem to stern, from pilot's house to cook's galley," Ferber once recalled. "I got out my yellow pad and hoped he'd never stop talking." Hunter talked for a year and a half, providing Edna with the richly researched background for her novel *Show Boat,* published in 1925. Much of Hunter's personality found its way into Ferber's own Cap'n

Andy; and Hunter's story of a famous white show boat performer married to an African-American woman gave life to the poignant relationship between Edna's fictional Steve and the mulatto Julie, shocking to readers living at a time when interracial marriages were illegal in many states. The book was Ferber's first commercially successful novel and the basis for the 1927 Jerome Kern-Oscar Hammerstein operetta that redefined American musical theater. It was one of the few adaptations of her works of which Ferber wholeheartedly approved. She called it "the most beautiful and important light opera music that has ever been written in America." Audiences ever since have agreed; the show has enjoyed numerous major stage revivals and three film treatments over the last 70 years.

The year 1927, it seemed, was Ferber's. Just one night after *Show Boat* first set sail on Broadway, her latest collaboration with George S. Kaufman, *The Royal Family,* opened to great acclaim. The show was a thinly veiled sendup of the nation's most famous acting family, the Barrymores. Edna had been smitten with Ethel Barrymore ever since her *Mrs. McChesney* days and

From the movie So Big, *starring Jane Wyman.*

was distressed when the great lady sued to close the show. Critics were glad the attempt was unsuccessful. "The play is one of the most enjoyable of the season," enthused the *Times*' Brooks Atkinson. "Nothing could make for a completer [*sic*] exploitation of its theme than this collaboration of a fiction writer . . . and a satirist." Ferber, now the toast of New York and pursued by editors, agents and Hollywood moguls, merely settled down to write her next novel, 1929's *Cimarron*. It was another piece of meticulously researched Americana, dealing this time with the settling of the Oklahoma Territory in the late 19th century. As usual, Edna intended the plight of the women in her story to be its focus, and was disdainful of both film versions of the story—RKO's 1931 adaptation (that year's Oscar winner for Best Picture) and MGM's 1960 release—for missing the real significance of the work. "*Cimarron* has been written with a hard and ruthless purpose," she took pains to remind her public. "It contains paragraphs and even chapters of satire and, I am afraid, bitterness, but I doubt more than a dozen people ever knew this."

Satire was the aim of her next project with Kaufman, 1932's *Dinner at Eight,* a sly attack on high society manners and morals (filmed by George Cukor in 1933), while their 1936 play *Stage Door* skewered the show business world. (*Stage Door* was filmed in 1937 and starred *Katharine Hepburn, *Lucille Ball, *Eve Arden, *Ann Miller, and *Ginger Rogers.) By 1939, Ferber had published *Come and Get It,* a novel about the lumber industry in Wisconsin (filmed in 1936 with *Frances Farmer); was researching a new novel set in New Orleans; and had published her first autobiography, *A Peculiar Treasure.* The financial security she had so sorely lacked in her younger days was now so solid that, in the midst of the Depression, she was able to build an imposing, two-story stone house near Westport, Connecticut, which she called Treasure Hill. All that was lacking, friends observed, was a husband and a family.

Ferber had once described herself as "a stagestruck Jewish nun," and Dorothy Rodgers suggested that Edna's single state was because "she probably couldn't find anyone smart enough." But Ferber, in more serious moments, claimed she enjoyed the company of men more than women. "[Men] act more directly, they have not been obliged for centuries, as women have, to dissemble, to resort to subterfuge," she said. "I find their company more stimulating, more challenging, no matter how old or young." Nonetheless, Ferber never publicly acknowl-

edged more than an admiring friendship with any man, although her sister Fanny claimed that an editor for *American Magazine* once proposed during Edna's early career. Ferber does mention Bert Boyden in *A Peculiar Treasure,* but gives no hint of a romantic attachment in her laudatory few sentences about Boyden's sensitivity to others and skills as an editor. Boyden died shortly after World War I. There has also been speculation about Ferber's relationship with William Allen White, 20 years her senior and the father of two children, but there is no evidence that anything other than a deep respect for each other's intellectual gifts passed between them. In her writings, Edna remained ambivalent, even somewhat awestruck, about the married state. "I'm glad I never married," she wrote near the end of her life. "But I should have married. Marriage is a real experience in life no one should miss. If you are born, and can stand it; live, and can stand it; die, and can stand it, one should be able to marry and stand it." But she never did, sharply telling anyone who inquired that she was not the least bit lonely. "The people in my books are my friends," she claimed. "They never let me down."

World War II was ravaging Europe by the time Ferber's New Orleans saga, *Saratoga Trunk,* was published in the early 1940s. Despite the insecurity of her telephone call to Kaufman, Edna found plenty to do to help the war effort, from writing war-bond speeches for actors to touring Europe as a reporter for national magazines. At the war's end, she personally sponsored the immigration of four German-Jewish children whose parents had perished in concentration camps, supporting all four financially for much of her life. Although not a practicing Jew, the depth of Ferber's feelings is revealed by an unused dedication to her first autobiography found among her papers: "To Adolph Hitler, who has made of me a better Jew and a more understanding and tolerant human being . . . this book is dedicated with loathing and contempt." She did not endear herself to America's Jewish community, however, with her criticism of the new Israeli state that had been established in 1948. It was, she said, "arrogant, uninformed, self-complacent, regarding the world outside itself as definitely second best," and she pointed as proof to a statement by Israel's first president, David Ben-Gurion, that any Jew who lived outside of Israel was not truly Jewish. She was particularly troubled, too, by the sentiment expressed by a character in Leon Uris' *Exodus* who notes how wonderful it is to be in a country where everyone is of the same extraction. Ferber reveled in America's ethnic variety and found the lack of it in many European countries she had visited stultifying. "It is like eating one of those steam-table meals in which every dish tastes like every other dish," she wrote, "or one in which every dish has its own flavor—piquant or sweet or bland." It was precisely this fascination with America's immigrant heritage that informed her last two collaborations with George S. Kaufman, *The Land Is Bright* and *Bravo!*

In 1952, Ferber published the book that would do for her later career what *Show Boat* had done for her earlier years. *Giant* was the result of five lengthy visits to Texas, starting in 1939, sparked by a national fascination with the fortunes being made and lost during the oil boom of the 1930s and '40s. Ferber had at first felt that Texas history was a man's subject ("Let Michener write it," she was heard to say), but by the late 1940s she found it irresistible. Texans, on the other hand, found *Giant* libelous. It was, said one reviewer, "a vicious attack on the beauty and chivalry of our state," while the review in

The Dallas Morning News bellowed that "Ferber Goes Both Native and Berserk: Parody, Not Portrait, of Texas Life!" Even critics who had been more kindly disposed to Edna in the past felt that her sprawling, earthy and boisterous novel dealt more in stereotypes than in actual characters. Ferber's own comment that "The State of Texas is as big as the Texans minds are small" did not help matters. As with *Show Boat*, the book's legacy survives thanks to another medium, in this case George Stevens' 1956 film starring James Dean, Rock Hudson and **Elizabeth Taylor*. (It was Dean's last screen appearance. He was killed in a car crash as production was being completed.) For the first time, Ferber participated directly in the film as a financing partner and pronounced herself satisfied with Stevens' work. No doubt Stevens was, too, for he was awarded an Oscar for Best Director.

Ferber was already completing work on her next novel as *Giant* opened in movie theaters. She had been working for five years on *Ice Palace,* about America's purchase of Alaska

From the movie Giant, *starring James Dean and Elizabeth Taylor.*

from the Russians and the territory's subsequent, tumultuous history. The book, published in 1958, was not a critical success. "Miss Ferber seems definitely more interested in the facts that her research has turned up than in the perfunctory structure she has thrown together to hang them on," wrote one critic. "Her story is too repetitious and disorderly to win a prize in the world of literature," agreed *Times* literary reviewer Charles Poore. "But I shouldn't be surprised at all to hear that it had helped measurably to win statehood for Alaska." Ferber always claimed later that she had not written the book with statehood in mind, but it seems hardly a coincidence that Alaska was admitted to the Union as the 49th state the same year that *Ice Palace* was published.

Although now in her 70s, Ferber refused to slow her pace. She began research on a new novel about Native Americans, inspired by the first of many months-long visits to a health spa in Arizona during which she met and talked with Hopis and Navajos. When not in Arizona, she gave elegant dinner parties at her Park Avenue apartment in New York (she had sold Treasure Hill in 1949) and attended the theater. She lectured her friends about the importance of proper diet and exercise, allowed herself one cigarette a month (which she did not inhale), only took an occasional sherry before dinner, and made sure she enjoyed eight hours of sleep a night. She had long suffered from an agonizing facial tic ("The Face," as she called it) which she refused to cure with surgery that would have left one side of her face paralyzed, and was delighted when the affliction seemed to cure itself and disappear in the mid-1960s, although glaucoma and cataracts remained troublesome. She seemed particularly voluble and bright at the opening of a 1966 revival of *Dinner at Eight*. Few beside herself knew by then that she was dying of an incurable cancer that had been diagnosed earlier that year. She stopped work on her Native American novel only when she was no longer able to travel or concentrate on her voluminous notes and was confined to her bed. Even so, it was reported that she counted aloud to keep her mind active as she lay on her deathbed. On April 17, 1968, Edna Ferber died at the age of 83.

The eulogies at her memorial service all called to mind Kaufman's image of her relentless advance on whatever topic or issue was at hand. Random House publisher Bennett Cerf remembered her as a "gallant, dauntless, irrepressible champion of causes she believed in. When she went on the warpath, tomahawk in hand," he said, "sovereign states like Texas and Oklahoma crumbled and arrogant adversaries . . . were reduced to a quivering glob of Jello." But for Edna Ferber, writing was something much more profound than a soapbox for her personal views. "I should love to think," she once wrote, "that when I am dead, the chronicles of my own country written by me, because I so wanted to write them, will be descendants, however puny and short-lived." Neither adjective is appropriate to describe her work, which remains as strong and vital as the beloved country that inspired it.

SOURCES:

Atkinson, Brooks. *Broadway*. NY: Macmillan, 1970.

Ferber, Edna. *A Kind Of Magic*. London: Victor Gollancz, 1963.

———. *A Peculiar Treasure*. NY: Doubleday, Doran, 1939.

Gilbert, Julie Goldsmith. *Ferber*. NY: Doubleday, 1978.

RELATED MEDIA:

Cimarron (131 min. film), starring Richard Dix, *Irene Dunne, RKO, 1931.

Cimarron (140 min. film), starring *Maria Schell and Glenn Ford, MGM, 1960.

Come and Get It (99 min. film), starring Frances Farmer, Edward Arnold, and Joel McCrea, produced by Samuel Goldwyn, 1936.

Dinner at Eight (113 min. film), starring *Marie Dressler, John Barrymore, Wallace Beery, *Jean Harlow, Lionel Barrymore, *Billie Burke, Madge Evans, *May Robson, produced by David O. Selznick, directed by George Cukor, screenplay by *Frances Marion, Herman J. Mankiewicz, and Donald Ogden Stewart, MGM, 1933.

Giant (201 min. film), starring Elizabeth Taylor, Rock Hudson, James Dean, *Mercedes McCambridge, *Jane Withers, Dennis Hopper, Sal Mineo, Carroll Baker, directed and produced by George Stevens, Warner Bros., 1956.

Ice Palace (143 min. film), starring Richard Burton, Robert Ryan, Martha Hyer, Warner Bros., 1960.

The Royal Family of Broadway (68 min. film), based on the stage play *The Royal Family,* starring *Ina Claire, Fredric March, *Mary Brian, directed by George Cukor, Paramount, 1930.

Saratoga Trunk (135 min. film), starring *Ingrid Bergman, Gary Cooper, *Flora Robson, produced by Hal B. Wallis, directed by Sam Wood, Warner Bros., 1945.

Show Boat (130 min. film), starring *Helen Morgan, *Alma Rubens, produced by Carl Laemmle, Universal, 1929.

Show Boat (110 min. film), starring Irene Dunne, Helen Morgan, Allan Jones, *Hattie McDaniel, produced by Carl Laemmle, Universal, 1936.

Show Boat (107 min. film), starring *Kathryn Grayson, *Ava Gardner, Howard Keel, Gower and Marge Champion, *Agnes Moorehead, produced by Arthur Freed, directed by George Sidney, MGM, 1951.

So Big (90 min. film), starring *Barbara Stanwyck, George Brent, *Bette Davis, Dickie Moore, produced by Jack L. Warner, directed by William A. Wellman, Warner Bros., 1932.

So Big (101 min. film), starring ***Jane Wyman**, Sterling Hayden, produced by Henry Blanke, directed by Robert Wise, Warner Bros., 1953.

Stage Door (83 min. film), starring Katharine Hepburn, Ginger Rogers, ***Constance Collier**, Lucille Ball, Eve Arden, Ann Miller, RKO, 1937.

Norman Powers,
writer/producer, Chelsea Lane Productions, New York

Fergusa (fl. 800s)

Queen of Dalriada. Flourished in the 800s; daughter of Fergus, king of Dalriada; maternal niece of two kings of the Picts, Kenneth II and Alpin II; married her cousin Eochaid IV, king of Dalriada; children: Alpin, king of Kintyre (d. 834).

Ferguson, Cathy Jean (1948—)

American swimmer. Born on July 17, 1948.

Bested five other world-record holders to win the 100-meter backstroke and also took gold in the 4x100-meter medley relay at Tokyo Olympics (1964); retired from competitive swimming at 19 and became a coach.

Born in 1948, Cathy Ferguson became serious about swimming at age ten. At twelve, fueled by an internal drive rather than parental pressure, she began training with Peter Daland at the Los Angeles Athletic Club. "I didn't want to be just 'C-Average Cathy,'" she commented. But she also listened when Daland, whom she admired enormously, convinced her that athletics were temporary while education had permanency. "It's lonely at that pool," she said. "Just think of the countless hours in the water when you scarcely talk to another human being. All you have is that black line. It becomes your best friend. . . . I can remember being so tired at the end of the day that there was no way I had any energy left over to talk to other kids."

In 1964, Ferguson participated at the Olympic Games in Tokyo, along with a strong American team that included ***Sharon Stouder**, **Kathy Ellis**, **Martha Randall**, **Sharon Finneran**, ***Donna de Varona**, and **Claudia Kolb**. Ferguson's roommate, → **Jenny Duenkel**, was also her competitor. "That is the essence of the Olympic Games," said Ferguson, "to be able to separate when it's time to work and when it's time to play. We understood this."

The women of the 1964 Olympics broke a series of world swimming times. Australia's ***Dawn Fraser** took the 100-meter freestyle with a stunning 59.5. In the preliminary heats for the 100-meter backstroke, Duenkel broke the world record. Ferguson then broke Duenkel's record, followed by **Christine "Kiki" Caron** of France who broke Ferguson's record. Only a fraction of a second separated each new winning time. In the holding area, while waiting for the 100-meter backstroke the following day, Ferguson was numb. She was also slow off the mark, typical for her. But during the race, she felt strong. At the finish, her gold-medal time was 1:07.7, a new Olympic and world record. Caron finished second for the silver; Duenkel came in third.

Ferguson married and ended her competitive swimming career before the 1968 Olympics. The 19-year-old felt free. But the transition was difficult because swimming had been her cocoon, and the marriage fell victim to the painful change. Eventually, Ferguson went on to college, married again, had children, and became a swimming coach. "Now that I'm coaching," she remarked, "I include breaks within my practices so that my swimmers have structured social time. . . . [Y]oungsters must learn how to make decisions and relate to one another if they are going to become functioning human beings. . . . Being an Olympic champion doesn't make life simpler. It opens the door and lets you get your foot in. But if you don't produce after that, you're gone the same as anybody else."

SOURCES:
Carlson, Lewis H., and John J. Fogarty. *Tales of Gold.* Chicago and NY: Contemporary Press, 1987.

Karin L. Haag,
Athens, Georgia

Ferguson, Helen (1901–1977).
See Stanwyck, Barbara for sidebar.

Ferguson, Ma (1875–1961).
See Ferguson, Miriam A.

Ferguson, Margaret Clay (1863–1951)

American botanist. Born in Orleans, New York, on August 20, 1863; died in San Diego, California, in

---

→ **Duenkel, Jenny (1947—)**

American Olympic swimmer. Name variations: Virginia Duenkel. Born Virginia Duenkel on March 7, 1947.

Jenny Duenkel won the bronze medal in the 100-meter backstroke at the Tokyo Olympics in 1964; she then took the gold medal in the 400-meter freestyle with a time of 4:43.3. Her U.S. teammates, **Marilyn Ramenofsky** and **Terri Lee Stickles**, took the silver and bronze, respectively.

1951; fourth of six children; attended Genesee Wesleyan Seminary in Lima, New York; attended Wellesley College as a special student in botany and chemistry; earned Ph.D. at Cornell University, 1899.

Head of science department at Harcourt Place Seminary in Gambier, Ohio (1891–93); spent the rest of her career at Wellesley, heading the botany department by 1902.

Margaret Clay Ferguson graduated in 1899 from Cornell University and later became head of the department of botany at Wellesley College, where she spent close to 40 years. While at Wellesley, she planned, designed, and raised the money for a botany building and two greenhouses; she also studied the genus of higher plants. Ferguson, who retired in 1938 from Wellesley at age 75, was elected a fellow by the American Association for the Advancement of Science. Her writings consist mainly of papers on plant embryology and physiology.

SUGGESTED READING:

Hart, Sophie C. "Margaret Clay Ferguson," in *Wellesley Magazine.* June 1932, pp. 408–10.

Ferguson, Miriam A. (1875–1961)

*Texan who was the first woman in the U.S. to be elected to a full term as a state governor. Name variations: Ma Ferguson. Born Miriam Amanda Wallace in Bell County, Texas, on June 13, 1875; died on June 25, 1961, in Austin, Texas; daughter of Joseph Lapsley and Eliza (Garrison) Wallace (well-to-do rancher-farmers); attended Center Lake School, Bell County, Texas, around 1879; later studied with a tutor; enrolled in Salado College, a preparatory school, in 1888; entered Baylor Female College in Belton, Texas, in 1890; married James Edward Ferguson, on December 31, 1899; children: two daughters, Ouida Wallace Ferguson Nalle and **Ruby Dorrace Ferguson**.*

Husband "Farmer Jim" Ferguson inaugurated governor of Texas (1915); husband reelected (1916); husband impeached and removed (1917); became Democratic Party candidate for U.S. Senate but withdrew when her husband ran and lost (1922); elected governor of Texas (1924); inaugurated (1925); lost renomination (1926); lost nomination for governor (1930); won nomination and was elected governor for second term (1932); announced she would not run again (1934); lost nomination for governor (1940); retired to Austin (1944); supported Lyndon B. Johnson candidacy for U.S. senate (1948).

Life at the head of a prosperous middle-class family in Texas appealed to Miriam Aman-da Wallace Ferguson. She was an educated woman, quiet and cultivated, comfortable as a small-town matron, jealous of her privacy, and home oriented. When her husband entered politics, she had already been married for 15 years. Two years later, after Governor James E. ("Farmer Jim") Ferguson made the political mistake that cost him statewide office, he began to take the political steps that were to propel Miriam onto the political playing field. Ironically, Texas had been among the last states to embrace the voting franchise for women, and Miriam Ferguson had not been its advocate. She voiced suspicion of women as voters, in fact, preferring that "men shall attend to all public matters." But when she saw running for office as a means of aiding her husband, she declared herself "eager to help her Jim."

When Miriam met Jim Ferguson, he was a wily and ambitious young lawyer. Both had attended a Texas preparatory school, Salado College; Miriam had gone on to Baylor Female College in Belton, Texas, but Jim had left in his mid-teens to wander as far as California, working as a miner, bellhop, vineyard laborer, roustabout in a barbed-wire factory, teamster, lumberjack, and railroad employee. In the late 1890s, he was back in Texas, where he settled down to the study of law.

Following the death of Miriam's well-to-do father, Joseph Lapsley Wallace, Jim (who was indirectly related to the Wallaces) became the family's financial and legal advisor. On New Year's Eve, 1899, he and Miriam were married. Soon afterward, in partnership with another man, Jim Ferguson opened the Farmers' State Bank in Belton, Texas. Next, he organized the Temple (Texas) State Bank, a larger venture that also did well.

Jim Ferguson's real political involvement began in 1914. Claiming that Texas needed a businessman as governor, he half-heartedly tried to persuade a well-known Texas investor to run, but after the older man refused because of age and a lack of interest, Jim filed for the office. A teetotaler, Jim Ferguson was adamantly opposed to Prohibition, claiming that it diverted the energies of government away from fundamental problems. With a canny instinct for the issues that could engage the people of his state, he turned his campaign into a struggle over the Prohibitionist sentiments then sweeping the country. By adroitly opposing anti-liquor laws, gaining financial support from liquor companies, and promising a new land-rent law, he won the Democratic nomination and then the general election.

As governor, Jim Ferguson began to compile a strong record, with policies that were an odd amalgam of regular Democratic Party issues as well as Populist and Progressive reforms, involving improvements in education and the state penitentiary, and a bonded warehouse where farmers could store grain and cotton at reasonable rates to wait for an improvement in market prices. In 1916, "Farmer Jim" was reelected for a second two-year term, but during the campaign, he was charged with various misuses of state and campaign funds. Then, by miscalculating the power of the regents who ran the University of Texas, the governor committed the mistake that would cost him his office. When he showed his displeasure with certain administrators and professors by trying to have them fired, Will C. Hogg, the son of a well-respected former governor and brother of *Ima Hogg, led the resistance among the regents, prompting the governor to veto the university's annual appropriation, which forced the institution to run on deficiency warrants. In reaction, the governor found himself accused of banking misconduct, then indicted for embezzlement and misuse of public funds.

The response of the governor was to post bail and announce that he would seek a third term in 1918, but in a special session of the legislature he was ousted from office, and the state senate took the further step of providing that he should thereafter "be disqualified to hold any office of honor, trust or profit under the State of Texas." When he still managed to get the Democratic nomination in 1918, he was easily defeated by the incumbent, his former lieutenant governor, William Hobby.

Since he was not disbarred by law from running for a national office, Jim Ferguson created his own party to run for the presidency of the United States in 1920 and polled about 50,000 votes as the American Party nominee. In 1922, he filed for the U.S. Senate race in Texas. To be on the safe side, however, he also filed candidate papers for Miriam, in case he should be ruled out of the race.

The Ku Klux Klan provided Farmer Jim with the issue he could exploit as he had with Prohibition. In the Senate race, he was defeated by the Klan candidate, former railroad commissioner and future senator Earl B. Mayfield. In 1924, he filed for the gubernatorial race as an anti-Klan candidate and was ready again—when the courts upheld his disbarment—for Miriam to step in.

If Miriam Amanda Ferguson seemed an unlikely candidate, ill-suited for Texas' raucous

Miriam
A.
Ferguson

election scene, she was in one sense perfect for the role. She was not a professional politician, and in most cases she was unwilling to speak ill of opponents, making her campaign appearances a respite from the rough and rowdy politics of the time. Still, her advisors made her seem a fool, and while she accepted their advice, she resented it. When a newspaper reporter could not fit MRS. FERGUSON in a headline and instead used her initials MA FERGUSON, she became "Ma" Ferguson, which she also hated. But her daughter **Ouida Ferguson Nalle** later wrote, "Mamma pitched into that campaign with a pep and fury no one suspected she had in her."

"Me for Ma, And I Ain't Got a Dern Thing Against Pa" soon became the campaign slogan. Ouida arranged for her mother to pose for photographs at a farm she owned, wearing a sunbonnet borrowed from the tenant farmer's wife, canning peaches and feeding the chickens. In rural Texas, the ploy was good politics: the bonnet became "Ma's" symbol. "Put On Your Old

Gray Bonnet with the Blue Ribbon on It" became her song, parodied by her supporters:

> Get out your old time bonnet
> And put Miriam Ferguson on it,
> And hitch your wagon to a star.
> So on election day
> We each of us can say
> Hurrah! Governor Miriam, Hurrah!

She despised the song, as well as the press' decision to dub the race as a contest between "the bonnet and the hood." As in many Texas elections without an incumbent, a multitude of candidates joined the field. Only four were serious contenders, and two were named Davidson. They took votes from each other, allowing Ferguson to enter the run-off primary against the Klan-backed hopeful, Judge Felix Robertson. Klan leaders, following the racist temper of the times, called it a contest between the K.K.K. and the J.J.J. (Jew, Jug, and Jesuit).

This grand old state is mighty great

too big for one to run it.

It takes a pair to run it fair

and Jim and Ma have done it.

—Texan jingle

Ma and Pa Ferguson (as Farmer Jim subsequently became known) often campaigned together, with Pa doing most of the talking. Their campaign slogan became: "Two Governors for the Price of One," and when opponents complained that the public was voting for Ma to make Pa governor, Pa would say, "I ask you, if your wife was governor, would you get mad and leave home or would you stick around and help her?" To his farmer friends he added that if Ma won he would be there "cuttin' wood and drawin' water" for her.

Ferguson's speeches usually began with an explanation of why she was running. In effect, it dealt first with Jim's disqualification:

> Mother, father, son or brother, won't you help me? Jim and I are not seeking revenge; we are asking for the name of our children to be cleared of this awful judgment. If any wrong has been done, God in heaven knows we have suffered enough. Though we have lost most of our earthly possessions in these years of trouble, we shall not complain if the people will keep us from losing our family name which we want to leave to our children.

At other rallies she might add:

> I have a little bright-eyed grandson that I love dearer than life itself. If somebody wants to point the finger of scorn at him and say, "Your grandfather was impeached by the senate of Texas," I want that grandson to be able to say: "Yes, and as a rebuke to that impeachment that denied Grandfather the right to go to the people, my dear Grandmother was elected governor."

Admitting that she knew little about governing, Ferguson would add that she had trust in her redeemer to guide her footsteps "in the path of righteousness for the good of our people and the good of our State."

Although she ran second to Robertson in the first primary, Ferguson beat him by a majority of 97,732 votes in the second. An abortive effort to keep her off the Democratic ticket failed in the courts; petitioners had asked that she be disqualified by the so-called common-law disability against women in office. In November, she easily defeated the Republican candidate, George C. Butte, dean of the University of Texas Law School. After the election, she reportedly said, "We departed in disgrace; we now return in glory!"

Norman D. Brown in *Hood, Bonnet, and Little Brown Jug* argues that "Mrs. Ferguson was governor in name only." Jim Ferguson set up an office next to hers in the capitol, and, when individuals arrived for an audience with the governor, the secretary would ask which governor the caller wanted to see, "Governor 'Ma' or Governor Jim?" Ma's private secretary, Ghent Sanderford, reported: "On the all-important things where there's lots at stake . . . [Pa] controlled that. But small matters, small matters, routines of the office and like that, she did it." Sanderford added, "If the people hadn't thought that [Pa] would be the governor himself, they never would have elected Mrs. Ferguson."

Although a number of constructive laws were passed during Miriam Ferguson's tenure, a variety of controversies developed. After a struggle, she succeeded in having the legislature restore her husband's rights to run for office. Her administration launched a road-building program under the auspices of Pa, who was then charged with seeking bribes; advertisements by road builders were said to increase dramatically in *The Ferguson Forum*.

Perhaps the most telling criticism concerned pardons. In the first 20 months, she commuted 2,000 sentences, and executive clemency was ultimately granted to 3,595 criminals. Apparently, Jim handled the "paperwork," allegedly taking "donations" from pardon attorneys. A joke popular in Austin described a day when a young man entered an elevator and accidentally stepped on Miriam's foot. "Pardon me, Governor," he said. "See my husband," she advised; "he handles those." According to another story, Pa, upon being approached by a man wanting clemency for his son, began talking about a horse he had for sale for $5,000. The father, missing the drift of the conversation, asked, "Well, why would I want a horse?" Pa answered, "I figured if you bought him your son might ride him home from the penitentiary."

In 1926, Miriam Ferguson sought reelection, running against a popular attorney general, Dan Moody, who, along with the Fergusons had almost ended the Klan in Texas. "Fergusonism" had come to symbolize corruption and demagoguery to many voters, and Ma was criticized for letting Pa be the state's governor. Ferguson promised to quit the race if Moody beat her in the first primary, but when he did, she didn't. Nevertheless, "Dan the Man" overwhelmed her in the run-off, and the Fergusons declared they were retiring from politics. A wiser small-town merchant said, "Old Jim will never be out of the political arena in Texas until he is placed four feet underground!"

In 1928, the Fergusons supported Alvin M. Owsley in the U.S. Senate race and Louis J. Wardlaw for governor. Two years later, Pa filed in his own right to be the state's chief executive, believing that the impeachment disqualification had been successfully lifted in 1925. To his chagrin, party leaders refused to certify his candidacy, and when he sued, the Texas Supreme Court ruled that the law granting him amnesty had been invalid; he was barred forever from office in Texas.

Once more, Miriam Ferguson was forced into duty. *The New York Times* had judged Ferguson "a good woman and a good wife" but not a "brilliant success as governor." She lost the second primary by 89,000 votes to millionaire publisher Ross Sterling, of the *Houston Post-Dispatch,* who had styled himself as the "Big Fat Boy from Buffalo Bayou." Governor Sterling had a miserable administration, and two years later Miriam beat him, by 3,798 votes.

This time, the Fergusons had a quieter, more productive administration, perhaps because of the Great Depression. They secured an issue of $20 million in "bread bonds" to help the destitute. Miriam supported the New Deal and took advantage of its relief programs; two days before Franklin D. Roosevelt declared a bank holiday nationally, she declared one locally, and sound Texas banks were ultimately reopened. She met the problems of overproduction in the oil industry

with a two-cents-per-barrel severance tax, and secured legalization of parimutuel betting on horse races to increase state revenue. She did not get a state sales tax or corporate income tax passed, and she again had trouble over pardoning.

In 1934, the Fergusons announced that Miriam would not seek reelection, claiming that she felt bound by the state's tradition against a third term. Jim had been elected a member of the Democratic National Committee for Texas, but when Vice-President John Nance ("Cactus Jack") Garner wanted the position, Jim resigned as a matter of courtesy.

The Ferguson family, however, was not yet finished with politics: Pa actively supported unsuccessful candidates in 1936 and 1938. When Franklin Roosevelt decided to run for a third term in 1940, the Fergusons backed him, and Miriam, now 65 years old, filed for the governor's office, facing an opponent who was possibly more colorful than Pa, the incumbent governor, Wilbur Lee O'Daniel. O'Daniel was a master trader who had built a financial empire on his Hill-Billy Flour enterprise and became widely known as "Pass the Biscuits Pappy" through his radio program. A guitar-playing troubadour, his nickname came from his theme song, sung to the tune of "I Like Mountain Music."

Jim, in his late 60s, was no match for the younger Pappy, who, when questioned closely by an audience, picked up his guitar and played "Beautiful Texas" or "The Boy Who Never Got Too Old to Comb His Mother's Hair." Miriam attacked him as a "medicine-man governor," and Jim called him a "slick-haired banjo picker," who answered questions by "grinning like a jackass in a thistle patch." Pappy was reelected, and Miriam ran a miserable fourth. The following year, in a special election to replace Senator Andrew Jackson Houston, Pa supported Pappy, his way of getting the political minstrel out of the state.

Jim Ferguson died in 1944. He had opposed Lyndon Baines Johnson in the 1941 senatorial race, but Miriam endorsed the future president when he ran for senator against Coke Stevenson in 1948; Governor Stevenson had not attended Pa's funeral.

In her last years, Ma lived in Austin doing what she liked most, keeping house and raising flowers. In 1955, she was feted by Texas Democrats on her 80th birthday, and three flowers were named for her: a new amaryllis and a new iris called "Governor Miriam A. Ferguson," and a new day lily, the "Ma Ferguson." Six years later, on June 25, 1961, she died of a heart attack and was buried in the state cemetery beside her beloved Jim.

In 1925, a popular joke in Texas asked, "How does it feel to have a woman governor?" The reply was, "I don't know; we haven't got one." Pa ran the show, as he always had. Still, the election of Miriam Amanda Ferguson was important. She was the first woman elected to a full term as governor in any American state, sharing the honor of being raised to the office that year with *Nellie Tayloe Ross of Wyoming; both women were elected on November 4, 1924, but Ross was chosen to complete the unexpired term of her husband, who had died, and was inaugurated on January 5, 1925, 15 days before Ferguson. In contrast to Texas, Wyoming had also led the United States in women's suffrage.

On November 7, 1924, *The New York Times* asked, tongue-in-cheek, whether Ma and the new governor of Wyoming should be called "Governine" or "Governette," since "Governess" wouldn't do. More to the point, the newspaper stated, "If they make good Governors it will be not because they are women, but because they have sense, intelligence and character."

SOURCES:

Brown, Norman D., *Hood, Bonnet, and Little Brown Jug: Texas Politics, 1921–1928*. College Station: Texas A&M Press, 1984.

Farrel, Mary D., and Elizabeth Silverthorne. *First Ladies of Texas: A History*. Belton, TX: Stillhouse Hollow Publications, 1976.

Gallagher, Robert S. "Me for Ma—and I ain't got a dern thing against Pa," in *American Heritage*. Vol. XVII, no. 6. October 1966, pp. 46–47, 105–106.

Gould, Lewis L. *Progressives and Prohibitionists: Texas Democrats in the Wilson Era*. Austin, TX: University of Texas Press, 1973.

Green, George Norris. *The Establishment in Texas Politics: The Primitive Years, 1938–1957*. Westport, CT: Greenwood Press, 1979.

Jones, Billy M. "Miriam Amanda Ferguson," in *Women of Texas*. Waco, TX: Texian Press, 1972, pp. 157–73.

Luthin, Reinhard H. *American Demagogues: Twentieth Century*. Boston, MA: Beacon Press, 1954.

Nalle, Ouida Ferguson. *The Fergusons of Texas or "Two Governors for the Price of One."* San Antonio, TX: Naylor, 1946.

The New York Times. May 31, 1922; November 7, 1924; January 23, April 5, 1925; February 13, August 3, 1926; July 26, 31, August 30, 1932; May 14, 1933; August 28, 1934; June 26, 1961.

SUGGESTED READING:

Alexander, Charles C. *Crusade For Conformity: The Ku Klux Klan in Texas, 1920–1938*. Houston, TX: Gulf Coast Historical Association, 1962.

———. *The Ku Klux Klan in the Southwest*. Lexington, KY: University of Kentucky, 1965.

Bolton, Paul. *Governors of Texas*. Corpus Christi, TX: Caller-Times, 1947.

Calbert, Jack Lynn, "James Edward and Miriam Amanda Ferguson: The 'Ma' and 'Pa' of Texas Politics," Doctoral Dissertation, Bloomington: Indiana University, 1968.

De Shields, James T. *They Sat in High Places*. San Antonio, TX: Naylor, 1940.

McKay, Seth S. *Texas Politics, 1906–1944*. Lubbock, TX: Texas Tech Press, 1952.

———. *W. Lee O'Daniel and Texas Politics, 1938-1942*. Lubbock, TX: Texas Tech, 1944.

———, and Odie B. Faulk. *Texas After Spindletop*. Austin, TX: Steck-Vaughn, 1965.

Robert S. La Forte, Professor of History, University of North Texas, Denton, Texas

Ferguson, Sarah (b. 1959).

See Elizabeth II for sidebar.

Fergusson, Muriel McQueen
(1899–1997)

Canadian legislator who was the first woman speaker of the Senate. Born Muriel McQueen in Shediac, New Brunswick, Canada, on May 26, 1899; died in Fredericton, New Brunswick, Canada, on April 11, 1997; graduated from Mount Allison University, 1921; received law degree from Dalhousie University; married a lawyer (died 1942).

A Canadian legislator for 22 years, and the first woman appointed speaker of the Senate (December 14, 1972), Muriel McQueen Fergusson is remembered as a wise and witty senator who was devoted to the causes of Canadian women.

A native of New Brunswick, Fergusson took up the study of law in 1921, even though her mother questioned spending the money to further her daughter's education when she was already engaged to be married. In 1925, after clerking in her father's law office, Fergusson was admitted to the New Brunswick Bar. Following her husband's death in 1942, she took over his law practice, slowly building the confidence of her mostly male clientele. Before her appointment to the Senate, Fergusson served as the director of the Family Allowance and the Old Age Security Programs in New Brunswick, during which time she was also at the forefront in the battle against sex discrimination in the workplace. She was the first woman elected to the Fredericton City Council and the first deputy mayor of that city.

Appointed as a Liberal to the Senate in 1953, Fergusson served on various Senate committees dealing with the rights of women and the welfare of all Canadian citizens. She was appointed speaker of the Senate on December 14, 1972. After serving in that capacity for three years, she retired in 1975, age 75. (Having voted in favor of mandatory retirement for senators at age 75 and although not bound by the legislation, Fergusson felt it was her duty to abide by the resolution.) Muriel Fergusson died in Fredericton, New Brunswick on April 11, 1997.

Fermor, Arabella (d. 1738)

English aristocrat who was the subject of "The Rape of the Lock." Name variations: Arabella Perkins. Died in 1738; daughter of James Fermor of Tusmore; married Frances Perkins of Ufton Court, near Reading.

Arabella Fermor became the subject of "The Rape of the Lock," a poem by Alexander Pope, when a lock of her hair was stolen by Lord Petre.

Fermor, Henrietta Louisa (d. 1761)

Countess of Pomfret and letter writer. Name variations: Fermour. Born Henrietta Louisa Jeffreys; died on December 15, 1761; daughter of John, 2nd baron Jeffreys of Wem, Shropshire; married Thomas Fermor, 2nd baron Leominster (later earl of Pomfret), in 1720.

Henrietta Louisa Fermor was lady of the bedchamber to Queen *Caroline of Ansbach until 1737. While in Rome, Fermor wrote a life of Van Dyck, and in 1805 her letters were published in *Correspondence between Frances, Countess of Hartford (afterward Duchess of Somerset) and Henrietta Louisa, Countess of Pomfret, between . . . 1738 and 1741.*

Fern, Fanny (1811–1872)

Pseudonym of Sara Willis Parton who protested American women's social, political, and economic inequality in both her fiction and her popular weekly newspaper column in the New York Ledger. *Name variations: Sara Willis Eldredge; Sara Willis Farrington; Sara Willis Parton; Sara Payson Willis; in childhood, spelled first name "Sarah"; name legally changed to Fanny Fern. Born Sara Willis on July 9, 1811, in Portland, Maine; died of breast cancer on October 10, 1872, in New York City; daughter of Nathaniel Willis (a printer and publisher of religious and children's periodicals) and Hannah Parker Willis (a homemaker); attended Catharine Beecher's Hartford Female Seminary, Hartford, Connecticut, 1828–31; married Charles Eldredge, on May 4, 1837*

(died 1846); married Samuel Farrington, on January 17, 1849 (divorced 1853); married James Parton, on January 5, 1856; children: (first marriage) Mary Eldredge (died in 1845 at age 7); **Grace Eldredge** *(d. 1862);* **Ellen Eldredge.**

Became first salaried woman newspaper columnist in America (1852); published bestselling novel, Ruth Hall (1854); offered record-setting payment of $100 a column by Robert Bonner, editor of the New York Ledger (1855); was a founding member of the women's club Sorosis (1868).

Newspaper columns published in Olive Branch (Boston, 1851–54); True Flag (Boston, 1852–54); Musical World and Times (New York, 1852); and the New York Ledger (1856–72). Newspaper columns collected and published in book form as: Fern Leaves from Fanny's Port Folio (1853); Fern Leaves from Fanny's Portfolio, Second Series (1854); Fresh Leaves (1857); Folly as It Flies (1868); Ginger-Snaps (1870); and Caper-Sauce (1872). Novels: Ruth Hall (1854); Rose Clark (1856). Children's books: Little Ferns for Fanny's Little Friends (1853); The Play-Day Book (1857); and The New Story Book for Children (1864).

Fanny Fern is often categorized as a "sentimental" novelist of the era and style of *Harriet Beecher Stowe. While Fern did write a bestselling novel, the 1854 *Ruth Hall*, in the somewhat melodramatic prose tradition of the mid-19th century, she had a long and successful career as a writer of nonfiction, and in her own day she was a national celebrity whose radical views were widely known. Fern was a pioneer of reform journalism and an early crusader for women's political and economic rights. In the newspaper columns she wrote from 1851 to 1872, she denounced what she saw as the ills of her society, from prostitution and domestic abuse to women's restrictive clothing and lack of the vote. While similar concerns were articulated in women's-rights publications of the day, such as the *Una* and the *Revolution*, Fern was the first journalist to regularly champion women's rights in a consumer medium with a large readership that cut across the divisions of gender and class—a weekly column in the *New York Ledger* that reached 400,000 readers, men as well as women, the working class as well as the upper classes.

The stances she took on political and social issues were a result of her own life experiences. The woman who became so well known as "Fanny Fern" was born Sara Payson Willis in 1811 in Portland, Maine, the fifth of nine children of a stern Presbyterian deacon who made his living as a printer and publisher of religious and children's magazines. After the Willises moved to Boston, Sara and her sisters were sent to boarding schools, including the Reverend Joseph Emerson's Ladies Seminary (run by a cousin of Ralph Waldo Emerson) and *Catharine Beecher's Hartford Female Seminary. During her three years in Hartford, the teenaged Sara received affection and support from her headmistress and began a lifetime friendship with Beecher's younger sister Harriet, who was one of Sara's classmates.

In 1837, when she was 26, Sara married Charles Eldredge, a young bank clerk with whom she lived happily until his death of typhoid fever nine years later. They had three daughters, one of whom died in childhood. Sara's relations with her in-laws, never good, disintegrated after Charles' death, and they offered no financial support for the 35-year-old widow and her two children. Neither did Sara's own family when she did not seem inclined to remarry, the course advised by her father (who had himself remarried within a year of Sara's mother's death in 1844). Sara and her daughters moved into a dismal Boston boardinghouse, where she took in sewing. This tedious and poorly paying work—she earned, at most, 75 cents a week—gave her, as one of her biographers notes, "a lifelong sympathy with working women" that she would later voice in her newspaper columns.

> [Fanny Fern] sails with all her canvas spread, by a chart of her own.
>
> —*Sara Clarke Lippincott

In 1849, she acquiesced to a match, made for her by her father, with Samuel Farrington, a Boston businessman. Farrington proved to be verbally abusive, and Sara left him two years later. He, in turn, spread stories that Sara had been unfaithful to him, following the lead of many other mid-19th-century husbands who used slander to keep their wives in line. Nevertheless, Sara refused to reconcile. Again in the position of breadwinner, she tried her hand at writing and immediately made a sale—a humorous essay on "model husbands"—to the editor of the Boston-based *Olive Branch,* a religious newspaper that, despite its small circulation, was read throughout the Eastern states. She was paid 50 cents. She sent other essays to her brother Nathaniel Parker ("N.P."), by then a successful poet and the editor of a magazine in New York, but he dismissed them as amateurish and told her she was "on a mistaken track."

Sara continued to contribute essays to the *Olive Branch,* using pseudonyms including "Clara," "Tabitha," and, finally, "Fanny Fern." Most women writers of the day wrote under pen names, and "flowery" ones were especially common (there were also, for instance, Essie Evergreen, Lottie Laurel, and Minnie Myrtle). But Sara had two additional incentives: the scandal associated with her second marriage, and her family's expressed disapproval of her writing. A pseudonym would hide her activity and income from all of them; what's more, she would be able to publish under a name that would not connect her to either her abusive second husband or her first husband's hostile parents. Sara began to use her new identity socially as well as professionally, and later she would legally change her name to Fanny Fern.

By early 1852, Fern was contributing to both the *Olive Branch* and another Boston-based newspaper, the *True Flag,* earning two dollars a column and producing a total of three columns a week. During the fall of 1852, she briefly wrote on an exclusive basis for the New York *Musical World and Times* (despite its title, a general-interest publication). Though this affiliation did not last long, it officially made her America's first woman "columnist"—someone paid a regular salary (not on an article-by-article basis) to write her opinion. When she resumed writing for the two Boston papers, they were forced to follow suit and put her on salary in 1853, the year Samuel Farrington divorced her on grounds of desertion.

Fern's articles were widely reprinted in newspapers all across the country, giving her a national audience and a national reputation. Her identity was becoming a matter of considerable speculation. In 1853, only two years into her journalism career, Fern accepted a publisher's offer to issue a collection of her columns in book form. It was called *Fern Leaves from Fanny's Port Folio,* and within one year it sold nearly 100,000 copies in the United States and Great Britain. The first volume was followed by a second, and its sales encouraged Fern to agree to the suggestion that she write a novel. During 1854, in only nine months, she produced *Ruth Hall,* a thinly veiled autobiography written in melodramatic language yet harboring a feminist theme: Ruth Hall learns that she cannot depend on men or other relatives to survive, but rather must look out for herself and earn her own living.

Like Fern's column collections, *Ruth Hall* was a popular success, selling more than 50,000 copies within eight months of its publication, but it was not a critical success. Dozens of reviews castigated Fern for being unfeminine and irreverent in her choice of story line (about a woman done wrong by self-important men). A rare positive review came from *Elizabeth Cady Stanton, who, writing in the feminist newspaper *Una,* praised the book's message "that God has given to woman sufficient brain and muscle to work out her own destiny unaided and alone."

What might have been a death blow to Fern's career was delivered the year after the publication of *Ruth Hall.* William Moulton, the editor of the Boston *True Flag,* who was angry because Fern had stopped writing for him, anonymously published a book called *The Life and Beauties of Fanny Fern* in 1855. Purportedly an official biography of Fanny Fern, *The Life and Beauties* not only personally and professionally slandered Fern—implying that as a divorcée she had loose morals and stating quite clearly that she had little talent and did not meet deadlines—but also revealed her real name. The final insult was that more than three-quarters of the book consisted of reprints of columns Fern had written for the Boston newspapers, each with a short, sarcastic introduction by Moulton; thus, he profited from her work while causing her pain and embarrassment.

Nevertheless, Moulton's "biography" served only to increase public interest in Fanny Fern. At the same time her star was rising, so was the ambition of Robert Bonner, the new publisher and editor of the *New York Ledger.* The *Ledger* was typical of the many mid-19th-century weekly newspapers in its content, which included essays, fiction, and poetry along with news. Bonner's paper was unique, however, in its publication of signed selections by well-known writers of the day. The first such scribe Bonner pursued was Fanny Fern. His 1855 promise to pay her $100 per column—not per article, but per *column* of type—was unprecedented. It was a one-shot deal for a piece of fiction rather than journalistic writing (the resulting story, "Fanny Ford," ran serially in the *Ledger* throughout June of 1855 and totaled ten columns of type, for which Fern was paid $1,000). But Bonner then offered Fern an exclusive contract to write a weekly opinion column in the *Ledger* at $25 a week.

Fern accepted the offer and moved to New York. Bonner announced his acquisition by buying a full page of advertising space in a rival paper, the *New York Herald,* filled with type repeating one sentence: "Fanny Fern writes only for the *Ledger.*" Soon her name was so widely known that it was used to promote merchandise

Fanny Fern

completely unrelated to her work or life—from railroad cars to songs to tobacco. Her early success in both journalism and letters earned her the respect and friendship of fellow writers including Horace Greeley and Walt Whitman, to whom she was an early mentor during the mid-1850s.

Fern was the first of a long list of celebrity conquests Bonner would make, and her record-setting fee was soon eclipsed by what he paid for the services of writers such as Henry Wadsworth Longfellow, John Greenleaf Whittier, Charles Dickens, and the Reverend Henry Ward Beecher. Other well-known writers who contributed to the newspaper included Harriet Beecher Stowe, *Louisa May Alcott, *Alice and Phoebe Cary, Edward Everett, *E.D.E.N. Southworth, *Lydia Sigourney, and James Gordon Bennett. Thanks to these famous bylines, as well as the booming population of New York City as America industrialized, the *Ledger's* circulation was soon the highest in the country, climbing to 400,000 in the 1860s.

The fact that many of the paper's new readers were women is evident in the voice and content of Fern's columns. She often began them by using a quote or maxim as a springboard for her commentary, or by summarizing and reacting to a news item—both devices that would be commonly used by 20th-century columnists. To choose these devices, she took her cue from the hundreds of letters she received each week from female readers, whose concerns ranged from parenting problems to dress styles to financial troubles. Fern's responses were sympathetic and yet full of humor and animation, written in a style Fern herself jokingly described as "popgun"—short, impassioned sentences broken up by dashes and exclamation points. Fern no longer worried about what people would think of her writing or her views. She had survived Moulton's attack with her popularity and paycheck intact. She and her daughters also had a happier home life by 1856, the year she married James Parton, a journalist and biographer who was supportive of her work.

While Fern's topics were many and varied during her 21-year career as a columnist, most of her journalism focused on the rights of women and other disadvantaged people. She categorically dismissed "the old cry of 'a woman's sphere being home,'" believing instead that women should get *out* of their homes, literally (through exercise) and figuratively (through reading, writing, and other mental stimulation). She crusaded against restrictive clothing and the "fashionable invalidism" of the day, urging women to don men's attire, as she and her eldest daughter, Grace, sometimes did. ("I've as good a right to preserve the healthy body God gave me, as if I were not a woman," she wrote in 1858.)

Her column was read not just by upper-class "literary ladies," but also by middle-class homemakers and working-class women, and she addressed all three groups in her many discussions of women and work. Remembering her own experience, she made plain the economic necessity that forced women to work and chided those who would fault such women for trying to earn a living—especially if they succeeded. "No matter how isolated or destitute [a woman's] condition," she wrote, "the majority would consider it more 'feminine,' would she unobtrusively gather up her thimble, and, retiring into some out-of-the-way place, gradually scoop out her coffin with it, than to develop [a] smart turn for business." She lamented the lot of domestic servants at the mercy of upper-class employers, taking the latter group to task for the unhappiness of their poorer sisters. Fern also championed women in the professions—even those whose husbands or fathers could support them—arguing that an accomplished working woman

"holds up her head with the best, and asks no favors." And she was ahead of her time in identifying and discussing problems such as sexual harassment and unequal pay.

Fern felt that women who worked at home were entitled to the same respect, and the same access to money, as women who worked in paid positions. In an 1869 column, she expressed the "disgust with which I am nauseated, at the idea of any decent, intelligent, self-respecting, capable wife, ever being obliged *to ask* for that which she so laboriously earns." She noted the exhausting work load of middle- and lower-class homemakers, calling the results "legal murder." Fern's then-radical position on housework and child care can be seen in passages like this:

> There are self-sacrificing mothers who need somebody to say to them, "Stop! you have just to make your choice now, between death and life. You have expended all the strength you have on hand—and must lay in a new stock before any more work can be done by you." . . . [L]et me tell you that if you think you are doing God service, or anybody else, by using up a year's strength in a week, you have made a sinful mistake. . . . [W]hen you are dead, all the king's men can't make you stand on your feet again, that's plain. Well, then—don't be dead. In the first place, go out a part of every day, rain or shine, for the fresh air, and don't tell me you can't; at least not while you can stop to embroider your children's clothes. As to "dressing to go out," don't dress. If you are clean and whole that's enough. . . . The moral of all which is, that if nobody else will take care of you, you must take care of yourself.

Several of Fern's columns addressed the relatively new campaign for women's suffrage, which she supported. She dismissed men's objections to giving women the vote; she also criticized women who opposed suffrage. In a column that linked women's political rights to their economic strength, she wrote, "I feel only pity, that, torpidly and selfishly content with her ribbons and dresses, [a woman] may never see or think of those other women who may be lifted out of their wretched condition of low wages and starvation, by this very lever of power."

Fern was also outspoken on women's legal rights during and after marriage. Again writing from personal experience, she acknowledged the horror of physical abuse within marriage but also noted the damage done by emotional abuse, even in the "best" marriages: "That the better educated husband murders with sharp words instead of sharp blows, makes it none the less murder." Fern believed that women in bad marriages should get out, not suffer nobly. She gave this advice in 1857:

> [T]here are aggravated cases for which the law provides no remedy—from which it affords no protection. . . . What I say is this: in such cases, let a woman who *has the self-sustaining power* quietly take her fate in her own hands, and right herself. Of course she will be misjudged and abused. *It is for her to choose whether she can better bear this at hands from which she has a rightful claim for love and protection, or from a nine-days-wonder-loving public.* These are bold words; but they are needed words—words whose full import I have well considered, and from the responsibility of which I do not shrink.

Just as Fern wrote about men's abuse of their power over women and children, she also scrutinized the ways in which wealthy New Yorkers viewed and treated the poor. In a column sympathizing with the life of a prostitute, Fern speculated that "They who make long prayers, and wrap themselves up in self-righteousness, as with a garment, turned a deaf ear, as she plead [sic] for the bread of honest toil." After an 1858 trip to a prison on Blackwell's Island (in New York City's East River), she wondered of its inmates, "How many times when their stomachs have been empty, some full-fed, whining disciple has presented them with a Bible or a Tract, saying, 'Be ye warmed and filled.'" Following her visit to a poor neighborhood in Manhattan, she graphically described the squalor of poverty and then questioned the priorities of a "democracy" divided, in 1864, by class as well as politics. She wondered what might be achieved, "if some of the money spent on corporation-dinners, on Fourth of July fireworks, and on public balls, where rivers of champagne are worse than wasted, were laid aside for the cleanliness and purification of these terrible localities which slay more victims than the war is doing."

In the later years of Fern's long tenure at the *Ledger,* her columns alternated between such grim subjects and her more reflective essays about nature and family life. She shared her joy at becoming a grandmother, when her daughter Grace had a baby girl in 1862, and her grief when Grace died of scarlet fever later that year, leaving Fern to raise the child. But she continued to write about "hard-news" topics such as crime and the war, and to make news herself. In 1868, when she and other women journalists, including *Jane Cunningham Croly, were excluded from a New York Press Club dinner to honor

Charles Dickens, they formed their own group, Sorosis, one of the first professional women's clubs in America.

By 1870, Fern knew she had cancer, and an operation in 1871 or early 1872—most likely, a mastectomy—failed to prevent its growth. Though weak and ill, she continued to write her weekly column until her death on October 10, 1872. Two weeks later, the editorial page of the *New York Ledger,* bordered in black, contained a eulogy written by Robert Bonner, who concluded, "Her success was assured, because she had something to say, and knew how to say it. . . . With all her intellect and genius, had there not been added to these her courage, her honesty of purpose, and her faithfulness of heart, she would not have been Fanny Fern."

SOURCES:

Fern, Fanny. *Fern Leaves from Fanny's Port Folio.* Auburn, NY: Derby & Miller, 1853.
———. *Fern Leaves from Fanny's Portfolio, Second Series.* Auburn & Buffalo, NY: Miller, Orton, & Mulligan, 1854.
———. *Folly As It Flies.* NY: G.W. Carleton, 1868.
———. *Ruth Hall and Other Writings.* Ed. Joyce W. Warren. New Brunswick, NJ: Rutgers University Press, 1986.
Greenwood, Grace. "Fanny Fern—Mrs. Parton." *Eminent Women of the Age.* Ed. James Parton. Hartford, CT: S.M. Betts, 1872.
Mott, Frank Luther. *American Journalism: A History, 1690–1960.* 3rd ed. NY: Macmillan, 1962.
Walker, Nancy A. *Fanny Fern.* NY: Twayne, 1993.
Warren, Joyce W. *Fanny Fern: An Independent Woman.* New Brunswick, NJ: Rutgers University Press, 1992.

SUGGESTED READING:

Adams, Florence Bannard. *Fanny Fern, or a Pair of Flaming Shoes.* West Trenton, NJ: Hermitage Press, 1966.
Baym, Nina. *Woman's Fiction: A Guide to Novels by and about Women in America, 1820–1870.* Ithaca, NY: Cornell University Press, 1978.
Wood, Ann Douglas. "The 'Scribbling Women' and Fanny Fern: Why Women Wrote," in *American Quarterly.* Vol. 3. Spring 1971, pp. 3–24.

COLLECTIONS:

Correspondence and manuscripts located in the Fanny Fern Collection, Barrett Library, University of Virginia; the Alma Lutz Collection, Schlesinger Library, Radcliffe College; the James Parton Papers, Houghton Library, Harvard University; the Sophia Smith Collection, Smith College; and other collections.

RELATED MEDIA:

Fanny Fern's Favorite [chapbook; songs]. London: Pattie, n. d. Microfilm, Cleveland, OH: Cleveland Public Library Preservation Office (most likely not authored by Fern but only marketed under her name).
Fern, Fanny. Lyrics. *Women's Rights* (sheet music). NY: William Hall & Son, 1853. The Alice Marshall Collection, The Pennsylvania State University at Harrisburg.

Jullien, Louis Antoine. *The Ruth Hall Schottische, Dedicated to Fanny Fern* (instrumental sheet music). New York, 1855.

Carolyn Kitch,
former editor for *Good Housekeeping* and *McCall's*,
and Assistant Professor at the Medill School of Journalism
at Northwestern University, Evanston, Illinois

Fern, Fanny (1866–1912).

See de Cleyre, Voltairine.

Fernandez, Gigi (1964—)

Puerto Rican tennis player. Born Beatriz Fernandez in San Juan, Puerto Rico, on February 24, 1964; one of four children, two girls and two boys, of Tuto Fernandez (a gynecologist) and Beatriz Fernandez; attended Clemson University, in Clemson, South Carolina.

A trailblazer in women's tennis doubles, Gigi Fernandez will be remembered as much for her on court antics as her substantial triumphs. Fernandez won two singles titles and 68 doubles titles, including two Olympic gold medals, before retiring from tennis in 1997 and taking up golf.

One of four children of **Beatriz Fernandez** and Tuto Fernandez, a gynecologist, Gigi was born in 1964 and raised in San Juan, Puerto Rico. She received tennis lessons as a gift from her parents on her seventh birthday. Possessing a natural talent for the game, she won the Puerto Rico Open doubles at age 12, at which time she also engaged in her first shouting match with the umpire, whom she felt was favoring her American partner. After considering athletic scholarships from three American universities, she chose (sight unseen) Clemson University in South Carolina. In 1983, while still in her freshman year, she reached the finals of the NCAA championships and turned pro at year's end. At the conclusion of her first full season on the tour (1984), Fernandez was ranked No. 27 in singles and was named *Tennis* magazine's "player to watch."

Fernandez's career was uneven for years, probably due to what she later identified as a lack of discipline. Still, she won three doubles titles with *****Martina Navratilova** in 1985, three titles with **Lori McNeil** in 1987, and her first major title, the U.S. Open doubles, with **Robin White** in 1988. That same year, with her game unsteady and 20 extra pounds on her 5'7" frame, she turned herself over to **Julie Anthony**, who became her long-time coach, mentor, and confidante. Fernandez later said that Anthony taught her the meaning of discipline. "I had no direction until I met Julie. She really helped me

with everything: my nutrition, my approach to tennis, my professionalism, my dedication." In an unintentional act of reciprocity, Fernandez turned Anthony into a coach. "I never would have been a coach if it weren't for Gigi," says Anthony. "I saw this wonderful, open person who wanted to learn. . . . We connected because she saw someone she could learn from, whom she could be more of an adult with. She was a child before, careening through life with lots of talent, but no game plan."

Fernandez won another U.S. Open doubles title with Navratilova in 1990 and the 1991 French Open with *****Jana Novotna**, before joining forces with **Natasha Zvereva** in 1992. Opposites in approach and personality, the two women complemented each other on the court. "Gigi's very fiery, while Natasha's more mellow, a more consistent player" said fellow pro **Lindsay Davenport**. "Together, they can do everything. They can dink, they can hit the ball hard, they can lob, they can hit sharp angles." The pair dominated women's doubles from 1993 to 1997, winning 20 grand slams, and ranking as Doubles Team of the Year in 1993, 1994, 1995, and 1997.

Fernandez was less successful with her singles game, although she won her first singles title in 1986 and another in 1991. In 1994, in addition to her doubles triumph, she reached the singles semifinals at Wimbledon, despite her No. 99 ranking. (Prior to Wimbledon, she had first-round losses in seven out of eight singles tournaments, prompting her to contemplate retiring from singles.) She lost to Martina Navratilova in the semifinals but gained some notoriety as the lowest-ranked women's semifinalist in Grand Slam history. "I always thought she was very talented and lived up to it in doubles but not singles," said Navratilova after the match. "This is definitely the best she has played."

Fernandez's candor and outbursts on the court made her one of the most enigmatic players on the pro circuit. "There's a real childish, narcissistic, selfish, controlling part of her," says coach Anthony, "but there's also a very sweet, bighearted, kind side to her." Fernandez maintained a love-hate relationship with some of her tennis peers as well as with the World Tennis Association (WTA), which on one hand deplored her behavior and on the other hand rejoiced over her contribution to popularizing the sport. But Fernandez topped herself at an event in Filderstadt, Germany in 1994, when, in a fit of pique, she turned away from her opponent, lifted up her skirt and started to bare her backside. She said later that she only pulled her panties down a few inches. "I was entertaining. The crowd loved it. They were laughing." The WTA was not amused, however, and fined her $2,000. In England, two weeks later, she repeated the panties episode and also destroyed a tennis racket, prompting a hefty fine of $4,000 that was later reduced to $250 after an appeal to the WTA Code of Conduct Committee. "I know the WTA is in financial trouble," commented Fernandez, "but they can't expect me to bail them out all by myself."

Fernandez won her first Olympic gold medal in 1992, competing for the United States and partnered with *Mary Joe Fernandez (no relation). The decision to play for America was a difficult one for Gigi, who understood she would by criticized back home in Puerto Rico, but she felt that it was the only way she would advance into the medal rounds. The win over the Spanish team dissipated any ill feelings. "I'm very proud for Puerto Rico. I'm very proud for the U.S. I'm very proud," Fernandez said about the victory. Fernandez won a second Olympic gold medal in 1996, paired again with Mary Joe Fernandez.

In September 1997, after she and Zvereva lost the U.S. Open women's doubles to Lindsay Davenport and Jana Novotna, Fernandez announced her retirement from tennis. Since then, she has devoted a great deal of time "giving back," as she puts it. She is active with the children's programs of the U.S. Tennis Association and with the Gigi Fernandez Charitable Foundation, which she established in 1992 to raise money for various Puerto Rican charities. She also is a long-time supporter of the National Hispanic Scholarship Fund. But Fernandez's greatest contribution to the young people of her homeland may be by example. As the first Puerto Rican athlete to turn professional and the first to win an Olympic gold medal, she has made athletics more acceptable for the women of her country. "In a way, it's kind of neat," she remarked in *Hispanic* magazine. "Before, it was taboo for a female to make a living out of a sport. Girls are supposed to get married and have kids, so now maybe this opens the door." As for sports, Fernandez, who occasionally played golf during her tennis career, has now

Gigi
Fernandez

FERNANDEZ

taken it up in earnest. "You can have a very successful amateur golf career playing six to twelve tournaments a year, which is what I hope to do," she said. In June 1998, she played in her first event, the San Diego Women's Amateur Championships, finishing fifth.

SOURCES:

Baccara, L. "An Interview with Gigi Fernandez," at www.dreamin.com.

Higdon, David. "Glamour," in *Tennis.* Vol. 31, no. 6. October 1995, pp. 50–53.

Johnson, Anne Janette. *Great Women in Sports.* Detroit, MI: Visible Ink, 1998.

O'Keefe, Kevin. "A New Approach Shot," in *Tennis.* Vol. 34, no. 5. September 1998, pp. 14–16.

Rachal, Janella. "Then and Now—An Interview with Gigi Fernandez," at www.dreamin.com.

Fernandez, Lisa (c. 1971—)

American softball player. Born in Long Beach, California, around 1971; daughter of Antonio Fernandez and Emilia Fernandez; attended St. Joseph High School, Lakewood, California; earned undergraduate degree in psychology from the University of California, Los Angeles.

Arguably the best all-around player in fast-pitch softball in the 1990s, Lisa Fernandez is a dazzling pitcher, a .400 batter, and plays third base like she owns it. Mike Downey of the *Los Angeles Times* called her "too unreal to be true" and compared her to Sandy Koufax, Fernando Valenzuela, and fictional baseball heroes such as Roy Hobbs, Joe Hardy, and Sidd Finch.

Fernandez was born into baseball. Her father Antonio played semi-pro baseball in Cuba before emigrating to the United States in 1962, and her mother **Emilia Fernandez**, a native of Puerto Rico, played in several softball leagues during the early years of her marriage. Fernandez grew up in Lakewood, California, where as a toddler she chased a rolled-up sock that her mother tossed around the house. "All I knew was softball," she recalled in *USA Today.* "We were always playing. I was the batgirl for my mom's slow-pitch team. When I was old enough, I started playing." Her early years were carefully supervised by her mother, who did not allow her daughter to play on teams she could dominate. "She didn't want me to be a big fish in a little pond," Fernandez explained. "So I always played on teams where there were better players, where I had to work hard to get better."

At age eight, during her first outing as a pitcher, Fernandez walked 20 batters and lost 28–0, but she improved quickly. She won her first American Softball Association championship at 11 and, during her high school career, pitched 69 shutouts, 37 no-hitters, and 12 perfect games (an impressive record considering that as a teen she was discouraged from pitching by a nationally recognized coach). Her college career at the University of California, Los Angeles (UCLA), was equally awesome. She was a four-time All-American and a two-time NCAA champion. She broke seven UCLA records and topped the NCAA record of winning percentages with a .930 average (93–7). In her senior year alone, she led the nation in hitting (.510) and had the lowest ERA (0.23). In addition to playing for her college team, she was also on Team USA and won six games and a gold medal at the 1991 Pan American Games. She also played on two gold-medal-winning Olympic Festival teams.

Since graduating from college, Fernandez has played for the Raybestos Brakettes, a championship amateur women's softball team based in Connecticut. In 1996, Fernandez fulfilled a long-time dream, pitching for the first-ever U.S. Olympic women's softball team. A leading force in the team's gold-medal victory, Fernandez delighted fans with a 68-mph rising fastball that is said to jump a foot as it buzzes through the strike zone. (It is only one of a six-pitch repertoire that includes a "backdoor changeup" which she throws backhanded.) "It will never be any better than this," she said of the team's victory at the Atlanta Games.

Most recently, Fernandez has served as an assistant softball coach at UCLA and has participated in a campaign to include women's softball, a provisional event in the 1996 Atlanta Games, in the Sydney Games in 2000. While at the top of her game and a success by any standards, Fernandez is still hard on herself. "God didn't give me that many physical talents," she told *USA Today*. "But one thing He did give me was a lot of heart and a lot of tenacity. I always tell myself never to be satisfied."

SOURCES:

Bender, Fran. "No Stopping the Brakettes," in *Women's Sports & Fitness*. Vol. 15, no. 5, August 1993, p. 17.

Johnson, Anne Janette. *Great Women in Sports*. Detroit, MI: Visible Ink, 1998.

Smith, Shelley. "Sports People," in *Sports Illustrated*. Vol. 78, no. 20. May 24, 1993, p. 52.

Fernandez, Mary Joe (1971—)

American tennis player. Born on August 19, 1971, in the Dominican Republic; daughter of José Fernandez and Silvia Fernandez; graduated from Carrollton School of the Sacred Heart, Miami, Florida.

Born in the Dominican Republic in 1971, Mary Joe Fernandez was raised in Miami, Florida, where her family settled when she was six months old. She began playing tennis at the age of three, frequently tagging along to her older sister's lessons. To keep her out of trouble, her father would bring along a bucket of balls that she could hit against the wall. Within two years, Fernandez was good enough for lessons of her own. She won a number of titles as a pre-teen and at 13 won her first professional tournament, competing as an amateur. At age 14, Fernandez considered turning pro and playing the professional circuit full time, but she concluded that school was more important. "I just decided that if I was going to go to school, I was going to do it right," she told an interviewer for *Sports Illustrated* in 1991. "And I wasn't ready to sacrifice being with my friends." For the next three-and-a-half years, she worked her tennis events, including four Grand Slam tournaments, around her high school classes, gaining valuable experiences and preventing the burn-out to which so many young players fall victim.

During her first full-time year on the women's pro circuit, Fernandez won 40 out of 50 singles matches and two tournaments, including her first professional tournament championship in the Tokyo Indoors. In 1990, her singles ranking was fourth in the world and her earnings topped $1 million, but she also suffered a number of injuries, including a knee sprain, a hamstring tear, and tendinitis in her shoulder. Overcoming her setbacks with a strength-training coach, she reached the high point of her career in 1992, when she and doubles partner *Gigi Fernandez (no relation) won the gold medal for the United States at the Summer Olympics in Barcelona, Spain, defeating Spain's own **Arantxa Sanchez Vicario** and **Conchita Martinez**. She also took home a bronze medal in Olympic singles competition. Fernandez then moved more into doubles play, frequently partnering with former opponent Sanchez Vicario.

SOURCES:

Johnson, Anne Janette. *Great Women in Sports*. Detroit, MI: Visible Ink, 1998.

Fernando, Sylvia (1904–1983)

Sri Lankan teacher and family planning advocate who was one of the founders in 1953 of the Family Planning Association of Ceylon. Born in 1904 in Colombo, Ceylon (now Sri Lanka); died in Colombo, Sri Lanka, in 1983; her father was a gynecologist and obstetrician and her mother was active in social work; had one brother; married; children: daughter, Nimali.

Opposite page

$\mathcal{L}$isa

$\mathcal{F}$ernandez

Sri Lanka, a lush tropical island nation situated off the southeastern tip of India, is a case study of rapid population growth. In its first census, taken in 1871 while it was the British Crown Colony of Ceylon, the population count was about 2.5 million. A century later the population had reached 13 million, and by the early 1990s it stood at over 17 million, making the nation of Sri Lanka one of the most densely populated non-industrialized nations in the world. A civil war that began in 1983 served to further impoverish and demoralize this land of stunning natural beauty.

After becoming an independent nation in 1948, few of its citizens looked upon family planning as a major priority of the new state. Virtually none of the men and only a small number of women had even heard of birth control. One woman, however, who appeared on the scene even before independence was achieved in 1948 was to prove herself a key player in a social and intellectual transformation that would bring about significant change. Sylvia Fernando was born in 1904 into an elite family in the capital city of Colombo; her father was a gynecologist and obstetrician and her mother was active in social work.

While growing up, young Sylvia would hear countless stories from her parents about the women whose families were sinking deeper and deeper into poverty because they were always pregnant, ill and exhausted. These were truly firsthand experiences, given the fact that her father was the medical superintendent at the De Sousa Maternity Hospital, while Sylvia's mother did social work at the Dean's Road Clinic. Sylvia Fernando was determined that when she grew up she would do something about this situation.

The obstacles to establishing an effective system of family planning in Ceylon/Sri Lanka were many and formidable. The new nation was composed of a great variety of ethnic groups and religions, with little trust between communities and much ingrained social conservatism deeply embedded in their thinking and life patterns. In the 1930s and 1940s, Fernando gained valuable experience as a leading member of the All Ceylon Women's Conference, an umbrella organization representing all of the colony's major women's and service organizations. During countless meetings and individual encounters with women representing the different ethnic and religious communities of Ceylon, she became sensitive to the hopes and fears of not only elite women but the masses who lived in tradition-bound villages and rural areas. Working alongside her mother at the Dean's Road Clinic, Fernando saw women who had become physically and emotionally drained by constant childbearing, and as time went by she began to seek solutions to this problem.

It was on a trip to the United Kingdom in 1946 that Fernando was able to obtain funding for a pilot program for family planning in Ceylon. She was particularly encouraged in her work on this occasion by meeting with the Norwegian champion of birth control, *Elise Ottesen-Jensen (1886–1973). Back in Colombo, a small group of women—at first, probably no more than 14 or 15—were organized by Fernando to build the foundations of a birth-control program. The obstacles facing the successful implementation of a national agenda of family planning were immense, particularly from conservative religious leaders, be they Roman Catholic, Buddhist, Hindu or Muslim. As a Christian, Fernando strongly believed that abortion should not be part of a family-planning scheme, not only because she was personally opposed to abortions but also because offering them to women would very likely engender even greater resistance to the idea of contraception and family planning. With these ideas as the basis of her projected campaign, in September 1953, at the De Sousa Hospital for Women, Fernando opened the first family planning clinic.

She received strong support in her work not only from her husband, who was "very enthusiastic" about her efforts, but from her entire family, including her mother, brother, and daughter **Nimali**. Her family's supportive attitude was psychologically essential during then early 1950s when her Family Planning Association (FPA) was still in its infancy and much of the population regarded Fernando and her associates as "vulgar and shameless people" who dared to meddle in the most intimate aspects of the lives of men and women. Fernando would serve as head of the FPA for the next 17 years. **Phyllis Dissanayake**, who would succeed Fernando in 1970, recalled how even after more than a decade of work some of the organization's officers still had dirt thrown at them in some communities because they had dared to discuss "dirty things" and interfered in a domain where not free human choice but "God gave children."

In the early years of the FPA, the political fallout from a family-planning program was such that the organization's first government grant had to remain a secret. By the early 1960s, however, the intense educational efforts of Sylvia Fernando and her national team had significantly changed attitudes so that in 1965 the Sri Lankan government officially recognized family planning as a national goal, taking over the clinics that had up to that time been run on a private basis. By this time, 85 clinics were in operation throughout Sri Lanka. Sylvia Fernando died suddenly in Colombo in 1983, passing away in the arms of Dr. **Siva Chinnatamby**, her trusted FPA medical expert and a woman who had been instrumental in introducing the newest contraceptive methods to Sri Lanka.

SOURCES:

Huston, Perdita. *Motherhood by Choice: Pioneers in Women's Health and Family Planning.* NY: The Feminist Press, 1992.

Linder, Doris H. *Crusader for Sex Education: Elise Ottesen-Jensen (1886–1973) in Scandinavia and on the International Scene.* Lanham, MD: University Press of America, 1996.

"Sylvia Fernando 1904–1983," in *People* [London]. Vol. 19, no. 1, 1992, p. 24.

John Haag,
Assistant Professor of History,
University of Georgia, Athens, Georgia

Ferner, Astrid (b. 1932).

See Oldenburg, Astrid.

Fernig, Félicité de and Théophile de

French soldiers.

Fernig, Félicité de (c. 1776–after 1831). Name variations: Felicite; Madame Van der Walen. Born at Montagne, Nord, France, around 1776; died after 1831; married M. Van der Walen, a Belgian officer.

Fernig, Théophile de (c. 1779–c. 1818). Name variations: Theophile. Born at Mortagne, Nord, France, around 1779; died in Brussels, Belgium, around 1818.

Known as the "Amazons of the Jemappes," Félicité and Théophile de Fernig were two French sisters who assumed male attire and enlisted in 1792 in a company of the National Guards commanded by their father. They distinguished themselves by their bravery in the battle of Jemappes which was fought in November between the victorious French, under Charles Dumouriez, and the Austrians, under Archduke Albert. Félicité rode in a charge by the side of the Duke of Chartres (afterward Louis-Philippe) and Théophile reputedly captured a Hungarian major. Félicité married M. Van der Walen, a Belgian officer, whose life she had saved. The sisters were celebrated by Lamartine in *Histoires de Girondins.*

Ferragamo, Fiamma (1941–1998)

Italian shoe designer. Born Fiamma di San Giuliano Ferragamo in Florence, Italy, in 1941; died of breast cancer at her home in Florence on September 28, 1998; eldest of three boys and two girls; daughter of Salvatore Ferragamo (d. 1960, founder of Salvatore Ferragamo Italia) and Wanda Ferragamo (chair of Salvatore Ferragamo Italia).

Born in 1941 in Florence, Italy, the daughter of Salvatore Ferragamo and **Wanda Ferragamo**, Fiamma Ferragamo began working for her father's famous shoe company when she was just 16. Three years later, her father, dying of cancer, handed her the reins of the prestigious shoe label. Though Salvatore Ferragamo Italia was making shoes for European royalty and Hollywood luminaries, Fiamma took the company even further—building it into a powerful international fashion influence.

As a designer for the company, Ferragamo valued elegance and comfort and in the 1960s created one of the most enduring upscale shoe designs, the "Vara." She was accorded the Neiman Marcus Award for Distinguished Service in Fashion in 1967. As executive vice president and company board member, she worked incessantly, promoting her shoes and masterminding acquisitions; in 1996, Salvatore Ferragamo Italia was doing so well it acquired the Emanuel Ungaro company.

In the late 1980s, Ferragamo was diagnosed with breast cancer and doctors thought the disease would take her life within months. But the active businesswoman defied the odds and ran her company with vigor for ten more years, even attending meetings just two weeks before her death at age 57. Fiamma Ferragamo also served on the Italian Environmental Fund board, which preserves historic Italian homes.

SOURCES:

"Fiamma Ferragamo, Shoe Designer," in *The* [New London] *Day,* September 30, 1998.

Jacquie Maurice,
Calgary, Alberta, Canada

Ferrara, duchess of.

See Leonora of Aragon (1450–1493).
See Borgia, Lucrezia (1480–1519).
See Renée of France (1510–1575).
See Sforza, Anna (1473–1497).
See Rovere, Giulia della.
See Medici, Lucrezia de (c. 1544–1561).
See Gonzaga, Margherita (1564–1618).

Ferrara, marquesa of.

See Este, Ricciarda d'.
See Gonzaga, Margherita (1418–1439).

Ferrari, Carlotta (1837–1907)

Italian pianist, poet, singer, and writer who was in great demand as a composer of operas and cantatas. Born in Lodia on January 27, 1837; died in Bologna on November 23, 1907.

When Carlotta Ferrari completed her first opera, *Ugo*, at age 20, she had to pay the entire expense of presenting it; no one would showcase an opera written by a woman. The performance was a success, however, and her work was soon in great demand. Ferrari studied piano and voice under Strepponi and Panzini, and composition under Mazzucato at the Milan Conservatory. Her strong grounding in music as well as her great talent made her much in demand. The Turin government commissioned her to write a cantata as well as a Requiem mass for the anniversary of the death of King Charles Albert. Considered one of the great masters of the canon form, Ferrari was extremely respected in the musical world. Her poetry was also highly regarded.

John Haag,
Athens, Georgia

Ferrari, Gabrielle (1851–1921)

French concert pianist and composer of five operas. Born Gabriella Colombari de Montègre in Paris, France, on September 14(?), 1851; died in Paris on July 4, 1921; married Francesco Ferrari, an Italian correspondent for Le Figaro.

Born in France in September of 1851, Gabrielle Ferrari first studied at conservatories in Naples and Milan before returning to her native Paris following her marriage to Francesco Ferrari, an Italian correspondent for *Le Figaro*. While in Paris, she studied with Théodore Dubois and H. Ketten, and François Leborne and Charles Gounod both championed her work. Ferrari was a concert artist, like many composers, and well known as a pianist. She concentrated on opera, completing five large works. Her first success was *Le dernier amour* in 1895 followed by *Le Cobzar* which created a great deal of debate among pro- and anti-feminists of the period. Her work used folk idioms and melodies.

John Haag,
Athens, Georgia

Ferraro, Geraldine (1935—)

American politician and vice-presidential nominee in 1984 who was the first American woman nominated for a major political office. Name variations: Geraldine Zaccaro. Pronunciation: fe-RAR-o. Born Geraldine Anne Ferraro in Newburgh, New York, on August 26, 1935; daughter of Dominick (a businessman) and Antonetta (Corrieri) Ferraro; graduated Marymount Manhattan College, B.A., 1956; J.D., Fordham Law School, 1960; married John A. Zaccaro, in 1960; children: Donna Zaccaro; John Zaccaro, Jr.; Laura Zaccaro.

Appointed assistant district attorney, Queens, New York (1975); elected to the House of Representatives (1978); reelected to the House of Representatives (1982); nominated for vice president at Democratic National Convention (1984); ran as unsuccessful candidate for U.S. Senate (1992); served as a public delegate (February 1993) and alternate U.S. delegate to the World Conference on Human Rights held in Vienna (June 1993); appointed U.S. ambassador to the UN Human Rights Commission by President Bill Clinton (1994), serving two years; was vice-chair of the U.S. delegation at the Fourth World Conference on Women held in Beijing (September 1955); was co-host of "Crossfire," a political interview program on CNN (1996–98); was a partner in the CEO Perspective Group, a consulting firm that advises top executives (1996–98); ran as unsuccessful candidate for U.S. Senate (1998).

On July 12, 1984, Congresswoman Geraldine Ferraro was named the vice-presidential running mate of Democratic presidential candidate Walter Mondale. It was the first time in U.S. history that a woman had been chosen to run on a major political ticket. "Mr. Mondale . . . announced his historic step before an ebullient crowd at the State Capitol," wrote Bernard Weintraub in a front-page story in *The New York Times*. "He introduced Mrs. Ferraro by saying, 'I looked for the best Vice President and I found her in Gerry Ferraro.'"

Across America, women cheered, while feminists, politicians and pundits jammed the airwaves with their reactions to the announcement. As the first woman nominated for vice president, Ferraro became the newest and most important member of an exclusive sisterhood of political pioneers dating back to 1917 when the first woman, Congresswoman *Jeannette Rankin of Montana, was elected to political office three years before women won the right to vote. Historically, the route for women to Washington was through widowhood. But Ferraro, who worked and campaigned her way into office, epitomized the new woman on Capitol Hill. Her increasing influence in Washington and subsequent nomination signaled the rising power of women in the sphere of American politics, a domain that traditionally had been restricted to men.

Geraldine Anne Ferraro was born on August 26, 1935, the last child and only daughter of Italian immigrant Dominick Ferraro and **Antonetta Corrieri Ferraro**, a first-generation Italian-American. The couple celebrated the birth of each of their four children, but the birth of Geraldine, a healthy baby girl, was cause for particular joyous and poignant family celebration. Before her birth, the Ferraros had experienced the sudden and tragic deaths of two boys; one infant died when he was six days old, another had died in his mother's arms at the age of three in a car accident. In between the two deaths, Antonetta Ferraro suffered a miscarriage.

This string of tragedies took an emotional toll on Ferraro's mother who suffered with severe depression. "I only have children to put them in the cemetery," Antonetta lamented to friends and family. To alleviate the depression, the family doctor urged her to become pregnant again. "I had been special to [my father] because I was the baby, the only girl after four boys, and because I had brought my mother back to life," Ferraro later recalled. My mother "delivered me at home in sheets sprayed with Lysol because she was afraid if she left my brother Carl to go to the hospital, something would happen to him."

Geraldine Ferraro spent the first eight years of her life in Newburgh, New York, where her parents earned a modest living running a restaurant and a five-and-dime business. But another tragedy soon struck the family, a blow from which they would never fully recover. When Geraldine Ferraro was eight, her father died suddenly at the age of 44 of a heart attack.

Faced with this personal and financial catastrophe, Ferraro's mother sold the house in Newburgh and moved with her two children to a tiny apartment in the South Bronx. Antonetta accepted a job as a crochet beader and eked out a marginal living, struggling to support her two children. The sudden reversal of fortune left a strong impression on the young girl. "My father's death changed my life forever," Ferraro later recalled. "I found out how quickly what you have can be taken away. From that moment on, I had to fight for whatever I wanted, to work and study my way out of the South Bronx and take my mother with me."

Determined to give her children every possible advantage, Antonetta Ferraro labored long hours to earn enough money to send them away to good schools. Geraldine was a hard-working, naturally gifted student who excelled at school and even skipped a couple of grades. She graduated from Marymount School in Tarrytown in 1952 and matriculated at Marymount Manhattan College where she graduated in 1956.

After a brief and unsatisfying stint as a legal secretary, Ferraro enrolled at Fordham Law School in 1957 where she was one of two women in her class. She attended classes at night and by day worked as an elementary school teacher. She graduated with honors in 1960 and a few days later married real-estate developer John A. Zaccaro. She settled down to domestic life in Queens, New York, and for the next 14 years played the dual role of wife and mother to her husband and their three children. Any career plans she might have had were put on hold; during that time, she practiced civil law sporadically and occasionally acted as a lawyer for her husband's real-estate company. The real-estate company prospered, and the family became wealthy.

In 1974, her cousin, a Queens district attorney, appointed Geraldine Ferraro an assistant district attorney. As such, she handled up to 40 criminal cases at a time. Then, in 1977, she was named bureau chief of a new sex-crimes division, which was responsible for handling all sex offenses in Queens county, including child abuse and rape. Her division was also charged with implementing recently passed battered-spouse legislation. Ferraro soon faced the inadequacies of the legal system to relieve the suffering of abused children, battered wives, and rape victims she encountered. The discovery that she was being paid significantly less money than the other bureau chiefs—all of whom were men—was another difficult lesson.

Based on her experiences, Ferraro began to contemplate a career in politics. "Working with victims of crime, I saw firsthand that there were real limitations on how much the current laws could help people with fewer resources or power: the elderly, poor mothers and their children, the undereducated. I wanted to make a difference in the most direct way I could, to create opportunities instead of neglect." In 1978, Ferraro ran for Congress in the Ninth District of Queens, New York, a historically conservative ethnic district. Using the slogan, "Finally . . . a tough Democrat" she ran on a law-and-order platform and with 54% of the vote won a seat in the House of Representatives.

When Ferraro arrived in Washington she was one of only 17 women in the House of Representatives and the Senate. She quickly realized that her male colleagues in the House regarded her with some suspicion and derision; her first committee assignment was to the inconsequential House Post Office and Civil Service Committee.

It was soon apparent to Ferraro that the lack of female representation in Congress was reflected in the paucity of legislation designed to benefit women. She was determined to change this by bringing the concerns of women to bear on policy making. To this end, Ferraro initiated a pension-equity bill in 1981 designed to make private pensions fairer and to legally recognize marriage as an economic partnership, thus giving women greater access to their husbands' pension plans and retirement benefits. Her bill also mandated that business allow women to participate in profit-sharing and retirement plans during certain job absences such as maternity leave. Another bill Ferraro sponsored would have given a two-year tax credit to employers who hired displaced homemakers. But with little support from other members of the House, the bills went nowhere.

$\mathcal{L}$adies and Gentlemen, my name is Geraldine Ferraro, and I'm proud to accept your nomination for vice president of the United States.

—Geraldine Ferraro, San Francisco, 1984

Ferraro was not the only woman in Congress frustrated by what she perceived as her male colleagues' indifference to women's issues. In 1983, acting together, the Democratic and Republican female members of the House sponsored a major piece of legislation called the Women's Equity Act. This act included Ferraro's two previous bills as well as other bills providing tax relief to single heads of households, civil service pension reform to aid wives and widows in receiving spouses' retirement benefits, funds for community child-care information and referral services, elimination of federal regulations that hampered women in business, and an improved system of child-support enforcement. Though not entirely successful, the Women's Equity Act scored some important victories, including the passage of Ferraro's pension-equity bill which President Ronald Reagan signed into law on August 23, 1984.

In 1981, Ferraro was also appointed to the Hunt Commission, a 70-member committee set up to review presidential delegate selection rules. She played a key role in devising a plan (known as the "Ferraro plan") under which a group of elected Democrats and party officials would go to the election convention as "superdelegates" uncommitted to any candidate. In a *Washington Post* story, her colleague on the commission, Mark Siegel, called Ferraro "a bridge between the new and old politics and between the feminists and the organization democrats."

In her six years in the House of Representatives, Ferraro established a voting record considerably more liberal than that of her largely conservative constituents. Early on, she earned a reputation as a team player, voting with the majority of House Democrats more than 90% of the time. She occasionally broke with the House leadership, however, on votes that aligned her more closely with her blue-collar constituents. For example, on social issues she advocated tax credits for parents who sent their children to private school and opposed mandatory busing of schoolchildren to achieve racial integration. But on matters of foreign policy, she consistently upheld the Democratic party line of noninterventionism and constrained defense spending, voting against American financing for Nicaraguan rebels, the financing of the MX missile, and the production of the B-1 bomber.

Ferraro gained influence in the House and made some powerful allies, including Speaker of the House, Thomas "Tip" O'Neill. Following her 1982 reelection, she was given a seat on the powerful House Budget Committee, which is responsible for allocating funds for every program before Congress. She was also named chair of the Democratic Platform Committee in 1984. Later that year when Senator Walter Mondale, the probable Democratic presidential nominee, began searching for a vice-presidential running mate, Geraldine Ferraro was a name roundly endorsed by Democratic Party officials. Mondale's decision to nominate Ferraro (who was not only the first woman, but the first Italian-American chosen to run on a major ticket) was in part a shrewd political calculation designed to gather support among blue-collar and trade-union voters. It was also a move intended to spark some excitement into what was generally considered a lackluster candidacy. Mondale's announcement of Ferraro as his running mate on July 12 and her official nomination as the Democratic vice-presidential nominee at the Democratic National Convention, one week later, did just that: it rejuvenated the Democratic Party and Mondale's flagging campaign. Her nomination also met with a deluge of media attention and a

Geraldine
Ferraro

groundswell of support from women voters and Democratic Party officials. "What a high that night was," wrote Ferraro of her nomination at the Democratic Convention in San Francisco. "As I looked out over the convention floor, I saw faces of America: farmers, factory workers, young professionals, the elderly, business executives, blacks, whites, Hispanics, Native Americans, people of Asian descent and women—so many women. No one wanted to leave. Even my normally more sobersided peers and colleagues were caught up in the euphoria."

Despite repeated Republican criticism of her as a political "novice" totally inexperienced in foreign affairs, Ferraro proved a tenacious, cool, and enthusiastic politician on the hustings. Campaigning throughout the country, she demonstrated a talent for rhetoric and a solid grasp of domestic issues and foreign policy. In speeches and in her televised debate with Republican vice president George Bush, she ably denounced the domestic policies of Ronald Reagan as damaging to women, middle-class families, and the poor, and criticized the Republicans' foreign policy as costly, short-sighted, and detrimental to world peace.

In the debate, Bush came across as condescending and repeatedly called her "Mrs. Ferraro" when "Congresswoman Ferraro" had been the agreed-upon appellation. In one rebuttal, Ferraro showed her annoyance: "I almost resent, Vice President Bush, your patronizing attitude that you have to teach me about foreign policy. I have been a member of Congress for six years."

Ferraro was the focus of more media attention than any other vice-presidential candidate in history. Although the American public and the press were initially supportive, she fell victim to an aggressive backlash of sentiment against her. As a woman, she was declared unfit; as an Italian-American, she was accused of having ties to organized crime; as a Catholic who personally opposed abortion but nevertheless upheld the right of women to choose, she was repeatedly attacked by Catholic leaders, including Archbishop John O'Connor of New York. Eventually her candidacy became jeopardized amidst growing speculation over husband John Zaccaro's alleged unlawful business practices. Questions were also raised about the financing of her 1978 campaign for Congress and whether she had violated the requirements of the Ethics in Government Act by not reporting the details of her husband's finances.

As Ferraro became bogged down in answering these charges and as Walter Mondale fended off growing concern about possible Democratic tax hikes and increased spending, the enthusiasm for the Mondale-Ferraro ticket began to evaporate. "More than once in the next four months, as the euphoria faded and the highs were equaled by the lows," wrote Ferraro, "I would remember my mother's words to me when I was young. 'Don't forget your name,' she would tell me. '*Ferro* means iron. You can bend it, but you can't break it.'" The Republican incumbents (Reagan/Bush) defeated the Democratic challengers (Mondale/Ferraro) in 48 of the 50 states and won the biggest electoral vote in U.S. history. The stunning sweep was in large part predictable since no incumbent U.S. president had ever lost an election following a year of economic growth.

Despite the Reagan/Bush landslide of 1984, the nomination of Geraldine Ferraro has had a lasting effect on American politics. As *Bella Abzug noted in an editorial in *The New York Times* three weeks after the election: "From now on the public will be more accepting when a woman runs for high office. All-male control of national political leadership is no longer written in stone or engraved on voting machines."

Following the election, Ferraro decided not to run for Congress in 1986, opting instead to spend more time with her family. Her autobiographical account of the campaign, *Ferraro: My Story,* was published a year later. In 1992, she was defeated in a close race for a seat in the U.S. Senate amid renewed allegations of ties to organized crime and illegal business dealings. She then signed on to co-host CNN's "Crossfire" for three years. In 1998, Ferraro made another bid for the Senate but lost in the primary to Charles Schumer. Though presently not in public office, Geraldine Ferraro remains a popular lecturer, a television analyst, and a visible and outspoken advocate for the rights of women and minorities, health care reform, and world peace.

Despite her subsequent losses, she has earned a respected place in history. Few women will forget that nominating night in San Francisco when a woman stood on the podium and said, "Ladies and Gentlemen, my name is Geraldine Ferraro, and I'm proud to accept your nomination for vice president of the United States." The crowd in the Moscone Center had gone wild.

A few days after the convention, Ferraro received a letter from one such woman. "I'm sitting here this morning with my coffee and this week's *Time* with you on the cover. As I begin to read, I find myself in tears. Tears of joy, of relief, of saying at last, I don't have to feel second class anymore. I'm thirty-six years old. I'm a Republican. For years something's burned inside me. Resentment about the way women are perceived in the world. Shame in halfway believing it. And now you've come along to say—never again do I have to feel this way. . . . You have changed my life—maybe even my vote."

SOURCES AND SUGGESTED READING:
Ferraro, Geraldine A. *Changing History: Women, Power and Politics.* Wakefield: Moyer Bell, 1993.
———, and Linda Bird Francke. *Ferraro: My Story.* NY: Bantam Books, 1985.
———, and Catherine Whitney. *Framing a Life: A Family Memoir.* Scribner, 1998.

Hartmann, Susan M. *From Margin to Mainstream: American Women and Politics Since 1960.* Philadelphia, PA: Temple University Press, 1989.

The New York Times. July 13, 1984; July 19, 1984; July 20, 1984; August 18, 1984; September 2, 1984; August 21, 1984; December 22, 1984; December 30, 1984; February 21, 1987; March 14, 1992; May 15, 1992; August 20, 1992; September 16, 1992.

Uglow, Jennifer S., ed. *The Continuum Dictionary of Women's Biography.* NY: Continuum, 1989.

Suzanne Smith,
freelance writer and editor, Decatur, Georgia

Ferrell, Barbara (1947—)

African-American runner. Name variations: Barbara Ann Ferrell Edmondson. Born on July 8, 1947, in Hattiesburg, Mississippi; attended Harrison Technical High School in Chicago and Los Angeles City College; received a B.A. in sociology at California State, Los Angeles, 1969; coached by Fred Jones; married Warren Edmondson; children: Malika and Maya.

Barbara Ferrell set the world record in the 100 meters in 1968. That same year, she won the silver medal in the 100 meters and the gold medal in the 4x100 meter relay in the Mexico City Olympics.

Ferrers, Anne (d. 1342)

*English noblewoman. Died in 1342; daughter of William Ferrers, 1st baron Ferrers of Groby, and *Margaret Segrave (c. 1280–?); married Edward Despenser; children: Edward Despenser, 1st baron Despenser.*

Ferrers, Elizabeth (1392–1434).

See Joan Beaufort (1379–1440) for sidebar.

Ferrers, Isabel.

See Mowbray, Isabel.

Ferrier, Kathleen (1912–1953)

English contralto who became one of the world's best-known and best-loved singers in the course of an all-too-brief career. Born Kathleen Mary Ferrier on April 22, 1912, at Higher Walton, near Preston, Lancashire, England; died of cancer on October 8, 1953; third surviving child of William Ferrier (a teacher) and Alice (Murray) Ferrier; married Albert Wilson, on November 19, 1935 (annulled 1947); no children.

Born into a musical family, Ferrier studied the piano from age nine and had established a reputation as an excellent amateur accompanist before she won a major singing competition when she was 25 (1937); *began to take regular voice lessons; within five years, had established her singing career in London and begun to win international acclaim (1937–42); from oratorio and folk songs, progressed to the songs of Schubert and Mahler and to the operas of Gluck and Britten; when she was 39, diagnosed with the cancer that would kill her (1951), but her voice was unimpaired; for two more years, continued to sing, retaining her infectiously joyous spirit until the end.*

Selected discography—the following Decca recordings were originally made between 1946 and 1952: Gluck, Orfeo ed Euridice (abridged), 417 182-1 DM (LP); Mahler, Das Lied von der Erde, 414 194-2 DH (CD); Mahler and Brahms Recital, 421 299-2 DH (CD); Bach and Handel Arias, 414 623-2 DH (CD); The World of Kathleen Ferrier, 430 096-4 (MC).

Having found no contralto who could adequately perform the taxing music of Mahler's *Das Lied von der Erde* which was to receive its first performance at the inaugural Edinburgh Festival in 1947, the distinguished 71-year-old conductor, Bruno Walter, somewhat reluctantly agreed to audition Kathleen Ferrier, whose singing career had been built primarily upon her interpretation of English folk songs and on oratorio. At 35, she had a well-established reputation in England but was almost unknown internationally. As Walter described the encounter in the *Sunday Times*, May 9, 1954:

> She came in dressed in a kind of Salzburg costume, a dirndl, looking young and lovely, pure and earnest, simple and noble, and the room seemed to become brighter for the charm of her presence. She had the charm of a child and the dignity of a lady.

It was "love at first sight," he wrote, only half in jest.

Kathleen Ferrier was of mixed Welsh, Scottish, Irish, as well as English blood. Her father William Ferrier, who ended his teaching career as headmaster of St. Paul's School, Blackburn, was an excellent bass singer with sound knowledge of music and a "calm and steady" temperament that his daughter was to inherit. Her mother **Alice Murray Ferrier**, who was possessed of a keen, instinctive love of music and a more volatile personality, was sometimes resentful that family responsibilities had never allowed her to pursue her own interests or develop her talents. Alice was 40 when Kathleen, her last child, was born; Kathleen's sister **Winnifred Ferrier** was eight years older and her brother George five years her senior.

It was at Alice's prompting that William applied for the headship of St. Paul's School in

1913. His new post brought a sorely needed increase in salary and allowed the family to move to Blackburn from the village where Kathleen had been born. Alice was determined that her children should have the better schooling and increased cultural opportunities that the thriving town could provide.

Kathleen showed her quick intelligence early; she was reading before she started school, and, from the first, there was music. Her mother sensed her natural talent and helped her to learn to read music before taking her to the best available local teacher for formal piano lessons. Unwilling to accept a beginner and suspicious of Kathleen's unorthodox fingering technique, **Frances Walker** soon discovered real ability in her new nine-year-old pupil. At age 12, Ferrier entered her first piano competition; she placed fourth out of 43 entrants.

No teaching, no musical associations, no help from whatever distinguished quarter could have worked this miracle. It was Kathleen herself, her great gift of voice, her hard work, artistry, sincerity, personality and, above all, her character that made her great.

—**Roy Henderson**

Kathleen loved performing; she acted in school plays and developed a talent for mimicry to entertain her friends. She began to sing in a choir, one of two that her father had joined, thereby connecting with that tradition of English choral and orchestral music that was particularly strong in the industrial north and especially dominant in an age before the emergence of rival entertainments such as radio and television. Regular choral performances of *Messiah* and *Elijah* endeared these works to Kathleen Ferrier, and the connection which she must have instinctively made between the musical and the sacred was probably reinforced by her mother's deep love and respect for music. When the family eventually acquired a radio, no one was allowed to talk while music was being broadcast; Alice insisted that it be listened to or switched off.

Apart from her fast-developing musical abilities, Ferrier did well at school and was so good at games that it was hoped that she might one day teach sport. However, neither music college nor teacher training were to materialize. While her older sister Winnifred had stayed at school until she was 18 and then went on to teachers' college, Kathleen left school at the age of 14 and started work for the Post Office as a telephone operator. Money had always been short, and her father was now about to retire. Her brother George, who had gone to Canada, remained a continual worry to the family and seemed likely to need habitual financial support. Vigorous objections from Kathleen's headmistress were brushed aside, and Alice found a job for her youngest child.

Ferrier's joyful, resilient temperament seems to have adapted easily to the working world. She impressed her fellow telephone operators with her ability to turn cartwheels, joined the Post Office tennis team, and began singing with a church choir. Nor did she let her new job hamper her piano studies; in 1928, at age 16, she won a piano in the area finals of a national competition, and at 17 she passed the Associate of the Royal College of Music exam, followed by the Licentiateship of the Royal Academy of Music two years later.

Ferrier continued to win prizes and became a much sought-after accompanist, never turning down a booking. Passing the LRAM exam meant that Kathleen had to devote less hours to practicing the piano, and it was at about this time that she began to take occasional voice lessons from her piano teacher and also to study elocution.

At age 21, Ferrier, who had never lacked boyfriends, started seeing one young man in particular who shared her love of dancing and cycling: Bert Wilson. They became engaged and were married on November 19, 1935. Well before the ceremony, Kathleen seems to have realized that she did not love the man she was to marry. Years later, she confided to her sister that she could not see any way of calling off the wedding once all the plans had been made, so she simply went along with them and hoped for the best. Optimism was not enough. Bert's conscription into the army in 1940 marked the effective end of the marriage; it was dissolved in 1947 on the grounds of non-consummation, and Ferrier rarely referred to it again.

Upon her marriage, she was forced to leave her job at the Post Office, which did not employ married women. Since Bert was working at Silloth, near Carlisle, the couple set up house there, and Kathleen occupied herself by giving piano lessons. However, she lacked the patience to really enjoy the challenge of teaching. The turning point in her career came in 1937 when she entered the prestigious Carlisle musical festival. To no one's great surprise, she placed first in the piano competition, but, responding to a half-joking challenge from her husband, she not only entered but won the vocal competition also.

Her success at Carlisle seemed to give her the confidence in her voice that she had previously lacked. It is likely also that her voice had taken time to mature, as is often the case with the darker contralto range; Ferrier was still only 25. She began singing lessons in earnest and started accepting professional singing engagements, winning still more vocal competitions and occasionally broadcasting on radio.

Following the outbreak of war in 1939, the Council for the Encouragement of Music and the Arts sponsored concerts throughout Britain to entertain the troops and to bring music to the lives of those who had little opportunity to hear it. In 1941, Ferrier was offered a contract, and for the next four years she traveled throughout the country, singing in church halls, basements, and barns: "anywhere it was possible to put a piano," observes her biographer Maurice Leonard, "and she soon established an extensive repertoire of English folk songs, along with works by Purcell and Schubert as well as offering numerous performances of Handel's *Messiah*."

In 1942, Ferrier auditioned for England's best-known conductor, Sir Malcolm Sargent, who advised her that she would have to go to London if she wanted to pursue a professional singing career. It was through Sargent that Kathleen secured an audition with John Tillett of Ibbs and Tillett, one of the most important concert agencies in the world. Tillett accepted her on first hearing and plans were soon made to make the essential move to London to launch her career. On Christmas Eve, 1942, the two sisters, along with their now-widowed father, moved into the small flat they had rented in Hampstead.

Kathleen had spent part of that same Christmas Eve on a train with the well-known tenor Roy Henderson, following a concert in which they had appeared together. Henderson was also represented by the Tillett agency, and he reported to John Tillett that he was unimpressed with this new contralto: "It was a good voice, but too dark. And she kept her nose buried in the score the whole time, terrified to look up. I told her she should learn her words and throw away the book." Ferrier realized the value of Henderson's advice and soon sought him out in London at the Royal Academy of Music, where he was teaching, to request some lessons.

Lessons with Henderson began in March 1943 and were to continue on a regular basis until 1947. Her new teacher's first focus was upon improving Kathleen's breath control, giving her exercises to strengthen her diaphragm.

Kathleen Ferrier

His methods proved effective; a new smoothness of line became apparent in her singing, and, in later years, Ferrier was to explain to her dressmaker that any gown she wore for a performance must allow for at least a three-inch expansion of the diaphragm. But Henderson in London, and J.E. Hutchinson in Carlisle before him, could only work to improve Kathleen's voice; they did not make it. Indeed, given her unusually large throat cavity, natural musicianship and the unique timbre of her "instrument," as well as what critic Alan Blyth called the "combination of dignity and radiance" evident in her performances, it might be argued that once her technique was secure, Kathleen had little more to learn.

Yet Ferrier was never one to rest content with herself; while she heeded Henderson's advice to avoid studying the theoretical aspects of voice production, she strove to be more spontaneous and less inhibited while on stage and to extend her performing repertoire. A down-to-earth north of England lass, she had been brought up far away from the rarefied world of opera and had never learned to care for it. Although she incorporated occasional Verdi arias into her concert performances and was advised by some to consider operatic roles, the more she saw of opera the less inclined she was to sing it. She told the soprano *Joan Hammond that she would feel foolish dressed up as somebody else.

In June 1944, Ferrier made her first recording for the Columbia Gramophone Company in a test performance to determine whether her voice would be suitable, given the limited technology of the time. The contralto voice was notoriously difficult to render faithfully, and the company decided that care would have to be taken with microphone placement in order to avoid distortion. Ferrier was not disturbed by the cautious verdict; she still regarded the recording studio as something of a novelty and believed records to be far less important than live performance.

That same year, Ferrier sang for the first time under the direction of Sir Malcolm Sargent, and she worked much of that summer to learn the *Four Serious Songs* of Brahms which Sargent had recently orchestrated. Ferrier found the songs, especially the poignant third in the cycle "O Death, How Bitter," deeply moving, and often both she and her accompanist would be overcome by tears. On such occasions, Kathleen would change the mood by breaking into one of the many bawdy songs or rhymes she knew, and, with emotions under control, the hours of practice would continue. Ferrier gave the first broadcast of the songs on August 26.

By the end of the war in 1945, Ferrier had achieved a national reputation, especially for her performances of religious works with England's major choral societies. She continued to be in great demand for radio broadcasts and had begun to record on a regular basis, although she remained dissatisfied with the results.

During the winter of that year, Benjamin Britten, England's best-known young composer, was at work on a new chamber opera, *The Rape of Lucretia,* which was to be premiered at the re-opening of the Glyndebourne opera house in 1946. Britten's friend, Peter Pears, suggested that Ferrier be considered for the title role, a heroine who, it was essential, should be "essentially pure and chaste." As unenthusiastic about opera as ever, Ferrier was convinced that she had not made a good first impression upon Britten and his librettist, Ronald Duncan. "She did not know," Duncan later wrote in *Opera* magazine, "that even while she was going down the stairs we were improvising a war dance of pleasure." In Ferrier's "natural simplicity and dignity," they had found "the precise quality" they wanted,

"and something no stage technique could ever achieve."

Working hard to overcome her nerves at being selected for the most important role of her career, Ferrier was cheered by winning the support of another of England's most influential conductors, Sir John Barbirolli, the outcome of her superlative performance with him in *The Dream of Gerontius*. Barbirolli became one of her staunchest admirers and most devoted friends; he was enchanted by her lack of pretentiousness, her humor, and her graceful beauty.

Ferrier did not feel graceful on stage; she continued to be painfully self-conscious. During the weeks of rehearsal for *Lucretia,* she sought advice from the soprano *Joan Cross about how best to move her arms and, especially, her large feet. As Cross recalled:

> My advice was simple. "Why don't you leave them alone? Your voice expresses all you need." After that she stood still on stage, and that was enough. If you confine acting to movement on stage then she was not brilliant, but if you define it as the ability to convey great depths of emotion, then she was a fine actress.

British reviews for the new opera were mixed and *Lucretia* attracted far more attention and praise in Holland, where it was performed at the end of a two-month tour following its month at Glyndebourne. The Dutch appearances marked the first of many overseas engagements. Her return to England saw her schedule crammed with bookings and several recording sessions for the Decca company with whom she had now signed a contract in the hope of achieving technically better results. Certainly her February 1946 recording of Gluck's "What is Life?" shows a vast improvement over her 1944 demo-disc for Columbia; the Decca recording sold well and remained at the top of the best-selling charts for several months.

The Gluck opera from which Ferrier's "hit" was taken, *Orfeo ed Euridice,* was presented to great acclaim, with Ferrier as Orfeo, at Glyndebourne during the 1947 season. It was no doubt this success would lead to Ferrier's audition for the German conductor, Bruno Walter, and to world fame as a singer of the songs of Gustav Mahler. Invited to launch the newly established Edinburgh Festival in 1947, Walter was determined to conduct the first performance of Mahler's *Das Lied von der Erde*. Scored for contralto, tenor, and orchestra, the work ends in an ecstatic contralto song, "Abschied," an impassioned farewell to the earth which can take 20 minutes to sing. Having been persuaded to audition Ferrier, the distinguished conductor was instantly won over. He believed that he had found the perfect Mahler voice, and he championed her career for the next six years, assisting her in establishing an international reputation.

Ferrier's triumph with Walter at the Edinburgh Festival was followed by her first American tour and a packed schedule of concerts at home and abroad during 1948. She had been experiencing occasional pain in her breast and arm, and, as she had always had a rather superstitious dread of cancer, she had a thorough medical check-up late in the year and was greatly relieved to be pronounced fit.

The year 1949 saw another taxing North American tour that also included appearances in Cuba. Before leaving, she recorded some of her best-loved English folk songs for Decca and had empowered her accompanist, **Phyllis Spurr**, and her sister Winnifred to agree to release them if they were satisfied with the quality. While the two deputies were pleased with the results, the recording was, as so often before, a great disappointment to Ferrier. However, she was too late to withdraw the record, and the songs have continued to delight listeners ever since.

Nor was Ferrier ever satisfied with her theatrical performances: during rehearsals for *Orfeo ed Euridice* in Holland during the summer of 1949, she wrote, in typically self-deprecating style:

> I'm working quite hard, but need every minute of it, as I'm *lousy* on stage. Can cope with expressing sorrow, happiness and fright on me old dial, but oh! my large extremities! I fall upstairs, downstairs, even over my own feet—there is a nice pet of a producer who's very patient and long suffering. And, it'll perhaps be alright on the night—I hope so!

It was indeed "alright on the night"; Kathleen was now a great favorite in Holland, as she was throughout Europe and, increasingly, in North America, where she toured again early in 1950.

Her full-packed performing schedule left her little time for anything else but music; a romance with Liverpool antique dealer Rick Davies petered out; "I don't mind him for a buddy for two days" she wrote to Winnifred, "then I've had enough and want to retire behind an iron curtain and not have to listen and make conversation!"

Given her punishing round of appearances, it was scarcely surprising that Kathleen showed signs of exhaustion between engagements. She also found the recurring pain in her breast spreading to her shoulder and neck and becoming more troublesome but, once again, a medical examination in the summer of 1950 revealed no apparent cause. However, in March 1951, she discovered a lump on her breast and, upon her return from a tour of Holland and Germany, received the diagnosis of cancer. All engagements were canceled for two months, and she had the breast removed in April.

From the first, Ferrier was determined to stay cheerful and make the best of things, telling her friends that she was glad of the rest and confident of recovery. Nine days after the operation, she wrote that she was "being spoiled to death and thoroughly enjoying myself" and on April 22, her 39th birthday, she held a lively party for friends in her hospital room, complete with oysters and champagne.

Radiation treatment followed with Ferrier remaining positive and optimistic throughout. Her assistant **Bernadine Hammond**, who, as it happened, was also a qualified nurse, observed to Kathleen's favorite accompanist, Gerald Moore:

> Kath enjoyed life from the moment she woke and purred over her morning cup of tea. . . . During the day she would say so often, "Lucky, lucky, Kath!" Troubles, and they were not infrequent, were never made much of. If there was anything she could do about it, then she did it smartly, otherwise she waited for it to blow over and turned her mind to something else.

Painting, gardening, playing the piano and singing for small groups of friends relaxed and restored her. Not contemplative by nature nor ostentatiously religious, she seems to have drawn strength from the beauty of the world around her and, most especially, from her music. She returned to the concert platform in June, and in July she embarked upon a strenuous series of performances in Holland, pronouncing herself "as fit as a flea." Further radiation treatment was fitted in between performances and broadcasts in England during the summer, but a projected North American tour in the autumn had to be canceled. Kathleen was suffering from exhaustion and experiencing continuing arm and back pain. In mid-November, she was forced to cancel her remaining engagements for the year, but by January 1952 she was once again touring England.

The following month, with pain and weakness continuing, she reentered the hospital and received yet more radiation treatment. Persuaded to seek other medical opinions, Ferrier refused to consider hormone injections, which might have altered her voice, and she eventually decided to opt only for further courses of radiation.

In May 1952 came Ferrier's long-awaited opportunity to record *Das Lied von der Erde* with Bruno Walter in Vienna. Despite her weakness and the taxing demands of the recording studio, she persevered and brilliantly executed all that was required of her, never once showing signs of tiredness or impatience. These songs, and the other three Mahler songs she recorded on this occasion, were an artistic triumph.

She rested for much of the summer, working on her garden and recovering her strength in time for the Edinburgh Festival at the end of August. Her performance of *Das Lied von der Erde* at Edinburgh was unanimously lauded by the press; *The Daily Despatch* was typical: "She is indeed a great singer—with the voice of a generation and intelligence and sensitivity to match." Engagements throughout England and Ireland followed, despite continuing back pain which Kathleen dismissed as "rheumatiz." The year also saw two private concerts for the newly crowned Queen *Elizabeth II and a November recital in London's Royal Festival Hall which prompted a rare negative review by Neville Cardus in the *Manchester Guardian*. Cardus was critical of Ferrier's mannerisms, particularly her overuse of her hands during the performance. While understandably disturbed, Kathleen wrote a graciously forgiving letter in response to a letter from Cardus: "I don't think you were 'unkind'—it's just made me think, and that doesn't do anybody any harm."

On December 23, Ferrier sang what was to be her last *Messiah*. A week later, on New Year's Day, 1953, she was honored by the queen with the title Commander of the British Empire in recognition of her services to music. The opening days of the new year left her little leisure to celebrate, for she was due to give four performances of *Orfeo ed Euridice* in a new production with Barbirolli at Covent Garden commencing on February 3.

Barbirolli had secured the best of everything for what he was determined would be the definitive production of the opera: scenery and costumes by **Sophie Fedorovitch**, choreography by Frederick Ashton, and ballet sequences by the Sadler's Wells Company. During the intensive rehearsals in January, Kathleen was receiving daily radiation treatment. She refused to consider the suggested removal of her ovaries in order to in- hibit the breast cancer once she learned that her voice might be altered as a result: "She said," reported her specialist, "that she regarded her voice as a divine gift and would go to the grave with the voice as it had been given her."

The press was unanimous in its praise following the first performance and, on this occasion, the *Manchester Guardian* pronounced that "certain passages touched the sublime." However, during the second performance Ferrier was overcome with a paralyzing pain in her leg and only managed to complete her role by a tremendous effort of will. She was injected with morphine and taken to hospital on a stretcher the moment the curtain fell. The remaining performances were rescheduled for April, when, it was hoped, she would be sufficiently recovered. Her sorrow at having to withdraw is evident in a letter she wrote from the hospital: "For the first time I really felt it had been done as I could have wished with a most lovely ballet and fine chorus and, between you and me, I wasn't so bad meself!!"

The two remaining performances of *Orfeo* never took place; on October 8, 1953, Kathleen Ferrier died at the age of 41. The capacious Southwark Cathedral was too small to hold all who wished to attend her memorial service. She had endeared herself to the elite in the international world of music; in a highly competitive profession, she seems to have made no enemies, only vast numbers of friends and admirers. Also, through her broadcasts and constant touring, she had touched the hearts of ordinary people, in Britain, Europe, and North America. And it was not merely Ferrier the glorious singer whom they mourned; her down-to-earth honesty and her warm-hearted spontaneity, qualities that seemed to shine through her every performance as they shone through her life, made "our Kath" a friend to thousands who had never had the chance to meet her.

SOURCES AND SUGGESTED READING:

Cardus, Neville, ed. *Kathleen Ferrier, 1912–1953: A Memoir*. Hamish Hamilton: London, 1954.

Henderson, Roy. "Ferrier, Kathleen Mary," in *Dictionary of National Biography, 1951–1960*.

Leonard, Maurice. *Kathleen: The Life of Kathleen Ferrier, 1912–1953*. Hutchinson: London, 1988.

(Dr.) Kathleen Garay,
Assistant Professor of History and Women's Studies,
McMaster University, Hamilton, Canada

Ferrier, Susan Edmonstone

(1782–1854)

Scottish novelist. Born Susan Edmonstone Ferrier in Edinburgh, Scotland, on September 7, 1782; died on

November 5, 1854, in Edinburgh; youngest of ten children of James Ferrier (a solicitor as well as agent and friend of the fifth duke of Argyll) and Helen Coutts; aunt to James Frederick Ferrier, a Scottish philosopher; never married; no children.

A bright child, given a solid education, Susan Ferrier was the daughter of James Ferrier, for some years factor to the duke of Argyll, and at one time one of the clerks of the court of session with Sir Walter Scott. Her mother was **Helen Coutts**, the beautiful daughter of a Forfarshire farmer. Susan was often a visitor to Inverary, the castle of the dukes of Argyll. While there, encouraged by the author Lady *Charlotte Bury, she began a satirical work of manners with the help of the duke's niece, **Charlotte Clavering**. The resulting novel *Marriage* (written around 1810), for which Clavering only wrote a few pages, was published anonymously in 1818. It portrayed far too many people of Edinburgh society for Ferrier to sign her name to it; many thought Sir Walter Scott had written it.

A woman of quick wit and warm heart, Ferrier was an intimate friend of Scott's as well as other eminent writers of her day, including *Joanna Baillie. Scott gave Ferrier a high place among the novelists of her time. In his diary entry of March 27, 1826, criticizing a new work that he had been reading, he wrote, "The women do this better. [*Maria] Edgeworth, Ferrier, [*Jane] Austen, have all given portraits of real society far superior to anything man, vain man, has produced of the like nature." In the conclusion of his *Tales of My Landlord*, Scott called Ferrier his "sister shadow."

Ferrier wrote three unsigned novels: *Marriage* (1818), *The Inheritance* (1824), and *Destiny* (1831), the last of which was dedicated to Scott who had engineered the deal with the publisher Robert Cadell. All these novels, though slim in plot, present lively pictures of Scottish life and character, written in clear, brisk English, with a keen sense of the ludicrous. Known as neither moralist nor cynic, Ferrier employed a wit that, though caustic, was not insensitive. Her novels portrayed the eccentricities and foibles of her society via strong characterizations like that of the Reverend Mr. M'dow in *Destiny*:

> The Reverend Duncan M'dow was a large, loud-spoken, splayfooted man, whose chief characteristics were his bad preaching, his love of eating, his rapacity for augmentations (or as he termed it *ougmentations*), and a want of tact in all *bienséances* of life which would have driven Lord Chesterfield frantic. . . . [T]he inward man was very

much of the same stamp. Mr. M'dow's principal object in this world was self, and his constant and habitual thoughts had naturally operated on his outward manners to such a degree as to blunt all the nicer perceptions of human nature, and render him in very truth his own microcosm. He was no dissembler; for a selfish dissembler is aware that in order to please, one must appear to think of others and forget self. This fictitious politeness he had neither the tact to acquire nor the cunning to feign; consequently he was devoid of all means of pleasing. Not that we mean to recommend dissimulation, or to insinuate that Mr. M'dow would in reality have been a better man had he been able and willing to form himself on the model of the Chesterfield school. He would merely have been less offensive. . . .

Because these works were issued anonymously, there were many conjectures about their authorship. James Hogg, in the *Noctes Ambrosianae* (November 1826), mentioned *The Inheritance* "which aye thought was written by Sir Walter, as weel's *Marriage,* till it spunked out that it was written by a leddy."

Though her novels were enormously popular, Ferrier did not relish the fame that came with professional writing. This notoriety, combined with dimming eyesight, a tendency to seek seclusion, and a growing religious preoccupation, caused her output to dwindle.

From the time of her mother's death in 1797, she kept house for her father until he died in 1829. For more than 20 years after her last work was published, she lived quietly at Morningside House and in Edinburgh. John Gibson Lockhart describes her visit to the dying Scott in May 1831 in which Scott talked as brilliantly as ever but sometimes, before he arrived at the point in a narrative, "it would seem as if some internal spring had given way." As he paused, he would gaze blankly and anxiously around him. "I noticed," remarked Lockhart, "the delicacy of Miss Ferrier on such occasions. Her sight was bad, and she took care not to use her glasses when he was speaking; and she affected to be also troubled with deafness, and would say, 'Well, I am getting as dull as a post; I have not heard a word since you said so-and-so,'—being sure to mention a circumstance behind that at which he had really halted. He then took up the thread with his habitual smile of courtesy—as if forgetting his case entirely in the consideration of the lady's infirmity."

It was not until a few years before her death on November 5, 1854, at her brother's house in Edinburgh, that Ferrier allowed her name on the title page of any of her novels. Among the papers she left behind was a short, unpublished article, "Recollections of Visits to Ashestiel and Abbotsford," her own account of her long friendship with Scott which contains some impromptu verses Scott wrote in her album at Ashestiel. Ferrier's complete works were published in 1882. Her letters to her sister were destroyed at Ferrier's request. In 1898, however, a volume of her correspondence with a memoir by her grandnephew, John Ferrier, was published.

SUGGESTED READING:

Cullinan, Mary. *Susan Ferrier*. 1984.

Ferrier, Susan Edmonstone. *Memoir and Correspondence.* Edited by A. Doyle. 1898.

Fetti, Lucrina (fl. 1614–1651)

Italian painter. Name variations: Giustina Fetti. Born Lucrina or Giustina Fetti in Rome; birth and death dates unknown; sister of painter Domenico Fetti (1589–1623); entered Franciscan convent of Sant Orsola, Mantua, Italy, 1614.

Paintings: Deposition; Adoration of the Shepherds; Adoration of the Magi; Annunciation; Crowning with Thorns; Visitation; Agony in the Garden; Margherita Gonzaga, duchess of Ferrara; Empress Eleanora I Gonzaga, wife of Emperor Ferdinand II; Eleanora II Gonzaga, wife of Emperor Ferdinand III; Caterina de' Medici, wife of Duke Ferdinando Gonzaga; St. Margaret; Mary Magdalene; St. Barbara *(1619).*

What little is known of Lucrina Fetti was recorded by Giovanni Baglione (c. 1573–1644), painter and biographer of 16th- and early 17th-century Roman artists. Referring to her as Domenico Fetti's "sister who likewise painted," Baglione noted that she was brought with her family to Mantua from Rome by Duke Ferdinando Gonzaga, ruler of the Mantuan court, who also provided money for her to enter the convent of Sant Orsola. As a painter and nun, Fetti created a body of religious work for the convent and its adjacent public church, as well as a group of state portraits of the distinguished women of the convent and the court of Mantua.

It was not until the second half of the 18th century that Fetti's paintings were identified, and only recently has she been singled out by critics as worthy of interest. (Questions remain regarding her dependence upon the style and collaboration of her brother, and some believe that Domenico not only taught her to paint, but retouched many of her paintings.) Of her religious works, six scenes (from a set of eight), depicting the lives of *Mary the Virgin and Jesus Christ

are housed at the Hospital of Mantua. Their quality suggests that they may be her earliest efforts or copies of them. A more developed style is seen in four life-size, full-length portraits of women, which reside in the Palazzo Ducale, Mantua. Although the portraits follow a conventional representation, they reveal a sensitivity and refinement in the modeling and textural differentiations. Fetti's *St. Barbara* (1619), which is currently part of an individual collection, is thought to be one of the best representations of her work. Although Domenico's lingering influence is apparent in this work, particularly in the Rubenesque fullness of the figure, Fetti's individual style makes itself known.

Barbara Morgan,
Melrose, Massachusetts

Feuchères, Sophie, Baronne de (c. 1795–1841)

Anglo-French courtier. Name variations: Feucheres; Sophia Dawes. Pronunciation: Fe-SHAR. Born Sophie Dawes or Daws at St. Helens, Isle of Wight, around 1795; died in London, England, on January 2, 1841 (some sources cite December 1840); married Baron Adrien Victor de Feuchères, in 1818 (separated 1822).

Considered to be of "low birth," Sophie Feuchères was born at St. Helens, Isle of Wight, in 1795, the daughter of an alcoholic fisherman named Dawes. She grew up in the workhouse, went up London as a servant, and in 1811 became the mistress of Louis Henri Joseph de Bourbon (1756–1830), the last of the Condé princes. Since Sophie was eager to improve her station, the prince saw that she was well educated not only in modern languages but also, as shown in her still extant exercise books, in Greek and Latin. The prince took her to Paris and, to prevent scandal and to qualify her to be received at court, had her married in 1818 to Adrien Victor de Feuchères, a major in the Royal Guards. The prince provided her dowry and made her husband his aide-de-camp and a baron.

Baroness Sophie, educated and attractive, became a person of consequence at the court of Louis XVIII. When de Feuchères, however, finally discovered her true relationship with Condé, whom he had been assured was her father, he left her and obtained a legal separation in 1827. He also apprised the king Louis, who thereupon forbade Sophie's appearance at court. Thanks to her influence, though, Condé was induced in 1820 to sign a will bequeathing about 10 million francs to her; he left the rest of his estate—more than 66 million—to the duc d'Aumale, the fourth son of Louis Philippe (I), the future king of France. Again, she was in high favor. Louis XVIII's successor Charles X received her at court, Talleyrand visited her, her niece married a marquis, and her nephew was made a baron. Condé, tired of Sophie's requests and displeased with the government, had made up his mind to leave France secretly. When on August 27, 1830, he was found hanging dead from his window, Sophie was suspected and an inquiry was held; there was no evidence of foul play, however, and she was not prosecuted. But life in Paris was no longer agreeable to her, and she returned to London, where she died on January 2, 1841.

Feuillère, Edwige (1907–1998)

French actress. Name variations: played minor roles early in career under stage name Cora Lynn. Born Caroline Vivette Edwige Cunati on October 29, 1907, in Vesorel, France; died on November 13, 1998; daughter of Guy (an architect) and Berthe (Koenig) Cunati; studied acting at the Conservatory of Dijon and the Conservatory of Paris, with Georges Le Roy; married Pierre Feuillère (an actor), in 1931 (divorced).

Made her stage debut at the Comédie Française, Paris, as Suzanne in Mariage de Figaro *(1931); remained with that company until 1933; her subsequent roles in French and international theater include: Marguerite Gautier in* La Dame Aux Camélias *(1940), Lia in* Sodome et Gomorrhe *(1943), the Queen in* L'Aigle à Deux Têtes *(1946), Ysé in* Partage du Midi *(1948), Paola in* Pour Lucrèce *(1953), Clothilde in* La Parisienne *(1957), La Périchole in* Le Carosse du Saint-Sacrement *(1957), title role in* Phèdre *(1957), title role in* Lucy Crown *(1958), title role in* Constance *(1960); later plays included Kopit's* Oh Dad, Poor Dad, Mamma's Hung You in the Closet and I'm Feelin' So Sad *(1963), Giraudoux's* La Folle de Chaillot *(1965), Williams'* Sweet Bird of Youth *(1971), Dürrenmatt's* Der Besuch der alten Dame *(1976), Arbuzov's* Old World, *known in French as* Le Bateau pour Lipaïa *(1977), Anouilh's* Léocadia *(1984).*

Selected films: La Fine Combine *(1931);* Mam'zelle Nitouche *(1931);* Le Cordon Bleu *(1931);* La Perle *(1932);* Une Petite Femme dans le Train *(1932);* Topaze *(1932);* Monsieur Albert *(1932);* Maquillage *(1932);* Toi que J'Adore *(1933);* Matricule 33 *(1933);* Les Aventures du Roi Pausole *(1934);* Le Miroir aux Alouettes *(1934);* Stradivarius *(1935);* La Route Heureuse *(1935);* Lucrece Borgia *(1935);* Golgotha *(1935);* Barcarolle *(1935);* Amore *(1935);* Mister Flow *(1936);* Marthe Richard, Espionne au Service

Edwige Feuillère

de la France *(1937);* Feu! *(1937);* La Dame de Malacca *(1937);* J'étais une Aventuriére *(1938);* Sans Lendemain *(1940);* Mayerling to Sarajevo *(1940);* L'Idiot *(1946);* L'Aigle à Deux Têtes *(The Eagle Has Two Heads, 1947);* Woman Hater *(1948);* Olivia *(1950);* Adorables Creatures *(1952);* Le Blé en Herbe *(1953);* En Cas de Malheur *(1957);* Le Crime ne paie pas *(1962);* Do You Like Women? *(1964);* Let's Make Love *(1968);* Clair de Terre *(1970);* La Chair de l'Orchidée *(1974);* Julia *(1977).*

After playing minor roles on the stage under the name Cora Lynn, French actress Edwige Feuillère joined the renowned Comédie Française in 1931, the same year she married actor Pierre Feuillère. Two years later, she parted with both her husband and the Comédie Française to pursue a film career. Eventually becoming the "first lady" of French cinema, the beautiful Feuillère excelled both in drama and comedy, playing desirable but heartless femmes fatales. Her classical style lent itself particularly well to costume roles. Feuillère returned to the Paris stage in 1934, where she added considerably to her stature as an actress. In 1946, Jean Cocteau wrote the play *L'Aigle à Deux Têtes* (*The Eagle Has Two Heads*) especially for her, and she recreated her stunning portrayal of the Queen in a later film version. The actress made several appearances on the London stage and also produced and directed for her own repertory company. She was named a Chevalier of the Légion d'Honneur and was honored by the French Film Academy with a César Award in

1984. Her autobiography, *Les Feux de la Mémoire*, was published in 1977.

Fewings, Eliza Anne (1857–1940)

British and Australian educational reformer. Born in Bristol, England, on December 28, 1857; died in Wales in 1940; daughter of Charles and Sarah (Twining) Fewings; trained as a teacher under her brother, headmaster of the King Edward VI Grammar School in Southampton.

Eliza Fewings, known for her dedication to educational reforms in England and Australia, began her teaching career at the Roan Girls' School in Greenwich, England. From 1886 to 1896, she was headmistress of Dr. Williams' Endowed High School for Girls in North Wales, and also served on the Council of Bangor and Aberystwyth University Colleges. During this time, she campaigned for and won equal status for women at Aberystwyth College.

In 1896, Fewings became headmistress of the Brisbane Girls' Grammar School in Australia, so appointed by Queensland Chief Justice, Sir Samuel Griffith and an all-male board of trustees.

Bobbi Fiedler

Concerned about standards at the school, in 1897 she petitioned for external assessment and the introduction of external examination, but was unsuccessful. She became the object of controversy in 1899, when she was dismissed on grounds of incompetence. The women in the community, among whom she was highly regarded, rallied on her behalf, writing to the newspapers in her defense and demanding public forums. Upon her dismissal, Fewings started a new school, the Brisbane State High School for Girls (later known as Somerville House). By 1903, it had secured external assessment and was the largest girls' school in Queensland, with 150 students.

Fewings, who made several trips overseas to study educational developments, served on the University's Extension Committee, and was a member of the Council of the Brisbane Technical College and of the board of Brisbane School of Arts. She returned to England in 1908, but traveled to Brisbane in 1921 to celebrate the 21st anniversary of Somerville House. She died in Wales in 1940.

SOURCES:

Radi, Heather, ed. *200 Australian Women*. NSW, Australia: Women's Redress Press, 1988.

Fichandler, Zelda (b. 1924).

See Women of the Regional Theater Movement in America.

Fiedler, Bobbi (1937—)

U.S. Republican Congresswoman from California who served three consecutive terms. Born Roberta Frances Horowitz in Santa Monica, California, on April 22, 1937; attended Santa Monica Technical School; attended Santa Monica City College, 1955–59.

Born and raised in California, Congresswoman Bobbi Fiedler worked in the pharmacy business and as an interior decorator before entering politics. She began her public career as the organizer of a citizens' group called BUSTOP, which opposed busing as a means of desegregating the Los Angeles schools. From 1977 to 1980, she served on the Los Angeles School Board, after which she entered her first congressional race, beating out ten-term incumbent and chair of the Democratic Congressional Campaign Committee James Corman by only 800 votes. Serving three consecutive House terms, Fiedler was a member of the Budget Committee where she advocated fiscal conservatism. She voted along party lines on most issues, but parted with her Republican colleagues in her support of feminist issues, including the Equal Rights Amend-

ment. In 1986, instead of pursuing another term in the House, Fiedler made an unsuccessful bid for a Republican Senate seat.

SOURCES:

Office of the Historian. *Women in Congress, 1917–1990.* Commission on the Bicentenary of the U.S. House of Representatives, 1991.

Field, Betty (1918–1973)

American actress. Born on February 8, 1918, in Boston, Massachusetts; died of a cerebral hemorrhage on September 13, 1973; only daughter of George Baldwin and Katherine Francis (Lynch) Field; studied acting at the American Academy of Dramatic Arts; married Elmer Rice (a playwright), on January 12, 1942 (divorced 1956); married Edwin J. Lukas, in 1957; children: (first marriage) John, Judith, and Paul.

Selected stage roles: reporter in Page Miss Glory *(1934);* Audrey in Three Men on a Horse; Susie in Boy Meets Girl *(1936 tour);* Hilda Manney in Room Service *(1937);* Nora in If I Were You *(1938);* Barbara Pearson in What A Life! *(1938);* Clare Wallace in The Primrose Path *(1939);* Rose Romero in Ring Two *(1939);* Mary Ward in Two on an Island *(1940);* Hope Nathan in Flight to the West *(1940);* Edith in A New Life *(1943);* Georgina Allerton in Dream Girl *(1945);* Helen Brown in The Rat Race *(1949);* Peter in Peter Pan *(1950);* Theodora in Not for Children *(1951);* Mildred Tynan in The Ladies of the Corridor *(1953);* Sally Ann Peters in Festival *(1955);* Madame Treplev in The Seagull *(off-Broadway, 1956);* Mlle. de Ste-Euverte in The Waltz of the Toreadors *(1958);* Yankee patrician in A Touch of the Poet *(1958).*

Filmography: What a Life! *(1939);* Of Mice and Men *(1940);* Seventeen *(1940);* Victory *(1941);* The Shepherd of the Hills *(1941);* Blues in the Night *(1941);* King's Row *(1942);* Are Husbands Necessary? *(1942);* Flesh and Fantasy *(1943);* The Great Moment *(1944);* Tomorrow the World *(1944);* The Southerner *(1945);* The Great Gatsby *(1949);* Picnic *(1956);* Bus Stop *(1956);* Peyton Place *(1957);* Hound-Dog Man *(1959);* Butterfield 8 (1960); Birdman of Alcatraz *(1962);* Seven Women *(1966);* How to Save a Marriage—and Ruin Your Life *(1968);* Coogan's Bluff *(1968).*

Betty Field (left) with Kim Novak, from the movie Picnic.

The only child of divorced parents, Betty Field grew up with her mother and stepfather in Newton, Massachusetts, Morristown, New Jersey, and Forest Hills, Long Island. Intent on acting from an early age, she attended the Academy of Dramatics Arts, where she was the first in her class to land an acting assignment. When Field was cast in a London production of *She Loves Me Not* (1934), her role as the debutante Frances Arbuthnot had to be rewritten as a subdebutante because she looked so young. She made her debut on Broadway in a one-line part in *Page Miss Glory* (1934). During the 1930s, Field became a popular ingenue in George Abbott productions, but it was her meeting with playwright Elmer Rice (who would later become her husband) that set her career in motion.

After appearances in Rice's *Flight to the West* (1940) and *A New Life* (1943), Field achieved her first genuine triumph in *Dream Girl* (1945), in which she played Georgina Allerton, a demanding role that required her to be on stage for all but three minutes of the production. For her performance, she won the 1945–46 New York Drama Critics Circle Award for the best performance by an actress. In his review, Lewis Nichols of *The New York Times* (December 15, 1945) wrote: "As Georgina Allerton she is wistful . . . fierce . . . amicably tough . . . amicably stately . . . and always a heroine." Field went on to play ingenue and character roles in both comedies and dramas, including Rice's *Not for Children* (1951), *Dorothy Parker's *Ladies of the Corridor* (1953), and *Festival* (1955), as well as the first American production of Eugene O'Neill's *A Touch of the Poet* (1958). Field divorced Rice in 1956 and remarried the following year.

Throughout her career, she appeared in many Hollywood films, most notably in *King's Row* (1942), opposite Ronald Reagan, and *Of Mice and Men* (1940), in which she portrayed the discontented wife of a rancher who falls victim to the farm hand Lennie. Subsequent film roles ranged from neurotic young women to slovenly but well-intentioned mothers. Betty Field died of a cerebral hemorrhage in 1973.

SOURCES:
Current Biography. NY: H.W. Wilson, 1959.

Field, Jessie (1881–1971)

American educator who founded the 4-H Club. Name variations: Jessie Field Shambaugh. Born Celestia Josephine Field on June 26, 1881, in Shenandoah, Iowa; died of pneumonia on January 15, 1971, in Clarinda, Iowa; fifth of eight children of Solomon Eli-
jah Field and Celestia Josephine (Eastman) Field (both educators); attended Western Normal College, Shenandoah, Iowa; married Ira William Shambaugh, in 1917; children: stillborn son (b. 1919); **Phyllis Ruth Shambaugh** *(b. 1922); (adopted) William H. Shambaugh; later had two more miscarriages.*

Educator Jessie Field devoted her career to encouraging young people to become involved in agricultural activities. While teaching at a one-room schoolhouse in Iowa, she helped her students form a Boys Corn Club and a Girls Home Club, the goals of which were to help the boys develop better farming techniques and to teach the girls home-management skills. In 1906, when she became superintendent of schools for Page County, Field established Corn Clubs and Home Clubs in all of the county's 130 schools. To promote the program, she designed a three-leaf-clover pin with the letter "H" on each leaf (for Head, Heart, and Hands). A fourth H, designating Home, was added in 1913 (it now stands instead for Health). In 1914, under the auspices of the Federal Extension Service of the U.S. Department of Agriculture, the clubs became a national organization, under the name 4-H Club.

Field resigned as superintendent in 1912 to become the national secretary for the Young Women's Christian Association (YWCA) in New York, a position she held until 1917, when she returned to her native Iowa. In her later years, she served as a national adviser to 4-H groups. Field wrote two autobiographies: *The Corn Lady: The Story of a Country Teacher's Life* (1911) and *A Real Country Teacher: The Story of Her Work* (1922).

Field, Kate (1838–1896)

American journalist, columnist, actress, lecturer, and publisher of the weekly **Kate Field's Washington.** *Born Mary Katherine Keemle Field on October 1, 1838, in St. Louis, Missouri; died in Honolulu, Hawaii, on May 19, 1896; daughter of Joseph M. (a well-known actor and playwright) and Eliza Lapsey (Riddle) Field (an actress); educated at Lasell Seminary.*

Selected writings: Adelaide Ristori *(1867);* Mad on Purpose, a Comedy *(1868);* Hap-Hazard *(1873);* Ten Days in Spain *(1875); also contributed to the Atlantic Monthly.*

Kate Field came from distinguished English stock, dating back to the time of *Elizabeth I. One of her forebears, Nathaniel Field, was an actor and friend to William Shakespeare. From

England, her ancestors migrated to Ireland, and in the rebellion of 1798 her grandfather Matthew Field, a leading Roman Catholic of Dublin, lost all his property. Emigrating to America, he settled in Baltimore, where he became a publisher and issued the first American Catholic almanac.

Matthew's son, Joseph M. Field, was educated in New York and became a popular stage actor in the West and in New Orleans, where he was one of the founders of the New Orleans *Picayune.* He also wrote plays (some of which he produced with success), founded and edited the "St. Louis Reveille," and built Field's Variety Theatre in St. Louis, Missouri. While playing Laertes in a stock production of *Hamlet,* he fell in love and married Ophelia: the actress **Eliza Lapsey Riddle.**

Their daughter Kate Field was born in St. Louis, on October 1, 1838. Her brother died when she was 11, but otherwise she enjoyed a carefree childhood. The little girl with red hair and blue eyes chose her own time for going to school, arranged to go there regularly, and then informed her parents that she had done so. Somewhat precocious, she also began to write at an early age and kept a journal: "I awoke at 5 finding the storm continuing unabated. . . . Did not rise til 6¼, lying until that time in bed wondering what the future might bring forth." Passionately fond of music and the stage, she aspired to become a successful opera singer— "Oh, how I long to be a follower of this divine art"—or a successful writer, or a successful entrepreneur. Successful seemed to be the motivating word.

In 1854, she journeyed to Boston to visit her wealthy Uncle Milton and favorite Aunt **Cordela "Corda" Sanford.** With a villa in Newport and glamorous friends that included *Julia Ward Howe, *Charlotte Cushman, and Edwin Booth, the Sanfords introduced their niece to Boston's social scene and put her through three years of school at Lasell Seminary. While she was there, her father died in January of 1856. Left with only a small insurance payment, the 17-year-old Kate and her mother moved in with the Sanfords.

In 1858, the Sanfords took Field abroad for a two-year stay in Florence, where she was placed under the charge of an Englishwoman, had tea with the Brownings, met George Eliot (*Mary Anne Evans) and *Frances Trollope, and flirted with Trollope's son Anthony and the 84-year-old author Walter Savage Landor while he gave her Latin lessons. Field also wrote a col-

Kate Field

umn for the Boston *Courier* and then the *Transcript.* She subsequently gained much of her reputation with her three-part reminiscence of "The Last Days of Walter Savage Landor" in the *Atlantic Monthly* (1861). Over the next seven years, other articles concerning her stay in Florence would appear in the *Atlantic,* including "A Study of *Elizabeth Barrett Browning."

At the start of the Civil War in 1864, the family returned home. Meanwhile, Field's relationship with her uncle was becoming contentious. Issues that divided the nation began to divide the household. He hated abolitionists; she thought John Brown a hero. At first, he only threatened to cut off her allowance; eventually, he would cut back on her financial aid and reduce her inheritance in his will. Another setback was a fall from her horse which seriously impaired her health.

But Field kept busy. In 1868, she helped found the first professional women's club, which she then quit because she hated the name Sorosis. On November 14, 1874, she opened on Broadway as *Peg Woffington in a revival of Charles Reade-Tom Taylor's *Masks and Faces.* The play closed the following night. Though she defied the critics and continued to tour, her ill health compelled her to give up acting. She was an excellent critic, however, and began writing articles on drama for the New York *Tribune.* When Dickens came to America, Kate Field heard him nightly and published *Pen Photographs of Dickens' Readings* which passed through several editions. About this time, Field and her friends purchased the farm in the Adirondacks where John Brown's body was buried and turned it into a memorial. She returned to New York and lectured on the subject, then followed up her first venture on the platform with a eulogy of Dickens.

Field then sailed for England and lectured abroad for several months. She traveled to Spain to meet President Emilio Castelar and wrote a series of letters for the *Tribune,* called "Ten Days in Spain," which eventually appeared in book form. She studied singing in London with Garcia and William Shakespeare, the English tenor; she also produced a play called "Extremes Meet," which had considerable success. She wrote many articles for leading journals and magazines, including an article about the telephone for the *London Times,* which led to her being considered an expert on the nascent invention. As a result, at Osborne House she sang "Kathleen Mavourneen" to Queen *Victoria over the telephone, and had a harp played into a telephone in Shakespeare's house in Stratford, which was heard in a London theater. Returning home, she wrote *Eyes and Ears in London,* which met with genuine success.

Traveling west in 1883, Field stayed a year in Salt Lake City, where she became interested in the study of Mormonism. The double standard of polygamy infuriated her. As noted by Helen Beal Woodward in *The Bold Women:*

> Kate claimed that the primary evil she fought was not polygamy but theocracy. It was what Jefferson had fought, and Andrew Jackson, and every real liberal since 1789; the union of church and state. This is plausible enough, but it does not quite explain the ardor with which she gathered statistics, tracked down the original lynchers of Joseph Smith in Nauvoo, Illinois, and interviewed Mormons, male and female. Basically a crack reporter, for all her bias, she concocted from her material her most eloquent lecture: *The Mormon Monster;* listening time, two hours.

When she returned East, her lectures on that subject and her evidence before a congressional committee brought about legislation that led to changed conditions and the admission of Utah as a State. Several years later (1887), Field visited Alaska and California and delivered the first lecture heard in Alaska to a crowd of miners; the subject was Charles Dickens. Her writing and lecturing were of great service to the Pacific slope. In 1890, she established a literary and critical journal in Washington, with a branch office in New York, which she entitled *Kate Field's*

Washington, a national weekly review in which she continued her brilliant criticism of literature, the stage, and politics. She wrote most of the articles herself. Through her efforts, the tariff on arts was reduced from 30 to 15% in the McKinley bill and subsequently abolished in the Wilson bill. She was decorated by the French government with the Palm of the Academy, the highest honor given to a woman, and named as Officier de l'Instruction Publique.

In the spring of 1895, Field accepted a commission from the Chicago *Times-Herald* to visit Hawaii and study conditions there. Her mission, short as it was, was eminently successful, and her letters were widely read. She secured the first press interview granted by Hawaii's president Sanford Dole, and her letters to her paper were read in Cabinet meetings in Honolulu.

Exposure in a storm brought on an illness that caused her death on board a steamer traveling from Kawaihae to Honolulu on May 19, 1896. Her last words were reputed to be: "Oh, yes—The Amherst Eclipse Expedition!" The day before her death, she had met members of a party en route to Japan to observe a total eclipse. The next day, ever the journalist, she roused herself from a coma as her new friends gathered round, and she asked one more time: "Who did you say you were?" When told they were from Amherst, she triumphantly blurted her words of recognition and died. Her body was brought to San Francisco for cremation, and her ashes were deposited by the graves of her parents in Mount Auburn Cemetery near Boston. Her friend and biographer, *Lilian Whiting,* placed over her grave a cross of purest Italian marble.

SOURCES:

American Biography. Vol II. NY: American Historical Society, 1918.

Edgerly, Lois Stiles. *Give Her This Day.* Gardiner, ME: Tilbury House, 1990.

Woodward, Helen Beal. *The Bold Women.* NY: Farrar, Straus, 1953.

Field, Mary (1896–c. 1968)

English filmmaker. Born Agnes Mary Field in Wimbledon, England, in 1896; died in 1968 or 1969; attended Bedford College for Women, London; received M.A at the Institute of Historical Research; married Gerald Hankin (a Ministry of Education official).

Filmography: Secrets of Nature (series, 1922–33); Strictly Business (1931); The King's English (1934); Secrets of Life (series, 1933–43); This Was England (1934); The Changing Year (1934); They

Made the Land *(1938)*; Shadow of the Stream *(1938)*; The Medieval Village *(1940)*; Winged Messengers *(1941)*; I Married a Stranger *(1944)*.

Mary Field was born in Wimbledon, England, in 1896 and began her professional life as a high school history teacher. In 1926, she accepted an offer from Bruce Wolfe to join British Instructional Films as education manager. The following year, Field moved to the production side of the company. Soon thereafter, she became a director on the acclaimed series *Secrets of Nature*. Field almost single-handedly invented cinematic techniques still used in nature cinematography.

In 1933, she went to work for Gaumont British Instructional Films (GBI) where she pioneered Britain's nascent children's film industry insisting that children need films about and for children. After making films for 11 years, Field headed the entire Children's Entertainment Division for GBI, while also acting as executive producer on Arthur Rank's Children's Cinema Clubs.

Her focus shifted during World War II, as it did with most documentary filmmakers, when she agreed to make a series of official films for the Ministry of Information. Immediately following the war, she lobbied for the establishment of the Children's Film Foundation and ultimately traveled the world lecturing and attending conferences on this subject. She wrote a book, *Good Company*, which analyzes children's responses to films (1952), and chaired Brussel's International Centre for Films for Children (1957). From 1959 to her retirement in 1963, Field worked as a children's programming consultant for ATV/ABC television. She was made CBE in 1951.

SOURCES:

Foster, Gwendolyn. *Women Film Directors: An International Bio-Critical Dictionary*. Westport, CT: Greenwood Press, 1995.

Kuhn, Annette, and Susannah Radstone, eds. *The Women's Companion to International Film*. Berkeley, CA: University of California Press, 1990.

SUGGESTED READING:

Field, Mary. *Good Company: The Story of the Children's Entertainment Film Movement in Great Britain, 1943-1950*. London: Longmans, 1952.

Deborah Jones,
Studio City, California

Field, Rachel Lyman (1894–1942)

American novelist and writer for children. Born on September 19, 1894, in New York City; died on March 15, 1942, in Beverly Hills, California; buried in Stockbridge, Massachusetts; youngest of five children of Matthew D. *(a physician) and Lucy (Atwater) Field; graduated from Springfield High School, Springfield, Massachusetts; attended Radcliffe College as a special student, 1914–18; married Arthur S. Pederson (a literary agent), on June 20, 1935; one adopted daughter,* **Hannah Pederson**.

Awards, honors: Drama League of America prize (1918), for Rise Up, Jennie Smith; *Newbery Medal, the first awarded to a woman (1929), for* Hitty: Her First Hundred Years.

Selected writings—all for children, except as noted: (illustrated by Allen Lewis) Calico Bush *(Macmillan, 1913); (self-illus.)* An Alphabet for Boys and Girls *(Doubleday, Page, 1926); (illus. by Elizabeth MacKinstry)* Eliza and the Elves *(Macmillan, 1926); (illus. by MacKinstry)* The Magic Pawnshop: A New Year's Eve Fantasy *(Dutton, 1927); (ed.)* Marie Catherine, Comtesse d'Aulnoy, The White Cat, and Other French Fairy Tales *(Macmillan, 1928); (self-illus.)* Little Toby *(Macmillan, 1928);* Polly Patchwork *(Doubleday, Doran, 1928); (ed.)* American Folk and Fairy Tales *(Scribner, 1929); (illus. by Dorothy P. Lathrop)* Hitty: Her First Hundred Years *(Macmillan, 1929);* Pocket-Handkerchief Park *(Doubleday, Doran, 1929); (self-illus.)* The Yellow Shop *(Doubleday, Doran, 1931); (illus. by Ilse Bischoff)* The Bird Began to Sing *(Morrow, 1932); (illus. by Allen Lewis)* Hepatica Hawks *(Macmillan, 1932); (self-illus.)* Just Across the Street *(Macmillan, 1933);* Susanna B. and William C. *(Morrow, 1934);* God's Pocket: The Story of Captain Samuel Hadlock, Junior, of Cranberry Isles, Maine *(Macmillan, 1934); (author of lyrics)* Ava Maria: An Interpretation from Walt Disney's "Fantasia" *(Random House, 1940); (illus. by Elizabeth Orton Jones)* Prayer for a Child *(Macmillan, 1944); (illus. by Adrienne Adams)* The Rachel Field Story Book *(Doubleday, 1958).*

Adult fiction: (play) Rise Up, Jennie Smith *(Samuel French, 1918);* Time Out of Mind *(Macmillan, 1935); (one-act play)* First Class Matter *(Samuel French, 1936); (with husband, Arthur S. Pederson)* To See Ourselves *(Macmillan, 1937);* All This and Heaven Too *(Macmillan, 1938);* All Through the Night *(Macmillan, 1940);* And Now Tomorrow *(Macmillan, 1942). Contributor of articles, stories, and verse to various periodicals, including* St. Nicholas, Horn Book, Saturday Review of Literature, *and* The New Yorker.

Film adaptations: All This and Heaven Too, *starring Bette Davis and Charles Boyer (Warner Bros., 1940);* And Now Tomorrow, *starring Loretta Young and Alan Ladd (Paramount, 1944);* Time Out of Mind, *starring* **Phyllis Calvert** *and Robert Hutton (United Artists, 1947).*

Writer Rachel Lyman Field was born in New York City on September 19, 1894, the youngest of five children of Matthew Field, a physician, and **Lucy Atwater Field**. She spent her early childhood in western Massachusetts, in Springfield and at Stockbridge, the ancestral home of the distinguished Field family. Her father was the nephew of three exceptional men: Cyrus Field, who laid the first Atlantic cable; David Dudley Field, an international lawyer; and Justice Stephen J. Field of the U.S. Supreme Court. Field, by her own admission, was not an early bloomer. "It is humiliating to confess that I wasn't one of those children who are remembered by their old school teachers as particularly promising," she wrote. "I was more than ten years old before I could read." After finally discovering the joy of words, however, Field soon developed a talent for poetry. In high school, she won $20 in an essay contest, and she was admitted to Radcliffe College as a special student on the strength of her writing ability. As a member of George P. Baker's famous "English 47" playwriting workshop, she scored her first success

Rachel Lyman Field

with *Rise Up, Jennie Smith,* which won the Drama League of America's prize for a patriotic play and was published by Samuel French in 1918. After college, Field went to New York, where for six years she worked in the editorial department of the film company Famous Players-Lasky, writing synopses of plays and books. While employed, she continued to work on her own poetry, short plays, and a novel.

Field made her mark through her work for young people, which encompassed poems, stories, and one-act plays. Considered especially noteworthy are her three juvenile novels, the first of which, *Hitty: Her First Hundred Years* (1929), tells of a quaint, 100-year-old doll, who also narrates the story. Particularly vivid are Field's descriptions of Maine, where she had spent many summers as a teenager. The book set a sales record for literature of its type and won a Newbery Medal, the first awarded to a woman. *Calico Bush* (1931) is also historical in nature, covering one year (1743) in the life of a French girl indentured to an English family who settle in

Maine. Field respected the intelligence of her young readers and paid particular attention to word choice. "So many juveniles today are too evidently written down to children," she explained, "with the words so simplified that all the spirit is lost in commonplaces."

In 1935, Field married Arthur Pederson, a literary agent, and also wrote her first full-length adult novel, *Time Out of Mind*, a romantic story set on the Maine coast during the decline of the shipbuilding trade. The couple moved to Beverly Hills, where they collaborated on the novel *To See Ourselves* (1937), a story about the "little people" living on the fringe of the movie capital. In 1938, Field achieved her greatest popular success with *All This and Heaven Too*, a fictionalized account of her great-aunt, the famous Mademoiselle D. (Mademoiselle **Henriette Deluzy-Desportes**, later Henriette Field) of Paris, who before her marriage to Henry M. Field was wrongly linked to the infamous murder of the **Duchess of Choiseul-Praslin**. The book was a national bestseller and was made into a highly successful movie starring *Bette Davis and Charles Boyer.

Despite her success and popularity, Field preferred to live quietly with her husband and baby daughter, cooking, taking care of her house, and "growing things." She died tragically in 1942, at age 48, having contracted pneumonia after an operation. Her last novel, *And Now Tomorrow*, was appearing serially in a national magazine at the time of her death and was published posthumously in book form. A poem, *Prayer for a Child*, written for her daughter Hannah, was also published after her death, in 1944. In a tribute to Field in the *Saturday Review of Literature*, **Laura Benét** called the author "a tonic and a stay to those who loved her."

SOURCES:

Commire, Anne. *Something about the Author.* Vol. 15. Detroit, MI: Gale Research.

James, Edward T., ed. *Notable American Women.* Cambridge, MA: Belknap Press of Harvard University Press, 1971.

Mainiero, Lina, ed. *American Women Writers.* NY: Frederick Ungar, 1980.

Barbara Morgan,
Melrose, Massachusetts

Field, Sara Bard (b. 1882).

See Bryant, Louise for sidebar.

Fielding, Sarah (1710–1768)

English novelist. Born in East Stour, Dorsetshire, England, on November 8, 1710; died at Bath, England, in 1768; daughter of Edmund Fielding (a general in the army) and Sarah Gould Fielding (daughter of Sir Henry Gould of Sharpham Park); sister of novelist Henry Fielding (1707–1754); never married; no children.

English novelist Sarah Fielding was the daughter of Edmund Fielding, an army officer, and **Sarah Gould Fielding**, the daughter of a judge. Among her six siblings was the novelist Henry Fielding, noted author of *Tom Jones* and *Joseph Andrews*, who frequently lent a helping hand in his sister's career. Sarah was eight when her mother died, and the Fielding children were put in the care of their maternal grandmother and great aunt. When her father married a Roman Catholic whom the children did not like, a family dispute erupted, and Sarah was sent off to boarding school in Salisbury. During the 1740s, she lived variously with Henry and his family and with her sisters, but she was frequently strapped for money. In the preface to her first and best-known novel, *The Adventures of David Simple* (1744), Fielding explained that the book was the result of "distress in her circumstances," a reference, no doubt, to her precarious financial situation.

The success of Fielding's first novel led to *Familiar Letters Between the Principal Characters in David Simple, and Some Others* (1747), which was financed by subscription and with some help from brother Henry. (Fielding's friend Samuel Richardson, of whom she was a great fan, also helped publish several of her books.) In 1749, Fielding published *The Governess: or Little Female Academy*, which is considered the first full-length children's novel in English, and in 1753 she created a sequel to her first novel titled *David Simple, Volume the Last*. She collaborated with her life-long friend **Jane Collier** (1710–1755) on *The Cry* (1754), described by **Joanne Shattock** as "an allegory about truth and falsehood, which is relevant to contemporary discussions about the nature of fiction." Two later novels, *The Countess of Dellwyn* (1759) and *Ophelia* (1760), like the earlier *David Simple*, follow the struggles of innocent protagonists in a hostile world. Fielding also wrote *Cleopatra and Octavia* (1757), in which the historical figures tell their own stories, and translated Xenophone's *Memoirs of Socrates: With the Defense of Socrates before his Judges* (1762), which was praised as having been "done with equal judgment and accuracy." Sarah Fielding died in Bath in 1768.

SOURCES:

Allibone, S. Austin. *A Critical Dictionary of English Literature and British and American Authors, Living and Deceased from the Earliest Accounts to the*

Middle of the Nineteenth Century. Philadelphia, PA: Childs and Peterson, 1854.

Buck, Claire, ed. *Bloomsbury Guide to Women's Literature*. NY: Prentice Hall, 1992.

Shattock, Joanne. *The Oxford Guide to British Women Writers*. Oxford: Oxford University Press, 1993.

Barbara Morgan,
Melrose, Massachusetts

Fields, Annie Adams (1834–1915).

See Jewett, Sarah Orne for sidebar.

Fields, Dorothy (1904–1974)

American lyricist for stage and screen who was the first woman to win an Academy Award for Best Song. Born on July 15, 1904 (some sources cite 1905) in Allenhurst, New Jersey; died on March 28, 1974, after suffering a stroke at her home in New York City; daughter of Lew Fields (Lewis Maurice Schanfield) and Rose (Harris) Fields; sister of Herbert Fields, a librettist (1898–1958), Joseph Fields, a playwright, producer and director, and Frances Fields Friedlander; graduated from the Benjamin School for Girls in New York; married Jack J. Weiner (a surgeon), in 1925 (divorced 1932); married Eli Lahm (a blouse manufacturer), in 1939; children: (second marriage) David Lahm (b. 1940); Eliza Lahm (b. 1944).

Awards and honors: Academy Award from the Academy of Motion Picture Arts and Sciences for "The Way You Look Tonight" from Swing Time *(1936); Screen Writers Guild Award for* Annie Get Your Gun *with Herbert Fields (1950); Tony Award for best lyrics for* Redhead *(1959); first woman elected to the Songwriters Hall of Fame.*

Filmography—worked as lyricist, screenwriter, or storywriter on the following: The Time, the Place, and the Girl *(1929);* Love in the Rough *(1930);* Dance Fools Dance *(1931);* Cuban Love Song *(1931);* Meet the Baron *(1933);* Dancing Lady *(1933);* Roberta *(1935),* Hooray for Love *(1935);* Every Night at Eight *(1935);* I Dream Too Much *(1935);* In Person *(1935);* The King Steps Out *(1936);* Swing Time *(1936);* When You're in Love *(1937);* The Joy of Living *(1938);* One Night in the Tropics *(1940);* Father Takes a Wife *(1941);* Let's Face It *(1943);* Something for the Boys *(1944);* Up in Central Park *(1948);* Mexican Hayride *(1948);* Annie Get Your Gun *(1950);* Excuse My Dust *(1951);* Mr. Imperium *(1951);* Texas Carnival *(1951);* Lovely to Look At *(1952);* The Farmer Takes a Wife *(1952);* Sweet Charity *(1969).*

Author of such standards as "On the Sunny Side of the Street," "The Way You Look Tonight," and "I Can't Give You Anything but Love, Baby," Dorothy Fields first made her mark in the mid-1920s. It was a pivotal time when musicals were evolving from naughty revues into plot-centered musical plays, such as Jerome Kern and Oscar Hammerstein's 1927 *Show Boat*, based on the novel by *Edna Ferber. Dorothy's mother was **Rose Harris Fields**. Her father Lew Fields was a legendary vaudeville and music-hall performer and half of the team of (Joseph) Weber and Fields. Soon after Dorothy, his youngest child, was born, Lew became a Broadway producer and starred in many of his own shows. He and Rose, who had both been raised on the Lower East Side, the children of Polish immigrants, urged their children to avoid show business and find "real" careers. With laughter, Dorothy recalled her mother saying, "You children must be extra polite to strangers because your father is an actor." However, Dorothy's elder sister Frances was the only one of the siblings to avoid working in the theater. Older brother Joseph became a playwright while Herbert became a noted librettist. Family friends were drawn from the worlds of celebrity and show business. At seven, Dorothy was the flower girl when actress *Lillian Russell married Colonel Alexander Moore, an industrialist. While pasting reviews into her father's scrapbooks, Dorothy became interested in what critics said about the plays themselves. She observed that a good story was essential, no matter how strong the acting, and never forgot this insight.

As a schoolgirl in New York, Fields occupied her spare time writing poetry and playing the piano. She considered becoming an actress and tried out for stock company, but her father dissuaded her. Her brother Herbert, meanwhile, was writing songs with Lorenz Hart and Fields' high-school sweetheart Richard Rodgers. Together the three of them put on amateur musicals and adapted their production of *If I Were King*, a romance about the poet François Villon, for Dorothy's annual high-school benefit. Starring as Villon, Dorothy made her debut in a Broadway theater on March 25, 1922.

Fields took a job teaching dramatic art at her alma mater, the Benjamin School for Girls, but her greatest enthusiasm was for writing lyrics. Then she met J. Fred Coots, later the composer of "For All We Know," "Santa Claus is Coming to Town," and "You Go to My Head," at a Long Island country club; he encouraged her and introduced her to music publishers. Shy and timid despite her expensive clothes, Fields made the rounds of seedy "Tin Pan Alley." The publishers thought she had talent but wanted to know why she didn't persuade her father to help her. When word of her rounds reached Lew Fields, he phoned the publishers and told them to throw his daughter out of their offices.

One, however, asked her to write a song for *Ruth Elder who was about to fly across the Atlantic. Sure this event would make Elder a celebrity and that the song would be a hit, the publisher told Dorothy the song must begin: "You took a notion to fly across the ocean." Though Dorothy objected that one did not just take a notion to do such a thing, she wrote some lyrics. Elder did not make it, and neither did Dorothy's song.

Lew Fields' economic hardships—he faced bankruptcy and the family was forced to sell their town house—gave her an understanding of people who were down on their luck. The feeling she later demonstrated in "I Can't Give You Anything But Love, Baby" and "If My Friends Could See Me Now" attests to her empathy. According to *From the Bowery to Broadway*, written by her cousins, Fields eloped with her fiancé Dr. Jack Weiner in 1925 to spare her father the expense of a wedding. She and her husband separated quickly, and Dorothy moved back home and began to establish her career. They divorced in 1932.

Fields had a great ear for contemporary speech idioms and was able to compress complex emotions into apt phrases, which helped her to portray character and plot through her lyrics. Jimmy McHugh asked her to write words for his song "Our American Girl" and paid her $50. Since she could write lyrics overnight, music publishers on Tin Pan Alley called her "the $50 a night girl." In 1927, when McHugh asked Fields to collaborate on some songs for The Cotton Club in Harlem, Lew Fields told Dorothy, "Ladies don't write lyrics." Dorothy countered, "I'm not a lady. I'm your daughter." On opening night, performers made her lyrics racier than those she had written, and both father and daughter were appalled. Lew, along with his friend the columnist Walter Winchell, forced the manager to announce that Dorothy Fields and Jimmy McHugh had not written those words to the music after all. Then Lew again told her to get out of show business.

The Cotton Club numbers brought McHugh and Fields a chance to write for the Delmar Revue, however, for which they produced "I Can't Give You Anything But Love, Baby," which Bert Lahr and *Patsy Kelly performed. Initially, the song was not successful,

but the team included it in their first Broadway show *Blackbirds of 1928*. Though critics called the song "sickening" and "puerile," its popularity with the audience made *Blackbirds* a hit that ran for 518 performances. In 1929, their *International Revue* included "Exactly Like You" and "On the Sunny Side of the Street."

As Fields continued to write single songs for revues, none of which had a plot, the lesson that she had learned from poring over her father's reviews stayed with her—songs had to advance the story line. "I'm not out to write popular song hits," she told writer Max Wilk, "though I've written songs that have become popular. I'm writing a song to fit a spot in the show, to fit a character, to express something about him or her, to move the story line forward."

I wrote "I Feel A Song Coming On," but anyone who tells you a song just comes on is wrong. It's slave labor—and I love it.

—**Dorothy Fields**

She began writing to fit plot lines when she and McHugh went to Hollywood to work first at MGM, where they produced *Cuban Love Song*. They then went over to RKO where Pandro Berman was producing the *Ginger Rogers-Fred Astaire films. Rogers and Astaire were beginning work on the musical film *Roberta*, which was set in the world of Paris couturiers. Berman gave Fields a melody written by Jerome Kern and asked her to do a lyric that would both introduce a fashion show and be a love song as well. She came up with "Lovely to Look At," and RKO filmed it without Kern's approval. He must have liked it, however, because when RKO asked him to write the music for *I Dream Too Much*, with the singer *Lily Pons, Kern asked Fields to collaborate. During the 1930s, a golden age for the Hollywood musical, Fields and Kern collaborated on other RKO productions, most notably *Swing Time*, again with Rogers and Astaire. To inspire them to write a song he could dance to, Astaire tapdanced around the room where they were working. The lively syncopated "Bojangles in Harlem" was the result. For that film, they also wrote "A Fine Romance" and "Pick Yourself Up." Uncharacteristically, Fields wrote the lyrics for those before Kern composed the music. "The Way You Look Tonight," also from *Swing Time*, earned Fields and Kern a 1936 Academy Award.

In 1938, she returned to New York to write *Stars in Your Eyes* with Arthur Schwartz for

Broadway. *Ethel Merman and Jimmy Durante starred and the young Jerome Robbins was in the chorus. Dorothy married Eli Lahm, a blouse manufacturer, in 1939. By that time, she had collaborated with her brother Herbert on many screenplays, including *Riviera* and *Love Before Breakfast,* both written in 1936. They also created Broadway musical-comedy librettos for Cole Porter, for such shows as *Something for the Boys* and *Mexican Hayride.*

At first it seemed that brother and sister might produce their best work with others. Herbert had written *Fifty Million Frenchmen* for Porter in 1929 and *DuBarry Was a Lady,* starring Merman and Lahr in 1939. The siblings first collaborated on a libretto for Broadway in 1941: *Let's Face It!* starred Danny Kaye, with music and lyrics by Cole Porter.

The two worked at Dorothy's home, either a succession of Manhattan apartments or her country house in Brewster, New York. In contrast to her brother, who was a bachelor, a Democrat, and an easy-going personality, Fields had a family, was a Republican, and was often intense. Tall and slender with chestnut hair and hazel eyes, she was an early riser and liked to write with a pencil and yellow pad on her bridge table. "I begin writing at 8:30 am and stop when the waste basket is full. By that time, I've had it," she said of her daily work schedule.

Fields worked until late afternoon, breaking only for noon-time soap operas. In the early years of World War II, the Fieldses explored the musical possibilities of the colorful, corrupt Boss Tweed era of the 1870s. They wrote a story of how one of the Tammany Hall swindles resulted in the creation of a beautiful park. One critic described *Up in Central Park,* for which Dorothy and Sigmund Romberg created the songs, as "quaint, colorful and spirited as a Currier and Ives print." The musical ran for 504 performances and was revived in the early 1950s.

Still more successful was their exploration of the dramatic possibilities of the Wild West. While working at the Stage Door Canteen in 1945, Fields heard an account of a decorated soldier who used his sharp-shooting skills to win prizes at Coney Island. Dorothy began thinking of the sharpshooter *Annie Oakley and came up with *Annie Get Your Gun,* for which the Fields team wrote the book. Dorothy and Jerome Kern were to have collaborated on the songs, but when the latter died suddenly that year, Irving Berlin stepped in. In 12 days, he wrote five songs, including "There's No Business Like

Show Business." Starring Ethel Merman, *Annie Get Your Gun* became one of the greatest musicals ever, running for 1,147 performances in New York and touring the U.S., Europe, and Australia. The Fieldses wrote film scripts for *Up in Central Park, Mexican Hayride* and *Annie Get Your Gun* (which starred *Betty Hutton), then returned to Broadway in 1950 with *Arms and the Girl,* starring **Nanette Fabray.**

Heroines dominated the Broadway stage of the 1950s and '60s. Fields wrote lyrics for many of them, notably *A Tree Grows in Brooklyn* and *By the Beautiful Sea,* both for *Shirley Booth. Though her brother Herbert and her husband died in 1958, she was still able to finish the lyrics for the 1959 musical *Redhead,* a box-office success, starring *Gwen Verdon, set in turn-of-the-century London. *Redhead* won six Tonys, including one for Dorothy.

Always working to be current, Fields joined with a talented trio of young men—the composer Cy Coleman, playwright Neil Simon, and choreographer Bob Fosse—to create the hit show *Sweet Charity,* starring Verdon in 1966. Although Fields had come of age personally and professionally in the late Flapper era, in the 1960s she produced lyrics like "Hey, Big Spender!," "Where Am I Going?" and "If They Could See Me Now," that reflected the sexually liberated world of contemporary New York. She and Coleman also teamed to produce the 1973 musical *Seesaw,* starring **Michele Lee.** It was Dorothy's ninth and final Broadway musical. On the evening of March 28, 1974, after attending a rehearsal for the road company of *Seesaw,* she had a stroke and died at her home in New York City.

SOURCES:

American Songwriters. NY: H.W. Wilson, 1987.
Current Biography. NY: H.W. Wilson, 1958.
Fields, Armond, and Marc L. Fields. *From the Bowery to Broadway.* NY: Oxford University Press, 1993.
Notable American Women: A Biographical Dictionary. Vol. IV. Cambridge, MA: Belknap Press of Harvard University Press, 1980.
Tape recording of "Lyrics and Lyricists: An Evening With Dorothy Fields," April 9, 1973, at the YMHA in New York City.
Wilk, Max. *They're Playing Our Song.* NY: Atheneum, 1973.

Kathleen Brady,
author of *Lucille: The Life of Lucille Ball* (Hyperion)
and *Ida Tarbell: Portrait of A Muckraker*
(University of Pittsburgh Press).

Fields, Gracie (1898–1979)

English singer, comedian, impersonator, and actress who rose from poverty in Lancashire to become one

of the best beloved performers in the world. Born Grace Stansfield on January 9, 1898, in the town of Rochdale, Lancashire, England; died on the Italian island of Capri on September 27, 1979; daughter of Fred Stansfield (an engineer) and Sarah Jane (Jenny) Bamford Stansfield (a housewife and laundress); attended Rochdale public schools until age 13; married comedian Archie Pitt (Archibald Selinger), on April 21, 1923 (divorced 1940); married Monty Banks (Mario Bianchi), in March 1940 (died 1950); married Boris Alperovici, on February 18, 1952; no children.

Made professional debut (1910); began touring with Archie Pitt (1916); first performance in London's West End (1924); made first command performance, recorded first record, took on first dramatic role, and began friendship with John Flanagan (1928); made first tour of U.S. (1930); took first trip to Capri, made first movie, Sally in Our Alley (1931); was informally separated from Pitt (1932); met Monty Banks (1935); made first film in Hollywood (1937); named Commander of the British Empire (1938); was operated on for cancer (1939); made wartime voyage with Monty Banks to the U.S. (1940); entertained Allied troops (1939–45); returned to England for BBC tour (1947); gave last public performance (1978); named Dame Commander of the Order of the British Empire (1979).

Films: Sally in Our Alley (1931); Sing As We Go (1934); Queen of Hearts (1936); We're Going To Be Rich (1937); Holy Matrimony (1943); Paris Underground (1945). Stage: S.O.S (1928). Television: "The Old Lady Shows Her Medals" (1956).

Gracie Fields, known to her millions of fans as "the Lancashire Lass" or, simply "our Gracie," was one of the most renowned stage-and-screen performers of the 20th century. Beginning in English music halls in their last years of prosperity around World War I, she moved on to the legitimate stage, radio, films, and eventually television. Fields made fifteen films during her career, including four in the United States, and more than 500 records. By the 1930s, she was the most highly paid entertainer in the world. Eventually, she would be asked to give ten Royal Command Performances.

The future star was born Grace Stansfield to a working-class family in northern England on January 9, 1898. Only a few steps removed from poverty, the Stansfields lived above a fish-and-chip shop, and, throughout her childhood, Gracie shared a bed with her two sisters. Fields never lost the speaking accent of Lancashire, where her birthplace, the mill town of Rochdale, was located. Her father Fred was an engineer

who had begun working on cargo ships and was now employed in Rochdale's textile mills, but her mother **Jenny Stansfield** was a devoted amateur singer who encouraged Grace, as well as her other children, to take up a career on the stage.

Gracie's untrained but powerful voice made an early impression on both the family's neighbors and her teachers at school. Jenny, who did laundry for theater companies that played at the Hippodrome, one of Rochdale's three theaters, timed the delivery of the finished wash so that she and Gracie could watch the shows. Jenny's enthusiasm for the stage led her to invite touring actresses to the family home, where young Grace was encouraged to sing for them. The child soon found herself participating in singing contests, winning a first prize when she was only seven. She also obtained unpaid roles in the performances of visiting theatrical troupes.

In 1908, when she was only ten, Gracie left home to join a troupe of juvenile performers, **Clara Coverdale**'s Boys and Girls. She lasted just a week, returning home with her body bruised and swollen from her first efforts to learn acrobatic dancing. A second try at joining a traveling group of young players, Haley's Garden of Girls, lasted for several months. Unfortunately, it led to an ugly encounter in which Gracie, still only ten but with the appearance of a mature teenager, barely escaped a sexual assault. She returned home emotionally distraught.

The talented youngster, like most of her classmates in the grim mill town, began work in a textile factory at the age of 12. But she soon started to make her escape. In August 1910, Gracie filled in at the Rochdale Hippodrome for a performer who had been taken ill. Success brought a two-week engagement, marking the start of her full-time stage career. Encouraged by the theater manager to find a short, memorable stage name, Gracie consulted with her mother. First, they changed "Stansfield" to "Fields." Then, after rejecting "Stana Fields" and "Anna Fields," they made the slightly formal "Grace" into "Gracie." It was destined to become one of the most widely known names in the world of British entertainment.

Jenny Stansfield continued to play a large role in Gracie's career, advising her on what bookings to accept. Roles came along often enough to provide money for her family, badly needed when her father was ill, and to keep Gracie from having to return to the hated job at the mill. During the grim wartime years, she sang for soldiers and Belgian refugees. In 1915, encouraged by her mother, Fields signed a long-term contract with a Manchester theatrical agent who had recognized her overflowing talent as a singer and impersonator. He also took advantage of the family's financial need to put a tight hold on half her future earnings.

She soon met the man who was to become her first husband. Archie Pitt, a modestly talented comedian from London with ambitions of becoming a producer, helped her to rehearse, informed her she would one day be a great star, and, despite his reputation as a ladies' man, made no sexual advances. Pitt also managed to break her disadvantageous contract with the Manchester theatrical agent.

Starting in 1916, Fields toured in Archie Pitt's shows. At Jenny's request, she found a place in the company for both her younger sisters and, eventually, her younger brother. By this stage in her career, she was a comedian, singer, and impersonator. She began to receive offers to appear in London, at five to ten times her current salary, but she remained loyal to Pitt and her touring companions. Appearing in Pitt's *Mr. Tower of London,* which began touring in 1918, Fields made herself famous throughout Great Britain. The show ran for more than nine years. Note her biographers Burgess and Keen, "It was the revue that gave Gracie Fields to the British Nation."

*S*he was, quite simply, the greatest female artiste we have ever produced. . . . She was, before the word had even been invented, a superstar.

—Roy Hudd

Meanwhile, in 1923, her longstanding working relationship with Archie Pitt led to their marriage. Fields had by now turned into a confident performer with a striking singing voice. On stage, she presented herself as loud and boisterous, but in real life she remained personally shy. Unlike her younger sisters, she was not beautiful, and the knowledge of this further undermined her confidence. Pitt's proposal came in harsh form. He reminded her of her age, "nearly twenty-five," adding that "you need a husband." Her newly married sister Betty urged her to accept. According to Betty, Fields needed someone to take care of her, destined as she was for stardom. Gracie's marriage was never a happy one. She later described Archie's motives in marrying her as financial: "I was just starting to make money and Archie wanted to consolidate his principal asset."

Her career blossomed. She was able to finance her parents' move from Rochdale to Lon-

don, and, starting in February 1924, she starred in *Mr. Tower of London* at the Alhambra Theater in Leicester Square, the center of London's stage district. Her performance dominated the critics' rave reviews.

In 1928, she gave her first Royal Command Performance, and the established stars of the London stage took time to observe this rising new star. A new opportunity soon appeared when the noted impresario Sir Gerald du Maurier offered her a part in an upcoming play. The music-hall performer transformed herself into a skilled actress under du Maurier's tutelage. Her first phonograph records began to appear, and she also played in nightclubs. But her many obligations drained her energy, and she had no occasion to enjoy the huge sums of money she was now making. When Archie took over her earnings, she found herself the reluctant owner of a mansion in the fashionable Hampstead suburb in north London. Adding to her discomfort was the fact that Archie invited **Annie Lipman** to live with them as his supposed secretary. It soon became clear to Gracie that Annie was Archie's lover.

Now a top ranking star, the young woman from Rochdale continued to feel she was an outsider in London's fashionable world. "School had been something to be sandwiched between helping Jenny do the actors' washing . . . or working in the mills," wrote Fields, "and I'd left at twelve anyway." She remained ill-at-ease even with her fellow stars: "I hadn't the faintest idea of how to behave or look like Gertrude Lawrence . . . or any of the other great names, and their sophisticated lives terrified me."

Fields found herself attracted to an Irish artist named John Flanagan whom she had met at one of her cabaret performances in 1928. When Flanagan convinced Fields to let him paint her portrait, she was soon confiding in him, detailing her unhappy marriage with Pitt. In time, their friendship developed into a romantic tie that lasted throughout the 1930s. Meanwhile in 1929, her unhappiness with Pitt's bullying and insensitive treatment pushed her to an almost unthinkable act: she walked off *The Show's the Thing* while in rehearsal in order to join Flanagan in southern France. In the end, her sense of obligation to her fellow performers overcame her personal feelings; she interrupted her trip in Paris and returned. The revue was a spectacular success, running in London for more than a year.

The year 1931 saw the young star's life turn in a number of new directions. She took a trip to Italy with Flanagan and another friend. Carry-

Gracie
Fields

ing an expired passport, she made it across the border into Italy by charming the customs officer with a rendition of "Santa Lucia," one of the few tunes she could sing in Italian. On this trip, she made her first visit to the island of Capri, immediately fell in love with the place, and soon bought a house there. Back in London, she moved into her own lodgings; while she intended to keep her professional tie to Archie Pitt, she no longer wanted an intimate relationship with him. Finally, she began her extensive film career with a part in *Sally in Our Alley*. The film's most important song, "Sally," went on to become a national hit. Audiences begged her to sing it for the remainder of her career.

Throughout the 1930s, Fields' film career boomed, and she became one of the industry's most famous and important stars. The medium gave her a chance to use her talents as a singer and comedian in front of a larger audience than ever. The films themselves rarely pleased the critics, but enthusiastic British audiences made them immensely successful financially. Her personality was so powerful that her screen roles did little beyond requiring her to be herself. Most of her characters were named "Grace" or "Gracie."

In 1935, her family introduced her to Monty Banks. An Italian, born Mario Bianchi, who had immigrated to the United States to become a leading film comedian, Banks became the director of her next film, *Queen of Hearts*. He also accompanied her to Hollywood when she was offered a lavish contract at Twentieth Century-Fox. In the course of her career, she made four films for the American studio.

By the time she was in her early 40s, Gracie Fields found herself an honored national figure. Debates in Parliament ended early so that the members could reach their radios to hear her sing. Her charitable activities, along with her work as an entertainer, led King George VI to name her a Commander of the British Empire in 1938. Meanwhile, her hometown of Rochdale formally honored her as its most distinguished citizen. The following year, she was stricken by cancer of the cervix and nearly died. The public was told only that she was seriously ill. All levels of British society showered her with tributes: a message from the queen, hundreds of thousands of letters delivered to her hospital, and an affectionate cartoon in one of London's largest newspapers. Her illness brought her closer than ever to Banks, who was her stalwart support throughout her ordeal. In place of hospital food, he brought her broth he had prepared, using prime beef from the kitchen of the elegant Dorchester Hotel.

In the aftermath of her hospital stay, Fields and Banks retired to Capri. The outbreak of World War II caught them there, and from her villa on the island they watched the lights in the harbor at Naples extinguished in Italy's first wartime blackout. They rushed back to Britain. Shortly after her arrival and despite her lingering weakness, she was on the radio singing songs taunting Hitler. Soon she was touring France to entertain the troops.

Fields began divorce proceedings against Archie Pitt in mid-1939, and the marriage ended in early 1940. That March, she wed Banks in California, after which the couple returned to Britain. But the war was taking a dramatic turn. Adolf Hitler's attack on Western Europe in May and June drove the British army out of France, and only the rescue operation at Dunkirk saved Britain's forces. As Hitler moved to finish off the French, fascist Italy prepared to enter the war. Monty, who was still an Italian citizen, received word from British government officials to leave the country before being interned as an enemy alien.

Fields and her husband sailed together for New York in circumstances that aroused public outrage back in Britain. She had seemingly deserted her country in its time of need and had taken a substantial sum of money along with her. Banks worsened the situation when he told newspaper reporters in New York, "I'm no Briton," and defended their right to pack their assets while fleeing a war zone. Fields went on to a previously scheduled concert tour in Canada to raise money for wartime charities, but her devotion to her husband made a poor impression on both sides of the Atlantic. Her tour in both Canada and the United States lasted until the fall of 1941 and raised more than a million dollars for charity. The singer's wartime image improved as a result of her tireless efforts. But the bitterness Britons felt toward her in 1940 lingered in some minds even though Prime Minister Winston Churchill came to her defense publicly.

During the war years, Fields continued to make movie and radio appearances in the United States. But she entertained troops throughout the war, spending the last months of the fighting singing for Allied forces in the Pacific. Even the news of the Japanese surrender, which she heard just before a concert for Australian forces on the island of Bougainville, did not put a halt to her efforts. She went on to entertain Allied military men and women and liberated prisoners of war for months thereafter. She and Monty then headed for their villa on Capri. Banks was soon urging her to transform their home into a tourist center complete with hotel and restaurant.

Fields and Banks returned to postwar London in 1947. The BBC planned a series of radio concerts with her in a starring role. The concerts were held in various locations starting in her home town of Rochdale and ending in East London. By the last one, she was wildly popular. As Burgess and Keen put it, "She'd given her heart to the English and in return they had laid their hearts at her feet."

Monty never lived to see the success of his plans for the villa. He died en route to Capri in January 1950, after a New Year's celebration in Paris. After a period of shock and loneliness, in 1952 Fields married for the third time. Her new husband was Boris Alperovici, a longtime resident of Capri. Although the British newspapers labeled him "a humble electrician" with a radio shop, he was in fact an inventor and, unlike his new wife, an accepted member of aristocratic Capri society.

Fields' career went on. She returned to England to perform in grand theaters like the Coliseum. In time, she went on to appear on television and made record albums almost to the year of her death. She returned to Rochdale in 1978 to open a theater named after her. That same year, she gave her tenth Royal Command performance, 50 years after her first one, and she made her last appearance before a London audience. In 1979, she received a final honor from her country as she was awarded the title of Dame Commander of the British Empire. To many observers, the award seemed long overdue. The delay may have come from some lingering clouds over her reputation in official circles from her trip to the United States in 1940. On September 27, 1979, having been hospitalized due to bronchitis, Gracie Fields died in Capri. Some sources indicate that the cause of death was pneumonia; others mention a heart attack.

A remarkably versatile performer, Gracie Fields could charm an audience with a ballad or a comic tune. She was the only music hall star of the 1920s to make a successful transition to the new media of radio and film. Her comic roles in the British films of the Depression era provided a rare opportunity for her beleaguered and impoverished compatriots to put aside their troubles for a brief moment.

SOURCES:

Burgess, Muriel, and Tommy Keen. *Gracie Fields.* London: W.H. Allen, 1980.

Fields, Gracie. *Sing As We Go: The Autobiography of Gracie Fields.* Garden City, NY: Doubleday, 1961.

Moules, Joan. *Our Gracie: The Life of Dame Gracie Fields.* London: Robert Hale, 1983.

SUGGESTED READING:

Hartnoll, Phyllis, ed. *The Oxford Companion to the Theatre.* 4th ed. Oxford: Oxford University Press, 1983.

Quinlan, David. *Quinlan's Illustrated Registry of Film Stars.* NY: Henry Holt, 1991.

Neil M. Heyman,
Professor of History, San Diego State University,
San Diego, California

Fields, Mary (c. 1832–1914)

African-American former slave, associated with the Ursuline nuns, who was one of the first women to drive a U.S. mail coach on a regular route and became a folk hero of the American West. Name variations: Black Mary; Stagecoach Mary. Born around 1832 in Hickman County, Tennessee, and celebrated her birthday on both March 15 and May 15; died in Cascade, Montana, on December 5, 1914; parents unknown; never married; no children.

Following the Civil War, worked at various jobs along the Mississippi River before finding work at the Ursuline convent in Toledo, Ohio; moved to St. Peter's mission, near Cascade, Montana (1885); forced by the area bishop to leave the mission because of her unruly temper, opened a restaurant in Cascade; became the second woman to drive a U.S. mail coach route (1895–1903); ran a laundry, became mascot and supporter of the Cascade baseball team, and a much-loved citizen.

When Mary Fields was born in Hickman County, Tennessee, slavery was still legal and birth records, especially of slaves, were poorly kept. In later years, the powerful six-foot woman, who became legendary as "Black Mary" and "Stagecoach Mary," claimed that the year of her birth was 1832, and she celebrated both March 15 and May 15 as her birth dates. These celebrations in her adopted hometown of Cascade, Montana, shut down the town's schools so that all the children could share in the party. Movie actor Gary Cooper recorded his vivid childhood recollections of Cascade's most famous black citizen in an account he gave *Ebony* magazine in 1959.

At the close of the Civil War, Fields was in her mid-30s when she apparently took a number of various jobs along the Mississippi River. One was as a chambermaid on the riverboat *Robert E. Lee*, and she loved to tell about the famous riverboat race held on June 30, 1870, between the *Robert E. Lee* and its rival, the *Natchez*. To build up extremely high levels of steam, the boat furnaces were stoked to their limits, and according to Fields, "They throw'd everything but the kitchen sink in that fire and it was so hot, we figured it was about to bust!" With the hearts of its passengers racing too, the *Robert E. Lee* was victorious.

By 1884, Fields was working at the Ursuline convent in Toledo, Ohio. Precisely how and when she arrived there is not clear. According to some reports, she met the convent's **Mother Amadeus** when she accompanied the children of the nun's brother to Toledo after the death of their mother. Other accounts say that Fields had been a slave and confidential servant in the house of the nun's oldest brother (her father, in some sources), Judge Edmund Dunne; still others say she had been a personal maid to the nun prior to her taking vows. At any rate, Mary found comfort and good work among the Ursulines, which she returned in good measure in her role as caretaker and handywoman.

She was a tart-tongued, gun-toting, hard-drinking, cigar-and-pipe-smoking, 6-foot 200-pound black woman who was tough enough to take on any two men. She was also a gentle, considerate person who won the hearts of many people in and near Cascade, Montana.

—Don Miller

In 1884, Mother Amadeus was sent to St. Peter's mission, near the small town of Cascade, Montana, where Jesuit priests had been working among the Blackfeet Indians for two decades. Her task was to open a school for Native American girls. When word reached the Ohio convent in 1885 that Mother Amadeus was extremely ill with pneumonia, Fields left for Montana to nurse her beloved benefactor. Mother Amadeus recovered, and Fields stayed on at the mission, handling deliveries, gardening, doing light construction work on the new convent, and other odd jobs. Put in charge of overseeing the washing, she preferred to do the church and sacristy linens herself.

Fields also raised chickens, doing a thriving business that amounted at one point to 400 birds. After a skunk got into the mission's coop one night and ate a number of chicks, Fields managed to kill it with a hoe. She then dragged the carcass a mile to the convent to show the nuns. A visiting army chaplain wrote her, asking about the odor of the skunk's "wrath." The practical Fields replied, "I killed him from the front not from the rear."

Fields carted goods for the mission, even in the harsh Montana winters when the roads were considered impassable. Mission annals of November 27, 1893, show: "Mary Fields returned today. She spent last night in a snowdrift about ½ way between here and Cascade and walked all night to keep from freezing." In one instance, when wolves frightened Mary's horses, causing her cart to be turned over, she stood guard over the supplies through the night, keeping the wolves at bay with her rifle and revolver.

Hardened to such conditions, and weighing well over 200 pounds, Fields could be fearless. She smoked a large cigar or pipe, and she always wore a man's cap, shoes and overcoat, as well as an apron and long dress. Contemporary accounts of her temper include an altercation with a ranch foreman over a broken harness for one of her draft horses, and the mission annals refer to a shootout between Fields and a hired hand, as well as a rifle standoff with another man. Eventually these displays of high temper brought so many complaints to the attention of Bishop John B. Brondel that he felt forced to direct that she be sent away. The order was received as a blow at the mission, where a great loyalty had developed between Mary and the nuns and children.

Moving into Cascade, 15 miles from the mission, Mary had the help of the townspeople and the mission in establishing a restaurant. Unfortunately, her kindness in extending credit to her customers caused the enterprise to fail. Help was provided to reopen the eatery, but Fields could not be hardnosed, and it failed again.

Then, in 1895, Mother Amadeus stepped in and donated a spring wagon and team of horses to help the 63-year-old Fields obtain a mail route. Fields is the second woman in the United States known to have held a regular mail stage route. After a bad accident with the larger wagon, Mother Amadeus gave Fields a one-horse buggy; later, when Fields drove a stagecoach, she earned the title by which she is best known, Stagecoach Mary.

For eight years, Fields covered the route from the town to the mission, until age finally forced her to give it up, in 1903. In that time, she met every train, and when snow made the route impassable, she would walk to the mission, carrying the mail bags herself. Contemporary reports indicate that she never missed a trip to St. Peter's.

After her official retirement, Fields took in laundry at her small house in Cascade. Though she had mellowed over the years, her rough temper never entirely evened out. She once grabbed a non-paying customer by the collar, then twirled him around and hit him in the jaw with her fist. "His laundry bill is paid!" she declared. Nevertheless, Fields was widely loved. She babysat many of the town children who shared in the celebration of her birthdays. As mascot of the baseball team, she provided boutonnieres for each member of competing teams from her well-known garden and presented large bouquets to hitters of home runs.

Opposite page

Mary Fields

In 1910, R.B. Glover leased the New Cascade Hotel with the understanding that Fields would receive free meals there. She had long enjoyed a nip at the local saloons and earned a reputation in some circles as a hard drinker. When a town ruling was passed forbidding women in the saloon, according to one recollection, it "almost broke her heart." Then D.W. Munroe was elected mayor and won Fields as a friend for life by rescinding the ruling. According to Cooper, this privilege, "if you want to call it one, [was] given to no other woman."

In 1912, when Fields was about 80 years old and her house and laundry burned, the people of Cascade rallied quickly to build her another house. Her popularity and spirit was commemorated by the renowned western artist Charles M. Russell, a resident of nearby Great Falls, in a pen-and-ink sketch entitled *A Quiet Day in Cascade*. The drawing shows Fields indignant at a kicking mule whose antics have caused a basket of eggs to be broken.

In early December 1914, a report appeared in the *Great Falls Tribune* that Mary Fields, "for more than a third of a century a resident of [Cascade] and believed to be the pioneer colored woman of the Chestnut Valley" had been brought to Great Falls' Columbus hospital, very ill, with "infirmities of old age . . . and . . . dropsy." On December 5, Fields died there, and, because there was as yet no Catholic Church in the town of Cascade, her funeral was held in the Pastime Theater. The *Tribune* reported "a large number of friends and acquaintances paid their last tributes of respect. . . . The casket was hidden from view by floral tributes," and the funeral was "one of the largest ever held in Cascade."

In the 1970s, as part of Cascade's bicentennial project, the wooden cross that had long marked Mary Fields' grave in Hillside Cemetery was replaced by a headstone, along the road to her beloved mission.

SOURCES:

"Great Crowd at Fields Funeral," in *Great Falls* [Montana] *Tribune*. December 6, 1914.

"Mary Fields Near Death," in *Great Falls* [Montana] *Tribune*. December 1, 1914.

McBride, Sr. Genevieve. *The Bird Tail*. NY: Vantage Press, 1974.

Miller, Don. "Mary Fields: Freight Hauler and Stage Driver," in *True West*. August 1982, pp. 52–55.

Rowe, Mrs. Clarence J., comp. *Mountain and Meadows: A Pioneer History of Montana, 1805 to 1925*. Great Falls, MT: Cascade County Historical Committee, n.d.

Mary
Fields

SUGGESTED READING:

Miller, Robert H. *The Story of "Stagecoach" Mary Fields: Stories of the Forgotten West Series*. Cincinnati, OH: Silver Burdett Press, 1994.

COLLECTIONS:

Contemporary papers and histories are held in the Cascade County (Montana) Historical Society Archives and in the archives of the Ursuline Center, both in Great Falls, Montana.

Margaret L. Meggs,
independent scholar on women's and disability
issues and on feminism and religion, Havre, Montana

Fields, Verna (1918–1982)

American film editor. Born Verna Hellman in 1918; died in 1982; daughter of Sam Hellman (a screenwriter); married film editor Sam Fields (died 1954); children: two.

Filmography—editor: The Savage Eye *(1960);* Studs Lonigan *(1960); (sound editor)* El Cid *(1961);* An Affair of the Skin *(1963); (sound ed.)* The Balcony *(1963);* Cry of Battle *(1963);* Nothing But a Man *(1964);* The Bus *(1965);* Country Boy *(1966);* Deathwatch *(1966);* Legend of the Boy and the Eagle *(1967); (sound ed.)* Targets *(1968);* Track of Thunder *(1968);* The Wild Racers *(1968);* Medium Cool *(1969);* What's Up, Doc? *(1972);* American Graffiti *(1973);* Paper Moon *(1973);* Daisy Miller *(1974);* The Sugarland Express *(1974);* Jaws *(1975).*

Known as the "Mother Cutter" among her colleagues, film editor Verna Fields was the daughter of screenwriter Sam Hellman, whose credits include *Little Miss Marker* (1934) and *My Darling Clementine* (1946). Fields insisted, however, that she entered the film business purely by chance. By her own account, she was visiting a studio with a friend when she met a "cute guy" working the studio gate and started hanging around just to see him. Director Fritz Lang wondered who she was and eventually hired her as a sound apprentice. She worked for four years and got her union card before quitting to marry the same attractive fellow, Sam Fields, and start a family. When Sam died suddenly in 1954, Fields went back to work as a sound editor on television, working on such series as "Death Valley Days," "Sky King," and "Fury." In 1960, she was hired to edit the full-length feature *Studs Lonigan,* directed by Irving Lerner, who became her mentor. *El Cid* followed in 1961, for which she received a Motion Picture Sound Editing Award.

Later in the 1960s, Fields worked for the U.S. Information Agency and also taught for a year at the University of Southern California, where she hired a young student by the name of George Lucas. (She did the final edit on Lucas' *American Graffiti* in 1973.) Fields went on to edit Steven Spielberg's first film, *The Sugarland Express* (1974), and worked with the director again on his breakthrough film *Jaws* (1975). At one point, Fields had a hand in saving the movie. "I was the liaison with the studio for Steven," she explained. "When there was thought of ditching the picture because the shark wasn't working, I told them, 'Keep doing it, even if you need to use miniatures.'" For her work on *Jaws,* Fields won an Academy Award and a new job as Universal's vice president in charge of feature productions, a post she held until her death in 1982.

SOURCES:
Acker, Ally. *Reel Women: Pioneers of the Cinema, 1896 to Present.* NY: Continuum, 1991.

Barbara Morgan,
Melrose, Massachusetts

Fiennes, Anne (d. 1595)

*English noblewoman. Name variations: Fienes; Lady Dacre. Pronunciation: Fines. Died in 1595; daughter of Sir Richard Sackville (cousin of *Anne Boleyn); married Gregory Fiennes.*

Fiennes, Celia (1662–1741)

British traveler and writer. Pronunciation: Fines. Born in Newton Toney, near Salisbury, in 1662; died in London in 1741; daughter of Nathaniel (member of the Council of State and the Keeper of the Great Seal under Cromwell) and Frances (Whitehead) Fiennes; never married; no children.

The travel journals of Celia Fiennes are prominent in the literature by women of the late 17th century. Born into a prestigious Puritan family, Fiennes undertook a series of journeys through England sometime between 1685 and 1702 (her accounts are not dated), supposedly in pursuit of good health and, in her own words, a "spirit of pure curiosity." Traveling mostly on horseback, accompanied by one or two servants, she made her way from one health resort to another, recording in detail the towns she visited, where she stayed, the food she ate, and what she paid for it. She visited coal mines, local work-shops, archeological sites, caves, cathedrals, and manor houses, and her observations provide a valuable source of English economic and social history. **Joanne Shattock** likens the journals to Daniel Defoe's *Tour through the Whole Island of Great Britain* (1724–26) and William Cobbett's later *Rural Rides* (1830). Fiennes' travel book *Through England on a Side Saddle in the Time of William and Mary* was first published in 1888 by a descendant who had acquired the manuscript. A modern edition, *The Journeys of Celia Fiennes,* edited by Christopher Morris, came out in 1947.

SOURCES:
Shattock, Joanne. *The Oxford Guide to British Women Writers.* Oxford: Oxford University Press, 1993.

Fieschi, Catherine (1447–1510).

See Catherine of Genoa.

Fieschi, Giacoma de.

See Este, Giacoma d'.

Fife, countess of.

See Isabel of Fife (c. 1332–1389).

Fife, duchess of.

See Alexandra of Denmark for sidebar on Louise Victoria (1867–1931).
See Alexandra Victoria (1891–1959).
See Carnegie, Caroline (b. 1934).

Figes, Eva (1932—)

German-born British feminist writer. Born in Berlin, Germany, in 1932; from age of seven, educated in London; graduated from University College.

Writings: (novels) Equinox (1966), Winter Journey (1967), Konek Landing (1969), B (1972), Days (1974), Nelly's Version (1977), Waking (1981); (non-fiction) Patriarchal Attitudes: Women in Society (1970), Tragedy and Social Evolution (1976), Sex and Subterfuge: Women Novelists to 1850 (1981).

Educated in England, German-born Eva Figes worked as an editor and translator before becoming a full-time writer in 1967. She is best known for her book *Patriarchal Attitudes: Women in Society* (1970), which examines the ideology of women's subordination in religious thought, liberal philosophy, capitalist economics, psychoanalysis, and popular custom. Along with **Germaine Greer**'s *The Female Eunuch,* it provided a descriptive base for the tenets of the women's movement in Britain. Figes is also a journalist and reviewer of note. In 1981, she examined the lives of British women writers in her *Sex and Subterfuge: Women Novelists to 1850.*

Figner, Vera (1852–1942)

Russian revolutionary whose work to free all Russian people led to her involvement in the assassination of Alexander II. Name variations: Vera Feigner; Verochka. Pronunciation: VEE-rah FIG-nur. Born on July 7, 1852, in Khristoforovka, Kazan Province, Russia; died in the USSR on June 15, 1942; daughter of Nikolai Alexandrovich Figner (a noble and local justice) and Ekaterina Khristoforovna Figner (daughter of a judge); sister of Olga Figner, Lydia Figner, and Evgenia Figner; attended Rodionovsky Institute at Kazan, 1863–69; attended medical school in Zurich and Bern, Switzerland, 1872–75; married Aleksei Victorovich Filippov, in 1870 (legally separated in 1876); no children.

Family moved to Nikoforovo, where Vera entered school (1863); graduated (1869); left for Swiss universities with husband and sister Lydia (1872); joined the Fritsche group (1872); returned to Russia (1875); passed exams for assistant physician in Yaroslavl (1876); became a member of the populist group Land and Liberty (1879); joined the radical insurrectionist group People's Will after the Voronezh conference (1879); took control of the People's Will group in Odessa, then recalled to St. Petersburg to become a member of the party's Executive Committee (1880); assisted in the assassination of Alexander II (1881); remained the last member of the People's Will Executive Committee at large in Russia (1882); arrested in Kharkov (1883); tried and sentenced in St. Petersburg (1884); incarcerated in the Schlüsselburg fortress (1884–1904); exiled in Russia (1904–06); lived abroad (1906–15). Publications: Polnoe sobranie sochinenii v shesti tomakh (Complete Works in Six Volumes, Moscow, 1929).

Vera Figner

The memoirs of Russian political revolutionaries of the late 19th century contain the names of many women who figured prominently in the movement; arrest totals show that some 15% were women. In these accounts, the name Vera Figner stands out as synonymous with a dedicated revolutionary. Indeed, her participation in the scheme to assassinate Tsar Alexander II,

her trial, and the ensuing years of imprisonment left an imprint on those who would follow a militant revolutionary path.

Figner was born into the Russia of the 1850s, a time of intense public debate in the country's history. Western Europe was in the process of evolving socially and politically to meet the challenges of a modern industrial state, while for the previous 70 years Russia had been fixated on the issue of serfdom and its eradication without changing existing social, economic, and political structures.

Figner's parents were members of the gentry class (or nobility). Her father Nikolai Figner was educated as a forester, a career he followed until the emancipation of the serfs in 1861. He then became a justice of the peace and moved his family to his estate in Nikoforovo when Vera was 12. Her mother **Ekaterina Figner** was the daughter of a judge and had received the type of home education usual for her time. Vera Figner would write about life in the provinces for women as "confined within the narrow boundaries of petty interests, and it seemed as though there were no escape from those boundaries." Her youthful dream was to become a tsarina.

During her childhood, Vera rarely had contact with her parents. As the eldest of six surviving children, she spent most of her time with nannies and siblings. In 1863, she was enrolled in the Rodionovsky Institute in Kazan, where she was taught little other than the usual finishing-school curriculum. During breaks from school, she read novels and journals recommended by her mother and uncle. As her six children grew up, Ekaterina had more time to spend with her older children. Vera formed a solid relationship with her mother and would remain devoted to her for the rest of her life. Although Nikolai Figner did not die until 1870, when Vera was 18 years old, he evidently had little impact on her life other than as an early political model. She described her parents, extended family members, and their close acquaintances as liberal democrats and not socialists of any type. They were basically utilitarians, who believed that each individual is responsible to do the greatest good to affect the greatest number of people. Her parents and many other liberals believed that the avenue to social change in Russia was through the gentry and its service to the state.

After graduation from the institute in 1869, Figner wanted to attend university; her parents, however, decided that she should have a debut in Kazan. There, she met her future husband Aleksei Victorovich Filippov, a legal investigator. Married in 1870, several weeks before her father died, Figner then moved forward with her plans to attend a university. She wanted to acquire a useful degree, hoping to find a cure for the social and economic ills that beset her country. Because medical degrees were unobtainable in Russia, Figner, her husband, and sister **Lydia Figner** decided to study abroad. The three left for Zurich, Switzerland, in 1872 when Figner was 21 years old.

Once installed in Zurich, she became involved with a Russian women's circle, a forum for women to learn to speak "logically" in order to articulate their ideas in front of men and thus undo centuries of Russian cultural practices as they pertained to women. The circle met only twice before breaking into smaller groups of likeminded women. One of these groups, the Fritsche, to which Figner and her sister belonged, espoused socialism and class warfare. Members of the group were to become the leading women in the political movements of Russia in the late 1870s and early 1880s. Figner absorbed the books of Proudhon, Fourier, Blanc, Bentham, and Bakunin. From these works, and discussions with the other women of the group, she formulated a new political identity. For the women of the Fritsche, their work was obvious: to return to Russia and live among the workers in order to bring social, political, and economic change to Russia. They firmly believed that the key to Russia's success would be a social revolution led by the urban workers. Figner pointed out that factory laborers should be the target group as "they were more highly developed mentally." She did not, however, believe she had the strength to live among the workers and survive the long days and arduous tasks of the factory.

As Figner evolved as a socialist, her husband Aleksei, never more than a liberal, became more conservative. She changed universities in 1873 as a result of a Russian government decree that female students in Zurich return to Russia at once or be barred from taking licensing exams. They were accused by the government of studying medicine in order to practice free love and obtain abortions. The decree said nothing, however, of women studying elsewhere, so Figner moved to Bern to continue her training. Aleksei did not go with her, and from that time forward they were separated. While she continued her studies, the Fritsche group put together a program before leaving Zurich, deciding on a populist approach for their ideas. They determined to live among the peasants, working at manual labor.

In 1875, after her sister Lydia's imprisonment in Moscow for possessing socialist litera-ture, Figner returned to Russia to work for the revolutionaries. She did not see or communicate with Lydia, however, for fear it would alert the authorities. In 1876, Vera stood for the state licensing exam for physician's assistant and midwife, passing both. License in hand, she continued to carry out the plan the Fritsche group had articulated, living among the people in order to raise their political awareness.

Prior to 1876, revolutionary groups were of two types—propagandists and insurrectionists. Propagandists believed that people were blank slates on which socialist principles could be etched. Insurrectionists believed that all methods of social upheaval were legitimate, and that the people would be able to create a new order only after the existing one was brought down. Out of the failures of both these groups came the *narodniki* or Populists. The basic program of the Populists was simple: by organizing petitions the tsar would not honor, they would prove his inability to take care of peasant needs and, thereby, foster discontent and insurrection among the peasants. Thus, they could gain ownership of the land for those who worked it. New groups, such as the Land and Freedom (Zemlya i volya) and the People's Will (Narodnaya volya), were formed to take this message to the people.

> To lose one's freedom means to lose the ownership of one's own body.
>
> —Vera Figner

Franco Venturi, a historian of political thought, claims that while the Populist program failed to incite the longed-for revolution, the peasants were exposed to different ideas: "Everywhere the peasants had listened to these strange pilgrims with amazement, surprise and sometimes suspicion. But the government understood that a new revolutionary movement had now been born." Believing in the Populist ideals, Figner picked up where those imprisoned had left off.

Her first opportunity came in August 1877. Taking a post as a physician's assistant at Studentsy in Samara province, she was in charge of the medical well-being of 12 peasant villages. For the first time, Figner was confronted with the realities of human suffering and deprivation. She lasted only three months. In 1878, she went to St. Petersburg, where she met and befriended *Sonia Perovskaya, a friendship that would last until Perovskaya was hanged for political terrorism. In the same year, Figner moved as a surgeon's assistant to the village of Vyazimo in Saratov province with her sister **Evgenia Figner**.

In order to practice in the countryside, Vera needed to win over the superstitious peasants and local officials. For most of the population, this was the first woman physician with modern medical training they had ever met. Figner estimated in her memoirs that she saw over 5,000 patients in the first ten months.

Beyond the use of her medical knowledge, Figner opened a school together with Evgenia, in which they taught reading, writing and simple mathematics to peasant children and parents. Over time, the local peasantry grew to respect them, requesting, on more than one occasion, that the sisters intervene for them with the local bureaucracy over issues such as taxation. During her sojourn in the countryside, Figner met Populist Alexander Soloviev, and together they talked about the futility of change in the peasant villages; they felt that the population, overall, was too backward to create a revolution. From this point on, Figner became an advocate for Soloviev's idea that political freedom was necessary for any change in Russia. Soloviev was hanged in May 1879 for an assassination attempt on Alexander II.

Ironically, Alexander II was known as the "tsar liberator." He had emancipated the serfs in 1861 and had instituted the first legal and political reforms in an effort to modernize Russia. "It is better to abolish serfdom from above," he said, "than to await the time when it will begin to abolish itself from below." But Alexander's reforms failed to produce the rapid social and economic growth that he had hoped they would achieve. After 1866, he gradually abandoned his liberal and reform program, partly as a result of the Polish rebellion of 1863–64. In addition, the profound disappointment of the peasants and radical intellectuals in the reforms led to widespread social unrest and even violence. A struggle developed between his government and the dedicated revolutionary elements that had been organizing even as he passed his reforms. On April 4, 1866, a student, Dmitri V. Karakazov, fired several shots at Alexander. Frightened and angry over the incident, Alexander moved steadily towards a reactionary response to the radicals. Several treason trials were held, and the police were given broad powers to keep order. These responses undermined Alexander's relationship with the Russian intellectuals, and the trials gave exposure to the radical cause.

In 1879, Figner became a member of the Land and Freedom movement, but when the group split over the method required to obtain political freedom, she chose the more radical People's Will, with its party platform centering on the legitimacy of political terror. She described the use of terror not as a goal but as a "weapon for protection." Leaving her work among the peasants, she became a terrorist revolutionary, involved with conspiracies to assassinate the tsar. Though several of the plans came to naught due to changes in the tsar's schedules, attempts continued to be made by Figner's colleagues. For the bombing of the Winter Palace in February 1880, Figner collected and stored the dynamite used. The dining room was blown up as the tsar, the empress *Marie of Hesse-Darmstadt, and their eight children entered, but the would-be assassin, Stepan Halturin, did not have a large enough charge to destroy the room.

Wrote Figner:

Society, at any rate its more intelligent element, greeted our activity with great enthusiasm, and offered us sympathetic aid and ardent approval. From this point of view we had the right to speak in the name of society. We constituted to a marked degree the front rank of a part of that society. Knowing that this group sympathized with us, we did not feel ourselves a sect, isolated from all the elements of the empire, and this contributed not a little to that "implacable quality" which we showed in our actions, and of which the public prosecutors used to speak at our trials.

For Figner and the others, the sacrifice of their lives, as well as the lives of the royals, was a small price to pay for delivering the Russian people from oppression.

In January 1880, she was given leadership of the People's Will group in Odessa. There, she organized an assassination attempt on a government official who had exiled many students and intellectuals for political crimes. That summer, after an abortive attempt on the governor of the province, she returned to St. Petersburg. Figner then took up secretarial work for the group and became a member of the Executive Committee, which made the decisions about targets and the methods to be used.

In the assassination of Alexander II, Vera Figner played a significant supporting role, while her friend, Sonia Perovskaya, orchestrated the event. Late in the morning of March 1, 1881, as Alexander rode through the streets of St. Petersburg, members of the People's Will Party hurled a bomb at his carriage. The tsar was uninjured, but when he left his coach to attend a wounded guard or check the damage, a second bomb was thrown that shattered both of his legs. At his request, Alexander was taken on a police sleigh to the Winter Palace to die that same day.

The group then sent a letter to the new tsar, Alexander III, demanding representative government, free press, free speech, and free elections. They also asked for amnesty for their crimes, asserting that they had only done their civic duty. The government response was to arrest those who could be found and track down the rest. Figner left St. Petersburg on April 3, the same day that Sonia Perovskaya was hanged for her part in the assassination. Figner and her group returned to Odessa in the hopes of rebuilding the party.

She had limited success. Figner believed that once outside the political center—where there had been an educated working population—the purpose of the group was not understood. By the end of 1881, only eight of the original twenty-three members of the Executive Committee were still at large. There were no longer enough leaders to plan, or carry out, any acts of terrorism. Angry that Russian society had failed to respond to the opportunity she felt it had been given with the tsar's assassination and realizing the impossibility of recreating the party as it had been, Figner began to recruit in the military. By June 1882, she was the only member of the Executive Committee still free. Continuing her work in Kharkov, Figner also helped to reestablish a printing operation in Odessa. Only five weeks later, the Odessa group was picked up by the police. Figner remained in Kharkov until February 10, 1883, when she was betrayed by her comrades and arrested on the street.

The following day, she was taken to St. Petersburg, questioned by the police and incarcerated in the Sts. Peter and Paul Fortress for 20 months while awaiting her trial. During this time, she refused to answer questions about her life after March 1, 1881, in order to protect those individuals still involved with party work. She saw no harm in discussing previous events, as the people involved were either dead or in prison.

Figner's life in prison was initially one of reflection upon the acts committed and the people who had committed them. As time passed, she did little besides read and wait for the bi-weekly 20-minute visits from her mother and her youngest sister **Olga Figner**. She lost the use of her vocal cords, became depressed, and no longer wished to be connected to the outside world. During this period of enforced silence and isolation, the only thing that kept her from going mad was her sense of duty to the cause: the chance to make a political statement at her trial. She was indicted with 13 others. The trial commenced in September 1884.

At the trial, Figner did not underplay her role or activities in the group and took full responsibility for her actions. Allowed to make her statement, she recounted her reasons for joining the group, justified her actions based on the existing political situation in Russia, and stated her resolve to take whatever punishment the court gave. She wrote later that when she ended her speech she felt that she had "outlived my spiritual and physical forces—there was nothing left— even my will to live had vanished." She sensed a liberation from her political duty, a freedom to become simply someone's daughter and sister. She was sentenced by the court to hang along with seven others. All, except Figner, asked for a sentence commutation.

After a final visit with her mother and sister, Figner was returned to the fortress to await execution. Eight days later, she was informed that her sentence had been commuted to penal servitude. Public sentiment was against the execution of women after Sonia Perovskaya's hanging three years earlier. Figner was well aware of what the altered sentence meant. "I had outlived all my strength," she said, "and I should merely have preferred a speedy death on the scaffold to a slow process of dying, the inevitability of which I recognized at that time."

In October 1884, Figner was moved north to the fortress at Schlüsselburg. She saw the bleached limestone towers, one with a gold key painted on its side, and later would remember that "the key rising to the sky, like an emblem, seemed to say that there would be no coming out." The only other inhabitants of the fortress were revolutionaries who were not to see, or speak to one another, for two years. Their guards were not allowed to communicate with the prisoners either, so they all lived in silence. Many went insane, which Figner feared above all else, or committed suicide. She felt they had been entombed alive; her only method for human contact was by tapping messages to other prisoners through the walls.

In January 1886, Figner was allowed to walk every other day for exercise with another prisoner, one of her codefendants, **Ludmila Alexandrovich Volkenstein**. Though the isolation was broken, the harsh punishments meted out to the prisoners continued. During 1887, Figner put herself in jeopardy to save one of her fellow inmates from severe punishment, when they were caught tapping on the walls and the guards intended to punish only the man. Fearing for his sanity, she demanded to be included. She was put in a punishment cell for seven days.

When a new commandant was brought in, the prison changed for the better. Starting in 1894, she petitioned the commandant for books from the public library. Prisoners were granted the use of a circulating natural history museum and prepared rock and plant collections. Their findings were used in the primary and secondary schools of St. Petersburg.

After 13 years of solitude, she was given the privilege of writing to her relatives. Still, she rarely exercised the option, not knowing how to avoid causing her family grief. Her mother died in 1903 having petitioned the tsar for mercy for Vera. By then, there were only 13 prisoners left in the fortress. Many had died, but several had served their sentences and been released into the world of exile. As for Figner, she never thought of leaving her prison existence and spent her days in introspection. At age 51, the revolutionary believed that the "mind and soul" must find equilibrium so the individual could live in harmony with the world around her even if it be prison.

On January 13, 1904, Figner was informed that her sentence had been commuted to 20 years and that her incarceration would end on September 28. Released 22 years after her arrest, she was exiled to Kazan province. In 1906, she left Russia to live abroad, raising money to help prisoners and convicts. She returned to Russia in 1915 and supported the program of the Bolsheviks during the revolutions of 1917.

The goal of her youth had been realized, a revolution for the freedom of the people. But before her death in 1942, at age 90, she would see the dream of freedom for all disintegrate first into civil war and later into Stalin's brand of totalitarianism. In the Soviet Union, Vera Figner remained a heroine in textbooks. Of what she thought about the radical changes wrought in her homeland after Stalin's rise to power, we know nothing.

SOURCES:
Berlin, Isaiah. *Russian Thinkers*. NY: Penguin, 1978.
Figner, Vera. *Memoirs of a Revolutionist*. NY: International Publishers, 1927.
————. *Polnoe sobranie sochinenii v shesti tomakh*. Moscow, 1929.
Venturi, Franco. *Roots of Revolution*. NY: Alfred Knopf, 1960.

SUGGESTED READING:
Engel, Barbara Alpern, and Clifford Rosenthal, eds. *Five Sisters: Women Against the Tsar*. NY: Alfred Knopf, 1975.

Linnea Goodwin Burwood,
Instructor in History, Memphis State University,
Memphis, Tennessee

Figueira, Josefa (1630–1684).

See de Ayala, Josefa.

Figueroa, Ana (1907–1970)

Chilean educator and UN representative who was the first woman to be elected chair of a major committee of the UN General Assembly and the first woman to be named an alternate delegate to the Security Council. Born in Santiago, Chile, on June 19, 1907; died in 1970; daughter of Miguel Figueroa Rebolledo and Ana Gajardo Infante; graduated from the University of Chile, 1928; attended Teachers College of Columbia University and Colorado State College; children: one son, Arturo.

An educator by profession, Ana Figueroa began her career as an English and philosophy teacher in various Chilean high schools. In 1938, she was named principal of the Liceo San Felipe and assumed the same position at the Liceo de Temuco the following year. In 1946, she was promoted to general inspector of secondary education, a position of national scope. In addition to her duties as a teacher and administrator, Figueroa taught psychology at the University of Chile and wrote a text on sex education (1934). An advocate of women's rights, she was a member of the board of the YWCA, president of the Federation of Women's Organization in Chile, and her country's delegate to the Inter-American Commission of Women.

Figueroa was appointed to the United Nations in 1948, as a delegate plenipotentiary to the third regular session of the General Assembly. In February 1950, she was appointed alternate permanent Chilean representative to the UN and later that year was elected to the Assembly's Trusteeship Committee. When the UN opened its Sixth General Assembly in Paris in November 1951, Figueroa was elected chair of the Social, Humanitarian and Cultural Committee, which dealt with problems of human rights, refugees, and migration. The first woman chosen to head a General Assembly committee, she downplayed any emphasis on the "feminine angle," believing that it was quite natural for a woman to be awarded a high post and that she should not receive special privileges. On January 22, 1952, her country named her an alternate delegate to the Security Council, a position never before filled by a woman. When General Carlos Ibáñez succeeded as president of Chile in November 1952, Figueroa, in keeping with Chilean custom, resigned as a representative to the UN.

SOURCES:

Current Biography. NY: H.W. Wilson, 1952.

Barbara Morgan,
Melrose, Massachusetts

Figuli, Margita (1909–1995)

Slovak novelist known for her work Three Chestnut Horses. *Born on October 2, 1909, in Vysny Kubin, Austria-Hungary (now Slovak Republic); died on March 27, 1995; the daughter of peasants.*

Born in 1909 in a poor mountain village in Slovakia when it was still under the jurisdiction of the Hungarian part of Austria-Hungary, Margita Figuli rose above the limitations imposed by her peasant upbringing and took advantage of the improved educational opportunities that were made available after 1918 under the new Czechoslovak Republic. After completing her studies at a commercial academy, in 1928 Figuli found employment in a bank in Bratislava, the Slovak capital. Her literary talents developed rapidly, and she began publishing in newspapers and journals. Her style was closely linked to two contemporary writers of the Slovak Lyrical Prose school of which she, Dobroslav Chrobak (1907–1951) and Frantisek Svantner (1912–1950) were the leading exponents. Her early short stories, written in an impressionist style, were published in 1937 under the title *Pokusenie* (*Temptation*).

In 1940, Figuli published what was to become her best-known work, *Tri gastanove kone* (*Three Chestnut Horses*), a short novel of little more than 100 pages which became a bestseller in Slovakia, appearing in seven reprint editions during the next seven years. In its lyrical descriptions of the unspoiled forest world of the Tatra mountains, and using the symbolism of three horses to depict the goodness, beauty and strength of the natural world, *Three Chestnut Horses* is also a love story of a simple peasant girl's dilemma over choosing which of two suitors she should marry. Although the happy ending of the book may appear naive and contrived to some contemporary readers and critics, the novel was an immense success and was hailed as representing a major step forward for Slovak literature.

Between 1939 and 1945, Slovakia was ostensibly a sovereign nation, but in reality it was a satellite state of Nazi Germany. The Fascist Slovak regime persecuted Jews, Marxists and democrats, and while Margita Figuli was not politically active her deeply held Christian and humanist beliefs brought her in conflict with the ideological dictates of the Bratislava regime.

Ana Figueroa

After having published several antiwar stories, including *Oloveny vtak* (*The Leaden Bird*) and *Tri noci a tri sny* (*Three Nights and Three Dreams*), her dissident views led to her being dismissed from her bank job in 1942. Although Slovakia remained an ally of Nazi Germany, an unsuccessful national uprising in 1944 left the nation traumatized in the spring of 1945 when it lost its "independence" and once more became part of Czechoslovakia.

Figuli had spent the final years of the war writing a massive historical novel, *Babylon,* which appeared in print in 1946. A detailed description of the rise and fall of the ancient Chaldean Empire filling over 700 pages, *Babylon* presented a rich tapestry of ancient life, wars and religious beliefs. Many readers detected analogies to the recently ended world conflict in the novel's colorful descriptions of savage warfare in the ancient Near East. Popular with the Slovak reading public, *Babylon* was viewed with suspicion and even hostility by the increasingly powerful arbiters of Marxist literary orthodoxy in what before 1948 was still a democratic but increasingly pro-Soviet Czechoslovakia. Stalinist critics then and later condemned *Babylon* as a book inappropriate to the times, and as an essentially escapist and "merely aesthetic" work of art that served to distract both the intelligentsia and the working masses from the urgent tasks at hand.

During the cultural and political terror that marked the final years of Stalinist rule in Eastern Europe (1948–1953), Slovak literature was forced to toe a line that was rigidly based on the doctrines of Socialist Realism. Although Figuli did not completely succumb to these pressures, neither could she afford to completely ignore what was required of her as a major writer. In her 1949 novella *Zuzana,* she attempted to portray the lives of two lovers in the 1930s whose happiness and survival were tied to a world sliding inexorably toward war and chaos. In the 1950s, both *Three Chestnut Horses* and *Babylon* appeared in revised editions that give credence to the notion that the author succumbed at least in part to the pressures of "constructive self-criticism" then in vogue. In 1974, Figuli published what would be her last novel, *Vichor v nas* (*The Whirlwind Within Us*). In this work, the artist attempted to fuse mythic and documentary styles in the story of a magical blacksmith and a girl suffering from hallucinations, hallucinations that had originated from her mother's rape by a Nazi soldier. Since the book ended in a factory that underlined the imperative of the "building of socialism," many readers as well as critics came to regard Figuli's last novel as a work sadly inferior to her earlier writings.

In the last decades of her life, Figuli continued to write, producing well-received children's books that enabled her to avoid grappling with the social concerns that, if "improperly" treated, could place one in danger of being blasted by official critics. In 1974, she was honored with the title of "National Artist of Slovakia" and, in the last decades of her long life, leading Slovak literary critics were crediting Figuli, along with Chrobak and Svantner, as having "created modern Slovak prose." Her mystical Christian ethics and elegant style continue to appeal to at least part of the Slovak reading public, with *Three Chestnut Horses* regarded as a classic work (a new edition appeared in print in 1996). Although Figuli's writings are virtually unknown beyond Central and Eastern Europe (her major works have been published in Czech, German, Russian, Magyar, Polish, Ukrainian, Slovenian, Rumanian, Latvian, and even Kazakh translations), perhaps the time will yet come when her best works are made accessible to the English-language world. Margita Figuli died on March 27, 1995.

SOURCES:

Cincura, Andrew, ed. *An Anthology of Slovak Literature.* Riverside, CA: University Hardcovers, 1976.

Fischerova-Sebestova, Anna. *Margita Figuli.* Martin: Matica Slovenska, 1970.

Jurco, Jan. *Tvorba Margity Figuli.* Bratislava: Tatran, 1991.

Jurik, Lubos. *Rozhovory o literature.* Bratislava: Smena, 1986.

Krcmery, Stefan. "A Survey of Modern Slovak Literature," in *Slavonic (and East European) Review.* Vol. 7, 1928, pp. 160–170.

Mamatey, Victor S. Personal communication, 1998.

"Na slovo s Margitou Figuli," in *Slovenske Pohl'ady na Literature a Umenie.* Vol. 84, no. 1, 1968, pp. 3–9.

"Odpoveda Margita Figuli," in *Slovenske Pohl'ady na Literature a Umenie.* Vol. 86, no. 11, 1970, pp. 53–58.

Pasteka, Julius. "Margita Figuli medzi tradicionalizmom a modernizmom: Pokusenie z odstupu a nadhl'adu," in *Slovenske Pohl'ady na Literature a Umenie.* Vol. 87, no. 10, 1971, pp. 40–52.

Petro, Peter. *A History of Slovak Literature.* Montreal and Buffalo: McGill-Queen's University Press, 1996.

Pisut, Milan. *Dejiny slovenskej literatury.* Bratislava: Obzor, 1984.

Pynsent, Robert B. and S.I. Kanikova. *Reader's Encyclopedia of Eastern European Literature.* NY: HarperCollins, 1993.

Rudinsky, Norma L. *Incipient Feminists: Women Writers in the Slovak National Revival.* Columbus, OH: Slavica Publishers, 1991.

———. "Margita Figuli 1909-1995," in Katharina M. Wilson, Paul Schlueter and June Schlueter, eds. *Women Writers of Great Britain and Europe: An Encyclopedia.* NY: Garland Publishers, 1997, pp. 155–156.

Strelinger, Peter. *Desat' autografov Slovesney jari 1974.* Martin: Matica Slovenska, 1974.

John Haag,
Assistant Professor of History,
University of Georgia, Athens, Georgia

Fikotová, Olga (1932—)

Czech-American discus thrower and winner of the gold medal in the 1956 Olympics. Name variations: Olga Fikotova; Olga Connolly. Born Olga Fikotová in Prague, Czechoslovakia, on November 13, 1932; entered School of Medicine at Prague's Charles University; married Harold Connolly (American gold medalist in the 16-pound hammer throw), in 1957 (divorced around 1972); children: four.

Won gold medal in discus at the Melbourne Olympics (1956); married, became an American citizen, and competed for the United States (1957); qualified for four consecutive Olympic Games (beginning 1960).

Olga Fikotová refused to accept the status quo. Growing up in Prague, she played soccer with the boys rather than practice the violin as her parents wanted. In high school, she played handball and basketball, representing Czechoslovakia in the top league. After she entered the School of Medicine at Prague's Charles University, Fikotová had philosophical differences with her team coach. In addition, team practice interfered with her studies, so she turned to the discus, an individual sport that gave her greater flexibility.

In 1955, Fikotová began to work with the hurdler "Father" Jandera who put "The Blue Danube" on the stadium's public-address system so that she could throw the discus to music. As she began to excel, Fikotová was given a monthly subsidy from the state (about the same amount her mother earned as a clerk). That same year, she competed in the Progressive Youth Festival in Warsaw but her performance was disappointing. Because of this, Fikotová was thankful when *Nina Ponomareva-Romashkova, the powerful Soviet thrower, spent an intense training period with her in Warsaw.

In the 1956 Melbourne Olympic Games, Fikotová won the gold medal, beating out her Soviet mentor Ponomareva, who was devastated by the defeat. The Soviet government insisted that the Czech and Soviet Olympic teams travel from Australia to Siberia by boat and then make a triumphal tour across the Soviet Union. Though the Czech athletes were not enthusiastic about the tour, they had little choice. Fikotová and Ponomareva were barely speaking when the ship left Australia. By the time the *Gruzia* reached chilly Siberia after warm Australia, Olga had developed a bad cold. It was Ponomareva who brought her a home remedy, a liquor predicted to "kill or cure." Two treat-

Olga
Fikotová

ments restored her health, as well as the friend-ship between the two champions.

Back in Czechoslovakia, Fikotová, now a national celebrity, received the title "supreme master of sports" and looked forward to a promising career. There was one obstacle. She was in love with Harold Connolly, the American gold medalist in the 16-pound hammer throw. The two had met at Melbourne, and their romance had been widely publicized throughout the world. Torn, Fikotová took several months before agreeing to marry Harold and move to the United States. A *New York Times* editorial on March 22, 1957, celebrated the decision:

> This poor old world of ours is quarreling, divided and perplexed. . . . The H-bomb overhangs us like a cloud of doom . . . but Olga and Harold are in love and the world does not say no to them. . . . Somehow this seems like a ray of light, intelligence and beauty in a world where ministers of state and heads of government go nervously back and forth in search of such things.

When Olga began competing for the United States, she discovered that with new freedoms came new restrictions. She resented, for example, that athletes were "treated as children" in America, with every glass of beer or wine monitored. The greatest difference, however, was in the attitude toward women's abilities. In New England, where the Connollys lived, she was often asked to speak to school groups, opportunities she took to encourage girls to go out for more strenuous sports as they did in Eastern block nations. "The hands of our girls are created to play the violin," one school principal told her. "Please do not put ideas in their heads about competition." An infuriated Fikotová replied, "For seven years I played the violin, and my hands were as good for that as for winning Olympic Games."

Another problem was a lack of major competitions for women. This was due, she felt, to the provincial reality that schools did not want women to compete, especially in events considered "unseemly." Despite the fact that she had less support in the United States than in Czechoslovakia, Fikotová qualified for four consecutive Olympic Games beginning in 1960. She was pregnant between each.

As an Olympic athlete, Fikotová often found she was in as much disagreement with her adopted government as she had been with her former government. In the 1968 Olympics, she was upset when Tommie Smith and John Carlos were castigated for raising their fists in a black-power salute in Mexico City. Fikotová felt their punishment smacked more of a communist dictatorship than of a Western democracy. In the 1972 Munich Olympics, she was an adamant opponent of the Vietnam War. The Olympic Committee ruled that no athletes could speak to the press unless supervised. Outraged, Fikotová filed a complaint with Senator Alan Cranston's office and the censorship was struck down.

Despite political protests, Fikotová loved participating in the Olympics. In 1972, at 39, she was one of the oldest athletes and, as the mother of four, had the most children of any competitor. Though she did not win a medal, she was the American standard holder at the 185'3" mark and was thrilled to be elected flag bearer for the U.S. team in Munich.

Olga Fikotová divorced Harold Connolly not long after the 1972 Olympics, but by this time she had adjusted to her adopted country. Eventually, Americans recognized that she had been right—women could and should participate in more strenuous sports.

SOURCES:

Carlson, Lewis H., and John J. Fogarty. *Tales of Gold.* Chicago: Contemporary Press, 1987.

Connolly, Olga. *The Rings of Destiny.* NY: David McKay, 1968.

Karin L. Haag, Athens, Georgia

Filatova, Maria (b. 1961).

See Comaneci, Nadia for sidebar.

Filipa.

Variant of Philippa.

Filipa de Lencastre (c. 1359–1415).

See Philippa of Lancaster.

Filipović, Zlata (c. 1981—)

Bosnian diarist. Name variations: Zlata Filipovic. Born in Sarajevo, Bosnia, around 1981; only daughter of Malik (a lawyer) and Alica Filipović (a biochemist).

Dubbed the *Anne Frank of the Bosnian War, Sarajevo schoolgirl Zlata Filipović was ten years old and looking forward to a new school year when she began a diary. The only child of a middle-class couple, she was a precocious student who took tennis and piano lessons and had a passion for pizza, American movies, and Michael Jackson. "I wanted to have a happy memory from a happy childhood," she said. "I wanted 20 years after to open that funny book and read the things that happened." By April of 1992, however, Sarajevo was under siege by Bosnian Serbs, and Filipović's diary, much like Anne Frank's (which she had read), turned into a heartwrenching chronicle of the horrors of war and a young girl's loss of innocence.

"Oh God! Things are heating up in Sarajevo," she wrote on March 5, 1992, as the conflict was in its early stages. "On Sunday, A small group of armed civilians (as they say on TV) killed a Serbian wedding guest and wounded the priest. On March 2 (Monday) the whole city was full of barricades." Within two months, conditions had deteriorated considerably. "Today was truly, absolutely the worst day ever in Sarajevo," began her entry of May 2, 1992, which was now addressed to an imaginary friend called "Mimmy." By this time, the constant gunfire had forced the family into the dark, smelly, rat-infested cellar. "We listened to the pounding shells, the shooting, the thundering noise overhead," she continued. "We even heard planes. At one moment, I realized that this awful cellar was the only place that could save our lives. Suddenly, it started to look almost warm and nice. We heard glass shattering in our street. Horrible. I put my fingers in my ears to block out the terrible sounds."

For two years, Filipović continued her poignant account of the war and the hardships of living without gas, electricity, or water, and subsisting on United Nations food packages. She mourned the death of her 11-year-old friend Nina, who was hit by shrapnel that lodged in her brain ("I cry and wonder why? She didn't do anything.") and denounced the politicians ("Ordinary people don't want this division because it won't make anyone happy, not the Serbs, not the Croats, not the Muslims. But who asks ordinary people? Politics only asks its own people.") As the war ground on, she described the toll it had taken on her parents. "Daddy . . . really has lost a lot of weight. I think even his glasses are too big for him. Mommy has lost weight too. She's shrunk somehow. The war has given her wrinkles." There were moments of despair ("There's a growing possibility of my killing myself. . . . I'm so sick of it all") and signs of youthful hope ("You had to have a light of life there, in that dark, in that hell and death").

In the summer of 1993, Filipović's diary was chosen from 100 others for publication by a peace group in Sarajevo and then found its way to French publishing house Fixot & Editions Robert Lafont, which released the diary and also arranged to get Zlata and her parents

out of Bosnia. The French edition became an instant bestseller, as did 25 foreign editions, including Viking's American translation by **Christina Pribichevich-Zorić**, *Zlata's Diary: A Child's Life in Sarajevo*. By Christmas 1993, when the Filipovićs were flown out of the war zone and landed in Paris, Zlata was already a literary sensation.

At age 13, Filipović was swept up in a celebrity whirl that left no time for the continuation of her diary. There were television appearances and a book tour, which included a visit to the United States. "When people read my book, when they see me on television, they may help the children of Sarajevo because we must not forget the children," she said in an interview, hoping to call attention to the 70,000 or so that were left in Sarajevo. To help those still in harm's way, Zlata and her publishers donated a portion of the profits from the diary to various relief projects, including distributing 5,000 ski jackets in the war-ravaged country. On a personal level, Filipović left a lasting impression on everyone she met. "She's very lovable, very modest and not remotely spoiled," said **Susanna Lee**, the director of foreign rights at Lafont/Fixot. "And her moral education is extraordinary."

SOURCES:
Chin, Paula, and Cathy Nolan. "Days of Despair," in *People*. March 21, 1994, pp. 66–68.
Filipović, Zlata. *Zlata's Diary: A Child's Life in Sarajevo*. Translated by Christina Pribichevich-Zorić. NY: Viking, 1994.
Krilic, Samir. "Schoolgirl's diary becomes a moving chronicle of war's terror, loss in Sarajevo," in *The Day* (New London, CT). July 20, 1993.
Publishers Weekly. February 21, 1994, p. 245.
Riding, Alan. "Teen-age Bosnian diarist is literary sensation," in *The Day* (New London, CT), January 6, 1994.

Fillmore, Abigail Powers

(1798–1853)

American first lady who established the White House library. Born on March 13, 1798, in Stillwater, New York; died on March 30, 1853, in Washington, D.C.; only daughter of Lemual (a Baptist minister) and Abigail (Newland) Powers; married Millard Fillmore, on February 5, 1826, in Moravia, New York; children: Millard Powers Fillmore (1828–1889, a lawyer); Mary Abigail Fillmore (1832–1854, often served as White House host).

Abigail Powers Fillmore was born on March 13, 1798, in Stillwater, New York, the only daughter of Lemual Powers, a Baptist minister, and **Abi-**

gail Newland Powers. She spent her girlhood in Cayuga County, New York, with her widowed mother and younger brother. Her father's death had left the family with limited funds but an extensive library, which Abigail used to educate herself. At age 16, with hopes of earning enough money to further her formal education, she began teaching school. In 1819, when Abigail was 21, Millard Fillmore, only slightly younger, appeared in her classroom. A "schoolbook romance" ensued and lasted for seven years, during which time Millard advanced steadily and began law studies. After the couple married in February 1826, Abigail continued to teach while her husband built his law practice. The couple began a family in 1828 with the birth of a son, Millard Powers Fillmore. A daughter, **Mary Abigail Fillmore**, followed in 1832.

Abigail Powers Fillmore

Fillmore's political career rose steadily from congressman to state comptroller. By the time he was elected vice president in 1849, Abigail's health was beginning to fail, and she spent as little time in Washington as possible. She was at home in Buffalo when she received the news of her husband's succession to the presidency following the death of Zachary Taylor just 16 months after taking office. Joining her husband in the White House, or as Millard dubbed it, "the temple of inconveniences," Abigail delegated many of the social duties to her daughter. Among the first tasks she chose for herself was overseeing the installation of water pipes and the first White House bathtub. She also upgraded the kitchen, replacing the open fireplace with an iron range.

More appalling to Abigail than the absence of running water was the lack of books in the mansion. She took immediate steps to have Congress appropriate modest funds for a library, which she established in the Oval Room. With her books, and the addition of a harp and piano, this became the most inviting room in the family quarters. On the social front, Abigail did make an effort to preside over Tuesday and Friday receptions, although a leg injury made it difficult for her to stand for long periods of time.

The signing of the Fugitive Slave Act proved to be Millard Fillmore's downfall, and he was not renominated by the Whigs in 1852. With plans to travel to Europe after they left Washington, the Fillmores attended inaugural ceremonies for Franklin Pierce. The foul weather that day is thought to have caused the bronchial pneumonia that took Abigail's life a few weeks later, at age 55. Millard Fillmore married *Caroline C. McIntosh, in 1858.

SOURCES:

Healy, Diana Dixon. *America's First Ladies: Private Lives of the Presidential Wives.* NY: Atheneum, 1988.
Melick, Arden David. *Wives of the Presidents.* Maplewood, NJ: Hammond, 1977.
Paletta, LuAnn. *The World Almanac of First Ladies.* NY: World Almanac, 1990.

Barbara Morgan,
Melrose, Massachusetts

Fillmore, Caroline C. (1813–1881).

See McIntosh, Caroline C.

Filomena or Filumena.

Variant of Philomena.

Finch, Anne (1631–1679)

Viscountess Conway and English philosopher. Name variations: Lady Anne Conway; Viscountess Conway. Born on December 14, 1631; died on February 23, 1679; daughter of Sir Heneage Finch (d. 1631, speaker of the House of Commons); sister of physician John Finch (1626–1682); educated at home; married Edward, 3rd viscount Conway, in 1651; children: one son, who died in infancy.

Selected works: The Principles of the Most Ancient and Modern Philosophy *(1690).*

Although in 17th-century England few women received much education, Anne Finch benefited from the intellectual environment of her home. The Finches were wealthy aristocrats who encouraged reading and philosophical discussion. In fact, the frequent and severe headaches Anne suffered from the age of 12 (probably a form of migraine) were at first attributed to too much reading, encouraged by the many gifts of books she received from her older brother John Finch. Her only education was at home, but she studied French, Greek, Hebrew, Latin, mathematics, and philosophy.

John was a good friend as well as a brother to Anne, and through him she encountered the intellectual circle with which she would be involved throughout her life. She was knowledgeable of the history of philosophy as well as the contemporary philosophy of Descartes, Hobbes and Spinoza. But John's introduction of her to his tutor at Cambridge, the Platonist Henry More, allowed her philosophical life to blossom. More adopted Anne as his own student (informally, as women of the day in England could not attend university), calling her his "heroine pupil." She became More's confidante and collaborator.

Both her intellectual and personal life were impacted by the relationship with More. At 19, Anne married Edward, Viscount Conway, who had also been More's student. Edward encouraged her friendship with More and the intellectual circle grew to include three other Cambridge Platonists, Ralph Cudworth, Joseph Glanvill and George Rust, as well as Francis Mercury van Helmont, a Kabbalist philosopher (involved with Jewish mysticism), who was known as "the gypsy scholar." All were frequently guests at the Conway home. Van Helmont also acted as Anne's doctor, as did many notable physicians of the day as her headaches worsened.

Anne Finch's only work, *The Principles of the Most Ancient and Modern Philosophy*, was published posthumously, but her ideas were discussed in her circle and reflected the concerns of the time. The dominant philosophical questions concerned science and the view of reality in terms of mechanisms. Finch endeavored to reconcile a mechanistic philosophy of nature with Platonism, the view that the form of the natural world is derived from the form of the heavens. She developed an understanding of nature that is both mechanistic (causation is the result of motion) and spiritual (motion is a spiritual emanation). Finch was one of the earliest proponents of vitalism, which claims that all of the material world is living and that there is only one substance that occurs on a continuum between the physical and the mental. She argued that God does not exist on the continuum, but outside it, and that Christ is the mediator between God and the natural continuum. This thinking had far-ranging philosophical implications, including the idea that sin is improper motion. Henry More rejected the implication that God contributes spirituality to nature because it seemed to lead to pantheism, the view that God exists in everything.

After the death of her only son as an infant, Finch's headaches became much worse. She spent the last 20 years of her life at her estate in the country, Ragley Hall. During her lifetime Finch's reputation as an intellectual grew. In her final years, when she was too weak to leave her bed or even to raise her head, she was visited by many famous scholars. Van Helmont, a Quaker, encouraged her conversion to Quakerism in the last days of her life, a move that was contrary to the advice of her friends and family, as Quakerism was then an obscure and unpopular sect. He also preserved her body in wine after her death in 1678 at the age of 47, until her husband Edward could see her. She was then buried at Warwickshire in a glass coffin inside another coffin.

The Principles of the Most Ancient and Modern Philosophy was written during a two-year period near the end of her life. What could be deciphered of her handwriting in the notebook was published posthumously by van Helmont. She was only credited in the preface as "a certain English Countess." More and van Helmont translated the work into Latin. The only English version remaining is a retranslation.

It is very likely that the text influenced the philosopher Gottfried Wilhelm Leibniz, who borrowed from her the concept of "monad," which is the basis of his most famous work, *The Monadology*. He admitted the similarities between their views, and he may have received a copy of her work from van Helmont, or the two may have discussed the ideas presented in Finch's text. It is possible, however, that the similarities between the two philosophers' views were simply the result of the type of ideas in general that were being discussed among intellectuals at the time.

SOURCES

Atherton, Margaret. *Women Philosophers of the Early Modern Period*. Indianapolis, IN: Hackett, 1994.

Kersey, Ethel M. *Women Philosophers: a Bio-critical Source Book*. NY: Greenwood Press, 1989.

Waithe, Mary Ellen, ed. *A History of Women Philosophers, vol. 3*. Boston, MA: Martinus Nijhoff, 1987.

SUGGESTED READING:

Hutton, Sarah, revised ed. Marjorie Hope Nicholson, ed. *The Conway Letters: The Correspondence of Anne, Viscountess Conway, Henry More, and their friends, 1642–1684*. NY: Oxford University Press, 1992.

Catherine Hundleby, M.A.
Philosophy, University of Guelph,
Guelph, Ontario, Canada

Finch, Anne (1661–1720)

Countess of Winchelsea and English poet. Born Anne Kingsmill at Sydmonton, in Hampshire, England, in April 1661; died at her home on Cleveland Row on April 5, 1720; daughter of Sir William and Anne (Haslewood) Kingsmill (d. 1664); married Heneage Finch (c. 1647–1719, became the 4th earl of Winchelsea, 1712, 1st earl of Aylesford, 1714), on May 15, 1684.

According to biographer **Barbara Mc-Govern**, Anne Finch, countess of Winchelsea, was "arguably, the best woman poet England produced before the 19th century." Five months after her birth as Anne Kingsmill, her father died and her mother remarried a younger man named Thomas Ogle. Three years later, her mother died. After a protracted estate and custody battle, the young Kingsmill was taken from her stepfather and put in the hands of guardians. Anne and her sister **Bridget Kingsmill** spent the next seven years with their paternal grandmother, Lady Kingsmill.

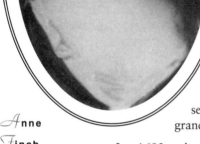

Anne Finch (1661–1720)

In 1683, along with ***Anne Killigrew**, **Catharine Fraser**, ***Frances Walsingham**, **Catharine Walters**, and ***Catharine Sedley**, Anne took up residence in the Stuart court at St. James's Palace as maid of honor to ***Mary of Modena**, second wife of James, duke of York (who would later be crowned James II). While there, Anne became devoted to the future queen, who was only three years her senior, and loyal to the Stuart monarchy; she also met and married Heneage Finch, groom of the bedchamber to the duke of York and future earl of Winchelsea, when she was 23. After her marriage, she resigned her court position, though her husband retained his.

For the first four years of their marriage all was bliss, and Finch, who had been dabbling with poetry for years, began to take up writing more seriously. But three years after James II assumed the throne in 1685, he fled to France (1688). Finch and her husband—both Anglicans and committed Royalists caught in the religious crossfire between James II and William of Orange—were exiled from court and sought refuge with friends and relatives. Fortunately, as they had no means of support, the 3rd earl of Winchelsea took them in at the family estate, Eastwell, in Kent.

After the death of the 3rd earl, the couple established a literary circle at this estate in Eastwell Park. Anne Finch's literary friendships included ***Katharine Philips**, ***Aphra Behn**, Alexander Pope, and Nicholas Rowe; she also had the affection and encouragement of Jonathan Swift.

Known to employ the "natural world in a distinctive and subtle way in her poetry," Finch is said by **Clare Buck** to link "landscape and state of mind in a way that blends the features of the inner and outer worlds, politics and place." But McGovern maintains that though she is best-known for her nature poetry—abetted by the high esteem with which William Wordsworth held her *A Nocturnal Reverie*—this is an unfortunate disservice. Finch's nature poems, remarks McGovern, are not her best; and they serve to thwart "recognition of the depth, the quality, and the diversity of her work."

It has long been reported that though her husband and friends delighted in her poetry, London society made it a subject of scorn. At the time, women who wrote often met with derision. Historians point to the satire *Three Hours After Marriage* which opened at the Drury Lane in January 1717 (co-authored by John Gay and Alexander Pope), in which Phoebe Clinket enters in an ink-stained dress, pens in her hair, while her maid has a desk strapped on her back in case her mistress should be inspired. The claim that Pope meant the character to be his good friend Finch was false, says McGovern. Rather, the claim was an attempt by an enemy to show that Pope had personally attacked known friends. Pope's biographer George Sherburn reaches a similar conclusion.

Anne Finch printed only one volume of verse in her lifetime, *Miscellany Poems on Several Occasions, Written by a Lady* (1713). Her long Pindaric ode, *The Spleen,* written in 1701, for which she was best known, contained a couplet that was echoed in Pope's *Essay on Man* and in Shelley's *Epipsychidion.*

SOURCES:

Buck, Clare, ed. *The Bloomsbury Guide to Women's Literature.* NY: Prentice Hall, 1992.

Goreau, Angeline. *The Whole Duty of a Woman: Female Writers in Seventeenth-Century England.* NY: Dial Press, 1984.

McGovern, Barbara. *Anne Finch and Her Poetry: A Critical Biography.* Athens, GA: University of Georgia Press, 1992.

Fine, Perle (1908–1988)

American abstract artist. Born in 1908; died in New York in 1988; studied at the Art Students League with Kimon Nicoläides and with Hans Hofmann at his Eighth Street School; married Maurice Berezov (an abstract artist).

Perle Fine knew as a child that she wanted to be an artist. As a teenager, she left her parents' dairy farm outside Boston and enrolled in New York's Art Students League, where she studied drawing with Kimon Nicoläides and met her future husband, abstract painter Maurice Berezov. After their marriage, Fine continued to use her maiden name to maintain her own artistic identity. In the 1930s, she studied with the abstract expressionist Hans Hofmann, although she did not agree entirely with his artistic philosophy. "Hofmann kept relating abstraction to the figure and to nature," she later said, "and I knew there was much more." She finally found a home at the Guggenheim Museum, as the recipient of a foundation grant. In return for enough money to pay for materials, she was required to bring in work once a month, which *Hilla Rebay, the foundation's director, showed to Solomon Guggenheim. One of her paintings was bought by Guggenheim architect Frank Lloyd Wright, although he reportedly disliked all painting.

Fine had her first solo exhibition at the Willard Gallery in 1945, followed by subsequent shows at the Nierendorf Gallery in 1946 and 1947. The paintings of this period were a balance of geometric curves and angles, solid forms, and connecting lines. One painting, *Polyphonic*, was described as looking like "an immobilized Calder mobile . . . using bright clear hues and a wiry black line." During the 1940s, Fine also joined the American Abstract artists, a group of primarily abstractionists devoted to the tradition of cubism. When she proposed membership for her friend Jackson Pollock (whom she met at the Guggenheim where he was working as a guard), the group objected, finding his work "impure." It was not until the Abstract Expressionists movement gained momentum a decade later that Fine, along with artists like Pollock and Willem de Kooning, found their niche.

In 1954, Fine moved from her large New York studio to the Springs, an art colony near East Hampton, Long Island. That year, she was also hired as an associate professor of art by Hofstra University, where she remained for 12 years. Fine, who had always considered herself something of a hermit, found teaching both a liberating and exhausting experience: "When I began to teach I discovered to my surprise that I enjoyed people. I took teaching very seriously but found that it drained most of my energy. Teaching is a creative commitment."

During a period of illness in the late 1960s, Fine experienced a change in style. Unable to work on large canvases, she began a series of collages, combining wood pieces with painted grids. These evolved into gridlike paintings which she called her "Accordment" series. Fine gave these works whimsical names like *The Dawn's Wind, A Woven Warmth,* and *Gently Cascading.* Her method is described by **Charlotte Rubinstein** in *American Women Artists*: "Using very minimal means (somewhat in the manner of *Agnes Martin)—vertical lines of color balanced against horizontal ones[—]she plays colors against one another, exploring the effects of color interrelationships on the overall field. Her paintings emit a kind of subtle inner luminosity." Perle Fine continued to paint at her studio on East Hampton into her late 70s. The artist died in 1988, at age 80.

SOURCES:

Bailey, Brooke. *The Remarkable Lives of 100 Women Artists.* Holbrook, MA; Bob Adams, 1994.

Rubinstein, Charlotte Streifer. *American Women Artists.* Boston, MA: G.K. Hall, 1982.

SUGGESTED READING:

Deichter, David. *Perle Fine: Major Works, 1954–1978 (A Selection of Drawings, Paintings and Collages).* East Hampton, NY: Guild Hall of East Hampton, 1978 (an exhibition catalog).

Barbara Morgan,
Melrose, Massachusetts

Fine, Vivian (1913—)

*American composer. Born in Chicago, Illinois, on September 28, 1913; eldest of three daughters of Rose (Finder) Fine and David Fine (both Russian-Jewish immigrants); studied with Djane Lavoie-Herz, Abby Whiteside, *Ruth Crawford, and Roger Sessions; married Benjamin Karp, in 1935; children: Margaret (Peggy) Karp; Nina Karp.*

*Began her career as an accompanist for dancers and then composed for ballet; wrote dance scores for Martha Graham, *Hanya Holm, and Charles Weidman; received the American Academy-National Institute of Arts and Letters Award (1979); served as musical director of the Bethsabee de Rothschild Foundation (1955–61); in addition to works for ballet and dance, composed many pieces for orchestra, chamber and choral groups.*

Vivian Fine was born in Chicago, Illinois, on September 28, 1913, the eldest of three daughters of Russian-Jewish immigrants **Rose Finder Fine** and David Fine. Influenced by her mother, Vivian Fine began her career on piano. An excellent pianist, she became the accompanist for *Doris Humphrey** and Charles Weidman at dance recitals and gradually began composing for the dance. She wrote her first large ballet, *The Race*

Vivian Fine

Fingerin, Agnes (d. 1515)

German textile merchant. Born in Gorlitz, Germany; died in 1515 in Gorlitz; married (husband died in 1465).

The child of a wealthy weaver, Agnes Fingerin was a textile merchant and an important townswoman in the German town of Gorlitz. Though she ran her own business even while she was married for a short time, the years after her husband's death in 1465 saw her greatest prosperity. Fingerin outlived her husband by 50 years, and during her widowhood she was one of the wealthiest textile merchants in the town. In addition to buying and selling in Gorlitz, like many merchants Fingerin did a fair amount of traveling, both for business and pleasure. After she had established her fortune, she even journeyed to Jerusalem on a pilgrimage.

However, most of the time she remained in Gorlitz, importing raw wool and selling it to cloth manufacturers. Although she was a shrewd manager of her money, out of a sense of piety she also felt a strong obligation to help those less fortunate. Toward this end, she gave generously to local hospitals and to other charitable causes. Fingerin used her considerable wealth to set up a permanent endowment to aid the needy by distributing bread; it remained active for hundreds of years, and its founder was remembered by the endowment's name, the *Agnetenbrot* (Agnes-bread).

Laura York,
Riverside, California

Fini, Leonor (1908–1996)

Italian-Argentinean artist. Born in Buenos Aires, Argentina, in 1908; died of pneumonia in Paris, France, on January 18, 1996; only child of an Argentine father and an Italian mother.

Selected paintings: Sphinx philagria *(1945);* Sphinx Regina *(1946);* The Angel of Anatomy *(1949);* The Two Skulls *(1950);* The Emerging Ones *(1958);* Capital Punishment *(1960);* Sfinge la Morte *(1973);* The Lesson on Botany *(1974).*

By the time of her death, Leonor Fini had achieved cult status in Paris art and theater circles. She was born in Buenos Aires, Argentina, in 1908, the only child of an Argentine father and an Italian mother who separated shortly after her birth. Fini spent her childhood with her mother in Trieste, Italy, although her father sought custody of her from time to time, and on one occasion supposedly hired thugs to kidnap her. Interested in painting from childhood, she was largely

of Life, in 1937 for Humphrey. This humorous, popular ballet was based on the drawings and story by James Thurber. The composer, Wallingford Riegger, suggested that Fine rescore *The Race of Life* as a concert number. Fine continued her work in the field of dance and in 1960 was commissioned by *Martha Graham to write *Alcestis.* Graham choreographed the work which received rave reviews. Although Fine once remarked, "I prefer a skilled conductor to direct my music because this conductor has the necessary training at realizing the intention of the composer," she began to conduct her own compositions. Speaking of the obstacles faced by women in composition, Fine noted, "I don't find any offensive attitudes toward myself as a composer but I do find a great many sexist attitudes toward women in general. I certainly can't point to myself as one who has suffered—I have a fine career." Several recordings have been made of Fine's work which continues to be widely performed.

John Haag,
Athens, Georgia

self-taught. In a 1954 interview, she described her visits to the local morgue, where she drew the cadavers, and remarked that her quasi-religious contemplation of the corpses stayed on in her spiritual life. In 1925, she went to Milan, where she was influenced by artists Carlo Carrà, Achille Funi, and Arturo Tosi. Later in Paris, she became friendly with the painters of the burgeoning Surrealist movement, including *Leonora Carrington, Salvador Dali, and Max Ernst. Although Fini occasionally exhibited with the group, she never completely aligned herself with their goals or the pronouncements of their leader André Breton. However, as **Nancy Heller** notes in *Women Artists,* her paintings often contain elements related to the movement: "Fini's realistic treatment of a strange world and the importance she attached to unconscious vision, whether it involves cruelty, eroticism, the fantastic, or bizarre metamorphoses, are compatible with Surrealism."

During World War II, Fini lived in Monaco, and then in Rome with artist Stanislau Lepri. In 1947, she returned to Paris, where in addition to painting she designed sets and costumes for the theater, opera, and films and illustrated books. Her painting continued to evolve, and her female form, with its shaved head and rigid body, became a trademark. Death, which Fini equated with stillness, immobility, and the ideal, was also a recurring theme. Skeletons and bones often appeared in her work, particularly during the decade following World War II. Sometimes presented as part of living beings (*The Emerging Ones* [1958] and *Sfinge la Morte* [1973]), they served as representations of not only death but metamorphosis, the change to something "other."

Leonor Fini cultivated a personal style that was as unique as her work. Beautiful and dramatic, she favored long skirts, thick dark eyeliner, large jewelry, and hats. She was said to take a number of cats wherever she went, and by one account delighted in donning masks that transformed her into a feline or birdlike creature. The artist died in Paris at the age of 87.

SOURCES:
Heller, Nancy. *Women Artists.* NY: Abbeville Press, 1987.
Sutherland, Anne, and Linda Nochlin. *Women Artists 1550–1950.* NY: Knopf, 1976.
Uglow, Jennifer S., comp. and ed. *The International Dictionary of Women's Biography.* NY: Continuum, 1985.

Barbara Morgan,
Melrose, Massachusetts

Finley, Martha (1828–1909)

*American author of stories and books for children, in particular the "Elsie Dinsmore" series. Name varia-*tions: (pseudonym) Martha Farquharson. Born Martha Finley on April 26, 1828, in Chillicothe, Ohio; died in Elkton, Maryland, on January 30, 1909; daughter of James Brown (a doctor) and Maria Theresa (Brown) Finley (a homemaker); educated at private schools in South Bend, Indiana.*

Taught school (1851–53); published first children's stories with Presbyterian Board of Publication (1853); published Elsie Dinsmore *and 27 subsequent "Elsie" books, all under name Martha Farquharson (1867–1905).*

In *All the Happy Endings,* **Helen Waite Papashvily** wrote that, with the exception of Huckleberry Finn, Elsie Dinsmore is probably the best-known character ever to appear in American fiction. If Elsie has been known to millions, her author, Martha Finley, remains a shadowy character. Possibly because many members of her family criticized fiction writing as a frivolous pursuit, Finley was something of a recluse during much of her adult life. Despite her family's objections, however, Finley supported herself comfortably with her stories for the Presbyterian Board of Publication and her 28 books in the Elsie series, publishing a new volume every year or two between 1867 and 1905. Like many other poor but genteel women of the late 19th century, Finley found her livelihood in the market for sentimental and children's fiction.

Martha Finley was born into a middle-class, staunchly Presbyterian family. Her parents were first cousins, of Scotch-Irish descent, who claimed two eminent ancestors. Her paternal grandfather, Samuel Finley, had a distinguished military career in the Revolutionary War and the War of 1812. Her great-uncle, also called Samuel Finley, had served as president of Princeton Theological Seminary. Both of these connections emerge in the Elsie books, as the characters read endlessly about the military exploits of the Revolutionary era and as the male characters who go to college inevitably attend Princeton.

When Martha was eight, her family moved to South

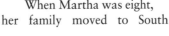

Martha Finley

Elsie Dinsmore, created by Martha Finley.

It is hard to imagine her relatives being offended by the substance of her work, as her early publications included such titles as *Ella Clinton; or "By Their Fruits Ye Shall Know Them," Clouds and Sunshine; or the Faith Brightened Pathway,* and *Elton, the Little Boy Who Loved Jesus.* During her lifetime, Finley would produce nearly 100 didactic books for children, such as the heavy handed "Do Good Library" published in 1868, and featuring, among others, *Anna Hand, the Meddlesome Girl; Grandma Foster's Sunbeam; Little Patience; Little Helper; Little Dick Positive; Loitering Linus; Milly, the Little Girl who Tried to Help Others;* and *Stupid Sally, the Poor House Girl.*

Martha Finley had suffered a serious back injury in the early 1860s. For a while, she was unable to work and had to depend on relatives for support. Praying for a miracle, Finley developed the character and the story line for *Elsie Dinsmore,* which she offered to the Dodd Publishing Company in 1867. The publishers decided to divide the book into two, *Elsie Dinsmore* (1867) and *Elsie's Holidays at Roselands* (1868). The decision to make two volumes out of one accounts for the fact that Elsie's redemption of her father—the central fact of the entire series—is fully accomplished in the second rather than the first book.

Although *Elsie Dinsmore* was the most widely read of the series, it really only introduced the major characters and set the stage for further adventures. As the story begins, the heroine is a motherless child of eight, living with her absent father's family on their plantation somewhere "in the South." The year must be approximately 1845. Although a good and beautiful Christian child, Elsie is harassed or ignored by everyone in the house except her faithful mammy, Chloe. Her father's return does not improve things, as he too neglects his loving daughter except to command or rebuke her. The climax of the story occurs when Horace, Elsie's father's orders her to play a secular song on the piano on the Sabbath. When Elsie's conscience compels her to refuse, he commands the child to remain on the piano stool until she obeys. It is only after Elsie faints and hits her head that Horace realizes his unreasonableness, although he still does not accept Elsie's strict notions of morality. Father and daughter are happy and loving as the book ends, but much unfinished business remains.

The second volume, *Elsie's Holidays at Roselands,* provides the indispensable chapter of the story. If Finley had shown any sense of

Bend, Indiana, where she attended private schools and apparently progressed far enough in her education to be able to teach school in Indiana (1851–53) and Pennsylvania (1853). Sources disagree about why Finley left home at the age of 25. Some say she moved East due to the death of both parents. Papashvily claims that Martha left Indiana after her mother died and her father remarried and started a new family. The latter version seems reasonable, as Finley definitely had a half-brother Charles to whom she left most of her considerable estate.

Martha Finley attempted to supplement her teacher's earnings by writing for the Presbyterian Publication Board. She wrote Sunday school stories and pamphlets which at first she published anonymously and later under the pseudonym, Martha Farquharson (her ancestral name, the Gaelic form of Finley). The use of the pseudonym seems to have been due to her family's objections to her writing. Whether they objected to writing as a profession for everyone or only as a profession for women is not apparent.

humor, the title might be considered ironic, as about half the book is taken up with Elsie's punishment when she refuses to obey her father's command to read a novel on the Sabbath. He undertakes a series of increasingly harsh measures to force her compliance—beginning with isolation from his company and culminating with the threat to dispatch Elsie to a convent school. The latter possibility drives Elsie to a complete physical and mental breakdown, verging on death. Seeing the results of his immovable attitude, Horace repents and becomes a fervent Christian. Elsie miraculously recovers, and father and daughter go on to enjoy a communion of spirit and what Finley apparently saw as an idyllic relationship. It is in *Elsie's Holidays* that the heroine reaches the high point of her redemptive role. Through her undeserved suffering, her father is saved.

With Horace Dinsmore's soul safely accounted for, Martha Finley devotes the next five volumes to Elsie's coming of age, courtship (including a narrow escape from a fortune-hunting scoundrel), marriage to her father's contemporary and best friend, Edward Travilla, the birth of eight children (each of whom seems to arrive as a surprise to all concerned), and Travilla's death. During those years, the Civil War occurred, but except for the deaths of several minor characters, it causes little change in the extremely affluent lives of Elsie's family.

After Elsie becomes a widow, the plots deteriorate further. Her daughter Violet marries a Captain Levis Raymond who assumes Mr. Dinsmore's role as wise father. The later volumes are almost totally didactic, consisting of lengthy lectures, attributed to Captain Raymond or Grandma Elsie, dealing with a bellicose version of American history or with Biblical texts.

Finley prefaced each of the earlier volumes in the Elsie series with a demurrer—each book, she asserted, was written in response to public demand, but it would end the series. The public must have continued to demand, however, for Finley continued to turn out Elsies, and after *Elsie's Widowhood,* she ceased to apologize for their publication.

At one level, Elsie appeared to embody the stereotyped female virtues—chastity, filial obedience, a world encompassed by her extended family, and an intense preoccupation with evangelical Christianity. Elsie seemed at first glance to be submissive in the extreme. Actually, she exerted great power over her family and friends through her virtuous example and preaching. In

the patriarchal setting of the stories, Elsie, a female Christ figure, was the instrument of salvation for dozens of characters. The message that women could exert a profound influence for good in the domestic sphere, and through their converts, in the wider world, is not far below the surface of the Elsie books.

> *Elsie spent her time alone with her Bible and her God, and there she found that sweet peace and joy which the world can neither give nor take away; and thus she gathered strength to bear her troubles and crosses with heavenly meekness and patience.*
> —**Martha Finley**

The series is reputed to have been read by 25 million readers and to have earned Finley a quarter of a million dollars. A century later, the reasons for its popularity are more elusive. Elsie was a character with a mixed message. Her redemptive powers made her powerful indeed, yet outwardly her behavior was docile. She was said to be "an apt scholar," but she had no formal education. Elsie was "quite capable of earning her own living," but she did no work. Papashvily finds several explanations for Elsie's attraction. She maintains that women envied her life of wealth and luxury, meticulously described by Martha Finley. In a rapidly changing industrial and urbanizing society, the Dinsmore plantations provided an idyllic version of "home." The moral absolutism of the books was echoed in a defense of existing social and economic arrangements. "Showers of gifts fell upon the deserving wellborn—ponies, gold watches, sets of pearls, lengths of real lace, silver spoons, complete wedding outfits—Elsie's generosity never slackened. The poor received soup and a flannel and a Bible," Papashvily notes. It may be the combination of orthodoxy and recognition of women's intangible power that accounts for the success of Elsie Dinsmore.

Some aspects of the books are particularly troublesome to the modern reader. Religious intolerance, racial stereotypes, and dialect date the series. The relationship between Elsie and her father must have seemed peculiar even to an audience in the pre-Freudian age. For example, on her wedding day: "'My darling!' murmured the father in low, half tremulous accents, putting his arm about the slender waist, 'my beautiful darling! How can I give you to another?' and again and again his lips were pressed to hers in long, passionate kisses."

The financial rewards from the Elsie series provided Martha Finley with economic independence and the resources to build a cottage in Elkton, Maryland. There she lived near her favorite half brother, Charles. While creating the Elsie series, Finley wrote other stories and novels, including "Little Books for Little Readers," the "Pewit's Nest" series, and the "Mildred" books (a seven-book spin-off of the Elsies). In addition, she wrote several novels for adults—the "Finley" and the "Honest Jim" series. Even though her work tended to be formula fiction, Finley's output was prodigious. Although all of her books sold well in the United States and England, none approached the popularity of the Elsie series, nor did Finley ever receive the attention of serious critics.

Martha Finley died at home of bronchopneumonia on January 30, 1909. Her will provided some further insights into her private life. Her half-brother Charles inherited most of her estate, but she also provided for a number of female relatives and her longtime maid, **Mary White**. She chose to leave nothing to some family members, apparently those who criticized her career as a writer. Perhaps most surprising, Finley's will revealed that she owned a women's bakery in Chicago.

SOURCES:

Atwell, Mary Welek. "Elsie Dinsmore . . . Haunting the Minds of Millions of Women," in *Women's Studies and the Curriculum*. Edited by Marienne Triplette. Winston-Salem, NC: Salem College, 1983.

Brown, Janet E. *The Saga of Elsie Dinsmore*. University of Buffalo Studies, Vol. 17, no. 3. Buffalo, NY: University of Buffalo, 1945.

Commire, Anne, ed. "Martha Finley," in *Something about the Author*. Vol. 43. Detroit, MI: Gale Research, 1986.

Kindilien, Carlin T. "Martha Finley" in *Notable American Women*. Vol. I. Cambridge, MA: Belknap Press, 1971.

Papashvily, Helen Waite. *All the Happy Endings*. NY: Harper & Brothers, 1956.

COLLECTIONS:

The Children's Literature Research Collection, University of Minnesota, has copies of twenty-six of the Elsie Dinsmore books and six of seven Mildred Keiths.

The Elkton Library, Elkton, Maryland, has a collection relating to Martha Finley and her work.

Mary Welek Atwell,
Associate Professor of Criminal Justice,
Radford University, Radford, Virginia

Finnbogadóttir, Vigdís (1930—)

President of Iceland. Name variations: Vigdis Finnbogadottir. Born on April 15, 1930, in Reykjavik, Iceland; daughter of Finnbogi Rutur (also seen as Ruter) Thorvaldsson (a civil engineer and professor at the University of Iceland) and Sigridur Eriksdóttir (a nurse and chair of the Icelandic Nurses Association

for 36 years); graduated from University of Iceland; attended University of Grenoble and the Sorbonne; married in 1953 (divorced, c. 1962); children: (adopted daughter) Astridur.

Vigdís Finnbogadóttir, who was elected president of Iceland in 1980, was born in 1930, the daughter of Finnbogi Thorvaldsson, a wealthy engineer, and **Sigridur Eriksdóttir**, a nurse. (First names are commonly used in Iceland, since surnames—a combination of the father's first name and the suffix *dóttir* [daughter] or *sson* [son]—are usually lengthy and complex.) Vigdís studied theater history in college before her marriage in 1953. She divorced nine years later and returned to Iceland where she hosted a television series about theater and, from 1972 to 1980, directed the Reykjavik Theatre Company. In 1974, she became interested in politics, when she helped organize a petition campaign for the removal of the U.S. naval base at Keflavik. Her run for the presidency was the result of a dare, and Vigdís attributed her victory to her country's growing awareness of women's issues. Reelected in 1984 and 1988, she used the largely ceremonial post to promote Icelandic culture and to better the status of women.

Firenze, Francesca da (fl. 15th c.)

Florentine artist and nun. Flourished in the 15th century in Florence; never married; no children.

Few artistic works have survived by the miniaturist Francesca da Firenze, and nothing is known of her birth or family. A highly educated nun who flourished as an artist in the scriptorium of a Florentine convent, Francesca represents a strong tradition of religious women who employed their artistic abilities for the benefit of their convents. Her miniature paintings and manuscript illuminations were well known in Florence, and the money generated from their sale helped support her conventual community.

Laura York,
Riverside, California

Firestone, Shulamith (1945—)

Canadian feminist. Born in Ottawa, Canada, in 1945; studied at the Art Institute of Chicago.

Selected writings: The Dialectic of Sex: The Case for Feminist Revolution *(1970); (with Chris Kraus)* Airless Spaces *(1998).*

Shulamith Firestone, who was active as a student in the civil rights and anti-Vietnam War movements, gained prominence in the women's movement through her controversial book, *The Dialectic of Sex: The Case for Feminist Revolution* (1970). During the early 1970s, Firestone also co-founded and was editor of the journals *Notes from the Second Year* and *Redstockings*, and she remained active in the New York feminist movement. In 1998, along with Chris Kraus, she published *Airless Spaces*, a collection of short stories about those who float in and out of institutions. Wrote one reader: "Refusing a career as a professional feminist, Shulamith Firestone found herself in an 'airless space'—since the publication of her first groundbreaking book." Writes **Eileen Myles**: "In her radical insider's tale, [Firestone] informs us repeatedly like lightly pelting rain that all of us are vanishing in a century of institutions [that] take and take until everyone has gone away and there is no one left to shut the door."

First, Ruth (1925–1982)

*White South African journalist, sociologist, and revolutionary activist whose outspoken opposition to the policy of apartheid drew her into political collaboration with Nelson Mandela and eventually led to her murder by letter bomb. Born Heloise Ruth First on May 4, 1925, in the Kensington section of Johannesburg, South Africa; died by letter bomb on August 17, 1982, in her office as director of research at the Center for African Studies, Eduardo Mondlane University in Maputo, Mozambique; daughter of Julius First (a furniture manufacturer) and Matilda First (both radical socialists and Jewish immigrants from the Baltic); attended Jeppe Girls' High School; graduated University of Witwatersrand, B.A., 1946; married Joe Slovo (a Communist defense lawyer and labor organizer), in August 1949; children: **Shawn Slovo** (b. 1950); **Gillian Slovo** (b. 1952); **Robyn Slovo** (b. 1954).*

At the University of Witwatersrand, founded a multiracial student group, joined the Communist Party, was secretary of the Young Communist League and secretary of the Progressive Youth Council (early 1940s); was one of only a handful of whites actively involved in the widespread black miners' strike (1946); exposed slavery-like labor conditions on a potato farm in Bethal, Transvaal, northern part of South Africa, prompting a successful countrywide potato boycott led by the African National Congress (1947); along with husband Joe Slovo, was "named by the government" and placed on a list of dangerous persons which made it illegal for them to be quoted in print (1950); visited China and Soviet Union as a member of the International Union of Students and

the World Federation of Democratic Youth (1954); banned from attending political gatherings (1954); became editor of Fighting Talk, *a radical political and literary journal (1955); along with Nelson Mandela and Walter Sisulu (leaders of the African National Congress) and her husband, was among 156 activists arrested and accused of treason in the mammoth Treason Trial (1956); detained in Marshall Prison (1956); acquitted of treason due to insufficient evidence (1958); banned from all journalistic activities (1960); arrested and held for 117 days in solitary confinement, the first white woman to be detained under the notorious 90-Day Detention Act (1963); with family, including father, went into exile never to return to South Africa (1963); started new career in London, teaching, lecturing, publishing and editing books on politics in southern Africa (1964); named Simon Research Fellow at the University of Manchester (1972–73); was lecturer in sociology of underdevelopment at the University of Durham, Durham, England (1973–79); began collaborative work with the Center* of African Studies, Eduardo Mondlane University, Maputo, Mozambique, directing the Youth Brigades on a research project studying the lives of migrant Mozambican miners who worked in gold and diamond mines in South Africa (1977); named director of research and co-director of Center of African Studies (1979–82); killed by letter bomb in her office at the Center for African Studies (1982).

Selected publications: South West Africa *(Penguin, 1963);* 117 Days: An Account of Confinement and Interrogation under the South African Ninety-Day Detention Law *(NY: Stein and Day, 1965);* The Barrel of a Gun: Political Power in Africa and the Coup d'Etat *(Allen Lane, 1970);* The South African Connection: Western Investment in Apartheid *(Maurice Temple Smith, 1972);* Libya: The Elusive Revolution *(Africana Publishing, 1974); (co-written with Ann Scott)* Olive Schreiner *(Schocken, 1980);* Black Gold: The Mozambican Miner, Proletarian and Peasant *(St. Martin's Press, 1983, published posthumously). Edited publications:* No Easy Walk to Freedom: Articles, Speeches and Trial Addresses of Nelson Mandela *(Basic Books, 1965);* South West Africa: Travesty of Trust *(Deutsch Publishing, 1967). Editor and contributor to journals and newspapers published in South Africa:* The Guardian, The Clarion, New Age, Spark, Fighting Talk; *contributor to journals published outside South Africa:* Ramparts, New Statesman, International Affairs, *and others.*

*R*uth
*F*irst

Ruth First spent 117 days in solitary confinement in 1963, the first white woman arrested and detained under the Republic of South Africa's notorious 90-Day Detention Act. "For the first 56 days of my detention in solitary," she wrote, "I changed from a mainly vertical to a mainly horizontal creature. A black iron bedstead became my world. . . . Without the naked electric bulb burning, a single yellow eye, in the center of the ceiling, the cell would have been totally black. . . . It was too cold to sit, so I lay extended on the bed, trying to measure the hours, the days and the weeks, yet pretending to myself that I was not." The sweep of First's life is intimately entwined with the major political movement of 20th-century South Africa—the struggle between the African National Congress (ANC) fighting for the self-determination of black South Africans and the apartheid legislation put in place by the Afrikaner National Party to disenfranchise blacks and protect white supremacy.

Born in 1925 in Johannesburg, South Africa, the daughter of radical-socialist Jewish immigrants from the Baltic, Ruth First died in

1982, the victim of a letter bomb sent to her office at Eduardo Mondlane University in Maputo, Mozambique, by the South African Bureau of State Security. Eulogized at her funeral by the general secretary of the South African Communist Party, Moses Mabhida, she was remembered as "one of the first citizens of a liberated South Africa." Mzala, another activist, wrote in 1982: "If our people ask what kind of relations the blacks and whites in a future South Africa will have, let them read the story of Ruth First and how she related to us and we to her." Sadly, First did not live to witness her passionate goal, a South Africa liberated from apartheid and governed by Nelson Mandela and the African National Congress. Nevertheless, her life is testimony to the enduring spirit of a Zulu woman's protest song: "*Wathinta abafazi, wathint'imbokodo, uzakufa*" (You have tampered with the women, you have struck a rock, you will be crushed).

Ruth First was introduced to politics at an early age. Her parents were members of the International Socialist League, a Marxist group that broke with the white South African Labour Party over support for World War I; they were also founding members of the South African Communist Party in 1921. Ruth attended neighborhood schools, belonged to the Junior Left Book Club, and graduated from Jeppe Girls' High School in Johannesburg, South Africa. At the University of Witwatersrand in Johannesburg, she studied social science (B.A. 1946), was a key figure in the newly created Young Communist League, editor of its newspaper, *Youth for a New South Africa*, and founder of the Federation of Progressive Students whose multiracial character was highly unusual. Writes First in her book, *117 Days:*

> What had influenced me? No one in particular. I had been able to read for myself. I didn't have any one teacher of politics; we students learnt from one another and from what was happening around us. There were Africans going to war carrying *assegais* (spears) and stretchers; there was bitterness that war-time costs of living were obliterating the buying-power of wages, that African trade unions were not recognized, that African strikes were illegal and the strikers prosecuted in mass trials.

Her university years, she noted, were "cluttered with student societies, debates, mock trials, general meetings, and the hundred and one issues of war-time and post-war Johannesburg that returning ex-service students made so alive. On a South African campus, the student issues that matter are national issues."

The African miners' strike of 1946 would be one of those issues. After graduation, First decided against the usual path of employment for a white woman with a university degree. "I turned my back firmly on the social worker's round of poor white families in Fordsburg," she wrote, "questioning them about what they did with their money to justify an application for State-aided butter or margarine." Instead, she landed a position working as a researcher for the social welfare department of the Johannesburg City Council only to discover that the research amounted to compiling mundane statistics on the number of supervisors for white children in white parks. Eventually, she became "bored and disgusted." When the miners' strike broke out in 1946, First immediately quit her job and joined the poverty-stricken migrant workers' effort to win a living minimum wage of ten shillings per day. When the top leadership of the Communist Party and the Mineworkers Union were arrested in conjunction with the strike, First stepped in and ran the party office for one year. She characterized the period of the mine strike as one of tumult:

> The strikers were enclosed in compounds under rule by the army, the mine and state police. A great squad of volunteers of all colors helped them set up strike headquarters in the most unlikely places, and from lodging rooms like the one I shared with a girl-friend, the handles of duplicating machines were turned through the night, while in the early hours before dawn white volunteers drove cars to the vicinity of the mine compounds and African organizers, hiding their city suits and their bundles of strike leaflets under colorful tribal blankets, wormed their way into the compounds.

The strike signaled a turning point in First's life as well as a new period for African political organizations. "The days of petitions and pleading were well and truly over," notes First, "and when the mine strike was over I became a journalist." She covered "the issues that rotted the lives of African people: unceasing police raids and arrests, continuous removal schemes to try and sort white from black according to the precepts of segregation, forced labor on the farms, a daily multitude of persecutions and indignities." She discovered her passion and her mission was "to write the news that no one else had the courage or will to print."

First quickly established herself as a fearless investigative journalist and published one of her most important pieces in 1947 in the radical weekly South African newspaper, *The Guardian* (later named *The Clarion*, then *Advance, New Age,* and *Spark,* due to successive bannings).

Notes historian Tom Lodge: First "initiated a style of campaigning reportage which at that time was unprecedented in South African journalism and which pushed *Guardian* sales into six figures." In collaboration with writer Wolfie Kodesh and photographer-writer Joe Gqabi, First broke the story of slave-labor conditions on potato farms in Bethal, Transvaal, north of Johannesburg. Risking her life, as well as those of her collaborators and informants, she wrote of starvation and death from exhaustion, of whippings, and of long days in the fields—sunup to sundown—bent over picking potatoes. Most important, First documented the sale of black farm labor by city police to rural white landowners. As a result of her text and Gqabi's searing photographs, the African National Congress organized a successful countrywide potato boycott. Historian Shula Marks claims that "the germ of Ruth's later concerns is to be seen in this earlier work: her clear understanding of the exploitative axis of the apartheid state, . . . her identification with the struggles of workers and peasants, her internationalism and the wider knowledge she gained of the problems of development and the transition to socialism." An obituary in *Sechaba* notes that "the Bethal farm labor scandal was more than a news scoop. It was in fact part of the whole two-way exchange between the *Guardian* and the liberation movement" and "was perhaps the most powerful illustration of the symbiosis between her own work and the mass people's movement which characterized all Ruth's best and most memorable activities."

Her work as a journalist and as a revolutionary activist drew the attention of the South African Bureau of State Security. In 1950, along with her husband, the Communist labor organizer Joe Slovo, Ruth First was "named" by the government and placed on a list of dangerous persons. It was now illegal to quote her in print. In 1954, she was "banned," thereafter forbidden to attend any political gathering. Despite this government pressure, First continued to be actively involved in the Communist Party leadership and took on the editorship of *Fighting Talk*, a radical literary political review that sponsored

From the movie A World Apart, *starring Jodhi May (right, and Barbara Hershey as Ruth First.*

a new generation of young black writers and brought together the black intelligentsia and the membership of the African National Congress. She recalled:

> I had been active on our newspapers and in the Congress of Democrats, founded when the African National Congress needed an organization of whites who would support its policies and break the front of solid white reaction ranged against it. I had been abroad to the founding conferences of the World Federation of Democratic Youth and the International Union of Students; I had visited the Soviet Union and China (and Britain, Italy, Yugoslavia, Germany and France) and had written and edited booklets about them.

By 1956, however, 156 anti-apartheid activists, including First, her husband Slovo, and both Nelson Mandela and Walter Sisulu, were charged with treason as a result of their activities with banned political organizations, such as the Communist Party and the African National Congress. Although only 30 people were eventually brought to trial, all were acquitted. Wrote First:

> Up to six months before my detention I had still been in our newspaper office. Over the years I had been served with banning orders that prohibited me from leaving Johannesburg, so that I could take part in no further exposés of forced labor like my work on Bethal; from entering African townships, so that I could no longer personally establish the contacts of African men and women who alerted our office first of all when some new vicious scheme of the police and the administration came to light; from attending meetings, so that others had to take the notes and the photographs; from writing anything for publication, so that I had to sit at my desk with a legal option that sub-editing someone else's copy might just slip past the ban. Working in the midst of these ministerial bans and under the continuous raids and scrutiny of the Security Branch was like going to work each day in a mine field, but we survived, and our editions continued to come out each week. Then finally the bans stopped every . . . printer, and the last one we could find in the country to publish our notoriously outspoken copy, gave us notice that he could no longer take the risk.

Their last publisher, Babla Saloojee, also detained under the 90-Day Detention Act, died after jumping out of a window while being interrogated by the South African Security Police.

Despite the obvious danger for herself and her family, as well as the seeming contradictions of a white, middle-class woman organizing for the emancipation of black male and female workers, First had no choice but to continue her political activism. "My steady involvement in politics seemed to be normal behavior, the only thing to do in South Africa," she explained. As the writer Albie Sachs noted, "South African society was manifestly, even grotesquely, oppressive and everyone had to do everything possible to replace it with something better. . . . She was a person fighting for her own right to live in a just society." First placed "at the disposal of the movement," continued Sachs, "all the accomplishments that her privileged upbringing had given her." Years later, while in prison, she told her interrogators:

> We Whites who embarked on protest politics side by side with Africans, Indians and Coloureds, led a vigorously provocative life. Our consciences were healthy in a society riddled with guilts. Yet as the years went by our small band led a more and more schizophrenic existence. There was the good living that white privilege brought, but simultaneously, complete absorption in revolutionary politics and defiance of all the values of our own racial group. As the struggle grew sharper the privileges of membership in the white group were overwhelmed by the penalties of political participation.

Her daughter, Shawn Slovo, confirmed the effect of this schizophrenic existence in an interview with the *Village Voice*. "We spent long summers by the sea, had private education, horseriding, and Spanish dancing lessons, and all the other privileges middle-class white South African children have, although one of the things my mother said in later years was that, had she and Joe known how the situation would develop, they would have thought twice about having a family." Because Joe Slovo's responsibilities as a lawyer for the Communist Party took him away from their home in Johannesburg for many months at a time, raising the couple's three girls was often left to First alone. Yet despite these difficulties, Slovo wrote in his memoirs, "One thing is clear, the world would be a poorer place if it was not peopled by children whose parents risked nothing in the cause of social justice, for fear of personal loss."

The ultimate challenge to First's professional career as a journalist and political activist and her role as mother to three daughters came in 1963 when she was arrested and held for 117 days in solitary confinement. The first white woman to be detained under South Africa's notorious 90-Day Detention Act, she was suspected of participating in an African National Congress meeting in Rivonia, Johannesburg, to plot a campaign to overthrow the government. Although the state was not able to convict First in the Rivonia trial, in truth she was the only woman in the inner circle of the secret sabotage group, Umkhonto we Sizwe (Spear of the Nation), the armed wing of the African National Congress which later attacked centers of state power such as police stations and army barracks. First never discussed her confinement with her family, though she wrote about it with eloquence and wit in her book. "She didn't talk about it, I think, because she wanted to protect us, and because she wanted us to live as normally as possible," remarked her daughter Shawn. "I think what she went through in the 117 days in prison was such a shock to her—a woman who had never had a spare minute during the day or been without books or writing paper—that she could never properly articulate it." Immediately upon release from her detention, First, her three daughters and her mother, joined her father and her husband in exile, first in Kenya, then in London in 1964. She never returned to South Africa.

In exile in England, First supplemented her investigative journalism with scholarly writing and shifted the focus of her political activism from organizing South African workers to petitioning European companies and governments to initiate economic sanctions against South Africa. In addition to many free-lance articles on the wars of liberation in Angola and Mozambique, she organized an international conference on South West Africa (now Namibia), edited Nelson Mandela's speeches, assisted Govan Mbeki with his book *The Peasant's Revolt*, and wrote a short book on Libya. In addition, her 1970 book, *The Barrel of a Gun*, was a passionate critique of despotic African rulers and explored the connections between imperialism, colonialism, and Africa's continuing underdevelopment. Shula Marks writes, "At a time when criticism of Africa's ruling elite was still muted on the left, this took the courage, intellectual integrity and independence of mind that characterized Ruth's approach to politics both within southern Africa and more widely." She was appointed lecturer in sociology of underdevelopment at the University of Durham from 1973 to 1979. In 1977, First began collaborative work with the Center of African Studies, at Eduardo Mondlane University in Mozambique, on a research project studying the lives of migrant Mozambican miners who worked in gold and diamond mines in South Africa. This produced over 1,000 interviews and resulted in the book, *Black Gold*, published posthumously in 1983.

At the same time, in collaboration with **Ann Scott**, First wrote one of the finest biographies to date of the South African writer, ***Olive Schreiner**, published in 1980. Marks suggests that First was attracted to the biography because both Schreiner and First "shared the isolation of exile, as well as the contradictions of personal and public lives." The book captures the full "paradox of Schreiner's achievements as a writer and radical as well as her personal suffering and failure, suggesting the integration in Ruth's own life of her socialism and feminism." Daughter Shawn's comments also reveal a new level of integration of First's personal and public lives in the late 1970s up to her death in 1982. "A couple of years before she was killed, we were beginning to talk about the past and forge a new kind of relationship. . . . For the first time—and this is something we both felt—we were each making efforts to stabilize the relationship, to confront and talk about the past, about the anger, about the guilt."

First's conclusion in her autobiography *117 Days*, describing her feelings about returning home after her long detention, proved strangely prophetic: "When they left me in my own house at last I was convinced that it was not the end, that they would come again." On August 17, 1982, they came again. The letter bomb, widely believed to be the work of the South African Bureau of State Security, was addressed to Ruth First at her office as director of research at the Center for African Studies at Eduardo Mondlane University. First was killed in the explosion, while the center's director Aquino de Braganca, lecturer **Bridget O'Laughlin**, and visiting ANC activist Pallo Jordan were injured. President Samora Machel and other political figures spoke to the more than 2,000 mourners at First's funeral in Mozambique. In London, more than 600 heard tributes to her life.

SOURCES:

Contemporary Authors. New Revision Series. Vol. 10. Detroit, MI: Gale Research, p. 169.

Dougherty, Margot, and Andrew Harvey. "A World Apart," in *People Weekly*. Vol. 30, no. 7. August 15, 1988, pp. 94–95.

First, Ruth. *117 Days: An Account of Confinement and Interrogation under the South African Ninety-Day Detention Law* (foreword by Albie Sachs, afterward by Tom Lodge). NY: Monthly Review Press, 1989.

Fuller, Graham. "White Woman's Burden," in *Village Voice*. Vol. 33, no. 23. June 7, 1988, pp. 59–60.

Kodesh, Wolfie. "Ruth First and New Age," in *Sechaba*. October 1982, pp. 29–32.

Marks, Shula. "Ruth First: A Tribute," in *Journal of Southern African Studies*. Vol. 10, no. 1. October 1983, pp. 123–128.

Mzala. "A Tribute to Comrade Ruth First: Why We Are With the Communists," in *The African Communist*. Vol. 93, 1983, pp 66–73.

Sechaba (obituary). October 1982, pp. 24–29.

Times (London, obituary). August 19, 1982.

SUGGESTED READING:

Bernstein, Hilda. *The World That Was Ours.* London: Heinemann, 1967.

Brown, Alasdair. *A World Apart: Film Study Guide.* London: BDAF, 1988.

Lazar, Carol (photographs by Peter Magubane). *Women of South Africa: Their Fight for Freedom.* Boston: Bulfinch Press, 1993.

Lazerson, Joshua. *Against the Tide: Whites in the Struggle Against Apartheid.* Boulder, CO: Westview Press, 1994.

Pinnock, Don. *They Fought for Freedom: Ruth First.* Cape Town, South Africa: Maskew Miller Longman, 1995.

Slovo, Gillian. *Every Secret Thing: My Family, My Country.* Boston, MA: Little, Brown, 1997.

————. *Ties of Blood.* NY: Morrow Press, 1990.

Slovo, Joe. *Slovo: The Unfinished Autobiography* (introduction by Helena Dolny). London: Hodder & Stoughton, 1996.

Slovo, Shawn. *A World Apart* (film script and diary). London: Faber and Faber, 1988.

Walker, Cherryl. *Women and Resistance in South Africa.* London: Onyx Press, 1982.

COLLECTIONS:

Correspondence, papers and memorabilia located in the Institute for Commonwealth Studies, University of London, London, England.

Colloquium on Ruth First held at the University of the Western Cape in Bellville, South Africa, in the early 1990s, papers available from The Mayibuye Center, UWC. Papers and other archival materials available from The Mayibuye Center, Institute for Historical Research, UWC.

RELATED MEDIA:

A World Apart (114 min.), starring **Barbara Hershey**, directed by Chris Menges, screenplay by Shawn Slovo, produced by Working Title, 1988 (special Jury Prize and Prize for Best Actress shared by **Jodhi May**, Barbara Hershey and **Linda Mvusi** at Cannes Film Festival, 1988).

"90 Days," BBC teleplay, directed by Jack Gold, based on First's book *117 Days*, in which Ruth First appears as herself.

Kearsley Alison Stewart,
Instructor, Department of Anthropology and
Women's Studies Program, University of Georgia,
Athens, Georgia

Fischer, Annie (1914—)

Hungarian pianist, particularly known for her Beethoven recordings. Born in Budapest, Hungary, on July 5, 1914.

Annie Fisher studied with Ernst von Dohnanyi at the Franz Liszt Conservatory in her native city of Budapest. In 1933, she won first prize in Budapest's International Liszt Competition. Over the years, she has mastered an imposing repertoire, communicating her ideas with impressive sonority and a powerful technique.

Fischer's recordings have usually received high marks, with her Beethoven performances being singled out as readings of extraordinary insight. Her interpretations of Mozart have also been highly rated.

John Haag,
Athens, Georgia

Fischer, Greta (1909–1988)

Child welfare worker with the Special Child Division of the UN Relief and Rehabilitation Agency who provided care for hundreds of orphaned and displaced children following World War II. Born Greta Fischerova in 1909 in Budisov, Czechoslovakia; died in Jerusalem, Israel, on September 28, 1988; youngest of six children of Leopold (a veterinarian) and Ida (Mayer) Fischerova; trained as a kindergarten teacher in the 1920s; graduated McGill School of Social Work in 1955; never married; no children.

Fled from Czechoslovakia (1939); first worked as a nanny in London, England, then with Anna Freud in the Wartime Hampstead Nursery; joined UNRRA Team 182 (1945) and was sent to Germany to establish an international children's center; served as chief child welfare officer at Kloster Indersdorf in Germany (1945–47); social worker for the Canadian War Orphans Project, Jewish Family and Children's Welfare Bureau in Montreal (1948–53); worked as a social worker in the autistic child program, Montreal Children's Hospital (1956–59); was a child resettlement worker for the American Joint Distribution Committee in Morocco and Israel (1960–62); served as social worker for the thalidomide children's program at Montreal's St. Justine's Children's Hospital (1963–67); established a department of social service at Hadassah Hospital in Israel (1970–80); organized a day center and home-care program for the elderly in Jerusalem (1981–88).

Smoke was still curling from the ruins of a vanquished Germany when Greta Fischer arrived in July 1945. Roads were clogged with barefoot, hungry refugees and freed prisoners of concentration camps. Dressed in khaki battle dress and driving an army lorry, Fischer was indistinguishable from the American soldiers, whose tracks she followed, except for the white UNRRA (United Nations Relief and Rehabilitation Agency) letters embossed on the scarlet flashes stitched on her shoulder and cap. Barely six miles away from where she finally parked her truck, near the walls of an abandoned monastery, the stench of the crematoriums still hung over the death camp of Dachau.

Fischer and her team of seven multilingual child welfare specialists had arrived in Bavaria to deal with a new kind of debris of modern war—"unattached or unaccompanied or stolen and lost children." No one could agree on a single word to name a condition so bizarre, and no one knew how many children there were. All that was known with certainty was that there were thousands of non-German children lost in the chaos.

This was the first time in history that the nations of the world had agreed to pool their resources to rescue and aid all the victims of aggression. Though far from being a high official in the vast enterprise that was UNRRA, Fischer knew that on its success depended not only countless lives but the future of international cooperation as an instrument of peace: it was a test of whether the world could cooperate in saving and rebuilding lives as well as it had in killing.

It was astonishing to see what a miracle could be worked for children orphaned by the Holocaust when the right thing was done.
—Greta Fischer

In the larger context of the history of the Second World War and its aftermath, the work of Fischer and her colleagues in establishing an international center for the recovery of children goes almost unnoticed. The grandiose language of victories and defeats in combat has little vocabulary to describe the battles waged against despair in the warmth of a kitchen where hungry children were fed, or the strategizing necessary to create dormitories where a comforting hand subdued the terror of recently lived nightmares. Greta Fischer's victories were small but profound ones, registered in her influence on the desperate young lives she touched. In her later years, she became well known for gently deflecting people who spoke of her as a heroine, often wondering aloud, "What is heroism?" and then answering, "Nothing more than the struggle to endure and overcome the circumstances that make us who we are. I happened to have lived in an unfortunate period of history."

Like the musician born to make music, or the artist to paint, Greta Fischer recognized at an early age that her vocation lay with caring for children, and she trained to become a kindergarten teacher. Born in Budisov, Czechoslovakia, in 1909, the youngest of six children, she managed to escape when the Germans overran Czechoslovakia in 1938. Fischer was among the fortunate few who were permitted to enter England where she found a position as a nanny, the only work then allowed women refugees. In London, her talent for working with children was quickly noticed, and she was recommended to *Anna Freud and invited to join her staff. At that time, Freud was establishing her wartime nurseries, the settings on which she based her ground-breaking studies in child psychology. These studies later became the foundations of the modern child-development movement.

The experience of working with Anna Freud and the high regard she earned during those years led to Fischer's assignment with the Special Child Division of UNRRA and to her subsequent posting to Bavaria. Locating themselves near Munich in order to have easy access to basic supplies from the American military headquarters there, Fischer and her co-workers of Team 182 lost no time in searching for a building to convert into a center for the care of children. The only suitable structure they could find was the abandoned 19th-century monastery of Kloster Indersdorf. The building was filthy and looked, wrote a regional officer, as "though many rooms were tossed up in a blanket and allowed to settle"; but at least it was solid, and it certainly had room for the hundreds of children expected to show up. Still legible over its front door was the motto placed there by the monastery's founding order of St. Augustine monks—*Liebe ist staerker als der Tod* (Love is stronger than death).

Within a short time, the kitchen was repaired, the larger rooms scrubbed and turned into dormitories, the smaller ones into classrooms. The graceful spire of the Kloster, rising high above the village and visible from a great distance, soon became known throughout Europe as a beacon of safety to orphaned and displaced children.

While most of Team 182 was billeted in the village, Fischer (officially a child welfare officer responsible for programming) lived in the Kloster. Many nights were spent trying to snatch a couple of hours sleep while looking after 25 to 30 babies demanding to be fed and comforted. It also meant that she was frequently the first member of the team that the new children would meet. The faintest drumming of small fists on the monastery's ancient door, even in the dead of night, would bring Fischer running from her bed, down the winding stairs and along the drafty corridor to the entrance. Pushing open the heavy door, she might find a group of young teenagers shivering in its shadow as a car or truck drove away; occasionally the darkness would reveal a single, lonely child looking up at her with frightened eyes.

The children who arrived at the Kloster were either brought there by military personnel or found their way on their own. Many had been snatched from their families, and sometimes from schools, on the pretext of being taken on a holiday. Brought to Germany from the occupied countries of France, Norway, Sweden, Yugoslavia, Hungary, and Poland, they were then handed over to German homes and institutions or given to farmers to be indoctrinated as Germans. Others were the sons and daughters of forced laborers who were not permitted to keep their families with them as they toiled in German factories and fields. Some were believed to be the illegitimate offspring of Nazi officers. There were also a number of Jewish children; some had survived the war in hiding, while others had been liberated from concentration and labor camps.

As the only center devoted entirely to the rescue and care of children, Kloster Indersdorf might be home at any one time to 300–350 Jewish, Catholic, and Protestant children of 22 different nationalities, covering an age span from birth to the late teens. Once the absolute basics of shelter and food had been provided, it became urgent to help the older children tell their stories—stories of pain and suffering beyond the scope of a civilized imagination, but which had to be told. Fischer struggled to find the inner resources to try to understand and communicate with these children, whose personal histories were so far removed from the kindergartens and nurseries of her previous experience. In what manual was it explained how a child worker should react to the words of a youngster who had been dragged out of the gas chamber by the hair and flung into the mountain of corpses, who had found the courage and cunning to lay there for a day and a half until it was safe for him to crawl away? Fischer learned to function with just the right amalgam of empathy and numbness. "To cry with the children would not have helped them," she said many years later.

Greta Fischer

Quite apart from its emotional demands, the workload taken on by the team was extremely heavy. An UNRRA memo from December 1945 notes that "the objective of an 8-hour day, with one day off a week has not been achieved . . . rather a burden of responsibility has fallen on the staff out of all proportion to a normal day's work. Staff was obliged to assume something of the role of the martyr." But Fischer's comment on the matter was a laconic, "Being so busy every minute helped to keep us normal." A visiting journalist praised the workers at Kloster Indersdorf: "Here one sees men and women from seven different countries far removed in habits and customs who are working together in harmony with a spirit seldom seen."

Team 182 worked hard to give the children as normal a life as possible, and educational and social programs of surprising variety were improvised under Fischer's responsibility. Douglas Glass, the chief official photographer for UNRRA in Europe wrote: "It is a wonderful sight to see these children eating good food in the refectory. Seeing them so gay it is hard to believe that this is the first kindness they have known since they were seized by the Germans and torn from their homes."

When something was needed for her children there was no bureaucracy too strong to be challenged or flouted by Fischer, and she collected a number of official reprimands for obtaining supplies through improper channels. While ample food supplies were provided by the American military, procuring articles that children require was a constant challenge. The absurdity of requisitioning baby bottles and training potties from the military was always a good source for levity. In later years, Fischer could laugh about escapades such as the "faulty telephone connection" which somehow caused her to hear that there was room for one more child at a time when the Kloster was officially full. Or the time she was threatened with a prison sentence for concealing a baby pig which some children had taken for a pet.

She acquired the ironic nickname "Step-and-Fetch-It" for some of her unorthodox methods of procuring supplies and felt flattered when she was reprimanded for obtaining supplies from the army that it did not have. Once, when fabric was unavailable through official channels, she decided to ignore the strictly enforced prohibition against asking for supplies from the local villagers. Her search led her to a deserted barn that had once belonged to a member of the Nazi Party. In it, she found bales of red Nazi flag fabric. The success of her foraging (and her sewing skills) can be seen today in snapshots of her well-nourished children smiling for the camera, each one dressed in overalls made of red Nazi flag fabric and trimmed with blue-and-white checked material once used as bed linen by camp guards.

An integral part of the team's work was ascertaining the national origin of the children so that they could be returned to their home country. However, since most of the children had been abducted at very young ages and had been living with new names in another language during their most formative years, it required a rare blend of ingenuity and intuition to succeed.

In an interview shortly before she died in 1988, Fischer described a practical example of this in which one of her UNRRA colleagues, despite the protestations of the German "mother," believed a child to be of French origin. In a last effort, the UNRRA worker sang a French Christmas song known to all French children and watched as the child's lips moved unconsciously to the long-forgotten words—the first piece of evidence in what became a solid case.

Fischer and the children expected their stay at Kloster Indersdorf to be short, merely a processing step before moving homeward or to new lands, and for many it was. But there were no homes for the Jewish children to return to, and no new lands wanted them. That was particularly hard during outings organized by the team, for the Jewish children saw in each passing stranger the suspected murderer of their parents and families. Looking back nearly half a century later, Fischer said, "It took the two long years of 1945 to 1947, of pleading, of waiting, of trying to convince the world of the Jewish children's membership in the human race. The world was closed to these children; nobody wanted them. Each nation was fearful that the children would have been so damaged that they could never be assimilated into normal life and would always be a burden on the state."

Finally, early in 1947, a first offer to accept a small group of Jewish children came from France, followed by a similar offer from Sweden. Then a group of 42 was accepted by England. But almost everyone that agreed to welcome an orphan preferred young children, particularly girls of five, but in fact most survivors by that time were aged 15 to 18 and older. In the summer of 1947, persuaded by the Canadian Jewish Congress who accepted full responsibility for their care, the Canadian government granted permission for 1,000 child survivors of the

Holocaust to enter the country. Since the agreement only allowed one small group at a time to enter, it wasn't until January 1949 that Fischer arrived in Montreal accompanying one of the last groups of child survivors to leave Kloster Indersdorf for Canada. On the last leg of the journey, on a train trip from New York to Montreal, they were placed in a locked car with a sign saying "dangerous cargo."

The years were to prove these fears unfounded. With a few exceptions, the child survivors of the Holocaust, despite the fears of governments, were able to establish normal lives wherever they went, with some achieving distinguished careers.

With her arrival in Montreal, Fischer's work was not yet complete. A bureaucratic blunder had sent her children onwards to Toronto while she was assigned work in Montreal. It was a great loss to be separated from them, but nothing could be done to rectify the oversight. Fischer's new assignment with the Canadian war orphans as an employee of the Jewish Family and Children's Welfare Bureau was important and engrossing, but she nonetheless found ways to stay in touch with her charges. "Those remarkable children," as she would say, with an "indescribable rage to live," had triggered her faith in their inner resources to realign their shattered lives. Fischer had found a way to help them become children again.

Forty years later, the walls of her Jerusalem apartment crowded with colorful drawings sent by her young charges, Fischer laughingly confessed that she still remembered the children's shoe sizes. She saw herself as the guardian of precious lives that had been entrusted to her. The fact that these children had somehow managed to survive imbued her with the feeling that she was engaged in a sacred trust and would tolerate no compromises in their care.

When the Canadian War Orphans Project came to an end, Greta Fischer entered the McGill School of Social Work as a 43-year-old student. After graduating, she worked at the Montreal Children's Hospital in one of the first programs in Canada for the study and treatment of autistic children. In 1960, the American Joint Distribution Committee sent her on a special child resettlement project in Morocco and Israel. In 1963, she returned to Canada to join the staff of Montreal's St. Justine's Hospital where a special program was being developed to serve the needs of children born with abbreviated limbs due to their mothers' use of the drug thalidomide.

In the 1970s, Fischer was invited to Israel to establish a Department of Social Service at Hadassah Hospital, where she worked until she reached retirement age in 1984. In her last years, she set up a day center and a home-care program for the elderly in Jerusalem.

SOURCES:

Fischer, Greta. *The Story of Kloster Indersdorf* (an unpublished report), and interviews with Greta Fischer.

Macardle, Dorothy. *Children of Europe: a Study of the Children of Liberated Countries*. London: Victor Gollancz, 1949.

United Nations Archives, NY. UNRRA Archive Records.

SUGGESTED READING:

Eisenberg, Azriel, ed. *The Lost Generation: Children in the Holocaust*. NY: Pilgrim Books, 1982.

Dwork, Deborah. *Children With A Star: Jewish Youth in Nazi Europe*. New Haven, CT: Yale University Press, 1991.

Moskovitz, Sarah. *Love Despite Hate: Child Survivors of the Holocaust and Their Adult Lives*. NY: Schocken Books, 1983.

Fraidie Peritz Martz,
freelance writer, Vancouver, British Columbia, Canada

Fischer, Ruth (1895–1961)

German-born American political commentator and scholar, founding member of the Austrian Communist Party and major personality of the German Communist Party in its formative years, who became a fierce anti-Stalinist and was regarded as one of the leading experts on Communism in the Western world. Name variations: Elfriede Eisler; "Fritzi" Eisler. Born Elfriede Eisler in Leipzig, Germany, on December 11, 1895; died in Paris, France, on March 13, 1961; daughter of Rudolf Eisler (1873–1926, a professor of philosophy) and Ida Maria (Fischer) Eisler; had brothers, Gerhart and Hanns Eisler; married Paul Friedländer; married Gustav Golke; married Edmond Pleuchot; companion to Arkadi Maximovich Maslow (1891–1941, original name Isaac Yefimovich Tshemerinsky); children: (first marriage) Gerhard Friedländer.

One of Central Europe's most militant revolutionary leaders from the end of World War I to the era of the Third Reich in the 1930s, Ruth Fischer was born Elfriede Eisler into a comfortable bourgeois family; her father Rudolf Eisler was a noted professor of philosophy who accepted a professorship at the University of Vienna when his daughter was still an infant. She grew up in Vienna with her parents and two brothers, Gerhart and Hanns. Fischer's environment was rich in intellectual stimulation, and from their earliest years she and her brothers wanted to not only understand the world, but to change it for the better. Still in her teens, Fischer joined the Austrian Social Democratic Party soon after the start of World War I. Dissatisfied with the pro-war policies of the party leadership, she quickly gravitated to the movement's left wing. At the same time, her brothers Gerhart and Hanns also became politically active as opponents of a war they condemned as imperialistic.

By war's end in the autumn of 1918, Fischer had become a convinced revolutionary Marxist who found inspiration in Vladimir Lenin's Bolshevik revolution in Russia. In early November, along with a handful of fellow radicals, she became a founding member of the Austrian Communist Party. Although she was now married to Paul Friedländer and had given birth to a son Gerhart, she was also a student at the University of Vienna and threw herself into revolutionary activities with enthusiasm, editing the women's supplement of the Communist newspaper *Die soziale Revolution*. As a left-wing Communist, Fischer believed that the world proletarian revolution, predicted more than a generation earlier by Karl Marx, was now at hand. But, after an initial phase of violent working-class discontent, the tide of popular militancy was now rapidly ebbing in Vienna, and in September 1919 Fischer decided to move to Berlin to be at the heart of Central Europe's revolutionary ferment. Her brother Gerhart followed her to Berlin the next year.

There, Fischer quickly found herself at the heart of Germany's most radical political environment and adopted the name Ruth and her mother's maiden name, Fischer, as her nom de guerre (*Kampfname*), a name she would bear for the rest of her life. Brashly outspoken, Fischer emerged almost overnight as a major personality in the German Communist Party (KPD), having by 1920 secured a post on the editorial board of the influential ideological journal *Die Internationale*. In 1921, she was elected to the important KPD post of director of the party's organization in Berlin-Brandenburg, the all-important District I of the Communist movement in Germany. Her political collaborator and intimate companion, Ukrainian-born Arkadi Maslow, was also regarded as a rising star in the KPD. Known to Fischer and other intimates as "Issya," Maslow used "Max" as his party name. Born into an assimilated bourgeois Jewish family, he was brought to Germany as a child, where he grew up in Dresden. Maslow could boast of considerable talent both in the areas of mathematics and music. For several years before he decided to devote his life to the cause of world revolution, he had toured Europe as a piano virtuoso.

By early 1923, as leader of the Left Opposition within the KPD, Fischer became a member of the party's Central Committee. Her rapid rise to power was not without controversy, for none other than Lenin himself had criticized Fischer for the ideas contained in her book *Sexualethik und Kommunismus*, a confident manifesto of the absolute nature of personal sexual freedom for both men and women in a future socialist world commonwealth. At heart a bourgeois conservative in his sexual views, Lenin cast scorn on Fischer's notions as being little more than a green light for a reckless reign of promiscuity that could easily distract the working class from its revolutionary agenda.

No less fanatical in her Communist beliefs than was Lenin, Ruth Fischer propagated her revolutionary perspective at meetings as well as in print. An attractive young woman, she was an inspiring orator who could often sway an audience, but when enmeshed in bitter struggles within the KPD executive circles, her uncompromising nature made her many enemies, including such "rightists" as the venerable *Clara Zetkin. The German government also began to take notice of the dynamic revolutionary leader, initiating measures to deport her to Austria. Having already obtained a divorce, Fischer averted expulsion by entering into a marriage of convenience with Gustav Golke, a functionary of the Moscow-dominated Communist International (Comintern), thus becoming a German citizen.

In May 1923, the Comintern placed KPD leadership in the hands of the "rightist" Heinrich Brandler, but the party remained deeply factionalized. Convinced that Germany was on the brink of revolution, Fischer challenged Brandler by initiating a campaign to forge a coalition between KPD leftists and nationalist radicals on the political right, including Adolf Hitler's fledgling National Socialist movement. Simultaneously, she made attempts to create an alliance with left-wing Social Democrats to work toward a German revolution that would destroy both capitalism and the shackles of the Versailles Treaty. Communist-led uprisings in Hamburg and Saxony were quickly suppressed by the authorities.

By the end of 1923, Fischer's grand strategy had failed utterly, ending Lenin's hope of a German revolution. But the political debacle led to her emergence by April 1924 as the undisputed leader of Germany's Communist movement. Since her lover Maslow was in prison at the time, Fischer was now the unchallenged head of the largest and most important Communist Party outside the Soviet Union. Continuing to regard her as a dangerous radical, German authorities issued an arrest warrant for "Elfriede Golke, né Eisler, known as Ruth Fischer." She was prepared to live underground, already having been provided with a false passport under the name of "Liane Bosshardt, teacher." But Fischer was saved from a term of incarceration by being elected to the Reichstag from the second electoral district (Berlin) on the KPD ticket in May 1924. As a parliamentary deputy, she enjoyed a salary, a free railroad pass, and could once again carry on a "legal" existence.

In the course of the speeches she delivered as a Reichstag deputy starting in June 1924, Fischer gave vent to her deep and abiding hatred of bourgeois society and politics. She lived up to her reputation as an unreconstructed Bolshevik, describing Germany's national Parliament as "a comedy theater" and its (non-Communist) members as "capitalist puppets," and she doubtless enraged many of her Reichstag colleagues by declaring, "We Communists are all guilty of high treason." But not all on the left approved of KPD ultra-leftism. The independent leftist journal *Die Weltbühne* (*The World Stage*) noted critically in May 1924 that Communist obstructionism in the Reichstag's sessions, which included KPD deputies blowing horns and beating drums, ultimately were the fault of Fischer, "this volcano of radicalism . . . a will free of all reflection and considered thought."

Although Communism in Germany remained unable to capture the allegiance of the bulk of the working class, most of whom remained loyal to their trade unions and the Social Democrats, Fischer could point to her achievements on the international front. Voted a candidate member of the Executive Committee of the Comintern in July 1924, she now appeared to enjoy the approval of the highest Bolshevik ruling circles in the Kremlin. Not surprisingly, Fischer found herself in prison in November 1924, when the Reichstag was dissolved to allow new elections to be held. But once again she was in luck, being reelected in December to her parliamentary seat by thousands of enthusiastically loyal working-class constituents. As a result, officials grudgingly released Fischer from prison.

Almost from the start, Ruth Fischer's leadership of the German Communist movement was characterized by controversy and bitter struggles. Valiantly, she fought attempts by the Comintern—increasingly under the control of Joseph Stalin—to control the KPD. On her left, a group of dissidents emerged who criticized her leadership as not being radical enough. Fischer was

Ruth Fischer

able to retain her control during the party congress that took place in July 1925, but by November her faction was in disarray and she was removed from her post as party leader. Summoned to Moscow by the Comintern leadership, Fischer soon realized that she was a virtual prisoner of the Stalinists. Her departure from Moscow without Comintern approval led to her denouncement for "a serious breach of discipline." Ominously, she was summarily removed from her high Comintern post.

Few observers of the German radical political scene were surprised when an announcement appeared in the official KPD newspaper *Die Rote Fahne* on August 20, 1926, revealing the expulsion of both Ruth Fischer and Arkadi Maslow. Although Fischer would remain a Reichstag deputy until spring 1928, heading an anti-Stalinist Left Opposition group challenging the KPD, her influence was now vastly reduced. In early 1928, she played a key role in founding the Leninbund, an organization conceived as a last-ditch effort to prevent the total Stalinization of the German Communist movement. Within a year, it became clear that this desperate effort had failed, with the forces of Stalinism celebrating triumph in both the Soviet Union and Germany.

By the middle of 1928, Fischer decided to drop out of political life, although she made an attempt to rejoin the KPD in 1929, when a new party line moved it radically leftwards; her membership application was rejected. Withdrawing completely from politics and needing to earn a living to support her son Gerhard, Fischer found employment as a social worker and teacher in the Berlin working-class district of Prenzlauer Berg. It was here that she observed the sufferings inflicted by the poverty and unemployment of the Great Depression. Fischer and fellow anti-Stalinist Franz Heimann studied the daily lives of working-class families and published the results of their observations in *Deutsche Kinderfibel* (*German Children's Primer*) in early 1933, only a few weeks before the establishment of the Nazi dictatorship. The suffering, including malnutrition, of countless thousands of unemployed Germans was documented in detail in a book that remains a classic study of German society on the eve of the Third Reich.

Although no longer politically active, Fischer remained distinct in the minds of many Nazi leaders who recalled her time of leadership as a "Bolshevik Jewess" within the hated KPD. When Adolf Hitler was appointed chancellor of Germany on January 30, 1933, it was obvious that radicals like Fischer could only look forward to severe treatment in a Nazi state. The February 28 fire that destroyed the Reichstag building, used by the Hitler government to immediately scrap constitutional guarantees and initiate a reign of terror, was the signal for Fischer, Maslow and many other anti-Nazis to flee for their lives. Fischer's apartment was vandalized by a gang of Nazis, and her teenage son Gerhard Friedländer was held as a hostage for several weeks, refusing to divulge his mother's hiding place despite being mistreated by brownshirted Nazi thugs. After his release, Gerhard went to Vienna, where he found temporary refuge with his grandparents. Fischer, determined to find a safe haven for her son, established contact with the Jewish Refugees Committee in London, securing safe passage. Gerhard arrived in London in August 1934 and was able to begin a new life in the United Kingdom where he eventually became a mathematics professor at Cambridge University.

Fischer and Maslow fled to Paris, where many refugees from Nazism hoped to organize an effective movement against Hitlerism. Infuriated because they had not been able to capture her, the Nazi regime stripped Fischer of her German citizenship in August 1933. In order to remain in France, she entered into a marriage of convenience with a French Marxist, Edmond Pleuchot. Both Fischer and Maslow were founding members of the militantly anti-Stalinist splinter organization, Gruppe Internationale. Working with other oppositional Communist groups, Fischer established alliances with the Fourth International of Leon Trotsky. By 1936, ideological and personal differences led Fischer and Maslow to break with the Trotskyites. That same year, she was sentenced to death in absentia by one of Stalin's purge trials.

The start of World War II in September 1939 impressed upon Fischer the urgent necessity of escaping from a European continent controlled by two dictators, Hitler and Stalin, who regarded her as a mortal enemy. After the German conquest of France by Blitzkrieg in late spring 1940, Fischer and Maslow fled for their lives, living briefly in Marseille, then going across the Pyrenees through Spain and Portugal. Arriving in Cuba in late 1940, Fischer and Maslow applied for admittance to the United States, but only she received permission to actually enter the favored land of refuge for anti-Nazi activists. Remaining behind in Cuba, Maslow died there suddenly in November 1941. Although his death certificate specified a heart attack as cause of death, he had in fact been discovered in an unconscious state on a street near his hotel. To the end of her life, Fischer remained convinced that Maslow had been murdered by Soviet intelligence agents.

The fact that Hitler's attack on the Soviet Union transformed the Stalinist dictatorship into an ally of the Western democracies did not change Fischer's attitude toward the Soviet system and its domination of the world Communist movement. Working as an independent scholar and journalist, she took an often unpopular position during the war years by reminding readers of the cynicism and brutality of Stalin's brand of "socialism." She supported herself by writing articles for anti-Stalinist publications like *Politics*, while also editing several limited-circulation but influential journals, including *The Network: Information Bulletin about Stalinist Organizations and Organizational Forms* as well as *The Russian State Party: Newsletter on Contemporary Communism.*

Fischer's dramatic break with Stalinism during her years in Germany resulted in profound personal as well as political changes in her life. Whereas she rejected the ideals and regime of Joseph Stalin, her brothers Gerhart and Hanns Eisler remained dedicated orthodox Communists, adhering loyally to the party line as propagated from Moscow. Gerhart was a professional revolutionary, and both he and Hanns—who achieved world fame as a film composer—settled in the United States in the late 1930s. By the early 1940s, the break between the Eisler siblings had become permanent and bitter. Settling in New York City, but often found at Harvard University, where she carried out her research projects, Fischer lived a life based on the premise that the world movement that claimed her brothers' loyalty was capable of carrying out her own assassination. She informed friends that since she had been found to be in good health by three physicians, if she were to die suddenly such an event would have to be regarded with deep suspicion. For her personal security, Fischer requested a special telephone number from the New York police so that she could contact them if she feared for her life.

By 1945, the world Ruth Fischer saw from such a distrusting perspective had in fact been proven to be evil beyond measure. The discovery of the Nazi death camps revealed aspects of human depravity few had believed possible. Fischer was personally as well as philosophically impacted by these revelations. She now was informed of the deaths in Nazi captivity of several men who played important roles in her earlier life. Her first husband Paul Friedländer lost his life in Auschwitz, while Werner Scholem and Ernst Thälmann, friends and foes within the KPD, were killed at the Buchenwald concentration camp. In the Soviet Union, Stalinist purges led to the death of her Communist party comrades Hugo Eberlein, Heinz Neumann and Hermann Remmele.

Far from blood-drenched Europe, Fischer fought her battles with a pen, working in libraries and archives to find materials to unmask the evil at the heart of Stalinist socialism. Still regarding herself privately as a Communist, Fischer rapidly achieved a reputation as one of the best-informed individuals in the European, and particularly the German, Communist movement. Unlike many political emigrés who lived a life of financial deprivation, Fischer was able to command handsome royalties and lecture fees, and received a generous monthly stipend from Harvard University Press. In 1948, the Harvard Press published Fischer's massive study *Stalin and German Communism*. Although regarded from the beginning by most historians as a problematical work because it represents an attempt to combine historical assessments with autobiography, the book nevertheless remains an important source for any serious investigation of the Stalinization of Europe's largest Communist Party in the interwar period.

In 1947, Ruth Fischer became a naturalized citizen of the United States. That same year, she became a media personality when she appeared as a friendly witness before the House Committee on Un-American Activities. Earlier that day, February 6, 1947, Fischer's brother Gerhart Eisler had appeared before the committee in response to a subpoena and refused to be sworn in unless he could make a public statement; because of the position he took, Eisler was cited for contempt. Later that day, Ruth Fischer testified about several matters, including her "hostile" relationships with her brothers Gerhart and Hanns, then described Gerhart as "a most dangerous terrorist, both to the people of America and to the people of Germany." Among his many crimes, she claimed, was his role in the deaths of the German Communist leader Hugo Eberlein, as well as the Russian Communist intellectual Nikolai Bukharin, during Stalin's purges. Magnifying her brother's influence considerably, she announced that were he to appear in Germany, he would play a key role in the creation of "another Nazi system" whose only difference from the Third Reich would be that its "Fuehrer's name will be Stalin."

One of the more interesting aspects of Ruth Fischer's February 1947 testimony was a question from committee member Richard M. Nixon, who voiced his suspicion that, while she appeared to disagree vehemently with Stalinist methods of achieving socialism, Fischer gave the impression that she still retained "some sympathy with the Marxist philosophy and the ends which Communism attempts to achieve." Fischer sidestepped Nixon's comments by calling for a struggle against Stalinist terrorist methods, urging that the United States "do everything in [its] power to hinder that movement." Privately, she was disturbed by a growing anti-Communist hysteria in America that did little to distinguish between Stalinist totalitarianism and independent radical and socialist movements. Although she continued to publish and lecture, and even served for a while as a consultant to the U.S. Department of State, Fischer felt less and less at home in an adopted country that had succumbed to the chill winds of Cold War paranoia.

In 1955, Fischer left New York for Paris, where she had lived for most of the 1930s and where she would now remain for the rest of her life. She was highly critical of developments in both German states. East Germany, which she regarded as the very embodiment of Stalinist rigidity, responded in kind when the official newspaper of the ruling Socialist Unity Party,

Neues Deutschland, attacked her as "Enemy Number 1." West Germany, which had become a staunchly anti-Communist member of the Western world, also was regarded critically by Fischer, particularly when Communists who had spent years in Nazi concentration camps once again found themselves in prison because of their beliefs.

Now a doting grandmother to her son Gerhard's children, Fischer became increasingly hopeful about the prospects for change that would come from the next generation. A small but growing radical student movement in West Germany was viewed positively by Fischer, who remained convinced that the course of history would always be changed by small groups of dedicated idealists. Developments in Yugoslavia, where experiments in worker-based socialism were being attempted in the 1950s and 1960s, seemed to meet with her approval. Her intellectual independence seems to have come to the attention of both French and American intelligence services, which discreetly kept tabs on the aging ex-revolutionary's activities.

During the last decade of her life, Fischer remained active as a journalist and commentator. Her perspective on the world became less and less Eurocentric and more global, at least in part because of her extensive travels, which included trips to Asia in 1951–52 and 1955. The post-Stalinist evolution of the Soviet Union also made her increasingly hopeful concerning the prospects of a renewal of a socialist construction of society that was essentially democratic and humane. Respected in France in scholarly circles as well as by the educated public, in 1957 she began to teach a course at the Sorbonne on the history of Soviet Communism, which in 1960–61 resulted in her also teaching a seminar on the problems of imperialism and colonialism, an issue that was highly topical in view of France's continuing conflict in Algeria. Though Fischer enjoyed her work, decades of stress and personal tragedies began to take their toll on her body. A sanatorium visit to Germany in the summer of 1960 appeared to have a restorative effect, but Fischer died suddenly in Paris on March 13, 1961. She was buried in the cemetery of Montparnasse, where her grave is decorated with a work of sculpture by her friend Joseph Erhardy.

SOURCES:

Angress, Werner T. *Stillborn Revolution: The Communist Bid for Power in Germany, 1921–1923.* Princeton, NJ: Princeton University Press, 1963.

Bentley, Eric, ed. *Thirty Years of Treason: Excerpts from Hearings before the House Committee on Un-American Activities, 1938–1968.* NY: Viking Press, 1971.

Deak, Istvan. *Weimar Germany's Left-Wing Intellectuals: A Political History of the Weltbühne and Its Circle.* Berkeley and Los Angeles: University of California Press, 1968.

Degras, Jane, ed. *The Communist International 1919–1943: Documents.* 2 vols. London: Oxford University Press, 1971.

Fischer, Ruth. "The Comintern in Hollywood," in *New York Journal American.* November 23, 1946.

———. *Die Umformung der Sowjetgesellschaft: Chronik der Reformen, 1953–1958.* Düsseldorf: Eugen Diederichs Verlag, 1958.

———. *Stalin and German Communism: A Study in the Origins of the State Party.* Cambridge, MA: Harvard University Press, 1948.

———. "Stalin's German Agents," in *American Mercury.* Vol. 63, no. 275. November 1946, pp. 563–570.

———. *Von Lenin zu Mao: Kommunismus in dere Bandung-Ära.* Düsseldorf: Eugen Diederichs Verlag, 1956.

———. "You Can't Retire from the N.K.V.D.," in *New York Journal American.* November 20, 1946.

———, and Arkadij Maslow. *Abtrünig wider Willen: Aus Briefen und Manuskripten des Exils.* Edited by Peter Lübbe. Munich: R. Oldenbourg Verlag, 1990.

———, and Franz Heimann. *Deutsche Kinderfibel.* Berlin: Ernst Rowohlt Verlag, 1933.

Gruber, Helmut, ed. *International Communism in the Era of Lenin: A Documentary History.* Garden City, NY: Anchor Books, 1972.

Hering, Sabine, and Kurt Schilde. *Kampfname Ruth Fischer: Wandlungen einer deutschen Kommunistin.* Frankfurt am Main: Dipa-Verlag, 1995.

Lüdtke, Alf. "Hunger in der Grossen Depression: Hungererfahrungen und Hungerpolitik am Ende der Weimarer Republik," in *Archiv für Sozialgeschichte.* Vol. 27, 1987, pp. 145–176.

Schrecker, Ellen. *Many Are the Crimes: McCarthyism in America.* Boston, MA: Little, Brown, 1998.

Schumacher, Martin. M.d.R. *Die Reichstagsabgeordneten der Weimarer Republik in der Zeit des Nationalsozialismus: Politische Verfolgung, Emigration und Ausbürgerung 1933–1945.* Düsseldorf: Droste Verlag, 1991.

Stephan, Alexander. *Im Visier des FBI: Deutsche Exilschriftsteller in den Akten amerikanischer Geheimdienste.* Stuttgart: Metzler Verlag, 1995.

Theoharis, Athan. "Fischer, Ruth," in John A. Garraty, ed., *Dictionary of American Biography, Supplement Seven: 1961–1965.* NY: Scribner, 1981, pp. 244–245.

Weber, Hermann. *Die Wandlung des deutschen Kommunismus: Die Stalinisierung der KPD in der Weimarer Republik.* 2 vols. Frankfurt am Main: Europäische Verlagsanstalt, 1969.

Wieland, Karin. "Lenins Hoffnung: Ruth Fischer und der deutsche Kommunismus," in *Merkur: Deutsche Zeitschrift für europäisches Denken.* Vol. 51, no. 7. July 1997, pp. 608–617.

Zimmermann, Rüdiger. *Der Leninbund: Linke Kommunisten in der Weimarer Republik.* Düsseldorf: Droste Verlag, 1978.

COLLECTIONS:

Ruth Fischer Papers, Houghton Library, Harvard University.

John Haag,
Assistant Professor of History,
University of Georgia, Athens, Georgia

Fisher, Cicely Corbett (1885–1959)

*British suffragist and women's rights activist. Born Cicely Corbett in Danehill, Sussex, England, in 1885; died in Danehill, Sussex, in 1959; youngest of two daughters of Charles (a lawyer) and Marie (Gray) Corbett; younger sister of *Margery Corbett-Ashby (1882–1981); educated at home; attended Sommerville College, Oxford; married Chambers Fisher (a journalist), in 1913; no children.*

The youngest daughter of suffragist *Marie Corbett and radical lawyer Charles Corbett, Cicely Corbett, along with her older sister Margery, was educated by her parents at home with the assistance of a local woman who taught French and German. At 15, no doubt influenced by her mother's politics, she joined with her sister and some friends to form the Younger Suffragist. Cicely went on to study modern history at Sommerville College, Oxford, where she was also active in the local branch of the National Union of Women's Suffrage Societies. When the Liberal Party failed to sufficiently support women's suffrage, she and Margery broke from the Women's Liberal Federation and, with their mother, formed the Liberal Women's Suffrage Group.

After college, Cicely went to work for *Clementina Black at the Women's Industrial Council, an organization that campaigned for improved pay and working conditions for women. She was also active in the Anti-Sweating League, which sought improved working conditions and wages in certain trades that primarily employed women and children, and for which she organized several conferences. Her programs often included speeches and demonstrations from women who were exploited in the work force. In 1914, Cicely married Chambers Fisher, a radical journalist. In her later years, she was active in the Labor Party and the Women's International League. She died at Danehill, Sussex, in 1959.

SUGGESTED READING:

Black, Clementina. *Married Women's Work*, 1993.

Corbett-Ashby, Margery. *Memoirs*, 1996.

Roberts, Marie, ed. *The Reformers Socialist Feminism*, 1995.

Fisher, Clara (1811–1898)

English-born American actress. Name variations: Clara Fisher Maeder. Born on July 14, 1811, probably in London, England; died in Metuchen, New Jersey, on November 12, 1898; fourth daughter and youngest of six children of Frederick George Fisher (proprietor of a library and later an auctioneer at Covent Garden, London); married James Gaspard Maeder (an Irish composer and music teacher), on December 6, 1834 (died 1876); children: seven, two of whom (Edward and Helen) died in infancy; four of the children—Frank Chickering, Amelia, James Gaspard, and Frederick George—were connected with the theater; the eldest daughter, Clara, married a physician and settled in England.

Made London debut at age six as Lord Flimnap in a children's adaptation of David Garrick's Lilliput (Drury Lane Theater); made New York debut as Albina Mandeville in The Will (September 11, 1827, Park Theater); appeared as the Singing Witch in Macbeth (May 10, 1849, Astor Place Opera House, on the occasion of the famous Astor Place riot); appeared as the Nurse in Romeo and Juliet (April 30, 1883, closing of the Booth Theater, New York); gave final performance at Ford's Theater, Baltimore (1889).

Encouraged by her father's interest in the theater, Clara Fisher was just six when she made her debut as Lord Flimnap in a children's adaptation of David Garrick's *Lilliput* at London's Drury Lane, a production that also included two of her sisters. In an afterpiece, she also performed excerpts from Shakespeare's *Richard III* and sang a comic song. Precocious and probably endearing, she subsequently became a famous child actress, touring Great Britain for a decade in children's parts and serious adult roles. She later admitted that she felt isolated and lonely in the regimented life of rehearsals and performances and hated being paraded around as a child prodigy.

Fisher came to America in 1827, accompanied by her mother and several of her siblings. Now an ingenue, she made her debut at the Park Theater, New York, as Albina Mandeville in *The Will*, a lackluster piece in which her rendition of a Scottish patriotic song, "Hurray for the Bonnets of Blue," was a high point. Audiences adored her, while the critics called her "fresh" and "captivating." For the next seven years, Fisher appeared in theaters in every major city in the country, playing to overflowing houses. Her repertoire encompassed a wide range of both male and female roles, including Cherubino in *The Marriage of Figaro*, Clari in *The Maid of Milan*, Helen Worrett in *Man and Wife*, Gertrude in *The Loan of a Lover*, and Letitia Hardy in *The Belle's Stratagem*, in which she sang her famous song "Buy a Broom." Notable among her Shakespearean roles were Juliet in *Romeo and Juliet* and Ophelia in *Hamlet*. During the height of Fisher's popularity, adoring fans named babies, ships, race horses, and even stage coaches after her.

Clara
Fisher

After Fisher married James G. Maeder in 1834, she appeared less frequently, probably due in part to the births of her seven children. For a period following the depression of 1837, she left her home in Harlem and retired to Albany. However, she was playing the Singing Witch in William Macready's *Macbeth*, on the occasion of the Astor Place riot of May 10, 1849. The riot, the result of a long-standing feud between Macready, an English star, and his American counterpart Edwin Forrest, was further fueled by anti-English sentiment among the Irish residents of the Bowery area. The militia was eventually called in to quell the melee, with orders to shoot into the crowd. As a result, over 20 people were killed and 150 were wounded in the incident. Evidently, Fisher was ushered to safety before the shooting began.

During her many semi-retirements, Fisher taught dramatics and elocution. In 1850, she took up her career again, primarily playing elderly women. In her later years, she toured with a number of stock companies, including *Louisa Lane Drew's Arch Street Theater in Philadelphia, and the Boston Globe Theater. In April 1883, Fisher portrayed the Nurse in *Romeo and Juliet* in her final performance at the Booth Theater in New York. Her last appearance was with Augustin Daly's company at Ford's Theater in Baltimore, in 1889. The actress died at her daughter's home in Metuchen, New Jersey, on November 12, 1898.

SOURCES:

James, Edward T., ed. *Notable American Women 1607–1950.* Cambridge, MA: The Belknap Press of Harvard University Press, 1971.

McHenry, Robert, ed. *Famous American Women.* NY: Dover, 1983.

Wilmeth, Don B., and Tice L. Miller, eds. *Cambridge Guide to American Theatre.* NY: Cambridge University Press, 1993.

SUGGESTED READING:

Autobiography of Clara Fisher Maeder, New York, 1897.

Barbara Morgan,
Melrose, Massachusetts

Fisher, Dorothy Canfield

(1879–1958)

Popular American author in the early 20th century who attacked intolerance in all its forms. Name variations; Dolly; Dorothy Canfield; (pseudonym for some magazine articles) Stanley Cranshaw. Born Dorothea Frances Canfield on February 17, 1879, in Lawrence, Kansas; died in Arlington, Vermont, on November 9, 1958; daughter of James Hulme Canfield (1883–1959, a professor and writer) and Flavia (Camp) Canfield; graduated from Ohio State University, 1899; graduated from Columbia University, 1904; married John Redwood Fisher; children: **Sally Fisher** *(b. 1909) and James (b. 1913)*

Awards: elected to the National Institute of Arts and Letters; was awarded an honorary Doctor of Letters from Middlebury College (1921), University of Vermont, Dartmouth, and Columbia (1929), Northwestern (1931), Rockford College (1934), Ohio State, Swarthmore, and Williams College (1935); given the Constance Lindsay Skinner Award from the Women's National Book Association (1951); the Vermont Congress of Parents and Teachers and the Free Public Library Commission established the Dorothy Canfield Fisher Children's Book Award (1956); the American Library Association in conjunction with the Book-of-the-Month Club began an annual Dorothy Canfield Fisher Award (1958) to aid libraries in small communities.

Selected writings: Gunhild *(1907);* What Shall We Do Now? *(1907);* The Squirrel Cage *(1912);* A Montessori Mother *(1912);* The Montessori Manual *(1913);* Mothers and Children *(1914);* The Bent Twig *(1915);* The Real Motive *(1916);* Self-Reliance *(1916); (with S.L. Cleghorn)* Fellow Captains *(1916);* Understood Betsy *(1917);* Home Fires in France *(1918);* The Day of Glory *(1919);* The Brimming Cup *(1921); (translator)* Life of Christ *(1921);* Rough Hewn *(1922);* Raw Material *(1923);* The French School at Middlebury *(1923);* The Home-Maker *(1924);* Her Son's Wife *(1926);* Why Stop Learning? *(1927);* The Deepening Stream *(1930);* Basque People *(1931);* Bonfire *(1933);* Tourists Accommodated *(1934);* Fables for Parents *(1937);* Seasoned Timber *(1939);* Nothing Ever Happens and How It Does *(1940);* Our Young

Folks *(1943)*; American Portraits *(1946)*; *(short stories)* Four-Square *(1949)*; Vermont Tradition *(1953)*.

Dorothy Canfield Fisher was a novelist, short-story writer, essayist, translator, lecturer, philosopher, educator, historian, and children's book writer. She was also a member of the editorial board of the Book-of-the-Month for 25 years, an enthusiastic advocate on the virtues of Vermont, and a beloved humanitarian, known for her unselfish integrity.

Born in Lawrence, Kansas, on February 17, 1879, the daughter of **Flavia Camp Canfield**, an artist, and James Hulme Canfield, a professor, Dorothea Canfield was named after one of her mother's favorite literary characters: Dorothea Brooke of George Eliot's (*Mary Anne Evans) *Middlemarch*. As a child, Dorothy built towers with books in her father's study; before long, she was immersing herself in their contents. She loved Thackeray, Fielding, Hakluyt, and Dickens. Though she received *Ivanhoe* for her sixth birthday, she preferred her book on America's first settlers, most especially the chapter on the Quakers' exile at the hands of the Pilgrims. Dorothy was bewildered by the behavior of those who came to America to seek freedom of religion, only to turn around and impose their beliefs on others. Her father gave her a dose of reality, explaining that freedom of thought was often the freedom to "bully everybody else into thinking as they do."

An energetic young girl, with blue eyes and brown hair, Dorothy played on the grounds of the State University of Kansas where her father taught. Her summers were spent in Arlington, Vermont, with her great-grandfather and her father's aunt and uncle, listening eagerly to stories of earlier Canfields. The ten-year-old wrote back to Kansas: "The reckless way these people talk of years is perpetually astonishing to me. 'How long ago did that happen, Uncle Zed?' I asked him yesterday. 'Oh, a few years, fourteen or fifteen maybe.' Why that's more than my whole life!" Instead of dolls, she had chickens, dogs, and horses to while away her days; she explored the countryside, the mountain roads, the sugar maples, and visited her neighbors on a Morgan colt called Don. In the evenings, she read of Indian raids, but the Native Americans depicted in the books were not like those she had seen on the Kansas plains or on the green mountains of Vermont. Dorothy had always been puzzled by the way the Indians in Lawrence were treated as outcasts. For the first time, she had doubts about the veracity of some of her readings.

At home in Kansas, all was not idyllic. Her mother, absorbed in art and tending toward the radical, was chafing under the confines of a settled marriage, while her father, who preferred a well-ordered household, was content to keep on teaching for the rest of his life. Dorothy was "beginning to understand something of the differences bound to exist between scholarly exactness and artistic irresponsibility," wrote **Elizabeth Yates**. Since she felt helpless to change the situation, Dorothy turned to the violin for consolation and escaped into her music.

In 1890, at age 11, she spent a year with Flavia in Paris, living in rooms in a girls' boarding school on the Rue de Vaugirard. Dorothy's mentor was the 23-year-old American *Emily Balch, something of an intellectual, who also lived there while attending the Sorbonne. While her mother studied art at a nearby studio, Dorothy attended the girls' school and easily absorbed French. Rainy days were spent in the Cluny Museum, where her mother made copies of the greats, or restlessly posing for her mother, while listening eagerly to the art talk of her mother's friends—of colors, of light and shadow, of Breughel's red.

Dorothy took care of Flavia, calmed her nerves, and did most of the interpreting as her mother did not take to languages. Eventually, Dorothy would be able to speak and write in French, German, Italian, and English, allowing her to do translations. That fall, she was to attend the Sorbonne herself, majoring in philology (at that time, a wide-ranging study of literature), but her mother, often described as self-absorbed, followed the Parisian art world on a mid-winter quest to Spain in search of Velasquez, dragging Dorothy behind her. Flavia was ready to sacrifice all to art and would have no truck with anything second-rate. Her daughter seemed to understand: "She's reaching for the only stars she sees," she wrote. "What better can any of us try to do."

Mother and daughter returned to America in 1891. That same year, when Dorothy was 12, the family moved to Lincoln, Nebraska, where James was made chancellor of the university. By then, he was president of the National Education Association and, as a dedicated feminist, instrumental in introducing athletics for girls. With the encouragement of her father, Dorothy took boxing lessons along with fencing lessons from an instructor named John James Pershing, the future general. James Canfield wanted to break the chains of over-protection, even when it came to criticism. Some take criticism so personally, he once told his daughter, that they can't profit from it. He taught her to make it serve her: take it in, appraise it, then use what you've learned.

In 1895, the family moved on to Columbus, Ohio, where James Canfield became president of Ohio State University. Flavia rang doorbells to some success, trying to pry the women of Columbus out of the house to hear her series of lectures on art while James took on the industrial community with his belief in free trade. Dorothy continued her music studies, playing second violin in a string quartet, but she was beginning to suspect that her talents as a musician would soon plateau. Rather, she wanted to spend her energy on a profession where growth would be unlimited; at first, it was teaching.

There was one drawback. At age 19, Dorothy, who had been experiencing noises in her head for some time, learned that her hearing was impaired and that she would have to live with the noises for the rest of her life. An infection of the inner ear had been caused by swimming in a warm-water pool. She told no one, but, from then on, she relied on a little lip reading to aid her hearing.

*H*er novels attack materialism, social discrimination, religious and racial intolerance, and all forms of brutality and fraud. Far ahead of her times, she wrote of the waste of human resources implicit in consigning women to limited roles of social usefulness.

—Ida H. Washington

In the spring of 1899, she graduated from Ohio State; that fall, when her father took a position as librarian at Columbia University in New York, she followed him to Manhattan, then studied languages in Europe for the next two years. *Willa Cather was also in Europe, and the two friends chummed around together. In 1902, Fisher entered Columbia, pursuing her doctorate in philology in order to teach. She graduated in 1904.

Dorothy began writing articles for *The New York Times* and, in the tradition of both parents, was becoming something of a nonconformist; she adamantly refused to wear corsets, proclaiming them implements of the Inquisition. She wrote stories and became a final reader for William Morrow's *American Magazine*; she also did some freelance editing. Along the way, she met John Fisher, then a law-school student. A handful of wild flowers cemented the relationship, and they were married on May 9, 1907. With saved earnings and a small house on a quarter-acre lot acquired as a wedding present, they located to Arlington, Vermont, determined to live simply and write. Dorothy became close friends with **Sally Cleghorn**, a writer living nearby. Wrote Cleghorn in her biography *Three-score:*

> When I'd begun genuinely to know Dorothy I made the fundamental discovery that she really meant it. All those gracious welcoming ways, that lighted-up look when you came in, weren't forms of politeness at all. They were Vermontishly honest and real. . . . I saw her meet other people, welcome them, and when they had gone retain the same kind of look for them, as she told me about them in the same cordial voice. Then I saw that these were fast colors. . . . She felt that way.

Fisher signed with a New York agent, and her first novel *Gunhild,* one she had been working on for about a year, came out that October. The critics found it promising; it sold 600 copies and sunk out of sight. But her short stories of Vermonters, stories of simplicity and courage, were being scooped up by *Munsey's, McClure's, Ladies' Home Journal, Good Housekeeping,* and *American Magazine.* Though cosmopolitan, she often wrote about a rural region. She had become the voice of the taciturn.

In May 1909, Fisher's first daughter Sally was born. The year 1912 saw the publication of *The Squirrel Cage,* a protest against conformity and materialism. With monies received, the Fishers took their second winter in Europe, baby Sally in tow. Before Fisher left, William Morrow had asked her to contact *Marie Montessori while in Rome, regarding a chapter in a book Morrow intended to publish on the Montessori method. Fisher was bowled over by what she saw at the Casa di Bambini and made several visits. Montessori maintained that children should be given complete freedom to learn in their own time in their own way as long as they did not hurt or annoy others. Fisher, writes Yates, "had long been convinced that totalitarian authority was wrong, in teaching and governing, as it strangled the natural growth of the individual. Step by step these children were being led from self-control, through self-discipline, to self-government." Back home, Fisher wrote *The Montessori Mother,* one of the first books in English on the Montessori system of education. Her next book, *Mothers and Children,* challenged child-rearing theories of the time. Fisher began to lecture on progressive education. Once asked if she would spank a child who refused to obey, she replied, "How big is a house?" "Which house?" asked the questioner. "Well then, which child?" replied Fisher.

Dorothy
Canfield
Fisher

Fisher would write a great deal on education. *Why Stop Learning?*, published in 1927, would be one of the first popular works in the U.S. on adult education. Writes Yates:

> The more she wrote, the more there was to say, and though she felt that writing on edu-

cational matters was distinctly worthwhile she was far more interested in the attempt to convey her ideas through fiction. She felt that one of her early observations was constantly being confirmed: fewer converts were made by straight exhortation than by apt parables. She knew that she could best express abstract truths in the form of human drama. Her love of liberty and fair play, her hatred for cruelty and the tyranny of caste, her contempt for the spirit of competition that carried one to the top by pushing another down, made their way through her writing to a widening and increasingly articulate circle of readers.

By 1913, most of the ancestral Canfield land had been willed to Dorothy or her brother. Some of the land was rented to farmers. To bring back the poorer land, the Fishers chose reforestation, with the help of neighbors, planting 10,000 white pines. That year, during Christmas week, their son James was born. In 1914, *The Bent Twig*, published under her maiden name Dorothy Canfield, met with success. She followed that with the children's book *Understood Betsy*, but Fisher was not taken seriously by critics.

In 1916, John joined the American Field Service and traveled to Paris to run an ambulance section during World War I; she and the family followed. There, Fisher established a Fund to Aid French Children, ran a Refugee Children's Home, worked on books for the blinded soldiers under the aegis of *Winifred Holt, and grew homesick. The family endured the zeppelin raids over Paris, and young Sally survived a bout of typhoid fever. All this resulted in the publication *Home First in France*. The family returned to Arlington in May 1919.

Dorothy Canfield Fisher's writing was simple, honest, and direct. In 1920, she published *The Brimming Cup*, known as the obverse of Sinclair Lewis' *Main Street* because of her positive view of village life. The two books shared the bestseller list, and *The Brimming Cup* went through eight printings in its first year. Fisher was fascinated with human behavior. She combined this with her reformer's mentality, thus *The Deepening Stream* was about Quakers and against war.

On the eve of World War II, she published *Seasoned Timber* (1939), warning of the growing threat to freedom. She formed a group to welcome German and Austrian refugee children in Bennington County (soon expanded to include Danish, Chinese, etc.), cajoling the American publisher of Hitler's *Mein Kampf* to contribute the royalties to the project. Though there were those that protested using schools to aid foreigners, she launched a Children's Crusade in schools across the nation, collecting pennies for the cause, totaling $140,000 (an enormous sum in 1940). But Fisher had more in mind than the raising of money; she was bent on teaching children that the only way to keep the freedoms of America was to safeguard the freedoms of other nations. For her work, she was awarded the *Ella Flagg Young Medal.

Fisher also served on the original prestigious committee selecting books for the Book-of-the-Month Club: it was at her urging that *Pearl S. Buck*'s *The Good Earth* was pulled out of nowhere; she also championed *Life with Father* and *Native Son* and wrote the introduction for Richard Wright's *Black Boy*. Along with *Eleanor Roosevelt, Fisher was the only other white woman on the board of the largely black Howard University.

In February 1945, Fisher and her husband received word that their son, 31-year-old Captain James Fisher, had been killed in the Philippines when he led his Ranger battalion on a successful attack at a Japanese prison camp, freeing 500 American prisoners of war. "We are struggling with what strength we have to reconstruct our lives without Jimmy," she wrote a friend. "To the eye I am the same gray-haired, deaf writer as ever, bent over the desk, the weary old hand still driving the old pen." In 1953, she finished a long-cherished enterprise, *Vermont Tradition: The Biography of an Outlook on Life*. Soon after, in December, she suffered a cerebral hemorrhage, what she called the "Canfield" stroke, and was confined to bed. Though she recouped, Dorothy Canfield Fisher died five years later, on Sunday, November 9, 1958, of another stroke.

SOURCES:

Washington, Ida H. *Dorothy Canfield Fisher: A Biography*. Shelburne, VT: New England Press, 1982.

Yates, Elizabeth. *The Lady from Vermont: Dorothy Canfield Fisher's Life and World*. Brattleboro, VT: Stephen Greene Press, 1958.

SUGGESTED READING:

Madigan, Mark J, ed. *Keeping Fires Night and Day: Selected Letters of Dorothy Canfield Fisher*. University of Missouri Press, 1993.

McAllister, Lois. *Dorothy Canfield Fisher: A Critical Study*. Ph.D. thesis, Case Western Reserve University, 1969.

COLLECTIONS:

Papers and manuscripts in the Wilbur Library at the University of Vermont.

RELATED MEDIA:

The Homemaker was filmed.

Fisher, Kate (fl. 1881).

See Elder, Kate.

Fisher, Mary (b. 1946).

See Glaser, Elizabeth for sidebar.

Fisher, M.F.K. (1908–1992)

American writer and gastronome who was one of her century's great prose stylists. Name variations: Mary Frances Parrish (1939–41); (joint pseudonym with Dillwyn Parrish) Victoria Berne. Born Mary Frances Kennedy on July 3, 1908, in Albion, Michigan; died on June 22, 1992, in Glen Ellen, California; one of four children of Rex Brenton (a newspaper editor) and Edith Oliver (Holbrook) Kennedy; sister of **Norah K. Barr**; *attended public schools in Whittier, California, and private boarding schools in southern California; attended Illinois College, Occidental College, University of California, University of Dijon, Dijon, France; married Alfred Young Fisher, in 1929 (divorced 1938); married Dillwyn Parrish (a writer), in 1939 (died 1941); married Donald Friede (a book editor), in 1945 (divorced 1951); children: Anne (b. 1943); (third marriage) Mary Kennedy (b. 1946).*

Selected writings: Serve It Forth *(1937);* Consider the Oyster *(1941);* How to Cook a Wolf *(1942);* The Gastronomical Me *(1943);* Here Let Us Feast: A Book of Banquets *(1946);* Not Now but NOW *(1947); (trans.)* Brillat-Savarin's Physiology of Taste, or, Meditations on Transcendental Gastronomy *(1949);* An Alphabet for Gourmets *(1949);* A Cordiall Water *(1961);* The Story of Wine in California *(1962);* Map of Another Town: A Memoir of Provence *(1964);* The Cooking of Provincial France *(1968);* With Bold Knife and Fork *(1969);* Among Friends *(1971);* A Considerable Town *(1978, reprinted in 1985 with* Map of Another Town, *as* Two Towns in Provence*);* As They Were *(1982);* Sister Age *(1983);* Spirits of the Valley *(1985);* The Standing and the Waiting *(1985);* Dubious Honors *(1988);* Answer in the Affirmative and The Oldest Living Man *(1989);* Boss Dog *(1990);* Long Ago in France: The Years in Dijon *(1991);* Stay Me, Oh Comfort Me: Journal and Stories, 1933–1945 *(1993).*

In a career that spanned almost six decades, M.F.K. Fisher changed the style of culinary writing in America and delighted readers with what W.H. Auden called "one of the best prose styles in America." In addition to writing over two dozen books, Fisher contributed short stories, articles, and some poems to the nation's top magazines, including *Harper's, Harper's Bazaar, Gourmet, Atlantic Monthly, Wine and Food Quarterly,* and *House Beautiful.* "I was never a food writer," she always insisted. "I just wrote about life."

Fisher was born in Albion, Michigan, the eldest of four children. She grew up in California, an Episcopalian in a Quaker community. A lonely child, she developed a love of words and of

the kitchen, which became her domain on the cook's day off. She attended public school in Whittier and private boarding schools in California, then sampled several colleges before her marriage to Alfred Young Fisher in 1929. She then sailed to France with her new husband to study at the University of Dijon, where she acquired her knowledge and love of French food and culture. Returning to California in 1932, Fisher began writing articles and essays based on old cookbooks. By the time her first book, *Serve It Forth* (1937), was published, she had separated from her husband (they divorced in 1938) and was living in Switzerland with writer Dillwyn Parrish (a son of artist Maxfield Parrish), with whom she collaborated on a novel, *Touch and Go.* In 1939, when Parrish was diagnosed with a fatal disease, the couple moved back to California and married. Parrish died in 1941. In 1943, Fisher had a daughter out of wedlock, whom she claimed was adopted. Two years later, she married book editor Donald Friede, with whom she had a second daughter. The press of deadlines, the death of her mother, and Friede's business and health problems caused the end of that marriage in 1951, after which Fisher moved to the family ranch in Whittier. In 1953, following her father's death, she took the children to Aix-en-Provence, then Lugano, where they lived for five years.

In the period after her second husband's death, Fisher wrote five books that comprise the core of her gastronomic works: *Consider the Oyster* (1941), *How to Cook a Wolf* (1942), *The Gastronomical Me* (1943), and *An Alphabet for Gourmets* (1949). The books were republished in 1954 as *The Art of Eating.* From her first effort, Fisher drew praise from the critics who found her writing unique and beguiling. *The New York Times* called *Serve It Forth* "a delightful book . . . stamped on every page with a highly individual personality." *Consider the Oyster* was termed "a sort of crunchy oyster cracker of a book." Particularly witty was the tongue-in-cheek *How to Cook a Wolf,* which came out during the World War II food shortages and offered ways to keep the proverbial wolf from the door. Among the unorthodox recipe suggestions was an exotically prepared meal of weeds.

Fisher's first novel, *Not Now But NOW* (1947), the story about Jenny, a harlot of a girl, was equally well received. "Like her other works, *Not Now But NOW* defies the ordinary rules of structure and direction," writes **Rose Feld**. "And like them it demands attention and

M.F.K.
Fisher

Toth, Emily. "Food is Love," in *Belles Lettres,* Summer 1995, p. 11.

SUGGESTED READING:

Barr, Norah K., Marsha Moran, and Patrick Moran, comp. *M.F.K. Fisher: A Life in Letters, Correspondence 1929–1991.* Counterpoint, 1997.

Reardon, Joan. *M.F.K. Fisher, Julia Child, and Alice Waters: Celebrating the Pleasures of the Table.* NY: Harmony Books, 1994.

COLLECTIONS:

The papers of M.F.K. Fisher are at the Schlesinger Library, Radcliffe College.

RELATED MEDIA:

"M.F.K. Fisher: Writer with a Bite" (color, 28 min.), conversations with the author with excerpts from her writings, produced by **Kathi Wheater**, distributed by Cinema Guild, New York, 1992.

Barbara Morgan,
Melrose, Massachusetts

Fisher, Minnie (1882–1964).

See Cunningham, Minnie Fisher.

Fiske, Minnie Maddern

(1865–1932)

American actress. Name variations: Minnie Maddern. Born Marie Augusta Davey on December 19, 1865, in New Orleans, Louisiana; died on February 15, 1932, in Hollis, Long Island, New York; only daughter of Thomas W. Davey (a theatrical manager) and Elizabeth "Lizzie" (Maddern) Davey (an actress); briefly attended convents in Cincinnati and St. Louis; married LeGrand White, around 1882 (divorced 1888); married Harrison Grey Fiske (a playwright, manager, and journalist), on March 19, 1890; children: (adopted son in 1922) Danville Maddern Davey.

Appearances as Minnie Maddern: Sybil in A Sheep in Wolf's Clothing *(New York debut, French Theater, May 30, 1870); Little Fritz in* Fritz, our German Cousin *(Wallack's Theater, July 1870); Dollie in* Chicago Before the Fire *(Theater Comique, June 1872); Prince Arthur in* King John *and Richelieu in* The Two Orphans *(Booth's Theater, May 1874); Widow Melnotte in* The Lady of Lyons; *Ralph Rackstraw in* HMS Pinafore *(1979); Chip in* Fogg's Ferry *(Park Theater, May 1882); Mercy Baxter in* Caprice *(New Park Theater, August 1884); Alice Glendenning in* In Spite of It All *(Lyceum Theater, September 1885 and on a subsequent U.S. tour); Mrs. Coney in* Featherbrain *(Madison Square Theater, May 1889).*

Appearances as Minnie Maddern Fiske: title role in Hester Crewe *(Tremont Theater, Boston, November 1893); Nora in* A Doll's House *(Empire Theater, February 1894); Gilberte in* Frou-Frou *(Garden Theater, March 1894); Césarine in* Marie Deloche *(Garden*

respect as the product of a richly civilized and fearless mind." Fisher's vast output included a translation of Brillat-Savarin's 1925 classic *Physiology of Taste* (1949), of which she was particularly proud, and a small book of folk cures and superstitions called *A Cordiall Water* (1961), which she wrote during the five years she lived in France with her daughters. During the 1960s, she wrote articles under exclusive contract to *The New Yorker,* including a series about her Whittier childhood, republished as *Among Friends* (1971).

Although interest in the author flagged for a time, she enjoyed a revival in the 1980s, at which time her popularity rivaled that of her earlier career. Just before her death in 1992, Fisher was the subject of a short film in which she reminisced about her career and her three marriages.

SOURCES:

Current Biography 1948. NY: H.W. Wilson, 1948.

Green, Carol Hurd, and Mary Grimley Mason, eds. *American Women Writers.* NY: Continuum, 1994.

Theater, March 1896); wrote and appeared in A Light from St. Agnes *(1896 or 1897);* Tess *in* Tess of the d'Urbervilles *(Miner's Theater, March 1897); Cyprienne in* Divorçons *(Miner's Theater, May 1897); Saucers in* A Bit of Old Chelsea *(Miner's Theater, 1898); Madeleine in* Love Finds the Way *(Miner's Theater, 1898); Magda Giulia in* Little Italy *(Miner's Theater 1899); Becky in* Becky Sharp *(Miner's Theater, 1899); title role in* Miranda of the Balcony *(Manhattan Theater, 1901); title role in* The Unwelcome Mrs. Hatch *(Manhattan Theater, 1901); title role in* Mary of Magdala *(Manhattan Theater, 1902); title role in* Hedda Gabler *(Manhattan Theater, 1903); title role in* Leah Kleschna *(Manhattan Theater, 1904); Heroine in* Dolce *(Manhattan Theater, April 1906); Cynthia Karslake in* The New York Idea *(Milwaukee, October 1906); Rebecca West in* Rosmersholm *(Lyric Theater, December 1907); Nell Sanders in* Salvation Nell *(Hackett's Theater, November 1908); Lona Hessel in* The Pillars of Society *(Lyceum Theater, March 1910); title role in* Hannele *(Lyceum Theater, April 1910); title role in* Mrs. Bumpstead-Leigh *(Chicago, November 1910); toured in* The New Marriage *and* Julia France *(1911–12); Lady Patricia Cosway in* Lady Patricia *(New York Theater, February 1912); Mary Page in* The High Road *(Hudson Theater, November 1912); Juliet Miller in* Erstwhile Susan *(Gaiety Theater, January 1916); George Sand in* Madame Sand *(Criterion Theater, November 1917); toured America with all-star cast in* Out There *for the Red Cross (1918); Madame Eulin in* Service *(Cohan Theater, April 1918); Nellie Daventry in* Mis' Nelly o' New Orleans *(Henry Miller Theater, 1919); Marion Blake in* Wake Up, Jonathan *(January 1921); Patricia Baird in* The Dice of the Gods *(National Theater, April 1923); Mary Westlake in* Mary, Mary, Quite Contrary *(Belasco Theater, September 1923); Helen Tilden in* Helena's Boys *(Henry Miller Theater, April 1924); Mrs. Alving in* Ghosts *(Mansfield Theater, January 1927); Mistress Page in* The Merry Wives of Windsor *(Knickerbocker Theater, March 1928); toured as Beatrice in* Much Ado About Nothing *(1928); gave final performance on tour in* Against the Wind *(Chicago, November 1931).*

Born into the theater, actress Minnie Maddern Fiske was the only child of Thomas Davey, a theatrical manager. Her mother, **Elizabeth "Lizzie" Maddern**, was one of seven children of Richard Maddern, a musician who had brought his family to America from England and had organized them into the Maddern Family Concert Company. As a three-year-old, Minnie accompanied her father's troupe on tour, first appearing on stage in Little Rock, Arkansas, as the young

Minnie Maddern Fiske

Duke of York in Shakespeare's *Richard III.* Not long after, the Daveys separated, and little Minnie and her mother continued to pursue their careers as a duo. On May 30, 1870, at age four, Minnie made her New York debut, appearing in *A Sheep in Wolf's Clothing* at the French Theater. Billed as "Little Minnie Maddern," she became a popular child actress and, at 13, was adding adult roles to her repertoire, including the elderly Widow Melnotte in *The Lady of Lyons.* By the 1880s, she had graduated to ingenue roles and appeared in a variety of popular plays of the decade, including *Fogg's Ferry, Caprice,* and *Featherbrain.*

In 1882, while touring in *Fogg's Ferry,* she married LeGrand White, a handsome young theater musician who served for a while as her manager. The couple soon separated, however, and were divorced on June 25, 1888. Two years later, in 1890, she married Harrison Grey Fiske, the wealthy young owner of the New York *Dramatic Mirror,* and she retired from the stage to become a lady of leisure. Finding herself bored with domesticity, she began writing one-act plays, of which *The Rose, The Eyes of the Heart,* and *A Light for St. Agnes* became quite popular. Now using the name Minnie Maddern Fiske, she returned to the stage in 1893, as the heroine in her husband's unsuccessful play *Hester Crewe.* The next year, she played Nora in a charity production of Henrik Ibsen's *A Doll's House,* and the performance, which won critical acclaim, not only signaled Fiske's return to the stage, but a new commitment to plays of substance.

Throughout the next two decades, Fiske gained a reputation as a serious actress as well as a champion of Ibsen, whom she considered the genius of the age. It was largely through her efforts that Ibsen and the realistic movement gained a foothold in America. In addition to *A Doll's House*, she starred in Ibsen's *Hedda Gabler* (1903), *Rosmersholm* (1907), *The Pillars of Society* (1910), and *Ghosts* (1927). Fiske reached the height of her popular success, however, in two adaptations of English novels: Lorrimer Stoddard's dramatization of the Thomas Hardy novel *Tess of the d'Urbervilles* (1897) and *Becky Sharp* (1899), a play based on William Thackeray's novel *Vanity Fair*. Fiske's performance as Becky Sharp, which ultimately became her favorite role, was glowing. Though Lewis C. Strang thought the play was colorless, he nonetheless rhapsodized over the actress: "One is tempted to spread on paper a synonym book of adjectives—brilliant, sparkling, scintillating, that sort of thing—but these, after all, are merely superficialities . . . they give no notion of the spirit of Mrs. Fiske's characterization."

Fiske, a wisp of a woman, with red hair and intense blue eyes, was generally noted for her understated "realistic" acting and impeccable technique, though there were some who considered her more of a personality than a great talent. Her wit and style were most apparent in her comic portrayals, which, like her more serious roles, were subtle and controlled. She was most often criticized for her staccato diction, and occasionally was accused of downright unintelligibility. Franklin Pierce Adams wrote in the *New York Tribune*:

> Somewords she runstogether
> Some others are distinctly stated.
> Somecometoofast and s o m e t o o s l o w
> And some are syncopated.
> And yet no voice—I am sincere—
> Exists that I prefer to hear.

In 1923, fledgling actress *Helen Hayes had the opportunity to see Fiske in *Mary, Mary, Quite Contrary*. Hayes recalls in her autobiography the absolute perfection of Fiske's performance. "It was immediately apparent," she wrote, "that I was witness to one of those performances of which every actor dreams, and which he may achieve only once in a lifetime." Hayes was so impressed that she returned to the theater every Thursday for the rest of the play's run. The consistency of Fiske's performance amazed her. "There wasn't a smile or a shrug that was a fraction of a second early or late. A crumb was brushed off her jabot at precisely the same moment as she was fashioning a particular syllable. All that incredible spontaneity was calculated to a sigh."

Fiske, who until 1899 performed almost exclusively at the Fifth Avenue Theater, was engaged in a running battle with the Theatrical Trust or Syndicate, which had a monopoly on most of the nation's major theaters by 1896. In 1901, weary of competing with Trust productions and seeking independence, she asked her husband Harrison Fiske to acquire the lease on the Manhattan Theater and had it renovated at great cost. Minnie Maddern Fiske opened the attractive new facility with a production of *Miranda on the Balcony*. For the next six years, she appeared there, and occasionally elsewhere, in a string of modern plays that included *The Unwelcome Mrs. Hatch* (1901), *Mary of Magdala* (1902), *Hedda Gabler* (1903), *Leah Kleschna* (1904), *The New York Idea* (1906), *Rosmersholm* (1907), and *Salvation Nell* (1908), the first play to make it to Broadway from George P. Baker's famous "47 Workshop" at Harvard. Although Fiske continued to attract large audiences, the prolonged fight with the syndicate had cut deeply into finances, and in 1911 her husband was forced to sell the *Dramatic Mirror*. By 1915, he had declared bankruptcy and was increasingly unfaithful, leaving Fiske both emotionally and financially stranded. After a brief foray into films—*Tess* (1913) and *Vanity Fair* (1915)—she returned to the theater, appearing in a string of hits, including an American tour of *Out There* (1917), an all-star fund-raiser for the Red Cross.

In 1922, perhaps regretting an earlier decision not to have children, Fiske adopted a baby boy, Danville Maddern Davey. Although she took him on tour when he was a baby, she later entrusted his care to her secretary. Much of her life outside the theater was involved in the prevention of cruelty and abuse to animals, the only cause to ever rival Fiske's devotion to her career. During her later years, the actress was honored with several honorary degrees and was named as one of the 12 greatest living American women by the League of Women Voters in 1923, and again by *Good Housekeeping* magazine in 1931.

Fiske revived the 1910 *Mrs. Bumpstead-Leigh* in April 1929 and, despite increasing ill health, embarked on a two-year tour. In November 1931, she collapsed during a performance of *Against the Wind* in Chicago and died three months later, on February 15, 1932, at her home in Hollis, Long Island. By her direction, funeral services were private and her body was cremated. Summing up her extraordinary career, the New York critic Brooks Atkinson called it "one of the most honorable on Broadway. At a time when nearly everyone else was content with humbug, she acted on the stage in a sharp, naturalistic style, and she was the champion of intelligence in the theater." Her fame, however, came at a price. At the end of his tribute, Atkinson wrote: "A brilliant public figure had a joyless private life and few of the comforts of companionship and devotion."

SOURCES:

James, Edward T., ed. *Notable American Women.* Cambridge, MA: The Belknap Press of Harvard University Press, 1971.

McHenry, Robert, ed. *Famous American Women.* NY: Dover, 1983.

Morley, Sheridan. *The Great Stage Stars.* London: Angus and Robertson, 1986.

Wilmeth, Don B., and Tice L. Miller. *Cambridge Guide to American Theater.* NY: Cambridge University Press, 1993.

SUGGESTED READING:

Binns, Archie. *Mrs. Fiske and the American Theater.* NY: Crown Publishers, 1955.

Barbara Morgan,
Melrose, Massachusetts

Fittko, Lisa (1909—)

Austrian-born activist who, with her husband, played a crucial role in helping almost 1,500 endangered refugees, many of them world-famous artists and intellectuals, flee Nazi-occupied France over a perilous but effective Pyrenees escape route known as the F-Route. *Born Lisa Eckstein in Uzhorod (then Austria-Hungary, now Ukraine), on August 23, 1909; had a brother Hans Eckstein; married Johannes (Hans) Fittko.*

In partnership with her husband, was active in resisting Nazism as exiles (1930s); played a crucial role in saving the lives of almost 1,500 endangered refugees, many of them world-famous artists and intellectuals (1940–41), helping them flee Nazi-occupied France over a Pyrenees escape route known as the F-Route (Fittko-Route); with husband, escaped to Cuba (1941), finally settling in U.S.; lived in Chicago and was active in the peace movement; awarded the Distinguished Service Medal, First Class, by the Federal Republic of Germany in recognition of her role in the resistance (1986).

Born in the town of Uzhorod in the Carpathian mountains in 1909, Lisa Eckstein grew up in Vienna and Berlin where her assimilated Jewish parents exposed her to the liberal humanist values that had flourished in 19th-century Central Europe. The optimistic ideals that made possible the emancipation of Jews in the

century before 1914 suffered grievously during World War I and its traumatic aftermath in defeated Germany and Austria. As a young student in Berlin, Lisa witnessed the rise of Nazi intolerance and racism as brown-shirted storm troopers insulted and physically assaulted their political enemies, particularly if they were Jews. Like many young people from bourgeois homes, Lisa was drawn to the organized working class as the only possible bulwark against the triumph of Adolf Hitler's National Socialist movement. A committed Social Democrat from an early age, she was convinced that only in a society based on socialism and egalitarianism could people transcend the narrow tribalism that had spawned wars, ethnic hatreds and exploitation throughout human history.

By the early 1930s, Lisa was putting her strongly held ideals into practice as an active member of Berlin's Socialist Student League. As soon as the Nazi dictatorship began to be erected in early 1933, Lisa and her young colleagues started to engage in highly dangerous underground activities, particularly the writing and dissemination of anti-Nazi literature. While producing their illegal leaflets, Lisa and her small band of resisters worked efficiently but they were always in fear of being discovered by the police or neighborhood Nazis. To hide the sound of their typewriter, they played the triumphal march from *Aïda* at high volume on their phonograph. The flyers, optimistically inscribed DEATH TO FASCISM—THE STRUGGLE GOES ON!, were left in the entrance halls of apartment buildings or under doors. Within months, however, the Nazi regime became increasingly efficient at discovering and crushing opposition cells like Lisa's, and she fled to the safety of Prague, in a Czechoslovakia that remained an island of democracy in the heart of Europe. There, Lisa met Hans Fittko.

An active Social Democrat from a working-class setting, Hans had pushed his way up from poverty to become a noted journalist and anti-Nazi publicist in Germany. When the Nazis took over the German government in the first months of 1933, Hans became a marked man, charged with "intellectual authorship" of the murder of a Berlin Nazi. Subject to the death penalty that he was convinced would be carried out if he found himself in Nazi hands, Hans had fled to Prague in the still-free Czechoslovak Republic. There, he met fellow refugee Lisa Eckstein. Hans and Lisa fell in love and became inseparable, sharing the hardships and dangers of political exile from the Third Reich.

As one of the most talented of the anti-Nazi journalists, Hans continued the struggle even as Hitler's Germany went from triumph to triumph throughout the 1930s. Lisa assisted his work and served as a full partner in their often materially and psychologically difficult life of exile. The Fittkos were high on the Nazi wanted list and never felt safe from assassination or kidnapping by Hitler's agents. They lived a precarious existence in Czechoslovakia, then Austria, Switzerland, the Netherlands, and France. Although she developed a deeper sense of her Jewish identity during these years, Lisa regarded herself as essentially a socialist political emigré from Nazi tyranny. Despite the hardships both endured, she and Hans often found their morale strengthened by the shared work of their anti-Nazi colleagues, be they German emigrés or the politically alert citizens of the nations that offered them refuge.

The start of World War II in September 1939 brought entirely new challenges to the Fittkos. A panicky French government arrested and interned all of the German refugees, incarcerating them in concentration camps under harsh conditions. Lisa found herself imprisoned in Gurs, a camp near the Pyrenees that quickly became known not only for its inadequate facilities but also for the often remarkable spirit of endurance that emerged among its prisoners. French paranoia about ubiquitous "German spies" made officials arrest not only *les indésirables* like the Fittkos who had as anti-Nazis and foreigners never been viewed with sympathy by a conservative bureaucracy, but others as well who fell under a blanket definition of potential traitors. These improbable "threats to the national security of France" included some French-speaking nuns who had lived in the province of Alsace, which had been part of the German Reich until 1918, as well as a Frenchwoman who had been briefly married to a German almost two decades earlier.

Although she was able to simply walk out of the Gurs camp after the military collapse of France in June 1940, Lisa Fittko remained at great risk from the Nazis who continued to occupy the northern region of France, leaving the rest of the country to be administered by the collaborationist French regime headquartered in the southern resort town of Vichy. Both Hans Fittko and Lisa's brother Hans Eckstein had been released from imprisonment some time before the German invasion in May. By the end of 1940, Vichy-controlled France was swarming with frightened refugees from Nazi tyranny, as well as many individuals who, out of conviction or greed, were willing to report on the whereabouts of these same refugees to the Vichy authorities who were now enforcing laws hostile to Jews and anti-Nazis.

With the vast majority of the French people traumatized and concerned with personal survival, a rescuer now appeared from far away in the form of an improbable hero, a young American named Varian Fry. The son of a wealthy stockbroker, Fry had graduated from Harvard and become a successful magazine editor in his home city of New York. After a trip to Berlin, he grew alarmed by the Nazi threat to modern civilization but soon discovered that most of his fellow Americans remained complacent about foreign developments that did not immediately impact on their daily lives.

Varian Fry found it impossible to remain indifferent. In the fall of 1939, he and the Austrian emigré Karl Frank raised funds to enable refugees from Nazism to leave France for the United States. The situation became much more desperate in June 1940 when France was conquered by the Nazis. Carrying papers identifying himself as a YMCA relief worker, and with a list of several hundred names of intellectuals threatened by the Nazis, Fry arrived in Marseille in August 1940. He also brought along $3,000 in cash taped to his leg. By the time Fry arrived, French authorities handed over to the German Gestapo all requests for exit visas—thus making it impossible for political or racial refugees from Nazism to leave France. Relying on the refugee grapevine, Fry quickly established contact with hundreds of potential escapees. With a staff of two—German-born refugee economist Albert Hirschman (called "Beamish" by Fry) and Boston-born art history student **Miriam Davenport**—Fry sought a viable escape route for increasingly desperate men and women.

The most obvious course—by sea—was also the most perilous, many of the available boats being unseaworthy and traffic being closely monitored by the French authorities. That left the Pyrenees. Although the Spanish and Portuguese dictatorships were clearly sympathetic to Hitler's Germany, they were nevertheless willing to allow refugees to travel through their countries provided they had proper transit visas and ultimate destinations, such as the United States, that would accept them. The snag was to find a way to get out of France illegally. Since the refugees did not have exit visas, Fry had to provide them with forged ones. These were brilliantly executed by another refugee, the Viennese cartoonist Bill

Freier, who spent his days doing portraits on the Marseille waterfront, while spending his evenings altering passports. Fry's rescue system was inaugurated in the fishing village of Cerbere, where the frontier posts were so positioned that neither the French nor Spanish officials could see each other, thus providing a golden opportunity for slipping refugees into Spain.

Unfortunately, after a while the Germans became suspicious of the Cerbere area and stationed troops there; a new route had to be found. Fortunately, Beamish had heard about the long years of experience Lisa and Hans Fittko had had in eluding Nazi pursuers during the 1930s. The Fittkos had already been scouting the mountain passes of the Pyrenees to plan their own escape in the near future. Now, Beamish brought them to Fry, who was able to persuade the couple to delay their own departure from France in order to help guide others over the border.

By the end of September 1940, the Fittkos had left Marseille for Banyuls-sur-Mer, a town a few kilometers up the coast from the now-abandoned escape route at Cerbere. Using identity papers forged by Freier, the Fittkos moved into a large house and were able to find work in local vineyards along the border. The house occupied by Lisa and Hans Fittko was to become a transit hotel for an extraordinary collection—nearly 1,500 in all—of writers, artists and scholars fleeing from Hitler's Europe. The caliber of talent can only be hinted at in the following names: the artists Marc Chagall, Jacques Lipchitz, and Max Ernst; musicians such as *Wanda Landowska; writers such as *Hannah Arendt and André Breton; and scholars such as the courageous anti-Nazi statistician and publicist Emil Julius Gumbel.

Before they departed from Marseille, refugees were given half of a torn strip of colored paper; a number was on the end of each strip. Lisa Fittko had the other half, with the same number on it. If the numbers matched and the two pieces fit together perfectly, she knew that the refugee had been sent by Fry. After a few days, Lisa or Hans would take some of their "visiting friends" into the nearby fields, either to work for a while in the vineyards or participate in a picnic. Then, when the coast was clear, the refugees would one by one fade into the hills. Amazingly, none who escaped the Nazis via what soon came to be known as the "F-Route" (Fittko-Route) were ever caught.

Only one incident marred these triumphs: the tragic death of the brilliant German critic and philosopher Walter Benjamin. On September 26, 1940, Lisa Fittko was the guide for a group of three refugees that included the unworldly Benjamin, whom she referred to half-fondly, half-mockingly as "Old Benjamin." Because of a serious heart condition, Benjamin was compelled to take a one-minute break for every ten minutes or so of strenuous hiking. Unfortunately on that day the Spanish border police had been given new orders, and the group's transit visas were declared to be invalid. Benjamin's will to live crumbled while spending the night in the Spanish border village of Port-Bou, and he took a fatal dose of morphine. Ironically, his two companions were able to proceed through Spain and on to the United States when authorities decided to waive their new regulations immediately after Benjamin's suicide, perhaps because of the philosopher's tragic escape from life.

Only when Varian Fry was taken into custody on August 29, 1941, did the Fittkos again seriously plan for their own escape. They had worked from the town of Banyuls-sur-Mer for more than six months. Now, in November 1941, Lisa and Hans succeeded in themselves escaping from Vichy France. By the end of 1941 time had virtually run out on Jews and anti-Nazis in Hitler's Europe, where the machinery of mass annihilation began to function with ever greater efficiency with each passing day. In their nation of refuge, Cuba, the Fittkos were soon able to create a new life for themselves.

But Lisa and her husband never gave up the hope of returning to Germany after the defeat of Hitlerism. Remaining ardent socialists, both believed that they could be of use in a defeated Germany, helping to build a democratic socialist society that would never again be able to threaten either its own citizens or humanity at large. But fate decreed that the Fittkos were never to return to a shattered Europe. Concerned that a radically democratized Germany might become overly pro-Soviet or neutralist, American occupation authorities in Germany soon after 1945 took measures to prevent the return of leftist exiles like the Fittkos. As a result, although they still resided in Cuba, they found themselves frustrated in their efforts to receive authorization papers for a return to Europe.

In 1948, Lisa and her husband left Cuba for the United States. They settled in Chicago, which had a large community of Jewish Holocaust survivors. Soon after their arrival Hans Fittko became seriously ill, and after a number of years of declining health he died. Refusing to become permanently depressed, Lisa Fittko continued her lifelong political and social activism in the context of her adopted country. She took a strong stand against the Vietnam War, was active in the Nuclear Freeze movement of the 1980s, and on countless occasions spoke out for racial and economic justice. She began writing her memoirs, which first appeared as articles in German magazines, and finally as books published in Munich in 1985 and 1992 (French and Spanish translations appeared in print in 1987 and 1997, respectively). In 1991, her memoir *Escape Through the Pyrenees* appeared in print, followed in 1993 by her account of the years of exile and resistance, 1933–40, entitled *Solidarity and Treason*. Published by Northwestern University Press, both volumes received enthusiastic reviews. In these books, Fittko paid tribute not only to the courage of her late husband as her partner in the difficult struggle against fascism, but also provided examples of the moral tenacity of thousands of other now largely forgotten anti-Fascist exiles of the 1930s who refused to accept as inevitable the victory of Hitler's barbarous hordes.

Determined to keep alive the ideals that had in dark times served to inspire her and her late husband, Fittko gladly took on the role of teacher and witness to history. In the final decades of her life, she chose to spend some of her most rewarding hours answering questions posed by the next generation, which included her youngest niece, Marlene. Growing up in a world of peace and prosperity, Marlene and her contemporaries were often ignorant of the terror, war and suffering that dominated the youth of Lisa and Hans Fittko. Lisa's answer to her niece's question of "Can it happen again?" was as simple as it was eloquent, "The same as before? Hardly. Although the breeding grounds of fascism have neither temporal nor geographical borders." When asked by Marlene as to where her homeland was now, Lisa Fittko answered, "Now my home is here. Although the dream of peace and freedom lives everywhere."

SOURCES:

Brodersen, Momme, and Martina Dervis. *Walter Benjamin: A Biography.* Translated by Malcolm R. Green and Ingrida Ligers. London: Verso, 1996.

Caron, Vicki. "The Missed Opportunity: French Refugee Policy in Wartime, 1939-40," in *Historical Reflections/Reflexions Historiques.* Vol. 22, no. 1. Winter 1996, pp. 117–157.

Dornhof, Dorothea. "'Nur nicht stillschweigen müssen zu den Verbrechen seines Landes': Gespräch mit Lisa Fittko, Chicago, 14. Dezember 1992," in *Exilforschung: Ein internationales Jahrbuch.* Vol. 11, 1993, pp. 229–238.

Fittko, Lisa. "'Der alte Benjamin': Flucht über die Pyrenäen," in *Merkur: Deutsche Zeitschrift für europäisches Denken.* Vol. 36, no. 1. January 1982, pp. 35–49.

———. *Escape Through the Pyrenees.* Translated by David Koblick. Evanston, Illinois: Northwestern University Press, 1991.

———. *Solidarity and Treason: Resistance and Exile, 1933–1940.* Translated by Roslyn Theobald in collaboration with the author. Evanston, IL: Northwestern University Press, 1993.

Fry, Varian. *Surrender on Demand.* Boulder, CO: Johnson Books, 1997.

Glayman, Claude. "Une adversaire irréductible du nazisme," in *La Quinzaine littéraire.* No. 495. October 16–31, 1987, p. 17.

Jasper, Willi. *Hotel Lutetia: Ein deutsches Exil in Paris.* Munich: Carl Hanser Verlag, 1994.

Mühlen, Patrik von zur. *Fluchtziel Lateinamerika—Die deutsche Emigration 1933–1945: Politische Aktivitäten und soziokulturelle Integration.* Bonn: Verlag Neue Gesellschaft, 1988.

Sharon, Lynn. "Zealous assistance," in *Jerusalem Post.* January 10, 1992.

John Haag,
Assistant Professor of History,
University of Georgia, Athens, Georgia

Fitton, Doris (1897–1985)

Founder of the Independent Theatre, Sydney, Australia. Name variations: Dame Doris Fitton. Born in Manila, the Philippines, in November 1897; died on April 2, 1985; daughter of Walter (an English accountant, broker, and manufacturer of cigars) and Janet (Cameron) Fitton (an Australian); early schooling was in Melbourne; attended Loreto convents in Portland and Ballarat; studied acting with Gregan McMahon and at the Melbourne Repertory Theatre; married Norbert "Tug" Mason (a lawyer), in 1922; children: two.

Doris Fitton, who presided over the Australian theatrical scene for four decades, was born in Manila of an English father and an Australian mother. Brought to Melbourne for her early education, she also attended convents in Portland and Ballarat and was infinitely more interested in the school plays than scholastic achievement. After leaving school, she worked as a secretary before beginning classes with the renowned Gregan McMahon. Her first acting role in 1915 led to engagements with J.C. Williamson Ltd. and the Melbourne and Sydney Repertory Societies. After her marriage in 1922, she continued to combine domestic and child-rearing duties with her acting career, taking small roles in the newly formed Sydney Repertory Company and other productions around the city.

In 1930, Fitton joined 19 other actors and 100 associated members to launch the Independent Theatre. Modeled after Constantin Stanislavsky's Moscow Arts Theatre, the Independent operated for the next 47 years, closing in May 1977 due to lack of funding. Through the Independent's long history, Fitton was at the helm, acting variously as director, producer, actress, and drama teacher. (During financial slumps, she was also known to sweep floors when necessary.) The theater, which received no government support, provided exposure for countless young playwrights and fostered the careers of numerous Australian actors. Productions sometimes sparked controversy; in 1948, the staging of *Sumner Locke's *Rusty Bugles* resulted in the play's temporary banning by the New South Wales government. Fitton, a beloved figure despite her dictatorial nature, was made Dame of the British Empire (DBE) in 1981. She died on April 2, 1985. Her autobiography, *Not Without Dust and Heat: My Life in Theatre* (1981), is also a history of the Independent.

Fitton, Mary (c. 1578–1647)

English noblewoman, doubtfully identified as the "dark lady" of Shakespeare's sonnets. Name variations: Mary Logher or Lougher. Born in 1578; baptized on June 24, 1578; died in 1647; daughter of Sir Edward Fitton the Younger of Gawsworth, Cheshire, England; married Captain W. Polwhele, in 1606 or 1607 (died 1609 or 1610); married a Captain Lougher or Logher (d. 1636); children: (first marriage) a son and daughter; (with Sir Richard Leveson) possibly two illegitimate daughters.

Identified by some as the "dark lady" of Shakespeare's sonnets, Mary Fitton was born in 1578, the daughter of Sir Edward Fitton the Younger of Gawsworth, Cheshire. When she was 14, her elder sister **Anne Fitton** married John Newdigate. Around 1595, Mary became maid of honor to Queen *Elizabeth I, and her father put her under the care of Sir William Knollys, comptroller of the queen's household, who promised to defend the "innocent lamb" from the "wolfish cruelty and fox-like subtlety of the tame beasts of this place." Though 50 and already married to *Elizabeth Knollys, Sir William soon became Mary's suitor, and he appears to have received a great deal of encouragement.

It is doubtful that Fitton is the basis for Shakespeare's "dark lady." There is no hint in her authenticated biography that she was acquainted with Shakespeare. William Kemp, a clown in Shakespeare's company, dedicated his *Nine Daies Wonder* to Mistress Anne Fitton, "Maid of Honour to Elizabeth" (possibly confused with her sister); and there is a sonnet ad-

dressed to Mary in an anonymous volume, *A Woman's Woorth defended against all the Men in the World* (1599). In court festivities in 1600, Mary Fitton led a dance at which William Herbert, also rumored to be the subject of Shakespeare's sonnets, was present; shortly afterwards, she became his mistress. In February 1601, Herbert, later the 3rd earl of Pembroke, was sent to the Fleet in disgrace because of the affair. Fitton, who appears to have been simply dismissed from court, went to stay with her sister, Lady Newdigate, at Arbury. It is also said that she gave birth to a child who died soon after.

A second scandal has been attributed to Fitton by George Ormerod, author of *History of Cheshire*. Ormerod asserts that she had two illegitimate daughters with Sir Richard Leveson, a friend and correspondent of her sister Anne.

In Gawsworth church, there is a painted monument of the Fittons, in which Anne and Mary are represented kneeling behind their mother. From what remains of its coloring, Mary is shown to be a dark woman, which is of course essential to her identification with the lady of the sonnets, but in the portraits at Arbury described by Lady Newdigate in her *Gossip from a Muniment Room* (1897), Mary has brown hair and grey eyes. The identity of the Arbury portrait with Mary Fitton was challenged by Thomas Tyler, however. Arguments in favor of Mary Fitton as the false mistress of Shakespeare's sonnets can be found in Tyler's *Shakespeare's Sonnets* (1890) and his *Herbert-Fitton Theory of Shakespeare's Sonnets* (1898).

Fitzalan, Alice (fl. 1285)

Countess of Arundel. Name variations: Alice of Saluzzo. Flourished around 1285; married Richard Fitzalan (1267–1302), 6th earl of Arundel; children: Edmund Fitzalan (1285–1326), 7th earl of Arundel.

Fitzalan, Alice (d. around 1338)

*Countess of Arundel. Name variations: Alice de Warrenne. Died around 1338; daughter of William de Warrenne (son of John, 3rd earl of Surrey) and Joan de Vere (daughter of 5th earl of Oxford); married Edmund Fitzalan, 7th earl of Arundel, in 1305; children: Richard Fitzalan (c. 1313–1376), 8th earl of Arundel; *Joan Fitzalan (fl. 1325, who married John Bohun).*

Fitzalan, Alice (1352–1416)

Countess of Kent. Name variations: Alice Holland. Born in 1352 in Arundel Castle, West Sussex, England; died on March 17, 1416; daughter of Richard Fitzalan (c. 1313–1376), 8th earl of Arundel, and *Eleanor Plantagenet (c. 1318–1372); sister of *Joan Fitzalan (d. 1419); married Thomas Holland, 2nd earl of Kent, on April 10, 1364; children: *Alianor Holland (c. 1373–1405); Thomas Holland, 3rd earl of Kent; Edmund Holland, 4th earl of Kent; *Margaret Holland (1385–1429); *Joan Holland (c. 1380–1434); *Elizabeth Holland (c. 1383–?); *Eleanor Holland (c. 1385–?).

Fitzalan, Amy (fl. 1440)

Countess of Ormonde. Name variations: Amy Butler. Flourished around 1440; daughter of John Fitzalan, 11th earl of Arundel, and Maud Lovell; second wife of James Butler (1420–1461), 5th earl of Ormonde.

Fitzalan, Anne.

See Percy, Anne.

Fitzalan, Eleanor (c. 1318–1372).

See Eleanor Plantagenet.

Fitzalan, Elizabeth (d. 1385)

Countess of Arundel. Name variations: Elizabeth Bohun; Elizabeth de Bohun. Died in 1385; daughter of William Bohun, 1st earl of Northampton, and *Elizabeth Badlesmere; married Richard Fitzalan, 9th earl of Arundel, in 1359; children: Thomas Fitzalan (1381–1415), 10th earl of Arundel; *Elizabeth Fitzalan (d. 1425); Margaret Fitzalan (who married Sir Rowland Lenthall); Alice Fitzalan (who married John Charlton, 4th Lord Charleton of Powis); Richard Fitzalan.

Fitzalan, Elizabeth (d. 1408).

See Despenser, Elizabeth.

Fitzalan, Elizabeth (d. 1425)

Duchess of Norfolk. Name variations: Elizabeth Mowbray. Died in 1425; daughter of *Elizabeth Fitzalan (d. 1385) and Richard Fitzalan, 9th earl of Arundel; married William Montacute, before 1378; married Thomas Mowbray, 1st duke of Norfolk, in 1384; children: (second marriage) Thomas Mowbray, 7th baron Mowbray (1385–1405); John Mowbray, 2nd duke of Norfolk (1389–1432); *Isabel Mowbray; *Margaret Mowbray.

Fitzalan, Elizabeth (fl. 1408–1417)

English noblewoman. Name variations: Elizabeth Berkeley; Lady Maltravers. Flourished around 1408 to

1417; married John Fitzalan (1385–1421); children: John Fitzalan (1408–1435), 11th earl of Arundel; William Fitzalan (1417–1487), 13th earl of Arundel.

Fitzalan, Isabel (fl. 1267).

See Mortimer, Isabel.

Fitzalan, Joan (fl. 1325)

Countess of Hereford and Essex. Name variations: sometimes referred to as Alice; Joan Bohun. Flourished around 1325; daughter of Edmund Fitzalan, 7th earl of Arundel, and *Alice (de Warrenne) Fitzalan (d. around 1338); sister of Richard Fitzalan (c. 1313–1376), 8th earl of Arundel; aunt of *Joan Fitzalan (d. 1419); married John Bohun, 5th earl of Hereford, 4th of Essex, in 1325.

Fitzalan, Joan (d. 1419)

Countess of Hereford, Essex, and Northampton. Name variations: Joan Bohun. Born before 1351; died on April 7, 1419; buried in Walden Abbey, Essex, England; daughter of Richard Fitzalan (c. 1313–1376), 8th earl of Arundel, and *Eleanor Plantagenet (c. 1318–1372); sister of *Alice Fitzalan (1352–1416); married Humphrey Bohun, earl of Hereford, Essex, and Northampton; children: *Eleanor Bohun (1366–1399); *Mary de Bohun (1369–1394, first wife of Henry IV, king of England).

Joan Fitzalan's daughter *Mary de Bohun married Henry IV, a few years before he became king of England. In the beginning of Henry's reign, there was a plot to restore Richard II to the throne. One of its ringleaders was John Holland, Richard II's half-brother, who was captured and fell into Joan Fitzalan's hands. Joan was very loyal to Henry, despite the fact that her daughter, the queen, had already died in childbirth in 1394. Joan had Holland beheaded on February 9, 1400, without trial.

Fitzalan, Joan (fl. 1480s).

See Neville, Joan.

Fitzalan, Katherine (b. around 1520)

Countess of Arundel. Name variations: Catherine or Katherine Grey. Born around 1520; daughter of Thomas Grey (1477–1530), 2nd marquess of Dorset, and *Margaret Wotton; married Henry Fitzalan (1512–1580), 16th earl of Arundel; children: *Mary Fitzalan (d. 1557).

Fitzalan, Katherine (fl. 1530s)

English noblewoman. Flourished around 1530; daughter of William Fitzalan, 15th earl of Arundel, and *Anne Percy; *first wife of Henry Grey (c. 1517–1554), later duke of Suffolk (created in 1551). In 1535, Henry Grey married his second wife* *Frances Brandon; *their daughter was Lady* *Jane Grey.*

Fitzalan, Margaret (b. around 1388)

English noblewoman. Name variations: Margaret Roos; Baroness Ros. Born around 1388; daughter of John Fitzalan (1365–1391) and *Elizabeth Despenser *(d. 1408); married William Roos (d. 1414), 7th baron Ros; children:* *Margaret Roos *(who married Reginald Grey); Thomas Roos, 9th baron Ros (d. 1431).*

Fitzalan, Margaret (fl. 1450s).

See Woodville, Margaret.

Fitzalan, Mary (d. 1557)

Countess of Arundel. Name variations: Mary Howard. Died after June 28, 1557; daughter of Henry Fitzalan (1512–1580), 16th earl of Arundel, and *Katherine Fitzalan *(b. around 1520); married Thomas Howard, 3rd duke of Norfolk, in 1556; children: Philip Howard, 17th earl of Arundel. Thomas Howard also married* *Margaret Audley *(d. 1564) after August of 1557 and* *Elizabeth Leyburne *(d. 1567).*

Fitzalan, Maud (fl. 1200s)

English noblewoman. Name variations: Maud de Verdun. Born Maud de Verdun; daughter of Roesia de Verdun; married John Fitzalan (who, though not known as an earl of Arundel, occupied the castle of Arundel from 1243 to 1267); children: John Fitzalan (d. 1272); grandmother of Richard, 6th earl of Arundel.

Fitzalan, Philippa (1375–1401).

See Mortimer, Philippa.

Fitzclarence, Amelia (1807–1858)

Viscountess Falkland. Born on November 5, 1807 (some sources cite 1803); died on July 2, 1858, in London; interred at Hutton-Rudby, Yorkshire; legitimized daughter of William IV (1765–1837), king of England (r. 1831–1837), and *Dora Jordan *(1761–1816); married Lucius Bentinck, 10th viscount Falkland, on December 27, 1830; children: Lucius*

William (b. 1831); Plantagenet Pierrepoint, 11th viscount Falkland (b. 1836); Byron Charles.

Fitzgerald, Lady Edward (1773–1831).

See Genlis, Stéphanie-Félicité, Comtesse de for sidebar on Pamela Fitzgerald.

Fitzgerald, Elizabeth (c. 1528–1589)

English noblewoman who was celebrated in verse. Name variations: Lady Elizabeth Fitzgerald; The Fair Geraldine. Born at Maynooth, Ireland, around 1528; died in 1589; youngest daughter of George Fitzgerald, 9th earl of Kildare; married Sir Anthony Browne (d. 1548); married Edward Fiennes de Clinton, earl of Lincoln, around 1552.

Lady Elizabeth Fitzgerald, member of the household of the Princess Mary (*Mary I) and later Queen *Catherine Howard, was married at age 15 to Sir Anthony Browne. He died five years later in 1548. She then married Edward Fiennes de Clinton, earl of Lincoln, around 1552. Fitzgerald has been celebrated in verse by Michael Drayton and Sir Walter Scott. Henry Howard, earl of Surrey, addressed a series of songs and sonnets to her, first published in Tottel's *Miscellany* in 1557.

Fitzgerald, Ella (1917–1996)

Jazz and pop world's "first lady of song," the most honored female vocalist in modern music history. Born Ella Jane Fitzgerald out of wedlock on April 25, 1917, in Newport News, Virginia; died at her home in Beverly Hills, California, on June 15, 1996; daughter of William Fitzgerald and Temperance Williams; had a half-sister Frances who died in 1960; educated in local schools in Yonkers, New York; married Benjamin Kornegay, in 1935 (annulled 1937); married Ray Brown (a bassist), in 1947 (divorced 1953); children: (second marriage) one adopted son, Ray Brown, Jr.

Discovered by bandleader William "Chick" Webb in Harlem, who gave her her first paid singing engagements with his band (mid-1930s); later became a noted jazz stylist with Dizzy Gillespie's band, known for her "scatting" and her emotive interpretations of pop and jazz standards; remained the most popular female vocalist of international stature from the end of World War II to the mid-1980s, winning 12 Grammy Awards before retiring because of poor health.

One night in 1935, at Harlem's Savoy Ballroom, bandleader Chick Webb was presented with an odd vision as he sat backstage between sets. Standing before "the king of the Savoy" was a gawky young girl of 18, wearing an ill-fitting dress and shoes much too large for her. "Don't look at her," his master-of-ceremonies said. "Just listen to her sing." With that, Ella Jane Fitzgerald took a deep breath and, unaccompanied, sang "The Object of My Affection" with such perfect pitch and subtlety of expression that not another sound could be heard until she had finished. Even though the last thing he had been thinking about was a vocalist for his band, Webb hired her on the spot, sensing instinctively what one biographer would later describe as Ella's "superb blend of musicianship, vocal ability, and interpretive insight."

I just sing as I feel, man. Jazz ain't intellectual.

—Ella Fitzgerald

Ella Fitzgerald's remarkable talents seemed completely spontaneous, since she had no formal vocal training, grew up in a distinctly non-musical household, and harbored a secret desire as a girl to become a dancer. She was born out of wedlock in Newport News, Virginia, in 1917, and while her father—a truck driver named William Fitzgerald—acknowledged paternity, he disappeared when Ella was only three. Her mother **Temperance ("Tempie") Williams** supported her daughter by taking in laundry before marrying a retired fisherman, Joseph Da Silva, and moving with him in 1920 to Yonkers, just north of New York City. By then, radio had become a major form of entertainment, and Ella grew up listening to the big bands of Fletcher Henderson, Jimmy Lunceford, and Jack Teagarden, many of whom appeared regularly just a train ride away at Harlem's nightclubs and ballrooms.

Her only musical training was in junior high school, where she sang in the Glee Club and was told by friends that she was good enough to make a living at it. Too shy to even consider such a thing, Ella would only go so far as to take the train into Harlem as often as she could to hang around the clubs and get autographs from stars like *Billie Holiday. When her mother died of a heart attack in 1932 and her stepfather turned to drink and became abusive, Ella moved to Harlem to live with an aunt. But when her new guardian found out that Ella had been making extra money by running numbers between illegal betting parlors and, worse, serving as a police lookout for one of Harlem's brothels, she disowned her niece and packed her off to the Riverdale Orphanage, where Fitzgerald learned to type and seemed destined for a drab life of secretarial work.

But there was always music—on the radio, in the movies, and best of all, live on stage. A favorite spot for hearing live music for not much money was the Harlem Opera House, and it was there one night in 1934 that Ella Fitzgerald first sang for a paying audience. Arriving for the Opera House's weekly amateur night, she and two friends dared each other to get up on stage and perform, drawing straws to decide which one of them was the victim. Ella drew the short straw. Shaking with stage fright, she stepped onto the stage intending to dance, but her body refused to cooperate; instead, she asked the pianist to play a number she'd heard *Connee Boswell sing on the radio, "The Object of My Affection." "I didn't know one key from another," she said many years later. "I just sang . . . in the key they picked for me." In only a few moments, the raucous audience had fallen silent before Fitzgerald's apparently effortless, silky, perfectly tuned singing, and asked for three encores before she was awarded the $25 first prize. (Another young hopeful named *Pearl Bailey, also born in Newport News, was in the audience.)

Encouraged by her success, not to mention the $25, Fitzgerald entered as many amateur night shows as she could, adding two other numbers—"Believe It, Beloved" and Hoagy Carmichael's "Judy"—to her repertoire. She won again the next year at the Opera House, this time for $50 and a week's work singing with Tiny Bradshaw's house band, all of whom chipped in to buy her a dress to wear. By now, word was getting around about the Fitzgerald girl with the velvet voice, and when Ella sang at the Apollo's amateur night (which she won), Chick Webb's M.C. Bardu Ali was in the audience and promptly got her to sing before his boss.

William "Chick" Webb had one of the most popular swing bands in New York City at the time, although he was unable to lead the musicians himself because of a crippling childhood bout with spinal tuberculosis that had left him partially paralyzed. While Ali worked the front of the band, Chick was content to sit at the back as drummer. But the band was his baby, and it was Chick who paid Fitzgerald out of his own pocket when he first used her as vocalist at a fraternity dance at Yale University. The collegians went wild for her, and Webb was certain he'd been right—so certain that he and his wife legally adopted Ella, then just 18, so she could work professionally. Back in Harlem, he and Charlie Buchanan, the Savoy Ballroom's manager, each chipped in ten dollars to pay Ella's salary for the next week. "We gave her fifty bucks the second

week," Buchanan recalled. "The third week, we dressed her up."

Webb wisely cautioned Fitzgerald not to be too anxious for success and to develop slowly, telling her that the ones who rose too fast were the ones who fell the quickest. "I felt I wanted to be a big success in a hurry," Fitzgerald recalled, "and I found all through the years you never appreciate anything if you get it in a hurry." Webb would only let her sing one number per set at first, as a way of getting her used to performing, and taught her everything she lacked in terms of deportment—how to stand at the mike, what to do with her hands, and so on. Even with her limited exposure in those early days, a young dancer at the Savoy one night in 1935 remembered, "She was so young and beautiful that we all fell in love with her before she opened her mouth. We were all captivated." So were the judges of 1935's famous "Battle of the Bands" between Chick Webb's group and Benny Goodman's ensemble. Fitzgerald went up against the Goodman Quartette, singing "Big Boy Blue" and "You Showed Me The Way" (a number she had written herself). The Chick Webb Band emerged the winner. Later that year, she made her first recording with Webb for Decca, "Love and Kisses," although she never heard her own voice until some months later, when she had to pay someone of legal drinking age to go into a bar and crank up the jukebox while she stood outside and listened. Early in 1936, she appeared with Webb on radio for the first time, Chick having been invited to appear on a regional radio program called "Gems of Color."

Fitzgerald's talent for "scat singing"—that is, improvising new melodies and harmonies over existing ones using onomatopoeic phrases and nonsense words—emerged early on in her career. In 1936, she recorded a song officially called "If You Can't Sing It, You'll Have to Swing It," although it became known by the more convenient title "Mr. Paganini." Addressed to the famous concert violinist, the lyrics ask him to "play my favorite rhapsody"; and if he can't play it . . .

> Won't you sing it?
> And if you can't sing it,
> You'll simply have to swing it.

And Ella was off on a soaring, swooping musical game with Webb's band that made the record enough of a bestseller that her next recordings were under her own name, as "Ella Fitzgerald and the Savoy Eight." It was typical of Chick Webb to be content in the background, just as he was when the band played before a live audience. "He never felt he was the only star," Fitzgerald said. "Anyone who could do something, he gave them the chance to do it." In 1937, Ella was named *Down Beat*'s female vocalist of the year, topping Billie Holiday—whose autograph she had shyly sought less than ten years before.

On tour in Boston with Webb in 1937, Fitzgerald picked out a tune on the piano one night between sets. It was a children's song she had learned in school years before, "A-Tisket, A-Tasket," about the little girl with the yellow basket. An arranger traveling with the band worked it up for her, and Fitzgerald sang it for the first time as a novelty song the next night, with an enthusiastic response. It was a year for novelty songs, one of the top tunes on the charts then being Slim Galliard's and Slam Stewart's "The Flat Foot Floogie with the Floy Floy." Decca was skeptical about recording Fitzgerald's invention, but Webb convinced them to release it, adding some business in which the band and Fitzgerald traded information about the basket in question:

> Was it green?
> No, no, no, no.
> Was it red?
> No, no, no, no.

. . . and so on, until Fitzgerald broke into a scat again when they finally worked their way down to the color yellow. The little song about the basket sold a million copies, went to number one on the Hit Parade, and made Ella Fitzgerald a star of national proportions. Later that year, Webb had to hustle Fitzgerald down to court to annul a marriage she'd made on a bet. ("The guy bet me I wouldn't marry him," claimed Fitzgerald; she also claimed to have forgotten his name, though he appears to have been a shipyard worker named Benjamin Kornegay.) At the hearing, the judge told her, "You just keep on singing 'A-Tisket, A-Tasket' and leave those men alone."

By 1939, five years after her nervous debut at the Harlem Opera House, Fitzgerald was earning $125 a week, was being pursued by the likes of Benny Goodman and Jimmy Lunceford, had won *Down Beat*'s poll for the third year in a row, and was working—either on tour or in the studio—nearly constantly. Her professionalism seemed almost nonchalant, especially when it came to her growing fondness for food. Sammy Cahn remembered one session in 1938 in which Fitzgerald was about to record a sensitive ballad, "a song," he said, "that required some kind of feeling, some personal involvement. She was standing at the mike with a hot dog in one hand and a bottle of Coke in the other, and she couldn't wait to get at the song so she could eat." Studio sidemen, who were paid per song, loved to record with Fitzgerald, since she rarely required more than one take for a tune, and several numbers could be laid down at each session. Jazz critic Whitney Balliet once described Fitzgerald's apparently effortless technique as one "that enables her to slide effortlessly up and down the scales, manage long intervals, and maintain perfect pitch. She is a peerless popular singer." The legendary perfect pitch was actually something much more rare, what musicologists call "relative" pitch—an ability to not only hit the correct pitch for each individual note, but for its relationship to the notes immediately before and after it. Chick Webb didn't bother much with such analyses, however. He merely changed his marquees in 1939, to read: "Ella Fitzgerald and the Chick Webb Band."

Few people besides Fitzgerald knew that Webb had been in nearly constant pain for most of his life because of his childhood tuberculosis, but during the first half of 1939, the pain seemed to be getting worse. Webb died that June, when he was only 29 years old. At the funeral, Ella stood next to his casket and sang "My Buddy" in tribute to the mentor who had brought her from the streets of Harlem to national prominence. Her eulogy for him was even simpler. "There was so much music in that man," she said.

Although Fitzgerald took over the band, renaming it Ella Fitzgerald and her Famous Orchestra, she must have wondered at times over the next six years if Webb's warning about succeeding too quickly had come true for her. With the onset of World War II and the draft, the band slowly began to break up, as the musicians were called up, one after another. Before long the band's manager, Moe Gale—who had taken over Fitzgerald's personal management as well—suggested that Ella begin to appear separately from the orchestra; and by 1942, with the coming of a bitter strike by the American Federation of Musicians against the record industry over royalties, the band finally gave up the ghost. Fitzgerald did a good deal of radio work and continued to record with all the big bands for Decca, with whom Gale negotiated a new contract with a $15,000 guarantee (although some insiders said she could have easily gotten $40,000). But her career seemed stalled, and for the first time since the mid-30s, she failed to appear on *Down Beat*'s annual poll.

After the war, however, things changed. Dizzy Gillespie had been a fan of Fitzgerald's since her days with Webb, and when the war ended and America was ready to let its hair down again, Fitzgerald went on tour with Gillespie and his band. Dizzy gave her, she later said, her "education in bop"—that happy blend of jazz and pop of which Gillespie was such a brilliant stylist. On tour, Ella said, "we would have some real crazy experiences, but to me it was what you call growing up in the music." The new, jazz-oriented Fitzgerald burst on the national charts with her recording of "Lady Be Good" in 1947, her first major hit built almost entirely around her trademark scat singing. Also in that year, she made her initial Carnegie Hall appearance with Dizzy, singing "Stairway to the Stars" and "How High the Moon." Not everyone was happy with her new style. *Melody Maker,* in an article bannered "Ella Switches To Sweltering Swing," wondered if she had gone too far for her traditional audience to follow. But follow her they did, loyally and in greater and greater numbers, for the next 40 years.

Fitzgerald's personal life also took a new turn. Ray Brown played bass with the Gillespie band, and, during the 1947 tour, he and Fitzgerald grew increasingly close. On December 10, the two were married in Mexico. During their six years together, most of it on the road, they adopted a son, Ray Jr., who remained with Fitzgerald when she and Ray were amicably divorced in August of 1953. The two continued to work together professionally for many years thereafter, including countless gigs with the Oscar Peterson Trio, for which Ray was the bassist.

It was Brown who introduced Fitzgerald to the man who would bring her, and so many other jazz artists, to international prominence. Norman Granz had loved being around musicians since his childhood in Los Angeles, and he was the first to realize the potential of a paying audience at what was then the novel idea of a "jam session." He staged his first such sessions while he was in college in Los Angeles in the late 1940s, paying the musicians six dollars a night—but he added a social dimension to these evenings by always stipulating to the club owners that the audience had to be integrated. The jams were such a success that Granz moved them to Los Angeles' Philharmonic Hall and instituted, in 1949, "Jazz at the Philharmonic." JATP, as the cognoscenti came to call it, would become a jazz tradition for the next eight years and tour the country to sellout audiences which were always, at Granz's insistence, racially mixed—not an easy proposition in America in the 1950s, particularly in the South, and especially if you were a Jewish jazz promoter from Los Angeles. In Houston, Granz and his musicians were the victims of a setup by the police, who tried to jail Granz, Fitzgerald and the band on gambling charges (Granz sued and won). Hotels that refused to accept black musicians were routinely taken to court or subjected to sit-down strikes organized by Granz, who also did not hesitate to sue the airline that refused to honor Fitzgerald's first-class ticket on a flight from California to Hawaii.

Granz was determined to add Ella to the growing roster of jazz performers that he managed. He tried to convince her of the half-hearted support she was getting from Decca and Moe Gale, who were content with her earlier work's royalties and were doing little to actively promote her. Loyal to anyone who had known Chick Webb, however, Fitzgerald refused to cancel her contract with either Decca or Gale and resisted Granz's pleas until 1954, when her current contracts expired. Signing with Granz in that year, she immediately found herself playing better clubs for higher salaries and, in 1956, became the cornerstone artist of the most prolific jazz label ever created, Granz's Verve Records. (He would later sell Verve to MGM, in 1960, only to return with a new label, Pablo, which recorded and released many of Fitzgerald's live performances.) It was Granz who first presented Fitzgerald singing with the Oscar Peterson Trio, after pianist Peterson joined the JATP tour in the early 1950s. Fitzgerald and Peterson would appear together for the next 30 years, and few will forget their first appearance at the inaugural Newport Jazz Festival in 1954. "I have never truthfully played with a musician," Peterson says, "who frightened me as much as playing for Ella. Because she has the kind of gift you can't describe."

Ella grew to trust Granz implicitly. "It was a Svengali relationship," says keyboardist Paul Smith. "She rarely bucked him." While it is true that Granz chose nearly all of Fitzgerald's material and the musicians who played for her, he is more unassuming about his influence over Fitzgerald. "She didn't always agree with me," Granz says, "and in some cases, rather than push it, I thought she should do what she wanted." It was Fitzgerald's and Granz's idea for her to record the classic "Songbook" series, each record dedicated to a particular composer, from Harold Arlen to Duke Ellington to Cole Porter—many of whom Fitzgerald had known personally.

By 1960, there were few places in the world where the name Ella Fitzgerald was unknown. But outside of her singing and touring, Fitzgerald had very little private life. She relaxed on tour by avidly watching movies or simply going to sleep. "I'm insecure," she had told an interviewer for *Ebony* in 1961, "because I feel that I'm not glamorous enough." She thought nothing of working seven days a week, doing several shows a day, but the grueling schedule began to take its toll. During a concert in Munich in 1965, she suddenly lost her breath in the middle of a lyric and had to be led from the stage; and for some years previously, her eyes had become increasingly trou-

blesome, first with cataracts and, later, with the glaucoma that accompanied the diabetes with which she was diagnosed. Often weighing 200 pounds or more, she had increasing difficulty negotiating stairs or standing in front of a band for long periods of time; and in the studio, she often took to singing while sitting down.

But sing she did, along with keeping up with the "new" music, telling an interviewer during the late 1960s, for example, that the Beatles "proved they know some kind of music. I'd love to make an album of their songs." She won her 12th Grammy award in 1984 and received the Honors Medal from the Kennedy Center for the Performing Arts that same year. Throughout the 1980s, as she approached 70 years of age, her voice retained its velvety spontaneity and its uncanny pitch.

By the late 1980s, Fitzgerald's eyesight had deteriorated so badly that she once inadvertently stepped off the stage during a concert at the Hollywood Bowl and toppled into a row of empty chairs, hurting her leg. After being helped back on stage, she brought the house down when she immediately launched into "Since I Fell for You." From then on, her schedule began to slow. Her last released recordings were in 1989—for Quincy Jones' "Back On The Block," teaming up with artists such as Bobby McFerrin and Al Jarreau, and a Pablo release, "All That Jazz." By 1990, jazz commentator Dan Morganstern noted that she had to be led on and off stage and had to sit throughout each concert. "But, boy," he went on, "does she still have energy. And she just does not want to let go!" Her last public performance was in Florida in 1992 (although she sang a few verses of "Lady Be Good" at a party in her honor at the University of Southern California School of Music in Hollywood later that year). In 1993, her worsening diabetes forced the amputation of both her legs below the knee. On June 15, 1996, Ella Fitzgerald died of complications of diabetes at her Beverly Hills home.

No doubt critics, composers, musicians, and fans will keep trying to define what Chick Webb felt instinctively that night in Harlem in 1935, though Fitzgerald would probably discourage such ruminations. "Listen, brother," she once said, "I sure get all shook up when folks start theorizing about my singing. I just tell 'em to sit back and relax. Yeah, that's it. Relax."

SOURCES:

Colin, Sid. *Ella: The Life and Times of Ella Fitzgerald.* London: Elm Tree Books, 1986.

Fidelman, Geoffrey. *The First Lady of Song: Ella Fitzgerald for the Record.* NY: Birch Lane Press, 1994.

Holden, Stephen. "Ella Fitzgerald, the Voice of Jazz, Dies at 79" (obituary) in *The New York Times*. June 16, 1996.

McDonough, John. "Tales from Ella's Fellas," in *Down Beat*. Vol. 62, no. 9, September 1995.

Nicholson, Stuart. *Ella Fitzgerald: A Biography of the First Lady of Song.* NY: Scribner, 1994.

SUGGESTED READING:

Cocks, Jay. "The Voice of America," in *Time*. June 24, 1996.

"The Scat lady," in *Newsweek*. June 24, 1996.

Norman Powers,
writer-producer, Chelsea Lane Productions,
New York, New York

Fitzgerald, Geraldine (1912—)

Irish-American actress nominated for an Academy Award for her performance in Wuthering Heights. *Born in Dublin, Ireland, on November 24, 1912; daughter of Edward (an attorney) and Edith Fitzgerald; studied at Dublin Art School and Queen's College, London; married Edward Lindsay-Hogg (a songwriter), in 1936 (marriage dissolved, 1946); married Stuart Scheftel (president of Museum of Famous People and co-founder of Pan-Am Building), in 1946 (died 1995); children: (first marriage) Michael Lindsay-Hogg (b. 1940, a film and theater director); (second marriage) one daughter Susan Scheftel (b. 1948).*

Awards: Handel Medallion (New York City, 1974); nominated for an Academy Award for Best Supporting Actress in 1939 for Wuthering Heights.

Made debut at the Gate Theater in Dublin (1932); made New York debut as Ellie Dunn in Heartbreak House, *Mercury Theater, New York (1938); appeared as Rebecca in* Sons and Soldiers, *Morosco Theater, New York (1943), Tanis Talbot in* Portrait in Black, *Shubert, New Haven (1945), Jennifer Dubedat in* The Doctor's Dilemma, *Phoenix Theater, New York (1955), Goneril in* King Lear, *City Center, New York (1956), Ann Richards in* Hide and Seek, *Ethel Barrymore Theater, New York (1957), Gertrude in* Hamlet, *American Shakespeare Festival, Stratford, Connecticut (1958), the Queen in* The Cave Dwellers, *Greenwich Mews Theater, New York (1961), the Mother in* Ah, Wilderness!, *Ford's Theater, Washington D.C. (1969), Mary Tyrone in* Long Day's Journey into Night, *Promenade Theater, New York (1971); (actress and co-author with Brother Jonathan OSF)* Everyman *and* Roach, *Society for Ethical Culture Auditorium (1971); appeared as Jenny in* The Threepenny Opera, *WPA Theater, New York (1972), Juno Boyle in* Juno and the Paycock, *Long Wharf, New Haven (1973), Amy in* Forget-Me-Not-Lane, *Long Wharf (1973), Aline Solness in* The Master Builder, *Long Wharf (1973), Essie Miller in* Ah, Wilderness!, *Circle in the Square Theater,*

New York (1974), Felicity in The Shadow Box, *Long Wharf and Morosco Theater, New York (1977), Nora Melody in* A Touch of the Poet, *Helen Hayes Theater, New York (1978); appeared in one-woman show* Songs of the Streets: O'Neill and Carlotta, *Public Theatre, New York (1979); made theatrical history as the first woman to appear as the Stage Manager in* Our Town *at the Williamstown Festival in Massachusetts. Founded the Everyman Street Theatre; directed* Mass Appeal *at the Manhattan Theatre Club (1980) and* The Lunch Girls, *Theatre Row (1981).*

Selected filmography: The Turn of the Tide *(1935);* Three Witnesses *(1935);* Blind Justice *(1935);* Radio Parade of 1935 *(1935);* Department Store *(1935);* The Mill on the Floss *(1936);* Dark Victory *(1939);* Wuthering Heights *(1939);* A Child Is Born *(1939);* Till We Meet Again *(1940);* Flight from Destiny *(1941);* Shining Victory *(1941);* The Gay Sisters *(1942);* Watch on the Rhine *(1943);* Ladies Courageous *(1944);* Wilson *(1944);* Uncle Harry *(1945);* Three Strangers *(1946);* O.S.S. *(1946);* Nobody Lives Forever *(1946);* So Evil, My Love *(1948);* The Late Edwina Black *(1951);* 10 North Frederick *(1958);* The Fiercest Heart *(1961);* The Pawnbroker *(1965);* Rachel, Rachel *(1968);* Believe in Me *(1971);* The Last American Hero *(1973);* Harry and Tonto *(1974);* Echoes of a Summer *(1976);* The Mango Tree *(1977);* Arthur *(1981);* Easy Money *(1983);* Pope of Greenwich Village *(1984);* Poltergeist II *(1986);* Arthur 2 *(1988);* King of the Hill *(1993).*

Television: Violet Jordan in "The Best of Everything" *(1970);* "Yesterday's Child" *(1976);* Orogon's Mother in "Tartuffe" *(1977);* "Street Songs" *(1979); also appeared in "Our Private World," "The Moon and Sixpence," "Dodsworth," and "The Jilting of Granny Weatherall."*

Geraldine Fitzgerald's family was closely involved in the Irish theater. Her aunt, *Shelah Richards, who later became a director and television executive, acted with the Gate Theater company which had been founded by Micheál MacLiammóir and Hilton Edwards in 1928. Richards was married to the playwright and poet Denis Johnston and their daughter is the novelist **Jennifer Johnston**. Fitzgerald and her sister **Pamela** began acting professionally while both were in their teens. They performed at the Gate in the early 1930s and came to know Orson Welles when he spent a season there. Geraldine came to public attention when she played Isabella Linton in the **Ria Mooney**-Donald Stauffer stage adaptation of *Wuthering Heights*. In his memoir *All for Hecuba* (1961),

MacLiammóir described her as: "Geraldine with her tawny hair and laughing gold-flecked eyes, her radiant youth, and the funny little break in her voice."

In 1934, she went to England where she appeared in a series of low-budget films, among them *The Ace of Spades, Radio Follies,* and *Turn of the Tide.* In 1936, she appeared in *Café Mascot* which was produced by Gabriel Pascal and the following year she starred in the film of George Eliot's (*Mary Anne Evans) *The Mill on the Floss.* Fitzgerald had married Edward Lindsay-Hogg in 1936, and in 1938 they left for New York where she played Ellie Dunn in *Heartbreak House.* Orson Welles then invited her to appear in the Mercury Theater's production of *Wuthering Heights.* In 1939, she moved to Hollywood where her career got off to an auspicious start in William Wyler's film of *Wuthering Heights* in which she again played Isabella Linton. Her performance received an Academy Award nomination. She also appeared in *Dark Victory* in which she played *Bette Davis' friend Ann King.

Fitzgerald had a busy film career over the next decade, with her best work in *Flight from Destiny* (1941), *Watch on the Rhine* (1943), *Wilson* (1944), and *Three Strangers* (1946). But she became increasingly frustrated by the kind of roles she was being offered and fought with the studio executives for better parts. In the early 1950s, she returned to New York to appear on television and revive her stage career, which she did triumphantly. Between 1955 and 1961, she played Jennifer Dubedat in *The Doctor's Dilemma,* Gertrude in *Hamlet,* Goneril in *King Lear,* and the Queen in William Saroyan's *The Cave Dwellers.* Her film career was also revived with *Ten North Frederick* (1958), *The Pawnbroker* (1964) and *Rachel, Rachel* (1968).

In 1971, Fitzgerald got the best notices of her career when she played Mary Tyrone in *Long Day's Journey Into Night* on Broadway. The following year, she was Jenny in *The Threepenny Opera,* and in 1973 she was again acclaimed for her performance of Juno in *Juno and the Paycock.* She gave other memorable performances in that decade in *The Glass Menagerie, The Shadow Box,* and *A Touch of the Poet.* In 1979, she devised her one-woman show *Songs of the Streets: O'Neill and Carlotta.* She also returned to Ireland to make the film *Tristan and Isolde* in which she played the role of Bronwyn. In 1980, she directed *Mass Appeal* for the stage. During the 1980s, Fitzgerald continued to act on stage and on television, but she also made successful cameo film appearances in *Arthur*

(1981), *The Pope of Greenwich Village* (1984), *Poltergeist II* (1986) and *Arthur 2* (1988). In 1993, she made her debut as a lyricist and librettist in *Sharon*, a musical based on *Sharon's Grave* by the Irish playwright John B. Keane which she also directed. She made her last film, *King of the Hill*, in 1993, after which she retired from acting. Fitzgerald was an active member of the New York State Council for the Arts, the Screen Actors' Guild and Actors' Equity. Her son is the film and theater director Michael Lindsay-Hogg.

Deirdre McMahon,
Lecturer in History, Mary Immaculate College,
University of Limerick, Limerick, Ireland

Fitzgerald, Katherine (c. 1500–1604)

Countess of Desmond. Name variations: The old Countess of Desmond. Born around 1500; died in 1604; daughter of Sir John Fitzgerald, lord of Decies; married Thomas Fitzgerald, 12th earl of Desmond, after 1505 (d. 1534, at age 80); children: one daughter.

Katherine Fitzgerald, countess of Desmond, was the second wife of Thomas Fitzgerald, 12th earl of Desmond. Legend has it that she lived to be 140; it is more likely, however, that she lived to be around 104. In his *Itinerary*, published in 1617, Fynes Morison states that "in our time" she had lived to be "about" 140 but was still capable of walking three or four miles to market. To add to the myth, stories abounded that she died of concussion after being hit by an apple, sometimes a walnut, sometimes a cherry, that fell from a tree.

Fitzgerald, Pamela (1773–1831).

See Genlis, Stéphanie-Félicité, Comtesse de for sidebar.

Fitzgerald, Scottie (1921–1986).

See Fitzgerald, Zelda for sidebar on Frances Scott Fitzgerald.

Fitzgerald, Zelda (1900–1948)

Southern society beauty, artist, writer, and dancer whose works were overshadowed by those of her husband, the novelist F. Scott Fitzgerald. Name variations: Zelda Sayre (1900–20); Zelda Fitzgerald. Born on July 24, 1900, in Montgomery, Alabama; died in a fire at Highland Hospital, a clinic in Asheville, North Carolina, on March 11, 1948; sixth child of Anthony Sayre (an Alabama Supreme Court judge) and Minnie (Machen) Sayre; attended high school in Alabama; married F. Scott Fitzgerald (a novelist), in 1920; chil-

dren: one daughter, Frances "Scottie" Fitzgerald (1921–1986).

Zelda Fitzgerald, beautiful, capricious, and wildly high-spirited, was the first and most famous flapper of what her husband F. Scott Fitzgerald named "the Jazz Age." But her moment of triumph as a rich, carefree bride was followed by years of disillusionment, alcoholism, and a descent into chronic schizophrenia.

Her family, the Sayres of Montgomery, Alabama, were eccentrics in the grand Southern manner and would have suited the plot of a Faulkner novel. Her father, Judge Anthony Sayre of the Alabama Supreme Court, was an icy, reserved man of unvarying habits, who went to and from work at exactly the same time every day throughout his life and always went to bed on the stroke of eight o'clock. Her mother **Minnie Machen Sayre**, a Southern belle from a leading Confederate family, had hoped to become an opera singer but had met and married the judge instead, with whom she had five children. Minnie's mother and sister had both committed suicide, and she too suffered frequent bouts of mental illness, a family trait passed on to Zelda.

Zelda, born with the century, was a mischievous child, vivacious and impulsive. As a ten-year-old, she called the fire department to rescue someone from the roof, then climbed up there until they arrived to "save" her. She grew up into a striking beauty and challenged local convention by bobbing her hair and smoking in public. One of her childhood friends, **Virginia Durr**, recalled later that "she was like a vision of beauty dancing by. She was funny, amusing, the most popular girl; envied by all others, worshipped and adored, besieged by all the boys." Durr recalled a Christmas dance when Zelda had pinned mistletoe to the back of her dress, in effect punning on the phrase "kiss my ass." But, as Durr added, Zelda was so used to being the constant center of attention that she found it difficult to adjust, later, to being a mother and to letting her writer-husband have uninterrupted time in which to work. Some of Zelda's admirers founded a fraternity at nearby Auburn University, using the Greek initials of her name, Zeta Sigma, and requiring for membership evidence that a man had dated her at least once. She had a reputation for being "fast" and flirtatious and often deliberately provoked her dates' jealousy by suddenly turning cold towards them and amorous towards others. She was also the center of attention with aspiring officers who came to Alabama for training during the war. Two avia-

Opposite page

Geraldine Fitzgerald

tion cadets, flying aerobatics over her house in tribute to her, crashed in mid-air and were killed.

Zelda met Scott Fitzgerald at a dance when she was 18, just after she had graduated from Sidney Lanier High School. Four years her senior, he was stationed near Montgomery with his army regiment, having recently left Princeton University without a degree. Zelda was impressed, and they began to meet frequently. When she invited him for dinner with the family for the first time, Zelda, annoyed at her father's impassivity, teased and provoked him until he jumped up, brandishing a carving knife, and chased her around the table. Other family members were oblivious. Though Fitzgerald could see he had encountered a highly unusual family, he did not realize (and no one told him) that they had a long history of certified mental illness.

Zelda was soon in love with Fitzgerald, smitten with his good looks and charm, his Ivy League education, and the contrast between her Southern Protestantism and his Midwest Irish Catholicism. In the spring of 1919, she accepted his proposal of marriage, noting that they also

Zelda Fitzgerald

had much in common: privileged upbringings, high spirits, love of drink and fun, and similar blond good looks. She then slept with him and later confided that she had first had sex at age 15 with another beau. Her family was worried, however, by the aspiring author's carefree ways, his reluctance to get a steady job, and his love for hard liquor. Zelda also had second thoughts, and she broke off the engagement after a few months when it seemed that Fitzgerald's *talk* about becoming a great writer would not be matched by the reality. Stung by this rejection, and by her apparent requirement that he be a success before he could marry her, he returned to his hometown of St. Paul, Minnesota, and in a burst of creative energy completed *This Side of Paradise*. Published the following year, this first novel was an instant success, prompting Zelda to revive the romance. The couple married in St. Patrick's Catholic Cathedral, New York, in April 1920, even though Scott had lapsed from the practice of his faith.

This Side of Paradise and the sale of dozens of short stories to mass circulation magazines like the *Saturday Evening Post* made Scott a lot of money, and the young couple at once took up an extravagant way of life in New York City. Zelda jumped into a fountain in Union Square one night and paid a taxi driver to let her ride around town on the hood of his cab. She also flirted outrageously with Fitzgerald's friends, jumping into bed with one, asking another if he would give her a bath, and often kissing men passionately on the lips, just after meeting them. Edmund Wilson, a former college friend of Fitzgerald and one of many men to admire Zelda, wrote that "she talked with so spontaneous a color and wit, almost exactly the way she wrote, that I very soon ceased to be troubled by the fact that the conversation was in the nature of free association of ideas and one could never follow up anything. I have rarely known a woman who expressed herself so delightfully and freshly." At first, Fitzgerald encouraged her wildness, which he later incorporated into stories, but he soon found that she sulked if she did not enjoy a steady stream of costly gifts, pampering attention, and opportunities to act outrageously. All who met them in the early years of the marriage agreed that she demanded to be the center of attention. Scott quickly reached the point of being unable to write if she was in their apartment (because she would not leave him alone) and unable to write if she was *not* there (because of anxiety at what she might be doing, and with whom). She confessed to him that she was selfish and useless, and that she was completely inept as a housekeeper.

The birth of their baby daughter ❧➤ **Frances "Scottie" Fitzgerald** in 1921 hardly slowed the couple down. They hired nannies and continued the wild round of parties, moving frequently, never having their own home, and often leaving disgruntled landlords and damaged properties in their wake. Zelda took abortifacient pills when she found she was pregnant again, but they caused internal injuries and began the long series of gynecological illnesses that contributed to her decline. (In 1926, when she wanted another child, she was unable to conceive.) Meanwhile Fitzgerald's second novel, *The Beautiful and the Damned* (1922), appeared, gaining him more critical admiration and more strong sales. Zelda's own first publication was an article about it for the *New York Tribune*. She noted that her husband had incorporated several passages from her letters and diaries into his new novel. "Mr. Fitzgerald," she added, "seems to believe that plagiarism begins at home."

> *Try to understand that people are not always reasonable when the world is as unstable and vacillating as a sick head can render it.*
>
> —**Zelda Fitzgerald**

The couple made frequent visits to Europe in the early 1920s where they befriended a group of talented and wealthy American expatriates who had gone in search of a richer cultural life and the chance to drink alcohol without break-

---

❧➤ **Fitzgerald, Frances Scott** (1921–1986)

American writer. Name variations: Scottie; Frances Scott Fitzgerald Lanahan Smith. Born in 1921; died in 1986; only child of F. Scott Fitzgerald (the novelist) and Zelda Fitzgerald (1900–1948); married Jack Lanahan (a lawyer; divorced); married Grove Smith, in 1967; children: four, including Tim and Eleanor Lanahan (an artist and illustrator).

The daughter of F. Scott and *Zelda Fitzgerald, Scottie Fitzgerald was a playwright, composer, *Washington Post* columnist, and Democratic insider. As depicted by her daughter **Eleanor Lanahan**, Scottie adored her alcoholic father and blocked out her mother's bouts of insanity, but she was burdened with their fame. Also a heavy drinker, Scottie became a controlling and manipulative mother, writes Lanahan, whose four children eventually rebelled. A son Tim, who had been mentally unstable for years, shot himself in 1973.

SUGGESTED READING:

Lanahan, Eleanor. *Scottie: The Daughter of . . . : The Life of Frances Scott Fitzgerald Lanahan Smith*. NY: HarperCollins, 1995.

---

ing the law (these were the Prohibition years in America). Among them were Ernest Hemingway, John Dos Passos, *Gertrude Stein, *Edith Wharton, T.S. Eliot, and many prominent British writers, including James Joyce. These new friends were fascinated by Zelda's beauty and impulsive behavior but dismayed by her drunkenness, which often led to public fights with the equally outrageous Fitzgerald, and sometimes to her undressing in public and throwing sexual taunts at him. When he met and was admired by the dancer *Isadora Duncan one evening, Zelda, in a jealous rage, flung herself down a long stone staircase in an apparent suicide attempt. On a trip to France and Italy, during which he completed *The Great Gatsby*, his masterpiece, she had a brief love affair with a French naval officer, Edouard Jozan, and then asked Fitzgerald for a divorce. But her intensity frightened her lover away. For him it was just a holiday romance; he was not seeking a wife. Zelda again responded by trying to kill herself, this time with an overdose of sleeping pills, and had to be kept forcibly awake by her husband and friends. She began to accuse Fitzgerald of being a homosexual and of being in love with Hemingway, then confided to friends that she found him sexually inadequate.

After the Jozan episode, which did permanent damage to the Fitzgeralds' marriage, she began writing articles, many of which were published in *Metropolitan Magazine, McCall's,* and the *New York Tribune*. They showed her to be a perceptive observer as well as a wild participant in the expatriates' lives, but she still felt overshadowed by her husband's talent and success, even though he encouraged her to write. Ironically, she found that she could get far more money for her articles if they were published under his name rather than her own, and she often settled for the money instead of the recognition. He, meanwhile, was forced to turn out masses of inferior stories for quick money rather than concentrating on his next novel, because the couple's way of life was so costly and wasteful.

In 1927, Zelda conceived a sudden passion for ballet dancing and began to study it with obsessive intensity, even though she was 27 and had started too late in life to hope for success as a ballerina. Often she practiced for seven or eight hours per day, exhausting herself and aggravating her medical problems, but making steady progress. She took dancing lessons first in Philadelphia from **Catherine Littlefield** and then in Paris from Madame **Lyubov Egorova**, a Russian ballerina and friend of Sergei Diaghilev, who

told her that she was good enough to play minor roles in the corps de ballet even if she could not expect to be a soloist. Dancing became Zelda's only interest, turning her, Fitzgerald wrote, into "more and more an egotist and a bore." Zelda herself became madly devoted to her teacher, sending her flowers every day, and cold towards nearly everyone else. She won a few brief dancing engagements in Cannes and Nice yet declined the offer of a better, solo role with the San Carlo Opera Ballet in Italy, where she would have danced *Aïda* as her debut. This refusal is a baffling one, which her biographers are unable to explain, unless it indicates that she was expecting an appointment with the world-famous Diaghilev company in Paris.

In 1930, in any case, she suffered a severe nervous breakdown, brought on partly by the strain of dancing for eight or more hours per day, partly from the knowledge that her husband, now at work in Hollywood, had had an affair with a young actress, *Lois Moran. Zelda's French doctors investigated her family's history of madness, diagnosed her as suffering from schizophrenia, hospitalized her, and forced her to give up dancing. Aware that she was unbalanced, she wrote to Fitzgerald: "I seem awfully queer to myself. . . . I see odd things, people's arms too long or their faces as if they were stuffed and they look tiny and far away, or suddenly out of proportion." She moved from Paris to a clinic in Switzerland, suffering from acute insomnia and sudden outbreaks of eczema and asthma. Fitzgerald visited her regularly and wrote constantly when traveling, showing that he was still passionately attached to her despite their destructive behavior towards each other. She wrote to him: "I am infinitely sorry that I have been ungrateful for your attempts to help me. Try to understand that people are not always reasonable when the world is as unstable and vacillating as a sick head can render it— That for months I have been living in vaporous places peopled with one-dimensional figures and tremulous buildings until I can no longer tell an optical illusion from a reality."

Sufficiently recovered by 1931, Zelda was able to leave the hospital, and the Fitzgeralds sailed to America. Scott returned to Hollywood, while Zelda went back to Montgomery for a time. In five months of hard work, despite suffering a mental relapse that took her to the Johns Hopkins Psychiatric Clinic in Baltimore, she wrote the text of a novel, *Save Me the Waltz*. It appeared in 1932 after a bitter squabble with Fitzgerald during which he called her "a third-rate writer and a third-rate ballet dancer." He had planned to use much of the same material (including the story of her breakdown) in his own work-in-progress, *Tender is the Night. Save Me the Waltz,* like Fitzgerald's novels, certainly was unmistakably autobiographical, even after the couple had settled their dispute and edited the text. It provides the best avenue to understanding Zelda Fitzgerald's frame of mind and her idea of herself. Its heroine, Alabama Knight, is married to a painter, rather than a writer, but like Zelda she longs to become a dancer, moves back and forth restlessly between America and Europe, feels overshadowed by her husband's achievements, and finally seeks solace in her old Southern home. Zelda tried unsuccessfully to write another novel and to stage a play but finished neither project, and she published no more articles after 1934.

By then, she and Fitzgerald were living apart nearly all the time but continuing to write and exchange pledges of their love. In 1933, Zelda's brother committed suicide by jumping from a hospital window in Mobile, Alabama. Zelda herself was in and out of mental hospitals then and for the next several years, suffering recurrent episodes of schizophrenia. For one long period, she experienced violent hallucinations and came to believe that God was talking to her directly, ordering her to preach His word. She followed her doctors' encouragement to take up painting, which she had studied in 1925 on the Mediterranean island of Capri, and had dabbled in ever since. She first contributed to an exhibition, in Baltimore, in 1933, selling a few paintings while giving away many more to family and friends. Her initial solo exhibition, in Manhattan, coincided with the publication of Fitzgerald's *Tender is the Night* (1934), but her paintings were not well reviewed. For a while, she became almost as obsessed with painting as she had been with dancing five years before, but this work too was interrupted by frequent stays in clinics and sanitariums.

From 1936 to 1940, Zelda lived almost constantly at Highland Hospital, a clinic in Asheville, North Carolina, and saw the decaying Fitzgerald only on his occasional visits from Hollywood, when he was often incapacitated with drink. He died suddenly from a heart attack at age 44, during one of her hospital stays, so that she was unable to attend his Maryland funeral. At the height of his fame, in the mid and late 1920s, he had been earning over $30,000 each year from writing, but by the time he died his entire estate left Zelda with an annuity that yielded only about $50 per month.

She returned to Montgomery and went to stay with her mother, who was also living in reduced circumstances. Zelda was now a born-again Christian and gained a reputation as a local eccentric, dressing in woolen alpine clothes and cycling around town despite the terrific summer heat, once falling to her knees and beginning to pray aloud at a garden party. She sent long, evangelical letters to old literary friends, instructing Edmund Wilson, for example: "You should redeem yourself; pray and repent. . . . You are much to be respected and handsome and have a genius for interesting people. You must look to your salvation." She continued to paint, mostly in a surrealist or semi-abstract style: dancers, scenes from Paris, and religious themes. Friends who visited her said she talked constantly of the past and of Fitzgerald, who she now feared would be forgotten. Worsening health forced her to return to the asylum in November 1947, where she was an experimental patient with new insulin treatments. A fire broke out there late one night in the spring of 1948, killing nine of the women inmates, Zelda among them.

In her last years Zelda wrote to her daughter Scottie, who had herself married a Princeton graduate and army officer cadet: "I wish that I had been able to do better at one thing and not [been] so given to running into cul-de-sacs with so many." Scottie herself lived to see a reevaluation of her mother's life by feminist scholars in the 1960s and 1970s, but she denied their claim that Zelda should be regarded as the victim of a dominating patriarchal husband. It "will probably remain a part of the 'Scott and Zelda' mythology" she wrote, "but is not, in my opinion, accurate," because "my father greatly appreciated and encouraged his wife's unusual talents and ebullient imagination."

SOURCES:

Bruccoli, Matthew, ed. *The Collected Writings of Zelda Fitzgerald.* NY: Scribner, 1991.

Fitzgerald, Zelda. *Save Me the Waltz.* NY: Scribner, 1932.

Lanahan, Eleanor, ed. *Zelda—An Illustrated Life: The Private World of Zelda Fitzgerald.* NY: Abrams, 1996.

Meyers, Jeffrey. *Scott Fitzgerald: A Biography.* NY: Harper-Collins, 1994.

Milford, Nancy. *Zelda: A Biography.* NY: Harper and Row, 1970.

COLLECTIONS:

New York Public Library; Princeton University Library.

Patrick Allitt,
Professor of History, Emory University,
Atlanta, Georgia

Fitz-Gibbon, Bernice (c. 1895–1982)

American advertising pioneer. Name variations: Mrs. Herman Block. Born around 1895 in Waunakee, Wisconsin; died in a Wisconsin nursing home in 1982; one of four children of William Fitz-Gibbon (a dairy farmer) and Nora (Bowles) Fitz-Gibbon; attended Sacred Heart Convent, Madison, Wisconsin, 1903–13; graduated from the University of Wisconsin, B.A., 1918; married Herman Block (an attorney), on July 6, 1925; children: Elizabeth Bowles Block; Peter Block.

Bernice Fitz-Gibbon, who struck it rich revolutionizing department-store advertising, grew up on a Wisconsin dairy farm. Educated in a convent and paying her own way through the University of Wisconsin, she taught school for two years in Chippewa Falls. She then sold advertising for the *Register-Gazette* in Rockford, Illinois, and worked for a year at Chicago's Marshall Field and Company before arriving in New York in the early 1920s. After a summer at Wanamaker's in New York, Fitz-Gibbon joined the staff of Macy's. During her 12 years there, beginning in 1923, she came up with several of her most imaginative and successful ad campaigns and coined the slogan, "It's smart to be thrifty," which Macy's used for years.

In the mid-30s, when Macy's wanted to cut her salary, Fitz-Gibbon returned to Wanamaker's, helping to transform it from a sleepy downtown emporium to a lively up-to-the-minute competitor. In 1940, when Fitz-Gibbon left for Gimbels, her loyal stable of copy writers resigned from Wanamaker's and went with her.

Fitz-Gibbon established her own small agency, Bernice Fitz-Gibbon, Inc., in 1954, and subsequently became a member of the board of directors of Montgomery Ward and Company. She was named Business Woman of the Year by the women editors of the Associated Press and was cited as one of the seven top businesswomen in the United States by *Fortune* magazine. She also contributed many articles to *McCall's, Good Housekeeping, The New York Times Magazine,* and *Glamour* and was in demand as a speaker. Fitz-Gibbon closed her office in 1964 to take life a little easier, though she continued to write ads and articles to "push people up." (Always the teacher, she took great joy in mentoring.) She never left New York, the city she loved, and after her husband's death she lived alone in a four-room apartment overlooking the East River.

SOURCES:

Fitz-Gibbon, Bernice. *Macy's, Gimbels, and Me.* NY: Simon and Schuster, 1951.

Barbara Morgan,
Melrose, Massachusetts

Fitzgibbon, Catherine (1823–1896).

See Irene, Sister.

Fitzgibbon, Irene (1823–1896).

See Irene, Sister.

Fitzhammon, Amabel (d. 1157)

*Countess of Gloucester. Died 1157; married Robert, 1st earl of Gloucester (illegitimate son of Henry I and *Nesta Tewdwr), in 1109 (died 1147); children: William Fitzrobert, 2nd earl of Gloucester.*

Fitzhenry, Mrs. (d. 1790?)

Irish actress. Maiden name Flannigan; first name is unknown. Died around 1790; daughter of a man named Flannigan who managed the Ferry Boat tavern in Abbey Street, Dublin; married a Captain Gregory; married a man named Fitzhenry (a lawyer), around 1757; children: (second marriage) one son, one daughter.

Now lost, Mrs. Fitzhenry's first name was a casualty of the theatrical custom of dropping actresses' given names in favor of the title "Mrs." She worked as a seamstress before marrying Captain Gregory who operated a ship trading between Dublin and Bordeaux. Following the death of her husband by drowning, Mrs. Fitzhenry moved to London and appeared at Covent Garden (1754). Her theatrical reputation, however, was made at the Smock Alley Theater in Dublin. In 1757, she appeared once more at Covent Garden as Lady Macbeth (*Gruoch) and reprised the role of Hermione in *The Distressed Mother.* She married a lawyer by the name of Fitzhenry around the same year, and later gave birth to a daughter and a son. From 1759 to 1764, she appeared in Dublin in Shakespearean roles, as well as in the role of Calista in *The Fair Pentitent.* In 1765, she worked at the Drury Lane. In Ireland, her chief rival was *Elizabeth Yates.

Fitzherbert, Maria Anne (1756–1837)

Illegal wife of King George IV of England. Name variations: Mary Ann; Mrs. Fitzherbert. Born Maria Anne Smythe in Hampshire, England, on July 26, 1756; died on March 27, 1837, in Brighton, Sussex; daughter of Walter Smythe and Mary (Errington) Smythe; married Edward Weld of Lulworth Castle, Dorset, in 1775 (died 1776); married Thomas Fitzherbert of Swynnerton, Staffordshire, in 1778 (died 1781); married George IV (1762–1821), king of England (r.

1820–1830), on December 21, 1785 (marriage declared illegal in 1787); children: (with George IV) ten.

Two early marriages and two early deaths left Maria Anne Fitzherbert well provided for by the time she met George (IV), the prince of Wales, in early 1785. Six years her junior, the 23-year-old prince fell head over royal heels and attempted to convey his passion by stabbing himself, presumably in a suicide attempt. Fitzherbert, a deeply religious Catholic, was terrified by George's demands that she become his mistress and fled to the Continent. Crazed with grief, the prince offered to marry her. With that, she returned to London, and they were wed secretly by an Anglican minister on December 21, 1785. Since the 1772 Royal Marriage Act prevented any of the royal family under the age of 25 from marrying without the king's permission, specifically the prince's father George III, theirs was a sham wedding performed by a cleric who had been bailed out of debtor's prison and promised a bishopric. The prince did not quarrel when Parliament declared the marriage illegal in 1787.

Nonetheless, for the decade after their wedding, the prince and Maria Fitzherbert lived as man and wife in the eyes of their friends. Eventually, as she gave birth to each of their ten children, she also added poundage, and the prince began to stray. Worse, he would arrive home an angry drunk, once chasing her with a drawn sword. Deeply in debt, he fell behind in her allowance. King George III offered to retire his son's debt if the prince assented to an arranged marriage to *Caroline of Brunswick, and the prince, though he despised Caroline, agreed.

The royal marriage took place on April 8, 1795; if anything, the nuptials pushed the prince back into the arms of Maria Fitzherbert, and he continued with his retinue of mistresses while privately settling miscellaneous paternity suits. In an early will, written in 1796, he described Fitzherbert as "his true and real wife," adding, to Caroline, "who is called the Princess of Wales, I leave one shilling." It was not until George had finally progressed to the station of prince regent in 1811 and had become infatuated with **Lady Hertford** that he left Fitzherbert, dismissing her with a final, "Madam, you have no place."

At the time of King George IV's death in 1830, Maria Fitzherbert was among the few who mourned. The late king obviously had shared the same affection, having requested that Fitzherbert's miniature portrait be hung round his neck and buried with him. She died seven years later, at age 81.

Maria Anne Fitzherbert

Fitzhugh, Anne (fl. 1466)

*Viscountess Lovell. Flourished in 1466; daughter of Henry Fitzhugh, 5th Lord Fitzhugh of Ravensworth, and *Alice Neville (fl. 1480s, sister of the Kingmaker); married Francis Lovell, Viscount Lovell, in 1466.*

Fitzhugh, Louise (1928–1974)

American author, illustrator, and artist, best-known for Harriet the Spy. *Born Louise Perkins Fitzhugh in Memphis, Tennessee, on October 5, 1928; died of an aneurism in New Milford, Connecticut, on November 19, 1974; daughter of Millsaps Fitzhugh (an attorney) and Louise (Perkins) Fitzhugh; attended Southwestern College, Florida Southern College, Bard College, and New York University; studied painting at Art Students League and Cooper Union, New York, and in Bologna, Italy.*

Fitzhugh's oil paintings were exhibited at several galleries, including Banfer Gallery, New York City (1963).

Awards: New York Times *Outstanding Books of the Year (1964) and Sequoyah Children's Book Award (1967), both for* Harriet the Spy; The New York Times *Choice of Best Illustrated Books of the Year (1969)* and Brooklyn Art Books for Children citation (1974), both for Bang, Bang, You're Dead; Other Award from Children's Book Bulletin (1976) for Nobody's Family Is Going to Change; Emmy Award for children's entertainment special (1979) for "The Tap Dance Kid."

Writings—all for children, all self-illustrated, except as noted: (with Sandra Scoppettone) Suzuki Beane (Doubleday, 1961); Harriet the Spy (ALA Notable Book, Harper, 1964); The Long Secret (Harper, 1965); (with S. Scoppettone) Bang, Bang, You're Dead (Harper, 1969); Nobody's Family Is Going to Change (Farrar, Straus, 1974); I Am Five (Delacourt, 1978); Sport (Delacourt, 1979); (illustrated by Susanna Natti) I Am Three (Delacorte, 1982); (illustrated by Susan Bonners) I Am Four (Delacorte, 1982).

Adaptations based on her work: "The Tap Dance Kid" (television; based on Nobody's Family Is Going to Change), NBC "Special Treat," 1978; "The Tap Dance Kid" (film), Learning Corporation of America, 1978; "The Tap Dance Kid" (play), first produced at Broadhurst Theater, New York, N.Y., December 21, 1983 (won two Tony Awards).

Nordstrom, Ursula. See Brown, Margaret Wise for sidebar.

Louise Fitzhugh

Children's author and illustrator Louise Fitzhugh was raised in Memphis, Tennessee, and began writing stories at the age of 11. Hers was not a happy childhood. ◀ **Ursula Nordstrom**, a former editorial director for Harper junior books, recalled, "There were many things in Louise's well-born southern upbringing and experiences that she did not like, including her horrified remembrance of teenage friends who, after a date, decided it would be fun to go down to 'coon town' and throw rocks at the heads of young Negro boys and girls. She got out of the South as soon as she could, came north, went to Bard College, and concentrated on losing every single trace of her southern accent—and prejudices."

Among the schools Fitzhugh attended were Hutchison School, Southwestern College, Florida Southern College, and New York University's School of Education. She left New York University six months before completing her degree in literature to pursue her interest in art. She studied at New York's Art Students League and Cooper Union, and also in Bologna, Italy. Her

oil paintings, realistic in style, were exhibited in several galleries, including Banfer Gallery, New York City, in 1963.

Fitzhugh first attracted attention with her satiric illustrations—including renderings of beatniks, society poets, and dancing teachers—for *Suzuki Beane,* written in collaboration with **Sandra Scoppettone** and published in 1961. An agent submitted pages of what would become Fitzhugh's classic and controversial work of children's literature, *Harriet the Spy,* to Harper. **Charlotte Zolotow**, then senior editor, wrote in her report of the manuscript: "You have to get this writer to come in and talk. This isn't a book but could be." When Harper and Row published *Harriet the Spy* in 1964, it was greeted with mixed reviews. It is now considered a major milestone in children's literature. Self-illustrated, the novel, set in New York, is the story of young Harriet M. Welsch. Aspiring to become a famous writer, Harriet dons her spy equipment, eavesdrops, and records her observations and thoughts in her notebook. Speaking of her classmates, Harriet notes in typically blunt fashion, "They are just bats. Half of them don't even have a profession." About mothers, she notes: "I wouldn't like to have a dumb mother. It must make you feel very unpopular." Harriet's observations expose the hypocrisy of the adult world and cause her trouble when her classmates discover the notebook.

The New York Times Book Review called Fitzhugh "one of the brightest talents of 1964," and praised the book as "vigorous" and "original in style and content." **Ellen Rudden**, in *Library Journal,* called Harriet "one of the meatiest heroines in modern juvenile fiction." However, critics like **Ruth Hill Viguers** of the highly respected *Horn Book* strongly objected to the story's "disagreeable people and situations" and questioned its "realism" and suitability for children, while others considered it "devastatingly" real. In 1974, 20 years after it was published, the book was still periodically removed from the shelves of school libraries out of fear that children might imitate Harriet's behavior.

Harriet's sequel, *The Long Secret* (1965), was less controversial and received particularly high praise for its sensitive treatment of young girls' reactions to the onset of puberty. Nordstrom remarked of her first reading of the manuscript: "When I came to the page where the onset of Beth Ellen's first menstrual period occurred, and it was written so beautifully, to such perfection, I scrawled in the margin, 'Thank you, Louise Fitzhugh.' It was the first mention in junior books of this tremendous event in a girl's life." At the end of a glowing review, *School Library Journal* commented: "This second book may be less of a bombshell to timid librarians and reviewers, but its impact may be more durable than that of *Harriet the Spy.*"

In 1969, Fitzhugh collaborated again with Scoppettone on *Bang, Bang, You're Dead,* an anti-war story. It was followed by *Nobody's Family Is Going to Change* (1974), which centers around a black, middle-class New York family with a maid and two private-school children, Emma and Willie. The story, about what happens when children do not live up to parental expectations (Willie wants to be a dancer and Emma a lawyer), was turned into a television movie called the "The Tap Dance Kid" in 1978 and also became a Broadway musical in 1983.

Fitzhugh suffered a fatal aneurysm in 1974, age 46, at the peak of her career. She was buried in Bridgewater, Connecticut, in accordance with her wishes to be interred north of the Mason-Dixon line. Recalled Nordstrom: "Louise Fitzhugh adored music and was a superb dancer. She was also a brilliant painter. One of her canvases of a little girl standing alone in a meadow expressed all the essential loneliness I think Louise always felt. She was a brilliant, erratic, moody, often extremely thoughtful and endearing person. And she was intensely committed to her writing and to her drawing and painting." At the time of her death, she was working on the text and illustrations of *I Am Five,* part of an uncompleted series. The book and its sequels were published posthumously in 1978, 1979, and 1982. In 1996, a movie was made of her most memorable book, *Harriet the Spy,* starring **Michelle Trachtenberg** and **Rosie O'Donnell**.

SOURCES:

Commire, Anne. *Something About the Author.* Vol. 45. Detroit, MI: Gale Research.

Barbara Morgan,
Melrose, Massachusetts

Fitzmaurice, Mrs.

See Hippisley, E.

FitzOsbern, Emma.

See Emma of Norfolk (d. 1100).

Fitzrobert, Amicia (d. 1225)

Countess of Hertford, countess of Gloucester. Name variations: Amicia of Gloucester. Died in 1225; daughter of William Fitzrobert, 2nd earl of Gloucester, and *Hawise Beaumont (daughter of Robert, 2nd *earl of Leicester); married Richard de Clare, 4th earl of Hertford, about 1180; children: Gilbert de Clare, 5th earl of Hertford, 1st earl of Gloucester (born around 1180); Richard also known as Roger de Clare; **Matilda de Clare** (who married William de Braose and Rhys Gryg).*

Fitzroy, Charlotte (1664–1717).

See Villiers, Barbara for sidebar.

Fitzroy, Isabel (1726–1782)

*Marquise of Hertford. Born in 1726; died in 1782; daughter of Charles Fitzroy, 2nd duke of Grafton, and *Henrietta Somerset; granddaughter of *Barbara Villiers; married Francis Seymour, 1st marquis of Hertford; children: Hugh Seymour (1759–1801).*

Fitzroy, Mary (c. 1519–1557)

*Duchess of Richmond. Name variations: Mary Howard. Born around 1519; died in 1557; daughter of Thomas Howard, 2nd or 3rd duke of Norfolk, and *Elizabeth Stafford; married Henry Fitzroy, duke of Richmond, in 1533 (died 1536).*

Though Mary Howard married Henry Fitzroy, duke of Richmond, around 1533, she never lived with him. He died of poisoning in 1536, rumored to have been administered by *Anne Boleyn and her brother. In 1546, Mary gave evidence incriminating her brother, the poet Henry Howard, the earl of Surrey, on charges of treason, for conspiring to usurp the throne and having encouraged her to become King Henry VIII's mistress.

Fitzwilliam, Fanny Elizabeth (1801–1854)

English actress. Born Fanny Elizabeth Copeland in Dover, England, in 1801; died in London on November 11, 1854; daughter of a theater manager; married Edward Fitzwilliam (an actor).

Fanny Elizabeth Fitzwilliam was a child actress in Dover, where her father managed a theater. In 1817, the 16-year-old Fanny appeared at the Haymarket. She performed at the Drury Lane (1821–22) and leased the Sadler's Wells in 1832. Fitzwilliam visited the United States in 1837, appearing to great acclaim in *The Country Girl*. On her return to England, at the height of her fame, she appeared in *Green Bushes* and *Flowers of the Forest*.

Flaccilla (c. 355–386)

*Roman empress. Name variations: Aelia Flavia Flaccilla; Flacilla; named "Augusta" (empress), probably around 383. Born around 355; died in 386 or 387 in Thrace at a spa where she had retired to take the medicinal waters; daughter of aristocratic parents whose families had long held Roman citizenship; aunt of Nebridius; became first wife of Theodosius I the Great, emperor of Rome (r. 379-395), between 376 and 378; children: Pulcheria (c. 376–385); Arcadius, emperor of Rome (r. in the East, 395–408); Honorius emperor of Rome (r. in the West, 395-423). Following the death of Flaccilla, Theodosius I married *Galla.*

Flaccilla was born and bred in Spain of aristocratic parents whose families had long held Roman citizenship. Flaccilla probably met and married her husband, Theodosius (I), between 376 and 378 when he went into temporary Spanish exile as a result of the political fall of his father, also named Theodosius. The years of Flaccilla's youth were troubled times for Rome, with sustained frontier pressures being exacerbated by civil and religious rivalries within the empire itself. Men of ambition, standing, and occasionally of conscience all too frequently saw in themselves the solution to the manifold problems of the age.

The elder Theodosius had been a good general who had restored Roman authority in Britain after an invasion of Saxons, Picts and Scots. Subsequently, he was assigned to the Continent where he served with distinction against the Alans and the Alamanni. Success in these theaters warranted the confidence of Valentinian I, who trusted Theodosius to suppress a revolt in the province of Mauritania (in Africa) led by one Firmus. There Theodosius was also victorious, but his rapidly rising star engendered jealousies in court circles and capital charges were laid against him. Whether Theodosius harbored imperial ambitions after his string of successes is not known, but it mattered little once those in the emperor's confidence suspected disloyalty: he was executed in 376. This fall from grace threatened to engulf all near him, especially his son, who was only able to escape the father's fate by "retiring" to family estates in Spain, where, as noted, he probably met and married Flaccilla, a marriage that appears to have consolidated the interests of an influential political faction with a Spanish base.

Flaccilla's husband did not languish long in disgrace, having already demonstrated military promise before his father's fall. When disaster struck the empire in the form of the Visigoths' victory at Adrianople in 378 (made a double catastrophe when the Emperor Valens died on the field), the contemporary emperor of the West, Gratian, promoted Theodosius I to the position of "Master of the Military" in the hopes that the latter could restore Rome's authority along the mid and lower Danubian frontier and throughout the northern Balkans. By early 379, Theodosius I had at least enough success against the Goths to save these regions from being completely overrun. As a result, given the magnitude of the crisis, Gratian promoted him to the status of emperor. After checking the Goths' advance, Theodosius' first order of business as an Augustus was to consolidate his control over the vast area that they imperiled. In order to do so, he established his initial base at Thessaloniki in northern Greece. After 380, however, he relocated the seat of his authority to Constantinople, thus laying personal claim to the city that Constantine had developed earlier in the century as the "New Rome" of the East.

Although Theodosius I struggled mightily against the Visigoths, he never succeeded in expelling them from the empire. Making a virtue out of a necessity, in 382 he officially recognized by way of a treaty their status as legal inhabitants of the empire. Some four years later, Theodosius also concluded a peace with Persia, Rome's ever-pesky rival along the Euphrates frontier. These only partial successes permitted Theodosius to concentrate on the empire's domestic political, military, and religious affairs. The biggest threats to the domestic peace lay in the political and military threats posed to those in power by would-be usurpers—a threat made all the more palpable because of the questionable legitimacy (in the eyes of many) of such emperors as Theodosius, who had been elevated to imperial authority neither through an ancestral claim nor through some universally recognized constitutional process, but only because of expediency. As such, those who considered themselves Theodosius' equals in terms of breeding and talent felt few qualms about putting his legitimacy to the test. A second problem facing Theodosius I was a religious one. A Christian who devoutly embraced the Nicene Creed, Theodosius faced a host of contemporaries who followed alternative theological creeds, especially the Arians, who, as a result, thought that Theodosius' authority was illegitimate on religious grounds alone.

Thus, the importance of Flaccilla. By the time she had made her way with her husband to Constantinople, she had already given birth to two children: a daughter *Pulcheria (c. 376–385) and a son Arcadius. As a result, although the process was only in its initial phase, a dynasty was beginning to take form thanks to Flaccilla's fertility: Pulcheria would one day be used to secure political alliances for her father, while Arcadius would be deemed Theodosius' political heir. In addition to these two children, in 384 at Constantinople's imperial palace another son, Honorius, was born to the imperial couple. Theodosius' line therefore seemed assured.

Flaccilla, however, was more than an imperial brood-mare. She too was a rabid follower of the Nicene Creed whose faith reinforced that of her husband in his war to keep the forces supporting the Arian interpretation of Christianity at bay. These were especially legion in the eastern empire. Moreover, Flaccilla provided more than just moral support, for she actively, and very publicly, cared for the sick, the orphaned (especially virgin girls), the widowed, the poor, and the hungry. The social manifestations of her faith were not lost on her contemporaries, and it is clear that her Christian actions helped to legitimize her husband's authority in the eyes of those he would have follow him willingly. In addition, she was especially praised for her *philandria* (wifely love) and thus became a kind of model for the age's "ideal woman." Although not as vaunted as her husband's military or political successes, Flaccilla's services went at least as far as anything Theodosius did to win over the hearts of his subjects, and to insure that her two sons would succeed their father with a minimum of fuss.

In short, Flaccilla was so popular that Theodosius consciously brought her image more into the limelight. This is especially seen through her elevation to the status of "Augusta" ("Empress"), probably at the same time (383) that Arcadius was officially proclaimed an Augustus, and thus his father's heir. Flaccilla's new status brought no real political authority, but the influence it implied far exceeded its constitutional perquisites. In fact, Flaccilla was the first woman to hold this title since the time of Constantine the Great, whose wife ❧➤ **Fausta** (d. 324) had last been so honored over a half-century before. Thus, not only did Theodosius' bestowal of this status affirm his commitment to the life of Christian service Flaccilla embodied, but it also worked as propaganda, for it confirmed a tangible link between his reign and that of the hugely popular Constantine, who was both the first Christian emperor and the refounder of the

❧➤
Fausta (d. 324).
See Helena
(c. 255–329) for
sidebar.

city Theodosius had adopted as his imperial capital. As an Augusta, Flaccilla's visage appeared, in imperial regalia, on all denominations of Roman coinage. Her numismatic portraits especially associated her with fertility as if to say, just as she had produced the beginnings of a dynasty for Theodosius, so would she help bear the fruits of peaceful prosperity for the entire empire. So much was her image used to promote the achievements of the new era that her full title, liberally broadcast throughout the realm was, "The Eternal and God-Loving Augusta Aelia Flavia Flaccilla, Mistress of the Inhabited World."

Flaccilla's kinship connections should not be overlooked as Theodosius struggled to become the sole master of the Roman world. Among the influential in her family was her nephew, Nebridius, the son of Flaccilla's sister (name unknown). After Theodosius' reign, Nebridius would be executed for favoring the interests of Arcadius and the eastern empire over those of Honorius and the west, but before this unfortunate end, Nebridius loyally and competently served both the elder and younger Theodosius. As a result, he was one of the more celebrated imperial servants of his day. Undoubtedly, more of Flaccilla's kin and their connections served her husband in this fashion, making her a vital linchpin in the faction that saw Theodosius triumphant over his rivals.

It should come as no surprise, then, that when Flaccilla died in 386 in Thrace at a spa where she had retired to take the medicinal waters (a death that came no more than two years after the death of Pulcheria, and thus a double-blow to the new "dynasty"), the news of her demise created shock-waves. In fact, Gregory of Nyssa in his consolation address at the time of her funeral compared her loss to the effects of earthquakes and disastrous floods. Gregory also painstakingly cataloged the virtues that enshrined Flaccilla as the ideal Christian empress and wife—a model which was revisited many times in subsequent generations. Hyperbole, perhaps, but clearly those Flaccilla left behind strongly felt the pain of her premature passing.

William Greenwalt,
Associate Professor of Classical History,
Santa Clara University, Santa Clara, California

Opposite page

𝒦irsten
𝒥lagstad

Flaccilla (d. 431)

Roman noble. Name variations: Flacilla. Died in childhood in 431; daughter of Theodosius II, East Roman emperor, and *Eudocia (c. 401–460).

Flagstad, Kirsten (1895–1962)

Norwegian singer who was the greatest Wagnerian soprano of the mid-20th century. Pronunciation: KEER-sten. Born Kirsten Malfrid Flagstad on July 12, 1895, in Hamar, near Oslo, Norway; died of cancer in Oslo on December 7, 1962; daughter of Michael (a violinist and conductor) and Marie (Nielsen) Flagstad (an organist, pianist, and operatic coach, known as the "musical momma of Norway"); sister of Karen Marie Flagstad Orkel, an opera singer; graduated from the ninth grade; took private singing lessons from Ellen Schytte-Jacobsen in Oslo and Dr. Gillis Bratt in Stockholm; married Sigurd Hall, in May 1919 (divorced 1930); married Henry Johansen, in 1930; children: (first marriage) Else-Marie Hall (b. 1920).

Made her debut as Nuri in d'Albert's Tiefland at the National Theater in Oslo (1913), where she also sang her first Isolde (1932); sang in Bayreuth (1933–34); made U.S. debut at the Metropolitan Opera (February 1935); returned to America after the war; gave farewell performance at Covent Garden with Tristan (1951), at the Met in Gluck's Alceste (1952), at the Mermaid Theater in London (1953) and at Oslo (December 1953); made numerous recordings with Edwin McArthur and Gerald Moore; served as director of the Norwegian State Opera (1958–60).

Opera appearances: Tiefland, Les Choches de Corneville, En hellig Aften, Vaarnat, Der Evangelimann, I Pagliacci, Der Zigeunerbaron, Die Schöne Galathee, Die Nürnberger Puppe, Abu Hassan, La Belle Hélène, Die Lustigen Weiber von Windsor, Die Zauberflöte, Otello, Un Ballo in maschera, Das höllisch Gold, La Fanciulla del West, Orphée aux enfers, Boccaccio, Carmen, Die Fledermaus, Les Brigands, Sjömandsbruden, Faust, Orfeo ed Euridice, Der Freischütz, Saul og David, Aïda, La Bohème, Tosca, Lohengrin, La Rondine, Die Meistersinger, Jonny spielt auf, Schwanda der Dudelsackpfeifer, Rodelinda, Tristan und Isolde, Die Walküre, Götterdämmerung, Tannhauser, Fidelio, Parsifal, Siegfried, Der fliegender Holländer, Oberon, Alceste, and Dido and Aneas.

Kirsten Flagstad grew up as the eldest child of four in a very musical family. To put food on their table, her father Michael worked as a Parliament stenographer, but he was also engaged as a violinist and later a conductor at the Central Theater in Oslo. Her mother **Marie Nielsen Flagstad** played the piano in the orchestra, besides coaching the chorus and giving private voice and piano lessons. Her brothers played the violin and cello, and, her sister, **Karen (Flagstad Orkel)**, who as the youngest was unable to eke out her turn at the piano, sang. Kirsten started playing the piano at six. Though she quickly became skilled, it occurred to no one, including herself, that she would make either playing or singing a career. Her mother wanted her to become a doctor, and she dutifully enrolled in high school as a preparatory step towards university studies. Always a hard worker, Flagstad tried to complete the course in two rather than three years but fell ill and had to discontinue her schooling temporarily. Though she made a brief return, she did not graduate. Content to think of herself as someone's future wife, she remained at home, helping her mother with the housework. From the age of ten, she had taken charge of the household when Marie Flagstad was on tour with the theater company.

At ten, Kirsten also had her first introduction to Wagner, given the score of *Lohengrin* as a birthday present. Having been taught French, English, and German in school, she knew German fairly well; so, she memorized the role of Elsa to sing and play for her own amusement and for the pleasure of her father. From time to time, her mother also asked her daughter to sing duo with one of her voice pupils. At 11, when Kirsten was asked to sing Senta for a man who was studying Wagner's *Fliegender Holländer,* she did so from score and, in that way, "slowly came to work with opera," she said. "It came as naturally as breathing, with no conscious effort on my part."

At 16, Flagstad started voice lessons with **Ellen Schytte-Jacobsen**, who had heard her sing and offered to coach her free of charge. With Madame Schytte-Jacobsen, Flagstad would do exercises, while studying a variety of roles by herself, though not planning to bring them to a stage. She paid little attention to her teacher's prediction that she would be ready to sing in public within three years, but she beat that prophecy by a year. On December 12, 1913, only two years after she had started her training, Flagstad made her debut in Eugen d'Albert's *Tiefland* at the Oslo National Theater, beginning a career that would span 40 years and make her famous worldwide as one of the greatest Wagnerian singers ever.

The outbreak of World War I prevented Flagstad from following the traditional course of those pursuing a singing career, going to Germany for further studies. Instead, she went to Stockholm. Acknowledged as having a promising, nice little voice, she had been offered a private donation to use as she wished. She invested her funds in four years of study with Dr. Gillis Bratt, a famous Stockholm throat specialist who

taught singing as a sideline. He immediately diagnosed Flagstad's "little" voice to be a result of her vocal cords not closing and thus letting air pass between them. Bratt taught her to close those cords, and in three months her voice had tripled in size. In March 1918, she sang her first recital in Oslo, planning to make her debut at the Stockholm Opera the following spring.

Plans changed when she married a businessman not especially interested in music on May 14, 1919. Instead of returning to Stockholm, Flagstad joined the newly opened Opera-Comique in Oslo, singing operettas by Lehar and Offenbach. Soon pregnant, she gave up singing and stayed home to await the birth of her baby. **Else-Marie Hall** arrived on May 17, 1920. Life as a wife and mother so contented Kirsten that she did not sing the entire summer, despite her mother's protestations and repeated urgings that she return to the Opera-Comique. Almost desperate on behalf of her daughter's lost opportunities, Marie Flagstad brought her the score of Lehar's *Zigeunerliebe,* insisting she sing it. Flagstad did as directed, then suddenly stopped, staring in disbelief at her mother. Her voice had doubled in volume. At that discovery, she accepted the role and went back to her career at the Opera-Comique where she would sing light soprano parts for the next eight years.

I am not an artist except when I am dealing with art, and when I am not dealing with art, I am the most commonplace person in the world.

—Kirsten Flagstad

In the spring of 1928, after Flagstad and her husband separated, she accepted an invitation to sing in Finland for the summer and spent the season there in the company of her daughter. Together they departed for Gothenburg, Sweden, where, that autumn, Flagstad was engaged to sing in *Aïda, La Bohème,* and *Tosca.* She was an unqualified success; Else, however, found it difficult to adjust to school in another country and returned to Norway to stay with her aunt and uncle.

In June of 1929, Flagstad was booked to sing in *Lohengrin* at the Theater in Oslo, an engagement that would yield a real life counterpart to her role as Lohengrin's bride. A friend introduced her to Norwegian business magnate Henry Johansen, who was in the audience. It was love at first sight for both, and, though she may not have been conscious of her feelings, Flagstad wrote her husband that night request-

ing a divorce. About the same time, the first inquiries from the Metropolitan Opera in America arrived. Eric Simon, the Met's European representative, invited her to send reviews, lists of roles, and photos. As before, Flagstad was not sufficiently interested to renounce her marriage plans and did not bother to answer Simon. The Metropolitan seemed as far away as the moon, and she had work to do in Norway. Above all, she was engaged to marry a man she loved. On a spring day in 1930, she became Mrs. Johansen in the office of the Norwegian consul general in Antwerp. The couple had been touring Germany, Austria, and Belgium and among other events had seen *Tristan and Isolde* at the Vienna Opera. At the end of that performance, Johansen had told his future bride, "This is something you could never sing." She agreed. "It's much too big for me." Both would eat their words some four months later when she sang in Handel's *Rodelinda* in Gothenburg, and they recognized a potential Isolde.

Flagstad had not planned to go to Gothenburg. Happily married, she felt she had earned a long rest and saw no need to go on singing. She was content to be Mrs. Henry Johansen who accompanied her husband on business trips. But a frantic call had come from Gothenburg. They were in a pinch, could she come and sing in Weinberger's *Schwanda* within a week. *Rodelinda* followed it, and two weeks later, by some strange coincidence, the National Theater in Oslo invited her to sing Isolde there the following June.

With her mother for a coach, Flagstad learned the part, "plunging into it like an exciting adventure." Her sister and sister-in-law acted as prompters, and together the four of them rehearsed in the Johansen home. In the evening, her husband would return from the world of business, and they would entertain friends and family, sitting around talking or playing music. Her daughter Else and Henry Johansen's daughter from a previous marriage studied together in Oslo, so for a short while Flagstad had everyone she loved within reach. She found life "complete and satisfying in every way" and could "easily have done without the singing." But her response to the frantic call from Gothenburg had set her feet on a path she would follow for another 23 years.

One role led to another. After one of the Isolde performances, *Ellen Gulbranson, who for 18 years had been singing *Brunnhilde at Bayreuth, approached Flagstad, insisting that she audition there. Thus, in July of 1932, with the urging of her husband, Flagstad tried out for Bayreuth and was engaged for the following two summers. The world of Wagner opened to her.

Nor did Henry Johansen object when an offer to sing came from the Metropolitan. Together they left for America at the end of December 1934, and Flagstad made her American debut on February 2, 1935, as Sieglinde in *Die Walküre*. Her next role was the *Walküre* Brunnhilde followed by the *Götterdämmerung* Brunnhilde, a total of 125 performances. On April 21, she made her first radio debut before a live audience of 4,000. By the summer of 1935, she was so overworked she had to cancel her engagements in South America, but she had sung to full houses and rave reviews. Flagstad had been deeply moved by the kindness and cooperation of her colleagues: at a flower show at the Grand Central Palace in New York, a flower had been named after her. Her first season in America, she felt, had been worth the price of exhaustion.

Rested after a summer in Norway, she returned to America on September 26 to commence a series of concerts. Thousands attended her performances, even in smaller cities; she found her audiences enthusiastic and receptive to unfamiliar songs, which encouraged her to make increasingly bolder choices for her repertoire. Only one thing troubled her: the American habit of turning celebrities into public property. Shy, with a deep need for privacy, Flagstad felt haunted by the attention. She refused to meet members of the audience backstage and frequently left the opera house with applause still ringing in her ears.

After five years of touring America, Australia, and Europe, she experienced a severe bout of homesickness and longed to return to Norway. She was concerned, too, about losing her daughter to another country. Else had accompanied her mother on her second trip to the States and had fallen in love with an American whom she wanted to marry. Hoping she would reconsider, Flagstad persuaded her daughter to return with her to Kristiansand, and Else agreed. They packed their bags and set their departure date for April 20, 1940.

On the morning of April 9, however, they learned that the Germans had invaded Norway and Denmark, and the *Bergensfjord* on which they were to sail remained at dockside. Her husband cabled around April 18 to tell her to stay where she was, so she made herself available for bookings through the next twelvemonth. In the middle of her tour, she received a different message: "Why don't you come home? I am waiting for you." She cabled back that her commitments demanded she stay, but she was growing exceedingly anxious about conditions in Norway and worried about every move she made, fearful of what the Germans would do to her family, all of whom had received notoriety due to her success. Flagstad was torn between her duty to go home and her obligation to honor her contracts running through April of 1941.

In October of 1940, her stepdaughter arrived in San Francisco, bringing with her the devastating truth that not only were Germans in command of her country, but Norwegians were arrayed against Norwegians in a war as serious as the one between them and the Nazis. Americans, among them Herbert Hoover, urged her to stay rather than return to a country occupied by Germans, but Flagstad could bear the agony of uncertainty no longer. She thought it her duty as a wife and a Norwegian to return to her homeland and made plans for leaving on April 19, 1941.

Her journey home took a circuitous route, involving visas and permits at every stage of the road through Portugal, Spain, France, Germany, and Sweden. At her hotel in Portugal, she had her first intimation of something being terribly wrong. There she learned, in the company of three Norwegian businessmen, that Henry Johansen, as a member of Quisling's political party, was thought to be keeping very strange company. Vidkun Quisling was vaguely familiar to Flagstad as a man who had formed his own political party, the National Union, ten years earlier. She also knew that, as a political conservative, her husband had joined the party some years before, believing it was a businessman's best defense against radicalism in Norway. What she did not know was that Quisling, who was friendly with the Nazis, had collaborated in the German invasion of her country and become head of the only party permitted in wartime Norway, Nasjonal Samling. When she finally reached Oslo after numerous delays, she decided to stay until the war was over.

The Johansens moved to their home in Kristiansand to live quietly together with friends and family. Again the issue of Henry Johansen's membership in Quisling's party surfaced when his daughter asked Flagstad to plead with her father to leave the party. Flagstad did, and her husband allowed that he was waiting for an opportunity to do so, realizing the danger connected with resigning at this time. He nonetheless ventured his resignation and bought them some quiet years at Kristiansand, interrupted only by

Flagstad's performances in Stockholm and Zurich. The Norwegians in Stockholm protested her presence there—a privilege they interpreted as a signifier of her collaboration with the enemy—by boycotting her performance. So she sang to a half-empty house and an audience that gradually and finally enthusiastically let themselves be won over. In Switzerland, her audiences were supportive and appreciative from the start, and she returned there in the summers of 1942 and 1943, after which traveling became prohibitive. Though she sang at home, the times were getting increasingly difficult. Norwegians were seized and sent to concentration camps, reprisals for slaying of members of the Quisling party were conducted, and finally Henry Johansen was arrested and kept a prisoner for eight days before being released.

The end of the war brought only a few days of respite for the Johansens. Henry Johansen was again arrested, this time by Norwegian patriots, and taken to a detention camp. He fell ill there and was refused hospital care until it was too late. He died in June of 1945.

Tied no longer with bonds of love and matrimony, Flagstad was free to leave and resume her career. She discovered she still had a voice—more voluminous than ever for the enforced rest—and she sang in Cannes, Paris, London, and Milan before returning to America on March 14, 1947. After a press conference on March 15, she went straight to her daughter in Bozeman, Montana. Else had married her American and, six months before, had made Kirsten Flagstad a grandmother, "the nicest thing that could happen to me," as she put it. Her first concert was in Boston on April 6. Flagstad had been told to expect picket lines protesting the performance of an alleged collaborator, but there were none, and the response of those who lent their presence to the half-full house was a welcome so encompassing it threw her "completely off balance." Two weeks later, she appeared in Carnegie Hall, looking regal in a black gown and a white lace collar, and received a standing ovation from a crowd of loyal friends and music lovers. As the great singer *Elisabeth Rethberg commented afterwards, she had on that afternoon experienced perfection. "The audience, the artist, the gown she wore, the way she walked on the stage, the way she acted, the applause, the program and the way she sang it—it was the whole thing." But the newspapers were cool, carrying references to her husband's arrest. Flagstad thus felt under constant scrutiny, but she made up her mind to sing as she had never sung before. She knew she was innocent of betrayals, or she could

not have faced her public or sung at all. So she said nothing about the "Kirsten Flagstad case"—she just sang. Putting up with booing and picket lines, she kept on singing.

She was sought-after everywhere but the Metropolitan Opera. In 1948, she returned to England to sing at London's Covent Garden, then on to Paris, Switzerland, Italy, and South America. Finally in July of 1949 came the coveted invitation. The Metropolitan cabled: could she do the Brunnhildes and Kundry there in 1950 and tour in Boston and Cleveland. Flagstad, however, had to refuse because she was fully booked for the 1950 season. Her reply resulted in furious letters from friends and admirers wondering how she dare say no to such an institution, but she felt she had no choice. Ahead of her she had a season with the San Francisco Opera, whose management had replied to objections over her appearance from war veterans: "If we cannot have Kirsten Flagstad, we won't have any opera season at all." She sang to "packed houses" both there and three times at Carnegie Hall as well. In December, she was approached again by the Metropolitan and agreed to do *Tristan*, *Fidelio* and the *Ring Cycle*. She appeared there for the last time in Gluck's *Alceste* on April 1, 1952.

Flagstad's last public appearance prior to her retirement as a singer was on December 12, 1953, at the National Theater of Oslo where she had made her debut 40 years earlier. Five years later, in 1958, she opened her first season as director of the Norwegian State Opera with d'Albert's *Tiefland*. She had come full circle. Returned home both as an artist-director and a daughter of Norway, she gave the State Opera's official welcome to King Olav V whose father, back in 1937, had honored her with his country's highest distinction, the St. Olav decoration.

Flagstad's voice of gold had thrilled audiences worldwide and brought her vast acclaim; yet, she would write in her memoirs that "fame, glory—they are empty meaningless words. One does what one can." Her "doing" was of gargantuan proportions, too great for the conventional life she so craved of wife-mother. Flagstad accepted that, but she never ceased blaming herself for the accusations levelled against "Flagstad's husband."

Kirsten Flagstad died of cancer in Oslo on December 7, 1962. In his tribute to the famous singer, Edwin McArthur, her American accompanist for 17 years, calls her a "great lady—a great artist—a simple woman—a complex individual—sweet and bitter like all human beings—

but above all, a true personification of uncompromising integrity." On December 12, 1963, 50 years to the day after Flagstad made her first appearance on stage, he presented her life-size portrait to the Metropolitan Opera Association. She had bequeathed it to her grandson Sigurd, who in turn donated it to the Association and thus ensured his grandmother a place in the company of other greats who together record the history of music on the walls of New York's Lincoln Center.

SOURCES:

Biancolli, Louis. *The Flagstad Manuscript*. NY: Putnam, 1952.

McArthur, Edwin. *Flagstad*. NY: Alfred A. Knopf, 1965.

Sadie, Stanley, ed. *The New Grove Dictionary of Music and Musicians*. NY: Macmillan, 1980.

Inga Wiehl,
Yakima Valley Community College,
Yakima Valley, Washington

Flahaut or Flahault, countess of.

See Souza-Botelho, Adélaïde-Marie-Émilie-Filleul, Marquise of (1761–1836).

See Elphinstone, Margaret Mercer (1788–1867).

Flaherty, Frances Hubbard

(c. 1886–1972)

American photographer, specializing in documentation, who worked with her husband on the heralded film Nanook of the North. *Born Frances Hubbard in Cambridge, Massachusetts, around 1886; died in Dummerston, Vermont, in 1972; graduated from Bryn Mawr College, Bryn Mawr, Pennsylvania, 1905; married Robert Joseph Flaherty (a prospector and supervisor for the Canadian Grand Trunk Railway and motion-picture director), on November 12, 1914 (died 1951); children:* **Barbara Flaherty** *(b. 1916); Francis Flaherty (b. 1917);* **Monica Flaherty** *(b. 1920).*

Frances Hubbard Flaherty worked almost exclusively with her husband Robert Joseph Flaherty, whom she met while he was a student at Michigan College of Mines (now Michigan Technological University). Between 1910 and 1916, when Robert headed exploratory expeditions for the Canadian Northern Railroad, Frances photographed geological formations and made documentary films focusing on life in the North. She also assisted on many of her husband's subsequent films, including the silent *Nanook of the North* (1924), about the life of the Eskimo (Inuit), which was hailed as the first documentary that attempted to interpret the lives of its subjects. Frances made still photographs for *Nanook of the North*, and the film

was a huge success internationally. Frances was co-editor on the film *Moana* (1926), their study of life in the South Seas. She also served as photographer on *Man of Aran* (1934) and co-writer of *Louisiana Story* (1948). Following her husband's death in 1951, she co-founded the Robert J. Flaherty Foundation, now the International Film Seminars. Frances Flaherty died in Vermont in 1972.

Barbara Morgan,
Melrose, Massachusetts

Flanagan, Hallie (1889–1969)

Experimental and innovative director, producer, and teacher of American theater. Born Hallie Ferguson in Redfield, South Dakota, on April 27, 1889; died in a nursing home in Beacon, New York, on July 23, 1969; daughter of Frederic (a traveling salesman) and Louisa (Fischer) Ferguson; attended public school through the twelfth grade; graduated from Grinnell College in 1911; studied with George Pierce Baker at Harvard theater workshop; received Guggenheim Foundation grant in 1926–27 to tour theaters of Europe and Russia; married Murray Flanagan, on December 25, 1912 (died 1917); married Philip Davis, on April 27, 1934 (died 1940); children: (first marriage) Jack (1914–1922) and Frederic; (stepchildren) Joanne, Jack, and Helen.

Taught English and theater at Grinnell College (1920–25); taught playwriting and dramatic production at Vassar College (1925–34); served as director of the Federal Theater of the Works Project Administration (1935–39); was theatrical director at Vassar College (1940–42); served as dean at Smith College (1942–52).

Selected publications: Shifting Scenes of the Modern European Theatre *(NY: Coward McCann, 1928);* Arena *(NY: Duell, Sloan and Pearce, 1940);* Dynamo *(NY: Duell, Sloan and Pearce, 1943).*

Hallie Flanagan, the object of controversy, criticism, and admiration, profoundly affected the American theater. Appointed by Harry Hopkins to head the Federal Theater Project in 1935, she created innovative and provocative entertainment during an era when political sentiment was shifting toward a conservatism that disparaged liberal expression in the arts. Hallie Flanagan never allowed expediency to compromise her dramatic vision or integrity.

She was born Hallie Ferguson in Redfield, South Dakota, on April 27, 1889. The economic fluctuations of the time forced Flanagan's parents to move frequently during her early years. Finally settling in Grinnell, Iowa, the family enjoyed a degree of prosperity and a harmonious and stable life. Flanagan's perhaps idealized memories of a leisurely and serene existence in the small town are complimented by her recollections of her father's gregarious charm and her mother's reserved calm. Her father Frederic engaged her in conversations about the world, challenging her to achieve, convincing her that she could do anything she chose to accomplish. Her mother **Louisa Fischer Ferguson** epitomized a life in service to her family. Flanagan admired and loved both her parents; their examples set her standards and were the foundation for her lifelong struggle to balance career and family. It was a struggle clearly weighted in favor of career but not without soul-searching. Even at age nine, Hallie seemed unusually mature and confident. She had a kind, lively spirit that was moderated by a somewhat excessive sense of propriety.

Flanagan attended Grinnell College in Iowa. Attractive, bright and enthusiastic, she participated in all aspects of college life except athletics, and her friends deferred to her as the natural leader. Some accused her of collecting admirers, but her charm was forthright and irresistible. The college fostered a strong sense of public service, and Flanagan's idealism flourished. She took strong stands against injustice and racism despite the underlying apathy of the time.

Years later, Hallie would maintain that the only significant occurrence for her at Grinnell was meeting Murray Flanagan, but she insisted they delay their marriage until she had taught high school English for a year. From the beginning, Flanagan's lack of interest in domestic chores and her growing restlessness contributed to a less than idyllic relationship. Tuberculosis killed Murray Flanagan in 1917, leaving Hallie with two young sons to raise.

To earn a living, she returned to instructing, first teaching high school English, then freshman English at Grinnell College in the fall of 1920. That was the year Grinnell, under William Bridge's direction, introduced playwriting and dramatic production into its curriculum. By the spring of 1921, Flanagan had become his assistant, was writing her first play, and had begun to seriously consider a career in theater. But everything came to a momentary halt the following year when Jack Flanagan, her seven-year-old son, contracted spinal meningitis; at the time, there was no cure. When the boy died in 1922, Flanagan was devastated, and only her younger son Frederic's needs compelled her to resume her career.

The loss of her husband and son convinced Flanagan that she had failed as a wife and mother; it also fueled her resolve to succeed. In January of 1923, she took over the theater courses at Grinnell and became head of the dramatic council; she was determined to create a substantial theater program, and her vision gained the support of both students and administration.

Influenced by the lectures of George Pierce Baker, an important figure in the "new theater" movement, and intent upon studying with him, Flanagan was accepted into Baker's playwriting classes at Harvard for the 1923 academic year. She later credited Baker with teaching her everything she knew about theater. Her eagerness and acumen earned his respect and recognition, and she became his assistant by midterm. Baker recommended she spend a year seeing plays in Europe and wrote glowingly of her abilities to the Guggenheim Foundation.

Returning to Grinnell, Flanagan reorganized the Dramatic Club and took charge of a production that assured her future: *Romeo and Juliet*. The staging, the costumes, and the spectacular lighting held the audience spellbound. The president of the Carnegie Foundation, Frederick Keppel was so impressed by the production that he promised his support for her Guggenheim fellowship.

In 1925, Flanagan was offered and accepted the job of teaching playwriting and dramatic production at Vassar College. Both the salary increase and the proximity to New York theater convinced her to make the move, though she was less comfortable with the snobbish superiority she perceived in the Vassar students and faculty. Nevertheless, Vassar was a lively cultural center where liberal thinking, innovation, and feminist ideals were encouraged, and Flanagan flourished. Finally awarded a Guggenheim fellowship for 1926–27, she was quick to receive permission from Vassar's president for a year's leave of absence. More difficult was the decision regarding her son Frederic. Her parents moved into her Poughkeepsie, New York, apartment to be near him while he boarded at Oakland School. Seemingly carefree and happy, the boy never complained about the continual separations.

Traveling through England, Ireland, Sweden, Denmark, and Germany, Flanagan met with celebrated members of the theatrical community of each nation, but she was less than excited by the works being done. Their days of innovation seemed over. In Russia, however, Flanagan found a theater in ferment. Artists

Hallie
Flanagan

were still experimenting and developing. After the 1917 Russian Revolution, theater had become a national obsession, and, though much that was being done was mediocre and merely propaganda for the Soviet regime, theater had become a vital part of the lives of the Russian people. It addressed their concerns and expressed their hope for a better social system. Konstantin Stanislavsky and Vsevolod Meyerhold were still working in comparative freedom; Stalinist suppression had not yet begun. Flanagan's response to Russia was entirely idealistic, based upon her hopes rather than reality. Stanislavsky and Meyerhold would have tremendous impact on Flanagan's future work and vision.

On her return to Vassar, she set forth an ambitious, innovative program of plays. Her class in dramatic production quickly became a catalyst for controversy among the more academically staid members of the faculty. Perhaps there was resentment over the enthusiasm of her students and the regard in which they held their teacher. Hallie Flanagan had become the center of an admiring, loyal following.

The quality of theater she produced justified the admiration. Flanagan's plays were reviewed favorably by *Theatre Arts Monthly, Theatre Magazine, Woman's Journal* and *The New York Times Magazine*. Writes biographer **Joanne Bentley**, she "won the respect of a profession ever derisive of the academic theater." She was the first to use Meyerhold's constructivist techniques in an American production, and it created a stir that spread far beyond the Vassar campus. New York writers, critics, and theater professionals would continue to attend her plays in the years that followed.

Flanagan's romance with Philip Davis began in 1930 when she cast him in a play. Davis, who was depressed and drinking heavily after the death of his wife, was as taken by Flanagan's magic and charisma as were her students, and he finally persuaded her to marry him in 1934 in Greece. Though she was hesitant to the last moment, the union proved a success. Davis, who brought three children into the marriage, was unfailingly supportive, encouraging and understanding of her need for independence.

During the 1930s, a growing number of playwrights turned their focus on the condition of the world's economy. Flanagan had been one of the first non-Communists in America to use the theater to stimulate public reaction to the issues of poverty, unemployment, and injustice. Publication of *Shifting Scenes* in 1928 and the articles she had written about Russia for *Theater Arts Monthly* had established her as an authority on Russian theater. Those credits, coupled with her productions of *Can You Hear Their Voices?, American Plan,* and *Miners on Strike,* had gained her a reputation as a theatrical propagandist for leftist causes. She was accused of being a "disseminator of Communist propaganda" in a Hearst editorial in February 1935. Flanagan repudiated Communism as being too simplistic an approach, but she believed in motivating students and audiences to become involved in world issues. Because of her unflinching willingness to create controversial, engaging theater of social relevance, the accusation would follow her throughout her career.

Flanagan's appointment as Federal Theater director was announced in July 1935. Harry Hopkins, who had been a classmate of Flanagan's in high school and college, was the head of the Works Progress Administration (WPA), created by Franklin Roosevelt to put the jobless to work during the Depression. It was Hopkins' idea to include the arts projects for writers, directors, musicians, painters, and thespians in the WPA. After their years together, Hopkins had followed Flanagan's career and admired her accomplishments. Both loved the arts and shared a vision of artists developing their craft while exposing audiences nationwide to affordable theater.

From the beginning, Flanagan tried to build the foundation for a national federation of theaters that would continue to function even when the federal subsidy was withdrawn. Her plan included five production centers in New York, Los Angeles, Chicago, Boston, and New Orleans. Resident companies would train actors and technicians in modern production techniques, provide a research center, commission plays, and perform new and classical plays that commercial theater could ill afford to try. Contemporary events were to be dramatized in a series of Living Newspapers. Touring companies would reach a circuit of smaller theaters throughout the country. Each region would enjoy dramatic autonomy, with Flanagan directing general policy from Washington. Hopkins was enthusiastic.

Flanagan was immediately faced with pressure from Washington to put 12,000 to 15,000 unemployed to work at once while trying to surmount a frustratingly cumbersome bureaucracy unaccustomed to dealing with artists. Furthermore, the theatrical unions were troublesome and uncooperative to the spirit of the project. It was only after imaginative negotiations that she was able to win their participation. Generally, those in commercial theater were unwilling to work for the minimal wages offered by the project, and most of Flanagan's appointments came from regional theaters. Thus, a younger and less established set contributed most to the Federal Theater.

Dedicated to the ideal of producing plays that provoked public debate, Flanagan was constantly in the spotlight defending Federal Theater presentations. Whether it was government bureaucrats fearful for national security or conservatives offended by the leftist examination of traditional policies, the Federal Theater and Hallie Flanagan were attacked and criticized. Politics also played an important part; conservatives were interested in discrediting the Roosevelt administration in every conceivable way. Called to testify before the House Un-American Activities Committee, Flanagan's patriotism and integrity were questioned and denigrated. She conducted herself with dignity and honesty in defense of both her own and the project's reputation.

Despite these attacks, the Federal Theater, under Flanagan's guidance, continued to produce plays that received critical acclaim and played to full houses. But by 1938 Congress was determined to dismantle the New Deal and was aggressively cutting relief spending. Though Flanagan fought hard to save the Federal Theater, the Senate and House passed a compromise relief bill which eliminated funds after June 30, 1939.

The next seven months following the close of the Federal Theater were surprisingly happy ones for Flanagan. She worked on her book about the project, *Arena*, and enjoyed more time with her family than had been possible during the preceding years. Then, in February 1940, Philip Davis died of coronary thrombosis. Though Flanagan felt the loss deeply, she submerged her grief with work: writing and teaching playwriting at Vassar. When her book was completed in mid-1940, she returned to the directing of experimental theater at Vassar and to the question of how to make a college theater responsive to the larger community.

Offered the post of dean at Smith College, she readily took the job, intrigued with the idea of creating a theater department and glad for an opportunity to distance herself from the memories of her life with Davis that surrounded her in Poughkeepsie. In 1942, when Flanagan relocated to Smith, in Northampton, Massachusetts, with her stepchildren, she was unaware that her appointment caused a furor on the campus. Many of the faculty opposed the idea of a nonacademic theater department and were annoyed that they had had no say in the selection of the new dean. Flanagan did not fit the staid image the college promoted in faculty members. She enjoyed easygoing, informal relations with the students in contrast to the reserved tradition other faculty members encouraged. Flanagan found herself surrounded by supporters and detractors. Those who worked closely with her were impressed with her ability and intelligence. It was a debate that continued throughout her tenure at Smith.

In 1944, Flanagan began to experience the early symptoms of Parkinson's disease. Upon her retirement from Smith in 1952, she returned to Poughkeepsie. For many years, she enjoyed her retirement: reading, seeing plays, keeping up a large correspondence, and visiting with friends. An automobile accident in 1963, however, necessitated her admission into a nursing home. During her last days, her son Frederic, who had long suffered from bouts of depression, committed suicide. Flanagan was never told. Following her death on July 23, 1969, a memorial service was held at the Vivian Beaumont Theater in Lincoln Center.

SOURCES:

Bentley, Joanne. *Hallie Flanagan: A Life In the American Theatre*. NY: Alfred Knopf, 1988.

Leaming, Barbara. *Orson Welles*. NY: Viking, 1985.

Jan Holden,
freelance writer, Los Angeles, California

Flanagan, Sinéad.

See Milligan, Alice for sidebar.

Flanders, countess of.

See Martel, Judith (c. 844–?).
See Elfthrith (d. 929).
See Matilda of Flanders for sidebar on Adela Capet (c. 1010–1079).
See Eleanor of Normandy (fl. 1000s).
See Gertrude of Saxony (fl. 1070).
See Joan of Montferrat.
See Margaret of Alsace (c. 1135–1194).
See Teresa of Portugal (1157–1218).
See Maria of Champagne (c. 1180–1203).
See Johanna of Flanders (c. 1200–1244).
See Margaret of Flanders (1202–1280).
See Yolande of Burgundy (1248–1280).
See Margaret of Brabant (1323–1368).
See Margaret of Flanders (1350–1405).
See Marie of Hohenzollern-Sigmaringen (1845–1912).

Flanner, Janet (1892–1978)

American novelist and journalist who chronicled 50 years of life in Europe for The New Yorker *magazine.*
Name variations: (pen name) Genêt. Born on March 13, 1892, in Indianapolis, Indiana; died on November 7, 1978, in New York City; daughter of William Francis Flanner (a mortician and real-estate developer) and Mary-Ellen (Hockett) Flanner; attended University of Chicago, 1912–14 (no degree); married William Lane Rehm, on April 25, 1918 (divorced 1926); no children.

Served as assistant drama editor, Indianapolis Star (1917–18); moved to New York with husband

(1918); moved to Greece with lover Solita Solano (1921); settled in Paris (1922); published The Cubical City *(1926); had published first "Letter from Paris" for* The New Yorker *(October 10, 1925); lived in New York (1939–44); returned to France (November 1944); broadcast for the Blue Network (later ABC) from Paris (1945–46); awarded the Legion of Honor (1947); given honorary degree, Smith College (June 1958); was a member, National Institute of Arts and Letters (1959); received National Book Award for* Paris Journal, 1944–1965 *(1966).*

Janet Flanner once described herself as "a midwesterner whose life began at the age of thirty, when she first went to Paris." Writing under the "androgynous, anonymous, invented" name of Genêt, she chronicled the history of Europe for 50 years in her fortnightly "Letter from Paris" for *The New Yorker* magazine. This "gentleman of the press in skirts" wrote eloquent, incisive prose, loved women and France, admired traditional European civilization, and hated war and the men who made it. Having fled the puritanical, restrictive America of the 1920s, Flanner became the stereotypical expatriate; an American who lived in Paris, alienated from her homeland, she identified with European Old World culture but never became European. She explained her decision to live abroad through one of her fictional characters: "I didn't leave home to have lovers. But I left home to be free."

Born in 1892, Janet Flanner was the second of three daughters whose parents were active, respected members of the community. William Flanner owned a mortuary and speculated in real estate. **Mary-Ellen Flanner** was interested in the theater and "schooled her daughters in English poetry and good manners"; the eldest daughter, Mary Emma (**Marie Flanner**), became a pianist; the youngest, **Hildegarde Flanner**, was an accomplished writer. Janet entered Tudor Hall, a private school, at age 11. The family's upper-middle-class lifestyle provided a secure, stable environment. The women of the family often felt "uncomfortable," however, about William Flanner's profession and seldom alluded to it.

Janet was a precocious child, outspoken and strong-willed; repudiating her self-righteous and repressed Protestant relatives, she lost her religious faith at age 14, she claimed, and became an adult. Never a brilliant student, she enjoyed school and was elected class president in 1905. Her mother, a frustrated actress, encouraged her to pursue a stage career, but Flanner had decided

at age five that she wanted to be a writer. And that is what she would be for over 60 years.

Instead of attending college, Flanner accompanied her family to Europe in 1910. William Flanner, overworked, anxious, and exhausted, had lost considerable money through bad investments which put a strain on his marriage. Janet was aware of the tension, but it did not affect her appreciation of the cultural richness of Europe. The family lived in Berlin, where Marie was already studying music, and traveled in France and England. Flanner readily adapted to her new surroundings and formed her own opinions on what she observed; from this time on, she associated Germany with "beer, militarism, and the rudeness of soldiers" who "assumed they were superior beings." And in contrast to the prudish American attitude towards sex, Berliners openly discussed, and practiced, homosexuality. Lesbians, called "congenital inverts," were generally considered dangerous to society, a threat to traditional gender roles. It was in this city that Flanner first experienced a conscious attraction to another woman, the young wife of an officer, whose picture Flanner kept for the rest of her life.

When their financial situation worsened, the Flanners returned home. Though the mortuary was doing well, William Flanner's bad investments tormented him. On Saturday, February 17, 1912, he committed suicide. Janet Flanner refused to view his desperate act as one of "heroic liberation" and, it seems, was not much affected by his death. The family continued to live comfortably, and, in the fall of 1912, Flanner entered the University of Chicago.

For two years, she enjoyed an active social life, avoided attending classes, and did poorly in her academic subjects, which fazed her not at all. She also "enjoyed flouting convention," and it is possible that she was expelled from the university; she later vaguely alluded to the fact that she was considered "lawless." So, in 1914, Flanner grudgingly returned home, despite despising "Indianapolis manners and mores." That same year, she worked at a Quaker girls' reformatory in Philadelphia; not temperamentally suited to social work, she left after nine months. Flanner's desire to be a writer was partially fulfilled when she was hired by the *Indianapolis Star*. She reviewed vaudeville and burlesque shows and, in 1917, was promoted to assistant drama critic. Her belief that the appreciation of art could not be learned and that "those who made art or appreciated it were in a class by themselves" served as a motif in her reporting over the next 60 years. This attitude

Janet Flanner, with Ernest Hemingway.

is obvious in her disdain for the taste of "puritans" and "common people." However, during World War I, the Germans, rather than American philistines, were targets of her attacks. Vilified as "absurd, savage, and crudely insensitive to the finer things in life," she accused them of destroying civilized Europe. This was, of course, in stark contrast to the cultured French.

Flanner had kept in touch with college friends, one of whom, William Lane Rehm, she suddenly, and inexplicably, married in April 1918. A "decent" young man, he was, according to **Brenda Wineapple**, "a Victorian, a puritan, a sentimentalist," qualities no one would expect Janet Flanner to find appealing. Why then did she marry him? Perhaps to get out of Indianapolis, but she never revealed the real reason. The couple moved to New York where Rehm worked in a bank. Curiously, Flanner was back in Indianapolis, working at the *Star* in May 1918, and did not return to New York until August. They moved to Greenwich Village, but it was soon evident that marriage and domesticity were an alien

world to which Flanner could not, or would not, adapt—she never mastered the use of a can opener or door locks. Flanner realized, much to her consternation, that she was not in love with her husband and that she was physically and emotionally attracted to women. Moreover, marriage interfered with the independent life she envisioned, a life built around her own friends and social circle. Fortunately, Flanner had an income from her father's estate which freed her from financial dependence on her husband, and a prenuptial agreement guaranteed her control of it. That she could not love Rehm, a "good man," as she admitted, caused her great anguish.

In New York, Flanner met prominent writers and journalists, including Alec Woollcott and **Jane Grant**, and achieved some social prominence in her own right. Two of her published short stories from this time illustrate her concerns and interests: "As It Was" relates "how women stirred her imagination," and "Portrait of Our Lady" looks at Adam and God and the creation of woman. Years later, she could write that "Men are strong and women are necessary," and pondered, "Why can't there be a third sex . . . a sex not dominated by muscle or the inclination to breed?" Flanner liked New York yet felt the urge to leave but wondered how she could abandon the man who was "too good for me?"

In the early twenties, when I was new there, Paris was still yesterday.

—Janet Flanner

Meeting the exotic-looking, 30-year-old *Solita Solano was the catalyst that determined and affected the rest of Flanner's life. Solano was drama editor of the *New York Tribune* but wanted, like Flanner, to be a novelist. These two unconventional, independent, spirited women fell in love. For almost 60 years, Solano was Flanner's confidante, her friend, her family. "Rarely does a day go by that I don't think of you," Flanner wrote to Solano in 1974, 56 years after they met. Their relationship is crucial to understanding Janet Flanner as a woman; the chaos of her private life is the antithesis of her structured, successful career in journalism. More immediately, Flanner's dilemma was three-fold—she was in love with a woman, she was married to a man her family adored, and she was pregnant. Whether she miscarried or had an abortion is not known. Flanner also agonized over hurting Rehm and how her mother and sisters would react. Obviously, she could not reveal her relations with Solano, and, in fact, Flanner's sexual orientation was never openly acknowledged or discussed with her family. Acceptance, not overt approval, was the basis of family harmony.

In 1921, Solano accepted an assignment for *National Geographic,* and Flanner accompanied her to Greece without informing her mother or sisters. She and Solano knew they could not live in the United States, and Flanner "wanted freedom from the sexual, personal, and professional restrictions" in America. While in Athens, Flanner wrote a travel article for the *New York Tribune,* "Hoi Polloi at Close Range," in which she declared that "the civilization of today, influenced by bourgeois self-interest, is moving away from an ideal," and she further deplored "the crudity and vulgarity of modern America." Janet Flanner had found her journalistic voice and the central theme of her future work. In Rome, she wrote poems celebrating her new-found freedom. From Vienna in 1922, she dispatched a letter to Woollcott at *The New York Times* about witnessing anti-Semitic demonstrations there. She was impressed with the elegance of Vienna but equally touched by the effects of war on the

people. And war was the fault of men who "are absurd enough to believe they are superior for doing it." The events leading to hostilities in 1939 only gave credence to her view.

Janet Flanner had found a world for the future "Genêt" to inhabit: old, traditional, refined and graceful, her home and her refuge from the "puritanism, materialism, hypocrisy," and "standardization" that characterized her native land. Flanner and Solano settled in Paris in the fall of 1922, where "we were able to begin anew," wrote Flanner. For 16 years, they lived in the historic quarter of Saint-Germain-des-Prés in the sparsely furnished rooms of an old, nondescript hotel. They lived as part of the lively neighborhood inhabited by the French and expatriate intelligentsia; they frequented the famous cafés, Deux Magots and Flore, and became part of the fecund French cultural scene. Their world was peopled with women who loved women—writers, artists, publishers, who "lived together, worked together, and were openly sexual with one another." F. Scott Fitzgerald, Ernest Hemingway, and *Gertrude Stein also became close, lifelong friends. Neither Flanner nor Solano was monogamous, and soon a third person joined them; *Nancy Cunard, the tormented, self-destructive English aristocratic "crusader" for social causes, became one of the "three happily married women" who, as Solano wrote, "survived all the spring quarrels and the sea changes of forty-two years of modern female fidelity."

In 1924, Flanner was working on her novel, *The Cubical City,* "her symbolic farewell to America," which is largely autobiographical. Writing was a slow, laborious process for Flanner, and she struggled all of her life to create and perfect the style that finally brought her international recognition and acclaim. Published in 1926, the novel was judged by one critic as too masculine to allow comparison to other women novelists. Undaunted, she began a second novel set in California but soon lost interest and abandoned it. Janet Flanner was about to embark on a new career and a new identity; *The New Yorker* magazine was launched, and Genêt was created in 1925.

Flanner had been writing letters from Paris to Jane Grant, and when Grant and her husband Harold Ross started *The New Yorker,* Grant asked Flanner to be their Paris correspondent. Ross wanted the author of the "Letter from Paris" to be French-sounding, and he invented what he considered a Frenchified version of Janet, Genêt. A steady income and deadlines gave structure, direction, and meaning to Flanner's life that had been missing. And she was able to maintain contact with New York while living in Paris. The "Letters" were meant to appeal to those familiar with all aspects of French life, not the typical tourist who came to "Yurrup" to satiate "their thirst for licker and bargains," as Flanner noted. Her task was to inform, not to educate, and to avoid analyzing, explaining, or editorializing. As an active participant in the Paris scene, Flanner, chic and fashionable, wrote intimate, amusing, and intelligent observations on all manner of subjects, art, literature, fashion, and the French themselves. A keen observer of the nuances of Parisian life, "Genêt portrayed each event, person, place, against a background of muted disdain for American plumbing, household appliances, puritanism, and prosperity," wrote one biographer. Her first fortnightly "Letter" appeared in the October 10, 1925, issue of *The New Yorker;* 50 years later, she penned the last of them.

Each day Flanner read about a dozen French newspapers, and she frequently attended cultural events, happy to partake of "the finest civilization had to offer," elegant taste, money, and wit. Writing her 1,000-word "Letter" required concentrated effort; alone in her hotel room, she often wrote and revised for 48 hours, "deliberately crafting materials into well-shaped vignettes edged in sharp humor." Her editors wanted her to submit additional pieces, and Flanner decided to attempt a "Profile" of a living person; she chose *Isadora Duncan, "a heroic woman whose art was . . . beyond the bourgeois stuffiness of those Americans bred. . . on 'Turkey in the Straw'." Janet/Genêt never missed an opportunity to satirize American taste. She and the magazine editors thought it an excellent portrait, and Flanner went on to write on the fashion designer Paul Poiret and the American expatriate novelist *Edith Wharton.

Flanner was proud of her success and recognition and her ability to earn a living. But the stability of her professional life in no way resembled the turbulence of her private affairs. It was essential that the nature of her relationships with Solano and other women be kept from her mother. And in 1926, her husband arrived in Paris. Flanner had, in fact, not given much thought to divorce, or to Rehm. When she and the "dear boy" met, they decided to divorce on the grounds that he had deserted Flanner. Actually the opposite was true. Freed from her non-marriage to Rehm, Flanner's personal life only became more complicated. After 1926, she saw less of Solano who was now a member of a com-

mune outside of Paris, founded by the Russian mystic Gurdjieff, and Nancy Cunard was involved in an affair with Louis Aragon, a Surrealist, whom Flanner did not like personally. Nor did she like Dadaism or Surrealism for she believed their objective was to destroy the culture she loved. But Flanner was not alone. In early 1932, she fell in love with the elegant, proud Noel Murphy, a woman from a wealthy, socially prominent New York family. Murphy had a house in Orgeval, near Paris, which became a refuge for women, and Flanner's second home. Flanner was still living with Solano in their hotel, but Solano also had another woman friend, as did Murphy. Monogamy was not an essential part of their relationships; love and loyalty bound them together over the years.

Flanner had love, a successful career, and a regular, comfortable income. But she had not been able to write a second novel, to be a "real" writer. As Europe plunged into economic depression and fascism, Harold Ross asked Flanner to expand her coverage of events in and around France. She neither knew nor cared much about politics, however, and felt unsure of herself on the subject. Her 1930 profile of François Coty, perfumer and financier, concentrated on character and business, avoiding reference to his fascist sympathies. Her world was changing, and her visits to Berlin, in 1931 and 1933, disturbed her. She admired the crisp, smart pageantry of the Nazi processions but objected to having her papers checked and being told she "must wear skirts, not trousers, not wear powder, lipstick or smoke in public." Further, bloody political riots in Paris in 1934 caused her to fear for the future. Violence and repression, which she hated, were rampant. More and more, her "Letters" covered political events, often sounding, she said, like "horrifying thrillers." But, she wrote her mother, she enjoyed being a journalist now more than ever before. "She had found her subject matter, her niche, her purpose," Wineapple noted. Flanner contributed articles to *Fortune, Arts and Decoration,* and *Vanity Fair,* in addition to "Letters from Paris" for *The New Yorker.* Periodically she returned to the United States but never considered living there: "If you don't go home after ten years, you know you're hooked. . . . And you won't go home. You won't want to go home." Flanner had a home—an austere hotel room in Paris.

In 1935, Flanner traveled again to Germany to gather material for a "Profile" on Adolf Hitler. She read *Mein Kampf* three times and intended to write an objective, politically neutral portrait of the "Führer," the title of her three-part essay. The first lines are an encapsulation of the nation and the Führer: "Dictator of a nation devoted to splendid sausages, cigars, beer, and babies, Adolf Hitler is a vegetarian, teetotaller, nonsmoker, and celibate." Fully cognizant of the Nazi persecution of the Jews, she did not mention it in the profile. This omission prompted some Americans to consider Flanner fascist, and the piece was viewed as pro-Führer in Germany. But Flanner refused to identify with the political Right or Left; French politics were irrational, she concluded, and she was disgusted with "men who arrogantly and stupidly presumed to govern, who abstractly theorized about the lives of others, particularly women." Flanner received several job offers after her Hitler profile appeared in January 1936, and even turned down *Time*'s offer to hire her as a foreign correspondent in 1937. She began, however, to think of returning to the United States if war broke out; she was admittedly afraid but would stay as long as she could, and she did—"I shall be the last to leave," she defiantly declared, "The last Middle-Westerner on this peninsula of Europe, of Eurasia."

If Flanner had little acquaintance with European politics, she knew even less about sports, but she was sent on assignment to cover the 1936 Olympics in Berlin. The spectacle impressed her as did the "aristocratic" Nazi SS troops. Exhausted and ill from traveling, meeting deadlines, and trying to keep some kind of order in her personal life, Flanner resigned her "Letters from Paris" assignment in 1937, and she had no interest in going to Spain to report on the civil war there; she hated war as fervently as her friend Hemingway gloried in bloody conflicts. Flanner was fond of the macho Hemingway but regarded his "male histrionics [as] childish."

Friends were leaving France, but Flanner still held tenaciously to her hope that war would be averted. Her editors wanted her to stay in Europe, and there was nothing for her in the United States. Depression and recurring sciatica made travel and working increasingly difficult for her. While attending music festivals in Germany and Austria, Flanner saw firsthand the reality of Nazi anti-Semitism, calling it "reprehensible." When Hitler invaded Czechoslovakia, Flanner and Solano packed their bags and hid their jewelry and gold coins at Orgeval. But the summer of 1939 saw Paris alive with theater, nightclub life, and balls which fortified her belief that war was not imminent. On September 1, Hitler invaded Poland, and Parisians prepared for an attack. *The New Yorker* wanted the experienced Flanner to stay in France, but she refused. She and Solano borrowed Murphy's car and drove to Bordeaux; they sailed for New York on October 5, 1939; Murphy remained in France. On June 13, 1940, Paris surrendered to the Germans.

Flanner intended to return to France no later than January 1940. In the United States, she felt uncomfortable, unattached, and had trouble concentrating: "The symbols of her life were gone; so were her friends, her community, her routine of work and pleasure." Janet/Genêt had lost her "home," her bearings. She experienced feelings of guilt and depression; she had abandoned France, her friends, and Noel Murphy. Flanner frequently lectured on what was happening in France, wrote articles on France, the French Resistance, General Charles de Gaulle, and war, all under her own name—she had left Genêt in France. She also continued to struggle with her profile of Thomas Mann whom she thought "stiff . . . and pompous." But her four-part study of Marshal Philippe Pétain, 87-year-old head of the collaborative Vichy government in France, was published as a book in July 1944; she thought it her best work.

Sharing a more settled life in New York with **Natalia Danesi Murray**, with whom she was in love, could not relieve her distress on hearing Noel Murphy had been arrested; she was released three months later. And Solano felt neglected, though their bonds remained solid. Natalia Murray was more demanding than Flanner's other lovers, and Solano was jealous. Paris was to Flanner what Rome was to Murray, and both longed to end their years of exile in America.

Finally *The New Yorker* arranged for Flanner to fly to London in November 1944 as an official war correspondent. In late November, she joined Murphy at Orgeval; three days later, she was in Paris. Flanner frequently saw Hemingway who boasted about "liberating" Paris and read her his poems. But Flanner had changed, as had France. Her fellow journalists at the Hotel Scribe regarded her as an experienced "old hand," but Flanner worried that she had nothing to say as she wandered around the "charnel house" that had been Europe. Out of this devastation Genêt was reborn with Flanner's first postwar "Letter from Paris" in December 1944. The deprivation endured by the war-weary civilians made her depressed, lonely, restless, and feeling out of touch. She traveled to assuage her anxiety and to have something to write about. In Cologne, she saw the "people starving, frightened, and still mouthing Nazi propaganda." She reported on concentration camps, Ravensbrück and Buchenwald, and on the Nuremberg trials where she made evident her feelings for what she called "the 'unreconstructed' German mind"; "I hate them," she wrote to her sister Hildegarde. Flanner also began broadcasting for the Blue Network, later ABC, despite extreme nervousness that caused her hands to shake. She enjoyed the freedom of voicing her own opinions, unlike the impersonal, neutral tone of her "Letters."

"I wish nothing had happened that has happened in our lives," Flanner sadly wrote to Solano. Her Paris, her France, her Europe no longer existed, and Janet/Genêt felt adrift. She appeared confused about her work and disjointed in her relations with her three lovers; she depended on, and needed, each in a different way. Wineapple explains that Flanner seemed to be losing faith in herself—she had always felt inadequate as a writer—and in the world. A belief in what she termed "civilization" had always sustained her, but her belief now wavered, and she was not certain about anything. It was difficult to have "faith in governments, politics, religion, God, and even man himself. He is full of the wicked *proof* of the rightness of not purely believing in anything." Only Solano and *The New Yorker* remained as bulwarks against the alien, uncertain world in which she lived.

Travel to Warsaw, Berlin, and Vienna in 1947 and receiving the Legion of Honor from the French government could not mitigate her sense of not belonging, of not recognizing her once-familiar surroundings. At age 56, she felt "desperate and homeless," she said. "I have now no place to go, to remove me from myself." In spring 1948, Flanner wrote Ross that she intended to resign in January 1949, but, when the time arrived, she had changed her mind. She was Genêt, and *The New Yorker* was her mainstay. Working on a profile of Léon Blum, the first Jewish and socialist prime minister ever in France, pleased her. Flanner admired the socialists as the party of pacificism, humanism, as the most "female-minded party." Her "Letters" must have revealed her political sympathies and her estrangement from postwar Europe; Ross remarked on her lack of faith in the French and asked her to return to the States, to "reorient" her, Flanner thought. All she could say was that "no one . . . felt the same way about anyone anymore," and offered to resign. But, once again, she remained, picking up her work and life in Paris.

Obviously, Europe had changed for the worse, but so had America in her eyes. McCarthyism was rampant, and Flanner's writer friend *Kay Boyle and her husband were accused of being security risks, "Red" sympathizers, in 1952. Flanner associated McCarthyism with Fascism and was highly critical and ashamed of her homeland. Her friends were to be tried by American officials in Germany where Flanner testified on their behalf in October 1952. *The New Yorker* had not renewed Boyle's accreditation with the magazine and refused to support her at the trial. Flanner was badly shaken by this violation of "an almost sacred trust," as she saw it. Kay Boyle was blacklisted in America, and, as a result, Flanner had certain papers removed from her own French dossier. McCarthy's witch hunt was aided by FBI agents who could search through any American's files in Paris.

Disillusioned and disappointed in *The New Yorker*'s lack of response to Boyle's situation, Flanner remained on the staff. After a five-month hiatus, she resumed writing her "Letter" and did several excellent, insightful profiles of artists Henri Matisse, Pablo Picasso, and Georges Braque, and one of General de Gaulle's close associates, André Malraux, whom she regarded as a genius. Several of her perceptive profiles appeared in a book, *Men and Monuments*, in 1957. Flanner's life remained hectic and demanding; every other month, she flew to New York; in Paris and Orgeval, she divided her time and attention among "present and former lovers" trying to avoid creating discord and ill will among them. Flanner's opinion of France and its future improved when General Charles de Gaulle took over the government and established the Fifth Republic in 1958. She regarded the authoritarian former war leader as "France's savior" and the "Frenchman of sacrifice," but became more critical of his policies as the bloody Algerian war dragged on.

Further recognition of her journalistic writing brought Flanner an honorary degree from Smith College in 1958; the following year, she was elected a member of the National Institute of Arts and Letters and was invited to speak to the Overseas Press Club. She was flattered to be so honored and felt she deserved the recognition. Still her success as a journalist could not compensate for her sense of failure—she wanted to be considered a writer, not a journalist. When approached about writing her memoirs, she flatly refused. To the public she was Genêt, a mask that concealed her true identity. Her "Letters" for *The New Yorker* revealed as much about her as she was willing to divulge.

Age did not interfere with or affect Flanner's frenetic lifestyle, but her energy was flagging, and she often felt disconnected from Paris and the younger generation. Flanner continued to fill her "Letters" with the latest happenings, but it was obvious she preferred the past with its elegance, grace, and *politesse*. These qualities are reflected in her writings which began to appear in collected form. *Paris Journal, 1944–1955* was published in 1965; as Wineapple wrote, "Janet re-created the drama and inconsistencies of twenty years of French life in a prose that read like poetry." It won the National Book Award in 1966, and Flanner became a celebrity, appearing on the "Today" show (1966), among others, to publicize her book. Back in Paris she found it increasingly difficult to relate to "modern" France, which was reflected in her writing for the magazine. The Paris skyline was changing, and she disliked the new literature and plays, the strident, long-haired youth, the politics of the New Left, and the presence of American slang and "franglais." Genêt evinced no empathy for the massive student revolt and workers' strikes of May 1968. She wrote scathingly of the rioting youth as "a generation of malcontents" engaged in "nihilistic tribal warfare," but her coverage of the "Days of May" was, nevertheless, objective and lucid. In August, she suffered a mild stroke yet managed to send off her fortnightly Paris dispatch. The success of her earlier *Paris Journal* was followed by two more volumes and the evocative *Paris Was Yesterday, 1925–1939*, for which she wrote the preface. "Memories are the specific invisible remains in our lives of what belongs in the past tense," she informed her readers. She was showered with accolades "which I frankly deserved," she remarked.

Heart problems did not prevent her from frequently traveling between Paris and New York, between Murray in New York and Solano and Murphy in France; "our poor ⅓ darling Nancy" Cunard had died in 1965. In October 1975, Flanner moved permanently to New York. Solano died in November, and Genêt's last Paris letter was posted that year.

Janet Flanner was, as Glenway Wescott recalled, "the foremost remaining expatriate writer of the Twenties." When she died in November 1978, on her way to the hospital in an ambulance, her *New Yorker* obituary noted that "She caught history as it raced by and before others knew that it was history." And Genêt also captured and forever preserved in her "Letters" the Paris that would always be yesterday.

SOURCES:

Flanner, Janet. *Darlinghissima: Letters to a Friend*. Edited and with commentary by Natalia Danesi Murray. NY: Random House, 1985.

Rood, Karen Lane, ed. *Dictionary of Literary Biography*. Vol. 4, "American Writers in Paris, 1920–1939." Detroit, MI: A Bruccoli Clark Book, 1980.

Wineapple, Brenda. *Genêt: A Biography of Janet Flanner*. NY: Ticknor & Fields, 1989.

SUGGESTED READING:

Flanner, Janet (Genêt). *Janet Flanner's World: Uncollected Writings, 1932–1975*. NY: Harcourt Brace Jovanovich, 1979.

———. *Men and Monuments*. NY: Harper and Brothers, 1957.

———. *Paris Journal, 1944–1955*. Vol. I. William Shawn, editor. NY: Harcourt Brace Jovanovich, Publishers, 1988.

———. *Paris Journal, 1956–1964*. Vol. II. William Shawn, editor. NY: Harcourt Brace Jovanovich, Publishers, 1988.

———. *Paris Journal, 1965–1970*. Vol. III. William Shawn, editor. NY: Harcourt Brace Jovanovich, Publishers, 1988.

———. *Paris Was Yesterday, 1925–1939*. NY: Viking Press, 1975.

COLLECTIONS:

Papers and letters are located in the Library of Congress, Washington, D.C.

Jeanne A. Ojala,
Professor of History, University of Utah,
Salt Lake City, Utah

Flavia (d. 324).

See Helena (c. 255–329) for sidebar on Fausta.

Flavia Domitilla (fl. 39 CE)

*Roman noblewoman. Flourished 39 CE; daughter of Flavius Liberalis (a Roman freedman, meaning freed slave) and a mother who was the daughter of a Roman freedman; married Titus Flavius Vespasianus (Vespasian), a general and emperor of Rome (r. 69–79 CE), in 39 CE; children: *Flavia Domitilla (fl. 60 CE); Titus, Roman emperor (r. 79–81 CE); Domitian (51–96), Roman emperor (r. 81–96 CE); grandchildren: *Flavia Domitilla (c. 60–96 CE). See Flavia Domitilla (c. 60–96 CE) for family history.*

Flavia Domitilla (fl. 60 CE)

*Roman noblewoman. Flourished around 60 CE; daughter of *Flavia Domitilla (fl. 39 CE) and Titus Flavius Vespasianus (Vespasian), a general and Roman emperor (r. 69–79 CE); married Q. Petillius Cerialis Caesius Rufus known as Petillius (a partisan of Vespasian), by 60 CE; children: (stepchildren) two sons, Rufus and Firmus; daughter *Flavia Domitilla (c. 60–96 CE). See Flavia Domitilla (c. 60–96 CE) for family history.*

Flavia Domitilla (c. 60–96 CE)

Roman noblewoman. Born around 60 CE; executed in 96 CE; daughter of Q. Petillius Cerialis Caesius Rufus, known as Petillius, and Flavia Domitilla (fl. 60 CE); married T. Flavius Clemens; children: sons T. Flavius Domitianus Caesar and T. Flavius Vespasianus Caesar.

Flavia Domitilla was the third woman in three generations of her family to bear the same name. Her grandmother, *Flavia Domitilla (fl. 39 CE), was the daughter of Flavius Liberalis (a Roman freedman, meaning freed slave), who attracted an offer of marriage from Titus Flavius Vespasianus. Vespasian was a general when he married Flavia Domitilla (39 CE). In 68, the emperor Nero was deposed, initiating civil war. In this conflict, three military rivals preceded Vespasian to the throne, but by the end of 69 he had secured his imperial claim through violence. Flavia Domitilla had three children with Vespasian: another *Flavia Domitilla (fl. 60 CE), Titus, and the notorious Domitian (the first two of whom were of adult age by 69). Flavia Domitilla (fl. 60 CE) married Petillius (a partisan of Vespasian) by 60 and thereafter remained loyal to Vespasian's cause. Vespasian rewarded Petillius with a suffect consulship (his second) in 74. At the time of his marriage, Petillius already had two sons (Rufus and Firmus), both of whom also supported the Flavian imperial house (the former serving as consul ordinary in 83 under Domitian). In about the year 60, a daughter was born to Petillius and Flavia Domitilla, who was the third to bear the name Flavia Domitilla. This Flavia Domitilla, who was the granddaughter of one emperor (Vespasian) and niece of two others (Titus and Domitian), was about ten when her family began its imperial odyssey.

A political prize of the first order because of her connections, this Flavia Domitilla married T. Flavius Clemens probably early in the reign of Domitian (r. 81–96). Several political reasons were behind this union. First, the angst-ridden Domitian, conscious of his family's lowly social background (his grandmother was the daughter of a Roman freedman), was loathe to marry his niece to someone of loftier ancestry, lest such a son-in-law threaten his imperial authority. Clemens made an excellent choice, for, far from creating political problems, his marriage to Flavia Domitilla actually helped to consolidate Flavian power, because Clemens was the grandson of the older brother of Emperor Vespasian. In addition, Clemens was likely to remain Domitian's trustworthy ally since he was neither particularly gifted in the political arena nor ambitious. A "solid" citizen, Clemens rose through the imperial ranks under the patronage of his imperial relative Domitian until Clemens reached the acme of his career in 95, at which time he became one of Rome's consul ordinaries.

Flavia Domitilla's marriage to Clemens was a successful match. They had two sons: T. Flavius Domitianus Caesar and T. Flavius Vespasianus Caesar. Because Emperor Domitian's own marriage to *Domitia Longina produced no offspring, these sons were adopted by their great-uncle Domitian as his heirs. Had things thus remained, at least one of Flavia Domitilla's sons would have become the next Roman emperor. However, such was not to be, and Flavia Domitilla's hopes for the future were dashed during the year of her husband's consulship. Domitian suffered from a deep-rooted sense of social inferiority, while possessing an autocratic personality. He styled himself *dominus et deus* ("lord and god") to distance himself from everyone else, and exhibited a cruel streak throughout his reign, especially against the senatorial class upon which he ironically had to rely heavily for help to rule the vast Roman Empire. Executions for treason (some *were* guilty) began as early as 87, but the real storm broke out in 93. As a result, a reign of terror enveloped the powerful throughout the empire which caused Domitian's popularity to plummet sharply. It is little wonder that by 95 Domitian felt the need to staff important offices with "safe" occupants, like Clemens.

Not even Clemens' disposition and marriage, however, would save him from the increasingly paranoid Domitian when Domitian learned of Clemens' intellectual interest in an "atheistic" religious doctrine. It is not known for certain which of these sects attracted Clemens, whether it was in Christianity or in Judaism that he began to dabble, but from Domitian's perspective it mattered little: both religions rejected all but one God, undermining (among other things) Domitian's claim to be "[the] lord and [a] god." Whether or not Clemens understood the political ramifications of his religious interests, Domitian interpreted his pursuits as treasonous, since they called into question one very real prop (the "divinity" of the emperor) to his imperial power. Equally unknown is whether or not Flavia Domitilla shared her husband's nascent religious explorations (although it is quite possible she did—later Christians claimed that she maintained an interest in their religion). Nonetheless, preferring to err on the side of rigor, Domitian acted as though she did for certain. The emperor "suitably" punished both: Clemens was executed immediately and Flavia Domitilla was exiled to the small island of Pandateria before her own execution in 96. Further, their sons—Domitian's erstwhile heirs—disappear at this time from the historical record, almost certainly the victims of Domitian's deadly paranoia.

Flavia Domitilla's story, however, did not end there. One of her stewards, a man named Stephanus, both remained at Domitian's court after her fall and loyal to her memory. Seeking revenge for the unjust murder of his mistress, her husband, and (probably) her sons, and perhaps fearing his own death as a party to their "illegal" religious activities, Stephanus plotted Domitian's overthrow. Feigning injury so as to wrap one of his arms in a bandage, Stephanus hid therein a knife. He then picked his time carefully and attacked Domitian in his bed. However good a steward Stephanus was, he was a terrible assassin. Making an initial mess of Domitian's murder, he needed help from fellow conspirators before the emperor was physically overcome. Regardless, the plot succeeded. Ironically, the act that avenged Flavia Domitilla simultaneously transferred the empire to another dynasty and killed the last living scion of her house.

William Greenwalt,
Associate Professor of Classical History,
Santa Clara University, Santa Clara, California

Flavia Valeria Constantia (c. 293–?).

See Constantia.

Fleeson, Doris (1901–1970)

American journalist who was a Washington political columnist for 20 years. Born in Sterling, Kansas, on May 20, 1901; died on August 1, 1970; youngest of six children and second daughter of William (manager of a clothing store) and Helen (Tebbe) Fleeson; University of Kansas, B.A., 1923; married John O'Donnell (a political reporter), on September 28, 1930 (divorced 1942); married Dan A. Kimball (a corporate president and former secretary of the navy), in August 1958; children: (first marriage) one daughter, Doris Kimball (b. 1932).

Acknowledged as one of the toughest journalists in Washington from 1940 to 1960, Doris Fleeson was one of the first women to gain respect as a political columnist. She was born in 1901 and raised in Sterling, Kansas, where her father ran a clothing store. Fleeson left her rural hometown to study journalism at the University of Kansas and graduated in 1923. After working for two midwestern newspapers, she moved to New York where she worked as city editor for

the *Great Neck* (Long Island) *News.* She then landed a job as reporter for the *New York Daily News,* where she covered crimes, trials, and scandals. Fleeson claimed her early tabloid experience taught her to hook the reader with the lead sentence. "We belonged to the who-the-hell-reads-the-second-paragraph school," she once quipped. As a result of her city reporting, Fleeson won a coveted assignment at the Albany bureau, where she began the political reporting that would become her stock in trade.

In 1930, Fleeson married fellow political reporter John O'Donnell, a tall, handsome Irish fellow described by colleagues as "brilliant and unpredictable." Three years later, after the birth of their daughter, the couple was assigned to the *Daily News*' newly opened Washington office, where they co-wrote a provocative political column called *Capital Stuff*. Fleeson, however, did not share her husband's political views, and her growing commitment to Franklin Roosevelt's foreign and domestic policies made the couple's professional and personal relationship increasingly difficult. They divorced in 1942, after which O'Donnell was kept on as a Washington correspondent while Fleeson was recalled to the New York office to write radio news. She left the paper in 1943 to become a roving war correspondent for *Woman's Home Companion*. In the 1940s, the magazine was broad in scope; its work included editorials for women doctors in the military and an investigation of rationing fraud. In a series of ten articles appearing in 1943 and 1944, Fleeson covered the Italian and French fronts during World War II.

After the war, she returned to Washington and launched a new phase in her career, that of syndicated columnist. Beginning with commitments from only the *Washington Evening Star* and *The Boston Globe*, she was soon carried in over 100 newspapers. According to a longtime friend, columnist *Mary McGrory, "She roamed the Capitol, a tiger in white gloves and a Sally Victor hat, stalking explanations for the stupidity, cruelty, fraud, or cant that was her chosen prey." One of her early columns became front-page news when it exposed the open feud between Supreme Court justices Robert H. Jackson and Hugo Black. Additional journalistic coups brought more and more subscribers to her column until she was eventually writing five days a week for the United Features Syndicate. Fleeson covered the administrations of five presidents and never hesitated to criticize or offer advice. Her barbs were fairly and evenly distributed. As *Newsweek* reported in 1957: "There is, in fact, almost no Washington figure, Republican or Democrat, who has not felt the sharp edge of her typewriter."

In 1958, Fleeson married Dan Kimball, secretary of the navy under President Harry Truman, and they settled in a century-old house in Georgetown. The columnist also worked tirelessly for liberal causes and helped young journalists like McGrory get started. "To be a woman reporter in the man's world of Washington in the 1940s and 1950s was to be patronized or excluded," wrote McGrory. "She knew that few of the men were her peers and none her superior, and she was, well in advance of the women's liberation movement, a militant feminist." Earlier, in 1933, Fleeson was a leader in the founding of the American Newspapers Guild and fought for a minimum wage of $35 a week for reporters. Later, she fought for the installation of women's restrooms in congressional galleries and, in 1953, sponsored the first African-American applicant for membership in the Women's National Press Club.

Doris Fleeson was semi-retired in 1967, suffering from circulatory problems. She died on August 1, 1970, just 36 hours after her husband's death on July 30. The couple had a joint funeral service and were buried together at Arlington Cemetery.

SOURCES:

Belford, Barbara. *Brilliant Bylines*. NY: Columbia University Press, 1986.

Current Biography. NY: H.W. Wilson, 1959.

Weatherford, Doris. *American Women's History*. NY: Prentice Hall, 1994.

Barbara Morgan,
Melrose, Massachusetts

Fleetwood, Bridget (1624–c. 1660).

See Cromwell, Bridget.

Fleischer, Leontine (1889–1974).

See Sagan, Leontine.

Fleischmann, Trude (1895–1990)

German-born photographer who specialized in portraits and fashion. Born in Vienna, Austria, in 1895; died in Brewster, New York, in 1990; studied art history in Paris.

Born into a well-to-do Viennese-Jewish family in 1895, Trude Fleischmann took up photography at age nine. After briefly studying art history in Paris, she apprenticed in a Vienna portrait studio before opening her own studio in 1920. Her well-known sitters during this period included actresses *Katharine Cornell and *Hedy

Lamarr, architect Adolf Loos, conductor Bruno Walter, and dancers *Tilly Losch, Claire Bauroff, and *Grete Wiesenthal. In 1938, after Germany annexed Austria, Fleischmann moved to Paris for six months, then went to London. Two of her students, *Marion Post Wolcott and Marion's sister Helen Post Modley, persuaded her to go to the United States. Setting up a studio in New York City around 1940, Fleischmann continued to photograph celebrities, including singer *Lotte Lehmann, physicist Albert Einstein, and conductor Arturo Toscanini. The portraits of her early period, soft and brown-tinted, eventually gave way to a more modern, focused style. Fleischmann also did fashion spreads for *Vogue* and other publications. She retired in 1969, moving to Lugano, Switzerland. In 1990, she died at her nephew's home in Brewster, New York.

Fleisser, Marieluise (1901–1974)

German playwright and writer, confidante of Bertolt Brecht, and controversial innovator in the area of the

Doris
Fleeson

Volksstück (folkplay), who is now viewed as one of the most important female playwrights of the 20th century. Name variations: Fleißer. Born Luise Marie Fleisser in Ingolstadt, Bavaria, on November 23, 1901; died in Ingolstadt on February 1, 1974; daughter of Heinrich and Anna (Schmidt) Fleisser; had three sisters, Anny Fleisser, Ella Fleisser, and Jetty Fleisser, and two brothers, Heinrich (died aged two) and Heinrich Fleisser; married Josef (Bepp) Haindl.

Produced a small but original body of work—particularly the plays Fegefeuer in Ingolstadt *(Purgatory in Ingolstadt) and* Pioniere in Ingolstadt *(Soldiers in Ingolstadt)—that in recent years has been critically reevaluated; was one of the most discussed women writers in the Weimar Republic; saw her books burned by the Nazis and was punished with a publication ban; after a decades-long silence that persisted even after 1945, resumed writing (1960s), enjoying in final years a long-overdue public recognition.*

The Bavarian garrison city of Ingolstadt, in which Marieluise Fleisser was born in 1901 and in which she would die 73 years later, was her often-turbulent home for most of her life. Born Luise Marie Fleisser into a large lower-middle-class family (her father Heinrich combined the trades of jewelry maker and ironmonger), the young girl was enrolled in 1914 at the Roman Catholic girls' high school (*Mädchengymnasium*) in the town of Regensburg. Here she revealed a strong literary curiosity which included secretly reading some of the works of August Strindberg. Although her father insisted that she embark on a "realistic" course of study to qualify for high school teaching, from the very start of her enrollment in 1919 at the University of Munich, Fleisser made it clear that she had other interests. At the university, besides enrolling in a Germanistics course, she was particularly drawn to Arthur Kutscher's popular lectures on various aspects of the theater.

Crucial to Fleisser's later development as a writer were two events that took place in 1922. One was her encounter with the gifted, young novelist Lion Feuchtwanger, who discerned undisciplined talent in the young student from Ingolstadt. Feuchtwanger unsparingly criticized Fleisser's writings but also told her that she had so much talent she needed to write more, and better, pieces. He also insisted that she change her name from Luise Marie to Marieluise.

One evening she attended a performance of the Expressionist play *Trommeln in die Nacht* (*Drums in the Night*) by a fellow Bavarian three years her senior, Bertolt Brecht (1898–1956).

Written by a supremely confident author who saw himself as both a literary and political revolutionary (he had already embarked on his life-long allegiance to Marxism and the Communist movement), Brecht's play was a savage exposé of the republican Germany's corruption and despair. Fleisser was overwhelmed by the exuberance of the play and was even more enthralled by Brecht himself when she was finally introduced to him in March 1924 by her mentor Lion Feuchtwanger. By the end of 1924, Fleisser was under Brecht's spell, having decided to terminate her university studies to embark on a writing career. Penniless, she had no choice but to return home to Ingolstadt where she found it impossible to explain her decision to an enraged father.

Although physically unprepossessing, Brecht had an intellectual aura that made him highly seductive to many women; Marieluise Fleisser was no exception. His encouragement, like that of Feuchtwanger, gave the shy young woman from "unenlightened" Ingolstadt confidence in her artistic abilities that did not come naturally to her. From 1924 to 1925, Fleisser, who wrote slowly and painfully, worked on the short story "Adventure from the English Garden" and on the play *Die Fusswaschung* (*Washing of the Feet*). The play, clearly autobiographical in nature, was an unsparing portrait of a thinly disguised Ingolstadt held in the grip of a patriarchal regime of ignorance, violence, and self-satisfied provincialism. On opening night, her audience found itself fascinated by a drama that examined how German regional society repressed the desires of the young. Fleisser's characters documented in stunning detail the grief of a group of teenagers who internalized the authoritarian controls of a social environment that was as unthinking as it was conservative and religion-based. Fleisser described her work as simply being "a play about the law of the herd and about those forcefully excluded from it."

On April 25, 1926, the play, renamed *Fegefeuer in Ingolstadt* (*Purgatory in Ingolstadt*) and championed by Brecht, received its premiere performance at the Deutsches Theater in Berlin. It was a huge success. Berliners were amazed when the city's two most influential drama critics, Herbert Ihering and Alfred Kerr, who rarely agreed on anything, wrote wildly enthusiastic reviews. Fleisser was given a small monthly subsidy by the prestigious Ullstein publishing firm, enabling her to purchase a typewriter. During the late summer and autumn of 1926, her relationship with Brecht was at its most intense, and she visited him on numerous occasions in his hometown of Augsburg. Late in the year, she moved to Berlin, remaining there until the summer of 1927.

In early 1926, Fleisser began writing another play set in her hometown. In *Pioniere in Ingolstadt* (*Soldiers in Ingolstadt*), she probed, in an even more unsparing fashion, the soul-crushing hypocrisies and repressive atmosphere of lower-middle-class life in the German provinces. In writing it, she followed Brecht's advice to closely observe people in Ingolstadt, going for walks with the town's soldiers and noting their dialogue. Premiered in Dresden in March 1928 to mixed reviews, this new play had been written by Fleisser in close collaboration with Brecht. Finding it difficult to steer her talent on a clear course and overwhelmed by Brecht's powerful personality, she not only allowed him to play a dominant role in both conceiving and writing *Soldiers in Ingolstadt,* but offered little or no resistance to Brecht when he began to plan for a Berlin production of the play. Following on the heels of his enormously successful *Threepenny Opera* (with a brilliant musical score by Kurt Weill), Brecht intended to present *Soldiers in Ingolstadt* at Berlin's Theater am Schiffbauerdamm in such a way that the production would create a public scandal guaranteed to attract attention not only to Fleisser but to himself.

The play's premiere in Berlin in early 1929 triggered furiously negative reviews not only from the pugnacious and growing Nazi press, but from the capital's conservative and nationalist newspapers as well. *Soldiers in Ingolstadt* was viewed as slanderous and obscene, deliberately staged to insult and dishonor venerable German patriotic and family ideals. One reviewer called upon Ingolstadt's mayor to "marry the girl off—maybe then she will give up writing plays, which seems to be the result of unresolved complexes. Bind her hands so she cannot hold a pen anymore!" Positive responses were in a distinct minority, even though some of the laudatory ones included the cultural critic Walter Benjamin's commendation of the drama for so clearly displaying the collective power of the masses in uniform as well as emphasizing its provincial roots.

Rejection and outrage was heard not only in Berlin but in other towns and cities including Fleisser's own Ingolstadt, where the mayor protested at a national mayors' conference about a play he regarded as a "vulgar and inferior work, a slanderous, disgraceful and infamous piece." With much of Ingolstadt up in arms against his daughter, Fleisser's father forbade her from ever again entering his home. Feuchtwanger urged her to sue the mayor for libel (she declined to do so). Brecht's response to the scandal, however, was one of satisfaction and triumph, for he had succeeded in detonating a cultural bombshell, thus bringing Fleisser to national attention and making her probably the best-known (but certainly not the best-loved) female dramatist in German literary history. Deeply upset by what had happened and feeling that she had been cynically used by Brecht largely for his own agenda, Fleisser broke off her relationship with him even before the dust from the scandal had settled.

By the end of 1929, Marieluise Fleisser had become engaged to Josef (Bepp) Haindl, a local swimming champion and tobacco-shop owner who had been courting her for several years in Ingolstadt. Now resigned to working long hours in his tobacco shop, she rarely had the time to devote to new writing projects. Concerned that she might never again write anything of value, Lion Feuchtwanger urged Fleisser to break off her engagement. She did this, but it brought her little happiness, making her feel more vulnerable than ever. To find some degree of stability, Fleisser entered into what turned out to be an extremely self-destructive relationship with Hellmut Draws-Tychsen. A journalist of little talent, Draws-Tychsen was an egomaniac, and his extremely reactionary political views placed him squarely on the other side of Fleisser's political spectrum. The abusive affair would last more than five years during which she was able to write several noteworthy works, including reportage of a trip she and Draws-Tychsen took to the Pyrenees mini-state of Andorra and, more important, the novel *Mehlreisende Frieda Geier* (*Frieda Geier, Traveling Flour Saleswoman*).

The early 1930s were difficult years for Marieluise Fleisser. Not only did the unsatisfactory relationship with Hellmut Draws-Tychsen leave her with permanent emotional scars and a lack of confidence as a writer, the rise of Nazism made it impossible for her to feel secure either as a woman or as a well-known leftist. By the end of 1932, Germany's crisis was reflected in Fleisser's own personal travails. Short of funds, she decided to return to Ingolstadt after having made a halfhearted attempt to commit suicide. The onset of the Nazi dictatorship in 1933 brought about the immediate end of intellectual freedom in Germany. Fleisser's books and those of scores of other "un-German" writers were consigned to public bonfires. The self-proclaimed German Rebirth of the new National Socialist state was in fact a reign of terror against all manifestations of freethinking and liberal culture. In Ingolstadt, Fleisser had long been a notorious figure in the minds of religious conservatives, nationalists and Nazis. All considered her to be a scandalous personality, made even worse by the environment she had been exposed to during her years in a culturally alien "Red Berlin."

In 1935, Fleisser was informed that she was under a partial *Schreibverbot* decreed by Nazi cultural officials; she could no longer publish any books or articles in journals, being only permitted to publish six newspaper articles each year. The same year, she married Bepp Haindl, not out of love but out of economic necessity and even physical fear. (Many of her fellow Ingolstadters regarded Fleisser with great hostility as a *Nestbeschmutzerin,* a person who had fouled her hometown's nest by revealing its dirty linen to a gawking outside world.) Utterly incapable of understanding his wife's desire to write, Haindl showed no sympathy for Fleisser's avocation, simply informing her, "Writing you can do at night." Later, she would describe the Nazi years as a time when she was "chained up like a dog." Hitler's national tyranny was echoed by Bepp's domestic tyranny, which demanded of Fleisser that she not only put in long hours in the tobacco shop but carry out her domestic chores as well. During the first years of her marriage to Haindl, Fleisser continued to write, even though it proved to be increasingly difficult for her both physically and emotionally. By 1937, despite these difficult conditions, she had been able to complete a working draft of the drama *Karl Stuart.* The next year, however, Fleisser suffered a serious nervous breakdown. Although she recovered, her health was never to be completely restored. This period of Fleisser's life was recounted in her powerful autobiographical story, "A Quite Ordinary Antechamber to Hell," written in 1963 and revised in 1972.

By 1943, a deteriorating German war situation led to increased dependence on women in the work force even though this obviously contradicted Nazi ideology. Fleisser was assigned unskilled duties in a local factory, but the physical and emotional demands of the job brought her to the brink of another breakdown. Her husband was finally able to pull some strings to release her from these demands. Though Fleisser and Haindl survived the war, both were physically diminished. Haindl, once a perfect physical specimen, returned from the war thin and suffering from heart disease. From 1945 to 1958, Fleisser had neither the leisure time nor the emotional distance from daily cares to carry out major writing projects. Haindl's sudden death in January 1958 led within a few days to Fleisser being stricken with a heart attack. For days, she hovered close to death but eventually began to recover. By the end of 1958, Fleisser had liquidated her husband's business affairs, selling the tobacco shop.

The 1960s witnessed the start of a Marieluise Fleisser renaissance. Although she had received a number of awards in the previous decade, now both scholars and the younger generation of authors took notice. Encouraged by the changing atmosphere, in the early 1960s Fleisser began to write new short stories and even a Bavarian-dialect comedy, *Der starke Stamm (Of Sturdy Stock).* Toward the end of that turbulent decade, she was working on revisions of both of her Ingolstadt plays. In 1968, the prestigious Suhrkamp publishing house released a new edition of *Soldiers in Ingolstadt,* and two years later, in March 1970, the new version received its premiere in Munich's prestigious Residenztheater. In 1972, Fleisser's return to the center of German literary life reached an apotheosis when her collected works (*Gesammelten Werke*) appeared under the Suhrkamp imprint to enthusiastic reviews.

During the last years of her often-frustrated career, Marieluise Fleisser was able to enjoy not only fame but the satisfaction of knowing that a number of Germany's most talented young writers now looked to the entire body of her work for inspiration. Unlike the men of the Weimar and Nazi period who had often manipulated and misused her talent, these mostly male writers—which included Martin Speer, Rainer Werner Fassbinder and Franz Xaver Kroetz—used her plays as models when writing their own sociocritical folk plays. While Fassbinder proclaimed that he would never have begun writing had he not seen *Soldiers in Ingolstadt,* Kroetz noted with approval the contrast between Fleisser's unflinchingly realistic assessment of the working class and Brecht's naive idealizations. Speer, too, gave Fleisser her due as a playwright who had important things to say even in her last drama, *Of Sturdy Stock.* These and other post-1960 writers were thus able to bring into the next generation of German letters at least some of the raw energy found in the writings of Marieluise Fleisser. She died in Ingolstadt on February 1, 1974.

SOURCES:

Brady, Philip. "Small Town, Small Minds, Small Stage," in *The [London] Times Literary Supplement.* No. 4590. March 22, 1991, p. 15.

Demetz, Peter. *After the Fires: Recent Writing in the Germanies, Austria and Switzerland.* NY: Harcourt Brace Jovanovich, 1986.

Fleisser, Marieluise. *Pioniere in Ingolstadt*. Edited by David Horton. Saarbrücken and Manchester: Universität des Saarlandes-Manchester University Press, 1992.

Fuegi, John. *Brecht and Company: Sex, Politics, and the Making of the Modern Drama*. NY: Grove Press, 1994.

Kraft, Friedrich, ed. *Marieluise Fleisser: Anmerkungen, Texte, Dokumente*. Ingolstadt: Verlag Donau Kurier, 1981.

Ley, Ralph. "Beyond 1984: Provocation and Prognosis in Marieluise Fleisser's Play *Purgatory in Ingolstadt*," in *Modern Drama*. Vol. 31, no. 3. September 1988, pp. 340–351.

———. "Liberation from Brecht: A Marieluise Fleisser in Her Own Right," in *Modern Language Studies*. Vol. 16, no. 2. Spring 1986, pp. 54–61.

Marieluise Fleisser Nachlass, Städtarchiv Ingolstadt an der Donau, Bavaria, Germany.

McGowan, Moray. *Marieluise Fleisser*. Munich: C.H. Beck Verlag, 1987.

Meyer, Marsha Elizabeth. "Marieluise Fleisser: Her Life and Work" (Ph. D. dissertation, University of Wisconsin—Madison, 1983).

Pfister, Eva. "'Unter dem fremden Gesetz': Zu Produktionsbedingungen, Werk und Rezeption der Dramatikerin Marieluise Fleisser" (Ph. D. dissertation, University of Vienna, 1981).

Schmidt, Henry J. *How Dramas End: Essays on the German Sturm und Drang, Büchner, Hauptmann, and Fleisser*. Ann Arbor, MI: University of Michigan Press, 1992.

Sieg, Katrin. *Exiles, Eccentrics, Activists: Women in Contemporary German Theater*. Ann Arbor, MI: University of Michigan Press, 1994.

Tax, Sissi. *Marieluise Fleisser: Schreiben, überleben: Ein biographischer Versuch*. Basel and Frankurt am Main: Stroemfeld Verlag-Roter Stern, 1984.

Text + Kritik: Zeitschrift für Literatur. Vol. 64. October 1979 (Special Fleisser issue).

John Haag,
Assistant Professor of History,
University of Georgia, Athens, Georgia

Fleming, Amalia (1912–1986)

Greek bacteriologist and political activist who stood up against the military dictatorship that ruled Greece. Name variations: Lady Fleming. Born Amalia Koutsouris in 1912 in Constantinople, Ottoman Empire (now Istanbul, Turkey); died in Athens, Greece, on February 26, 1986; daughter of Harikios Koutsouris (a physician); had a brother Renos; married Manoli Vourekis (an architect); married Sir Alexander Fleming (the discoverer of penicillin), in 1953 (died March 11, 1955); children: (stepson) Robert.

Became Lady Fleming when she married Sir Alexander Fleming, discoverer of penicillin (1953); opposed the military dictatorship that ruled Greece (1967–74); was arrested and briefly imprisoned (1971), then expelled from the country; continued her activities from exile in the United Kingdom; returned to Greece to become highly visible in that nation's newly revived democracy.

Born two years before the start of World War I in the fabled city of Constantinople, Amalia Koutsouris could reasonably look forward to a life of comfort and ease as the child of a physician in the Ottoman Empire. Unfortunately, she was born into the most violent century in history, into an age of world wars, ethnic cleansing, and genocide. By the time she reached age two, her idyllic existence had been forever crushed. In 1914, Amalia's family fled the racially intolerant Pan-Turkish state which would in due course destroy and deport its Armenian and Greek minorities. Her family lost its home and her father's laboratory was seized, material losses that would seem trifling later in Amalia's turbulent life. Growing up in Athens, Greece, she studied medicine at the University of Athens, with a specialty in bacteriology. After graduation, she accepted a position at the Athens municipal hospital, then married Manoli Vourekis, whose career path was architecture.

Normal work patterns and private life were demolished for Amalia and Manoli Vourekis in April 1941, when Greece was defeated and occupied by Nazi Germany while it assisted its hapless Fascist Italian ally. Harsh Nazi rule soon included the repression of resistance activities and the rounding up of Jews to be shipped to death camps. Like many patriotic Greeks, both Amalia and her husband joined the resistance movement. The risks of being captured were great and punishments draconian, but in the anti-Nazi underground they met remarkable women and men from various backgrounds whose only goal was to rid their nation of the hated German and Italian aggressors. Amalia hid British and Greek officers and arranged their escape routes to Egypt. She also transcribed and distributed BBC broadcasts and helped prepare false identity cards for endangered Greek Jews so that they would appear to be members of the Greek Orthodox faith. After a member of her resistance group succumbed to torture and revealed Amalia's name along with several dozen others, she was arrested by the Italians. An attempted breakout from a prison hospital by feigning appendicitis resulted in the unnecessary removal of her appendix but did not facilitate her escape. Instead, she was transferred to a jail, sentenced to death, and served six months behind bars before advancing British troops caused the Germans to flee and abandon the facility.

The end of foreign occupation brought peace neither to Amalia nor her husband nor indeed to the people of Greece. Fascist inhumanity had destroyed 14,000 villages and resulted in the death of one in ten of the Greek population. A civil war between Communist-led forces and conservative royalists, started in 1947 by the United States and backed by the British, plunged the already ravaged nation into a fratricidal struggle. Estranged from and soon to divorce her husband, Amalia had little to return to after the war. With her marriage in tatters, and her husband's prewar house, studio and laboratory completely destroyed, a discouraged Amalia hoped to start a new life elsewhere. Almost miraculously, her application for a British Council scholarship to study bacteriology at St. Mary's Hospital, London, was approved. An additional aspect of her remarkable good fortune was the fact that the director of the hospital's highly regarded Wright-Fleming Institute of Microbiology was none other than Nobel Prize-winner Sir Alexander Fleming, known throughout the world as the discoverer of penicillin.

Amalia was ushered into Sir Alexander Fleming's office on October 1, 1946. Because of a misunderstanding and her shaky English, Alexander did not place her on the allergy team as had been planned but informed her that she could work directly with him. Thus, she would be the first woman physician ever to work in Alexander Fleming's laboratory. Alexander and his staff were quickly impressed by her research, and before long her name appeared on several research studies published in such world-class scientific periodicals as the *British Medical Journal* and *The Lancet*. Alexander and Amalia developed an excellent professional and personal relationship over the next few years, but it did not involve romance until after the death of Alexander's first wife in 1949.

By the end of 1950, Sir Alexander had fallen in love with his much younger medical colleague, but his timidity hampered his ability to articulate a marriage proposal. When Amalia returned to Greece for the Christmas holidays, she received a job offer from an Athens hospital. Not until November 1952, when he was in Athens for a UNESCO conference, did Sir Alexander find the courage to propose to her. After their 1953 marriage in London, the Flemings resumed their joint research work at the Wright-Fleming Institute. Their union was to be happy but brief. Sir Alexander Fleming died of a heart attack in London on March 11, 1955.

Immobilized by her grief for two years, Lady Amalia Fleming decided against living the life of leisure that would have been possible for her as the widow of a world-famous medical pioneer. Instead, she determined to return to the world of bacteriological research, even refusing the widows' pension that was rightfully hers from the Wright-Fleming Institute. Although she regularly made short visits to Greece, she spent the great bulk of her time in London concentrating on her scientific work, relatively oblivious of Greek political life.

Although she had taken on dual Greek and British citizenship when she married her late husband, Lady Fleming did not spend much time in Greece until 1962; in 1963, she spent seven months in Athens, and from 1964 through 1966 it was nine months a year. At this point, she considered herself a resident of Athens. On March 15, 1967, her last belongings from London arrived. As it turned out, the time Amalia Fleming had chosen to return home was indeed to be a fateful one in modern Greek history. For several years prior to 1967, an already volatile Greek political scene had grown ever more unpredictable. At the same time, a popular leftist leader, George Papandreou, led his party to an impressive electoral victory of 53% of the national vote. The extreme right, backed by the young and inexperienced King Constantine, became increasingly alarmed that their interests would suffer if the popularity of the leftist parties should further increase. When it became clear that elections scheduled for May 28, 1967, would likely result in a landslide victory for Papandreou's forces, the Greek military struck against the constitutional order.

On April 21, 1967, the military proclaimed Greece to be under their rule. Constitutional guarantees and liberties had been revoked in order, they argued, to save the country from chaos and Marxist upheaval. Within days, real or imagined enemies of the dictatorship found themselves behind bars. Torture and intimidation became standard methods of control for the police and bureaucracy. As soon as the enormity of what was happening sank in on Lady Fleming, she began to find ways to resist the dictatorship. The moral basis of her opposition was her powerful sense of right and wrong. In a 1971 interview, she recalled that she had been "ashamed that a dictatorship should take over in Greece—that a few self-appointed people should decide to 'save us' without our permission when there was really nothing to save us from."

From her tiny one-room apartment in Athens which she shared with a large number of cats (sometimes as many as eight), Lady Fleming organized humanitarian efforts. Of particular concern to her was the fate of political prisoners and their families. Not only were most of the prisoners subject to extreme forms of physical and psychological torture, their families were usually reduced to poverty. "When the bread-winner suddenly disappears," Fleming told a *New York Times* reporter, "the family has to face a terrible financial strain." Her activities on behalf of the persecuted political opposition quickly brought Lady Fleming to the attention of the military regime, but although she doubt-less irritated and even angered them, they decid-ed not to arrest her. She could claim dual British and Greek citizenship, and furthermore as the widow of a man who had been greatly respected in Greece she enjoyed a name recognition few could match. Conscious of maintaining a posi-tive public-relations image, the Greek military kept Fleming under surveillance but hesitated to take more drastic action against her.

By 1970, Fleming's defiant acts of opposition were testing the dictatorship's patience. After tes-tifying forcefully as a defense witness at the trial of 34 anti-regime intellectuals, her passport was revoked. But worldwide protest made the regime reconsider its action, and within two weeks her passport had been restored. At the end of 1970, about 200 anti-regime activists were arrested and held for months without trial, the main reason for their detention being a police attempt to link them to Lady Fleming's activities. In August 1971, she was "invited" by the police for an in-terrogation which lasted for 13 hours. Although she was threatened and bullied, Fleming refused to provide her captors with any important infor-mation they might use against their foes.

But that same month, after attempting for several years to pin specific charges of anti-state activities on Lady Fleming, the military dictator-ship was finally able to make a case against her. For years, she had been particularly concerned about the fate of one political prisoner, Alexan-der Panagoulis. Convicted in 1968 of a failed at-tempt to assassinate the leading figure of the dic-tatorship, Premier George Papadopoulos, Panagoulis was considered a dangerous foe of the regime and was held in maximum security. It was also generally believed that he was being tortured on a routine basis, and it was reported that he had made several desperate attempts to escape his tormentors. Lady Fleming was con-vinced that only an immediate rescue of Panagoulis would save his life and sanity. When another rescue plot was hatched, she chose to get involved in it, helping to arrange for a get-away car. The planned escape, scheduled for Au-gust 31, 1971, did not take place, because an in-formant betrayed the plan to the police. Four of the plotters were arrested outside the prison, while Lady Fleming was arrested at home. At first, the police did not know of her involve-ment, but once the connection was established they were delighted that at long last a specific charge of criminally subversive activity could be linked to her.

The trial began on September 27, 1971, with Lady Fleming and her accomplices brought be-fore a military tribunal. Speaking in her own de-fense, Fleming proudly admitted her role in the plot to free the prisoner, emphasizing the years of incarceration and torture he had already en-dured. She was convicted of the charges the next day and sentenced to 16 months in prison. Be-cause she was in poor health and suffering from diabetes and its complications, the regime be-lieved she would accept their offer of being de-ported. But she refused to play along, insisting she intended to remain and serve her prison term: "If I leave, they will take away my Greek citizen-ship. I am a Greek and I intend to stay." The in-ternational press reports of the trial, almost al-ways to the disadvantage of the Greek military, persuaded an embarrassed dictatorship to sus-pend the remainder of her sentence on October 21. Permitted to return to her apartment, she was awakened there by police on the morning of No-vember 14 and told she was being taken to the chief of police. In reality, however, Fleming was driven to the Athens airport where she was forced on board a plane bound for London.

Arriving in England some hours later, a defi-ant Lady Fleming at first refused to leave the plane, informing the press that if necessary she was planning to "walk back to Greece." Simul-taneously with her physical expulsion from Greece, Fleming was stripped of her Greek citi-zenship, the charges being for ill-defined "anti-national activities." Over the next several years, until the Athens dictatorship collapsed in 1974 because of its ineptitude, Amalia Fleming re-mained one of the most passionate defenders of Greek democracy in exile. Along with two other women, *Melina Mercouri and *Helen Vlachos, who stood up against the dictatorship estab-lished on April 21, 1967, Fleming embodied the unbroken spirit of Greek independence. A patri-ot through and through, she defined her identity as a Greek as "an incurable disease that nothing and no one can treat or change."

After returning to Greece in 1974, Amalia Fleming became active in national politics. Fiercely independent, she at first feuded with Papandreou but in 1977 he asked her to join the national list of his Panhellenic Socialist Movement (Pasok). She was elected to Greek Parliament in 1977 and re-elected in 1981 and 1985. She was also a delegate to the Council of Europe Assembly and was proud of having been chosen first chair of the Greek chapter of Amnesty International. Although a conscientious parliamentary deputy, Fleming thought of herself as being more of a humanitarian than a politician, often describing her career in terms of having been "a reluctant political campaigner, interested in social reforms, not public offices." Both during the seven years of dictatorship and the twelve years of life that remained to her after 1974, Lady Fleming tended to neglect her own fragile health, more concerned with what she could do for others. In 1971, she had compared her work during the Nazi occupation of World War II with her efforts to end the military dictatorship: "In those days I was working for humanitarian ideals. I thought I was right then, and I think I'm right now."

SOURCES:

Anastasi, Paul. "Lady Fleming Dies in Athens; Foe of Nazis and Army Junta," in *The New York Times Biographical Service*. February 1986, p. 296.

Becket, James. *Barbarism in Greece*. NY: Walker, 1970.

Clogg, Richard, and George Yannopoulos, eds. *Greece Under Military Rule*. NY: Basic Books, 1972.

Council of Europe. *European Commission on Human Rights. The Greek Case: Report of the Commission.* 4 vols. Strasbourg: Council of Europe, 1969.

Danopoulos, Constantine P. "Military Professionalism and Regime Legitimacy in Greece, 1967-1974," in *Political Science Quarterly*. Vol. 98, no. 3. Fall 1983, pp. 485–506.

Fleming, Amalia. *A Piece of Truth*. Boston: Houghton Mifflin, 1973.

Korovessis, Pericles. *The Method*. London: Allison and Busby, 1970.

"Lady Fleming: Greek Patriot and Politician," in *The Times* (London). February 27, 1986, p. 14.

Macfarlane, Gwyn. *Alexander Fleming: The Man and the Myth*. Cambridge, MA: Harvard University Press, 1984.

John Haag,
Assistant Professor of History,
University of Georgia, Athens, Georgia

Fleming, Jane (fl. 1550s)

English royal mistress of French king. Flourished in the 1550s; mistress of Henry II (1519–1559), king of France (r. 1547–1559); children: (with Henry) Henri (b. 1551), Grand Prieur.

Fleming, Margaret (1803–1811)

British writer. Name variations: Marjory, Marjorie, or Marjarie. Born on January 15, 1803; died at age eight of measles on December 19, 1811; daughter of James Fleming of Kirkcaldy, Scotland.

Although she lived only a brief span of eight years, Margaret Fleming is remembered for her charming diary, in which, as noted by **Mary Jane Moffat** and **Charlotte Painter**, she "wrote of the difficulties of achieving an ideal of feminine goodness even before she had learned to punctuate." Fleming's daily writing assignments were imposed by her cousin and tutor **Isabella Keith**, who also served as the paradigm of virtue little Margaret aspired to. However, as might be expected, she frequently—and some might say delightfully—failed in her attempts at piety:

> To Day I pronounced a
> word which should never
> come out of a ladys lips it was
> that I called John a Impu-
> dent Bitch and Isabella afterwards told
> me that I should never say
> it even in joke but she kindly
> forgave me because I said
> that I would not do it again.

In the Spring of 1911, the year of her untimely death, Margaret's thoughts turned to love:

> Love I think is in the fashion for
> every body is marrying there
> is a new novel published nam-
> ed selfcontroul a very good
> maxam forsooth yesterday
> a marrade man name Mr
> John Balfour Esq offered
> to kiss me, & offered to marry
> me though the man was es-
> pused, & his wife was present, &
> said he must ask her per
> -mission but he did not I
> think he was ashamed or con-
> founded before 3 gentelman.

Following Margaret's death, her diary remained with her family until the 1850s, when it was edited and published by Dr. John Brown, as *Pet Marjorie: A Story of Child Life Fifty Years Ago*. Even though Margaret's original work was heavily censored in reproduction, she gained worldwide notoriety, and was the youngest subject listed in Sir Leslie Stephen's *Dictionary of National Biography*. Her childhood musings remain timeless and universal in their appeal.

SOURCES:

Moffat, Mary Jane and Charlotte Painter, eds. *Revelations: Diaries of Women*. NY: Random House, 1974.

Fleming, Peggy (1948—)

American figure skater and Olympic gold medalist who is generally credited with popularizing competitive ice skating for American audiences and turning it into the most closely watched event at the winter Olympic Games. Born July 27, 1948, in San Jose, California; attended Colorado State College; daughter of Albert Fleming (a pressman) and Dorothy Fleming; had three sisters: Janice, Maxine, and Cathy Fleming; married Gregory Jenkins (a dermatologist), in 1970; children: two sons, Andrew and Todd.

Began skating competitively at the age of nine (1957); by age 16, had won the first of five successive U.S. figure skating championships, being much admired for her combination of technical precision and artistic sensibility; captured and held the world title for three years running (1966, 1967, 1968) and capped her amateur career by winning her country a gold medal at the Winter Olympic Games in Grenoble, France (1968), the only American to do so; began competing professionally after her Olympic win; starred in several television specials and major ice shows and continued to serve as a network sports commentator.

In 1957, nine-year-old Peggy Fleming began taking skating lessons at a rink in Cleveland, Ohio, under the watchful eye of the rink's resident instructor, **Harriet Lapish**. A few months later as Fleming came off the ice, Lapish asked the young girl if she would like to enter a competition. She would be required to demonstrate her knowledge of the basic exercises and figures she had been learning, warned Lapish, yes, even Peggy's favorite, the "sit-spin," in which she crouched to the ice on one leg with the other extended, twirling gracefully and smiling serenely. Some weeks later, Peggy Fleming skated perfectly through the Preliminary Test of the U.S. Figure Skating Association (USFSA), her first step on the path that would lead, ten years later, to an Olympic Gold medal and world attention as figure skating's first superstar.

Until the day of Lapish's suggestion, skating had been just another of the athletic activities Fleming's parents had devised for the most active of their four daughters. "I used to play baseball and golf with [my father]," Peggy says. "I roller skated, and I just loved to run around, dancing and looking at my shadow." All the girls—**Janice**, the oldest, along with Peggy's younger sisters **Maxine** and **Cathy**—had been born in San Jose, California, Peggy arriving on July 27, 1948. Albert Fleming, a World War II veteran, had moved his family to the Midwest to take advantage of a job-training program as a pressman for

the *Cleveland Plain Dealer*. The long winters added a whole new category of outdoor activities for a family that could rarely be found sitting still, for Albert and **Dorothy Fleming** made sure the girls were exposed to a wide variety of pursuits. "My father loved all kinds of athletic activity," said Fleming, "and my parents offered us all the things they could." Although violin and flute lessons were among the offerings, neither helped to dissipate Peggy's apparently limitless energy. She discovered skating on her own and fondly recalls the silence of an empty rink, the whisper of skates on clean, glistening ice, and the sense of effortless movement. "She took to it right away," Maxine says. "She started skating as though she had been at it for a long time."

I think I'll always be connected to skating. It's a change from housework.

—Peggy Fleming

Less than a year after passing her Preliminaries, Fleming sailed through the USFSA's First Level test by demonstrating her knowledge of school figures, the elementary circles and figure-eights upon which even the most complicated maneuvers are based. Her father had by then completed his training, and the Flemings moved back to San Jose where Peggy's penchant for skating led her to her second coach, Eugene Turner, in nearby Berkeley. Turner drilled his students relentlessly in perfecting their school figures, going so far as to require them to skate their routines in the dark. Under his careful eye, Peggy passed her Second Level test just after her tenth birthday and was entered in the Juvenile Girls event of the USFSA's Central Pacific regional trials in San Francisco. It was her first exposure to a major audience, but few could have judged from her flawless performance in the school figures how nervous she had been. Her standing after skating the required three figures was high enough to qualify her for the second phase of the event, her first competitive freestyle performance in public, skated to music and combining school figures and maneuvers in any way the competitor wished. When all the scores were in, Fleming had placed first.

But her next competition provided a lesson she never forgot. Jubilant at her regional championship and swelled with confidence, Fleming skated onto the ice at the next week's finals for the Pacific Coast championship sure that winning was as natural to her as breathing. She placed last. "I think that whole experience helped me quite a bit," she said years later. "It was no fun finishing last, and I decided if I was going to compete, I'd better get serious about it." From that point on, Fleming would never be out of the top five contenders at any event; at the next year's Pacific Coast championships at Squaw Valley, she easily placed first to become the West Coast's Juvenile Girls champion. By now, she had begun to think more about her freestyle and had already set herself apart from her competitors by adding graceful arm movements taken from ballet to her routine, as well as a difficult "double salchow"—a jump from the back inside edge of her left skate to the back outside edge of her right, with two airborne spins on the way. Her stunning performance at Squaw Valley attracted the attention of Bill Kipp, who was about to be named coach of the U.S. figure skating team headed for the 1961 World Games in Prague. Kipp agreed to take Fleming on as a student at his rink in Pasadena.

Bill Kipp successfully guided Peggy through her Fourth Level test, began preparing her for the USFSA's next level of competition, Novice Girls, and even found Fleming a summer job as a solo skater for the Arctic Blades Ice Review tour of the western United States. More important, Kipp encouraged Fleming to start thinking more seriously about the image she wanted to present on the ice, urging her to watch his older skaters for ideas on a personal style. What Fleming observed, she later said, was a lack of any sort of style at all in the older group. In 1960, ladies figure skating was characterized, as it had been for 30 years, by what one sports commentator called the "Ice Follies approach," all spectacle and little substance. Fleming's older peers, said fellow competitor Dick Button, were "clumping around, skating fast like hockey players, flailing the ice with quick stops and trying to overpower you with gimmicks. The crowd may like it, but it's not beautiful and it's not good skating." Fleming told Kipp she wanted to leave her audience with a sense of grace and elegance, so that "everything blends smoothly as you flow across the ice." It was under Kipp's guidance that the Peggy Fleming style, a sophisticated blend of ballet and skating that would revolutionize women's figure skating, began to develop.

By late 1960, Fleming had won her first Novice Girls title at the Pacific Coast championships and looked forward to beginning her training for the Fifth Level tests on Kipp's return from the World Games. In February 1961, she arrived home from school to be told by her mother that the plane carrying the entire United States skating team and six coaches, Bill Kipp

among them, had crashed en route to Prague. There were no survivors. (American figure skating coach *Maribel Vinson Owen and her medal-winning daughters *Laurence Owen and *Maribel Owen were also killed.) Added to the personal tragedy of the crash was the fact that the United States was left with no skating team in place for the Olympic Games three years hence, while Fleming's own progress seem blocked. Her decision to quit skating resisted the pleas of her family, Peggy arguing that the Flemings could ill afford to support what now seemed to her merely a hobby. It took a former student of Kipp's familiar with his teaching methods to talk Fleming back onto the amateur circuit.

Doriann Swett's encouragement and coaching got Peggy successfully through her Fifth Level test, the Southwest Pacific regional Junior Girls championship, and to Great Falls, Montana, to skate for the 1961 Pacific Coast Junior Girls title. As she advanced up the USFSA's competition ladder, Fleming worried constantly about the expense placed on her family's already strained finances. "You already have the best equipment that money can buy—yourself and your two legs," Swett reassured her. Fleming's extraordinary talent was so obvious to everyone that even the severe viral infection that struck her during the Great Falls competition, and forced her to leave the ice before completing her freestyle, could not stop her advancement. Her skating up to that point had been so flawless that the USFSA's Pacific Coast regional committee agreed to issue a letter qualifying her to compete at the 1962 National championships in Boston, normally awarded only to the top three scores at each regional level. Fleming skated well, but not well enough, ranking second and missing the National championship title. It was only the second time in her nearly four years of competing that she failed to take first place.

Back in Pasadena, the Flemings rallied to give Peggy another chance at the Nationals. Her father, who had already taken a second part-time job in addition to his night shift at Pasadena's *Star News*, drove her to the rink every morning at 5:30 and even learned how to operate the ice-scraping machinery so Peggy would have a clean surface for her morning practice. Her mother made all of her daughter's skating outfits by hand, despite the increasing sophistication and style needed for the higher levels of competition, while her sisters screened music for her freestyle program. Peggy herself skated every morning from 5:30 to 8:30, put in a full day at school, then skated again from 3:30 to 5:00 be-

fore returning home for dinner. She often ended her day with another two hours of evening practice. By late 1962, she had qualified again for the National championships, held that year closer to home, in Long Beach, California. She scored well on her compulsory program but placed third in the freestyle and for the second time in two years went home empty-handed, again convinced that her skating dreams were ended.

But just as they had done a year before, the family convinced her otherwise. Over the next ten months, Peggy passed the Eighth and final USFSA test, allowing her to compete at the Senior Ladies level; and by late 1963, she qualified once again for the Nationals. The reward this time, however, was much more than just the National title. The three highest scorers would automatically be placed on the U.S. Olympic Team at the 1964 Winter Games in Innsbruck, Austria, which began little more than a month after the Nationals. Fleming was delighted to hear that the Nationals would be held at the same rink in Cleveland where she had trained five years before with Harriet Lapish. The Flemings solved the considerable expense of traveling halfway across the country by sending Peggy alone by air, while Dorothy and Albert left by car ahead of her for the four-day drive from Pasadena.

The competition began hopefully, with Peggy completing her compulsory program in third place; and from her first movement as the music began for her freestyle, Fleming's work over the past year with skater-turned-choreographer Bob Turk became immediately apparent. The audience was riveted by her balletic movements, balancing athletic strength with an artistic sensibility that was more performance than program, and to which the graceful leaps and spins seemed organically connected as part of a flowing, elegant whole. The judges agreed, awarding her near perfect scores and making Peggy Fleming, at 15½, the youngest competitor up to that time to win the National Senior Ladies title. Even better, Fleming was on her way to the Olympics.

With the tragic loss of the expected 1964 team three years earlier, Innsbruck provided the world its first opportunity to watch the new crop of skaters that would normally not have been considered ready for international competition. Fleming, it was thought, had a chance at the bronze medal, even after she placed eighth at the end of her compulsory school figures. All she needed to advance in the rankings, said her fans, was a repeat performance of her Nationals freestyle. But as 11,000 spectators and an international television audience watched, Fleming fell to the ice halfway through the program during a routine maneuver. She completed the program to generous applause and, as evidence of her superlative style despite the fall, finished sixth in the overall rankings. She offered no excuses, even though she had been suffering from a severe cold during the competition. Privately, Fleming told friends that the higher altitude at Innsbruck, higher than any other venue at which she had skated, affected her endurance and left her exhausted going into the freestyle event. Her suspicions were confirmed at the World Games in Germany the next month, where she placed seventh. Nonetheless, she was asked by the International Skating Union to join 30 of the world's top skaters for its World Championships Tour of Europe. She skated two performances a night at the tour's stops in Italy, Germany, France and Switzerland, where her All-American charm and graceful routine was widely praised. But as she skated off the ice after a performance in Germany, Fleming could tell by the look on her mother's face that something was terribly wrong. Her father, she learned, had suffered a heart attack.

Back in Pasadena, Peggy stayed off the ice while her father recuperated and would have quit skating once and for all if Albert hadn't convinced her otherwise. Absent from the circuit for several months, Fleming reentered the skating world by way of an exhibition at Sun Valley in the late summer of 1964, where she met Bob Paul, a gold medalist in the Pairs competition at the 1960 Olympics. Paul devised a training routine to build up her endurance and refined Fleming's freestyle even further. "I want everyone else to enjoy the performance as much as I do," she told him, "whether they like athletics or ballet or music. It should be a combination of all three." By the time of the Nationals in Lake Placid, Fleming successfully defended her National title with scores as high as 5.9 (out of a maximum 6.0) but slipped to third place in the World Games held just a month later at Colorado Springs. Again, Fleming felt it was her lack of altitude training that had hurt her. As they had done several times over the past nine years, the Flemings found a solution by moving permanently to Colorado Springs, where Albert arranged for Peggy to practice at the famed Broadmoor Hotel under the coach who would make her the most famous skater in the world.

Italy's Carlo Fassi had been the World Champion before turning full-time to coaching and settling at the Broadmoor, with its Olympic-sized indoor and outdoor rinks. Fassi and Fleming focused on the upcoming 1966 World Games in Davos, Switzerland, where Peggy would again be exposed to an outdoor rink at a high altitude. It was Fassi who strengthened Fleming's school figures, always her weaker discipline, by forcing her to make her turns and figures mathematically precise. Fleming remembered this training period as the happiest of her career. Her father's health was strong enough for the family to ski and hike together; the pressure of school work had been eased somewhat by enrolling in the Professional High School in Hollywood, which allowed her to study by correspondence and receive her diploma; and Fassi's mix of stern disciplinarian and good-humored mentor were immensely appealing to her. "I owe him so much," Fleming said after Fassi's death from a heart attack in 1997. "He was like your father, your mentor, your strength when you didn't feel you could do it. He always brought out the best in me, like no one else has ever done." It was through Fassi that Fleming had met, in Europe while touring with the ISU, a young admirer named Greg Jenkins. As she began her training at the Broadmoor, she was delighted to discover that Jenkins was just entering Colorado State University and living in Colorado Springs. Fassi was only too happy to reintroduce them. As Fleming headed for the 1966 Nationals in Berkeley, Jenkins awarded her with the first in a long series of good-luck charms—a green chewing-gum wrapper that Peggy never failed to pin inside her costume before entering the rink.

Fleming skated to her third Nationals title at Berkeley and left almost immediately for the World Games in Davos, Fassi mentioning on the journey to Switzerland that a defending World champion (that year, Canadian ❧ **Petra Burka**) had only been defeated four times in the history of the international competition. Peggy, meanwhile, knew from Fassi that her chief rival in Davos would be the European Ladies Champion, East German ❧ **Gabriele Seyfert**. But at the end of the compulsories, Fleming led Seyfert by 49 points, proof that Fassi had been right to concentrate on her school figures. Her final weapon was the opening figure developed by Fassi for her freestyle, skated to Tchaikovsky's *Pathétique*. It was a spread eagle and double axel, followed quickly by a double flip—a daring combination never before seen at the World Games. At the end of the judging, Fleming had captured first place in the overall competition by 62 points, becoming, at 17, the best woman skater in the world.

The 1966 World championship, the first of three consecutive World titles, marked the beginning of Fleming's second try for a spot on the U.S. Olympic team. She trained with Fassi six hours a day, six days a week, in preparation for the 1967 Nationals in Omaha, Nebraska, taking time off only to help defray the expenses of her career by going once again on the ISU's World Champions tour in Europe. One day in Moscow, as Fleming and her mother hurried to catch a plane for the tour's next stop in Germany, an at-

taché from the American Embassy stopped them just as they were about to board. The embassy had received a call, he said, and it was tragic news. Albert Fleming, who had always remained behind in the States to look after things while Peggy and Dorothy were away, had died. Fleming had last seen him in Boston at a benefit event, little more than a month before, when Albert had driven all the way from Colorado to visit with her before she returned to Europe for the ISU tour. He had died in Cleveland, where he had stopped to visit relatives on his way back to Colorado. "He worked so hard to help me," Fleming told the press on her return to the United States, recalling how Albert had thought nothing of changing jobs so that she could be

---

❧▶ **Burka, Petra** (1946—)

Canadian figure skater and the first woman to perform a triple Salchow in competition. Born on November 17, 1946, in Canada; daughter of Ellen Petra Burka (a skating coach born in Amsterdam, Holland, August 11, 1921).

Petra Burka was born in Canada in 1946, the daughter of **Ellen Petra Burka**, a skating coach who produced 26 Canadian Olympic and World champions and medalists, including Toller Cranston, Christopher Bowman, Elvis Stojko, and her own daughter. Petra Burka began skating at age six. At 14, she won the Canadian junior figure skating title. In 1962, she placed fourth at the World championships and made history that year as the first female to perform a triple Salchow in competition. Two years later, Burka won an Olympic bronze medal in figure skating in Innsbruck, Austria; *Sjoukje Dijkstra of Holland took home the gold. The following year, Petra won the Canadian national title, along with the North American and World championships. The first ladies champion in Canada since *Barbara Ann Scott, she was voted Canada's top female athlete two years in a row. In 1997, Petra Burka was inducted into the Canadian Figure Skating Hall of Fame. Her mother had been inducted the preceding year.

❧▶ **Seyfert, Gabriele** (c. 1948—)

East German figure skater. Name variations: Gaby. Born around 1948; daughter of Jutta Mueller (her mother and also her coach).

In 1968, Gaby Seyfert won the Olympic silver medal in figure skating at the Grenoble Winter Games. Seyfert went on to win the World championships in 1969 and 1970. She was also European Ladies Champion in 1967.

SUGGESTED READING:

Seyfert, Gaby. *Da muss noch was sein. Mein Leben, mehr als Pflicht und Kür* (an autobiography), 1998.

near the best coaches and facilities. "He was so instrumental. He taught me how to take care of my body, to warm up and warm down, not to overtrain, and to take care of injuries."

Although publicly Fleming sidestepped questions about her future, she privately told Dorothy and her sisters that she wanted to quit skating, complete her courses for an education degree at Colorado State, and help support the family. Greg Jenkins, who became something of a big brother to the younger girls in the absence of their father, joined with Dorothy and Carlo Fassi in urging her to continue long enough to reach the Olympics in Grenoble, France, just a year away. Fleming reluctantly agreed after insisting she would retire after the Winter Games. The public never knew how much Peggy missed her father, but everyone noticed the difference in her form at the 1967 Omaha Nationals, technically perfect but without the artistic spark that usually ignited her time on the ice. She won her fourth consecutive National title nonetheless, followed by the North American Ladies title in Montreal, and her second World title in Vienna, which she won despite a bad spill during the freestyle that sent her spinning into the rink's sidewall.

Fassi stepped up her training as soon as Fleming returned from Vienna, where the European press had called her "America's shy Bambi" and had noted with much speculation the presence of Greg Jenkins at every event. Gaby Seyfert, whom Peggy had once again defeated in the World championships, noted that "Peggy has no weaknesses. [She] lands softly and everything she does is connected. It's pure ballerina." Former men's champion Dick Button called her the "Audrey Hepburn of skating. With some skaters," he said, "there's a lot of fuss and feathers, but nothing is happening. With Peggy, there's no fuss and feathers, and a great deal is happening."

By the time of the 1968 Nationals in Philadelphia, Fleming seemed unstoppable. The judges all awarded her 5.9's for technical method in her freestyle, while two of them gave her perfect 6.0's for interpretation and style. With her fifth consecutive National championship behind her, Fleming set off for Grenoble. Bothered by an incipient cold that threatened to race through the Olympic Village, Peggy set tongues wagging when she obtained permission from the Olympic Committee to move out of the Village and into a nearby hotel with her mother. Some observers put the blame on Dorothy as the instigator, pointing out Dorothy's reputation as an assertive and sometimes overly protective stage mother. Fleming always bristled at the talk,

remembering that in 1968 the days of professional management and corporate sponsorships were still in the future. "At the time my mother was like my agent-manager. She made all my costumes, she was a buffer. To hire someone to do that was considered amateurish, and we didn't have the money anyhow."

After the opening ceremonies on February 6, with Fleming marching behind the American flag in the parade of athletes, she settled down to work. Those around her at the time remember that she spoke little and, as was her usual habit, found a quiet corner of the dressing room to spend the tense period before her turn on the ice was called. She skated in 17th position out of more than 30 competitors, gliding onto the ice in Dorothy's chartreuse costume for her compulsory school figures as millions watched on television, the event being broadcast for the first time live and in color. When the compulsories were over, Fleming led Gaby Seyfert by 77 points. Since compulsories in those days accounted for 60% of a competitor's total score, Fleming was virtually assured of first place in the overall scores. But it was her freestyle that captivated the world, was replayed over and over for days following, and catapulted figure skating into a major spectator sport. During those four minutes, Fleming stunned her audience by opening with two double loops and a double axel, gliding through a back spiral and layback spin, soaring through two splits and a double lutz, and finishing with the spread eagle and double axel she had introduced in Davos. Spectators could hardly tell where one movement ended and the next began. Fleming knew her program had not been flawless and anxiously scanned the judge's booth amid the cheers and bouquets thrown to the ice after her performance. But her concern evaporated when the judge's cards went up. There were unanimous 5.9's for artistic quality, while all but three of the judges gave her the same rating for technique. First place was hers, by 88 points. Two days later, the gold medal was draped over Peggy Fleming's neck, the only American in any discipline at Grenoble to be so honored.

Just a month after the Olympics, Fleming won her third World championship title in Geneva, returning to the United States with her position as the world's best women's figure skater secured. At a White House ceremony at the end of that month, then-President Lyndon Johnson expressed a nation's thanks for "helping us with the gold drain by bringing back the gold medal." In early April, as she had vowed, Fleming announced her retirement from amateur competition. Shortly afterward, she signed with NBC for a series of television specials and with a management and promotion company for live events, including her own "Concert On Ice" and as the star for four seasons running of the Ice Follies tour. Her 1973 NBC special, "Peggy Fleming Visits the Soviet Union," was the first Soviet-American television venture; and in 1975, she became the youngest inductee of the Skating Hall of Fame. Of more significance to Fleming, however, was her marriage in 1970 to Greg Jenkins and the arrival of two sons, Andrew and Todd, over the next ten years.

More than 30 years after her stunning victory in Grenoble, Peggy Fleming remained an influential and respected voice in both amateur and professional sports. The 1998 Winter Olympics in Nagano, Japan, would have marked her 21st year as a network commentator had she not undergone an operation for breast cancer on February 10, 1998, 30 years to the day after she had won her gold medal in Grenoble. "The doctor said I'm going to be fine," she told reporters.

Fleming is also a well-known spokesperson for such organizations as the Women's Sports

Peggy Fleming winning the free skate at the 1968 Olympics at Grenoble.

Foundation and the President's Council on Physical Fitness. She has been invited to the White House by four separate administrations and became the first skater to perform there, in 1980. She has never, in fact, stopped skating. The Boston Globe's Dan Shaughnessy, reporting on the 1994 "Skates of Gold" tour, with Fleming leading a roster of 38 Olympic champions, noted that "it's about the grace and beauty of athleticism, and it appears that Peggy Fleming will still have her fastball long after Nolan Ryan's plaque is gathering dust in the Hall of Fame." Because of that grace and beauty, figure skating has become the most closely watched event at the Winter Olympics, and hundreds of hopeful young skaters, from *Dorothy Hamill to **Michelle Kwan**, have been inspired by her example. Fleming, however, has often stressed the wider significance of competitive sports at any level: "I guess you could say that skating taught me to be true to the best that's within me."

SOURCES:

Eldridge, Larry. "Peggy Fleming—Elegant Skating with Less Pressure," in The Christian Science Monitor. February 15, 1979.

Swift, E.M. "Peggy Fleming," in Sports Illustrated's Forty for the Ages. Vol. 81, no. 12. September 19, 1994.

Van Steenwyck, Elizabeth. Peggy Fleming: Cameo of a Champion. NY: McGraw-Hill, 1978.

Young, Stephanie and Bruce Curtis. Peggy Fleming: Portrait of an Ice Skater. NY: Avon Books 1984.

Norman Powers,
writer-producer, Chelsea Lane Productions, New York

Fleming, Williamina Paton

(1857–1911)

Scottish-American astronomer who discovered the stars of extremely high density known as "white dwarfs" and became the first American woman elected to the Royal Astronomical Society. Name variations: Mina. Born Williamina Paton Stevens on May 15, 1857, in Dundee, Scotland; died of pneumonia on May 21, 1911, in Boston, Massachusetts; daughter of Robert (an artisan) and Mary (Walker) Stevens; attended Dundee public schools, where she also taught, 1871–76; married James Orr Fleming, on May 26, 1877; children: Edward Pickering Fleming (b. October 6, 1879).

Immigrated to America, where she was abandoned by her husband (1878); hired as temporary employee at Harvard College Observatory (1879); observatory employment made permanent (1881); began Draper Memorial classification project (1886); developed improved stellar spectra classification system published in the "Draper Catalogue of Stellar Spectra" (1890); spoke about women's work in astronomy at the Chicago World's Fair (1893); in first board appointment of a woman at Harvard, made observatory's curator of astronomical photographs (1898); helped co-found the Astronomical and Astrophysical Society (1898); elected to Royal Astronomical Society (1906); published study of variable stars (1907); discovered the "white dwarf" stars (1910); was starred in the first edition of American Men of Science; final paper, "Stars Having Peculiar Spectra," published posthumously.

Selected publications: "Detection of New Nebulae by Photography," in Annals of Harvard College Observatory (Vol. 18); "Description and Discussion of the Draper Catalogue," in Annals of Harvard College Observatory (Vol. 26); "The Draper Catalogue of Stellar Spectra," in Annals of Harvard College Observatory (Vol. 27); "A Field For 'Woman's Work' in Astronomy," in Astronomy and Astrophysics (Vol. 12, 1893, pp. 683–689); "A Photographic Study of Variable Stars, Forming a Part of the Henry Draper Memorial," in Annals of Harvard College Observatory (Vol. 47); "Stars Having Peculiar Spectra," in Annals of Harvard College Observatory (Vol. 56).

Few careers in science have had as unlikely a beginning as that of the astronomer Williamina Paton Stevens Fleming, who became one of the most eminent women scientists of the late 19th century. A 22-year-old Scottish immigrant, pregnant and abandoned by her husband soon after her arrival in Boston, she took a job as a household servant in the home of Edward C. Pickering, the director of the astronomical observatory at Harvard University. Accounts vary as to exactly how the job that took her life in a new direction came about, but essentially Pickering had become so dissatisfied by the performance of his scientifically trained workers that he began to claim that his Scottish maid with a high-school education could compute figures more competently than they did. In 1879 (according to most sources), he brought her into the observatory as a temporary employee; two years later, in 1881, she was made a permanent member of his research staff. During her 30-year career, she discovered 10 novae, 59 nebulae, and the stars of extremely high density known as "white dwarfs." She established the first photographic standards of magnitude for the measurement of the variable brightness of stars, became the curator of astronomical photographs at the Harvard College Observatory and the first woman at Harvard to receive a corporation appointment, and was the first American woman elected to the British Royal Astronomical Society.

Williamina Paton Stevens, known as Mina to family and friends, was born at Dundee, Scotland, on May 15, 1857, the daughter of **Mary Walker Stevens** and a gifted and prosperous artisan named Robert Stevens. In her early years, Mina's educational and cultural opportunities were far different from those that led other women, who were to be prominent female astronomers, into the scientific field. Mina's father was a carver of wood frames, which he gilded with gold leaf and sold in a shop. He also experimented with photography, introducing daguerreotypes to the citizens of Dundee. Robert Stevens died when Mina was seven, but the photographic techniques she learned from her father were preparation for her later astronomical work.

Raised in the home of her mother's family, the young girl developed qualities of "energy, perseverance, and loyalty" that characterized her career. She attended the common schools of Dundee and became a pupil-teacher at age 14, helping with the schooling of the younger children while she continued her own studies. Her teaching career ended when she married James Orr Fleming on May 26, 1877.

In December 1878, the couple immigrated to America, where they settled in Boston. Mina Fleming was soon forced to cope with an unreliable husband as well as an unfamiliar environment, and she was pregnant by the time James deserted her. Seeking support for herself and her unborn child, she applied for a job as a maid. Serendipitously, Edward C. Pickering was in need of a housekeeper, and the hiring that transformed her misfortune into good luck became a lifelong benefit to Pickering and the entire astronomical profession. Mina traveled home briefly to Scotland, where she gave birth to her son Edward Pickering Fleming, on October 6, 1879, named in honor of her benefactor. She then returned with the child to Boston and took up work again in the home of Pickering.

Pickering, who had become director of the Harvard Observatory in 1877, was deeply impressed by Fleming's intelligence, and he made her his first woman research assistant. "Her duties were at first of the simplest character, copying and ordinary computing," wrote Pickering. The skill she soon demonstrated in the handling of mathematical calculations and other complex responsibilities encouraged him to create more opportunities for women in the field, and Pickering became a pioneer in hiring women for careers in astrophysics. Annoyed that some male astronomers limited talented and intelligent women to routine tasks such as filing, he opened up many positions in astronomical research to women that had traditionally been restricted to males.

One of the most important programs under Pickering's direction was in celestial photography, funded by the Draper Memorial. Henry Draper was a New York physician who had been the first to experiment with stellar spectrum photography, establishing the largest collection of astronomical photographic plates in the world. After Draper's death, Pickering had secured his equipment as well as funding to continue the work.

Pickering's first assistant in studying stellar spectra was **Nettie A. Farrar**, who left the job in 1886, after instructing Fleming, who was by then in charge of the observatory's photograph library, as her replacement. In collaboration with Pickering, Fleming studied plates of stars photographed through prisms to produce spectrums. In a student-teacher partnership with Pickering, Fleming became engaged in the large-scale but non-theoretical work of examining each fragile photographic glass plate in the collection, identifying the peculiarities of the star, indexing it and storing the information.

Sparkling and friendly though she was, her reputation as a strict disciplinarian lived after her, and as late as the 1930s, elderly ladies who had worked with her in their youth still regarded her with awe.

— E. Dorrit Hoffleit

As Pickering became aware of Fleming's scientific and analytical capabilities, she was given more responsibility for devising an empirical classification system to catalogue the stars according to the evidence of the spectra on the photographic plates. Up to this time, celestial classification had been based on a system developed by Angelo Secchi, who gauged the brightness of spectral lines through visual observations made through telescopes, and devised a category system that included four classes of stars. Pickering's aim was to adapt the relatively new technology of photography for astronomical research, securing a permanent record of the sky and its phenomena by photographing numerous stars through a prism onto one plate. Since the plates recorded wavelengths that the human eye could not see, the results demanded a newer and more complex classification.

Examining these photographs of refracted starlight under a magnifying glass, Fleming expanded the classification to 17 classes of stars.

"With a naturally clear and brilliant mind," according to *Annie Jump Cannon, "Mrs. Fleming at once evinced special aptitude for this photographic investigation, which was so novel that precedents could not be found for its execution."

The results were not flawless. The poor quality of the plates caused some defects to lead to the creation of extra classes, and Fleming experienced some difficulties in placing her classes in consistent order. But her characteristics of the star groups were well defined and yielded an improved arrangement, reliable for the time. In the 1890 *Draper Catalogue of Stellar Spectra,* more than 10,000 stars were described according to the new Pickering-Fleming System, establishing a new foundation for astronomical classification.

Because Pickering was the observatory's director, many of Mina's early works were published under his name, but by 1890 "M. Fleming" was frequently appearing as author along with him in astronomical publications. In the preface to the 1890 *Draper Catalogue,* Pickering emphasized that Fleming had conducted the groundwork for the new celestial classification, and when notices were published in *Astronomical Journal* about the unusual spectra she had discovered, her mentor took responsibility but credited her for the studies.

In the October 1891 issue of *Observatory,* a reviewer wrote, "The name of Mrs. Fleming is already well known to the world as that of a brilliant discoverer; but the present volume shows that she can do real hard work as well." In 1895, Fleming published two papers in the prestigious *Astrophysical Journal,* and she became prolific at penning articles for the *Harvard Annals* and college circulars, claiming her work in her own name rather than Pickering's when she could.

At a Harvard conference in 1898, Pickering read Fleming's paper, "Stars of the Fifth Type in the Magellanic Clouds," about stars with bright line spectra, before a predominantly male crowd. Pickering stated that although Fleming had not credited herself for the discovery of the stars discussed, he felt that she should be recognized for her achievements, "whereupon Mrs. Fleming was compelled by a spontaneous burst of applause to come forward and supplement the paper by responding to the questions elicited by it." During that meeting, she was named a co-founder of the Astronomical and Astrophysical Society.

In her examination of the photographic plates, Fleming observed spectral peculiarities in brightness that suggested celestial bodies that did not fit into her classification scheme. Scrutinizing these more closely, she discovered more than 300 variable stars, including long-period variables which became known as Mira stars. She also established the first photographic standards for measuring the variable brightness of stars, and explained astronomical techniques for locating them. In 1907, she published "A Photographic Study of Variable Stars," in the *Annals of Harvard College Observatory,* a study of 222 of the celestial bodies she had discovered, each patiently measured for its positions and magnitudes of comparison as a guide for astronomers to their placement in the universe. According to British astronomer H.H. Turner, "Many astronomers are deservedly proud to have discovered one variable, and content to leave the arrangements for its observation to others; the discovery of 222, and the care of their future on this scale, is an achievement bordering on the marvelous."

Fleming also discovered 59 gaseous planetary nebulae—and was the first astronomer to utilize photography for this purpose—as well as ten novae, the majority of new stars discovered during her lifetime. In 1910, she was the first astronomer to discover the stars of extremely high density, known as "white dwarfs," which are believed to be in their final evolutionary stage. She also identified new stars in the constellations Norma and Carina. In her 1912 article, "Stars Having Peculiar Spectra," she listed Wolf-Rayet stars, which were hard to interpret because of highly ionized atmospheres. Such skillful zeal for star hunting won her international respect and praise as a "brilliant discoverer" in *Astronomische Nachrichten* and the British *Observatory.*

In 1898, Mina Fleming was named curator of astronomical photographs, the first woman to receive an official appointment from the governing board of Harvard College. With the assistance of a primarily female staff that grew to include several dozen, she examined, approved, and catalogued all photographic plates taken at Harvard observatories, in Cambridge and Arequipa, Peru, amounting to almost 200,000 by the time of her retirement. A stern supervisor, Fleming monitored the scrutiny of every plate and verified the work of her assistants. She also acted as secretary to Pickering, handling his correspondence and editing the observatory's publications, including the tedious technical work of proofreading the *Annals.* Pickering freely praised Fleming for her organizational and technical skills, declaring, "Her diligence and patience were combined with great self-reliance and courage." He also acknowledged that paperwork "occupied so much of her time that it interfered seriously with her scientific investigations."

Fleming's state of mind remained divided over her priorities. In 1900, as part of a university history project, she kept a diary in which she wrote that she wanted to be assigned more scientific work and less administrative tasks. She rarely took vacations and worked late into the night to complete projects for Pickering. She also found it "very trying" that her mentor preferred that she prepare the work of others for publication instead of her own. Some staff members did not communicate well, requiring revisions that usurped time she might have spent in research.

Despite Pickering's rhetoric regarding the advancement of women, few actually advanced very far within the observatory. And, although her mentor stated in his memorial to Fleming that she "occupied one of the most important positions in the Observatory," her most serious complaint against her job continued to revolve around the issue of unfair compensation. As much as Fleming respected Pickering, she observed:

> He seems to think that no work is too much or too hard for me, no matter what the responsibility or how long the hours. . . . Sometimes I feel tempted to give up and let him try some one else, or some of the men to do my work, in order to have him find out what he is getting for $1500 a year from me, compared with $2500 from some of the other assistants. . . . Does he ever think that I have a home to keep and a family to take care of as well as the men? But I suppose a woman has no claim to such comforts.

Fleming's concern at this time was the expense of educating her son Edward, a student at the Massachusetts Institute of Technology (MIT). "I am told that my services are very valuable to the Observatory," she confided in her diary, "but when I compare the compensation with that received by women elsewhere, I feel that my work cannot be of much account." Angry at Pickering, and frustrated by the long hours, stress, and sacrifices she made for her job, she wrote, "I feel almost on the verge of breaking down." Ironically, the only significant raise Pickering offered to a woman during Fleming's tenure was to *Henrietta S. Leavitt, who departed due to an out-of-state family emergency.

If Pickering remained stingy toward Fleming regarding income, he was generous in promoting the attention toward her that drew professional awards and numerous honors. For her discovery of new stars, she received the Guadalupe Almendaro gold medal from the Sociedad Astronómica de Mexico; she was named an honorary fellow in astronomy by the Astronomical and Astrophysics Society and at Wellesley College, and an honorary member of the Société Astronomique de France. In 1906, she was the first American woman (and the fifth woman internationally) elected a member of the British Royal Astronomical Society, and was starred in the first edition of *American Men of Science*. The *Dictionary of American Biography*, which included few women, profiled Fleming's life. Frequently compared to her professional predecessor, *Maria Mitchell, Mina Fleming was considered the most famous American woman astronomer of her lifetime.

Despite misgivings about her own career, Mina supported other women in her field. According to historian Owen Gingerich, "Mrs. Fleming's keen eyesight, remarkable memory, and industrious nature enabled her to advance to a position of considerable authority at the observatory," which she used to influence and inspire fellow women employees. Her administrative promotions, without raises, permitted her to supervise corps who sorted stellar spectra photographs, surveyed glass plates with magnifying glasses, and recorded data in notebooks. Fleming recruited and interviewed workers, hiring women such as Annie Jump Cannon and *Antonia Maury who became notable astronomers working on the Henry Draper Star Catalog, the same project that gave Fleming her professional fame.

Performing at rates of 25–35 cents an hour, the women did the work at a wage level men refused to accept, while the observatory acquired its international reputation primarily on the basis of this work in classification. And while her supervisory work impeded Fleming's independent work so that some of her disciples, like Cannon, eventually surpassed her in classification, she remained greatly respected by her staff. According to *E. Dorrit Hoffleit, "Sparkling and friendly though she was, her reputation as a strict disciplinarian lived after her, and as late as the 1930s, elderly ladies who had worked with her in their youth still regarded her with awe."

In 1893, Fleming spoke about the future of women in astronomy, emphasizing their "natural talent for astronomical work," at the Congress of Astronomy and Astrophysics of the Chicago Columbian Exposition, known today as the World's Fair. She stressed that women had enhanced "positive contributions to our knowledge of the universe." Focusing on the Draper Memorial work that day, she praised Pickering for his hiring of women and encouraged other observatory directors to follow suit, because "if granted similar opportunities [they] would un-doubtedly devote themselves to the work with the same untiring zeal." Mentioning women's colleges that taught astronomy and employment opportunities in the field, Fleming continued:

> While we cannot maintain that in everything woman is man's equal, yet in many things her patience, perseverance and method made her his superior. . . . Therefore, let us hope that in astronomy, which now affords a large field for woman's work and skills, she may, as has been the case in several other sciences, at least prove herself his equal.

The talk, "A Field for Woman's Work in Astron-omy," received nationwide coverage in contem-porary magazines.

Outside her work, Fleming's life revolved around her son, who graduated from MIT in 1901 and became chief mining engineer and metallurgist for a copper company in Chile. A woman of "a large-hearted, sympathetic nature" who "won friends easily," Fleming enjoyed cooking and needlework, and often sewed dolls costumed in Scottish Highland dress for her em-ployees. When she embraced the suffragist movement, it benefitted from her international stature. And according to colleagues, there was "no more ardent champion of the Harvard eleven" in the stands than Mina Fleming, who especially cheered for the Crimson football team against rival Yale. After Edward left home, Fleming often hosted guests in her home at 52 Concord Avenue, near the observatory.

During her three decades at Harvard, Mina encountered changing astronomical methodolo-gy and professional expectations. Career-minded and determined to remain proficient, she worked long hours even as she aged. In Septem-ber 1910, despite intense illness, she attended the Union for Solar Research at Mount Wilson, California. By the next spring, she had devel-oped serious pneumonia and was hospitalized in May. She died that month, on May 21, 1911, at the New England Hospital.

Expressions of sympathy arrived at the ob-servatory from colleagues around the world. Obituaries eulogized Fleming as one of the world's best astronomers, claiming that she had discovered more stars than any other person at that time. Her final paper, "Stars Having Pecu-liar Spectra," which she wrote while ill, was published posthumously in the *Annals of Har-vard College Observatory*. At the time of her death, it was said, she had created enough data "to fill several quarto volumes of the *Annals*."

Annie Jump Cannon, appointed by Picker-ing as Fleming's successor as the Harvard Ob-servatory's curator of astronomical pho-tographs, recalled Mina Fleming as a petite woman with brown hair. "Mrs. Fleming was possessed of an extremely magnetic personality and an attractive countenance, enlivened by re-markably bright eyes," Cannon later wrote. "Her bright face, her attractive manner, and her cheery greeting with its charming Scotch accent, will long be remembered." Cannon completed the Draper Catalogue and further refined Flem-ing's classification system.

At Harvard, Fleming's legacy influenced stu-dents who never even met her, including *Cecilia H. Payne-Gaposchkin, who reflected that Flem-ing "must have been an excellent organizer, a strenuous worker, a martinet." "When I first went to Harvard, several years after her death," wrote Payne-Gaposchkin, "she was still spoken of with respect, with a kind of awe; but to say that she had not been beloved was an under-statement." Nevertheless, this self-taught scien-tist set precedents in her field that opened the way for later women to have even more profes-sional impact, and for this reason, according to biographer **Doris Weatherford**, Mina Fleming's "life amid the stars should not be forgotten."

SOURCES:

Cannon, Annie Jump. "Williamina Paton Fleming," in *Science*. Vol. 33. June 30, 1911, pp. 987–988.

———. "Williamina Paton Fleming," in *Astrophysical Journal*. Vol. 34, 1911, pp. 314–317.

Gordon, Anne. "Williamina Fleming: 'Women's Work' at the Harvard Observatory," in *Women's Studies Newsletter*. Vol. 6, no. 2. Spring 1978, pp. 24–27.

Mack, Pamela E. "Women in Astronomy in the United States, 1875-1920." B.A. honors thesis, Harvard University, 1977.

Pickering, Edward C. "In Memoriam: Williamina Paton Fleming," in *Harvard Graduates Magazine*. Vol. 2. September 1911, pp. 49–51.

Weatherford, Doris. *American Women's History*. NY: Prentice Hall, 1994.

SUGGESTED READING:

Bailey, Solon I. *The History and Work of Harvard Obser-vatory*. NY: McGraw-Hill, 1931.

Jones, Bessie Z., and Lyle Boyd. *The Harvard College Observatory: The First Four Directorships, 1839–1919*. Cambridge, MA: Harvard University Press, 1971.

Kass-Simon, Gabriele, and Patricia Farnes, eds. *Women of Science: Righting the Record*. Bloomington, IN: Indiana University Press, 1990.

Rossiter, Margaret W. *Women Scientists in America: Struggles and Strategies to 1940*. Baltimore, MD: Johns Hopkins University Press, 1982.

COLLECTIONS:

Williamina Paton Stevens Fleming's journal, her corre-spondence, and a scrapbook of her obituaries are available in the Harvard University Archives, Cambridge, Massachusetts. Collections of Harvard College Observatory's and Edward C. Pickering's correspondence, letter books, astronomical photographs, and other material are also preserved by the archives.

Elizabeth D. Schafer, Ph.D.,
freelance writer in the history of
technology and science, Loachapoka, Alabama

Flemming, Mary (fl. 1540s).

See Diane de Poitiers for sidebar.

Fletcher, Alice Cunningham
(1838–1923)

American anthropologist who did some of the first ethnographic field work among Native Americans, primarily the Omaha, and acted as government agent on the Indian allotment program. Born Alice Cunningham Fletcher on March 15, 1838, in Havana, Cuba; died on April 6, 1923, at her home in Washington, D.C.; daughter of Thomas Fletcher (a lawyer) and Lucia Adeline (Jenks) Fletcher; attended the Brooklyn Female Academy (later the Packer Collegiate Institute); never married; no children.

Raised in Brooklyn; at age 18, moved to New Jersey as a governess to the Claudius B. Conant family (1856); returned to New York City; joined the Sorosis Club; helped found the Association for the Advancement of Women (1870); began educating herself and lecturing in anthropology (1878); began ethnographic field work among the Omahas (1881); joined the Lake Mohonk Conference of the Friends of the Indian (1883); began work for U.S. government on allotting land on the Omaha, Winnebago, and Nez Perce Reservation (1884); carried on survey for the Senate report on Indian Education and Civilization issued 1888; received the Thaw fellowship in anthropology at Harvard University and began to devote full time to the science (1890); elected to first term as president of the Woman's Anthropological Society (1890); informally adopted Francis La Flesche (1891); worked on the World's Columbian Exposition (1893); was founding member of American Anthropological Association (1902); served as president of the Anthropological Society of Washington (1903); served as president of American Folklore Society (1905) and also presiding officer of the anthropology section of the American Academy of Science; served as chair of American Committee of Archaeological Institute of America (1907); elected vice-president of American Anthropological Association (1908); continued active association with Archaeological Institute of America until 1912.

Alice Cunningham Fletcher

Publications: extensive, many in the Peabody Museum publications, Proceedings of the American Association for the Advancement of Science, American Anthropologist, *and the Bureau of American Ethnology publications; several have been reprinted, including* Indian Song and Story *(Peabody Museum, 1893),* The Hako *(BAE, 1904),* Handbook of North American Indians *(BAE, 1907, 1910).*

In 1907, Alice Cunningham Fletcher was 69 years old when she systematically destroyed all material relating to her private life, choosing, as she said, to "avoid gossip," and expressing her desire to be remembered as an anthropologist and scientist. There is not much information, therefore, about her early years, although the public part, once she began to support herself, is well documented, as is the final phase, in which she became widely recognized as an anthropologist. To cover the early years, therefore, her biographer **Joan Mark**, author of *A Stranger in her Native Land*, has resorted to *Gertrude Stein's notion of "repeatings" to assist in identifying the character of Fletcher and understanding her life. Mark's work suggest that two major themes reappear through Fletcher's writings: the concepts of "struggle" and "alone in the world." The struggle is either against male power and authority wrongfully used or against the Victorian gender constructs that limited what Fletcher could do. In Mark's view, Fletcher's gender was the "single most significant factor in explaining the course of her career." The second of the "repeatings," Fletcher's sense of being alone in the world, reflected her alienation from her family and the feeling she had that, unlike indigenous Americans, Euro-American immigrants had not yet, as Mark puts it, "developed a sense of the sacred geography of America, of nature and their place in it."

Alice Cunningham Fletcher was born in Havana, Cuba, where her parents, who belonged to a prominent New England family, were residing because of her father's health. The family returned to New York, and her father died before she was two years old. Raised in Brooklyn, she attended the Brooklyn Female Academy, where she was called "little Alice" by classmates, including E. Jane Gay, with whom she formed an association 40 years later. Fletcher said of these years only that she attended "the best schools." Following her mother's remarriage, Alice was apparently unhappy at home and may have suffered unwanted sexual overtures from her stepfather. At 18, she took a job as a governess for several years, residing at the home of Claudius B. Conant and traveling extensively in Europe with his family while apparently having no contact with her own. She later taught literature and history at private schools in New York.

Around 1870, Fletcher returned to New York City "to sample the cultural life" and to teach literature and history in private schools, although she still received support from Conant. In her association with a number of women's clubs, she worked on issues such as temperance, anti-tobacco, and the "woman problem." She became a member of the Sorosis Club, which was primarily a social club, although many of its members—including such prominent figures as *Julia Ward Howe, *Mary Livermore, and *Maria Mitchell—were later involved in forming the Association for the Advancement of Women. The women organized study committees, sponsored Congresses of Women in different cities, and generally worked for women's rights, and Fletcher's name appears often in connection with the association and its annual meetings, as well as other congresses held at the time for discussion and the presentation of papers. The association had six committees (science, statistics, industrial training, reform, art, and education). Members were to gather facts about women, their education and training; encourage women and assist them in preparing for work; and create women's jobs in business and industry. Fletcher was chair for several of the congresses up to 1882, when her involvement in anthropology curtailed her participation.

Conant continued to provide Fletcher with financial support until his death in 1877, apparently paying her well. He also provided investments for her future, but the financial depression of the mid-1870s in the United States limited her financial resources. At age 40, she was partly in pursuit of financial security when she began to make a serious effort at establishing herself in a profession. By 1878, her name had begun to appear on the lecture circuit, first in New York City, then elsewhere. Gradually, her selection of topics settled on prehistoric America and the emerging field of anthropology, until she had developed a series of 11 lectures on ancient America, which included specimens, maps and watercolor illustrations. In preparing for these presentations, Fletcher established contacts that included Frederic W. Putnam, director of the Peabody Museum of American Archaeology and Ethnology in Cambridge, Massachusetts, who invited her to study at the museum and offered to assist in her anthropological education. Her initial work at the Peabody appears to have centered on archaeological work related to shell middens and included raising money for research and the protection of key sites such as the Serpent Mound in Ohio. Putnam assisted Fletcher in joining the American Institute of Archaeology when it was founded in 1879, encouraged her to present papers before the American Association for the Advancement of Science, and remained a strong supporter of her until the end of her life. In their extensive correspondence, Fletcher initially tended to seek his guidance and approval, but their later relationship was characterized by collegiality and mutual respect.

Sometime in early 1880, Fletcher met the young Omaha Indians Francis and *Susette La Flesche, and Thomas Henry Tibbles (whom Susette eventually married), who were touring the East to protest the removal of Native Americans from Dakota reservations to Indian Territory. When Fletcher made plans for a field study of Native American women to add to what she called the "historical solution of the woman question," as well as to gather scientific facts on contemporary Native Americans, she asked Susette to assist her in traveling to Nebraska to live on the reservation. Over the next several years, she produced extensive writings that suggest she was heavily influenced by the work of anthropologist Lewis Henry Morgan, author of *Ancient Society* (1877), and by visits with the La Flesche family and other Native Americans, including the Sioux chief Sitting Bull.

In 1881, Fletcher made an autumn camping trip to Nebraska that turned out to be the first important step in what would become a distinguished career in anthropology. While there, she told a group from the Omaha tribe: "I came to learn, if you will let me, some things about your tribal organization, social customs, tribal rites, traditions and songs. Also to see if I can help you in any way," anticipating her work both as a field ethnographer and as an agent of the U.S. government directly involved with Native American issues.

Fletcher arrived in Nebraska at a critical time in Indian and government relations. The federal government was in the process of shifting its philosophy toward the country's Native Americans from one of "armed conflict with aliens" with stated aims of "clearing Indians from the land" and "separating Indians from the whites" to one that proposed the assimilation of Native Americans into the surrounding society through such policies as offering them the right to vote, attend public schools, and own their own plots of land. There was, of course, a government incentive for this policy: by allocating each Native American a parcel of land for "farming," called allotments, the "surplus" reservation land could then be opened to settlement by whites.

The Omahas encountered by Fletcher were mostly educated people, associated with Christian missions, who were working to get Congress to agree to allotments as a means of protection against their removal from the reservations. Her views on public policy were further shaped by association with the Lake Mohonk Conference of the Friends of the Indians, a Quaker-based group that included influential individuals then lobbying for Indian citizenship, assimilation, and the proposed Dawes Act (General Allotment Act). Fletcher planned to follow the tradition of Morgan, James Owen Dorsey, Frank Hamilton Cushing, and *Matilda Stevenson, who were just beginning to pioneer scientific field work in this area. There were many others on the reservations, however, who were deeply opposed to allotment, but the government quickly saw allotment as a solution to several problems and passed the Omaha Severalty Act in 1882. In 1883, because of her lobbying efforts with the Lake Mohonk group, Fletcher was appointed special agent to carry out the allotment of Omaha land.

Although Fletcher had been able to obtain some funds from private sources, the job had become the only means available to continue her ethnographic work and limited the time she was able to devote to her field studies. With Francis La Flesche as her interpreter, Fletcher worked hard to assure that the Omahas were given the best land on their reservation and that individuals received their allotments before any land was sold. While the government work was under way, she suffered for months with inflammatory rheumatism, and when La Flesche had some of his people visit her and sing ritual healing songs, she used the opportunity to begin collecting material on ceremonial activities. Her efforts to collect the songs of the Omaha also led to her being credited with initiating ethnomusicology studies for Native Americans; she also recognized La Flesche as a valuable resource for her ethnographic work.

I learned to hear the echoes of a time when every living thing even the sky had a voice. The voice devoutly heard by the ancient people of America I desired to make audible to others.

—Alice Cunningham Fletcher

Fletcher continued to work with groups like those at Lake Mohonk that assisted young Indians in building homes when they completed their education. She also lobbied for the Dawes Act, and its final form reflected many of her beliefs. She has often been criticized for what are now seen as patriarchal views that Native Americans were like children and needed "assistance" to "grow up" to civilization, and many have since seen allotment as responsible for the loss of Indian lands and the destruction of many tribes. At the time, however, Fletcher and others truly concerned about the welfare and physical survival of Native Americans believed that allotment was the only way to secure them some land. She went on to negotiate the allotment for both the Winnebagos (1887–89) and the Nez Perce (1890–93), working in each case to get the best land terms for Native Americans despite tremendous pressure from many sides. Her allotment work is documented by E. Jane Gay, who accompanied Fletcher as photographer and "tent" keeper during her work among the Nez Perce. Gay's letters refer to Fletcher as "Her Majesty," a nickname apparently applied because she so resembled Queen *Victoria.

During those years of documenting Omaha culture, when the tribe was suffering from the breakdown of its traditional tribal system, Fletcher and La Flesche arranged for the removal of many tribal artifacts for safe-keeping with the Peabody Museum. Fletcher's government work was also extended to include a firsthand survey of all Native American Reservations, including those in Alaska, and an account of the history, current situation and educational facilities for a report on Education and Civilization to the U.S. Senate. This 700-page summary established Fletcher as the period's foremost authority on Native Americans and led almost singlehandedly to huge increases in the budget for Native American education.

In 1886, Fletcher was named to an unsalaried position as an assistant at the Peabody. In 1888, she was back lobbying Congress, with Matilda Stevenson, for laws guaranteeing the preservation of archaeological monuments. She wrote popular accounts of her work for *Century Magazine* and other publications, measured Native Americans for physical studies being done by anthropologists including Franz Boas, and worked on museum exhibits as she "made herself into an anthropologist."

In 1890, Fletcher's hard work began to pay off in recognition both in the United States and abroad. That year **Mary Copley Thaw** donated money for a fellowship to the Peabody Museum at Harvard, in honor of her late husband William Thaw, to support Fletcher's "scientific and philanthropic researches." The Thaws had backed some of Fletcher's prior research and philanthropic activities through the Peabody Museum, but the fellowship became the first ever given to a woman at Harvard. The fact that Putnam chose to earmark the fellowship for the study of "anthropology" rather than archaeology or ethnology was also an important milestone in the emergence of such studies as a science. The new scientific stature acknowledged by the fellowship also enhanced the position of its first recipient in scientific, philanthropic, and social circles. Over 800 attended the reception in Washington to mark its bestowal, which established Fletcher as the most preeminent woman scientist in the country.

In 1897, however, when Fletcher revisited the Omaha reservation after an absence of seven years, her feelings about the government's work are believed to have undergone a change. Although she never publicly addressed the issue, there is evidence that she recognized that the allotment policy had been a mistake, and Fletcher's biographer suggests that this recognition is accompanied by a withdrawal from philanthropic activities in favor of concentration on her scientific work. In 1905, she wrote in a letter:

> The revelation of the Indian's thought, of his ancient attempts to express ideals of life and of duty are not only helpful to an under-

standing of his conditions today but they are also encouraging to those who are trying to assist him to cross over into our community. There is much in his past that should be conserved. . . . It is just here that the Ethnological student can become a practical helper to the philanthropist.

For the last 23 years of her life, Fletcher devoted herself to science and an active social life. Although she was never wealthy, she was financially secure and able to establish a home. In 1892, with the assistance of Mary Thaw, she purchased a house in Washington, where she resided with her unofficially adopted son, Francis La Flesche, and various female companions (first E. Jane Gay and later Emily Cushing, the widow of anthropologist Frank Cushing). The house became an important place for anthropologists and Native Americans, and Fletcher's "at homes" were famous for attracting visiting scientists, artists, congressional representatives, and many members of Washington society.

Fletcher's papers written during this period reflect a move from reporting and observations to a new maturity and depth reflected in serious theoretical analysis. In 1890, for example, she presented an insightful paper to the American Folklore Society which treated the "Ghost Dance" phenomenon as a result of the cultural crisis on American Indian Reservations. Despite Boas' description of the ceremony as a "nervous reaction," Fletcher's analysis was later verified by studies identifying the Ghost Dance as part of "revivalistic or cargo cult" movements among societies under the pressures of assimilation. In 1895, her paper on "totemism," a belief that ancestral spirits are connected with animals, challenged the interpretation accepted among European armchair anthropologists that Native Americans actually believed they were descended from the animals. Fletcher's paper, along with a similar one by Boas, led to the establishment of the "American theory" on totemism. Her in-depth analysis of Omaha Indian music established her as a leading ethnomusicologist.

Although her trips to the field became less frequent, Fletcher continued to work with informants who came to Washington, and she and La Flesche completed their Omaha ethnography in 1911. By this time the field of anthropology was coming under the control of a new generation of academics, and the younger generation, often trained by Franz Boas, established the tradition of ignoring earlier works on Native Americans such as Fletcher's, while crediting Boas with bringing anthropology to America in the 1890s. Although the 1911 Omaha study was controversial, criticized by American reviewers but often praised by major Europeans in the field such as Hadden, Durkheim, and Mauss, it remained a very popular report.

From 1903 to 1905, Fletcher had worked extensively on articles for the *Handbook of North American Indians*; it is a sign of her influence that she was asked to contribute 35 entries to this major publication. In 1904, she published, along with two Pawnee men, J. Murie and Tahirussawich, a major monograph on Pawnee ceremonial, *The Hako*. During this period, she also occupied major leadership roles in several professional associations. Probably her most prestigious position was that of vice-president and presiding officer of the anthropology section of the American Association of the Advancement of Science. Following her address at one of its meetings, she attended a meeting of the Association for the Advancement of Women in Canada with her lifelong compatriots, Howe and Livermore, and was greeted there as a heroine. She was president of the Women's Anthropology Society in Washington for several years, and, after it merged with its male counterpart, she served as president in 1903. In 1902, she was a charter member, and the only woman, of the new American Anthropology Association and served on its council. She was also president of the American Folklore Society in 1905.

By 1900, anthropology was at a critical turning point. The early death of one of the leaders in the field, Frank Cushing, stunned the scientific community, and especially Fletcher, who noted that the two had shared field methods which included "unconscious sympathy" with Native Americans. Recognizing her own limitations due to age, gender, and lack of a Ph.D., she also saw a vacuum developing in the leadership of American anthropology. A few years earlier, she had written to Putnam at the Peabody: "I am sometimes tempted when I think of the Museum and of what I could possibly do there, to wish what I never did wish, to be a man! I am aware that being a woman I am debarred from helping you as I otherwise could—but the bar is a fact."

Nevertheless, through her association with several wealthy female patrons, especially
❧ **Sara Yorke Stevenson**, *Phoebe A. Hearst, and Mary Thaw, she began to enhance the future of the science from "behind the scenes." Through Hearst, Fletcher played a major role in the establishment of the important Department of Anthropology at Berkeley by Alfred Kroeber. She traveled in the United States, Mexico, and Europe on scientific business, and in 1910 she addressed the British Association for the Advancement of Science, where she was elected vice-president for the anthropology section.

Some of her most important activities were associated with the Archeological Institute of America (AIA), when she lobbied for the Lacey Bill in 1904 to protect American antiquities and the bill creating Mesa Verde park and when she became chair of the AIA's committee on American archaeology in 1906, establishing a strong association with the archaeologist Edgar Hewett. Fletcher led the forces for the AIA to create an American School for archaeology in the United States as they had in Greece and Italy, seeing this as an opportunity to develop a new force in American archaeology. Although her work in this field eventually led to alienation from her old friend Putnam, her foresight in recognizing the important role the southwest would play in future anthropological studies in the United States proved correct. The School of American Archaeology established in 1907 at the Old Palace of the Governors in Santa Fe, New Mexico, with Hewett as its head, eventually lived up to Fletcher's vision and became a major center for study of anthropology and American Indian art by the mid-20th century. Fletcher served on the board of regents for the school until 1912 and spent several summers in Santa Fe. This work led her to choose the school's original location as the site for her ashes.

In the last 12 years of her life, Fletcher served mostly in the role of a research associate to Francis La Flesche as his own career as an ethnographer matured. She worked on Osage songs for his study. La Flesche escorted her to Santa Fe and the Omaha reservation for the last time in the summer of 1922, and she fell ill the following February. Alice Cunningham Fletcher died on April 6, 1923.

❧ **Stevenson, Sara Yorke** (1847–1921)
American archaeologist. Born Sara Yorke in Paris, France, in 1847; died in 1921; granted Sc.D., University of Pennsylvania; married Cornelius Stevenson, 1870.

Sara Yorke came to America from Paris in 1862 and, in 1870, married Cornelius Stevenson. She was later awarded the degree of Sc.D. by the University of Pennsylvania, the first ever conferred on a woman by that institution. In 1898, she was sent to Egypt for the American Exploration Society to investigate archaeological work in the Nile Valley. Her books include *Maximilian in Mexico* and *The Book of the Dead.*

SOURCES:

Mark, Joan. *A Stranger in Her Native Land.* Lincoln: University of Nebraska Press, 1988.

———. *Four Anthropologists.* NY: Science History Publications, 1980.

Mark, Joan T., and Frederick Hoxie, eds. *With the Nez Perce: Alice Fletcher in the Field, 1889–92 by E. Jane Gay.* Lincoln: University of Nebraska Press, 1981.

SUGGESTED READING:

Gacs, Ute, Aisha Khan, Jerrie McIntyre, and Ruth Weinberg, eds. *Women Anthropologists: A Biographical Dictionary.* NY: Greenwood Press. 1988.

Lurie, Nancy Oestreich. "Women in Early American Anthropology," in *Pioneers of American Anthropology.* Edited by June Helm. Seattle: University of Washington Press. 1966.

Janet Owens Frost, PhD,
Anthropology, Eastern New Mexico University,
Portales, New Mexico

Fletcher, Jennie (1890–1968).

See Durack, Fanny for sidebar.

Fletcher, Mrs. Maria Jane (1812–1880).

See Jewsbury, Maria Jane.

Flexner, Jennie M. (1882–1944)

American librarian who directed the first readers' advisory service of the New York Public Library. Born in Louisville, Kentucky, in 1882; died in 1944; one of five children of Jacob (a physician) and Rosa (Maas) Flexner; graduated from Western Reserve Library School.

Jennie Flexner entered the library system at the turn of the century, just as it was expanding under the favorable conditions of the Carnegie grants. Hired by the Louisville Free Public Library because she could type and was "a great reader," she realized before long that she would need training. Flexner graduated from the newly established Western Reserve Library School and then returned to Louisville, where she spent the next 16 years. Heading the circulation department from 1912 to 1928, she played a major role in the development of the library and its work within the community.

In 1928, she was invited to join the New York Public Library, where Flexner created and ran the institution's first readers' advisory service. This department was established to provide counseling and assistance for adult readers, including guiding them through the immense reference department and through the general collection that was dispersed through the 65 branches of the circulation department. The advisory service was opened in March 1929 in a makeshift office with a staff of two. Flexner developed and expanded the department over the next 15 years, until her death in 1944 at age 62. While aiding individual readers, Flexner also worked with community and national organizations. During the Depression, she assisted the Adjustment Service for the Unemployed, creating book lists to help the unemployed prepare for new jobs. Throughout the 1930s and early 1940s, she joined with the National Refugee Service to provide books that would help immigrants master the language and culture of their adopted home. Her book list "Interpreting America" was used throughout the country. Flexner supplied reading lists to "Town Meeting of the Air" and other early educational radio programs and worked with the library's many discussion groups, including the original Great Books Group. She collaborated with the Book Mobilization Committee in preparing a list of 50 books that had helped the war effort, and chaired the Library Committee of the Council on Books in Wartime. Flexner also wrote a layman's guide to the use of libraries called *Making Books Work.* (1943).

Flexner's enthusiasm for connecting books with people was most apparent to those who had the opportunity to sit with her one-on-one. A frequent visitor to her office remarked: "I always came away from a talk with her feeling that I was a little brighter than I am. I may have trudged in, but I came out on tiptoe."

SOURCES:
Pioneering Leaders in Librarianship. American Library Association, 1953.

Barbara Morgan,
Melrose, Massachusetts

Flikke, Julia O.

See Blanchfield, Florence for sidebar.

Flintoff, Debra (1960—)

Australian runner. Name variations: Debbie Flintoff-King. Born Debra Flintoff in Kew, Melbourne, Australia, on April 20, 1960; married Phil King (her coach).

Won gold medals in the Commonwealth Games (1982, 1986); won Olympic gold medal in 400-meter hurdles in Seoul, Korea (1988).

A hard-working and determined athlete, Australian Debbie Flintoff-King had an early interest in netball and the heptathlon before turning her attention to the demanding 400-meter hurdles. After winning gold medals in the Commonwealth Games of 1982 and 1986, she further

Opposite page

Emilie
Flöge

honed her skills under the careful eye of her husband-coach Phil King. At the 1988 Olympic Games in Seoul, Korea, she overcame physical and personal setbacks to win a gold medal in Olympic record time: 53.17. **Tatyana Ledovskaya** of the Soviet Union took the silver; **Ellen Fiedler** of East Germany took the bronze.

Flöge, Emilie (1874–1952)

Austrian fashion designer, owner and manager with her sisters of one of Vienna's leading fashion salons, who was immortalized in Gustav Klimt's stunning **Art Nouveau.** *Name variations: Emilie Floege; Emilie Floge. Born Emilie Louise Flöge in Vienna, Austria, on August 30, 1874; died in Vienna on May 26, 1952; daughter of Hermann Flöge and Barbara Flöge; sister of Helene Flöge Klimt, Pauline Flöge, and Hermann Flöge.*

For over ten years, considered the most important person in the life of artist Gustav Klimt (1897–1918); with sisters, owned and managed one of Vienna's leading fashion salons (c. 1910–1938); portrayed in Klimt's Art Nouveau (1902).

One of the most remarkable women of fin-de-siècle Vienna, Emilie Flöge was born into a Viennese artisan family that had only recently ascended the ladder of social respectability. Her father Hermann was a master turner who had founded a firm that exported Meerschaum pipes, mostly to the British market. In 1892, barely 18, Emilie first met the man who would make the strongest mark on her life, the artist Gustav Klimt. Twelve years older and already a successful artist, Klimt met Emilie because his brother Ernst, also a talented painter, was married to Emilie's sister **Helene Flöge Klimt.** Ernst Klimt died at the age of 28 in 1892, leaving behind a pregnant widow. Gustav extended generous assistance to his sister-in-law and her infant daughter. In 1895, Klimt chose the strikingly attractive Emilie as a model in one of his works, the ceiling painting *Hanswurst at the Fair,* a composition that had been begun but not completed by his late brother Ernst.

By 1897, Emilie Flöge and Gustav Klimt had become inseparable, and most Viennese close to the couple assumed that she had in fact become his mistress. While there can be no doubt that the couple were passionately attached emotionally, and would spend countless hours in each other's company over the next two decades, some scholars have raised the possibility that their relationship always remained platonic. Klimt's strong physical attraction to a large number of women other than Flöge is,

however, an undisputed fact; he had innumerable liaisons with artists' models and other young women and by the time of his death in 1918 was alleged to have fathered no less than 14 children.

Starting around 1898, Klimt and Emilie spent their summer vacations together at the Flöge family villa near the village of Weissenbach on the Attersee in Upper Austria. Inspired both by the presence of his beloved Emilie and the breathtaking scenery of the lake, Klimt began to paint landscapes, either of the area around Weissenbach or of nearby Unterach, where other relatives of Emilie also spent their summers. Of Klimt's 225 known paintings, there are 54 landscapes, and most of these depict the area around the Attersee. In the closing decades of the 20th century, Gustav Klimt's paintings had become incredibly popular—and expensive. With very few of his works remaining in private hands, they fetched fabulous amounts whenever they came up for auction. On one such occasion, in October 1997, his 1909 depiction of a romantic villa, *Schloss Kammer am Attersee II,* sold for an astonishing £14.5 million at Christie's in London. The four other paintings from the highly praised series are to be found hanging in the national art galleries of Prague and Vienna.

Although Emilie Flöge often served to inspire Klimt, particularly during the summer months when they could be together for an extended period of time, he only rarely painted his beloved. When she was 17, he had painted her looking dreamy and rather withdrawn. In *Art Nouveau,* Klimt's famous 1902 portrait of Emilie, she is depicted with much greater psychological complexity. Unlike many of his commissioned portraits in which the woman wears a white tea gown, here Emilie wears a stunning bright blue dress ornamented with gold and silver. Appearing confident and determined, she has her hand on her hip to create a memorable and eye-catching composition. First exhibited in 1903 at Vienna's Secession, *Art Nouveau* was popular with the public but neither Klimt nor Emilie liked the portrait. In 1908, it was sold to the Historical Museum of the City of Vienna, where it still hangs to delight countless visitors every year.

Along with her sisters Helene and **Pauline Flöge,** Emilie served several years of apprenticeship, finally obtaining her master diploma in dressmaking. Encouraged by their father and assisted financially by their brother Hermann, the three sisters set up a fashion shop registered under the name "Schwestern Flöge" (Flöge Sisters). This was at a time when few Austrian women ventured into the world of commerce, but the Flöge establishment, located at the Casa Piccola at Mariahilferstrasse 1c, soon began to prosper. Upon entering the Flöge sisters' shop, Vienna's elite women found themselves in a stunning reception room decorated in art nouveau style by the Wiener Werkstätte, the innovative crafts guild headed by the painter and designer Koloman Moser and the architect Josef Hoffmann. In the years just before 1914, the clientele of Schwestern Flöge included most of the cream of Vienna's stylish women. A sign of their shop's popularity with Viennese upper crust was the fact that Emilie and her sisters employed as many as eighty seamstresses and three cutters.

The success of the Flöge sisters' business resulted in the entire first floor of the Casa Piccola eventually being used by their flourishing enterprise. While the reception room was in a striking black-and-white design, the walls of the next room were covered in felt. Samples of embroidery and lace were displayed in vitrines situated between the windows. The collapse of the Habsburg monarchy in 1918, and the ensuing years of impoverishment that gripped Vienna, represented a severe economic test for Emilie Flöge and her sisters, but they displayed remarkable business skills and were able to survive into a new era in which the pre-1914 world of aristocracy and *Grossbürgertum* became a vanished epoch of elegance and leisure.

Despite the horrific inflation of the early 1920s and the depression of the 1930s, Schwestern Flöge was able to remain in business. Although no longer as wealthy as they had once been, many customers remained loyal to an establishment that signified stylishness often raised to the level of art. Only with the Anschluss, the annexation of Austria by Nazi Germany in March 1938, was the venerable shop forced to close down. With the loss of their Jewish clientele, Emilie and her sisters could no longer remain in business. The new Nazi rulers of Vienna regarded the shop as a symbol of an undesirable decadent era dominated by cosmopolitan Jews and haughty aristocrats, and were pleased when it expired.

Emilie Flöge's *haute couture* shop was shuttered forever in 1938; in many ways, her personal ambitions had died two decades earlier. On January 11, 1918, Gustav Klimt was struck down by a stroke. The first recognizable words that he was able to utter were "*Die Emilie soll kommen*" {"Emilie must come"}. After Klimt's death from pneumonia on February 6, 1918, Emilie collected her letters to him, burning several laundry baskets full. But she never forgot their love for each other, and after the closure of her business, she retained a small room looking onto a courtyard at the Casa Piccola, turning it into a private and intimate museum in which the furnishings of Klimt's studio were kept. Emilie Flöge never wrote her memoirs, but despite the paucity of sources historians have been able to reconstruct the story of her powerful influence as the muse of one of fin-de-siècle Vienna's greatest artists. Among the last survivors from an utterly vanished world, she died in Vienna on May 26, 1952.

SOURCES:

Brix, Emil, and Lisa Fischer, eds. *Die Frauen der Wiener Moderne.* Vienna: Verlag für Geschichte und Politik, 1997.

Emilie Flöge, und Gustav Klimt: Doppelporträt in Ideallandschaft: 112. Sonderausstellung des Historischen Museums der Stadt Wien, Hermesvilla, Lainzer Tiergarten, 30. April 1988 bis 28. February 1989. Vienna: Das Museum, 1988.

Fischer, Wolfgang G., and Dorothea H. Ewan. *Gustav Klimt and Emilie Flöge: An Artist and His Muse.* Woodstock, NY: Overlook Press, 1992.

Fliedl, Gottfried. *Gustav Klimt, 1862–1918: The World in Female Form.* Cologne and London: Taschen Verlag, 1998.

Hildebrandt, Irma. *Hab' meine Rolle nie gelernt: 15 Wiener Frauenporträts.* Munich: Eugen Diederichs Verlag, 1996.

Joll, James. "Tales from the Vienna Woods," in *New York Review of Books.* Vol. 39, no. 16. October 8, 1992, pp. 28–31.

Nebehay, Christian Michael. *Gustav Klimt: Sein Leben in zeitgenössischen Berichten und Quellen.* 2nd ed. Munich: Deutscher Taschenbuch Verlag, 1976.

Partsch, Susanna. *Gustav Klimt: Painter of Women.* Munich and NY: Prestel Verlag, 1994.

Powell, Nicolas. "Emilie Flöge and her Lover Gustav Klimt," in *Apollo.* Vol. 116, no. 246. August 1982, pp. 112–114.

Schorske, Carl E. *Fin-de-Siècle Vienna: Politics and Culture.* NY: Alfred A. Knopf, 1980.

Vereinigung Secession LXXXVIII. Inselräume: Teschner, Klimt & Flöge am Attersee. Rev. ed. Seewallchen a. A.: Die Vereinigung, 1989.

John Haag,
Assistant Professor of History,
University of Georgia, Athens, Georgia

Flora.

Variant of Florence.

Flora and Maria of Cordova

(d. 851)

Saints and martyrs of the Roman Catholic Church.
Flora (d. 851) was born in Cordova, Spain, of a Mohammedan father and a Christian mother; both died on November 24, 851.

Little is known of the lives of saints Flora and Maria, aside from their deaths together on November 24, 851, in Cordova, Spain. Flora, born of a Mohammedan father and a Christian mother, practiced her Christian religion in secret, but, following the death of her parents, she was turned over to the authorities, the cadi, by her brother. When she would not denounce her religion, she was "whipped til the blood ran, struck on the head," and then returned to the custody of her brother. She eventually escaped from him, finding temporary refuge with her sister at Ossaria. But the Moors of the Cordova caliphate were then unleashed against the Christians, and those who hid them were in danger. Flora's sister, fearing that harboring a Christian would jeopardize her own family, asked Flora to return to Cordova.

In Cordova's Church of St. Acicle, Flora met Maria, a Christian woman who was also concerned for her life following the execution of her brother, the deacon Valabonse. The two women, seeing no way out of their dilemma, decided to face their inevitable death together. Presenting themselves to the authorities and declaring that they would never deny their faith, they were imprisoned and martyred together on November 24, 851. St. Eulogius, in his *The Memorial of the Saints,* credit the two women with his own deliverance from prison and certain death. His was a short-lived reprise, however, for he too later died defending his faith.

Florence of Cartagena (d. 7th c.).

See Florentina of Cartagena.

Florentina (d. 7th c.)

Saint. Name variations: Florence of Cartagena. Born at Cartagena (Andalusia), around the middle of the 6th century; died in the early 7th century; daughter of Severianus and Turtur; sister of St. Fulgentius, bishop of Ecija, St. Leander, and St. Isidore of Seville.

Of Greco-Roman ancestry on her father's side, Saint Florentina lived between the 6th and 7th century and was a cloistered nun. What little else is known about her comes from an extant letter she received from her brother, St. Leander. In it, he extols her virtue. "Nothing that I have seen under the sun is worthy of you," he writes; "I have found above the skies that great treasure which is the gift of holy virginity, ineffable and mysterious gift which I cannot possibly praise highly enough." He also tells her that the nuns that were born slaves are now her equals. "Those who fight with you for Christ under the banner of virginity should taste the same joyful liberty that is yours." Finally, Leander recalls the memory of their mother, who also ended her days in a cloister. "Rest now on the breast of the Church, that mystic dove, as you used to sleep upon the heart of her who tended your infancy." Upon her death, Florentina was laid to rest next to her brother Leander in the cathedral of Seville.

Florenzi, Marianna Bacinetti
(1802–1870).

See Bacinetti-Florenzi, Marianna.

Flores, Lola (1924–1995)

Spanish stage actress and flamenco singer-dancer, who was the best-loved singer in Spain for decades.
Name variations: Dolores Flores Ruiz. Born Dolores Flores Ruiz on January 21, 1924 (some sources cite 1928), in Jerez de la Frontera, Spain; died in Madrid, Spain, on May 16, 1995; daughter of Pedro Flores and Rosario Ruiz; married Antonio González (a Gypsy [Roma] guitarist), in November 1957; children: Rosario, Lolita, Antonio.

Born in Jerez de la Frontera, Spain, on January 21, 1924, Lola Flores was the daughter of Pedro Flores and **Rosario Ruiz**. She grew up in Andalusia, the Spanish home of flamenco song and dance, and although not a Gypsy (people of Romany) herself Lola was fond of saying that the Rom were her cousins. As a child, she frequented the convivial bars of Sevilla and Jerez, where her father often worked, and began singing and dancing with Rom friends.

By the 1940s, she had attracted the attention of Manolo Caracol, a great flamenco singer, and began touring with him. Caracol sang while Flores danced, like "thunder and lightening" according to one observer. Flores and Caracol formed a very successful team that evolved into a fiery relationship. She also appeared in a movie, *Maringala*, made in 1943. When Flores and Caracol finally broke up, she formed her own company, as one of the foremost flamenco performers in the Hispanic world.

Her ability as a dancer outshone her singing. Trained by flamenco guitarists Javier Molina and Sebastián Núñez and by the dancer **María Pantoja**, Flores was nonetheless an instinctual artist rather than a highly choreographed performer. She possessed *duende*, what the Rom call mysterious, emotional, instinctive

genius. Such dancing with *duende* harkened back to the traditional roots of flamenco.

A popular idol in Spain, Flores was the subject of constant media attention. Gossip about her tours and love affairs attracted readers. In November 1957, she married Antonio González, a Gypsy guitarist in her company. They soon had three children, continued to tour, and even starred together in movies, including *La Venta de Vargas*. In 1989, the Spanish bureaucracy caught up with Flores' free-wheeling ways because she had never filed an income-tax report. Lola Flores died in 1995.

SOURCES:

Medina, Tico. *Lola, en carne viva: Memorias de Lola Flores.* Madrid: Ediciones Temas de Hoy, 1990.
Pohren, D. E. *Lives and Legends of Flamenco.* Sevilla: Society of Spanish Studies, 1964.
Umbral, Francisco. *Lola Flores: Sociología de la petenera.* Barcelona: DOPESA, 1971.

SUGGESTED READING:

"Lola Flores," in *The Times* [London]. May 29, 1995, p. 19.
"Lola Flores, 72, Spain's Definitive Flamenco Singer", in *The New York Times.* May 17, 1995, p. C18.
"Spain Mourns Its Flamenco Diva," in *The New York Times.* May 18, 1995, p. C19.

Kendall W. Brown,
Professor of History, Brigham
Young University, Provo, Utah

Flower, Eliza (1803–1846).

See Adams, Sarah Flower for sidebar.

Flower, Lucy (1837–1921)

American welfare worker. Born Lucy Louisa Coues on May 10, 1837, probably in Boston, Massachusetts; died on April 27, 1921, in Coronado, California; adopted daughter and one of eight children of Samuel Elliott Coues (a merchant and reformer) and his second wife, Charlotte Haven (Ladd) Coues; attended local schools in Portsmouth, New Hampshire; attended Packer Collegiate Institute, Brooklyn, New York, 1856–57; married James M. Flower (a lawyer), September 4, 1862 (died 1909); children: two sons and a daughter.

The daughter of a wealthy merchant, Lucy Flower was born on May 10, 1837, probably in Boston, Massachusetts, and grew up in Portsmouth, New Hampshire. After a year of college, she went to work for the U.S. Patent Office in Washington. In 1859, she moved to Madison, Wisconsin, where she taught high school and, from 1862 to 1863, operated a private school. In September 1862, she married a

Madison lawyer, James M. Flower, and during the next ten years had three children. After the couple moved to Chicago in 1873, she went to work for the social betterment of Chicago, focusing much of her attention on the city's underprivileged children.

Flower became a member of the board of the Half-Orphan Asylum and later of the Chicago Home for the Friendless. In 1880, joining with Dr. *Sarah Stevenson and others, she helped found the Illinois Training School for Nurses, the first school of its kind in the city. Flower remained president of the institution for 11 years and was a director until 1908. In 1886, she joined other Chicago welfare societies to work for a state industrial school for dependent boys, and, though legislation was defeated, a school was opened in Glenwood, Illinois, in 1889 with funds raised by the Chicago Woman's Club. In 1887, she took part in organizing the Protective Agency for Women and Children and in the following years helped form the Lake Geneva Fresh Air Association, organized to provide poor urban children with a respite from the city.

For three years beginning in 1891, Flower served on the Chicago board of education, during which time she devoted herself to making schooling more relevant to the city's poor children. She helped establish kindergartens and domestic and manual training classes in the lower grades, and also worked to provide better training programs and salaries for teachers. In 1894, she was elected by a wide margin as a trustee of the University of Illinois, thus becoming the first woman to hold an elective office in the state. In her capacity as a trustee, she labored unsuccessfully to secure legislation to expand facilities for women students (she opposed, however, unlimited suffrage for women, believing that the illiterate and uneducated of both sexes should be excluded from the polls). Also in 1894, seeking to centralize private charitable efforts, Flower helped establish the Chicago Bureau of Charities and was elected its first vice president.

In the late 1890s, she reorganized support for the establishment of a juvenile court system in Chicago, a cause that had earlier failed. Flower won the support of the Illinois social-welfare leaders and assisted a committee of the Chicago Bar Association in drafting legislation. Her efforts were rewarded in 1899, with the formation of the Cook County Juvenile Court, the first of its kind anywhere in the world. Flower then founded a Women's Juvenile Court Committee which, headed by *Julia Lathrop, raised money to provide salaries for probation officers.

She also continued to serve the court in an advisory capacity.

In 1902, Flower and her husband moved to Coronado, California, where he died in 1909. After years spent as an invalid, Flower died of a cerebral hemorrhage, on April 27, 1921. Chicago's Lucy Flower Technical High School for Girls bears her name.

SOURCES:

James, Edward T., Editor. *Notable American Women.* Cambridge, MA: The Belknap Press of Harvard University Press, 1971.

McHenry, Robert, ed. *Famous American Women.* NY: Dover, 1983.

Barbara Morgan,
Melrose, Massachusetts

Flügge-Lotz, Irmgard (1903–1974)

German engineer. Name variations: Flugge-Lotz. Born Irmgard Lotz in Germany on July 16, 1903; died in 1974; daughter of Oscar (a mathematician) and Dora Lotz (daughter of a wealthy family in the construction business); graduated from the Technische Hochschule in Hanover, Germany, 1927, Ph.D. in thermodynamics, 1929; married Wilhelm Flügge (an engineer and professor at Stanford), in 1938; became a naturalized American citizen in 1954.

Because her maternal relatives were highly successful builders, Irmgard Lotz spent an inordinate amount of time viewing construction sites during her childhood. In her college years, engineering appealed to her, and, after obtaining advanced degrees, Lotz became a research engineer at the Aerodynamische Versuchsanstalt at Göttingen, working with Ludwig Prandt. By age 30, she had invented the "Lotz" method, a new way of calculating the distribution of the lifting force of airplane wings of disparate sizes. With this discovery, she was soon heading her own research program at the institute.

In 1938, she married fellow engineer Wilhelm Flügge, who, in opposing the rise of the Nazi regime, had lost out on a promotion. But Hermann Göring, commander-in-chief of Hitler's Luftwaffe, felt research should supersede politics, and he hired the newlyweds to work at the Deutsche Versuchsanstalt für Luftfahrt. Though anti-Nazi, Irmgard Flügge-Lotz worked for Göring's aeronautics research institute throughout World War II. After the war, frustrated by her inability to secure a position at a German university, she and her husband moved to the United States in 1948, where she became the first woman professor of engineering at Stanford (1960). She remained at Stanford for the rest of her career, establishing graduate programs in mathematical aerodynamics and hydrodynamics. Her book on flight-control systems for aircraft, *Discontinuous Automatic Control,* was published in 1953.

Flygare-Carlén, Emilie (1807–1892).

See Carlén, Emilia.

Flynn, Elizabeth Gurley

(1890–1964)

American radical, labor organizer, and Communist Party official who dedicated her life to the overthrow of capitalism. Name variations: Elizabeth Gurley; the Rebel Girl. Pronunciation: Flin. Born Elizabeth Gurley Flynn on August 7, 1890, in Concord, New Hampshire; died of acute gastroenterocolitis on September 5, 1964, in Moscow, USSR; daughter of Annie Gurley Flynn (a seamstress) and Thomas Flynn (a civil engineer and mapmaker); attended public schools in New Hampshire and New York City through the 10th grade; married John Archibald Jones, in January 1908 (divorced 1920); children: John Vincent (1909–1909); Fred (1910–1940).

After several moves, the Flynn family settled in the South Bronx (1900); gave first speech at age 15 before the Harlem Socialist Club; joined the Industrial Workers of the World (IWW, 1906); led the IWW free speech fights in Missoula, Montana, and Spokane, Washington; arrested twice for conspiracy; was an organizer for the IWW during the Lawrence strike (1912) and Paterson strike (1913); helped found the Workers' Defense Union (1918) and American Civil Liberties Union (1920); was active in Sacco and Vanzetti defense movement (1920s); elected to American Communist Party (CPUSA) national committee (1938); elected to CPUSA political bureau (1941); served as delegate to Women's Congress in Paris (1945); indicted by federal government under the Smith Act (1951); imprisoned at the federal penitentiary for women at Alderson, West Virginia (January 1955–May 1957); elected national chair of CPUSA (1961).

Selected publications: Thirteen Communists Speak to the Court *(1953);* I Speak My Own Piece: Autobiography of "The Rebel Girl" *(1955);* The Alderson Story: My Life as a Political Prisoner *(1963); numerous articles and regular columns in the* Daily Worker, Sunday Worker *and* Political Affairs.

On Wednesday, January 31, 1906, the Harlem Socialist Club gathered to hear that evening's speaker. She was a slender, serious 15-year-old who had regularly attended the club's meetings and had already won a gold medal in her grammar school debate club for a speech demanding women's suffrage. Although still in high school, Elizabeth Gurley Flynn felt quite confident about her talk, entitled "What Socialism Will Do For Women." She had recently read *Mary Wollstonecraft*'s *Vindication of the Rights of Women* and August Bebel's *Women and Socialism.*

That night, a career was born. Flynn, also known as "The Rebel Girl" after the 1915 song written about her by Industrial Workers of the World (IWW) songwriter Joe Hill, went on to make many more speeches, inspiring countless men and women to organize for their rights as workers. She played an active role in some of the most violent labor strikes from the early 1900s through the Red Scare of the 1920s and was a Communist Party leader during the heady days of the Popular Front in the 1930s and during the anti-communist reaction of the McCarthy era of the 1950s. Through it all, Elizabeth Gurley Flynn never lost the spark that sustained her radicalism.

She was born in Concord, New Hampshire, on August 7, 1890. Her mother **Annie Gurley Flynn** came to America from Ireland in 1876 and worked as a seamstress. Her father Thomas Flynn was born in Maine and worked in granite quarries there and in New Hampshire. Though he attended Dartmouth College, he never graduated; shortly before he was to earn his degree in engineering, his older brother died, forcing him to support his widowed mother and sisters. Thomas Flynn found work as a civil engineer in several New England towns as well as in Cleveland, Ohio. By 1900, he and Annie Flynn had three other children in addition to their first born, Elizabeth. After living in several cities, the family finally moved to New York City, settling in the South Bronx. Given her father's apparent inability to hold one job for any length of time, Elizabeth Gurley Flynn's childhood was marked by economic uncertainty, even poverty. So too did the political radicalism of both her parents leave a mark.

Annie Gurley was an Irish nationalist and an ardent feminist. Tom Flynn was also a supporter of Irish nationalism and a devout Socialist. Both the Flynns encouraged their daughter Elizabeth to become politically involved at an early age. As a young teenager, she attended Socialist club meetings in the company of one or both her parents. At her mother's suggestion, Flynn read Edward Bellamy's socialist utopian novel, *Looking Backward,* when she was just 15. A year later, she was reading the work of Marx and Engels. Thomas Flynn was also quite taken by socialist theory and its attack on capitalism. However, it was Annie Gurley Flynn who, through her emotional and financial support, made it possible for her eldest daughter to try to turn theory into practice.

In the era before television, much less radio, public speaking was not only a convenient way to air ideas, it was also a form of entertainment. From her first speech, Flynn proved herself to be one of the most effective speakers of her day. The aspiring novelist Theodore Dreiser wrote an article in 1906 in which he likened Flynn to *Joan of Arc, saying "she electrified her audience with her eloquence, her youth and loveliness."

She took her message to the streets, speaking on New York City streetcorners to passersby who gathered in increasing numbers to hear her simple yet powerful condemnation of capitalism. While Flynn was well aware of the social and political oppression of women in the early 20th century, she sought a greater change. From 1906 until her death in 1964, she truly believed that only with the overthrow of capitalism would women ever achieve real equality. Socialism

Elizabeth
Gurley
Flynn

would also address the exploitation of men as workers as well. Seeking change and feeling that the Socialist Party was "too stodgy," in 1906 Flynn joined the Industrial Workers of the World (IWW), a radical working-class organization founded the previous year. For the next ten years, she toured the country as one of their most powerful and beloved speakers and organizers.

Flynn was soon on the front lines. During the summer of 1907, while still a high-school student, Flynn participated in her first strike, aiding the Metal and Machinery Workers Union in Bridgeport, Connecticut. Later that summer, she traveled to Chicago for the annual IWW convention where she came to the attention of several IWW leaders. On her return to New York, Flynn stopped along the way, making speeches in Cleveland and Pittsburgh. She also visited factories and coal mines, gathering first-hand impressions of the difficult, even dangerous conditions under which American industrial workers labored. When the Pittsburgh IWW local paid her two weeks' salary for her organizing efforts there, Flynn suddenly realized she could make a living at what she loved best—speaking and organizing workers. Although she had planned on continuing her education and becoming a constitutional lawyer, the now 17-year-old Flynn quit high school and began her career as an IWW "jawsmith."

Socialism was a great discovery—a hope, a purpose, a flame within me, lit first by a spark from anthracite.

—Elizabeth Gurley Flynn

With her parents' reluctant permission, she traveled to the iron ore mines in Minnesota's Mesabi Range. Flynn had been invited to come there by a fellow IWW organizer and miner, John A. Jones, whom she had met at the previous summer's convention. A handsome man in his early 30s, Jack Jones represented everything that Flynn found so appealing about miners, the West and the IWW. As she later remembered in her autobiography, "I romanticized the life—so different from New York—and the organizer who lived and worked there, under conditions of hardship. I fell in love with him and we were married in January 1908."

Despite the romantic beginnings, the marriage was troubled from the start, and the two rarely lived together, separating for good in 1910. The young couple were both dedicated to their IWW work, and, during two pregnancies, the first of which ended in the birth of a premature infant who lived only a day, Flynn refused to quit. While Jones continued to focus on organizing Western miners, Flynn became involved in the free-speech fights that brought the IWW and its fiery young orator to national attention.

Local governments sought to limit the spread of the IWW by denying organizers the right to speak in public. First in Missoula, Montana, and then in Spokane, Washington, IWW members from across the country came to challenge local ordinances they saw as oppressive despite the risk of arrest and even police brutality. Most notable perhaps was the 19-year-old Flynn who was arrested in Missoula for her efforts there. Later in Spokane, she was arrested again in November 1909, visibly pregnant with her second child. The IWW won their right to free speech after a long and difficult struggle. However, by the spring of 1910, Flynn realized that her marriage to Jones was a struggle not to be won. In April, she traveled home to be with her mother in the South Bronx. There, in May 1910, Fred Flynn was born. Although Jack Jones came East and lived briefly with his wife and newborn son during the summer, the couple could not reconcile and soon separated permanently. They were officially divorced in 1920.

Flynn took a few months off but soon returned to organizing and speaking for the IWW. Her mother and her sister, **Kathie**, cared for Fred during Flynn's many absences. She felt guilty about the long periods away from her son. In turn, her son expressed his resentment more than once. But Flynn was passionate about her work. As a self-providing woman, she also needed the salary she received as an organizer.

The 1912 textile strike in Lawrence, Massachusetts, was the next major IWW campaign. Flynn was one of several IWW leaders who spent months in Lawrence during what was also known as the Bread and Roses strike. She was particularly effective in organizing women textile workers, many of whom spoke little English. From IWW leader William D. (Big Bill) Haywood, Flynn perfected the art of plain yet impassioned speaking that could reach even those workers who spoke little English. Along with the future birth-control advocate *Margaret Sanger, Flynn organized the placement of hundreds of the strikers' children in temporary foster homes outside of Lawrence. The underfed and underclothed appearance of these children as they arrived in New York and Vermont generated national headlines and helped to bring a successful settlement to the strike in March 1912.

It was in Lawrence that Flynn met the Italian anarchist, Carlo Tresca. Tresca, a handsome man who had been forced to leave Italy in 1904 because of his radical politics, was married to someone else, as was Flynn. However, the two fell in love and would live together for the next dozen years. They appeared to be the perfect couple, passionate about their work for the IWW and for each other. Yet, as time went on, Tresca increasingly urged Flynn to be less active, to stay home and care for him and her son Fred. As she had refused to give up her work for Jones, she now refused to do the same for Tresca who sought revenge through unfaithfulness. In 1925, after Flynn's youngest sister, **Bina**, gave birth to Tresca's son, the couple separated. Still, for the rest of her life, even after his murder by an assassin in 1943, Flynn considered Tresca to be her greatest love. From Lawrence to the less-successful IWW strikes in Paterson, New Jersey, in 1913 and on the Mesabi Range in 1916, Flynn and Tresca publicly and privately represented the passion of the IWW.

After a disagreement between Flynn and Haywood developed in late 1916, she changed her focus. When the United States entered World War I in April 1917, persecution of workers began on the federal level. Flynn, along with the radical Socialist *Ella Reeve Bloor, helped organize the Workers' Defense Union (WDU) in 1918. The WDU raised money and provided legal assistance for the thousands of workers arrested as suspected revolutionaries. In 1920, as the post-World War I "Red Scare" went into high gear, Flynn was a founding member of the National Civil Liberties Bureau, later the American Civil Liberties Union (ACLU). As a leader of both the WDU and ACLU, Flynn was a prominent part of the Sacco and Vanzetti defense movement during the 1920s. The two Italian anarchists were, many felt, falsely accused of murder because of their radical politics. Until Sacco and Vanzetti were finally executed in 1927, many liberals and radicals such as Flynn devoted themselves to freeing the pair. However, before that struggle ended in failure, Flynn collapsed in 1926.

She had just applied for membership in the recently formed Communist Party (CPUSA) and wanted to return to organizing workers rather than focus on their legal problems. At the same time, she was coping with the painful end to her long relationship with Carlo Tresca. While speaking in Portland, Oregon, Flynn became ill and was told by doctors she had heart disease and needed immediate and complete rest. An old friend and fellow radical, Dr. **Marie Equi**, took her in and nursed her back to health. It would be

ten years before Flynn returned to public life. Although she regained her strength within a couple years, she stayed in Portland caring for Equi after she became ill in 1928. Flynn increasingly felt trapped in this relationship and in 1937 finally broke away. Her brother Tom had just committed suicide, and Flynn used his death and the need to be with her mother as an excuse to return East.

Resuming political life was even more difficult as so much had changed. During her absence, Flynn had gained 70 pounds; she was now in her late 40s. So much of her public persona had been based on her youthful good looks as well as her radical politics. Further, during her ten-year stay in Portland, the Great Depression had begun in 1929. As part of the New Deal, labor organizing had received a new lease on life with the passage of the Wagner Act in 1935. Finally, the Communist Party was attempting to enter mainstream American politics through its efforts known as the Popular Front.

The broad-based policies of the CPUSA appealed to Flynn as well, and in 1937, sponsored by her old friend Bloor and Communist Party official William Z. Foster, she reapplied for membership. The application was immediately accepted and the party appointed Flynn to a salaried position. Still, she worried that her effectiveness as a radical had peaked. In a poem from 1939, Flynn wrote: "My ten lost years, the broken thread of work.... Frightened—was I a ghost, a passing legend?"

Although the first phase of her political career may have passed, Flynn would achieve much more in the years ahead. She quickly rose through the upper levels of the CPUSA hierarchy and was elected to the party's national committee in 1938. As a national organizer, she spoke across the country, often to the children of workers she had organized 30 years earlier. She wrote a regular column for the party newspaper, the *Daily Worker,* focusing on issues pertaining to women; she was also a member of the party's women's commission.

Yet, Flynn's life during the days just before the United States entered World War II was not without difficulty, even tragedy. Despite the efforts of the Popular Front, the CPUSA fell into disfavor with many American liberals in 1939 after the Soviet Union signed a treaty with Nazi Germany. What was to be a very brief alliance between fascism and communism affected Flynn a year later. In 1940, the executive board of the ACLU voted to expel her because of her activities for the CPUSA. Flynn was not only a member of the ACLU executive board, she had been one of the organization's founders in 1920. She refused to resign, publicly arguing that the ACLU condemnation of her was in violation of its own, most basic principles.

Flynn was finally expelled after a bitter internal trial made even worse by the recent death of her son. Fred Flynn died from lung cancer before his 30th birthday. Since her return from Portland a few years earlier, she had worked hard at reestablishing a relationship with the son she barely knew. Nonetheless, his early death caused her to lament all the years she had spent away. While she never once regretted her lifelong efforts to improve conditions for the American working class, she grieved over the effect her career had on her son. That grief, along with the trauma of her ex-lover Carlo Tresca's death in 1943, haunted her the rest of her life.

Flynn's work sustained her through these personal crises. In 1941, she was elected to the highest level of leadership in the CPUSA, the party's national board. Now that the United States and the Soviet Union were allies in the fight against fascism, the CPUSA joined the war effort on the home front. Flynn continued to speak and write, placing particular emphasis on women's role in ridding the world of fascism. When World War II ended, she went to Paris in November 1945 as a delegate to the Women's Congress where she opposed the fight for the Equal Rights Amendment (ERA), fearing that its passage would erase vital protective labor legislation for women.

At the end of the war, the CPUSA was divided by internal disputes over leadership and the direction the party should take in postwar America. Flynn did her best to avoid involvement in party factionalism. However, she did not escape the growing anti-communist reaction of the period that came to be known as the McCarthy era. In 1948, she led defense efforts for several top party officials arrested under the Smith Act for conspiring to teach or support the overthrow of the U.S. government through force or violence. In 1951, Flynn and 12 other party leaders were also indicted on the same charges.

Perhaps harkening back to her youthful ambitions to be a constitutional lawyer, Flynn acted as her own attorney during the nine-month trial. In her closing statement to the court, she stressed her love of America, arguing that she and her co-defendants sought not to overthrow the country, merely to improve it. Flynn also argued for the principles of free speech, much as she had more than 40 years earlier during her IWW days. She

told the court, "My body can be incarcerated but my thoughts will remain free and unaffected." She was sentenced to three years and, after numerous appeals failed, served her time in the women's federal penitentiary in Alderson, West Virginia, from January 1955 to May 1957.

Upon her release from prison, the now almost 66-year-old radical continued to play an active role in the CPUSA. As the Civil Rights movement grew in the early 1960s, Flynn urged her fellow American communists to support the efforts of African-Americans demanding their rights as citizens. She traveled to the Soviet Union in 1960 and again in 1961. Before her second visit, she was elected national chair of the CPUSA, the first woman to hold the office. During her third trip to the Soviet Union, she became ill and died there September 5, 1964. She received a state funeral and some of her ashes were placed beneath the Kremlin Wall. The rest of her ashes were returned to the United States and interned in Waldheim cemetery in Chicago, the final resting place of several other American radicals including Big Bill Haywood, Eugene Debs, and *Emma Goldman.

Elizabeth Gurley Flynn dedicated her life to bringing the message of socialism to the American people. Shortly before her release from prison in 1957, she wrote her sister Kathie, "I love this country and her varied people and I know them well. For over fifty years I have traveled back and forth across the broad bosom of my country, to make it a happier, more prosperous place to live in for our people."

SOURCES:

Baxandall, Rosalyn Fraad. *Words on Fire: The Life and Writing of Elizabeth Gurley Flynn*. New Brunswick, NJ: Rutgers University Press, 1987.

Flynn, Elizabeth Gurley. *The Rebel Girl: An Autobiography, My First Life, 1906–1926*. NY: International Publishers, 1973 (first published as *I Speak My Own Piece*, 1955).

SUGGESTED READING:

Dubofsky, Melvin. *We Shall Be All: A History of the Industrial Workers of the World*. Chicago, IL: Quadrangle Books, 1969.

Gallagher, Dorothy. *All the Right Enemies: The Life and Murder of Carlo Tresca*. New Brunswick, NJ: Rutgers University press, 1988.

RELATED MEDIA:

"Elizabeth Gurley Flynn: The Rebel Girl" video, directed by Leah Siegel, 1993.

COLLECTIONS:

Correspondence, papers, and memorabilia located in the Tamiment Library, New York University.

Kathleen Banks Nutter,
Manuscripts Processor at the Sophia Smith Collection,
Smith College, Northampton, Massachusetts

Fogerty, Elsie (1865–1945).

See Ashcroft, Peggy for sidebar.

Foix, Anne de (fl. 1480–1500)

*Queen of Bohemia and Hungary. Name variations: Anne de Fair. Flourished between 1480 and 1500; possibly daughter of *Madeleine of France (1443–1486) and Gaston de Foix, prince of Viane or Viana; possibly sister of *Catherine de Foix (c. 1470–1517); married Vladislav II also known as Ladislas II of Bohemia, king of Hungary (r. 1490–1516), king of Bohemia (r. 1471–1516); children: Louis II, king of Bohemia (r. 1516–1526), king of Hungary (r. 1516–1526); *Anna of Bohemia and Hungary (1503–1547, who married Ferdinand I, Holy Roman emperor, r. 1556–1564).*

Foix, Catherine de (c. 1470–1517).

See Margaret of Angoulême for sidebar.

Foix, Françoise de (c. 1490–1537).

See Châteaubriant, Comtesse de.

Foix, Germaine de (1488–1538).

See Juana la Beltraneja for sidebar.

Foix, Janine-Marie de (fl. 1377)

French soldier. Flourished in 1377 in France.

Few facts are available about the remarkable life of Janine-Marie de Foix, a French peasant who fought for King Charles V. Most medieval women's military careers involved planning and leading troops as feudal landholders or queens. Janine-Marie, however, was a common footsoldier, who held no special place in Charles' army but fought alongside her compatriots for three years.

Laura York,
Riverside, California

Foix, Margaret de (d. 1258).

See Margaret de Foix.

Foix, Marguerite de (fl 1456–1477).

See Marguerite de Foix.

Fokina, Vera (1886–1958)

Russian ballerina. Born Vera Petrovna in 1886; died in New York on July 29, 1958; graduated from the St. Petersburg Ballet School in 1904; married Michel Fokine, in 1905 (died 1942); children: one son, Vitale Fokine.

Vera Fokina supported the reforms of her husband Michel Fokine and danced in many of his ballets under the aegis of the Diaghileff company. In 1918, she formally resigned from the Maryinsky Theatre and, in 1924, settled with her husband in New York, where they formed their own company. During the 1920s, Fokina made many concert appearances in America, while also traveling widely with her husband who worked for numerous companies. She retired from the stage around 1928. After her husband's death in 1942, her health began to deteriorate, and she died in 1958.

Folcheid

*Duchess of Bavaria. Married Theodebert of Bavaria, duke of Bavaria; children: Hucbert, duke of Bavaria; *Guntrud of Bavaria; *Sunnichild (d. 741).*

Foley, Margaret (c. 1827–1877)

American sculptor. Born around 1827; died in Merano in 1877; grew up in rural Vergennes, Vermont.

Margaret Foley whittled and carved as a young girl in Vergennes, Vermont. She then worked in a textile mill in Lowell, Massachusetts, before moving to Boston in 1848 where she specialized in cameo portraits. In 1860, Foley immigrated to Rome and began to work on larger marble medallion portraits; one of her sitters was William Cullen Bryant. Despite a neurological disorder, she won international recognition; her marble fountain base, supported by three children, was unveiled at the 1876 Philadelphia Centennial Exposition; it now resides in Horticulture Center, West Fairmount Park, Philadelphia.

Foley, Martha (c. 1897–1977)

American editor and writer who was co-founder and co-editor of the magazine Story. *Born Martha Foley around 1897 in Boston, Massachusetts; died of heart disease on September 5, 1977, in Northampton, Massachusetts; daughter of Walter Foley and Margaret (McCarthy) Foley; married Whit Burnett (an editor, writer) in 1930 (divorced 1942); children: David Burnett (b. 1931).*

Worked as a Paris reporter for New York Herald *(1927); served as European correspondent for* New York Sun *(1929); was co-editor of* Story *(1931–42); lectured at University of Colorado (1935–36), Columbia University (1936), and New York University (1937); taught at Columbia University (1945–66).*

Works include: The Story of Story Magazine: A Memoir *(posthumously published, 1980); contributed short stories to periodicals; (co-editor)* A Story An-thology, 1931–1933: Thirty-three Selections From The European Years of "Story," the Magazine Devot-ed Solely to the Short Story *(1933); (co-editor)* Story in America, 1933–1934: Thirty-four Selections From The American Issues of "Story," the Magazine Devot-ed Solely to the Short Story *(1934); (co-editor)* U.S. Stories: Regional Stories from the Forty-eight States *(1949); (co-editor)* The Best of the Best American Short Stories, 1915–1950 *(1952); (co-editor)* Two Hundred Years of Great American Short Stories *(1975); editor or co-editor of the annual* The Best American Short Stories *(1942–76).*

A writer and editor who dedicated her career to the short-story genre, Martha Foley was born around 1897 in Boston, Massachusetts. Her fa-ther Walter Foley, a doctor, wanted Martha to be a teacher like her mother **Margaret McCarthy Foley**, but Martha displayed an early desire to be a writer. Her first short story was published in her school magazine when she was only 11. From 1909 to 1915, Foley attended the Boston Girls' Latin School; she then attended Boston University for two years before moving to New York to work. In 1922, she relocated to southern California, where she met editor Whit Burnett.

By 1926, Foley and Burnett were both working in New York, and by 1927 in Paris—she as a writer, he as an editor. In 1929, they worked in Vienna, Austria, for the Consolidated Press, for which Foley was Central European correspondent. In 1930, they married in a Vien-na town hall, and in 1931 their son David Bur-nett was born. Foley had recognized a need for a magazine devoted to short stories, and in the spring of 1931 she and Burnett published the first issue of *Story* magazine. The couple made no profit on the 167 mimeographed copies but were undaunted; their magazine was a literary "crusade" more than a business venture. Their dedication to fresh, top-quality stories, and aver-sion to the "too slick . . . pseudo O. Henry school of writing" paid off, and *Story* quickly garnered recognition and more readers.

In 1933, they relocated their reputable mag-azine to New York City. Maintaining high stan-dards and rejecting superficial stories with "trick endings," they introduced such writers as *Tess Slesinger, Richard Wright, and William Saroyan. Then in 1941, Foley accepted an offer to edit *The O'Brien Memorial Best Short Story Yearly Anthology* after the death of its editor Edward J. O'Brien, whom Foley counted among the people she "loved best in the world." The story of *Story*

parallels that of Foley and Burnett, and her res-ignation from their magazine hurt Burnett enough to precipitate their divorce in 1942.

Foley went on to edit *The Best American Short Stories* for Houghton-Mifflin for the next 34 years, co-editing it with her son David from 1958 until his death in 1971. She taught at Co-lumbia University from 1945 to 1966, where she encouraged young writers, and died in Massa-chusetts on September 5, 1977. Whit Burnett re-married in 1942, and his second wife *Hallie Southgate Burnett edited *Story* with him. *Story* magazine struggled after 1948, disappeared in 1951, resurfaced in 1960, and, lacking reader support, finally perished four years later.

SOURCES:
Current Biography, 1941. Edited by M. Block. NY: H.W. Wilson, 1941.

SUGGESTED READING:
Foley, Martha. The Story of STORY Magazine: A Mem-oir. Edited by J. Neugeboren. NY: Norton, 1980.

Jacquie Maurice,
Calgary, Alberta, Canada

Follett, Mary Parker (1868–1933)

American visionary of modern management theory and a proponent of democratic governance in organi-zations who worked as a social worker, political thinker, researcher, consultant, and author. Born Mary Parker Follett in Quincy, Massachusetts, on Sep-tember 3, 1868; died in Boston on December 18, 1933; daughter of Charles Allen Follett (a skilled tradesman) and Elizabeth Curtis (Baxter) Follett; had one younger brother; graduated from Thayer Acade-my in 1884 at age 15; attended the Society for the Col-legiate Instruction of Women in Cambridge, then an unaffiliated annex to Harvard University which be-came Radcliffe College; spent a year abroad in 1890-91 at Newnham College in Cambridge, England; at-tended intermittently and graduated summa cum laude from Radcliffe College in 1898 in economics, government, law and philosophy; also did postgradu-ate work in Paris; involved in long-term relationship for 30 years with Isobel Briggs (died 1926).

Returned to Boston after post-graduate studies in Paris to do social work and social service for 25 years; concurrently advised local and national organizations on management issues; pioneered the organization and management of vocational guidance centers in the pub-lic schools in Boston, the first program of its kind na-tionally (1917); served as chair of School Houses Sub-Committee to Women's Municipal League of Boston (around 1909); represented the people of Massachu-setts in various public bodies, including minimum-wage boards, arbitration boards, and public tribunals; served as vice president of the National Community Center Association (1917–21); worked as consultant to business, analyzing problems in factories and organizations (1920s); lectured on business organization and management (1925–33) at annual conferences of the Bureau of Personnel Administration in New York; moved to London (1929), where she continued to study industrial conditions and lecture; lived with Dame Katharine Furse until shortly before Follett's death.

Selected publications: The Speaker of the House of Representatives *(1896);* The New State—Group Organization, the Solution for Popular Government *(1918);* Creative Experience *(1924);* Freedom and Coordination *(1949); numerous papers in* Dynamic Administration—The Collected Papers of Mary Parker Follett *(1973).*

Unknowingly, modern management leaders have expressed the ideas of Mary Parker Follett—who never managed a business—decades after she pioneered the effective practice of management. After her death in 1933, her ideas, harbingers of contemporary management concepts, disappeared into the annals of management literature. She has since been acknowledged as a "prophet of management." Her ideas about flatter organizations, participative management, conflict resolution, and leadership derived from ability rather than position are ideas whose time came after their creator. When Follett introduced them in the 1920s, they did not reflect management trends of her day. Follett's fundamental abiding interest was in the individual in the group and society. Her innovative approach to social work was a point of departure for her philosophical and practical ideas about organizational management.

Mary Parker Follett was born on September 3, 1868, in Quincy, Massachusetts, to a family of English-Scottish-Welsh heritage. Her parents were Charles Allen Follett and **Elizabeth Baxter Follett**. After her adored father, a skilled tradesman, died, responsibility for the household, its financial affairs, and her younger brother fell to Mary since her mother was an invalid. After graduating from the Thayer Academy in 1884, she studied English, political economy, and history for two years at the Society for the Collegiate Instruction of Women, which would become Radcliffe College. During a year of classes abroad at Cambridge University in England, where she studied history, law, and political science, she wrote a paper that would be the core of her first book, *The Speaker of the House of*

Mary Parker Follett

Representatives (1896), which described in practical terms how the U.S. Congress worked and how effective representatives exert their power and influence. Her time at Cambridge instilled an interest in English life and matured her, but before she could take exams she was called home because of her mother's illness. Returning to Radcliffe after finishing her book, she received her bachelor's degree in 1898, graduating summa cum laude at the age of 29.

An inheritance from her mother's father made Follett financially independent. She spent the next 25 years as a volunteer doing social work in Boston, initially with clubs for boys and men in Roxbury, a poor section of Boston. In 1902, she chaired a committee that sponsored clubs in local schools, which she thought a better location than the patronizing environment of a settlement house. A series of community centers resulted. In 1908, Follett joined as chair of the Committee on Extended Use of School Buildings sponsored by the new Women's Municipal League of Boston, which focused on plans of action for solving community problems in cooperation with city agencies. Her innovative approach to management problems was apparent even in her social work activities. To get young people off the streets at night, her committee pioneered evening programs in the public schools. By 1914, the Boston School Centers had spread to six high schools with an attendance of around 7,000 young people. To address the need of school dropouts who attended the evening programs, she developed a vocational Boston Placement Bureau, working with a coalition of local community agencies, which expanded to serve all of Boston. Eventually this became part of the school system. Follett served as vice president of the National Community Center Association from 1917 to 1921. Her pioneering work has been acknowledged as a major influence on the emerging field of social work.

Follett's social-service activities that addressed management problems became a foundation for her later work in industrial management. Her second book, *The New State* (1918), began as a report on her work but became a critique of American institutions and political theory. She proposed the gradual replacement of various governmental institutions by a network of occupational, local, regional, state, national, and international groups. Follett introduced a theme that would inform her life work—group dynamics, which she had observed at the school centers. In light of corrupt practices of government officials, her ideas were new and welcome, and the book built her reputation.

The potentialities of the individual remain potentialities until they are released by group life. Thus, the essence of democracy is creating. The technique of democracy is group organization.

—Mary Parker Follett

Her books reflect an evolving perspective, from philosophical idealism to the new psychology of the day with its emphasis on group experience. She recognized that social life is constantly changing and is built on interrelationships and interwoven experiences; her recognition of the social life of organizations anticipated by decades similar observations of many in the industrial management field.

Follett's next book, *Creative Experience* (1924), concentrated even more on the subject of group experience. Through Henry Dennison, a board member of the Boston Placement Bureau, she observed the Dennison Manufacturing Company's progressive personnel policies in action at the Framingham, Massachusetts, headquarters. She also studied Filene's department store in Boston, Rountree and Co., Ltd., in York, England, and the Economic Division of the League of Nations. Insights about business that she published in *Creative Experience* popularized her ideas among business leaders and brought her invitations to lecture and consult. Her work at the Rountree Cocoa Works led to lecture conferences for managers and supervi-

sors that took place at Balliol College, Oxford, on weekends.

Follett developed her ideas against a backdrop of the popular early 19th-century scientific management theory of Frederick Taylor, who focused on time-and-motion studies to determine how workers could do their jobs better; the worker, at the low end of a stratified organization that operated in a command style, was seen by Taylor as a tool of industry. Follett's approach was to use workers' firsthand experience to learn about management. Proponents of Taylorism, she said, "ignore one of the fundamental facts of human nature, namely, the wish to govern one's own life."

Because the study of organizations alone was not enough, she used participant observation to understand how people behave in groups. Follett's research involved everyone she met; from industrialist to maid, she engaged everyone in conversation to understand a range of perspectives. By 1925, she was lecturing on business organization and management. A year later, at a lecture for a British audiences at Oxford, she explained the rationale for her involvement:

> The most profound philosophers have always given us unifying as the fundamental principle of life. And now business men are finding it is the way to run a successful business. Here the ideal and the practical have joined hands. That is why I am working at business management, because, while I care for the ideal, it is only because I want to help bring it into our everyday affairs.

Her lectures featured at annual conferences of the Bureau of Personnel Administration in New York between 1925 and 1932 were part of a series presented by leaders from a range of fields. They were designed to bridge the gap between the academic education of managers and administrators and their need for pragmatic information related to their changing industrial environments. Follett's lectures were later collected in the book *Dynamic Administration*.

According to Elliot Fox and L. Urwick, the editors of her collected papers, Follett had two fundamental concepts that were "at once simple, profound, and far-reaching." The first was the "universal fact," a circular or reciprocal response, to which Follett assigned numerous other terms as well. She did not believe that a simple stimulus-response existed between parties to an interaction in real life; rather, the parties influence each other and together produce a situation. Situations were always multifaceted, influenced by all the relationships that have bearing on the thoughts of the parties involved. Each situation was a dynamic process.

The second basic concept was the universal goal of integration, a harmonious synthesis of differences to produce a new result (she also referred to this as unifying, synthesis or coordination). Each solution has seeds of new differences, but they, in turn, contain the seeds of new solutions; thus the continuous environment of change is a fact of life.

Peter Drucker observes that of Follett's work, the most well known concerns her ideas about conflict management: "Constructive Conflict." She wrote, "As conflict—difference—is here in this world, as we cannot avoid it, we should, I think, use it to work for us." Assuming that both sides are right, they will give right answers, but to different questions. Follett believed that accurate information and expertise could only inform difference: "the object is not to do away with difference but to do away with *muddle*. . . . Difference based on inaccuracy is meaningless." According to Follett, the resolution of conflict hinges on using the understanding of each side's perspective to integrate the interests of both positions. This creative adjustment to different interests leads to "plus-values," new values that represent creative responses to social conflict. This is different from compromise, where each side gives something away. However, Follett did acknowledge that all disputes can be settled by integration and that irreconcilable differences can exist.

There are three types of leadership, suggests Follett: leadership of position, leadership of personality, and leadership of function, which she called the most important. She saw the leader's basic focus as organizing and integrating experience; the effective leader provides opportunities for participation, showing others how to meet their own responsibilities, and each individual assumes responsibility for a piece of the whole. Follett saw organizations evolving so leadership would assume "horizontal rather than a vertical authority," spurring easier exchange of information within organizations, which echoes modern management theory. In *Creative Experience,* she associated exercising leadership with cultivation: discovering a purpose in a situation was like finding an unfamiliar plant one cultivates without knowing what to expect; when it bears fruit, the purpose of the work comes clear.

Follett also was a proponent of worker participation, which encourages integration of the differences she promoted for resolving conflicts. She saw employee participation in management as a way of increasing collective responsibility but with limitations. Labor would assist management not by sharing existing power, but by developing joint power, therefore creating new power. Follett saw "power over" or domination as an obstacle to integration. She defined power as "the ability to make things happen." Integrated situations were characterized by "power with," which meant that individual power would be unified for the total power of the group. The power-with model is inherent in Follett's concept of conflict resolution as well as cooperation.

Some have criticized Follett for too much idealism in management. Her work suggests that everything is possible at the same time, e.g. collectivism can exist with individualism and freedom. However, Follett saw her idealism as reflecting a possible world, not an ideal world. She expressed in her work a belief in the potential for change in human nature and that education can change attitudes. Critics also note that her belief in the potential to integrate interests depends on a particular configuration of interests, and objectives and means to achieve integrative solutions may differ. Supporters, like Fox and Urwick, say she was in the vanguard of applying social science findings to the practice of management. By the time of her death in 1933 during the Depression era, sheer survival characteristics of management thinking had supplanted the interest of the 1920s in creative use of human potential.

According to **Rosabeth Moss Kanter**, Follett's long-term influence was not assured because she was neither an academic nor a chief executive who could sustain the impact of her work through a base of student disciples or an exemplary organization. Peter Drucker has noted that her ideas were against the management trends of the 1930s and 1940s. Making government more controlling and more powerful was in opposition to Follett's focus on the individual and reinventing the citizen; because of this, Follett was perceived as a subversive.

Commenting on the continuing respect for Follett's work in England and Japan since its introduction decades ago, Kanter writes in *Mary Parker Follett: Prophet of Management* that she was less of an immediate threat given the greater geographic distance. The Japanese started a Follett association in the 1950s to study her work. Her perspective of individuals as interdependent and interconnected reflects Japanese sensibilities about group membership, according to Tokihiko Enomoto. In 1991, the Society of Professionals in Dispute Resolution, whose members are involved in mediation and arbitration in the public and private sectors in the United States, established a Mary Parker Follett Award.

Follett has been described as a plain woman with an engaging manner who had little taste for power and prestige. She read Latin, Greek, French and German, and her interests included music, painting, nature and travel. Her circle of friends and acquaintances encompassed intellectual and social leaders of Boston, and leading industrialists—all of whom provided her with numerous connections. For three decades, Follett had a long-term relationship with **Isobel L. Briggs**, an Englishwoman 20 years her senior. They lived at Otis House in Boston until Briggs' death in 1926. Two years later, Follett met Dame *Katharine Furse, head of the World Association of Girl Guides and Girl Scouts, during trips to Geneva to study the League of Nations. In 1929, Follett moved to London and lived with Furse in her Chelsea home.

Follett continued to study British industry and lecture in England, including a series at the London School of Economics, and in America. In 1933, she returned to Boston on financial business. In poor health, Mary Parker Follett died in Boston after an operation on December 18, 1933. Her ashes were taken to Putney, Vermont, where she had enjoyed enlightening conversation with friends in the summer home she had shared with Isobel Briggs.

SOURCES:

Follett, Mary Parker. *Creative Experience*. NY: Longmans, Green, 1924.
———. *Freedom and Coordination*. London: Management Publications Trust, 1949.
Fox, Elliot M. and L. Urwick, eds. *Dynamic Administration—The Collected Papers of Mary Parker Follett*. NY: Pittman, 1973.
Graham, Pauline, ed. *Mary Parker Follett—Prophet of Management; A Celebration of Writings from the 1920s*. Boston, MA: Harvard Business School Press, 1995.
Linden, Dana Wechler. "The Mother of Them All," in *Forbes*. January 15, 1995, pp. 75–76.

Laurie Norris,
intercultural relations consultant who works
with immigrants and refugees encountering U.S. culture
and making work transitions, New York, New York

Follin or Folline, Miriam (1836–1914).

See Leslie, Miriam Folline Squier.

Foltz, Clara (1849–1934)

American political and social reformer who was the first woman admitted to the California bar. Born Clara Shortridge in Indiana, possibly in New Lisbon, Henry County, on July 16, 1849; died in Los Angeles, California, on September 2, 1934; second child and only daughter of five children of Elias Willets Shortridge (a druggist, minister, and lawyer) and Talitha Cumi (Harwood) Shortridge; attended Howe's Female Seminary, Iowa, 1840–43; briefly attended Hastings College of Law, San Francisco; married Jeremiah Richard Foltz (a businessman), on December 30, 1864 (widowed or divorced, 1877); children: two sons and three daughters.

A pioneering lawyer and the first woman to be admitted to the California bar, Clara Foltz was also a political and social reformer, particularly in the area of women's rights. Her hard-won career was combined with caring for five children, which, despite her feminism, she considered to be her primary responsibility in life. Foltz was admired for her wit, her charm and spirit, and her intelligent, elegant courtroom demeanor.

Born in New Lisbon, she grew up in Wayne County, Indiana, and Mount Pleasant, Iowa, where she attended Howe's Female Seminary for three years. She taught school until her marriage to businessman Jeremiah Foltz in December 1864. The couple lived for a short time in Portland, Oregon, then moved to San Jose, California. There Jeremiah ran a grocery store and sold real estate, and Clara gave birth to five children, wrote newspaper articles, and occasionally gave lectures on women's suffrage. After her husband's death in 1877 (by one account, the couple divorced), Foltz was left to provide for the children. With the help of her parents, who had followed her to San Jose in 1876, she began to read law with a local attorney and soon discovered that the California constitution admitted to the bar only "white male" citizens. Foltz drew up an amendment striking out these limitations and, aided by *Laura de Force Gordon and other suffragists, pushed it through the California legislature, where it was passed in April 1878. In September of that year, Foltz was admitted to practice in the 20th District Court at San Jose. The following year, when she and Gordon were denied admission to the state-supported Hastings College of Law in San Francisco, they each filed suit to force the college to accept women. Both women, acting as their own counsel, successfully argued their case through the 4th District Court and eventually the California Supreme Court. Foltz enrolled at Hastings but due to the demands of her growing law practice was only able to attend for a short time. On December 6, 1879, she and Gordon became the second and third women to be admitted to the bar of the state supreme court. Foltz also served as clerk of the state assembly's judiciary committee (1879–80), the first woman so appointed.

Foltz successfully practiced law for over 20 years but not without interruptions. For two years, beginning in 1887, she lived in San Diego, where she founded a daily newspaper, the *San Diego Bee*. After winning admittance to the New York bar in 1896, she briefly opened an office in New York City. Although she was primarily a divorce and probate lawyer, her growing business interests also led her into corporate law, and in 1905 she organized a women's department for her client the United Bank and Trust Company of San Francisco. That year, she also founded and published a trade magazine, *Oil Fields and Furnaces* (later merged into the *National Oil Reporter*).

From 1906, Foltz lived and worked in Los Angeles, where, in addition to her busy law practice, she continued to pursue interests in women's rights, social welfare, and politics. Having organized the Portia Law Club in San Francisco in 1893, she also helped found the Women Lawyers Club in 1918 and for several years conducted a law school for women in her Los Angeles office. An active suffragist, she was president of the California Woman Suffrage Association in the 1880s and, in 1884, ran for the office of presidential elector on the Equal Rights ballot headed by *Belva Ann Lockwood. Foltz played an important role in the campaign that secured the vote for women in state elections in 1911. From 1916 to 1918, she published the feminist magazine *New American Woman*. She also championed legislation that allowed women to serve as the executors and administrators of estates and to hold commissions as notary publics.

Much of Foltz's social-welfare work centered on penal reform and the administration of justice. She was a leader in the movement to appoint public defenders for indigent defendants and worked for the segregation of adult and juvenile prisoners, as well as for modification of the parole system. In 1910, she was the first woman appointed to the State Board of Charities and Corrections, a post she held until 1912.

Foltz was active in both state and national politics, usually in conjunction with the Republican Party. In 1886, however, she left the party to support Democratic gubernatorial candidate Washington Bartlett, who, when elected, appointed her a trustee of the State Normal School. In Los Angeles, she was the first woman appointed deputy district attorney and served two terms. In 1921, she refused an appointment as

assistant U.S. attorney general. In 1930, at age 81, Foltz entered the Republican primary as a candidate for governor, receiving a respectable 8,000 votes. Two years later, plans for a second run for governor were cut short by a heart attack. Clara Foltz died on September 2, 1934, and was buried in Hollywood Park Cemetery in Los Angeles.

SOURCES:

James, Edward T., ed. *Notable American Women*. Cambridge, MA: The Belknap Press of Harvard University Press, 1971.

McHenry, Robert, ed. *Famous American Women*. NY: Dover, 1983.

Barbara Morgan,
Melrose, Massachusetts

Fonseca, Marchesa de (c. 1768–1799).

See Pimentel, Eleonora.

Fontaine, Joan (b. 1917).

See joint entry under de Havilland, Olivia.

Fontaine, Mlle de la (1655–1738)

French ballerina. Born in 1655; died in 1738.

It wasn't until 1630 that the public was admitted to France's court ballets. Before long, they had their first premiere ballerina, *la première des premières danseuses*, the "Queen of Dance." Not much is known about Mlle de la Fontaine. Historians have more information about her audience: rowdy, demanding, drunk, and often accompanied by dogs. Mlle de la Fontaine left the stage and her audience for a life in the church.

Fontana, Lavinia (1552–1614)

*Bolognese painter, mainly of portraits and holy scenes, who gave a successful example of Italian painting during the Counter-Reformation. Name variations: Lavinia Fontana Zappi; Lavinia Fontana de Zappis. Born Lavinia Fontana in August 1552 in Bologna, Italy; died in Rome, Italy, on August, 11, 1614; daughter of Prospero Fontana (a painter) and Antonia De Bonardis (who came from a printer's family in Parma); married Giovan Paolo Zappi, in 1577; children: Emilia (b. 1578); Orazio (b. 1578); Orazio (b. 1579); **Laura Zappi** (b. 1581); Flaminio (b. 1583); Orazio (b. 1585); Severo (b. 1587); Laodamia or **Laudomia Zappi** (1588–1605); Prospero (b. 1589); Severo (b. 1592); **Costanza Zappi** (b. 1595).*

Major paintings: Self-Portrait in the Studio (Florence, Galleria degli Uffizi, 1579); (first known public

Lavinia Fontana, self-portrait.

(1593–c. 1652), the unlucky Bolognese painter *Elisabetta Sirani (1638–1665), the Florentine miniaturist **Giovanna Garzoni Domenica Maddalena Caccia**, daughter of Moncalvo, and Fontana's contemporaries **Barbara Longhi** from Imola (1552–1638) and Venetian **Marietta Robusti**, whose father was Tintoretto. Undoubtedly, at least in Italy, birth into an artistic household was the only way for a woman to become an artist. It was unacceptable for women to enter the *botteghe,* run by well-known male painters, as students. Generally speaking, as painters' daughters their learning occurred naturally during their early years, in an informal way, within the walls of their homes. In fact, women belonging to artists' families often aided their fathers and husbands, grinding, mixing and preparing colors, painting in backgrounds on canvases, and even painting unimportant portions of major paintings, but of course without signing their contributions. The private lives of Italian women who became recognized artists often offered only difficulties, failures, or tragic ends. (Artemisia Gentileschi was raped; Elisabetta Sirani died of poison; and many spent their lives wandering in foreign courts.) A conventional life with a husband and a family was not the rule. Lavinia Fontana was an exception, even among women painters: she had an independent, successful career and an ordinary life as a wife and mother.

Bologna, in Fontana's time, was the second largest city of the Papal State. A well-known university town with 50,000 inhabitants, its bourgeoisie and nobility were wealthy but rather provincial. Rome attracted many of the Bolognese who entered a religious career or made a living from related activities, often in decorative arts. Moreover, the mid-16th century was turbulent: after a period of wars culminated in the Sacco di Roma (1527), the Italian peninsula was rife with political and religious tensions. Following the establishment of Spanish influence (which directly governed the State of Milan and the Kingdom, later to be called Kingdom of the Two Sicilies), the Council of Trent (1545–1563) ended the period of theological disputes, but it affected the rest of the century by its strict vision of the world. Even painting was strongly controlled (as well as sponsored) by the Roman Catholic Church. In arts, the Renaissance was over, Mannerism was fashionable, and Baroque was on the horizon. It was in such an atmosphere that Prospero Fontana's daughter was to reach her artistic maturity.

Young Lavinia was baptized on August 24, 1552, in the Metropolitan church of St. Pietro.

commission) Assumption of the Virgin with Saints Peter Crisologus and Cassian *(Imola, Pinacoteca Comunale, 1583);* Portrait of the Gozzadini Family *(Bologna, Pinacoteca Nazionale, 1584);* Portrait of Lady with Dog *(Baltimore, Walters Art Gallery, c. 1584);* Ritratto del frate Panigarola *(Florence, Uffizi, 1585);* Portrait of a Noblewoman from the Ruini family *(Florence, Galleria di Palazzo Pitti, 1593);* Judith and Holophern *(Bologna, Museo Davia Bargellini, 1600);* Conversation-piece *(Milan, Pinacoteca Nazionale di Brera, c. 1600);* The Queen of Sabah Visiting King Solomon *(Dublin, National Gallery of Ireland, c. 1600);* Cleopatra *(Rome, Galleria Spada);* Dressing Minerva *(Rome, Galleria Borghese, 1613). Signs works: Lavinia Fontana virgo (before her wedding); Lavinia Fontana de Zappis (most frequently later).*

Lavinia Fontana has to be considered a *figlia d'arte,* for she was the daughter of a painter, Prospero Fontana. This was the rule for the vast majority of Italian women painters of the 16th and 17th centuries, the only exception being the noblewoman *Sofonisba Anguissola (1532–1625). Other artists who grew up in artistic households were the Milanese still-life painter *Fede Galizia (1578–1630), the famous *Artemisia Gentileschi

WOMEN IN WORLD HISTORY

Born a few days before (date unknown), she was the daughter of the celebrated painter Prospero (1512–1597) and Antonia di Bartolomeo De Bonardis (d. 1607), who were married in 1539. Her only mentioned brother and sister were Flaminio and Emilia, both of whom died before 1577 (in fact, in her wedding contract Lavinia is said to be Prospero Fontana's only daughter). It is, however, impossible to state if Prospero's family had been larger, but heavily hit by the high infant mortality rate in an age when only 50% of children born made it to adulthood. It is known that Lavinia grew up in material comfort. Her father had been a well-known artist since the early 1540s, even outside of Bologna; he worked with Perin del Vaga and the brothers Zuccari, all three major artists of the Mannerist movement, and he was patronized by Pope Julius III Ciocchi del Monte (1550–1555), who gave him an annual pension of 60 scudis. Despite his frequent absence during Lavinia's childhood (in 1553–55, he was working in Rome; in 1560, probably in Fontainbleu, France; in 1563–65, in Florence; in 1665–70, in the Tuscan Citta' di Castello), Prospero owned a *bottega* (studio) in Bologna. In 1569, he founded a new guild for painters in that city and became its leader. In 16th-century Bologna, any artisan (including painters, who were considered manual workers until the end of that century) needed citizenship, a license and guild membership, in order to run a studio with pupils and helpers. In such a position, Prospero was at the center of local Bolognese artistic life and many major painters were among his pupils, including Lorenzo Sabbatini (1530–1577), Orazio Samacchini (1532–1577), the Flemish Denis Calvaert (1540–1619), Bartolomeo Passarotti (1529–1592), the French sculptor Giambologna (Jean de Boulogne, 1529–1608), Bartolomeo Cesi (1556–1629) and, above all, the young brothers Ludovico (1555–1619), Agostino (1557–1602) and Annibale Carracci (1560–1609). Prospero was also well-positioned within the town's intellectual milieu and was a close friend of the naturalist Ulisse Aldrovandi, who taught at Bologna University. Moreover, he personally collaborated with Bologna bishop, Cardinal Gabriele Paleotti, who had been an adviser to the Council of Trent in its last days and an intimate friend of Carlo Borromeo, the Milanese archbishop and future saint. Thanks to Prospero's technical support, in 1582 Paleotti was able to publish his treatise on holy images and paintings, defined by the historian Roberto Zapperi as the Inquisition's handbook on images.

It is possible to claim that Lavinia took advantage of her privileged position, breathing art, as she did, from the cradle, and, more practically, inheriting her father's ambient connections, patrons and clients. Documents do not provide any details about Lavinia's childhood and adolescence until the year 1577, and no information exists about her instruction. One century later, in 1678, Lavinia's first historian Carlo Cesare Malvasia (whose lengthy work on Bolognese painting is of lasting importance) states that Lavinia's father personally took care of her artistic education, but we know for certain that she never worked in the *bottega*. Apart from painting and drawing, she learned reading and writing, and it is unknown whether or not she entered a convent as a boarder, a usual course for well-brought-up girls. In any case, she received a good education, which also provided her with proper manners, typical of an upper-class girl and useful in dealing with important clients, as would later occur. Her few preserved letters attest to a polished and skilled Italian. Art historian Cantaro points out that Lavinia writes in an elegant and cultivated hand. In her *Portrait of Alfonso Lorenzo Strozzi* (Florence, Collection of the Earls Dal Pero), painted in 1579, the gentleman holds in his left hand a long, beautifully written, business letter. Finally, in all her self-portraits *(Self-portrait at a Clavichord with Servant,* 1577, *Self-Portrait in the Studio,* 1579, and the *Self-portrait,* drawing, 1595), she underlines her lady-like attitude and social status, showing elegant, jewel-ornate dresses. In the first, she paints herself playing an instrument, as did Sofonisba Anguissola (whom Lavinia knew and appreciated) in one of her own self-portraits. In the second, she is holding a pen and sitting at her desk.

On February 14, 1577, Prospero promised Lavinia to the son of his friend Severo Zappi, a grain merchant. Giovan Paolo Zappi, who in correspondence was identified as "very wealthy and almost a gentleman," was an amateur painter and one of Prospero's students. He was to marry Lavinia before June 1577. As a present to her groom's family, Lavinia sent her *Self-portrait at a Clavichord with Servant.* Upon viewing the painting, Severo Zappi, who had never met Lavinia, wrote that the bride was "not fair and not ugly, but just in the middle, as women have to be." The wedding contract (Lavinia presumably was not there, for she did not sign it) stated that the new couple were to live with Prospero and Antonia, and contribute to the family and share the income from Lavinia's work. On his part, Prospero willingly provided them with housing, food, and clothing, as well as Lavinia's dowry, composed of a house and property.

In the first 15 years of marriage, Lavinia gave birth to a series of children, but, as we know from Giovan Paolo's notebook of *Ricordanze,* of the eleven children, only four reached adulthood. The children's godfathers' and godmothers' names (all belonging to Bologna's high nobility, like the Gozzadini, Boncompagni and Paleotti) make apparent the high status enjoyed by the Fontana-Zappi family, thanks to Lavinia's art. Since the number of her commissions was increasing significantly in these years (she was living in Bologna, only traveling in the neighborhood), it seems probable that she did not nurse her babies (breastfeeding was the first, primitive form of contraception, but usually upper-class women avoided it and preferred to give their babies to wetnurses). Her *Birth of the Virgin* (c. 1590, Bologna, church of SS. Trinita), which is considered among her greatest paintings, represents the scene of a delivery. While lying in bed eating an apple, St. *Anne recovers from the birth assisted by a serving girl who holds a bed warmer; the baby *Mary the Virgin is being washed near the fireplace; completing the domestic scene are a dog and a cat in a corner. Although this subject belongs to a strong icono-

Portrait of a Lady with a Lapdog, *by Lavinia Fontana.*

graphic tradition, the way Lavinia paints it suggests her personal participation and experience.

During the years of her maternities, Lavinia continued to work hard with great success. Though she was still not admitted to the Bolognese painters' guild—usually Italian women were not, unless they were widowed—Lavinia certainly belonged to the painters' world. Her remarkable production of paintings—oil on canvas, wood and copper—(and a few drawings) testify to her busy creative life. The full catalogue of her work, assembled by the art historian **Maria Teresa Cantaro** in 1989, identifies about one-hundred works as incontestably attributed, usually dated and signed, and now located in Italian and foreign museums. In her early period, Lavinia's style is strongly influenced by her father's, but shows as well the influences of Emilian painters, like Correggio or the less famous Lelio Orsi, and the Fontainbleau school, revisited in a Flemish use of light, and, later, of the Carraccis' naturalism.

The first historical evidence of Lavinia's work dates from the early 1570s. At the beginning of her career, she preferred small formats, representing holy scenes for domestic and private piety. In the same period, and particularly in the following two decades, she was cultivating her real talent, portraiture. This field often brought women painters success for one practical reason: gentlemen preferred having their wives and daughters pose for long hours in front of a woman painter, within their palaces. In general, portraits provided the only way to capture and preserve people from the oblivion of the death. Often portraits pictured people who had died long before, as happens in the beautiful *Portrait of the Gozzadini Family*, where the gentleman sitting at the center of the table, as well as his daughter who gives him her hand, had died in 1561 and 1581, respectively. Lavinia painted this picture in 1584. Moreover, since portraits testified to the importance (and wealth) these individuals had reached during their lives, the subjects were usually painted with objects and in an atmosphere that indicated their professions. At the same time, it was crucial to protect people who asked for portraits from the Counter-Reformation accusation of *superbia*: only kings and Popes were allowed to have themselves painted. When, probably in 1578, Lavinia portrayed Carlo Sigonio, the famous historian and professor at Bologna University, she was fulfilling the request made by the Dominican Spanish father Alfonso Chacon, who was collecting portraits of eminent men and women "who were relevant for their holy lives, . . . their bravery in the army or the liberal arts."

More precisely, Lavinia possessed a certain talent in realistically capturing the physiognomy of her subjects. She paid much attention to small details, such as embroidery, lace and jewels that women and men wore when they posed, showing all possible status symbols. Even dogs, besides the significance of fidelity, were proof of a high status. Furs had the same aim (beside the practical one of attracting lice from the clothes and bodies of the ladies), as in the sable worn by the *Noblewoman* (painting now in Washington D.C., National Museum of Women in the Arts).

> *Pittora singolare tra le donne . . . che andava al pari delli primi huomini di quella professione.* (A unique painter among women . . . who was at the same level of the most excellent men painters in that profession.)
>
> —Roma, Archivio Segreto Vaticano, Avvisi Urbinati, Lat. 1077, f. 428.

In the same years, Lavinia did several public commissions. In 1584, she painted the 1.5 meters by 2.5 *Assumption of the Virgin with Saints Peter Crisologus and Cassian* for the Municipal Council in Imola. This painting is an oil on canvas, for, since it was not acceptable for women to paint in public places (even in churches), the commissioned frescoes could not be done in loco. Lavinia's success culminated in 1589, when she painted a *Holy Family with the Sleeping Child and Young St. John the Baptist* for the Escorial monastery, Pantheon of the Infants (still on the main altar, for which it was commissioned). King Philip II of Spain paid the enormous price of 1,000 ducats for this picture (whereas in the same period the now very famous Annibale Carracci received only 800 ducats for paintings of similar size). This altar-piece is considered one of Fontana's masterpieces.

Lavinia moved with her family to Rome (1603–04), the last step of her successful career. The center of life was now in the capital. She was famous enough to survive without the Boncompagni family's patronage, which had protected and helped her from the beginning of her career, when Ugo Boncompagni was sitting on St. Peter's chair as Pope Gregory XIII (1572–1585). Throughout her life, Lavinia had strong supporters, and in Rome she lived in Cardinal d'Este's palace. The beginning of her stay brought criticism of the huge pala she did for the church of San Paolo fuori le Mura (destroyed in the 1823 fire). This was her last public commission. Still, in the following years Lavinia preserved a certain amount of success. She portrayed a number of important people, including Pope Paul V and the Persian ambassador (both portraits have been lost); and she painted small paintings on mythological (rather rare in her work) or historical subjects, like the famous *Cleopatra (VII) (Rome, Galleria Spada). Between 1611 and 1614, in the church of Santa Maria della Pace, she painted four full-length saints (the virgins *Cecilia, *Agnes, Claire, and *Catherine of Siena; oil on slate), decorating the Rivaldi Chapel, designed by the architect Carlo Maderno.

On August 13, 1614, Lavinia Fontana died in Rome, at the age of 62, and she was buried in the Dominican church of St. Maria sopra Minerva. Only three of her eleven children outlived her. Her sons, Flaminio, Orazio and Prospero, wrote the text of the engraved tombstone, now destroyed, which told of her being a proved painter whose "fame reached outside the feminine sphere." Her husband Giovan Paolo, who is not mentioned there, died in his native town Imola two years later. He had spent all his life as Lavinia's personal manager. With her death, the glory of the rest of the family was over, and they all moved back to Imola.

In the following centuries, the fame Lavinia Fontana enjoyed in life disappeared. She was remembered more as being a prodigy of nature, a woman painter as skilled as a man painter. Only in recent times has her talent been discovered again, in the wake of the recent attention to women's history.

SOURCES:

Cantaro, Maria Teresa. *Lavinia Fontana bolognese "pittora singolare."* Milano-Roma: Jandi Sapi, 1989.

Fortunati, Vera, ed. *Lavinia Fontana, 1552–1614.* Milano: Electa, 1994.

Fortunati Pietrantonio, Vera. "Lavinia Fontana—Bologna 1552—Roma 1614." in *Nell'eta' di Correggio e dei Carracci. Pittura in Emilia dei secoli XVI e XVII.* Bologna, Pinacoteca Nazionale e Accademia di Belle Arti Museo Civico Archeologico, September 10–November 10, 1986. Bologna: Nuova Alfa Editoriale, pp. 132–135.

Galli, Romeo. *Lavinia Fontana pittrice.* Imola: Tipografia P. Galeati, 1940.

Ghirardi, Angela. "Una pittrice bolognese nella Roma del primo Seicento: Lavinia Fontana," in *Il Carrobbio.* Vol. 10, 1984, pp. 146–181.

Harris, A. Sutherland, and L. Nochlin. *Women Artists, 1550–1950.* (Italian translation, Milan, Feltrinelli, 1979, pp. 21–32).

Malvasia, Carlo Cesare. *Felsina pittrice. Vite dei pittori bolognesi.* Vol. 1. Bologna: D. Barbieri, 1678, pp. 215–224.

Zapperi, Roberto. "La corporation des peintres et la censure des images a Bologne au temps des Carrache," in *Revue d'histoire moderne et contemporaine.* Vol. 38, 1991, pp. 387–400.

Francesca Medioli,
Lecturer in Italian Studies at the University of Reading, Reading, United Kingdom, has published and lectured widely on cloistered women in Early Modern Italy

Fontanges, Duchesse de (1661–1681).

See Montespan, Françoise for sidebar.

Fontanne, Lynn (1887–1983)

British-born star of the American stage who, together with her American husband Alfred Lunt, formed the most celebrated acting couple in the history of the American theater. Born Lillie Louise Fontanne in Woodford, Essex County, England, on December 6, 1887; died on July 30, 1983; youngest of five daughters of Jules Pierre Antoine Fontanne (a French designer of printing type) and Frances Ellen (Thornley) Fontanne; attended local schools in various parts of London; studied acting under Ellen Terry (1903–05); married Alfred Lunt, Jr., on May 26, 1922; no children.

First visited the U.S. (1910); came permanently to appear with Laurette Taylor (1916); teamed for the first time with Alfred Lunt (1919) and together they joined the Theater Guild (1924), where their participation in its productions was vital to its success; after Lunt's death (1977), spent her last years between her New York City apartment and her retirement home in Genesee Depot, Wisconsin.

Awards: American Academy of Arts Gold Medal for Diction (1935); Delia Austrian Medal (1943); (with Alfred Lunt) Drama League of New York (1943); honorary degrees from Russell Sage College, Troy, New York (1950), New York University, Beloit College, Wisconsin, Carroll College, Waukesha, Wisconsin, Yale University, Brandeis University, Dartmouth College, and the University of Wisconsin; Globe Theater, New York City, renamed Lunt-Fontanne Theater (1958); received the President's Medal of Freedom from President Lyndon B. Johnson (1964); Emmy award (1965).

Made first stage appearance in London as a child extra in Edwin Drood (1899); appeared in London in the Christmas Pantomime Cinderella (December 1904); toured in Alice Sit-by-the-Fire (1905); appeared as an extra in several London productions over the next four years; toured as Rose in Lady Frederick (1909); appeared in London in Where Children Rule and as Lady Mulberry in Billy's Bargain (both, 1910); made American debut as Harriet Budgeon in Mr. Preedy and the Countess in Washington, D.C. (fall, 1910) and then at Nazimova's 39th Street Theater

(November 7, 1910); back in London as Gwendolyn in The Young Lady of Seventeen (February 1911); as Mrs. Gerrard in A Storm in a Tea Shop (September 1911); toured as Gertrude Rhead in Milestones (1912–13); in London as Liza and Mrs. Collison in My Lady's Dress and as Gertrude Rhead in Milestones (1914); in London in Searchlights; in the title role in The Terrorist, as Ada Pilbeam in How to Get On, and in The Starlight Express (all, 1915); The Wooing of Eve (in Rochester, NY, and then in New York City) and The Harp of Life (1916); Out There, The Wooing of Eve and Happiness (all, 1917), A Pair of Petticoats, Someone in the House (both 1918); A Young Man's Fancy (Chicago, 1919); in New York, as Mary Blake in Made of Money (1919); in Chris (Chicago, 1920); in London in One Night in Rome (1920); in Philadelphia in Chris (1920); as Dulcinea in Dulcy (Chicago, 1921); Lady Castlemaine in Sweet Nell of Old Drury and In Love with Love (1923); in New York as the wife in The Guardsman (1924); in New York as Raina in Arms and the Man (1925); in New York as Stanja in The Goat Song and At Mrs. Beam's (both, 1926); in New York in The Second Man, as Eliza Doolittle in Pygmalion, Agrafina in The Brothers Karamazov, and as Jennifer Dubedat in The Doctor's Dilemma (all, 1927); in London, as Nina Leeds in Strange Interlude and Ilsa von Lisen in New York in Caprice (1928); in Meteor (1929); in New York as Queen Elizabeth in Elizabeth the Queen (1930), as Gilda in Design For Living (1933); in New York, as Elena in Reunion in Vienna (1934), as Linda Valaine in Point Valaine (1935), as Katherine in The Taming of the Shrew (1935), Irene in Idiots Delight (1936), Alkmena in Amphitryon 38 (1937), Madame Arkadina in The Seagull (1938), Miranda Valkonen in There Shall Be No Night (1940), Manuela in The Pirate (1942), Olivia Brown in O Mistress Mine (1946), The Marchioness of Heronden in Quadrille (1952), Essie Sebastian in The Great Sebastians (1955), and Claire Zachanassian in Time and Again which toured in England and New York under title The Visit (1958).

Films: Second Youth (1931); The Guardsman (1931); (cameo) Stagedoor Canteen (1943). Radio (for the Theater Guild): "The Guardsman" (September 30, 1945); "Elizabeth the Queen" (December 2, 1945); "Strange Interlude, Part 1" (March 31, 1946); "Strange Interlude, Part 2" (April 7, 1946); "Call It a Day" (June 2, 1946); "The Great Adventure" (January 5, 1947, and November 20, 1949); "There Shall Be No Night" (September 24, 1950); "Pygmalion" (October 21, 1951); "I Know My Love" (January 6, 1952); "The Old Lady Shows Her Medals" (February 3, 1952). Television: "The Great Sebastians" (1957); "The Old Lady Shows Her Medals" (June 12, 1963, the last Theater Guild TV production); "The Magnificent Yankee" and "Anastasia" (both, 1964), and a 90-minute guest appearance on the "Dick Cavett Show" (1972).

Lynn Fontanne was born Lillie Louise Fontanne in Woodford, Essex, England, on December 6, 1887. Her father Jules Fontanne, a French printer and designer of printer type, was descended, he claimed, from a noble family that had been ruined in the French Revolution. An unsuccessful businessman, more devoted to tinkering with his inventions than earning a living, Jules seems to have been devoted to literature and the arts and to have introduced his daughters to Shakespeare. Her mother **Frances Thornley Fontanne** appears to have been a hot-tempered Irish woman. Lynn Fontanne freely admitted that she had come from an unhappy home from which each of her sisters as well as herself had extricated themselves as soon as they were able to leave. Years later, she chided the playwright Eugene O'Neill for his sentimental portrayals of mothers and urged him to write a play about another kind. The result was Strange Interlude, one of his more remarkable plays.

Determined to be an actress, Fontanne made her stage debut at age 12 as one of a bevy of children in the play Edwin Drood, starring Sir Herbert Beerbohm Tree in 1899. Until then, her parents had discouraged her from pursuing her theatrical goal, but, after seeing her live on a London stage, they relented. Thereafter, she appeared in similar bit parts with the French actor Coquelin and with Lewis Waller in a revival of Monsieur Beaucaire. At 17, Fontanne managed to secure an introduction to Dame *Ellen Terry, then the leading actress of the English stage, who, impressed by Lynn's reading of one of Portia's scenes from The Merchant of Venice, allowed Fontanne to join a select group of young women to whom she taught acting, and who then secured her a role in a London Christmas Pantomime at the Drury Lane Theater in 1904. Fontanne's first appearance outside of London was on tour with Terry in the popular Alice-Sit-by-the-Fire.

Fontanne's big break came shortly thereafter, when she was one of 15 who read for the title role in Somerset Maugham's Lady Frederick. Cast in the part, she appeared in the "first" (main) company to take the popular play on tour (1909). After a season touring the provinces, Fontanne secured another tour with Weedon Grossmith in Mrs. Preedy and the Countess. In 1910, she journeyed to America to appear in Mrs. Preedy, which opened at the long-gone Belasco Theater on Lafayette Square in Washington, D.C., and then moved to New York. There it lasted a scant 24 performances, after which Fontanne returned to London.

Her first London lead was in *A Young Lady of Seventeen*, which was unsuccessful but which led to her being engaged to tour in *Milestones* (1912–13), and a dual role of a poor girl and a young lady in *My Lady's Dress* (London, 1914). Meanwhile, at a London garden party in 1913, Fontanne met the famed American actress *Laurette Taylor, who at that time was making her London debut in her great New York success, *Peg o' My Heart*. A casual conversation led to an invitation from Taylor to join her in America where she planned to stage a number of plays in repertory. The invitation arrived when Fontanne was patriotically driving a munitions truck during the First World War. Arriving in New York in 1916, Fontanne immediately began performing and received favorable notices. Laurette Taylor was delighted at the success of her discovery and soon the two women became fast friends—if not more. "Lynn became Miss Taylor's constant companion, the satellite to the planet," writes Maurice Zolotow, "the confidante of Miss Taylor's problems and pleasures, the eternal protégée. She was backstage at the Globe every matinee and evening. She lived in Laurette's dressing room and dined regularly at Laurette's house."

The story of Lynn Fontanne is inseparable from that of her husband, colleague, co-star and life's companion, Alfred David Lunt. Born in Milwaukee, Wisconsin, on August 8, 1893, he was the son of a lumber and railroad man, who was 70 at the time and died when Alfred was two. Lunt's mother, 32 years younger than her husband, was remarried in 1898 to a Finnish doctor who took the family back to Finland every summer, while allowing Alfred to spend his winters at school in the Wisconsin. While attending Carroll College in Waukesha, Wisconsin, he became exposed to theatricals and, as soon as he graduated, he secured a position as a performer in the John Craig Stock Company in Boston. He then toured with the celebrated actress, *Margaret Anglin, appearing in such plays as *Green Stockings, Beverly's Balance, As You Like It, Medea* and *Iphigenia in Tauris*. He made his New York debut at the Standard Theater in 1916, then toured with the famed British stage star of the previous century, *Lillie Langtry, in a vaudeville sketch called "Ashes." In 1918, Lunt joined the Tyler Stock Company. It was during their summer season in Washington, D.C, the following year that he met Fontanne. The joint career of the Lunts thus began when the producer George C. Tyler, planned a series of five new plays at the National Theater, featuring Lunt, Fontanne, *Helen Hayes, *Cornelia Otis Skinner, Glenn Hunter, and Sydney Toler, ultimately to be remembered as Charlie Chan. One of the five plays, *Made of Money,* marked the first occasion on which the Lunts ever worked together. Lynn Fontanne's first outstanding success was in the role of Dulcinea in *Dulcy* (1921), after which producers showered her with scripts from which she chose whatever role she wished; Lunt's first success, was in Booth Tarkington's *Clarence* (1922). Their first success together would be in Ferenc Molnar's *The Guardsman*. Lynn Fontanne always joked that she knew she had arrived as an actress when the press finally got her surname right and stopped spelling it Fontaine.

After their marriage, the Lunts took an apartment at 969 Lexington Avenue in Manhattan, complete with their own cook. Unencumbered by children, they were great gadabouts in their early years together. These were the "roaring '20s" and both Lynn and Alfred were not averse to parties and long nights on the town, but they always kept these activities well within limits; they were too professional to do otherwise.

In 1924, Alfred Lunt and Lynn Fontanne joined the Theater Guild, under whose auspices they were to have most of their greatest successes. Consisting of a group of dedicated artists determined to raise the level of the American theater, the Theater Guild was a producing organization founded in New York City in 1918. So successful was the Guild in achieving its goals that by 1931 all respectable theatrical producers had adapted its standards, and plays of intellectual depth and unusual construction had become commonplace. In the words of New York critic Brooks Atkinson: "The modern American theater began with the appearance of one dramatist and one producing organization. The dramatist was Eugene O'Neill. The producing organization was the Theater Guild." Many of the finest actors in America joined the Guild or at least appeared with it, and several began their careers under its aegis. The names of the numerous performers associated with it in its greatest years form almost a who's who of the American and British stages between the wars: *Stella Adler, *Sara Allgood, *Tallulah Bankhead, *Ethel Barrymore, *Ina Claire, *Gladys Cooper, *Jane Cowl, *Clare Eames, Jose Ferrer, Margalo Gillmore, *Ruth Gordon, Sydney Greenstreet, Helen Hayes, *Katharine Hepburn, *Josephine Hull, *Eva Le Gallienne,

Lynn Fontanne, with Alfred Lunt.

Gene Lockhart, *Pauline Lord, Helen Menken, Philip Merivale, Paul Muni, *Alla Nazimova, Claude Rains, Edward G. Robinson, Joseph Schildkraut, *Sylvia Sidney, Franchot Tone, Lucille Watson, Clifton Webb, *Helen Westley, Margaret Wycherley, *Blanche Yurka, and, of course, the Lunts. Through careful selection of plays (Shakespeare, Shaw, Strindberg, Molnar, Pirandello, Galsworthy, O'Neill, Werfel, Odets, Sherwood, Behrman, Anderson, Wilder, Hecht, Rice, Saroyan, etc.), directors (Rouben Mamoulian, *Theresa Helburn), composers (Lorenz and

Hart, George and Ira Gershwin), set designers, costume designers and lighting experts, the Guild, while not always successful with the critics or at the box-office, succeeded in making the New York stage one of the most brilliant in theatrical history.

The Lunts were noteworthy for having been responsible for a great deal of the success of the Theater Guild in its first two decades. Under its auspices, they appeared in well over a dozen Guild productions, both light and serious, including Molnar's *The Guardsman* (1924, one of the Lunts' greatest hits and which marked the debut of the celebrated theatrical setting and lighting designer, Jo Mielziner), Shaw's *Arms and the Man* (1925), Werfel's *Goat Song* (1926), Behrman's *The Second Man* (1927), Shaw's *The Doctor's Dilemma* (1927), Sil-Vara's *Caprice* (1928), Behrman's *Meteor* (1929), Anderson's *Elizabeth the Queen* (1930), Sherwood's *Reunion in Vienna* (1931), Sherwood's *Idiot's Delight* (1936), Giradoux's *Amphitryon 38* (English adaptation by S.N. Behrman, 1937), and Sherwood's *There Shall Be No Night* (1940). Among the most memorable of their teamings was the rollicking production of *The Taming of the Shrew* (1935), the Guild's first attempt at a Shakespearean classic, and widely considered to be the best production of the comedy ever seen. In their spirited and hilarious performance, Lunt and Fontanne squeezed laughs out of lines where none had been detected, and filled the stage with ingenious interpretations and bits of business that left the audience in tears and the critics groping for superlatives.

Lawrence Langner, one of the founders of the Theater Guild, said of the Lunts:

> Alfred Lunt and Lynn Fontanne had written a vivid page in the history of the American theater. . . . The couple brought such zest and vitality to their acting, and there was such interplay of point and counterpoint in their scenes together, that soon one began to think of them as one personality . . . capable of endowing every couple that they played with the qualities of beauty, charm, wit, gaiety and enormous interest in one another. . . . [No film] can convey the sheer delight which the audiences of our time have enjoyed in watching their virtuoso acting, which can range, as occasions demand, from delicate sentiment to deep emotion and tragedy, from moods of gaiety and light laughter to the savage laughter of satire or irony. . . . They work without sparing themselves, paying attention to the minutest details.

Alfred Lunt and Lynn Fontanne were described by New York drama critic, Brooks Atkinson, as two perfectly matched geniuses, the secret of their success together being the way that they were so perfectly attuned to one another. When playwright Robert E. Sherwood was asked the secret of his success, he replied: "I write plays for the Lunts."

The Lunts were known both for their professionalism and their search for perfection, and Laurence Olivier, meeting them for the first time in 1931, confessed to having been overwhelmed by their total absorption in the theater. Fontanne's contribution to this perfectionism was demonstrated by her attention to every detail of a particular production, spending weeks and months selecting designs for costumes and then choosing the appropriate fabrics and color to suit the characters, the roles, and the particular demands of theatrical lighting. Lunt's professionalism was shown when, distraught at the deterioration of a cast's performance, he called for a full rehearsal two days before the play was to close, and, on another occasion, even went so far as to try out new bits of business at a final performance just to see how they would work. The success of the Lunts' teaming did not keep them from appearing solo. Fontanne singled in Eugene O'Neill's *Chris,* an earlier version of his later success *Anna Christie.* Later, she starred in his ground-breaking *Strange Interlude,* in which the cast froze when each character voiced his or her thoughts aloud, and as Eliza in Shaw's *Pygmalion,* a part in which she was favorably compared to *Mrs. Patrick Campbell, for whom Shaw had written the role in 1914. This was one of Fontanne's greatest successes and the hit of the Theater Guild in its 1926–27 season. For his part, Lunt appeared solo in O'Neill's *Marco Millions,* in Werfel's *Juarez and Maximillian,* and as Mosca in Ben Jonson's *Volpone,* among other plays.

In 1931, the Lunts went to Hollywood to do a screen version of *The Guardsman* for producer Irving Thalberg, the "Boy Wonder" of MGM. The story has it that the film was shot in as few as 21 days simply because the Lunts insisted on rehearsing each scene before it was filmed, a feat achieved a year later when *Mae West brought in *She Done Him Wrong* in three weeks using the same device. *The Guardsman* was a critical success but predictably not a popular one. Nevertheless, Thalberg offered the Lunts a three-year contract at $990,000 to do a number of films, some of them based on their stage successes, the rest to be chosen by the studio. To Thalberg's astonishment, the Lunts declined, refusing to give up control in regard to directors, casting, costumes, and other aspects of the production over which they had always had control on the stage. *The Guardsman,* thus, was the only film the Lunts ever made together, and this, along with their rare television appearances, are the only record of their art.

In 1933, the Lunts sailed to Europe specifically to appear in a London production of *The Guardsman,* but to also travel to the Soviet Union, France, Italy, and Egypt. The Soviet portion of the trip was to last five days but was extended to two weeks as the Soviet government, only just recently recognized by the United States, outdid itself with its lavish hospitality for two bright lights of the American theater. As with George Bernard Shaw, who had visited the Soviet Union the year before, the Lunts were carefully screened and insulated from the realities of Soviet life. The London opening of *The Guardsman* in January 1934 was a great success, and the Lunts found themselves the toast of the season, the most desired guests in the social whirl. They made many trips to Europe, usually in connection with the London opening of one of their New York successes.

Not everything went smoothly for the Lunts with the Theater Guild. There were many artistic disputes of one kind or another and, in 1940, they terminated their association with the company. In later years, however, they continued to do occasional plays for the Guild and always spoke well of the organization. Not until the Guild produced the musical *Oklahoma!,* however, would it have a success to surpass that of the Lunts in *The Guardsman.*

One of the last plays that the Lunts did before leaving the Theater Guild was Sherwood's *There Shall Be No Night,* a play written in protest of Russia's invasion of Finland in the so-called "Winter War," an event that had deep personal significance for Alfred Lunt who knew Finland from his boyhood. A deliberate piece of propaganda, written to arouse Americans to the growing threat of Nazi and Soviet aggression, the production co-starred Sidney Greenstreet, Thomas Gomez, and a young but soon-to-be-famous Montgomery Clift. One of the few "message plays" in which the couple had ever appeared, it won the Pulitzer Prize for best play of 1940 and served them well for a triumphal tour of the United States, Canada, and England. In the full fury of the war, the Lunts pulled the necessary strings to get themselves back to England with *There Shall Be No Night,* hoping to give war-weary audiences a sense of what they were fighting and suffering for. Back in America, the Lunts toured army bases with their production of

Terence Rattigan's *O Mistress Mine* while the war was on, demonstrating, as *Sarah Bernhardt had done in World War I, that ordinary soldiers, many of whom had never seen a live production, could become enthralled by serious theater.

> *B*ecalmed in the middle of the stage she looks like some exquisite ship turning all about her to anchorage.
>
> —James Agate

Lynn Fontanne and Alfred Lunt were the most successful acting couple of all time, their 40 years performing together having broken the records of Henry Irving and Ellen Terry in England and E.H. Sothern and *Julia Marlowe in the United States. After their retirement, no acting couple even came near to replacing them, not Laurence Olivier and *Vivien Leigh, nor Fredric March and *Florence Eldridge. When rehearsing a play, the Lunts learned their parts in a way that somewhat approximated the idea of improvisation popularized by the method acting technique that became popular after the Second World War. Acting together, they played with one another to perfection, artfully overlapping their lines in such a way that no meaning was lost and in a manner that became a kind of trademark. Although there is no question that the Lunts excelled in light and sophisticated comedy, they took great pride in their versatility and deliberately chose to alternate between comedy and more serious plays. Performers in the old tradition, they could never reconcile themselves to the idea that the theater had become limited to New York and to a handful of other large cities, and continued to tour the country. In 1940, at the end of a major tour with *Idiot's Delight, The Seagull, The Taming of the Shrew,* and *Amphitryon 38,* done in repertory, they estimated that they had traveled over 39,000 miles in a five-year period, appearing before 300,000 in 80 cities. Everywhere, their names meant packed houses, delighted audiences, and rich box-office returns. It was said of the Lunts that they never once let down an audience, a producer, a director, a playwright or a fellow actor. If the town was snowed in, they played to however few managed to get to the theater. If the scenery failed to arrive, they played without it. In every town, drama teachers could be counted on to haul their students down to see two real "pros" at work.

The marriage of Lynn Fontanne to Alfred Lunt seems to have been on the order of that between *Katharine Cornell and Guthrie McClintic, in each case, the lady in question concealing her preference for her own gender by marrying a man who preferred his. In both cases, however, the partners appear to have been genuinely devoted to one another and the arrangement would seem to have suited both concerned. The Lunts lived together, worked together, took their vacations together, had their friends in common, and seem to have had no special interests that the other did not share. Their lives were also enriched by many friendships. Noel Coward was their oldest and dearest, but they were also close to the photographer and costume designer Cecil Beaton, another Brit, like Coward, known for his attraction to his own sex. Naturally they knew well and counted as good friends many of their own generation in the theater, including **Laura Hope Crewes**, Ina Claire, George and **Beatrice Kaufman**, Irving and **Ellen Berlin**, Alexander Woolcott, as well as George Burns and *****Gracie Allen**, whom they had seen on the stage and whom they admired enormously for their incredible timing. They were devoted to Olivier and Leigh, consoling them all night after their disastrous *Romeo and Juliet*. As they grew older, however, the Lunts kept themselves apart from the hurley-burley of theatrical life. Whenever they finished a play or a tour, it was off to Ten Chimneys, their 110-acre farm that Alfred had purchased in Genesee Depot, Wisconsin, early in their marriage and which became their permanent home after they retired.

Lynn Fontanne was not a beauty and made no bones about it, once saying, "I am picturesque in a gauche and angular way. With lots of trouble, with infinite care in the choice of clothes, I contrive to look smart." In appearance, she had brown eyes and dark brown hair, which for a long time she kept carefully dyed. She was tall and rather gaunt, and, with the addition of high heels, her height (5'6") made her an imposing figure on the stage. Like all good actresses, however, she could command beauty when the part called for it, and, if the part called for her to look smart, she certainly achieved the desired results and was reckoned one of the best-dressed women of the stage, some of her costumes even setting fashion trends. Her perennial youthfulness was a legend, and it was joked that Alfred would soon look too old to play with her. Fontanne was lively, with a vivaciousness that stood her well in the comedy roles she preferred, and she had a bright and sparkling sense of humor. She hated writing letters, loved wines and liqueurs (she once shilled for the Wine Growers of California in the '40s), and claimed that her favorite role was always the one in which she was currently appearing. At 90, however, she would admit that the highpoint of her

career was her appearance with Lunt in *There Shall Be No Night*.

After World War II, the Lunts continued to perform in New York and London, though with decreasing frequency, and so closely were their names associated now that they never appeared apart. Among their later successes were Noel Coward's *Quadrille* (1952) and *The Great Sebastians* (1955) by Howard Lindsay and Russell Crouse. In 1957, upon their return from a road tour with the last named play, the Lunts announced their retirement, a little too soon as it turned out, capping this with a protracted visit to Paris, where Alfred studied cooking at the Cordon Bleu School. The following year, however, the Lunts returned to the stage one final time for a production of *The Visit*, a dark comedy by the Swiss dramatist Friedrich Dürrenmatt, that had captured their imagination. After an initial and unsuccessful production in London, the play was taken to New York, where, despite its unpleasant subject matter, tone and mood, those who believed in its quality, including the Lunts, were willing to give it another chance. Far from softening the essentially evil character of the woman Lynn was playing or that of the decadent, depraved old villain portrayed by Alfred, the Lunts played their parts as written. Upon the opening of the play at the newly restored Globe Theater on 47th Street on May 5, 1958, it was announced that the playhouse was to be renamed in their honor. The glittering opening night was followed by a ball at which the Lunts were greeted with a red carpet and serenaded by *****Mary Martin**. (The demolition of the Lunt-Fontanne Theater in the 1980s, one of Broadway's most beautiful venues, together with the Helen Hayes Theater next door, was greeted with protests and demonstrations.)

Alfred Lunt died on August 3, 1977, age 84, and only then did Lynn Fontanne acknowledge the coming of old age. She stopped dyeing her hair and admitted frankly that she was 90, claiming that even her husband had gone to his grave thinking her to be a year younger than she actually was. Fontanne never fully recovered from her husband's death, which effectively ended any chance of her resuming her long career. In an interview for *The New York Times* in 1978, she said of Alfred: "I miss him every second of every day."

Offers continued to arrive, but she had reached the point where her memory had begun to fail her, and she could no longer remember lines. She flew to London with the idea that she might live out her last years in her native land, but a few months away taught her that after so many decades her home was in America, and she returned to Ten Chimneys. There, in the summer, she enjoyed her walks with her poodle, getting her exercise from a stationary bicycle in the winter. Otherwise, tended by a live-in cook, a maid and a manservant-cum-butler, who had been in the Lunts' employ for 50 years, she passed her time enjoying the company of her niece and nephew, who lived on the grounds, and weekly visits from her brother-in-law, whiling away the hours making her own clothes, watching television, reading novels, playing cards, and keeping in touch with the world by phone. Occasionally, she would suddenly fly off to New York or Denver to visit with old friends.

Lynn Fontanne's last public appearance took place in 1979 when, at 92, she was the guest of honor at the American College Theater Festival at the Kennedy Center in Washington, D.C., the city where she had made her American acting debut 69 years before. She died on July 30, 1983, at the age of 95.

SOURCES:

Coe, Richard L. "Fontanne always had perfection and poise," in *Washington Post*. August 2, 1983.

Current Biography, 1941. NY: H.W. Wilson, 1941.

The Free Library of Philadelphia, Theater Collection.

Zolotow, Maurice. *Stagestruck: The Romance of Alfred Lunt and Lynn Fontanne*. NY: Harcourt, Brace & World, 1965.

SUGGESTED READING:

Nadel, Norman. *A Pictorial History of the Theater Guild*. NY: Crown, 1969.

Young, William C. *Famous Actors and Actresses of the American Stage*. Vol. 2. NY: R.R. Bowker, 1975.

Robert H. Hewsen,
Professor of History, Rowan University, Glassboro, New Jersey

Fonteyn, Margot (1919–1991)

British star of the Royal Ballet and one of the world's leading ballerinas from the 1930s through the 1970s. Name variations: Peggy Hookham; Margot de Arias. Pronunciation: Fon-TAIN. Born Margaret Hookham on May 18, 1919, at Reigate, Surrey, England; died on February 21, 1991, in Panama City, Panama, of cancer; daughter of Felix John Hookham (an engineer) and Hilda Fontes Hookham; educated by governesses, tutors, and in local schools in England and China to 1933, then studied ballet at Vic-Wells Ballet School, 1933–34; married Roberto Arias (an attorney and Panamanian diplomat), on February 6, 1955 (died 1989); no children.

Began dance training (1924); moved to U.S. (1926); lived in China (1927–32); made professional debut (1934); became prima ballerina of Sadler's Wells Company, succeeding Alicia Markova (1936);

escaped from German invasion of Holland (1940); toured provinces in reduced ballet company (1939–45); toured U.S. and Canada (1949–50); endured period of illness (1952–53); named president of Royal Academy of Dancing (1954); made first American television performances and husband named Panama's ambassador to Great Britain (1955); named Dame Commander of the Most Excellent Order of the British Empire and saw Sadler's Wells Company receive royal charter and become Royal Ballet (1956); toured Australia and New Zealand (1957); began guest status with Royal Ballet (1959); danced first performance with Rudolf Nureyev (1962); informed husband paralyzed by gunshot wound (1964); made triumphal appearance with Nureyev in Romeo and Juliet *at Covent Garden (1965); appeared at Royal Ballet gala in her honor and gave final performance with Nureyev (1979); death of Rudolf Nureyev (1993).*

Selected roles: title role in Giselle; *Odette-Odile in* Swan Lake; *Aurora in* The Sleeping Beauty; *title role in* Ondine; *Marguerite in* Marguerite and Armand; *Juliet in* Romeo and Juliet.

Margot Fonteyn has been called the personification of the British ballet. With a career that spanned more than four decades, she danced especially memorable roles in numerous ballets created for her by choreographer Frederick Ashton. Two turning points marked her professional life. In 1936, at age 17, she became the successor to *Alicia Markova in the Sadler's Wells Ballet Company (subsequently the Royal Ballet), starting a period in which she emerged as the best-known British ballerina of the era. In 1962, she began what **Susan Au** has called "a second spring" in her career when she became the partner for Rudolf Nureyev. Despite the difference in their ages, they became the most famous duo in the ballet world.

Following the death of Sergei Diaghilev in 1929 and the demise of his Ballets Russes, the ballet world became increasingly decentralized. Since Diaghilev's success in taking the Russian ballet to Western Europe in 1909, a closely knit group of Russian ballet stars and choreographers had played the dominant role in this branch of the arts. This Russian preeminence now gave way to a resurgence of national ballet companies in a number of European countries. For example, under the leadership of the noted ballerina *Ninette de Valois, a veteran of the Diaghilev troupe, a lively British tradition began to emerge. She had opened a school in London, then obtained the support of leaders of the Old Vic Theater and by the mid-1930s organized the

Margot
Fonteyn

Sadler's Wells Ballet. Margot Fonteyn, in conjunction with the choreographer Frederick Ashton, soon became its dominant female star.

The future Margot Fonteyn was born Margaret Hookham, in Reigate, Surrey, on May 18,

1919. Her father was Felix Hookham, an English engineer from a family with a longstanding
interest in music, who had grown up in Brazil.
Margot's mother **Hilda Fontes Hookham** had a
Brazilian father and an Irish mother. In later
years, some observers attributed Margot

Fonteyn's dark-haired good looks to her Brazilian heritage.

Felix Hookham's professional career made his two children, Margaret and her older brother, world travelers at an early age. The future ballerina grew up in England, the United States, and China. She claimed not to know why she began dance lessons at the age of four. "The circumstances of my initial attendance at Miss Bosutow's Academy," she wrote in her autobiography, "are too indistinct in the minds of those concerned for anyone to be really sure." Nonetheless, under her mother's firm direction, she pursued ballet training wherever the family settled for long. In China, her teachers included Russian emigrés trained in the classic traditions of the pre-1917 Russian ballet.

Margaret's return to England allowed her to see the great stars of the ballet world such as *Olga Spessivtzeva in live performances. In 1934, the future ballet star entered the school of the Vic-Wells Ballet. The company, soon renamed the Sadler's Wells Ballet, would receive a charter from Queen *Elizabeth II and become the Royal Ballet Company in 1956. When Margaret Hookham, then 15, became a student, Ninette de Valois was the company's director and Alicia Markova its star dancer. Young Margaret appeared in a number of roles starting in late 1934, and her chance for stardom came only a year later.

In late 1935, Markova left the company to start her own dance troupe, and de Valois decided that Fonteyn could fill the vacancy. In short order, the young woman rose to become the prima ballerina, the dominant female dancer, for the company. Her career soon became linked with choreographer Ashton, who created new roles for her; meanwhile, Michael Somes became her principal partner for the next two decades. By now, she had dropped her birth name. Margaret became the more glamorous "Margot." Though she had thought of adopting her mother's maiden name Fontes in place of Hookham, as she put it, "the English branch of the family shied off connections with the stage." In response to their objections, she chose the variant "Fonteyn" as the name she would make famous.

The team of Fonteyn and Ashton had its first great success in the Romantic ballet *Apparitions* in 1936. In 1939, she danced the most notable role of the first half of her career, Aurora in *The Sleeping Beauty*. The style that Fonteyn perfected lacked the flamboyance of other ballet stars. Her best qualities have been described as a

mixture of skill as an actress, personal warmth, and effortless motion. Her great musical sense became legendary; claiming to have a tape recorder in her head, she invariably matched her flowing movements precisely to the course of the musical score.

The years of World War II began with a notable adventure. Touring Holland, Fonteyn and the rest of the company were almost caught by the German invasion of that country in the spring of 1940. With German paratroops landing nearby, the dancers fled by bus from Arnhem, where they were giving a performance, to the port of Ijmuiden. There they were lucky enough to find a freighter to take them back across the English Channel. (*See Hepburn, Audrey for more on this event.*)

The remaining years of the conflict found Fonteyn and a shrunken company, lacking most of its male dancers, touring Great Britain. In a time of rationing, fans of the ballet donated their portions of sugar and chocolate to Fonteyn and

Margot Fonteyn in Les Sylphide.

the other dancers to give them the energy needed for their strenuous performances. Along with other members of the company, Fonteyn traveled to France and Belgium in 1945 to entertain Allied forces. Ashton was able to steal some time from his duties in the Royal Air Force to write a new ballet for her, *The Quest*. At the close of the war, the young ballerina had her first encounter with serious illness, which she attributed to physical stress and wartime diet.

Her combination of personal beauty, talent and feminine charm was irresistible.

—Alexander Bland

Her career, and the reputation of the Sadler's Wells Company, grew in the postwar period. Sadler's Wells was chosen to reopen Covent Garden's Royal Opera in 1946 with a performance of *The Sleeping Beauty*, which now became its most renowned ballet. Fonteyn, along with Robert Helpmann, who had been her principal partner during the war years, danced the starring role. Her tours took her as far as Prague and Warsaw, and the United States and Canada in 1949–50. During this tour, her performance in *The Sleeping Beauty* once again entranced audiences. One New York critic hailed her as "a ballerina among ballerinas" who had just "conquered another continent." She remembered the occasion vividly: "Unimaginable success! It was unlike anything we had ever experienced before." A sign of the times would be her appearance on television when NBC broadcast a performance of *The Sleeping Beauty* to an American audience in late 1955.

In 1948, the star ballerina hurt a ligament in her ankle, and, in the early 1950s, she found her work increasingly burdened by ill-health. A fortuneteller had once predicted 1952 would be a bad year in her life. Late that year, she contracted diphtheria. One of the disease's frightening symptoms was a temporary paralysis of her feet, and it took her five months to recover completely.

In 1953, Fonteyn's personal life took a happy turn when Roberto ("Tito") Arias reappeared in her life. She had known the Panamanian lawyer and diplomat since the late 1930s when he was a student at Cambridge. Her career ambitions and his reputation as a playboy had seemingly ended their relationship then, but he reappeared in New York as she toured the United States. At their first meeting, he abruptly asked her to marry him, even though he was already married and the father of three. Arias courted her throughout her tour. After his wife

agreed to a divorce, he and Fonteyn were married on February 6, 1955. Arias became his country's ambassador to Great Britain upon returning from their honeymoon and held the position until 1958. Thus, Margot Fonteyn took on the social duties of an ambassador's wife while continuing her dancing. In a more stimulating involvement in her husband's political career, she was briefly held by the police in Panama in 1959 when Arias became involved in an attempted revolution.

By 1961, the Russian influence in ballet was reasserting itself as the Soviet government permitted leading Russian companies to tour Western Europe. That year, one of the male stars of the Kirov Ballet, the young, rebellious, and talented Rudolf Nureyev, deserted his touring company in Paris and received asylum in the West. Stifled by the artistic conformity of the ballet world in his homeland, he now plunged into the European dance scene.

Now in her early 40s, Fonteyn enjoyed the position of a reigning star on the ballet stage and a model for younger dancers like ⚜➤ **Antoinette Sibley** and ＊**Marcia Haydée**. Nonetheless, Fonteyn's career seemed in its last years. Her longtime partner Michael Somes was now retired, and Fonteyn herself seemed anxious to cut down on her artistic responsibilities. She was now only a guest artist on the roster of the Royal Ballet.

Margot Fonteyn was at first skeptical about dancing with the mercurial young Russian. "I think it would be like mutton dancing with lamb," she commented to Ninette de Valois when the idea of a joint appearance first came up. But she put aside her concerns about the 20-year difference in their ages, and she and Nureyev received a wildly favorable welcome when they danced together in *Giselle* in London in early 1962. They repeated their success to equally lavish acclaim in New York in the spring of 1963. For the remainder of the decade, they became the most famous and popular ballet team in the world. As Alexander Bland put it, "Their presence together on the dance scene was immediately electrifying and lastingly dominant." Over a period of 17 years, from 1962 to 1979, the two were to dance together on a relatively small number of occasions: fewer than 200. Nonetheless, their partnership dominated the dance stage of the era.

Dancing with Nureyev not only extended Fonteyn's career, it brought out new facets of her talent. "With him she exhibited new daring," writes **Sarah Montague**, "performing everything from bravura pas de deux . . . to erotic Op-Art spectacles." One New York critic noted the magical combination of the Russian's "smoulder, mystery, [and] dynamic presence" and "the beauty, the radiance, the womanliness, the queenliness" of Fonteyn. "The youthful Nureyev, almost twenty years her junior, has given her new theatrical inspiration," he wrote. In this stage of her career, her great role as Juliet in *Romeo and Juliet* was as much a high point of her work as *The Sleeping Beauty* had been in earlier years. In all, Fonteyn and Nureyev danced 26 ballets together. These ranged from classic roles to short duets. Their signature ballet was *Marguerite and Armand,* a retelling of the story of Camille (***Alponsine Plessis**), which they performed for the first time in London in March 1963. In all, the partnership of the serene and vulnerable Fonteyn and the flamboyant and athletic Nureyev created an unlikely but matchlessly effective dance combination.

Their partnership was sometimes colorful in unexpected ways. Photographers caught them in local dance halls and night clubs doing the ballroom steps of average partygoers. On one occasion in San Francisco in July 1967, they were arrested together at a post-performance gathering in a local home. The police had received word of the presence of drugs, and the newspapers ran pictures of the two ballet stars in handcuffs. In the end, the charges were dropped.

Inevitably, journalists tried to discover a romantic link despite Fonteyn's insistence that she was happily married. But a tragic occurrence marred her personal life when, in June 1964, her husband was severely wounded in a shooting in Panama: a former political associate had attempted to kill him. Fonteyn, who received the news in the English city of Bath following a rehearsal, rushed to his side. Arias, who had been near death, was paralyzed by his injuries.

Fonteyn's career stretched into the 1970s. Her appearances with Nureyev came less frequently as he became involved with experimental dance companies and she engaged in worldwide tours and a long affiliation with the Australian Ballet. In a remarkable display of longevity, she continued to perform brief selections in touring companies until she was 60. The noted duo made their last major appearances together at the Royal Ballet in 1976. In 1979, at the close of her career, the two danced together for the last time.

As her professional life came to a close, Fonteyn turned to writing about ballet. She pub-

---

&▶ Sibley, Antoinette (1939—)

English ballerina. Born in Bromley, England, in 1939; married Michael Somes; studied at Arts Educational School until 1949, then the Royal Ballet School.

Antoinette Sibley entered the company of the Royal Ballet in 1956. In 1959, she became a soloist; by 1960, she was a principal. Her roles include Odette/Odile, Giselle, and the betrayed girl in *The Rake's Progress.* Sibley also created the role of Titania for Frederick Ashton's *The Dream* and was one of the Juliets in Kenneth Macmillan's *Romeo and Juliet.*

---

lished her autobiography in 1975 and followed it in 1979 with a volume designed to aid parents whose children desired ballet training, *A Dancer's World: An Introduction for Parents and Students.* At the start of the 1980s, she reached a larger audience than ever before with her six-part BBC-TV series entitled "The Magic of Dance," which she accompanied with a book of the same name.

Fonteyn also received the acclaim of the Royal Ballet where she had danced with matchless distinction. The company put on a gala performance on May 23, 1979, to mark her 60th birthday. The program listed 77 roles that she had performed in her years there. In the early 1980s, she retired to her husband's cattle ranch in Panama. There she nursed her husband, who had never recovered from the gunshot wounds of 1964, until his death in 1989.

Margot Fonteyn died of cancer in Panama City on February 21, 1991. She was followed in short order by her great partner of the 1960s and 1970s, when Rudolf Nureyev died of complications from AIDS on January 6, 1993.

SOURCES:

Au, Susan. *Ballet & Modern Dance.* London: Thames and Hudson, 1988.

Bland, Alexander. *Fonteyn and Nureyev: The Story of a Partnership.* NY: Times Books, 1979.

Clarke, Mary, and Clement Crisp. *Ballerina: The Art of Women in Classical Ballet.* London: BBC Books, 1987.

Fonteyn, Margot. *Autobiography.* NY: Alfred A. Knopf, 1976.

Montague, Sarah. *The Ballerina: Famous Dancers and Rising Stars of Our Time.* NY: Universe Books, 1980.

SUGGESTED READING:

Bland, Alexander. *The Royal Ballet: The First Fifty Years.* Garden City, NY: Doubleday, 1981.

Monahan, James. *Fonteyn: A Study of the Ballerina in Her Setting.* London: Adam & Charles Black, 1957.

Money, Keith. *The Art of Margot Fonteyn*. Northampton, England: Reynal, 1965.

Stuart, Otis. *Perpetual Motion: The Public and Private Lives of Rudolf Nureyev*. NY: Simon & Schuster, 1995.

Walker, Katherine Sorley. *Ninette de Valois: Idealist without Illusions*. London: Hamish Hamilton, 1987.

Neil M. Heyman,
Professor of History, San Diego State University,
San Diego, California

Foot, Philippa (1920—)

British philosopher. Born Philippa Ruth Foot on October 3, 1920; daughter of **Esther Cleveland Bosanquet**; graduated B.A. Somerville College, Oxford University, 1942, M.A., 1946.

Lecturer in Philosophy, Somerville College (1947); fellow and tutor (1950–69); visiting professor, Cornell University, Massachusetts Institute of Technology, University of California at Berkeley, Princeton University, City University of New York; fellow, Center for Advanced Studies in Behavioral Sciences, Stanford University (1981–82); senior research fellow, Somerville College (1970—); professor of philosophy, University of California at Los Angeles (1974—).

Selected works: "The Philosopher's Defence of Morality," in Philosophy *(October 1952, pp. 311–328); "Freewill as Involving Determinism," in* Philosophical Review *(October 1957, pp. 439–450); "Moral Arguments," in* Mind *(October 1958, pp. 502–513); (ed.)* Theories of Ethics *(London: Oxford University Press, 1967); "The Problem of Abortion and the Doctrine of Double Effect," in* Oxford Review *(Trinity, 1967);* Morality and Art *(Henrietta Hertz Trust, Annual Philosophical Lecture, London: Oxford University Press, 1970); "In Defence of the Hypothetical Imperative," in* Philosophic Exchange *(Summer 1971, pp. 137–145); "Morality as a System of Hypothetical Imperatives," in* Philosophical Review *(July 1972); "Euthanasia," in* Philosophy and Public Affairs *(Winter 1977, pp. 85–112);* Virtues and Vices and Other Essays in Moral Philosophy *(Berkeley: CA: University of California Press, 1978);* Moral Relativism *(Lindley Lecture, 1978, Lawrence: University of Kansas Press, 1979); "Killing, Letting Die and Euthanasia: A Reply to Holly Smith Goldman," in* Analysis *(June 1981, pp. 159–160); "Moral Realism and Moral Dilemma," in* Journal of Philosophy *(July 1983, pp. 379–398); "Utilitarianism and the Virtues," in* Proceedings of the American Philosophical Association *(November 1983, pp. 273–283); "Nietzsche's Immoralism," in* The New York Review of Books *(June 13, 1991, pp. 18–22);* Justice and Charity *(The Gilbert Murray Memorial Lecture, 1992, Oxford:* Oxfam, 1993); "Does Moral Subjectivism Rest on a Mistake?," in* Oxford Journal of Legal Studies *(1995, pp. 1–14);* The Grammar of Goodness *(Oxford: Oxford University Press, 2000).*

Philippa Foot has spent most of her life in England, particularly at Oxford University, but in her later career she has been associated with some of the more prestigious American academic institutions, including Cornell University, Massachusetts Institute of Technology, University of California at Berkeley, Princeton University, City University of New York, and Stanford University. In 1974, she became a professor of philosophy at the University of California, Los Angeles, but continued to reside in Oxford, England. Foot has published prolifically in philosophical journals during her career as an academic philosopher, especially on the subject of ethics.

Catherine Hundleby,
Guelph, Ontario, Canada

Foote, Maria (c. 1797–1867)

English actress and countess of Harrington. Born, probably at Plymouth, England, around 1797; died on December 27, 1867; daughter of Samuel Foote (a descendant of the great actor Samuel Foote, 1720–1777); married Charles Stanhope, 4th earl of Harrington.

An English actress whose amatory and matrimonial affairs were somewhat sensational, Maria Foote appeared as Amanthis in ***Elizabeth Inchbald**'s *The Child of Nature* at Covent Garden in 1814. She remained at Covent Garden until 1825, then did a stint at the Drury Lane before touring England and Ireland. Foote retired from the stage, after a relatively notorious career, in 1831, on her marriage to Charles Stanhope, earl of Harrington.

Maria Foote previously claimed that she had been seduced by a militia colonel named Berkeley who would not marry her. She also sought and won £3,000 damages for breach of promise from one Joseph Hayne, Esq., also known as "Pea Green" Hayne because of the color of his coat. A report of the 1824 trial of *Foote* v. *Hayne*, wherein the sympathy of the public was squarely behind her, sold for sixpence on the streets of London.

Foote, Mary Hallock (1847–1938)

American author and illustrator. Born Mary Anna Hallock in Milton, New York, on November 19, 1847, of English Quaker ancestry; died in Hingham,

Massachusetts, on June 25, 1938; attended the Pough-keepsie (NY) Female Collegiate Seminary and the Cooper Institute School of Design for Women; married Arthur De Wint Foote (a mining engineer), 1876.

Mary Hallock Foote was born in Milton, New York, on November 19, 1847, the daughter of English Quakers. She was educated at the Poughkeepsie (NY) Female Collegiate Seminary and at the Cooper Institute School of Design for Women, in New York. In 1876, she married Arthur De Wint Foote, a civil and mining engineer, and subsequently lived in the mining regions of Idaho, Colorado, California, and Mexico. As a popular illustrator, she was a frequent contributor to *Scribner's Monthly, Harper's Weekly,* and *Century,* but she was best known for her stories and drawings depicting the mining life of the West. Though later tending toward the formulaic, some of her finest drawings appear in her own books, the best of which, some say, rival the works of Bret Harte. Among her publications are *The Led-Horse Claim* (1883), first serialized in *Century, John Bodewin's Testimony* (1886), *The Last Assembly Ball* (1889), *The Chosen Valley* (1892), *Coeur d'Alene* (1894); *The Prodigal* (1900), *The Desert and the Sown* (1902), *The Royal Americans* (1910), *The Valley Road* (1915), *Edith Bonham* (1917), and *The Ground Swell* (1919). Foote also produced several collections of short stories, including *In Exile* (1894) and *A Touch of Sun* (1903).

Forbes, Esther (1891–1967)

American historical novelist and short-story writer. Name variations: Mrs. A.L. Hoskins. Born in Westborough, Massachusetts, on June 28, 1891; died in Worcester, Massachusetts, on August 12, 1967; youngest of five children of William Trowbridge (a judge) and Harriette (Merrifield) Forbes (a historian and author); graduated from the Bradford (Massachusetts) Academy, 1912; attended the University of Wisconsin, 1916–1918; married Albert Learned Hoskins, Jr., in 1926 (divorced 1933).

Esther Forbes was uniquely qualified to write about the history of her native New England. One of five children of an old and respected Eastern family, she was born in Westborough, Massachusetts, on June 28, 1891, and spent much of her childhood in the family attic, poring over ancestral manuscripts and dusty books. She was encouraged in these early explorations by her mother **Harriette Forbes**, a noted researcher and the

author of *Gravestones of Early New England and the Men Who Made Them* (1927).

Mary Hallock Foote

Esther attended the University of Wisconsin for two years before leaving to aid the war effort as a farmhand in Harper's Ferry, Virginia. Returning to New England after the World War I armistice, she joined the editorial staff of Houghton Mifflin and worked in her spare time on her first novel, *O Genteel Lady!* (1926). In 1926, following her marriage to Albert Learned Hoskins, she traveled abroad and continued to write. By the time of her divorce in 1933, she had published her second book *A Mirror for Witches* (1928) and had established her reputation as a historical novelist.

Forbes focused on New England in both her novels and nonfiction and was known for her meticulous research and vibrant, well-drawn characters. In her early works, she was preoccupied with the development of heroines of various types and fates. *O Genteel Lady!* concerns a Boston editor and writer of the late 19th century who gives up her writing, and her love for an adventurer, to marry a staid Harvard professor. In *A Mirror for Witches,* set in the late 17th century, the heroine Doll Bilby has a love affair with a "devil" and dies an accused witch in a Salem prison. (One of Forbes' ancestors was accused of witchcraft and died in a Cambridge jail.) The title character in *Miss Marvel* (1935) is a spinster who leads a romantic inner life depicted in letters to an imaginary lover.

Forbes reached the height of her fame in 1943 with the publication of a book for children, *Paul Revere and the World He Lived In,* which captured that year's Pulitzer Prize for History. Reviewer John Chamberlain claimed the book went "straight to the heart of life in old Boston without sacrificing an iota of universal quality." Close on the heels of this success came *Johnny Tremain* (1943) which won the Newbery Medal. Both books reflect Forbes' interest in individuals caught up in important historical events. Written during World War II, the books also reveal her immediate concern with the nature of human freedom in the context of war. A third children's biography, *America's Paul Revere* (1948), like its distinguished predecessors, won critical acclaim and continues to be a standard in juvenile literature.

Esther Forbes was honored as the first woman member of the American Antiquarian Society and was also a member of the Society of American Historians and the American Academy of Arts and Science. She died on August 12, 1967, while working on a study of witchcraft. In her obituary in *The New York Times*, she was referred to as "a novelist who wrote like a historian and a historian who wrote like a novelist" and was praised as "one of the most exciting and knowledgeable authors on the Revolutionary War." Forbes' last published work, *Rainbow in the Road* (1954), was adapted as a musical in 1969.

SOURCES:

Dictionary of Literary Biography. Vol. 22. Detroit, MI: Gale Research.

Kunitz, Stanley J. *Twentieth Century Authors.* NY: H.W. Wilson, 1942.

Esther Forbes

Mainiero, Lina, ed. *American Women Writers*. NY: Frederick Ungar, 1980.

COLLECTIONS:

The Richard Hutchings Goddard Library at Clark University, Worcester, Massachusetts, holds an uncatalogued collection of Forbes' papers from 1906 to 1967, including manuscripts, historical notes, and essays.

Barbara Morgan,
Melrose, Massachusetts

Forbes, Kathryn (1909–1966).

See Dunne, Irene for sidebar on Kathryn McLean.

Forbes, Rosita (1893–1967)

English traveler and writer. Born Joan Rosita Torr in Swinderley, Lincolnshire, England, in 1893; died in 1967; daughter of Herbert J. Torr; educated privately; married Col. Ronald Forbes, around 1910 (divorced 1917); married Col. Arthur T. McGrath, in 1921.

Selected works: Unconducted Wanderers *(1919);* The Sultan of the Mountains: The Life Story of Raisuli *(1924);* A Fool's Hell *(1924);* From Red Sea to Blue Nile *(1925);* If the Gods Laugh *(1925);* Sirocco *(1927);* Adventure *(1928);* King's Mate *(1928);* One Flesh *(1930);* Conflict: Angora to Afghanistan *(1931);* Ordinary People *(1931);* The Secret of the Sahara! Kufara *(1931);* Eight Republicans in Search of a Future *(1933);* Women Called Wild *(1935);* Forbidden Road: Kabul to Samarkand *(1937);* These Are Real People *(1937);* India of the Princes *(1939);* A Unicorn in the Bahamas *(1940);* These Men I Knew *(1940).*

Born in Lincolnshire, England, in 1893, and consumed by maps at an early age, Rosita Forbes traversed the world several times during her lifetime, turning out novels and nonfiction based on her experiences. She began her phenomenal career in 1915, driving an ambulance for the French Societé de Secours aux Blessés Militaires and winning two medals for valor. Her travels took her to every country in the world with the exception of Tibet and New Zealand, and on one of her trips around the world, she covered 30 countries in 13 months. Her adventures included an attempted pilgrimage to Mecca disguised as an Arab; a journey to the Atlas Mountains to write the life of Ahmed Raisuli, a Moroccan brigand and kidnapper, and a 14,000-mile trip around Central and South America, flying her own plane.

Forbes' first book *Unconducted Wanderers* (1919) was a chronicle of a trip to the Far East with a woman friend. Later books were the results of her visits to remote areas of the world, where she liked to live among the people. Her narratives unite a firm grasp of international politics with a gift for racy, exhilarating writing; her stories about real people and events are considered by some to be more interesting and romantic than her novels. In two of her later books, *These are Real People* (1937) and *These Men I Knew* (1940), Forbes described some of the many people she had met. She also enjoyed speaking about her travels. In 1924, she crossed the United States, giving 88 lectures in 91 days. In 1940, in Canada, she gave 64 lectures and 9 broadcasts under the auspices of the National Council of Education.

Forbes, described as a slender, almost frail-looking woman, was married twice, although neither marriage curbed her wanderlust. She wrote under the name of her first husband, Colonel Ronald Forbes, whom she married around 1910, age 17, and divorced in 1917. Her second husband, Colonel Arthur T. McGrath, was with the British War Office. In her later years, Forbes lived and worked in the Bahamas. She died in 1967.

Forbes-Robertson, Gertrude.

See Elliott, Gertrude.

Force, Juliana (c. 1888–1948).

See Whitney, Gertrude Vanderbilt for sidebar.

Ford, Betty (b. 1918)

American first lady from 1974 to 1977, known for her candor, who established the Betty Ford Center in Rancho Mirage, California. Born Elizabeth Ann Bloomer on April 8, 1918, in Chicago Illinois; youngest of three children and only daughter of William Stephenson (an industrial supply salesman) and Hortense (Neahr) Bloomer; attended Fountain Street Elementary School; graduated from Central High School, Grand Rapids, Michigan, 1936; attended the Bennington School of Dance at Bennington College, Vermont, for two summers; studied with Martha Graham in New York; married William C. Warren (a furniture dealer), in 1942 (divorced 1947); married Gerald Ford (president of the United States), on October 15, 1948; four children by second marriage: Michael Ford (b. 1950); John Ford (b. 1952); Steven Ford (b. 1956); Susan Ford (b. 1957).

In the course of ten months, Betty Ford went from being the wife of the House Minority Leader, to being the wife of the vice-president of the United States, to being the wife of the president of the United States, to being a sought-after first lady, a dramatic rise to national prominence by any standard. Entering the White House under the cloud of the Watergate scandal and the subsequent resignation of Richard Nixon, Ford called the day of her husband's oath of office the saddest of her life. During the next three years, Betty Ford not only blossomed into a gracious and capable first lady, but she became an outspoken and tireless crusader for women's rights. Daughter **Susan Ford**, credits her mother with almost single-handedly jump-starting the Equal Rights Amendment (ERA) movement. However, it was through her courage and honesty in dealing with her own personal tragedies, first breast cancer, then addiction to alcohol and drugs, that Betty Ford made her most significant and lasting contributions.

Born in Chicago in 1918, Betty Ford was raised in Grand Rapids, Michigan, where she enjoyed what she referred to as a "sunny childhood" and an easy transition into adolescence. A round-faced, chubby child, she grew up in a comfortable house in the city and spent summers at the family cottage at Whitefish Lake. She took ballet lessons from the age of eight and while in high school gave dancing lessons and modeled for a local department store to help her family through the Depression. Her carefree girlhood ended abruptly at the age of 16, when her father died of carbon monoxide poisoning in a freak accident while fixing the family car.

After high school Ford studied modern dance for two summers at Bennington College in Vermont and decided to make it her career. She spent several years in New York City, studying and performing with *Martha Graham's auxiliary concert troupe while supporting herself with modeling assignments for John Robert Powers. Graham has remained her idol through the years. "She was a great disciplinarian," she told Jerry Tallmer of the *New York Post* (December 15, 1973), "and that has given me the strength to carry on. Had I not had that association with her I might not have been able to do as well." At the persistent urging of her mother **Hortense Neahr Bloomer**, Betty returned to Grand Rapids for what was to be a six-month trial period. She stayed on, becoming a fashion coordinator for Herpolsheimer's Department Store and forming her own dance troupe. At age 24, she married William Warren, her high-school sweetheart. Warren, however, did not share her desire for a home and children. The marriage was dissolved in 1947, on the grounds of incompatibility.

Soon after, she began dating former football player Gerald Ford, one of the most eligible bachelors in Grand Rapids at the time. After a nine-month courtship, they were married during his 1948 Congressional campaign, and began their life together in a small apartment in Washington, D.C.; they would later move to Alexandria, just outside the beltway. Ford worked in her husband's office, entertained constituents, and absorbed the ways of Washington. As her husband rose up in the Congressional ranks, she stayed home to care for her rapidly growing family. (Four children, three boys and a girl arrived between 1950 and 1957.) In her husband's absence (an estimated 258 days in some years), Ford was den mother, Sunday School teacher, PTA volunteer, and full-time mom and dad. "I couldn't say, 'Wait till your father comes home,'" she recalls in her autobiography *The Times of My Life*, "their father wasn't going to come home for maybe a week." It was a lonely life that sapped her self-esteem. She began, in a controlled manner, to lean on alcohol to relieve her feelings of inadequacy.

In 1964, Ford suffered a pinched nerve in her back which caused debilitating pain, and she began to take medication. As she developed tolerance for one drug, the doctors prescribed another; before long, she was taking pills in advance of the pain to ward it off. She learned much later that some of the pain she was trying to ward off was emotional. In her book, *A Glad Awakening*, which traces her recovery from alcoholism and drug addiction, Ford admits that her pride in her husband's success was tempered with self-pity. "I was beginning to feel sorry for myself. It was poor me, who do they think is making it possible for him to travel all over the United States giving all those speeches? He gets all the headlines and applause, but what about me?" In 1965, about a year after she began mixing pain medication with alcohol, Ford had what she refers to as a minor crack-up and began to see a psychiatrist. Although he treated her low self-esteem, he did not suggest that she stop drinking.

Gerald Ford became president through a series of bizarre events that began in 1973, when Spiro Agnew resigned as vice president during an investigation into kickbacks he had allegedly taken while governor of Maryland. Chosen by Richard Nixon to succeed Agnew, Gerald Ford was in office less than a year when Nixon resigned. For Betty Ford, the transitions were swift and terrifying, from her first interview with **Barbara Walters** as the wife of the vice president, to the moment on August 9, 1974, while they were

Betty
Ford

still living in Alexandria, when her husband was sworn in as president. "The words cut through me, pinned me to the floor," she later said. "I felt as though I were taking the oath with him, promising to dedicate my own life to the service of my country."

The day after the swearing in, she wrote in her diary:

August 10. At 7 AM., the President of the United States, in baby-blue short pajamas, appears on his doorstep looking for the morning paper, then goes back inside to fix his orange juice and English muffin. Before leaving for his office, he signs autographs on his lawn.

At 10 AM, an aide from the White House phones the wife of the President of the United States in Alexandria, and says, "What are you going to do about the state dinner?"

"What state dinner," I say.

Despite dire warnings from *Pat Nixon that she might grow to hate life in the White House, Betty enjoyed her new-found celebrity. "I flowered," she later wrote. "Jerry was no longer away so much. And I was somebody, the First Lady. When I spoke, people listened. I could campaign for women's rights and against child abuse. I began to enjoy a reputation for candor, and was able to do some good." Indeed, from her initial insistence on sharing a White House bedroom with her husband, Betty Ford brought an openness and honesty to the White House that had been missing for years.

Less than two months into her stay at the White House, Ford was diagnosed with a malignant breast tumor and underwent a radical mastectomy. Speaking openly about her ordeal, she spurred hundreds of women to go to their doctors for check-ups. Within weeks of Ford's operation, **Marguerite (Happy) Rockefeller**, the wife of the vice president, also had a mastectomy and credited Ford with saving her life. **Jane Howard**, of *The New York Times Magazine* (December 8, 1974), praised Ford for bringing cancer out of the closet. "If she achieves nothing else during her husband's Administration, the light her trouble has shed on a dark subject would be contribution enough."

Ford unabashedly sought to influence her husband at every opportunity. "I used everything," she wrote in her autobiography, "including pillow talk at the end of the day, when I figured he was most tired and vulnerable." She championed the appointment of *Carla Hills as secretary of Housing and Urban Development (HUD), and *Anne Armstrong as ambassador to Great Britain. In January 1975, when Gerald signed an executive order establishing a National Commission on the Observance of International Women's Year, Betty celebrated it as a moral victory; a president of the United States was standing up for women and against "legal inequities between sexes." Most passionate in her support of the Equal Rights Amendment, Ford did a great deal of stumping for the ERA, phoning and writing legislators, making speeches. Eager to make her opinions known, she never dodged subjects or played it safe. "I felt the public had a right to know where I stood," she wrote later. "Nobody

had to feel the way I felt, I wasn't forcing my opinions on anybody, but if someone asked me a question, I gave that person a straight answer." One of Ford's straight answers to a hypothetical question, her pronouncement on the "60 Minutes" television show that she would not be surprised if her daughter Susan had an affair, brought such a swarm of controversy that she feared becoming a political liability.

In addition to visits to China, Russia, and Japan, and the constant round of state dinners and parties (including one for Martha Graham, who received a Presidential Medal of Freedom), Ford supported the Washington Hospital for Sick Children and worked for an organization called No Greater Love, which helped children of soldiers who were missing in action. She was involved with the Heart Association, Goodwill Industries, and the cancer and arthritis foundations. In 1976, she added campaigning to her hectic schedule, an activity she grew to enjoy, although initially speech-making churned her stomach. Any fears that she would be a liability because of her outspoken views were short-lived; she was often greeted with signs and buttons that read "Betty's Husband for President" or "Keep Betty in the White House." When Gerald lost to Jimmy Carter in a very close election, Ford was bitter and depressed. "In a sense, I was out of office too. As First Lady, there had been a lot of demands made of me. I had been equal to most of them, performed well and enjoyed my moment in the sun. People with low self-esteem crave reassurance from the outside world."

After leaving the White House, the Fords moved to Palm Springs, California, where Betty's neck condition worsened, exacerbated by developing arthritis. While building a new house and beginning her autobiography, Ford's dependence on pain killers increased; a doctor at the University of Southern California declined to treat her because of all the drugs she was taking. With her children and husband often away, she also began to drink again, a habit she had given up when her husband was vice president and president. The medication, mixed with alcohol, had debilitating effects. In the fall of 1977, when Ford narrated *The Nutcracker* ballet for Moscow television, critics tagged her performance as "sloe-eyed," and "sleepy-tongued." Finally her worried family held an intervention, and two weeks after moving into her new home, Betty Ford was on her way to the Long Beach Naval Hospital where she underwent a four-week detoxification program. As with her breast cancer, Ford chose to speak openly about her alcohol and drug addiction and, in doing so, gave countless people the courage to openly seek help.

In the four years following her recovery, Ford, along with Joe Cruse and Leonard Firestone, raised nearly $6 million in private funds to build the 14-acre Betty Ford Center, located at the Eisenhower Medical Center, in Rancho Mirage, California. Since its opening in October 1982, many celebrities, inspired by Ford's courage and honesty, arrived for treatment. "Betty Ford is responsible for taking the life-crippling stigma and shame out of what we now know to be a disease," said actress **Ali Mac-Graw**, one of the center's famous alums. As president of the center, Ford continues to work tirelessly to expand and improve the facility, which she admits has become the focus of her life. "The nice thing is that now I know I can make a mistake or two before I'm through with this world," she writes, "and it won't mean I'm unfit to live."

SOURCES:
Ford, Betty, with Chris Chase. *Betty: A Glad Awakening.* NY: Doubleday, 1987.
———. *The Times of My Life.* NY: Harper and Row, 1978.
"The First Lady of Recovery," in *Entertainment Weekly.* May 10, 1996.
"Generations," in *People.* March 7–14, 1994, p. 229.
Moritz, Charles, ed. *Current Biography 1975.* NY: H. W. Wilson, 1975.
Paletta, Lu Ann. *The World Almanac of First Ladies.* NY: World Almanac, 1990.

Barbara Morgan,
Melrose, Massachusetts

Ford, Eileen (1922—)

*American entrepreneur who, with her husband, established the Ford Model Agency. Born Eileen Otte on May 25, 1922, in New York City; daughter of Nathaniel Otte and Loretta Marie (Laine) Otte; graduated from Barnard College, B.S., 1943; married Gerard William Ford, known as Jerry Ford (an entrepreneur), on November 20, 1944; children: Gerard William Ford, known as Bill Ford (president of Ford's licensing division); A. **Lacey Ford** (who married John Williams); M. Katie Ford (who married André Balazs); Margaret Ford, also known as **Jamie Ford** (who married Robert Craft).*

Selected writings: Eileen Ford's Book of Model Beauty, Eileen Ford's Secrets of the Model World, A More Beautiful You in 21 Days, *and* You Can Be Beautiful *(1977).*

Eileen Ford was born in New York City on May 25, 1922, the daughter of a wealthy Long Island couple, Nathaniel and **Loretta Laine Otte**.

She credited her parents with giving her a strong dose of self-confidence. "My family believed I could do no wrong," she recalled. "That's probably why I have utter confidence in myself—even when I shouldn't have." A graduate of Barnard College, she had a brief modeling career before eloping with Jerry Ford, with whom she started the Ford Model Agency in their Manhattan walkup in 1948. The Fords revolutionized modeling by establishing standardized fees and acting as agents for models by collecting fees and handling bookings. Over the years, the agency grew into a multimillion-dollar business which also included the Fords' three children.

Eileen Ford's flair for spotting charismatic models was highly regarded in the industry; her discoveries include **Lauren Hutton**, *****Jean Shrimpton, Capucine, Jane Fonda, Candice Bergen, *****Suzy Parker, Christie Brinkley, Jerry Hall, Cheryl Tiegs, Brooke Shields, Ali Mac-Graw, Penelope Tree, Christy Turlington**, and **Rachel Hunter**. Described in *People Weekly* as "part pit bull, part den mother and all business," Ford was known to mother her models and frequently took teenager models into her home if she felt they were not mature enough to handle New York City on their own. Ford, who "often slouched through the corridors of high fashion with her hem unraveling," notes *People Weekly*, unabashedly accepted her role as an arbiter of beauty and style, and claimed that American women—particularly those of her generation—meant a great deal to her. "They never have anyone to turn to. I help them understand how they can look better, how to do this, do that, get a job. And they're very trusting. Like little lost kids." Of her husband and long-time business partner, she said: "He's the brains, I'm the noise."

In 1995, to the surprise of many, the Fords assumed the title of co-chairs and handed the agency over to their middle daughter **Katie Ford**. "We were getting old," Ford said. "What were we going to do, let her be like Prince Charles and wait for us to die?" Katie increased the staff by 15%, moved the agency downtown, added an on-line service, and created a more culturally diverse stable of models. "The definition of beauty is much broader today," said Katie. "The ideal American is no longer considered Swedish."

SOURCES:
Blackwell, Earl. *Celebrity Register.* Detroit, MI: Gale Research, 1990.
"Katie Ford," in *People Weekly.* September 8, 1997.
Martin, Jean, ed. *Who's Who of Women in the Twentieth Century.* Greenwich, CT: Brompton Books, 1995.

Barbara Morgan,
Melrose, Massachusetts

Ford, Elizabeth Bloomer (b. 1918).

See Ford, Betty.

Ford, Isabella O. (1855–1924)

British feminist. Born in Leeds, England, in 1855; died in 1924; one of eight children of Robert (a solicitor) and Hannah (Pease) Ford.

One of eight children in an upper-middle-class Quaker family, Isabella Ford was raised in an enlightened environment. Her parents taught their children to treat everyone, including the servants, with "esteem, equality and friendship." They also believed in gender equality and educated their children in both the sciences and the arts. Politically, the Fords supported John Bright, the Quaker MP for their district, and his campaign for repeal of the Corn Laws. They also championed other progressive causes such as prison reform and the protection of wild life. Their home (Adel Grange), outside of Leeds, became a gathering place for political radicals, and

Isabella O. Ford

Isabella came in contact with prominent feminists, such as *Josephine Butler and *Elizabeth Garrett Anderson. In 1857, Ford met Edward Carpenter, a former Anglican priest who introduced her to socialist ideas. In 1883, the two of them joined the Fabian Society, a newly formed organization whose aim was to "reconstruct society in accordance with the highest moral possibilities through political means."

In 1885, Ford began a long campaign to reform conditions for the women textile workers in Leeds, who endured low pay and deplorable working conditions. Joining with *Emma Paterson, president of the Women's Protective and Provident League, Ford helped form a Machinists' Society for tailors. In 1889, she established the Leeds Tailoresses' Union and was elected president.

Continuing her work for women's rights, in 1890 Ford, her sister **Bessie Ford**, and her sister-in-law **Helen Cordelia**, helped form the Leeds Women's Suffrage Society. Three years later, Ford was involved in organizing the Leeds branch of the Independent Labor Party. By 1900, she had gained a national reputation as a speaker and organizer for the women's movement. She also wrote books on the struggle for equality, including *Women's Wages* (1893), *Industrial Women* (1900), and *Socialism* (1904).

Ford's political involvement grew in 1903, when she became a member of the national executive committee of the Independent Labor Party. In that role, she helped persuade party leaders to support women's suffrage. In 1907, despite the objection of some suffragists to her socialist ties, Ford was elected to the executive committee of the National Union of Women Suffrage Societies (NUWSS). In 1912, she persuaded the NUWSS to support Labor Party candidates in the parliamentary elections, which did not sit well with the Liberal Party.

A life-long pacifist, Ford became concerned about growing hostilities between Britain and Germany and, in 1914, helped organize a peace rally in London for August 4. During the rally, which was supported by the NUWSS, the Women's Labor League, and the International Women's Suffrage Alliance, news came that Britain had declared war on Germany, effectively launching World War I.

As the conflict wore on, the women's movement was split over the role women should play in the war. While some factions supported Britain's effort to defeat Germany, others, including Ford, argued that the women's movements should work to try and secure a cease-fire. As the schism deepened, Ford found herself more and more isolated, and in 1915, she was forced to resign from the executive committee of the NUWSS. In her later years, she put all her effort into the peace movement, serving as a delegate to the Women's International League Congress from 1919 to 1922. Isabella Ford died in 1924.

SUGGESTED READING:

Middleton, Lucy. *Women in the Labour Movement,* 1977.

Roberts, Marie, ed. *The Reformers: Socialist Feminism,* 1995.

———, ed. *The Workers,* 1995.

Rowbotham, Sheila. *Hidden From History,* 1972.

Ford, Mary (1924–1977)

American popular singer who, with partner Les Paul, achieved fame during the 1950s. Born Colleen Summers on July 7, 1924, in Pasadena, California; died on September 30, 1977; married Les Paul, in 1949 (divorced); married Dan Hatfield (a contractor); children: (first marriage) one son and one daughter.

Partial discography: Lover/Brazil *(Cap. 15037);* Little Rock Getaway/Tennessee Waltz *(Cap. 13316);* How High the Moon/Walkin' and Whistlin' Blues *(Cap. 1451);* Whispering/The World Is Waiting for the Sunrise *(Cap. 1748);* Just One More Chance/Jazz Me Blues *(Cap. 1825);* It's a Lonesome Old Town/Tiger Rag *(Cap. 1920);* Smoke Rings/In the Good Old Summertime *(Cap. 2123);* Meet Mister Callaghan/Take Me in Your Arms *(Cap. 2193);* Sleep/I'm Sitting on Top of the World *(Cap. 2400);* Vaya Con Dios/Johnny *(Cap. 2486);* I Really Don't Want to Know/South *(Cap. 2735); additional hits on* Columbia *(1958–61).*

Mary Ford was a country-and-western singer on Gene Autry's Sunday night radio program when she met guitarist Les Paul, who changed her singing style and both of their careers. From their first record together, "Lover," released in 1949, the duo remained at the top of the charts throughout the 1950s. Much of their success was due to Paul's innovative use of echo and multiple-track recording techniques (considered years ahead of their time), which made many of their renditions of old songs sound new. Their single of the standard "How High the Moon" was number one in the nation from April 21 to June 16, 1951. Their enormous hit, "Vaya Con Dios," sold four million copies.

Married in 1949, the couple was at the height of their fame when they announced their divorce in 1963. The news sent such shock waves across the country that their commercial for a clothing store was pulled off the air. Ford later married her high-school sweetheart, Don Hatfield, and settled in Monrovia, California. After the split, Les Paul also abandoned his career to concentrate on inventing, then became active once more in the mid-1970s, performing and promoting guitars. Mary Ford died on September 30, 1977.

Ford, Michelle Jan (1962—)

Australian swimmer. Born in Sans Souci, Sydney, Australia, on July 15, 1962.

Won six Australian individual championships (in the 200-meter butterfly, 200-, 800-, and 1500-meter freestyle), and one relay championship; won a gold medal in the Commonwealth games in Edmonton (1978) and Brisbane (1982); won the bronze medal in the 200-meter butterfly and the gold medal in the 800-meter freestyle in the Moscow Olympics (1980).

By the age of 12, Australian swimmer Michelle Jan Ford had already broken a record, swimming the fastest-ever 100-yard freestyle in the world for her age. From that auspicious start, she went on to win six Australian individual championships in the 200-meter butterfly, 200-, 800-, and 1500-meter freestyle, and one relay championship. She competed in two Commonwealth games, winning a gold medal in Edmonton in 1978 and another in Brisbane in 1982. Although Ford swam in the 1976 Olympic Games in Montreal, it was at the Moscow Olympics in 1980, that she peaked, winning a gold medal in the 800-meter freestyle and a bronze in the 200-meter butterfly. That same year, Ford won the first gold sport Australia Award as the best female athlete.

Forlí, Countess of (1462–1509).

See Sforza, Caterina.

Fornalska, Malgorzata (1902–1944)

Polish revolutionary who was one of the leaders of the Left in the 1930s and during the Nazi occupation. Name variations: (underground alias) "Jasia." Born on June 10, 1902, in Fajslawice; shot by her Nazi captors in Warsaw, Poland, on July 26, 1944.

A powerful revolutionary tradition has characterized much of modern Polish history, and by the early 20th century women were playing an increasingly influential role in both the Socialist and nationalist movements. Once Polish independence was restored in 1918, a Communist

XROCZNICA POWSTANIA PPR

1¹⁵ ZŁ M. FORNALSKA

POCZTA POLSKA

M.R. POLAK   P.W.P.W.   ST. ŁUKASZEWSKI

Malgorzata Fornalska

Party arose on the extreme left in opposition to the more moderate Social Democratic Party. Inspired by the Bolshevik revolution in Russia, some Polish radicals hoped to create a Communist regime in their country that would be closely linked to Lenin's revolutionary state, thus facilitating the onset of a general revolutionary upheaval in Central Europe. These dreams were never realized, and Polish Communists were regarded by most of their compatriots as being political adventurers at best and, more likely, as representing the forces of subversion and upheaval. Individually, however, each Polish Communist had a unique life story to tell, and that of Malgorzata Fornalska is well worth telling.

Fornalska was born in a poor village and early in her life she became active in the workers' movement. During World War I, she and her family were evacuated to Russia, where she became an enthusiastic supporter of the revolution. Living in Tsaritsin in 1918, she joined the Marxist Social Democratic Party of the Kingdom of Poland and Lithuania. Determined to save the revolution from its enemies, she joined a Red Guard detachment and soon became a member of the Red Army. Returning to Poland in 1921 after the end of hostilities, she settled in

Lublin where she became a member of the Communist Party of Poland (KRPR). As a revolutionary activist, her activities were noted by the local security police and after being arrested in 1922 Fornalska was found guilty of subversive activities and sentenced to four years and three months imprisonment.

Released from prison, Fornalska went to Moscow where she worked in the international revolutionary organization, the Communist International. Returning to Poland in 1934, she took a post in the agricultural section of the KRPR. Again the Polish political police decided that her activities represented a threat to the internal security of the dictatorial regime, and in August 1936 she was again arrested. Held without a trial, she was still in the Warsaw prison when Nazi Germany attacked Poland on September 1, 1939. Although she suffered considerably as a political prisoner, Malgorzata Fornalska did not share the fate of her brother Aleksander, who had remained in the Soviet Union where he lost his life in Josef Stalin's bloody purges. A few days before Warsaw surrendered to German forces, the prison governor decided to release a number of prisoners including Fornalska. Eluding the Germans, she was able to escape to the city of Bialystok in the newly annexed territories of the Soviet Ukraine. Here she worked as a teacher until June 1941, when Hitler's forces attacked the USSR.

Fleeing the advancing Germans, Fornalska worked with Soviet forces behind the front lines to establish resistance groups to free Poland from Nazi occupation. She parachuted into occupied Poland in 1942, immediately joining up with local underground elements. Fornalska concentrated on organizing printing facilities that produced all-important forged documents. Her luck ran on out November 14, 1943, when she and Pawel Finder, another leader of the Communist underground apparatus, were arrested in Warsaw and incarcerated in the infamous Pawiak prison. As Soviet forces neared Warsaw, the Nazis decided to systematically liquidate their prison system and on July 26, 1944, Fornalska was shot. After 1945, she became one of the martyrs celebrated in the People's Republic of Poland, with streets, squares and schools named in her honor. A commemorative postage stamp of Fornalska was issued on January 18, 1952.

SOURCES:

Fornalska, Marcjanna. *Pamietnik matki.* Warsaw: "Ksiazka i Wiedza," 1988.

Partington, Paul G. *Who's Who on the Postage Stamps of Eastern Europe.* Metuchen, NJ: Scarecrow, 1979.

Simoncini, Gabriele. "The Communist Party of Poland: 1918–1929" (Ph.D. dissertation, Columbia University, 1991).

Toranska, Teresa. *"Them": Stalin's Polish Puppets.* Translated by Agnieszka Kolakowska. NY: Harper & Row, 1987.

John Haag,
Assistant Professor of History,
University of Georgia, Athens, Georgia

Fornari, Maria Victoria

(1562–1617)

Founding member of the order of Celestial Annunciades, honoring the Annunciation of the Blessed Virgin (1604). Born Maria Victoria Fornari in 1562 in Genoa, Italy; died in 1617; married Angelo Strata, in 1579 (died 1587); children: six.

Blessed Maria Victoria Fornari, born in 1562 in Genoa, Italy, was happily married for eight years to Angelo Strata. Then, with five small children and a sixth on the way, she was widowed in 1587. In desperation, she prayed before a statue of the ***Mary the Virgin**, who, as she later recounted, held out her arms and said: "Victoria, my daughter, do not fear; it is I who will henceforth take care of your home." Over the course of the next 16 years, Fornari raised her family and devoted her life to good works. When all her children had grown and entered the religious life, she carried out her long-time dream of endowing her native town with a convent consecrated to the honor of the Annunciation of the Blessed Virgin. After approval from **Clement VIII**, the convent was erected, and on August 5, 1604, Fornari and several companions received the white tunic, blue scapular, belt, and cape that would define the order of Celestial Annunciades. (Another order of Annunciades—the Franciscans—was founded by ⚜ **Jeanne de France**, the spurned wife of Louis XII.) Fornari served for six years as abbess of the convent before retiring from her official duties to live out her life as a nun. Five convents of the Celestial Annunciades are still in existence today, three in Italy and two in France.

Fornia, Rita (1878–1922)

American mezzo-soprano, particularly known for her secondary roles at the Metropolitan Opera. Born Regina Newman in San Francisco, California, on July 17, 1878; died in Paris, France, on October 27, 1922.

Rita Fornia has been called a "useful and adaptable artist." From 1907 to 1922, she appeared at the Metropolitan Opera, often in secondary roles. Trained by Emil Fischer, **Sofia Scalchi**, **Selma Nicklass-Kempner**, and Jean de Reszke, Fornia was a coloratura soprano. In 1901, she made her debut in Hamburg, then joined Henry Savage's Opera Company in America. In 1907, she made her debut at the Met and remained there for most of her career.

Forrest, Helen (1918–1999)

American popular singer of the big-band era whose signature song was "I Had the Craziest Dream." Name variations: sang under Helen Trees, Helen Farraday, Fran Helene, Hilda Farrar, and Bonnie Blue. Born on April 12, 1918, in Atlantic City, New Jersey; died of congestive heart failure on July 11, 1999, in Los Angeles, California; married drummer Al Spieldock (divorced); married actor Paul Hogan (divorced); married businessman Charlie Feinman, in 1959 (divorced); children: (third marriage) one son.

Epitomizing the big-band singer of the swing era—the years during and following World War II—Helen Forrest was a vocalist for three of the top bandleaders of her day: Artie Shaw, Benny Goodman, and Harry James. Known for her warm, flexible voice, Forrest could handle any expressive mood or rhythmic style and was one of a handful of band singers who could project the lyric of a ballad without losing the dance beat. Forrest reached the peak of her career in the early 1940s with hits such as "I Had the Craziest Dream," "Skylark," I Cried for You," "I've Heard That Song Before," and "I Don't Want to Walk Without You," and won both the *Down Beat* and *Metronome* polls as the number-one female singer in the country in 1942 and 1943.

Helen Forrest was born on April 12, 1918, in Atlantic City, New Jersey, and started her career in her hometown, singing with her brother's small band and on local radio stations. In 1939, she was Artie Shaw's lead vocalist for 15 months, until he suddenly decided to disband and quit the business. Ten days later, she was hired by Benny Goodman, who, according to Forrest, was a cold and difficult man to work for. She left him after two grueling years and went to work for trumpeter Harry James, who had also deserted Goodman to form his own band. Forrest and James were romantically involved for most of the two years she was with his band and were engaged to be married at one point. But then, as she explained later to columnist Earl Wilson, "He met Betty Grable—and how could I compete with the pinup girl of the world? The next thing I knew I was standing

Jeanne de France. See Anne of Beaujeu for sidebar.

outside the window of my apartment on a ledge about three stories high and people were yelling at me not to do anything foolish." In her 1982 autobiography, *I Had the Craziest Dream,* Forrest says she is glad she did not jump. "I've had a pretty good life and a lot of laughs since then."

Forrest left James' band and went out on her own in 1943. Despite a thriving radio show with Dick Haymes from 1944 to 1947, she was not as successful as other erstwhile band singers, such as *Jo Stafford and *Peggy Lee. She blamed it on not being beautiful enough and the coming of rock and roll. Forrest, who was married and divorced three times, quit show business in the mid-1960s, when she moved to Phoenix, Arizona, in hopes that a dryer climate would help her son's sinus condition. After running an Indian jewelry shop for a time, she made a brief comeback in 1979, participating in big-band fundraisers for public-television stations and rejoining Haymes for a tour of *The Fabulous '40s.* After suffering a mild stroke in 1980, she returned to singing two months later on a limited schedule. "I think every time I step on a stage I am young again," she once said. "I think my performances prove I can still sing with anyone, even those many years younger. What scares me is being alone."

SOURCES:

Clarke, Donald, ed. *The Penguin Encyclopedia of Popular Music.* NY: Viking, 1989.

Hemming, Roy and David Hajdu. *Discovering Great Singers of Classic Pop.* NY: New Market Press, 1991.

Barbara Morgan,
Melrose, Massachusetts

Förster-Nietzsche, Elisabeth

(1846–1935)

Celebrated literary figure, notorious anti-Semite, who wrote books and articles on the life and ideas of her brother, Friedrich Nietzsche, and participated in the founding of the New Germany colony in Paraguay. Name variations: Elisabeth Nietzsche; Elisabeth Forster-Nietzsche; Lisbeth or Lichen or Eli Förster. Pronunciation: Ee-LIZ-ah-beth FURstur-NEET-chee. Born Elisabeth Therese Alexandra Nietzsche on July 10, 1846, in Röcken, Saxony; died on November 8, 1935, following a bout of influenza, at Villa Silberblick, Weimar; daughter of Karl Ludwig Nietzsche (a Lutheran pastor) and Franziska (Oehler) Nietzsche; attended Fräulein von Pareskis' private school for young ladies in Naumburg, Germany, and finishing school in Dresden; married Bernhard Förster, on May 22, 1885; no children.

Major works: Dr. Bernhard Förster's Kolonie Neu-Germania in Paraguay (Dr. Bernhard Förster's New Germany colony in Paraguay, 1891); Das Leben Friedrich Nietzsches (The Life of Friedrich Nietzsche, 2 vols., 1895–1904); Das Nietzsches-Archiv, seine Freunde und seine Feinde (The Nietzsche-Archive, his Friends and his Enemies, 1907); Der junge Nietzsche (The Young Nietzsche, 1912); Der einsame Nietzsche (The Lonely Nietzsche, 1914); Wagner und Nietzsche zur Zeit ihrer Freundschaft (Wagner and Nietzsche: Their Times and Their Friendship, 1915); Friedrich Nietzsche und die Frauen seiner Zeit (Friedrich Nietzsche and the Women of His Times, 1935).

When Elisabeth Förster-Nietzsche entertained Adolf Hitler at the Nietzsche Archive after his accession to power in 1933, there was fixed in the popular mind a connection between the philosophy of Friedrich Nietzsche and Nazism. That association in large part was the result of Elisabeth Förster-Nietzsche's unrelenting and successful effort to project and disseminate her renditions of her dead brother's ideas.

In a sense, Friedrich Nietzsche had been the focus of Elisabeth's life from the time they were children. Both of them grew up in a house that exposed them to strong conservative and anti-democratic views. Their father, a Lutheran pastor, maintained the 17th-century view that monarchs had a divinely ordained right to rule and that monarchy's logical partner, the aristocracy, were to be honored. Elisabeth, who grew up in a middle-class environment, always aspired to join the ranks of nobility. With regard to the masses, she wrote later in life that "an abyss separates us from them; they are and remain common."

When Elisabeth was christened, she was given the names of the three young princesses— *Elisabeth of Saxe-Altenburg (1826–1896), Therese, and *Alexandra of Saxe-Altenburg (1830–1911)—daughters of *Amelia of Wurttemberg and Joseph, duke of Saxe-Altenburg, whom her father had tutored before he assumed his pastoral duties in the town of Röcken. Tragically, her father died in 1849, when she was three years old, of what was described as a "softening of the brain." **Franziska Nietzsche**, Elisabeth's mother, could not support her family on the inadequate pension of her dead husband and had to move in with relatives in the town of Naumburg. Biographers describe Naumburg as a staunchly conservative, devoutly Christian town; they describe the family environment as curious at best. Historian Ben Macintyre notes that they shared a large apartment with Franziska's mother-in-law and two aunts. Aunt Rosalie, "devout and dotty and opposed to Shakespeare," Aunt Augusta and her gastric problems, and Grandmother Erdmuthe who "couldn't stand noise." The children, according to H.F. Peters "grew up in secret alliance against being dominated by women. They had no playmates, shared one room for play and sleep, and declared . . . that they would become husband and wife when they were grown up."

Elisabeth doted on, deferred to, and defended her brother Friedrich. By age six, she was in the habit of collecting every scrap of paper on which Friedrich had written and storing them in her treasure drawer. His nickname for her was Llama, according to Peters, because of her habit of spitting at him when she was angry. Elisabeth found no reason to challenge the ruling 19th-century assumption that women were subordinate to men, who were the makers of history. Throughout her life, according to Macintyre, she opposed the idea of women's suffrage and wrote that "feminism is a movement of spinsters and its adherents are generally childless women." A woman, in Elisabeth's view, "tries to lighten her husband's burdens . . . refresh him of the petty worries of daily life, and shows some understanding of his higher aspirations." Elisabeth, however, would follow this advice only when it suited her, or advanced her own agenda.

Fräulein von Pareskis' private school for young ladies was the venue for Elisabeth's early education. There, she was immersed in the art of good manners and exposed to arithmetic, French, English, reading and composition. In a revealing comment to her brother, she said that while in school she could "talk about anything without understanding much of it." While brother Friedrich, known as Fritz, was enrolled at the Royal Boarding School at Pforta, Elisabeth attended finishing school in Dresden. Young women in their teenage years were expected to show an interest in prospective husbands. Elisabeth did not, to the consternation of her mother. At least one Nietzsche biographer, Ronald Hayman, suggested that her indifference to marriage was a reflection of her fixation on her brother. That Elisabeth and Friedrich were close was clear, how close has been a matter of conjecture, some of it scurrilous.

A crisis in Elisabeth's relations with her brother occurred as he moved away from Christianity. While she wanted to trust Fritz's "superior judgment," she was also, in Peter Bergmann's words, "disturbed by this threat to the 'most holy, at least most believable' aspect of her faith and fled to her clerical uncle for fortification of

her piety and for a 'reconversion' to the correct path." Elisabeth's intellect was narrow, and her ideas were based on a number of set and rigidly held beliefs that would influence her views of politics, culture, and race.

Elisabeth's view of the world in combination with her biases and bigotry set the stage for turmoil in the Nietzsche family. She glowed in 1869 when Friedrich become a professor at the University of Basel at age 24 and asked for her assistance to index 24 volumes of the *Rheinische Museum,* a scholarly journal. She beamed when Fritz struck a friendship with the great German composer Richard Wagner. Peters notes that Elisabeth was "determined not to be left behind" in Friedrich's "rise to fame." She occasionally watched the Wagner children and was delighted when they called her "Aunt Elisabeth." To be part of Wagner's inner circle played to her ambition.

Throughout the 1870s, Elisabeth alternately cared for and fought with Friedrich, who by

Elisabeth Förster-Nietzsche

1871 was suffering the effects of syphilis, the disease that would ultimately destroy his mind and take his life. When Friedrich broke with Wagner in 1876, it was partly because of his failing health—but it was also a realization of his dissatisfaction with Wagner's anti-Semitism, his loud, arrogant nationalism, and his pompous self-centeredness. Elisabeth was distraught with the break, because she thought it might harm her chances for advancement. Her simple explanation for Fritz's defection from the inner circle was that her brother had fallen under the influence of a cynical Jew, Paul Rée. Elisabeth had embraced the anti-Semitism that surrounded Wagner and his friends.

Present at Bayreuth, the site of Wagner's self-glorifying festivals, was Bernhard Förster, who was attracted to Elisabeth and shared with her his dreams for a rebirth of the German spirit. That German spirit had no room for capitalism, communism, or democracy, which he perceived in negative terms and blamed on Jews. Bernhard's anti-Semitism served to enforce that of Elisabeth. In 1880, Bernhard circulated a petition that demanded government action to "cleanse" Germany of Jewish corruption. Elisabeth willingly helped to gather signatures.

My mission in the next ten years is to plant the personality of Nietzsche, as the noblest figure of light, firmly into the hearts of people.

—Elisabeth Förster-Nietzsche

Elisabeth also continued to monitor her brother's writings and escapades. In 1882, his dalliance with the beautiful and intelligent *Lou Andreas-Salomé sparked an explosion of indignation from Elisabeth, especially when Lou suggested a sexless *menage à trois* that would see Friedrich, Paul Rée and Lou living together in what they described as a "Holy Trinity." As Elisabeth wrote: "I cannot deny that [Lou] really personifies my brother's philosophy: that rabid egotism which tramples on anything in its way, and that complete indifference to morality." Historian Bergmann suggests that Elisabeth reacted as strongly as she did because she was upstaged by Andreas-Salomé and "affected indignant outrage to the younger woman's provocative manner, melodramatically declaring that were she a Catholic she would enter a nunnery to atone for her brother's philosophy of sin." Friedrich Nietzsche wrote to Elisabeth after his breakup with Lou: "Souls like yours, my dear sister, I do not like, especially when they are morally bloated."

While the Andreas-Salomé affair absorbed much of Elisabeth's attention, Bernhard responded to the rejection by the German government of his anti-Semitic petition with a pledge to found a New Germany in a different part of the world, on "a soil unadulterated by Jewish influences." Elisabeth was again attracted to a man she saw as "visionary." In a letter of 1883, she wrote that Bernhard was "filled with a magnificent enthusiasm for Wagner's efforts to regenerate our country. We feast on compassion, heroic self-denial, Christianity, vegetarianism, Aryanism, southern colonies. I find all this so sympathetic and feel so much at home in it." In February, Bernhard departed for Paraguay intent on the forging of a new fatherland.

In the meantime, Elisabeth's relationship with her brother blew hot and cold. While she was horrified by Friedrich's assertions that he was the Anti-Christ, she reveled in his growing fame, especially after the publication of *Also Sprach Zarathustra (Thus Spoke Zarathustra)*. When he was apprised not only of Elisabeth's strong attraction to Bernhard but also of her intention of joining him in Paraguay, he exploded with rage. In Peters' words: "That his own sister was considering making common cause with a man whose ideas he abhorred was incredible. Elisabeth knew how much he detested Förster's vulgar anti-Semitism, and as for Förster's Aryan ideals, they were patently absurd." Elisabeth "was betraying him and his philosophy by embracing it." She, on the other hand, wrote to Bernhard that Friedrich's goal "is not my goal, his entire philosophy goes against my grain." While his "striving for the superman seemed something admirable and I thought that you with your colonizing venture had taken the first step toward it," after reading the second part of *Zarathustra* "my excitement is gone. I see now that superman is not my ideal."

Bernhard and Elisabeth were married on Wagner's birthday, May 22, 1885. Together they would reconstitute the old Germany in the New World. To that end, she helped him author a book on Paraguay that served as a prospectus for the envisaged colony and bombarded friends and acquaintances with requests for financial support. It was in February 1886 that Bernhard, Elisabeth, and a disappointingly small group of colonists sailed for South America. In typical fashion, Elisabeth recreated Paraguay in the paradisal image she imagined it to be. In time, land was acquired and by 1888 enough acreage was cleared to establish the first town of New Germany, Försterrode. But both financial backing and families of immigrants failed to materialize, which jeopardized the colony's existence. Under the terms of the contract signed by Bernhard Förster with the Paraguayan government, should he fail to settle 140 families on the land it would revert to the state. Moreover, Elisabeth found that as her husband lacked the ability to manage the colony's day-to-day affairs she was forced to take control.

Not surprisingly, as the colony teetered on the verge of failure, charges were raised by some colonists as well as critics in Germany that Bernhard was a fraud and that the colonists had been willfully deceived. Elisabeth took the offensive, simultaneously defending her husband and assailing his critics. Bernhard in the meantime had become increasingly moody and distant. Paraguay presented Elisabeth with one set of problems; the declining state of her brother's health raised others. In 1888, Friedrich Nietzsche drifted into insanity and, despite the harsh words that had been exchanged, wrote to his sister for help. Although she was fully absorbed with the New Germany colony, Elisabeth began, in Macintyre's words, "the long process of reinventing her own relationship with Fritz. . . . Instead of being a bad-tempered burden with a taste for Jewish company, she started to turn him back into the idolized figure of her childhood."

Clearly, Elisabeth was torn between her obsession to make a success of New Germany and her deepening concern over brother Fritz. The burdens of the colony proved insurmountable for Bernhard Förster and on June 3, 1889, he committed suicide. In true fashion, according to Peters, Elisabeth transformed his death into "a patriotic apotheosis." She could not accept failure, and this would not be the first time that Elisabeth changed the historical record to bring events into conformity with her beliefs. In August, she was forced to give up ownership of New Germany to a consortium, most of whose members were non-German. But she was intent on regaining control and traveled to Germany to raise the necessary funds and silence her dead husband's critics. The culminating effort of her campaign was the authorship, in just five months, of a book on the colony. *Bernhard Förster's Colony New Germany in Paraguay* was published in 1891 and cast her husband, according to Macintyre, as "a battling hero worthy of Valhalla, in the image of whose face the true Christ is united with the real German race, who has fallen on a foreign field for his belief in the German spirit."

To raise money for the colony, she determined to take advantage of her brother's grow-

ing fame in German intellectual circles. To this end, she attempted to gain control of the publication of Friedrich Nietzsche's works. Peters wrote that those she found blasphemous, such as the fourth part of *Zarathustra,* she tried to suppress, to the consternation of the editor of the manuscripts, Peter Gast. In essence, Elisabeth wanted a publisher who would print all of her brother's works in exchange for a lifetime annuity for Friedrich and the assurance that the publisher would assume liability for any legal actions taken against the author.

A suitable publisher was located, and, given the appeal of Nietzsche, she promoted an inexpensive edition for the use of students. Having secured a reasonable source of support, Elisabeth returned to Paraguay in July 1892. Her return was not a cause for celebration on the part of the colonists. While most of the settlers kept quiet for fear of reprisals, some lashed out at Elisabeth. "Germany had not cured Frau Förster of her sickness, almost amounting to megalomania," one wrote. "On the contrary, she appears to be even more domineering and deluded." The situation was beyond salvation, but Elisabeth managed to find a way to cut her losses and simultaneously save face. She sold her home, the largest in New Germany, and published an official farewell that, in Peters' words, spoke of courage in the forests and the glories of the transplanted fatherland. She appealed for further financial support for New Germany but noted that she was no longer involved. "I must say farewell to all colonial affairs because another great task now awaits me—the care of my dear and only brother, the philosopher Friedrich Nietzsche."

Elisabeth's plan was simple: "to preside over the execution of [Friedrich's] literary estate, which was rapidly increasing in value, and to establish herself as his representative." With this in mind, she had her name legally changed to Förster-Nietzsche. Phase one of her scheme was to pen a biography of Friedrich which would "present a picture to the world in a manner that would appeal to his admirers and enhance his reputation." Then she would supervise the publication of his works with an eye to the maximization of profits. Manipulative and self-centered, Elisabeth explained her actions in other terms: "My mission in the next ten years is to plant the personality of Nietzsche, as the noblest figure of light, firmly into the hearts of people." Macintyre is convinced that Elisabeth was "incapable of distinguishing between what she wanted and what was actually true." Once she gained control of Nietzsche's writings, there was little doubt that her will would triumph over that of the bed-ridden philosopher. However, the caveat expressed by Bergmann is worth repeating: "the political complications facing the prophet emergent cannot be simply or solely blamed on Elisabeth Nietzsche, as extensive and as stupid as were her later forgeries and insinuations." Nietzsche was profoundly anti-democratic and elitist and provided the material with which Elisabeth worked.

Elisabeth completed the first volume of her biography of Nietzsche in 1895, and it enjoyed immediate popular success. Nietzsche became the prophet and his sister an object of reverence as his "only true confidant and supporter." Nietzsche's philosophy was significantly recast by Elisabeth; his anti-nationalism became patriotism and his anti-Christianity masked "a tender love for the founder of Christianity."

By the end of 1895, Elisabeth had wrested control of the Nietzsche archive from her mother, and in the following year it was moved to Weimar where Nietzsche's notes were edited into her version of the truth. One editor complained that "she did not understand her brother at all, that she was falsifying him, that everything she did was a sham and that she had organized the archives only to satisfy her personal vanity." In 1897, after the death of their mother, the insane Nietzsche was moved to Villa Silberblick in Weimar, which in time became a shrine for his devotees. Elisabeth delighted in the visits of intellectuals, artists, poets, and aristocrats to the archive. She lived the life of royalty to which she had always aspired.

Even Nietzsche's death by stroke on August 25, 1900, was manipulated to further Elisabeth's ends. The funeral was an event, and Nietzsche was buried with the blessings of the Christian church. Elisabeth completed volumes two and three of Nietzsche's biography by 1904. Those critics who dared challenge the assertions of the author were rudely dismissed. The popular view of Nietzsche's philosophy had gained the high ground. A close friend of Nietzsche's was dismayed by Elisabeth's biography. "One often hears that the world wants to be deceived, and yet rarely has the reading public been so duped as in Förster's book," he wrote. "It reads sometimes as though Frau Förster wants to prove that she is far wiser than her brother. She is often praised now as a saint among sisters. But this will change. The time may come when she will be considered a prime example of the type: dangerous sisters."

Elisabeth's extravagant spending habits always placed a strain on the resources of the Nietzsche archive. Ironically, it was a Jew, the Swedish banker Ernst Thiel, who put the archive on a firm financial footing and remained a friend until her death. He had Elisabeth painted in 1906 by Edvard Munch and entertained her entreaties for his support in her quest for the Nobel prize for literature in 1908.

When World War I shattered Europe's peace, Elisabeth rejoiced at the sight of a nation in arms. "This war shows the force of my brother's words—'become hard.'" Not surprisingly, she opposed any movement toward peace and firmly believed that the armistice of 1918, made by unpatriotic politicians, had stabbed the German army in the back. The establishment of the Weimar Republic, the very real prospects for revolution in 1919, and chaos in the streets of Germany—all of these were anathema to Elisabeth. She wrote to Thiel in 1921: "My brother wished us dangerous times. Well, we are now living dangerously enough. Let us hope that a great star will arise out of this chaos, a truly great man and leader like Napoleon. . . . Our young people want to worship, venerate and love someone." Elisabeth looked for heroes to save Germany. Fortunate Italy had been saved by Benito Mussolini. Who would save Germany?

Elisabeth met Adolf Hitler in 1932 and was struck by his eyes, "which stare right through you." She had approved of his attempted *putsch* in Bavaria in 1923 and when he assumed power in 1933 she rejoiced at this manifestation of her brother's triumph of the will. Hitler welcomed her support and promised financial backing for the archive. Superman had been found: "[W]e have suddenly achieved the one Germany which for centuries our poets have depicted longingly . . . and which we have been waiting for: one People, one Empire, One Leader." The Nietzsche Archives, she announced, had become the center of National Socialist, i.e. Nazi, ideology. Blind to Nazi ambition and naive as to the means by which Nazism would be spread, Elisabeth willingly subordinated her brother's name and philosophy to the cause of the fatherland. Days after she was informed that Hitler's government planned to build a memorial to Nietzsche, complete with an auditorium and library, Elisabeth Förster-Nietzsche died after a bout with influenza. She did not live to see the horrors that her superman would unleash on the world.

SOURCES:

Bergmann, Peter. *Nietzsche, "the Last Antipolitical German."* Bloomington, IN: Indiana University Press, 1987.

Hayman, Ronald. *Nietzsche: A Critical Life.* NY: Oxford, 1980.

Macintyre, Ben. *Forgotten Fatherland: The Search for Elisabeth Nietzsche.* NY: Farrar, Straus & Giroux, 1992.

Peters, Heinz F. *Zarathustra's Sister: The Case of Elisabeth and Friedrich Nietzsche.* NY: Crown Publishers, 1977.

SUGGESTED READING:

Hayes, Carlton J.H. *A Generation of Materialism, 1871–1900.* NY: Harper & Row, 1941.

Kaufmann, Walter. *Nietzsche: Philosopher, Psychologist, Antichrist.* 3rd ed. Princeton, NJ: Princeton University Press, 1968.

RELATED MEDIA:

"Forgotten Fatherland: The Search for Elisabeth Nietzsche" (2-part, BBC documentary), shown on Arts & Entertainment network, 1992.

Paul B. Goodwin, Jr.,
Professor of History, University of Connecticut,
Storrs, Connecticut

Fort, Cornelia (1919–1943)

Member of Women's Auxiliary Ferrying Squadron (WAFS) in World War II and first American woman killed on active duty. Born Cornelia Clark Fort on February 5, 1919, in Nashville, Tennessee; died in a plane crash near Abilene, Texas, on March 21, 1943; daughter of Rufus E. Fort, Sr. (a doctor and insurance executive) and Louise (Clark) Fort (a homemaker); graduated from Ward-Belmont private school and Sarah Lawrence College; never married; no children.

Began flight instruction and became second woman to receive commercial pilot's license (1940); served as private flight instructor and taught in Civilian Pilot Training Program in Colorado and in Hawaii (1941); witnessed Japanese attack on Pearl Harbor from the air (1941); became second volunteer accepted into WAFS (1942); assigned to Long Beach, California, to ferry planes to Dallas, Texas (February 1943).

"I knew I was going to join the Women's Auxiliary Ferrying Squadron before the organization was a reality, before it had a name, before it was anything but a radical idea in the minds of a few men who believed that women could fly airplanes," wrote Cornelia Fort in a 1943 article for *Woman's Home Companion.* "But I never knew it so surely as I did in Honolulu on December 7, 1941."

Fort was born in 1919 and had grown up in a 24-room mansion, known as Fortland, overlooking the Cumberland River in Nashville, Tennessee. In the warm and wealthy household that included her four brothers and two sisters, she was exposed to books, art, travel and fine food; attended the best local private schools; and en-joyed the particular pleasures of living on a large farm where she could roam with her horses and dogs. A bright student with an excellent academic record, Fort was bookish but also popular among the "sub-debs," girls whose families would formally present them to society at a debutante ball. Her debut was a gala affair held at Nashville's most fashionable country club during her Christmas vacation from Sarah Lawrence College in 1938.

Sarah Lawrence, in Bronxville, New York, was far from Southern culture in distance as well as thought. The choice of this liberal women's institution had dismayed Fort's traditionalist father, but he must have recognized her yearning for something different. At the school, her talents were rewarded with the position of chief editorial writer for the newspaper, *The Campus.* In an editorial published in November 1938, when the attention of the American public was being drawn to events in Europe, Fort wrote of Hitler's atrocities:

> But surely this campaign of horror will turn on its creator and smash him also. Surely this wave of barbarism will weaken the ranks of Fascism and restore the faculty of healthy criticism to the mobs blinded with enthusiasms—We shall aid the persecuted Jews with one hand and try to hasten retribution with the other.

At the time, such sentiments were still somewhat strange to family and friends in Tennessee and to the majority of Americans. Hitler's campaign had not directly affected most people and isolationists in Congress were struggling to keep it that way. Fort's progressive college experience, and increasing questions about the situation in Europe, probably furthered her vague sense of dissatisfaction when she returned to Nashville. As a member of the clubs and organizations appropriate for a young woman of means and social breeding, she felt something missing. She understood that idealism was part of the privileged existence that she led. Fort believed she had a responsibility to uphold the integrity, loyalty, and freedom her family life had taught her to value.

In 1940, flying lessons provided Fort with the focus she sought; she was immediately hooked. "None of us can put it into words why we fly," said Fort. "I can't *say* exactly why I fly but I *know* why as I've never known anything in my life." Her sister Louise once suggested that "flying apparently added a sense of wonder and joy to her life."

On her first flight, she had difficulties handling the control stick; within a month, she had soloed. The Fort family admired her achievements but could not quite understand the passion that had enveloped her. Rushing home to announce that she had soloed, she found her mother working among the roses. "How very nice, dear," **Louise Clark Fort** replied. "Now you won't have to do that again." Shortly after Fort's first lesson, Rufus Fort, Sr., died. For all his conventional outlook, he was a much-loved figure in the family, and the loss was a crushing blow.

In those days, aviation was still a novelty and very expensive. A private pilot's license cost between $500 and $750, and a pilot's average income was less than $2,000 a year. Since the first planes buzzed low over the landscape, however, America had a love affair with flying; Charles Lindbergh and *Amelia Earhart were national heroes, and the barnstorming pilots of the Great Depression had been romanticized as the ultimate in escapist entertainment. But Earhart was not the only woman to tackle the rigors of guiding an airplane buffeted by the wind, maneuvering through clouds, rain and fog while relying on landmarks along the ground for direction. By 1928, there had been enough female pilots to form an international organization called the Ninety-Nines.

I, for one, am profoundly grateful that my one talent, my only knowledge, flying, happens to be of use to my country when it is needed.

—**Cornelia Fort**

During June 1940, Fort earned her private pilot's license. In the first week alone, she logged over 2,000 miles visiting friends around the southeast. Within a few months, she earned her commercial pilot's license, and by March 1941—just a year after she began flying—she earned an instructor's rating. This made her the first female flight instructor in Nashville and the only one in Tennessee. Fort continued her own flight training in larger aircraft. She was certain that aviation was a growing field, and she intended to be a part of it.

As the war in Europe escalated and American armed services began preparing for the possibility of engagement, more planes were manufactured and more pilots were needed. In early 1941, President Franklin Roosevelt authorized the Civilian Pilots Training Program (CPT), administered through colleges and universities, to financially assist those of college-age to learn flying. While the program did not exclude women, the ratio of acceptance was one woman for every ten men. When Fort was hired to teach in the CPT at Ft. Collins, Colorado, she planned to drive from Nashville with her dog, but her mother was scandalized by the idea of her daughter making such a long journey unchaperoned. So, despite the long and complicated solo flights Fort had undertaken, she gave in to her mother's insistence that she be accompanied by the family chauffeur.

One reason for taking the position in Colorado was to get altitude experience, "the hardest flying there is." In the Rocky Mountains, a plane took off at a height above what most small planes achieved taking off at sea level, and the winds could be a real challenge. "One learns plenty and fast," she wrote, noting that a year before she would have laughed had anyone suggested she would be willing to "get up at 4:30 AM and work straight through until almost 8:00 PM daily for six months." In fact, she loved it.

In October 1941, Fort accepted a position in Hawaii, where she was one of two female flight instructors. The beauty of the islands impressed her but not the boom-town atmosphere and press of people from the defense industry and military bases. She wrote her brother that she missed the seasonal changes of home and the ability to get away to someplace different. Still, she continued, it was the best job she could have "unless the national emergency creates a still better one."

On December 7, a beautiful Sunday morning, Fort and a student pilot were flying above the island, preparing to make a landing, when she realized she was on a collision course with a military plane. Grabbing the controls, she pulled up, and the passage of the military aircraft caused a violent shaking in the windows of her airplane. Fort looked for the aircraft's identification to report the incident and was astonished to see orange circles, the Japanese emblem of the Rising Sun. She wrote:

> I looked quickly at Pearl Harbor and my spine tingled when I saw billowing black smoke. Then I looked way up and saw the formations of silver bombers riding in. Something detached itself from an airplane and came glistening down. My eyes followed it down, down and even with knowledge pounding in my mind, my heart turned convulsively when the bomb exploded in the middle of the harbor.

Having witnessed the bombing of Pearl Harbor, she landed the plane and ran to safety, as "a shadow passed over" her and "simultaneously bullets spattered all around." Three months later, Fort returned to Nashville a celebrity and was asked to recount her experience over and over to newspapers, clubs, and on the radio. She made a short film to sell war bonds and became a speaker at war-bond rallies. The periodical *Calling All Girls* requested permission to base a comic strip on the story of her life, and she was offered a contract for lectures and radio appearances by the company that had managed Earhart and others. Fort, however, had other plans.

While waiting to return from Hawaii, she had missed a telegram from *Jacqueline Cochran, a well-known pilot who was forming a group to fly with the Royal Air Force Air Transport Auxiliary in Britain. In Nashville, Fort returned to instructing, waiting for another such opportunity. She would be in Binghamton, New York, enrolled for a three-month, instrument-training course, when she would finally receive the telegram for which she'd been hoping.

Meanwhile, a struggle was under way involving Cochran and another prominent pilot, ✍➤ **Nancy Harkness Love**, who were working from different directions to persuade the U.S.

Love, Nancy Harkness. *See Cochran, Jacqueline for sidebar.*

Cornelia Fort

Army Air Force that women pilots were an answer to the drastic shortage of pilots needed to ferry newly manufactured planes to destinations around the country. Military leaders resisted, because many were not convinced that women had the strength to fly military craft, and many were simply uncomfortable with women in military work. Congress also resisted; on the floor of the House of Representatives there was an impassioned plea in 1941: "If we take women into the Armed Service, who then will do the cooking, the washing, the mending, the humble homey tasks to which every woman has devoted herself? . . . Think of the humiliation! What has become of the manhood of America!" But something had to be done soon. Men were being drafted into the infantry and joining other services that would engage in direct combat, leaving fewer and fewer to fly or be trained as pilots.

Cochran's small group of women flyers joined the Royal Air Transport Auxiliary, setting an example that was hard for the American armed forces to ignore. Cochran continued to push for a group in the States, using her personal influence with the president and *Eleanor Roosevelt. In fact, Eleanor used her weekly radio address to support the use of women pilots in the war effort. Meanwhile, Love and her husband, who was in the Army Air Forces' Air Transport Command (ATC), began to lobby harder for the use of women to take some pressure off the ATC. Eventually, the competition and resulting bitterness between Cochran and Love did serious injury to their mutual cause, but without their efforts the American military might never have accepted the active support of American women pilots during World War II.

By 1942, the need for ferry pilots was so drastic that the army brass capitulated to Love's lobbying and authorized the Women's Auxiliary Ferrying Squadron (WAFS), with Nancy Love as their non-military commander. In September 1942, Love sent out a telegram to the most qualified women pilots in the country, inviting them to report within 24 hours to New Castle Army Air Base near Wilmington, Delaware, at their own expense. Fort received her telegram on September 6 and left Binghamton immediately, wiring her mother, "The heavens have opened up and rained blessings on me. The army has decided to let women ferry ships and I'm going to be one of them." A few days later, she became the second woman to be accepted into the WAFS.

Quarters for the women were not finished when the first recruits arrived. Initially, the candidates had to pay not only for their transportation to Wilmington but for their hotel, meals and transportation to and from the base for testing and early training, all without a salary. Even when they moved in, they had to pay for the facilities, meals and flying gear checked out to them. The salary for women was $250 per month plus a $6 per diem, significantly less than civilian men received for the same jobs. Love warned her squadron that they must adhere to the strictest codes of conduct at all times lest there be any appearance of fraternizing with the enlisted men or of actions that cast doubt on their integrity. Such behavior would result in instant dismissal from the WAFS; similar behavior in a man would call for simple army discipline.

The WAFS attracted great public attention, receiving coverage from newsreel film and magazine photographers. Not all the attention from men at New Castle could be labeled friendly. The WAFS were resented by some who believed the women were getting better treatment and who believed women should not be doing "a man's job." Other men simply thought of the WAFS as whistlebait. Love watched the situation with an eagle eye, seeing the dangers to her program if the group should get a "loose" reputation.

Fort's marching partner, **Adela R. Scharr**, wrote in her memoirs that Fort was simply pleased to be in the company of other distinguished female pilots. Fort had a look, she said, "of austere bookishness and her long handsome face did not correspond to the pretty-pretty face so beloved by moviegoers of the era." She had plenty of friends, but her purpose in the WAFS was to fly in support of her country.

On October 22, 1942, Fort was included in the first WAFS plane delivery from the Piper airplane factory at Lockhaven, Pennsylvania, to Long Island, New York. With difficult weather closing in, flight leader **Betty Gillies** wired the airfield of their arrival because there had been word that flights were being grounded due to aerial target practice near the area. The telegram was dangerously delayed. By the time it arrived, the women pilots had landed and were waiting for rides into the city, an incident that was only the first of many hazards and difficulties WAFS had to overcome.

Even so, the squadron was soon ferrying planes throughout the country. Cochran returned to the States and began to campaign for a place within the program, and a period of political maneuvering by Love, Cochran and their various supporters finally resulted in a compromise that allowed each woman her own sphere of influence. Love continued to command the WAFS, and Cochran established a school near Houston, Texas, to train pilots for the WAFS, an arrangement that was only partially satisfactory.

Occasionally, WAFS would ferry planes to locations near family and friends. Fort visited her brother Rufus, a recruiter for the Women's Army Corps in Atlanta. Sometimes she would arrange to meet her mother and sister at the Nashville airport, and at Christmas she managed a short visit home. Just after she returned to Delaware, she received word that a fire had damaged her beloved Fortland, destroying her childhood treasures and all her diaries, letters, and books. After learning of the loss, Fort appeared at the door of her room in the barracks "so stupefied it was difficult for her to speak," wrote Scharr. Fort compared this loss to the death of her father, for much of her life had been wrapped up in her home and her writings. The journals she had kept since her first flight were also gone. Many pilots are very superstitious and believe tragedies come in threes. Tragedy had now struck close to Fort twice, at Pearl Harbor and at home; many members of the WAFS began to wonder what would be next.

Change was about to take place for the "originals," as the first WAFS were called. They were split into small groups and reassigned, creating the nucleus of a squad that was to be developed with Cochran's graduates. Fort was assigned to Long Beach, California, where she arrived on February 18, 1943, after a one-day visit to Nashville en route. Ferrying planes to Dallas, she soon became so familiar with the route she felt it was a path cut into the sky. On March 21, she was on a routine trip with a squadron that included male pilots. One was a young hotshot, Frank W. Stamme, Jr., who teased, flirted with, and harassed Fort during the flight, fairly standard behavior when it came to the male pilot's attitude toward the WAFS. Just outside Abilene, Texas, he tried a particular stunt, perhaps not realizing that evasive maneuvers was not included in the women's training. As he dived toward her aircraft, a section of his plane hit her wing. Fort's plane went into a spin then plunged, diving nose into the ground to a depth of two feet. Apparently, Fort was either knocked unconscious or killed instantly for there was no evidence of an attempt by her to control the aircraft or to use the parachute. In the ensuing Army Air Force inquiry, no pilot error was found on her part. Stamme was found at fault, but the need for pilots was so great that he was not court-martialed and continued to fly.

Almost three years to the day after the burial of her father, Fort was laid to rest in Nashville, at age 24. The downtown church was packed for the funeral, and Nancy Love and Betty Gillies attended. Three weeks later, Gillies led a ferry mission from Hagerstown, Maryland, to Calgary, Canada—a 2,500-mile trip made in four days—an extraordinary feat for the WAFS Ferrying Division seen both as a morale booster for the women pilots and a tribute to Fort from her peers.

The "boys will be boys" attitude about dangerous flying habits continued for some time until a larger pool of pilots made individuals less important to the service. The Army Air Force commander, General H.H. Arnold, finally directed that disobeying safety regulations would mean dismissal or severe punishments, meaning the possible loss of military benefits—an ironic punishment, since women were not allowed military benefits. Not eligible to be taken under the Women's Army Corps as originally planned, the WAFS and the Women's Flying Training Detachment (WFTD) of Cochran's school watched efforts to militarize their own divisions undermined by the rivalry between their leaders. In 1943, the two groups were combined into the Women's Air Service Program (WASPs). The WASPs were deactivated in December 1944, without receiving military status or veterans benefits. In 1977, the efforts of former WASPs and their supporters finally rectified this injustice when Congressional legislation certified WASPs as military personnel eligible for veterans benefits. The U.S. Air Force gave the first official recognition in 1979, and in 1984 each woman pilot was awarded the Victory Medal while those with over one year of duty received the American Theater Medal.

The contribution of Cornelia Fort to her country has been recognized in several ways, including a private air park in Nashville that is named for her. During the wait to leave Hawaii after Pearl Harbor in 1941, she had written to her mother, reflecting on the possibility of her death while flying: "I was happiest in the sky— at dawn when the quietness of the air was like a caress, when the noon sun beat down and at dusk when the sky was drenched with fading light. Think of me there and remember me, I hope as I shall you, with love."

SOURCES:

Fort, Cornelia. "The Twilight's Last Gleaming," in *Woman's Home Companion.* July 1943.

Fort, Homer T., Jr., and Drucill Stovall Jones. *A Family Called Fort: The Descendants of Elias Fort of Virginia.* Midland, TX: West Texas Printing, 1970.

Scharr, Adela Riek. *Sisters in the Sky*. Vol. I, *The WAFS*, and Vol.II, *The WASP*. St. Louis, MO: Patrice Press, 1986, 1988.

Tanner, Doris Brinker. "Cornelia Fort: A WASP in World War II: Part I," in *Tennessee Historical Quarterly*. VOL. XL. Fall 1981; "Part II." Vol. XLI. Spring 1982.

Verges, Marianne. *On Silver Wings, 1942–1944: The Women Airforce Service Pilots of World War II*. NY: Ballantine Books, 1991

SUGGESTED READING:

Cochran, Jacqueline, with Floyd Odlum. *The Stars at Noon*. Boston, MA: Little, Brown, 1954.

Cole, Jean Hascall. *Women Pilots of World War II*. Salt Lake City, UT: University of Utah Press, 1992.

Fisher, Marquita O. *Jacqueline Cochran: First Lady of Flight*. Illustrated by Victor Mays. Champaign, IL: Garrard, 1973.

Simbeck, Rob. *Daughter of the Air: The Short Soaring Life of Cornelia Fort*. Boston, MA: Atlantic Monthly, 1999.

RELATED MEDIA:

"Women of Courage of World War II" (video with Student-Teacher Companion Guide). Ken Magid, Executive Producer. Lakewood, CO: KM Productions, 1992.

COLLECTIONS:

Documents about the Women's Auxiliary Ferrying Squadron (WAFS) and Women's Air Service Program (WASP) are located in the Air Force Historical Research Center at Maxwell Air Force Base, Alabama.

Margaret L. Meggs,
independent scholar on women's and disability issues,
and a member of the Fort family

Forten, Charlotte (1837–1914).

See Grimké, Charlotte L. Forten.

Forten, Harriet (1810–1875).

See Purvis, Harriet Forten.

Forten, Margaretta (1808–1875)

*African-American abolitionist and educator. Born in Philadelphia, Pennsylvania, in 1808; died of pneumonia on January 14, 1875; daughter of James Forten and his second wife Charlotte (Vandine) Forten; aunt to *Charlotte Forten Grimké (1837–1914); educated at home and at the school set up by her father and Grace Douglass; never married; no children.*

Sarah Mapps Douglass. *See Grimké, Angelina E. for sidebar.*

Born in 1808 as the eldest child of James Forten and **Charlotte Vandine**, Margaretta was named for her paternal grandmother Margaret Forten who died two years before her granddaughter's birth. Both James and Charlotte, his second wife, were freeborn. Charlotte, a native of Pennsylvania, married James in 1805 when he was 39 and a widower. James' great-grandfather arrived in Pennsylvania as a slave brought from West Africa in the 1680s. James' grandfather became a free man, most likely by self-purchase, and James' father Thomas was a skilled artisan who worked as a sailmaker. James learned the trade from his father who also made sure that his son was educated. In 1796, James took over the business of Robert Bridges, a white sailmaker who had employed both James and his father. Soon well established in the trade, Forten was known for the quality of his workmanship and fair dealing, and he refused to fit out vessels that he suspected were employed with the slave trade. As Philadelphia prospered in the 1790s and early 1800s from trade, James Forten too prospered and invested his profits in real estate, moneylending, and in time in railroad and bank stocks.

By 1808 when Margaretta was born, the family lived in an elegant brick house on a main thoroughfare in Philadelphia, at 92 Lombard Street. The three-story house was home to Margaretta, her parents and siblings as well as domestic servants and apprentices and journeymen from James' sail loft. The number of occupants grew during the early 19th century, with the federal census recording 15 members in 1810 as compared to 22 in 1830.

The Fortens had six children by 1819, and Margaretta had three sisters and two brothers (two more Forten sons would follow). Securing a decent education for the children was of concern in an age when the schools that were open to black children were church and charity enterprises; these schools could teach the Forten children the basics but were not equipped to provide them with the advanced education that James Forten wanted for his children. **Grace Douglass**, who was an old friend of James' and now had five children of her own, worked with James to open a school. They hired a teacher in 1819, Britton E. Chamberlain, and the school would eventually be taken over by Grace's daughter **Sarah Mapps Douglass** when Chamberlain left. Margaretta attended this school and also received additional education at home. She learned to both speak and read French. When taking tea with the Forten family, the Reverend Breckinridge, a member of the American Colonization Society, was discussing Haitian politics with James Forten. To prove a point, James handed a letter from an acquaintance about Haiti to Breckinridge who could not read French. Margaretta was called to translate the letter. As **Julie Winch** writes in *Notable Black American Women*: "[T]he editor of an abolitionist journal, in recounting this incident, observed that Breckinridge went from the Forten home to a meeting at which he argued that black people should leave the United States because they were intellectually inferior to whites."

Upon visiting the Forten home in 1833, the white abolitionist Samuel J. May was impressed by how "lovely [and] accomplished" the daughters were. He insisted upon escorting Margaretta to an antislavery meeting, to the mortification of some of his acquaintances.

From an early age, Margaretta was called to assist her father in his business affairs and witnessed a deed for him at age nine (1817). When James Forten drew up his will in 1836, she was appointed one of three executors. In this position, she would later complete property deals that had been begun by her father and initiate several court cases to protect her own interest as well as those of the other heirs.

Drawn into the abolitionist fold by her upbringing, her community, and her own perceptions of American societal injustices, Margaretta had grown up in a home that was a place of calling for committed opponents to slavery. Her father provided a good deal of the early funding for the *Liberator,* an antislavery journal edited by William Lloyd Garrison who was a welcome guest at the Forten home. Other guests Margaretta met included James and *Lucretia Mott, Arthur and Lewis Tappan, George Thompson, Benjamin Lundy, Edward Abdy, and J. Miller McKim.

When the American Anti-Slavery Society was created in Philadelphia in December of 1833, Margaretta expressed her emotions in verse. Her poem, published in the *Emancipator* (January 14, 1834), was addressed to the organization's founders, her brother-in-law Robert Purvis among them, and included the lines:

> Ye blessed few! who have stood the storm
> Of persecution, in its direful form;
> Unmov'd have faced the foe in stern array
> Clad in bold armor for the dread affray;
> Your banner floats—its motto may be read,
> "DOWN WITH OPPRESSION! FREEDOM
> IN ITS STEAD!"

Signed "M.T.F.," the poem was identified by the editor as having been written by "the daughter of a highly respected colored gentleman of Philadelphia." This is the only poem attributed to Margaretta with certainty, though it is possible that she wrote others under a pseudonym.

Female abolitionists were initially denied full membership in the Anti-Slavery Society and so formed their own societies. Forten, along with her sisters **Sarah** and **Harriet Forten**, traveled to New York in 1837 and attended the Women's Anti-Slavery Convention. They also attended two subsequent conventions in Philadel-

phia. Organizing at the local level, Forten participated in drawing up the constitution that formed the Philadelphia Female Anti-Slavery Society, an interracial organization. She was also present when the Society disbanded, and it was she who moved the adoption of a preamble and resolution that dissolved the society on March 24, 1870.

With a keen interest in promoting the education of black children, for more than 30 years Margaretta Forten ran a successful private school. She served as principal of the Lombard Street Primary School from 1845. Her influence on her niece *Charlotte Forten Grimké (the daughter of Margaretta's brother Robert Bridges Forten) was profound, and, after the death of Robert's wife, Charlotte was apparently entrusted to his mother and Margaretta. Charlotte owed much of her early education to her aunt, with whom she corresponded while away at school. "Wrote a letter to my dear aunt," wrote Charlotte in her journal. "I can always write more freely to her than to any one else" (Stevenson, November 19, 1854). Margaretta was responsible for identifying her niece as the author of a poem in the *Liberator* (1855), a disclosure that annoyed Charlotte. Forten visited her niece in Salem, and they attended antislavery celebrations together. The close ties between the two continued, with Forten shaping Charlotte's literary tastes. During the Civil War, when Charlotte went to the Sea Islands to teach at the Freedmen's School, Forten received letters from her which included requests for clothing for the freedmen and toys for Charlotte's younger students.

In time, the running of the Lombard Street household fell to Margaretta Forten. She took care of her elderly mother and brothers Thomas and William, bachelors. William Forten continued the family's tradition of activism by aiding fugitives in the 1850s, achieving notoriety for his coordination of the defense of those charged with a Southern slaveholder's death in the Christiana riot, helping recruit black troops during the Civil War, and as an officer of the Pennsylvania Equal Rights League. He was instrumental in Philadelphia politics during the 1870s when his ability to deliver the black vote for the Republican Party proved crucial. Never married, Margaretta took on the roll of political hostess, and her running of the household facilitated her brother's political career.

Evidently suffering from recurrent respiratory problems, possibly from tuberculosis, Margaretta Forten had to take absences from school a number of times. Two of her sisters as well as her nieces and nephews also suffered respiratory problems. She remained a teacher and dedicated advocate of social reform until her death from pneumonia on January 14, 1875.

SOURCES:

Smith, Jessie Carney, ed. *Notable Black American Women*. Detroit, MI: Gale Research, 1992.

Forten, Sarah (c. 1811–1898).

See Purvis, Sarah Forten.

Fortibus, Isabella de (1237–1293).

See Isabella de Redvers.

Forz, Avelina de (1259–1274).

See Isabella de Redvers for sidebar.

Forz, Isabella de (1237–1293).

See Isabella de Redvers.

Fosburgh, Minnie Astor (1906–1978).

See Cushing Sisters.

Fossey, Dian (1932–1985)

Controversial American primatologist who waged an unrelenting battle to save the mountain gorillas of central Africa. Name variations: Nyirmachabelli (The Woman Who Lives Alone on the Mountain). Born on January 16, 1932, in Atherton, California; murdered on the early morning of December 27, 1985, at Karisoke, in the Virunga mountains, Rwanda; daughter of George Fossey III (an insurance agent) and Kathryn Fossey; attended Marin Junior College, 1949, and University of California at Davis, 1950; graduated San Jose State College, 1954; granted doctorate from Cambridge, 1976; never married; no children.

Directed the Occupational Therapy department at the Kosair Crippled Children's Hospital (1955–65); went on first tour of Africa (September–October, 1963); attended Louis Leakey lecture in Louisville (March 1966); left for Africa (December 15, 1966); set up camp in the Kabara Meadow (January 14, 1967); escorted off the mountain by soldiers because of outbreak of hostilities in the Congo (July 9, 1967); set up Karisoke Research Camp in Rwanda (September 24, 1967); except for intermittent periods, remained at Karisoke for the rest of her life; traveled to states for dental work (September 24, 1968); attended Darwin College at Cambridge for three months (1970); was visiting professor at Cornell in Ithaca, New York (1980–82).

Dian Fossey was born on January 16, 1932, near San Francisco. Three years later, her father, an alcoholic, moved out of the house, and her mother Kitty eventually married Richard Price, a building contractor. Under the stern rules laid down by Price that children should rarely be seen, much less heard, Fossey shared her evening meal in the kitchen with the housekeeper and was often left with her aunt and uncle. To offset her loneliness, she turned her affection to animals and, in her teens, took up horse riding.

Her mother, a petite blonde alarmed by her daughter's growing height, took Dian to a doctor. The doctor's diagnosis was that Dian was just, well, tall. Full grown, she would reach 6'1". Though the Prices were comfortably off, Fossey was pretty much on her own—financially and emotionally—when she finished high school. In 1950, she enrolled at the University of California at Davis as a preveterinary student and did well in most subjects, but she failed her second year, tripped up by the "hard" sciences: chemistry and physics. Transferring to San Jose State College, she graduated in 1954 with a degree in occupational therapy (OT).

Fossey then moved to Louisville, Kentucky, to run the OT department at the Kosair Crippled Children's Hospital and remained there for ten years. She loved working with children; she also took in stray dogs and continued riding horses, but Fossey longed to be with animals in their natural state, where they had not, she wrote, "been driven into little corners." Determined to go on safari in Africa, she borrowed from a loan company, at exorbitant interest rates, the $5,000 needed for a six-week trip to Kenya, Tanganyika (now Tanzania), Uganda, Rwanda, and the Belgian Congo (known as Zaire, 1976–97, now Republic of Congo). At the time, $5,000 was her yearly salary.

Because she suffered from allergies, asthma attacks, and frequent bouts of pneumonia, Fossey traveled with a well-packed medicine chest when she departed for Africa on September 26, 1963. She endured a sprained ankle and frequent bouts of dysentery, fever, nausea, and vomiting. Even so, she gamely pressed on. At the suggestion of her guide, she visited Olduvai Gorge, near the Kenya-Tanzania border, home of paleoanthropologist Louis Leakey and archaeologist *Mary Leakey, and found them home and welcoming. When Fossey told Louis that her dream was to live and work with the mountain gorillas, he heartily encouraged her, calling it a sorely neglected field of study. Louis Leakey was convinced that women were better suited for animal field study than men; he felt that women were more prone to patience and had a higher capacity to give fully. Six years earlier, he had launched *Jane Goodall in her study of chimpanzees. (He would later sponsor *Biruté Galdikas' work with orangutans.)

Spurred on by Leakey's enthusiasm, Fossey headed for the home of the mountain gorilla, a four-day journey from Nairobi by Land Rover. "Right in the heart of central Africa, so high up that you shiver more than you sweat," writes Fossey, "are great, old volcanoes towering up almost fifteen thousand feet, and nearly covered with rich, green rain forest—the Virungas." Composed of eight volcanoes, including Mt. Karisimbi, Mt. Visoke, and Mt. Mikeno, the Virungas mountain range spans three African nations: the Congo on its western slopes, Rwanda on its southwestern slopes, and Uganda on its northern slopes. (The Parc des Volcans in Rwanda had been established in 1929 to protect gorillas and wildlife. On the Congo side, a counterpart, the Parc des Virungas, was established in 1922; the British did the same in Uganda.)

After six hours of high-altitude climbing on Mt. Mikeno, by way of the Congo, Fossey arrived at a base camp at Kabara Meadow, high up in the Virungas. From there, she was invited to join photographers Alan and **Joan Root** on a trek to find

gorillas. "The terrain was unbelievable," writes Fossey, "almost straight up, and we had to hang on to vines to get along or go on hands and knees." Dian, who was, and would remain, terrified of heights, found herself panting behind the others. "For a long time we found no sign of gorillas, but then we came upon a bedding place where thirteen of them had slept the night before."

Back in the States, Fossey longed to return to Africa. She wrote of her explorations but, except for the Louisville *Courier Journal*, found no buyers. Then in March 1966, Louis Leakey arrived in Louisville on a lecture tour, and she was in attendance. Pleased to see her, Leakey again urged Fossey to begin observing the gorillas. She reminded him that she had not finished her preveterinary studies and had no background in the "oligies," but he waved her off. He preferred that those who entered the work be without academic prejudices. She then reminded him of her age, 34. Perfect, he said, all she had to do was have her appendix removed. Appendicitis in the bush, as Mary Leakey could testify, was dangerous.

Dian Fossey

As she waited for funding, Fossey devoured books on Africa, especially George Schaller's *The Year of the Gorilla*. Schaller had spent extended time in the Virungas only a few years earlier. With Louis Leakey's prodding, the Wilkie Foundation, which had supported Goodall, offered a grant to establish Fossey's project; National Geographic also kicked in. Against the advice of parents and friends, Fossey left for Africa on December 15, 1966, visited Goodall's camp to check out the setup, then purchased a used Land Rover.

> *I* heard a noise in the foliage by my side and looked directly into the beautifully trusting face of Macho, who stood gazing up at me. . . . On perceiving the softness, tranquillity, and trust conveyed by Macho's eyes, I was overwhelmed by the extraordinary depth of our rapport.
>
> —Dian Fossey, *Gorillas in the Mist*

On January 14, 1967, leaving their cars in the tiny village of Kibumba, Fossey, Alan Root, and 41 African porters hauled equipment 4,000 feet up the mountain. Fossey would spend two years in a tent at this camp on the edge of the Kabara Meadow, where the days were dark and generally enveloped in rain or mist, and the trails were difficult. The day after Root left, Fossey found herself celebrating her 35th birthday alone; she was depressed, listless, and lonely. Because of her limited knowledge of Swahili, she could barely talk to the three Africans who stayed in their own quarters. But that day also brought the sighting of a gorilla near the camp; it was a sign, she thought. Five days later, she made contact with her first band of gorillas, a family of nine. She named them Group 1 and began her log.

At first, Fossey was too eager, and the gorillas were disturbed. She learned to avoid sudden appearances and to maintain a submissive posture. She began to mimic their mannerisms, imitate their sounds. She also learned to track them expertly, thereby discovering other groups. After six months, despite staff insubordination and poachers, problems encountered by all primatologists undergoing similar studies, she was getting nearer the gorillas for longer periods of time; she had also acquired a workable knowledge of Swahili.

Though she had no expertise as a cook and limited options because of the paucity of food in the Kibumba market, Fossey was beginning to enjoy the isolation. She surrounded herself with animals, caring for her pet rooster Dezi, her beloved boxer Cindy, her ravens Charles and Yvonne, and her monkey Kima, despite Kima's tendency to bite. But disaster struck on July 9, 1967, when soldiers arrived to escort her off the mountain, seemingly for her protection, because of an outbreak of hostilities in the Congo. European mercenaries fighting on the side of Moise Tshombe were provoking a backlash against whites. The week before, Joseph Mobotu had authorized Congolese radio to warn that foreigners were trying to take over the country and the borders were about to be closed. Fossey was in "protective" custody for 16 days and kept in a cage for the last two. She would later confide only to close acquaintances that she had been raped repeatedly. "She knew very well that the second anybody suspected what she had been through, she would have been sent straight home," said **Anita McClellan**, her editor at Houghton Mifflin. "She wasn't about to let that happen. What had become more important to her than anything else on earth were those gorillas." Using bribes and a ruse, Fossey was one of the last whites to escape the eastern Congo alive. (Three Europeans of her acquaintance would be tortured and killed by the Congolese.)

Now in Rwanda, she was unemployed, penniless, close to a nervous breakdown, and fearful that Louis would think she had not tried hard enough. Leakey, on the contrary, was amazed at her courage. Then Fossey met **Rosamond Carr**, a 53-year-old white American who owned property at the forested lower slopes of the Virungas on the Rwanda side. The two became fast friends, and Carr suggested the home of **Alyette de Munck**, a Belgian woman and recent widow who lived a mile or two near, for a base camp. (Contrary to the media's depiction of her as a loner who only knew gorillas, Fossey had many close friends throughout the world and was known for her spontaneous generosity.)

With Louis' backing, Fossey began to track on the Rwandan side of Mt. Karisimbi. Two days out, she discovered her "old" Group 2—a group she had not seen for 19 weeks—but she was 30 minutes inside the Congolese border, a dangerous place to be. On the tenth day, she found a site for her camp which she would name Karisoke: a 10,000-foot-high plateau where the saddle that joins mounts Visoke, Karisimbi, and Mikeno reaches its tallest point. On September 24, 1967, as she helped pitch her tent (which would eventually be replaced by a two-room cabin), Fossey could hear the beating of gorilla chests on the slopes behind the camp.

But there were far more poachers and there was far more corruption with park officials on the Rwandan side. Fossey was soon going head to head with tradition. Though poaching and hunting was illegal in the park, Tutsi and Batwa tribes had been hunting on the slopes from time immemorial and had an understanding with the park guards. Despite admonishments from her friends to respect the traditions of the locals, Fossey demanded that the park rules be enforced: she would protect her gorillas at all costs. She complained to the L'Office Rwandais du Tourisme et des Parcs Nationaux (ORTPN), and they agreed to increase patrols.

Before Fossey, little was known about the birth and death rates of mountain gorillas, nor about their social behavior, their interaction within the group. She learned that play, a trait that gorillas generally concealed from observers, was far more important than early ape studies realized. By the end of summer 1968, she had located and was tracking nine gorilla groups and was familiar with 80 named gorillas. The outside world began to take note of the 36-year-old Fossey with her salt-and-pepper hair. There were offers of Ph.D. studies at Cambridge, publishers asking for books, adventurers hiking to her camp, bent on meeting her. Many thought her brave for mingling with gorillas; Fossey disagreed. Her bravery, she felt, was in going head to head with her acrophobia (fear of heights): she found that "sliding across a moss-slippery rock face of seventy percent slope, something a two-year-old could jump across," reduced her to "shivering weakness."

But her fears for the gorillas were not imaginary. In 1960, Schaller had estimated there were 400 mountain, as opposed to lowland, gorillas left in the world. Infant gorillas wanted by zoos were captured at high cost. In 1948, locals had killed 60 adult gorillas in order to capture 11 infants. None of the 1948 infants survived in captivity. In 1969, Fossey received word that ten adults in a group were found slaughtered by poachers intent on capturing a baby gorilla for Germany's Cologne zoo. Alerted by authorities who now had the dying baby gorilla on their hands, Fossey brought the 3-year-old male back to camp, named him Coco, and nursed him day and night. Then another baby, a three-year-old female, was captured for the zoo and brought to her for nursing. Despite her protestations, the babies were eventually crated by Rwandan officials and sent off to Cologne.

A white African warned her that, as a woman, she could not stay alone on a mountain, hunt down poachers, and live. Throughout Africa, he said, European women have lived alone on farms while their husbands went off to war. His mother was one of them. "The only way they survived was to become known as some sort of banshee." He advised her to become a spiritual witch. Since *Sumu* (native sorcery) was prevalent in Africa, he told her to play to it—exude toughness, create terror, wail, shriek, make crazy faces, and strike poachers if need be. In a decision that possibly led to her death, Fossey took his advice to heart, terrifying poachers, even killing the cattle of Tutsi herders because they were illegally grazing in the park. For years, it served her and it served the gorillas. It did not, however, do much for her reputation when each stupefied researcher saw the display without benefit of the explanation. Despite some who accused her of racism, those that knew Fossey said it was never about race, that she would shoot at a white poacher as fast as an African.

There were other problems in 1969. Her cabin caught fire, her chickens died. Bitten by a dog, she came down with rabies and had to be carried off the mountain to the local French hospital and endure days of rabies injections. Fossey was also having severe chest pains, and she suspected TB. Short-handed, she requested census takers to keep tabs on the dwindling gorilla population. Her first student census-taker, however, dabbled in hashish. Of all the students and researchers who would work at Karisoke, Fossey found only four who lived up to her criteria. These were the ones who treated the gorillas "with respect," writes her biographer Farley Mowat, those who recognized that "these superb creatures were according them a great privilege by tolerating the human presence." One early favorite was Sandy Harcourt; he would later become a major nemesis.

By then, Bob Campbell had also joined her off and on to do the photography. On January 1, 1970, with Campbell in tow, Fossey went in search of gorillas once more and encountered Group 8. Then, Peanuts, a young blackback, "left his tree for a bit of strutting," she wrote in *Gorillas in the Mist:*

> He beat his chest, he threw leaves in the air, he swaggered and slapped the foliage around him, and then suddenly he was at my side. . . . I lay back in the foliage to appear as harmless as possible and slowly extended my hand. I held it palm up at first, as the palms of an ape and a human hand are more similar than the backs of the hand.

When I felt he recognized this 'object,' I slowly turned my hand over and let it rest on the foliage. Peanuts seemed to ponder accepting my hand, a familiar yet strange object extended to him. Finally he came a step closer and, extending his own hand, gently touched his fingers to mine.

It was the first friendly physical contact ever recorded between a wild mountain gorilla and a human, and the event was captured on film by Campbell, prompting a January 1970 cover story in *National Geographic* which contributed to her fame. Soon, physical contact between the gorillas and Fossey would become routine.

A week later, Fossey was attending Darwin College at Cambridge, England, for a three-month term as a doctoral student in natural science. Though she felt out of her element, she knew that she "had to obtain a union card in the scientific field" to give her findings validity and obtain grant support or student help in the bush. "Without that Big Degree, you don't cut much ice no matter how good you are," she wrote. But she needed someone to watch the camp during her forays in academia; replacements would be a constant problem and cause her endless worry. Even so, with periodic excursions into academia, she would be granted a doctorate from Cambridge in 1976.

Throughout 1972, she spent much of her time with Group 4 whose population included a non-mature male that she had named Digit because of his twisted broken finger; she had been observing him since he was five in 1967. Writes Mowat:

Dian was often mobbed by the youngsters of Group 4, who treated her almost as one of themselves. Digit in particular seemed to welcome her presence. On such occasions note-taking would be forgotten and Dian would revel in the pure joy of being accepted. She groomed her friends and allowed them to groom her. She dozed with them in the sun. She tickled the infants and exchanged commiserative belches with the older females. These intimate contacts she described as 'just too thrilling for words,' and she was often moved to tears by them."

"I received the impression that Digit really looked forward to the daily contacts with Karisoke's observers as a source of entertainment," writes Fossey in *Gorillas in the Mist:*

"He seemed pleased whenever I brought strangers along and would completely ignore me to investigate any newcomers by smelling or lightly touching their clothing and hair. If I was alone, he often invited play by flopping over onto his back, waving stumpy legs in the air, and looking at me smilingly as if to say, 'How can you resist me?' At such times, I fear, my scientific detachment dissolved."

As Digit grew older, though their bond also matured, she gave him his space. One rainy day, with Digit off to the side and the group braced against the cold of the downpour, Fossey intentionally sat on the opposite edge of the huddled forms. "After a few minutes she felt an arm around her shoulders and looked up into Digit's warm, gentle brown eyes," wrote Mowat. "He stood pensively gazing down at her before patting her head then settling down by her side." She then laid her head on his lap. The entire sequence was captured by Campbell, and Digit became a poster child for the preservation of the gorillas. The episode would be an integral part of a widely viewed National Geographic television special, "The Search for the Great Apes," aired in 1973.

Fossey adored Campbell. The two had become close, and she dreaded his time away. But Campbell was married and each time he left with promises to talk to his wife, each time he returned without having done so. In November 1971, Fossey learned she was pregnant. A Belgian woman doctor drove from the Congo to handle the abortion. Four days later, Fossey began hemorrhaging and was near death by the time she was carried off the mountain and into surgery. The tension between Campbell and Fossey became unbearable until he left for good on May 29, 1972. During the next two months, she often drank throughout the day. By July, she was back at work.

Fossey had continual money worries. Though Leakey had promised her a salary, she never received one for all her years in the forest. By now an expert speaker who could obtain grants without his aid, Fossey kept the camp going from grant to grant. With National Geographic checks inevitably months late, Fossey would live on potatoes and borrow from friends to pay her staff. By Christmas 1976, the financial uncertainties as well as the extended living, climbing, and hiking at high altitude was taking a toll on Fossey's health. Besides an acute case of acrophobia, she suffered from insomnia, severe sciatica in her right hip, chronic pneumonia, chronic emphysema (which her heavy smoking did not help), and severe calcium deficiency (she snapped a bone in her ankle, set it herself, but it was never again quite right); she would later add hepatitis. Because of these ills and the endless paperwork, Fossey was finding it harder to get to the gorillas.

In August 1977, she trekked down the mountain to see doctors about the great pain in her chest. Rwandan physicians thought they saw tubercular lesions on the lungs, and she was packed off to Brussels. But experts there discovered an undiagnosed splintered thoracic rib that had caused bone splinters to be set adrift in her pleural cavity. The problem was corrected with surgery.

Four months later, on January 2, 1978, Ian Redmond, one of her favored researchers, came upon a "black and shapeless mound hazed with an aura of blowflies—the huge corpse of a gorilla, mutilated almost beyond recognition," writes Mowat. "The head was missing and the arms terminated in blood-encrusted stumps from which shattered slivers of bone protruded. Belly and chest had been deeply ripped and gashed. Everywhere the once-sleek black hair was matted and spiked with coagulated blood and fouled with body fluids." Digit had been massacred by poachers who had been offered $20 for the head and hands of a silverback for the tourist trade. "There are times when one cannot accept facts for fear of shattering one's being," wrote Fossey. "As I listened to Ian's terrible words, all of Digit's life since my first meeting with him as a playful little ball of black fluff ten years earlier, poured through my mind. From that dreadful moment on, I came to live within an insulated part of myself." It was the first time poachers had attacked any gorilla in her working groups.

By chance, a BBC film crew arrived on the day of Digit's burial. Fossey convinced them to film the story and distribute photos of Digit's mutilation in hopes that she might save the rest of the gorillas. Soon, two other members of Digit's group were killed, including Macho, the mother of a three-year old who was wounded and later died from gangrene. The gorillas were dying in large numbers: 36 heads had been brought down the mountain in 1976. After failing to resuscitate another baby gorilla who was gangrenous because of the snare around its foot, Fossey fell into a deep depression. In an effort to fight Rwandan indifference to the gorillas plight, she launched the Digit Fund to staff and train antipoacher patrols, a course of action that separated her from the scientific community.

Back in England, Sandy Harcourt had founded the Mountain Gorilla Project and agreed to hold and collect the money for Fossey's Digit Fund. Fossey would later learn that monies given to the fund were diverted by Harcourt and given to the Rwandan government. Harcourt insisted his group was better qualified to decide how to save the gorillas. (To Dian's fury, his group used the money to fly a committee to Rwanda for a consultation with park authorities.) In the United States, another supposed friend, Robinson McIlvaine, was also diverting Digit Fund monies into his own American Wildlife Fund. In her fury and frustration, Fossey used her own money from a personal inheritance to fund patrols.

Fossey felt under siege. Her energy now went to protecting her gorilla groups; the research, the writing, came second. She was "tough but fair," wrote Harold Hayes. She was hard on those she thought did not carry their load, compassionate to those in trouble. But she hated to be taken advantage of and those that did became the enemy. As the years in the dark and the mist wore on—18 in all—and she was beaten down by conservationist infighting, poachers, and the loss of gorillas, Fossey began to distrust everyone, even those who wanted to help. She became more reclusive and more demanding, and some students and researchers left embittered and spread rumors: that she was an alcoholic (untrue though she did drink), that she was a manic-depressive, that her gorillas were being killed because she was the target of a vendetta. Some posited that it might be easier to eject the target of the vendetta to protect the gorillas. On hearing that others were suggesting that she was the cause of the killings, she awoke, she wrote, at 1 AM, "got up and lit the gas lamp and sat in bed; went into a sweat, then a chill, then threw up and felt I was going berserk."

Fossey's reputation was suffering irreparable damage, but her patrols worked. Her African staff of nine men proved to be far more loyal than her students and researchers. They confiscated thousands of snares and traps and captured spears, bows, and other weapons. In her outrage, Fossey could be high-handed. She regularly destroyed poacher snares and ransacked or demolished their shelters; she once burned the belongings of an aggressive poacher and was handed a $600 fine. Fossey took a herder's cow hostage and threatened to kill it when a herder kidnapped her dog Cindy. Cindy was returned that same evening. In four months, her African patrol had found 987 traps. The park guards had found none. Soon, there were few poachers in her area.

But there were many who were now actively trying to get Fossey out of Rwanda, some because they honestly thought she had "gone bushy," others, including the U.S. State Department and the Belgian Aid organization in Rwanda, because she was causing diplomatic discomfort. Some of her ex-researchers were hopeful she'd be removed and that they would be funded instead to run Karisoke. Sandy Harcourt announced that she was too close to her subjects and accused her of anthropomorphism, a destructive label in the scientific community and one that would also be used against Jane Goodall. Writes Hayes:

> Many scientists take a less circumspect view of anthropomorphism than Harcourt. These experts say that the projection of the observer's attributes and emotions onto the study animal is not necessarily bad. They believe that anthropomorphism can be a useful tool. Frans de Waal, the author of *Chimpanzee Politics*, does not apologize for his anthropomorphic bias. There is no other way, he says, to look at these animals, they're so close to humans.

Even the highly respected Schaller, wrote Hayes, suggested that "these animals behaved in certain ways very much like people." A talented scientist, Schaller also stood to lose his reputation by incurring the charge of anthropomorphism, "of crossing the line that separates man from beast." But Schaller, wrote Hayes, thought it was "impossible to observe animals, particularly gorillas, without interpreting their behavior in human terms." "If a person thinks he understands a creature," Schaller maintained, "he must be able to predict its behavior in any given situation, and with gorillas I was able to do this only if I followed the bare outline of my own feelings and mental processes." By the end of his study, Schaller felt he had come to regard gorillas as he might a "human child." He also came off the mountain very concerned about the survival of the mountain gorilla; in frustration, he, too, had threatened poachers.

As Fossey saw it, there were two schools of thought when it came to conservation: theoretical conservation and active conservation. Once a gorilla was caught in a wire snare, Fossey felt they should help free it from the snare and nurse it; the theorists felt that nature should take its course, the scientist should not interfere. In Fossey's mind, poaching snares were not the work of nature.

In her view, the most important role for Karisoke was to "ensure that the creatures of the park continued to exist *in life,* rather than in the abstract as mere accumulations of information." Harcourt was a scientist and wanted the camp to be a compilation of data. Dian maintained that without the anti-poacher crusade there would be nothing left to study. "Data gathering surely is important," wrote Fossey, "but things haven't changed that much from the days when scientists shot everything in sight to gather data. They built their reputations then on mainly dead animals. Now they use live animals too, but the principle is the same. Alive or dead, you use the data to pile up a lot of research papers until you've got enough to get 'silverback' status. Nothing terribly wrong with that, except that many modern scientists, just like their predecessors, don't seem to care if the study species perish, just so that they get all the facts they need about them first." Ironically, Fossey's work had the disadvantage of turning gorillas into a tourist attraction. And there were those, including Harcourt, who were convinced that that was the way to go. He wanted to take tourists to see the gorillas.

By 1979, National Geographic was threatening to withdraw funding and advising Fossey to come home for a year and finish her book and research. Crippled by pain in her hip, she could barely visit the gorillas except when they were close to camp, but she dug in. Her patrols had been very effective: poachers had abandoned the region central to the three southern volcanoes. Elsewhere, the killing went on; other conservancies had no effect on the problem.

While on an African tour to further his studies in primatology, Dr. Glenn Hausfater from Cornell University in Ithaca, New York, came to visit; they became friends, then lovers, and he invited her to Cornell as a visiting professor. Intermittently from mid-March 1980 to 1982, Fossey taught at Ithaca and seemed to bandage wounds. "I feel myself falling into place again for the first time since Digit was killed," she wrote a friend. Her students voted her best professor of the year.

During her absence from Karisoke, her beloved Kima died, and ex-researchers attempted to take over the research center. The powers that be put Harcourt in charge. Under his management, the camp was neglected, most of the equipment was stolen or ruined from neglect, and the poaching was back in full swing. Harcourt proved to be so demanding a manager that the board turned to Fossey to bail them out. She returned to Karisoke in June 1983, having been away three years. Within three months, she had restored the camp and her men had destroyed 1,701 traps.

To save her gorillas, Fossey finished the book that she had been working on for years. Published in 1983 by Houghton Mifflin, who hated the title, *Gorillas in the Mist* enjoyed worldwide sales but was poorly received by the scientific community; the loudest condemnation came from those same ex-researchers.

In 1984, Fossey was finally enjoying good press from all three of Rwanda's newspapers, but two gorillas died of diseases contacted from tourists or researchers, her parrots were being poisoned, and she found a wooden puff adder on her doorstep late one night in October. Native sorcery had planted the curse of death.

On the morning of December 27, 1985, a member of Fossey's African staff found her sprawled on her back in her cabin, her skull split from forehead to mouth on a diagonal by a *panga* (machete). Lamp chimneys were smashed, furniture upturned, cupboard doors flung open, only the Christmas tree with its presents for her staff sat untouched. Since nothing was missing, it was not a burglary.

The murder is still unsolved, though the Rwandans determined it was a researcher who happened to be there at the time. Wayne McGuire hardly fit the portrait of a killer, and there was little evidence, mostly contrived. Then Fossey's chief tracker, Emmanuel Rwelekona, was arrested as an accomplice. He was later found hanged in his prison cell and deemed a suicide by the authorities, though that verdict is now widely doubted. Mowat contends that she was not murdered by a vengeful poacher but by a hired assassin, because she was interfering with the exploitation of the park. She had just been granted a two-year extension on her visa. Nicholas Gordon, in his book *Murders in the Mist*, charges that the trail of guilt for both deaths leads to the highest levels of Rwanda's government, including the king's wife and her brother.

Near her campsite, in a graveyard that she had set aside for the gorillas, Dian Fossey was buried in a plywood coffin next to her beloved Digit. As of 1990, because of her determination, there were 310 gorillas in the mist.

SOURCES:

Fossey, Dian. *Gorillas in the Mist*. Boston, MA: Houghton-Mifflin, 1983.
Hayes, Harold T.P. *The Dark Romance of Dian Fossey*. NY: Simon and Schuster, 1990.
Mowat, Farley. *Woman in the Mists*. NY: Warner Books, 1987.

SUGGESTED READING:

Gordon, Nicholas. *Murders in the Mist: Who Killed Dian Fossey?* Trafalgar, 1994.

RELATED MEDIA:

Gorillas in the Mist (125 min.) film, screenplay by **Anna Hamilton Phelan**, based on the work of Dian Fossey, starring **Sigourney Weaver**, *Julie Harris*, and Bryan Brown, produced by Warner Bros.-Universal, 1989.

Foster, Abigail Kelley (1810–1887).

See Kelley, Abby.

Foster, Hannah Webster
(1758–1840)

American author. Born Hannah Webster in Salisbury, Massachusetts, on September 10, 1758; died in Montreal, Canada, on April 17, 1840; married John Foster (a Unitarian minister); children: six.

Little is known about Hannah Webster Foster aside from her enduring 45-year marriage to a Unitarian minister and the publication of one highly successful novel. In 1789, signing herself simply "A Lady of Massachusetts," Foster published *The Coquette; or The History of Eliza Wharton*, a sentimental novel loosely based on a scandal involving a prominent Connecticut family, and including seduction, elopement, and tragic death. Reminiscent of Samuel Richardson's *Clarissa Harlowe* in its epistolary form, the book reached its peak of popularity between 1824 and 1828. It went through 13 reprints, though it was not until the 1866 edition, published decades after Foster's death, that her name finally appeared on the title page. Foster's second book, *The Boarding School; or, Lessons of a Preceptress to her Pupils*, published in 1798, failed to find an audience.

Foudy, Julie.

See Soccer: Women's World Cup, 1999.

Fourquet, Jeanne (c. 1454–?).

See Hachette, Jeanne.

Fowler, Katharine (1631–1664).

See Philips, Katharine.

Fowler, Lydia Folger (1822–1879)

*Physician who was the second American woman to receive an M.D. degree. Born Lydia Folger in Nantucket, Massachusetts, in 1822; died in London, England, in 1879; daughter and one of seven children of Gideon (a businessman and farmer) and Eunice (Macy) Folger; attended Nantucket schools; attended Wheaton Seminary, Norton, Massachusetts, 1838–39; attended Central Medical College, Syracuse, and later Rochester, New York, 1849–50, M.D., 1850; married Lorenzo Fowler (a noted phrenologist), in 1844; children: one daughter, **Jessie Fowler**.*

One of seven children, Lydia Folger Fowler was born in 1822, grew up on Nantucket Island, Massachusetts, and attended Wheaton Seminary, where she stayed on as a teacher. In 1844, she married Lorenzo Fowler, a noted phrenologist (one who studies character and mental capacity through the conformation of the skull), after which she became a writer and itinerant lecturer, speaking to women on health and phrenology. In 1849, she enrolled at Central Medical College, receiving her M.D. in 1850, and thus becoming the second American woman after *Elizabeth Blackwell to receive that degree. While still a student, Fowler had been appointed head of the school's "Female Department," and upon graduation she became a "demonstrator" of anatomy to female students. In 1851, one year before Central Medical College closed its doors, she was promoted to professor of midwifery and diseases of women and children.

From 1852 to 1860, Fowler practiced medicine in New York City, lectured, and became involved in a number of reform causes, including women's rights and temperance. In 1860, she left for a yearlong study of medicine in Paris and London, returning to New York to teach midwifery at the New York Hygeio-Therapueutic College. Around 1864, she and her husband moved to London, where she spend the rest of her life engaged in various causes. She died there of pneumonia at the age of 56.

Fowler's writings include *Familiar Lessons on Astronomy, Designed for the Use of Children and Youth* (1948), *Familiar Lessons on Phrenology, Designed for the Use of Schools and Families* (n.d.), and *Familiar Lessons on Physiology, Designed for the Use of Children and Youth in Schools and Families* (1948). Much of her work, however, especially in her later years, writes Marilyn Ogilvie, "involved medical ideas that were not acceptable to most physicians at the time and have since been dismissed." Even so, notes Ogilvie, Fowler was a trailblazer in opening up the medical profession to women and providing health education to those who might not otherwise have received it.

SOURCES:

Ogilvie, Marilyn Bailey. *Women in Science*. Boston, MA: Cambridge Press, 1993.

Barbara Morgan,
Melrose, Massachusetts

Fox, Beatrice (1887–1968).

See Auerbach, Beatrice Fox.

Fox, Beryl (1931—)

Canadian documentary filmmaker. Born in Canada in 1931.

Television: "Balance of Terror" (1962); "Servant of All" (1962); "One More River" (1963); "Three on a Match" (1963); "The Single Woman and the Double Standard" (1963); "Summer in Mississippi" (1963); "The Chief" (1964); "The Mills of the Gods: Vietnam" (1965); "The Honourable Rene Levesque" (1966); "Saigon: Portrait of a City" (1967); "Last Reflections on a War" (1968); "A View from the 21st Century" (1968); "Memorial to Martin Luther King" (1969); "Be a Man—Sell Out!" (1969); "North with the Spring" (1970); "Here Come the Seventies" (series, 1970–72); "Travel and Leisure (1971); "Jerusalem" (1973); "Habitat 2000" (1973); "Man into Superman" (1974); "Wild Refuge" (series, 1974); "Take My Hand" (1975); "How to Fight with Your Wife" (1975); "The Visible Woman" (1975); "Return to Kansas City" (1978). Film: Images of the Wild *(1978);* Fields of Endless Days *(1978);* Dr. Elizabeth *(1978);* Rose's House *(1979);* Hot Wheels *(1979);* By Design *(1981).*

Beryl Fox began her career in the early 1960s at the Canadian Broadcasting Company (CBC) as a script assistant in the sports department. "I was so bad at it they never let me do hockey, only bowling," said Fox. "The only reason I advanced was because . . . I never refused any kind of work." "No matter how scared you are," she advises women filmmakers, "never say no."

She learned fast. By 1965, Fox had produced and directed *The Mills of the Gods*, an hour-long documentary, shot on location, about combat in Vietnam. Besides being cited as Film of the Year by the Canadian Film Institute, the documentary also won the prestigious George Polk Memorial Award. Fox continued to cover Vietnam, the first Canadian to do so, with *The Mill of the Gods, Saigon*, and *Last Reflections on a War: Bernard Fall*, concerning the war correspondent who was killed there.

During the turbulent '60s, Fox was not only at the right place at the right time, but she had a knack for capturing the feeling of an era. Her coverage of black voter registration and race relations in the South in "One More River" and "Summer in Mississippi" contains some of the best documentary footage of the time.

Fox left the CBC in 1966 though she continued to produced documentaries for television throughout the '70s. She began producing feature films for theatrical release in the 1980s, including *By Design*, starring American actress **Patty Duke.**

SOURCES:

Kuhn, Annette, and Susannah Radstone, eds. *The Women's Companion to International Film.* Berkeley, CA: University of California Press, 1990.

Smith, Sharon. *Women Who Make Movies.* NY: Hopkinson and Blake, 1975.

Deborah Jones,
Studio City, California

Fox, Carol (1926–1981)

American opera producer who co-founded and managed the Lyric Theater of Chicago, which was reorganized in 1956 as the Lyric Opera of Chicago. Born in Chicago, Illinois, on June 15, 1926; died in Chicago, on July 21, 1981; only daughter of Edward (an office supply company executive) and Virginia (Scott) Fox; attended Girls Latin School in Chicago; studied acting at the Pasadena Playhouse, Pasadena, California; studied voice with Edith Mason and Vittorio Trevisan in Chicago and Virgilio Lazarri and Giovanni Martinelli in New York and Italy; coached in operatic repertory by Fausto Cleva; never married.

Credited with restoring Chicago's pre-Depression operatic glory, Carol Fox was the co-founder and general manager of the Lyric Opera of Chicago, often called "La Scala West" because of its international reputation. Fox was largely responsible for the American operatic debut of *Maria Callas and many European opera stars, and also helped establish the Lyric's apprentice artist program for American singers. Involved in every aspect of the company's operation, from the mailroom to casting, Fox was described by a colleague as "formidable," exuding "enough authority and confidence to give the word *chutzpa* a new meaning."

The only child of a wealthy couple, Fox was born in Chicago, Illinois, on June 15, 1926, and encouraged in the performing arts by her mother **Virginia Scott Fox**, who had longed for a theatrical career. As a child, Carol studied voice, piano, ballet, drama, and opera, as well as several foreign languages. She passed the entrance exams for Vassar but convinced her father to let her study acting at the Pasadena Playhouse and take voice lessons instead. After two years in Italy, studying with voice coach Giovanni Martinelli and taking minor roles in some amateur opera productions, she returned to the United States intent on starting her own opera company.

In 1952, with seed money from her father and in collaboration with business promoter Lawrence Kelly and conductor Nicola Rescigno, Fox founded the Lyric Theater of Chicago and took over the empty Civic Opera House, which remains the company's home. Recruiting a group of 30 young people, called the Lyric Guild, Fox began fund-raising and promotion campaigns. In February 1954, the fledgling company presented a "calling card" performance of *Don Giovanni.* **Claudia Cassidy** of the *Chicago Tribune* later recalled the performance: "I could not believe that stage. The Lyric did not exist, except in faith, hope and a vast amount of charity. Yet on that . . . stage was true, luminous Mozart."

For the Lyric's first full season, Fox traveled to Europe and signed Maria Callas, Tito Gobbi, *Giulietta Simionato, and Giuseppe de Stefano, none of whom had ever performed in the United States. Callas made her enormously successful American debut at the Lyric in November 1954, in the title role of *Norma.* (In a later performance during the Lyric's first three-week season, Callas drew a 12-minute standing ovation for her mad scene in *Lucia di Lammermoor.*) That premiere season, the company played to 84% capacity. (In later years, capacity reached 99%, with audiences totaling more than 60,000.) In 1956, when Kelly and Rescigno left Chicago, the Lyric Theater was reorganized as the Lyric Opera of Chicago, with Fox as general manager.

Having established her company, Fox faced new hurdles, among them the aesthetic conservatism of her public and the fiscal caution of the board of directors. There were ongoing complaints that the repertory was dominated by older, particularly Italian, operas, with not enough balance of modern works. With new artistic co-directors, Pino Donati and Bruno Bartoletti, Fox attempted to include more adventuresome productions (Berg's *Wozzeck,* Ravel's *L'Heure Espagnole,* and Prokofiev's *Angel of Fire*) but found that they were enormously expensive to produce and were not particularly popular with audiences. She maintained that her first duty was to please the public, "to get them to come and bit by bit to indoctrinate them to the new. It takes some time to make someone enjoy an unknown piece, even a new boom-boom-boom piece." In the continuing battle to meet the Lyric's staggering $5 million annual budget, Fox developed into the consummate fund raiser and could be tightfisted when it came to spending. Attempting to cut costs, she entered into arrangements for the interchange of costumes and sets with other opera houses. Known as firm and exacting, Fox also had a generous heart. Each Thanksgiving, she held a huge dinner at her apartment and was always available to offer encouragement or listen to grievances. She made it a point to know everyone's name, down to the last stagehand.

In 1973, the Lyric inaugurated its apprentice program, taking into residence ten young American singers for a year of training and choral experience. Apprentice productions were showcased at a small theater next door. In 1974, the Lyric's 20th anniversary, the company hosted the Fourth International Verdi Congress, culminating in an all new production of *Simon Boccanegra*. That season also included Chicago premieres of *Peter Grimes* and *Don Quichotte*, as well as the first production in almost half a century of *Götterdämmerung*. In 1976, the Lyric enjoyed one of its most brilliant seasons with company premieres of Offenbach's *Les Contes d' Hoffmann* and Prokofiev's *The Love of Three Oranges*. In celebration of the American Bicentennial in 1978, the Lyric commissioned Krzysztof Penderecki's *Paradise Lost*.

Among numerous honors, Carol Fox received the Steinway Award and the Chicago medal of Merit. She was also recognized by Italian and American organizations for promoting goodwill between the two countries. Ill health and budgetary pressures forced her to resign in January 1981, just months before her death on July 21, 1981.

SOURCES:

Moritz, Charles, ed. *Current Biography 1978*. NY: H.W. Wilson, 1978.

———. *Current Biography 1981*. NY: H.W. Wilson, 1981.

Warrack, John, and Ewan West. *Oxford Dictionary of Opera*. Oxford, England: Oxford University Press, 1992.

Barbara Morgan,
Melrose, Massachusetts

Fox, Caroline (1723–1774).

See joint entry on Lennox Sisters for Caroline Lennox.

Fox, Caroline (1819–1871)

English diarist. Born in Falmouth, Cornwall, England, on May 24, 1819; died in Falmouth on January 12, 1871; daughter of Robert Were Fox (a physicist and mineralogist); sister of Anna Maria Fox (also a writer).

An English diarist, Caroline Fox was born in Falmouth, England, in 1819, the daughter of Robert Were Fox, a physicist and mineralogist. Extracts from her diary, which she began at age 16, covering the period of 1835 to 1871, were published in 1881 as *Memories of Old Friends* (edited by H.N. Pym), with a third edition published in 1882. She also translated religious works into Italian. She was the friend of John Stuart Mill, Thomas Carlyle, and other noted personages, and in love, but made no mention of it, with John Sterling, a married cleric, writer, and friend of Carlyle. Following Sterling's death in 1844, her lively writings were laced with a mild melancholy.

Fox, Charlotte Milligan (1864–1916).

See Milligan, Alice for sidebar.

Fox, Della (1870–1913)

American actress and singer, known as a light-opera comedian. Born Della May Fox on October 13, 1870, in St. Louis, Missouri; died on June 15, 1913, in New York City; daughter of Andrew J. (a photographer) and Harriett (Swett) Fox; married Jacob D. Levy (a New York diamond broker), in December 1900.

Selected plays: title role in Editha's Burglar *(1883);* Yvonne in *The King's Fool* (Niblo's Garden, 1890); *Blanche in* Castles in the Air *(Broadway Theater, 1890);* Wang *(Broadway Theater, 1891);* Panjandrum *(1893);* The Lady or the Tiger *(1894);* Clairette Duval in *The Little Trooper* (Casino Theater, 1894); *Fleur-de-lis* (Palmer's Theater, 1895); The Wedding Day *(Casino Theater, 1897);* Margery Dazzle in *The Little Host* (Herald Square, 1898).

Briefly the highest paid performer on the American variety stage, musical star Della Fox started her theatrical career while still a schoolgirl, appearing in a juvenile production of Gilbert and Sullivan's *H.M.S. Pinafore*. At 13, she made her professional debut in *Editha's Burglar*, a one-act farce based on a story by ***Frances Hodgson Burnett** and adapted by Augustus Thomas; Thomas also appeared in the play. The production toured throughout the Midwest and Canada between 1883 and 1885, after which Fox performed with a succession of touring opera companies. Much of her most valuable professional experience was gained in the company of Heinrich Conried, who taught her acting and oversaw her New York debut in *The King's Fool* (1890). She went on to play opposite DeWolf Hopper in the operetta *Castles in the Air*. Fox's diminutive size and Hopper's tall, lanky stature made them truly a comic duo, and they were paired again in *Wang* (1891), *Panjandrum* (1893), and *The Lady or the Tiger* (1894). Her first starring role in *The Little Trooper* (1894) led to a number of successful productions, including a turn with ***Lillian Russell** in *The Wedding Day* (1897). As Margery Dazzle in the musical *The Little Host* (1898), Fox crossed the continent with her own company, reaching the pinnacle of her popularity. Blonde, plump, and baby-faced, she popularized the "Della Fox curl" throughout the United States.

Fox suffered an attack of peritonitis in the spring of 1899, followed a year later by a nervous breakdown brought on by alcohol and drugs. She had recovered sufficiently by 1900 to marry Jacob D. Levy, a New York diamond broker, after which she made only sporadic appearances on stage. She returned for the 1912 season and in April 1913, shortly before her death, appeared in a revival of the comedy *Rosedale.* Della Fox died in a private sanitarium in New York City, at the age of 42.

SOURCES:

James, Edward T., ed. *Notable American Women.* Cambridge, MA: Belknap Press of Harvard University Press, 1971.

McHenry, Robert, ed. *Famous American Women.* NY: Dover, 1981.

Barbara Morgan,
Melrose, Massachusetts

Fox, Elizabeth Vassall (1770–1845)

*Lady Holland. Name variations: Elizabeth Webster. Born Elizabeth Vassall in Jamaica in 1770; died in 1845; married Sir Godfrey Webster (divorced); married Henry Richard Vassall Fox, 3rd baron Holland, 1797; children: Henry Edward Fox, 4th and last Lord Holland (who married *Mary Fox).*

Born in Jamaica in 1770, Elizabeth Fox presided over the Whig circle at Holland House as Lady Holland. She was an adroit, lively, but slightly haughty host, censured by Lord Byron in his *English Bards and Scotch Reviewers.* Sympathetic to Napoleon, Fox sent a message to him during his exile at Elba and some books for him during his exile at St. Helena. In return, Napoleon bequeathed her his gold snuff-box given to him by Pope Pius VI.

Fox, Kate and Margaret

Canadian-born spiritualists and mediums.

Fox, Kate (c. 1839–1892). Name variations: Catherine or Katie Fox; Kate Fox-Jencken. Probably born in 1839, in Bath, New Brunswick, Canada; died on July 2, 1892, in New York City; youngest of six or more children of John Fox (a farmer) and Margaret (Rutan) Fox; sister of Margaret Fox (c. 1833–1893); married Henry D. Jencken (an international lawyer and legal scholar), on December 14, 1872 (died 1881); children: Ferdinand (b. 1873) and Henry (b. 1875).

Fox, Margaret (c. 1833–1893). Name variations: Margaretta Fox; Maggie Fox. Possibly born on October 7, 1833, in Bath, New Brunswick, Canada; died on March 8, 1893, in Brooklyn, New York; one of six or more children of John Fox (a farmer) and Margaret (Rutan) Fox; sister of Kate Fox (c. 1839–1892).

Modern spiritualism and mediumism dates from the mid-19th century, the time of the Fox sisters, Kate and Margaret, who quite innocently set into motion a social and religious movement that encompassed millions in America and thousands in Europe and England. Two of six children of John and Margaret Fox, the girls were born in the province of New Brunswick, Canada, near Nova Scotia, but moved with their parents to an isolated farm in Hydesville, New York, in 1847. In the spring of 1848, strange rappings and knockings began to emanate from the girls' bedroom. Many, including Kate and Margaret, attributed the sounds to spirits, and as news of the manifestations at Hydesville spread, the house was besieged by visitors—believers and skeptics alike—who came to observe the phenomenon. In one of many efforts to get the emanations to stop, the Foxes decided to separate the girls. An elder sister, *Leah Fox, married and living in Rochester, took Margaret to live with her, while Kate was taken in by her married brother David in Auburn. (David eventually devised a complicated code by which believers could spell out messages by means of the rappings.) The spirit sounds, however, appeared to follow the girls, and droves of people now flocked to Leah's and David's houses, hoping to communicate with the departed.

In 1849, Eliab W. Capron, an ardent believer, joined Leah in managing the sisters and arranging public demonstrations. To early observers, the girls, who were small, delicate, and shy, often appeared confused and uncertain about their powers and the reactions of those around them. In 1850, Leah took her sisters to New York City where they held regular seances that were often attended by prominent intellectual and literary figures. As a result, spirit circles began to appear; one such group included James Fenimore Cooper and William Cullen Bryant, while another was attended by editor Horace Greeley, who not only endorsed the girls' gifts in the *New York Tribune,* but also provided for Kate's education.

In 1852, while giving a public demonstration in Philadelphia, Margaret met the famous Arctic explorer Elisha Kent Kane. Outraged by what he felt was exploitation, Kane encouraged both girls to give up spiritualism. He subsequently arranged for Margaret's support and education at a school near Philadelphia, although much about the rest of their relationship is shrouded in mystery. After Kane's death in 1857, Margaret claimed that they had exchanged marriage vows, and that as his common-law wife, she was due an annuity he had left her. When she later filed suit for the money, his family offered to honor the annuity if she surrendered letters Kane had written to her. Years later, claiming that the family had not carried out their end of the bargain, Margaret published anonymously

an edited version of the letters titled *The Love-Life of Dr. Kane* (1865), a questionable publication at best. She continued to use the name Margaret Fox Kane for the rest of her life, and in 1858, maintaining that it was Kane's wish, she converted to Catholicism and, for the most part, gave up spirit-rapping.

Kate remained the most active medium. In 1855, inventor and reformer Horace H. Day established the Society for the Diffusion of Spiritual Knowledge and hired her at a salary of $1,200 a year to give free public sittings. By now, the

Margaret and Kate Fox

Fox sisters, as well as countless imitators, were offering seances that included not just simple rappings, but music, materializations, spirit writing, and other manifestations. Kate also gave extended seances for wealthy patrons, the first of which was banker Charles F. Livermore, whose dead wife, accompanied by Benjamin Franklin, often spoke to him through Kate.

Public life took a heavy toll on Kate and Margaret and both suffered from alcoholism until their deaths. In 1865, Kate underwent the Swedish Movement Cure, invented by Dr. George Henry Taylor, who also made use of Kate's skills as a medium to call forth two of his dead children. In 1871, she traveled to England, where she held seances attended by highly respected people of letters and science. There, she met and married Henry D. Jencken, an international lawyer and legal scholar, who also wrote articles for the English Spiritualist press. Kate had two sons, the first of which was said to have displayed mediumistic powers at the age of three months. Jencken died in 1881, and Kate returned to America in the spring of 1885. Within a short time, she again succumbed to the drinking disease. In 1888, she was arrested, and her children were taken away from her by the Society for the Prevention of Cruelty to Children.

It was Margaret who came to her sister's defense, telling reporters that Spiritualism was the cause of Kate's downfall. She admitted that she and Kate had devised the rappings to fool their mother, and at an appearance at the New York Academy of Music on October 21, 1888, she demonstrated how the sounds were made by throwing her fingers and toes out of joint. She further charged that her sister Leah had forced her and Kate to perpetuate the fraud. (Leah refused to publicly address the accusation.) Ranks of confirmed Spiritualists denounced Margaret as a drunken liar, who would do anything to get money, while opponents praised her for debunking a practice that they felt to be a dishonest hoax. Soon thereafter, however, Margaret retracted her confession and once again turned to Spiritualism, although her subsequent lecture tours were failures. Both she and Kate spent their final years in poverty. Kate died in New York City on July 2, 1892; Margaret died in Brooklyn, New York, on March 8, 1893. They were both buried at Cypress Hill Cemetery, in Brooklyn.

SOURCES:

Brandon, Ruth. *The Spiritualists: The Passion for the Occult in the Nineteenth and Twentieth Centuries.* NY: Alfred A. Knopf, 1983.

James Edward T., ed. *Notable American Women.* Cambridge, MA: The Belknap Press of Harvard University Press, 1971.

McHenry, Robert, ed. *Famous American Women.* NY: Dover, 1983.

RELATED MEDIA:

Telegrams from the Dead (documentary film), 1994.

Barbara Morgan,
Melrose, Massachusetts

Fox, Leah (c. 1818–1890)

Canadian-born medium who was the sister of spiritualists Margaret and Kate Fox. Name variations: Leah Fish. Born Ann Leah Fox around 1818, in the state of New York; died on November 1, 1890, in New York City; eldest of six or more children of John Fox (a farmer) and Margaret (Rutan) Fox; sister of Margaret Fox (c. 1833–1893) and Kate Fox (c. 1839–1892); married to a man named Fish, in the 1840s (possibly died); married Calvin Brown, 1851 (died, 1853); married Daniel Underhill (an insurance executive and a spiritualist), 1858; children: three by first marriage; possibly more.

In most accounts of the spiritualists *Margaret and *Kate Fox, the role of a third sister, Leah, is significant. She is portrayed variously as opportunistic and ambitious, or concerned and protective, depending on the source. **Ruth Brandon,** in her book *The Spiritualists,* quotes one commentator as explaining that Leah exploited her sisters in the interest of founding a new religion. Whatever her motives, Leah appears to have been the most robust and well adjusted of the three sisters, and seemingly capable in dealing with the notoriety that surrounded the family. She was living in Rochester, New York, with her first husband and family around the time of the first rappings at the Fox home in 1848 and, with Eliab W. Capron, managed her sisters during the years of their public demonstrations. After either the death or desertion of her first husband, she remarried twice, and from 1858 lived a quiet life. One source indicates that Leah often providing sanctuary for her troubled sisters, while another maintains that she eventually disowned them. Leah was said to be an adept medium herself, although she only gave private seances, never for money. Upon her death in 1890, she was mourned by spiritualists around the world.

SOURCES:

Brandon, Ruth. *The Spiritualists.* NY: Alfred A. Knopf, 1983.

James, Edward T., ed. *Notable American Women.* Cambridge, MA: The Belknap Press of Harvard University Press, 1971.

Fox, Margaret (1614–1702).

See Fell, Margaret.

Fox, Margaret (c. 1833–1893).

See joint entry on Fox, Kate and Margaret.

Fox, Mary (b. 1817).

Lady Holland. Born Lady Mary Augusta Coventry in 1817; daughter of the 8th earl of Coventry and Lady Mary Beauclerk (daughter of the 6th duke of St. Albans); married Henry Edward Fox, in 1833 (died 1859); daughter-in-law of Elizabeth Vassall Fox (1770–1845).

Mary Fox was born Mary Augusta Coventry in 1817 and spent her early years on the Continent before marrying Henry Edward Fox, son of *Elizabeth Vassall Fox and minister plenipotentiary at the court of Tuscany. The couple lived primarily in Naples, Italy, after their marriage. When her husband died in 1859, Lady Holland inherited Holland House in Kensington and St. Ann's Hill near Chertsey (once the home of Charles James Fox) where she divided her summer months, returning to Naples for the winter. She was known as a gracious hostess to diplomats, distinguished foreigners, and the accomplished. Her annual garden parties, writes George W.E. Russell, "combined all the solemn dignity which clings to one of the most historical of English houses, with the fantastic grace and sprightly merriment of an Italian *Festa*." In her later years, she remained in England. "Her most conspicuous trait was the extraordinary brightness of her piercing eyes," writes Russell. "Her mental gaze was of penetrating power. She saw through unreality, vanity, and pretence at a glance; but she was full of the most genial charity towards mere error, ignorance, or indiscretion. For some years she suffered grievously, but her patience and courage in bearing pain . . . were models to all like sufferers."

SOURCES:

Russell, George W.E. *Portraits of the Seventies.* 1916.

Foyle, Christina (d. 1999)

British businesswoman who was managing director of the famous Foyle's Bookshop in London. Born Christina Agnes Lillian Foyle; died in London, England, age 88, in June 1999; daughter of William (a bookseller) and Christina (Tulloch) Foyle; attended the Aux Villas Unspunnen, Wilderswil, Switzerland; married Ronald Batty, in 1938 (died 1994).

As managing director of Foyle's Bookshop (W. & G. Foyle, Ltd.), in London, Christina Foyle represented the second generation to run one of that city's oldest and most revered businesses. The bookshop, co-founded by her father William Foyle and his brother Gilbert in 1904, became known as the largest in the world and by 1954 boasted an art gallery, a literary agency, a record shop, a publishing house, and a lecture bureau. In 1928, at age 17, Christina had the idea for the famous Foyle Literary Luncheons, which were inaugurated in 1930, under her management. Occurring monthly and honoring distinguished personalities from every walk of life, the luncheons were originally held at Holborn Restaurant, with 350 to 400 guests. By the late 1930s, attendance had climbed to nearly 1,800, and the event was moved to the classy Dorchester Hotel. Through the years, guests of honor have included such diverse personalities as John Drinkwater, *Sophie Tucker, Lord Louis Mountbatten, Jimmy Durante, Anthony Eden, T.S. Eliot, Randolph Churchill, the archbishop of Canterbury, and Chico Marx. Since 1949, one luncheon each year has been devoted to poets and poetry. Recipients, who receive a cash prize, have included Edwin Muir, Christopher Fry, the late Dylan Thomas, Roy Campbell, and Walter de la Mare.

At the end of the 20th century, Foyle's remained unchallenged as the largest bookstore anywhere, occupying several connecting buildings on Charing Cross Road. It houses five floors of books, 50 specialized departments, and 13 miles of ramshackle shelves from which customers are welcome to browse. The saying went, "If Foyle's doesn't have it; nobody will." Christina Foyle, married in 1938 to the Ronald Batty, wrote *So Much Wisdom* (1984) and contributed articles to various books and journals. She died in London, age 88, in June 1999, having run Foyle's for almost 70 years. Bookseller Tim Waterstone described her as "a most proud and determined woman."

Barbara Morgan,
Melrose, Massachusetts

Fradon, Ramona (b. 1926).

See Messick, Dale for sidebar.

Fragonard, Marie Anne (1745–c. 1823)

French artist. Born Marie Anne (also seen as Anne-Marie) Gérard in Grasse, France, in 1745; died in Paris, France, in 1823 or 1824; sister of Marguerite Gérard (1761–1837); married Jean Honoré Fragonard (an artist); children: several.

A student of her husband Jean Honoré Fragonard, Marie Anne, a miniaturist, was soon eclipsed by her younger sister *Marguerite Gérard, who joined the Fragonard household at the age of eight. Marie Anne exhibited at the Salon des Correspondance in 1779 but gradually gave up painting to run the household and care for her many children. She remained devoted to her husband and family until her death in 1823 or 1824.

Frame, Janet (1924—)

New Zealand writer who survived a childhood of poverty and misfortune and many years of incarceration in mental hospitals to write a wealth of novels, poems and short stories, as well as an autobiography. Born Janet Patterson Frame on August 28, 1924, in Dunedin, New Zealand; third of five children of Lottie Clarice Godfrey (a dental nurse and housemaid until her children were born) and George Samuel Frame (a railway worker); attended public school before entering Dunedin Training College for teachers and Otago University (no degree); never married, no children.

During final year of teacher's training was committed for six weeks to Seacliff mental hospital (1945); submitted first collection of stories for publication (1945); worked as housemaid and waitress (1946); recommitted to psychiatric hospital, where she stayed for most of the next eight years (1947); won the Hubert Church award for The Lagoon (1951); released from psychiatric hospital (1955); completed her first novel, Owls Do Cry, and, with a grant from the New Zealand Literary Fund, traveled to Europe, where she spent seven years and completed three novels and two volumes of stories (1957); returned to New Zealand (1964), where she wrote seven more novels, another volume of stories, a volume of poetry, and a children's book.

Selected publications: The Lagoon and Other Stories (Caxton, 1951); Owls Do Cry (Pegasus, 1957); Faces in the Water (Pegasus, 1961); The Edge of the Alphabet (Pegasus, 1962); The Reservoir, Stories and Sketches (Braziller, 1963); Snowman, Snowman: Fables and Fantasies (Braziller, 1963); Scented Gardens for the Blind (Pegasus, 1963); The Adaptable Man (Braziller, 1965); A State of Siege (Braziller, 1966); (poems) The Pocket Mirror (Braziller, 1967); The Rainbirds (W.H. Allen, 1968); Intensive Care (Braziller, 1970); Daughter Buffalo (Braziller, 1972); Living in the Maniototo (Braziller, 1979); (selected short stories) You Are Now Entering the Human Heart (Victoria University Press, 1983); The Carpathians (Braziller, 1988). *The three-volume* An

Autobiography *was collected in one volume (Braziller, 1991) and issued separately as* To the Is-Land *(1982),* An Angel at My Table *(1984), and* The Envoy from Mirror City *(1985).*

Janet Frame survived a life marked by hardship and bereavement to become one of the most prolific and innovative of New Zealand's writers. She grew up during the Depression and spent much of her life in poverty. One of the few in her family ever to complete a formal education, Frame was misdiagnosed as schizophrenic as a young adult and spent many years incarcerated in a mental hospital. Despite these and other misfortunes, she went on to write eleven novels, three volumes of stories, a book of poetry, and a children's story. Words were a lifelong source of mystery and fascination to her, and it was as a writer that she found her place in the world.

Janet Frame was delivered by the first woman medical graduate in New Zealand, Dr. **Emily Seideberg McKinnon**, at St. Helen's Hospital in Dunedin. She was known as "the baby who was always hungry." The third of what was soon to be five children, Janet moved with her family for the first time when she was three weeks old. Her father was a railway engineer, and the family was uprooted often. They lived in trackside huts and ramshackle housing furnished by the railroad; much of it was cramped and uncomfortable, without running water, heat, or electricity. Janet and her sisters slept four to a bed; it wasn't until she went away to college that she experienced sleeping on sheets. Labor was exhaustive: milking cows, washing and mending clothes, carrying water.

Frame was extremely shy. In her *Autobiography,* she describes herself as "an anxious child full of twitches and tics, standing alone in the playground at school, wearing day after day the same hand-me-down tartan skirt that was almost stiff with constant wear." With her unruly, bright-red hair and tattered, patched uniform, she felt unattractive and different from her schoolmates. She was awkward in her body and around other children. Her life at home was also troubled: in addition to the ever-present threat of financial doom, Janet's older brother began having epileptic seizures when she was eight. This cast a shadow of unreality and fear over the house. It also added to the discord between Janet's parents: her mother **Lottie Clarice Frame** devoted herself to caring for the boy and began a fervent and never-ending search for a cure, while her father George blamed his son, claiming that he could stop the seizures if he really tried.

There were also pleasures and escapes. Frame enjoyed the companionship of her sisters, and together they told stories, wrote poems, and explored the countryside. The natural world was a source of wonder and refuge; though she felt ill-at-ease with her schoolmates, Frame was at home outdoors. Throughout her life, she loved the New Zealand landscape: the rivers and creeks, the ocean, fields, and woods.

And there were words. From early childhood, Frame was intrigued by them: what they meant and didn't mean, how they looked and sounded, their relationship to the objects, people and feelings around her. Lottie, who had always dreamed of being a poet, often recited verse to her children, poems inspired by her surroundings—the lighthouse at Waipapa, the Aurora Astralis, the Southern Lights in the night sky, shipwrecks, tidal waves. Frame's imagination was captured; at an early age, she and her siblings began composing poems and entering them in competitions. In her autobiography, she describes her earliest poems as "a mixture of conventional ideas about 'poetic' vocabulary and the cowboy and prison songs recorded in my other notebooks and the contents of the small popular song books brought home by [my sister] Myrtle and the songs sung by my parents and grandparents."

I did not know my own identity. I was burgled of body and hung in the sky like a woman of straw.

—Janet Frame, *Faces in the Water*

In New Zealand, as in the rest of the world, the Depression was a time of hardship. There was talk of bankruptcy, of wage cuts, of being on the dole. Doctor bills mounted in the Frame household as Janet's brother continued to suffer from epilepsy and Lottie searched for effective treatment. Before air travel became common, New Zealand was remote from the rest of the world. News traveled by radio and film. The Frame girls were avid movie fans; in contrast to the bleak economic landscape around them, the luxury and glamour that appeared on screen was enticing. They practiced singing and dancing and dreamed of being "discovered" and going to Hollywood.

Janet learned at an early age about the unexpectedness of death, of the finality of loss, of the grief of parting. In 1936, when Janet was 12, her 16-year-old sister drowned at the public pool. Nine years later, this same lesson was reemphasized when her younger sister also drowned in a swimming accident.

Frame did well in school, though she continued to feel different from her classmates and suffered embarrassment because of her clothes, her hair, and her developing body. "There were the usual worries about money," she writes in her autobiography. "And an increasing worry for me about my school tunic, which was now too tight over my growing breasts but which had to last me until I left school," a total of six years. There were "the dramatic terrifying continuing episodes" of her brother's illness, and a growing climate of fear, prejudice, and anticipation in the country as the speeches of Adolf Hitler began to be broadcast over the airwaves and talk of war in Europe escalated. "I did my best to smooth the surface of life," Frame wrote. "To be, in a sense, invisible, to conceal all in myself that might attract disapproval or anger. I had no close girlfriends at school and no boyfriends."

Frame finished high school, and, unlike most of the girls around her who went to work in the nearby woolen mill, she applied and was accepted to teacher's training college. Once again clothes were a problem; looking at the list of essential clothing, Frame was "overcome by a hopeless feeling of unreality. Where, except in films, did people own so many dresses, costumes, shoes, coats?" In an effort to raise money, she wrote to a Member of Parliament. When he didn't respond, she appealed to relatives and accelerated her submission of stories and poetry to competitions.

At Dunedin Teacher's College and at Otago University where she took courses in French and English, Frame found both freedom and loneliness. "The gradual learning of the language, the attitudes, the customs of behavior and dress [of the college] produced in me a euphoria of belonging which was intensified and contradicted by my actual feeling of isolation," she wrote. Her ignorance of the outside world made everyday tasks, such as posting a letter, seem challenging. Her shyness caused her to refuse meals that the aunt with whom she was boarding offered; consequently, she was often hungry. Though she wanted very much to contribute to the college magazine, she lacked the courage even to pick up a copy from the rack outside the school. Not surprisingly, she didn't make friends and spent most of her time alone. Her only romance was with poetry and literature; among those she read were James Joyce, *Virginia Woolf, W.H. Auden, Dylan Thomas, and T.S. Eliot.

Nineteen forty-five was a pivotal year in Janet Frame's life. She was completing her probationary year as a teacher; at the end of the

Janet Frame

term, she hoped to receive her certificate. She would turn 21 in August of that year, the same month that the atom bomb was dropped on Japan and World War II ended. She had also begun to take courses in psychology at the university and had published her first story in the *Listener* for which she was paid two guineas. But while she enjoyed teaching, she secretly dreamed of becoming a poet. And while she was good at understanding and encouraging her students, she failed at being accepted as a member of the staff. She dreaded the final classroom evaluation, which was required for her certificate, and devised a method for postponing it as long as possible. One spring day toward the end of the term, the headmaster and inspector appeared in her classroom, and Frame knew she could no longer delay the inevitable. She simply excused herself and walked out the door, never to return.

"I felt completely isolated," Frame writes. "I knew no one to confide in, to get advice from; and there was nowhere I could go. What, in all the world, could I do to earn my living and still live as myself, as I knew myself to be." Desperate, believing that she had no other escape, she cleaned her room, swallowed a package of aspirin, and laid down to die.

When she woke the next morning with a roaring in her ears and a bloody nose, her failure at school seemed minor. She was delighted and thankful just to be alive. She resigned from teacher's college and found a job washing dishes but continued her course at the university. When she mentioned in a school assignment that she had attempted suicide, concerned teachers persuaded her to check into the hospital for a rest. Frame agreed. It was only after she was admitted that she learned she was in the psychiatric ward.

This began a period of about eight years during which Frame spent most of her time incarcerated in mental hospitals. In her novel *Faces in the Water,* she describes this part of her life in great and moving detail, evoking the sights, smells, events and torments that she and a great many other women suffered. Istina Mavet, the protagonist of this novel, says:

> I will write about the season of peril. I was put in hospital because a great gap opened in the ice floe between myself and the other people whom I watched, with their world, drifting away through a violet-colored sea where hammerhead sharks in tropical ease swam side by side with the seals and the polar bears. I was alone on the ice.

The conditions in which Frame and the other patients lived and the treatment they received were often terrifying, cruel, and painful. They were stripped of their belongings with, as Frame writes, "no clothes of their own to wear, no handbags, purses, no possessions but a temporary bed to sleep in with a locker beside it, and a room to sit in and stare." Food was often rotting and inedible, hygiene was lax. Many patients suffered from tuberculosis. Doctors spent little time treating, or even talking to or observing, patients, many of whom were forgotten, with little hope of ever resuming life outside the institution.

Frame had been diagnosed with schizophrenia after only the briefest consultation with a doctor. She, like many of her fellow patients, was subjected to electroshock treatments, which were often administered as punishment for being uncooperative or not having the proper attitude. In Frame's case, she received over 200 applications of electroshock, each one, she says, "the equivalent, in degree of fear, to an execution."

Janet Frame had always been different from many of those around her and had often felt outside the normal flow of life, but she was not insane. Neither, she discovered, were a great many of the women who were incarcerated along with her, though they would most likely spend their lives committed to a mental hospital. More than ever before, Frame experienced society's intolerance for people who are different; each day she witnessed the misery accorded to those who cannot or will not conform to established expectations. This knowledge informed her writing for the rest of her career.

The institution was often like a foreign land, with a language and customs of its own. Frame learned the routines. She made friends, was moved from ward to ward, and endured weeks in solitary confinement. At times it seemed that there was no way out, that she would spend the rest of her life behind locked doors. It was her writing that finally saved her. In 1951, the doctors decided that Frame's condition would be improved by a lobotomy—a procedure that was becoming popular at the time—and scheduled her for surgery. Then one of the doctors at the hospital happened to read a notice in the newspaper announcing that Frame's first collection of stories, *The Lagoon*—which had been published without her knowledge during her stay in the hospital— had won the Hubert Church Award. The doctor decided that Frame's mind was unique and should remain intact. The surgery was canceled, and Frame was released shortly after.

Once again Frame was confronted with the necessity of earning a living. She still wanted to write. She worked for awhile as a housemaid in a boardinghouse, then as a waitress in the Grand Hotel in Dunedin. She struggled to afford a room, meals, a typewriter, and time to write. She published a few poems in the *Listener* and completed several short stories. She discovered Kafka and Faulkner and began to take an avid interest in the literature of her native land. In the volumes of slim books published by small New Zealand presses, she found stories and poetry that spoke of the mountains, sea, and rivers that she had known and loved all her life.

In 1954, when Frame was 30, she moved north to Auckland to live with her sister. There she met the writer Frank Sargeson, who offered to let her live in an army hut in his garden. He arranged for her to receive £3 a week in disability assistance and encouraged her to write every day. Frame recalls:

> I had an army hut containing: a bed, a built-in desk with a kerosene lamp, a rush mat on the floor, a small wardrobe with an old curtain strung in front, and a small window by the head of the bed. . . . I thus had everything I desired and needed, as well as the regret of wondering why I had taken so many years to find it.

She had a place to live and work undisturbed, with no one to dictate how she should eat, dress, act, or speak. Sargeson treated her like a writer and introduced her to such authors as Proust and Tolstoy. When she completed her first novel, *Owls Do Cry,* Sargeson helped her apply for a grant from the Literary Fund to "travel overseas and broaden her experience."

Frame's novel was accepted and published; that same year, her mother died. Her travel grant was awarded and the day after her 32nd birthday, after a month of devastating seasickness, Frame landed in London. She stayed several weeks before traveling to the Spanish island of Ibiza where, she had been told, life was cheap and her grant money would last the longest.

She was captivated by the beauty of the island, and the warmth of its inhabitants. She wrote during the day, took long walks, and learned Spanish. And, for the first time in her life, she fell in love. Bernard was a young American visiting on the island. "I thought Bernard's laughter was the most joyous I had ever heard," Frame wrote. "The sound seemed to have the right assembly to connect with a jagged shape inside my heart. I could not otherwise explain the delight of listening to his laughter."

When Frame left Ibiza, she was pregnant. Bernard had left before her, not suspecting that he was the father of her child. On the advice of friends, Frame—whose funds were now low—traveled to Andorra, where she had been told her money would last even longer. She arrived in the snow of the Pyrenees feeling the loss of her lover, and with both wonder and dread at the thought of the life she now carried inside her. She miscarried, however, and, in the confusion of feelings that followed, accepted the marriage proposal of an Italian resistance fighter she had met in Andorra. She was not in love. Realizing her mistake, and under pretense of collecting belongings she

had left in England, she returned to London, where she stayed for the next seven years.

In London, she took a job as an usher at the Regal Theater; she also found a literary agent. Feeling that she wanted to know the truth of her past mental condition, she checked into the Maudsley Hospital—known for its progressive and distinguished psychiatric work—and stayed as a patient for six weeks, undergoing all manner of tests. The doctors were unanimous in confirming what Frame had suspected: that she had never suffered from schizophrenia, that she should never have been admitted to a mental hospital, that most of the problems she experienced were a direct result of her stay there. Most important, her doctor felt that Frame genuinely needed to write, and that she should arrange her life in a way that would make this possible. She should feel free to live alone, to join in activities with others only if she were so inclined.

Frame entered a very productive period. She signed on for National Assistance and with this financial support was able to write every day. While *Owls Do Cry* was being published, she completed *Faces in the Water,* a novel drawn from her experience in the mental hospital. The book was a success, selling more than her previous novel and earning her a £100 advance, with a similar sum from her American publisher. Reviews were favorable, and Frame immediately began work on her next novel, *The Edge of the Alphabet.*

Every six months the National Assistance inspector arrived, and Frame held her breath, hoping to be funded for another half year. During the course of one winter, she wrote two volumes of stories from which *The New Yorker* and other magazines chose. Suddenly her bank account held £600; she was making a living as a writer. She finished another novel, *Scented Gardens for the Blind.*

Frame was reviewed widely and often favorably; still, she had to learn to cope with the ups and downs of critical opinion. "Likely a work of genius," one reviewer said. "Unreadable in the worst sense," said another. Both were reviewing the same book. Frame tried to guard herself from being inflated by the good reviews, devastated by the bad. More and more she lived in the world of fiction: writing by day, going to the cinema in the late afternoon, taking solitary walks.

In 1963, when Frame received a letter from her sister telling of her father's death, she realized that she wanted to return to live and work in New Zealand, in her own words "the country where [I] first saw daylight and the sun and the dark.... Now that writing was my only occupation, regardless of the critical and financial outcome, I felt I had found my 'place' at a deeper level than any landscape of any country would provide." She took the long sea journey back and was startled to find members of the press waiting to meet her. She had become a celebrity, an author with a reputation.

The following year, 1964, Frame was awarded a Scholarship in Letters, which allowed her to live and write without financial worry for a year. In 1965, she was made a Burns Fellow at the University of Otago, which enabled her to buy a cottage. She went on to write more novels and to become one of the few non-U.S. writers awarded honorary membership in the American Academy of Arts and Letters. In 1989, she won the Commonwealth Writer's Prize for *The Carpathians*. In the early 1980s, the three volumes of her autobiography, titled *To the Island, An Angel at My Table*, and *The Envoy from Mirror City*, appeared. The London *Sunday Times* called it "one of the greatest autobiographies written this century." She was now widely considered the finest novelist New Zealand had ever produced.

SOURCES:

Frame, Janet. *An Autobiography*. NY: George Braziller, 1991.

The Oxford History of New Zealand Literature. Oxford: Oxford University Press.

RELATED MEDIA:

An Angel at My Table (motion picture) directed by **Jane Campion**, starring **Kerry Fox**, screenplay by **Laura**

Celia Franca

Jones, produced by Hibiscus Films (the film portrays Frame's life from early childhood on).

Leslie Larson,
Copyrighting and Catalog Manager at the
University of California Press, Oakland, California

Franca, Celia (1921—)

British ballerina and choreographer who was founding director of the National Ballet of Canada and its director for 24 years. Born in London, England, on June 25, 1921; studied dance at the Guildhall School of Music and the Royal Academy of Dancing.

The daughter of a British tailor, Celia Franca was born in London, England, on June 25, 1921, and studied ballet from the age of four with the aid of scholarships and loans. She attended the Guildhall School and the Royal Academy of Dancing, where she apprenticed with famed British ballet teacher, *Marie Rambert. She was also the student of Stanislas Idzikowski, **Judith Espinosa**, and Antony Tudor. Franca made her debut at age 15, performing in *The Planets* with the Ballet Rambert, and in 1939, as a member of the Ballet des Trois Arts, she choreographed her first piece, *Midas*. Franca went on to dance and choreograph with Sadler's Wells, the Metropolitan Ballet, the Ballet Jooss, and other companies. In 1951, she was recommended as a possible founding director of a Canadian classical company by Dame *Ninette de Valois, the founder of Sadler's Wells, who called Franca "the greatest dramatic dancer the Wells ever had" (*Maclean's*, August 20, 1955).

Franca, who was once described as "a mite of a creature," achieved the almost impossible, pulling the Canadian company together in ten months. While working as a file clerk to support herself, she recruited and trained dancers, selected an artistic staff, staged some Promenade Concerts, and organized a summer school. The troupe made its debut on November 12, 1951, in Toronto, including in its first program Franca's staging of Michel Fokine's *Les Sylphides*. Overcoming financial difficulties and "technical roughness" during its fledgling years, Franca deftly guided her new company. She brought in guest artists and in 1959, with **Betty Oliphant**, founded the National Ballet School. In building a repertoire, Franca relied on the classics and created her own ballets when necessary, including *Cinderella* (1968), which won an Emmy in 1970, and several versions of *The Nutcracker* (1955 and 1964). Mindful of the need to encourage Canadian choreography, she included 30 Canadian ballets in the company's repertoire and started the National Ballet's Choreographic Workshops. Under Franca's directorship, the company toured throughout Canada, the United States, Mexico, Japan, and Europe, establishing an international reputation of note.

Franca has received countless honors for her achievements and contributions to the arts in Canada, including the Canadian Conference of the Arts' Diplome d'Honneur in 1986. In 1987, she received the St. George's Society of Toronto award and was among the first to be honored with the Order of Ontario. Since her retirement in 1975, Franca has lived in Ottawa, where she has remained active in civic and national artistic programs. She is a former member of the board of Theatre Ballet of Canada and has served as an artistic director of The School of Dance in Ottawa and on the board of directors of the Canada Dance Festival Society. She has also supervised a popular lecture series in dance at the University of Ottawa.

SOURCES:
Current Biography 1956. NY: H.W. Wilson, 1956.
Information from The National Ballet of Canada, The Walter Carsen Centre, Toronto, Ontario, Canada.

SUGGESTED READING:
Neufield, James. *Power to Rise: The Story of The National Ballet of Canada.* Toronto: University of Toronto Press, 1996.

Barbara Morgan,
Melrose, Massachusetts

France, empress of.
See Josephine (1763–1814).
See Marie Louise of Austria (1791–1847).
See Eugénie (1826–1920).

France, queen of.
See Ermengarde (c. 778–818).
See Ansgard (fl. 863).
See Ermentrude (d. 869).
See Richilde of Autun (fl. 870).
See Adelaide Judith (fl. 879).
See Theodorade.
See Richilde (d. 894).
See Frederona (d. 917).
See Beatrice of Vermandois (880–931).
See Emma of Burgundy (d. 939).
See Edgifu (902–951).
See Gerberga of Saxony (c. 910–969).
See Emma of Italy (948-after 990).
See Adelaide of Poitou (c. 950–c. 1004).
See Adelaide of Anjou.
See Constance of Arles (c. 980–1032).
See Matilda of Flanders for sidebar on Bertha of Burgundy (964–1024).
See Anne of Kiev (1024–1066).
See Matilda of Germany.

See Bertha of Holland (1055–1094).
See Bertrada of Montfort (d. after 1117).
See Adele of Maurienne (1092–1154).
See Constance of Castile (d. 1160).
See Eleanor of Aquitaine (1122–1204).
See Adele of Champagne (1145–1206).
See Isabella of Hainault (1170–1190).
See Ingeborg (c. 1176–1237/38).
See Agnes of Meran (d. 1201).
See Blanche of Castile (1188–1252).
See Margaret of Provence (1221–1295).
See Isabella of Aragon (1243–1271).
See Marie of Brabant (c. 1260–1321).
See Joan I of Navarre (1273–1305).
See Margaret of Burgundy (1290–1315).
See Jeanne I of Burgundy (c. 1291–1330).
See Clemence of Hungary (1293–1328).
See Jeanne of Burgundy (1293–1348).
See Blanche of Burgundy (1296–1326).
See Mary of Luxemburg (1305–1323).
See Blanche of Boulogne (1326–1360).
See Joan of Evreux (d. 1370).
See Blanche of Navarre (1331–1398).
See Jeanne de Bourbon (1338–1378).
See Isabeau of Bavaria (1371–1435).
See Marie of Anjou (1404–1463).
See Charlotte of Savoy (c. 1442–1483).
See Anne of Beaujeu for sidebar on Jeanne de France (c. 1464–1505).
See Anne of Brittany (c. 1477–1514).
See Mary Tudor (1496–1533).
See Eleanor of Portugal (1498–1558).
See Claude de France (1499–1524).
See Maria Teresa of Savoy.
See Medici, Catherine de (1519–1589).
See Elisabeth of Habsburg (1554–1592).
See Louise of Lorraine (1554–1601).
See Medici, Marie de (c. 1573–1642).
See Anne of Austria (1601–1666).
See Maintenon, Françoise d'Aubigne, marquise de (1635–1719).
See Maria Teresa of Spain (1638–1683).
See Marie Leczinska (1703–1768).
See Marie Antoinette (1755–1793).
See Maria Teresa of Savoy (1756–1805).
See Maria Amalia (1782–1866).

Frances.
Variant of Francesca.

Frances, Lady Mar (1690–1761).
See Mar, Frances, countess of.

Frances Evelyn (1861–1938), countess of Warwick.
See Greville, Frances Evelyn.

Frances Mary Theresa, Mother
(1794–1861).

>*See Ball, Frances.*

Frances of Rome (1384–1440)

Saint. Name variations: St. Frances the widow. Born in Rome in 1384; died in 1440; daughter of Paul Bussa and Jacobella de' Roffredeschi; married Laurence Ponziani, a young noble; children: son (b. 1400), son (b. 1404), and daughter (b. 1407).

Born into an illustrious family, Frances of Rome gave signs of exceptional piety at an early age and rejected childhood amusements. At 11, she asked to enter a convent, but her parents coaxed her into a marriage with the young, equally pious, noble, Laurence Ponziani. The successful 40-year marriage was based on mutual respect. "A married woman must, when called upon," wrote Frances, "quit her devotion to God at the altar, to find him in her household affairs." Though she was known to be kind and indulgent to her household, treating her servants well, she imposed mortifications on herself, including making mouldy bread her staple diet. She wore a coarse serge dress, a hairshirt, and a horsehair girdle.

Her sister-in-law, **Vanozza Ponziani**, was of a similar persuasion. Together, they met to pray in a grotto in the garden, cared for the sick of the Sancto Spirito, and gave money to the poor. With her husband's approval, Frances founded a monastery for nuns, named the Oblates, in 1425, and gave them the rule of St. Benedict and the statutes of the Olivetan monks. When many flocked to join the mission at Tor di' Specchi, she had it enlarged in 1433. Following her husband's death, Frances entered the monastery but was soon ill. She died, age 56, while on a visit to the bedside of her son John Baptist who was also ill at the Palazzo Ponziani. Immediately following her death, Frances was canonized by Pope Paul V. St. Frances of Rome left behind 97 visions, dictated to her confessor. Her feast day is on March 9.

Frances Xavier Cabrini, Mother
(1850–1917).

>*See Cabrini, Frances Xavier.*

Francesca.

>*Variant of Frances.*

Francesca da Firenze (fl. 15th c.).

>*See Firenze, Francesca da.*

Francesca da Rimini (d. 1285?)

Italian noblewoman. Name variations: Francesca Malatesta. Born Francesca da Polenta; slain around 1285; sister of Bernardino da Polenta; married Gianciotto (Giovanni) Malatesta.

Francesca da Rimini is one of history's ill-starred lovers. Married to Gianciotto Malatesta, she fell in love with his younger brother Paolo Malatesta, captain of the commune in Florence from 1282 to 1283, while the two jointly read a French romance, *Lancelot du Lac*. When a third brother informed Gianciotto, he killed Francesca and Paolo in a "crime of honor." The story, immortalized by Dante, has also been the subject of many artists, including Germany's Anselm Feuerbach, Holland's Ary Scheffer, and Italy's Amos Cassioli.

Francis, Arlene (1908–2001)

American television personality and actress. Born Arlene Francis Kazanjian in Boston, Massachusetts, in 1908; died in 2001; only child of Aram Kazanjian (a portrait photographer), and Leah (Davis) Kazanjian; attended grade school in Boston; graduated from the Academy of Mount St. Vincent, Riverdale, New York; attended Finch School, New York; attended the Theater Guild School for a year; married Neil Agnew (a movie executive), in 1935 (divorced 1945); married Martin Gabel (an actor-producer), on May 14, 1946 (died 1979); children: one son, Peter Gabel.

A popular television personality of the 1950s, Arlene Francis might have inherited her flare for performing from her maternal grandfather, a Shakespearean actor who taught her to recite. After displaying a talent for dramatics in school plays, she attended the Theater Guild School for a year. Her father, possibly hoping to lure his daughter away from the stage, then opened a gift shop for her on Madison Avenue, but Francis turned it into a meeting place for her friends, and it closed in less than a year. After a brief turn in Hollywood and a name change, she returned to New York where she took bit parts on radio and on Broadway. Her first major stage role was in George Abbott's *All that Glitters* (1938), followed by featured roles in Orson Welles' Mercury Theater production of *Danton's Death* (1938) and Maxwell Anderson's *Journey to Jerusalem* (1940). Her early radio assignments also included serials and appearances with Jack Benny, Fred Allen, and George Burns and *Gracie Allen. She also did soundtrack commentary for fashion newsreels.

In 1942, Francis landed the role of Natalia, a Russian lady sniper, in Joseph Fields' comedy *The Doughgirls,* which ran for a year and a half. For several years, she continued on Broadway and on the radio, where her show "Blind Date" became popular and was later transferred to television. In 1954, she was selected over 30 other actresses to host the "Home" show, a daytime television program for women, the first NBC show to be broadcast in color; she was also the first woman to guest-host the "Jack Paar Tonight Show." Francis became best known, however, as a regular panelist on "What's My Line?" (CBS-TV), a game show on which a panel of celebrities guessed the occupations of various contestants by asking them questions. The success of the show caught her by surprise. Its charm, she later recalled was "its simplicity." Francis briefly had her own television show, the "Arlene Francis Show," and hosted a radio program, "Arlene Francis at Sardi's." As late as 1981, she was co-hosting the "Prime of Your Life" on WNBC-TV, New York.

Francis was married to Neil Agnew, a movie executive, for ten years. They divorced in 1945, and she married actor-producer Martin Gabel, with whom she had a son, Peter, in 1947. On their first wedding anniversary, Gabel presented her with a diamond heart pendant, which she wore so constantly that it became her trademark.

SOURCES:

Brown, Les. *Les Brown's Encyclopedia of Television.* Detroit, MI: Visible Ink, 1977.

Candee, Marjorie Dent, ed. *Current Biography 1956.* NY: H.W. Wilson, 1956.

Barbara Morgan,
Melrose, Massachusetts

Francis, Connie (1938—)

Popular American singer of the 1950s and early 1960s who had 25 records in the top 100. Born Concetta Marie Franconero on December 12, 1938, in Newark, New Jersey; only daughter and one of two children of George (a former dockworker and roofing contractor) and Ida (Ferrara) Franconero; attended Bergen Street school and the Arts High School in Newark; graduated from Belleville (New Jersey) High School, 1955; thrice married (thrice divorced); children: (adopted) son, Joey.

Discography—singles: "Freddy"/ "Didn't I Love You Enough?"; "(Please) Make Him Jealous"/ "Goody Good-bye"; "Are You Satisfied?"/ "My Treasure"; "My First Real Love"/ "Believe in Me (Credimi)"; "Forgetting"/ "Send for My Baby"; "My Sailor Boy"/ "Everyone Needs Someone"; "I Never Had a

Arlene Francis

Sweetheart"/ "Little Blue Wren"; "No Other One"/ "I Leaned on a Man"; "Faded Orchid"/ "Eighteen"; "The Majesty of Love"/ "You My Darlin' You"; "Who's Sorry Now?"/ "You Were Only Foolin' (While I Was Fallin' in Love)"; "I'm Sorry I Made You Cry"/ "Lock Up Your Heart"; "Heartaches"/ "I Miss You So"; "Stupid Cupid"/ "Carolina Moon"; "Happy Days and Lonely Nights"/ "Fallin'"; "My Happiness"/ "Never Before"; "If I Didn't Care"/ "Toward the End of the Day"; "Lipstick on Your Collar"/ "Frankie"; "You're Gonna Miss Me"/ "God Bless America"; "Mama"/ "Teddy"; "Everybody's Somebody's Fool"/ "Jealous of You (Tango della Gelosia)"; "My Heart Has a Mind of Its Own"/ "Malagueña"; "Many Tears Ago"/ "Senza Mamma e Innamorato"; "Where the Boys Are"/ "No One"; "Breakin' in a Brand New Broken Heart"/ "Someone Else's Boy"; "Atashi-no ("Where the Boys Are"—Japanese)"/ "Swanee" (Limited release); "Together"/ "Too Many Rules"; "(He's My) Dreamboat"/ "Hollywood"; "When the Boy in Your Arms"/ "Baby's First Christmas"; "Don't Break the Heart That Loves You"/ "Drop It Joe"; "A Second Hand Love"/ "Gonna Git That Man"; "Vacation"/ "The Biggest Sin of All"; "I Was Such a Fool"/ "He Thinks I Still Care"; "I'm Gonna Be Warm This Winter"/ "Al Di La"; "Follow the Boys"/ "Waiting for Billy"; "If My Pillow Could Talk"/ "You're the Only One Can Hurt Me"; "Drownin' My Sorrows"/ "Mala Femmina"; "Your Other Love"/ "Whatever Happened to Rosemarie?"; "In the Summer of His Years"/ "My Buddy"; "Blue Winter"/ "You Know You Don't Want Me"; "Look-

ing for Love"/ "This Is My Happiest Moment"; "Don't Ever Leave Me"/ "We Have Something More"; "Whose Heart Are You Breaking Tonight?"/ "C'mon Jerry"; "For Mama (La Mamma)"/ "She'll Be Comin' Round the Mountain"; "Wishing It Was You"/ "You're Mine (Ho Bisogno di Vederti)"; "Forget Domani"/ "No One Ever Sends Me Roses"; "Roundabout"/ "Bossa Nova Hand Dance (Deixa Isso P'rá Lá)"; "Jealous Heart"/ "Can I Rely on You?"; "When the Boys Meet the Girls"/ "Exodus"; "Love Is Me, Love Is You"/ "I'd Let You Break My Heart"; "It's a Different World"/ "Empty Chapel"; "A Letter from a Soldier"/ "Somewhere, My Love"; "A Nurse in the U.S. Army Corps" (Promotional); "So Nice (Summer Samba)"/ "All the Love in the World"; "Spanish Nights and You (Noches Españolas)"/ "Games That Lovers Play"; "Another Page"/ "Souvenir D'Italie"; "Time Alone Will Tell (Non Pensare a Me)"/ "Born Free"; "My Heart Cries for You"/ "Someone Took the Sweetness Out of Sweetheart"; "Lonely Again"/ "When You Care a Lot for Someone"; "My World Keeps Slipping Away"/ "Till We're Together Again"; "Why Say Goodbye"/ "Addio Mi Amore"; "Somebody Else Is Taking My Place"/ "Brother Can You Spare a Dime?"; "The Welfare Check"/ "I Don't Want to Play House"; "The Wedding Cake"/ "Over the Hill Underground"; "Gone Like the Wind"/ "Am I Blue?"; "Invierno Triste Azul (Blue Winter—Spanish)"/ "Noches Españolas (Spanish Nights)"; "Zingara"/ "Mr. Love."

Filmography: Where the Boys Are *(1960);* Follow the Boys *(1963);* Looking for Love *(1964);* Where the Boys Meet the Girls *(1965).*

The undisputed queen of the popular music scene in the late 1950s and early 1960s, Connie Francis is probably best remembered for "Where the Boys Are," the title song from her 1960 hit movie. Francis, who sold over 88 million records globally, made a smooth transition from teen queen to cabaret singer before a series of highly publicized tragedies in the 1970s and 1980s halted her career.

Born Concetta Marie Franconero on December 12, 1938, in Newark, New Jersey, the daughter of George and **Ida Ferrara Franconero,** Francis made her debut at age four playing "Anchors Aweigh" on a miniature accordion given to her by her father. George Franconero would diligently promote her career. By 11, she was a veteran of a number of juvenile variety programs and, shortly before her 12th birthday, won first place on Arthur Godfrey's TV talent show, singing "Daddy's Little Girl." (It was Godfrey

who suggested she change her name.) For four years during the early 1950s, Francis appeared on George Scheck's weekly "Star Time" television show and toured the borscht circuit in the Catskills during the summers. It was a difficult period for the young teenager, who felt out of place with the other more sophisticated girls in the "Star Time" show and began to overeat out of loneliness. "I never mixed socially with these other kids," she later recalled. "I just sat around by myself and ate." Through Scheck, Francis met and fell in love with Bobby Darin, a rising young singer whom her father did not like. George Franconero maneuvered his daughter out of the relationship and pressured Scheck to stop managing the singer. Though she was separated from Darin, he remained the one true romance of her life. Her devotion endured through his two marriages and his untimely death from heart disease in 1973.

When "Star Time" ended, Scheck became Francis' manager, and in 1955, after she had been rejected by several labels and had spent years making demos for music publishers, he negotiated a contract for her with MGM Records. Following another 18 months of flops, Francis recorded an uptempo version of one of her father's favorite tunes, "Who's Sorry Now?" Released in November 1957, the record went nowhere until it was plugged by Dick Clark on his "American Bandstand" television show in January 1958. Within six months, it had sold a million copies and kicked Francis' career into high gear.

Over the next five years, she had 25 records in the top 100, including "Stupid Cupid" (1958), "My Happiness" (1959), "Lipstick on Your Collar" (1959), "Mama" (1960). and "Vacation" (1962), which she co-wrote. She also made four films, including *Where The Boys Are,* appeared as a guest on most of the popular television variety programs (including a bittersweet reunion with Bobby Darin on "The Ed Sullivan Show"), and starred on her own TV special. As her record sales increased, she was booked at Carnegie Hall and began concert tours around the world. Francis won a variety of awards, including *Billboard*'s Most Programmed Vocalist of the Year and *Cashbox* magazine's Best Female Singer of the Year. In 1960, she became the first female singer to have two consecutive singles on the charts, "My Heart Has a Mind of Its Own" and "Everybody's Somebody's Fool." Francis also gained international stature by recording a number of singles and albums in foreign languages. In a clever merchandizing scheme, each

Connie Francis

of the multilingual albums featured a photograph of the singer on the album cover, dressed in appropriate native garb.

With the emergence of the Beatles in 1964, Francis had fewer hit records, although she continued to perform for several years at the Sahara Hotel in Las Vegas. In 1967, she underwent cosmetic nasal surgery that left her unable to sing in air-conditioned facilities and further limited her bookings. After two failed marriages and several unsuccessful attempts to jump-start her career, Francis appeared to be on the comeback trail when tragedy struck again. On November 7, 1974, after a performance at the Westbury (Long Island) Music Fair, she returned to her motel room, where she was held at knife point for two-and-a-half hours and beaten and raped. Her attacker was never found, and Francis, who was thoroughly traumatized by the ordeal, was eventually awarded $2.5 million dollars in damages from the Howard Johnson's motel chain. In the ensuing years, she underwent frequent psychiatric treatment and additional nasal surgery which caused her to lose her voice from 1977 to 1981. "It's a sad admission," she wrote later, "but gone with my voice was my already badly damaged self-esteem. Even though after the rape I was unable to face the public, I always knew in my heart that someday when I put my life back together again, singing was always an option for me—the only option really."

In 1981, Francis' 40-year-old-brother George, a former law partner of New Jersey Governor Brendan Byrne, was gunned down in front of his home, the result of his cooperation in a federal investigation of mob infiltration into the state's banking industry. Claiming that the incident was "a turning point," she regained her voice and wrote her autobiography *Who's Sorry Now?* (1984). In 1985, she undertook an elaborate two-performance concert in Los Angeles and also announced that she was going to record again. However, she continued to be plagued with emotional problems, which led to four years in and out of mental institutions. In 1989, she finally resumed her career with an engagement at the Diplomat Hotel in Hollywood, Florida, followed by a successful run at the Aladdin Hotel in Las Vegas. Divorced from her third husband, Joseph Garzilli, and the mother of a grown adopted son, Joey, she appeared to be emerging into the spotlight again. In 1996, she made a triumphant return to the Westbury Music Fair and also signed a recording contract with Click, the new label started by her longtime friend Dick Clark.

SOURCES:

Clarke, Donald, ed. *The Penguin Encyclopedia of Popular Music*. NY: Viking, 1989.

Francis, Connie. *Who's Sorry Now?*. NY: St. Martin's Press, 1984.

Moritz, Charles, ed. *Current Biography 1962*. NY: H.W. Wilson, 1962.

Parish, James Robert, and Michael R. Pitts. *Hollywood Songsters*. NY: Garland, 1991.

Romanowski, Patricia, and Holly George-Warren. *The New Rolling Stone Encyclopedia of Rock & Roll*. NY: Fireside, 1983.

Scott, Walter. "Personality Parade," in *Parade Magazine*. September 1, 1996, p. 2.

Barbara Morgan,
Melrose, Massachusetts

Francis, Kay (c. 1899–1968)

American film actress of the 1930s. Born Katherine Edwina Gibbs in Oklahoma City, Oklahoma, on January 13, 1899 (some sources cite 1903 or 1905); died of cancer at her home in New York City on August 26, 1968; daughter of Katherine Clinton (a vaudeville star); educated in a convent; four marriages, all ending in divorce, including third husband, actor Kenneth MacKenna (1931–33).

Selected filmography: Gentlemen of the Press *(1929);* The Coconuts *(1929);* Dangerous Curves *(1929);* Illusion *(1929);* The Marriage Playground *(1929);* Behind the Makeup *(1930);* Street of Chance *(1930);* Paramount on Parade *(1930);* A Notorious Affair *(1930);* For the Defense *(1930);* Raffles *(1930);* Let's Go Native *(1930);* The Virtuous Sin *(1930);* Passion Flower *(1930);* Scandal Sheet *(1931);* Ladies' Man *(19131);* The Vice Squad *(1931);* Transgression *(1931);* Guilty Hands *(1931);* Twenty-Four Hours *(1931);* Girls About Town *(1931);* The False Madonna *(1931);* Strangers in Love *(1932);* Man Wanted *(1932);* Street of Women *(1932);* Jewel Robbery *(1932);* One Way Passage *(1932);* Trouble in Paradise *(1932);* Cynara *(1932);* The Keyhole *(1933);* Storm at Daybreak *(1933);* Mary Stevens MD *(1933);* I Loved a Woman *(1933);* The House on 56th Street *(1933);* Mandalay *(1934);* Wonder Bar *(1934);* Doctor Monica *(1934);* British Agent *(1934);* Living on Velvet *(1935);* Stranded *(1935);* The Goose and the Gander *(1935);* I Found Stella Parish *(1935);* The White Angel *(1936);* Give Me Your Heart *(1936);* Stolen Holiday *(1937);* Another Dawn *(1937);* Confession *(1937);* First Lady *(1937);* Women Are Like That *(1938);* My Bill *(1938);* Secrets of an Actress *(1938);* Comet Over Broadway *(1938);* King of the Underworld *(1939);* Women in the Wind *(1939);* In Name Only *(1939);* It's a Date *(1940);* When the Daltons Rode *(1940);* Little Men *(1940);* Play Girl *(1941);* The Man Who Lost Himself *(1941);* Charley's Aunt *(1941);* The Feminine Touch *(1941);* Always in My Heart *(1942);* Between Us Girls *(1942);* Four Jills in a Jeep *(1944);* Divorce *(1945);* Allotment Wives *(1945);* Wife Wanted *(1946).*

One of the most glamorous and highly paid film stars of the 1930s, Kay Francis worked as a stenographer and a real-estate agent before deciding to become an actress. Summer stock and a few Broadway roles led her to a film contract and the role of a vamp in *Gentlemen of the Press* (1929), followed by a supporting part in the first Marx Brothers film *The Coconuts* (1929). Despite a slight speech impediment, her popularity grew during the 1930s, partly due to her doll-like features and her reputation as the best-dressed star in Hollywood. With Paramount, then with Warner Bros., she typically portrayed stylish, worldly women in romantic melodramas and an occasional comedy. Her best-known films were *Trouble in Paradise* (1932), *Cynara* (1932), *The White Angel* (1936), and *The Feminine Touch* (1941). Francis was eventually passed over for brighter stars in the Warner's hierarchy and by the mid-1940s was relegated to B pictures. From 1945 to 1946, Francis co-produced and starred in three low-budget films for Monogram and then toured in stock for several years before retiring.

Kay Francis was married and divorced four times, once to actor Kenneth MacKenna. By most accounts, she ended her career on a bitter note and in later years would not grant interviews. She died of cancer, age 65, leaving her considerable estate to The Seeing Eye, founded by *Dorothy Eustis, to help allay costs for dogs for the blind.

Barbara Morgan,
Melrose, Massachusetts

Francisca of Portugal (1800–1834)

*Duchess of Molina. Born Maria Francisca de Assis on April 22, 1800, in Queluz; died on September 4, 1834, in Alberstoke Rectory, Gosport, Hampshire, England; daughter of *Carlota Joaquina (1775–1830) and Joao or John VI, king of Portugal; married Charles also known as Don Carlos (1788–1855), duke of Molina, on September 22, 1816; children: Charles of Molina (1818–1861), count of Montemolin; Johann also known as John of Molina (1822–1887); Ferdinand of Molina (b. 1824).*

Francisca of Portugal (1824–1898)

*Princess of Brazil. Name variations: Francisca de Braganca. Born on August 2, 1824, in Rio de Janeiro, Brazil; died on March 27, 1898, in Paris, France; daughter of *Leopoldina of Austria (1797–1826) and Peter IV, king of Portugal (r. 1826), also known as Peter I of Brazil or Pedro I, emperor of Brazil (r. 1826–1831); married François or Francis (1818–1900), duke of Joinville, on May 1, 1843; children: *Françoise d'Orléans (1844–1925); Peter (b. 1845), duke of Penthievre.*

Franco, Carmen Polo de
(1902–1988)

Spanish wife and adviser of Francisco Franco, dictator of Spain. Name variations: María del Carmen Polo y Martínez Valdés de Franco. Born María del Carmen Polo y Martínez Valdés in Oviedo, Spain, in 1902; died in 1988; married Francisco Franco (head or Caudillo of the Spanish state), in October 1923; children: María del Carmen, called Carmencita (who married Cristóbal Martínez Bordiu).

A native of Oviedo, Spain, Carmen Polo was born in 1902 to parents from the provincial aristocracy. When Carmen's mother died and left her father Felipe with several young children, his sister Isabel helped raise the family. Convent-educated, Carmen met a young military officer, Francisco Franco, in 1917. He

Kay
Francis

began courting her, despite opposition from her family, which considered him socially inferior. Franco's military successes in Morocco and his persistence eventually won the family's support, and they were married in October 1923.

Carmen played her chosen part well as devoted wife of, depending on one's political inclinations, a hero or rogue destined to transform his country. In 1926, she had the couple's only child, María del Carmen, called **Carmencita Franco**. Meanwhile, she endured postings to Morocco. Their fortunes apparently receded in 1931, with the abdication of Alphonso XIII and the proclamation of Spain's Second Republic. The liberal government distrusted the military, and abolished the Academy, which Franco headed. She fed his bitterness, and her religious conservatism confirmed her dislike of the liberals. As social and political chaos descended on Spain in the mid-1930s, the government posted the Francos to the Canary Islands and placed him under surveillance, hoping to prevent him from plotting against the Republic.

Civil war erupted in July 1936. Carmen took her daughter to France aboard a German ship while Franco successfully led the Foreign

Legion into Spain. They rejoined him two months later. On October 12, Carmen performed one of her most famous acts. Present at *Día de la Raza* (Day of the Hispanic Race) celebrations in Salamanca when the great Spanish philosopher and educator Miguel de Unamuno publicly challenged the anti-intellectual ravings of General Millán Astray, Carmen protected the writer by escorting him to his home. Franco's victory in 1939 made her supreme in Spain for the next 35 years.

She and Franco moved into El Pardo palace on the outskirts of Madrid. He insisted that Spaniards treat her almost like a queen: they played the royal march for her at state functions and called her *La Señora*. Carmen attempted to rewrite her husband's ancestry to make it more aristocratic. Her avarice knew few bounds. She melted down the gold medals presented by cities and provinces to her husband and collected jewelry and antiques from sycophants and influence seekers. She secured her daughter's marriage to Cristóbal Martínez Bordiu in a royally ostentatious wedding and revelled in her granddaughter's marriage to Alphonso de Borbón-Dampierre, member of Spain's old royal family.

When Franco died on November 20, 1975, King Juan Carlos allowed her to stay on in El Pardo palace for several months. Carmen then moved to an apartment in Madrid, where she lived quietly until her death in 1988.

SOURCES:

Garriga, Ramón. *La Señora de El Pardo*. Barcelona: Editorial Planeta, 1979.

Preston, Paul. *Franco*. London: HarperCollins, 1993.

Kendall W. Brown,
Professor of History, Brigham Young University,
Provo, Utah

Francois, Elma (1897–1944)

Political activist in the Caribbean, founder of the National Unemployed Movement and Negro Welfare Cultural and Social Association in the 1930s, and first woman charged for sedition in the history of Trinidad and Tobago, who was acquitted after her own defense. Born Elma Constance Francois on October 14, 1897, in Overland, on the Caribbean island of St. Vincent; died on April 17, 1944, from complications of the thyroid, in Port-of-Spain, Trinidad and Tobago; daughter of Stanley and Estina (Silby) Francois (agricultural laborers); received only primary level schooling, but self-educated and well-read; lifetime companion James Barrette; children: one son, Conrad James.

Migrated from St. Vincent to republic of Trinidad and Tobago, where she worked as a domestic servant (1919); became a member of the Trinidad Workingmen's Association (1920s); with others, founded the National Unemployed Movement (NUM, 1934); participated in NUM "hunger marches" to draw attention to unemployment and destitution (1934); with others, founded the Negro Welfare Cultural and Social Association (NWCSA, 1935); with the NWCSA, led the local agitation against Mussolini's Italian invasion of Ethiopia, then known as Abyssinia (1935–36); with the NWCSA, led the labor disturbances in the north of Trinidad and was charged for sedition (1937); tried for sedition and acquitted after her spirited self-defense (1938); with other members of the NWCSA, was involved in founding the Federated Workers Trade Union, the Public Works and Public Service Workers Trade Union, and the Seamen and Waterfront Workers Trade Union (1937–40); campaigned against local support for and participation in World War II (1939); one of three women out of 25 island citizens named National Heroes of Trinidad and Tobago (September 25, 1985).

Along with the suppression of the events of the radical and labor-oriented political struggle that took place in the West Indies republic of Trinidad and Tobago before the 1950s, there has also been the obliteration from memory of the stories of hundreds of women who took part in the struggles resulting in benefits for the people of these islands that are now taken for granted. Of these women, Elma Francois is one whose life was dedicated to the social movement through her work in organizations like the Negro Welfare Cultural and Social Association (NWCSA).

The land of her birth was St. Vincent, a tiny Caribbean island grouping, presently referred to as St. Vincent and the Grenadines. There, from an early age, Francois joined her mother **Estina Silby Francois** in the fields to pick sea island cotton on the Arnos Vale and Cane Garden estates, near the capital of Kingston. The family had moved to the city in 1902, after losing their home and belongings during the eruption of the Soufrière volcano. According to Jim Barrette, her longtime comrade and companion, Francois would sit and talk to him for hours about the conditions for agricultural laborers in her homeland and the few opportunities, especially for poor women, to earn a living. Before leaving St. Vincent, she became involved in the St. Vincent Representative Government Association, a group that sought to introduce elected representation into the local legislature.

Elma Francois

Francois was 22 in 1919 when she migrated to Trinidad, leaving her only son, Conrad James, with her mother. In the republic's capital at Port-of-Spain, she found work as a domestic servant in the home of a wealthy white upper-class family and sent weekly packages back to St. Vincent containing money, clothing or other items bought with her meager earnings. She also joined the Trinidad Workingmen's Association (TWA) then led by Captain Arthur A. Cipriani, a Trinidadian of Corsican origin, although she was critical of the leader's accommodationist style; Cipriani resisted worker confrontation, seeking instead to represent the workers before the colonial authorities and the employers of laborers. For Francois, political activity meant working among the people. Reading often by candlelight, she gathered the information she would use for "rap sessions" with working-class men and women in the city squares and streets. On occasion, she also spoke on platforms of the TWA, but she was known to challenge Cipriani publicly on topical issues.

In the early 1930s, Francois was strongly influenced by Jim Headley, a Trinidad seafarer who had been involved in the National Maritime Union and Young Communist League of the United States, as well as by publications emanating from the local chapter of the Comintern's International Trade Union Committee of Negro Workers, led by another Trinidadian, George Padmore. In early 1934, Francois joined Headley, Barrette, and others, in forming the National Unemployed Movement (NUM), which coordinated a series of hunger marches, and a register of the unemployed, to bring attention to the plight of the increasing numbers of the destitute in the country during this period of severe economic depression.

At the end of 1934, NUM was converted into the NWCSA, as the membership sought to expand its activities beyond the issue of unemployment. Another woman, **Christina King**, was among those helping to found the new organization, and their combined presence may have contributed to the importance women would have in the association for some time to come.

In 1935, the hunger marches continued despite the opposition of Cipriani, who was now the mayor of Port-of-Spain. In addition, the NWCSA highlighted international issues for the local populace, including the racist trial of the Scottsboro Boys in Alabama. Most of their activities, however, involved what was known as the Anti-Abyssinian Agitation, against the recent Italian invasion of Ethiopia. Interest in the African war developed after copies of the *Ethiopian Times* edited by *Sylvia Pankhurst, the British Socialist-feminist, reached the island. The NWCSA corresponded with Pankhurst and became knowledgeable on the Ethiopian issue, and during that year, anti-Italian feeling ran high, as many in the country, including middle-class groups joined in the activities. On Friday, May 29, 1935, Francois was the main speaker at a meeting at Woodford Square, the main political center in Port-of-Spain. She criticized the League of Nations, noting that Ethiopia had been a loyal observer of the covenant of the League, and denounced Italy's barbaric attacks in Ethiopia against an innocent and defenseless black people. During that period, even the Roman Catholic Church was affected by the censure, as many denounced the pope for blessing the Italian troops.

At a local level, NWCSA activities were often concentrated on improving the quality of life for the country's poor and unemployed. One issue taken up by the group was the price of condensed milk, a staple, at the time, in the working-class diet. In 1936, to press their case, a Condensed Milk Association was registered under the Trade Union Ordinance. The group gathered research on the cost of living, nutritional standards, hospital services, old age pensions, school meals, and health services, in preparation for a memorandum to be presented to the governor by a high-powered delegation. Discussions were also held with local trade unions and popular religious groups.

On November 8, 1936, Francois led the delegation that met with the governor on the issue of condensed milk-prices, the first time in the history of the country that a political delegation included a large proportion of women. According to one respondent, the initial reaction of one member of the governor's team was, "What is this I am seeing, West Indian women on a political delegation?"

The year 1937 saw the efforts of the NWCSA concentrated on workers' struggles and the formation of the early trade unions. In June of that year, the culmination of years of disaffection and labor protest resulted in riots and disturbances to the south and north of the country. The starting point was the village of Fyzabad, in South Trinidad, where a protest meeting on June 19th turned into a riot when an attempt was made to arrest the labor leader Uriah Butler. While much has been known and documented about Butler, little was known until recently about the related activities of Francois and her colleagues in the NWCSA.

According to her son Conrad, the events of June 19th took his mother by surprise. He recalls being awakened by her at about 3:00 AM on the morning of the 20th and being told that she was leaving immediately for Fyzabad where there was rioting. His attempts to discourage her were useless. Francois spent the following day in Fyzabad investigating the situation and returned in the evening to Port-of-Spain. The very next day, June 21, on her instigation, the NWCSA went into action in North Trinidad. By June 28, Francois, Barrette and two other colleagues were arrested and held in jail for seven days.

In February 1938, Francois was brought to trial on charges of sedition, the first woman in the history of the country to be formally accused of insurrection. The jury, as was customary in those days, was all male, and drawn from classes that met with property qualifications. The witnesses against the defendant were police officers, and the case became the central focus of all the sedition trials that year growing out of the same event. Unlike the other defendants, and against the advice of the barrister, Francois undertook the greater part of her own defense, giving an extended speech after the first witness had been cross examined:

> In keeping with the aims and objectives of our Association, we hold meetings. I keep in touch with local affairs, I follow the local politics as best I can. We particularly pay attention to the underdog.
>
> The subject of my address was "World Imperialism and the Colonial Toilers". . . . In dealing with my subject, I dealt with world conditions linking them up to local conditions; I dealt with land reservations in the Kenya colony. I explained that a certain amount of land was reserved for the working-class and often they were deprived of it and they decided there to organize in order to get their wrongs righted with regard to the subject of land reservations, by a Royal Commission. They succeeded in getting a Royal Commission.
>
> I dealt with Nigeria. I dealt with the natives there protesting against increased taxations. I further told them that only by organized unity can we gain better conditions. I discussed Germany and Russia also. I pointed out the effective method the workers of England used by organizing and what they gained. I spoke about Negro and East Indian workers who sleep under the Town Hall in the Square through poverty. I wanted their conditions to be bettered.

When asked by the Court to define "World Imperialism and Colonialism," Francois described the relationship between the ruling classes of the world and the exploited workers of the colonies. When asked what the German workers had to do with her, she replied that "they meant something to her as a worker." On the third day of the trial, after the judge's summation, the jury returned the unanimous verdict of not guilty, and Francois was released. Her colleagues were not so fortunate: all depended on the barrister, and all were found guilty.

In the following period, just prior to World War II, the Caribbean economic situation declined even further. With the formation of early trade unions in the aftermath of the 1937 labor disturbances, Francois and the NWCSA were extremely busy, coordinating the Committee of Industrial Organisation (CIO) in the north, a forerunner to the national trade union council which was to be formed a few years later.

I don't know that my speeches create disaffection, I know that my speeches create a fire in the minds of the people so as to change the conditions which now exist.

—Elma Francois

As a British colony, Trinidad and Tobago was actively involved in World War II. In return for four old destroyers, four large areas of the island country had been leased by the British to the United States for military bases, and after an initial ambivalence about Britain's role in the war, the trade unions were mobilized by the colonial authorities to support the war effort. Indeed, as in World War I, a number of local men sought enlistment in the British army, and a number of trade unions agreed to put their labor disputes on hold for the duration of the war. Francois and other NWCSA members publicly disagreed with this position. In their analysis, the Western allies had initially seen the rise of Adolf Hitler as a counter to Joseph Stalin in the Soviet Union. It was only when Hitler turned his military might against them that they sought to defend themselves and draw on the colonials— whom they discriminated against racially—to die with them in their war. The NWCSA therefore called for working people to withdraw their support for the war and not to enlist, but the position they had taken was extremely unpopular and served to isolate the group even from their radical allies in the labor movement, who supported the British war effort.

Then Francois received a personal shock that may have contributed to her early and untimely death: her only son, Conrad, had joined the British army and was leaving for the front. Conrad was frankly attracted by warfare. He recalled the "sweets available during the early war years whose wrappings carried slogans such as 'I like war'" and noted that he even "wore war slogans on his shirt." On April 16, 1944, as Conrad was about to leave for the front, Francois went to a farewell dance at the Princes Building Port-of-Spain to say goodbye. Though not a dancer, she danced with her son at his request; it was the last time he was to see her alive. The following day, Elma Francois died of complications of the thyroid. When the news reached Conrad at his military barracks, he managed to get permission to attend the funeral, before setting sail for the war in Europe and North Africa.

As with other members of the NWCSA, Francois received a "socialist" funeral. The body was dressed in a red shroud and association members all wore their full uniform of red blouses or shirts, flannel trousers or skirts and red felt or panama hats. Among those watching the procession was her old political adversary, Captain Cipriani. Friends of Francois remained convinced that her death was the result of grief at the decision of her only son, going against everything for which she stood. Stress is known to have a negative affect on diseases of the thyroid.

SOURCES:

Calder-Marshall, Arthur. *Glory Dead*. London: Michael Joseph, 1939.

Henderson, Thelma. "The Role of Women in Politics in Trinidad and Tobago" for the Caribbean Studies Project, 1973. The University of the West Indies, St. Augustine.

Interviews with Jim Barrette, Christina King, Conrad James and others.

Reddock, Rhoda. *Elma Francois, The NWCSA, and the Workers Struggle for Change in the Caribbean*. London: New Beacon Books, 1988.

Rennie, Bukka. *The History of the Working-Class in the 20th Century (1919–1956): The Trinidad and Tobago Experience*. Tunapuna: New Beginning, 1973.

SUGGESTED READING:

Ramdin, Ron. *From Chattel Slave to Wage-Earner*. London: Martin Brian and O'Keefe, 1982.

Rhoda E. Reddock,
Senior Lecturer and Head of the Centre for Gender and Development Studies at The University of the West Indies, St. Augustine Campus, Trinidad and Tobago, and author of *Women, Labour and Politics in Trinidad and Tobago: A History* (Zed Books, London, 1994)

Françoise d'Orleans (fl. 1650)

*Duchess of Savoy. Name variations: Francoise of Orleans; Mlle de Valois. Flourished around 1650; daughter of Gaston d'Orleans (1608–1660), duke of Orléans (brother of Louis XIII, king of France) and *Marguerite of Lorraine; first wife of Charles Emmanuel II (1634–1675), duke of Savoy (r. 1638–1675).*

Françoise d'Orleans died a few months after her marriage to Charles Emmanuel II, duke of Savoy; he then married *Jeanne of Nemours (d. 1724).

Françoise d'Orleans (1844–1925)

*Duchess of Chartres. Name variations: Francoise d' Orleans; Frances of Orleans; Francisca d'Orleans. Born on August 14, 1844; died on October 28, 1925; daughter of *Francisca of Portugal (1824–1898) and François or Francis (1818–1900), duke of Joinville; married Robert (1840–1910), duke of Chartres, on June 11, 1863; children: *Mary Oldenburg (1865–1909); Robert (1866–1885); Henry (1867–1901); Margaret of Chartres (b. 1869, who married Patrice de MacMahon, duke of Magenta); John (1874–1940), duke of Guise.*

Françoise-Marie de Bourbon (1677–1749), Countess of Blois and duchess of Orléans.

See Montespan, Françoise for sidebar.

Françoise of Guise (1902–1953)

*Princess of Greece. Name variations: Francoise of Guise, princess of Guise. Born on December 25, 1902; died on February 25, 1953; daughter of *Isabella of Orleans (b. 1878) and John (1874–1940), duke of Guise; married Prince Christopher Oldenburg of Greece (1888–1940), on February 11, 1929; children: Michael Oldenburg (b. 1939). Christopher Oldenburg's first wife was *Anastasia Stewart (1883–1923).*

Frank, Anne (1929–1945)

Dutch girl, one of the millions of Jews killed by the Germans, who became a symbol of brutalized innocence through the power of her diary. Born Anneliese Marie Frank on June 12, 1929, in Frankfurt am Main, Germany; died of typhus in the concentration camp at Bergen-Belsen in March 1945; daughter of Otto Frank and Edith Frank-Hollander; sister of Margot Betti Frank.

"The diary of Anne Frank has taken on a kind of mystical quality . . . ," wrote **Anna Quindlen** in 1993. "I read the diary first when I was twelve, reread it just last week. . . . Its power is so enormous that, looking at the pictures of the actual diary, with its plaid cover and impotent little lock, a shiver took hold of me as though the thing was a relic, as indeed it is."

Anneliese Marie Frank was born on June 12, 1929, in Frankfurt am Main. Long before others were prepared to act, Otto and **Edith Frank** were leery of the growing anti-Semitism in Germany. In 1933, they moved from Frankfurt to Amsterdam, Holland, in the Netherlands, where their daughters—four-year-old Anne and six-year-old ✥▸ **Margot Frank**—could lead a normal existence. There, Anne would attend the Sixth Public Montessori School (now named the Anne Frank School) for six years.

Otto Frank managed Opekta, the Dutch division of a company that produced pectin for the preparation of jam. As the firm grew, it moved to a building facing the Prinsengracht, one of the many canals that wind through old Amsterdam. Prinsengracht 263 was a five-story, narrow, red-brick building which, shoulder to shoulder, shared the street with other small factories or businesses. Among his employees were two woman: *Miep Gies and a young typist, ✥▸ Bep Voskuijl.

On Friday, May 10, 1940, the Germans invaded the Netherlands. Two days later, Queen *Wilhelmina and her family fled to England, and the nation's surrender came within a week. Holland was now a part of the Third Reich, commanded by Arthur Seyss-Inquart. At first, the Germans tried to woo the Dutch with their civility, but the theaters showed only German movies, the radio played only German music, and the newspapers contained only German news. At Otto Frank's factory, life went on as usual. Each day, the bells from the church down the block rang out on the quarter hour while seagulls bobbed on the canal. But Hollanders made a mental list of all their Dutch acquaintances: those with Nazi sympathies, known as NSBers, would prove to be dangerous.

The changes in Amsterdam were gradual. In August 1940, Dutch Jews were told to register. That September, Jews in the Civil Service—teachers, professors, mail deliverers—lost their jobs. The Old Jewish Quarter was sealed off. Opekta was ordered to register as a business having one or more Jewish partners. When 400 Jews were trucked off in a punitive move and met with accidental death, the Dutch called a general strike of docks, transportation, and industry for February 25, 1941; it lasted for three days. There were brutal reprisals from the Nazis.

Jews were now forbidden accommodation in hotels and restaurants, and could no longer attend movies, frequent public parks, or ride streetcars. Jews could shop only between the hours of three and five and only in Jewish stores. Jews had to turn in their radios. With their assets frozen, Jews could no longer use their bank deposits or valuables. Yanked out of public and private schools, Jewish children were told to attend all Jewish schools with all Jewish teachers. Thus, in September 1941, Anne and Margot Frank were transferred to the Jewish Lyceum (secondary school). Anne's schoolfriend **Jacqueline van Maarsen** confided: "I don't dare do anything anymore, 'cause I'm afraid it's not allowed." Then came the yellow star; it was now a crime for a Christian to mix with a Jew. The Germans had successfully separated the Dutch Jews from their neighbors.

Aware that his position as managing director was threatening the company, Otto Frank announced that, though he would run the business as usual, he would legally resign and transfer the corporate papers to a partner. In the meantime, he was secretly filling a hiding place with necessities for living: canned goods, soap, linens, sacks of dried beans, furnishings, and cooking utensils. The ground floor of the Opekta company faced the canal; the first floor contained the offices, a kitchen, and a small storeroom; the second floor was used for warehousing; the third floor was an attic. Toward the back of the second floor, down a small corridor, there was an annex. Containing five small rooms, the annex was a separate section in the rear of the building that butted against the

✥▸ **Frank, Margot** (1926–1945)
Sister of Anne Frank. Born Margot Betti Frank in February 1926 in Frankfurt am Main, Germany; died of typhus in the concentration camp at Bergen-Belsen in March 1945; daughter of Otto Frank and Edith Frank-Hollander; sister of Anne Frank.

An excellent student and unfailingly polite, Margot Frank was pretty, bookish, and much more introspective than her sociable younger sister Anne.

✥▸ **Voskuijl, Bep** (d. 1983)
Young typist who helped the Franks. Name variations: Elli Vossen in the original diary. Born Elisabeth Voskuijl; died in 1983.

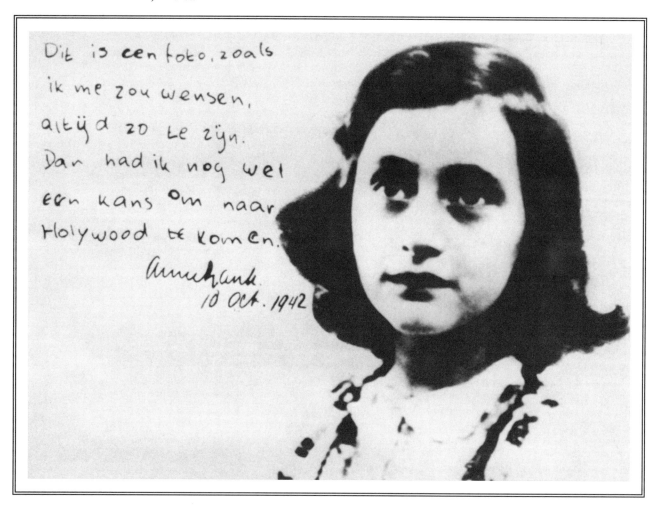

Dit is een foto, zoals
ik me zou wensen,
altijd zo te zijn.
Dan had ik nog wel
een kans om naar
Holywood te komen.

Anne Frank.
10 Oct. 1942

Anne
Frank

second and third floor. Though Margot and Anne were unsuspecting, their parents had been preparing for their disappearance into this annex for more than a year.

As the Nazis tightened their grip, Otto called Miep Gies into his office and told her he was taking his family into hiding. Since only a few walls would separate the Frank family from Miep's work station, he wanted to know if she objected. She said she did not. He then asked if she would be willing to assume the responsibility of their care. When she replied that she would, Otto reminded her of the punishment for those who helped Jews, but Gies cut him off. "I said, 'of course.' I meant it." They did not discuss details.

On June 12, 1942, for her 13th birthday, Anne Frank received a diary, a stiff-backed notebook with a red-plaid cover. "I hope I will be able to confide everything to you, as I have never been able to confide in anyone," she wrote that first day, "and I hope you will be a great source of comfort and support." She longed to be a writer and, despite the fact that no one would be

"interested in the musings of a thirteen-year-old schoolgirl," she had an even greater need to get things off her chest since "paper has more patience than people." Though Anne hastened to point out that she had many friends, including ❦▸ Hannah Goslar, she would make her diary her one good friend. She would call it Kitty.

Three weeks later, on the first Sunday in July 1942, 16-year-old Margot received a postcard, summoning her to report to a work camp in the East, a euphemism for German forced labor. That night, Miep and her husband Jan made several trips to the Frank house and spirited out goods that they would smuggle into the hiding place at a later date. The following morning, on July 6, thankful for the pouring rain, the family—minus Anne's mourned-for cat Moortje—moved into the "Secret Annex" behind the business. By planting clues, they fostered the rumor that they had escaped to Otto's mother's home in Basel, Switzerland. A week later, the Franks were joined by the van Pelses (known as the van Daans in the diary). The agreeable Hermann van Pels worked with Otto Frank, overseeing the new spices division; he was accompanied by his wife ❦➤ **Auguste van Pels**, their son, 16-year-old Peter, and Peter's cat Mouschi. Wrote Anne:

> No one would ever suspect there were so many rooms behind that plain gray door. There's just one small step in front of the door, and then you're inside. Straight ahead of you is a steep flight of stairs. To the left is a narrow hallway opening onto a room that serves as the Frank family's living room and bedroom. Next door is a smaller room, the bedroom and study of the two young ladies of the family. To the right of the stairs is a windowless washroom with a sink. . . . If you go up the stairs and open the door at the top, you're surprised to see such a large, light and spacious room in an old canal-side house like this. It contains a stove . . . and a sink. This will be the kitchen and bedroom of Mr. and Mrs. van [Pels], as well as the general living room, dining room and study for us all. A tiny side room is to be Peter van [Pel]'s bedroom. Then, just as in the front part of the building, there's an attic and loft.

Eventually, the group added a hinged bookcase in front of the Annex door that would swing out to open, sealing off the rooms and the stairs from view.

From the moment the workers arrived downstairs in the morning to the time they left, there was no noise from the tiny, three-floor Annex: no toilet flushed, no floorboard creaked. Miep would climb the stairs for the day's shopping list, then, using forged ration cards obtained from the underground, return with the groceries in the afternoon and stay for a visit. Once a week, she and Jan Gies would deliver a stack of books from a lending library. Otto Frank's business partners would also visit.

The two families made the Annex as liveable as possible. Anne, who initially shared a tiny first-floor bedroom with Margot, covered the wall with magazine photos: Ray Milland, *Greta Garbo, *Norma Shearer, Dutch actress **Lily Bouwmeester**, England's then Princess *Elizabeth (II)**, and Michelangelo's Pietà. Anne loved movies and was adept at mimicking voices; she also loved being the center of attention and was once dubbed a chatterbox by her teacher. With her deep set, gray-green eyes and keen intelligence, she had been popular at school. "Five admirers on every street corner," she wrote, "twenty or so friends, the favorite of most of my teachers, spoiled rotten by Father and Mother, bags full of candy and a big allowance. What more could anyone ask for?"

❦➤ **Goslar, Hannah** (1928—)
Childhood schoolmate of Anne Frank, known as Lies Goosens in the original diary. Name variations: Hannah Pick-Goslar; Hanneli Goslar; Lies Goslar; Lies Goosens in the original diary. Born Hannah Elisabeth Goslar in Berlin, Germany, in 1928; daughter of Hans Goslar (before moving to the Netherlands, was deputy minister for domestic affairs and press secretary of the Prussian Cabinet in Berlin) and Ruth Judith Klee (a teacher); married; children: three, including son Chagi (an officer in the Israeli army).

Born in Berlin in 1928, Hannah Goslar was the daughter of **Ruth Klee Goslar**, a teacher, and Hans Goslar, who was deputy minister for domestic affairs and press secretary of the Prussian Cabinet in Berlin before moving to Amsterdam, the Netherlands, in 1933. The Goslars lived diagonally across from the Franks, and Anne and Hannah were very close. One day Hannah arrived at the Franks' door to borrow a scale and was told they had moved to Switzerland.

As reported in Anne's diary, in October 1942 Hannah's mother died in childbirth. On November 27, 1943, Anne wrote that she dreamed that Hannah was dead. In reality, Hannah, her sister, and her father were part of a large Nazi roundup on June 20, 1943. On February 15, 1944, they were transported from Westerbork to Bergen-Belsen. A year later, Auguste van Pels fetched Hannah and told her that Anne was in the same camp in a section composed of large tents. The friends met and talked through the barbed wire. Unaware that Otto Frank was still alive, Anne was tearful and told Hannah that her parents were both dead. After the war, with the help of Otto Frank, Hannah Goslar moved to Israel.

❦➤ **Pels, Auguste van** (1900–1945)
Known as Petronella van Daan in Anne Frank's diary. Name variations: known as Petronella van Daan in diary. Born on September 9, 1900; died in 1945; married Hermann van Pels; children: Peter.

Known as Petronella van Daan in the original diary, Auguste van Pels was transferred to Bergen-Belsen from Auschwitz, then to Buchenwald, then to Theresienstadt on April 9, 1945. Though it is certain that she died in the camps, the date is not known. Her son Peter was on the forced "death march" from Auschwitz to Mauthausen (Austria) where he died on May 5, 1945, three days before the liberation of the camp.

Between June 12, 1942, and August 1, 1944, Anne was attentive to her diary. The earlier sections list the travails of a budding teenager. Anne was indignant when all occupants of the Annex (especially her mother and Mrs. van Pels) felt obliged to aid in her upbringing, pointing

out her many shortcomings. Though Margot and Anne both had their every mood analyzed, Margot, that "paragon of virtue," got off easier. Then, on November 17, 1942, the debonair dentist Fritz Pfeffer (named Albert Dussel in the diary) joined them in the Annex. Pfeffer brought news of the fate of friends in the outside world that made the Annex inhabitants gloomy for days. Unfortunately for Anne, Pfeffer, who now shared her bedroom (Margot had moved into the room with her parents), turned out to be another disciplinarian, a long-winded one, at that. It was not easy to rebel against two sets of parents and a visiting dentist.

"Everyone thinks I'm showing off when I talk, ridiculous when I'm silent, insolent when I answer, cunning when I have an idea, lazy when I'm tired, selfish when I eat one bite more than I should, stupid, cowardly, calculating, etc., etc.," lamented Anne. "All day long I hear nothing but what an exasperating child I am, and although I laugh it off and pretend not to mind, I do mind."

Their day-to-day routine seldom varied. In the August 4–5, 1943, entries, Anne wrote:

Nine in the evening. Bedtime always begins in the Annex with an enormous hustle and bustle. Chairs are shifted, beds pulled out, blankets unfolded—nothing stays where it is during the daytime. I sleep on a small divan, which is only five feet long, so we have to add a few chairs to make it longer. . . . *Ten o'clock.* Time to put up the blackout screen and say good-night. For the next fifteen minutes, at least, the house is filled with the creaking of beds and the sigh of broken springs. . . . *Approximately three o'clock.* . . . Sometimes the guns go off during the night, between one and four. I'm never aware of it before it happens, but all of a sudden I find myself standing beside my bed, out of sheer habit. . . . Then I grab a pillow and a handkerchief, throw on my robe and slippers and dash next door to Father.

Each day started at 6:45 with an alarm. All householders prepared for the silent hours when the workers were downstairs. "Margot and mother are nervous," wrote Anne.

"Shh . . . Father. Be quiet, Otto. Shh! . . . It's eight-thirty. Come here, you can't run the water anymore. Walk softly!" A sample of what's said to Father in the bathroom. At the stroke of half past eight, he has to be in the living room. No running water, no flushing toilet, no walking around, no noise whatsoever. As long as the office staff hasn't arrived, sounds travel more easily to the warehouse.

At 12:30, when the workers leave for lunch:

The whole gang breathes a sigh of relief. . . . Upstairs you can hear the thud of the vacuum cleaner on Mrs. van [P].'s beautiful and only rug.

Visitors would sometimes join them from below to listen to the BBC. Over Radio Orange, the underground radio, Queen Wilhelmina broadcast hope from England. "The time will come when we'll be people again and not just Jews!" wrote Anne. "Who has inflicted this on us? Who has set us apart from all the rest?"

In the prolonged existence in close quarters, all of the inmates inevitably got on each other's nerves. "I wonder if everyone who shares a house sooner or later ends up at odds with their fellow residents," wrote Anne. "Or have we just had a stroke of bad luck? At mealtime, when Pfeffer helps himself to a quarter of the half-filled gravy boat and leaves the rest of us to do without, I lose my appetite and feel like jumping to my feet, knocking him off his chair and throwing him out the door."

They lived with terror. Air-raid warning sirens blared outside; planes with bellies filled with bombs droned overhead, anti-aircraft guns boomed, rooms shook under the bombing. Since the Nazis had shipped Dutch food and goods to Germany, rations had dwindled, leaving Netherlanders with a meager monthly allotment. Most of Holland was starving. Crime increased. On two different nights, there were break-ins in the warehouse below; in their helplessness, those in the Annex did not know whether the intruders were burglars or the Gestapo. The nights grew longer.

Anne had two diaries. The first version (version *a*) was written for herself. But in 1944, she heard Gerrit Bolkestein, the minister of education of the Dutch government in exile, broadcasting from London, exhorting the Dutch to keep accounts of the Nazi occupation, specifically letters and diaries. After the war, he said, a collection would be made. So Anne began to rewrite and edit her diary, adding passages from memory, cutting passages of little interest (version *b*). In the *b* version, she also revisited passages as a 15-year-old that she had written as a 13-year-old and commented upon them. She longed to be a journalist:

I finally realized that I must do my schoolwork to keep from being ignorant, to get on in my life, to become a journalist. . . . I can't imagine having to live like Mother, Mrs. van [Pels] and all the women who go about their work and are then forgotten. I need to have something besides a husband and children to devote myself to! I don't want to have lived in vain like most people. I want to be

useful or bring enjoyment to all people, even those I've never met. I want to go on living even after my death! And that's why I'm so grateful to God for having given me this gift.

When Anne looked downcast, her mother exhorted her to think of those more miserable, "be grateful you're not in Poland." "This is where Mother and I differ greatly," wrote Anne. "Her advice in the face of melancholy is: 'Think about all the suffering in the world and be thankful you're not part of it.' My advice is: 'Go outside, to the country, enjoy the sun and all nature has to offer.'"

She longed to be outside.

Is it because I haven't been outdoors for so long that I've become smitten with nature? I remember a time when a magnificent blue sky, chirping birds, moonlight and budding blossoms wouldn't have captivated me. . . . [S]everal months ago, I happened to be upstairs one night when the window was open. I didn't go back down until it had to be closed again. The dark, rainy evening, the wind, the racing clouds, had me spellbound; it was the first time in a year and a half that I'd seen the night face-to-face. . . . [L]ooking at the sky, the clouds, the moon and the stars really does make me feel calm and hopeful. . . . Nature makes me feel humble and ready to face every blow with courage!

Anne grew out of her clothes; her eyes weakened. Clearly maturing, she began to see her mother's side of things a little more often, began to be less jealous of Margot's relationship with their father; even her attitude toward the van Pelses began to change. The girl she called "the good Anne" was coming to the fore more often.

"I think spring is inside me," she wrote on Saturday, February 12, 1944. "I feel spring awakening, I feel it in my entire body and soul. I have to force myself to act normally. I'm in a state of utter confusion, don't know what to read, what to write, what to do. I only know that I'm longing for something." Until then, she had longed for a girlfriend, for someone to confide in; now she noticed Peter van Pels. In the beginning, she had found Peter obnoxious, but something was changing. Despite protestations to Kitty of not being in love, Anne began to have something to look forward to: seeing and talking to Peter—every minute of every day, seeing and talking to Peter.

But events drove the group nearer the precipice. On March 1, 1944, there was another break-in downstairs, and Hermann van Pels may have inadvertently been seen by the thief. On March 14, those that supplied Miep with extra

Opposite page

The Franks hid in the loft of this warehouse for almost two years.

food coupons were arrested. Those in the Annex now dined on potatoes and kale. On Sunday, April 9, there was another break-in, and the night watchman alerted the police who searched the house. Anne and others in the Secret Annex had lain frozen through night, sure they had been found out.

They lived for the news of Allied victories: Tunis, Casablanca, Sicily. Mussolini resigned; Italy capitulated. And finally, on June 6, 1944, the invasion they had long been waiting for began. Over the BBC, they heard the words: "This is D-Day." One week later, Anne turned 15 and began to think it possible that she might be returning to school in October.

The world's been turned upside down. The most decent people are being sent to concentration camps, prisons and lonely cells, while the lowest of the low rule.

—Anne Frank

Sometime between 10 and 10:30 in the morning, on August 4, 1944, the Annex was raided by the German SD and Dutch members of the Security Police who had been tipped off by an anonymous caller. All eight in hiding were arrested, as well as two of their Dutch supporters. Four days later, the Franks were transported to Westerbork, a holding camp for the Jews in the north of Holland. On September 3, with the Allies 120 miles away, the Franks were herded onto a transport train for the two-day journey to Auschwitz-Birkenau; it was the last transport from the Netherlands to Auschwitz and contained 1,019 people (127 would survive).

On arrival, 549 were immediately sent to the gas chamber, including all children under 15 years of age. Since Anne had turned 15 that June, she escaped the selection and was sent to Barracks 29 along with her mother Edith and sister Margot. Since the women had been separated from the men, they did not know of Otto's fate. For the next two months, because Anne had scabies, most of their time was spent in what was known as the Krätzeblock (scabies barracks). Probably on October 28, 1944, the sisters were shipped to Bergen-Belsen, but Edith was forced to remain behind. Edith Frank died in Auschwitz of grief, hunger, and exhaustion, it is said, on January 6, 1945.

At this point in the war, living conditions were so terrible at Bergen-Belsen that 10,000 died without the help of gas chambers. It was winter; there was no food; the camp was notoriously overcrowded and disease was rampant.

Margot and Anne had their hair chopped off and were put in a section composed of large tents. Shortly after, their tent blew down in a severe storm, and they were moved to an overcrowded barrack. "The Frank girls were so emaciated. They looked terrible," said **Rachel van Amerongen-Frankfoorder** who was in the camp at the same time. "They had those hollowed-out faces, skin over bone. They were terribly cold. They had the least desirable places in the barrack, below, near the door, which was constantly opened and closed." In early March 1945, Anne and Margot Frank died of typhus within days of each other. Anne "stayed on her feet until Margot died," said **Janny Brandes-Brilleslijper,** who was also there as a political prisoner, "only then did she give in to her illness." The British liberated the camp a few weeks later.

The day the Franks were abducted, Miep Gies and Bep Voskuijl found Anne's diary, copy books, and papers strewn about the Secret Annex floor. Fortunately, Gies did not read the diary. If she had, she later claimed, she would have burned it to keep it out of the hands of the Gestapo: the diary contained the names of those who had helped the Franks. Instead, she hid it in her desk drawer throughout the last months of the war. After learning of Anne's death, Gies handed the diary over to Otto Frank who had survived and returned home.

Otto honored his daughter's wish by publishing the diary. Selecting material from both versions (which became version *c*), he omitted many of Anne's references to her emerging sexuality, her teenage angers, and her rejection of her mother. He also cut negative passages regarding others in the Annex. Published as *Het Achterhuis* (The Annex) in the Netherlands in 1947, the diary was eventually released in over 50 countries in 55 languages, and the Annex at No. 263 Prinsengracht became a museum.

When Otto Frank died in 1980, he willed Anne Frank's manuscripts to the Netherlands State Institute for War Documentation in Amsterdam. Since there were those who denied the authenticity of the diaries, the Institute did a thorough investigation, found the documents to be authentic beyond question, and released them in their entirety, including the Institute's examination of Anne's handwriting and materials concerning the Franks' arrest and deportation. In 1991, the Anne Frank Foundation (Anne Frank-Fonds) in Basel, Switzerland, decided to publish an unexpurgated edition of the diary, containing 30% more of the original. In the new version, the actual names of those in the Annex and those who assisted the Franks are used, while those who wished to remain anonymous are represented by initials.

"The struggle for identity, the fears, the doubts, above all the everydayness in the diary entries," writes Quindlen, "the worries about outgrown shoes, the romantic yearnings, and the ever-present conflicts with Mama and Margot reflect, mirror, and elevate the lives of millions who went about the business of studying, romancing, cooking, sewing, and struggling to live in the world until the Nazis ended their millions of ordinary, individual lives."

SOURCES:

"As She Was," in *People Weekly*. May 13, 1996, p. 73.

Frank, Anne. *The Diary of a Young Girl: The Definitive Edition*. Edited by Otto Frank and Mirjam Pressler. NY: Doubleday, 1995.

Gies, Miep, with Alison Leslie Gold. *Anne Frank Remembered*. NY: Simon and Schuster, 1987.

Lindwer, Willy. *The Last Seven Months of Anne Frank*. NY: Random House, 1991.

van der Rol, Ruud, and Rian Verhoeven for the Anne Frank House. *Anne Frank, Beyond the Diary: A Photographic Remembrance*. Introduction by Anna Quindlen. NY: Viking, 193.

SUGGESTED READING:

Graver, Lawrence. *An Obsession with Anne Frank: Meyer Levin and the Diary*. Berkeley, CA: University of California Press, 1995.

Rittner, Carol, ed. *Anne Frank in the World: Essays and Reflections*. M.E. Sharpe, 1997.

RELATED MEDIA:

The Diary of Anne Frank, dramatization of the diary in two-acts by **Frances Goodrich** and Albert Hackett (winner of the Pulitzer Prize and Drama Critics Circle Award), directed by Garson Kanin, starring **Susan Strasberg** and Joseph Schildkraut, opened at the Cort Theater on October 5, 1955.

The Diary of Anne Frank, produced on Broadway at the Music Box Theater, opened on December 4, 1997, starring **Natalie Portman, Linda Lavin,** and George Hearn, adapted by **Wendy Kesselman** from the Goodrich-Hackett script, directed by James Lapine.

The Diary of Anne Frank, 20th Century-Fox film, 1959, starring *Millie Perkins, Joseph Schildkraut, *Shelley Winters** (who received an Academy Award for Best Supporting Actress), directed by George Stevens; screenplay by Frances Goodrich and Albert Hackett.

Anne Frank Remembered, written and directed by Jon Blair, distributed by Sony Pictures Classics (winner of an Academy Award for Best Documentary Feature, 1996).

The Last Seven Months of Anne Frank, documentary by Willy Lindwer, first televised in the Netherlands, May 1988.

Franken, Rose (c. 1895–1988)

American playwright, producer, director, and screenwriter, who was best known for her popular "Clau- *dia" series. Name variations: (joint pseudonyms) Franken Meloney and Margaret Grant. Born Rose Dorothy Lewin on December 28, 1895 (some sources cite 1898), in Gainesville, Texas; died on June 22, 1988, in Tucson, Arizona; daughter of Michael and Hannah (Younker) Lewin; attended the Ethical Culture School, New York City; married Sigmund Walter Anthony Franken (an oral surgeon), in 1915 (died 1933); married William Brown Meloney (an author, playwright, and producer), in 1937; children: (first marriage) three sons, Paul, John, and Peter.*

Selected works: Pattern (1925); Another Language; a Comedy Drama in Three Acts (1932); (with J. Lewin) Mr. Dooley, Jr.; a Comedy for Children (1932); Twice Born (1935); (with W.B. Meloney) Call Back Love (1937); Of Great Riches (1937); Claudia (1939, dramatization, 1941, screenplay, 1943); Claudia and David (1939, screenplay, 1946); (with W.B. Meloney) Strange Victory (1939); (with W.B. Meloney) When Doctors Disagree (1940, dramatization by Franken, 1943); (with W.B. Meloney) American Bred (1941); The Book of Claudia (1941); Another Claudia (1943); Outrageous Fortune; a Drama in Three Acts (1943); (with W.B. Meloney) Beloved Stranger (1944); Soldier's Wife; a Comedy in Three Acts (1944); Young Claudia (1946); The Hallams; a Play in Three Acts (1947); The Marriage of Claudia (1948); From Claudia to David (1950); The Fragile Years (also published as Those Fragile Years: A Claudia Novel, 1952); Rendezvous (English title, The Quiet Heart, 1954); Intimate Story (1955); The Antic Years (1959); The Complete Book of Claudia (1958); Return to Claudia (1960); When All Is Said and Done: An Autobiography (1963); You're Well Out of a Hospital (1966).

Rose Franken was a prolific writer who turned out plays, short-stories, magazine serials, novels, and motion-picture scripts, frequently in collaboration with her second husband, author, playwright, and producer William Brown Meloney. Franken was the author of the enormously popular "Claudia" novels, which she also adapted into a hit play, two movies, and a radio serial. In addition to writing, she directed her own plays, some of which she also co-produced with Meloney.

Franken was born Rose Dorothy Lewin on December 28, 1895, in Gainesville, Texas. Her parents were separated when she was very young, and she grew up in New York's Harlem with her mother, grandparents, three siblings, and other members of the extended family. In 1915, she left high school to marry Sigmund

Rose
Franken

Franken, a prominent oral surgeon some ten years her senior. But Sigmund was diagnosed with tuberculosis just two weeks after the wedding and, after a year in a sanitarium, remained in ill health until his death in 1933. To ease her constant concern about her husband, Franken began writing, publishing her first novel *Pattern* in 1925. Her first dramatic effort, *Fortnight,* was not produced, but her second play, *Hallam Wives,* was staged in Greenwich, Connecticut, in the summer of 1929. The play, a comedy-drama focusing on a middle-class American family dominated by a possessive matriarch, was later revised and produced as *Another Language* (1932). Received favorably by critics and audiences alike, it ran for 453 performances on Broadway—a record for a first play—and was included in Burns Mantle's *Best Plays of the Year.* (Several of Franken's subsequent plays were also included in this annual review.)

After her husband's death, Franken, now the mother of three sons, moved her family to California, where she met William Meloney when they collaborated on a screenplay. They courted during subsequent writing assignments. Following their marriage in 1937, the couple moved to a Connecticut farm, where they con-

tinued to produce novels and magazine serials, using the joint pseudonyms Franken Meloney and Margaret Grant.

Franken began her "Claudia" novels in 1939, as a series for *Redbook* magazine. The series expanded into eight novels which sold well in the United States and in 20 countries abroad. The novels chronicle the youthful marriage of Claudia to David Naughton and take the reader through Claudia's maturation from child-wife to mature partner. Writes **Felicia Londrè** in *American Women Writers:* "Although the Claudia novels rely heavily upon illness, accidents, and death for the emotional upheavals that lead Claudia toward increasing self-awareness, they are essentially the saga of a blissful marriage." Franken, in her autobiography *When All Is Said and Done* (1963), admitted that Claudia eventually became burdensome, writing that "the sheer technical task of remaining within her consciousness became increasingly onerous and demanding."

The first two stories of the Claudia series formed the basis for Franken's hit play *Claudia,* which was produced in 1941. Purportedly, Franken, who directed the play, auditioned close to 200 actresses before choosing 23-year-old *Dorothy McGuire for the title role. An unknown, McGuire was catapulted to fame by the play, which received a chorus of good reviews. "The best new American play of the season by all odds," proclaimed Richard Watts of the New York *Herald Tribune.* After a run of 477 performances on Broadway, the play toured under the auspices of three separate companies, while McGuire went on to recreate her role in the film version in 1943 and again in a film sequel, *Claudia and David,* in 1946.

Franken's next play, *Outrageous Fortune* (1943), was a serious drama dealing with homosexuality and anti-Semitism as well as a number of other social issues. Although it was criticized as theme-heavy, most reviewers felt that it was her best theatrical work. Audiences supported the production for ten weeks, making it a moderate success. Franken suffered her first solid failure with her next attempt, *When Doctors Disagree,* based on a "Franken Meloney" novel of the same name. She got back on track, however, with *Soldier's Wife* (1944), a drama which examined the problems caused when a husband returns from the war. Starring *Martha Scott, Glenn Anders, and Myron McCormick, the play was praised by **Willela Waldorf** of the New York *Post* as "simple, unpretentious, intelligent, and full of a warm understanding of human and decent values, plus a consistently diverting sense of humor."

Franken resurrected the middle-class Hallam family from *Another Language* for her last professionally produced play, *The Hallams* (1947), after which she concentrated on fiction and her autobiography. Rose Franken did not publish after 1966; she died on June 22, 1988, in Tucson, Arizona.

SOURCES:

Kunitz, Stanley J., ed. *Twentieth Century Authors.* NY: H.W. Wilson, 1942.

Mainiero, Lina, ed. *American Women Writers: From Colonial Times to the Present.* NY: Frederick Ungar, 1980.

Moritz, Charles, ed. *Current Biography.* NY: H.W. Wilson, 1988.

Rothe, Anne, ed. *Current Biography.* NY: H.W. Wilson, 1947.

Wilmeth, Don B., and Tice L. Miller, eds. *Cambridge Guide to American Theatre.* NY: Cambridge University Press, 1993.

Barbara Morgan,
Melrose, Massachusetts

Franklin, Christine (1847–1930).

See Ladd-Franklin, Christine.

Franklin, Deborah (1707–1774).

See Bache, Sarah for sidebar on Deborah Read.

Franklin, Eleanor (1795–1825).

See Franklin, Jane for sidebar.

Franklin, Jane (1792–1875)

English social reformer and traveler who gained international fame for her relentless efforts to locate and rescue her husband's ill-fated Arctic expedition. Name variations: Lady Jane Franklin. Born Jane Griffin in 1792 (some sources cite 1791) in Spitalfields, England; died at Phillimore Gardens, her London home, on July 18, 1875; daughter of John Griffin (a silk-weaving magnate) and Mary Guillemard (Griffin); educated at a boarding school in Chelsea; married Sir John Franklin (an explorer), 1828; children: none.

After marriage, traveled and lived in Van Diemen's Land and New Zealand (1828–33); was the first woman to travel overland from Melbourne to Sydney in Australia (1829); financed five vessels to the Arctic to search for her husband's expedition (1850–57); awarded the Founder's Gold Medal from the Royal Geographical Society (1860).

Jane Franklin was an incurably restless woman who traveled extensively and recorded voluminous notes on everything she observed—first with her father, later with explorer-husband John Franklin, and finally as a solitary adventurer. Belying the stereotype of the Victorian woman of means, parlors, and needlework, she took ocean voyages, climbed mountains, visited dignitaries, and sponsored exploratory expeditions. Though she married late, she loved her husband and fought until her death to assure his reputation in the history of Arctic exploration.

Jane Griffin was born in 1792 at Spitalfields, England. She was the third of four children of John Griffin of Bedford Place, a magnate in the silk-weaving industry and a liveryman in the Worshipful Company of Goldsmiths, and **Mary Guillemard Griffin** who died in 1795 when Jane was three years old. The children's early upbringing was provided by a Miss Peltrau, the daughter of John Griffin's housekeeper. When Jane's only brother John died in 1804, Jane and her two sisters were sent to Miss Van den Enden's small boarding school in Chelsea for the proper education of young ladies of their class. Jane was an intelligent child who excelled in reading, memorization and arithmetic. Though well-behaved, she was by nature a mischievous and romantic young lady.

At age 17, Jane wrote her name on the inside cover of her first daybook and added, "A Journal of a Visit to Oxford, in June, 1809." Although none of her work was published during her lifetime, she would be a voluminous writer who recorded her extensive travels and adventures, leaving behind over 200 travel diaries and nearly 2,000 letters. Her writing is extremely neat despite the fact that she sometimes squeezed 40 lines onto a single page and often wrote sideways around the margins. With her father, she traveled extensively in England and Europe while noting everything in her journals—every monument, church, plaque, tombstone, historic object, landscape, industry, geographic location, and travel distance.

During her late teens, Jane established a schedule for enriching her mind through almost continuous study. In one three-year period, she read nearly 300 books on religion, travel, education and various other subjects. She also pursued a multitude of activities of educational value. She attended lectures at the Royal Institution, visited Vauxhall Gardens, was a member of the Book Society, visited Newgate Prison, and regularly attended British and Foreign School Society meetings. A serious-minded young woman, Jane Griffin had no time to devote to needlework, society balls or novels, which she considered to be frivolous. Her incessant intellectual growth continued to expand during her travels with her father.

On November 5, 1828, Jane married Captain John Franklin (1786–1847), the Arctic explorer. She had been friends with John and his first wife ◄❧ **Eleanor Franklin**, who died in 1825 while her husband was in the Arctic. Shortly after his return to England, the world-renowned explorer had presented Jane with exotic gifts from his explorations. They fell in love and the 36-year-old Jane became the wife of the 42-year-old John. Their adventurous natures made them kindred spirits. During the period of their engagement, Jane had traveled to Russia with her father and written to John that she would never wear a conjugal ring as a badge of slavery nor be a wretched wife who obliged her husband as a sense of duty. Other than their spirit of adventure, Jane was the opposite of her placid, sober and humorless husband. Unlike his wife, he wrote an unimaginative prose and communicated his experiences in an almost apologetic style. Even in appearance they seemed an odd couple. He was short, bald and portly while Jane was a tiny, blue-eyed beauty with a lovely complexion.

John, who had served in the navy at the Battle of Trafalgar (1805) and the Battle of New Orleans (1814), had subsequently been on three expeditions to the Arctic region. His last overland expedition (1825–27) had added over 1,200 miles of new knowledge about the Arctic coastline and earned him a knighthood in 1829. Following their marriage, the Franklins lived in the Mediterranean where he was assigned peacetime duties as commander of the H.M.S. *Rainbow*.

Franklin spent the years in the Mediterranean traveling through Turkey, Greece, Egypt, Syria and the Holy Land. She described in her journals being in an earthquake in the Greek Isles, bandit attacks in Arabia, crossing the Nile River during a hurricane, and observing a revolution in Spain. When Sir John returned to England in 1833, Lady Jane was in Alexandria preparing for a trip up the Nile River. On her advice, John met with Sir James Graham, first lord of the admiralty, to request a new naval command. Since

❧► Franklin, Eleanor (1795–1825)

English poet. Name variations: Mrs. Eleanor Anne Franklin. Born Eleanor Anne Porden in July 1795; died on February 22, 1825; married John Franklin (afterwards Sir), in 1823.

Eleanor Franklin was a poet and invalid and a magnet to London's literary society. Her major work was the epic *Coeur de Lion*, written in 1822. The following year, she married the explorer John Franklin.

nothing was available, Jane joined John in England so that they could continue to pressure the authorities for a meaningful appointment.

Jane Franklin believed that another Arctic expedition was much more preferable to an assignment to a ship or station. Since there was talk of reviving the search for the Northwest Passage, the couple concluded that John should seek command of an expedition for that ultimate prize. The Admiralty, which had supported two unsuccessful Arctic expeditions, was forced into a hiatus in Arctic exploration due to economic restraints. Deeply disappointed, John accepted an appointment as governor of Van Diemen's Land (Tasmania), a colonial island near Australia.

Van Diemen's Land in 1836 was a dumping ground for English convicts and impoverished settlers. Franklin earned the good will of the inhabitants for her private benevolence and support of her husband's public policies. She campaigned for improved conditions for the convicts and poor emigrants. She formed commissions to examine conditions and treatment of aborigines, female convicts, and prostitutes. Her actions resulted in an avalanche of criticism from the colonial aristocracy. Her failure to follow the conventional role of a governor's wife also created dissatisfaction in official circles. Somewhat blunted in her humanitarian efforts, Franklin began to travel extensively as an outlet for her restless nature. She was the first woman to climb Mount Wellington, a mountain of over 4,000 feet near Hobart. In April 1839, she became the first woman to travel the overland Australian route from Melbourne to Sydney. On a visit to New Zealand in 1841, she studied Maori language and customs. Her room at Government House in Van Diemen's Land looked like a museum with her collections of fossils, geological specimens, stuffed birds, and aboriginal weapons obtained during her journeys.

The Franklins' six years in Van Diemen's Land were not happy. They did not fit into the conservative, snobbish clique of British public servants. The bureaucrats considered John Franklin to be a weak, inept, inexperienced governor with a liberal reform-minded mentality. They despised Jane Franklin's activism and considered her to be a meddling power behind her husband's throne. In 1841, the Franklins and Captain John Montagu, his colonial secretary, became such enemies that they hardly spoke to one another. After an open act of insubordination, John suspended Montagu. With the support of the Tasmanian press, Montagu took his anger back to London where he utilized his con-

Jane
Franklin

nections to eventually have John removed as governor. Although personally popular with the general public, the Franklins sailed for England on January 12, 1844.

Sir John felt that his honor had been stained, but he had virtually no success in reclaiming his official reputation in England. In reality, he was still a hero for his Arctic exploits with the general public. He, however, felt that he must do something daring to relieve his demoralization from the Van Dieman's Land experience. Jane convinced him to again appeal to the Admiralty for an appointment for Arctic exploration. Although John was 58 years old, Lord Haddington, first lord of the admiralty, decided to give him command of 138 handpicked sailors for a major Arctic expedition.

The instructions from the Admiralty were that he should go through Lancaster Sound and Barrow Strait until he reached Cape Walker, north of Prince of Wales Island, then proceed on a course directly towards the Bering Strait as far as ice or land presently unknown would permit. Sir John was given two vessels, the 370-ton *Erebus* under his command and the 326-ton *Terror* under Captain Francis Rawdon Crozier. Both vessels were veterans of Arctic exploration and, in addition to their three masts, were the first polar vessels equipped with emergency screw-steam power engines. Their commissary contained provisions for three years. There was tinned mutton, pork, chocolate, condiments, biscuits and spirits. The vessels, almost like floating palaces, even contained silverware, crystal, a barrel organ, and a library of nearly 3,000 volumes. Jane Franklin embroidered a silk Union Jack flag for him to place at the Arctic Circle. When she playfully tossed it over his face as he napped, a startled John reminded her that the flag was placed over a corpse who died on duty.

This monument was erected by Jane, his widow, who after long waiting and sending many in search of him, herself departed to seek and to find him in the Realms of Light.

—Second Inscription on Franklin Memorial, Westminster Abbey

Sir John's expedition sailed from London on May 18, 1845. The ships were last sighted by a Scottish whaling vessel in Upper Baffin Bay, west of Greenland, at the entrance of Lancaster Sound on July 25. There was little concern when nothing was heard of John at the end of the 1846 sailing season in the Arctic. He himself had warned his superiors that he expected to be out of touch for at least two years. When no word came in 1847, however, both Lady Franklin and the Admiralty began to worry. The Admiralty launched a massive rescue search in 1848. Three vessels were sent to the eastern Arctic, three more ships advanced eastward from the Bering Sea, and an overland expedition was sent to the Canadian Arctic coast. Although the expeditions failed to find any trace of John, they spurred new and greater efforts to locate the lost explorers. The Admiralty offered a reward of £20,000 and Lady Franklin added £3,000 to the sum. She also financed a supply of coal and provisions that were marked and placed on the coast of Lancaster Sound for the use of the missing explorers.

In 1849, she appealed for rescue efforts to U.S. President Zachary Taylor, Russian Tsar Nicholas I, French Emperor Napoleon III and British Prime Minister Lord Palmerston. While international public and private expeditions searched for the explorers, Lady Franklin waited in hope that they were still alive. She had dispatched letters to John with each expedition. Publicly, she continued to discuss issues such as popery and to distribute anti-chartist pamphlets.

Jane Franklin was committed in every way to finding her husband. She visited seaports to encourage whalers heading for Baffin Bay to carry extra provisions for the lost expedition. The Admiralty, somewhat tardy after its early response, finally launched more expeditions and even sought help from the Hudson's Bay Company. Franklin had used her own funds to send out the *Isabel* in 1852, but it found nothing. Another expedition financed by her was the *Prince Albert* under the command of Captain Charles C. Forsyth. This expedition brought back news that one of Franklin's camps on Beechey Island had been discovered.

In 1854, Dr. John Rae of the Hudson's Bay expedition found traces of Sir John's expedition at Boothia Peninsula. This encouraged Lady Franklin to outfit and dispatch the *Fox* under Sir Francis Leopold McClintock. He sailed in 1857 and in two severe Arctic winters discovered written accounts left behind by the lost expedition ten years earlier. When McClintock brought the documents back to her, she learned that her husband and some members of the expedition had died in June 1847. The notes described a successful first year before the *Erebus* and *Terror* were permanently beset by ice near King William's Island. John died on June 11, but, mysteriously, his body had never been found. In April 1848, Crozier and the 105 survivors abandoned their base and supplies in an effort to reach the Hudson's Bay Company posts over 1,000 miles away. In time, over 30 bodies would be found in the wastelands northwest of the Back River. None of John Franklin's expedition ever left the Arctic.

While waiting for McClintock's return, a restless Jane Franklin traveled by boat and train through France, Greece, the Crimea, and North Africa. In Athens, she had an audience with the queen of Greece (*Amalie of Oldenburg). Franklin was resting for her health in a Pyrenees mountain resort when word reached her that McClintock had come back from the Arctic. She returned to England and the admiration of her nation because she had always maintained that her husband, unfailingly obedient to orders, would be found in the exact area searched by McClintock. In her way, she was as stubborn and consistent as John had been. The expedition relics were displayed before massive crowds in London. Working behind the scenes, Franklin obtained an award of £5,000 for the crew of the *Fox*, but she declined a reimbursement for the funds she had expended on the expeditions. Queen *Victoria invested McClintock with a knighthood and the Royal Geographical Society awarded its Patron's Gold Medal to him.

Based on the information in the notes discovered by McClintock, Lady Franklin established that before his death, her husband had proven the existence of the Northwest Passage between Victoria Strait and Bering Strait. For her support of polar exploration and the tireless efforts to solve the disappearance of her husband's expedition, the Royal Geographic Society awarded Lady Franklin with the Founder's Gold Medal in 1860. She was the first woman ever to be honored with that prestigious award.

Franklin continued her travels, perhaps as solace for the tragic loss of her husband, perhaps because of her natural curiosity and love of adventure. In the fall of 1860, she visited the United States, Canada, Brazil, Patagonia, and Chile. She then spent two years in Hawaii, Japan, China, Singapore, Penang, and India. On this trip, she met Brigham Young in Salt Lake City, had an audience with King Kamehameha IV in Hawaii, climbed the column of Kutb-Minar near Delhi, and had "Lady Franklin Pass" named for her in the gold fields of British Columbia. After attending the dedication of a monument honoring her husband at Waterloo Place in London, she was off to France, Spain, Switzerland, Italy, Dalmatia, and Germany. She had an audience with Pope Paul IX and attended the Paris Exhibition of 1867. Still another trip to India was followed by visits to Northwest Africa and the Canary Islands before returning to London in 1869. Her later travels were limited to visits to Europe.

Her last years were spent in perpetuating the reputation of her husband. Shortly before her death in 1875, she arranged for a Carrara marble statue to be placed in Westminster Abbey, proclaiming her husband as the discoverer of the Northwest Passage. The epitaph at the base of the statue was written by the Franklins' friend, Alfred, Lord Tennyson, poet laureate of England. A second inscription paid homage to Jane Franklin's love and devotion to her husband. Jane Franklin died at her Phillimore Gardens home in London on July 18, 1875, at the age of 83.

SOURCES:

Franklin, Jane. *A Letter to Viscount Palmerston, K.G.* London: James Ridgway, 1857.

Gell, Edith Mary. *John Franklin's Bride*. London: John Murray, 1930.

Rawnsley, Willingham Franklin. *The Life, Diaries and Correspondence of Jane Lady Franklin*. London: MacDonald, 1923.

Woodward, Francis. *Portrait of Jane: A Life of Lady Franklin*. London: Hodder and Stoughton, 1951.

SUGGESTED READING:

Berton, Pierre. *The Arctic Grail: The Quest for the North West Passage and the North Pole, 1818–1909*. NY: Viking, 1988.

Cyriax, Richard J. *Sir John Franklin's Last Arctic Expedition: A Chapter in the History of the Royal Navy*. London: Methuen, 1939.

Fitzpatrick, Kathleen. *Sir John Franklin in Tasmania, 1837–1843*. Melbourne: Melbourne University Press, 1949.

Neatby, Leslie H. *The Search for Franklin*. London: Barker, 1970.

Rasky, Frank. *The North Pole or Bust*. Toronto: McGraw-Hill Ryerson, 1977.

Wright, Noel. *Quest for Franklin*. London: Heinemann, 1959.

COLLECTIONS:

Journals of Lady Jane Franklin are located in the Scott Polar Research Institute, Cambridge, England; Sir John Franklin's Papers are located in the National Maritime Museum, London, England.

Phillip E. Koerper,
Professor of History, Jacksonville State University,
Jacksonville, Alabama

Franklin, Martha Minerva

(1870–1968)

African-American nurse who founded the National Association of Colored Graduate Nurses (NACGN). Born on October 29, 1870, in New Milford, Connecticut; died on September 26, 1968, in New Haven, Connecticut; middle child and one of two daughters of Henry J. and Mary (Gauson) Franklin; graduated from Meriden Public High School, Meriden, Connecticut, 1890; graduated from Woman's Hospital Training School for Nurses of Philadelphia, December 1897; postgraduate course at Lincoln Hospital, New York City, 1920s; attended Teachers' College, Columbia University, 1928–30.

In 1895, Martha Minerva Franklin was the only black woman in her class at the Woman's Hospital Training School for Nurses of Philadelphia. After graduating in 1897, she worked as a private-duty nurse in her hometown of Meriden, Connecticut, and later in New Haven. Although of fair complexion and often mistaken for white, Franklin became more and more sensitive to the color barriers in nursing. In 1906, she began to devote her spare time to studying the status of black graduate nurses in the United States. She concluded that black nurses needed to work together to overcome racial biases, and that they might best do so through a national organization. In 1908, she sent out 1,500 handwritten letters at her own expense, asking nurses to consider uniting for a meeting.

Fifty-two nurses responded and attended the first three-day organizational meeting of the National Association of Colored Graduate Nurses, held at St. Mark's Methodist Episcopal

Church in New York City, at the invitation of
*Adah B. Thoms, president of the Lincoln
School of Nursing Alumnae Association. Beginning on August 23, 1908, the fledgling group set
forth the following goals: to wipe out discrimination in the nursing profession; to develop
leadership among black nurses; and to improve
standards in administration and education. They
also unanimously elected Franklin as their
leader, a position she held for two years, after
which she served as the organization's permanent historian and honorary president.

In 1912, the organization was represented
at the International Council of Nurses meeting
in Cologne, Germany, integrating the older organization for the first time. By the end of World
War I, the NACGN had a membership 2,000,
which by 1940 had reached 12,000. As membership increased, a national registry was established to help black nurses find work.

In the 1920s, Franklin, who never married,
relocated to New York City, where she enrolled in
a postgraduate course at Lincoln Hospital, a pre-
requisite for status as a registered nurse in New
York State. At age 58, she spent two years at Columbia University's Teachers' College, studying to
qualify as a public-health nurse. After living and
working in New York for many years, she returned to New Haven, where she resided with her
sister. She lived until the age of 98, dying of natural causes on September 26, 1968.

SOURCES:
Smith, Jessie Carney. *Notable Black American Women.*
Detroit, MI: Gale Research, 1992.

SUGGESTED READING:
Carnegie, Mary Elizabeth. *The Path We Tread: Blacks in
Nursing 1854–1984.* Philadelphia, PA: J.B. Lippin-
cott, 1986.

Barbara Morgan,
Melrose, Massachusetts

Franklin, Miles (1879–1954)

*One of Australia's most authentic voices, whose first
novel, the semi-autobiographical* My Brilliant Career
*(1901), and later works of fiction and nonfiction
brought her enduring fame in the English-speaking
world. Name variations: (pseudonym) Brent of Bin-
Bin. Born Stella Maria Sarah Miles Franklin in Australia at Talbingo, near Canberra, New South Wales,
on October 14, 1879; died at home of a heart attack in
Carlton, near Sydney, on September 19, 1954; eldest
child of John Maurice Franklin (a grazier and farmer)
and Susannah Margaret Lampe Franklin (a cultivated
woman who raised seven children and worked hard
throughout her life); educated at home by her mother*

*and a private tutor until age ten, after which she com-
pleted her formal studies at age fourteen in a one-
teacher school; never married; no children.*

*Dreams of a musical career were dashed when an
extended drought ruined the family's fortunes (1889);
worked long and toil-laden hours helping her parents
run a small dairy farm (1889–99); completed her first
and best-known novel,* My Brilliant Career *(1899);
moved to Sydney and Melbourne, where she continued
writing and became interested in social and economic
reform movements (1901); left Australia for U.S. (late
1905), settling in Chicago (1906) where she became
secretary of the Women's Trade Union League and
helped edit its publication,* Life and Labor; *had her
third novel,* Some Everyday Folk and Dawn, *published
by Blackwood (1909); rejected by publishers for only
novel to take place in the U.S.,* On Dearborn Street
*(1914); moved to England (1915), working with re-
form groups in London and serving for six months
(1917–18) as a volunteer with the Scottish Women's
Hospital in the Balkans; during the most intense creative period in her life, wrote six novels about pioneering days in 19th-century Australia under the pseudonym Brent of Bin-Bin, which mystified only strangers
to her previous fiction (1925–31); returned to Australia (1932) where she published what is regarded as
her masterpiece,* All That Swagger *(1936); devoted the
last 18 years of her life to promoting Australian literature and keeping up a voluminous correspondence
with friends in Australia, U.S., and Great Britain.*

*Publications: Miles Franklin was a prolific but
uneven writer who completed some 16 novels, 13 of
which were published in her lifetime or after her
death. Of these, her first and last novels,* My Brilliant
Career *(1901) and* All That Swagger *(1936), are universally regarded as her best fiction. Her posthumously published memoir,* Childhood at Brindabella *(1963)
is considered her finest work of nonfiction.*

Miles Franklin, one of Australia's best-
known and most original writers, was, as she
herself noted, a child of the mighty bush. Born
Stella Maria Sarah Miles Franklin at Talbingo,
north of Canberra in New South Wales, she
spent the first ten years of her life on a large
property at Brindabella some 70 miles from Talbingo. There her parents, John Maurice Franklin
and **Susannah Lampe Franklin,** raised and sold
cattle and sheep. Franklin's posthumously published memoir, *Childhood at Brindabella,* chronicles the idyllic life she and her siblings lived there.
The Franklins were well-off and could afford servants as well as a private tutor for their children.
At Brindabella, Miles Franklin learned to ride a

Opposite page

ℳiles
𝒥ranklin

horse almost as soon as she was able to walk, and she enjoyed horseback riding into her 70s. She spent part of each day working alongside the station workers and the rest of the day studying, reading, and learning to play the piano her mother had brought to Brindabella as a bride.

Australia has only one large river system, and even well-watered regions, as Brindabella, are subject to periodic and devastating droughts. In 1889, an extended dry spell brought the idyll at Brindabella to an end, and the Franklins were forced to sell their dwindling stock and the ranch. They moved to Thornburn, northeast of Canberra and near the cathedral city of Goulburn. There John Franklin took up dairy farming on a relatively small property of about 1,000 acres which they called Stillwater for its nearby lagoons. In Franklin's first and best-known novel, *My Brilliant Career,* she ruefully noted that her parents "had dropped from swelldom to peasantism." Miles and her siblings continued their education at a one-teacher school and then spent hours each day helping their mother milk the cows, tend the garden, prepare meals, clean the house, and do the laundry. Franklin never forgot how their hands and arms swelled from the milking. In fact, the pain from milking was so extreme as to disturb their sleep.

Franklin grew up loving books and music, but the family's poverty prevented her from pursuing a musical career or attending a university. She found an outlet for her rage and frustration over the "lifeless life" she and her family endured at Stillwater by writing about it. When she was barely 20, Franklin completed a semi-autobiographical work that she ironically entitled *My Brilliant(?) Career.* (The question mark was later dropped by the publisher.) Franklin characterized it as neither a romance nor a novel, "but simply a yarn—a *real* yarn." This assertion was to haunt Franklin for the rest of her days, and when *My Brilliant Career* was published in 1901 many of her relatives and neighbors and other bush Australians were upset and outraged, not so much by the rebelliousness of its feminist heroine, Sybylla Melvyn, as by the novel's negative depiction of many of Sybylla's family, relatives, neighbors, and other bush dwellers.

In *My Brilliant Career,* Franklin not only railed against the narrowness, monotony, and absolute uncongeniality of life in Possum Gully, as she called Stillwater, but also rebelled against the circumscribed role and unequal position of women in late 19th-century Australian society. Franklin expressed her antipathy to marriage time and again in her narrative, stating emphati-

cally that "marriage to me appeared the most horrible tied-down and unfair-to-women existence going."

While Miles Franklin had harsh things to say about men in her first works, it was men who came to her aid early in her career. When she was unable to find a publisher in Australia for *My Brilliant Career,* she appealed to Henry Lawson, Australia's leading poet and short-story writer, to take the manuscript with him on his return to England. While Australian publishers found the story of an angry and rebellious young woman too frank, too daring, and too uncompromising in its feminism, Lawson and Blackwood's of Edinburgh were charmed and captivated by the spontaneity, originality, vitality, and earthiness of *My Brilliant Career.* There was not a trace of pretentiousness, affectation, or humbug in it, nor, for that matter, in any of her later novels and other writings.

When Blackwood's of Edinburgh published *My Brilliant Career* in 1901, with an appreciative introduction by Lawson, the novel received enthusiastic reviews by mostly male critics in England and Australia. In September of 1901, A.G. Stephens, critic and editor of Australia's leading literary journal, *The Bulletin,* praised *My Brilliant Career,* calling it the first truly Australian novel. Stephens noted that "the author has the Australian mind; she speaks Australian language, utters Australian thoughts and looks at things from an Australian point of view absolutely." Another champion was Joseph Furphy, author of the classic novel, *Such Is Life,* who encouraged Franklin to keep on writing and to ignore negative reactions to her work.

Franklin kept on writing, but she was deeply hurt by the continuing controversy over *My Brilliant Career.* Mortified by the uproar she had caused, she left Stillwater and moved, first to Sydney and then to Melbourne. She hoped to become a journalist, but to pay her way and gather firsthand information about domestic service, she became, for a time, a "Mary Anne," that is, a maid. In both Sydney and Melbourne, Franklin found the praise, the appreciation, and the congeniality that she had longed for. In both cities, she was befriended by the literary elite, social reformers and feminists, and made the first of a series of lifelong friendships. *Rose Scott (1847–1925) who labored long and hard for woman suffrage (granted in 1902), prison reform, as well as decent wages, hours and working conditions, welcomed Franklin to her literary salon and introduced her to Sydney's leading writers, poets, philanthropists and politicians.

Another lifelong friend was *Vida Goldstein (1869–1949) also a prominent reformer who, like Rose Scott, found that life was too short to devote to the service of one man. These and other prominent single women were important role models for Franklin, and they strengthened her resolve to devote her life to writing, to social reform, and to the encouragement of Australian literature.

By 1904, Franklin had completed her second novel, *My Career Goes Bung,* which satirized the pretentiousness of the social and political elites of Sydney and Melbourne. However, no Australian publisher would touch it for fear of libel suits, and the sequel to *My Brilliant Career* did not appear until 1946, by which time Franklin was universally honored as one of Australia's leading writers.

Discouraged by her foundering career in journalism and her inability to publish *My Career Goes Bung* in her native country, in April 1906 Franklin sailed from Melbourne to San Francisco. She was urged on by her friend Vida Goldstein, who provided Franklin with letters of introduction to reformers and suffragists whom Goldstein had met in San Francisco and Chicago a few years before. Franklin stayed in San Francisco briefly, and then moved to Chicago, where she came under the wing of a compatriot, *Alice Henry. Henry was one of the leading reformers of her day, and she introduced Franklin to *Jane Addams, *Mary Anderson, *Lillian Wald, *Margaret Dreier Robins (*see Dreier Sisters*), and other outstanding champions of progressive causes, including women's rights, prison reform, and social legislation protecting all workers.

In 1907, Margaret Dreier Robins, leader of the National Women's Trade Union League, invited Franklin to serve as the League's secretary, a position she held until 1915. In addition, between 1912 and 1915 Franklin helped Alice Henry edit the League's influential publication, *Life and Labor.* Despite her many duties with the League, Franklin continued to write fiction and in 1909 Blackwood's published *Some Everyday Folk and Dawn,* a plea for sexual equality set in contemporary Australia. However, she could find no publisher for her fourth novel, *On Dearborn Street,* which was one of only two of the thirteen novels she published which were set outside Australia. Despite Franklin's inability to find an American publisher for *On Dearborn Street,* she always looked back on her nine years in the United States as a time of excitement, struggle and camaraderie. After Franklin left the states in 1915, she continued corresponding with her American friends to the end of their days or hers.

The coming of World War I weakened and derailed the Women's Trade Union League, the pacifist movement, and most American reform movements in general. Franklin had a falling out with Robins (they reconciled later and wrote to each other until Robins' death in 1948), left the league, and in 1915 decided to move to England. In London, Franklin became involved with reform groups and eventually found work with the National Housing and Planning Council, a phil-

anthropic organization located in Bloomsbury. Australian poet and novelist *Mary Fullerton, and Fullerton's patron and friend **Mabel Singleton**, befriended Franklin and invited her to share their London home. Franklin later repaid their kindness by championing Fullerton's writing and seeing to the publication of her poetry in their native Australia.

In the latter part of 1917, Franklin, a lifelong pacifist, decided to join the Scottish Women's Hospital, serving as a cook and then an orderly in battle-scarred Salonika in Macedonia.

From the movie My Brilliant Career, *starring* Judy Davis.

Unfortunately, she had to leave her post in February 1918 (and forfeit her year's salary of £25) when she contracted malaria. While recovering in London, Franklin wrote an account of her experiences in the Balkans. *Ne Mari Nishti (It Matters Nothing)* is one of about 30 of Franklin's manuscripts—plays, short stories and three novels—that in 1999 remained unpublished.

> *I* am proud that I am an Australian, a daughter of the Southern Cross, a child of the mighty bush. I am thankful I am a peasant, a part of the bone and muscle of my nation, and earn my bread by the sweat of my brow.
>
> —Miles Franklin

In late 1923, Franklin returned to Australia for the first time in 18 years to visit her aging parents and her surviving siblings. Years before, in 1915, Franklin's parents had given up farming and bought a home in the modest suburb of Carlton, near Sydney. From Carlton, Franklin made visits to Brindabella and Stillwater. This visit and a subsequent one in 1927 unleashed a creative flood that, between 1927 and 1933, resulted in the writing of six novels about pioneering life in 19th-century Brindabella, Talbingo, and other locations in the high Monaro region of New South Wales. Most of them were written at a desk in the British Museum, where Franklin could work undisturbed. Wishing to avoid any association with her controversial first novel, Franklin adopted the pseudonym of Brent of Bin-Bin. When close friends asked her why, Franklin replied that mysteries and secrets were great for publicity and aroused the reading public's curiosity. In 1928, *Up the Country,* the first of the six Bin-Bin novels to be published, won universal praise in Australia. *Ten Creeks Run* (1930) and *Back to Bool Bool* (1931) were not as enthusiastically received but sold relatively well despite the onset of the Great Depression. The remaining three Bin-Bin novels, *Prelude to Waking, Cockatoos,* and *Gentlemen at Gyany Gyang,* did not appear until the 1950s.

In 1931, Franklin learned of the death of her father, and the following year she returned to Australia for good to take care of her ailing mother. After Susannah Franklin died in 1938, her daughter Miles lived alone at Carlton until her own death 16 years later. The Bin-Bin novels and Franklin's masterpiece *All That Swagger* (1936), a novel inspired by the life of her Irish grandfather Joseph Franklin, elevated her to celebrity status. She used her fame to advance her last great cause: Australian literature. Between 1936 and 1954, Franklin joined many groups and associations that encouraged all writers, young and old. She lectured on Australian literature at Perth's university and, with **Kate Baker,** co-authored a biography of the novelist Joseph Furphy. In addition, she single-handedly revived interest in the poetry and prose of another dear friend, Mary Fullerton. Lastly, Franklin lived very frugally to endow a Pulitzer-like annual literary award. After Franklin's death, the first recipient of the Miles Franklin Award was Patrick White, author of the highly acclaimed novel *Voss.* Years later, White was awarded the Nobel Prize in literature. Franklin passionately believed, as she told one of her many friends, the writer **Florence James,** that "without an indigenous literature people can remain aliens on their own soil." Thanks to Miles Franklin's pioneering novels set in Australia's vast interior, and to the work of subsequent writers, Australians are not strangers in their own land.

After the posthumous publication of a memoir that is regarded as Franklin's third masterpiece, *Childhood at Brindabella* (1963), interest in her work declined by the late 1960s. However, the revival of feminism in Australia in the early 1970s brought a renewed interest in Franklin's work. The international acclaim accorded the 1979 cinema version of *My Brilliant Career,* a film written, directed and produced by Australian women, brought back into print a number of Franklin's best novels. In addition, since 1979 dozens of scholarly articles and reviews, two biographies and two editions of Franklin's letters have appeared. Miles Franklin, who prized friendship above all other human relationships, would have been delighted to know how many more friends she has made since her passing.

SOURCES:

Barnard, Marjorie. *Miles Franklin: The Story of a Famous Australian.* St. Lucia, Queensland: University of Queensland Press, 1988.

Coleman, Verna. *Miles Franklin in America: Her Unknown (Brilliant) Career.* Sydney: Angus and Robertson, 1981.

Ferrier, Carole, ed. *Gender, Politics, and Fiction: Twentieth Century Australian Women's Novels.* St. Lucia, Queensland: University of Queensland Press, 1992.

Modjeska, Drusilla. *Exiles at Home: Australian Women Writers, 1925–1945.* Sydney: Angus and Robertson, 1981.

Roderick, Colin Arthur. *Miles Franklin: Her Brilliant Career.* Adelaide: Rigby, 1982.

Roe, Jill, ed. *My Congenials: Miles Franklin and Friends in Letters.* 2 vols. Sydney: Angus and Robertson, 1993.

Baker, Kate (1861–1953)

Australian teacher and literary benefactor. Born Catherine Baker on April 23, 1861, in Cappoquin, County Waterford, Ireland; died in 1953 in Australia; educated in Australian public schools; never married; no children. Awarded the Office of the Order of the British Empire (OBE, 1937).

Selected works: (editor) The Poems of Joseph Furphy *(1916); (with Miles Franklin)* Joseph Furphy: The Legend of a Man and His Book *(1944).*

Kate Baker is known to Australians for her unflagging support of author Joseph Furphy. Without Baker, Furphy may well have remained an unknown; without Furphy, Baker most certainly would have. Born in Ireland in 1861, she was the youngest of a large Irish brood, whose father died within three months of her birth. Shortly thereafter, the family moved to Williamstown, Victoria, Australia, where Baker's mother brought up her children with a firm hand and urged conformity; thus Kate dedicated herself to teaching rather than poetry. Trained in the public schools of her region, she began to teach for the Victoria School Department in 1881.

Rural Australia offered ample opportunity for young teachers to gain experience, and Baker was sent to head the Wanalta Creek State School in January of 1886. There, she lodged with Isaac Furphy, taking on the schooling of four of his six children. The large Furphy family was close-knit, and Baker met them all except the elusive Joseph. After one year boarding with Isaac and traveling six miles a day to and from her school, she moved to patriarch Samuel Furphy's home, where she was treated like a daughter.

When Baker met Joseph Furphy in October of 1887, "He talked and I listened and questioned," Baker wrote. "In this opportunity to talk to a congenial listener he seemed like a thirsty man at a spring of cool water." The 44-year-old Joseph Furphy, whose wife **Leonie** was not intellectually inclined, found a malleable, intelligent mind in the 25-year-old Baker, and they became frequent correspondents.

Though no evidence exists that their relationship was improper, at least one love letter, written by Baker during a near-death illness, caused such scandal that she lost the friendship of every Furphy but Joseph, who staunchly de-fended her. Though many letters were destroyed and defaced, no overtly amorous ones exist. Baker was certainly in love with Furphy, but knew him to be married and generally uninterested. As her friend *Miles Franklin noted, Kate "lives and breathes and thinks only of Furphy. He is her monomania."

Baker was Furphy's critic, editor and benefactor. Until he became financially independent with the bestseller *Such is Life*, which introduced the character of Tom Collins, she provided funding for early publications. Teaching remained her livelihood until 1913, but Furphy was her life. His death of a cerebral hemorrhage when she was 51 caused her to have an emotional breakdown. But perpetuating his work gave her new purpose. Baker spent her remaining 40 years editing and publishing his poetry, and she reissued his most famous book. The biography, *Joseph Furphy: The Legend of a Man and His Book*, written with Franklin and released in 1944, created a glorified picture of Furphy, in part, because Franklin did not wish to hurt Baker or her subject's family, in part, because Franklin was blinded by their vision of Furphy as a hero.

For her efforts on behalf of Furphy, an Australian national legend, Baker was awarded the Office of the Order of the British Empire (OBE) in 1937. She lived well into her 90s as Furphy's literary widow.

SOURCES:

Barnes, John. *The Order of Things*. Melbourne: Oxford University Press, 1990.

Franklin, Miles, and Kate Baker. *Joseph Furphy: The Legend of a Man and His Book*. Sydney: Angus and Robertson, 1944.

Furphy, Joseph, and John Barnes, ed. *Joseph Furphy*. St. Lucia: University of Queensland Press, 1981.

Wilde, William H., Joy Horton, and Barry Andrews, ed. *Oxford Companion to Australian Literature*. Melbourne: Oxford University Press, 1994.

Crista Martin,
freelance writer, Boston, Massachusetts

James, Florence (b. 1904)

New Zealand-born writer. Born in Gisborne, New Zealand, in 1904; graduated from the University of Sydney.

Florence James, and her co-author *Dymphna Cusack, published the children's book *Four Winds and a Family* in 1947 and the novel *Come in Spinner* in 1951.

SUGGESTED READING:

Franklin, Miles. *Childhood at Brindabella*. Sydney: Angus and Robertson, 1963.

———. *My Brilliant Career*. Edinburgh: Blackwood and Sons, 1901.

———. *My Career Goes Bung*. NY: St. Martin's Press, 1981.

RELATED MEDIA:

My Brilliant Career (98 min. film), starring **Judy Davis** and Sam Neill, New South Wales-GUO-Analysis, 1980.

Anna Macias,
Professor Emerita of History,
Ohio Wesleyan University, Delaware, Ohio

Franklin, Rosalind (1920–1958)

English chemist and molecular biologist who played a central role in the discovery of the structure of DNA. Born Rosalind Franklin in London, England, on July 25, 1920; died in London on April 16, 1958; daughter of Muriel (Waleys) Franklin and Ellis Franklin; graduated from St. Paul's Girls' School (1938); enrolled Newnham College, Cambridge University (1938); graduated from Cambridge University (1941); never married; no children.

Stayed on at Cambridge after graduation as researcher; joined the British Coal Utilization Research Association (CURA, 1942); awarded Ph.D., Cambridge University (1945); hired by the Laboratoire Central des Services Chimique de État, Paris (1947); awarded Turner Newall Fellowship (1951); joined King's College Medical Research Council Biophysics Unit, London (1951); moved to Birkbeck College, London (1953); Francis Crick, James Watson, and Maurice Wilkins awarded Noble Prize in Medicine and Physiology (1962).

Publications: "A Note on the True Density of Chemical Composition and Structure of Coal and Carbonized Coals," in Fuel (1948); "The Interpretation of Diffuse X-Ray Diagrams in Carbon," in Acta Crystallographica (1950); "The Structure of Graphite Carbons," in Acta Crystallographica (1950); "Molecular Configuration in Sodium Thymonucleate," in Nature (1953); "Evidence for 2-Chain Helix in Crystalline Structure of Sodium Deoxyribonucleate," in Nature (1953); "Structure of Tobacco Mosaic Virus," in Nature (1955); "X-ray Diffraction Studies of the Structure of the Protein in Tobacco Mosaic Virus," in Symposium on Protein Structure (1957).

Born in London, England, into a family of wealthy merchant bankers on July 25, 1920, Rosalind Franklin experienced a progressive upbringing. The second child and first daughter, she was encouraged by her parents to cultivate her own interests, rather than conform to the rigid model of feminine behavior that the era imposed. When her father brought home a carpenter's workbench so that his children might learn practical skills, Rosalind took up woodworking along with her brothers. Her inclination towards the practical aspects of science were evident in later life, when she was often seen in the workshops of the British Coal Utilization Research Association.

Her father Ellis Franklin was a noted educator and vice-principal of the Working's Men's College, founded by Frederick Denison Maurice in 1854. Her mother **Muriel Waleys Franklin** was involved in the socialist movement. From an early age, Rosalind showed herself to be strong-willed and complex. Writes Muriel:

> Rosalind felt passionately about many things, and on occasion she could be tempestuous. Her affections both in childhood, and in later life, were deep and strong and lasting, but she could never be demonstrative, or readily express her feelings in words. This combination of strong feeling, sensibility, and emotional reserve, often complicated by intense concentration on the matter of the moment . . . could provoke either stony silence or a storm. But when she was a child, frustration tended to produce vehement protest, with sudden angry tears. . . . These storms were as a rule quickly over, even if sometimes too easily provoked. But the strong will, and tempestuousness of temper, remained characteristic all her life.

At St. Paul's Girls' School, Rosalind Franklin received a privileged education. St. Paul's offered courses in physics and chemistry which were on a par with the finest boys' schools in England. It was here that Franklin first discovered her love for the sciences; by the age of 15, she had already decided that this would become her profession. At St. Paul's, she also took courses in French.

Career opportunities in the sciences were extremely limited for women prior to the Second World War. While not wholly dismissive of his daughter's interests, Ellis Franklin was nonetheless concerned about her future prospects. He suggested that she become involved in social causes. Although by no means blind to the injustices of the world, Rosalind showed no strong inclination to follow her father's advice.

In 1938, she entered Cambridge University. However, as *Virginia Woolf remarked a year later in the *Three Guineas*:

> At Cambridge in the year 1939, the women's colleges . . . are not allowed to be members of the university; and the number of educated men's daughters who are allowed to receive a university education is still strictly limited. . . . The total number of students at recognized institutions for the higher education of women [is not allowed to] exceed five hundred, [though] the number of male students who were resident at Cambridge in 1935 was 5,328.

At that time, women's colleges at Cambridge offered only "titular" degrees. This practice excluded the degree holder from university government, and meant that women were unable to influence university policy. Neither Cambridge nor Oxford, both institutions with historic connections to the Church of England and the British government, were prepared to accept women within their hallowed walls.

This was the atmosphere in which Franklin found herself as an undergraduate. Many of her fellow female students were faced with a central dilemma of university life at the time—the choice between marriage or the career for which they had been trained. Women were not allowed to hold an academic post and marry. Franklin's desire to pursue an academic career led to her decision not to marry. In return, she hoped to be treated simply as a scientist, rather than as a woman, though she was a dark-haired, if unconventional, beauty.

In the Cavendish Laboratory, possibly the best in England, Rosalind Franklin received her undergraduate training. Wartime conditions at Cambridge dictated that students be more independent, and these conditions suited Franklin's temperament ideally. She excelled in physical chemistry and wrote to a friend that she was spending "8¼ hours a day in the lab." The diligence with which Franklin pursued her academic career had its price. In her final year at Cambridge, she wore herself out with a self-imposed workload that far exceeded that of her classmates. As a result, she did not receive a first-class degree and settled instead for a high second. Nevertheless, she received a research fellowship to Newnham College and went on to study gas-phase chromatography under Professor Ronald Norrish.

Franklin was passionate about research but only mildly attracted to teaching. At 22, she was appointed an assistant research officer of the British Coal Utilization Research Association (CURA), a body founded in 1938 to undertake research and development for the coal industry. It was during this period, while working under D.H. Bangham, that Franklin first became acquainted with crystallography and molecular biology. At an age when most young scientists are still emerging from graduate school, her research output was impressive. Between 1942 and 1946, Franklin published no less than five scientific papers, three as sole author. Her research on coal, Professor Peter Hirsch of Oxford University wrote in 1970, was "remarkable. She brought order into a field which had previously been in chaos." Franklin's work on the structure of coal is still used by scientists.

In 1945, Rosalind Franklin completed her Ph.D. thesis and was awarded a doctorate from Cambridge University. By 1946, however, she was restless and bored with her work at CURA. She wrote to Adrienne Weill, a friend from Cambridge and a fellow scientist working in Paris:

> In spite of the effort to move, I am still at CURA, which is still in its usual state of crisis. I am free to leave as soon as I can find another job. If ever you hear of anybody

anxious for the services of a physical chemist who knows very little about physical chemistry, but quite a lot about the holes in coal, please let me know.

Weill did not take the letter lightly. When Marcel Mathieu, in charge of the French government agency that oversaw most scientific research, came to London, Weill suggested he look Franklin up. As a result, in February 1947 Rosalind Franklin was appointed to the position of researcher at the Laboratoire Central des Services Chimique, or the Central Laboratory of Chemical Services, in Paris, where she found the French attitude towards women refreshing. As Canadian writer Mavis Gallant noted:

> Frenchmen do not seem to resent women or be afraid of them, they are not bored by feminine company. . . . [T]he war between the sexes scarcely exists. Equal pay for equal work is the law of the country, and women often hold more important jobs than do women in America. A woman's intelligence is respected, her professional status accepted, and as to her personal life, the French are notorious for an indifference to others that is also a form of minding one's business.

In Paris, Franklin made friends easily. She spoke French well and eventually became completely fluent. Unlike CURA, the laboratory staff in Paris formed a closed society of equals. They lunched together, exchanged dinner invitations, picnicked on weekends, and took camping and hiking holidays together. Working with Jacques Méring, Franklin was introduced to the techniques of X-ray diffraction, a method by which X-ray beams are passed through a crystal and are recorded on film. The pattern can then be analyzed. Franklin and Méring subsequently collaborated extensively and published a series of papers on graphitizing and nongraphitizing carbons. Franklin also began to apply X-ray diffraction to biological substances.

It was the possibility of applying X-ray diffraction to such substances that attracted her back to England. In 1951, Professor J.T. Randall offered her the Turner-Newall Research Fellowship at King's College in London. She had little biological experience. "When Randall offered Rosalind a Turner-Newall Research Fellowship," writes **Anne Sayre**, "it was on the understanding that she would be put in charge of building up an X-ray diffraction unit within the laboratory, which at the time lacked one. . . . She was not brought to King's College to work upon DNA or any other specific problem."

A great deal of research had been done on DNA in England between the 1920s and the

1940s. By the early 1950s, scientists were preparing to test a central hypothesis—that DNA was a carrier of genetic information. In order to do so, the structure of DNA had to be identified. While X-ray photography had failed to yield much in the way of insight, X-ray diffraction held out greater promise. Unfortunately, King's College suffered from the same institutional intolerance towards women to which Cambridge and Oxford were prey. Originally a theological college, the male staff lunched in an exclusive dining room, while female staff members were relegated to the students' canteen. This arrangement deprived Franklin of the convivial professional atmosphere that she had been accustomed to in Paris and that was an essential medium of exchange for scientific information.

Describing her work at King's College, Franklin wrote in a report to Randall in 1950 that, "the greater part of the first eight months was taken up with the assembling of the necessary [X-ray] apparatus." Soon after, however, Franklin's research began to stray into the area of DNA X-ray diffraction analysis, as she was the only staff member qualified to undertake such work.

Maurice Wilkins was the most prominent of her colleagues at King's College. A talented physicist who had worked on the Manhattan Project and for the University of California, he and Franklin's research on DNA began to overlap. This caused friction between the two, which eventually verged on outright hatred. As well, Wilkins did not appreciate the presence of a female colleague. Throughout his long and distinguished career, Maurice Wilkins never supervised a female student.

In the autumn of 1951, Rosalind Franklin discovered the B form of DNA and produced a significant amount of experimental data on the subject. She divined the density of B form DNA and located the sugar-phosphate backbone of the molecule. "The highly crystalline fibre diagram given by DNA fibres is obtained only in a certain humidity range, about 70% to 80%," she noted. "The general characteristics of the diagram suggest that the DNA chains are in a helical form."

Without Franklin's knowledge, Maurice Wilkins shared much of her research with Francis Crick and James Watson, who were undertaking similar research at Cambridge. In April 1953, Crick and Watson published their findings, which conclusively identified the structure of DNA. In their 1953 article in *Nature,* which announced the discovery, Crick and Watson were less than forthcoming about the role Franklin played in these events: "We have also been stimulated by a knowledge of the general nature of the unpublished experimental results of and ideas of Dr. M.H.F. Wilkins, Dr. R.E. Franklin, and their co-workers at King's College, London," they wrote. For their efforts, Crick, Watson, and Wilkins would be awarded the Noble Prize in 1962. Had Rosalind Franklin been alive at the time, her contribution could not have been overlooked. As her colleague Aaron Klug, a young South African, wrote: "Rosalind Franklin made crucial contributions to the solution of the structure of DNA. She discovered the B form, recognized that two states of the DNA molecule existed and defined conditions for the transition."

Unwittingly, Franklin's research contributed decisively to the understanding of DNA, but recognition of her contribution was largely obscured by personal antipathy between her and Maurice Wilkins. This lack of recognition was only deepened by a discredited and self-serving account of events published by James Watson in *The Double Helix.* Franklin's reaction to the discovery of the structure of DNA was one of pleasure, for she did not know how much her work had contributed to that of Crick and Watson. Had she known, her attitude would likely have been different. Because of her devotion to science, however, the solution of one problem led inexorably to the exploration of other fields.

By 1954, the atmosphere at King's College had become intolerable, and Franklin decided it was time to move on. When Birkbeck College offered her a position, she accepted. The head of research at Birkbeck, Professor J.D. Bernal, was a Marxist who believed in equality of the sexes. In a typically understated fashion, Franklin wrote: "Birkbeck is an improvement over King's, as it couldn't fail to be." At Birkbeck, Franklin applied X-ray diffraction techniques to the analysis of the Tobacco Mosaic Virus, one of the most difficult viruses of the day to unravel. Her research was initially supported by the British Agricultural Research Council and later by the U.S. Department of Health.

Franklin was joined at Birkbeck by Klug, beginning a collaboration which was to last until the end of her life. Klug described Rosalind Franklin in glowing terms:

> As a scientist Miss Franklin was distinguished by extreme clarity and perfection in everything she undertook. Her photographs are among the most beautiful X-ray photographs of any substance ever taken. . . . She did nearly all this work with her own hands. At the same time she proved to be an

admirable director of a research team and inspired those who worked with her to reach the same high standards.

In her final years, Franklin's prominence and reputation were growing. She was asked to produce an exhibit on the structure of small viruses for the Royal Society, to present her work before the Royal Institution, and to prepare a model of the Tobacco Mosaic Virus as a central feature of the Brussels World Fair.

In the autumn of 1956, Rosalind Franklin's health began to falter. Nevertheless, she continued working, although cancer was taking its toll. In public, she bore her illness stoically, insisting that she would soon be well again. In private, her reaction was somewhat different. Her friend **Mair Livingstone**, a medical doctor, wrote:

> She was indignant that there was not the technical skill available to avert death. She felt her mental power, and bitterly grudged its achievement being curtailed. She was saddened, but not depressed, I would say, since she remained combative to the end.

Rosalind Franklin died in London on April 16, 1958, age 37. "The importance of Franklin's work has been lost sight of," Klug noted, "partly because of her untimely death." Despite the fact that death cut short her early promise, she was a tireless scientist who produced exemplary results in whichever field she chose to apply herself. Her flexibility and her ability to assimilate new skills was extraordinary. From her work on coal structures at CURA, to her exploration of graphites with X-ray diffraction in Paris, her work on DNA, and her efforts to unravel the mysteries of the Tobacco Mosaic Virus, Rosalind Franklin undertook each challenge with a determination and a professionalism that distinguished her among British scientists.

Sayre wrote that Rosalind Franklin "was, indeed, one of the world's great experimental scientists." Nonetheless, it is unfortunate that her most important contribution, her discovery and analysis of the structure of B-form DNA, has been misunderstood and obscured. Others have seemingly claimed credit for the work that she undertook, and although Franklin was not one to seek the public limelight, it nevertheless seems a pity that other scientists have deliberately pushed her into the shadows.

SOURCES:
Gillispie, Charles C., ed. *Dictionary of Scientific Biography*. NY: Scribner, 1972.

Hamilton, L.D. "DNA: Models and Reality," in *Nature*. London: Macmillan, 1968.

Klug, Aaron. "Dr. Rosalind E. Franklin," in *Nature*. London: Macmillan, 1958.

———. "Rosalind Franklin and the Discovery of the Structure of DNA," in *Nature*. London: Macmillan, 1968.

Watson, James D. *The Double Helix*. Edited by Gunther S. Stent. London: Weidenfeld and Nicolson, 1981.

SUGGESTED READING:
Sayre, Anne. *Rosalind Franklin and DNA*. NY: W.W. Norton, 1975.

Hugh A. Stewart, M.A.,
University of Guelph, Guelph, Ontario, Canada

Franklin, Stella (1879–1954)

See Franklin, Miles.

Franks, queen of the.

See Chunsina.
See Clotilda (470–545).
See Aregunde.
See Ingunde (fl. 517).
See Radegund of Poitiers (518–587).
See Guntheuca (fl. 525).
See Fredegund (c. 545–597).
See Beretrude (d. 620).
See Nanthilde (610–642).
See Bilchilde (d. 675).
See Ragnetrude (fl. 630).
See Balthild (c. 630–c. 680).
See Clotilde (d. 691).
See Tanaquille (d. 696).
See Edonne.
See Bertha (719–783).
See Himiltrude.
See Desiderata (d. 773).
See Hildegarde of Swabia (c. 757–783).
See Fastrada (d. 794).
See Luitgarde (d. 800).

Frantz, Virginia Kneeland
(1896–1967)

American physician, surgeon, and researcher. Born Virginia Kneeland in New York City in 1896; died in 1967; daughter of Yale and Anna Isley Ball Kneeland; attended Brearley School for girls, New York City; graduated from Bryn Mawr College; medical degree from the College of Physicians and Surgeons at Columbia University, 1922; married Angus MacDonald Frantz (a physician), in 1920 (divorced); children: Virginia Frantz (b. 1924); Angus Frantz, Jr. (b. 1927); Andrew Frantz (b. 1930).

A pioneering woman in the field of medicine, Virginia Kneeland Frantz grew up in an upper-class Manhattan family and attended the exclusive Brearley School for girls in New York City. She graduated at the head of her class at Bryn Mawr and was one of only five women in a class of 74 at Columbia University's College of Physicians and Surgeons. In 1922, already married to her classmate Angus Frantz (they were later divorced), she became the first woman to undertake a surgical internship at the Columbia-affiliated Presbyterian Hospital. In 1924, along with giving birth to her first child, she was appointed an assistant surgeon and a member of the Columbia faculty. Specializing in surgical pathology, she became one of the first women to test the prevailing theory, among male doctors, that women physicians were unable to withstand the rigors of surgery.

Frantz also excelled in research, gaining national renown for her work on pancreatic tumors. She conducted some of the earliest studies on breast disease, including chronic cystic disease and cancer. In 1940, she was one of the first to demonstrate that radioactive iodine was effective in treating thyroid cancer, and during World War II she discovered that oxidized cellulose used on wounds controlled bleeding and was absorbed into the body. For this discovery, she received the Army-Navy Certificate of Appreciation for Civilian Service (1948).

Frantz, who became a full professor at Columbia in 1951, was also a highly effective and popular teacher. She was equally well-respected among her peers, twice serving as president of the New York Pathological Society (1949 and 1950), and once as the first woman president of the American Thyroid Association (1961). Throughout her career, she disliked recognition that focused on her gender rather than her contributions. "I'm not a medical oddity," she would say. Dr. Frantz retired from Columbia in 1962 and died of cancer in 1967, age 65.

Fraser, Dawn (1937—)

Australian swimmer, the greatest of her day, who was the first Olympian—male or female—to win the same event in three consecutive Games. Born Dawn Lorraine Fraser on September 4, 1937, in Balmain, Sydney, Australia; married Gary Ware (a bookmaker), in 1965 (divorced); children: one daughter.

Won gold medals in the 100-meter freestyle and the 4x100-meter freestyle relay and the silver medal in the 400-meter freestyle in the Melbourne Olympics (1956); won the gold medal in the 100-meter freestyle and silver medals in the 4x100-meter medley relay and the 4x100-meter freestyle relay in Rome Olympics (1960); won the gold medal in the 100-meter freestyle and the silver in the 4x100-meter freestyle relay in the Tokyo Olympics (1964); held 39 world records (27 individual and 12 team); held the record for the 100 meters for 16 years (1956–72); won 30 Australian championships (23 individual and 7 team); won eight medals (six gold and two silver) for the British Empire and Commonwealth Games; awarded the OBE.

On the night of October 28, 1962, after Dawn Fraser broke the 60-second mark in the 100 meters, one of the oldest records in swimming, a reporter asked how she planned to celebrate. Fraser, knowing she was at an emotional pitch and would be unable to sleep, replied: "I'll go to a party. And I'll drink a fair bit of beer. . . . I've worked so bloody hard for this night; now it's come, I'll have to unwind." It would be better, she was informed by a nearby official, to do her beer drinking away from the press. The incident typified the constant struggle between the rough-hewn, working-class Fraser and an elite sporting establishment that frowned on her behavior for the length of her career. Dawn Fraser was "the lone female representation of the happy-go-lucky, party-going images that characterized her male counterparts," wrote Bud Greenspan, and one of the greatest swimmers in the history of the sport.

Fraser was born on September 4, 1937, the youngest of four brothers and three sisters, and grew up in an old, semi-detached house that sat opposite an abandoned coal mine in Balmain, Australia, "the bleak, tired suburb," she wrote, "fronting the docks in Sydney." Her father was a shipwright who had immigrated to Australia from Scotland as a boy; her mother was from Balmain. At an early age, Fraser took up residence at the local pool, the Elkington Park Baths, swimming elbow to elbow with other kids and riding the back of her older brother Don off the high-diving tower. She idolized Don, eight years her senior, who taught her to swim. By age ten, Fraser was bouncing off the springboard so often that earaches kept her awake at night.

"I was a very ordinary kid," she wrote, "except maybe a bit cheekier, a bit sicklier." Fraser suffered from chronic asthma, possibly from the coal dust, and "other assorted chest troubles," including pleurisy. She was also allergic to chlorine; it made her eyes itchy. Otherwise, she had a "strange kind of affinity with the water," she wrote; "it makes me feel relaxed and content just to be in it. If I'm upset or in a cranky mood, I take a good long swim. . . . [B]y the time I haul myself out, I've forgotten what it was that was bothering me." Swimming also helped her asth-

ma, though she did not immediately put the two together. She only knew that swimming made her feel good; unconsciously, she was learning to discipline her breathing. She would spend the day at the pool breathing free then return home to wheeze and cough through the night.

According to Australian standards, Fraser began to swim seriously relatively late. Her cousin Ray Miranda, an amateur swim coach, urged her into competitive swimming; he also recommended that she join the Leichhardt-Balmain League, a professional swimming club. By age 11, Fraser was in her first serious race, beating out women three times her age.

Fraser was so athletically adept that her football-loving brothers let her play fullback when they practiced. But it was brother Don who was her pal, Don who stopped other boys from calling her "Dawn the prawn." When Fraser was 13, 21-year-old Don died of leukemia, three months after he had taken ill. "I thought I'd never recover from it," she wrote. Within weeks, she began to consider a serious career as a swimmer; it was Don who had told her if she worked at it, she could "finish up a champ." She would do it for Don.

With both parents laid up and Dawn the only unmarried daughter at home, she was given permission to quit school to take over the household responsibilities; she also took a part-time job at the local teen hangout, a milk bar. At 14, in 1951, Fraser entered the Western Suburbs championship with little hope of beating *Lorraine Crapp, then a highly publicized up-and-comer. When Dawn narrowly beat Lorraine, Crapp's coach protested Fraser's association with the Leichhardt-Balmain League, and Fraser was stripped of the championship and her amateur status. For 18 months, she was not allowed to compete in amateur swimming. Instead, she enrolled at the Leichhardt Home Science School, but Fraser had become rebellious, contemptuous of authority. So she quit school at age 15 and took a job in a dress factory. As far as she was concerned, her career in swimming was over; she started smoking and acquired a rugged vocabulary.

Then the secretary of the Australian Swimming Union (ASU) looked over the books of Leichhardt-Balmain, ascertained that she had never won money for swimming, only trophies, and brought her case before the ASU, arguing that a child could not be expected to know the difference between amateur and professional. Throughout the controversy, she felt "puzzled and alone," a feeling she would experience "quite a lot" during her career. When she was told that she could compete once more, she was not sure she wanted to.

Enter Harry Gallagher. Gallagher, who coached champion Jon Henricks at his Golden Dolphins amateur swimming club at Drummoyne, only two miles from her house, had seen Fraser at the local pool and was impressed with her ability. He was less impressed with her boysterism. The smooth, manicured coach listened to his future protege "screeching around" the pool and it made him "shudder." She was like "a wild race horse out

of the hills," he said, "with stacks of power and completely uncontrollable." Gallagher was a strict disciplinarian; Fraser hated authority in all forms. He agreed to train her for a year for free; she agreed to abide by his rules. Fortunately, for both of them, he gave her a little slack.

At that time, the sport of swimming in Australia was undergoing a massive change. Gallagher was one of four coaches on the frontline who had discovered the value of conditioning. For the rest of her swimming career, Fraser trained six months a year, five days a week, swimming seven or eight miles a day, sometimes with her ankles bound while towing an empty, open, four-gallon oil drum to build arm strength. Her enthusiasm for the sport began to get the best of her.

The summer of 1953 (in Australia, midsummer is in December–January), Fraser entered her first State championships for New South Wales (NSW) in the 110 and 220-yard races. In the 110, she finished third to Lorraine Crapp's first; in the 220, with Crapp out of the race, Fraser placed first by a touch, earning her a trip to Melbourne and the nationals in February 1954, but she did not place in Melbourne. The following year, Fraser made the reserve team for NSW to compete at the nationals in Adelaide. During the competition, when Crapp pulled out of the 220 because of ear trouble, Fraser entered the pool and won with a new Australian record of 2:29.5.

In September 1955, Gallagher took a coaching job in Adelaide and asked 18-year-old Dawn to continue her training there for six months. At first, her father was adamantly against letting her go that far from home, but he relented. In Adelaide, Fraser literally lived at the pool with Gallagher and his parents and took a job selling sportswear in a department store. She worked out continually, at the pool and in the weight room. "It was the most concentrated swimming buildup of my life. I honestly believe that it benefitted me for years afterward." Gallagher took blood samples of each of his swimmers, gave them heart-rate tests, fed them vitamins by the pound, tailored their diet, filmed them through observation windows at the pool, then analyzed the film. On weekends, Fraser took mountain hikes and chopped down trees on a piece of land Gallagher owned. That summer in Adelaide, she won every South Australian freestyle championship: the 110 yards, 220 yards, 440 yards, and 880 yards.

The 1956 nationals in Sydney would decide the Olympic trials squad. In the 110 and 440,

Crapp was favored, having just broken five world records. ❧▶ **Faith Leech** was also expected to have a strong showing; Fraser was a dark horse. While Crapp took the 440, Fraser amazed the crowd by taking the 110 at 64.5, beating the women's world record of 64.6 set by ❧▶**Willie den Ouden** for the Netherlands in 1936. This was a remarkable feat. In 1956, women swimmers were still wearing cotton swimsuits that weighed 10 pounds when wet. That week, she also won the 220-yard freestyle, smashing two 18-year-old world records in the 200 meters and 220 yards—2:20.6 and 2.21.2, respectively. (The 220-yard freestyle and the 200-meter freestyle are a difference of inches; the 220 being slightly longer; thus, a participant in the 220 could be clocked for both). Though she missed her family, Fraser returned to Adelaide with Gallagher following the games. Except for short visits, she never lived at home again.

On Saturday, December 1, 1956, at the summer Olympics held in Melbourne, 19-year-old Fraser mounted the block, extremely nervous, and heard the murmur of the crowd abruptly silenced. "You can almost hear a gigantic intake of breath," she wrote. As the gun sounded, her nerves disappeared, but at the halfway turn Crapp was ahead. The two swimmers raced at a dead heat, stroke for stroke, hitting the wall, at least by human eye, at the same time. Fraser had won her first gold medal at a world-record time of 62.0; Crapp was second, Faith Leech third—a clean sweep for the Aussies. Crapp, Leech, Fraser, and **Sandra Morgan** also took gold in the women's 4x100-meter freestyle relay.

In the 1958 Australian nationals, to everyone's surprise, Fraser won the 440 yards at 4:55.7, beating the favorite ❧▶ **Ilsa Konrads**. She also took the 110 yards and the 220 yards at 61.5 and 2:14.7, respectively. Fraser kept battering away at the 110-yard record, determined to break the minute mark, to go below 60 seconds. At the Empire Games in Cardiff, she won the 110-yard freestyle at 61.4, another world record, and was a member of the winning Australian relay squad who set a record of 4:17.4 in the 4x110; she then won in France and in Rotterdam, breaking the world record in the 110 at 61.2.

In 1959, despite a bout of hepatitis and a 14-pound weight loss, Fraser won the 110 in the Australian nationals at 61.7 and the 220 at 2:15.3. A year later, Gallagher suggested she enter the butterfly at the Sydney nationals. She did, breaking four world records within two days: the butterfly (70.8), the 100-meter and 110-yard free styles (60.2) and the 220-yard (2:11.6). "You have just seen the greatest performance of any woman athlete, in any sport, the world has yet known," the president of the Australian Swimming Union told the crowd.

The next time Fraser attempted the butterfly, however, she suffered from agonizing stomach cramps, and a doctor recommended that she drop the event from her agenda. She readily agreed. Though she had qualified for the butterfly for the 1960 Rome Olympics, she told the manager of the Australian Olympic team that she would no longer swim that race; she did not want to take the chance of bringing on stomach cramps that might knock her out of the race she really cared about, the 100-meter sprint.

Just before she left for the Rome Games, Fraser began to hear rumors questioning her sexual orientation; her morale plummeted. "For one thing," she wrote, "I stopped hugging girls who won races . . . and I've never done it since." She also became engaged to Ken Robinson. On the flight to Rome, the team had an unscheduled stopover in Bahrain, drank the water, and suffered what they dubbed "Rome tummy." To add to the tension, Lorraine Crapp had secretly married a divorced doctor Bill Thurlow who had been attending the Australian team during their

---

❧▶ **Leech, Faith** (1941—)
Australian swimmer. Born on June 18, 1941.

Faith Leech won the bronze medal in the 100-meter freestyle and the gold medal in the 4x100-meter freestyle in the Melbourne Olympics in 1956.

❧▶ **Ouden, Willemijntje den** (1918—)
Dutch swimmer. Name variations: Willie den Ouden. Born in January 1918 in the Netherlands.

Dutch swimmer Willie van Ouden won silver medals in the 4x100-meter freestyle relay and the 100-meter freestyle at the 1932 Olympic Games in Los Angeles. In Berlin in 1936, she won a gold medal in the 4x100-meter freestyle relay. Her teammates were **Catherina Wagner** (b. 1919), **Johanna Selbach** (b. 1918), and ***Rie Mastenbroek**.

❧▶ **Konrads, Ilsa** (1944—)
Australian swimmer. Born on March 29, 1944.

In 1960, Ilsa Konrads won a silver medal in the Rome Olympics in the 4x100-meter freestyle relay.

pre-Olympic training. Crapp was supposed to be rooming with Fraser and **Ruth Everuss**, but she skipped out at night to be with her new husband, and they covered for her, having to lie about her whereabouts to their chaperon **Joyce Ross**. Fraser began to chafe under the arrangement and begged Crapp to tell Syd Grange the team manager. Lorraine confessed, the Australian Federation demanded she stay in the women's village at night, the reporters broke the story, and Crapp lost her fighting form and swam badly.

That same week, Fraser had to defend her title in the 100-meter freestyle from American ❦▶ **Chris von Saltza** who had broken Fraser's record with a 61.9 in an earlier heat. But Fraser was one of those with Rome tummy; she had constant dysentery, no energy, couldn't eat, and lost weight. Even so, she swam hard and recouped the record in her heat at 61.4. In the finals, Fraser beat von Saltza for the gold medal with a 61.2 world record. An ecstatic Fraser was now the first woman to win the sprint gold medal twice in a row and the only Australian woman to win in Rome. Her ecstasy lasted for about 24 hours.

The next day at 2:00 in the afternoon, as she sat in the dining hall eating a platter of pasta after a day of walking the town, Roger Pegram, manager of the Australian swimming team, hurried in and told her to get to the pool, that she was to swim the butterfly leg in the medley heat that afternoon. Knowing she was ill-prepared, Fraser protested that to her knowledge she was to swim the freestyle leg in the final. He was adamant; they argued, and she refused. What she did not know, and he did not tell her, was that ❦▶ **Jan Andrew**, who was supposed to swim the butterfly leg, had made the butterfly finals set for that evening, and the coaches wanted to save her energy. As a result of Fraser's balk, her team did not speak to her for the rest of the week (which included the day of her 23rd birthday on September 4). The Australian women's team won a disappointing silver medal in the 4x100-meter medley relay, which Fraser competed in, and returned home despondent.

In February 1961, on the strength of Pegram's report to the committee, the ASU branded Fraser a person unworthy to represent her country because she did not do her best "in and out of the water" and pulled her from the Australian teams competing in South Africa and New Zealand. Without warning or an offer to hear her side, the ASU charged in the media: 1) she did not try to win in the Olympic 4x100-meter freestyle championship (Fraser claims she

gave it her all but, by that time, was an emotional and physical mess); 2) she clobbered Jan Andrew who won a bronze medal in the butterfly for Australia (the swimmers had been sitting around a room, gossiping; at one point, there was a violent exchange and Fraser leveled a pillow at Andrew; it was reported that she socked her); 3) she refused to wear an Australian tracksuit, even on the dais when receiving her gold medal (hers, she says, was wet); 4) she took part in an unauthorized exhibition in Switzerland (after the Olympics, on the way to the Paris Games, Fraser stopped off in Zurich, used the community pool to unwind, and there were onlookers). Then the secretary of the ASU said to the press, "that's not all she did," and left it at that, leading to a heyday for speculators, especially those concerned with her sexual preferences. Fraser was devastated by the ASU stance. She wrote a letter of apology, but the ASU told the press it was not apologetic enough. Even so, she took the 100-meters in 61 seconds and the 400-meter in 4:49.7 at the Brisbane nationals.

There were many on Fraser's side, including a hefty portion of the population of Australia who greeted her at poolside with "Good on ya, Dawnee." They loved her, not despite her resistance to authority, but because of it. The ASU, and most of Australian sport, was considered snobbish, using its might against one of the working-class. One critic described the Pegram report as "one of the most vindictive documents ever penned." An Australian senator called the actions of the ASU petty. The South Australian Swimming Association was more sympathetic and had Fraser represent them in meets out of the country. Nothing seemed to go right in 1961. There was a misunderstanding with a police officer in Adelaide, and she was arrested for loitering and spent the night in jail. At trial, the police prosecutor apologized, announcing that she was "innocent of any offense." Fraser was at her lowest ebb; she felt trouble-prone. Two days after Christmas, her father died of lung cancer.

In the 1962 Melbourne nationals, Fraser won four more titles, bringing her Australian championship tally up to 20. ❦▶ **Judy Joy Davies** had held the record at 18.) Despite the titles, Fraser was intent on breaking the minute. By the end of 1962, though there had been no official announcement from the ASU that she was through being punished, there were a few hints that her ostracism might be over—just in time for the British Empire Games in Perth, Western Australia. During the trials in Melbourne on October 28, 1962, she won the 440 and finally broke the minute at

59.9 in the 110. "I can't say how much that performance meant to me. Swimming officials described it as one of the greatest sporting achievements of the century. For me, four years of bloody-hard striving were suddenly ended. I sat around in the dressing room afterward feeling half stunned. . . . I remember wondering if that crummy little tenth had been worth all of four years." Oddly enough, once she proved to herself that she could get inside the one-minute barrier, "it stopped being any sort of barrier for me." At Perth, she covered the 110 at 59.6. She then swam two relay legs under a minute and took the 440. Fraser won four gold medals in the Empire games.

The year 1964 held much more promise. In February at the Australian nationals in Sydney, Fraser again clocked a world record of 58.9 in the 110 yards and took the 220 at 2:13.0 and the 440 at 4:50.6, equaling Chris von Saltza's Olympic record. With the ASU sanctions at an end, she looked forward to the Tokyo Olympics in October. If she won, and to do so she would have to beat an upcoming American named *Sharon Stouder, Fraser would be the first Olympian—male or female—to win a gold medal in the same event three times in succession.

After the nationals, Fraser and her mother stayed in Sydney for a holiday. Since her father's death, Fraser and her mother had grown close, and the two looked forward to Tokyo; it would be her mother's first trip overseas. While driving back from a dinner party at the Balmain Rugby League club, having swilled nothing stronger than orange juice, Fraser came around a curve at 40 mph and rear-ended a truck that had been parked out into the road while the driver went fishing. Fraser's mother was killed; her sister Rose was injured, and a friend, **Wendy Walters**, was facially scarred. Fraser, who had a chipped vertebrae, spent nine weeks with her neck in a steel brace, battling depression and overwhelming guilt. It took her brothers and sisters to convince her to prepare for Tokyo; their mother, they said, would want her to go for the biggest record of them all.

At the Tokyo Olympics, Fraser was in hot water from the very first day when she marched in with her team. No swimmer with a meet within three days could march, but Fraser, who had missed the opening march in the Rome Olympics and wasn't about to do that again, did so anyway. She also bucked wearing the official swimsuit, preferring one of the same color and pattern made by another company that didn't chafe and hamper her breathing. Her rebellion might not have been arbitrary for someone with asthma. Breathing was as important to a swimmer at it was to a singer. *Kathleen Ferrier wore gowns that would allow for at least a 3" expansion of the diaphragm.

On the day of the 100 meters on October 13, though her asthma had kicked up, Fraser clipped more precious seconds off her record, coming in at 59.5. Fifteen-year-old Stouder, who took the silver, became the second woman ever to break the minute. Though Fraser missed her parents looking down from the stands, it was, she wrote, a "mighty night." That mighty night, still keyed up, Fraser, with the help of others, was caught by the Japanese police while trying to cop an Olympic flag from the grounds of Emperor Hirohito's Palace, a prank known only to the Japanese police and the pranksters until the publication of her autobiography. Despite her apparent rebellion, there were those in the official ranks who quietly championed her. For the closing ceremony, she was asked to carry the Australian banner (the first Australian woman to do so) and the Japanese constabulary privately gave her the confiscated Olympic flag.

When she arrived back home all of Australia rejoiced with Fraser fever. Just before Tokyo, Fraser had met Gary Ware, a bookmaker; within weeks, he had proposed, and they agreed to wed after the Games. The marriage, though brief, took place on January 30, 1965. Then, the ASU issued a press release:

❧▶ **von Saltza, Chris** (1944—)
American swimmer. Born on January 3, 1944.

Chris von Saltza won four swimming medals during the Rome Olympics in 1960: the silver for the 100-meter freestyle, the gold in the 400-meter freestyle, and two golds in the relays, the 4x100 medley and 4x100 freestyle.

❧▶ **Andrew, Jan** (1943—)
Australian swimmer. Born on November 25, 1943.

Jan Andrew won a bronze medal in the 100-meter butterfly and a silver medal in the 4x100-meter medley relay in the Rome Olympics in 1960.

❧▶ **Davies, Judy Joy** (1928—)
Australian swimmer. Born in June 1928.

Judy Joy Davies won the bronze medal in the 100-meter backstroke in the London Olympics in 1948. She also held 18 Australian championships.

The Union . . . is determined that it will maintain a strong discipline especially among the members of its teams who represent Australia overseas. It is with deep regret that the Union finds it necessary to take strong action arising out of incidents which occurred in Tokyo.

They then suspended "Mrs. Dawn Fraser Ware" from all forms of competitive swimming for ten years, and three other women swimmers were given lighter suspensions. Though the charges were not specific, it was understood that all four were suspended for marching in the opening day ceremony and Fraser for her nonregulation swimsuit. The ASU was then unaware of the incident with the Japanese police. Though the suspension lasted only four years, by then, Fraser was 31, too old to compete.

In 1988, 23 years later, Dawn Fraser was elected to the New South Wales (NSW) Parliament, where she represented Balmain until 1991. That same year, she was named Australia's greatest female athlete. The Elkington Park Baths were renamed the Dawn Fraser Pool.

SOURCES:

Fraser, Dawn, with Harry Gordon. *Below the Surface: The Confessions of an Olympic Champion.* NY: William Morrow, 1965.

Greenspan, Bud. *100 Greatest Moments in Olympic History.* Los Angeles, CA: General Publishing, 1995.

Oxford Companion to Australian Sport. Melbourne, Oxford University Press, 1992.

Fraser, Eliza (c. 1798–1858)

Legendary Australian heroine. Born Eliza Anne Slack, possibly in Ceylon, around 1798; died in 1858 in Melbourne, Australia; married Captain James Fraser (died 1836); married Captain Alexander John Greene, on February 23, 1837; children: (with first husband) three.

The true and extraordinary adventures of Eliza Fraser, the wife of Captain James Fraser, began in 1835, when, age 37 and pregnant with her fourth child, she left her three children in Scotland to accompany her ailing husband on a voyage from London to Sydney Australia. In May 1836, their ship, *Stirling Castle,* foundered and sank on the Great Barrier Reef off New South Wales. Set adrift in a leaky longboat with her husband and several crew members, Eliza delivered a "born drowned" baby, which was buried at sea. After 28 days, during which time they were unable to land except on small sections of reef exposed at low tide, the survivors went ashore on what was then Great Sandy Island, where they were subsequently captured by a tribe of Stone Age Aborigines described as "of rude habits and cannibalistic tendencies." After witnessing the death of her husband who was speared in the back, Eliza was made a slave of the tribe and forced to endure ritualistic punishments carried out at the will of her captors. She and the remaining survivors were eventually rescued by John Graham, an ex-convict and member of the 14th Regiment from Moreton Bay. A member of the rescue party, a Lieutenant Otter, later wrote a letter to his sister in England in which he described Eliza's condition at the time of her rescue.

You never saw such an object. Although only thirty-eight years of age, she looked like an old woman of seventy, perfectly black, and dreadfully crippled from the sufferings she had undergone. . . . She was a mere skeleton, the skin literally hanging on her bones, whilst her legs were a mass of sores, where the savages had tortured her with firebrands.

Recuperating in New South Wales, Eliza remarried in haste and returned to England, where she petitioned the Secretary of State for the Colonies for "charity" money. (She was turned down by the Treasury, although she did receive private funds raised on her behalf.) There is also evidence that for a time Eliza hired out as a sideshow attraction. Henry Stuart Russell, in *Genesis of Queensland* (1888), related that while walking near Hyde Park in London, he encountered a man carrying a show advertisement displaying crude artwork representing savages with bows and arrows and some dead bodies of white men and women, under which was written: "'STIRLING CASTLE' WRECKED OFF THE COAST OF NEW HOLLAND, BOTANY BAY, ALL KILLED AND EATEN BY SAVAGES: ONLY SURVIVOR A WOMAN: TO BE SEEN: 6d. ADMISSION." Eventually, Eliza, Captain Greene, and the Fraser children settled in Auckland. Eliza was reportedly killed in a carriage accident in Melbourne in 1858.

Years after her death, Eliza's ordeal inspired a number of books, including Robert Gibbings' *John Graham, Convict* (1937), Charles Barrett's *White Blackfellows* (1948), Michael Alexander's *Mrs. Fraser on the Fatal Shore* (1971), and Patrick White's *A Fringe of Leaves* (1976). The dust jacket on the original edition of White's novel featured the Eliza Fraser painting by Sidney Nolan that inspired yet another novel, *An Instant in the Wind* (1976), by South African Andre Brink. An Australian film, *Eliza Fraser,* scripted by David Williamson, was also made in 1976. The history of Great Sandy Island, which was later named Fraser Island, is told in *Written in Sand* (1982) by Fred Williams.

SOURCES:

Alexander, Michael. *Mrs. Fraser on the Fatal Shore.* NY: Simon and Schuster, 1971.

Wilde, William H., Joy Hooton, and Barry Andrews, eds. *Oxford Companion to Australian Literature.* Oxford: Oxford University Press, 1985.

Barbara Morgan,
Melrose, Massachusetts

Fraser, Gretchen (1919–1994)

American skier. Name variations: Gretchen Kunigk. Born Gretchen Kunigk in Tacoma, Washington, on February 11, 1919; died of natural causes, at age 75, in Sun Valley, Idaho, on February 17, 1994; daughter of William Kunigk and a Norwegian skier (name obscure); married Donald Fraser (a skier), in 1939.

Won the National and Combined Downhill Championships (1941); was National Slalom champion (1942); won the gold medal in the women's special slalom event in the Olympics in St. Moritz, Switzerland (1948), the first American to win a gold medal in skiing since 1924.

Gretchen Fraser's mother, Norwegian by birth, was a ski enthusiast on the slopes in the Northwest who worked for the development of Mt. Rainier as a public ski resort and encouraged many to try this new sport. Though her daughter Gretchen skied, she did not enter competition until she was 16. When Gretchen met Donald Fraser, a member of the 1936 Olympic team, they fell in love and were married in 1939. A year later, both qualified for the 1940 Olympic team. The Games were canceled, however, with the outbreak of World War II, and Donald joined the Navy, leaving for four years.

Fraser continued to ski, winning the Diamond Sun event in Sun Valley, Idaho, in 1940 and 1941. She also won the National Combined and Downhill championships in 1941. In 1942, after she became the National Slalom champion, Fraser left competitive skiing to work as a volunteer in army hospitals teaching swimming, riding, and skiing to amputees. Then Donald came back from the war and encouraged his wife to begin skiing again.

By the time Gretchen Fraser entered the 1948 Winter Olympics, much was against her: she was 29, not the youngest athlete, and no American had won a gold medal in skiing since 1924. She was also the first of 31 skiers on Mt. Piz-Nair in St. Moritz, Switzerland. Although her first run was flawless, her caution had cost her precious

Gretchen Fraser

seconds. On her second run, because of a foul up with a telephone connection from below, she stood in the starting gate for 17 minutes, a mass of raw nerves. At last given the signal, she took off downhill, reaching the finish line in 57.7 seconds, giving her a combined time of 1:57.2. (The next best time was 1:57.7, posted by Switzerland's **Antoinette Meyer**; **Erika Mahringer** of Austria won the bronze, with 1:58.0). To everyone's surprise, an "unknown American housewife" had upset the Europeans. Gretchen Fraser was, in fact, a skilled professional when she shocked the competition. She then went on to take a silver medal in the slalom-downhill combined (an event discontinued in 1988).

SOURCES:

Hollander, Phyllis. *100 Greatest Women in Sports.* NY: Grosset and Dunlap, 1976.

Porter, David L., ed. *Biographical Dictionary of American Sports: Basketball and Other Indoor Sports.* NY: Greenwood Press, 1989.

Karin L. Haag,
Athens, Georgia

Fratianne, Linda (1960—)

American skater. Born in Northridge, California, on August 2, 1960.

Held the American national title four times (1977–80); was world champion (1977 and 1979); won a silver medal in the winter Olympics in Lake Placid, New York (1980).

In the 1970s, East Germany emerged as a major powerhouse in the sports arena. *Anett Pötzsch was the first East German to win a gold medal in Olympic ice skating, followed by the celebrated *Katarina Witt. American contenders in this Cold War on ice were *Dorothy Hamill and Linda Fratianne. From 1977 to 1980, Fratianne won the national title four times, having first competed in the 1976 Olympics placing 8th. An athletic skater known for her jumps and spins, Fratianne won the world title in 1977, lost the title to Pötzsch in 1978, then won again in 1979.

In the 1980 winter Olympics in Lake Placid, the battle lines were drawn. Political tensions were high and the summer games would be boycotted by the United States when the Soviet Union invaded Afghanistan. Fratianne, who had worked to develop a more artistic style, skated brilliantly, defeating Pötzsch in the free skate. But Fratianne was placed so low in the compulsories that it was impossible for her to win the top spot. In the end, Pötzsch beat the American by a fraction of a point, the closest competition in 60 years, and a disappointed Fratianne went home with the silver. The following month, she finished third in the world championships. Fratianne then retired from competitive skating, appeared in several ice shows and pro competitions, then moved to Sun Valley, Idaho, where she works as a skating coach.

Karin Loewen Haag,
Athens, Georgia

Frechette, Sylvie (1967—)

Canadian synchronized swimmer who won the gold medal in the Barcelona Olympics. Name variations: Sylvié Fréchette. Born on June 27, 1967, in Montreal, Quebec, Canada; coached by Julie Sauvé and Denise Sauvé.

Began involvement in synchronized swimming (1975); was a member of the Canadian National Team (1983–92); won the Commonwealth Games championship (1986 and 1990); won the World championship (1991); won the silver medal at the Atlanta Olympics (1996).

Canadian Sylvie Frechette won a highly contested silver for synchronized swimming (solo) in the 1992 Barcelona Olympics. When one judge pushed the wrong button by mistake, giving her a lower score, she was inched out of a gold medal. Frechette's total score of 191.717 was topped by America's **Kristen Babb-Sprague**'s 191.848. Though the judge immediately admitted the error, the Olympic Committee would not change the outcome. It took 18 months of determined appeals by indignant Canadians for Sylvie Frechette to receive her gold medal. Kristen Babb-Sprague also retained hers.

Known as a superb technician in the water, Frechette had won many international championships, including the 1986 and 1990 Commonwealth Games. She was the only athlete to receive seven perfect 10's at the 1991 World Aquatic championships for solo event. She was chosen female athlete of the year by the Aquatic Federation of Canada in 1989, 1990, 1991, and 1992. In 1996, Frechette came out of retirement for the Atlanta Olympics and placed second for the silver medal.

Fredegar (c. 547–597).

See Fredegund.

Fredegund (c. 547–597)

Merovingian queen whose talent for political intrigue in late 6th-century Gaul resulted in the elevation of her son Lothair II to the position of sole king of the previously divided Frankish territories. Name variations: Fredegond or Fredegonde or Frédégone; Fredegar; Fredegonda, Fredegunde or Fredegunda; Fredegundis or Fredigundis. Born, presumably in Neustria, around 547 (some sources cite 545); died in 597; daughter of unknown, non-noble parents; became concubine and then third wife of Chilperic I, king of Soissons, king of the Franks (r. 561–584), in 567; children: (with Chilperic) one daughter, Riguntha, and sons Chlodobert (d. 580); Samson (d. 577); Dagobert (d. 580); Theodoric (d. 584); Chlothar also known as Clotaire or Lothair II (584–629), king of Neustria (r. 584–629), king of the Franks (r. 613–629).

Was mistress to Chilperic I (prior to 567); engaged in feud with her husband's sister-in-law Brunhilda due to Galswintha's murder (567–97); instigated murder of King Sigibert of Austrasia (575); endured deaths of four infant sons (577–84), and Chilperic (584); acted as regent for infant son Lothair II upon Chilperic I's death (584).

As the consort of Chilperic I, called "the Nero and Herod of our time" by the 6th-century chronicler Gregory of Tours, Fredegund is one of the most vilified and well-known Merovingian queens. Her career cast her in roles from concubine to queen mother, and the political instability of her period made ruthless maneuvering an absolute necessity. The contemporary accounts of 6th-century Gaul generally look disparagingly on Fredegund's remarkable talent for maintaining her personal interests against all threats, yet it was this very quality that allowed her to protect and champion her son Lothair II's interests, enabling him to unite the several warring Frankish states under his sole control by 613. To accomplish this, Fredegund engaged in a bitter feud with another forceful Merovingian queen, ❧▶ **Brunhilda**. Their enmity lasted for nearly a quarter of a century, and the sensationalism of their prolonged struggle captured chroniclers' attention.

Understanding the political climate of the 6th-century Frankish territories allows one to appreciate the difficulties faced by Fredegund and helps to place her forceful actions in their proper context. By the late 5th century, Western Roman imperial power in Gaul was virtually nonexistent. Around this time, a Germanic tribe, the Franks, led by Clovis (466–511), began its conquest of Gaul; within five years, they controlled Paris, Rouen, Reims, and other major centers. Clovis' military success in Gaul was strengthened by his fortuitous religious policy: although by the late 400s all the other Germanic tribes had converted to the Arian form of Christianity, the Franks had remained pagan. But in the early 490s, Clovis married the orthodox Burgundian princess *Clotilda, who succeeded in converting her husband (and thus his entire tribe) to her form of Christianity. With the East Roman Empire increasingly unable to assert imperial control in the West and the papacy's consequent need to

❧▶ Brunhilda (c. 533–613)

Merovingian queen. Name variations: Brunechildis; Brunehilde, Brunhilde, Brunnhilde, or Brunehaut, queen of Austrasia. Born around 533; died in 613; daughter of Athanagild (Athangild), king of the Visigoths, and Queen **Goinswintha** *of Spain; sister of Galswintha; married Sigibert I, king of Austrasia (r. 561–575, assassinated, 575); married Merovech (son of Chilperic I and Audovera); sister-in-law of Fredegund (c. 547–597); children: Childebert II, king of Austrasia (r. 575–595), king of Burgundy (r. 593–595).*

The marriage of Brunhilda to Sigibert I, the king of Austrasia who was reigning at Metz, took place in 567. The Italian poet Fortunatus, then at the Frankish court, composed the epithalamium (the nuptial song). Sigibert's younger brother Chilperic I, king of the west Frankish kingdom of Neustria, was jealous of the renown that the marriage brought Sigibert, and so Chilperic soon married Brunhilda's sister *Galswintha. This marriage was brief. Chilperic, following the instructions of his paramour *Fredegund, assassinated Galswintha. Brunhilda set out to avenge her sister's death, and bloody deeds, provoked by the enmity of Brunhilda and Fredegund, fill the annals of the next half century in Gaul. Sigibert was also anxious to avenge the death of his sister-in-law, but on the advice of Duke Guntram, Sigibert accepted the compensation offered by Chilperic, namely the cities of Bordeaux, Cahors and Limoges, with Béarn and Bigorre.

Even so, war soon broke out between Sigibert and Chilperic. In 575, Sigibert was murdered at the instigation of Fredegund, and Brunhilda was captured by Chilperic and held captive. Brunhilda managed to escape from the prison at Rouen, assisted by Chilperic's son Merovech whom she married. After Merovech was put to death by his father, Brunhilda returned to Austrasia, where she ruled in the name of her son Childebert II and engaged in a desperate struggle against the nobles who also wished to govern in her son's name. Bettered in the conflict, Brunhilda had to seek refuge in Burgundy for some time. After the death of her son Childebert II in 597, she was bent on governing Austrasia and Burgundy in the name of her grandsons Theudebert and Theuderich II. Expelled from Austrasia, she incited Theuderich II against his brother, whom he defeated at Toul and Tolbiac and put to death. Soon after the victory, Theuderich II died, and Brunhilda had one of her great-grandchildren proclaimed king. But the nobles of Austrasia and Burgundy now summoned Fredegund's son Lothair II, king of Neustria, to support them against the queen. Lothair overthrew the armies of Austrasia in 613, and the aged Brunhilda was handed to him. After being held captive for three days and subjected to torture, she died a horrid death, being dragged at the heels of a wild horse in 613.

Considered a great queen, Brunhilda was responsible for the construction of many old castles, and a number of Roman roads are known by the name of *Chaussées de Brunehaut*. She had also been a protector of the church. In a series of letters addressed to her, Pope Gregory I (590–604) showered her with praise, even though she had taken it upon herself to supervise the bishoprics and monasteries, until she came into conflict with Columbanus, abbot of Luxeuil.

manage the political affairs as well as spiritual needs of the West, Frankish orthodoxy proved to be a very significant factor. Clovis' Franks were able to provide a cultural bridge between the desire of the Gallo-Roman population to maintain their traditions, and the Germanic desire to "fit in" with the Roman world.

In many ways, Clovis strove to preserve Roman imperial institutions; he accepted the East Roman emperor's offer of the consular title, maintained the imperial currency, and attempted to continue the administrative machinery of the empire. Still, he retained Germanic ideas about the personal nature of his office, for upon his death in 511, he allowed his four sons to inherit his kingdom as if it were family property. Before long, the brothers began to wage war against each other to expand their personal inheritances. Each of their kingdoms was also subjected to further partitions by the brothers' sons. These internal Frankish struggles, combined with the ever-present need to fight off other Germanic threats, produced an extremely violent climate in 6th-century Gaul.

When Clovis died, the Frankish kingdom was not ruled by one king again until his youngest son Lothair I managed to outlive his brothers, and he was the sole king of the Franks from 558–561. But like Clovis, Lothair I was survived by four sons, each one eager to increase his own inheritance. Civil war broke out almost immediately among the brothers Charibert, Sigibert, Gunthram, and Chilperic, who controlled Aquitaine, Austrasia, Burgundy, and Neustria, respectively. When Charibert died in 567, the remaining three brothers divided his inheritance, even partitioning the city of Paris. With each brother possessing territories scattered throughout Gaul, the stage was set for constant turmoil over the arrangement.

Besides war, marriage was a useful way to enhance royal prestige and wealth, and Sigibert was the first of the brothers to employ this advantageous method of aggrandizement. The 6th-century chronicler Gregory, bishop of Tours, who favored the cause of this Austrasian king— for Sigibert was the bishop's patron—wrote of how "King Sigibert, seeing his brothers take to themselves unworthy wives and even wed serving maids, sent an embassy to Spain with many gifts to demand in marriage Brunhilda, daughter of King Athanagild." Gregory's observation on the undistinguished marital taste of his brothers constitutes an oblique reference to Fredegund, who became Chilperic I's third wife.

Fredegund was probably born around 547, but her birth attracted no special attention from chroniclers for her background was ordinary rather than noble. Two additional references corroborate her humble origins: Gregory of Tours gave an account of Bishop Praetextatus of Rouen castigating Fredegund for not properly educating her son. This suggests that Fredegund lacked the kind of education that noble Frankish women sometimes received, a benefit that could facilitate their potential careers as regents. The slightly later *Liber Historiae Francorum* flatly states that Fredegund "was from a family of low rank." Her relationship with King Chilperic I at the time of Sigibert's marriage is thus the first reference to the woman who would play an extraordinarily powerful role in late 6th-century Frankish affairs.

Chilperic I was married to ❧▶ **Audovera**, with whom he had at least three sons and one daughter **Basina**; concurrently, he maintained Fredegund as a concubine. Although there are no records of how Fredegund initially captured the royal Frank's attention, there are two different accounts of her acquisition of the title of queen. The Neustrian chronicle *Liber Historiae Francorum* describes a plot devised by Fredegund to displace Chilperic's legitimate wife Audovera, occurring some time before 567. Audovera had given birth to Basina while her husband was on campaign against the Saxons. Knowing the church's ban on marriage between parents and godparents of a child, Fredegund tricked Audovera into standing as Basina's godmother, thus allowing Chilperic I to set her aside and marry Fredegund instead. Audovera and her daughter were ordered to enter a convent.

The story told by Gregory of Tours concerning Fredegund's ascension to the position of legitimate queen is situated in the period immediately following Sigibert's spectacular wedding to the Visigothic princess Brunhilda. Chilperic I, awed by the Spanish riches Brunhilda brought her new husband, promised to give up his other women if Brunhilda's older sister *Galswintha would marry him. According to Gregory, when Galswintha came to King Chilperic, "he received her with great honour, and was joined to her in marriage, loving her dearly, for she had brought with her great treasures." But "because of his passion for Fredegund," Chilperic I was a cold husband to his Visigothic wife. Galswintha complained of her treatment and requested permission to return to Spain, offering to leave behind the riches she had brought. But Chilperic I responded to this request by having her strangled by a slave (according to Gregory of Tours), or, as the author of the *Liber Historiae Francorum* suggested, by strangling Galswintha himself. A short time later, he made Fredegund his queen.

There followed a series of military clashes between Chilperic I and his brother Sigibert; their wives encouraged the fraternal enmity, as Brunhilda considered Fredegund's role in Galswintha's murder to be a personal affront. Audovera and Chilperic's sons were involved in many of the campaigns on their father's behalf, yet Fredegund viewed Chlodovech, Theudebert, and Merovech with dislike and distrust, as they represented rivals to the sons she hoped to produce. For example, after Theudebert was killed by Sigibert's duke Guntram Boso, Fredegund later secretly protected Guntram in gratitude for the service he had rendered by removing one of her children's rivals. She was also responsible for the deaths of Chilperic I's other two sons.

Brunhilda, Sigibert's consort, had serious reasons for her hatred of Fredegund. Brunhilda not only held Fredegund responsible for her sister Galswintha's death, but, according to Gregory of Tours and the *Liber Historiae Francorum*, for Sigibert's death in 575 as well. Both sources agree that Fredegund instructed two of her men to disguise themselves as envoys from Chilperic I in order to approach Sigibert with false offers of peace from his warring brothers. Both sources state that Fredegund had to use extraordinary measures to entice the two into this treacherous act, and the queen is thus portrayed as unreservedly evil: Gregory says she "bewitched" her agents, and the other source elaborates by insisting that the queen had to get them drunk and promise to take care of their survivors if the plot failed. They were successful, and Brunhilda found herself widowed by the very woman who was responsible for her sister's death. Brunhilda's five-year-old son Childebert (II) succeeded his father, and she acted as regent.

King Chilperic I seized Brunhilda's treasury and forced her to live in banishment at Rouen. Merovech, ordered by his father to occupy Poitiers, instead pretended to visit his discarded mother Audovera, but traveled to Rouen and married his aunt Brunhilda. Bishop Praetextatus, who performed the service, was later murdered by Fredegund's agents in retaliation for his assistance to Brunhilda. Chilperic I forced his son Merovech to separate from his wife, and he was tonsured and forced into religious life, from which he escaped several times in his desire to reunite with Brunhilda. When at last he was captured and killed, his death was attributed to Fredegund.

Chilperic I's last son with Audovera, Chlodovech, would also die because of his stepmother's desire to remove all potential threats to her children. Four of Fredegund's sons died in infancy, and the sources reveal a distraught maternal reaction in nearly every case. A curious exception was the queen's seeming lack of concern for her son Samson, who died in 577. Gregory of Tours observed that, perhaps due to an illness suffered by Fredegund at the time of Samson's birth, she "cast him away from her, and would have let him die" if Chilperic I had not rebuked her for her negligent attitude. Nevertheless, little Samson died before his fifth birthday. But the deaths of her three infant sons, Dagobert, Chlodobert, and Theodoric, would elicit enormous grief from Fredegund, and the deaths of the former two would provide the opportunity for her to execute their elder half-brother Chlodovech. In 580, when two of her infant sons Dagobert and Chlodobert were ill with dysentery, Fredegund suspected that their imminent deaths were a sign of God's displeasure at the rapacious tax policies she had urged her husband to pursue. Gregory of Tours recounts her impassioned plea to Chilperic I to bargain with God for their sons' lives:

> The divine goodness has long borne with our bad actions; it has often rebuked us with fevers and other evils but repentance did not follow and now we are losing our sons. . . . We have no hope left now in gathering wealth. . . . [W]e are losing what we hold more dear. Come, please, let us burn all the wicked tax lists and let what sufficed for your father king [Lothair I], suffice for your treasury.

Despite the drastic measure of burning tax records in atonement for their past sins, both

---

❧ Audovera (d. 580)

Merovingian queen. Name variations: Audovere or Audovère. Flourished in the 560s; put to death by orders of Fredegund (c. 547–597) around 580; first wife of Chilperic I, king of Soissons (Neustria, r. 561–584); children: one daughter **Basina** *(who became a nun at Poitiers) and three sons, Chlodovech also known as Clovis (d. 580); Theudebert also known as Theodobert (d. 575); Merovech (d. 577 or 578, who married his aunt,* ***Brunhilda**).

Because of the machinations of ***Fredegund** Audovera, wife of Chilperic I, was ordered to a convent with her daughter Basina sometime before 567. Fredegund had her put to death around 580.

of their sons died of their illness. Chlodovech was accused of employing witchcraft to bring about his half-brothers' deaths, and Fredegund not only had him killed for this offense, but prevailed upon Chilperic I to put his former wife Audovera to death as well. When her fourth infant son died in 584, Fredegund commanded all of his personal belongings to be burned so that her immense mourning would not be intensified by the presence of baby Theodoric's effects.

Fredegund, the enemy of God and man.
—King Gunthram to Bishop Gregory of Tours, *Historia Francorum*

Fredegund's determination to manage events that affected her was not restricted to bargaining with God and reactive burnings; she often played a more direct role, as is seen by her responsibility for her stepsons' deaths. When her daughter *Riguntha was betrothed to the Visigothic prince Reccared, Fredegund raided the Frankish treasury to send her off with an appropriately showy dowry, deceitfully reassuring her thrift-minded husband that the wealth came from her own personal treasury. When Riguntha, robbed of her riches en route to Spain, had to turn back, Fredegund tried to kill her own daughter by bringing the heavy lid of a treasure chest down upon the young woman's neck, and only the protest of a slave saved Riguntha from death at her mother's hands. In addition, Fredegund tried unsuccessfully to kill Brunhilda, Childebert, and her brother-in-law Gunthram, who wavered between his two brothers' sides in futile attempts to play peacemaker. She was even accused by the author of the *Liber Historiae Francorum* of killing her own husband in order to protect herself when Chilperic I discovered she had been committing adultery with the mayor of the palace Landeric:

> One day very early in the morning the king went out to exercise at hunting at the villa of Chelles near Paris. Since he loved [Fredegund] too much, he returned from the horse stable to the palace bedroom. [Fredegund] was in the bedroom washing her hair with her head in the water. The king came up behind her and whacked her on the buttocks with a stick. She, thinking that it was Landeric, said: "Why do you do this, Landeric?" Then she looked up and . . . saw that it was the king; she was very scared.

Knowing that punishment would surely follow, she bribed two men both to kill Chilperic I and to publicly proclaim that Childebert of Austrasia was responsible. Gregory of Tours, gloating over the death of his great enemy Chilperic I, nevertheless did not blame Fredegund for her husband's death.

Fredegund spent her 13 years of widowhood, from 584 to 597, as regent for her only surviving son Lothair II, who was four months old at the time of his father's death. The Burgundian king Gunthram expressed some doubt as to whether the child was indeed his slain brother's son, but Fredegund was able to swear an oath with three bishops and 300 nobles that Lothair II was indeed Chilperic I's son. Despite her cruel measures, Fredegund enjoyed considerable support in the Frankish realm. The author of the *Liber Historiae Francorum* even credits her with devising an ingenious military plan involving camouflage of her troops, resulting in a military victory over King Childebert's forces.

Though her ruthless attention to details could potentially thwart her son Lothair II's future career, Fredegund managed to keep his position as Neustrian king intact. When in 597 Fredegund died a natural death—"old and full of days," according to the *Liber Historiae Francorum*, although she was only 50—her son buried her body at St. Vincent the Martyr's basilica in Paris, but he kept alive her hatred for Brunhilda and his rival Austrasian cousins. In 613, Lothair II defeated them, and, assuming the title of sole king of all the Franks, he tortured and had the octogenarian Brunhilda torn limb from limb by wild horses. Fredegund's son was one of the last effective Merovingian kings, and he ruled over a united realm that helped to inspire the Carolingian dynasty's appetite for unity nearly 200 years later.

SOURCES:

The Fourth Book of the Chronicle of Fredegar, with its continuations. J.M. Wallace-Hadrill. NY: Thomas Nelson, 1960.

History of the Franks by Gregory, Bishop of Tours. Selections translated with notes by Ernest Brehaut. NY: W.W. Norton, 1969.

The History of the Franks by Gregory of Tours. Translated with an introduction by O.M. Dalton. 2 vols. Oxford: Clarendon Press, 1927.

Liber Historiae Francorum. Edited and translated with an introduction by Bernard Bachrach. Lawrence, KA: Coronado Press, 1973.

SUGGESTED READING:

Deanesly, Margaret. *A History of Early Medieval Europe, 476–911.* NY: Barnes and Noble, 1963.

Queens, Concubines, and Dowagers: The King's Wife in the Early Middle Ages. Athens, GA: University of Georgia Press, 1983.

Wemple, Suzanne Fonay. *Women in Frankish Society: Marriage and the Cloister, 500 to 900.* Philadelphia, PA: University of Pennsylvania Press, 1981.

Cathy Jorgensen Itnyre,
Associate Professor of History,
Copper Mountain College, Joshua Tree, California

Frederica.

Variant of Fredericka or Frederika.

Frederica Amalie (1649–1704)

Duchess of Holstein-Gottorp. Born on April 11, 1649; died on October 30 1704; daughter of **Sophie Amalie of Brunswick-Lüneberg (1628–1685)* and Frederick III (1609–1670), king of Denmark and Norway (r. 1648–1670); married Christian Albert, duke of Holstein-Gottorp, on October 24, 1667; children: Frederick (b. 1671); Christian Augustus (b. 1673), duke of Holstein-Gottorp.

Frederica Dorothea of Baden (1781–1826)

Queen of Sweden. Born Frederica Dorothea Wilhelmina on March 12, 1781; died on September 25, 1826; daughter of Charles Louis of Padua (b. 1755), prince of Padua and Baden, and Amalie of Hesse-Darmstadt (b. 1754); married Gustavus IV Adolphus (1778–1837), king of Sweden (r. 1792–1809), on October 31, 1797 (divorced 1812); children: Gustavus of Sweden, prince of Vasa (b. 1799); **Sophia of Sweden (1801–1875)*; Charles Gustavus (b. 1802); **Amelia Marie Charlotte** (1805–1853); **Cecilie** (1807–1844, who married Frederick Augustus, grand duke of Oldenburg).

Frederica Louise (1715–1784)

Margravine of Anspach. Born on September 28, 1715; died on February 4, 1784; daughter of **Sophia Dorothea of Brunswick-Lüneburg-Hanover (1687–1757)* and Frederick William I (1688–1740), king of Prussia (r. 1713–1740); married Charles William, margrave of Anspach, on May 30, 1729; children: Christian Frederick, margrave of Anspach (b. 1736).

Frederica Louise (1770–1819)

Princess of Brunswick-Wolfenbuttel. Born Frederica Louise Wilhelmina on November 28, 1770; died on October 15, 1819; daughter of **Wilhelmina of Prussia (1751–1820)* and William V, prince of Orange; married Charles Augustus, prince of Brunswick-Wolfenbuttel, on October 14, 1790.

Frederica of Hesse (1751–1805)

Queen of Prussia. Name variations: Fredericka; Louisa of Hesse-Darmstadt. Born Fredericka Louise on October 16, 1751, in Prenzlau, Brandenburg, Germany; died on February 25, 1805, in Berlin, Germany; daughter of **Caroline of Birkenfeld-Zweibrucken*

(1721–1774) and Ludwig also known as Louis IX, landgrave of Hesse-Darmstadt; became second wife of Frederick William II (1744–1797), king of Prussia (r. 1786–1797), on July 14, 1769; children: Frederick William III, king of Prussia (1770–1840); Christine (1772–1773); Frederick Louis Charles (1773–1796, who married **Frederica of Mecklenburg-Strelitz*); **Frederica Wilhelmina of Prussia (1774–1837, who married William I, king of the Netherlands)*; Augusta (1780–1841, who married William II, elector of Hesse); Charles (1781–1846); William (1783–1851), prince of Prussia; Henry. Frederick William II's first wife was **Elizabeth of Brunswick (1746–1840).*

Frederica of Hesse-Darmstadt (1752–1782).

See Louise of Prussia for sidebar.

Frederica of Mecklenburg-Strelitz (1778–1841)

Duchess of Cumberland and queen of Hanover. Name variations: Frederica Caroline of Mecklenburg-Strelitz. Born on March 2, 1778, in Hanover, Lower Saxony, Germany; died on June 29, 1841, in Hanover; interred at Chapel of Schloss Herrenhausen, Hanover; daughter of Charles II Louis Frederick, grand duke of Mecklenburg-Strelitz, and **Frederica of Hesse-Darmstadt (1752–1782)*; sister of **Louise of Prussia (1776–1810)*; married Frederick Louis Charles (1773–1796), prince of Prussia, on December 26, 1793 (divorced 1796); married Frederick-William, prince of Salms-Branfels, on January 10, 1798; married Ernest Augustus I (1771–1851, son of King George III of England), duke of Cumberland and king of Hanover, on August 29, 1815; children: (first marriage) two boys who died in infancy; **Frederica Wilhelmina Louise** (1796–1850, who married Leopold Frederick, duke of Anhalt-Dessau); (second marriage) Frederick William Henry (b. 1801); **Augusta Louisa of Salms-Branfels** (1804–1865, who married Albert, prince of Schwarzbourg-Roudolstadt); Alexander Frederick (b. 1807); Frederick William (b. 1812); (third marriage) Frederica (1817–1817, stillborn); another daughter (1818–1818); George V (b. 1819), king of Hanover.

Frederica of Prussia (1767–1820)

Prussian princess and duchess of York and Albany. Name variations: Fredericka; Frederica Charlotte, princess royal of Prussia. Born Frederica Charlotte Ulrica Catherine on May 7, 1767, in Charlottenburg,

Berlin, Germany; died of water on the lung on August 6, 1820, in Oatlands Park, Weybridge, Surrey, England; daughter of *Elizabeth of Brunswick *(1746–1840) and Frederick William II, king of Prussia (r. 1786–1797); married Frederick Augustus (1763–1827), duke of York and Albany (son of George III and* *Charlotte of Mecklenburg-Strelitz*), on September 29, 1791 (separated).*

Frederica Wilhelmina of Prussia

(1774–1837)

Queen of the Netherlands. Name variations: Wilhelmina of Prussia; Wilhelmina Hohenzollern. Born on November 18, 1774, in Potsdam, Brandenburg, Germany; died on October 12, 1837, in The Hague, Netherlands; daughter of Frederick William II, king of Prussia (r. 1786–1797), and *Frederica of Hesse *(1751–1805); married William I (1772–1843), king of the Netherlands (r. 1813–1840, abdicated in 1840), on October 1, 1791; children: William II (1792–1849), king of the Netherlands (r. 1840–1849, who married* *Anna Pavlovna*); Frederick Orange-Nassau (1797–1881); Charlotte (1800–1806);* *Marianne of the Netherlands *(1810–1883). Following the death of Frederica Wilhelmina of Prussia, William I married* *Henrietta Adrienne*, on February 17, 1841, in Berlin, Germany.*

Frederick, Empress (1840–1901).

See Victoria Adelaide.

Frederick, Pauline (c. 1906–1990)

American journalist, television and radio news reporter and analyst. Born in Gallitzin, Pennsylvania, around 1906 (date of birth has been cited as late as 1920); died in Lake Forest, Illinois, on May 9, 1990; daughter and second of three children of Matthew P. (an official of the Pennsylvania State Department of Labor) and Susan (Stanley) Frederick; American University, B.A. in political science, M.A. in international law, Washington, D.C.

Pauline Frederick, a pioneering television journalist born around 1906 in Gallitzin, Pennsylvania, was filing reports to newspapers in Harrisburg while still in high school. Though originally headed for law school, she was persuaded by a college history professor to try journalism instead. After receiving a B.A. in political science and M.A. in international law from American University, Frederick stayed in Washington to work as a freelance journalist for various newspapers and radio stations. During the late 1930s,

she also did Washington interviews for the National Broadcasting Network (NBC). Her first big break came in 1945, when she became a globe-trotting war correspondent for the North American Newspaper Alliance. She later covered the Nuremberg trials of Nazi officials and the "Big Four" conferences in New York and Paris.

In 1946, Frederick joined the news staff of the American Broadcasting Company (ABC), where she had an early morning radio show and occasionally worked on the evening television news. Beginning in 1947, she shared the United Nations "beat" with commentator Gordon Fraser and, in 1948, covered the Democratic and Republican conventions, the presidential campaign, and the inauguration. During the 1950s, she covered the Korean War as well as the revolutions in Africa and the Middle East.

In June 1953, she rejoined NBC, where she ultimately became a star and the first woman to report serious television news. Frederick remained NBC's "man at the UN" for the next 21 years, appearing in a wide range of programs that included reporting, commentary, and interviews. Leaving NBC in 1974, one year past mandatory retirement age, Frederick bristled over having to quit: The networks "can accept a man who looks his age; but not a woman." She later joined National Public Radio as an international affairs analyst. During the election campaign of 1976, she moderated the debate between Jimmy Carter and Gerald Ford.

Frederick received numerous honors for her trailblazing work, including the Alfred DuPont Award for "meritorious service to the American people." The 1953 citation praised Frederick for "avoiding the slickness, automatic orthodoxy and superficial sensationalism characteristic of much news commentary today . . . without making concessions to a vulgarization of either thought or style." She also received 23 honorary degrees and was the first woman to be elected president of the UN Correspondents Association. Pauline Frederick died on May 9, 1990.

SOURCES:
Candee, Marjorie Dent, ed. *Current Biography 1954.* NY: H.W. Wilson, 1954.
Moritz, Charles, ed. *Current Biography Yearbook 1990.* NY: H.W. Wilson, 1990.
Slater, Charlotte. "She's still got that voice—ever steady and rich," in *Detroit News.* September 15, 1974.

Barbara Morgan,
Melrose, Massachusetts

Fredericka.

Variant of Frederika.

Fredericka (1917–1981)

Queen of Greece. Name variations: Frederika or Frederica; Fredericka Louise of Brunswick; Queen of the Hellenes. Born Fredericka Louise Thyra Victoria Margaret Sophia Olga Cecily Isabel Christa on April 18, 1917, in Blankenburg, Hanover, Lower Saxony, Germany; died on February 6, 1981, in Madrid, Spain; the third of five children and only daughter of *Victoria Louise *(1892–1980) and Ernest Augustus of Cumberland, duke of Brunswick-Lüneburg; attended North Foreland Lodge Girls' School, near Broadstairs, Kent, England; attended schools in Obernkirchen, Germany and Florence, Italy; married Paul I, king of the Hellenes, January 9, 1938 (died, March 6, 1964); children: Sophia of Greece (b. 1938), queen of Spain; Constantine II (b. 1940), king of Greece (r. 1964–1973); Irene (b. 1942).*

Called "passionately charitable" and "almost irresistibly charming," Queen Fredericka, the German-born consort of Paul I, king of Greece, from 1947 until his death in 1964, was devoted to her adopted country, particularly during and after World War II and during the Communist war when she played a crucial role in the country's rehabilitation. "We must put ourselves at the disposal of the people," she once said. "We are not to be served, but to serve."

The only daughter of the Duke and Duchess of Brunswick-Lüneburg, Fredericka was born in Blankenburg, Germany, on April 18, 1917, and christened Fredericka Louise Thyra Victoria Margaret Sophia Olga Cecily Isabel Christa. She grew up in Gmunden, Austria, where her family moved when she was one year old. Described as "a bright, alert, gay and affectionate tomboy," she received her early education at home and, at 17, was sent to the North Foreland Lodge Girls' School, near Broadstairs, Kent, in England. After two years, she went to a girls' agricultural school in Germany, then later attended a school in Florence, Italy. While there, she frequently visited her relatives, Princess *Helen of Greece (1896–1982) and Princess *Irene (b. 1904), sisters of George II, then king of the Hellenes. It was there that the dimpled, blue-eyed princess caught the attention of the king's brother, Crown Prince Paul, whom she wed on January 9, 1938, in a splendid royal ceremony attended by 55 princes and princesses and 40 bishops.

Following the wedding, Fredericka learned the language of her new country and was received into the Greek Orthodox Church. The prince and princess first resided at a small villa at Psychico, outside Athens, where their first two children were born: ***Sophia of Greece** (b.

1938) and Constantine (b. 1940). When the war broke out in 1940, the family went first to Crete, then to Egypt, and finally settled in South Africa, where their third child, *Irene, was born in 1942. While in South Africa, Fredericka organized the Crown Princess' Relief Fund, which had branches throughout the Western world. The funds raised were used for the immediate relief of the Greek people following the liberation of the country in October 1944, although the Royal Family was unable to return to Greece until 1946, when a plebiscite restored King George II to the throne. Fredericka arrived home to find her country completely devastated and under a new threat from the Communists.

Following the death of King George on April 1, 1947, Paul succeeded him as king and Fredericka became queen. The royal couple now devoted themselves to ending the war with the Communists and creating solidarity between the Greek people and their government. Fredericka, in addition to her welfare projects, traveled with the king throughout Greece, even to the battle front. In 1948, while the king was ill with typhoid fever, the queen visited the Greek troops in his place and was the first to enter the town of Kónitsa, after a fierce but successful battle against enemy forces. The tired Greek soldiers greeted her with cheers. "My husband is sick and I belong at his bedside," she told them, "but I think he must love you more than he does me, for he sent me to be with you in his place."

In 1949, the Communist rebellion was put down and peace was restored. Fredericka then embarked on a massive effort to rehabilitate her country, coordinating philanthropic organizations and taking an active role in establishing hospitals and social institutions to serve the needs of orphaned children. Later, calling education in her country "prehistoric," she led a campaign for a more modern Greek School that would instill a personal responsibility to the community. "In our country, freedom has come to be considered as a piece of personal property of the citizen, rather than as a personal responsibility," she told *Look* magazine (October 20, 1953). "An ideal democracy is one in which every person carries his share of the burden." In educating their son Constantine, the immediate heir to the throne, the queen and king endeavored to balance his book learning with practical life experiences. In addition to military school, they sent him to work in the mines and factories in order to learn about the lives and problems of the Greeks. The two princesses attended a school in Germany.

In 1962, when the United States cut off economic aid to Greece, the royal family began to be viewed as a drain on an already depleted treasury, and they suffered a sharp decline in popularity. By 1964, when the king died of stomach cancer and Constantine succeeded to the throne, the country was entering a volatile period under the newly elected prime minister George Papandreou, a liberal parliamentarian. As queen-mother, Fredericka had little influence in her country, now in the grip of conflict. Following the Greek military coup d'état in 1967, she fled to Rome with her son where she continued to live in self-imposed exile following the overthrow of the monarchy in 1973. Fredericka died in Madrid on February 6, 1981, while visiting her daughter, Sophia of Greece, now queen of Spain.

SOURCES:

Candee, Marjorie Dent, ed. *Current Biography 1955.* NY: H.W. Wilson, 1955.

Moritz, Charles, ed. *Currently Biography 1981.* NY: H.W. Wilson, 1981.

SUGGESTED READING:

Frederica, Queen of the Hellenes. *A Measure of Understanding.* London: 1982.

Barbara Morgan,
Melrose, Massachusetts

Fredericka of Hanover (1848–1926)

*Princess of Hanover. Born Fredericka Sophia Mary Henrietta Amelia Theresa on January 9, 1848, in Hanover, Lower Saxony, Germany; died on October 16, 1926, in Biarritz, France; daughter of George V, king of Hanover, and *Mary of Saxe-Altenburg (1818–1907); married Alphonso, 6th baron von Pawel-Rammingen, on April 24, 1880; children: one.*

Fredericka of Mecklenburg-Strelitz (1778–1841).

See Frederica of Mecklenburg-Strelitz.

Frederika.

Variant of Frederica or Fredericka.

Frederika Louise of Brunswick (1917–1981).

See Fredericka, Queen of Greece.

Frederika of Hesse-Darmstadt (1752–1782).

See Louise of Prussia for sidebar.

Frederona (d. 917)

Queen of France. Name variations: Frederuna. Died in 917; sister of Bovo, bishop of Chalons; married Charles III the Simple (879–929), king of France (r.

898–923); children: *Gisela Martel (d. 919). Charles' second wife was *Edgifu (902–951).*

Fredesendis (fl. 1000)

*Frankish noblewoman. Flourished around 1000; second wife of Tancred of Hauteville; children: Robert Guiscard (d. 1085, duke of Apulia and Calabria, count of Sicily, r. 1057–1085); William, count of the Principate (d. 1080); Roger the Great, count of Sicily (r. 1072–1101); *Fredesendis (fl. 1050); and others.*

Fredesendis (fl. 1050)

*Princess of Capua. Flourished around 1050; daughter of *Fredesendis (fl. 1000) and Tancred of Hauteville; married Richard I, prince of Capua.*

Freeman, Alice (1857–1936)

Canadian columnist who wrote under the pseudonym Faith Fenton. Name variations: (pseudonym) Faith Fenton. Born Alice Freeman in Bowmanville, Ontario, Canada, in 1857; died in 1936; third of twelve children; graduated from Toronto Normal School; spent 20 years as a teacher in the Toronto school system.

Canadian columnist *Kit Coleman once referred to Faith Fenton's column as "one of the brightest, tenderest, most sympathetic pages ever written by any woman." When Alice Freeman, alias Faith Fenton, died in 1936, she was hailed as a pioneer Canadian journalist and "one of the glamorous figures of the gold rush of '98." Unlike Coleman, however, her name became obscure for a time in Canadian history.

One of 12 children, Freeman was born in Bowmanville, Ontario, Canada, in 1857 and grew up wanting to be a writer. Instead, she became a schoolteacher. During much of her career, she led a double life, teaching elementary school by day and plying the less respectable trade of reporter by night under the name of Faith Fenton. She covered polite society as well as the down-and-out and once posed as a homeless woman to write an exposé. A social activist and avid feminist, Freeman wrote about child abuse, sexual discrimination and harassment, and wage disparity long before they were considered legitimate media topics. One of her early assignments was a prison visit, undertaken she said, "that readers of the Empire might know something of the daily lives of those restless, broken-winged birds, the imprisoned women of Ontario." Freeman had a wide range of readers and received mail from regular citizens as well as notable personalities such as Prime Minister Sir Wilfrid Laurier, the diva *Emma Albani, and the poet *E. Pauline Johnson. At age 40, Freeman lost her teaching job and fled to the Klondike, where she gained notoriety for her stories on the Gold Rush.

SOURCES:

Naves, Elaine Kalman. "Exhumed from past: woman journalist who joined gold rush," in [Montreal] *Gazette*. June 29, 1996.

SUGGESTED READING:

Downie, Jill. *A Passionate Pen: The Life and Times of Faith Fenton*. HarperCollins, 1996.

Barbara Morgan,
Melrose, Massachusetts

Freeman, Alice E. (1855–1902).

See Palmer, Alice Freeman.

Freeman, Emma B. (1880–1927)

American photographer. Born Emma Belle Richart in Nebraska in 1880; died in San Francisco, California, in 1927; married Edwin R. Freeman (a salesman for the garment industry), in 1902 (divorced 1915); married Edward Blake (a bookkeeper), in 1925; no children.

Nebraska-born, Emma B. Freeman married in 1902 and moved with her husband Edwin to San Francisco, where he ran an art goods and handicrafts store while she took drawing and painting classes. When the store was destroyed by the earthquake in 1906, the couple moved to the small town of Eureka, California. Edwin became a photographer and eventually opened Freeman Art Company, selling his scenic views along with the art supplies. Emma also took up photography around 1910 but concentrated on portraits. In 1913, she was involved in a local scandal when she took a train to San Francisco with former governor of Illinois Richard B. Yates, who had been speaking in Eureka. She was subsequently divorced from Edwin (1915) and began to seriously pursue her interest in photography.

Widely acclaimed among Freeman's photographs were a series of 200 Indian studies called the Northern California series, which were displayed at the Panama-Pacific International Exposition in San Francisco, in 1915. She also made her mark in the male-dominated world of photojournalism with her coverage of the USS *Milwaukee*, when it sank while attempting to salvage the submarine H-3 in Eureka Bay, in 1916. In 1919, Freeman moved her art company back to San Francisco but went bankrupt in 1923. She married Edward Blake, a bookkeeper, in 1925, just two years before her death.

Freeman, Mary E. Wilkins
(1852–1930)

American novelist and short-story writer. Name variations: wrote under Mary E. Wilkins Freeman and Mary E. Wilkins. Born Mary Eleanor Wilkins in Randolph, Massachusetts, on October 31, 1852; died on March 15, 1930, in Metuchen, New Jersey; one of two daughters of Warren E. Wilkins (an architect and storekeeper) and Eleanor (Lothrop) Wilkins; attended Brattleboro (Vermont) high school; attended Mt. Holyoke Seminary and Mrs. Hosford's Glenwood Seminary in West Brattleboro; married Charles Manning Freeman (a physician), 1902 (separated, 1921); no children.

Principal works—short stories: The Adventures of Ann *(juvenile, 1886);* A Humble Romance *(1887);* A New England Nun *(1891);* The Pot of Gold *(1892);* Young Lucretia *(1892);* Comfort Pease and Her Gold Ring *(1895);* The People of Our Neighborhood *(1898);* Silence *(1898);* The Jamesons *(1899);* The Love of Parson Lord *(1900);* Understudies *(1901);* Six Trees *(1903);* The Wind in the Rose Bush *(1903);* The Givers *(1904);* The Fair Lavinia *(1907);* The Winning Lady *(1909);* The Green Door *(1910);* The Yates Pride *(1912);* The Copy-Cat *(1914);* Edgewater People *(1918). Novels:* Jane Field *(1893);* Pembroke *(1894);* Madelon *(1896);* Jerome: A Poor Man *(1897);* The Heart's Highway *(1900);* The Portion of Labor *(1901);* The Debtor *(1905);* "Doc" Gordon *(1906);* By the Light of the Soul *(1906);* The Shoulders of Atlas *(1908);* The Butterfly House *(1912);* An Alabaster Box *(with F.M. Kingsley, 1917). Miscellaneous:* Decorative Plaques *(verse, 1883);* Giles Corey: Yeoman *(play, 1893);* Once Upon a Time and Other Child Verses *(1897).*

Called one of the last great genre writers in New England, Mary Eleanor Freeman was born in Randolph, Massachusetts, in 1852 and received what little education she had in Brattleboro, Vermont, where the family moved in 1867. Obliged to leave Mount Holyoke Seminary (now Mount Holyoke College) due to poor health, her last formal schooling included a few months at a boarding school in West Brattleboro. In 1883, after the death of her parents and her only sister, Freeman returned to Randolph to live with a friend, although in ensuing years she also traveled around the United States and in Europe. After her marriage to Dr. Charles Freeman in 1902, she moved to Metuchen, New Jersey, where she resided for the rest of her life. (Freeman was legally separated from her husband in 1921, after he was committed to an institution for alcoholism.)

By the 1880s, Freeman had established herself as a children's writer. Her early work, *Decorative Plaques* (1883), was a collection of 12 poems from the children's magazine *Wide Awake*. After her first adult story, "A Shadow Family" (since lost), won a prize in a contest sponsored by a Boston newspaper, she began to concentrate on adult fiction, and her work was regularly featured in *Harper's Bazaar* and *Harper's Weekly*. Freeman's stories and novels about New Englanders, rich with themes of pride, endurance in the face of poverty and adversity, and religious fervor, are thought to be her best, particularly in their direct style and lack of sentimentality. As John Macy once pointed out: "Her material was close at hand, plain and simple; she had the genius to see it and render it objectively." The novel *Pembroke* (1894) may best represent Freeman's New England works and is considered by some to be her greatest achievement.

Mary E. Wilkins Freeman

As her career progressed, Freeman became more elaborate and elegant in her style, not always with good results. She began to write not only of New England, but of the prosperous suburban life in New Jersey, where she lived. Attempting to keep up with the fashionable trend of the times, she also tried her hand at a historical romance, *The Heart's Highway* (1900), and a labor novel, *The Portion of Labor* (1901). Both failed miserably.

In 1926, Freeman was awarded the Howells medal for distinction in fiction by the American Academy of Letters and was elected to membership in the National Institute of Arts and Letters. Once extremely prolific, she wrote very little in the decade before her death in March 1930. Mary Freeman was then largely forgotten, though there has been renewed interest in her work.

SOURCES:

Kunitz, Stanley J,. and Howard Haycraft. *Twentieth Century Authors*. NY: H.W. Wilson, 1942.

Mainiero, Lina. ed. *American Women Writers*. NY: Frederick Ungar, 1980.

SUGGESTED READING:

Showalter, Elaine, ed. *Modern American Women Writers*. NY: Scribner, 1991.

Barbara Morgan,
Melrose, Massachusetts

Freier, Recha (1892–1984)

German-born Israeli Zionist leader, teacher, and writer who, as the founder of Youth Aliyah, rescued thousands of young Jews from Nazi Germany. Born Recha Schweitzer in Norden, Ostfriesland, Germany, in 1892; died in Jerusalem in 1984; married Moritz Freier; children: Shalhevet Freier; Amud Freier; Zerem Freier; Maayan Freier.

Married to Rabbi Moritz Freier (1889–1969) and the mother of four children, Recha Freier was living a busy and contented life in Berlin in the early 1930s. But for Jews like the Freier family, there were darkening clouds on the German horizon. The impact of the world economic depression devastated all sectors of German life, and many Jews who had once been prosperous were now struggling or out of work. For Jewish youth, prospects of finding jobs were dim. In the streets of Berlin and other German cities and towns, hate-filled Nazi brownshirts attacked at will those political and racial foes they deemed to be "un-German." What could one woman do to respond to this bleak situation? As it turned out, a great deal. Throughout Recha Freier's long life, people unacquainted with her passionate determination greatly underestimated her willpower and many tal-

ents. A lover of music and poetry and a gifted poet herself, Freier gave every impression of being a rather sheltered member of Berlin's cultivated German-Jewish bourgeoisie. She dressed in an old-fashioned way, wearing long white dresses and wide-brimmed hats (she continued to dress in this distinctive fashion in her 80s in Israel).

The opportunity to leap from her sheltered life into the turmoil of a society in the throes of political and moral upheaval presented itself in February 1932, when 16-year-old Nathan Höxter, acting as the leader of five friends in one of Berlin's Zionist youth groups, appealed to Freier to help them find work. She had long nursed the hope that, instead of passively remaining in a Europe increasingly threatened by Nazi racism, young Jews could take the lead in an exodus to the Zionist homeland of Eretz Israel (at that time the British-controlled Mandated Territory of Palestine). After a meeting with Enzo Sereni, the representative in Germany of one of Palestine's leading kibbutz movements, boosted her confidence, she told Höxter that young Jews had no future in Germany; their true home was Eretz Israel.

But turning ideas into reality entails much time and effort, as well as a great deal of luck. Freier met with skepticism if not downright hostility when she brought her idea of creating an organization that would enable young Jews to immigrate to the Palestine's kibbutzim, where they would submit themselves to a regimen of Zionist-inspired agricultural training (*hachsharah*). It was a common belief among many German Jews that they were a community that was too assimilated, too urban, and simply too "soft" to ever thrive in a harsh land like Palestine. On a visit to Dr. Georg Landauer, director of the Palestine division of Berlin's Zionist organization, she chanced to read a circular intended to be mailed to the organization's branches in which they were warned to beware of her "reckless" plan of *aliyah* (emigration to Palestine) for German-Jewish youth. Incensed by what she had just read, Freier slipped the entire printing of the circular into her handbag, then triumphantly dumped them into a garbage pail on her way home.

Refusing to be discouraged, Recha Freier worked countless hours intent to organize a mass movement of youth to Palestine. The odds against her were enormous, not the least of which was the passive attitude that characterized the assimilated, complacent majority of Germany's Jewish community. Feeling themselves to be patriotic citizens who had sacrificed more than 12,000 of their sons in World War I, many German Jews refused to believe that their beloved Fatherland would ever turn on them.

Many Jewish parents were extremely skeptical of a plan to send their young sons and daughters, aged 14 to 17, to a far-off desert territory, cut off from parental authority and prey to countless dangers and temptations. Even before the scheme received its official name, Jugendaliyah (Youth Aliyah), the first tiny vanguard of thousands to come—Nathan Höxter and his group of five—arrived in Jaffa, Palestine, on December 2, 1932.

On January 30, 1933, the day that Adolf Hitler was appointed chancellor of Germany, Freier announced the official establishment of the Society for Youth Aliyah. Despite the rapid establishment of a Nazi dictatorship based on terror and propaganda, Freier and her husband decided not to flee Germany. Instead, she traveled to Palestine in May 1933 in an attempt to win over for her plans the most powerful woman in the Zionist movement, American-born *Henrietta Szold. Despite her passionate pleas on behalf of the Youth Aliyah concept in the face of the now poisonously anti-Semitic German environment, Szold remained unconvinced of the viability of the idea. She told her visitor from Germany that the fragile Palestinian economy could not possibly absorb urban, middle-class youth without skills when impoverished refugees from Eastern Europe were already to be found sleeping on the beaches of Tel Aviv. The most encouraging response Freier got from Szold was her endorsement of preliminary agricultural training of young Zionists in Germany, who would then at least bring useful skills along when they finally arrived in Eretz Israel at some undetermined date in the future. Although Szold remained largely hostile to the practical possibilities of Freier's work, she was by no means indifferent to the potential power that would accrue by being linked to an organization that might one day achieve success; thus she became director of a still largely theoretical Youth Aliyah organization in Palestine on November 27, 1933.

Disappointed but by no means stopped by Szold's skepticism, Freier returned to Germany in July 1933 to build a strong alliance with an older, stronger organization, Jüdische Jugendhilfe (Jewish Youth Assistance). Her efforts to convince Jewish youths (and their parents) of the desirability of settling in Palestine brought about concrete results: on February 19, 1934, the first organized group of young emigrants from Germany arrived in Haifa harbor on board the S.S. *Martha Washington*.

A victory of sorts was achieved for Freier at the World Zionist Congress held in Lucerne,

Switzerland, in 1935 when Szold publicly acknowledged her as leader of the Youth Aliyah movement. But Szold also saw to it that Freier would have neither power nor influence within the Palestine branch of the organization. Undeterred, Freier continued to concentrate on what really mattered to her—the rescue of Jewish youth from the increasingly hostile environment of Nazi Germany. Working without rest, she was able to raise the funds to instruct hundreds of youth in training courses lasting from four-to-six weeks so as to prepare them for *aliyah* to Eretz Israel.

The number of emigrants who were able to gain entrance to Palestine during the first two years of the Youth Aliyah program was relatively modest: 363 in 1934, increasing to 550 in 1935. In the second half of the 1930s, however, these numbers would jump dramatically. By the outbreak of World War II in September 1939, 5,012 had been able to immigrate to Palestine; during the war, 1939–45, an additional 9,342 lives were saved by Youth Aliyah. From 1945 until the establishment of the State of Israel in 1948, an additional 15,999 youth left Europe for Palestine. Having been responsible for the emigration to Palestine of a total of 30,353 from 1934 to 1948, by any criterion Youth Aliyah must be recognized as the most successful rescue project of young Jews during the entire Holocaust period. The Youth Aliyah organization not only rescued these individuals, but created programs designed to integrate them into a new life in Jewish Palestine. The members of over 50 kibbutzim not only made these refugees feel welcome in a strange new environment but tutored each of them so that they would succeed in learning a new language, absorbing new cultural traditions and mastering practical agricultural and industrial skills.

In 1938, Youth Aliyah headquarters had been transferred from Berlin to London but Freier remained in the German capital to direct the work of her organization. In 1939, her husband immigrated to Great Britain, taking with him three of their four children. The youngest child, daughter **Maayan Freier**, remained in Berlin with Recha. Only in 1940 did Freier decide to leave Germany. This remarkable woman, often dismissed as "an impractical poet and dreamer" by her critics within Zionist circles, fled the borders of the Reich to Yugoslavia, eluding the Gestapo with a group of 120 children as well as her daughter.

Realizing that she, Maayan, and her band of youth were still in danger in Yugoslavia, Freier worked to secure immigration certificates valid for travel to Palestine. By the time Nazi Germany attacked Yugoslavia in April 1941, she had been able to secure passage for herself, her daughter, and 90 of her brood. In Palestine during the war years, Freier grieved for the 30 she had been forced to leave behind, but a near-miracle took place in the depths of the Holocaust when she received word in 1945 that they had all survived the war, due at least in part because of the remarkable abilities of their Youth Aliyah leader, Joseph Indyk.

Recha Freier's tense relationship with Henrietta Szold did not improve when she arrived in Palestine. In early 1941, Szold simply informed her that there were no positions open for her anywhere within the Youth Aliyah organization in Palestine. The historical record of Freier's achievements was also either grossly ignored or even falsified on several occasions, including a Jewish Agency exhibition in 1944 in which a decade of Youth Aliyah work was commemorated without a single mention of her rescue efforts in the heart of Nazi Germany. These slights, along with the normal stresses that invariably accompany acculturation to a new environment by someone who was entering middle age, left their mark on Freier. During these difficult years, she was often depressed and at times suicidal. But her continuing work among underprivileged children in kibbutzim, and the fact that her daughter needed a mother, finally enabled her to evolve toward a more hopeful life. The war also served to alienate Freier from her husband, who remained in Europe after 1945 to serve as rabbi to the remnants of post-Nazi Berlin's Jewish community. Moritz Freier would die in Zurich, Switzerland, in 1969, at age 80.

In the 1960s, Freier took on a new role, that of music patron. In 1966, she collaborated with Polish-born Israeli composer Roman Haubenstock-Ramati to found a concert series designed to reflect the various Jewish traditions throughout history. Naming it "Testimonium," Freier emphasized that it was her wish that the concerts would bring together both non-Jewish as well as Jewish artists. The series was a success from the start, and by the early 1980s had become an internationally recognized institution. Among those who composed works that were first performed at Testimonium festivals in Israel were such internationally recognized composers as Luigi Dallapiccola, Lukas Foss, Alexander Goehr, Mauricio Kagel, George Rochberg, Karlheinz Stockhausen, and Iannis Xenakis. Recha Freier the poet was proud to see some of her own texts used in compositions performed in Testimonium festivals.

Despite having been born and raised in the conservative Germany of Kaiser Wilhelm II, Freier remained receptive to new cultural and artistic experiences even in the final decades of her long life. In 1983, when she was 90 years old, she attended a Testimonium concert at which *Pleuk* was performed, an aggressively modernist work by the German composer Hans Joachim Hespos. His home was Friesland, the North Sea island on which Freier had herself been born. In her final years, she rekindled her relationship with Germany and in the 1970s witnessed the publication in Hamburg of two volumes of her poetry. Recha Freier's death in Israel in 1984 ended a remarkable odyssey begun half a century earlier. In April 1990, the West German ambassador to Israel and the mayor of what was then still East Berlin attended the cornerstone laying ceremony for the Recha Freier Educational Center at Kibbutz Yakum near Herzliya. Partially funded by the German government, the center honors not only Recha Freier but was designed to house part of the archives of the pre-Holocaust Berlin Jewish community.

SOURCES:

Eliav, Mordechai. "German Jews' Share in the Building of the National Home in Palestine and the State of Israel," in *Year Book XXX of the Leo Baeck Institute* (1985), pp. 255–264.

Erel, Shlomo. *Neue Wurzeln: 50 Jahre Immigration deutschsprachiger Juden in Israel*. Gerlingen: Bleicher Verlag, 1983.

Freier, Recha. *Auf der Treppe*. Hamburg: Hans Christians Verlag, 1976.

———. *Fensterladen*. Hamburg: Hans Christians Verlag, 1979.

———. *Let the Children Come: The Early History of Youth Aliyah*. London: Weidenfeld and Nicolson, 1961.

———, and Alexander Goehr. *Sonata About Jerusalem: Cantata/Music Theatre III*. London and NY: Schott Music Corporation, 1976.

———, and Meir Gottesman. *Out of the Fire*. Edited by Alan Sillitoe. London: Children and Youth Aliyah Committee, 1979.

———, and Josef Tal. *Amnon und Tamar: Oper in einem Akt, vier Szenen*. Wiesbaden: Impero-Verlag, 1959.

Gelber, Yoav. *Moledet hadashah: Aliyat Yehude merkaz Eropah u-kelitatam, 1933–1948*. Jerusalem: Yad Yitshak Ben-Tsevi/Mekhon Leo Bek, 1990.

———. "The Origins of Youth Aliyah," in *Studies in Zionism*. Vol. 9, no. 2. Autumn 1988, pp. 147–171.

Gill, Dominic. "Testimonium in Israel," in *Financial Times* [London], March 17, 1983, section I, p. 19.

Kol, Moshe. *Masekhet Aliyat ha-noar*. Jerusalem and Tel Aviv: M. Nyuman, 1961.

Landauer, Georg. *Der Zionismus im Wandel dreier Jahrzehnte*. Edited by Max Kreutzberger. Tel Aviv: Bitaon-Verlag, 1957.

Leshem, Perez. *Strasse zur Rettung: 1933–1939 aus Deutschland vertrieben, bereitet sich jüdische Jugend auf Palästina vor.* Tel Aviv: Verband der Freunde der Histadrut, 1973.

Levin, Marlin. "The Foundation of Youth Aliya," in *Jerusalem Post.* November 28, 1995, p. 6.

Luft, Gerda. *Heimkehr ins Unbekannte: Eine Darstellung der Einwanderung von Juden aus Deutschland nach Palästina vom Aufstieg Hitlers zur Macht bis zum Ausbruch des Zweiten Weltkrieges.* Wuppertal: Hammer Verlag, 1977.

Walk, Joseph. *Kurzbiographien zur Geschichte der Juden 1918–1945.* Munich: K. G. Saur Verlag, 1988.

John Haag,
Assistant Professor of History, University of Georgia,
Athens, Georgia

Frémont, Jessie Benton

(1824–1902)

American writer and wife of explorer John C. Frémont who chronicled the American scene during the 19th century. Name variations: Jessie B. Fremont. Born Jessie Ann Benton on May 31, 1824, near Lexington, Virginia; died on December 27, 1902, in Los Angeles, California; second of four daughters and five children of Thomas Hart Benton (a senator from Missouri) and Elizabeth (McDowell) Benton; educated by private tutors; attended Miss English's school, Georgetown, Washington; married Lieutenant John Charles Frémont (an explorer), on October 19, 1841; children: Elizabeth Benton (b. 1842); Benton Benton (b. 1848); John Charles Benton (b. 1851); Anne Beverley Benton (b. 1853); Frank Preston Benton (b. 1854).

*Jessie
Benton
Frémont*

Outspoken and strong-willed from childhood, writer Jessie Frémont witnessed and chronicled the changing American scene during the final half of the 19th century from a woman's perspective. The daughter of Thomas Hart Benton, the famous senator from Missouri, and **Elizabeth McDowell**, whose family was active in Virginia politics, Jessie was born on May 31, 1824, near Lexington, and raised in a richly social atmosphere and schooled by private tutors at home. She described a happy childhood, dominated by her father, whom she called "a companion and a friend from the time almost that I could begin to understand." Jessie was 16 and attending Miss English's academy for girls in Georgetown, when she met and fell in love with the brilliant and handsome Lieutenant John Charles Frémont, 11 years her senior and an ill-paid member of the army's Topographical Corps. Although her parents disapproved of the match, Jessie continued to see John Frémont during weekends at home. (At one point, her father attempted to end the relationship by having John sent off to map the Des Moines, but the young man returned as ardent as ever.) Jessie and John were married by a sympathetic Catholic priest in a secret ceremony in October 1841. Although initially furious, Benton eventually bestowed his blessings on the union and then became active in promoting John Frémont's career as an explorer. Jessie, in addition to giving birth to five children, two of whom died in infancy, channeled her own ambition into her husband's future.

During the 1840s, John headed up a series of government expeditions to the West, designed to prepare for and encourage future expansion to the Pacific. He returned home from the first expedition to the Wind River Range in October 1842, just a month before the arrival of the couple's first child, a daughter. Jessie used her considerable literary talent to help him prepare his notes and recollections of the expedition into an extremely lively and widely acclaimed report, which was published as a Senate document in 1843. It was the beginning of a collaboration with her husband that would become her life's work.

As John Frémont was preparing to leave on a second expedition in May 1843, Jessie intercepted a letter sent to him from the War Department, which she interpreted as a threat to his command. Sending him a message to leave immediately, she then wrote to authorities in Washington telling them what she had done. Upon John's return in 1844, after a successful tour in Oregon and California, she was once again influential in the preparation of the account of the expedition, which was printed as a Senate document in an edition of 10,000 copies and widely sold in a commercial edition as well. Entitled simply the *Report,* it was said to have influenced Far Western settlement more than any other single book.

In 1845, while on his third expedition, John Frémont became involved with the American settlers in California in their Bear Flag Rebellion against Mexico. His battalion of volunteers, composed of some of the settlers and voyagers from his topographical party, became known as

Jessie Benton Frémont, 1891.

the California Battalion and served during the Mexican War under the command of Robert F. Stockton, who became chief of naval and land operations on the Pacific Coast and who later appointed Frémont governor of the conquered territory. The arrival in California of Brigadier General Stephen Watts Kearny, however, created problems for John Frémont. Caught in the middle of the struggle between Kearny and Stockton for supremacy of command, Frémont chose the wrong side, was ordered to march east behind Kearny's army and, despite his father-in-law's efforts, was ultimately court-martialed and convicted on charges of mutiny, disobedience, and conduct prejudiced to military discipline. President James K. Polk remitted the penalty and ordered him to duty again, but Frémont, unwilling to admit in any way the justice of the decision, resigned from the army.

Throughout his ordeal, Jessie and her father stood staunchly by him. In June 1847, Jessie defended him in an interview with President Polk. In 1849, while John led yet a fourth expedition westward to chart a railroad route, Jessie and her daughter underwent a grueling crossing of the Isthmus to meet him in California. The family eventually settled on the Mariposas estate, a large tract of land that John had acquired in the Sierra foothills, east of San Francisco, where they lived under primitive frontier conditions. Upon her husband's election as senator from California in 1850, Jessie accompanied him to Washington for a brief term that ended in March 1851. After another year in California, they traveled to London to raise money to develop the gold mines on the Mariposas property.

In 1855, having grown quite wealthy, they moved to New York City, where John further promoted his mining interests and his plans for the Pacific railroad. He also became involved in politics and was nominated as the first Republican candidate for president. Jessie, unfortunately, was limited by custom to a small role in her husband's campaign, mainly assisting with the official biography and entertaining supporters, but her contribution was a major factor in his strong showing. She was devastated by his defeat and took a vacation to France before returning to California.

Jessie also served as her husband's ally during his troubled Civil War service, first as commander of the Department of the West, headquartered in St. Louis, and later in field command in Virginia. She supported his controversial proclamation emancipating the slaves of Missourians bearing arms against the Union and stood by him through criticism of his policies and attempts to take over some of his command. At one point, she traveled to Washington to argue her husband's case before President Abraham Lincoln, but her efforts proved unsuccessful. John was eventually stripped of his command. Jessie wrote about the uncompleted campaign in a series of impassioned articles for the *Atlantic Monthly*, which were published in book form in 1863, titled *The Story of the Guard: A Chronicle of the War.*

During the later war years, the Frémonts returned to New York, where Jessie, who had been instrumental in establishing the Western Sanitary Commission in New York and St. Louis, was active in raising money and recruiting volunteers for Sanitary Commission hospitals in the West. Unwise railway and mining speculations brought financial hardship, which increased with John's unsuccessful run as a Radical Republican candidate for the presidency in 1864. In 1873, when John was forced to declare bankruptcy, Jessie turned to writing to support the family, which now included their three children and the daughter of a friend whom they had adopted. While living in a small house on Staten Island, Jessie produced a flood of reminiscences, travel sketches, and stories for leading magazines. The best of her work was collected in *A Year of American Travel* (1878), *Souvenirs of My Time* (1887), *Far-West Sketches* (1890), and *The Will and The Way Stories* (1891). She was also the principal author of her husband's *Memoirs of My Life* (1887).

Jessie Frémont spent her final years in Los Angeles, California, where, after her husband's death, she lived with her daughter in a house presented to her by the women of the city. She continued to write until two years before her death, at age 78, in 1902.

SOURCES:

James, Edward T., ed. *Notable American Women.* Cambridge, MA: The Belknap Harvard University Press, 1974.

McHenry, Robert, ed. *Famous American Women.* NY: Dover, 1983.

Randall, Ruth Painter. *I Jessie: A Biography of the Girl Who Married John Charles Frémont.* Boston, MA: Little Brown, 1963.

SUGGESTED READING:

Herr, Pamela, and Mary Lee Spence, eds. *The Letters of Jessie Benton Fremont.* Urbana, IL: University of Illinois, 1993.

COLLECTIONS:

The Frémont Papers, which include the letters and autobiographical writings by Jessie Frémont, are in the Bancroft Library, University of California, and in the Southwestern Museum in Los Angeles.

Barbara Morgan,
Melrose, Massachusetts

Fremstad, Olive (1871–1951)

Swedish-born American mezzo-soprano. Name variations: Olive Fremstadt. Born Anna Olivia Fremstad in Stockholm, Sweden, on March 14, 1871; died in Irvington, New York, on April 21, 1951; studied in Berlin with Lilli Lehmann.

Born in Stockholm, Sweden, Olive Fremstad received her early musical training as pianist, organist, and singer in Christiania, Norway (now Oslo), and continued to study music in Minneapolis, Minnesota, where her parents settled when she was 12 years old. In 1890, she studied as a contralto in New York City, and in 1893 she studied with the celebrated German singer *Lilli Lehmann, who trained her as a soprano. Fremstad made her debut in grand opera at Cologne in 1895, when she sang the role of Azucena in Verdi's *Il Trovatore.* She was a member of the Munich Opera from 1900 to 1903 and of the Metropolitan Opera Company, New York City, from 1903 to 1914; she also sang with many other important opera companies. Fremstad was particularly noted for her interpretation of Wagnerian roles, which included those of Venus in *Tannhaüser,* Kundry in *Parsifal,* and Brünnhilde in both *Siegfried* and *Götterdämmerung.* Her most successful part was that of Isolde in *Tristan und Isolde.* Frenstad's repertoire also included Carmen in Bizet's *Carmen* and Tosca in Puccini's *La Tosca;* and she was celebrated for her performances as Salome in Richard Strauss' opera of the same name.

$\mathcal{O}$live
$\mathcal{F}$remstad

French, Evangeline (1869–1960) and Francesca (1871–1960).

See joint entry under Cable, Mildred.

French "Witches"

(14th–16th centuries)

On August 9, 1390, two women, ❧ **Margot de la Barre** and ❧ **Marion la Droiturière**, were sentenced by the judges of the Châtelet in Paris to the pillory and then to be burned at the stake. Their case, carefully recorded in the *Registre du Châtelet de Paris* by the notary Aleaume Cachemarée, offers a telling example of the shift in attitudes toward sorcery that occurred as the Middle Ages drew to a close. Sorcerers—both men and women—who had long been a traditional part of the social fabric of their communities were increasingly finding themselves targets of the judicial system. Clever women skilled in divination, magic love philters and the uses of herbs, were now carried off to the torture chamber, where they were tormented into confessing their allegiances to the Devil and participation in a celebration of evil known as the witches' Sabbath. Under the condemnation of ecclesiastical and lay prosecutors, the formerly accepted figure of the sorcerer was now transformed into a demonic puppet of Satan.

In the case of Margot de la Barre and Marion la Droiturière, the two women were first interrogated at the end of July 1390. The accusation against them was the casting of a spell on Ainselin, the former lover of Marion, and his wife **Agnesot**. To regain her lover, Marion had been advised by a friend to share a drink with Ainselin, made of a few drops of her menstrual blood mixed with red wine; from Margot de la Barre she had obtained two recipes, the first based on herbs gathered during the magical night of Saint John, which was to provoke impotence in Ainselin with his wife. The second, intended to arouse his desire for Marion, involved roasting the testicles of a white rooster, grinding them into powder, and putting it into Ainselin's pillow for nine days before mixing it in his food and wine.

By themselves, these misdeeds, which were confessed by the accused at their first questioning, did not merit the death penalty. But after sessions in the torture chamber, both admitted to their abjuration of Christ and invocations of the Devil, crimes subject to redemption if confessed, but which still called for capital punishment.

A few months later, at the end of October 1390, two other women, known as skilled in divination and magic arts, similarly fell victims of the judiciary. ❧ **Jehenne de Brigue**, described in the *Registre* as a soothsayer, specialized in the recovery of lost objects, a respectable enough vocation in the Middle Ages. Some six years earlier, she had been approached by the priest of a neighboring village for aid in recovering a sum of money and a silver cross stolen from his church. It was not uncommon for a parish priest of the time to share his parishioners' beliefs in such a woman's gifts, as well as a deeper understanding of her social function. The priests themselves were mediators of the supernatural, endowed with powers of healing and exorcising evil spirits, and subject themselves to accusations of exercising magic.

What brought Jehenne de Brigue to trial at the Châtelet was an exchange of recipes of love and disenchantment with ❧ **Macette de Ruilly**, who was accused as her accomplice. Jehenne had shown Macette how to cast a spell on her husband, using three toads, fed with the milk of a woman and then tormented with pins, as well as a puppet made of wax and of the husband's hair melted in a copper pan. Macette, in return, was accused of helping Jehenne, who wanted to marry the father of her children; in this case, the melted wax was to be rubbed between the man's shoulders for nine nights, while he slept. Under torture, Jehenne admitted to having been introduced to the Devil, under the name of Haussibut, by her godmother, while Macette's account of invoking her personal demon, Lucifer, involved a curious mix of the magic recipes de-

❧ **Barre, Margot de la** (d. 1390)
French woman. Name variations: Du Coignet. Lover of Ainselin, tried and burned in 1390.

❧ **Droiturière, Marion la** (d. 1390)
French woman. Name variations: Droituriere or L'Estalee. Tried and burned in 1390.

❧ **Brigue, Jehenne de** (d. 1391)
French soothsayer. Name variations: Jehenna; La Cordière. Tried in 1390; died in 1391; married Hennequin Le Cordier.

❧ **Ruilly, Macette de** (d. 1391)
French woman. Tried in 1390; died in 1391; married Hennequin de Ruilly.

scribed above, along with the liturgically ortho-dox *Pater* and *Ave* and the sign of the cross.

Cachemarée's precise and detailed transcriptions of the trials of the four women are exemplary. Their intention was to produce test cases and judicial models for the "inquisitorial" procedure that had been gradually put in place by the ecclesiastical courts since the year 1230. Implemented at first as an exceptional method for use against heretics, the procedure had replaced the older "accusatory" method, which depended on accusation by a private citizen rather than an inquiry initiated by authority. With its main objective being to obtain the suspect's confession, the inquisitorial process was conducted in private, without defense counsel, and judicial torture played a central role. Appearing at the very end of the 14th century, the trials of the Châtelet are therefore historically revealing for demonstrating a new attitude toward witchcraft, in which the traditional magic arts tended to become demonized, and the clever woman who practiced them ostracized as an outcast. The process was to take decades, and the first actual witch hunts did not take place before the end of the 15th century. When they did, they became a symptom of a profound cultural mutation and the widening gap between popular traditions and the doctrines developed by a university-trained class.

*A*s far back as the records go, people had always been apt to imagine troublesome or eccentric old women as being linked in a mysterious and dangerous way with the earth and with the forces of nature, and as themselves uncanny, full of destructive power. But from the twelfth century onwards a new element appears—at first amongst monks, then amongst other literate elements in the population: the need to create a scapegoat for an unacknowledged hostility to Christianity.

—**Norman Cohn**

In 1431, the trial of **Joan of Arc* at Rouen represented just such a gap, when her judges wanted to discredit her crusade on behalf of the French king Charles VII, and against the English, by condemning her as heretic and sorcerer. In the indictment against her, Joan's participation in spring rituals with the youngsters of her village of Domrémy was construed as diabolical idolatry. On the second Sunday of Lent, it was the young Joan's habit to dance with them around a big oak called the "fairy tree" and to picnic at a healing fountain. In their efforts to cast suspicion on customs of pagan origin that were outside the control of the church, her prosecutors systematically distorted her answers, until the collective rite took on the appearance of a solitary act of conjuration. According to their version, she danced by herself at night, offering herb garlands hung off the branches of the oak to attract evil spirits.

Apart from the gap between traditional popular culture and learned official culture, the cases of Joan of Arc and the witches condemned at the Châtelet indicate the type of woman who now became susceptible to being targeted. While the virgin Joan might seem at first to have little in common with the sexually promiscuous Margot, Jehenne, and their friends, all are bound by their situations of being outside the bonds of marriage; all also behave as independent women, without the protection of a husband or, more precisely, of a family structure in the context of a well-defined community. Joan, leading an army dressed as a man, and in virtually every other aspect of her conduct, transgressed what was expected of her sex; Margot de La Barre went from towns to villages as a prostitute; neither Marion la Droiturière nor Jehenne de Brigue were officially married, and Macette was unfaithful to her husband with the parish priest. Following patterns of behavior that excluded them from the class of respectable women who complied to the sacred rules of marriage or else devoted themselves to monastic life, all became similarly vulnerable to slandering, marginality, and collective rape, and easy scapegoats for inquiries of heresy or witchcraft.

In 1439, less than a decade after the death of Joan, the case of **Catherine David** offers an example of another trend making its appearance at the end of the Middle Ages, when private conflicts brought into the hands of the inquisitor became transformed into an accusation of witchcraft. Following her father's disinheritance of her three sisters in her favor, Catherine was brought to trial on the word of the sisters, who claimed that their parent's decision had been made under the influence of a magical potion Catherine had prepared. According to the inquisitor's indictment, Catherine was under the influence of the demon Barrabas, thus transforming a domestic quarrel into a major crime of the Church.

In another case involving sexual promiscuity, **Martiale Espaze** was brought before the inquisitor in 1491, for conduct believed to have caused a series of deaths among children and domestic animals. By this time, at the end of the 15th century, attitudes toward witchcraft had evolved so that the stereotype was fully in place, of the witch murderer of children, who was a member of an underground diabolic sect conducting nightly meetings where the host was desecrated and the Devil worshiped.

Again, torture disclosed the accused's contacts with the Devil. Martiale admitted to encounters under different demonic shapes: a tall man named Robin with whom she had intercourse, or a goat when she met him at the Sabbath. The list of her confessed crimes also established her responsibility for the community's disasters. She had abjured Jesus and *Mary the Virgin, provoked the death of her neighbor's pigs, and exerted her malevolence against infants and children (the usual designated targets of witches). She was held responsible for the poisoning of an 18-month-old girl, lameness in another girl, casting a lethal spell on two baby boys in their cradle, and, finally, the bewitching of a neighboring woman to death. All these crimes, supposedly committed under the instructions of Satan's minion, were characteristic of recognized witches' work at the end of the 15th and throughout the 16th centuries. Martiale's account of the unholy Sabbath also conforms to the typical depiction of those hellish assignations, still widespread in modern-day representations. Her demon transports her nightly through the air to a place where women are gathered with their personal demons, dancing around a big fire. They pay homage to the Devil in the shape of a goat, with their flying broomsticks burning like candles.

Viewed in another way, Martiale's case defines those activities that transgress the fundamental values of society and traditional faith. Usually, there is a suggestion of ritual sex performed by the demons and other witches, without consideration of gender or family ties, and thereby violating the main societal taboos; rites of infanticide and cannibalism are further transgressions of what is most sacred for humanity, culminating in devil worship and abjuration in one's faith in God.

The prevalence of such conventions at the end of the Middle Ages—the ritualistic gatherings, witches' sects and worshipers of the Devil—bring certain questions to mind: If there were no such sects, what is the origin of the belief in them? Were they a consequence of popular fears, or the result of a growing obsession among clerics with the Devil and his demons?

David, Catherine
Name variations: Malavesse. Tried in 1439; married Jacques Blanc.

Espaze, Martiale
Married Jean Dumas; tried in 1475.

One part of the answer can be found in a treatise published by two Dominicans, Henry Institoris and James Sprenger, with papal approval, in 1486. The title, *The Witches' Hammer* (*Malleus Maleficarum*), clearly expresses the intention of its authors, who prepared it as a kind of textbook for inquisitors. After naming the evil deeds of witches under the influence of the Devil, they describe exorcisms and other means of protection; beyond that, their main objective is to provide inquisitors with the means for a correct trial that will unmask the culprit. The *Malleus Maleficarum* had an enormous influence, appearing in at least 34 editions before the 17th century. It was referred to and quoted in trials of both Protestants and Catholics and served as a model for many subsequent treatises.

One of the effects of the *Malleus* was to reinforce the view of women as dangerous forces of great power, able to reduce men to impotency. Institoris and Sprenger attribute much importance to sex-related crimes, the relationship of witches to incubi and succubi, and the procreation of children through the collection and injection of semen; women are viewed as more likely to be witches than men, and men are considered to be more often bewitched than women.

With the invention of the printing press, the treatises elaborating the principles of the diabolic witch theory became widespread. Some of the ideas thus disseminated could be traced back to pagan beliefs in ceremonial magic, evil women, and nocturnal flights, which were useful to the inquisitors for the prosecution of heretics when combined with fears of Devil influence. During the great period of the European witch hunts, lasting from the late 15th to the end of the 17th centuries, the practices that came under suspicion were of both popular and learned origin. To give two examples, both the rituals of the Sabbath and the accusations of infanticide and cannibalism can be seen as revivals of ancient stereotypes, formerly used against early Christians, medieval heretics, and Jews, all of whom were held responsible at one time or other for secret nightly meetings, sexual orgies, infanticide and ritual anthropophagy of babies. Treatises perpetuating these stereotypes, and linked to Satanic sects, date from the beginning of the Christian era. In 1575, pagan rituals were at the root of a trial held in the northern Italian province of Friuli, where the accused described their ancestral beliefs. They maintained that certain men and women could travel to the world of the dead during an ecstatic trance, often induced by narcotic drugs, where they could do battle against evil spirits to ensure the fertility of crops.

In 1682, witch hunts in France finally ended with a royal ordinance issued by Louis XIV forbidding prosecution for witchcraft. By that time, those who had been suspected or condemned are said to have numbered in the hundreds of thousands, a figure impossible to assess accurately and probably greatly exaggerated. Without question, however, the inquisitors' methods had helped to multiply the accusations; torture could make it difficult to resist denouncing even one's relatives and neighbors.

Viewing the trends identifiable in such records, the first question to arise concerns the predominance of women among the prosecuted. One explanation could be a new criminalization of women, previously considered the responsibility of their fathers or husbands in the case of standard crimes like violent aggression or theft. Significantly, however, most of the women labeled as witches also correspond to a specific stereotype, which identifies witchcraft as a rural phenomenon as well as a sex-related crime. A great percentage of the accused were old women, often widows, and living in the countryside. Freed from both patriarchal control and protection, they were easy targets, while their role in the transmission of traditional wisdom and culture tended to be seen by both lay and clerical authorities as associated with superstition. Both aspects contributed to an image of old women as potentially dangerous and threatening, and as such they became perfect scapegoats in a profoundly changing world.

In the difficult transition from the medieval to the modern period, as a predominantly rural culture became subjected to urban values, witch hunts can thus be considered a symptom of the times. Politically and socially, as the bonds of community and family were challenged by new power structures, and societies grew increasingly centralized and bureaucratic, those in charge attempted to impose strict controls on beliefs and behaviors. Churches tried to eradicate superstitions and strands of animist belief, and the absolutist monarchy in France was increasingly disseminating its authority through civil servants. Finally, for those feeling the threat of witchcraft, the judicial system provided both its doctrine of diabolism and a procedure of accusation, supported by the infallible techniques offered by the treatises on demonology for detecting Satan at work. Since, for instance, the Devil made certain parts of the witch's body insensitive to pain, such a Satanic spot could be systematically searched for with the help of long needles; another method of proof was to throw bound suspects into water: one who was guilty of a pact with the devil would float, while the innocent sank.

In such a context of transformation, the old woman labeled a witch lived at the margins of society, designated a deviant by a community in the process of redefining its values and norms. She symbolized the local, traditional way of life then yielding to a more centralized law and order. During the 16th century and the first half of the 17th, the social emphasis was on the necessity for women to find their place within patriarchal families, which were the model for the society as a whole. Authority was seen as coming from God, the rulers of the Church and the king, from which it passed to male heads of families; and the role of female healers was being overtaken by university-trained male professionals.

Swept up and crushed by the waves of such transformation, hundreds of victims were deprived of protection by their lower-class status. In contrast to these mostly rural cases, however, there were also a few instances of women of aristocratic or high bourgeoisie stature who became celebrated for their relations with the Devil. In 1611, there was the case of ✥➤ **Madeleine Demandols de la Palud**, a young nun in Aix-en-Provence, who claimed she had been bewitched by her confessor, Louis Gaufridy. Madeleine was subjected to several public sessions of exorcism, and the priest was tried and executed. Afterward, Madeleine lived a saintly life on her estate as a recluse, until February 1653, when she in turn found herself accused of bewitchment. Held responsible for the strange illness of a neighbor's daughter, who was struck with convulsions and vomited pins and straw, Madeleine was indicted by a tribunal for sacrilege and casting an evil spell and condemned to life imprisonment.

In the city of Nancy, another famous episode of diabolic possession occurred from 1618 to 1625, when ✥➤ **Élizabeth of Ranfaing**, a young widow, endured sessions of public exorcism leading to the denouncement, among others, of her doctor, who was burned at the stake in 1622. In 1631, Élizabeth founded a congregation for repentant prostitutes, which was condemned by the pope as a sect shortly before her death in 1649.

In 1632, in the small town of Loudun, near Poitiers, the convent of the Ursulines became famous when it was struck by an epidemic of diabolic possession among its nuns, beginning with the prioress, ❧▸ **Jeanne des Anges**. The prioress then named a priest of the area, Urbain Grandier, who was renowned for his profligacy, and the possessed women appeared for months before fascinated crowds, in their convulsions and numerous attempts at exorcism. After the torture of Grandier, sentenced to death on August 18, 1634, the public displays of possession continued for another three years while Jeanne's ordeal developed into a successful struggle with the Demon, demonstrated in a series of mystical trials. In 1635, she displayed her palms, marked with red stigmata, to the populace; in 1638, she began performing cures with a holy ointment of her own composition.

Beginning in March 1643, the convent of the town of Louviers, in Normandy, became the site of an outburst of possession cases similar to those at Loudun. After revelations made by several nuns in the course of exorcism, one of them, ❧▸ **Madeleine Bavent**, was sentenced to life imprisonment by the bishop of Evreux. Again, the person named responsible for the possessions was a priest, Mathurin Picard, who had been Madeleine's spiritual director, and had since died, but was exhumed for investigation. Picard's vicar, Thomas Boullé, was also later incriminated. A legal action taken by Picard's family led to years of controversy between those under the direction of the bishop, who accepted the possession theory, and a group of skeptics who were mainly doctors. On August 21, 1647, the saga ended when a tribunal sentenced the surviving priest to the stake; the nuns were dispersed to other convents, and Madeleine Bavent remained in jail.

The notoriety of these incidents helped to induce other episodes sharing similar characteristics, of struggle with the demon, exhibitions of its manifestations, competition among the exorcists and—most interestingly—debates between believers in the devil and skeptics. As members of the medical profession became involved, their presence indicated a new tendency toward a search for rational explanations. Medical interpretations, of melancholia or hysteria, now came into use to explain the nuns' behavior, and

by the end of the 17th century, such "natural" or "profane" explanations brought the criminalization of witchcraft to an end. But the determining factor in the passage of the royal decree of 1682, abolishing witchcraft as a crime, was also the most sensational criminal case of the century. Known as the Affair of the Poisons, it culminated in the arrests of hundreds in 1679, when 34 persons were sentenced to death and executed.

The affair was the last and most famous of several cases involving the higher circles of the aristocracy, reaching right up to the monarchy itself. They began as early as 1617, under the young king Louis XIII, when ❧▸ **Leonora Galigaï**, the close friend and maid of the queen mother, *Marie de Medici, fell victim to the political rivalries between her mistress, the king, and certain lords. One issue at stake involved the Italian origin of Marie de Medici, who raised Leonora and her husband, Concini, to high positions in the kingdom. Concini had become marshal of Ancre, but once he fell victim to a plot led by Louis XIII himself, nothing could protect his wife, who was accused of witchcraft and executed on the grounds of cures she took against her constant bad health.

In the case of Leonora Galigaï, witchcraft was clearly put forward as justification for a political trial; it was probably an important component in the indictments in two scandalous episodes during the reign of Louis XIV, both known as "affairs of the poisons." The first occurred in 1676, when *Marie de Brinvilliers was

---

❧▸ **Demandols de la Palud, Madeleine**
Main victim in an episode of possession lasting 1609–1611.

❧▸ **Ranfaing, Élizabeth of** (d. 1649).
Name variations: Elizabeth de Ranfaing. Victim of possession in case lasting 1618–1625.

❧▸ **des Anges, Jeanne**
Mother of the Ursulines of Loudun, possessed, along with others in her order, in 1634.

❧▸ **Bavent, Madeleine**
Accused of witchcraft at Louviers in 1642.

❧▸ **Galigaï, Leonora** (c. 1570–1617)
Close friend of Marie de Médici. Name variations: Leonora Galigai. Born around 1570; tried and executed in 1617; married Concino Concini, marshal of Ancre.

---

found guilty of having poisoned her father and two brothers with the help of her lover. Her trial brought to light the existence in Paris of a ring of poison dealers, the magnitude of which was revealed during the second "Affair of the Poisons," beginning in 1679 with the incrimination of ✤ Catherine Deshayes, Madame Monvoisin, also known as La Voisin. Three years of inquiry and 210 sessions of a special tribunal brought to light the numerous members of the higher nobility, as well as ordinary folk, who applied to La Voisin for fortunetelling, drugs, poisons and black masses. La Voisin was burned to death on February 22, 1680, in the Place de Grèves. It was the alleged participation of the *Marquise de Montespan, however, the favorite mistress of the king, which brought the prosecutions to an end. When word circulated that the marquise had used love charms to win the king's love, had taken part in black masses, and had tried to poison her rival and Louis himself, it took the king's personal intervention to protect her.

Rational explanations were meanwhile gaining ground over the supernatural, but belief in sorcery, possession and diabolism was not at an end. The last trial to actually involve accusations of witchery took place in 1731, in Aix-en-Provence. ✤ Catherine Cadière had been seduced by her spiritual director, Jean-Baptiste Girard, a Jesuit, and underwent an abortion in 1729. Her confession to her brothers led to a series of judicial battles between the Jesuits and Catherine, involving mutual accusations of bewitchment and possession, which some of the judges were still inclined to consider on criminal grounds. A divided tribunal resulted in a double acquittal, arousing the indignation of the great 19th-century historian Jules Michelet for the leniency it showed toward the debaucher.

SOURCES:

Aubenas, Roger. *La sorcière et l'Inquisiteur: Épisode de l'Inquisition en Provence (1439)*. Aix-en-Provence: La pensée universitaire, 1959.

✤ Deshayes, Catherine (d. 1680)

French poisoner. Name variations: Madame Monvoisin; Catherine Monvoisin; La Voisin. Burned at the stake on February 22, 1680; main figure accused in the Affair of the Poisons, lasting 1679–1682.

✤ Cadière, Catherine (b. 1709)

French woman. Born in 1709; went to trial in 1731.

Barrett, Wilfred Phillip. *The Trial of Jeanne d'Arc*. NY: Gotham House, 1932.

Bligny-Bondurand, M. "Procédure contre une sorcière de Boucoiran (Gard), 1491," in *Bulletin historique et philologique*. 1907, pp. 380–407.

Mandrou, Robert. *Magistrats et sorciers en France au XVIIe siècle*. Paris: Seuil, 1980.

Registre criminel du Châtelet de Paris du 6 septembre 1389 au 18 mai 1392. Edited by H. Duplès-Agier. 2 vols. Paris: Lehure, 1861 and 1864.

Sprenger, Jacob, and Heinrich Institoris, *Malleus Maleficarum*. Trans. by Montague Summers. London: Reider, 1928 (reprinted NY: Dover, 1970).

SUGGESTED READING:

Cohn, Norman. *Europe's Inner Demons: An inquiry inspired by the Great Witch-hunt*. London: Chatto-Heinemann, 1975.

Hester, Marianne. *Lewd Women and Wicked Witches: A Study of the Dynamics of Male Domination*. London: Routledge, 1992.

Kieckhefer, Richard. *European Witch Trials: Their Foundations in Popular and Learned Culture, 1300–1500*. Berkeley, CA: 1974.

Larner, Christina. *Witchcraft and Religion*. Oxford: Blackwell, 1984.

Quaife, G.F. *Godly Zeal and Furious Rage: The Witch in Early Modern Europe*. London and Sydney: Croom Helm, 1987.

Madeleine Jeay,
Professor of Medieval Literature,
McMaster University, Hamilton, Canada

Freni, Mirella (1935—)

Italian lyric soprano. Born Mirella Fregni on February 27, 1935, in Modena, Italy; studied at Mantua and at Bologna Conservatory with Ettore Campogalliani; married Leone Magiera; married Nicolai Ghiaurov (a bass), in 1981; children: (first marriage) one daughter.

Made debut in Modena (1955), Covent Garden (1961), Teatro alla Scala (1962), Metropolitan Opera (1965); appeared at Salzburg (1966–72 and 1974–80).

Known for her performances of Handel and Mozart, Mirella Freni established her operatic reputation performing works from the 18th and 19th centuries. In 19th-century repertoire, Freni performed French, Italian, or Russian roles with equal aplomb. One of her best roles was as Tatyana in Tchaikovsky's *Eugene Onegin*, described by one critic as "the Tatyana of one's dreams." She was equally praised for performances of Verdi's *Aïda*. Her rich tone and intelligent phrasing were hallmarks of her art. Freni brought great energy to her portrayals, whether they were light and cheerful or dark and tragic. She sang recitative as if it meant something, with real pathos in her voice. Freni's acting abilities were considerable and enabled her to bring characters to life.

John Haag,
Athens, Georgia

Frenkel-Brunswik, Else

(1908–1958)

Jewish-Austrian psychologist. Born Else Frenkel in Poland in 1908; died of drug overdose in 1958; daughter of Abraham (a bank owner) and Helene (Gelernter) Frenkel; University of Vienna, Ph.D. in psychology; married Egon Brunswik, a psychologist (died 1955); no children.

The author of *The Authoritarian Personality*, a pioneering synthesis of social psychology and psychoanalysis, Else Frenkel-Brunswik introduced American behaviorists to the nuances of psychoanalysis. Unfortunately, her brilliant career was cut short by her suicide at the age of 49.

She was born Else Frenkel in Poland in 1908. When she was six, her family escaped Jewish persecution in Poland and settled in Vienna. At age 22, she earned a Ph.D. in psychology at the University of Vienna and, against her parent's wishes, married her psychology professor Egon Brunswik, who was not Jewish. She stayed on at the University with her husband, working as an assistant professor until the Nazi invasion of Austria in 1938. At that time, she and her husband fled to the United States, where Egon had secured a position at the University of California at Berkeley. Although Frenkel-Brunswik could not be considered for an academic position because of rules against nepotism, she worked out of the university as a lecturer and researcher in psychoanalysis, a relatively new subject to American psychologists. In the 1940s, she and three other researchers undertook a ground-breaking study on prejudice, which was underwritten by the American Jewish Committee in 1945. The project culminated in the publication of *The Authoritarian Personality* (1950), which presented an extremely controversial model of the relationship between ideology and child rearing. Else Frenkel-Brunswik's continuing work on prejudice in children and on aging was interrupted by her husband's illness and subsequent suicide in 1955. She was so devastated by the loss that even a position as a full professor at Berkeley and a Fulbright scholarship were of no consolation. She was found dead of a drug overdose in 1958.

Barbara Morgan,
Melrose, Massachusetts

Freud, Anna (1895–1982)

Pioneering psychoanalyst who made important theoretical contributions to child development and ego psychology and established a model for training analysts that remains the standard. Born Anna Freud in

Vienna, Austria, on December 3, 1895; died in London, England, on October 8, 1982; daughter of Sigmund Freud (doctor, founder of psychoanalysis) and Martha Bernays (homemaker); graduated Cottage Lyzeum, Vienna, 1912; LL.D., Clark University, 1950; Sc.D., Jefferson Medical College, Philadelphia, 1964; LL.D., University of Sheffield, England, 1966; lived with her lifelong companion and collaborator, Dorothy Burlingham.

Commenced analysis with her father (1918); began psychoanalyzing adults and children and delivered her first paper before the Vienna Psychoanalytic Society (1922); met Dorothy Burlingham and became a training analyst at the Vienna Psychoanalytic Institute (1925); established the Jackson Nursery for children (1937); immigrated to London (1938); established the wartime nurseries (1941); opened the Hampstead Child Therapy Clinic (1951).

Publications: Introduction to the Technic of Child Analysis *(1927);* The Ego and the Mechanisms of Defence *(1936);* Infants Without Families *(with Dorothy Burlingham, 1944);* Normality and Pathology in Childhood *(1965).*

When an aging Sigmund Freud needed to find a guardian to protect his most important

Mirella Freni

creation—psychoanalysis—he turned to Anna Freud, the youngest of his six children. For more than 50 years, Anna Freud worked tirelessly to secure the future of psychoanalysis and safeguard its principles. The effects of her work are far reaching. As a gifted clinician and theoretician, her work in ego psychology and child development remain a part of the foundation upon which current psychoanalytic thought is built. And in the schools and research centers she established, she trained and influenced a generation of future analysts.

In 1895, the year of Anna Freud's birth, her father was an undistinguished neurologist who was plagued by physical ailments and financial worries. Sigmund Freud was only beginning to formulate his theories about the origins of hysteria and the existence of an unconscious. (The publication of *The Interpretation of Dreams* was still four years away.) Anna's mother **Martha Bernays Freud** was exhausted mentally and physically from the demands of the five children she had given birth to over the previous seven years. When their sixth child, Anna, arrived on December 3rd, it was with heavy hearts that the baby was welcomed into the house.

*S*he was a strong moral and intellectual force in psychoanalysis for half a century.

—Robert Coles

That Anna Freud's mother was ambivalent toward her youngest child from the start is evident from her behavior. She chose not to nurse the baby as she had her previous children, and took her first vacation away from the family when Anna was only ten months old. Martha Freud was also a strict, idiosyncratic disciplinarian. "My mother observed no rules, she made her own rules," Anna Freud later remarked. Her mother's remote harshness caused the young Anna to seek comfort from her beloved nursemaid, **Josefine Cihlaiz**, and from her father, whom she adored.

As a young child, Anna Freud was adventurous and mischievous, traits that her father evidently encouraged. When Anna was two, Sigmund wrote to his friend Wilhelm Fleiss: "Recently Anna complained that [her eldest sister] Mathilde had eaten all the apples and demanded that [Mathilde's] belly be slit open (as happened to the wolf in the fairy tale of the little goat). She is turning into a charming child."

Anna Freud attended good private schools and graduated from high school at 15. Though she had been an imaginative, brilliant student, her professional ambitions were modest. She de-

cided to become a schoolteacher and in 1914, at age 19, began an elementary school apprenticeship. For six years, she worked as an assistant and then as a certified teacher. She was genuinely fond of children and immensely interested in the way they learned. That keen interest would remain, and her later work in child psychoanalysis was always marked by a pedagogical imperative.

When Anna's school schedule allowed, she traveled with her father on the Continent and abroad, acting as his companion and secretary. She had always loved her father with a single-minded devotedness; not surprisingly, she began taking an interest in psychoanalysis. She read her father's books and discussed psychoanalytic ideas and methods with him. During the war, she began writing German translations of English psychoanalytic articles in an effort to help her father keep the psychoanalytic journals in print. Anna Freud was quickly absorbing her father's work and in the process was becoming his closest, most trusted confidante. Perhaps most significantly, she became his patient, a training analysand, in October 1918 when she was 23 years old.

Anna Freud discontinued teaching at the elementary school in 1920 and gave herself over fully to the study of psychoanalysis. She attended lectures at the Vienna Psychoanalytic Society and accompanied other analysts, former patients, and students of her father on ward rounds at the Psychiatric Clinic of the Vienna General Hospital. Later she remarked on her education in psychoanalysis: "We were trained by our personal analysts, [and] by extensive reading, by our own unsupervised efforts with our first patients, and by lively interchange of ideas and discussion of problems with elders and contemporaries."

In 1920, she attended a lecture by Siegfried Bernfeld which had an enormous impact on her life. Bernfeld had initiated a project called the Baumgarten Children's Home which provided food and shelter to Viennese Jewish war orphans. Anna Freud was deeply impressed with his work and realized that his interests in working with children, particularly those in crisis, mirrored her own. As an apprentice teacher, she had worked in a *Kinderhort,* a day care for working-class children, and more recently she had performed some volunteer work with young victims of the war. She initiated a study group that included, among others, Bernfeld and August Aichhorn. Aichhorn, a former teacher like Anna, was pioneering a new approach of applying psychoanalytic techniques to his work with delinquent adolescents. Aichhorn became a men-

tor of sorts for Anna Freud, and with him she began an informal apprenticeship.

In 1922, Anna Freud began analyzing children and adults. In May of that year, she delivered her first paper, "Beating Fantasies and Daydreams," to the Vienna Psychoanalytic Society. The paper identified the repression of the "love fantasy" a child possesses for his/her father as the origin of post-Oedipal beating fantasies, and seems to have been based largely on her own analysis with her father. Shortly after delivering the paper, Sigmund Freud suffered the initial symptoms of an illness that required serious medical attention, and Anna Freud's analysis was suspended until 1924, when it resumed for another year or so.

In 1925, Anna Freud encountered for the first time the woman who would become her lifelong companion and collaborator, **Dorothy Burlingham**. Burlingham, accompanied by her four children, had arrived in Vienna from the United States as a training analysand of Sigmund Freud. Her eldest child underwent analysis with Anna Freud, as

did subsequently all the Burlingham children. The two women became inseparable, eventually sharing a house and a life together. Anna had never shown the slightest romantic interest in any man; her affection and loyalties had remained directed to her father exclusively. Yet she loved children and seemed to desire companionship and a familial arrangement. By all accounts, the relationship was not homosexual in nature, but was "the ideal friendship" as Anna Freud referred to it, loving and nurturing, and one that offered her the challenging dual role of analyst and stepparent to the Burlingham children.

That same year, Anna joined the executive board of the Vienna Psychoanalytic Institute and began work as a training analyst. The Institute was set up by the Vienna Psychoanalytic Society to function as a training academy where students could systematically learn psychoanalytic theory and techniques. For Anna Freud, herself a lay analyst with no formal medical background, establishing the place of lay analysts in psychoanalysis was of paramount importance. A debate was then raging within the international psychoanalytic community over the advisability of placing psychoanalysis in the hands of those who did not possess a medical degree. When in 1927 she was elected secretary of the International Psychoanalytic Association, she became a key player in the debate.

As a training analyst at the Institute, Anna Freud had the opportunity to teach classes in child development to nursery and primary school teachers. She hoped to influence education by bringing the principles of psychoanalysis to bear on pedagogical practice. In 1927, with the help of Dorothy Burlingham and another friend, **Eva Rosenfeld**, Freud initiated her first independent educational experiment: a private school where young children could learn in a psychoanalytically informed environment. Future analysts such as Erik Erikson and Peter Blos taught there.

Her first book, *Introduction to the Technic of Child Analysis,* was published that same year. In it, she set about establishing the parameters of child analysis, putting forth new theories and techniques based on her own clinical work. The book called for a modification of the classic psychoanalytic technique of dream interpretation and free association pioneered by her father in favor of a technique of analysis which sought to exert an educational influence over the child. She defended this strategy by emphasizing the important differences between the psyches of adults and of children, namely the structure of the superego (which Anna Freud believed was weak in a child and subject to external influences), the inability of a child to develop a transference neurosis (due to its extreme dependence on its parents and environment), and the inability of the child to perceive itself as sick. "Everything is lacking in the situation of the child which seems indispensable to that of the adult: insight into illness, the voluntary decision to be cured and the will to be cured."

Anna Freud went a step further and encouraged therapists to try to gain the child's confidence. She stressed the importance of working with the parents, thus extending the work that is accomplished in the analytic hour to the home and school. These views differed sharply from the theories being developed by *Melanie Klein, a child psychoanalyst who had worked in Berlin and was now practicing in England. Klein applied Sigmund Freud's classic psychoanalytic technique to children by analyzing and interpreting their play. Moreover, Klein believed children could develop a transference

neurosis and that analyzing it was an important part of the analysis. Throughout *Introduction to the Technic of Child Analysis,* Freud systematically refuted Klein's theories using her own case histories and novel theories of child development. The debate between Freud and Klein would eventually move to England and play out more dramatically at the British Psycho-Analytical Society.

The publication of the book as well as her subsequent lectures based on it in Berlin and Budapest established Anna Freud's reputation in the international psychoanalytic community. Freud's techniques and theories of child analysis (along with those of her colleagues Aichhorn and Bernfeld) came to be known as the "Vienna School" and quickly dominated Continental Europe and America. The Vienna School from its inception was marked by pedagogical interests and involved in efforts to help delinquents and working-class children. Part of the efforts of Freud and her colleagues was to bring psychoanalysis out of the parlors of the bourgeois and into the tenements of the poor. A belief that parental and environmental factors influence child development and a conviction that altering environments can improve psychic development of children were hallmarks of the Vienna school.

Freud continued with her enormous work load of psychoanalysis, teaching and writing despite increasing political upheaval in Vienna. In 1935, at the age of 40, she began work on her most ambitious project, *The Ego and the Mechanisms of Defence.* The book, published in May 1936 on Sigmund Freud's 80th birthday, is a major study of the ego's activity, particularly in adolescence, and expands the concepts of the ego, id and superego.

In *The Ego and the Mechanisms of Defence,* Anna Freud explores the conflicts that arise when the instinctual drive of the id comes into direct conflict with the ego, the psychic apparatus that experiences and reacts to the outside world and is governed by the conscience (or superego). She discusses the various mechanisms and effects of the ego's defense and cites two examples in particular: first, "identification with the aggressor" in which "by impersonating the aggressor [an outside anxiety-object], assuming his attributes or imitating his aggression, the child transforms himself from the person threatened into the person who makes the threats"; and second, "altruistic surrender," a projection of dangerous or forbidden wishes onto other people. The book is still considered one of the standard works in psychoanalysis and remains her most important theoretical contribution.

In February 1937, Freud established the Jackson Nursery for children under the age of two. The school admitted children from the poorest families in Vienna and provided these desperate youngsters with a nurturing environment. In addition to its charitable aim, the nursery offered Freud and Burlingham the opportunity to observe child development and behavior outside a clinical or laboratory setting. The childcare experiment came to an end in March of 1938 when Hitler invaded Vienna and the nursery was shut down. The Gestapo raided the Freud home on March 22, and Anna Freud was taken in for questioning, though she was quickly released. The Freuds realized that escape from Vienna was necessary. Psychoanalysts from Berlin and Vienna had already fled the Continent and resettled in London, finding refuge at the British Psycho-Analytical Society. On June 4, the Freuds left Vienna for England.

Anna Freud and her family settled at 20 Maresfield Garden in Hampstead where she would live the rest of her life. She spent much of the first year analyzing patients and caring for her father who was now in the advanced stages of cancer. (Sigmund Freud would die on September 23, 1939.)

In 1938, at the request of the head of the East London School district, Anna Freud gave a series of three public lectures on psychoanalysis. The lectures were received enthusiastically by London educators as well as by the band of Viennese emigre analysts. Certain members of the British Psycho-Analytical Society were less impressed. The theories of Melanie Klein dominated the intellectual life of the Society. Klein, however, had recently come under fire from some members of the Society for "unorthodox" views. The influx of emigre analysts from the Continent, particularly the appearance of Anna Freud, added to the friction, and the old theoretical debate between Freud and Klein flared up again. Eventually, unpleasant ideological disputes over training methods broke out at the British Psycho-Analytical Society. A compromise with the Kleinians seemed impossible and a split occurred in the Society, from which Freud attempted to distance herself.

In January 1941, she opened The Children's Rest Center, an evacuation residence for working-class children. By summer, she was operating two more centers: A Babies' Rest Center in Hampstead and an evacuation center for older children in Essex. In the wartime nurseries, Freud and Burlingham observed firsthand the effects of institutional life and maternal separation on children.

Based on her observations, Anna Freud became convinced that children's development depends less on instinctual repression (as her father had believed) and more on their ability to form attachments to adults. In particular, she believed the bond between mother and child was crucial, and this theory set her on a course of pioneering a more mother-centered therapeutic approach. Within a year, Freud had restructured the nursery into family-like groups composed of four or five children and one "mother." Under the new arrangement, the children thrived. (Freud's family grouping system was later incorporated into postwar British childcare legislation.)

This emphasis on family was based, in part, on a theory of Aichhorn's that children brought up in a family setting fared much better than those raised in institutions. Anna Freud arrived at the same conclusion and attributed delays in language development and toilet training to the negative effects of institutional life on children. The institutional child, she noted "is at a disadvantage whenever the emotional tie to the mother or to the family is the mainspring of development."

Anna Freud and Dorothy Burlingham elaborated on their approach to institutional life in the 1942 booklet, "Young Children in War-time: A Year's Work in a Residential War Nursery." It was later expanded into a book, *Infants Without Families: The Case For and Against Residential Nurseries,* and published in 1944.

Freud's wartime nurseries closed in the summer of 1945, and she stopped analyzing children in 1949. But, in 1951, she opened the Hampstead Child Therapy Clinic which became one of the most famous training and research centers in the world. As with Freud's earlier projects, the emphasis was on research into normal and abnormal childhood development based on the direct observation of children. Services at the Hampstead Clinic included psychoanalysis and training, a well-baby clinic, a kindergarten for working-class children, and a research unit. Freud devoted her time to training analysts, supervising the clinic's activities, writing and lecturing in the United States.

Based on her work with the wartime nurseries and on the research at the Hampstead Clinic, Anna Freud concluded that development involves gradual mastery of the id by the ego, or "the socialization of the drives." Although she believed that the presence of the mother was crucial to the success of this process, she shied away from identifying the mother as the root of all developmental problems.

Freud identified "lines of development" that constituted psychological growth, including gradual independence from the mother, maturation of drives and ego, and adaptation to the environment and object relations. She believed pathology in children was manifested in arrested development and produced not conflict but defects in a child's psychic structure and personality. She urged analysts to pay attention to these lines of development and not focus entirely on unconscious drives and ego functions. Anna Freud used this model in developing the Hampstead Diagnostic Profile which assessed pathology along developmental lines rather than by reference to adult psychiatric categories. Another important contribution of the Hampstead Clinic was the Hampstead Index, which aggregated individual case material thus providing "a collective psychoanalytic memory" of clinical examples of transference, acting out, reactions to interpretations and so on.

In the early 1960s, Freud's sphere of influence broadened to the area of childcare policy when she was invited to participate in seminars in family law at Yale University. Two books based on these seminars, *Beyond the Best Interests of the Child* and *Before the Best Interests of the Child*, were published, recommending child custody decisions be based on psychological rather than biological ties and that government minimize its interference in family matters.

Anna Freud suffered a stroke in March 1981 which seriously curtailed her activity. She remained confined to her home under the care of relatives and former students until her death on October 8, 1982, at the age of 86.

SOURCES AND SUGGESTED READING:

Coles, Robert. *Anna Freud: The Dream of Psychoanalysis.* Reading: Addison-Wesley, 1992.

Freud, Anna. *The Writings of Anna Freud.* Vols 1–8, London: Hogarth. Vol 1: *The Introduction to Psychoanalysis* (1927), 1974; Vol 2: *The Ego and the Mechanisms of Defence*, 1936; Vol 3: *Infants Without Families* (1944), 1968; Vol 4: *Indications for Child Analysis and Other Essays* (1945–1956), 1968; Vol 5: *Research at the Hampstead Child Therapy Clinic and Other Papers* (1956–65), 1969; Vol 6: *Normality and Pathology in Childhood* 1965; Vol 7: *Problems of Psychoanalytic Technique and Therapy* (1966–70), 1971; Vol 8: *Psychoanalytic Psychology of Normal Development* (1970–80), 1982.

Sayers, Janet. *Mothers of Psychoanalysis.* NY: W.W. Norton, 1991.

Young-Bruehl, Elizabeth. *Anna Freud.* NY: Summit, 1988.

Suzanne Smith,
freelance writer and editor, Decatur, Georgia

Freund, Gisèle (1912—)

German-born French photographer. Name variations: Gisele Freund. Born in Berlin, Germany, in 1912; studied sociology and art history, Albert-Ludwigs-Universität Freiburg, Breisgau, Germany, 1932–33; studied at the Sorbonne, France, 1933–36, receiving Ph.D. in sociology and art; married Pierre Blum, in 1937 (divorced 1948).

Became a naturalized citizen of France (1936); moved to Lot, France, to escape Nazis (1940–42); was photographer and assistant film producer in Argentina and Chile with the Louis Jouvet Theatre Company (1943–44); worked for France Libre, Argentina (1944–45); lived in New York City (1947–49); lived and worked in Mexico (1950–52); became a member of Magnum Photos in Paris (1947–54); honored with the Grand Prix National des Arts, France (1980).

Born in Germany in 1912, Gisèle Freund arrived in Paris in 1933 to study sociology and the history of art. She underwrote her schooling with portraits and photo-journalism taken with a small Leica, a present from her father. In 1936, Freund received her doctorate at the Sorbonne and saw her first published photographs appear in *Life* magazine. She soon became known for her photo portraits, many in color as early as 1938, of literary and artistic greats, including James Joyce, Jean-Paul Sartre, *Colette, *Virginia Woolf, *Elsa Triolet, *Sylvia Beach, André Malraux, and Matisse. As a freelance photojournalist for *Life, Weekly Illustrated, Picture-Post,* and *Paris Match,* Freund produced photoessays on everyone from unemployed workers to *Evita Peron. Her books include *Photography and Society, The World and My Camera, Three Days with Joyce,* and *Gisèle Freund: Photographer.*

Freundlich, Emmy (1878–1948)

Austrian Social Democratic leader and women's rights activist who advocated social reforms in cooperatives, women's suffrage, and adult education. Born Emma Kögler in Aussig, Bohemia, Austria-Hungary (now Usti, Czech Republic), on June 25, 1878; died in New York City on March 16, 1948; daughter of Adolf Kögler and Emma Kögler; had sister Martha and brother Karl; married Leo Freundlich (a Social Democratic journalist), in 1900; children: Gertrude Freundlich; Hertha Freundlich.

Born into an elite German-speaking family in the city of Aussig, Bohemia, Emmy Kögler was far removed from the poverty and insecurity of the workers who toiled in the factories of her hometown and other industrial centers of the Austro-Hungarian monarchy. Her father, whom Emmy deeply respected for his energy and achievements, was a successful engineer whose career had been linked to the growth of railroads and industry in Bohemia. Adolf Kögler was also deeply involved in local politics, being a leader of the Liberals in his city; he was eventually elected the mayor of Aussig. Despite the family's affluence, Emmy (the name she would always be known by) and her siblings were brought up in a simple if not spartan environment that emphasized the virtues of studiousness and service.

At 13, Emmy was sent to a girls' boarding school with a reputation for its strictness; her life's path was to be one of middle-class propriety and, eventually, a "good" marriage. Emmy regarded her regimen irrelevant and her classmates frivolous, spending much of her free time voraciously reading, particularly about politics (at age 11, she became a confirmed newspaper reader). Her youth ended in 1895 with the death of her father. Devastated, Emmy's mother died the next year, and at the age of 18 Emmy became the head of her family of three orphans.

By 1899, Emmy had spent an extended period in Vienna and now viewed Aussig as being too provincial for her expanding intellectual interests, which centered around the radical reforms advocated by the Social Democratic Party. She had also met and fallen in love with Leo Freundlich, a Social Democratic journalist. As editor of Mährisch-Schönberg's *Volkswacht,* one of the party's provincial Moravian newspapers, Freundlich was able to secure the publication of Emmy's first article. In view of the hostility of Emmy's extended family to her relationship with Leo Freundlich, to whom they objected because he was both Jewish and an ardent Marxist, the couple eloped and in 1900 were married far away from Central Europe, in Gretna Green, Scotland.

Although Emmy Freundlich was busy raising two daughters over the next several years, by 1904 she was becoming increasingly involved in the educational activities of Mährisch-Schönberg's Arbeiterheim (Workers' Center). Here she helped her husband, the center's director, in organizing various educational activities including language courses and vocational training in cooking and sewing. The election of Leo Freundlich as a Social Democratic deputy in 1907 to the Austrian Reichsrat (parliament) only strengthened Emmy's determination to make her own significant contribution to social progress, particularly in the area of women's political and economic rights. She became increasingly active

in the women's trade union movement in Moravia, organizing women textile workers, particularly those working at home in substandard dwellings under miserable conditions. The problems she confronted on a daily basis included employer resistance and the growing tensions between the German-speaking and Czech-speaking sections of the population. Despite immense difficulties, by 1914 she could point to the creation of almost two dozen organizations that had a total membership of about 1,300 women.

The final months of 1911 marked some decisive changes in Emmy Freundlich's life. She and her husband moved to Vienna, ostensibly because their daughter **Gertrude Freundlich**'s delicate health necessitated the high quality of medical care found in the Austrian capital. Other reasons, however, were behind the move as well. Emmy's marriage to Leo Freundlich was in decline, and they divorced in 1912. She also desired a larger stage on which to carry on her political and educational work within the Social Democratic movement. Inherited wealth made it possible for Freundlich to live as a divorced woman without any financial worries, and once settled in Vienna she threw herself into her work with greater enthusiasm than ever before.

In 1912, Freundlich heeded a recommendation from party leader Karl Renner by becoming active in the Social Democratic cooperative society (*Konsumgenossenschaftsbewegung*). Here, she was soon convinced, was a key factor that would help to empower working-class women both economically and politically. As the energetic editor of the newspaper of the Austrian women's cooperative society, by 1914 she had been able to increase that journal's circulation to an impressive 120,000 copies per printing. The cooperative movement enabled women to develop managerial skills as well as helping them to improve their family's standard of living. Convinced that the rise of the working classes was not simply a matter of economic improvements, Freundlich emphasized various educational programs aimed at both proletarian youths and adults.

For the next two decades, she would be an indefatigable campaigner for both the cooperative idea as well as for new working-class educational programs. Starting in 1915, she became one of the leaders of the Social Democratic Kinderfreunde (Friends of Children) organization, which emphasized not only general education but the inculcation of humanistic, secular working-class ideals that would guarantee the lifelong loyalty of Austrian youth to the Social

Democratic Party. Like most Social Democrats, Freundlich was profoundly saddened by the onset of World War I, which signalled a significant failure of the workers of the world to prevent a terrible global conflagration. She refused, however, to be demoralized and continued her editorial and educational work of advocating cooperative schemes throughout the war. In 1915, she also began to work for the government as a specialist in the Ministry of Nutrition.

The end of World War I in Vienna signalled not only the end of the Habsburg monarchy and the disintegration of multinational Austria-Hungary but a troubling new era as well. Small and economically weak, the new Austrian Republic appeared to many to be a stillborn commonwealth. Not surprisingly, many Austrians yearned for *Anschluss* (union) with the much larger German Republic. In this new state, the Social Democratic Party quickly emerged as the only major party on the left (the Communists remained an ineffectual sect). Strongly supported by industrial workers and intellectuals, the Social Democrats controlled the municipal government of Vienna from 1920 to 1934, quickly initiating in "Red Vienna" a sweeping program of public housing projects, comprehensive child care and educational reforms. Emmy Freundlich now emerged as one of Red Vienna's best-known leaders, enjoying a public forum not only through her writings but also by virtue of being a member of the City Council, as well as a deputy to the new National Assembly in which she represented Vienna's districts 2, 20 and 21—all of which were solidly working class and solidly Social Democratic in their voting patterns.

Despite the poverty of postwar Vienna in the early 1920s, for Social Democratic idealists like Emmy Freundlich it was a city brimming with new ideas and much optimism, particularly among its young people. As one of the best-known and influential women within the Social Democratic Party, she was constantly in demand as a lecturer. Her editorial work, and the writing of books, pamphlets and articles, kept her schedule full for months at a time. What leisure time she did have was spent with her two daughters, who continued to live with her into adulthood (neither daughter would ever marry).

As one of Europe's most respected experts on the cooperative movement, Emmy Freundlich was elected president in 1921 of the International Cooperative Women's Guild (ICWG), a global organization with headquarters in London. Her work both within Austria and internationally was highly regarded, and Freundlich was to retain this post until her death. Her privileged upbringing was now of great value to her, since as a child and young woman she had achieved mastery of both English and French. Being able to not only read in these languages but to converse in depth with visitors from abroad enabled her to closely study in the original sources those developments that other party leaders could only discover at second hand. Because of these advantages, Emmy Freundlich was generally regarded as one of the best-informed individuals within the ranks of the Social Democratic leadership. Freundlich was a major asset to her party not only because of her intellectual gifts, but because on at least one occasion her personal wealth enabled her to save the day for Social Democracy. When the leading party newspaper, Vienna's *Arbeiter-Zeitung,* found itself deep in debt, Freundlich resolved the crisis by making a gift of funds she raised by selling one of her valuable Viennese properties.

Despite the successes of Red Vienna, Austria slid into the abyss of dictatorship in 1934. Although he was opposed to Hitler's Germany, Chancellor Engelbert Dollfuss was an ally of Benito Mussolini and a foe of democracy and socialism. In February 1934, a brief but bloody civil war brought about the demise of parliamentary government in Austria and the destruction of the experiment of Red Vienna. As one of the most prominent leaders of the Social Democratic movement in Austria, Freundlich had long been hated by the country's political and social reactionaries. While some Social Democrats fled abroad and others were executed, a large number found themselves imprisoned. Emmy Freundlich was one of these prisoners, and she was released only because of the strong protests that came from abroad demanding that she be freed forthwith. Although her disdain for the Austrian regime was common knowledge, Freundlich now concentrated her efforts not on the dismal political landscape but instead on broader issues of social change that would one day again prove useful in a free society. It was in this spirit that she wrote in 1936 a study for the International Labor Office of the League of Nations on the role of women in nutritional issues. Three years later, she produced another report for the same body, this time on the status of working women.

The Nazi annexation of Austria in March 1938 was a profound shock to humanistic internationalists like Emmy Freundlich. Nazism was not only a political evil for her, but represented a direct threat to her family as well because under the anti-Semitic Nuremberg racial decrees both of her daughters were at great risk, being defined as "half-Jewesses." Fortunately, they were able to escape to Geneva, where their father lived. In May 1939, Emmy was reunited with her daughters in London, where all three had now been able to attain a permanent refuge from persecution. Both daughters found employment in London and were soon able to send their aging father, who lived in poverty in Geneva, a small monthly subsidy. Emmy spent some of her time at the headquarters of the ICWG, where she remained its respected president. Although she took pains to be well-informed on the basic issues, Freundlich chose to avoid involvement in the heated political debates that usually raged within the Austrian exile community. Enjoying respect from the various factions, and with the end of the war beginning to appear an eventual reality rather than merely a wish, in December 1943 she was chosen to chair the economic commission of the representative bodies of the Austrian Committee for Relief and Reconstruction.

It was with a mixture of joy and sadness that Emmy Freundlich celebrated the liberation of Austria that took place only weeks before the end of the war in Europe in May 1945. The shattered condition of occupied Vienna made an immediate return an impossibility but significant relief efforts could be assisted by exiled Austrians living abroad. Freundlich now struggled with achieving a balance between stimulating a broad process of democratization for Austria's Nazi-contaminated population and at the same time successfully addressing the immediate challenges of a defeated people's day-to-day physical survival. Despite her advancing years, Freundlich remained active in London's Austrian exile community. Neither did she neglect her activities in the cooperative movement, returning to the continent in 1946 when she traveled to Zurich to celebrate the 25th anniversary of her election as president of the ICWG. The same year, she participated in the plenary meetings of UNESCO.

In the summer of 1947, the ICWG was granted an advisory role in the Economic and Social Council of the newly formed United Nations. As ICWG president, Freundlich chose to represent her organization in the United States at the end of the year. Arriving in a nation that was prosperous, confident and physically untouched by the recent war, Freundlich soon found herself investigating the details of the American way of life, particularly as it affected women. In an article she wrote for a Viennese women's magazine, Freundlich praised the labor-saving devices enjoyed by American women, whom she described as living in a veritable *"Hausfrauenparadies"* (Housewives' Paradise). Even though she was in declining health and appeared to some to be increasingly fragile in appearance, she refused to slow down her activities. Her friends and admirers were shocked and saddened when Emmy Freundlich died suddenly in New York City on March 16, 1948. "In looking back on my life," she wrote, "I think of the words I read once: Your life's span is three score and ten years, and its worth is measured by the work and the effort you put into them. And I believe that my life was worth while, for it has given me the chance to work and to apply my efforts in a great movement from which I received more than I gave."

SOURCES:

Arbeitsgemeinschaft "Biografisches Lexikon der österreichischen Frau," Dokumentationsstelle Frauenforschung im Institut für Wissenschaft und Kunst, Vienna.

Bechtel, Beatrix. "Emmy Freundlich," in Edith Prost and Brigitta Wiesinger, eds., *"Die Partei hat mich nie enttäuscht . . . ": Österreichische Sozialdemokratinnen.* Vienna: Verlag für Gesellschaftskritik, 1989, pp. 88–132.

File 2600, Dokumentationsarchiv des österreichischen Widerstandes, Vienna.

Freundlich, Emmy. "Frau und Staatsbürgertum" (unpublished manuscript), Nachlass Alma Motzko, Österreichisches Institut für Zeitgeschichte, Vienna.

Gruber, Helmut. *Red Vienna: Experiment in Working-Class Culture, 1919–1934.* NY: Oxford University Press, 1991.

———. "Sexuality in Red Vienna: Socialist Party Conceptions and Programs and Working Class Life," 1920-1934," in *International Labor and Working Class History.* Vol. 31. Spring 1987, pp. 37–68.

King, Linda J. "The Woman Question and Politics in Austrian Interwar Literature," in *German Studies Review.* Vol. 6, no. 1, 1983, pp. 75–100.

Magaziner, Alfred. *Die Wegbereiter.* Vienna: Volksbuchverlag, 1975.

Richter, Annette. "Emmy Freundlich," in Norbert Leser, ed. *Werk und Widerhall: Grosse Gestalten des österreichischen Sozialismus.* Vienna: Verlag der Wiener Volksbuchhandlung, 1964, pp. 159–167.

Weinzierl, Erika. *Emanzipation? Österreichische Frauen im 20. Jahrhundert.* Vienna and Munich: Verlag Jugend & Volk, 1975.

John Haag,
Assistant Professor of History,
University of Georgia, Athens, Georgia

Freytag-Loringhoven, Baroness von
(1875–1927).

See Abbott, Berenice for sidebar.

Frideswide (d. 735?)

English saint and princess. Name variations: Fredeswitha or Fritheswith. Died possibly in 735; was buried in St. Mary's Church, Oxford; her shrine was destroyed in 1538.

An English saint, Frideswide was a royal princess, according to legend, who fled from the persecution of her lover, a king, to Oxford, where she founded the monastery of St. Frideswide. The monastery was refounded by Roger, bishop of Salisbury, then suppressed in 1524 and put in the hands of Cardinal Wolsey. Her feast day is on October 19.

Friedan, Betty (1921—)

Author of The Feminine Mystique, *the book that launched the feminist movement in the United States, who fought for equal rights for women and founded the National Organization for Women (NOW). Name variations: Bettye. Pronunciation: FREE-dan. Born Bettye Naomi Goldstein on February 4, 1921, in Peoria, Illinois; daughter of Harry Goldstein (owner of a jewelry store) and Miriam Horwitz (local newspaper reporter and housewife); attended Smith College, B.A. in psychology, 1942; married Carl Friedan, in June 1947 (divorced 1969); children: Daniel Friedan (b. 1948); Jonathon Friedan (b. 1952);* **Emily Friedan** *(b. 1956).*

Family lived in Peoria, Illinois; graduated Central High School (June 1938) as one of five valedictorians; attended and graduated Smith College with honors (1942); attended graduate school at University of California at Berkeley for one year; moved to New York City after father's death (1943); married (1947) and had three children; founded NOW (1966) and became its first president; served as head of unofficial NOW delegation to final U.N. Conference for Women in Kenya (1985); death of her mother (1988).

Selected writings: The Feminine Mystique *(W. W. Norton, 1963);* It Changed My Life *(Random House, 1976);* The Second Stage *(Summit Books, 1981):* The Fountain of Age *(Simon and Schuster, 1993).*

Women were granted the right to vote in the United States in 1920, when the 19th amendment was passed. Despite this major breakthrough, women's lives were very different then. Few women worked. Those who had jobs expected to keep them only until they married. Most people were sure that women's place was in the home and that women were unsuited for work. As a result, even if they had to work, there were few positions available for them outside domestic labor. Major universities excluded women or segregated them in special courses, and there were only a handful of women's colleges. Although individual women did some-

times get an education and find productive work, those who did so rarely married. The majority of women in the Western world accepted the role of wife and mother, subservient to their husbands and dependent on them for support.

Betty Naomi Goldstein was destined to change this world. She was born on February 4, 1921, less than one year after women were granted the right to vote. Not a pretty child, she found growing up in the small midwestern town of Peoria, Illinois, difficult. She needed glasses for her weak eyes, and braces to straighten her teeth and legs. Friedan excelled in school work, however, and that interest compensated for what she and her family perceived as her lack of good looks. But when she became a teenager, intellectual success seemed less important. Her friends were going out on dates and joining high school sororities.

One of Betty's biggest disappointments at the time was not being invited into a sorority. The reason had nothing to do with her appearance, or her popularity. In fact, she had many friends and had organized clubs of her own throughout her school years. Her exclusion was due to the fact that she was Jewish. For that same reason, her family could not join the local country club, even though her father was a successful and respected merchant in Peoria. That kind of prejudice had a lasting effect on Friedan and made her feel like an outsider. At Smith, a fine women's college in New England, she excelled in her studies but still felt unpopular and unloved. She longed for a boyfriend of her own, someone that "loved her best," but she rarely had a date and felt too insecure to develop relationships with young men.

As she had during her high school years, Friedan concentrated all her energies on academics. She organized a literary magazine, worked on the college newspaper, and took interesting summer courses. When she decided to major in psychology, she became a favorite of the department. At graduation, she was singled out as one of the four top students who finished *summa cum laude* (with highest praise). She was elected to two academic honor societies and was awarded a fellowship at the University of California at Berkeley to continue her studies in psychology.

Despite all these positive developments, however, Friedan's life was crammed with tension and conflicts. She had never gotten along with her mother. Now, the relationship with her father was also deteriorating. When Harry Goldstein died in 1943, only three weeks after

Betty
Friedan

their last bitter quarrel, Betty was hurt and confused. It took her many years to make sense of
the profusion of emotions she felt at his death.

In addition to family problems, Friedan was
frightened and worried about her choices as an
adult woman. These fears led her to abandon
her graduate studies after only one year, leaving
behind a promising career in psychology. Part of
the reason for this decision was Betty's own
doubts about her life. Following the prevailing
thinking of the time, Friedan believed that a

woman could not combine a career with marriage and family; a woman who chose to work had to give up the love of a man and the satisfaction of motherhood. Friedan was not prepared to make that choice. Instead, she left Berkeley and traveled across the country to New York City, joining a group of women friends from college who were working in Manhattan, the center of the city, and sharing an apartment.

It was not difficult for a woman to find a job in 1943. Because so many young men were off fighting in World War II, women were now being encouraged to enter the work force—at least temporarily. Friedan found employment as a reporter for a small newspaper published by an electrical union. She even managed to keep her job after the war was over.

During those postwar years, Betty Goldstein met Carl Friedan, newly returned from the army. The two liked each other immediately and soon Carl moved into her apartment. In 1947, they were married and within a year their first son, Daniel, was born. Though problems in the marriage surfaced almost immediately, Betty pushed them aside, hoping things would improve.

Once Daniel came along, there was no room in their tiny Manhattan apartment, and the family moved to Queens, a suburb of New York City. Here, Friedan got her first taste of being a full-time housewife and mother. She soon learned it was not what she wanted; she needed the challenge and excitement of the work world. Friedan returned to her old job at the union newspaper, but when she became pregnant for the second time she knew she would have to stop working. In the 1940s and '50s, pregnant women were not accepted in the workplace, and there was no arrangement for pregnancy leave.

Jonathon was born in 1952; four years later, a daughter, Emily came along. Friedan found a lovely old house for her growing family in a suburb north of New York City. She kept herself busy decorating their new home, doing freelance journalism, and organizing programs in the children's school. Her relationship with Carl was not perfect, but it was eclipsed by involvement with the children. Though the days were filled with productive activities, Friedan felt dissatisfied and unsuccessful. These feelings influenced her to take on a new project.

In 1957, she was asked by the alumnae association of Smith to prepare a questionnaire for her classmates at their 15th college reunion. The purpose of this survey was to find out how a Smith College education had affected the lives of the graduates. What had they done with that education? Did it make them happier? Were they better wives and mothers as a result of it? Friedan plunged into the project. She was sure the answers to her questions would refute the popular beliefs that had surfaced in the 1950s. Many prominent sociologists and psychologists were insisting that education was bad for women; it made them unhappy with their natural role and caused them to compete with men. Friedan would prove otherwise. She would show that education was good for women; that it made them happier, more productive, better wives and mothers. She worked hard preparing the questionnaire and her old classmates responded with honest and thoughtful answers.

Back home, after the reunion was over, Friedan began to analyze the results. She discovered that most of the Smith alumnae she interviewed had lives very similar to hers and felt very much the same as she did. Each woman seemed to be asking the question: "Is this all there is to my life?" Friedan began thinking: Was it possible that all the theories of the modern day experts were wrong? Did women need more than the support of a man and children to care for? Such a revolutionary idea contradicted centuries of established tradition and volumes of expert opinion. Forging ahead with more research and analysis, she spent five years reading articles and interviewing women from all walks of life.

"We had no image of our own future, of ourselves as women," wrote Friedan. Women were taught to identify themselves as someone else's wife or someone else's mother. If they had a loving husband and a family, they were supposed to be happy. But most women found that insufficient. Whether they knew it or not, women needed their *own* identity, their *own* accomplishments. Friedan first called this feeling of conflict and unease "the problem that has no name." Later, she dubbed it "the feminine mystique," a phrase that became the title of her book. For many women, *The Feminist Mystique,* published in 1963, turned the world upside down.

As word of her new ideas spread throughout the country, Friedan's life changed. Suddenly, she was a celebrity, invited to speak at universities and major organizations and asked to write articles and grant interviews. Not all the reaction was positive. She was often jeered on the lecture platform and attacked on radio and television talk shows. Newspapers made fun of her looks with cruel remarks, calling her "the feminine mistake." Friedan took it all in stride. There was enough positive reaction to satisfy her. Many reviews praised her book and her ideas. But most important for her were the letters of gratitude she received from individual women whose lives had changed because of her work.

The Feminine Mystique was published at a time when the United States was experiencing many changes. The civil-rights movement, organized in the 1950s, had succeeded in passing several new laws guaranteeing equality for African-Americans. This success had brought the concept of equal rights to the forefront. Women began to demand changes in laws and in social customs that would allow them increased opportunities.

At first, neither the government nor private groups took women's demands seriously. The thought that women could fill the same jobs as men and mingle in what were then all-male business associations seemed preposterous. Although women had managed to be included in the new civil-rights law passed in 1964, that law was not being enforced for them. Friedan kept hearing complaints from women working in government jobs and in universities. Despite the legal guarantees, they were still being passed over for promotions and paid less wages than men for the same work. Women feared that if they complained they would be fired.

It was time to organize. At a National Conference of State Commissions on the Status of Women, held in Washington, D.C. in June 1966, a small group of women got together. Realizing that the government did not intend to do anything tangible about their needs and complaints, they decided to do it themselves. They would create a movement parallel to the civil-rights movement for blacks. Betty Friedan seemed to be the natural choice to lead such a group. She had no job to lose and could speak independently.

At the final luncheon of the National Conference, while the official presentations were being made, Friedan and a handful of other women delegates sat together at a table whispering and jotting down ideas. When the luncheon was over, they had written out, on a paper napkin, the goals of their new organization: ". . . to take the actions needed to bring women into the mainstream of American society now. Full equality for women, in full and equal partnership with men. NOW—the National Organization for Women."

As national president of NOW, Betty Friedan was launched on a new career. Together with her executive board, she tackled some of the problems that had faced women for centuries. As she said in her first press conference:

"Discrimination against women is as evil and wasteful as any other form of discrimination."

At a National Convention, the organization drafted its own Bill of Rights. It included support for the Equal Rights Amendment as well as federal tax deductions for child care and money to aid women who wanted to return to school. Friedan did not want to include the right to choose an abortion, considering it too controversial. Other members insisted, however, and that, too, was included in NOW's Bill of Rights.

> *After tonight, the politics of this nation will never be the same. By our numbers here tonight . . . we learned . . . the power of our solidarity, the power of our sisterhood.*
> —**Betty Friedan**

Women from all over the country responded to the goals of NOW. Among those goals was a commitment to end discrimination of women in the workplace and grant them equal opportunity for jobs. In order to accomplish this, Friedan and her colleagues launched a campaign to end listing jobs in newspapers by sex. As a result of that effort, "Help Wanted, Male" and "Help Wanted, Female" disappeared from the want ads and were replaced in all publications by "Help Wanted."

Young women began to demand—and get—access to all-male specialty high schools and colleges. Consciousness-raising groups were organized, allowing women to share problems and ideas with other women and to become sensitized to the social patterns that had created those problems. NOW fought for pregnancy leaves and for the right of a married woman to continue working. Members organized sit-ins in major restaurants and private clubs, demanding that women be allowed to enter and be served with or without a male escort.

At the first of those sit-ins, at the Oak Room of New York's Plaza Hotel, Friedan showed up late. After a violent fight with her husband, she needed extra time to hide a black eye, and numerous other bruises, under make-up and dark glasses. But she was too busy and too frightened to deal with a divorce. It took her several more years before she gathered the courage to divorce Carl and face life as an unmarried woman.

After two years as national president, it was time for Friedan to step down and make room for new leaders. However, her commitment to NOW did not end. One of her greatest successes was the March for Women's Equality which she planned and helped organize. It was set for August 26, 1970, the 50th anniversary of the women's suffrage amendment. With a budget of only $10,000, she managed to organize women's marches and related events in several major cities throughout the country.

The most important and well-attended march was in New York City. Friedan arrived in time to lead "a sea of people" down Fifth Avenue from Central Park to the 42nd Street Library where a grandstand had been set up. Ignoring the rush-hour traffic and the orders by police that the group must stay on the sidewalks, Friedan shouted as loud as she could: "Take the streets!" Thousands followed her. They filled the broad avenue with a solid wall of marching women and urged those on the sidelines to join them. By the time they reached the speaker's podium, 15 blocks away, it was estimated that more than 10,000 women and a small number of men had marched in support of women's rights. As Friedan ascended the platform to address the cheering crowd, she felt a new pride and excitement in being a woman. "After tonight," she said, "the politics of this nation will never be the same. By our numbers here tonight . . . we learned . . . the power of our solidarity, the power of our sisterhood."

The Women's March for Equality was a high point for the women's movement and for Betty Friedan. It also marked the end of what later would be called the "Golden Age" of feminism. The March, along with the other early successes of NOW, attracted many more women to the struggle for equal rights. Those who joined often had a variety of ideas and differing opinions about how to achieve their goals—opinions with which Friedan disagreed. For example, support for lesbians, an open animosity towards men, and political alliances with the liberal left were ideas that tended to divide the women's movement and make it more vulnerable to outside attack from mainstream, anti-feminist groups.

Friedan objected to these developments. Even her divorce from Carl in 1969 could not make her condemn all men. "This is not a bedroom war," she insisted. "Men are not the enemy." Despite her protests—or perhaps because of them—Friedan found herself being squeezed out of the inner circle of NOW and rejected by new feminist organizations and projects. These were being led by more charismatic and outspoken women such as journalist *Gloria Steinem and Congresswoman *Bella Abzug. Friedan was excluded from involvement in *Ms.,* the first feminist magazine. She did maintain

some influence in the early organization of the Women's Political Caucus but was soon excluded from its leadership, too.

An open conflict with Steinem and Abzug at the Democratic National Convention in 1972 marked the beginning of the end of Friedan's public role in the movement. Though she remained involved for a few more years, her position was eroding. When she lost an open election at the First National Women's Conference held in Houston, Texas, in 1977, Friedan accused the organizers of altering the election results so that she would not be on the steering committee. She retained a lawyer and fought for new elections, but the case could not be proved outside of court and Friedan dropped the issue.

Those years were the most difficult. Friedan had thrown her considerable energy and talent into the women's movement. Now it had rejected her and her efforts. Her reputation as a woman who was difficult to work with, who always demanded the limelight and had to have things her way, became a major excuse for her rejection. Another reason was her identification with the upper-middle class. Friedan and NOW were both accused of a lack of interest in the problems of minority and poor women.

Throughout the 1970s, Friedan maintained a column in *McCall's,* a mainstream woman's magazine, and traveled in the United States, Europe, and the Middle East, lecturing and visiting foreign dignitaries and feminist leaders. She wrote a second book, *It Changed My Life,* which was published in 1976. However, her early accomplishments seemed to have been forgotten.

Betty Friedan never rejected the basic philosophy of the women's movement that she had been so instrumental in shaping. She remained optimistic about the goals of feminism and was active in trying to pass the Equal Rights Amendment in her home state of Illinois, but those years, from the mid-1970s until 1980, represented a low point in her life. She overcame her disappointments and insecurities partly through group encounter, a method of self-exploration which was popular at that time. Urged on by her son Jonathon, she also developed a renewed interest in Judaism. Another support for Friedan during that time was a small group of friends with whom she shared a vacation home and holiday celebrations. This group, which she would later refer to as "a family of friends," largely replaced her own family.

By the beginning of the 1980s, as she approached her 60th birthday, Friedan's life had changed once more. She was less in the limelight, no longer on the cutting edge of feminism, but she was more at peace with herself, and comfortable and respected in the academic world. From her new vantage point, she perceived feminism as a movement that had gotten off track, creating a false dichotomy between women's interests and the interests of the family. As a result, she began writing a third book about women and the direction of the women's movement. Published in 1981, *The Second Stage* drew a tirade of criticism from feminists throughout the country. Friedan wrote that women have to move on to a new partnership with men. Women should not be imitating men or competing with them. Both sexes had to work together for a just society.

Many feminists saw Friedan's philosophy as a betrayal of their goals. Most women were not yet ready for the "second stage," they claimed. Friedan made it seem as if the battle was won, and there was no longer a need for feminism. Her opinions turned the leadership of the movement solidly against her, but the mainstream now began to feel more comfortable with Betty Friedan and her ideas. She was welcomed into the literary and academic world, chosen as author of the year by the American Society of Journalists and Authors, and granted a fellowship at the John F. Kennedy School of Government at Harvard University. Friedan realized that her strong point was in organizing and inspiring others. She was not good at "fighting defensive battles where I simply tried to hold on to my own power."

In 1985, Betty Friedan was asked to lead the unofficial NOW delegation to the final U.N. Conference on Women in Nairobi, Kenya. That same year, she accepted an offer from the University of Southern California to be joint visiting professor at the School of Journalism and Women's Studies. Friedan now began an alternating schedule, with half a year in California and the other half in New York, where she maintains a permanent residence.

Friedan was in California in the spring of 1988 when news of her mother's death reached her. Organizing the memorial service, she attempted, with the help of her friends, to make peace with her negative feelings about her mother.

Betty Friedan reached her 70th birthday in February 1991. Called the "Mother Superior" of the women's movement, her popularity was once again on the rise. To mark the 25th anniversary of the last wave of feminism, Friedan was invited to speak, debate and write articles for major publications. Now a grandmother as well as a recognized founder of the movement, she remains optimistic and positive about women's accomplishments.

Friedan's most recent book, *The Fountain of Age,* appeared in 1993 and suggests that she has moved into new territory but has retained the old lessons. In *The Feminine Mystique,* she wrote that men and women need the same things to be happy: "work and love." Now she is demanding that same privilege for another group. "Old age is a new period for human growth," she wrote, pointing out that "work and love" should be a goal for older people also. Now in the last stages of her own life, Betty Friedan claims to have achieved that goal. "When you love your work," she says, "you have everything."

SOURCES:

Friedan, Betty. *It Changed My Life.* NY: Random House, 1976.

Henry, Sondra, and Emily Taitz. *Betty Friedan: Fighter for Women's Rights.* Hillside, NJ: Enslow Publishers, 1990.

SUGGESTED READING:

Cohen, Marcia. *The Sisterhood: The True Story of the Women Who Changed the World.* NY: Simon & Schuster, 1988.

Hennessee, Judith. *Betty Friedan: Her Life.* NY: Random House, 1999.

COLLECTIONS:

Correspondence, papers, and memorabilia located in the Schlesinger Library, Radcliffe College, Cambridge, Massachusetts.

Emily Taitz,
Professor of Women's Studies at Adelphi University,
Garden City, New York, and co-author of
several biographies and collections, including
Remarkable Jewish Women (Jewish Publication Society)

Friederike.

Variant of Frederica or Fredericka.

Friederike of Hesse-Cassel

(1722–1787)

*Duchess of Oldenburg. Born on October 31, 1722; died on February 28, 1787; daughter of Maximilian, prince of Hesse-Cassel; married August (1711–1785), duke of Oldenburg (r. 1777–1785), on November 21, 1752; children: *Charlotte of Oldenburg (1759–1818), queen of Sweden; Wilhelm, duke of Oldenburg (b. 1754); Luise (1756–1759).*

Friedman, Elizebeth (d. 1980)

America's "premier" cryptographer who devised a code system for the Office of Strategic Services and deciphered messages from German spies in Allied lands during World War II. Born Elizebeth Smith; died in 1980; graduated from Hillsdale College, Michigan, 1915; married William Friedman (a cryptographer), in May 1917; children: John Friedman; Barbara Friedman.

Elizebeth Friedman never planned a career as a codebreaker, and as a young girl probably never imagined herself testifying against smugglers. After graduating from Hillsdale College in Michigan with an English degree, she went to work at the Newberry Library in Chicago. Through a member of the library staff, she obtained a position as well with George Fabyan, the eccentric millionaire who ran the Riverbank Laboratory, a think tank located on a 600-acre estate west of Chicago. At Fox Hill, Fabyan supported a stable of top scientists who worked on whatever projects he found interesting, from cryptology to plant genetics. Elizebeth was teamed with **Elizebeth Wells Gallup**, a woman who had convinced Fabyan that Francis Bacon was the real author of Shakespeare's sonnets and plays, and that Bacon had hidden a number of coded messages in the original printed copies. (Gallup also claimed that Bacon was the illegitimate son of Queen *Elizabeth I and the rightful heir to the throne.) At Fox Hill, Elizebeth met William Friedman who at the time was performing experiments in plant genetics and also assisting on the Bacon project. In 1916, he left his work in genetics and joined Elizebeth in studying everything they could find on secret writings. "We had a lot of pioneering to do," Elizebeth later recalled. "Literary ciphers may give you the swing of the thing, but they are in no sense scientific. There were no precedents for us to follow."

In May 1917, at the height of World War I, Elizebeth and William married and began working on decoding diplomatic messages from unfriendly powers that were sent to Fox Hill from the government. For a year, Riverbank was the only organization in the country capable of carrying out work on secret messages. In late 1917, when the U.S. Army created its own Cipher Bureau, Fabyan arranged for the Friedmans to conduct classes in cryptography for the army officers. When the classes ended, William left for France, where he served as a lieutenant in the army.

In 1920, the Friedmans broke with Riverbank and went to work for the army for a six-month trial period as civilian "code experts," and in 1921 began military contract work in Washington D.C. Early in 1922, the War Department hired William permanently as chief codebreaker, and he went on to become recog-

nized as the greatest maker and breaker of secret codes and ciphers in history. His papers brought cryptology into the scientific age, and the team he trained and headed broke into Japan's highest diplomatic cipher just before World War II. Overworked to the breaking point during World War II, William suffered bouts of depression that required hospitalization. After the war, William served as a top-ranking cryptanalyst in various agencies, including the National Security Agency. He retired in 1955 but continued to work on special and highly secret missions.

Elizebeth's career advanced in the 1930s, during Prohibition. In 1927, now the mother of two, she became a "special agent" on loan from the Department of Justice to the Coast Guard and Navy. Her job was to unravel the secret messages sent by rumrunners to establish rendezvous points and prices and to send warnings. Although the early messages were simple to decipher, as time went on and more sophisticated syndicates took over the distribution network, the coding systems became more complex and difficult to break. In three years, she and her staff solved 12,000 messages using dozens of different schemes. During the 1930s, her work led to a number of important convictions of narcotics traffickers, but also put her family on edge. Her daughter remembers being quite aware of the dangers her mother faced. "I remember Dad jesting once, when Mother was late getting home, that she might have been taken for a ride," she recalled. During World War II, Elizebeth devised a code system for the Office of Strategic Services, and deciphered messages from German spies in Allied lands.

Although the Friedmans shunned publicity and never discussed their work, even with each other, their passion for cryptology spilled over into their home life. William created cipher games for the children and sent holiday greeting cards with cipher messages. The couple were well-known for their progressive dinner parties, which would begin at a restaurant where the guests would have their first course and divide into teams. "While they were eating," recalled the Friedmans' son John, "the restaurant owner gave them a piece of paper containing a clue about the next place to go. They'd go to five or six restaurants. . . . The first team to return home, won a prize."

Late in her career, Elizebeth set up a secure communications system for the International Monetary Fund. After their official retirement, the couple returned to the Shakespeare problem, which had lured them into cryptography in the first place. In 1955, they published an award-winning book, *The Shakespearean Ciphers Examined*, in which they included a hidden biliteral cipher. On page 257 of the book, buried in an italicized phrase, using two different typefaces, they offered their opinion on the lingering controversy. The cipher read, "I did not write the plays. F. Bacon."

SOURCES:

Chiles, James R. "Breaking codes was this couple's lifetime career," in *Smithsonian*. Vol. 18, no. 3. June 1987, pp. 128–144.

Barbara Morgan,
Melrose, Massachusetts

Friedman, Esther Pauline and Pauline Esther.

Syndicated columnists.

Friedman, Esther Pauline (b. 1918). Name variations: (pseudonym) Ann Landers; Mrs. Jules Lederer; (nickname) Eppie. Born on July 4, 1918, in Sioux City Iowa; identical twin of Pauline Esther and one of four daughters of Abraham (a motion-picture exhibitor) and Rebecca (Rushall) Friedman; graduated with honors from Central High School, Sioux City, 1936; attended Morningside College, Sioux City; married Jules William Lederer (a businessman), July 2, 1939, in a double wedding ceremony with her twin sister (divorced); children: one daughter, Margo.

Friedman, Pauline Esther (b. 1918). Name variations: (pseudonym) Abigail Van Buren; Mrs. Morton Phillips; (nickname) Popo. Born on July 4, 1918, in Sioux City, Iowa; identical twin of Esther Pauline and one of four daughters of Abraham (a motion-picture exhibitor) and Rebecca (Rushall) Friedman; graduated with honors from Central High School, Sioux City, 1936; attended Morningside College, Sioux; married Morton Phillips (a businessman), July 2, 1939, in a double wedding ceremony with her twin sister; children: Jeanne and Eddie.

The identical twin sisters, known to millions of readers as columnists Ann Landers (Esther Pauline) and Abigail Van Buren (Pauline Esther), have led strikingly similar lives, even given the circumstances of their birth. Growing up in Sioux City, Iowa, they were both honor students in high school and attended a local college before marrying in a double ceremony just short of their 21st birthdays. Esther (Landers) then moved to Chicago, where she raised her daughter and was active in political and philanthropic causes. Pauline (Van Buren) lived in Minneapolis, Eau Claire, Wisconsin, and San Francisco. She had two children, a boy and a girl, and, like

her sister, devoted her spare time to charitable causes and politics.

In 1955, Esther entered a contest run by the *Sun-Times* to find a successor to columnist **Ruth Crowley**, who wrote an advice column for the newspaper under the pen name of Ann Landers. The only non-professional out of 29 women who sent in entries, Esther landed the job. Her first column appeared on October 16, 1955, and was an immediate success. In the manner of **Dorothy Dix*, Landers offered insightful, straightforward, and sometimes acerbic replies to questions from readers. "When you sit down and cry with people, you don't help them," she once explained. "Some people have to be shook." Even as mores changed and problems became more complex, she rarely sidestepped an issue. In one of her early columns, she declared that "hot potatoes are my specialty—and I've never run from a 'controversial' issue yet."

One month after Landers began her column, Pauline (Van Buren) launched her own journalistic career by submitting a sample column to the *San Francisco Chronicle,* which at the time was publishing an advice column by **Molly Mayfield**. (Pauline insisted that her sister's success was

Esther Friedman (Ann Landers)

Pauline Friedman (Abigail Van Buren)

never a factor in her career choice.) The editors were so impressed that they dropped Mayfield and turned the job over to Pauline, who, writing under the by-line of Abigail Van Buren, enjoyed the same extraordinary success as her sister. Although similar in style to Landers, Van Buren was cited in *Time* (January 21, 1957) as "slicker, quicker and flipper than her twin sister."

Both columnists, still working at age 81, had also published books based on their columns. To Van Buren's credit: *Dear Abby* (1958); *Dear Teen-Ager* (1959); *Dear Abby on Marriage* (1962); *Dear Abby on Planning your Wedding* (1988); and *The Best of Dear Abby* (1991). From Landers: *Since You Ask Me* (1961); *Ann Landers Talks to Teen-Agers About Sex* (1964); *Truth is Stranger* (1968); and *Where Were You When President Kennedy Was Shot* (1993). Although the rivalry between the sisters has been a factor in their success, it has also exacted a toll. Van Buren once advised, "Parents of identical twins should not dress them alike. Break up the vaudeville act. It may be good for the parents' ego but for the sisters it means double trouble."

SOURCES:
Candee, Marjorie Dent, ed. *Current Biography 1957.* NY: H.W. Wilson, 1957.

Moritz, Charles, ed. *Current Biography 1960.* NY: H.W. Wilson, 1960.
McHenry, Robert, ed. *Famous American Women.* NY: Dover, 1983.

RELATED MEDIA:
"Take My Advice: The Ann and Abby Story" (television movie), starring **Wendie Malick**, Lifetime channel, first aired July 1999.

Friedman-Gramatté, Sonia
(1899–1974).

See Eckhardt-Gramatté, S.C.

Frietschie, Barbara (1766–1862)

American Civil War hero. Name variations: Barbara Fritchie. Pronunciation: Frich-ee. Born Barbara Hauer on December 3, 1766, in Lancaster, Pennsylvania; died at her home in Frederick, Maryland, on December 18, 1862; daughter of German immigrants; married John Frietschie.

According to legend, Barbara Frietschie defied the Confederate troops under General "Stonewall" Jackson as they advanced through Frederick, Maryland, by waving a Union flag from an upper window of her home (September 1862). After subsequent investigations, it was determined that Jackson never did pass by her home, but it is possible that a germ of truth was enlarged out of recognition by writers John Greenleaf Whittier (*Barbara Frietchie*, 1863) and Clyde Fitch (*Barbara Frietchie*, a play, 1898). In October 1863, Whittier had Frietschie defiantly yelling to Jackson, after her flag was riddled with bullets, "Shoot, if you must, this old gray head/ But spare your country's flag."

Frings, Ketti (1909–1981)

American screenwriter, playwright, novelist. Name variations: (pseudonym) Anita Kilgore. Born Katherine Hartley on February 28, 1909, in Columbus, Ohio; died in 1981; one of three daughters of Guy Herbert Hartley (a Quaker paper-box salesman) and Pauline (Sparks) Hartley; attended the Lake School for Girls, Milwaukee, Wisconsin; attended Principia College, St. Louis, Missouri, for one year; married Kurt Frings (a lightweight boxer turned actors' agent), on March 18, 1938; children: son Peter; daughter Kathie.

Screenplays: Hold Back the Dawn *(1941);* Guest in the House *(1945);* The Accused *(1949);* Thelma Jordan *(1950);* Dark City *(1950);* The Company She Keeps *(1951);* Come Back, Little Sheba *(1953);* About

Mrs. Leslie *(1954)*; The Shrike *(1955)*; Foxfire *(1955)*; By Love Possessed *(1961)*; Mr. Sycamore *(1975)*.

Other works: *(novel)* Hold Back the Dawn *(1940)*; R. Ayre's Mr. Sycamore *(dramatization by Frings, 1942); (novel)* God's Front Porch *(1944); (novel)* Let the Devil Catch You *(1947)*; Thomas Wolfe's Look Homeward Angel *(dramatization by Frings, 1957, musical version, with P. Udell, 1978)*; R. Wright's The Long Dream *(dramatization by Frings, 1960); (with R.O. Hirson)* Walking Happy *(musical version of the play* Hobson's Choice *by H. Brighouse, 1966)*.

Playwright, screenwriter, and novelist Ketti Frings produced an impressive number of plays, novels, and screenplays during her 35-year career, but *Look Homeward Angel* (1957), her adaptation of Thomas Wolfe's autobiographical novel, remains the work for which she is best known. For this play, she received the Pulitzer Prize in Drama, the New York Drama Critics' Circle Award, and was named by the Los Angeles *Times* as "Woman of the Year."

Frings was born in 1909, the daughter of a paper-box salesman, and grew up in 13 different cities spanning the East and West coasts. Following her mother's death, she and her two sisters settled with an aunt in Milwaukee, Wisconsin, where she attended the Lake School for Girls. After graduating, she enrolled at Principia College in St. Louis, but was there for only a year. Frings believed that it was her early desire to be an actress that spawned her writing career. "When I was in school," she recalled, "I wrote plays so that I could write myself the best parts."

After leaving college, Frings wrote advertising copy, radio scripts, and articles for movie magazines, then decided to spend a year in the South of France, ostensibly to write her first novel. Although the book never materialized, she did meet her future husband Kurt Frings, a German-born lightweight boxer. (It was Kurt who called Frings "Ketti," the name that she eventually came to use professionally.) Following their marriage in 1938, the couple spent two years in Mexico waiting for Kurt to be allowed to enter the United States. The hiatus inspired Frings' first novel *Hold Back The Dawn* (1940), which the *New Republic* called "a moving and disturbing book, written in clipped, vivid sentences." Almost simultaneously, she adapted the novel for a film with the same title. (Released by Paramount in 1941, it starred Charles Boyer and *Olivia de Havilland.)

Frings had less success with her first Broadway play *Mr. Sycamore* (1942), a fantasy about a disgruntled postman who turns himself into a tree. Despite an encouraging review from Brooks Atkinson, who called it "mildly imaginative," the play lasted for only 19 performances. "I was not too bruised by its lack of success," Frings said later. "You can only learn from your mistakes."

After a second novel, *God's Front Porch* (1944), Frings turned out a series of screenplays, including *Guest in the House* (1944), *The Accused* (1949), *Thelma Jordan* (1949), and *The Company She Keeps* (1951), the last of which was inspired by a visit she made to Tehachapi Women's Prison. In 1952, she wrote the screenplays for two successful Paramount pictures: *Because of You*, which at the time was labeled a "woman's picture," and *Come Back, Little Sheba*, a critically acclaimed adaptation of the William Inge play that earned an Academy Award for its star, *Shirley Booth*. Frings' next screenplay was also an adaptation of a popular play, *The Shrike*, by Joseph Kramm, and was released by Universal-International in 1955. During the shooting of the film, which was directed by José Ferrer, who also played the lead opposite *June Allyson*, Frings served as an assistant to Ferrer for those scenes in which he acted.

Ketti Frings began working on the adaptation of *Look Homeward Angel* in 1955, after receiving dramatic rights from Edward C. Aswell, Wolfe's last editor and literary executor. The project took two years, not an unusual length of time for Frings, who was known to spend 10 to 12 hours a day at her typewriter. "The greatest mistake anyone can make is to undertake a play as a casual excursion in creative work, to treat it as an alternate occupation," she said about the craft of playwriting. "It's quite the other way. It demands the most complete dedication. And even with that kind of dedication you can't be sure of the result, but you have to possess it anyway."

Although Frings condensed Wolfe's 626-page novel into two hours' playing time, altered the time span to three weeks, and reduced the number of characters to 19, she nevertheless, in

$\mathcal{B}$arbara
$\mathcal{F}$rietschie

the words of Richard Watts, Jr. (New York *Post,* November 29, 1957), "captured the letter and spirit of the Wolfe novel in completely dramatic terms." He felt that Frings adaptation had "truth, richness, abounding vitality, laughter and compassion, and enormous emotional impact." John McCain called the play "quite simply, one of the best evenings I've ever had in the theatre."

Frings and her husband, who became a well-known actor's agent with such clients as *Elizabeth Taylor, *Audrey Hepburn, and *Maria Schell, had two children and lived in Beverly Hills, where they had an ultra-modern home that Cleveland Amory called "one of Hollywood's most showy showplaces." Although the house appeared to be made entirely of glass, one of the rooms had no windows at all, only a skylight. It served as Frings' office, because it kept her focused. "You can't look out! You have to look in. It's a darn good thing, too, not only for writing but for everything else."

Frings' later work for the stage never quite clicked. Her 1960 dramatization of Richard Wright's novel, *The Long Dream,* was not well received, and *Walking Happy,* a 1966 musical adaptation of Harold Brighouse's play *Hobson's Choice,* received mixed reviews. Her last work for the stage was a collaboration with Peter Udell on a musical version of *Look Homeward Angel,* retitled *Angel.* The ill-fated production opened on Broadway on May 10, 1978, but closed after only five performances. Frings' final screenplay was also resurrected from the past, an adaptation of her earlier play *Mr. Sycamore* (1975).

SOURCES:

Katz, Ephraim. *The Film Encyclopedia.* NY: Harper-Collins, 1994.

Mainiero, Lina. *American Women Writers: From Colonial Times to the Present.* NY: Frederick Ungar, 1980.

Moritz, Charles, ed. *Current Biography.* NY: H.W. Wilson, 1960.

Wilmeth, Don B., and Tice L. Miller, eds. *Cambridge Guide to American Theatre.* NY: Cambridge University Press, 1993.

Barbara Morgan,
Melrose, Massachusetts

Frink, Elizabeth (1930–1994)

English sculptor. Born in Suffolk, England, in 1930; died in 1994; convent educated; studied at the Guildford School of Art (1947–49), and later at the Chelsea School of Art (1949–53), under Bernard Meadows and Willi Soukop; married Michael Jamnet (1956–62); married Edward Pool (1968–1974); married Alex Csaky, in 1975.

During her early career, sculptor Elizabeth Frink taught at her alma mater, the Chelsea School of Art (1953–60), and at the St. Martin's School of Art (1955–57). She lived in France from 1967 to 1972, and later returned to England, living and working in Dorset. Her early works are characterized by their rough surfaces and aggressive quality, reflecting the influences of artists such as **Lynn Chadwick** and Kenneth Armitage. Frink, who exhibited regularly from 1955, is best known for a series of heads, begun in the mid-1960s, which reflect her interest in war and the military. In the mid-1970s, her warriors and soldiers gave way to victims of suffering. Frink also executed a number of public and religious commissions, including the *Alcock Brown Memorial,* for Manchester Airport (1962), *Horse and Rider* (London, Dover Street), and *Walking Madonna,* for Salisbury Cathedral (1981). She also painted and produced etchings illustrating *Aesop's Fables* (1967), *The Canterbury Tales* (1971), and the *Odyssey and Iliad* (1974–5). Elizabeth Frink was made a CBE in 1969.

Frissell, Toni (1907–1988)

American photographer who specialized in fashion, children, documentary, and sports. Born Antoinette Wood Frissell on March 10, 1907, in New York City; died on April 17, 1988, in Saint James, New York; third child and only daughter of Dr. Lewis Fox (teacher of clinical medicine at Columbia University and medical director of St. Luke's Hospital) and Antoinette Wood (Montgomery) Frissell; attended private school in New York City; graduated from Miss Porter's School, Farmington, Connecticut, 1925; married Francis McNeill Bacon III (a broker), in 1932; children: son, Varrick Bacon (b. 1933); daughter, Sidney Bacon (b. 1935).

The daughter of a socialite and a New York doctor, photographer Toni Frissell's early interests were art history and the theater. After graduating from the fashionable Miss Porter's School, she played bit parts in several Max Reinhardt productions, then toured with his company both in the United States and Europe during the late 1920s. Returning to New York in 1930, she wrote advertising copy for Stern's department store before joining the staff of *Vogue* as a caption writer. "They finally fired me," she later recalled, "because I couldn't spell." The magazine, however, did publish some of her early fashion photographs in 1931 and, in 1933, offered her a contract. Innovative in approach,

Frissell was the first to photograph her formally dressed models outside, in natural sunlight, instead of in the usual studio setting. Striving for a natural look, she didn't pose her subjects either. "I try to make them look not like Powers girls modeling," she explained, "but like human beings." Frissell was with *Vogue* for 11 years, before signing on with *Harper's Bazaar*.

In 1932, Frissell married Francis McNeill Bacon, III and had two children, Varrick and Sidney, who, with their friends, were often the subjects of her "photo-illustrated" books, notably *A Child's Garden of Verse* (1944). Reviewers praised her photographs of children for their natural unposed quality, although Edward Steichen once complained that her youngsters were too scrubbed and too well dressed, and their parents made too much money.

Frustrated with fashion and wanting a true reporting job, Frissell volunteered to serve as a pictorial historian for the Red Cross when the war began. She spent ten weeks photographing in England and Scotland in 1941 and later covered assignments in other parts of the world for the American Army Air Forces and as a freelancer for a number of publications. Employed by the Office of War Information, Frissell also served as official photographer of the Women's Army Corps. She received a star and two overseas stripes for her work at the front as a wartime correspondent.

Frissell was under contract to *Harper's Bazaar* from 1941 to 1950 and worked for *Life* and *Sports Illustrated* in the 1950s. Her photographs and illustrated articles also appeared in a number of national magazines, including *Collier's, Good Housekeeping, Ladies' Home Journal, Holiday, McCall's, Fortune, This Week,* and *Arts and Decoration.* Her work was part of Steichen's *Family of Man* exhibition at New York's Museum of Modern Art in 1955. Her fashion photographs appeared in the exhibit *Fashion Photography: Six Decades,* sponsored by the Emily Lowe Gallery, at Hofstra University, 1975–76, and in *History of Fashion Photography,* at the International Museum of Photography, George Eastman House, Rochester, New York, 1977–78.

SOURCES:

Moritz, Charles, ed. *Current Biography 1988.* NY: H.W. Wilson, 1988.

Rosenblum, Naomi. *A History of Women Photographers.* NY: Abbeville Press, 1994.

Rothe, Anna, ed. *Current Biography 1947.* NY: H.W. Wilson, 1947.

Barbara Morgan,
Melrose, Massachusetts

Fritchie, Barbara (1766–1862).

See Frietschie, Barbara.

Frith, Mary (c. 1584–1659)

British pickpocket and highway robber who formed her own gang. Name variations: Moll Cutpurse; Molly Cutpurse; Mary Markham; Molly Frith. Born in London, England, around 1584; died in 1659; daughter of a shoemaker.

One of Britain's most infamous and powerful outlaws, Mary Frith started down the wrong path early in life, defying her parents and teachers. A homely girl by conventional standards and scorned by her female peers, Frith took to competing with the boys in her neighborhood, often winning her way with her fists. While still in her early teens, she abandoned dresses for breeches and a doublet, the costume she wore until her dying day.

Frith worked unsuccessfully as a domestic servant and fortuneteller before coming to the attention of the Society of Divers, who, noting her long middle finger, pegged her as a natural pickpocket. Finding her niche, she excelled in her new profession, flaunting her success by obtaining the finest men's wardrobe available, smoking a pipe, and frequenting the local pubs. Around 1605, she took to the stage of London's Fortune Theater, belting out bawdy songs and making lewd speeches. Her performances gained her dubious acclaim as the first professional actress in England and also brought her to the attention of Elizabethan playwrights Thomas Dekker and Thomas Middleton, who made her a character in their 1907 drama, *The Roaring Girl.* Five years later, dramatist Nathan Field also immortalized Frith as a despicable character in his play *Amends of Ladies.*

After being caught picking pockets several times and having her hands branded, Frith moved on to highway robbery. At first operating within other bands, she later formed her own gang and terrorized the area until she wounded a prestigious military figure during a robbery and was jailed and condemned to death. Able to bribe her accuser and free herself but spooked by the incident, Frith decided to open the Globe Tavern, which soon became a gathering place for criminals who used the premises to guzzle ale and plan their capers. In addition to running the establishment, Frith became a master fence, receiving and selling stolen goods at enormous profit. In return for exclusive contracts, she provided her thieving partners with lists of the great merchants and

Mary Frith

grave, because, she said, "I am unworthy to look upwards, and that as I have in my life been preposterous, so I may be in my death."

SOURCES:

Concise Dictionary of National Biography. Oxford: Oxford University Press, 1992.

Nash, Jay Robert. *Look for the Woman.* NY: M. Evans, 1981.

Barbara Morgan,
Melrose, Massachusetts

Frith, Molly (c. 1584–1659).

See Frith, Mary.

Fritheswith (d. 735?).

See Frideswide.

Frithpoll, Margaret (d. 1130)

Queen of Norway and queen of Denmark. Died on November 4, 1130; daughter of *Helen (fl. 1100s) and Inge I the Elder, king of Sweden (r. 1080–1110, 1112–1125); married Magnus III Barelegs, king of Norway (r. 1093–1103), in 1101; married Niels, king of Denmark (r. 1104–1134), around 1105; children: (second marriage) Magnus (b. around 1106); Inge of Denmark (d. around 1121).

Froman, Jane (1907–1980)

American band singer of the 1930s and 1940s. Born in St. Louis, Missouri, on November 10, 1907; died at her home in Columbia, Missouri, on April 22, 1980; attended the University of Missouri and the Cincinnati Conservatory of Music; married twice; no children.

Selected discography: singles: "Lost in a Fog"/ "My Melancholy Baby" (De 180); "I Only Have Eyes for You"/ "A New Moon Is Over My Shoulder" (De 181); "But Where are You?"/ "Please Believe Me" (De 710); "If You Love Me"/ "It's Great to Be in Love Again" (De 725); "Tonight We Love"/ "What Love Done to Me" (Co 36314); "Baby Mine"/ "When I See an Elephant Fly" (Co 36460); "You, So It's You"/ "Linger in My Arms a Little Longer, Baby" (Maj 1048); "I Got Lost in His Arms"/ "Millionaires Don't Whistle" (Maj 1049); "For You, for Me, for Evermore"/ "A Garden in the Rain" (Maj 1086); "The Man I Love" (Vi [12"] 12333); "I'll Walk Alone"/ "With a Song in My Heart" (Cap 2154); "Wish You Were Here"/ "Mine" (Cap 2154); "My Love, My Life"/ "No!" (Cap 2219); "My Shining Hour"/ "If I Love You a Mountain" (Cap 2496); "Robe of Calvary"/ "The Sound of Love" (Cap 2639); "I Solemnly Swear"/ "Backward, Turn Backward." Movie soundtrack: With a Song in My Heart (Cap T-309).

tradespeople in England, which she obtained through high-placed government contacts.

During her long career, Frith also dabbled in procurement and blackmail. Aside from her single incarceration, she avoided further confrontations with the law until early in February 1612, when she was arrested, not for any of her serious crimes, but for wearing male attire in public. Tried and convicted, she was sentenced to do public penance by standing in the square at St. Paul's Cathedral during a morning sermon and proclaiming her remorse. Not only did Frith perform her penance (supposedly drinking herself into oblivion so as to appear properly contrite), but arranged to have her best pickpockets present in the square to loot the pockets of the onlookers. For the next two decades, she reigned supreme among London criminals, adding to her already great fortune. At the time of her death at age 73, however, she had gone through most of her money and left what little there was to three maids in her employ. At her request, she was buried face downward in her

Jane Froman was born in St. Louis, Missouri, on November 10, 1907. Formally trained, with a strong melodious voice and excellent phrasing, she started her career on the radio in Cincinnati and with Paul Whiteman in Chicago. By the mid-1930s, she had established herself in New York, with successful radio and club appearances as well as recordings (notably, "I Only Have Eyes For You"). On Broadway, she appeared in *Ziegfeld Follies of 1934, Keep off the Grass* (1940), and the vaudeville show *Laugh, Town, Laugh* (1942) with Ed Wynn. Her early movie musicals included *Movie Stars Over Broadway* (1935) and *Radio City Revels* (1938). In February 1943, while on tour entertaining troops during World War II, Froman was seriously injured in a plane crash off the coast of Portugal. She would undergo numerous operations for her badly damaged legs throughout her life. Froman returned to Broadway in 1943 in *Artists and Models* (which closed after 28 performances) and played New York's Copacabana in 1945. Her career then slumped until the 1950s, when she reappeared on the television show "USA Canteen" and also had some solid hit recordings, including "I'll Walk Alone," from the movie *Follow The Boys* (1944). *Susan Hayward portrayed Froman in *With a Song in My Heart,* the 1952 movie about the singer's life; Froman dubbed the soundtrack.

Fry, Elizabeth (1780–1845)

English activist who was a practicing Quaker and early advocate of prison reform. Born Elizabeth Gurney on May 21, 1780, at Earlham Hall, near Norwich, England; died on October 12, 1845, at Ramsgate, Kent; fourth daughter of John Gurney (a wool merchant and banker) and Catherine Bell; no formal education; married Joseph Fry, in 1800; children: eleven, including Katherine Fry *(b. 1801),* Rachel Fry *(b. 1803), John ((b. 1804), William (b. 1806),* Richenda Fry *(b. 1808), Joseph (b. 1809),* Elizabeth Fry *(b. 1811),* Hannah Fry *(b. 1812),* Louisa Fry *(b. 1814), Samuel (b. 1816), and Daniel (b. 1822).*

Outbreak of the French Revolution (1789); food riots in London (1801); final defeat of Napoleon (1815); Queen Victoria crowned (1837).

Selected writings: Observations on the Visiting, Superintending and Government of Female Prisoners *(1827);* Memoir of the Life of Elizabeth Fry *(1847).*

Born on May 21, 1780, Elizabeth Gurney (Fry) and her 11 brothers and sisters grew up on an affluent country estate, Earlham Hall, a few miles from Norwich on the east coast of England.

Jane Froman

Her father John Gurney had made his fortune in the then burgeoning wool trade. In fact, his business was so financially lucrative that he was eventually able to diversify his interests and become owner of a successful private bank in Norwich. He and his wife **Catherine Bell Gurney** (who died when Elizabeth was 12 years old) were Quakers, although neither appears to have taken their religious beliefs very seriously. By all accounts, both thoroughly enjoyed music and the pleasures of frequently entertaining friends and guests.

Like all her other siblings, Elizabeth received no formal education. Rather, the children obtained their schooling from private governesses and tutors. Although when she was in her late teens Elizabeth lamented her lack of a more substantial education, it is clear in retrospect that she was exposed, at an early age, to many of the most important intellectual debates of the period. Her father maintained an extensive private library where she read the works of such important social and political theorists as Jean-Jacques Rousseau, Voltaire, William Godwin, and the great democratic theorist, Thomas Paine. This was the age of the American and French Revolutions, and radical republican principles were regularly and keenly discussed.

Elizabeth
Fry

can Quaker then visiting other Quakers (or "Friends") in England. Fry was entranced by Savery's "soft, pleasing manner" and how he enabled her "to feel a little religion." This initial stirring of what was soon to become a deeply held faith was perceived by her father as little more than a passing enthusiasm. Deciding that Elizabeth needed a change of scene, he packed her off to her cousin Amelia's house in Hampstead, London.

For the next few months, under the guidance of Amelia, Elizabeth participated in a wide assortment of social activities, including dancing which she particularly enjoyed. More significantly, she became aware for the first time of the extent of poverty, degradation, and misery that the lower classes then endured. Britain's war with revolutionary France was reaching its peak, causing depressed wages and high prices. When this was combined with the endemic state of illiteracy, crime, and drunkenness among the working class, the result was a city where brutality and cruelty were everyday facts of life. Fry was deeply affected by what she witnessed in London, and when she returned to Earlham Hall, she was noticeably more serious and reserved.

Deciding that her first consideration was to supplement her education, she embarked on an intensive private study of grammar and literature. Fry's principal concern, however, was not simply to improve her self. Rather, she began to look for opportunities of using her acquired skills to assist others, and this she found in the large numbers of uneducated and illiterate children that inhabited the villages around her family's home. Elizabeth, who was not yet 20, inaugurated a small school at Earlham Hall which soon was providing a rudimentary education to about 70 local children from poor and distressed families. She supplemented this endeavor by visits to the children's homes where she took further steps to alleviate the hunger and sickness she discovered.

As a child, Fry suffered from recurring illness. When she was 16, her poor health was aggravated following an unfortunate love affair with the son of another prominent local Quaker banker. Following the dissolution of their informal engagement, Elizabeth was deeply hurt and suffered what would probably now be identified as a nervous breakdown. It was several months before she fully recovered.

During her convalescence, she began to keep a personal journal. The early entries testify to a general feeling of regret that, in her opinion, she possessed no distinctive talents or abilities. At the same time, however, Fry began to express a growing understanding that, thanks to her fortuitous social circumstances, she was perhaps in a position to do something to help those less fortunate than herself.

Elizabeth, like the rest of her family, had never displayed any strong attachment to her religious faith. This began to change in February 1798 when she met William Savery, an Ameri-

After a great deal of self-examination, Fry decided, in 1799, to more closely embrace her religious faith. She adopted the lifestyle of, what is known as, a "Plain" Quaker which meant that she relinquished music and dancing and assumed a more simple form of dress. It was at this time also that Joseph Fry, the son of yet another prominent Quaker banking and merchant family in Norwich, asked for her hand in marriage. Though Elizabeth initially refused his offer (on the grounds that it would be incompatible with her new religious calling), she eventually agreed.

Joseph had indicated that he was willing to support his prospective wife in her vocation, and so the couple were married in August 1800.

Following their marriage, they moved to a home in Mildred's Court, London. Initially, Fry was extremely homesick, and it was some time before she fully adjusted to her situation. The situation improved after the birth of Katherine (the first of her 11 children) the following year. Shortly afterwards, Fry was invited by an acquaintance to visit a new school that had recently been opened in nearby Southwark. This school had been founded by Joseph Lancaster and was the first of a series of institutions (known later as Lancastrian schools) which were to spring up all over England, in the next few decades, in order to provide educational opportunities for poor children. Lancaster divided the pupils at his schools into small groups each of which was under the charge of an older pupil or monitor. The task of the monitor was to assist the appointed teacher to instruct the younger pupils and generally help to keep order in the classroom.

During her next few years in London, Fry became increasingly aware of the plight of the poor and destitute. Due to her growing family, however, she was unable to take any practical steps towards addressing their problems. In 1809, Joseph's father died, and he inherited a country estate, Plashet House, which was situated near Epping Forest outside London. There Elizabeth had to cope with managing a large house, an attached local farm, extensive gardens as well as dealing with the problem of educating her own children. Despite these responsibilities, she also realized that rural poverty was an important and pressing issue. She began a soup kitchen to help alleviate the widespread hunger and did what she could to provide medicines for the sick. Fry also initiated a small school and hired a teacher trained in Lancastrian principles to begin educating local children.

Two years later, she moved even closer to her religious calling by becoming, what was termed, an "approved minister" of the Quaker faith. This designation did not signify any official license or credential to preach in public. Rather, it conveyed the approval and support of other Friends to her speaking at various Quaker gatherings. With her husband's encouragement, Fry then followed the path of other committed Quakers and began to travel widely throughout the country to meet and discuss matters of religious concern with other Friends. This inevitably meant that she was separated from her young family for extended periods of time. As her journal amply demonstrates, Fry lamented her absence from Joseph and the children but attempted to atone by means of long and frequent letters.

During one of her visits to London in 1813, she met Stephen Grellet, a Quaker of mixed French and American extraction. It was Grellet who first introduced her to the appalling conditions that were then to be found in Newgate, the largest and most notorious of the city's prisons. Newgate was indeed a grim place. It was literally bursting with men, women and children (both juvenile offenders and the offspring of adult prisoners) who lived in wretched windowless conditions without sanitation. Many of the inmates were awaiting transportation to serve their sentences in New South Wales, Australia, and they lived in an atmosphere of constant violence and drunkenness (the latter courtesy of the beer sold at a handsome profit by the prison staff). Shortly after her first visit to Newgate, Fry wrote that in this institution "all the courtesies of civilized society are laid aside and human nature . . . stalks . . . in naked, horrible deformity."

I know now what the mountain is I have to climb.

—Elizabeth Fry

Although Fry was made aware of the seriousness of the problems in Newgate, it would be another four years before she visited the prison again because of a number of domestic reasons. During this time, she gave birth to two more children while one of her daughters, Elizabeth, born in 1811, died. Moreover, following the victory over Napoleon I in 1815, a severe economic crisis ensued that had grave impact on the family's fortunes. Joseph's bank, which he had inherited from his father, became embroiled in serious financial difficulties. Indeed, the Frys feared for some time that they would have to give up Plashet House in order to pay their outstanding debts. In the meantime, they felt it better to send some of their older children to stay with relatives. Although the crisis eventually passed without serious consequence, the strain and worry of these events took a serious toll on Elizabeth's health.

Early in 1816, the Official Society for Reform of Prisons was founded in London with the express purpose of pressuring Parliament to conduct much-needed reforms of the country's prisons. Fry followed the formation of this society with interest but concluded that such an approach would take too long to have any practical effect. More direct measures were required. She returned to Newgate and made preparations to establish a school for the child inmates. Al-

though the prison authorities were initially reluctant to allow her to proceed, they soon recognized the importance of Fry's initiative and allowed her to install a young woman named **Mary Connor** as teacher. Approximately 30 children were enrolled in Connor's first class (most of whom were no more than seven years of age) where they were taught the basic rudiments of reading and writing.

Fry's next act was to form a support committee composed of ten close, Quaker friends which was called the Ladies' Association for the Improvement of the Female Prisoners in Newgate (more commonly referred to as the Ladies' Newgate Committee). The purpose of this association was to help supervise and fund sewing classes for the female inmates and to arrange the sale of the work produced. In addition, they helped to offset the salary of a nurse who was permanently employed by the committee to take care of the women inmates health needs. As a condition of their participation in this program, the female prisoners had to promise to stop drinking and

agree to attend a twice-daily Bible reading. This initiative was an immediate success and quickly came to the favorable attention of the Lord Mayor and town councillors of London.

In 1818, Fry furthered her work by appearing before a special committee of the House of Commons in Parliament to submit evidence on the state of the nation's prisons. She argued that the current system of mixed prisons, then under the sole supervision of male warders, should be abandoned, and that special women's prisons be built staffed by newly trained female guards. Fry also suggested that inmates should be given the possibility of partaking in some useful occupation that would increase their chances of rehabilitation and the possibilities of finding employment at the conclusion of their sentences.

In the next few years, Fry (and an increasingly larger and more vocal Ladies' Newgate Committee) supplemented their work by attempting to improve conditions on the transport ships to Australia and to alleviate conditions at the convict settlement in New South Wales. In addition, they sought a reform of the death penalty which, at that time, was regularly applied to an extremely wide range of offenses. In a short book written in 1827, *Observations on the Visiting, Superintendence and Government of Female Prisoners* (a text primarily intended for women interested in prison reform), Fry put forward what was at that time the radical proposition that "punishment is not for revenge, but to lessen crime and reform the criminal."

Although she was not without critics among people in authority, Fry's work gained wide public approval, allowing her to extend the network of prison committees throughout England, Scotland, and Ireland. This work was interrupted, however, by another financial panic in 1825 which again seriously threatened the stability of her husband's bank. Although Joseph managed to weather that crisis in the short term, he was unable to avoid bankruptcy three years later. Fortunately, he managed to retain his other business, importing tea, but was forced to sell Plashet House in order to pay his debts. The family then acquired a more modest property in Upton Lane just outside London.

Fry's public standing had brought her to the attention of the highest circles in society. She became, what can only be described as a kind of spiritual advisor to many members of the English aristocracy, including the young Princess *Victoria (who would later be crowned queen in 1837). Some years later in his memoirs, the influential and powerful Duke of Argyll would write of his own meetings with Elizabeth: "She was the only really very great human being I have ever met with whom it was impossible to be disappointed."

Despite the adulation and attention, Fry remained true to her Plain Quaker beliefs and her calling to assist those unfortunates in prison. Between 1838 and 1843, she made five extended tours of France, Germany, and Holland in order to promote the cause of prison reform. She quickly became as well known in Europe as she was in Britain and was enthusiastically welcomed wherever she went. In 1842, the king of Prussia, Frederik Wilhelm IV (then on an official visit to the United Kingdom) requested that he be allowed to accompany Elizabeth on one of her trips to Newgate. There, it is said, he was so moved by her Bible reading to the inmates that he broke down and wept.

During these years, Fry also formulated the first plans to put nursing on a professional basis. In 1840, she established a training home in London that provided up to 20 women with living quarters, a uniform, and a small salary while they received instruction at one of the city's main hospitals. Although their standard of training was rudimentary in comparison to modern-day standards, these women, who became known as the Fry Sisters, were the true pioneers of the modern nursing profession.

These numerous activities gradually began to exact a heavy toll on Fry's health. Throughout the 1840s, she was frequently ill, suffering from respiratory problems and a heart ailment. Despite her condition, she insisted, in June 1845, on attending a meeting of the Ladies' support committee where she advocated the establishment of a new home for the rehabilitation of former prostitutes. This home, known as the Elizabeth Fry Refuge, came into being shortly afterwards and continued for many years to offer support and counselling to these women.

Elizabeth Fry, however, did not live to see the realization of her last project. Shortly after the June meeting, she was advised in the interest of her health to leave London and spend some time taking the sea air at Ramsgate in Kent. There her health rapidly deteriorated. On October 12, 1845, she died peacefully in her sleep.

SOURCES:
Fry, Elizabeth. *Memoir of the Life of Elizabeth Fry*. Edited by Katherine and Richenda Fry. London: Charles Gilpin, 1847.

———. *Observations on the Visiting, Superintending and Government of Female Prisoners*. London: 1827.

Lewis, Georgina King. *Elizabeth Fry*. London: Hendley Bros., 1910.

Whitney, Janet. *Elizabeth Fry*. London: George G. Harrap, 1937.

SUGGESTED READING:
Quinlan, Maurice. *Victorian Prelude*. London: Frank Cass, 1965.

Swayne, Kingdon. *Stewardship of Wealth*. Wallingford, PA: Pendle Hill Publications, 1985.

Dave Baxter,
freelance writer, Waterloo, Ontario, Canada

Fry, Margery (1874–1958).

See Hodgkin, Dorothy for sidebar.

Fry, Mrs. Maxwell (1911–1996).

See Drew, Jane.

Fry, Shirley (1927—)

American tennis player. Name variations: Mrs. K.E. Irvin. Born Shirley June Fry in June 1927 in Akron, Ohio; married K.E. Irvin.

Won the French Open (1951), beating Doris Hart; won the French Open doubles championship with Doris Hart (1950, 1951, 1952, 1953); won Wimbledon's women's doubles with Doris Hart (1951, 1952, 1953); won the U.S. Open (1956); won the U.S. Open doubles championships with Doris Hart (1951, 1954); with Vic Seixas, won the mixed doubles Wimbledon championship (1956); won the Australian singles title (1957).

An outstanding all-round player, Shirley Fry's chief competitors were ***Doris Hart**, ***Louise Brough**, and ***Maureen Connolly**. Twelve years after starting her career, Fry took the Wimbledon singles title in 1956, beating England's **Angela Buxton**. She had more success in doubles play at Wimbledon, winning the women's doubles with Doris Hart in 1951, the longest set played in the event to that point, as well as in 1952 and 1953 when they triumphed 6–0, 6–0 in the finals. Hart and Fry also took the U.S. women's doubles title in 1951 and 1954. In all, the duo took 12 major doubles events. Fry won two other singles titles, beating ***Althea Gibson** in each final contest, the U.S. and Australian Opens.

Fuchs, Ruth (1946—)

East German javelin champion. Born in East Germany on December 14, 1946.

Won the gold medal for the javelin throw in Munich Olympics (1972); won the gold medal in Montreal Olympics (1976).

Called the "queen of javelin throwing," East Germany's Ruth Fuchs dominated the sport from 1972 to 1980. At Potsdam in 1972, she broke her first record, bettering the 62.70 meters of Poland's **Ewa Gryziecka** with a throw of 65.06 meters. Fuchs went on to win gold medals at both the 1972 Olympics in Munich and the 1976 Games in Montreal, where she was also the only woman to retain her Olympic title in the javelin event. In April 1980, she narrowly missed the 70-meter mark with a throw measuring 69.96 meters, although at the 1980 Olympics in Moscow, she surprised everyone by finishing in ninth place. During her career, Fuchs also won the European title (1974 and 1978) and the World Cup (1977 and 1979).

Fuertes, Gloria (1918—)

Twentieth-century Spanish poet. Born in Madrid, Spain, in 1918; youngest of eight children of working-class parents

The youngest of eight children, Gloria Fuertes was born in Madrid in 1918 to working-class parents. She attended convent school and had a generally happy, if poor, childhood. By age 15, she had begun writing poetry and short stories and also attended an institute where she studied literature and grammar in addition to the traditional subjects for women, such as cooking and embroidery. When the Spanish Civil War began in 1936, Fuertes worked as a bookkeeper in a munitions factory, which made artillery shells. She fell in love with a fellow worker and would have married, but he was killed in the war. The sorrows and malnutrition of those years were fundamental in her decision to become a writer.

When the war ended, she published poems and children's stories and read some of her works on the radio. Friendship with the poet Carlos Edmundo de Ory drew her into the *Postisto* literary movement, an offshoot of surrealism. She published her first book of poetry, *Isla ignorada*, in 1950. Continuing to write and publish, she co-founded the poetry journal *Arquero* in 1952. Her small earnings from her poetry, however, convinced her to study English and library science with the intention of obtaining more secure employment. She gained a position in a public library. Meanwhile, in 1955 Fuertes became friends with **Phyllis Turnbull**, a professor of Spanish at Smith College, who helped her gain a Fulbright grant in 1961 to teach Spanish at Bucknell University.

After three years, she returned to Spain, teaching Spanish to foreign students in Madrid's International Institute. In 1968, *Poeta de guardia* appeared, one of her best works. As her own literary works drew greater renown, their sales enabled Fuertes to devote her full energies to writing. She toured Spain, giving readings of her poetry, an effort reflecting her love of Spain and its people more than a desire for profits. Around 1970, she also began appearing on children's programs on Spanish television and was voted both the best writer for children and the children's most popular TV personality. In all, she published more than a dozen volumes of poetry and two dozen children's books.

SOURCES:

Cano, José Luis. *Vida y poesía de Gloria Fuertes*. Madrid: Colección Torremozas, 1991.

Kendall W. Brown,
Professor of History, Brigham Young University,
Provo, Utah

Fugger, Barbara Baesinger (d. 1497)

German textile merchant. Name variations: Barbara Baesinger; Barbara Basinger. Born in Augsburg, Ger-

many; died in 1497 in Augsburg; married Ulrich Fugger, a textile merchant of Augsburg (died 1469); children: 11, including sons Ulrich, George, and Jacob, and eight daughters (names unknown).

Barbara Baesinger Fugger was a wealthy German merchant. Born into the affluent Baesinger family of Augsburg, Germany, she married Ulrich Fugger, a textile merchant, as a teenager. Barbara was widowed after bearing 11 children. Because her sons were too young to succeed their father, she proceeded to take over the management of the family business herself. She had phenomenal success, eventually dealing internationally in wool and linen.

Fugger was a careful manager of her children's futures as well; she planned for them, providing each daughter with a suitable dowry and saving enough money to establish each son in his own business. Two of her sons remained with her to learn the textile trade, while her youngest, Jacob, was sent to Rome to become a priest. Before he had completed his studies Barbara called him home due to the deaths of several other children. Jacob remained in Augsburg and eventually, with his mother's capital and training, was able to establish a tremendously profitable banking company. "Jacob the Rich" became one of the most successful of all medieval bankers, acting as principal banker to the ruling Habsburgs of Austria. Barbara Fugger continued transacting business until advancing age forced her to retire.

SOURCES:

Anderson, Bonnie S., and Judith P. Zinsser. *A History of Their Own*. Vol. I. NY: Harper and Row, 1988.

Gies, Frances, and Joseph Gies. *Women in the Middle Ages*. NY: Harper and Row, 1978.

Laura York,
Riverside, California

Fu Hao (fl. 1040 BCE)

Earliest woman general of the ancient Shang dynasty, more than 3,000 years ago, and queen consort of Emperor Wu Ding, whose recently unearthed tomb contained a wealth of funerary objects symbolic of her royal and military power. Name variations: Lady Hao. Pronunciation: FOO HOW. Lived during China's bronze age, late in the second millennium around 1040 BCE; consort of the Emperor Wu Ding of the Shang dynasty and a leading general in her own right, whose remarkable activities were known only through oracle bone inscriptions until the 1976 discovery of her tomb; children: one known son, Xiao Yi, who preceded her in death.

In the winter of 1976, on the outskirts of Anyang in China's Henan province, an ancient tomb was discovered at Yi Au, site of one of several capitals of the ancient Shang dynasty, dating back more than 3,000 years. Among the wealth of fabulous objects unearthed in the excavation were several large bronze vessels, unsurpassed in their size and artistry, of the kind known as *jue*. On one *jue* appeared the two Chinese characters, "Fu Hao," identifying the site as the burial tomb of Lady Hao, the earliest woman general of the Shang dynasty, and consort of the Emperor Wu Ding. Before this find, Fu Hao was barely known except for the appearance of her name on a few pieces of ox bone or tortoise shell from the Shang period, when they had been used in the art of "scapulimancy," or bone divination. At the Gulbenkian Museum of Oriental Art and Archaeology in England, one record of Lady Hao, scratched into a fragment of tortoise-shell, was as commander of a force of 3,000 troops, one of two columns sent to fight a regional enemy.

At the time of its opening, the tomb was intact; inside, in addition to the sarcophagus of Fu Hao, were the remains of 16 slaves buried alive with her to attend to her after her death; some 440 smaller bronze vessels, bells, mirrors and weapons; 560 hairpins and arrowheads made of bone; 700 pieces of jade; and articles of opal, ivory, or stone standing amidst pieces of pottery. Clearly Fu Hao's was a tomb of great importance, The fact that a woman had been given such an elaborate burial tomb in ancient China was unusual in itself; the sizes of the *jue*—one vessel weighed nine kilograms, or almost 20 pounds, and another was only slightly smaller—were further signs of her powerful status. Many of the bronze vessels, inscribed with her name, were probably cast to hold offerings made in her honor at the time of her burial.

There were more than 20 different types of bronze vessels, 70 of which were inscribed with either her given name or her temple name, by which she would be remembered among her descendants; the jade carvings were reminders of China's neolithic past, when humans depended heavily upon animals for food or as protective totems signifying the nature gods. The figurines are of dragons, eagles, elephants, and phoenix, all zoomorphic figures holding cosmological significance. In addition there were a number of human figurines, carefully depicting the facial features and dress of the Shang upper class, which held a monopoly at the time on bronze military technology.

Archaeologists who have studied the burial site have concluded that Fu Hao was China's earliest woman general; her name was subsequently left out of the ancient classics written at later periods, beginning with the Zhou. Among the inscriptions found, some refer to Fu Hao as a royal consort, some as a military leader with the rank of general, and others as a feudal vassal. In a number of divinations undertaken on her behalf, questions appeared concerning childbirth, the success of her religious rituals and her military enterprises. Few facts are known about the venerated Fu Hao, but she was obviously of the aristocratic elite; mention of her appears on the oracle bones prepared by Wu Ding, the fourth king of the Shang to make his capital at Anyang. According to Hung-hsiang Chou, writing in the April 1987 issue of *Scientific American,* "The example of Lady Hao is only one of the fascinating glimpses into the lives and activities of the people of the Shang that the oracle bone inscriptions afford us, even though these lives are separated from our own by three millenniums."

*I*n the numerous divinations undertaken on [Lady Fu Hao's] behalf questions are asked not only about childbirth but also about the success of her religious rituals and even about her military enterprises.

—Hung-hsiang Chou

Fu Hao was not the only female militarist and commander of China during the Shang period. Oracle bones of the period indicate more than 100 women by name who were active in military campaigns. But her tomb has allowed us to know much more about her than other female commanders. Comparing the oracle bone inscriptions from the Shang dynasty with those of the later Zhou, it appears that Shang aristocratic women enjoyed much higher status than Zhou women, possibly due to the Confucian doctrines introduced in the later Zhou dynasty, which reduced and subordinated women's status.

According to oracle bone inscriptions, it has been estimated that at least 30 kings ruled during the Shang dynasty, which lasted from around 1766 to 1027 BCE, and that the last 14 ruled from Anyang, Henan province. At this time, during China's bronze age, there was as yet no tradition for naming the wife of a king as queen, and Fu Hao is referred to both as wife and consort. Recent findings have caused archaeologists to increase their estimates of the geographical area under the control of the Shang, well beyond the area of the Yellow River to include Zhengzhou, now believed to have been an earlier Shang capital. Artifacts similar to those of Zhengzhou found in the valley of the Yangtze River suggest that Shang control may have extended as far south as Panlongcheng, Hubei.

Wu Ding's father was Di Xiao Yi, and his grandfather had been Di Xiao Xin. Among the handful of facts we have about Wu Ding and his consort, is that the death of his father forced the emperor into a three-year period of mourning. During this time, he toured the countryside with Fu Hao, inspecting crops, assessing irrigation systems, and meeting the people under his rule. Wherever the couple traveled, they would call together local officials, who would in turn arrange a meeting of the local villagers, for an inquest into affairs of public and private interest. During this period, the Shang dynasty was faced both with reverses in agricultural productivity and challenges from the *hsiung-nu,* or "barbarians," waiting to invade the dynasty's frontiers.

At one rural gathering, an intelligent slave named Fu Yue was recommended by the local commoners to serve the king, because of his brilliant ability to make walls for defense. Wu Ding, eager to bring the lowborn but gifted man into his service, feared that the elitist members of his imperial court would not accept the slave. So Wu Ding concocted a story about a dream he'd had, in which God (T'ien) had informed him about a man named Fu Yue, who lived in the cave of a sage, and would save the country. Wu Ding related the many great virtues and astute knowledge of politics of the wise Fu Yue, all of which proved in fact to be true when Fu Yue reached the emperor's court.

During their tour of the provinces, Wu Ding and Fu Hao had left national affairs in the charge of the courtier Tian Guan Qin; but upon their return, they again took personal charge, named the clever Fu Yue premier and honored him with the title of Father of a Dream. As a hostile tribe of invaders, called the Tu Fang, began to threaten from the north, Fu Yue prepared for the defense of the Shang territories. Then while two leading Shang military commanders were away from the capital, one dispatched to the southeast and one to the southwest, the enemy began to threaten their boundaries. Recognizing the emergency, Fu Hao stepped forward, volunteering to lead the military campaign against the Tu Fang.

In her youth, Fu Hao had received military training; in her three-year tour of the countryside with her husband, she had gained firsthand knowledge of the geography of the land; and as a ruler she was kept in touch with the more sophisticated arts of war. Wu Ding understood his wife's capabilities, and, after consulting with Fu Yue, he was persuaded to grant her a bronze *jue,* the symbol that empowered her to lead a military campaign. When a diviner was brought in to judge if the omens were favorable, he wrote questions on tortoise shells which yielded positive answers, and Fu Hao had her commission to fight.

Marching northward to confront the Tu Fang, Fu Hao fought at the head of her troops, nursed the wounded off the battlefield, and inspired morale. Badly defeated by her leadership, the Tu Fang would never again challenge the military power of the Shang.

The next threat of war came from the Qiang Fang tribe, in the northwest. Again, Fu Hao was awarded a *jue* and a military commission and routed the cavalry units of the Qiang Fang. Exhausted upon her return to the capital Anyang, she was soon forced to respond to yet another threat. Without rest, she led a third force against the Yi Fang, who threatened from the southeast and southwest, and she was again triumphant. A fourth and final campaign against the Ba Fung tribe in the southwest gained Fu Hao another *jue;* this time, she shared command of the army, fighting alongside her husband. Cleverly, Wu Ding deployed his troops in an attack on a neighboring tribe allied with the Ba Fung, and, when the Ba Fung moved in to aid them, they fell into a trap laid by Fu Hao. With the Shang forces again victorious, Fu Hao was celebrated as the most outstanding military leader of the country.

But shortly after returning to Anyang, Fu Hao fell ill from exhaustion. While she was still ailing, her only son, Xiao Yi, died, leaving her deeply dispirited, and she died shortly thereafter. The *jue,* which honored her in life, were added to the grave of this remarkable woman warrior, commemorating her feats of daring, courage, and skill in what are now recognized as some of the most monumental and illuminating artifacts of Shang culture.

SOURCES:

Elisseeff, Danielle. *La Femme au Temps des Empereurs de Chine,* 1988.

"Fu Hao," in *Famous Women in Chinese History.* Shanghai People's Press, 1988 (translated from the Chinese by Fang Hong).

Neill, Peter, "New Light on Old China's Oldest Civilizations," in *Asia.* May–June, 1980.

SUGGESTED READING:

Chou, Hung-hsiang. "Chinese Oracle Bones," in *Scientific American,* April 1987.

Peterson, Barbara Bennett, "Fu Hao," in *Notable Women of China.* Fulbright Association, 1994.

Barbara Bennett Peterson, Ph.D.,
Professor of History, University of Hawaii, and editor of numerous biographical and historical compilations

Fukuda Hideko (1865–1927)

Japanese pioneer in the women's liberation movement during the Meiji era and one of the few women in the early socialist movement, who was editor of Japan's first feminist journal and author of the first autobiography of a woman to be written in her country. Name variations: Kageyama Hideko; Fukuda Hideko. Born Hideko Kageyama in 1865 in Okayama, Western Japan; died in May 1927; daughter of Katashi (a provincial samurai) and Umeko (a school teacher); left elementary school to become an assistant teacher in 1879; married Fukuda Yusaku, in 1892 (died 1900); children: (with Oi Kentaro) one son, (with Fukuda Yusaku) three sons.

Joined women's rights movement after hearing Kishida Toshiko speak (1882); opened a school for girls and women (1883); moved to Tokyo after school closed by authorities (1884); joined group of radical liberal activists, arrested and imprisoned for her role as an explosives courier (1885); tried and sentenced to jail for ten months (1887); after release from prison, lived with Oi Kentaro and gave birth to a son (1890); became a socialist and started school for women (1901); wrote autobiography Half My Life and began campaign against restrictions against women in Meiji Civil Code (1904); founded feminist magazine Women of the World (1907), which was banned by Tokyo court (1909); wrote article in feminist journal Seito, banned (1913); continued feminist and socialist activities up to year of death (1927).

For three days, the voice of *Kishida Toshiko had filled the Okayama lecture hall, thrilling the audience with her denunciation of Japan's "evil practice" of "respecting men and despising women." A former lady-in-waiting at the Japanese imperial court who had left her position because she found it "boring," Kishida declared Japan's need to build a new society based on equality between men and women. "Equality, independence, respect, and a monogamous relationship are the hallmarks of relationships between men and women in a civilized society," cried Kishida, while a teenage girl named Hideko and her mother, Umeko, sat enthralled.

Years later, Hideko Fukuda wrote of the effect of that speech, heard in 1882, that became her first step on the road to social activism as one of Japan's earliest feminists: "Listening to her speech, delivered in that marvelous oratorical style, I was unable to suppress my resentment and indignation . . . and began immediately to organize women and their daughters . . . to take the initiative in explaining and advocating natural rights, liberty, and equality . . . so that we might muster the passion to smash the corrupt customs of former days relating to women."

Hideko was born in 1865, in the Okayama prefecture, one of four children in the family of a low-ranking samurai named Katashi, who ran a small private school, raised vegetables, and later became a policeman. Hideko's mother Umeko was a teacher in a girls' middle school, who dressed and behaved like a "modern" woman and remained a strong influence on Hideko throughout her life.

Hideko grew up in the early years of the Meiji Period, which lasted from 1868 to 1912, when her country was undergoing a number of major reforms. At the beginning of the Meiji era, government policy was concerned with opening up Japan to Western influences, in the hope of making the country more modern and industrial. At the same time, some attention was also paid to the enlightenment of its women. In 1868, when Hideko was three, the Meiji government sent five young girls abroad to learn about Western life in order to become role models for Japanese women. Throughout the 1870s, the role of women in the family was an issue under frequent discussion. In particular, some debated that women should be treated with more respect, since mothers bore much of the responsibility for teaching a new generation of young Japanese to be more independent and think critically. According to this argument, women should be better educated and given more authority in the family. The "good wife, wise mother" was held up by reformers as the female ideal. The Popular Rights Movement of this period incorporated some ideas about women's political rights, and Hideko later became a member.

Hideko was a bright girl. After she finished elementary school, her parents encouraged her to become an assistant teacher, although they worried that the Western-style education she had received would not prepare her to become a traditional Japanese wife. At home, she was given traditional lessons in the tea ceremony, flower arrangement, sewing, and proper manners. Her parents also arranged for music lessons, as she said, "hoping to make me behave like a girl rather than a boy." In her autobiography, she wrote, "So I had to take daily lessons in how to play a string instrument like the two-string koto and the Chinese lute. . . . I worked at these lessons well into the night, day after day."

By the time Hideko was 16, she was receiving offers of marriage, which she rebuffed, placing her parents in an awkward position. She was making her own living by then, but she did not want to be pressured into marriage, so she proposed to her parents that she give them all her earnings, in return for being allowed to remain in their home. "I pleaded with my parents with all my heart," she wrote. "They must have concluded that I could not be easily dissuaded. . . . There are many women who, coerced by their parents, mechanically and ritualistically marry men who they do not love. After my experience, I vowed to help these unfortunate women so that they might follow the path of independence and self-reliance."

The year she was 17, she heard the speeches by Kishida Toshiko, expressing ideas that went far beyond the "good wife, wise mother" ideal. Following Kishida's appearances in Okayama, Hideko organized the first women's discussion and lecture groups ever held in Japan. At one of these meetings Hideko herself gave a speech called "The Theory of the Equality of Human Beings." She and her mother also joined in opening a private school for girls and older women who had never had the chance to receive a basic education.

In 1884, Hideko joined the Liberal Party, a reform group whose members clashed with the police that same year in an incident involving free speech. When the police retaliated by closing Hideko's school, she was ready to leave Okayama anyway and set off for Tokyo.

At the age of 20, Hideko quickly involved herself in the radical branch of Tokyo's liberal political circles. Her friends were activists who wanted to increase Japan's influence in the world. In 1885, she joined a plot to aid a liberal and revolutionary pro-Japanese movement involving Korean-born students in Japan who wanted their country to modernize along the same lines as Meiji Japan. When the Japanese government failed to support the group in their attempt to overthrow conservative rivals, Hideko became involved in a plan to supply the revolutionaries with explosives sent to Korea by ship. The plan was to create an incident that would undo a Sino-Japanese agreement whereby neither Japan nor China would maintain troops in Korea.

Inspired by a biography of *Joan of Arc she had just read, Hideko dreamed of becoming

Japan's St. Joan. But the radicals' plot was exposed, Hideko and her friends were arrested, and in May 1887, Hideko was sentenced to an 18-month term in prison as a state criminal in what became known as the Osaka Incident. "Even though I was a woman," Hideko later said about the episode, "I had decided to risk my life challenging the brutal government, and now I was learning the truth of the adage, 'If you win, you are a loyalist; if you lose, you are a traitor.'"

In prison, Hideko taught other female prisoners how to read and write, and sewed clothes to make money. In 1889, the group was awarded amnesty and released, and a huge crowd was present to greet them as they left jail, with banners congratulating them on their freedom. As the only woman in the group, Hideko became the focus of attention, made a public figure by the Osaka Incident.

That same year, Hideko began a relationship with a fellow conspirator, Oi Kentaro, who was a leader in the radical liberal movement. Promising to divorce his mentally ill wife, Oi proposed to Hideko, and meanwhile the two lived together. In 1890, the couple had a son, but Hideko later found out that Oi's wife was already dead, and that he was having several affairs while living with her. In Hideko's eyes, Oi's infidelities came to reflect the actions of a number of male activists who advocated the equality of the sexes while in reality holding women in low regard. Of her disillusionment, she wrote: "I could not understand how these men could party so, and I castigated them for their behavior. . . . I stayed awake, mulling over the fact that my comrades behaved as if we had enough money for them to spend their time in bordellos." Like other female reformers in the Meiji period, Hideko argued that the sanctioned practices of concubinage and prostitution were central to the question of women's status.

Hideko broke up with Oi in 1891. Eager to work for "women's rights and equality," she started a girls' vocational school with her family in Tokyo, but after the family suffered a series of misfortunes, she was forced to close the school. During this time, however, she met an American-trained scholar, Yusaku Fukuda, and despite the objections of his family, they married in 1892. In the years 1893–99, Hideko and Yusaku had three sons.

While Hideko was involved with raising her small sons, the Meiji government was backing away from its past support of reforms for women. As Japanese women insisted on a more public role for themselves and challenged the social institutions that blocked their opportunities for change, the government grew increasingly threatened by the democratic forces unleashed during the first two decades of Meiji period; then it was shocked by the involvement of women textile workers, who were the backbone of the textile industry, in a series of strikes. In an attempt to control the direction of change, the government began to crack down. In 1887, it passed the Peace Preservation Law, which placed strict police controls on political opposition. Article Five of the law was specifically aimed at women, allowing fines or imprisonment for women who tried to organize a political association, join a political group, or attend a political meeting. Women were also forbidden to attend the Japanese Diet as observers of legislative activities, to make political speeches, or even to take a course in political science. These were the harshest political regulations the country's women had ever faced.

> *When I look at the conditions currently prevailing in society, I see that as far as women are concerned, virtually everything is coercive and oppressive, making it imperative that we women rise up and forcefully develop our own social movement.*
>
> —Hideko Fukuda

In 1889, Japan's new Constitution went even further, with a Civil Code that recognized only men as legal persons. Married women, for example, were not allowed to bring legal action as independent beings, although husbands were free to dispose of their wives' property as they liked. The Code also shored up the patriarchal nature of Japan's family model by reinstating laws of primogeniture and patrilocality, while the status of Japanese women was reduced to that of mental incompetents and minors. The aim of public schooling for girls became more narrowly defined as a training for the roles of "good wives and mothers" who would manage the home skillfully and be obedient and submissive. By 1900, there were few reformers left in Japan who championed women's rights.

In 1900, Hideko Fukuda's husband died after a short illness, leaving her a widow with four children and her mother to support. In order to earn money, Hideko turned again to teaching, establishing a women's technological school to produce women who could be self-supporting. Helping her in the school was Ishikawa Sanshiro, a man 11 years younger than herself. That same year, Hideko moved in with Ishikawa.

In 1901, Hideko and Ishikawa joined the Japanese socialist movement, beginning the association that was to dominate her life from 1901 to 1907. Her primary work was through an organization called Heiminsha, or the Commoner's Society, which published a newspaper known for its pacifist stand against the Russo-Japanese War. It is not clear if Hideko wrote for the paper, but she helped raise funds for its support and advocated its antiwar position.

In 1904, Heiminsha published Hideko's account of her life up to the turn of the century. Called *Half of My Lifetime,* it was the first autobiography of a woman written in Japan, and described her involvement in the Osaka Incident, her years in jail, and her unhappy relationship with Oi Kentaro. The book was an immediate success and remains in print. The following year, Hideko published a novel called *My Reminiscences,* which was less well received.

Heiminsha was forced by the government to disband in 1905. The socialist movement was splintering into small, ideologically diverse groups at the time, and Hideko joined one that was leading a nationwide petition campaign to revise the "insulting" constitutional restrictions of Article Five. In 1908, the Lower House of the Diet responded by voting in favor of allowing women to join political parties, but the petition was rejected by the more conservative Upper House, and Hideko was furious. "What bigoted men they are! How ignorant!" she wrote. "They simply maintain their opposition, saying 'Observing the courts and the Diet, and reading political debate in the newspapers are acceptable, but women may not listen to political lectures.'"

Hideko was also upset by the position of her socialist colleagues, who claimed that women's liberation would automatically arrive with the economic liberation of everyone. Hideko feared that "economic liberation" might allow women to be treated even worse than before, unless attitudes about the roles of men and women changed first. Convinced of the need for women to become financially independent, she believed they must be allowed to earn money and to keep it.

In 1907, concluding that socialist journals never adequately covered women's concerns, Hideko formed a women's group and began publication of a journal called *Sekai Fujin,* or *Women of the World.* In its first issue, dated January 1, 1907, *Women of the World* proclaimed its goal: "To determine the real vocation of women by extracting it from the tangled web of law, custom, and morality that are a part of women's experience. Then, we hope to cultivate among all of you a desire to join a reform movement founded on what will be the true mission of women."

As the title suggests, the aim of *Women of the World* was to inform women about suffrage movements around the world, and of the important roles of women in historical events, like *Madame Roland during the French Revolution. Hideko also tried to attract women of diverse interests by covering practical topics, including recipes and advice on cooking and sewing. But the deeper purpose of *Women of the World* was to inspire women to action. At best, Hideko wanted to create a movement among women which would improve their status in Japanese society. At the very least, she wanted to draw them into the campaign against the hated Article Five. Hideko argued that it symbolized the "double burden" of oppression forced on women, by the wealthy and by men.

At age 43, Hideko had embarked on her most ambitious project to date, and the one for which she would be best known. Published bimonthly for more than two years, the journal has been cited by one scholar as the "beginning of the rise of a conscious, organized feminist movement in Japan." Beyond women's issues, *Women of the World* tackled other concerns, including the dangerous working conditions in the Japanese textile factories and the plight of people along the Watarase River, whose waters were being poisoned by the Ashio Copper Mine. After 1908, the journal became the target of systematic government harassment, with some issues banned or heavily fined. Hideko received cancellation letters from subscribers who were being pressured by family and friends to cut their association with the magazine. Young women in one school were forced to cancel their subscriptions under threat of punishment. Hideko tried to make the journal less political and more literary, but in 1909, the government officially banned it; as Hideko said, "beginnings are easy, it's continuing that's difficult." In 1910, Hideko ceased trying to keep the journal alive and retreated to Ishikawa's family home.

Hideko's efforts to keep the journal going left her penniless. But if *Women of the World* had proved to be a financial failure, it did succeed in opening up a new world of ideas for a number of women by raising issues and giving them a sense of purpose. Hideko herself became a role model for Japan's "second wave" feminists. In 1911, the next generation of young and well-to-do female intellectuals, calling themselves the "Bluestocking" Group, began their own magazine, called *Seito*. An article by Hideko appeared in *Seito* in 1913, advocating the establishment of a community system that would use "all scientific knowledge and mechanical power" for the "equality and benefit of all," and that issue of the journal was banned. That same year, Ishikawa left Japan to escape the government's harassment of socialists and used his departure to end his relationship with Hideko. In her later years, Hideko was much less involved in political affairs, and lived in extreme poverty. She died in 1927, at the age of 61.

SOURCES:

Hane, Mikiso, ed. and trans. *Reflections on the Way to the Gallows: Women in Prewar Japan*. Berkeley, CA: University of California Press, 1989.

Sievers, Sharon L. *Flowers in Salt: The Beginnings of Feminist Consciousness in Modern Japan*. Stanford, CA: Stanford University Press, 1983.

———. "Women in China, Japan, and Korea," in *Restoring Women to History: Teaching Packets for Integrating Women's History into Courses of Africa, Asia, Latin America, The Caribbean, and the Middle East*. Bloomington, IN: Organization of American Historians, 1988.

Ushioda, Sharlie C. "Fukuda Hideko and the Woman's World Of Meiji Japan," in *Japan in Transition*. Hilary Conroy et al., eds. London: Associated University Presses, 1984.

SUGGESTED READING:

Fujimura-Fanselow, Kumiko, and Atsuko Kameda, eds. *Japanese Women: New Feminist Perspectives on the Past, Present, and Future*. NY: Feminist Press, 1994.

Sproule, Anna. *Solidarity: Women Workers, Women History Makers Series*. London: Macdonald, 1987.

Tanaka, Yukiko. *To Live and to Write: Selections by Japanese Women Writers 1913-1938*. Seattle, WA: The Seal Press, 1987.

Lyn Reese,
women's history author and director of Women in the World
Curriculum Resources, Berkeley, California

Fuld, Carrie (1864–1944)

American philanthropist who co-founded the Institute for Advanced Study in Princeton, New Jersey. Born Carrie Bamberger on March 16, 1864, in Baltimore, Maryland; died on July 18, 1944, in Lake Placid, New York; fifth of six children of Elkan (a businessman) and Theresa (Hutzler) Bamberger; attended public and private schools in Baltimore; married Louis Meyer Frank (co-founder of L. Bamberger & Company, a department store), in the early 1980s (died 1910); married Felix Fuld (partner in L. Bamberger & Co.), on February 20, 1913 (died 1929); no children.

One of six children of German-Jewish parents, Carrie Bamberger, later Fuld, was born in 1864 and raised in Baltimore, Maryland, where her father ran a wholesale notions business. Her mother **Theresa Hutzler Bamberger** was the daughter of Moses Hutzler, who founded a well-known Baltimore department store. In the early 1880s, Carrie married Louis Meyer Frank, who, in 1893, joined Carrie's brother Louis Bamberger and a second partner, Felix Fuld, to open L. Bamberger & Company, a small store in Newark, New Jersey. After Frank died in 1910, Carrie married Felix Fuld, her brother's surviving partner. At the time of Fuld's death in 1929, L. Bamberger was the largest department store in the United States. Just prior to the stock-market crash, Carrie and her brother sold the concern to R.H. Macy & Company for $25 million.

A strong social conscience led Carrie and her brother to use their fortune to benefit the public—particularly the citizens of New Jersey. Originally interested in endowing a medical school, they met with Abraham Flexner, an educator and foundation executive, who persuaded them to use their money to promote basic research and advance the frontiers of knowledge. In 1930, Fuld and Bamberger donated $5 million to found the Institute for Advanced Study, which opened in Princeton, New Jersey, in 1933, with Flexner as its director. The first institute of its kind in the United States, it employed some of nation's finest minds to engage in research and creative scholarship. (The brilliant mathematician Albert Einstein was the first professor of the institute's school of mathematics.) Additional gifts from Bamberger and Fuld, eventually totalling $18 million, endowed a school of economics and politics and a school of humanistic studies. Fuld also served as vice president of the board of trustees of the Institute until 1934, when she felt her services were no longer needed.

Carrie Fuld contributed generously to other causes as well, although she carefully avoided publicity and made many of her donations anonymously. She was especially generous to the Jewish community, making large donations to the Beth Israel Hospital in Newark, and to the American Jewish Joint Agricultural Corporation to help train Russian Jews for work in factories and on farms. One of her pet charities was the Jewish Day Nursery and Neighborhood House, a settlement house in the Newark slums. It was renamed the Fuld Neighborhood House in 1941. She also supported Hadassah and was active the National Council of Jewish Women. A patron of the arts, Fuld backed the New York Philharmonic Society and made a gift of several paintings and sculptures to the Newark Museum. After her death in 1944, the works of art from her home in South Orange were given to the museum and to the New Jersey Historical Society.

SOURCES:

James, Edward T., ed. *Notable American Women.* Cambridge, MA: The Belknap Press of Harvard University Press, 1971.

Weatherford, Doris. *American Women's History.* NY: Prentice-Hall, 1994.

Barbara Morgan,
Melrose, Massachusetts

Fuller, Iola.

See McCoy, Iola Fuller.

Fuller, Loïe (1862–1928)

American-born music-hall performer whose innovations with shadows and light brought drama and mystery to the stage and elicited a strong following among French intellectuals. Name variations: Lois,

Loïe
Fuller

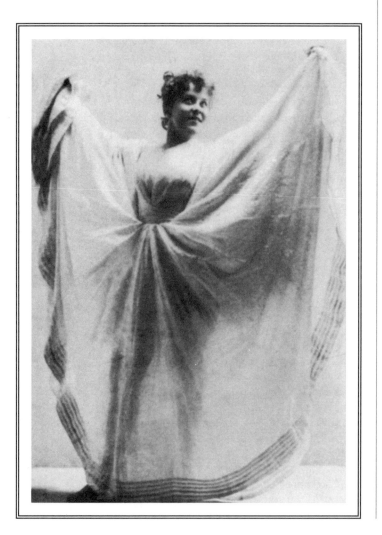

Loie, La Loïe. Pronunciation: LO-ee. Born Mary Louise Fuller, probably on January 22, 1862, in Fullersburg, Illinois; died in Paris, France, of pneumonia on January 1, 1928; daughter of Reuben (a well-known fiddler and tavern owner) and **Delilah Fuller** (a singer); self-taught; married Colonel William Hayes, in May 1889 (divorced 1892); lived with Gabrielle Bloch; no children.

Raised from childhood in vaudeville, stock companies, and burlesque shows; made Paris debut at Folies Bergère (1892); using innovative lighting techniques which became her trademark, created "Fire Dance" (1895); had her own theater at International Exposition in Paris (1900); recorded on film (1904); toured U.S. (1909–10); made honorary member of French Astronomical Society for her artistic uses of light.

Theatrical works: "Serpentine" (1891); "Butterfly" (1892); "Fire Dance" (1895); "Radium Dance" (1904); "La Tragédie de Salomé" (1907); "Danse Macabre" (1911); "La Feu d'Artifice" (1914); "Le Lys de la Vie" (1920); "La Mer" (1925).

When Loïe Fuller learned about the newly discovered element that gave off a magical light, she wrote directly to its discoverers, the scientists Pierre and *Marie Curie, to ask about the possibility of using radium in her theatrical performances. As a performer known in France as the "Fairy of Light," the dancer saw an opportunity in using the radioactive material to add to the effectiveness of her production numbers. When the Curies made it clear that radium was too expensive and impractical for use onstage, Fuller instead created her "Radium Dance" (1904) and arranged a performance for the Curies in their home. While modern understanding of the dangers of radioactivity might make Fuller's idea seem especially foolhardy, her original approach was typical of what made Fuller famous: her endless quest for technological and scientific innovations to enhance her theatrical ideas; her eagerness to use spectacle for artistic ends; and her hardworking but practical approach to creating the mysterious and shimmery vision she projected on stage.

Born Mary Louise Fuller on or around January 22, 1862, Loïe Fuller spent virtually all of her life onstage. Her parents, Reuben and Delilah, were vaudeville entertainers. Her father was a famous fiddler who later owned a tavern near Chicago, and her mother was an aspiring opera singer who eventually turned to singing in less-esteemed venues. Forever creating a legend to surround herself, Fuller recalled in her autobiography that she first went onstage at age two-

and-a-half because there was no babysitter in the dance hall.

Around age 13, Loïe appeared briefly as a child temperance lecturer. Keen about the effectiveness of dramatic techniques even then, she would call the town drunkard to come up onstage and then supplement his actions with colored charts of the liver to depict the evils of alcohol and its physical effects. In the last part of the 19th century, temperance lecturing drew large crowds as a popular nightly entertainment offering, and *Frances Willard, then president of the largest temperance organization, the Women's Christian Temperance Union, was a hero of Loïe's. The lecturers gave Fuller valuable lessons on how to capture and hold an audience's attention by forcing her to dramatize, and make visually interesting, a repetitive, moralizing tract.

From temperance lecturing, Fuller went on to perform in vaudeville, stock companies (which supplied the regional base of performers to appear with traveling stars), and even burlesque shows, gaining the experience she would turn to her own use in inventing a new kind of theatrical spectacle that was neither dance exactly, nor theater. By 1886, she had moved from the Midwest to New York, where she appeared in various theatrical productions, none of which yet distinguished her from many other performers. In 1889, she reached London, where a stint at the Gaiety Theater introduced her to the work of the popular dancer ⚘▸ Kate Vaughan, famous as the "Gaiety Girl" for her variation on the "Skirt Dances" then being performed in dance halls throughout England. The dances used a voluminous costume to enhance and exaggerate the movements of the dancer's body, while also leaving some parts of flesh exposed, if only briefly.

Back in the United States, Fuller experimented with her own version of the "Skirt Dance," introduced in 1891 in a production number called "Quack, M.D." There are as many as seven different versions of how she obtained her first silk dress and "discovered" its theatrical effect. In her autobiography, she claimed that she was looking for a costume for a dance about hypnotism, when she came across an old gift of Indian silk. Onstage, lit in pale green, she heard murmurs from the audience, saying, "It's a butterfly," from which she took her inspiration to create non-human visions through large, flowing costumes. While this version ignores the 18 months she spent at London's Gaiety Theater, there is no question that American audiences reacted well to a theatrical vision they took as completely new.

Soon after "Quack, M.D.," Fuller was hired as a specialty dancer in "Uncle Celestin," where she performed the "Serpentine Dances" that made her a soloist of some repute. To dramatize her version of the skirt dances, she also began to add more and more cloth, until the skirt became draperies around a small body. For "Le Lys du Nile," introduced in 1895, her costume contained 500 yards of fine silk and the hem measured close to 100 yards. In performance, the costume could become a 10-foot halo around her body, or be thrown 20 feet upward. Over the years, she created a system of wands sewn into the costumes to help her control the massive amounts of fabric. Still, the enormous strength and practice it took to manipulate them would leave her so weary that she would have to be carried home after a day of rehearsal and a night of performance.

Fuller also learned to utilize light and color for varying effects on the swirling material. The incandescent lamp invented by Thomas Edison in 1879 soon began to replace the gaslights that had illuminated theaters, and Fuller was one of the first to manipulate color onstage by placing a colored glass plate in front of the light projector. Each of her three dances in "Uncle Celestin" was illuminated by a single color, first blue, then red and yellow. Later on, she spent a great deal of time mixing chemicals to come up with the different gelatin covers to create various shades of color onstage.

As a shrewd businesswoman. Fuller knew how quickly and how often imitators sprang up. She made numerous attempts to patent her costumes, lighting ideas, and even her dances. While her dances were often denied copyright in court as mechanical movements, she would not

---

⚘▸ **Vaughan, Kate** (c. 1852–1903)

English actress and dancer. Born Catherine Candellon around 1852; died in Johannesburg, South Africa, in 1903.

Born Catherine Candellon around 1852, Kate Vaughan made her debut as a dancer in 1870. From 1876 to 1883, she was a headliner in burlesques at the Gaiety Theater in London. For two years, she worked with her own company, the Vaughan-Conway Comedy troupe, and inaugurated the modern school of skirt dancing, before performing on stage in the roles of Lady Teazle and Lydia Languish. In 1902, she sailed to Johannesburg, South Africa, in hopes of improving her declining health. She died there one year later.

Loïe Fuller,
poster by Jules
Chéret, 1893.

use some of her ideas until they were protected. Her plan to replace part of a stage floor with glass and light under the stage so that it would shine through the costume from below was patented in 1893, but not used until her "Fire Dance," first presented in 1895. Fear of imitation may not have been the only reason for the delay; the technique required making a hole in the stage, a measure few theater owners were willing to undertake, even for the "Fairy of Light." The "Fire Dance" also required 14 electricians to handle color changes.

At age 30, Fuller decided to build on her success by planning a tour of Europe. Accompanied as always by her mother, she set off with Paris as her goal, but first had to travel to Berlin, Hamburg, and Cologne, performing in various venues, even a circus. In late 1892, she finally reached the French capital, where she convinced Monsieur Marchand, head of the famous Folies Bergère music hall, to let her replace the serpentine dancer then performing the ubiquitous skirt dance. Fuller's debut appearance, on November 5, was received with reviews more glowing than the stage upon which she had appeared. In *Consideration on the Art of Loïe Fuller,* the writer Stéphane Mallarmé wrote:

> Her performance, *sui generis,* is at once an artistic intoxication and an industrial achievement. In that terrible bath of materials swoons the radiant, cold dancer, illustrating countless themes of gyration. From her proceeds an expanding web—giant butterflies and petals, unfoldings—everything of a pure and elemental order. She blends with the rapidly changing colours which vary their limelit phantasmagoria of twilight and grotto, their rapid emotional changes—delight, mourning, anger; and to set these off, prismatic, either violent or dilute as they are, there must be the dizziness of soul made visible by an artifice.

Mallarmé stood at the forefront of the Symbolist movement, which soon made Loïe Fuller an emblematic embodiment of its ideas. Symbolists revolted against the materialism and rationalism of Positivist thought, in which the rules of science and evolution governed morality and philosophy. Eschewing the machination of a world of ideas based on what can be empirically known, Symbolists sought to revivify the mysterious and the unprovable, heralding art "for art's sake," not as a purpose for something else; and they recognized a transcendence beyond literalness and what can be articulated. In Loïe Fuller, they identified the clear manifestation of what it meant to be a *symbol*: to represent something in its essence—fire, a butterfly, the sea—but not be the thing itself.

Fuller reveled in her Paris reception. Steeping herself in the scientific and mechanical techniques of the mysterious image, she maintained the theatrical illusions she created with a great deal of practicality. She set up a laboratory in Paris and eventually was made a member of the French Astronomical Society, which honored her for her artistic use of light. More often she was known from Symbolist and Art Nouveau depictions of her by contemporary artists and writers. Jules Cheret drew a famous poster of her, and

Henri Toulouse-Lautrec made a lithograph; La Loïe, as she became known, numbered among her admirers some of the most famous French artists and intellectuals of her day, including August Rodin, the Goncourt Brothers, Jean Lorrain, and Anatole France.

The peak of her success may have been the International Exposition held in Paris in 1900. Fuller by then had her own theater, designed by the Art Nouveau architect Henri Sauvage, which included a statue of herself. Here she gave her mystical performances and also hosted the Japanese actress **Sada Yacco** and her husband, Otojiro Kawakami, propelling them to international acclaim. The American dancers *Isadora Duncan and *Ruth St. Denis were inspired by her performances. In 1902, Fuller helped Duncan to tour Europe, sponsoring her appearances in Berlin and Vienna. In 1924, St. Denis choreographed "Valse à la Loie" to memorialize Fuller's performance at the International Exposition.

> *I* suppose I am the only person who is known as a dancer but who has a personal preference for Science.
> —Loïe Fuller

Fuller spent most of the rest of her life in Paris. "Well, I was born in America," she is said to have remarked, "but I was made in Paris." Around 1908, she formed a school and a company of 30 women, and in 1909–10 she took the company on a triumphant tour of the United States. The Metropolitan Opera House and the New Boston Opera House were among the places where "Loïe Fuller and Her Muses" appeared. Her forays into science also led her to experiment with motion pictures, a nascent technology at the beginning of the 20th century, and film clips recorded around 1904 still survive. Filmmaking was a logical outgrowth of Fuller's interest in lighting, and after World War I she began to produce her own films.

Fuller's career overshadowed her personal life. In 1889, she married Colonel William Hayes, a nephew of President Rutherford B. Hayes, but the couple never lived together. Since Hayes lent money to Fuller, she may have agreed to marry him in return. Three years later, in 1892, Fuller sued her husband for bigamy and was awarded $10,000. Fuller's lifelong companions, outside this marriage of convenience, were her mother (who died in Paris in 1908) and **Gabrielle Bloch.** In her autobiography, Fuller described her relationship with Bloch: "For eight years Gab and I have lived together on terms of the greatest intimacy, like two sisters. Gab is much younger than I and regards me with deep affection." Theirs was probably a sexual relationship as well as a significant friendship; certainly Fuller was surrounded with women, with no men in her home, school, or company.

Fuller's innovations in lighting, set, and costume designs shaped both theater and dance history. Neither a dancer of much skill (she took fewer than six dance lessons in her life) nor an actress of wide emotional range (her interest lay in displaying visual effects), she has often been overlooked, but her influence on artists and dancers has in fact been greater than that of some performers who immediately followed her. Alwin Nikolais, well-known for his work combining theater and dance in the 1960s, took off on Fuller's experimentation with gel slides, lighting plans, and sound. The theater of the future that Fuller dreamed of, calling it "The Temple of Light," was eventually created by Nikolais and others.

Fuller also initiated a creative migration to France made by many other artists and intellectuals from America. The warm reception French audiences gave to modern dance, particularly Isadora Duncan, was an offshoot of the affection and respect generated by "La Loïe." In her fusion of France and America, science and art, Fuller raised the level of music-hall entertainment while also popularizing the abstract notions of art of the Symbolist and Art Nouveau movements. Over the years, however, she grew increasingly obese and moved about with more and more difficulty, until the woman who had been described as "music of the eyes" by Anatole France, died penniless in Paris, of pneumonia, on January 1, 1928.

SOURCES:

de Morinni, Clare. "Loïe Fuller: The Fairy of Light," in *Dance Index*. Vol. 1, no. 3. March 1942, pp. 40–51.

Fuller, Loïe. *Fifteen Years of a Dancer's Life*. Boston, MA: Small, Maynard, 1913.

Harris, Margaret Haile. *Loïe Fuller: Magician of Light*. A loan exhibition at the Virginia Museum. Richmond: The Virginia Museum, 1979.

Sommer, Sally. "Loïe Fuller," in *The Drama Review*. Vol. 19. March 1975, pp. 53–67.

SUGGESTED READING:

Current, Marcia Ewing, and Richard Nelson Current. *Loie Fuller: Goddess of Light*. Boston, MA: Northeastern University Press, 1997.

Jowitt, Deborah. *Time and the Dancing Image*. NY: William Morrow, 1988.

Kendall, Elizabeth. *Where She Danced*. NY: Alfred A. Knopf, 1979.

COLLECTIONS:

Correspondence, reviews, film clips, and photographs located in the Dance Collection, Performing Arts Library, New York Public Library.

Julia L. Foulkes,
former Rockefeller Foundation Postdoctoral Fellow at the Center for Black Music Research, Columbia College, Chicago, Illinois, and author of numerous articles

Fuller, Lucia Fairchild (1870–1224).

See Bacon, Peggy for sidebar.

Fuller, Margaret (1810–1850)

Early feminist writer, central figure with the Transcendentalists, and one of the most intellectually gifted American women of the 19th century. Name variations: Sarah Margaret Fuller as a child; Margaret Fuller Ossoli, d'Ossoli, or Marchioness Ossoli after her marriage. Born Sarah Margaret Fuller in Cambridgeport, Massachusetts, on May 23, 1810; died in a shipwreck off New York harbor, on July 19, 1850; eldest child of Timothy Fuller (1778–1835, a lawyer, member of the state assembly and U.S. Congress) and Margaret (Crane) Fuller; may have been married to her lover Marquis Giovanni Angelo Ossoli in 1849 or 1850; children: one son, Angelo.

Taught school in Providence (1837–39); began "conversations" for educated women (1839); was editor of the Dial *(1840–42); wrote book reviews for Greeley's New York Tribune (1844–46); voyaged to Europe (1846); as a journalist, covered the Italian republicans and the revolution (1846–49).*

Selected writings: Günderode *(translation of the correspondence between *Karoline von Günderode and *Bettina von Arnim, 1842);* Summer on the Lakes in 1843 *(Boston: Little Brown, 1844);* Women in the Nineteenth Century *(NY: Tribune Press, 1845);* Papers on Literature and Art *(2 vols. NY: Wiley and Putnam, 1846);* Collected Works *(1855);* Life Without and Life Within *(collection of essays and poems, Boston, 1860).*

Margaret Fuller was one of the most intellectually gifted American women of the 19th century. Thwarted by her family's poverty and by the restrictions of her gender in early life, she matured into a superb speaker and writer in her 30s. Her work as a literary critic and historian of the Italian revolution was cut tragically short by her death in a shipwreck when she was only 40.

Fuller was the oldest of nine children, and her ambitious father Timothy Fuller decided to bring her up as though she were a son. He made her work hard at a difficult educational pro-

Margaret Fuller

gram while pursuing his own career, first as a lawyer, later as a U.S. congressional representative, and then as speaker of the Massachusetts Assembly. At age six, she began to learn Latin and soon showed prodigious intellectual gifts, devouring Shakespeare and Cervantes while still very young and reading all of Virgil, Horace, and Ovid by the time she was eight. The price of this forced learning and a harsh streak in her father's manner was a long series of gruesome nightmares, in which she dreamed of being trampled by horses, and of being lost in a blood-soaked forest. She spent two teenage years in Groton, Massachusetts, at Miss Prescott's boarding school, where her intellectual brilliance amazed the teachers and unnerved fellow students. Fuller had violent temper tantrums when other students mocked her eccentricities, followed by paroxysms of remorse when her petty vengeance was discovered. She returned to the family's home in Cambridgeport, near Harvard University, when she was 15. There, she befriended Oliver Wendell Holmes, Sr., William Ellery Channing, and Richard Henry Dana, soon to be famous men, who were then studying at Harvard, and advanced her education by discussions with such professors as the logician Henry Hedge.

The pleasures of Harvard life ended abruptly when her father decided to retire from law and politics to a country farm in 1833. The life did not suit Margaret Fuller, then aged 23; she was bored teaching her young siblings and looking after the family when her mother **Margaret Crane Fuller** became an invalid. Her father's death from cholera two years later made matters worse. Responsible for the entire family, Fuller decided to work in Boston as a teacher and send them money rather than remain immured in the countryside. She worked at Bronson Alcott's Temple School as a Latin and French teacher, amazing the father of *Louisa May Alcott with her brilliance and energy, and taking on extra teaching and translating work to earn money for the family. After a year, Bronson's eccentric methods of religious education scandalized the children's parents, most of whom abandoned his school and drove it into bankruptcy. Fuller's reputation was spreading, however, and the Greene Street School in Providence, Rhode Island, now offered her $1,000 per year to teach just four hours a day, which was the highest teaching salary offered to a woman up to that time. She accepted and spent her leisure time reading Goethe and translating works of German philosophy. Aware that she was not a beauty, Fuller worked hard to make striking dresses for herself and to cut a distinctive figure even if not a conventionally attractive one.

In 1841, the family sold its farm in Groton and moved back to the Jamaica Plain section of Boston. There Fuller became a central figure in the Transcendentalist Club, befriending Ralph Waldo Emerson, Henry David Thoreau, the ◀ Sturgis sisters, George and ❧ Sophia Ripley, and *Elizabeth Palmer Peabody. The Transcendentalists rebelled against the conventional, theologically dry religion of Unitarian Boston in favor of their own blend of German philosophical idealism and nature mysticism. A group of talented writers, they were also great conversationalists (Bronson Alcott tried to make a living as a traveling conversationalist), and many of them described Fuller as the greatest talker among them. Her friend James Freeman Clark wrote: "All her friends will unite in the testimony that whatever they may have known of wit and eloquence in others, they have never seen one who, like her, by the conversation of an hour or two, could not merely entertain and inform, but make an epoch in one's life."

From late 1839, Fuller led a series of women's "conversations," which were in effect seminars on contemporary issues. Developing an early feminist insight into the condition of her sex, she urged her "assistants," as the participants were known, to study with the same rigor showed by their men folk and to look on their intellectual lives as vocational rather than merely decorative. The conversations, two hours a week, lasted 13 weeks for each of four consecutive years, gaining steadily in repute and drawing larger audiences each time. Fuller profited from them (at $10 per "assistant") and became an intellectual celebrity in New England but found when she once tried a course of mixed "conversations" that the men dominated the talk and patronized the women. Never subject to false modesty, she told Emerson, who also admired her, "I now know all the people worth knowing in America and I find no intellect comparable to my own."

Relinquishing teaching, she became first editor of *The Dial*, the Transcendentalists' magazine. Widely renowned, with a large group of clever and influential friends and acquaintances, she had the intellectual, literary, and business skills to make the project succeed. Emerson and George Ripley helped her get the magazine going, but she wrote eight of the articles in the first edition and was *The Dial*'s most prolific contributor throughout its five-year life. When Ripley started the Brook Farm commune in the spring of 1841, he and his wife urged Fuller to join them as the farm's "presiding genius." Fuller was willing to visit for weekends and hold impromptu conversations but, recalling her earlier experiences, felt no attraction to farming and the countryside and refused to live there. She suffered from severe and disabling headaches nearly every afternoon and cherished the privacy she could not have enjoyed in the commune. Nathaniel Hawthorne, who did settle down at Brook Farm for a while, disliked Fuller and modeled his odious character Zenobia, in *The Blithedale Romance* (1852), on her. He also wrote later that she was "a great humbug with a strong, heavy, unpliable, and, in many respects, defective and evil nature."

Fuller always had her share of opponents, knew she was unattractive to many men, and never expected to marry. "From an early age" she wrote:

> I have felt that I was not born to the common womanly lot. I knew that I should never find a being who could keep the key to my character, that there would be none on whom I could always lean; that I should be a pilgrim and sojourner on the earth, and that the birds and foxes would be surer of a place to lay their heads than I.

❧▶
Sturgis sisters.
See Adams, Clover for sidebar on Ellen Sturgis Hooper; see also Tappan, Caroline Sturgis.

In the late 1830s, she had fallen in love with Samuel Gray Ward, a man seven years her junior who had studied art and literature in Germany and shared many of her philosophical enthusiasms. She was dismayed when Ward decided to join his family's banking business rather than take the risk of a writing career, and even more dismayed when she learned that he was marrying one of her young disciples, Anna Barker.

In 1843, Fuller took a break from overwork and emotional upset by visiting what was then the far western edge of white settlement, now Illinois, Michigan, and Wisconsin. Traveling to Niagara Falls and then by boat to the small settlement of Chicago, she met Native Americans for the first time and began to lament their displacement by acquisitive and often violent white settlers. In true Transcendentalist fashion, she also regretted that the evangelical missionaries who were often among the first settlers in a new frontier area were trying to extinguish the natives' nature-religion. In a book based on this summer's experiences, *Summer on the Lakes* (1844), Fuller expanded on themes she had been exploring in the *Dial*, particularly the sufferings of women on the frontier and the unjust disadvantages they faced. While completing it, she got permission to use Harvard University's library, the first woman ever admitted there. The book's success gave her confidence to press on with another, *Women in the Nineteenth Century*, based on her 1843 *Dial* article, "The Great Lawsuit: Man *versus* Men: Woman *versus* Women." It was an acute work of feminist criticism, demonstrating the unjust burdens borne by American women. It too had no American precedent, and it marked Fuller as a leading theorist in the cause of American feminism. She made the analogy between women and African-Americans which has since become a standard argument:

> As the friend of the Negro assumes that one man cannot by right hold another in bondage, so should the friend of Woman assume that Man cannot by right lay even well-meant restrictions on Woman. If the Negro be a soul; if the woman be a soul, appareled in flesh, to one Master only are they accountable. There is but one law for souls, and if there is to be an interpreter of it, he must come not as man or son of man, but as son of God.

Laced with Italian poetry, quotations from German and French philosophers, and occasional Transcendentalist asides, *Woman in the Nineteenth Century* attacked prostitution, criticized the psychological degradation of women, and argued that men and women would both benefit from equal social and legal treatment. It sold out within a week and spread widely through North America, scandalizing conventional readers but widening her circle of intellectual admirers.

One of her former conversational "assistants," **Mary Cheney**, now married to New York newspaper editor Horace Greeley, read and admired *Summer on the Lakes*, and when she showed it to her husband he also recognized its author's exceptional talent. Greeley had made famous the phrase, "Go West, Young Man!," which inspired frontier adventurers, and Fuller's learned discussion of the costs as well as the benefits of frontier life impressed him. He invited her to come to New York and work as literary critic on his crusading newspaper the *Tribune*, and she accepted with alacrity. There, Fuller was required to write three articles every week, many of them reviews of poor quality fiction. She could be scornful of inferior work and, even when reviewing the books of Boston friends like Emerson, was willing to make sharp reprimands.

Book reviewing took up most of her time on the *Tribune*, but she also wrote about the prison-reform movement in which she became involved. After visiting women's prisons at Sing-Sing and in New York City, she was convinced that many of the inmates, incarcerated for prostitution, could be rehabilitated if the prisons taught them working skills rather than simply keeping them off the streets. Articles advocating these and other reforms helped Greeley sell more newspapers, and he found his gamble in hiring her paying handsome dividends.

Ripley, Sophia (1803–1861)

American educator and Transcendentalist. Born on July 6, 1803; died in 1861; married George Ripley (1802–1880, a leading Transcendentalist); children.

A close friend of Margaret Fuller, Sophia Ripley also contributed to the *Dial*. She was the first in that periodical to touch on the "women's question," in her 1841 article "Woman," complaining that women lose themselves in marriage, becoming "an appendage . . . the upper nurse." Though Ripley carried on a traditional existence in her marriage to George Ripley, she was a leading spirit in developing with her husband their utopian Brook Farm, a model community based on the ideals of Christianity and Transcendentalism. Its members included Nathaniel Hawthorne, John Sullivan Dwight, Christopher Cranch, **Almira Barlow**, and Margaret Fuller's brother Lloyd. Wrote Ralph Waldo Emerson: "Sarah R is wonderfully free from egotism of place and time and blood."

As a personal friend of Greeley and his wife, Fuller lived with them in their house by the East River, but their relationship became strained when she fell in love with a man they considered unsuitable. He was James Nathan, a German-Jewish immigrant and merchant with literary and artistic tastes to match her own. He confided his hopes and plans to her during their frequent meetings, most of which had to take place outdoors because of the Greeleys' disapproval. At one point, he apparently made sexual advances that shocked her. They remained intimate, however, and it grieved her to learn that his family was sending him on an extended business tour to Europe. She wrote him almost every day during the first months of his absence. His replies were dutiful but a good deal less frequent.

> $\mathcal{L}$et Ulysses drive the beeves [cows] home, while Penelope there piles up the fragrant loaves; they are both well employed. . . . But Penelope is no more meant for a baker or weaver solely, than Ulysses for a cattle-herd.
>
> —Margaret Fuller

When Fuller was a child, her father had promised that she could conclude her education with a trip to Europe. Financial problems and his untimely death had made the trip recede from her horizon, and, at the age of 35, she had still not set foot on European soil. In 1846, her opportunity came at last when a pair of close friends, Marcus and **Rebecca Spring**, offered Fuller the chance to accompany them on a long European excursion, acting as companion to their son Edward. She agreed to go and arranged to write regularly for Greeley's paper, playing in effect the part of foreign correspondent for the *Tribune*. After a rapid but rough journey on one of the new Atlantic steamers which added seasickness to her already long list of infirmities, Fuller reached England. She toured the sights of the industrial revolution, many of them horrifying visions of poverty and degradation, and met several literary celebrities, including Thomas Carlyle and William Wordsworth. Her reputation had preceded her over the ocean, and many of the British writers recognized her as a luminous figure in American literature. The meeting that she most prized, however, came a few months later when she and the Springs had moved on to France. It was with *George Sand, a daringly bohemian woman who had had a string of well-publicized love affairs with some of Europe's greatest artists, had written controversial novels based on her experiences, and was

now "living in sin" with the composer and piano virtuoso Frederic Chopin. Sand saluted Fuller as a literary equal which went at least some way towards compensating her for the shattering news, learned just before she left London, that James Nathan had decided to marry another woman.

From France, the group moved on to Italy, visiting Florence, Pisa, Naples, Venice, and Rome. Italy held a special place in Fuller's affections, and she believed strongly in the cause of the Italian republican leader Giuseppe Mazzini, whom she had met during his exile in London. At Rome in a chance encounter, she met the Marquis Giovanni Ossoli, whose family were distinguished servants of the Vatican. Against their wishes, he had become a republican sympathizer, and in the political upheavals of the following two years was closely allied with the radical faction that planned to unify Italy and nullify the pope's political power. Fuller's friendship with Ossoli, who was ten years her junior, matured quickly, based on common political convictions, even though he did not share her literary and artistic tastes. She told the Springs that she would like to stay on when they moved from Rome, reassuring them that she could live for several months on her savings and that the steady flow of articles she was sending back to New York would enable her to make more money.

The events of the Italian crisis of 1848–49 are immensely complex, involving the country in invasions from France and Austria and dividing Rome between supporters and opponents of the papacy. As the crisis unfolded and as Mazzini returned to lead the provisional republican government of Rome, Fuller's fascination at being in the midst of a revolution gave way to dismay. She discovered that she was pregnant as a result of her love affair with Ossoli. They were devoted to one another but for the moment both agreed that they could not possibly marry. His family would cut him off penniless if he married an American Protestant, and she had no plans to become a Catholic, nor a conventional wife. She was convinced that her life was ending, that no one so ill and old as she (she was 38) could give birth. In any event, however, the baby boy was born safely in a mountain village away from Rome, and Fuller hired a wet nurse to look after him in the town of Rieta. She then spent several hectic months migrating back and forth between Rome and Rieta, watching the revolution unravel. Ossoli fought on the battlements of Rome against a French army that had besieged the city, and Fuller became involved in supervising a hospital for wounded republican soldiers on an island in the River Tiber. She also conceived the plan of writing a history of the Roman revolution as it unfolded before her eyes, comparing it to the American Revolution. Considering the two countries side by side she wrote:

> My friends write to urge my return; they talk of our country as the land of the future. It is so, but that spirit which made it all it is of value in my eyes, which gave all hope with which I can sympathize for that future, is more alive here [in Italy] at present than in America. My country is at present spoiled by prosperity, stupid with the lust of gain, soiled by crime in its willing perpetuation of slavery.

She was depressed to discover that the American republic refused to give diplomatic recognition to the Roman republic but instead stood by and watched it fall. The Romans, in the face of overpowering odds, surrendered unconditionally on July 4, 1849, after a prolonged French bombardment had shattered many familiar Roman landmarks. Fuller and Ossoli had survived but now feared reprisals and had to leave the city rapidly. Going to collect Angelo, their son, they found him sick and half starved because of recent privations brought on by the war.

Angelo recovered, and Fuller realized that she must now break the fact of his existence to her relatives and friends back in States. The news at once started rumors and gossip going in America; Greeley terminated her contract at the *Tribune*, and she found she was unable to get a contract for the book she was writing about the Roman revolution. With her son and Ossoli, whom she now introduced as her husband, she went to Florence where she found a temporary job as a governess and was befriended by Robert and *Elizabeth Barrett Browning*, the English poets. Aware that the authorities were seeking former republican soldiers, however, they were not safe anywhere in Italy, and Fuller decided they must return to America and face the risk of scandal and ostracism.

After borrowing the money for passage on the cheapest ship they could find, the family set sail for New York on the American merchant ship *Elizabeth* in May 1850. En route, the captain died and an inexperienced mate was forced to take over. Approaching New York harbor in high wind on the early morning of July 19, 1850, the ship ran aground on a reef off Fire Island. The storm worsened and the ship began to break up. The shore was in sight, but the lifeboats had been smashed, and one of the men who tried to swim ashore for help was swept away and drowned. Fuller and Ossoli, with their son Angelo, appar-ently resolved that they would stay together at all costs, and when the captain cried "Abandon ship" they stayed behind and were drowned.

Mourned by relatives and friends who had been waiting with eager anticipation to see her as a wife and mother and to meet her exotic husband, Fuller's death seemed tragic and, to many, unnecessary. Three of her Transcendentalist friends, Emerson, Clark, and Channing, published a eulogistic memoir of her life and work in 1852 and paid tribute to her lasting influence on their lives. Fuller was largely forgotten by the end of the 19th century, however, and only with the more recent feminist movement have her history and her work been thoroughly revived.

SOURCES:

Allen, Margaret V. *The Achievement of Margaret Fuller*. University Park, PA: Pennsylvania State University Press, 1979.

Capper, Charles. *Margaret Fuller: An American Romantic Life*. NY: Oxford University Press, 1992.

Slater, Abby. *In Search of Margaret Fuller*. NY: Delacorte Press, 1978.

Stern, Madeleine. *The Life of Margaret Fuller*. Westport, CT: Greenwood Press, 1991.

Wade, Mason, ed. *The Writings of Margaret Fuller*. NY: Viking, 1941.

SUGGESTED READING:

Blanchard, Paula. *Margaret Fuller: From Transcendentalism to Revolution*. NY: Delacorte Press, 1978.

Emerson, Ralph Waldo, W.H. Channing, and J.F. Clarke. *Memoirs of Margaret Fuller Ossoli*. Boston, MA: Phillips, Sampson, 1852.

Miller, Perry, ed. *Margaret Fuller: American Romantic*. Gloucester, MA: Peter Smith, 1969.

Von Mehren, Joan. *Minerva and the Muse: A Life of Margaret Fuller*. Boston, MA: University of Massachusetts, 1994.

COLLECTIONS:

Fuller Manuscripts and Works, Houghton Library, Harvard University; Margaret Fuller Papers, Massachusetts Historical Society.

Patrick Allitt,
Professor of History, Emory University,
Atlanta, Georgia

Fuller, Meta Warrick (1877–1967).

See Women of the Harlem Renaissance.

Fuller, Sarah (1836–1927)

American educator of the deaf. Born on February 15, 1836, in Weston, Massachusetts; died in Newton Lower Falls, Massachusetts, on August 1, 1927; youngest of six children of Hervey (a farmer) and Celynda (Fiske) Fuller; attended local schools in Newton Lower Falls, Massachusetts; graduated from the Allan English and Classical School of West Newton; never married; no children.

An early leader in the education of the deaf, Sarah Fuller was raised and educated in Newton Lower Falls, Massachusetts, and spent her early career teaching at schools in Newton and Boston. In 1869, after a period of training under *Harriet B. Rogers at the Clarke School for the Deaf in Northampton, Massachusetts, Fuller was named principal of the Boston School for Deaf-Mutes (renamed the Horace Mann School for the Deaf in 1877), which opened on November 10, 1869, with ten students. The first institution of its kind in the country to be operated on a day-school basis, the school flourished under her leadership. Fuller strongly advocated teaching deaf children to speak, rather than sign, and believed that instruction should begin at the earliest possible age, views that were not always popular with her professional colleagues. In 1870, after hearing of Alexander Melville Bell's system of "Visible Speech," which utilized graphic symbols to represent speech sounds, Fuller invited his son, Alexander Graham Bell, to visit the school and teach the new technique to the faculty. It was Bell's work with the deaf that contributed significantly to his later development of the telephone.

Throughout the 1870s and 1880s, Fuller attempted to promote her theories to the American Instructors of the Deaf and Dumb, a conservative professional organization that still favored manual speech. Receiving a cool reception from the group, partly because of her views and partly because she was a woman, Fuller, along with Dr. Bell, *Caroline A. Yale, and others, united to form the American Association to Promote the Teaching of Speech to the Deaf, of which she served as a director from 1896. Fuller's innovations did not always meet with resistance. In 1888, Mr. and Mrs. Francis Brooks, the parents of a deaf child who had benefitted from Fuller's approach, endowed the Sarah Fuller Home for Little Children Who Cannot Hear, the first school attempting to educate preschool-age deaf children. (The home closed in 1925, after which the endowment was used to establish the Sarah Fuller Foundation for Little Deaf Children, part of the Hearing and Speech Clinic of the Children's Medical Center, in Boston.) Fuller also designed charts of speech exercises and wrote *An Illustrated Primer* (1888), a manual to assist instructors in teaching speech to the deaf. When time allowed, she and some of her colleagues taught speech reading to hard-of-hearing and speech-impaired adults. She is said to have given ten-year-old *Helen Keller, who was both blind and deaf, her first speech lessons in 1890. Sarah Fuller retired in 1910 and died at her home in Newton Lower Falls at the age of 92.

SOURCES:

James, Edward T., ed. *Notable American Women.* Cambridge, MA: The Belknap Press of Harvard University Press, 1971.

McHenry, Robert. *Famous American Women.* NY: Dover, 1980.

Barbara Morgan,
Melrose, Massachusetts

Fullerton, Georgiana Charlotte
(1812–1885)

English novelist and philanthropist. Name variations: Lady Georgiana Charlotte Leveson-Gower; Lady Georgiana Fullerton. Born at Tixall Hall, Staffordshire, England, on September 23, 1812; died at Bournemouth, England, on January 19, 1885; youngest daughter of Granville Leveson-Gower, 1st earl Granville (an English diplomat); married Alexander Fullerton, 1833.

Daughter of a diplomat, Lady Georgiana Fullerton sponsored the sisters of St. Vincent de Paul in England and founded the Poor Servants of the Mother of God Incarnate. After converting to the Catholic faith in 1846, she wrote various biographies on the lives of the saints and stories, as she said, "with a purpose." She also took on translations, principally from the French. Her writings include *Ellen Middleton* (1844), *Grantley Manor* (1847), *Laurentia* (1861), *Rose Leblanc* (1861), *Too Strange Not to be True* (1864), *Constance Sherwood* (1865), *Life of St. Francis of Rome* (1885), *A Stormy Life* (1867), *Mrs. Gerald's Niece* (1869), *A Will and a Way* (1881).

Fullerton, Mary Eliza (1868–1946)

Australian poet, author, and socialist. Name variations: (pseudonyms) Alpenstock and Austeal; (pseudonym) "E". Born Mary Elizabeth Fullerton on May 14, 1868, at Glenmaggie, Victoria, Australia; died on February 23, 1946; one of seven children of Robert (a farmer) and Eliza (Leathers) Fullerton; attended local state school; never married; lived with Mabel Singleton; no children.

Selected writings: Moods and Melodies *(poetry, 1908);* The Breaking Furrow *(poetry, 1921);* Bark House Days *(childhood reminiscences, 1921);* Two Women *(novel, 1923);* The People of the Timber Belt *(novel, 1925);* A Juno of the Bush *(novel, 1930);* The Australian Bush *(a descriptive work, 1928);* Moles Do So Little With Their Privacy *(poetry, 1942);* The Wonder and the Apple *(poetry, 1946).*

Australian writer Mary Eliza Fullerton was an avid reader and independent thinker at an early age. Born in a bark house built by her father and largely self-educated, she was raised in a Scots-Presbyterian community but was later critical of religion, calling herself "a medley of beliefs." In the late 1890s, she became active in the suffrage movement, an interest ignited in her childhood when her mother was denied the vote. "I felt that somehow . . . my mother was slighted and, at large, women," she wrote. Later, she joined the Victorian Socialist Party and the Women's Political Association. During World War I, she became a member of Women Against War.

A self-described loner who never married, Fullerton made a living writing articles, stories, and poems for newspapers, often using the pseudonyms Alpenstock and Austeal. Her first collection of poems, *Moods and Melodies*, was published in 1908. From 1922, Fullerton lived in England, where she met and befriended writer *Miles Franklin, who arranged to have her poetry published during the 1940s. Fullerton won a prize for *Two Women* (1923), one of only three novels she wrote under her own name. Her use of the pseudonym "E," under which her later poetry was published, was said to be linked to her sensitivity about her lack of formal education and her belief in sex bias in publishing. Her true identity was the subject of much speculation in literary circles and was only revealed after her death in 1946.

SOURCES:

Wilde, William H., Joy Horton, and Barry Andrews, ed. *Oxford Companion to Australian Literature.* Melbourne: Oxford University Press, 1994.

Barbara Morgan,
Melrose, Massachusetts

Fulvia (c. 85/80–40 BCE)

Ambitious Roman aristocratic woman who engaged in political and military activities normally reserved exclusively for Roman men. Pronunciation: FULL-vee-ya. Born around 85/80 BCE; died in Greece in 40 BCE; daughter of Marcus Fulvius Bambalio and Sempronia; married Publius Clodius, in 62 BCE (died, January 18, 52 BCE); married Gaius Scribonius Curio, in 52 or 51 BCE (died, August 49 BCE); married Mark Antony, in 47 or 46 BCE; children (first marriage) Publius Clodius Pulcher; Clodia (b. around 60 BCE); (second marriage) Gaius Scribonius Curio; (third marriage) Marcus Antonius Antyllus; Iullus Antonius.

Made first public appearance on the political scene (52 BCE), testifying in court; led active political life (44–40 BCE); led troops against Octavian at Praeneste (41 BCE).

The daringly ambitious, sometimes outrageous, Roman aristocrat, known to history as Fulvia, lived during the Late Roman Republic, a chaotic era lasting from 130 BCE to 31 BCE that was characterized by turmoil and strife. During Fulvia's youth, Rome experienced the terror of a cruel dictatorship under Sulla as well as the tumult of the Catalinarian conspiracy, which left the fate of the people subject to politicians divided along the lines of two opposing factions—the *populares,* who looked out for the good of the people, and the *optimates,* who were out for the good of the leaders. The resulting rivalries would culminate in full-blown civil war. Fulvia was not only an active participant in these rivalries, she also led troops in a military siege against one of Rome's most historic leaders.

Writers of the period assert that Fulvia was not the traditional Roman woman of the Late Republic. In his *Life of Mark Antony,* Plutarch refers to Fulvia as a "woman who gave no thought to spinning or housekeeping"; on the contrary, he goes on to say, she preferred to accompany her husbands everywhere, even into their army camps. Another Roman writer of the 1st century BCE claimed that "Fulvia had nothing womanly about her except her body," and that "she mixed everything with arms and commotion." On the other hand, the men around Fulvia had reason to fear and despise the power that she achieved through her determined control of the careers of three husbands, and some of the denigrating accounts of her, written in her lifetime, were undoubtedly biased. Thus, it is not known how much of her behavior is concocted or if the stories that support such behavior are apocryphal.

Although highborn women of the Late Republic were exerting increasing influence in society, they were still having difficulty breaking out of the traditional domestic duties that had ruled the life of a Roman matron since the Early Republic. As the central figures in their households, such women had long been able to affect political endeavors through male relatives, particularly their sons, without attaining any public rights and generally receiving no recognition for their roles.

Fulvia's position in politics began with her links to two old Roman families—the Fulvii and the Sempronii Tuditani—both of whom had been active in government during the Middle Republic but had lost their political clout. Fulvia's father, Marcus Fulvius Bambalio, was a nobody in the scheme of politics, and her maternal grandfather, Gaius Sempronius Tuditanus, was recognized as insane, known for his habit of mounting the platform for public speaking in the Roman forum, dressed in tragic costume, to scatter coins among the people. His father, however, Gaius Sempronius Tuditanus, had served as consul—the highest political office in the Roman Republic—in 129 BCE and had written one of the earliest works on Roman law. The way had therefore been prepared for Fulvia to find a role in public life in a male-dominated society. But for her to achieve a first marriage to a man with political influence, she also needed something more to offer him.

In the Roman Republic, marriages were not made for love, but were a means of political manipulation, to cement alliances between influential families. When such an alliance was no longer beneficial, the marriage usually ended in divorce. Since Fulvia had no recent male blood relatives of political stature, scholars have suggested that she probably had money, inherited as the last in the family line on both sides. But wealth alone was not reason enough to marry a woman in Roman times.

Fulvia wished to rule a ruler and command a commander and she schooled Antony to obey women.

—Plutarch

Then, in 62 BCE, her mother Sempronia married the Roman consul. It was an opportune time for Fulvia to marry the first of her husbands, Publius Clodius Pulcher. Clodius was a politically ambitious young man, known for his spendthrift nature, so the marriage to a stepdaughter of a consul was a good move for him financially and politically. According to ancient sources, Fulvia accompanied Clodius everywhere, and in the ten years of their marriage she organized a *collegia*, or group of supporters, on his behalf. But Valerius Maximus wrote that the dagger Clodius wore was a sign of his subjection to a woman's *imperium* (absolute control).

In 52 BCE, Clodius was murdered, and Fulvia joined the Roman tribunes in making public speeches that exhorted others to avenge his murder. When a man named Milo was accused of the murder, Fulvia appeared in court as a witness against him, thus gaining both the recognition and the enmity of the famous orator and lawyer, Cicero. Cicero was the defense attorney for Milo, and he blamed Fulvia for his failure to acquit his client. Cicero made a practice of using verbal attacks against the female

relatives of his enemies to make the enemies look bad, and he was an adversary of all three of Fulvia's husbands. He would continue to slander Fulvia and publicly deride her until his death in 43 BCE.

Fulvia's second marriage was to Gaius Scribonius Curio, a man of some influence and military ambitions, but described by contemporary Roman authors as disorganized and weak. Cicero once wrote a letter to Curio, advising him to exercise more decisiveness and control. Since Curio's political career progressed upward in ways similar to Clodius', it is probable that Fulvia was behind the scenes, applying all that she had learned about political mastery during the years she was married to her first husband. The benefits of her forceful personality were short-lived, however, as Curio was killed in battle in 49 BCE.

Fulvia then married Mark Antony in 47 or 46 BCE. At that time, the command of the Roman state had passed into the hands of the first Triumvirate, or three-man rule, under Julius Caesar, Pompey, and Crassus. Far from resulting in a stronger government, the triumvirate had disintegrated into continual fighting among political factions divided at least three ways, and when Crassus died, the simmering opposition between Caesar and Pompey came to a head. Mark Antony and Fulvia were both supporters of Caesar against Pompey, and Mark Antony attempted to have Caesar declared the king of Rome. But the Romans had been ruled by kings some 600 years earlier and eschewed all talk of monarch. On March 15, 44 BCE, Caesar was brutally assassinated, setting off a struggle for succession to the position that under Caesar had become a dictatorship. Three men were contending for this power: Mark Antony, Octavian (the future Caesar Augustus), and Lepidus.

In the period of the Early Republic, the state was run by the people of Rome through their representatives in the Senate, and armies were loyal to the Roman state. By the Late Republic, however, soldiers gave their loyalty and devotion to their generals. Thus, individual Roman military leaders, seeking control of the state, built up their armies and took on other Roman military leaders, causing enormous civil strife. At the same time, the Romans were still involved in expanding their territories, meaning that the military leaders were also fighting foreign peoples they were out to subdue. Against this tumultuous backdrop, Rome was plagued with political back-stabbing, murders, treason, and other criminal activities, which may help to explain some of the events, following the assassination of Julius Caesar, described by both Cicero and Cassius Dio.

In one episode, Fulvia was with Antony at the port of Brundisium, on the Adriatic, where a mutiny of soldiers had occurred. According to Cicero and Cassius Dio, Fulvia watched as the mutinous soldiers were executed. Cicero's narrative went one step further, describing Fulvia as "that most avaricious cruel woman" who looked on while the blood of the men's lopped-off heads was spattering over her face. Later in that year, Cicero refers to Fulvia's influence in Antony's political affairs during the trial of Deiotarus, who had been governor of the Roman province Galatia. Because Deiotarus had been accused of planning to murder Caesar, his province had been taken from him. When Mark Antony restored Galatia to Deiotarus, Cicero wrote that "Deiotarus was worthy of any kingdom, but not of one bought through Fulvia."

Between September 2, 44 BCE, and March 20, 43 BCE, Cicero delivered his orations known as the *Philippics*. The second of these, in which Cicero expressed his resentment against Antony and Fulvia, was never actually delivered orally, but was spread by means of a political propaganda pamphlet during Antony's absence from Rome in November 44. As a supporter of Octavian, Cicero used his writing to slander the absent Antony and to persuade the Roman Senate to declare Mark Antony a public enemy of the state. While Cicero, Octavian, and other enemies of Antony were canvassing support for the declaration of Antony as a public enemy, Fulvia turned to the law in her husband's defense, raising a constitutional question that had been controversial since her great-grandfather wrote his law book. The issue was whether a person could be declared a public enemy without having an opportunity to present a defense.

The night before the Senate was to decide the issue, Fulvia, together with her son and Antony's mother **Julia**, visited the house of every senator in Rome. The next morning, Fulvia and her mother Sempronia stood in the road on the way to the Senate, wearing mourning clothes and wailing lamentations, following the practice used by relatives to arouse sympathy for persons accused of criminal charges. The Senate decided against Antony, however, and exiled him from Italy, while his enemies tried to rob Fulvia of her possessions and plotted to kill her children.

Later in the same year, Octavian, Mark Antony, and Lepidus restored peace among themselves and formed the Second Triumvirate. They divided the rule of the Roman provinces into three parts while they shared equal control in Rome.

Without Fulvia behind him, Antony did not stand a chance against Octavian. Historians of the time describe him as a playboy, who lacked the seriousness to be a military leader. It was Fulvia's strong will that was believed to be the cause of Antony's success. When Antony was on military campaigns in the East, Fulvia was in Rome gathering support for him against Octavian, acting as Antony's agent.

The months of November–December 43 BCE were the time of the triumviral proscription lists. Joined again in power, Octavian, Antony, and Lepidus had drawn up lists of their enemies and hired agents to kill them. The head was brought back to the triumvir who contracted for the person's death, then impaled and displayed in front of the rostra (speaking platform) in the forum. The historian Appian relates a story that indicates the level of personal power that Fulvia had reached. A man named Rufus had refused Fulvia's offer to buy his house; in retaliation, Fulvia added his name to the proscription list. According to Appian, she refused to remove his name even after he offered her the house for free. When Antony's agents brought him the head of Rufus, Antony responded that it should be taken to Fulvia. Abrogating power to herself as a fourth leader of the Roman state, Fulvia had it impaled in front of the dead man's house instead of in front of the rostra.

The name of Cicero had also been included on the proscription lists. On December 7, 43 BCE, Mark Antony's agents brought Antony the head of the dead senator. Fulvia was present. According to Dio Cassius, she spat on Cicero's head, pulled out his tongue and thrust a hairpin into it, and made cruel jokes against her longtime adversary.

In 42 BCE, 1,400 women who had lost male relatives as a result of the proscriptions approached the female relatives of the triumvirs for help. Antony's mother Julia and Octavian's sister *Octavia supported the women, who were being heavily taxed by the triumvirs, but Fulvia supposedly refused all help and treated the women rudely.

When Antony was drawn into a military campaign in Bithynia, and Octavian in Macedonia, Fulvia took a stronger hand in the affairs of Rome, despite the presence of Lepidus, the third member of the triumvir. The people of Rome, even members of the Senate, consulted Fulvia before acting. Dio Cassius remarks that Servilius Isauricus and Lucius Antonius were the consuls of the Roman Republic in name only, and that in reality Fulvia had taken on the powers of the consul. When Lucius Antonius requested a triumphal entrance into Rome to celebrate a military victory, Fulvia opposed the ceremonial event on the grounds that he had not killed the required 5,000 members of the enemy forces and convinced the Senate to deny his request. After Lucius Antonius personally persuaded Fulvia that he deserved the triumph, he brought the request before the Senate again, and this time a vote in favor of it was passed unanimously. Some historians speculate that Fulvia used the event to test her power over the Senate, and thus learned that she did indeed have control over the governing body.

Fulvia's apparent aim was to consolidate what power she could before Octavian returned to Rome. After his return, the two soon became embroiled over the issue of land distribution. Octavian's intention was to act on a triumviral plan that allowed confiscation of land in the areas of 18 cities of Italy for redistribution to military veterans as their reward for service. Fulvia opposed Octavian, claiming that she and Antony should be handling the land distribution. Dio Cassius reports that Octavian was so put out that he divorced Fulvia's daughter ◄⚶ **Clodia** and supposedly returned her to her mother still a virgin. Antony, through the advice of Fulvia, then decided to back the landowners whose lands were being confiscated. Appian in his *Bellum Civile* says that Fulvia appeared with her children before Antony's troops to encourage them not to forget Antony, nor to give credit to Octavian for the lands they received.

Fulvia's most daring act was to resist Octavian by military force. She first bribed his soldiers against him and then, together with Lucius Antonius, led an attack on his army, command-

ing her husband's troops while he was in Egypt. Cassius Dio relates that for this siege, "Fulvia girded on a sword, gave out the watchword, and even harangued the soldiers, although she relied on the advice of senators and knights to issue orders to the military network still ostensibly under Lucius' command."

Fulvia's prominence in the Late Republic cannot be doubted. Exactly what her role was cannot be fully determined, however, because two of her adversaries, Cicero and Octavian, wrote false and exaggerated stories to tarnish her reputation. Octavian wrote an obscene poem about her in which he claims that Fulvia acts the way she does because Mark Antony is elsewhere with other women. The poem even includes what he claims was her ultimatum, to "f—— or fight." Octavian was very effective in the use of propaganda, and in 27 BCE, long after the death of Fulvia, he had won the backing of the people enough to be declared Augustus, the first emperor of Rome.

Meanwhile, what had been written about Fulvia must be viewed to some extent as a measure of her prominence as a player in the events of her time. Archaeological evidence supports the extent of her influence in the military, social, and political arenas of the Late Roman Republic. Some coins minted in Rome during the triumviral period bore a likeness of Fulvia, appearing as the goddess Victory; the same face, matching Fulvia with Victory, has been found on coins minted in Eumeneia (later named "Fulvia"), a city of ancient Phrygia. It has been maintained that these coins were minted earlier than those bearing the likenesses of the triumvirs. The prominence and power that Fulvia held in Roman politics, paved the way for the role of a succession of powerful and manipulative empresses of the Roman Empire. In essence, Fulvia was the first empress of Rome, and Bauman states that none of the real empresses came close to achieving what Fulvia actually did politically.

Whatever her motives, Fulvia devoted herself fully to the advancement of Antony and suffered great rebuffs. In 40 BCE, Antony's relationship with *Cleopatra VII had begun when Fulvia joined Antony in Athens, where she fell ill. When Antony was summoned back to Italy to meet with Octavian, he apparently did not even visit his wife on her death bed; he was at Brundisium when he learned that Fulvia had died, in Greece.

SOURCES:

Babcock, Charles L. "The Early Career of Fulvia," in *American Journal of Philology*. Volume 86, no. 1, 1965, pp. 1–32.

⚶► **Clodia** (c. 60 BCE–?)

*Roman noblewoman. Name variations: Claudia. Born around 60 BCE; daughter of *Fulvia (c. 85/80–40 BCE) and Publius Clodius; stepdaughter of Mark Antony (80–30 BCE); became first wife of Octavian (63 BCE–14 CE), later known as Augustus Caesar, emperor of Rome (divorced). His second wife was *Scribonia; his third was *Livia Drusilla (58 BCE–29 CE).*

Bauman, Richard A. *Women and Politics in Ancient Rome*. NY: Routledge, 1992.

Broughton, T. Robert S. *The Magistrates of the Roman Republic: Volume II 99 BC–31 BC*. Atlanta, GA: Scholars Press, 1984.

Grueber, H.A. *Coins of the Roman Republic in the British Museum*. London: British Museum, 1910.

Hallett, Judith P. *Fathers and Daughters in Roman Society: Women and the Elite Family*. Princeton, NJ: Princeton University Press, 1984.

———. "Perusinae Glandes and the Changing Image of Augustus," in *American Journal of Ancient History*. Vol. 2, no. 2, 1977, pp. 151–171.

Hooper, Finley. *Roman Realities*. Detroit, MI: Wayne State University Press, 1980.

Lefkowitz, Mary R., and Maureen B. Fant. *Women in Greece and Rome*. Baltimore, MD: Johns Hopkins University Press, 1992.

Pomeroy, Sarah B., ed. *Women's History and Ancient History*. Chapel Hill, NC: University of North Carolina Press, 1991.

Shackleton Bailey, D.R., ed. *Cicero Philippics*. Chapel Hill, NC: University of North Carolina Press, 1986.

White, Horace, trans. *The Roman History of Appian of Alexandria: Volume II The Civil Wars*. NY: Macmillan, 1899.

Woodman, A.J. *Velleius Paterculus: The Caesarian and Augustan Narrative (2.41–93)*. Cambridge: Cambridge University Press, 1983.

SUGGESTED READING:

Roberts, John Maddox. *SPQR II: The Catiline Conspiracy*. NY: Avon Books, 1991.

Saylor, Steven. *Roman Blood*. NY: Ivy Books, 1991.

Syme, Ronald. *The Roman Revolution*. Oxford: Clarendon Press, 1939.

Marjorie Dearworth Keeley,
classics scholar and freelance writer,
Amherst, Massachusetts

Furbish, Kate (1834–1931)

American botanist. Born Catharine Furbish on May 19, 1834, in Exeter, New Hampshire; died on December 6, 1931, in Brunswick, Maine; only daughter and eldest of six children of Benjamin Furbish (a businessman and manufacturer of tinware and stoves) and Mary A. (Lane) Furbish; educated in Brunswick, Maine; studied drawing in Portland, Maine; briefly studied French literature in Paris.

Born in New Hampshire in 1834, the daughter of Benjamin and **Mary Lane Furbish**, Kate Furbish grew up in Brunswick, Maine. There, she developed an early fascination with botany that was encouraged by her father. Around 1860, after attending a series of lectures in Boston given by the young George L. Goodale, later a professor of botany at Harvard, Kate decided to document all the flora of her native region. First, she took a drawing course. Then in 1870 she embarked on her life's work. After 1873, she was financed by a large inheritance from her father.

Over the course of the next 35 years, Furbish traveled across the state and into the most inaccessible wilderness in search of specimens. Small in stature but determined in spirit, she paddled up rivers, sloshed through bogs, crawled through bushes, and trekked up mountain paths in search of yet another obscure flower to add to her remarkable collection. Her exquisite paintings, which she called "her children," were accurate in every detail and were widely praised by professional botanists who often relied on dedicated amateurs like Furbish to advance the science.

In 1895, Furbish founded the Josselyn Botanical Society of Maine and would later serve as its president (1911–12). Well into old age, she attended meetings and participated in excursions, often astounding her colleagues with her energy and enthusiasm. In 1908, she presented her 16-volume portfolio drawings, entitled "Illustrated Flora," to Bowdoin College. Her collection of dried plants (4,000 sheets) was given to the New England Botanical Club, which placed it in the Gray Herbarium at Harvard, and a collection of ferns (182 sheets) went to the Portland Society of Natural History. Furbish continued to classify specimens and work on painting right up until her death in 1931, at age 98. Two of her plant discoveries bear her name: *Pedicularis Furbishiae* and *Aster cordifolius* L., var. *Furbishiae*.

SOURCES:

James, Edward T., ed. *Notable American Women*. Cambridge, MA: The Belknap Press of Harvard University Press, 1971.

McHenry, Robert, ed. *Famous American Women*. NY: Dover, 1983.

SUGGESTED READING:

Graham, Frank and Ada. *Kate Furbish and the Flora of Maine*.

Barbara Morgan,
Melrose, Massachusetts

Furman, Bess (1894–1969)

American newspaper reporter. Born in Nebraska on December 2, 1894; died in 1969; one of five children of a journalist; married Robert B. Armstrong, Jr. (a reporter), 1932; children: twins, Ruth Eleanor and Robert Furman.

The daughter of a journalist, Bess Furman was born in 1894 and spent her early career as a schoolteacher before landing her first job with a Nebraska newspaper. Her coverage of the 1928 presidential election brought her to the attention of the Associated Press, who hired her just months before the stock-market crash of 1929. Furman married Robert B. Armstrong, Jr., a fellow reporter, in 1932, and returned to Nebraska after the birth of her twins at age 41. Taking advantage of the job openings that materialized for women during World War II, she joined the Office of War Information. In 1945, she was hired by *The New York Times,* working out of its Washington bureau until 1961. Not quite ready for retirement at age 67, Furman worked as an executive in press relations for the newly formed Department of Health, Education, and Welfare during the 1960s.

Bess Furman covered the White House from the time of the Hoover administration and knew every prominent woman of her time, including first ladies. Her position with the Associated Press gave her particular access to *Eleanor Roosevelt, who was especially amicable to women of the press. "To my continuous astonishment, I found myself riding in the White House car," Furman recalled in her autobiography *Washington By-Line* (1949), "lunching at the White House table, receiving Easter lilies from the White House green houses, carrying the cards of the President and Mrs. Roosevelt." Furman also authored *White House Profile* (1951).

SOURCES:

Furman, Bess. *Washington By-Line: The Personal History of a Newspaperwoman.* NY: Alfred A. Knopf, 1949.

Weatherford, Doris. *American Women's History.* NY: Prentice Hall, 1994.

Barbara Morgan,
Melrose, Massachusetts

Furneria of Mirepoix (fl. 13th c.)

French Albigensian. Flourished in the 13th century in France; married William Roger also known as Guillaume-Roger, count of Mirepoix.

Furneria of Mirepoix was an Albigensian leader in the 13th century. Born into the nobility of southern France, she married Guillaume-Roger, lord of Mirepoix, and became involved in a heretical movement sweeping southern France. Called Albigensianism, or Catharism, this radical sect anticipated many facets of the Protestant Reformation. Its adherents denied the truth of the Trinity, materialism, and the rituals of the Catholic service and perhaps, even more radically, preached an equality between the sexes. Women could become sect leaders, if they studied hard enough, and could then achieve the status of *perfecta,* the "perfect one" whom other believers had to serve. Lady Furneria achieved the title of *perfecta* and used her wealth to support and protect other Albigensians of fewer means, including providing refuge for them in her castles when Cathars were condemned as heretics.

Laura York,
Riverside, California

Furness, Betty (1916–1994)

American actress, broadcast journalist, and consumer advocate. Born Elizabeth Mary Choate on January 3, 1916, in New York City; died on April 2, 1994, in New York City; daughter of George Choate (a business executive) and Florence (Sturtevant Furness) Choate; attended the Brearley School, New York City, and Bennett Junior College, in Millbrook, New York; married John Waldo Green (a composer and conductor), on November 26, 1937 (divorced 1943); married radio announcer Hugh B. Ernst (d. 1950); married Leslie Midgeley (a television producer), on August 15, 1967; children: (first marriage) one daughter, Barbara Green.

The daughter of an executive for the Union Carbide Corporation, Betty Furness worked as a model before a screentest took her to Hollywood, where she appeared in around 35 films, mostly low-budget Bs. "They were appalling," she later said, "except for two—*Swing Time,* with Fred Astaire and *Ginger Rogers, and the first *Magnificent Obsession,* with Robert Taylor and *Irene Dunne." Furness moved on to stage roles, appearing in summer stock and in the road shows of *Doughgirls* and *My Sister Eileen,* the latter based on *The New Yorker* stories of *Ruth McKenney.

Discouraged with her theatrical career, Furness decided to try her luck in the pioneering television industry. In 1949, after spotting her in a CBS "Studio One" episode, Westinghouse hired her as an on-air spokesperson for their products; for the next 11 years, she demonstrated refrigerators and vacuum cleaners on live television commercials. In 1952, when Westinghouse signed on as one of the sponsors of the televised national political conventions, Furness was the pitchwoman. "I'd been opening refrigerator doors for three years," she later recalled, "but when I did it during the conventions I was famous overnight." She would continue selling refrigerators to Republicans and Democrats alike during the nominating conventions of 1956 and 1960. The caucuses made her the most recognized woman in America; they also sparked her interest in politics and public affairs.

After working for Lyndon Johnson's successful presidential campaign in 1964, Furness was hired as a recruiter for the Head Start and VISTA programs. In 1967, she became Johnson's special assistant for consumer affairs, an appointment that engendered a storm of protest from professional consumer-protection groups, who cited her lack of experience. Six months later, the very groups that had questioned her appointment were pleased with her development and praised her serious efforts to educate herself on the job. After Johnson left office, she was appointed executive director of the New York State Consumer Protection Board and then commissioner of the New York City Department of Consumer Affairs. In the 1970s, Furness joined NBC as a consumer specialist on the network's "Today" show, answering consumer complaints and later conducting her own investigations. Furness worked longer than most women on television, appearing on camera until she was 76. "She pioneered consumer TV news reporting," remarked fellow advocate Ralph Nader, "and she pursued it with intelligence, inquisitiveness and irrepressibility." Betty Furness was married three times and had a daughter, **Barbara Green**, with her first husband. Furness was diagnosed with stomach cancer in 1990 and died on April 2, 1994, while undergoing treatment.

SOURCES:

Martin Jean, ed. *Who's Who of Women in the Twentieth Century.* Avenel, NJ: Crescent Books, 1995.

Moritz, Charles, ed. *Current Biography 1968.* NY: H.W. Wilson, 1968.

"Obituaries," in *The Day* (New London, CT). April 3, 1994.

Furse, Katharine (1875–1952)

English pioneer who was the first commandant of the Women's Royal Naval Service (WRNS). Name variations: Dame Katharine Furse. Born Katharine Symonds in 1875; died in 1952; fourth daughter of John Addington Symonds; educated privately; married C.W. Furse, in 1900.

The fourth daughter of English scholar John Addington Symonds, Katharine Furse grew up in Davos, Switzerland, and in 1900, at age 25, married C.W. Furse. In 1909, she enrolled in the Voluntary Aid Detachment (VAD), an offshoot of *Florence Nightingale's "Naval Nursing Service," started in 1885. With the outbreak of the First World War, Furse, who had risen to the post of commandant of the VAD, was tapped as the first commandant of the newly formed Women's Royal Naval Service (WRNS), a special uniformed service for women, organized to provide shore support for the Royal Navy. Working with **Tilla Wallace** and ❧ **Rachel Crowdy**, Furse helped organized the WRNS from the ground up, drafting the terms of pay, allowance and regulation, and even designing the uniforms. The women chose to call themselves "Wrens" in hope of warding off any objectionable nicknames. Following approval from King George V, the service began recruitment in

November 1917. At that time Furse was appointed director and was also awarded a GBE for her outstanding work.

Response to the WRNS was overwhelming, and accommodations had to be expanded to handle all the applicants. At first, the Wrens primarily provided clerical and domestic support for naval officers, but as more men were sent abroad, the women took over more substantial jobs as telegraphers, signalers, designers, and coders. Soon they were involved in every aspect of onshore naval work, including preparing the blueprints for weapons, priming depth charges, and constructing submarine nets. By 1918, Wrens were stationed throughout the country, and in Malta, Gibraltar, Geneva, and Bizerta. At the end of the war, the service was disbanded, but when World War II seemed inevitable, the group reorganized. By that time, however, Furse had moved on to work with the Girl Guides.

As in 1917, women answered the call in record numbers, and by 1939 there were over 3,000 Wrens. The number grew to 74,620 by 1944, when *Vera Laughton Mathews, a former WRNS officer and pioneer of the Sea Rangers branch of the Girl Guides, was appointed director. During World War II, the Wrens became involved in even more complex jobs, including some very dangerous ones, like driving bomb disposal experts close to UXBs and working with flammable hydrogen balloons. Although the women became an irreplaceable part of operations, they remained a separate entity from the Royal Naval Service and were unable to

---

❧ **Crowdy, Rachel** (1884–1964)

English social reformer. Name variations: Dame Rachel Eleanor Crowdy. Born in 1884; died in 1964; educated at Hyde Park New College, London; trained as nurse at Guy's Hospital, 1908.

Rachel Crowdy joined the Voluntary Aid Detachment (VAD) in 1911. From 1912 to 1914, she was a lecturer and demonstrator at the National Health Society, then worked with *Katharine Furse to establish the Women's Royal Naval Service (WRNS) during the First World War. Crowdy was awarded the DBE in 1919, the same year she was appointed chief of Social Questions and Opium Traffic Section at the League of Nations. In 1920–21, she was stationed with the International Typhus Commission in Poland, then pursued social work in many nations from 1931 to 1939. From 1939 to 1946, Crowdy was regions' advisor to the Ministry of Information.

---

carry out crucial maneuvers or give orders. As the shortage of manpower grew, however, Wrens became more active at sea, sailing on troop ships as cypher officers and coders, often for months at a time.

At the end of the war, the government retained the WRNS as a permanent but still separate part of the Royal Navy. The service is represented all over the world, with Wrens serving with the Royal Marines in Northern Ireland and in research expeditions and military training units. In 1989, M.H. Fletcher, a former director of the WRNS, chronicled the history of the service in *The WRNS: A History of the Women's Royal Naval Service*.

SOURCES:

Dictionary of National Biography. Oxford: Oxford University Press, 1994.

This England. Winter 1989, p. 75.

Furse, Margaret (1911–1974)

British costume designer for films. Born in 1911; died of cancer on July 7, 1974, at her home in London, England; studied at the Central School of Art under Jeanetta Cochrane; married Roger Furse (an artist and set designer); married editor-critic Stephen Watts.

Films: (with Roger Furse) Henry V *(1944); (with Sophie Harris of Motley)* Great Expectations *(1946); (with S. Harris)* Blanche Fury *(1947);* Oliver Twist *(1948);* The Passionate Friends *(One Woman's Story, 1948);* Madelaine *(1949); (with Oleg Cassini)* Night and the City *(1950); (with Edward Stevenson)* The Mudlark *(1950);* No Highway *(No Highway in the Sky, 1951);* The House in the Square *(I'll Never Forget You, 1951);* Meet Me Tonight *(1952);* The Crimson Pirate *(1952);* Master of Ballantrae *(1953);* The Million Pound Note *(Man With a Million, 1953);* The Spanish Gardener *(1956); (with Olga Lehmann)* Inn of the Sixth Happiness *(1958);* Kidnapped *(1960);* Sons and Lovers *(1960);* Greyfriars Bobby *(1960);* The Horsemasters *(1960);* The Prince and the Pauper *(1962);* In Search of the Castaways *(1962);* Becket *(1963);* A Shot in the Dark *(1964);* Young Cassidy *(1964);* The Three Lives of Thomasina *(1964);* Return From the Ashes *(1965);* Cast a Giant Shadow *(1965);* The Trap *(1966);* The Lion in Winter *(1967);* Great Catherine *(1967);* Sinful Davy *(1968);* Anne of the Thousand Days *(1969);* Scrooge *(1969);* Mary, Queen of Scots *(1971);* A Delicate Balance *(1973).*

Eclipsed by her husband, noted artist and set designer Roger Furse, Margaret Furse was a talented costume designer who began her career at the Gaumont-British Studios as an assistant

designer. Her credits include such films as *The Mudlark* (1950), *Becket* (1963), *The Lion in Winter* (1967), *Scrooge* (1970), and *Mary, Queen of Scots* (1971), all of which were nominated for an Academy Award. She received the Oscar for *Anne of the Thousand Days* (1969). Furse's last movie, *A Delicate Balance* (1973), was made a year before her death.

Furtseva, Ekaterina (1910–1974)

Soviet government and party official who served as minister of culture for 14 years and was the only woman ever to sit on the Communist Party's ruling Presidium. Name variations: Catherine. Pronunciation: FURTS-ev-a. Born Ekaterina (or Catherine) Alekseevna Furtseva on November 24, 1910 (o.s.) in Vyshnii Volochek, Russia; died presumably of a heart attack on October 25, 1974, in Moscow; daughter of Aleksei Furtsev (a textile worker); attended elementary and trade schools in Vyshnii Volochek, Higher Academy of Civil Aviation, 1933–35, Lomonosov Institute of Chemical Technology, 1937–42, Higher Party School (by correspondence), 1948; married Nikolai Pavlovich Firiubin, mid-1930s; children: Svetlana and Margarita.

Worked as textile weaver (1925–30); joined Communist Party (1930); served as party organizer and instructor in Komsomol organization (1930–37); served as party official at Lomonosov Institute (1937–42); appointed secretary, Frunze District Party Committee in Moscow (1942–50); became second secretary (1950–54) and then first secretary (1954–57) of Moscow City Committee; served as deputy to the USSR Supreme Soviet (1950–62, 1966–74); was a candidate (1952–56) and then full member (1956–74) of the Central Committee of the Communist Party; was a candidate (1956–57) and then full member (1957–61) of the Central Committee's Presidium; served as a member of the Party Secretariat (1956–60); served as minister of culture (1960–74).

There were two defining moments in the political career of Ekaterina Furtseva. The first occurred on May 1, 1955, when she, like many Communist Party functionaries, was standing at the base of the Lenin-Stalin mausoleum waiting for the annual May Day parade to pass through Moscow's Red Square. Much to her surprise and that of correspondents covering the occasion, Nikita Khrushchev, the head of the Communist Party of the Soviet Union, summoned her to join him and the other male dignitaries on the official reviewing stand atop the marble mausoleum. His very public introduction of her to the other leaders of the Soviet state and the Communist Party was seen by some as evidence of his desire to bring women into the ranks of the ruling elite. It also was an indication that Furtseva, who at the time was a candidate or non-voting member of the Party's Central Committee and first secretary of the powerful Moscow Committee, was a rising political star.

The second event took place two years later when Furtseva returned Khrushchev's favor. On the evening of June 18, 1957, she stood up before an extraordinary meeting of the Central Committee and began to talk. And she talked and she talked some more. For six hours, she filibustered so as to provide time for other committee members to filter into Moscow from across the Soviet Union for one of the most important meetings in party history. Her tactic, while common in the U.S. Congress, had no precedent in Soviet politics, and it saved the political career of Khrushchev. By the time she finally finished speaking, a sufficient number of Khrushchev's supporters had arrived to overturn an earlier decision of the party's Presidium to remove him from office. This defeat of what has come to be known as the "Anti-Party Plot" also allowed gradual political reform to continue in post-Stalinist Russia. Furtseva was rewarded for her services. Shortly after this meeting, she was made a full or voting member of the Presidium—the first and only woman ever to sit on this, the most powerful body in the Soviet Union. For the next three years, she was part of the small inner ruling circle. In 1960, she gave up some of her political responsibilities when she became minister of culture. She was to remain the only woman on the Council of Ministers until her death in 1974.

Ekaterina Furtseva's origins, like those of most Soviet leaders, were humble, and they have remained obscure. She was born in the small town of Vyshnii Volochek, 175 miles northwest of Moscow, on November 24, 1910—seven years before the October Revolution brought the Bolsheviks to power. Her parents were both textile workers. In part because of her father Aleksei's death in the First World War, Ekaterina had to leave the local trade school at the age of 14 to help support her mother and family. From 1925 to 1930, she worked as a weaver at the Bolshevichka Factory in Vyshnii Volochek. She joined the Young Communist League or Komsomol at the relatively early age of 13 and, in 1930, became a member of the Communist Party.

For the next seven years, she held various party positions inside the Komsomol organiza-

tion: first as secretary of the Korenevo district committee, then of the larger Feodosia city committee, and finally as department head in the Crimean regional committee. While in the Crimea, she developed an interest in gliding, which in turn led her to enter the Higher Academy of Civil Aviation in Leningrad in 1933. Following graduation two years later, she was assigned by the Komsomol leadership to serve as deputy head of the political department of the Aeroflot Aviation High School in Saratov and then as instructor in the organization's Department of Student Youth in Moscow. In both positions, her "domineering disposition" was noted approvingly by her superiors. Sometime during these years, she met and married Nikolai Firiubin, an aviation official whose subsequent rise to political prominence paralleled her own.

In 1937, Furtseva (who kept her maiden name) enrolled in the Lomonosov Institute of Chemical Technology in Moscow ostensibly to be trained as a chemical engineer. She spent much of the next five years, however, working in the Institute's Party Bureau and then serving as secretary or head of its party organization. While she graduated from the Institute in 1942, she never pursued a career as an engineer any

Ekaterina Furtseva

more than she did one in aviation. This lends credence to the assumption that her attendance at both institutions was dictated by the party and designed more to contribute to her political résumé than to further her vocational training.

From 1942 to 1957, Furtseva rose steadily in the apparatus of the Moscow party organization as a result of what *The New York Times* subsequently called her "willingness to tackle any job with zeal and an ability to get things done." An initial assignment to the secretariat of Moscow's Frunze District Committee led to promotions to second secretary and then first secretary of the district. She rapidly gained a reputation of being a no-nonsense administrator who was able to produce results, particularly in the economic construction of the Frunze District, by bullying subordinates and bureaucrats into complying with the party's wishes. To improve her political credentials, she concurrently enrolled in the Higher Party School and completed its requirements by correspondence in 1948. Like other ambitious and opportunistic politicians during the murderous last years of Stalin's reign, she on occasion proved her own political vigilance by denouncing and dismissing academics and medical personnel in her district who might have been too honest in their research.

Her role in the highest echelons of the Party [was] more than that of a mere figurehead representing Soviet womanhood.

—The *Times* [London], October 26, 1974

In 1949, Nikita Khrushchev became head of the Moscow party organization and promptly took the energetic and capable Furtseva under his wing. In 1950, he was instrumental in having her named second secretary of the Moscow City Committee, and in that same year she was elected as a deputy to the Supreme Soviet—an honorific position in the rather meaningless Soviet Parliament which she was to hold for 20 of the next 24 years. Two years later, she and several other of Khrushchev's protégés were chosen to be candidate members of the Central Committee. When Khrushchev began to consolidate his position after Stalin's death in 1953, Furtseva rose with him. In 1954, she took over his old job as first secretary of the Moscow Committee, and she joined him as a member of a high-level Soviet delegation to Communist China. After Khrushchev denounced Stalin in his famous "secret speech" at the 20th Party Congress in 1956, Furtseva became a full member of the Central

Committee and a candidate member of the party's Presidium as well as one of eight secretaries on the influential Secretariat. She repaid Khrushchev's patronage by actively supporting his de-Stalinization campaign and his attempts to reorganize the inefficient Soviet industrial bureaucracy. When these reforms caused the majority of the Presidium to seek Khrushchev's ouster in June 1957, Furtseva filibustered long enough for the Central Committee to come to his rescue.

Inevitably, when women rise to political prominence, there are some who wish to credit their success to special personal relationships. Furtseva was no exception. Western correspondents, noting her presence at state functions and on foreign tours with Khrushchev, dubbed her the "unofficial first lady" of the Soviet Union. The Canadian ambassador reported rumors he had heard that she was Khrushchev's mistress, a fact that was "a secret only for deaf Muscovites" according to one Russian émigré. Some referred to her as "Catherine III"—an invidious comparison to *Catherine II the Great, the 18th-century Russian empress who also wielded immense political power in a man's world and was criticized for her many amours. Rumors and gossip may be unavoidable in cases such as this. Readers, however, should not necessarily accept them as the truth.

Madame Furtseva, as she was invariably called by the Western press, like Khrushchev himself, was a refreshing presence in an otherwise staid and conservative Moscow. She drove around the Russian capital in a sports car rather than a government limousine; she was an "expert and inexhaustible dancer" at balls held in the Kremlin; she had a Russian love of vodka and preferred tennis to dieting as a means of controlling her "robust Slavic figure." Western visitors described her as a "lively personality with a pleasant smile, blonde hair and blue eyes" who always "radiated euphoria and energy." In time, her conservative black business suits and twisted-bun hairstyle gave way to more stylish and attractive attire, especially when she was on one of her frequent trips abroad.

After her dramatic role in the defeat of the "Anti-Party Plot" in 1957, Furtseva was at the pinnacle of political power for a period of three years. At 46, she was the second youngest member of the party's Presidium and the only woman on either it or the Secretariat. It is unlikely that her youthful and effervescent qualities noted by Western observers appealed to all of her old-fashioned male colleagues. Her new positions meant that she had to give up her secretaryship of the Moscow organization, and thus she lost her personal powerbase. Moreover, her special responsibility inside the Secretariat for cultural affairs did not bring with it the appointment powers enjoyed by some of the other secretaries, but it did force her to deal with embarrassing issues such as the publication abroad of Boris Pasternak's *Dr. Zhivago.* Her removal from the Secretariat in 1960 may have been a result of these factors, or Khrushchev's colleagues may simply have sought to weaken his political grip by demoting one of his more vulnerable protégés. Her subsequent ouster from the Presidium in November 1961 was ironically justified by one of Khrushchev's own reforms that required the periodic replacement of one-quarter of the membership of all higher party bodies.

Under these circumstances, few would have predicted that Madame Furtseva would have lasted 14 years in her new position as minister of culture, especially after Khrushchev himself was removed from office in 1964. It was a difficult and sensitive portfolio. As minister of culture, she had immediate responsibility for a wide and diverse empire, encompassing book publishing, libraries, film production, ballet, music, folk dancing, television, and even the famed Moscow circus. She herself had neither formal training in the arts nor a real appreciation for Russian culture. Musicians shook their heads when she referred to one of Modest Musorgsky's famous symphonic works as an opera. Victor Sparre, a Norwegian critic, may have been partially correct when he claimed that "Furtseva had hardly opened a literary work until the day she was given absolute power over Russia's cultural life. She had little in common with the artistic leaders of her country except a liking for vodka." She did not in fact have "absolute power over Russia's cultural life." Overall cultural policy continued to be set by equally uncultured but even more conservative men in the Presidium and the Secretariat, bodies in which she was no longer represented. It was her job to execute these policies.

This was a difficult task; the 1960s were years of intellectual ferment in the Soviet Union. Khrushchev's earlier attacks on Stalinism, his relaxation of some of the state's authoritarian controls, and his expanding contacts with the West caused many intellectuals to question the need for any restraints on artistic creativity. These expressions of dissent were not appreciated by the party's increasingly reactionary leadership. Furtseva was caught in the middle. She tried to be flexible in meeting some of the demands of the artistic community by giving commissions to avant-garde sculptors, allowing musicians critical of the regime occasionally to perform abroad, and sanctioning exhibits of abstract art. She also did the bidding of her political masters by vehemently attacking the writings of Alexander Solzhenitsyn, condemning sexual overtones in new Soviet ballet productions, and closing down one modern-art exhibit when it offended the old-fashioned tastes of her former colleagues in the Presidium. Perhaps her most important contribution as minister of culture was dramatically expanding Soviet cultural exchanges with other countries. Not only did Russians get a chance to see Hollywood movies and hear Western jazz, but Western audiences were given an opportunity to see classical Russian ballet and hear superb Soviet musicians. The end of Stalin's self-imposed cultural isolation was itself a breath of fresh air for the Soviet artistic community, and indirectly it contributed to the pressures for further liberalizations.

Furtseva took advantage of her office to travel widely outside of the Soviet Union. Often accompanied by one of her daughters, she visited Queen *Elizabeth I in Buckingham Palace, had tea with *Pat Nixon in the White House, and revelled in "photo opportunities" with Western movie stars. Foreign travel was just one of the perquisites enjoyed by the "new class" of the Communist elite to which Furtseva and her family belonged. Her husband, who had held ambassadorial appointments to Yugoslavia and Czechoslovakia under Khrushchev, was deputy minister of Foreign Affairs throughout most of the Brezhnev period. Her daughter, **Svetlana Kozlov**, was married to the son of Frol Kozlov, one of the most powerful political figures in the early 1960s, and her granddaughter had one of the coveted places in the Bolshoi ballet school. Her salary, Furtseva once admitted, was more than 20 times that earned by a factory worker, and she had "other emoluments" worth thousands of rubles annually. She, like other members of the privileged elite, did her shopping in special stores stocked with otherwise unobtainable Western luxury goods. She had become a *dachnik* of the type she herself had once publicly criticized. Her family had one dacha or vacation home on the temperate shores of the Black Sea and another outside of Moscow. In 1974, she decided to pass on some of her new-found wealth by building a third dacha for her daughter Svetlana. Expense was not a concern, since the materials were purchased at government wholesale prices and the labor was provided by ministry workers. The finished "cottage," which included a marble-paved swimming pool, was worth $170,000.

Furtseva's privileged existence and questionable practices were hardly unique among the ruling class of the Brezhnev era. What was unusual is that she was caught and held accountable. Apparently, one of the builders of the dacha complained about its opulence and his own low pay. The ensuing publicity forced the government to investigate. Furtseva was reprimanded by the Party Control Commission, dropped from the list of delegates to be elected to the next session of the Supreme Soviet, and ordered to repay the state $80,000. Even Brezhnev's substantial eyebrows must have gone up when this relatively large sum was produced almost immediately. The rumored appointment of her husband to head the Soviet delegation at the United Nations did not materialize, and Furtseva's own job as minister of culture was said to have been in jeopardy. She saved it, at least temporarily, by twice personally pleading her case with Brezhnev himself. On October 25, 1974, shortly after attending a concert and just before a planned trip to Mexico for a film festival, Ekaterina Furtseva died at the age of 63. The announced cause of death was a heart attack. According to the Canadian ambassador, however, the aftereffects of the scandal of the previous spring had caused her to commit suicide. She was given a state funeral on the 29th and buried in the Novodevichi Cemetery alongside scores of writers and composers she never appreciated.

Furtseva was neither a feminist nor a figurehead. She showed no interest in women's causes, in protesting against the male domination of her party and state, or in serving as a spokesperson for her gender. She rose to power not because she was a woman but because she was a hard-nosed, devious, and opportunistic *apparatchik* or party functionary who produced results. Being a good politician, however, she recognized that her propaganda value to the state of what women could achieve in the Soviet Union was also a protection for her in changing political times. Unlike the few other women who rose to prominence under Khrushchev, Furtseva proved to have political longevity. She was a member or candidate of the Central Committee for 22 years, of its ruling Presidium for six years, and of its Secretariat for four. Her tenure of 14 years as minister of culture was longer than that of almost all of her male ministerial colleagues. This longevity is also explained by more than just her gender. Both as party secretary and as government minister she had shown herself to be a competent, hard-working and firm-spoken administrator who was politically reliable and ideologically flexible.

In 1974, *The New York Times* noted in its obituary that Furtseva was "the only woman in Soviet history to become a member of the inner ruling circle." Fifty-two years earlier, *Alexandra Kollontai, who had sought but did not achieve this status in the 1920s, stressed that while women enjoyed broad civil rights in the Soviet Union, "the Soviet state is run by men." The long career of Ekaterina Furtseva is the exception that proves this rule.

SOURCES:

Ford, R.A.D. *Our Man in Moscow: A Diplomat's Reflections on the Soviet Union from Stalin to Brezhnev.* Toronto, 1989.

Glazov, Yuri. *The Russian Mind since Stalin's Death.* Dordrecht, 1985.

Hangen, Wells. "Closeup of the 'Soviet Woman'," in *The New York Times Magazine.* March 11, 1956, pp. 26+.

Sparre, Victor. *The Flame in the Darkness: The Russian Human Rights Movement as I Have Seen It.* London: Grosvenor Books, 1979.

SUGGESTED READING:

Ciboski, Kenneth N. "A Woman in Soviet Leadership: The Political Career of Madame Furtseva," in *Canadian Slavonic Papers.* Vol. XIV, no. 1. Spring 1972, pp. 1–14.

Hull, Henry Lane. "Furtseva, Ekaterina Alekseevna," in *Modern Encyclopedia of Russian and Soviet History.* Vol. 12, 1979, pp. 47–49.

Mandel, William M. *Soviet Women.* Garden City, NY: Anchor Books, 1975.

Skorodumov, V. "Furtseva, Yekaterina Alekseevna," in *Portraits of Prominent USSR Personalities.* No. 105, Munich, 1967.

Taranov, E.V. "Pervaia dama Moskvy (Shtrikhi k politicheskomu portretu, E.A. Furtsevoi)" (Moscow's First Lady: Sketches for a Political Portrait of E.A. Furtseva), in *Kentavr* (Moscow). November–December 1992, pp. 59–75; no. 1, 1993, pp. 100–109.

R.C. Elwood,
Professor of History, Carleton University, Ottawa, Canada, and author
of *Inessa Armand* (Cambridge University Press, 1993)

Fusae or Fusaye Ichikawa (1893–1981).

See Ichikawa Fusae.

${\mathcal{A}}$CKNOWLEDGMENTS

Photographs and illustrations appearing in *Women in World History, Volume 5,* were received from the following sources:

Photo by James Abbe, **p. 5**; Courtesy of the American Program Bureau, **p. 89**; Artist unknown, **p. 139**; Courtesy of the Embassy of Australia, Office of Public Affairs, **p. 739**; Painting by Taddeo di Bartolo, **p. 165**; Photo by Cecil Beaton, **p. 664**; Belgian postage stamp, 1976, **p. 153**; Courtesy of the Bibliotheque Nationale (Paris), **p. 303**; From a photo by Matthew Brady, **p. 797**; Compliments of the British Embassy; photo by Anthony Buckley, **p. 141**; © Brooksfilms, **p. 391**; Courtesy of the Chris Evert Pro-Celebrity Tennis Classic, **p. 347**; Courtesy of Columbia Pictures, **p. 501**; Photo by Louis David, 1895, **p. 29**; Pastel by M.-Q. de LaTour, **p. 447**; Courtesy of The Digit Fund (Englewood, Colorado), **p. 693**; Courtesy of the Dwight D. Eisenhower Library, **p. 83**; Courtesy of Geraldine A. Ferraro, **p. 489**; Courtesy of Vivian Fine, **p. 534**; Courtesy of Frick Art Reference Library, painting by Edward Dalton Marchant, **p. 477**; Courtesy of George Braziller, **p. 709**; © GEPA Pressfoto, **p. 481**; German postage stamps, **pp. 81, 84, 253**; Courtesy of Glaxo Wellcome, Inc., **p. 125**; Courtesy of GUO-Analysis (New South Wales), 1980, **p. 741**; Courtesy of Haworth Productions, Ltd., 1968, **p. 98**; Courtesy of the Embassy of Iceland, **p. 539**; Courtesy of the International Museum of Photography at the George Eastman House, **p. 659**; Courtesy of the International Swimming Hall of Fame, **pp. 43, 224, 749**; Courtesy of the Jewish Historical Society of Greater Washington, **p. 364**; From the Photographic Archive of the Jewish Museum of Greece, **p. 261**; Photo by Douglas Kirkland, **p. 673**; *Art Nouveau,* painting by Gustav Klimt, **p. 635**; Courtesy of Bettye Lane, Studio Sold (New York City), **p. 789**; Photo by Harry Langdon, **p. 619**; Courtesy of the Library of Congress, **pp. 39, 766** (photo by Floride Green), **601**; Courtesy of Fraidie Martz, **p. 547**; Courtesy of the National Portrait Gallery (London), **p. 439**; Polish postage stamp, **p. 678**; Portuguese postage stamp, **p. 263**; Courtesy of the Schlesinger Library, Radcliffe College, **p. 330**; Courtesy of Reebok, **p. 482**; From the painting by George Romney, **p. 585**; Courtesy of Samuel Goldwyn Co., 1985, **p. 193**; Courtesy of The Seeing Eye, **p. 322**; Courtesy of Simon Schuster, **p. 463**; Photo by Susanne Singer, **p. 586**; Courtesy of the Sophia Smith Collection, Smith College (Northampton, Massachusetts), photo by Lemuel S. Ellis, **p. 771**; Courtesy of the Cultural Office, Embassy of Spain, **p. 222**; Courtesy of the Swarthmore College Peace Collection, **p. 676**; Painting by Titian, Kunsthistoriches Museum (Vienna), **p. 270**; Courtesy of the U.S. House of Representatives. **pp. 452, 459, 500**; Courtesy of Universal Press Syndicate, **p. 796**; Courtesy of the College of Environmental Design, Documents Collection, University of California, Berkeley, **p. 410**; Courtesy of the University Archives, University of California, Santa Barbara, **p. 257**; Courtesy of the Wilbur Collection, University of Vermont Library, **p. 559**; Courtesy of the Ursuline Centre Archives (Great Falls, Montana), **pp. 517–518**; Postage stamp from the U.S.S.R., 1957, **p. 251**; Photo by Pamela Valois, **p. 562**; Photo by Vandamm (New York), **p. 8**; Courtesy of Virago Press, **p. 333**; Photo by Vizzavona, **p. 233**; Photo by William Walling, **p. 387**; Courtesy of the Walters Art Gallery (Balimore, Maryland), **p. 654**; Courtesy of Warner Bros., **pp. 465, 467**; Courtesy of Mobil Masterpiece Theatre, WGBH-TV (Boston, Massachusetts), **p. 339**; Courtesy of Working Title Productions, **p. 542**.